HAND
NEW INSTITUTI

HANDBOOK OF
NEW INSTITUTIONAL ECONOMICS

Edited by

CLAUDE MÉNARD

University of Paris (Pantheon-Sorbonne), France

and

MARY M. SHIRLEY

The Ronald Coase Institute
Chevy Chase, MD, U.S.A.

Springer

Claude Ménard
Centre d'Economie de la Sorbonne (CES)
Université de Paris (Panthéon-Sorbonne)
106 Bd de l'Hôpital
75647 Paris Cedex 13
FRANCE
Claude.Menard@univ-paris1.fr

Mary M. Shirley
President
The Ronald Coase Institute
5610 Wisconsin Ave., Suite 1602
Chevy Chase, MD 20815
USA
mshirley@coase.org

ISBN: 978-3-540-77660-4

Library of Congress Control Number: 2008921400

© 2008 Springer-Verlag Berlin Heidelberg

This work is subject to copyright. All rights are reserved, whether the whole or part of the material is concerned, specifically the rights of translation, reprinting, reuse of illustrations, recitation, broadcasting, reproduction on microfilm or in any other way, and storage in data banks. Duplication of this publication or parts thereof is permitted only under the provisions of the German Copyright Law of September 9, 1965, in its current version, and permission for use must always be obtained from Springer. Violations are liable for prosecution under the German Copyright Law.

The use of registered names, trademarks, etc. in this publication does not imply, even in the absence of a specific statement, that such names are exempt from the relevant protective laws and regulations and therefore free for general use.

Cover Design: WMX Design GmbH, Heidelberg, Germany

Printed on acid-free paper

5 4 3 2 1 0

springer.com

Contents

	Contributors	ix
	Acknowledgement	xiii
	Introduction Claude Ménard and Mary M. Shirley	1
Section I	**The Domain of New Institutional Economics**	
1.	Institutions and the Performance of Economies over Time Douglass C. North	21
2.	The Institutional Structure of Production Ronald H. Coase	31
3.	Transaction Cost Economics Oliver E. Williamson	41
Section II	**Political Institutions and the State**	
4.	Electoral Institutions and Political Competition: Coordination, Persuasion and Mobilization Gary W. Cox	69
5.	Presidential versus Parliamentary Government John M. Carey	91
6.	Legislative Process and the Mirroring Principle Mathew D. McCubbins	123
7.	The Performance and Stability of Federalism: An Institutional Perspective Barry R. Weingast	149

Section III Legal Institutions of a Market Economy

8. The Many Legal Institutions that Support Contractual Commitments
   Gillian K. Hadfield 175

9. Legal Systems as Frameworks for Market Exchanges
   Paul H. Rubin 205

10. Market Institutions and Judicial Rulemaking
    Benito Arruñada and Veneta Andonova 229

11. Legal Institutions and Financial Development
    Thorsten Beck and Ross Levine 251

Section IV Modes of Governance

12. A New Institutional Approach to Organization
    Claude Ménard 281

13. Vertical Integration
    Paul L. Joskow 319

14. Solutions to Principal-Agent Problems in Firms
    Gary J. Miller 349

15. The Institutions of Corporate Governance
    Mark J. Roe 371

16. Firms and the Creation of New Markets
    Erin Anderson and Hubert Gatignon 401

Section V Contractual Arrangements

17. The Make-or-Buy Decisions: Lessons from Empirical Studies
    Peter G. Klein 435

18. Agricultural Contracts
    Douglas W. Allen and Dean Lueck 465

19. The Enforcement of Contracts and Private Ordering
    Victor P. Goldberg 491

Section VI Regulation

20. The Institutions of Regulation. An Application to Public Utilities.
    Pablo T. Spiller and Mariano Tommasi 515

21.	State Regulation of Open-Access, Common-Pool Resources Gary D. Libecap	545
22.	Property Rights and the State Lee J. Alston and Bernardo Mueller	573
23.	Licit and Illicit Responses to Regulation Lee Benham	591

Section VII   Institutional Change

24.	Institutions and Development Mary M. Shirley	611
25.	Institutional and Non-Institutional Explanations of Economic Differences Stanley L. Engerman and Kenneth L. Sokoloff	639
26.	Institutions and Firms in Transition Economies Peter Murrell	667
27.	Social Capital, Social Norms and the New Institutional Economics Philip Keefer and Stephen Knack	701
28.	Commitment, Coercion and Markets: The Nature and Dynamics of Institutions Supporting Exchange Avner Greif	727

Section VIII   Perspectives

29.	Economic Sociology and New Institutional Economics Victor Nee and Richard Swedberg	789
30.	Doing Institutional Analysis: Digging Deeper than Markets and Hierarchies Elinor Ostrom	819
	Subject Index	849
	Author Index	867

[Handwritten note: Q: How is global governance affecting private property transactions? CSR / Global Compact / HRIA]

Contributors

ALLEN, DOUGLAS W.
Burnaby Mountain Professor
  of Economics
Simon Fraser University

ALSTON, LEE J.
Professor of Economics, Director
  Program on Environment and
  Behavior, Institute of Behavioral
  Sciences
University of Colorado and
  National Bureau of Economic
  Research

ANDERSON, ERIN
John H. Loudon Chaired Professor of
  International Management and
  Professor of Marketing
INSEAD

ANDONOVA, VENETA
Professor of Business Administration
Instituto Tecnológico Autónomo
  de México

ARRUNADA, BENITO
Professor of Business Organization
Universitat Pompeu Fabra
Barcelona

BECK, THORSTEN
Senior Financial Economist
Development Research Group
The World Bank

BENHAM, LEE
Professor of Economics
Washington University in St. Louis and
  The Ronald Coase Institute

CAREY, JOHN M.
Associate Professor
Department of Government
Dartmouth College

COASE, RONALD H.
Clifton R. Musser Professor Emeritus
  of Economics
The University of Chicago

COX, GARY W.
Professor of Political Sciences
Department of Political Science
University of California, San Diego

ENGERMAN, STANLEY L.
Professor of Economics and History
Department of Economics and History
University of Rochester and Research
  Associate, National Bureau of
  Economic Research

GATIGNON, HUBERT
Claude Janssen Chaired Professor of
  Business Administration and Professor

of Marketing,
INSEAD

GOLDBERG, VICTOR P.
Thomas Macioce Professor of Law
Co-Director, Center for Law and
    Economic Studies
Columbia University

GREIF, AVNER
The Bowman Family Endowed Professor
    in Humanities and Sciences
Department of Economics
Stanford University, and Senior Fellow
Stanford Institute for International
    Studies

HADFIELD, GILLIAN K.
Professor of Law and Co-Director
Center for Law, Economics and
    Organization
University of Southern California

JOSKOW, PAUL L.
Elizabeth and James Killian Professor
    of Economics
Massachusetts Institute of
    Technology

KEEFER, PHILIP
Lead Research Economist
Development Research Group
The World Bank

KLEIN, PETER G.
Associate Professor of Agribusiness
    and Associate Director
Contracting and Organizations
    Research Institute
University of Missouri

KNACK, STEPHEN
Senior Research Economist
Development Research Group
The World Bank

LEVINE, ROSS
Curtis L. Carlson Professor of Finance
Carlson School of Management
University of Minnesota

LIBECAP, GARY D.
Anhenser Busch Professor,
Entrepreneurial Studies, Economics
    and Law;
Director Karl Eller Center
University of Arizona; and Research
    Associate, National Bureau of
    Economic Research

LUECK, DEAN
Bartley P. Cardon Professor of
    Agricultural & Resource Economics
Professor of Economics, and Professor
    of Law
The University of Arizona

McCUBBINS, MATHEW D.
Professor of Political Science
Department of Political Science
University of California, San Diego

MÉNARD, CLAUDE
Professor of Economics and
    Director Centre ATOM
Université de Paris (Panthéon-Sorbonne)
    and The Ronald Coase Institute

MILLER, GARY J.
Professor of Political Science
Department of Political Science
Washington University in St. Louis

Contributors

MUELLER, BERNARDO
Department of Economics
Universidade de Brasilia

MURRELL, PETER
Professor of Economics
Department of Economics and IRIS
 Center
University of Maryland

NEE, VICTOR
Goldwin Smith Professor of Sociology
Cornell University

NORTH, DOUGLASS C.
Spencer T. Olin Professor in Arts and
 Sciences
Department of Economics
Washington University in St. Louis,
 and Bartlett Burnop Senior Fellow,
 Hoover Institution
Stanford University

OSTROM, ELINOR
Co-Director Workshop in Political
 Theory and Policy Analysis
Co-Director, Center for the Study
 of Institutions, Population, and
 Environmental Change
Department of Political Science at
 Indiana University

ROE, MARK J.
Berg Professor of Corporate Law
Harvard Law School

RUBIN, PAUL H.
Samuel Candler Dobbs Professor
 of Economics and Law
Emory University

SHIRLEY, MARY M.
President
The Ronald Coase Institute

SOKOLOFF, KENNETH L.
University of California
Los Angeles and National Bureau
 of Economic Research

SPILLER, PABLO T.
Jeffrey A. Jacobs Distinguished
 Professor of Business and Technology
Haas School of Business
University of California, Berkeley, and
National Bureau of Economic Research

SWEDBERG, RICHARD
Professor of Sociology
Department of Sociology
Cornell University

TOMMASI, MARIANO
Chairman, Department of Economics and
 Director, Center of Studies for
 Institutional Development
Universidad San Andrés
Buenos Aires

WEINGAST, BARRY R.
Senior Fellow, Hoover Institution and
 Ward C. Krebs Family Professor
Department of Political Science
Stanford University

WILLIAMSON, OLIVER E.
Edgar F. Kaiser Professor of Business
 Administration, Economics,
 and Law at the
University of California, Berkeley

Acknowledgements

We are grateful to The Nobel Foundation 1991 for permission to publish the Prize Lecture "The Institutional Structure of Production" by Ronald H. Coase, with changes introduced by Professor Coase.

Each chapter in this book went through a very extensive review process. Beside a systematic review by the two editors, the following reviewers did a remarkable job and we are very grateful for their assistance:

Douglas Allen, James Alt, Wladimir Andreff, Nicholas Argyres, Benito Arrunada, Kathleen Bawn, Lisa Bernstein, Jean-Claude Berthelemy, Thomas Borcherding, George Clarke, Regis Coeurderoy, Robert Cull, Lance Davis, Bruno Deffains, Arthur Denzau, Philippe Desbrieres, Daniel Diermeier, Gregory Dow, John N. Drobak, David Epstein, Gillian K. Hadfield, Christian Harm, Pierre-Cyrille Hautcoeur, George Hendrikse, P.J. Hill, Jonathan Isham, Simon Johnson, Philip Keefer, Peter G. Klein, Charles Knoeber, Richard Langlois, Philippe Le Gall, Gary D. Libecap, Stephen Littlechild, Dean Lueck, Mary Morgan, Jackson Nickerson, Douglass North, Seth Norton, Jeffrey B. Nugent, John Nye, Bruce Rayton, Rudolf Richter, Gerard Roland, Alan Schwartz, Kenneth Scott, Andrei Shastitko, Kenneth A. Shepsle, Matthew Shugart, Brian Silverman, John Wallis, Scott Wallsten, Steven B. Webb, Oliver E. Williamson, Dean Williamson, Michael Woolcock, Bennet Zelner, and Decio Zylberstajn.

Introduction

CLAUDE MENARD and MARY M. SHIRLEY

1. WHAT IS NEW INSTITUTIONAL ECONOMICS?

New institutional economics (NIE) studies institutions and how institutions interact with organizational arrangements. Institutions are the written and unwritten rules, norms and constraints that humans devise to reduce uncertainty and control their environment. These include (i) written rules and agreements that govern contractual relations and corporate governance, (ii) constitutions, laws and rules that govern politics, government, finance, and society more broadly, and (iii) unwritten codes of conduct, norms of behavior, and beliefs. Organizational arrangements are the different modes of governance that agents implement to support production and exchange. These include (i) markets, firms, and the various combinations of forms that economic actors develop to facilitate transactions and (ii) contractual agreements that provide a framework for organizing activities, as well as (iii) the behavioral traits that underlie the arrangements chosen. In studying institutions and their interaction with specific arrangements, new institutionalists have become increasingly concerned with mental models and other aspects of cognition that determine how humans interpret reality, which in turn shape the institutional environment they build (North 1990, p. 3–6; Williamson 2000).

New institutional economics abandons the standard neoclassical assumptions that individuals have perfect information and unbounded rationality and that transactions are costless and instantaneous. NIE assumes instead that individuals have incomplete information and limited mental capacity and because of this they face uncertainty about unforeseen events and outcomes and incur transaction costs to acquire information. To reduce risk and transaction costs humans create institutions, writing and enforcing constitutions, laws, contracts and regulations—so-called formal institutions—and structuring and inculcating norms of conduct, beliefs and habits of thought and behavior—or informal institutions. They develop modes of organization embedded in these settings that provide different incentives that vary in their capacity to motivate agents. For new institutionalists the performance of a market economy depends upon the formal and informal institutions and modes of organization that facilitate private transactions and cooperative behavior. NIE focuses on how such institutions

1

C. Ménard and M. M. Shirley (eds.), Handbook of New Institutional Economics, 1–18.
© 2005 Springer. Printed in the Netherlands.

emerge, operate, and evolve, how they shape the different arrangements that support production and exchange, as well as how these arrangements act in turn to change the rules of the game.

Because NIE considers choices to be embedded in institutions, it has a much broader reach than neoclassical economics, which has been largely concerned with prices and outcomes. But unlike old institutional economics, NIE does not abandon neoclassical economic theory. While new institutionalists reject the neoclassical assumption of perfect information and instrumental rationality, they accept orthodox assumptions of scarcity and competition. Both Arrow and Williamson have attributed the rising influence of NIE to its acceptance of the successful core of neoclassical economics. As Kenneth Arrow observed, unlike the older institutionalist school, New Institutional Economics does "... not consist of giving new answers to the traditional questions of economics—resource allocation and the degree of utilization. Rather it consists of answering new questions, why economic institutions emerged the way they did and not otherwise..." (1987, p. 734).

NIE tries to answer questions that neoclassical economics does not address and this has given NIE a distinct identity and a strong following. As North has pointed out (North 2004, forthcoming) neoclassical economics was not created to explain the process of economic change, much less political or social change. Institutionalists in contrast aim to understand change by understanding human incentives and intentions and the beliefs, norms and rules that they create in pursuit of their goals (see North 2004, forthcoming).

Answering new questions requires institutionalists to devise new methodologies. Elinor Ostrom points out that unlike much of social science institutional analysis cannot simply hold constant other institutions because "the impact on incentives and behavior of one type of rule is not independent of other rules" (Ostrom, chapter 30). There are numerous examples of these interaction effects throughout this Handbook. For instance, the section on state institutions illustrates how electoral procedures, political party norms and constitutional laws and structures interact with one another to shape the incentives of politicians and voters and, ultimately, to influence policy decisions and organizational choices.

NIE's breadth and innovation have fostered a multi-disciplinary approach. Institutional analysts adapt useful concepts and methodology from political science, sociology, law, anthropology, cognitive science, evolutionary biology, and any other discipline that sheds light on the rules, norms and beliefs that govern human interactions in the process of production and exchange. A number of the authors in this Handbook are not economists, but all are social scientists who share an interest in the scientific analysis of institutions.

2. WHY A HANDBOOK ON NEW INSTITUTIONAL ECONOMICS?

New institutional economics (NIE) has grown rapidly over the last three decades. Since the term was first coined by Oliver Williamson in 1975 (1975) the subject has exerted rapidly increasing influence over scholarly research.[1] This influence is not limited to economists. Increasing numbers of legal scholars, political scientists, sociologists, anthropologists, management specialists, and others are doing research in new institutional economics. NIE is also attracting new researchers, from many different countries.

The time is ripe for a synthetic book that provides interested readers with an overview of recent developments and broad orientations of new institutional economics. Much institutional research is published in journals that may not be familiar to others working in the field, and new institutionalists may be unaware of discoveries from disciplines other than their own. This Handbook acquaints readers with the scope of NIE, the recent trends, and the progress made by scholars from other fields. Also, young researchers may want guidance about what the topic means and how it is being researched. This volume, written by some of the foremost NIE specialists, gives new researchers an introduction to the topic and a reference book for their research.[2]

The book opens with three chapters that give the reader a sense of the scope of new institutional economics and the issues fundamental to the study of economic institutions (Section I). One branch of NIE focuses on the macro institutions that shape the functioning of markets, firms, and other modes of organization: the state (Section II) and the legal system (Section III). Another branch concentrates on the micro institutions that govern firms (Section IV) and their contractual relations (Section V). New institutionalists are also much concerned with the interactions between state and firm (Section VI). Increasingly institutional economics has also focused on how institutions, both macro and micro, change: how they emerge, evolve and die (Section VII). Because NIE is addressing new questions or new aspects of old questions its future is being shaped by new methodologies and a multifaceted, multidisciplinary approach (Section VIII).

3. The Domain of NIE

Douglass North argues in his chapter that one of NIE's main inputs to economics has been to remove the fiction of the frictionless market by adding institutions, but that NIE has the potential to perform an equally, or more powerful service: changing neoclassical economics from a static to a dynamic theory. To understand economic change and how to improve economic performance it is not enough to understand the basic rules of the game or even customs, norms and habits, North maintains. We must also understand what people believe and how they arrive at those beliefs—how people learn. North has been leading the movement to study the broader institutional framework that shapes the functioning of markets, to add beliefs and norms to the study of institutions,

---

[1] Our thanks to Rudolf Richter for dating the use of the term.
[2] Useful background on NIE can be found in Furubotn and Richter, 1998.

and to incorporate aspects of cognition in order to understand institutional change.

Ronald Coase's chapter on the institutional structure of production hearkens back to his seminal work that lies at the heart of New Institutional Economics: "The Nature of the Firm" (1937) and "The Theory of Social Cost" (1960) (reprinted in Coase 1988). Coase describes his unwillingness to treat the firm as a "black box" that takes prices at one end and produces outputs at the other. This unwillingness led him famously to ask why firms exist, why are not all transactions done through the market? He famously answered that firms exist to economize on transaction costs. We find firms when it is cheaper to organize activities under a governing hierarchy than to try to conduct them in the market place and pay the costs to search, negotiate, monitor and enforce contracts. Coase's argument that the level of transaction costs depends upon the institutional setting within which economic actors operate set the stage for the NIE. Coase's emphasis on empirical analysis of real economic phenomena using practical, even if sometimes inelegant, methodologies has also been influential in the variety of themes, approaches and disciplines that characterize the NIE.

Transaction cost economics is a direct descendent of Coase's "Big Idea," as Oliver Williamson (following Varian) terms the theory of the firm in his chapter. Transaction cost economics is well named; it is concerned with transactions, specifically: (i) the extent to which the assets involved are specific to a transaction, (ii) how disturbances or changes may affect the transaction, and (iii) how frequently the transaction will reoccur. The nature of transactions affects contracts and the way in which economic activities are allocated between firms, markets or other modes of organization. These in turn affect whether incentives are high- or low-powered, whether administration is hands on or off; and whether dispute resolution relies on courts or private ordering. As a consequence, the relative advantages of a specific arrangement can only be assessed comparatively, taking into account the characteristics of the transactions at stake and the institutional environment within which they are conducted.

4. POLITICAL INSTITUTIONS AND THE STATE

The level of transaction costs depends upon the institutional setting according to Ronald Coase, and political institutions are among the foremost factors that shape that setting. As North has pointed out, political institutions can play an important role in reducing transaction costs by improving the security of property rights and enforcement of contracts (North 1997, p. 150). But states do not necessarily play this role; indeed, many are ineffectual at protecting rights or securing contracts and many others are themselves an important threat to the security of property rights and a prime violator of contracts. Understanding how polities affect the transactional environment, how economic and political markets interact, and how, when and why states enforce or violate property rights and contracts are important tasks for NIE research.

As Barry Weingast makes clear in his chapter on federalism, NIE approaches these themes by dropping the traditional economic assumption of government as benevolent and the opposite assumption of government as Leviathan, focusing instead on how different institutional arrangements affect the incentives and performance of government. In particular NIE considers a fundamental dilemma: investment increases when property rights are protected, but a state strong enough to protect property rights is also strong enough to expropriate them (Weingast 1993). An underlying theme of all the chapters in this section is how to strike a balance between a state powerful enough to act decisively yet limited enough to prevent abuse of authority. One way to limit government is to separate state powers into branches (executive, legislative, judicial) or hierarchies (federal, provincial, local) and require them to compete or balance each other.

These chapters show how state performance in a democratic system is strongly influenced by the rules governing elections, the executive branch, the legislative branch and the division of power between federal and local governments. The large variation in rules that govern a democratic system documented in these chapters helps explains why measures of democracy have an ambiguous effect on growth or other performance variables in cross country regressions.[3] To describe and measure democracy we have to understand the devil in the details.

Electoral rules are a good example of this variance. As the chapter on electoral institutions by Gary Cox makes clear, the variance in electoral rules is large and the effects of different designs, significant. Yet electoral rules are not often analyzed as determinants of outcomes and few papers compare the effects of different electoral rules. This is a major gap. Within democracies, electoral systems differ in how they allocate the number of votes per voter, the number of seats per district, and the proportionality of votes to seats. These three factors—number of votes, district magnitude, and proportionality—affect how electoral competitors try to coordinate, persuade and mobilize voters, and this in turn has implications for who gets elected, the types of promises politicians make to voters, and both the extent of turnout and which groups are likely to vote. Policy choices are strongly influenced by which groups of constituents a policy maker must account to during elections, and this ultimately has a profound effect on economic performance. To see an example of how this works, consider Pablo Spiller and Mariano Tommasi's chapter on utility regulation. Spiller and Tommasi illustrate how political incentives affect government's willingness to abide by its contractual obligations to private providers,

---

[3] This section does not include an analysis of the institutions of dictatorships. Recently, as Carey's chapter documents, dictatorships have been increasingly replaced by democracies. Yet understanding the fundamentals of coercion is part of NIE and later in the Handbook Greif suggests a theoretical framework for incorporating coercion institutions into institutional analyses.

such as whether politicians will allow contracted price increases when these adversely affect their constituents. The credibility of a state's commitments to honor its contracts determines in turn whether or not the government can employ the more efficient and flexible regulation that enhances utility performance.

The choice between a presidential or parliamentary government is also highly consequential for any democracy. This seems like a stark choice between two polar options, but it is not. As John Carey's chapter shows there are many hybrid arrangements, especially in new democracies. New democracies have overwhelmingly adopted systems that directly elect the chief executive, but many have also adopted mechanisms to try to ensure that the president maintains support from the legislative body, by adding an office of prime minister or requiring the president to survive confidence votes, for example. Even more striking are recent actions by legislatures in Latin America to replace presidents. These hybrids between presidential and parliamentary systems are attempts to preserve a separation of powers while reducing the risk that a president loses all cooperation from the legislature, which can threaten the very survival of a fragile democratic system. The stability and policies of presidential and hybrid systems are affected by electoral rules, such as whether the president and legislature are elected at the same time, and by the rules governing the power of the president to set the legislative agenda, issue decrees, veto laws, and be reelected.

Given the previous discussion, it should be no surprise that there are many ways to organize the internal activities of legislatures and these various legislative organizations have systematic policy consequences. The most obvious variance is in how policy decisions are taken: what voting procedures are used; what types of amendments are allowed; what provisions are made for debate; whether the public can participate; etc. But as Mathew McCubbins' chapter makes clear there are two other important elements in the legislative process that vary across countries. One is how the legislative agenda is controlled—by the executive, by the lower or upper house, etc. The other is, what happens when no new laws are passed—does the status quo continue or does a program end?— and who decides. These internal legislative processes emerge from a complex interaction between constitutional and electoral institutions and the political environment. The political environment, in turn, is influenced by the constitutional separation of powers and purpose. Constitutional institutions affect the influence of different factions in society, but they themselves also mirror these influences. Polities with many diverse interests and factions have less unitary government institutions with more separation of power than more unified and homogeneous polities.

The design of federal systems, as Barry Weingast shows in his chapter, is another complex source of variance. Federalism varies in the number and character of layers in the hierarchy of a country's governments, the types of power delegated to its sub-national governments, the extent and regulation of the common market shared by its different sub-national governments, and the institutions that protect the federal arrangement from encroachment. These choices have profound implications for performance since they affect whether governments serve private or public ends. For example, Weingast shows how federal revenue sharing rules can affect levels of corruption. When local governments raise funds locally they have a stronger incentive to focus on market enhancing public goods because it increases their tax base and allow local governments to provide more of these goods. To the extent that revenues are raised nationally and distributed to the local governments according to national political criteria, this incentive is reduced and local governments will focus more on private rents. The design of the federal rules also determines whether federalism itself can survive. The center of a federal state needs sufficient power to police common pool problems among the sub-national governments, yet the more powerful the center, the more likely it is to abuse its power. In addressing this puzzle, Weingast's chapter exemplifies how an institutional focus poses different questions and seeks new answers. Traditionally economists asked what powers should be assigned to what level of government and answered variously that power should be assigned to the level with the most information, to maximize competition, to produce public goods most efficiently, etc. NIE asks instead how different federalist designs affect the incentives and objectives of government officials to further citizens' welfare and whether federalism is self-enforcing.

5. Legal Institutions of a Market Economy

An important regularity in NIE, that goes back to Coase (Coase 1960), is the critical role played by rule of law in the development and health of a market economy. The chapters in this section focus on how legal institutions support market economies by enforcing contractual obligations and protecting private property from state predation. Contractual agreements can be enforced in many ways, as Gillian Hadfield's chapter describes, but many forms of enforcement are not credible to all parties or have high costs. When enforcement is not credible or too costly, many otherwise lucrative transactions will not occur and economic performance will suffer. Even though very few disputes are actually pursued in court, an effective and efficient legal system alters people's incentives to behave opportunistically, improves the efficacy of other forms of contract enforcement, and increases the number of profitable transactions. Hadfield shows that the term "legal system" covers a complex, interwoven structure of laws, doctrines, norms, organizations, professions, and individuals facing major incentive and coordination problems, nicely illustrating Ostrom's argument that interactions between institutions cannot be safely ignored. In identifying clearly the different components of a legal system, Hadfield also suggests ways to approximate its costs and to compare different systems.

Hadfield's chapter introduces us to a debate that is analyzed in all the chapters in this section: the effects of civil versus common law origins on the current performance of a country's economy and its legal, state, financial and other institutions. Common law, which originated in England and was implanted in its colonies, combines laws passed by the legislature with custom and rules made when judges decide cases that are treated by other judges as precedents for future decisions. Civil law requires judges to uphold laws as they were written by the legislature with less room for judicial interpretation or discretion. Civil code law is associated with Europe, originally the Roman Empire and subsequently France and the countries conquered by Napoleon and their colonies. A growing literature, summarized in the chapters by Paul Rubin and Thorsten Beck and Ross Levine, argues that civil law provides less protection for private property rights from state predation and is less flexible in the face of changing circumstances. All the chapters cite cross sectional studies that find common law is correlated with greater civil liberties, less government intervention, more developed financial systems, and higher rates of growth in per capita income. This remains a highly controversial issue.

Hadfield is skeptical about the claims for legal origin, noting that informal judicial norms of reasoning and the interaction of these norms with legal practice shape the character of legal systems far more than distant legal origins. She also points to the large body of code law present in common law countries today, and notes the potential inflexibility and bias of common law's precedent-based decisions.

Paul Rubin is more sympathetic to the argument that common law systems were once more efficient than civil law systems, although he too sees convergence between common and civil laws systems. In his discussion of the functions and mechanisms of a judicial system in a market economy, he emphasizes the protection of property rights from both private opportunism and state encroachment. It was the latter protection that functioned better in common law in his view, because judges were more independent of government. This argument has parallels with the previous chapters on the importance of separation of powers in limiting state predation. Rubin also cites intriguing evidence that some common law countries may have had more competition between different court systems and this may have been the source of their relatively higher efficiency.

Benito Arruñada and Veneta Andonova take up the same debate from a historical perspective. They document how common and civil laws were both attempts to install market-oriented legal systems and were both efficient in their particular circumstances during the 19th century. Civil law countries wanted to restrain judicial discretion because the judges were aristocrats who purchased or inherited their position; they were the intellectual product of the ancient regime and would not have respected private property or contractual freedom if given freedom to choose. England's common law emerged gradually over a longer period of development of a modern market; English judges were former barristers who, because they had defended clients in contractual disputes, had a personal appreciation for the market economy. Like Hadfield and Rubin, Arruñada and Andonova see a growing convergence between civil and common law systems in the 20th century. They are critical of this evolution (which they term an anti-market bias) because they view it as a restriction on market-oriented arrangements.

Beck and Levine trace the influence of legal origins on financial systems which they see as a prime mechanism by which law affects growth. They cite empirical evidence that common law origin is significantly correlated with indices measuring how much a country's current rules protect the rights of minority shareholders and creditors during reorganizations of firms. These indices are themselves highly correlated with measures of the development of equity markets and the availability and flexibility of financing for firms. They argue that historical difference in legal tradition led to differences in protection of investors, property and contractual rights and hence to differences in the willingness of savers to invest. They offer little empirical support for Rubin's view that the more important influence of legal origins is on protection of property rights from the state, perhaps because this is harder to measure.

All of these chapters suggest that imposition of legal rules in developing and transitional countries is fraught with problems. Rubin and Beck and Levine suggest that common law systems may export better than civil law systems because of their greater respect for jurisprudence and flexibility in the face of radically different circumstances. Nevertheless, Arruñada and Andonova note that most transitional countries chose civil law systems, perhaps because they face a problem of protecting the market from judicial encroachment similar to that of early Continental Europe, and perhaps because legal systems in developed countries, even the US and the UK, now resemble statute law more than common law.

The importance of legal institutions to market development has been soundly established, and new institutionalists have played a major role in putting that item on the research agenda. But this section suggests that the case for legal origins is still a matter for debate. The argument for common versus civil law origins suffers from a number of missing links. What is the causal path by which greater judicial discretion of judges in 19th century common law countries led to stronger rules protecting shareholders and creditors? The answer is not clear and much of the cross sectional evidence is correlation in search of a theory of causality. How well do the rules protecting shareholders and creditors predict actual enforcement of shareholder and creditor protection? An important strength of NIE is to search out the gap between de jure and de facto rules, but most of the studies of legal origin focus on rules-on-the-books, not rules-in-practice. Why does the convergence of legal systems in the 20th century not affect these correlations?[4] Are problems of adaptation (which are not measured) more important than legal origin in driving these outcomes? These chapters suggest that we have much to learn about the role and evolution of legal institutions.

---

[4] Mark Roe has argued that US protection of minority shareholders was done by code—the creation of the Security and Exchange Commission—because US common law was seen as weak in protecting shareholders' rights.

6. MODES OF GOVERNANCE

Ronald Coase's query as to why some transactions are done in markets and others in firms seems deceptively simple. An important achievement of NIE in the years since Coase asked that question is to show how complex both question and answer really are. Claude Menard's chapter explores how command, control and cooperation might give firms an advantage over markets and argues that we must understand the internal costs of firms as well as transaction costs if we want to explain when they have an advantage over markets. Menard explores the many different ways of organizing activities that fall between the polar choices of vertically integrating the transaction into a firm or conducting trades on the spot market. NIE differs from traditional economics not just by peering into the black box of the firms; it also opens the black box of markets. Menard points out that to a new institutionalist markets are not costless, identical, or immediate; they are diverse in their costs because they vary in how they are organized, the rules that support them, and how those rules are enforced.

As Menard's chapter suggests, there are still many unanswered questions in the study of transactions and governance. Many of the insights about inter-firm transactions could apply to intra-firm governance, but so far the internal structure of firms has received less attention from new institutionalists. Exceptions can be found in Gary Miller's chapter on principal/agent problems in firms and Erin Anderson and Hubert Gatignon's chapter on the creation of new markets. The market is an alternative to hierarchy, but that does not mean it is institution free; yet to date there has been relatively little work on the micro-analytics of market governance structures. (Ostrom lists the rules required for a competitive market in her chapter, and the list is quite long.) Another gap in the literature emerges from the failure of many empirical studies of transaction costs and the firm adequately to account for the effects of the broader institutional environment, even though regulation or norms may be as important determinants of the choice of governance structure as asset specificity or uncertainty.

An area where NIE has proved particularly powerful is in explaining vertical integration. Paul Joskow's chapter contrasts traditional and so-called "new property rights" explanations for vertical integration with transaction cost explanations. One clear advantage of transaction cost explanations over alternative theories is that they have produced testable hypotheses and spawned a wealth of empirical studies, which Joskow summarizes and critiques. Transaction cost theories start with the recognition that contracts are incomplete and subject to both ex ante and ex post opportunism, and that transaction costs will vary both with the nature of the transaction and with the different modes of governance. In choosing whether to rely on markets, vertically integrate, or use some hybrid mode of governance, transacting parties consider both how well the various options mitigate opportunism and at what cost. Asset specificity is an important factor in this calculus and Joskow shows the many guises and roles of asset specificity. Such choices are not static, but we do not yet have a dynamic theory of why governance modes change and how contractual relations and organizations adapt to changing circumstances.

The difficulties of negotiating, monitoring and enforcing contracts and the problems of opportunism apply equally to transactions within a firm as to trade between firms according to Gary Miller. He links principal/agent theory to a NIE perspective in his chapter to explain how incentives, monitoring and cooperation interact with the varying nature of intra-firm transactions and to show why different types of contracts work better for different kinds of transactions in different settings. Firms use different mixes of solutions to the problem of motivating agents to do what their principal wants, and that creates different kinds of firms. Firms that rely principally on high-powered incentives tend to be risk-taking innovators; those that use monitoring most are cautious and bureaucratic; and those that rely mostly on cooperation are more closely-knit and team oriented. The variety of firms that Miller portrays has its parallel in the diversity of hybrid forms Menard describes and the multifarious solutions to the make-or-buy problem revealed by Joskow.

Miller focuses on the agency problem for managers at each level of the hierarchy within a firm to motivate their subordinates; Mark Roe focuses instead on the agency problems at the top levels of a firm. Corporate governance tries to solve a vertical problem: how do stockholders prevent stealing and shirking and assure competent senior managers? Corporate governance must also deal with a horizontal problem: how can distant, minority shareholders prevent close, controlling shareholders from shifting value to themselves? Corporate governance institutions also affect an external problem: how can outside or inside interests be deterred from using political means to intervene in the corporation? Roe describes the different institutions that can deal with corporate governance problems, including markets; boards of directors; executive incentives and norms; information disclosure mechanisms; takeovers, proxy fights, and shareholder voice; capital structure; bankruptcy; and lawsuits. His approach is comparative and illustrates nicely how rules of the game on the books and in practice depend on their institutional environment. Roe also shows how more sophisticated institutions must rest on a functioning system of corporate law and property rights to work effectively. In that respect, corporate governance interacts in complex ways with the legal and political institutions in which it is embedded.

The final chapter in this section turns to the dynamic problem of how firms create new markets for both existing and new products. Erin Anderson and Hubert Gatignon consider markets as institutional arrangements resulting from interactions among firms and between firms and potential customers. Market creation thus results from both the internal challenge of governing to encourage innovation and the external challenge of acquiring innovations through acquisition or appropriation. New markets can be developed through in-house marketing efforts or by franchising or other forms of partnership, all requiring safeguards against the risk of opportunism. Uncertainty in the firm's environment as well as internally is a key issue here. This analysis substantiates the NIE perspective that markets should not be treated as black boxes: they can be analyzed as diverse outcomes of complex adjustments and innovations over time. Anderson and Gatignon show how NIE is the right analytical tool to understand the comparative business logic of these governance choices and the effects of path dependence and bounded rationality.

7. CONTRACTUAL ARRANGEMENTS

In the previous section we saw the many organizational forms that transactions can engender. New institutionalists also analyze the variety of contractual arrangements these organizations conclude. Much of the empirical literature on contracts has been concerned with the fundamental question—make or buy? As Peter Klein describes in his chapter on this literature, empirical studies of how transaction costs influence this decision have had to overcome serious data, methodology, and conceptual problems. Yet these problems have been far less formidable than those posed by rival theories. Property rights models focus exclusively on how inefficient ownership arrangements cause ex ante underinvestment in relationship-specific human capital. As Klein shows, few studies have managed to measure ex ante human capital investment, much less compare it to some optimal estimate. Transactions cost models, with their focus on ex post execution of the contract, are empirically more tractable, and in the few studies that have compared them, win out over rival theories, including market power, resourced-based, or strategic management explanations.

Douglas Allen and Dean Lueck reach similar conclusions for agricultural contracts. Agriculture is another area where transaction cost models have generated a large empirical literature and trumped rival explanations, such as principal/agent models, in comparative studies. For example, principal/agent theory argues that contracts such as sharecropping contracts are designed to balance risk against moral hazard incentives, yet empirical tests find no support for the hypothesis that share contracts are likely to be chosen over cash rent contracts as crop risk increases. Transaction cost analyses do not treat contracting parties as principal and agent, but instead examine the incentives of both parties to maximize wealth in an uncertain environment, where inputs and outputs are complex and hard to specify in the contract, options are limited by seasonality, and delays in some activities can raise costs and reduce yields or quality. Allen and Lueck argue that the focus of the transaction cost approach on incentives, realism, and testable hypotheses have generated robust and empirically supported explanations for the structure of agricultural contracts.

Notwithstanding the successes cited by Klein and Allen and Lueck, there is much room for further development. One problem, not unique to NIE, is that contracts are often confidential. Another problem is measurement. Recall that Williamson argued that three variables of a transaction affect transaction costs and the design of the contract: frequency, asset specificity and uncertainty. Frequency can produce ambiguous results, while both asset specificity and uncertainty have proved hard to measure leading many researchers to resort to proxies, with mixed success. Linking transaction costs to contractual design or contractual design to performance is also tough, and success varies. Moreover, few studies have connected contractual choice to changes in the broader institutional environment or tried to test transaction cost results against alternative theories. Recent research has begun to address these issues, by empirically testing competing theories (as Klein and Allen and Lueck describe), and by comparing the performance of similar contracts in different environments (as referenced by Spiller and Tommasi and Shirley).

The effects of contracts on performance depend not just on how they are written and implemented. How they are enforced is also significant as Victor Goldberg's chapter reminds us. NIE's emphasis on the importance of enforcement was an early development and made an important contribution to an issue largely ignored by the standard approach. The NIE view—that contracts are usually not fully self-enforcing and ex post conditions of implementation need to be seriously taken into account—has led to greater attention to the role of courts. While thus far the economic analysis of ex-post conditions has had limited effect on how courts interpret contracts, Goldberg is optimistic that the success of the economic approach as a framework for analyzing contracts will eventually have influence.

8. REGULATION

The chapters in this section show how NIE has proved a powerful approach for the study of regulation, both theoretically and in comparative empirical studies. We have already discussed how transaction costs analysis led to a reexamination of anti-trust regulation; it has begun to have a similar influence on other regulations as well, especially utility regulation. Institutionalists reject the notion that state ownership and state regulation of utilities are substitutes, arguing instead that they are polar options with radically different incentive and efficiency properties and that their feasibility depends on political circumstances. As Pablo Spiller and Mariano Tommasi discuss in their chapter, institutionalists also reject the traditional view that the only problem of utility regulation is opportunistic behavior of the regulated firm, and turn the spotlight on opportunism of politicians. Government opportunism is a general problem, but is especially relevant for poor countries trying to privatize their state owned utilities since these countries lack the institutions to enforce government commitments and ensure that policies are stable through regime changes. Spiller and Tommasi discuss the differences between regulatory governance regimes relying on formal administrative procedures, such as those that predominate in the US, and contract law, such as in the UK. They also examine the sorts of constitutional institutions that are required to make these governance modes function effectively and the options for countries that lack these supportive institutions. They show that in order to better understand regulations and their successes and failures we need to treat regulations as a mode of governance rather than pure incentive mechanisms, an approach distinct to NIE.

NIE is similarly distinct in its approach to open-access, common-pool resources, such as fisheries, aquifers, oil pools, and the atmosphere, and to problems of property rights more generally. Indeed, from the outset an important focus of the NIE research agenda was analysis of the issues surrounding the delineation, allocation and implementation of property rights. Many regulations deal primarily with these issues.

Gary Libecap describes in his chapter how transaction costs create the tragedy of the commons, which arises when it is too costly to put boundaries around the resource, secure agreement to limit individual actions, and obtain enough information to design, motivate and monitor possible solutions. The transaction costs of gathering, interpreting, and conveying information about the common resource and of negotiating among the relevant parties also help explain why private agreements and state regulations of common-pool resources take the forms they do. For example, side payments are often proposed as a way to mitigate opposition from those who might be harmed, but side payments are not feasible if it is costly to reach agreement on what is the magnitude of the harms involved, whether compensation is warranted, who should be compensated, and what should be the size, source, and form of the compensation. Some parties who may be harmed, such as politicians who lose constituents, cannot legally receive compensating side payments. Libecap illustrates how NIE analyses of regulation consider bargaining among all affected parties, as well as the role of cultural, legal, and political precedents in determining regulatory outcomes.

Libecap examines state regulation of resources where private property rights are not feasible; Lee Alston and Bernardo Mueller examine the state's role in the opposite case where private property rights **are** feasible. Early theories argued that scarcity in resources would make secure property more valuable and create demand for the state to protect property rights. But many states do not supply secure property rights nor do they change property rights when changes in scarcity value demand it. There are political and economic transaction costs associated with the state establishing or changing property rights that are very similar to those described in other chapters of this Handbook for other actions. Alston and Mueller's chapter shows how NIE illuminates the causes and consequences of insecure and inefficient property rights.

A hallmark of NIE is its concern with how and why ex post behavior differs from ex ante rules, assumptions or agreements. Lee Benham's chapter illustrates how regulation can have a number of consequences that were not anticipated in standard neoclassical models. Regulation can lead to a number of licit responses such as substituting unregulated goods for regulated ones, or barter for regulated money exchange, or altering the organization of the market in response to regulations that raise or lower transaction costs. Regulation also stimulates a number of illicit responses, such as extralegal activity (the informal or underground economy) or corruption. Benham shows how regulation is path dependent and its long-run consequences depend heavily on the context and time period, leading to outcomes in which the effects on allocation are only a small part of regulation's total impact. His conclusions substantiate a central theme of NIE: the effects of institutions need to be assessed comparatively.

9. INSTITUTIONAL CHANGE

The contributions in this section confront the challenge that Doug North posed at the outset: move economics from a static to a dynamic theory by explaining how institutions change. There is no clear evidence on how long institutions persist or why and how they change. Like North, Mary M. Shirley's chapter on institutions and development agrees that we have a long way to go in understanding how institutions change. Her chapter deals with two questions: why have so few countries been able to create and sustain institutions favorable to growth and how can institutions be changed to support economic development rather than hinder it? Although great strides have been made in identifying the core institutions that are correlated with economic growth and the historical circumstances that explain why these supportive institutions are weak or absent in some countries, her review shows how far we are from being able to answer the two questions she raises. Empirical studies exhibit significant regularities; in particular institutional variables systematically dominate other variables in explaining growth and social progress. But these studies lack a theory that would transform regularities into causal explanations. Her analysis also emphasizes the failure of outsiders in trying to reform institutions and the difficulty of introducing specific and sustainable micro reforms when the broader institutional framework and society's belief systems are hostile to change. Shirley argues that cross-sectional studies would need to become more specific about the institutions and settings they measure while case studies would need to become more comparative if we are to bridge the gap between observed regularities and adequate theorizing.

Stanley Engerman and Kenneth Sokoloff concur that institutions are critical to any explanation of economic development, but also find that institutions are to some extent endogenous to changing circumstances. They argue that colonists from Britain or Spain arrived in the New World with similar beliefs and cultural heritage to individuals in their home countries, but confronted different conditions and as a result evolved different institutions. If institutions are indeed endogenous, then those who make strong claims for the effects of institutions on economic growth face a challenge to defend their thesis. Advocates for institutional determinants of growth also face a challenge: to explain why very different institutional structures are sometimes equally conducive to growth and, symmetrically, why similar institutions lead to very disparate outcomes. Engerman and Sokoloff suggest that perhaps what matters for growth is not any particular institutional design but how well institutions are adapted to their specific settings and how flexible they are in adapting to changing circumstances.

Peter Murrell's chapter on transitional economies challenges the pessimism inherent in much of the literature, which assumes that basic institutions usually change only very slowly. Although he finds that the transition experience supports many of the premises of NIE, he also presents evidence that institutions in the transitional economies of Eastern Europe have improved very rapidly, thanks in part to political consensus on the need for change. The demand for institutional change from voters and businesses was an important stimulus in Eastern Europe, but it was influential politicians, academics, and state officials who designed the details of institutional transformation in these countries according to Murrell. These "institutional entrepreneurs," acting with advice from foreign actors, altered institutions in a process that was surprisingly insulated from politics and demand pressures. Even more strikingly at odds with the assumptions of much of the literature on development and institutions is his finding that firm governance changed more slowly than some state and state supported institutions such as political institutions (e.g. election processes), the legal system (e.g. laws protecting property rights, corporate governance, rules for courts), and regulation and enforcement by quasi-government bodies (e.g. central banks) and private bodies (e.g. arbitration courts or accounting standard boards).

Philip Keefer and Steven Knack analyze social capital and norms, which are often assumed to be among the most rigid of institutions. Looking in particular at norms of trust and trustworthiness, they find that these vary widely across countries and have a significant effect on economic outcomes and development. Although written laws and rules enforced by government, courts, or other third parties and by reputation can affect or substitute for trust, these are not the only explanation for why levels of trust and trustworthiness vary so widely. Social homogeneity and membership in groups or networks also affect trust norms. Although that suggests that norms of trust will be difficult to instill where these forces are absent, Keefer and Knack argue (as does Keefer, 2000) that family, religious or ethnic norms sometimes substitute for wider norms. They also point to evidence that income equality and education affect trust and other development-producing norms, suggesting that norms are not as immutable as they are sometimes portrayed.

In the last chapter of this section, Avner Greif examines the factors determining the dynamics of markets and market-supporting institutions. His analysis describes the key role played by two sets of institutions. First are "contract-enforcement institutions", the complex set of institutions required for securing exchanges. "Contract-enforcement institutions" can be organic, private-order institutions that arise spontaneously from the pursuit of individual interests or designed private- or public-order institutions that are intentionally created to secure contracts. Second are "coercion-constraining institutions," rules that constrain those with coercive power from abusing the property rights of others. Without coercion-constraining institutions economic actors will be unwilling to bring their goods to market for fear that the rulers or other powerful actors will expropriate them. Greif describes how markets and political institutions co-evolve through the dynamic interaction of these two sets of institutions. Referring to historical examples, such as the contrast in the organic institutions implemented by the Maghribi traders and the designed institutions used by the Genoese, he shows the different forms that contract enforcement and coercion constraining institutions can take and how they explain the dynamics of markets and political institutions. As we described earlier, this problem of controlling coercive power is an issue central to several other contributions as well.

10. Perspectives

The last section of the Handbook deals with new ideas and approaches, suggestive of NIE's future paths. A clear track toward greater interdisciplinary approaches is exemplified in both chapters in this section.

In their chapter, Nee and Swedberg examine the complex relationship between new institutional economics and economic sociology. They argue that there is much less interaction between these fields than there should be and that both sides would gain from deeper exchanges. A short review of recent developments in economic sociology confirms the existence of significant overlapping areas. Economic sociology's critical perspective on behavioral assumptions in mainstream economics and its emphasis on the need to embed individual choices in the social networks that shape them are surely mirrored in similar concerns among new institutionalists. Similarly the analysis of networks, markets, and firms as social constructions rooted in institutional settings, the sociological approach to law and economics or finance, and other recent themes in economic sociology overlap with ongoing research in NIE. Nee and Swedberg propose a sociological analysis of how formal and informal rules are shaped by norms and conventions, which themselves manifest shared mental models, an analysis that could substantiate North's concept of institutions. The authors conclude with a challenging model of interactions between institutional environments, modes of organization, and social groups that builds on and expands the model proposed by Williamson.

We conclude with Elinor Ostrom's chapter, which presents a challenge to new institutionalists as daunting as North's challenge at the outset of this Handbook. Ostrom calls for institutionalists in all social sciences to seek out universal components for markets and hierarchies and develop theories of human behavior in diverse settings. Ostrom draws on the foundations of many disciplines to devise a framework (IAD, Institutional Analysis and Development) that can be used in analyzing any type of institutional arrangement, which she and others have applied to a variety of different arenas. The theoretical and empirical tasks she sets are difficult and complex, but her own large body of research shows that they are feasible if social scientists are ready to rise above the specialized language, knowledge and assumptions of their sub-disciplines.

Reading these chapters, one gets a sense of the richness of new institutional economics. Notwithstanding the diversity in themes and approaches from different disciplines, a hard core emerges. Transaction cost is a key concept that has surpassed the limited role it initially played in economics, nurturing new avenues of research in political science, sociology, legal studies, management, etc. Also at the core of NIE is a common methodological concern with comparative analysis of institutions at all levels, from broad societal norms or rules governing the polity to specific details of contracts and firms and all that lies between. At the same time many puzzles are still to be solved and these chapters define an ambitious research agenda. From the outset this Handbook intended to summarize the developments in the subfields of New Institutional Economics, raise questions that leaders in the field consider crucial, and supply scholars with tools for exploring answers to these questions. The future task—to fill in the blanks—now belongs to the readers of this Handbook.

References

Arrow, Kenneth J. 1987. "Reflections on the Essays" in George Feiwel (ed). *Arrow and the Foundations of the Theory of Economic Policy*. New York: New York University Press, pp. 727–34.

Coase, Ronald H. 1960. "The Problem of Social Cost". *The Journal of Law and Economics* 3: 1–44.

―――. 1988. *The Firm, the Market and the Law*. Chicago: The University of Chicago Press.

Furubotn, Eirik G. and Rudolf Richter. 1998. *Institutions and Economic Theory: The Contribution of the New Institutional Economics*. Ann Arbor, MI: The University of Michigan Press.

Keefer, Philip and Mary M. Shirley. 2000. "Formal versus Informal Institutions in Economic Development" in Claude Menard (ed). *Institutions, Contracts, and Organizations: Perspectives from New Institutional Economics*. Cheltenham, UK: Edward Elgar, pp. 88–107.

North, Douglass C. 1990. *Institutions, Institutional Change, and Economic Performance*. New York: Cambridge University Press.

―――. 1997. "Transaction Costs through Time" in Claude Menard (ed). *Transaction Cost Economics: Recent Developments*. Brookfield, VT: Edward Elgar.

―――. 2004. *Understanding the Process of Economic Change*. Princeton, NJ: Princeton University Press (forthcoming).

Weingast, Barry R. 1993. "Constitutions as Governance Structures: The Political Foundations of Secure Markets". *Journal of Institutional and Theoretical Economics (JITE)* 149(1): 286–311.

Williamson, Oliver E. 1975. *Markets and Hierarchies. Analysis and Antitrust Implications*. New York: Free Press.

―――. 2000. "The New Institutional Economics: Taking Stock, Looking Ahead". *Journal of Economic Literature* 38: 595–613.

SECTION I

The Domain of New Institutional Economics

1. Institutions and the Performance of Economies Over Time

DOUGLASS C. NORTH

1. INTRODUCTION

The discipline of economics is made up of a static body of theory that explores the efficiency of resource allocation at an instant of time and under the restrictive assumptions of frictionless markets. Recent research has explored the nature of the frictions by incorporating institutions, transaction costs, and political economy into economic analysis thereby providing the theory with a bridge to the real world of real economies. But the first constraint of static analysis severely hinders our ability to analyze and improve the performance of economies in a world of continuous change. And, in fact, the employment of static theory as a source of policy recommendation in a setting of dynamic change is a prescription for the policies producing unanticipated and undesirable results. In this essay I intend to provide an approach to the study of the process of economic change. There is still much that we do not understand about the process but this essay provides an analytical framework that does, I believe, highlight the problems that must be confronted in order to understand and improve economic performance. I first describe the intentional nature of human interaction in a world of pervasive uncertainty (2) before going on to describe the process of economic change (3). I conclude with drawing some implications from this approach to the process of change which highlight the lacunae in our understanding of this process (4).

2. INTERACTIONS IN A WORLD OF UNCERTAINTY

[1] In contrast to standard theory that draws its inspiration from physics, modeling the process of change must derive its inspiration from evolutionary biology but in contrast to Darwinian theory in which the selection mechanisms are not informed by beliefs about the eventual consequences, human evolution is guided by the perceptions of the players in which choices—decisions—are made in the light of these perceptions with the intent of producing outcomes downstream that will reduce the uncertainty of the organizations—political, economic, and social—in

---

[1] This section is drawn from my essay "Five Propositions about Institutional Change", in Knight, J. and Sened, I., *Exploring Social Institutions*, Michigan: The University Press, 1995.

pursuit of their goals. Institutional change, therefore, is a deliberate process shaped by the perceptions of the actors about the consequences of their actions. The immediate vehicle by which the actors attempt to shape their environment is by altering the institutional framework in order to improve their (and their organizations') competitive position. Let me state five propositions that describe this process:

1. The continuous interaction between institutions and organizations in the economic setting of scarcity and hence competition is the key to institutional change.
2. Competition forces organizations continually to invest in new skills and knowledge to survive. The kind of skills and knowledge individuals and their organizations acquire will shape evolving perceptions about opportunities and hence choices that will incrementally alter institutions.
3. The institutional framework provides the incentive structure that dictates the kinds of skills and knowledge perceived to have the maximum payoff.
4. Perceptions are derived from the mental constructs of the players.
5. The economies of scope, complementarities, and network externalities of an institutional matrix make institutional change overwhelmingly incremental and path dependent.

Let Me Expand on These Propositions

1. Institutions are the rules of the game—both formal rules, informal norms and their enforcement characteristics. Together they define the way the game is played. Organizations are the players. They are made up of groups of individuals held together by some common objectives. Economic organizations are firms, trade unions, cooperatives, etc.; political organizations are political parties, legislatures, regulatory bodies; educational organizations are universities, schools, vocational training centers. The immediate objective of organizations may be profit maximizing (for firms) or improving reelection prospects (for political parties); but the ultimate objective is survival because all organizations live in a world of scarcity and hence competition.
2. New or altered opportunities may be perceived to be a result of exogenous changes in the external environment which alter relative prices to organizations, or a consequence of endogenous competition among the organizations of the polity and the economy. In either case the ubiquity of competition in the overall economic setting of scarcity induces entrepreneurs and the members of their organizations to invest in skills and knowledge. Whether through learning by doing on the job or the acquisition of formal knowledge, improving the efficiency of the organization relative to that of rivals is the key to survival.

While idle curiosity surely is an innate source of acquiring knowledge among human beings, the rate of accumulating knowledge is clearly tied to the pay-offs. Secure monopolies, be they organizations in the polity or in the economy, simply do not have to improve to survive. But firms, political parties, or even institutions of higher learning faced with rival organizations must

strive to improve their efficiency. When competition is muted (for whatever reasons) organizations will have less incentive to invest in new knowledge and in consequence will not induce rapid institutional change. Stable institutional structures will be the result. Vigorous organizational competition will accelerate the process of institutional change.
3. There is no implication in proposition 2 of evolutionary progress or economic growth—only of change. The institutional matrix defines the opportunity set, be it one that makes income redistribution the highest pay-off in an economy or one that provides the highest payoffs to productive activity. While every economy provides a mixed set of incentives for both types of activity, the relative weights (as between redistributive and productive incentives) are crucial factors in the performance of economies. The organizations that come into existence will reflect the payoff structure. More than that, the direction of their investment in skills and knowledge will equally reflect the underlying incentive structure. If the highest rate of return in an economy comes from piracy we can expect that the organizations will invest in skills and knowledge that will make them better pirates. Similarly if there are high returns to productive activities we will expect organizations to devote resources to investing in skill and knowledge that will increase productivity (the new growth economics literature can become relevant at this point).

   The immediate investment of economic organizations in vocational and on the job training obviously will depend on the perceived benefits; but an even more fundamental influence on the future of the economy is the extent to which societies will invest in formal education, schooling, the dissemination of knowledge, and both applied and pure research which will mirror the perceptions of the entrepreneurs of political and economic organizations.
4. The key to the choices that individuals make is their perceptions about the payoffs, which are a function of the way the mind interprets the information it receives. The mental constructs individuals form to explain and interpret the world around them are partly a result of the genetic evolution of the mind, partly of their cultural heritage, partly a result of the local everyday problems, they confront and must solve, and, partly a result of non-local learning. The mix among these sources in interpreting one's environment obviously varies as between for example a Papuan tribesman on the one hand and an economist in the United States on the other (although there is no implication that the latter's perceptions are independent of his or her cultural heritage).

   The implication of the foregoing paragraph is that individuals from different backgrounds will interpret the same evidence differently; they may, in consequence, make different choices. If the information feedback of the consequences of choices were complete then individuals with the same utility function would gradually correct their perceptions and over time converge to a common equilibrium; but as Frank Hahn has succinctly put it, "There is a continuum of theories that agents can hold and act upon without ever encountering events which lead them to change their theories." (Hahn, 1987, p. 324). The result is that multiple equilibria are possible due to different choices by agents with identical tastes.

5. The viability, profitability, and indeed survival of the organizations of a society typically depend on the existing institutional matrix. That institutional structure has brought them into existence; and their complex web of interdependent contracts and other relationships has been constructed on it. Two implications follow. Institutional change is typically incremental and is path dependent.

This institutional change is occurring in a world of pervasive uncertainty or ambiguity which by definition is one in which one cannot derive a probability distribution of possible outcomes-such as is possible with decision making in the face of risk (in the Knightian definitions). This uncertainty persists because the "human landscape" in which humans are interacting is continually undergoing change—change induced in part by non-human action (for example changes in climate, natural disasters) but primarily by the human actors themselves.

Humans attempt to reduce that uncertainty (or convert it into risk) by learning. The cumulative learning of a society embodied in language, beliefs, myths, ways of doing things—in short the culture of a society—not only determines societal performance at a moment of time but through the way in which it constrains the choices of the players contributes to the nature of the process through time. Humans scaffold both the mental models they possess—belief systems—and the external environment—institutions. The focus of our attention, therefore, must be on human learning, on what is learned and how it is shared among the members of a society, on the incremental process by which the beliefs and preferences change through time, and on the way in which they shape the performance of economies through time.

We can describe that performance by innumerable statistics on its demographic, economic, technological, and institutional features; but what we really need to know is what is the interplay between all these features that makes it work. The foundations of the interplay are three: the demography, which describes the quantity and quality of human beings; the stock of knowledge that the society possesses, which determines the human command over nature; and the institutional framework that determines the rules of the game. The demographic characteristics include not only the fertility, mortality, and migration characteristics and the labor force composition, but also the stock of human capital (derived from the stock of knowledge). The stock of knowledge includes not only the scientific knowledge that a society possesses, its distribution in the society, and its application to solving problems of scarcity, but also the beliefs that the society holds that influence the choices made. That stock of knowledge determines the potential upper bound of the well-being of the society. The institutional framework determines the incentive structure of the society. It is the interplay between these three that shapes the features of the economy. We know very little about this interaction, although we do have some limited hypotheses about parts of the interaction. Self conscious modeling of this interaction at a moment of time, much less over time, has not been part of the agenda of economists, development economists, or economic historians.

But with this background we are now ready to explore the process of economic change.

3. Process of Economic Change

A bare-bones description of that process is straightforward. The "reality" of a political-economic system is never known to anyone, but humans do construct elaborate beliefs about the nature of that "reality"—beliefs that are both a positive model of the way the system works and a normative model of how it should work. The belief system may be broadly held within the society, reflecting a consensus of beliefs; or widely disparate beliefs may be held, reflecting fundamental divisions in perception about the society. The dominant beliefs—those of political and economic entrepreneurs in a position to make policies—produce over time an elaborate structure of institutions—both formal rules and informal norms—that determines economic/political performance. The resultant institutional matrix imposes severe constraints on the choice set of entrepreneurs when they seek to introduce new or modified institutions in order to improve their economic or political positions. The resultant path dependence typically makes change incremental. But change is continually occurring (although the rate will depend on the degree of competition among organizations and their entrepreneurs) as entrepreneurs enact policies to improve their competitive position—policies that result in alterations of the institutional matrix described in the previous section. The result is revised perceptions of reality, and in new efforts by entrepreneurs to improve their position. The process of change is never ending. Change can also come from non-human induced changes in the human landscape, such as natural disasters; but overwhelmingly it is humans themselves who are incrementally altering the human landscape, as even the most cursory overview of human history will attest.

It is one thing to be able to provide a summary description of the process of economic change; it is something else to provide sufficient content to this description to give us an understanding of this process. What do we mean by reality? How do beliefs get formed? How do they change? What is the relationship between beliefs and institutions?

I have nothing to add to the age old question of philosophers—what is reality? But I do have a direct pragmatic interest in just what it is that we are trying to model in our theories, beliefs, and ideologies. The pragmatic concern is with the degree to which our beliefs coincide with "reality". To the extent that they do then there is some prospect that the policies we enact will produce the intended result. The model is always a very imperfect reflection of how the economy really works. In some cases the defects are fatal, as in the case of the communist economies that disintegrated in 1989.

Beliefs and the way they evolve are at the heart of understanding the process of change. For the most part economists, with a few important exceptions like Hayek, have ignored the role of ideas in making choices. While the rationality assumption has served economists well for a limited range of issues in micro-theory, it has devastating limitations in dealing with the process of economic change. The way we perceive the world and construct our explanations about that world requires that we delve into how the mind and brain work—the subject matter of cognitive science. We are some distance from a theory of learning that would account for how the mind works but we can at least outline the nature of the process.

The first level of learning entails developing a structure by which to make sense of the varied signals received by the senses. The initial architecture of the structure is genetic, but its subsequent development is a result of the experiences of the individual. This architecture can be thought of as generating an event space which gets us to interpret the data provided by the world. The experiences can be classified into two kinds—those from the physical environment and those from the socio-cultural linguistic environment (Hutchins and Hazlehurst, 1992). The event space structure consists of categories—classifications that gradually evolve from earliest childhood on in order to organize our perceptions and keep track of our memory of analytic results and experiences. Building on these categories, we form mental models to explain and interpret the environment, typically in ways relevant to some goals (Holland et al., p. 22). Both the categories and the mental models will evolve to reflect the feedback derived from new experiences—feedback that may strengthen and confirm our initial categories and models or that may lead to modifications. Thus, the event space may be continually redefined with experience, including contact with others' ideas.

Learning which preserves the categories and concepts intact but provides changed ideas about details and the applicability of the existing knowledge is the second level of learning. Together, learning within a given set of concepts and learning which changes the structure of concepts and mental models suggest an approach to the dynamics of learning.

The belief systems that evolve from learning induce political and economic entrepreneurs in a position to make choices that shape micro and macro economic performance to erect an elaborate structure of rules, norms, conventions and beliefs embodied in constitutions, property rights, and informal constraints; these in turn shape economic performance. This "scaffolding" not only constrains the choice set at a moment of time but is the source of path dependence. Thus when political or economic entrepreneurs seek to alter some aspect of economic performance they make choices that are constrained not only by the standard constraints of technology and income but also by this scaffolding. The process of institutional change described above is intended to alter performance in a particular direction. The aggregate of such institutional changes is continually altering the way the economy works. In turn that leads to gradual alterations of the models we devise in a never ending process of economic change.

Throughout history humans have typically gotten it (at least partly) wrong in 1) their understanding of the way the economy works, 2) the synthetic frameworks they construct, or 3) the policies they enact (at best blunt instruments to serve their purposes) which produce unanticipated consequences. We may write economic history as a great success story of the enormous increase in material well-being which has reflected the secular growth in the stock of knowledge. But it is also a vast panorama of decisions that have produced death, famine, starvation, defeat in warfare, economic decline and stagnation, and indeed the total disappearance of civilizations. And even the decisions made in the success stories have typically been an admixture of luck intermingled with shrewd judgments and unanticipated outcomes. Take American economic history. From the earliest attempts at settlement, through the colonial era, to the perceptions leading to the revolutionary war the colonists had it, at best, half right. The Constitution, surely a classic of shrewd judgment, was aided by chance (the events of the 1780s), luck (the boycott of the Convention by the anti-federalists), and unanticipated decisions (the development of the independent judiciary and the Marshall court).

I wish to emphasize the limits to our understanding because there is a certain amount of hubris evident in the annual surveys by the World Bank and in the writing of orthodox economists who think that now we have it right. But it is important that we understand that even if we did have it right for one economy it would not necessarily be right for another economy and even if we have it right today it would not necessarily be right tomorrow. I am not suggesting that we haven't learned a good deal about determinants of economic performance. We have; but the implications of my brief survey of the sequence of steps from our understanding of an economy, to the scaffold we erect, to the policies we then enact to alter economic performance are that there are innumerable junctures where we can and do get it wrong. Crucial junctures, critical to the issues of improving the performance of economies, have resulted from the way scaffolds have evolved and policies were formed as well as the way time has affected the formation of beliefs.

Scaffolds include the political structure that specifies how we develop and aggregate political choices, the property rights structure that defines the formal incentives in the economy, and the informal constraints of norms, conventions and internally held beliefs. They have evolved over many generations, reflecting, as Hayek has reminded us (1960), the trial and error process which has sorted out those behavioral patterns that have worked from those that have failed. Because the experience of every society has been unique, they will differ for each economy. They constrain the choice set not only because the organizations of that economy have been built on the foundations of that institutional structure and therefore their survival depends on its continuance but also, and perhaps more fundamentally, because the belief system that is a complementary part of that scaffolding tends to change very slowly. This scaffolding is what makes path dependence so important. When the scaffolding crumbles, as it did in eastern Europe in 1989, the problems of constructing a new framework have exposed our limited understanding of the process of change.

Equally crucial are the policies that we enact to alter the performance of an economy. Even when we have a "correct" understanding of the economy and the (more or less) "correct" theory about its operation, the policies at our disposal are very blunt instruments. They consist of alterations in the formal rules only, when in fact the performance of an economy is an admixture of the formal rules; the informal norms, and their enforcement characteristics. Changing only the formal rules will produce the desired results only when the informal norms that are complementary to that rule change and enforcement is either perfect or at least consistent with the expectations of those altering the rules.

Finally, time is important because it is the dimension in which human learning occurs and there is no implication in the foregoing brief description of the process of learning that suggests that we get it right. Indeed throughout history we have gotten it wrong far more often than we have gotten it right. The rise and fall of communism in the twentieth century is only a recent illustration. It is probably correct that if "reality" stayed constant the feedback from the policies we enacted would gradually lead us to get it right, but change and therefore persistent uncertainty is our lot which guarantees that we will continue to get it wrong at least part of the time.

4. Implications and Lacunae

The implications of the foregoing brief outline of the process of economic change are straightforward. If our objective is to improve the long run performance of economies we are in possession of the essential characteristics of successful economies. The best single predictor of the growth of an economy remains its investment rate. The new growth economics literature highlights some of the specific features of successful development. What is glaringly missing from this literature is the incentive structure to realize these objectives. But we do know a good deal about the institutional foundations of successful development. A number of recent empirical studies have made clear the importance of the institutional matrix (see Knack and Keefer, 1995 for a good summary). That matrix broadly comprises the incentive structure which will determine the quantity and quality of investment. What is still missing is how to get there. The key is the way path dependence will constrain the process of institutional and economic change.

The implication of the foregoing analysis is that path dependence can and will produce a wide variety of patterns of development depending on the cultural heritage and specific historical experience of the economy. Indeed the success of TVEs (township and village enterprises—a form of organization that is neither a firm nor a cooperative) in China does not fit our preconceptions about successful institutional/organizational structures and has been a sobering reminder of how much we still have to learn about the process. A description of that process in China from the enactment of the household responsibility system traces a unique path which has produced (so far) rapid economic growth (although even that success is tempered by growing problems of TVEs). I would hope that this paper puts to rest for good any simplistic general nostras such as "big bang" or "shock therapy" theories to magically overcome lack of development.

If path dependence can help us to understand the variety of development patterns, it also speaks forcefully to the constraints that the scaffolds erected in an economy impose on institutional change. The historically derived constraints are supported not only by the existing organizations that oppose change but also by the belief system that has evolved to produce those constraints. The rate and direction of change will be determined by the "strength" of the existing organizations and belief system.

The demise of communism in Eastern Europe in 1989 reflected a collapse of the existing belief system and consequent weakening of the supporting organizations. Policy makers were confronted not only by the problems of restructuring an entire society but also by the blunt instrument that is inherent in policy changes that can only alter the formal rules but cannot alter the accompanying norms and even have had only limited success in inducing enforcement of policies. The relative success of policy measures—such as the auctioning of state assets and the reestablishment of a legal system—in the Czech Republic compared to Russia resulted from the heritage of informal norms that made for the relatively harmonious establishment of the new rules (although even here the system for shifting assets from public to private hands in the Czech Republic produced some adverse and unanticipated downstream consequences).

One of the shortcomings of research is the lack of attention paid to the polity and the problem of aggregating choices through the political system. We simply have no good models of polities in third world, transition, or other economies. The interface between economics and politics is still in a primitive state in our theories but its development is essential if we are to implement policies consistent with intentions.

5. CONCLUSION

Let me conclude by talking again about time. If you accept the crude schematic outline of the process of change I laid out in section 3 above, it is clear that change is an ongoing continuous affair and that typically our institutional prescriptions reflect the learning from past experience. But there is no guarantee that the past experiences are going to equip us to solve new problems. Indeed an historic dilemma of fundamental importance has been the difficulties of economies shifting from a political economy based on personal exchange to one based on impersonal exchange. An equally wrenching change can be the movement from a "command" economy to a market economy. In both cases the necessity to restructure institutions—both economic and political—has been a major obstacle to development; it still is the major obstacle for third world and transition economies. The belief system that has evolved as a result of the cumulative past experiences of a society has not equipped the members to confront and solve the new problems.

We are just beginning systematically to explore the process of economic change. Our laboratory is not only our history but, particularly, what we are learning in the ongoing efforts to improve the performance of third world and transition economies. We have made some progress but we still have a long way to go.

REFERENCES

Hahn, Frank H. 1987. "Information, Dynamics, and Equilibrium". *Scottish Journal of Political Economy* 34(4): 321–34.

Hayek, F. A. 1960. *The Constitution of Liberty*. Chicago: The University of Chicago Press.

Holland, John H., Keith J. Idalyoak, Richard E. Nisbett, and Paul R. Thagard. 1986. *Induction: Processes of Inference, Learning, and Discovery*. Cambridge, MA: MIT Press.

Hutchins, Edwin and Brian Hazlehurst. 1992. "Learning in the Cultural Process" in C. G. Langston, C. Taylor, I. Farmer, and S. Rasmussen, (eds.), *Artificial Life II*. Redwood City, CA.: Addison-Wesley, pp. 682–706.

Knack, Stephen, and Philip Keefer. 1995. "Institutional and Economic Performance: Cross Country Tests Using Alternative Institutional Measures". *Economics and Politics* 7(3): 207–227.

2. The Institutional Structure of Production[1]

RONALD H. COASE

In my long life I have known some great economists, but I have never counted myself among their number nor walked in their company. I have made no innovations in high theory. My contribution to economics has been to urge the inclusion in our analysis of features of the economic system so obvious that, like the postman in G. K. Chesterton's Father Brown tale, "The Invisible Man," they have tended to be overlooked. Nonetheless, once included in the analysis, they will, as I believe, bring about a complete change in the structure of economic theory, at least in what is called price theory or microeconomics. What I have done is to show the importance for the working of the economic system of what may be termed the institutional structure of production. In this lecture I shall explain why, in my view, these features of the economic system were ignored and why their recognition will lead to a change in the way we analyze the working of the economic system and in the way we think about economic policy, changes which are already beginning to occur. I will also speak about the empirical work that needs to be done if this transformation in our approach is to increase our understanding. In speaking about this transformation, I do not wish to suggest that it is the result of my work alone. Oliver Williamson, Harold Demsetz, and Steven Cheung, among others, have made outstanding contributions to the subject, and without their work and that of many others, I doubt whether the significance of my writings would have been recognized. While it has been a great advantage of the creation of the Prize in Economic Sciences in Memory of Alfred Nobel that, by drawing attention to the significance of particular fields of economics, it encourages further research in them, the highlighting of the work of a few scholars, or, in my case, one scholar, tends to obscure the importance of the contributions of other able scholars whose researches have been crucial to the development of the field.

I will be speaking of that part of economics which has come to be called industrial organization, but to understand its present state, it is necessary to say something about the development of economics in general. During the two centuries since the publication of *The Wealth of Nations*, the main activity of economists, it seems to me, has been to fill the gaps in Adam Smith's system, to correct his errors, and to make his analysis vastly more exact. A principal theme

---

[1] This paper is published with minor changes made by Ronald Coase, with the kind permission of the Nobel Foundation, 1991.

of *The Wealth of Nations* was that government regulation or centralized planning were not necessary to make an economic system function in an orderly way. The economy could be coordinated by a system of prices (the "invisible hand") and, furthermore, with beneficial results. A major task of economists since the publication of *The Wealth of Nations*, as Harold Demsetz (1988, volume I, page 145) has explained, has been to formalize this proposition of Adam Smith. The given factors are technology and the tastes of consumers, and individuals, who follow their own interest, are governed in their choices by a system of prices. Economists have uncovered the conditions necessary if Adam Smith's results are to be achieved and where, in the real world, such conditions do not appear to be found, they have proposed changes which are designed to bring them about. It is what one finds in the textbooks. Harold Demsetz has said rightly that what this theory analyzes is a system of extreme decentralization. It has been a great intellectual achievement, and it throws light on many aspects of the economic system. But it has not been by any means all gain. The concentration on the determination of prices has led to a narrowing of focus which has had as a result the neglect of other aspects of the economic system. Sometimes, indeed, it seems as though economists conceive of their subject as being concerned only with the pricing system and anything outside this is considered as no part of their business. Thus, my old chief and wonderful human being, Lionel Robbins, wrote, in *The Nature and Significance of Economic Science*, about the "glaring deficiencies" of the old treatment of the theory of production with its discussion of peasant proprietorships and industrial forms: "It suggests that from the point of view of the economist 'organisation' is a matter of internal industrial (or agricultural) arrangement—if not internal to the firm, at any rate internal to 'the' industry. At the same time it tends to leave out completely the governing factor of all productive organisation—the relationship of prices and cost ... (Robbins, 1932, page 70). What this comes down to is that, in Robbins's view, an economist does not interest himself in the internal arrangements within organizations but only in what happens on the market, the purchase of factors of production, and the sale of the goods that these factors produce. What happens in between the purchase of the factors of production and the sale of the goods that are produced by these factors is largely ignored. I do not know how far economists today share Robbins's attitude but it is undeniable that microeconomics is largely a study of the determination of prices and output; indeed, this part of economics is often called price theory.

This neglect of other aspects of the system has been made easier by another feature of modern economic theory—the growing abstraction of the analysis, which does not seem to call for a detailed knowledge of the actual economic system or, at any rate, has managed to proceed without it. Bengt Holmstrom and Jean Tirole (1989) writing on "The Theory of the Firm" in the recently published *Handbook of Industrial Organization*, conclude at the end of their article of 63 pages that "the evidence/theory ratio ... is currently very low in this field" (page 126). Sam Peltzman (1991) has written a scathing review of the *Handbook* in which he points out how much of the discussion in it is theory without any empirical basis. What is studied is a system which lives in the minds of economists but not on earth. I have called the result "blackboard economics." The firm and the market appear by name but they lack any substance. The firm in mainstream economic theory has often been described as a "black box." And so it is. This is very extraordinary given that most resources in a modern economic system are employed within firms, with how these resources are used dependent on administrative decisions and not directly on the operation of a market. Consequently, the efficiency of the economic system depends to a very considerable extent on how these organizations conduct their affairs, particularly, of course, the modern corporation. Even more surprising, given their interest in the pricing system, is the neglect of the market or more specifically the institutional arrangements which govern the process of exchange. As these institutional arrangements determine to a large extent what is produced, what we have is a very incomplete theory. All this is beginning to change, and in this process I am glad to have played my part. The value of including such institutional factors in the corpus of mainstream economics is made clear by recent events in Eastern Europe. These ex-communist countries are advised to move to a market economy, and their leaders wish to do so, but without the appropriate institutions no market economy of any significance is possible. If we knew more about our own economy, we would be in a better position to advise them.

What I endeavoured to do in the two articles cited by the Royal Swedish Academy of Sciences was to attempt to fill these gaps or more exactly to indicate the direction in which we should move if they are ultimately to be filled. Let me start with "The Nature of the Firm." I went as a student to the London School of Economics in 1929 to study for a Bachelor of Commerce degree, specializing in the Industry group, supposedly designed for people who wished to become works managers, a choice of occupation for which I was singularly ill-suited. However, in 1931 I had a great stroke of luck. Arnold Plant was appointed Professor of Commerce in 1930. He was a wonderful teacher. I began to attend his seminar in 1931, some five months before I took the final examinations. It was a revelation. He quoted Sir Arthur Salter: "The normal economic system works itself." And he explained how a competitive economic system coordinated by prices would lead to the production of goods and services which consumers valued most highly. Before being exposed to Plant's teaching, my notions on how the economy worked were extremely woolly. After Plant's seminar I had a coherent view of the economic system. He introduced me to Adam Smith's "invisible hand." As I had taken the first year of university work while still at high school, I managed to complete the requirements for a degree in two years. However, University regulations required three years of residence before a degree could be granted. I had therefore a year to spare. I then had another stroke of luck. I was awarded a Cassel travelling scholarship by the University of London. I decided to spend the year in the United States, this being treated as a year's residence at the London School of Economics, the regulations being somewhat loosely interpreted.

I decided to study vertical and lateral integration of industry in the United States. Plant had described in his lectures the different ways in which various industries were organized, but we seemed to lack any theory which would explain these differences. I set out to find it. There was also another puzzle which, in my mind, needed to be solved and which seemed to be related to my main project. The view of the pricing system as a coordinating mechanism was clearly right, but there were aspects of the argument which troubled me. Plant was opposed to all schemes, then very fashionable during the Great Depression, for the coordination of industrial production by some form of planning. Competition, according to Plant, acting through a system of prices, would do all the coordination necessary. And yet we had a factor of production, management, whose function was to coordinate. Why was it needed if the pricing system provided all the coordination necessary? The same problem presented itself to me at that time in another guise. The Russian Revolution had taken place only 14 years earlier. We knew then very little about how planning would actually be carried out in a communist system. Lenin had said that the economic system in Russia would be run as one big factory. However, many economists in the West maintained that this was an impossibility. And yet there were factories in the West, and some of them were extremely large. How did one reconcile the views expressed by economists on the role of the pricing system and the impossibility of successful central economic planning with the existence of management and of these apparently planned societies, firms, operating within our own economy?[2]

I found the answer by the summer of 1932. It was to realize that there were costs of using the pricing mechanism. What the prices are have to be discovered. There are negotiations to be undertaken, contracts have to be drawn up, inspections have to be made, arrangements have to be made to settle disputes, and so on. These costs have come to be known as transaction costs. Their existence implies that methods of coordination alternative to the market, which are themselves costly and in various ways imperfect, may nonetheless be preferable to relying on the pricing mechanism, the only method of coordination normally analyzed by economists. It was the avoidance of the costs of carrying out transactions through the market that could explain the existence of the firm in which the allocation of factors came about as a result of administrative decisions (and I thought it did). In my 1937 article I argued that in a competitive system there would be an optimum of planning since a firm, that little planned society, could only continue to exist if it performed its coordination function at a lower cost than would be incurred if it were achieved by means of market transactions and also at a lower cost than this same function could be performed by another firm. To have an efficient economic system it is necessary not only to have markets but also areas of planning within organizations of the appropriate size. What this mix should be we find as a result of competition. This is what I said in

---

[2] A fuller account of these events will be found in Oliver E. Williamson and Sidney G. Winter (editors), 1991, pages. 34–47.

my article of 1937. However, as we know from a letter I wrote in 1932 which has been preserved, all the essentials of this argument had been presented in a lecture I gave in Dundee at the beginning of October, 1932 (see Williamson and Winter, 1991, pages 34–5). I was then 21 years of age, and the sun never ceased to shine. 1 could never have imagined that these ideas would become some 60 years later a major justification for the award of a Nobel Prize. And it is a strange experience to be praised in my eighties for work I did in my twenties.

There is no doubt that the recognition by economists of the importance of the role of the firm in the functioning of the economy will prompt them to investigate its activities more closely. The work of Oliver Williamson and others has led to a greater understanding of the factors which govern what a firm does and how it does it.[3] But it would be wrong to think that the most important consequence for economics of the publication of "The Nature of the Firm" has been to direct attention to the importance of the firm in our modern economy, a result which, in my view, would have come about in any case. What I think will be considered in the future to have been the important contribution of this article is the explicit introduction of transaction costs into economic analysis. I argued in "The Nature of the Firm" that the existence of transaction costs leads to the emergence of the firm. But the effects are pervasive in the economy. Businessmen in deciding on their ways of doing business and on what to produce have to take into account transaction costs. If the costs of making an exchange are greater than the gains which that exchange would bring, that exchange would not take place and the greater production that would flow from specialization would not be realized. In this way transaction costs affect not only contractual arrangements, but also what goods and services are produced. Not to include transaction costs in the theory leaves many aspects of the working of the economic system unexplained, including the emergence of the firm, but much else besides. In fact, a large part of what we think of as economic activity is designed to accomplish what high transaction costs would otherwise prevent or to reduce transaction costs so that individuals can freely negotiate and we can take advantage of that diffused knowledge of which Hayek has told us.

I know of only one part of economics in which transaction costs have been used to explain a major feature of the economic system, and that relates to the evolution and use of money. Adam Smith pointed out the hindrances to commerce that would arise in an economic system in which there was a division of labor but in which all exchange had to take the form of barter. No one would be able to buy anything unless he possessed something that the producer wanted. This difficulty, he explained, could be overcome by the use of money. A person wishing to buy something in a barter system has to find someone who has this product for sale but who also wants some of the goods possessed by the potential buyer. Similarly, a person wishing to sell something has to find someone who both wants what he has to offer and also possesses something that the potential seller wants. Exchange in a barter system requires what

---

[3] Amendment made by the author, R.H.C., June 2003.

W. S. Jevons called "this double coincidence." Clearly the search for partners in exchange with suitable qualifications is likely to be very costly and will prevent many potentially beneficial exchanges from taking place. The benefit brought about by the use of money consists of a reduction in transaction costs. The use of money also reduces transaction costs by facilitating the drawing up of contracts as well as by reducing the quantity of goods that need to be held for purposes of exchange. However, the nature of the benefits secured by the use of money seems to have faded into the background so far as economists are concerned, and it does not seem to have been noticed that there are other features of the economic system which exist because of the need to mitigate transaction costs.

I now turn to that other article cited by the Swedish Academy, "The Problem of Social Cost," published some 30 years ago. I will not say much here about its influence on legal scholarship, which has been immense, but will mainly consider its influence on economics, which has not been immense, although I believe that in time it will be. It is my view that the approach used in that article will ultimately transform the structure of microeconomics—and I will explain why. I should add that in writing this article I had no such general aim in mind. I thought that I was exposing the weaknesses of Pigou's analysis of the divergence between private and social products, an analysis generally accepted by economists, and that was all. It was only later, and in part as a result of conversations with Steven Cheung in the 1960's that I came to see the general significance for economic theory of what I had written in that article and also to see more clearly what questions needed to be further investigated.

Pigou's conclusion and that of most economists using standard economic theory was (and perhaps still is) that some kind of government action (usually the imposition of taxes) was required to restrain those whose actions had harmful effects on others (often termed negative externalities). What I showed in that article, as I thought, was that in a regime of zero transaction costs, an assumption of standard economic theory, negotiations between the parties would lead to those arrangements being made which would maximize wealth and this irrespective of the initial assignment of rights. This is the infamous Coase theorem, named and formulated by George Stigler, although it is based on work of mine. Stigler argues that the Coase theorem follows from the standard assumptions of economic theory. Its logic cannot be questioned, only its domain (Stigler, 1989, pages 631–3). I do not disagree with Stigler. However, I tend to regard the Coase theorem as a stepping stone on the way to an analysis of an economy with positive transaction costs. The significance to me of the Coase theorem is that it undermines the Pigovian system. Since standard economic theory assumes transaction costs to be zero, the Coase theorem demonstrates that the Pigovian solutions are unnecessary in these circumstances. Of course, it does not imply, when transaction costs are positive, that government actions (such as government operation, regulation, or taxation, including subsidies) could not produce a better result than relying on negotiations between individuals in the market. Whether this would be so could be discovered not by studying imaginary governments but what real governments actually do. My conclusion: let us study the world of positive transaction costs.

If we move from a regime of zero transaction costs to one of positive transaction costs, what becomes immediately clear is the crucial importance of the legal system in this new world. I explained in "The Problem of Social Cost" that what are traded on the market are not, as is often supposed by economists, physical entities, but the rights to perform certain actions, and the rights which individuals possess are established by the legal system. While we can imagine in the hypothetical world of zero transaction costs that the parties to an exchange would negotiate to change any provision of the law which prevents them from taking whatever steps are required to increase the value of production, in the real world of positive transaction costs, such a procedure would be extremely costly and would make unprofitable, even where it was allowed, a great deal of such contracting around the law. Because of this, the rights which individuals possess, with their duties and privileges, will be, to a large extent, what the law determines. As a result, the legal system will have a profound effect on the working of the economic system and may in certain respects be said to control it. It is obviously desirable that these rights should be assigned to those who can use them most productively and with incentives that lead them to do so and that, to discover (and maintain) such a distribution of rights, the costs of their transference should be low, through clarity in the law and by making the legal requirements for such transfers less onerous. Since this can come about only if there is an appropriate system of property rights (and they are enforced), it is easy to understand why so many academic lawyers (at least in the United States) have found so attractive the task of uncovering the character of such a property-rights system and why the subject of "law and economics" has flourished in American law schools. Indeed, work is going forward at such a pace that I do not consider it overoptimistic to believe that the main outlines of the subject will be drawn within five or ten years.

Until quite recently, most economists seem to have been unaware of this relationship between the economic and legal systems except in the most general way. Stock and produce exchanges are often used by economists as examples of perfect or near-perfect competition. But these exchanges regulate in great detail the activities of traders (and this quite apart from any public regulation there may be). What can be traded, when it can be traded, the terms of settlement, and so on are all laid down by the authorities of the exchange. There is, in effect, a private law. Without such rules and regulations, the speedy conclusion of trades would not be possible. Of course, when trading takes place outside exchanges (and this is almost all trading) and where the dealers are scattered in space and have very divergent interests, as in retailing and wholesaling, such a private law would be difficult to establish, and their activities will be regulated by the laws of the State. It makes little sense for economists to discuss the process of exchange without specifying the institutional setting within which the trading takes place, since this affects the incentives to produce and the costs of transacting. I think this is now beginning to be recognized and has been made crystal-clear by what is going on in Eastern Europe today. The time has surely gone in which economists could analyze in great detail two individuals exchanging nuts for berries on the edge of the forest and then feel that their analysis of the process of exchange was complete, illuminating though this analysis may be in certain respects. The process of contracting needs to be studied in a real-world setting. We would then learn of the problems that are encountered and of how they are overcome, and we would certainly become aware of the richness of the institutional alternatives between which we have to choose.

Oliver Williamson has ascribed the non-use or limited use of my thesis in "The Nature of the Firm" to the fact that it has not been made "operational," by which he means that the concept of transaction costs has not been incorporated into a general theory. I think this is correct. There have been two reasons for this. First, incorporating transaction costs into standard economic theory, which has been based on the assumption that they are zero, would be very difficult, and economists who, like most scientists, as Thomas Kuhn has told us, are extremely conservative in their methods, have not been inclined to attempt it. Second, Williamson has also pointed out that although I was correct in making the choice between organization within the firm or through the market the centerpiece of my analysis, I did not indicate what the factors were that determined the outcome of this choice and thus made it difficult for others to build on what is often described as a "fundamental insight." This also is true. But the interrelationships which govern the mix of market and hierarchy, to use Williamson's terms, are extremely complex, and in our present state of ignorance it will not be easy to discover what these factors are. What we need is more empirical work. In a paper written for a conference of the National Bureau of Economic Research, I explained why I thought this was so. This is what I said: "An inspired theoretician might do as well without such empirical work, but my own feeling is that the inspiration is most likely to come through the stimulus provided by the patterns, puzzles, and anomalies revealed by the systematic gathering of data, particularly when the prime need is to break our existing habits of thought (Coase, 1988, page 71). This statement was made in 1970. I still think that in essentials it is true today. Although much interesting and important research was done in the 1970's and 1980's and we certainly know much more than we did in 1970, there is little doubt that a great deal more empirical work is needed. However, I have come to the conclusion that the main obstacle faced by researchers in industrial organization is the lack of available data on contracts and the activities of firms. I have therefore decided to do something about it.

Believing that there is a great deal of data on contracts and the activities of firms in the United States available in government departments and agencies in Washington, DC, and that this information is largely unknown to economists, I organized a conference at the University of Chicago Law School in the summer of 1990 at which government officials presented papers in which they described what data was available and how to get access to it and also reported on some of the research being carried out within their departments. The audience consisted of academic economists. It was, as a colleague remarked, a case of supply meeting demand. The proceedings of this conference will be published in a special issue of the *Journal of Law and Economics*.[4] This availability of data

---

[4] Amendment made by the author, R.H.C., June 2003.

and the encouragement given to all researchers working on the institutional structure of production by the award to me of the Nobel Prize should result in a reduction in that elegant but sterile theorizing so commonly found in the economics literature on industrial organization and should lead to studies which increase our understanding of how the real economic system works.

My remarks have sometimes been interpreted as implying that I am hostile to the mathematization of economic theory. This is untrue. Indeed, once we begin to uncover the real factors affecting the performance of the economic system, the complicated interrelations between them will clearly necessitate a mathematical treatment, as in the natural sciences, and economists like myself, who write in prose, will take their bow. May this period soon come.

I am very much aware that many economists whom I respect and admire will not agree with the opinions I have expressed, and some may even be offended by them. But a scholar must be content with the knowledge that what is false in what he says will soon be exposed and, as for what is true, he can count on ultimately seeing it accepted, if only he lives long enough.

REFERENCES

Coase, R. H. 1988. *The Firm, The Market, and the Law*. Chicago: University of Chicago Press.

Demsetz, Harold. 1988. *Ownership, Control, and the Firm*, Vol. I. Oxford: Blackwell.

Holmstrom, Bengt and Jean, Tirole. 1989. "The Theory of the Firm" in Richard Schmalensee and Robert D. Willig (eds.), *Handbook of Industrial Organization*. Amsterdam: North-Holland, pp. 61–128.

Peltzman, Sam. 1991. "The Handbook of Industrial Organization: A Review Article". *Journal of Political Economy* 99: 201–217.

Robbins, Lionel. 1932. *The Nature and Significance of Economic Science*. London: Macmillan.

Stigler, George J. 1989. "Two Notes on the Coase Theorem". *Yale Law Journal* 99: 631–633.

Williamson, Oliver E. and Sidney G. Winter (eds.). 1991. *The Nature of the Firm, Origins, Evolution, and Development*. Oxford: Oxford University Press.

3. Transaction Cost Economics

OLIVER E. WILLIAMSON

Transaction cost economics is an effort to better understand complex economic organization by selectively joining law, economics, and organization theory. As against neoclassical economics, which is predominantly concerned with price and output, relies extensively on marginal analysis, and describes the firm as a production function (which is a technological construction), transaction cost economics (TCE) is concerned with the allocation of economic activity across alternative modes of organization (markets, firms, bureaus, etc.), employs discrete structural analysis, and describes the firm as a governance structure (which is an organizational construction). Real differences notwithstanding, orthodoxy and TCE are in many ways complements—one being more well-suited to aggregation in the context of simple market exchange, the other being more well-suited to the microanalytics of complex contracting and nonmarket organization.

I begin by contrasting the lens of contract (out of which TCE works) with the lens of choice (orthodoxy). Vertical integration, which is the paradigm problem for TCE, is then examined. The operationalization of TCE is discussed in Section 3. Variations on a theme are sketched in Section 4. Public policy is discussed in Section 5. Concluding remarks follow.

1. THE LENSES OF CHOICE AND CONTRACT[1]

Big Ideas

Hal Varian has recently distinguished between important ideas and Big Ideas and describes Ronald Coase's classic paper, "The Nature of the Firm" (1937) as a Big Idea (2002, p. C2). Although there is widespread agreement on this, the nature of the big idea took a long time to register. Thus as of 1972, thirty-five years after the publication of "The Nature of the Firm," Coase described his 1937 article as "much cited and little used" (1972, p. 63). It was much cited because it was onto something important, perhaps even big. But it was little used because the big idea was only dimly perceived and/or lacked operationalization (Coase, 1992, pp. 716–718).

---

[1] This subsection is based on Williamson (2002b).

The essence of the Coasian contribution has been variously described (Williamson, 1994, p. 202; North, 2000, p. 37; Werin, 2000, p. 45). For the purposes of TCE, I contend that the overarching big idea was to move from choice to contract: bring the lens of contract systematically to bear on economic phenomena of all kinds. For many transactions, of which the make-or-buy decision is one (Coase, 1937), the contractual structure is easily recognized. Other transactions, such as the externality problem (Coase, 1960), needed to be reformulated to bring out their latent contractual features. The object, in these and other cases described herein, is to uncover previously neglected but, often, consequential features, the discovery of which often leads to different and, sometimes, deeper understandings than the orthodox lens of choice affords. If, as James Buchanan declares, "mutuality of advantage from voluntary exchange is...the most fundamental of all understandings in economics" (2001, p. 29), then at least some of us should be thinking of economics as the "science of exchanges" (Buchanan, 2001, p. 28).[2]

The Sciences of Choice and Contract

Economics throughout the 20th century has been developed predominantly as a science of choice. As Lionel Robbins famously put it in his book, The Nature and Significance of Economic Science, "Economics is the science which studies human behavior as a relationship between ends and scarce means which have alternative uses" (1932, p. 16). Choice has been developed in two parallel constructions: the theory of consumer behavior, in which consumers maximize utility, and the theory of the firm as a production function, in which firms maximize profit. Economists who work out of such setups emphasize how quantities are influenced by changes in relative prices and available resources, a project which became the "dominant paradigm" for economics throughout the twentieth century (Reder, 1999, p. 48).

But the science of choice is not the only lens for studying complex economic phenomena, nor is it always the most instructive lens. The other main but less fully developed approach is the science of contract. Indeed, Buchanan (1975, p. 225) avers that economics as a discipline went "wrong" in its preoccupation with the science of choice and the optimization apparatus associated therewith. What was needed was the parallel development of a science of contract. Awaiting this, some phenomena would go unnoticed, others would be poorly understood, and public policy error would result.

---

[2] Students of the history of thought will remind us that catallactics—meaning "the science of exchanges"—has much earlier origins. Indeed, a book by E. B. de Condillac on this subject was published in 1776, which is when The Wealth of Nations first appeared (see Murray Rothbard (1987, pp. 377–378) for an historical sketch). Recurrent interest in the science of contract notwithstanding, it has operated in the shadows of the science of choice. Why the disparity? Here as elsewhere, good ideas need to be operationalized. Contractual analysis has gotten under way in a sustained way only during the past 40 years.

As perceived by Buchanan, the principal needs for a science of contract were to the field of public finance and took the form of public ordering: "Politics is a structure of complex exchange among individuals, a structure within which persons seek to secure collectively their own privately defined objectives that cannot be efficiently secured through simple market exchanges" (1987, p. 296; emphasis added). Thinking contractually in the public ordering domain leads into a focus on the rules of the game. Issues of a constitutional economics kind are posed (Buchanan and Tullock, 1962; Brennan and Buchanan, 1985).

Whatever the rules of the game, the lens of contract is also usefully brought to bear on the play of the game. This latter is what I refer to as private ordering, which entails self-help efforts by the immediate parties to a transaction to align incentives and craft governance structures that are better attuned to their exchange needs. John R. Commons' prescient statement on the nature of the economic problem provides the unifying theme: "the ultimate unit of activity... must contain in itself the three principles of conflict, mutuality, and order. This unit is the transaction" (1932, p. 4).[3] Not only does transaction cost economics take the transaction to be the basic unit of analysis, but governance is the means by which to infuse order, thereby to mitigate conflict and realize mutual gain.

Although market competition serves these governance purposes in the context of the "simple market exchanges" to which Buchanan made reference (which is wholly in the spirit of orthodox price theory), transaction cost economics is predominantly concerned with complex market exchange where there are small numbers of parties on each side of the transaction. Rather than examine such issues with the price-theoretic apparatus of oligopoly or oligopsony, transaction cost economics focuses instead on uncovering and explicating the strategic hazards that are posed by small numbers exchange in the context of incomplete contracting and the cost-effective deployment of governance to mitigate these hazards. Strategic issues that had been ignored by neoclassical economists from 1870 to 1970 now make their appearance (Makowski and Ostroy, 2001, pp. 482–483, 490–491).

Figure 1 sets out the main distinctions. The initial divide is between the science of choice (orthodoxy) and the science of contract. The latter then divides into public (constitutional economics) and private ordering parts, where the second is split into two related branches. One branch deals with ex ante incentive alignment (mechanism design, agency theory, the formal property rights literature) while the second features the ex post governance of contractual

---

[3] Not everyone associated with the lens of contract would agree. Coase, for example, contends that "American institutionalism," of which Commons was a prominent part, "is a dreary subject... All it had was a stance of hostility to the standard economic theory. It certainly led to nothing" (1984, pp. 229–230). My view is that Commons was ahead of his time. He had a lens of contract conception of economics as early as the 1920s.

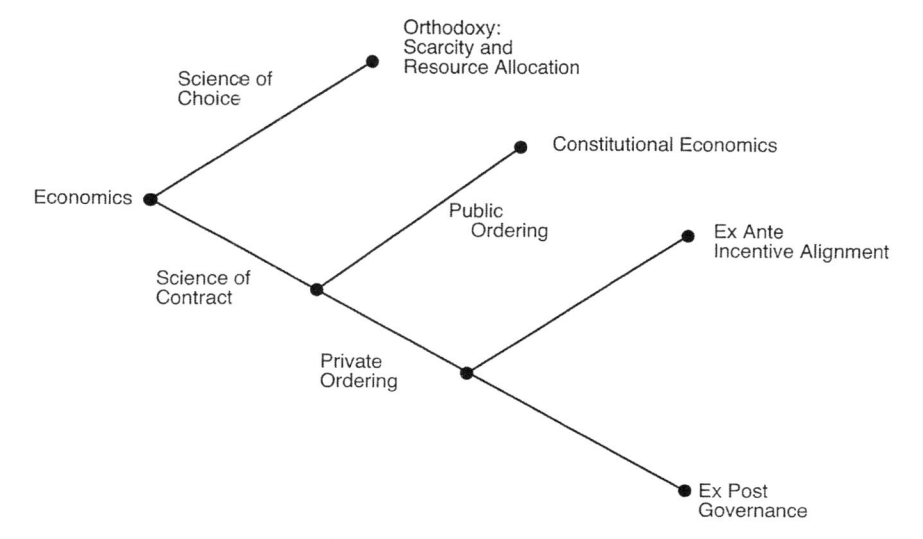

Figure 1. The sciences of choice and contract

relations (contract implementation). Albeit related, these two are in tension. Thus whereas transaction cost economics locates the main analytical action in the ex post stage of contract (where maladaptation problems appear), the formal incentive alignment literature annihilates ex post governance.[4] One device for accomplishing this is to assume common knowledge of payoffs and costless bargaining.

The use of strong assumptions (of which common knowledge of payoffs and costless bargaining are two) to strip away inessentials and get at the essence is, to be sure, vital to the scientific enterprise. Simplifications, however, that lose contact with core issues are deeply problematic: "A model can be right in ... [a] mechanical sense ... [yet be] unenlightening because ... [it is] imperfectly suited to the subject matter. It can obscure the key interactions, instead of spotlighting them" (Solow, 2001, p. 112). In the degree to which the core issues that are posed by contractual incompleteness are those of maladaptation,

---

[4] Contract theorists who concentrate the analytical action on the ex ante incentive alignment stage of contracting might complain that TCE makes strong assumptions also, the effect of which is to annihilate the ex ante incentive alignment stage. For example, TCE assumes that contracting parties in intermediate product markets are risk neutral, whence efficient risk bearing plays no role in incentive alignment. Contract theorists who rely on risk aversion for their main results might protest against risk neutrality.

Be that as it may, TCE also assumes that contracting parties look ahead, recognize consequential contractual hazards that arise during contract implementation, and factor these into the ex ante contractual design—by pricing out unrelieved contractual hazards and by introducing credible commitments (in cost effective degree)—so ex ante and ex post stages of contract are definitely joined. What TCE disallows are assumptions which vaporize maladaptation and strategizing during contract implementation—of which common knowledge of payoffs and costless bargaining are two.

formalizations that preserve rather than annihilate ex post governance are needed (Bajari and Tadelis, 2001).

2. THE PARADIGM PROBLEM: VERTICAL INTEGRATION

Contract is an encompassing concept. Rather than treat the issue in its full generality, it will be instructive to begin with a specific puzzle of economic organization, ideally one for which other contractual issues will turn out to be variations on a theme.

The obvious transaction with which to begin is that of vertical integration, or, in more mundane terms, the make-or-buy decision. Not only is the make-or-buy decision the transaction on which Coase focused in 1937, but it has a prior and continuing history of importance within economics. Examining the intermediate product market transactions (within and between firms) also has an advantage in that it relieves many of the asymmetry conditions—of information, budget, legal talent, risk aversion, and the like—that complicate the analysis of transactions in final product markets.[5]

Coase's classic article opens with a basic puzzle: Why does a firm emerge at all in a specialized exchange economy? If the answer resides in entrepreneurship, why is coordination "the work of the price mechanism in one case and the entrepreneur in the other" (Coase, 1937, p. 389)? Coase appealed to transaction cost economizing as the hitherto missing factor for explaining why markets were used in some cases and hierarchy in other cases and averred that "The main reason why it is profitable to establish a firm would seem to be that there is a cost of using the price mechanism, the most obvious...[being] that of discovering what the relevant prices are" (1937, p. 391). That sounds plausible, but is it truly comparative? How is it that internal procurement by the firm avoids the cost of price discovery?

The "obvious" answer is that sole-source internal supply avoids the need to consult the market about prices because internal accounting prices of a formulaic kind (say, of a cost-plus kind) can be used to transfer a good or service from one internal stage to another. If, however, that is the source of the advantage of internal organization over market procurement, the obvious lesson is to apply this same practice to outside procurement. The firm simply advises its purchasing office to turn a blind eye to the market by placing orders, period by period, with a qualified sole-source external supplier who agrees to sell on cost-plus terms. In

---

[5] Final product market transactions and transactions between suppliers and distributors need to be distinguished. The former refer to transactions between firms (as suppliers) and final consumers (buyers). Serious asymmetry conditions for which consumer protections are sometimes warranted arise for final product market transactions. By contrast, the transactions between the manufacturer and the distributor are between firms. Thus the manufacturer can sell outright to distributors (which is a market transaction). Or the manufacturer can integrate forward into distribution (so both stages are under unified ownership/hierarchy). Or the manufacturer can create franchisees (which are a hybrid mode of contracting).

that event, firm and market are put on a parity in price discovery respects—which is to say that the price discovery burden that Coase ascribes to the market does not survive comparative institutional scrutiny.

Even, however, if price discovery did survive comparative institutional scrutiny, that seems to be a thin basis upon which to rest the case for using firms rather than markets if, as I contend, firm and market differ in kind rather than in degree. What economic purposes are served by the discrete structural changes that distinguish market and hierarchy? Does the move from choice (where prices are focal) to contract implicate other, possibly more basic, considerations? What rudiments inform the logic of contract and comparative economic organization?

3. THE RUDIMENTS

This last invites the student of economic organization to step back and address contract "on its own terms." What are the attributes of human actors that bear on the efficacy of contract? What unit of analysis should be employed? Of the many purposes of contract, which are salient? How are alternative modes of governance described? What refutable implications accrue upon reformulating the problem of economic organization in comparative contractual terms? Are the data corroborative? What are the public policy ramifications?

(a) Human Actors

If "Nothing is more fundamental in setting our research agenda and informing our research methods than our view of the nature of the human beings whose behavior we are studying" (Simon, 1985, p. 303), then economists and other social scientists are well-advised to describe the key cognitive, self-interest, and other attributes of human actors on which their analyses rest. Simon's view of cognition is that the usual hyperrationality assumption be supplanted by bounded rationality—behavior that is "intendedly rational but only limitedly so" (1957a, p. xxiv). He further recommends that self-interest be described as "frailty of motive" (1985, p. 305). TCE concurs that bounded rationality is the appropriate cognitive assumption and takes the chief lesson of bounded rationality for the study of contract to be that <u>all complex contracts are unavoidably incomplete</u>. But TCE also takes a further step, which takes exception with the common view that bounded rationality implies that human actors are myopic. As against myopia, human actors are assumed to have the capacity to look ahead, uncover possible contractual hazards, and work out the contractual ramifications (Shultz, 1995).

TCE also pushes beyond frailty of motive to make provision for opportunism. This latter does not deny that most people will do what they say and some will do more most of the time. Opportunism, however, has reference to exceptions—outliers where there is a lot at stake and parties are often observed to defect from the spirit of cooperation to insist on the letter of the incomplete contract. Strategic considerations are introduced upon making provision for opportunism.

(b) Unit of Analysis

The natural unit of analysis for lens of contract purposes is the transaction. Naming a unit of analysis is always much easier, however, than identifying the critical dimensions for describing the unit of analysis—as witness the fact that the key attributes for so many would-be units of analysis are never identified.[6] Awaiting dimensionalization, transaction cost economics remained a largely tautological construction.

To be sure, transactions can be variously described—depending on the purpose. Transaction cost economics holds that three dimensions that have pervasive ramifications for governance are asset specificity (which takes a variety of forms—physical, human, site, dedicated, brand name—and is a measure of nonredeployability), the disturbances to which transactions are subject (and to which potential maladaptations accrue), and the frequency with which transactions recur (which bears both on the efficacy of reputation effects in the market and the incentive to incur the cost of specialized internal governance). The absence of asset specificity describes the ideal transaction in law and economics for which competition works well: "sharp in by clear agreement; sharp out by clear performance" (Macneil, 1973, p. 734). As asset specificity builds up, however, bilateral dependency develops and, in combination with uncertainty (which pushes incomplete contracts out of alignment), the aforementioned contractual complications set in.

(c) Main Purpose

Interestingly, both the economist Friedrich Hayek (1945) and the organization theorist Chester Barnard (1938) were in agreement that adaptation is the central problem of economic organization. Hayek (pp. 526–527) focused on the adaptations of economic actors who adjust spontaneously to changes in the market, mainly as signaled by changes in relative prices: Upon looking "at the price system as...a mechanism for communicating information," the marvel of the market resides in "how little the individual participants need to know to be able to take the right action." By contrast, Barnard featured coordinated adaptation among economic actors working through administration (hierarchy). The latter is accomplished not spontaneously but in a "conscious, deliberate, purposeful" way (p. 9) and comes into play when the simple market exchanges on which Hayek focused break down.

In effect, the adaptations to which Hayek refers are <u>autonomous</u> adaptations in which individual parties respond to market opportunities as signaled by changes in relative prices whereas the adaptations of concern to Barnard are <u>cooperative</u> adaptations accomplished through administration within the firm.

---

[6] Examples of would-be units of analysis for which operational content is missing include the role (see Simon's critique (1957a, p. xxx), the decision-premise (which is Simon's candidate, but which has found little application outside of cognitive psychology (Newell and Simon, 1972)), and the routine (Nelson and Winter, 1982). The next two paragraphs and Section 4 are based on Williamson (2002a).

Because a high performance economic system will display adaptive capacities of both kinds, an understanding and appreciation for both markets and hierarchies (rather than the comparative economic systems dichotomy between markets or hierarchies) is needed. The firm for these purposes is described not as a production function (which is a technological construction) but as a governance structure (which is an organizational construction). And the market is described similarly. The lens of contract, as against the lens of choice, is made the cutting edge.

One of the advantages of focusing on adaptation as the main case is that it brings added meaning to the idea of mutual gain. It is elementary that gains from trade will always be realized by moving onto the contract curve. But how is this to be accomplished in a world where complex contracts are incomplete and are implemented over time in the face of disturbances for which contingent provisions either have not been made or, if made, are often in error? Crafting governance structures that are attuned to the hazards and help the parties to restore efficiency (return to the shifting contract curve) where otherwise a costly impasse would develop is needed in these circumstances. More attention to designing processes that have good adaptive properties (and less to concentrating all of the action in the ex ante incentive alignment stage) is thus one of the central lessons of TCE.

(d) Governance Structures

Examining economic organization through the lens of contract both places the spotlight on ex post adaptation and, in the process, gives prominence to the role of governance. Specifically, TCE holds that each generic mode of governance is defined by a syndrome of internally consistent attributes to which different adaptive strengths and weaknesses accrue.

The three attributes of principal importance for describing governance structures are (1) incentive intensity, (2) administrative controls, and (3) contract law regime. Spot markets and hierarchy differ with respect to these attributes as follows: the high-powered incentives of markets are supplanted by low-powered incentives when transactions are organized within firms; market exchange is a hands-off control mechanism whereas hierarchy involves considerable hands-on administrative involvement; and whereas disputes in markets are treated in a legalistic way and rely on court ordering, courts refuse to hear (most) internal disputes, whereupon the firm becomes its own court of ultimate appeal. Firms have access to fiat that markets do not because of these dispute resolution differences.[7]

Governance, moreover, is an encompassing concept. Going beyond polar forms, all modes of organization within which (or with the support of which)

---

[7] One of the reasons why markets lack fiat is that attempts to award decision rights to autonomous agents by contract (e.g., A will decide disputed matters of type X; B will decided disputed matters of type Y; etc.) are commonly unenforceable. That is because one of the parties to a market contract can invoke (invent) a "technicality," the effect of which is to bring the dispute before the courts.

Table 1. Attributes of leading generic modes of governance

	Governance Modes		
Governance Attributes	market	hybrid	hierarchy
incentives	high-powered	less high-powered	low-powered
administrative support by bureaucracy	nil	some	much
contract law regime	legalistic	contract as framework	firm as own court of ultimate appeal (fiat)

transactions are managed come under scrutiny. Hybrid modes of contracting to which credible commitment supports have been crafted (penalties against premature termination, specialized dispute settlement mechanisms and the like) are especially important. Table 1 summarizes the key attributes of (spot) market, hybrids, and hierarchies. As developed in the text accompanying Figures 2 and 3 below, the clusters of attributes that define these three alternative modes of

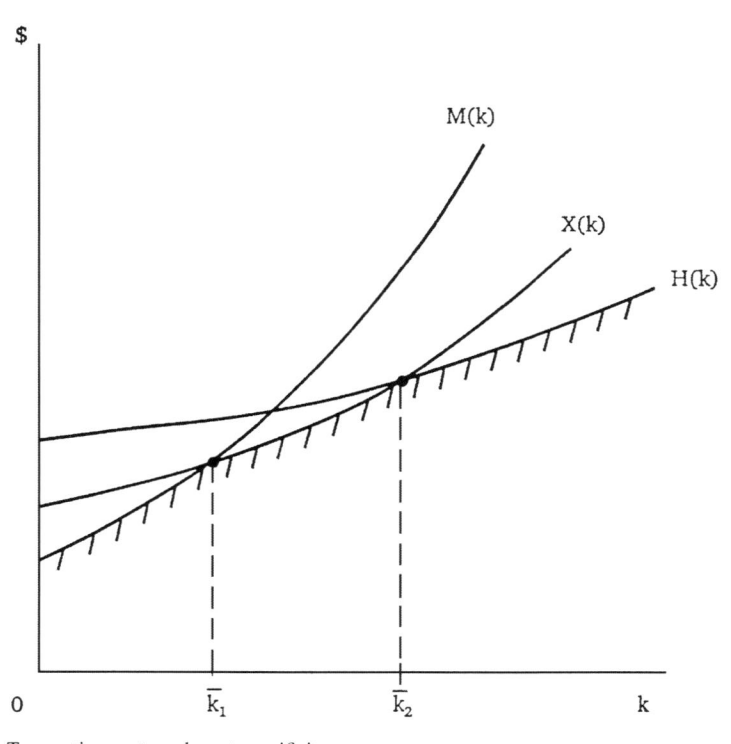

Figure 2. Transaction costs and asset specificity

50   *Oliver E. Williamson*

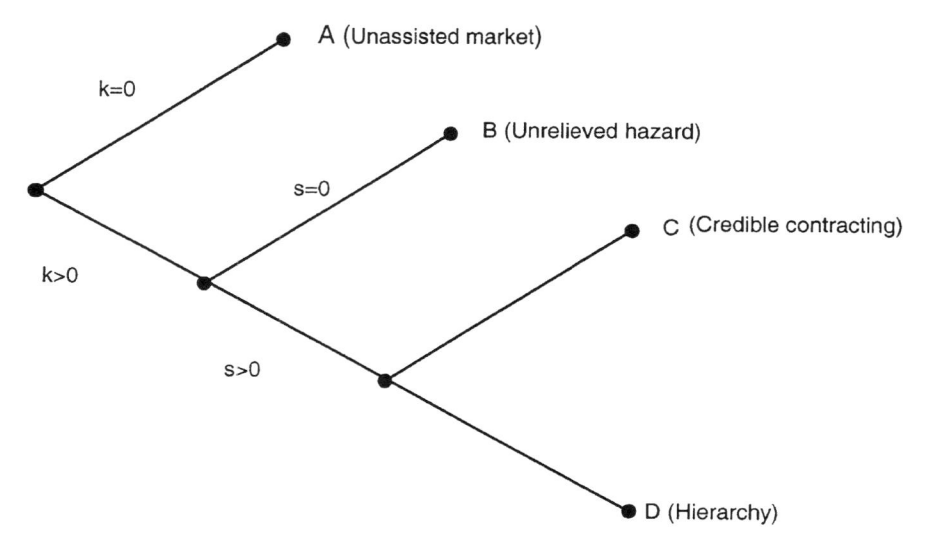

Figure 3. Simple contracting schema

[Tree diagram with nodes: k=0 leading to A (Unassisted market); k>0 branching to s=0 leading to B (Unrelieved hazard), and s>0 branching to C (Credible contracting) and D (Hierarchy)]

governance give rise to differential transaction costs among modes, conditional on the attributes of the transactions to be organized.

An unremarked governance complication also needs to be introduced. This is that organization, like the law, has a life of its own (Selznick, 1950, p. 10). Issues of internal organization that have been featured by organization theorists (Barnard, 1938; Simon, 1947; March and Simon, 1958) and by sociologists (Michels, 1912; Merton, 1936; Selznick, 1949; Scott, 1992) thus arise. Note in this connection that while it is relatively easy to show that internal organization is subject to incentive limits and bureaucratic distortions, it is much more difficult to show that *comparative* cost consequences accrue upon taking a transaction out of the market and organizing it internally (Williamson, 1985, Chap. 6). That is because the goods and services traded in a market are produced within firms. The question of make-or-buy is thus whether the costs (including bureaucratic costs) are greater in two autonomous firms than in one combined entity.

TCE uncovers and explicates the incentive and bureaucratic cost consequences that attend the move from market to hierarchy by postulating two processes: replication and selective intervention. Were it that the firm could replicate the market in all circumstances where market procurement works well and intervene selectively (if expected net gains can be projected) where markets break down, then the firm could never do worse than the market (through replication) and would sometimes do better (through selective intervention). As it turns out, it is impossible to realize this ambition. Incentives are unavoidably compromised[8] and added bureaucratic cots are unavoidably incurred upon taking a transaction out of the market and organizing it internally. The upshot is that the move from market to hierarchy is attended by tradeoffs. Discriminating alignment is thus needed.

(e) Predictions and Empirical Testing

The main engine from which the predictions of TCE are derived is that of discriminating alignment, according to which transactions, which differ in their attributes, are aligned with governance structures, which differ in their cost and (adaptive) competence, so as to effect a transaction cost economizing result. The upshot is that there is a place for each generic mode of governance, yet each should be kept in its place. The TCE answer to the Coasian puzzle of which transactions go where and why resides precisely in discriminating alignment, the efficacy of which relies in part on weak-form natural selection (Simon, 1983, p. 69) to penalize errors of inefficient alignment.

It will be convenient here to focus on three modes: spot markets (M), hybrid modes of contracting (X), into which credible commitments have been introduced, and hierarchies (H). The basic argument is that (1) markets are well-suited to making autonomous adaptations, firms enjoy the advantage for comparative adaptation purposes, and hybrids are located in between, (2) the needs for adaptation vary among transactions (especially with reference to asset specificity), and (3) bureaucratic cost burdens increase as transactions move from market, to hybrid, to hierarchy.

In a heuristic way, the transaction cost consequences of organizing transactions in markets (M) and hierarchies (H) as a function of asset specificity (k) are shown in Figure 2. As shown, the bureaucratic burdens of hierarchy place it at an initial disadvantage (k = 0), but the cost differences between M(k) and H(k) narrow as asset specificity builds up and eventually reverse as the need for cooperative adaptation becomes especially great (k $\gg$ 0). As indicated, moreover, the hybrid mode of organization X(k), is viewed as a market-preserving credible contracting mode that possesses adaptive attributes located between classical markets and hierarchies. Incentive intensity and administrative control thus take on intermediate values and Karl Llewellyn's (1931) concept of contract

---

[8] The issues here are rather involved. The interested reader is referred to Williamson (1985, Chap. 6) for a discussion. Briefly the argument is that (1) replication is essential if parity between firm and market is to be assumed, (2) such replication implies that incentives are unchanged in each of the separable stages upon taking a transaction out of the market and organizing it internally, yet (3) unchanged incentive intensity cannot be accomplished if the acquiring stage exercises control over the accounting system (to include transfer prices, overhead rates, depreciation, and the like) and cannot credibly commit to behaving nonstrategically, to include intervening always but only for good cause (selective intervention).

But there is more. Not only is incentive intensity unavoidably weakened when transactions move from market to hierarchy, but cooperative adaptation across successive stages is promoted by intentionally weakening incentive intensity within the firm.

as framework applies. As shown in Figure 2, M(0) < X(0) < H(0) (by reason of bureaucratic cost differences) while M' > X' > H' (which reflects the differential ability of these three modes to implement coordinated adaptation, the needs for which increase as asset specificity builds up).[9] The least cost mode of governance is thus the market for $k < \bar{k}_1$, the hybrid for $\bar{k}_1 < k < \bar{k}_2$, and hierarchy for $k > \bar{k}_2$.

Whereas many theories of vertical integration do not invite empirical testing, the transaction cost theory of vertical integration invites and has been the subject of considerable empirical analysis. Both the theory of the firm (Holmstrom and Tirole, 1989, p. 126) and the field of industrial organization (Peltzman, 1991) have been criticized for lack of empirical testing; yet empirical research in transaction cost economics has grown exponentially during the past 20 years. (For surveys, see Shelanski and Klein (1995), Lyons (1996), Crocker and Masten (1996), Rindfleisch and Heide (1997), Masten and Saussier (2000) and Boerner and Macher (2001).) Added to this are numerous applications to public policy, especially antitrust and regulation, but also to economics more generally (Dixit, 1996) and to the contiguous social sciences (especially political science). The upshot is that the theory of the firm as governance structure has become a "much used" construction.[10]

4. VARIATIONS ON A THEME

Vertical integration turns out to be a paradigm. Thus although many of the empirical tests and public policy applications have reference to the make-or-buy decision and vertical market restrictions, this same conceptual framework has application to contracting more generally. Specifically, the contractual relation between the firm and its "stakeholders"—customers, suppliers, and workers along with financial investors—turn out to be variations on the theme set out in the simple contractual schema.

---

[9] M', X', and H' refer to the marginal costs of market, hybrid, and hierarchical governance with respect to changes in asset specificity (k).

[10] Reprints of leading articles on vertical integration (by Benjamin Klein on Fisher Body-GM (1988), Paul Joskow on long-term coal contracting (1988), Kirk Monteverde and David Teece on automobile integration (1982), Scott Masten on aerospace production (1984), Erin Anderson and David Schmittlein on sales force organization (1984), George John and Barton Weitz on forward integration into distribution (1988), and Scott Masten, James Meehan, and Edward Snyder on the cost of organization (1991)) can be found in Williamson and Masten, Vol. II (1995).

This same volume includes empirical contracting articles (by Thomas Palay on rail freight contracting (1984), Victor Goldberg and John Erickson on long term petroleum coke contracts (1987), Paul Joskow on contract duration (1987), Harold Mulherin on natural gas contracting (1986), Scott Masten and Keith Crocker on take-or-pay provisions (1985), Keith Leffler and Randal Rucker on timber (1991), and Keith Crocker and Scott Masten on the long term contracting process (1991).

Empirical studies of regulation and positive political economy include Oliver Williamson (1976), Victor Goldberg (1976), George Priest (1993), Brian Levy and Pablo Spiller (1994), Barry Weingast and William Marshall (1988), and Rafael Gely and Pablo Spiller (1990). Antitrust applications include Oliver Williamson (1979), Roy Kenney and Benjamin Klein (1983), and Scott Masten and Edward Snyder (1993).

The Simple Contractual Schema

Assume that a firm can make or buy a component and assume further that the component can be supplied by either a general purpose technology or a special purpose technology. Again, let k be a measure of asset specificity. The transactions in Figure 3 that use the general purpose technology are ones for which k = 0. In this case, no specific assets are involved and the parties are essentially faceless. Those transactions that use the special purpose technology are ones for which k > 0. As earlier discussed, bilaterally dependent parties have incentives to promote continuity and safeguard their specific investments. Let s denote the magnitude of any such safeguards, which include penalties, information disclosure and verification procedures, specialized dispute resolution (such as arbitration) and, in the limit, integration of the two stages under unified ownership. An s = 0 condition is one for which no safeguards are provided; a decision to provide safeguards is reflected by an s > 0 result.

Node A in Figure 3 corresponds to the ideal transaction in law and economics: there being an absence of dependency, governance is accomplished through competitive market prices and, in the event of disputes, by court awarded damages. Node B poses unrelieved contractual hazards, in that specialized investments are exposed (k > 0) for which no safeguards (s = 0) have been provided. Such hazards will be recognized by farsighted players, who will price out the implied risks of contractual breakdown.

Added contractual supports (s > 0) are provided at nodes C and D. At node C, these contractual supports take the form of interfirm contractual safeguards. Should, however, costly contractual breakdowns continue in the face of best bilateral efforts to craft safeguards at node C, the transaction may be taken out of the market and organized under unified ownership (vertical integration) instead. Because added bureaucratic costs accrue upon taking a transaction out of the market and organizing it internally, internal organization is usefully thought of as the organization form of last resort: try markets, try hybrids, and have recourse to the firm only when all else fails. Node D, the unified firm, thus comes in only as higher degrees of asset specificity and added uncertainty pose greater needs for cooperative adaptation.

Note that the price that a supplier will bid to supply under node C conditions will be less than the price that will be bid at node B. That is because the added security features serve to reduce the risk at node C, as compared with node B, so the contractual hazard premium will be reduced. One implication is that suppliers do not need to petition buyers to provide safeguards. Because buyers will receive product on better terms (lower price) when added security is provided, buyers have the incentive to offer cost-effective credible commitments. Also note that whereas such commitments are sometimes thought of as a user-friendly way to contract, the analytical action resides in the hard-headed use of credibility to support those transactions where asset specificity and contractual hazards are at issue. Such supports are without purpose for transactions where generic technologies are employed.

The foregoing schema can be applied to virtually all transactions for which the firm is in a position to own as well as to contract with an adjacent stage—backward into raw materials, laterally into components, forward into distribution. But for some activities, ownership is either impossible or very rare.[11] For example, firms cannot own their workers or their final customers (although worker cooperatives and consumer cooperatives can be thought of in ownership terms). Also, firms rarely own their suppliers of finance. Node D drops out of the schema in cases where ownership is either prohibited by law or is otherwise rare. I begin with forward integration into distribution, after which relationships with other stakeholders of the firm, including labor, finance, and public utility regulation are successively considered.[12]

Applications

(a) Forward Integration into Distribution

I will set aside the case where mass marketers integrate backward into manufacturing and focus on forward integration into distribution by manufacturers of products or owners of brands. Specifically, consider the contractual relation between a manufacturer and large numbers of wholesalers and, especially, of retailers for the good or service in question.

Many such transactions are of a generic kind. Although branded goods and services are more specific, some require only shelf space, since advertising, promotion and any warranties are done by the manufacturer. Since the obvious way to trade with intermediaries for such transactions is through the market, in a node A fashion, what is to be inferred when such transactions are made subject to vertical market restrictions—such as customer and territorial restrictions, service restrictions, tied sales, and the like?

Price discrimination, to which allocative efficiency benefits were often ascribed, was the usual price theoretic (science of choice) explanation for such restrictions. Such efficiency claims, however, are problematic once the transaction costs of discovering customer valuations and deterring arbitrage are taken into account (Williamson, 1975, pp. 11–13). Not only are the benefits problematic, but price discrimination is a needlessly narrow interpretation.

---

[11] Closely complementary technologies are commonly relegated to the "core technology" (Thompson, 1967, pp. 19–23) and are effectively exempt from comparative institutional analysis, it being "obvious" that these are done within the firm.

[12] Natural monopoly and government bureaus can be interpreted in terms of the schema in Figure 3 as follows: First, given natural monopoly, the three "evils" to which Milton Friedman (1962, p. 128) referred—unregulated monopoly, regulation, and nationalization—correspond, roughly, to nodes B, C, and D, respectively. Also, for a good or service for which the government is the buyer, nodes A, B, and C are all market nodes (spot market, unrelieved hazard, and long-term (often cost-plus) contracting, respectively), while node D is the government bureau deciding to do the task itself. The government bureau has especially low-powered incentives, is highly bureaucratized (by design), and has its own dispute settlement machinery (Williamson, 1999).

Viewed through the lens of contract, vertical market restrictions often have the purpose and effect of infusing order into a transaction where the interests of the system and the interests of the parts are otherwise in conflict. For example, the Schwinn bicycle company imposed nonresale restrictions upon franchisees. The concern was that the integrity of the brand, which was a system asset, would be compromised by franchisees who perceived local opportunities to realize individual gain by selling to discounters, who would then sell a "bike in a box," without service or support (Williamson, 1985, pp. 183–189). More generally, the argument is this: in circumstances where market power is small, where simple market exchange (at node A) would compromise the integrity of differentiated products, and where forward integration into distribution (at node D) would be especially costly, the use of vertical market restrictions to effect credible commitments (at node C) has much to recommend it.

(b) Relationship with Labor

Because the firm is unable to own its labor, node D is irrelevant and the comparison comes down to nodes A, B, and C. Node A corresponds to the case where labor is easily redeployed to other uses or users without loss of productive value ($k = 0$). Thus although such labor may be highly skilled (as with many professionals), the lack of firm-specificity means that, transition costs aside, neither worker nor firm has an interest in crafting penalties for unwanted quits/terminations or otherwise creating costly internal labor markets (ports of entry; promotion ladders), costly information disclosure and verification procedures, and costly firm-specific dispute settlement machinery. The mutual benefits simply do not warrant the costs.

Conditions change when $k > 0$, since workers who acquire firm-specific skills will lose value if prematurely terminated (and firms will incur added training costs if such employees quit). Here, as elsewhere, unrelieved hazards (as at node B) invite governance responses to which mutual gains accrue. Because continuity has value to both firm and worker, governance features that deter termination (severance pay) and quits (nonvested benefits) and which address and settle disputes in an orderly way (grievance systems) to which the parties ascribe confidence have a lot to recommend them. These can, but need not, take the form of "unions." Whatever the name, the object is to craft a collective organizational structure (at node C) in which the parties have mutual confidence and that enhances efficiency (Baron and Kreps, 1999, pp. 130–138; Williamson, 1975, pp. 27–80, 1985, pp. 250–262).[13]

---

[13] The emphasis on collective organization as a governance response is to be distinguished from the earlier work of Gary Becker, where human asset specificity is responsible for upward sloping age-earnings profiles (1962). Becker's treatment is more in the science of choice tradition whereas mine views asset specificity through the lens of contract. These two are not mutually exclusive. They do, however, invite different public policy interpretations and redirect the empirical research agenda.

(c) Relationship with Sources of Finance

Viewed through the lens of contract, the board of directors is interpreted as a security feature that arises in support of the contract for equity finance (Williamson, 1988). More generally, debt and equity are not merely alternative modes of finance, which is the law and economics construction (Easterbrook and Fischel, 1986; Posner, 1986), but are also alternative modes of governance.

Suppose that a firm is seeking cost-effective finance for the following series of projects: general-purpose, mobile equipment; a general-purpose office building located in a population center; a general-purpose plant located in a manufacturing center; distribution facilities located somewhat more remotely; special-purpose equipment; market and product development expenses; and the like. Suppose further that debt is a governance structure that works almost entirely out of a set of rules: (1) stipulated interest payments will be made at regular intervals; (2) the business will continuously meet certain liquidity tests; (3) principal will be repaid at the loan-expiration date; and (4) in the event of default, the debtholders will exercise preemptive claims against the assets in question. In short, debt is unforgiving if things go poorly.

Such rules-based governance is well-suited to investments of a generic kind ($k = 0$), since the lender can redeploy these to alternative uses and users with little loss of productive value. Debt thus corresponds to market governance at node A. But what about investment projects of more specific (less redeployable) kinds?

Because the value of holding a preemptive claim declines as the degree of asset specificity deepens, rule-based finance of the above described kind will be made on more adverse terms. In effect, using debt to finance such projects would locate the parties at node B, where a hazard premium must be charged. The firm in these circumstances has two choices: sacrifice some of the specialized investment features in favor of greater redeployability (move back to node A), or embed the specialized investment in a governance structure to which better terms of finance will be ascribed. What would the latter entail?

Suppose that a financial instrument called equity is invented and assume that equity has the following governance properties: (1) it bears a residual-claimant status to the firm in both earnings and asset-liquidation respects; (2) it contracts for the duration of the life of the firm; and (3) a board of directors is created and awarded to equity that (a) is elected by the pro-rata votes of those who hold tradeable shares, (b) has the power to replace the management, (c) decides on management compensation, (d) has access to internal performance measures on a timely basis, (e) can authorize audits in depth for special follow-up purposes, (f) is apprised of important investment and operating proposals before they are implemented, and (g) in other respects bears a decision-review and monitoring relation to the firm's management (Fama and Jensen, 1983).[14] So construed, the board of directors is awarded to the holders of equity so as to reduce the cost

---

[14] It will not go unnoticed that this is a rather normative way to describe the board of directors. In practice, many boards are rubber stamps to the management (in exchange for handsome fees). Takeover by tender offer is important for precisely because it is a means by which to replace a protective/complacent/compliant board.

of capital by providing safeguards for projects that have limited redeployability (by moving shareholders from node B to node C).

(d)   Regulation and Natural Monopoly

The market-oriented approach to natural monopoly is to auction off the franchise to the highest bidder (Demsetz, 1968; Posner, 1972). But while this is an imaginative proposal, it is not an all-purpose construction. Viewed through the lens of contract, whether this works well or poorly depends on the nature of the transaction and the particulars of governance. The action, once again, resides in the details (Williamson, 1976)—although others counsel that to "expound the details of particular regulations and proposals... would serve only to obscure the basic issues" (Posner, 1972, p. 98).

Going beyond the initial bidding competition ("competition for the market"), the governance approach insists upon examining the contract implementation stage. Transactions to which the Fundamental Transformation applies—namely, those requiring significant investments in specific assets and that are subject to considerable market and technological uncertainty—are ones for which the efficacy of simple franchise bidding is problematic. If what had been a large numbers franchise bidding competition at the outset becomes, in effect, a small numbers supply relation during contract implementation and at the contract renewal interval, then the purported efficiency of franchise bidding is problematic.

This is not to say that franchise bidding never works. Neither is it to suggest that decisions to regulate ought not to be revisited—as witness the successful deregulation of trucking (which never should have been regulated to begin with) and more recent efforts to deregulate "network industries" (Peltzman and Whinston, 2000). I would nevertheless urge that examining deregulation through the lens of contracting is instructive for both—as it is for assessing efforts to deregulate electricity in California, where too much deference was given to the (assumed) efficacy of smoothly functioning markets and insufficient attention to potential investment and contractual hazards and appropriate governance responses thereto. As Joskow (2000, p. 51) observes: "Many policy makers and fellow travellers have been surprised by how difficult it has been to create wholesale electricity markets.... Had policy makers viewed the restructuring challenge using a TCE framework, these potential problems are more likely to have been identified and mechanisms adopted ex ante to fix them."

Here as elsewhere, the lesson is to think contractually: look ahead, recognize potential hazards, and fold these back into the design calculus. Paraphrasing Robert Michels (1962, p. 370) on oligarchy, nothing but a serene and frank examination of the contractual hazards of deregulation will enable us to mitigate these hazards.

5. Public Policy

The initial public policy applications of TCE were in the field of industrial organization, especially to antitrust and regulation. These were followed by public policy applications to labor, health, agriculture, public finance, economic development and reform, and the list goes on. If, indeed, any problem that arises as or can be reformulated as a contracting problem can be examined to advantage through the lens of contracting, then the list of applications is unending.

(a) Antitrust

A long-standing puzzle for antitrust was what to make of vertical integration. If the "natural" way to procure a good or service was in the market, why take a transaction out of the market and organize it internally? For that matter, what explained efforts by firms to go beyond simple market exchange and impose customer, territorial, and other vertical market restrictions on distributors? Issues of both kinds arose during the year that I spent as Special Economic Assistant to the head of the Antitrust Division of the U.S. Department of Justice (1966–67). Stringent vertical merger guidelines were issued by the Department in 1968. And the Justice Department mistakenly ascribed anticompetitive purposes to prohibitions against franchisee resale of bicycles in arguing the Schwinn case in 1967.[15] More generally, the prevailing view on vertical market restrictions was that these were to be interpreted "not hospitably in the common law tradition, but inhospitably in the tradition of antitrust."[16] If the natural boundary of the firm was defined by technology (the firm being viewed as a production function), then what useful purpose was served by interfering with nature?

All well and good in the context of simple market exchange. It overreaches, however, to prohibit node C governance by forcing all market transactions for which k > 0 onto node B because the "market is a marvel." Organization in all of its forms is a marvel—once we understand which transactions go where and why. Monopoly purpose enters into the calculus only when the requisite preconditions for monopoly are satisfied, which is a special case.

(b) Regulation/Deregulation

As discussed above, the obvious regulatory problem to which to bring TCE to bear was the imaginative proposal to use franchise bidding as the solution to natural monopoly. In a TCE world where all feasible forms of organization are flawed, it is not surprising that franchise bidding can be expected to work well in some circumstances but not in all.

Other applications of comparative contractual reasoning to regulation (broadly construed) include the much condemned sugar program (Williamson, 1996, pp. 197–210) and consumer health and safety and labor health and safety (Williamson and Bercovitz, 1996, pp. 343–347) issues. More generally, the lens of contract can be applied to the full range of regulatory issues (at local, state,

---

[15] For a discussion see Williamson (1985, pp. 183–189).
[16] The quotation is attributed to Turner by Stanley Robinson, 1968, N.Y. State Bar Association, Antitrust Symposium, p. 29.

and federal levels) and such uses have been growing. As matters stand presently, however, TCE is still underused in relation to its potential.

(c)   Other Public Policy

Avinash Dixit opens his monograph on *The Making of Economic Policy: A Transaction-Cost Politics Perspective* (1996) with a contrast with old-style public finance, where the government was described as an omniscient, omnipotent, and benevolent dictator (1996, p. 8), with the lens of contract approach, according to which all feasible forms of organization are flawed. This latter is an immediate ramification of describing human actors as boundedly rational, which disallows omniscience, and given to subgoal pursuit (opportunism), which disallows benevolence. Upon recognizing implementation obstacles, moreover, omnipotence also drops out.

Two crucial TCE moves endorsed by Dixit are the view of the firm as governance structure and to insist upon remediableness. He observes with reference to the first that the standard normative approach to policy analysis views the process as taking place within (1996, p. 9):

> ...a social welfare maximizing black box, exactly as the neoclassical theory of production and supply viewed the firm as a profit-maximizing black box. While some useful insights follow from this, it leaves some very important gaps in our understanding and gives us some very misleading ideas about the possibilities of beneficial policy intervention. Economists studying business and industrial organization have long recognized the inadequacy of the neoclassical view of the firm and have developed richer paradigms and models based on the concepts of various kinds of transaction costs. Policy analysis also stands to benefit from such an approach, opening the black box and examining the actual workings of the mechanism inside. That is the starting point, and a recurrent theme, of this monograph.

The remediableness criterion for evaluating public policy proposals is to be contrasted with that of the Pareto criterion. Whereas the latter typically scants issues of feasibility and implementation, the remediableness criterion makes express provision to both. Thus the remediableness criterion holds that an extant practice or mode of organization for which no <u>feasible</u> superior mode can be described and <u>implemented</u> with expected net gains is <u>presumed</u> to be efficient. Reference to feasibility disallows hypothetical ideals (costlessness in any of its forms, including costless bargaining, is thus disallowed). Reference to implementation entails looking ahead to uncover obstacles to implementation, after which the mechanisms are worked out. And presumptions of efficiency are rebuttable—possibly by showing that the initial conditions (often of a political kind) are not acceptable (Williamson, 1996, pp. 208–212).

Whereas lens of choice reasoning holds that a simple display of deadweight losses is dispositive of inefficiency, the lens of contract (remediableness) holds otherwise. Now the analyst is pushed to establish that the proposed reform is feasible (recall that hypothetical ideals are disallowed) and further to demonstrate that "legitimate" resistance can be overcome in a cost-effective way. Those are not impossible obstacles, but they are very demanding. Among other things, ready recourse to costless compensation of losers (of a Hicks-Kaldor kind) is disallowed.

6. Conclusions

Robert Solow's prescription for doing good economics is set out in three injunctions: keep it simple; get it right; make it plausible (2001, p. 111). Keeping it simple entails stripping away the inessentials and going for the main case (the jugular). Getting it right "includes translating economic concepts into accurate mathematics (or diagrams, or words) and making sure that further logical operations are correctly performed and verified" (Solow, 2001, p. 112). Making it plausible entails describing human actors in (reasonably) veridical ways and maintaining meaningful contact with the phenomena of interest (contractual or otherwise).

To this, moreover, I would add a fourth injunction: derive refutable implications to which the relevant (often microanalytic) data are brought to bear. Nicholas Georgescu-Roegen has a felicitous way of putting it: "The purpose of science in general is not prediction, but knowledge for its own sake," yet prediction is "the touchstone of scientific knowledge" (1971, p. 37).

Why the fourth injunction? This is necessitated by the need to choose among alternative theories that purport to deal with the same phenomenon—say vertical integration—and (more or less) satisfy the first three injunctions. Thus assume that all of the models are tractable, that the logic of each hangs together, and that agreement cannot be reached as to what constitutes veridicality and meaningful contact with the phenomena. Does each candidate theory then have equal claims for our attention? Or should we be more demanding? This is where refutable implications and empirical testing come in: ask each would-be theory to stand up and be counted.

Why more economists are not insistent upon deriving refutable implications and submitting these to empirical tests is a puzzle. One possibility is that the world of theory is set apart and has a life of its own. A second possibility is that some economists do not agree that refutable implications and testing are important. Another is that some theories are truly fanciful and their protagonists would be discomfited by disclosure. A fourth is that the refutable implications of favored theories are contradicted by the data. And perhaps there are still other reasons. Be that as it may, a multiplicity of theories, some of which are vacuous and others of which are fanciful, is an embarrassment to the pragmatically oriented members of the tribe. Among this subset, insistence upon the fourth injunction—derive refutable implications and submit these to the data—is growing.

TCE responds to the injunction of keeping it simple by taking economizing on transaction costs to be the main case. The logic of economic organization is that of discriminating alignment (the implementation of which requires that the key attributes of transactions and governance structures be named and the logic of efficient alignment be worked out). The main response to the plausibility injunction is to describe human actors in more veridical terms—in cognitive, self-interestedness, and feasible foresight respects. And TCE is insistent upon deriving refutable implications to which the data are thereafter brought to bear.

As described elsewhere, TCE has progressed from informal into preformal, semi-formal, and fully formal stages. As matters stand presently, however, some efforts at fully formal modelling lose contact with key issues.[17] Specifically, if adaptation (of autonomous and cooperative kinds) is truly the central problem of economic organization, then to annihilate ex post maladaptation (by making implausible assumptions of common knowledge of payoffs and costless bargaining), thereby to focus entirely on ex ante incentive alignment, is deeply problematic. Recent formal models have nevertheless begun to restore attention to ex post governance (Bajari and Tadelis, 2001).

However such fully formal modelling shapes up, there is broad agreement that work of a transaction cost economics kind has helped to transform our understanding of complex contracting and economic organization (in both theoretical and public policy respects) and that applications outside of economics are growing and will continue.

ACKNOWLEDGEMENTS

This is not the first time that I have attempted to describe the transaction cost economics project. For earlier treatments, see Williamson (1989, 1998). My thanks to Claude Menard and the referees for constructive suggestions and to the Rockefeller Study and Conference Center at Bellagio for tranquility.

REFERENCES

Anderson, Erin and David C. Schmittlein. 1984. "Integration of the Sales Force: An Empirical Examination". *Rand Journal of Economics* 15(3): 385–395.

Bajari, Patrick and Steven Tadelis. 2001. "Incentives Versus Transaction Costs: A Theory of Procurement Contracts". *Rand Journal of Economics* 32: 387–407.

Barnard, Chester I. 1938. *The Functions of the Executive*. Cambridge, MA: Harvard University Press.

Baron, James N. and David M. Kreps. 1999. *Strategic Human Resources: Frameworks for General Managers*. New York: John Wiley.

Becker, Gary. 1962. "Investment in Human Capital: Effects on Earnings". *Journal of Political Economy* 70: 9–49.

---

[17] I have reference to the Property Rights Theory of firm and market organization (Hart, 1995), which Bernard Salanié mistakenly describes as formalizing "the intuitions of transaction cost economics, as created by Coase and Williamson" (1997, p. 176). For a discussion, see Williamson (2002a).

Boerner, Christopher and Jeffrey Macher. 2002. "Transaction Cost Economics: A Review and Assessment of the Empirical Literature". Unpublished manuscript.

Brennan, G. and James Buchanan. 1985. *The Reason of Rules*. Cambridge: Cambridge University Press.

Buchanan, James M. 1975. "A Contractarian Paradigm for Applying Economic Theory". *American Economic Review* 65: 225–230.

———. 1987. "The Constitution of Economic Policy". *American Economic Review* 77: 243–250.

———. 2001. "Game Theory, Mathematics, and Economics," *Journal of Economic Methodology* 8: 27–32.

Buchanan, James M. and G. Tullock. 1962. *The Calculus of Consent: Logical Foundations of Constitutional Democracy*. Ann Arbor, MI: University of Michigan Press.

Coase, Ronald H. 1937. "The Nature of the Firm". *Economica* 4: 386–405.

———. 1960. "The Problem of Social Cost". *Journal of Law and Economics* 3: 1–44.

———. 1972. "Industrial Organization: A Proposal for Research" in V. R. Fuchs (ed), *Policy Issues and Research Opportunities in Industrial Organization*. New York: National Bureau of Economic Research, pp. 59–73.

———. 1984. "The New Institutional Economics". *Journal of Institutional and Theoretical Economics* 140: 229–231.

———. 1992. "The Institutional Structure of Production". *American Economic Review* 82: 713–719.

Crocker, Keith J. and Scott E. Masten. 1991. "Pretia ex Machina? Prices and Process in Long-Term Contracts". *Journal of Law and Economics* XXXIV(1): 69–99.

———. 1996. "Regulation and Administered Contracts Revisited: Lessons from Transaction-Cost Economics for Public Utility Regulation". *Journal of Regulatory Economics* 8: 5–39.

Demsetz, Harold. 1968. "Why Regulate Utilities?" *Journal of Law and Economics* 11: 55–66.

Dixit, Avinash K. 1996. *The Making of Economic Policy: A Transaction-Cost Politics Perspective*. Boston, MA: MIT Press.

Easterbrook, Frank and D. Fischel. 1986. "Close Corporations and Agency Costs". *Stanford Law Review* 38: 271–301.

Fama, Eugene F. and Michael C. Jensen. 1983. "Separation of Ownership and Control". *Journal of Law and Economics* 26: 301–326.

Friedman, Milton. 1962. *Capitalism and Freedom*, Chicago, IL: University of Chicago Press.

Gely, Rafael and Pablo T. Spiller. 1990. A Rational Choice Theory of Supreme Court Statutory Decisions with Applications to the *State Farm* and *Grove City* Cases". *Journal of Law, Economics, and Organization* 6(2): 263–300.

Georgescu-Roegen, Nicholas. 1971. *The Entropy Law and Economic Process*. Cambridge, MA: Harvard University.

Goldberg, Victor P. 1976. "Regulation and Administered Contracts". *Bell Journal of Economics* 7(2): 426–448.

Goldberg, Victor P. and John R. Erickson. 1987. "Quantity and Price Adjustment in Long-Term Contracts: A Case Study of Petroleum Coke". *Journal of Law and Economics* XXX(2): 369–398.

Hart, Oliver. 1995. *Firms, Contracts and Financial Structure*. New York: Oxford University Press.

Hayek, Friedrich. 1945. "The Use of Knowledge in Society". *American Economic Review* 35: 519–530.

Holmstrom, Bengt and Jean Tirole. 1989. "The Theory of the Firm" in R. Schmalensee and R. Willig (eds.), *Handbook of Industrial Organization*. New York: Oxford University Press.

John, George and Barton A. Weitz. 1988. "Forward Integration into Distribution: An Empirical Test of Transaction Cost Analysis". *Journal of Law, Economics, and Organization* 4(2): 337–355.
Joskow, Paul L. 1985. "Vertical Integration and Long-Term Contracts: The Case of Coal-Burning Electric Generating Plants". *Journal of Law, Economics, and Organization* 1(1): 33–80.
_____. 1987. "Contract Duration and Relationship-Specific Investments: Empirical Evidence from Coal Markets". *American Economic Review* 77(1): 168–185.
_____. 2000. "Transaction Cost Economics and Competition Policy". Unpublished manuscript.
Kenney, Roy W. and Benjamin Klein. 1983. "The Economics of Block Booking," *Journal of Law and Economics* XXVI(3): 497–540.
Klein, Benjamin. 1988. "Vertical Integration as Organizational Ownership: The Fisher Body-General Motors Relationship Revisited". *Journal of Law, Economics, and Organization* 4(1): 199–213.
Leffler, Keith B. and Randal R. Rucker. 1991. "Transactions Costs and the Efficient Organization of Production: A Study of Timber-Harvesting Contracts". *Journal of Political Economy* 99(5): 1060–1087.
Levy, Brian and Pablo T. Spiller. 1994. "The Institutional Foundations of Regulatory Commitment: A Comparative Analysis of Telecommunications Regulation". *Journal of Law Economics, and Organization* 10(2): 201–246.
Lyons, B. R. 1996. "Empirical Relevance of Efficient Contract Theory: Inter-Firm Contracts". *Oxford Review of Economic Policy* 12(4): 27–52.
Makowski, L. and J. Ostroy. 2001. "Perfect Competition and the Creativity of the Market". *Journal of Economic Literature* 32: 479–535.
Masten, Scott E. 1984. "The Organization of Production: Evidence from the Aerospace Industry". *Journal of Law and Economics* XXVII(2): 403–417.
Masten, Scott E. and Keith J. Crocker. 1985. "Efficient Adaptation in Long-Term Contracts: Take-or-Pay Provisions for Natural Gas". *American Economic Review* 75(5): 1083–1093.
_____. and S. Saussier. 2000. "Econometrics of Contracts: An Assessment of Developments in the Empirical Literature on Contracting". *Revue D'Economie Industrielle* 92: 215–236.
_____. and Edward A. Snyder. 1993. "United States versus United Shoe Machinery Corporation: On the Merits". *Journal of Law and Economics* XXXVI(1) (Part 1): 33–70.
_____. James W. Meehan, Jr., and Edward A. Snyder. 1991. "The Costs of Organization". *Journal of Law, Economics, and Organization* 7Z(1): 1–25.
Merton, Robert. 1936. "The Unanticipated Consequences of Purposive Social Action". *American Sociological Review* 1: 894–904.
Michels, R. 1962. *Political Parties*. Glencoe, IL: Free Press.
Monteverde, Kirk and David J. Teece. 1982. "Supplier Switching Costs and Vertical Integration in the Automobile Industry". *Bell Journal of Economics* 13(1): 206–213.
Mulherin, J. Harold (1986): "Complexity in Long-Term Contracts: An Analysis of Natural Gas Contractual Provisions". *Journal of Law, Economics, and Organization* 2(1): 105–117.
Nelson, R. R. and S. G. Winter. 1982. *An Evolutionary Theory of Economic Change*. Cambridge: Belknap Press.
Newell, A. and Herbert Simon. 1972. *Human Problem Solving*. Englewood Cliffs, NJ: Prentice-Hall.
North, Douglas. 2000. "A Revolution in Economics" in Claude Menard (ed.), *Institutions, Contracts, and Organizations*. Northampton, MA: Edward Elgar, pp. 37–42.
Palay, Thomas M. 1984. "Comparative Institutional Economics: The Governance of Rail Freight Contracting". *Journal of Legal Studies* XIII(2): 265–287.
Peltzman, Sam. 1991. "The Handbook of Industrial Organization: A Review Article". *Journal of Political Economy* 99: 201–217.
Peltzman, Sam and Michael Whinston. 2000. *Deregulation of Network Industries*. Washington, DC: Brookings Institution Press.

Posner, Richard A. 1972. "The Appropriate Scope of Regulation in the Cable Television Industry". *Bell Journal of Economics* 3: 98–129.
_____. 1986. *Economic Analysis of Law*, 3rd edn. Boston: Little Brown.
Priest, George L. 1993. "The Origins of Utility Regulation and the 'Theories of Regulation' Debate". *Journal of Law and Economics* XXXVI(1) (Part 2): 289–323.
Reder, M. W. 1999. *Economics: The Culture of a Controversial Science*. Chicago IL: University of Chicago Press.
Rindfleish, A. and Jan Heide. 1997. "Transaction Cost Analysis: Past, Present and Future Applications". *Journal of Marketing* 61: 30–54.
Robbins, Lionel. 1932. *An Essay on the Nature and Significance of Economic Science*. New York: New York University Press.
Rothband, Murray. 1987. "Catallactics" in J. Eatwell, M. Milgate, and P. Newman (eds.), *The New Palgrave: A Dictionary of Economics*, Vol. 1. New York: The Stockton Press, pp. 377–378.
Salanié, Bernard. 1997. *The Economics of Contracts: A Primer*. Cambridge, MA: The MIT Press.
Scott, R. W. 1992. *Organizations*. Englewood Cliffs, NJ: Prentice-Hall.
Selznick, Philip. 1949. *TVA and the Grass Roots*. Berkeley, CA: University of California Press.
_____. 1950. "The Iron Law of Bureaucracy". *Modern Review* 3: 157–165.
Shelanski, Howard A. and Peter G. Klein. 1995. "Empirical Research in Transaction Cost Economics: A Review and Assessment". *Journal of Law, Economics, and Organization* 11: 335–361.
Shultz, George. 1995. "Economics in Action". *American Economic Review* 85: 1–8.
Simon, Herbert A. 1947. *Administrative Behavior*. New York: The Free Press.
_____. 1957a. *Administrative Behavior*. New York: Macmillan.
_____. 1957b. *Models of Man: Social and Rational; Mathematical Essays on Rational Human Behavior in a Social Setting*. New York: Wiley.
_____. 1983. *Reason in Human Affairs*. Stanford, CA: Stanford University Press.
_____. 1991. "Organizations and Markets". *Journal of Economic Perspectives* 5: 25–44.
Solow, Robert. 2001. "A Native Informant Speaks". *Journal of Economic Methodology* 8: 111–112.
Thompson, J. S. 1967. *Organizations in Action: Social Science Bases of Administrative Theory*. New York: McGraw-Hill.
Varian, Hal. 2002. "If There Was a New Economy, Why Wasn't There a New Economics?" *New York Times*, January 17, C2.
Weingast, Barry and William J. Marshall. 1988. "The Industrial Organization of Congress: or, Why Legislatures, Like Firms, Are Not Organized as Markets". *Journal of Political Economy* 96(1): 132–163.
Werin, Lars. 2000. "Ronald Coase and the New Microeconomics" in Claude Menard (ed.), *Institutions, Contracts, and Organizations*. Northampton, MA: Edward Elgar, pp. 42–47.
Williamson, Oliver E. 1975. *Markets and Hierarchies: Analysis and Antitrust Implications*. New York: The Free Press.
_____. 1976. "Franchise Bidding for Natural Monopolies—In General and with Respect to CATV". *Bell Journal of Economics* 7(1): 73–104.
_____. 1979. "Assessing Vertical Market Restrictions: Antitrust Ramifications of the Transaction Cost Approach". *University of Pennsylvania Law Review* 127: 953–993.
_____. 1985. *The Economic Institutions of Capitalism*. New York: The Free Press.
_____. 1988. "Corporate Finance and Corporate Governance". *Journal of Finance* 43: 567–591.
_____. 1989. "Transaction Cost Economics" in Richard Schmalensee and Robert Willig, (eds.), *Handbook of Industrial Organization*, Vol. 1. New York: North Holland, pp. 136–184.
_____. 1994. "Evaluating Coase". *Journal of Economic Perspectives* 8: 201–204.

_____. 1996. *The Mechanisms of Governance*. New York: Oxford University Press.

_____. 1998. "Transaction Cost Economics: How It Works; Where It Is Headed". *De Economist* 146: 23–58.

_____. 1999. "Public and Private Bureaucracies". *Journal of Law, Economics, and Organization* 15: 306–342.

_____. 2002a. "The Theory of the Firm as a Governance Structure: From Choice to Contract". *Journal of Economic Perspectives* 16: 171–195.

_____. 2002b. "The Lens of Contract: Private Ordering". *American Economic Review* 92: 438–443.

Williamson, Oliver E. and Janet Bercovitz. 1996. "The Modern Corporation as an Efficiency Instrument" in Carl Kaysen (ed.), *The American Corporation Today*. New York: Oxford University Press, pp. 327–359.

SECTION II

Political Institutions and the State

4. Electoral Institutions and Political Competition
Coordination, Persuasion and Mobilization

GARY W. COX

In the Schumpeterian conception, democracy consists of regular and non-violent competition for control of government between alternative teams of elites (Schumpeter 1942). The question that much scholarship in electoral studies addresses, and on which this essay will focus, is: how does changing the rules of the electoral game change the strategies of parties and candidates, hence the outcome of elections?

Figure 1 illustrates both the sequence of events in a stylized democracy and some of the topics to be covered. In the beginning, there is a set of potential electoral competitors. These agents decide (at stage 1 of the diagram) whether to enter a particular electoral competition—that is, to formally nominate candidates for one or more elective offices. Since winning office requires amassing a sufficient number of votes, the nature of the entry game between potential competitors has a strong coordination game flavor to it.[1] For example, if fifteen right-of-center parties all enter the race as separate competitors, while the left unites behind a single option, the right is likely to do poorly (under most extant electoral systems). The right can do better if some potential competitors withdraw in favor of others, but each potential competitor may prefer that *it* remain and *the others* withdraw.

After a given set of competitors have entered the race, each decides to allocate effort to one or more of three vote-producing activities: (2.1) persuasion: providing voters with reasons, such as better policy positions or larger bribes, to prefer it to the other competitors; (2.2) vote coordination: convincing supporters of other parties that the expected utility of their vote, in terms of affecting the allocation of seats across competitors, will be higher if they support it than if they support their most-preferred competitor; (2.3) mobilization: boosting the probability that its known supporters will actually participate in the election.

---
[1] The essence of a coordination game is that the players would like to coordinate their actions on some one of n possibilities but disagree which of these possibilities is the best. For example, two allies, A and B, may wish to coordinate an attack on a third nation but disagree whether the attack should be launched from A's territory or B's.

n potential competitors
    ↓   (1) coordination of entry.

$m \leq n$ **actual competitors in the election(s)**
    ↓   (2.1) persuasion; (2.2) coordination of votes; (2.3) mobilization.

vote distribution across competitors
    ↓   (3) mechanical translation of votes into seats.

seat distribution across competitors
    ↓   (4) government formation process.

portfolio distribution across competitors

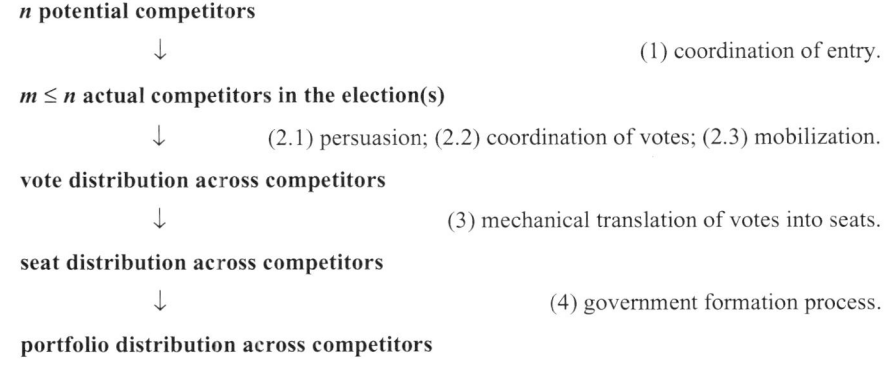

Figure 1. The office-seeking sequence in a hypothetical democracy

Each of these vote-producing activities is cost-effective under somewhat different conditions.

After the election has been held, an allocation of votes across the available competitors is determined. This allocation of votes is translated into an allocation of seats by a series of deterministic mathematical operations mandated by the relevant electoral rules (in particular, the electoral "formulas") of a system. Finally, after the allocation of offices has been determined, those competitors who hold seats in the national legislature can bargain among themselves over the distribution of portfolios (defined here to include both cabinet ministerial posts and, in those systems where such positions confer substantial authority over the legislative agenda, legislative committee chairs).

In this essay, I focus on the first three stages of Figure 1, leaving government formation to others. In order to simplify the exposition, I do not deal much with the detailed electoral rules. Rather, I categorize electoral systems by three broad architectonic features: the number of votes per voter; the number of seats per district; and the proportionality of the votes-to-seats translation. These features play the role of independent variables, with candidates' and parties' strategies of coordination, persuasion and mobilization in the role of dependent (or sometimes intermediate) variables.[2]

Although not the focus of this essay, it may be worth suggesting how parties' strategies in turn affect policy choices. A short answer is that parties' strategies help define the sort of actor they will be in government. In particular, the larger are the electoral aggregates that form (the greater is the equilibrium level of coordination), the broader are the interests those aggregates will represent; and the more that parties choose to persuade via promises to provide differing packages of public goods, rather than differing packages of private goods, the greater the pressure will be on them to deliver such goods when in office.[3]

---

[2] Throughout, I focus (albeit not exclusively) on formally derived institutional comparative statics results. For other reviews similar in spirit, see Myerson (1995, 1999).

[3] More elaborate answers along these lines can be found in Shugart (2001), Cox and McCubbins (2001), and Tsebelis (2002).

1. ELECTORAL RULES

There is an immense range of different electoral rules that can be combined into an even larger number of possible electoral systems. Here, I shall focus on the three main components of any electoral system: votes, seats and the rules translating votes into seats. Each of these components can be characterized in detail, by describing all the features of the particular electoral system at hand. Each can also be characterized in a more summary fashion—the approach taken here.

Translating Votes into Seats

One can characterize a given electoral system in terms of *where* and *how* votes are converted into seats. As far as *where* is concerned, votes can be translated into seats within electoral districts, within upper tiers and within electoral segments. Let's consider each of these in turn.

An *electoral district* is a geographical area within which votes are counted and seats awarded. For example, the U.S. House of Representatives has 435 districts, each returning a single member. Votes are counted at the district level and seats are awarded at the district level. There is no process by which votes from an election in California's 4th district can affect the outcome of the election in New York's 3rd or California's 5th.

Other electoral systems have provisions by which votes and sometimes seats are translated from their district of origin to a secondary district (a larger geographic area encompassing two or more districts), with an additional round of votes-to-seats conversions occurring at that level. For example, one could modify the U.S. system by stipulating that all votes not cast for a winning candidate in their district of origin transfer to the national level, where they can translate into seats according to stipulated rules.

Many electoral systems have *upper tiers* of secondary districts placed over their primary districts. In Belgium as of 1960, for example, votes were cast within 30 *arrondissements* (primary districts) which were in turn grouped into 9 provinces (secondary districts). A party's votes in a given *arrondissement* might suffice to "buy" one or more seats at that level, where the "price" in votes per seat was the so-called Hare quota (equal roughly to the total number of votes cast divided by M). Any unused votes cast for a party in a given *arrondissement* transferred to the provincial level, where they combined with the party's unused votes from the other *arrondissements* in the province, and might then suffice to "buy" some seats at the provincial level. The purpose of layering an upper tier of provinces over a lower tier of *arrondissements* was to increase the proportionality of the overall system (on which more below).

In addition to layering secondary districts over primary districts, another technique to affect overall proportionality that has become increasingly popular is to have two parallel segments of districts. An *electoral segment* consists of a set of electoral districts that together cover the entire nation, along with any associated upper tiers. The typical two-segment electoral designs combine one segment of single-member districts with one segment of multi-member districts operating under proportional representation (see Shugart and Wattenberg 2001). In Japan, for example, the 1993 electoral reform created one segment of 300 single-member districts (which together covered the entire nation); and one segment of 11 multi-member districts (which also collectively covered the nation) (see Reed and Thies 2001).

A full description of where votes are converted into seats thus involves a stipulation first of the number of segments (one or two) and then a characterization of each segment. In addition, one would wish to specify the procedures by which seats are apportioned to districts and tiers, as well as the procedures (if any) by which district boundaries can be redrawn. Here, however, the structure of districts, tiers and segments will be reduced to a single number (the effective magnitude; see the next section) and the procedures by which reapportionment and redistricting occur will be left in the background.

In addition to knowing *where* votes are converted into seats, one would also wish to know *how*. Particular mathematical formulas are used at each stage of seat allocation in an electoral system. In Belgium, for example, the electoral code stipulates a "price" for each seat (the Hare quota) and each party in a given *arrondissement* wins as many seats as its votes can buy at the stipulated price. A somewhat different formula (a different way of deciding the price per seat) is then used at the provincial level to award seats at that stage.

Individual electoral formulas can be arrayed along a continuum indicating their *proportionality*. At one extreme are the winner-take-all formulas: the candidate or list with the most votes wins all the seats available to be won in the particular district. Such formulas provide strong incentives to form "large" coalitions, in order to be able to compete seriously for the seats at stake. Opposed to these winner-take-all systems are those in which a list receives seats in strict proportion to its votes. Here, the larger parties receive no bonus seats (seats in excess of what they would get on a strictly proportional allocation).[4]

Because an electoral system may have more than one electoral formula operating at different levels (as in Belgium or Japan), it is not always easy to characterize the overall proportionality of a system. Putting this technical difficulty aside (as does most of the literature), I shall denote the overall proportionality of the votes-to-seats translation in a system by P, with higher values of P denoting more proportional systems.

---

[4] Of course, there are many different ways to define the gap between vote and seat shares, leading to different algorithmic embodiments of the proportional ideal (Cox and Shugart 1991). Conceptually, I prefer to characterize systems in terms of responsiveness or *big-party bias*, defined as the degree to which parties with larger vote shares tend also to receive higher-than-proportional seat shares (Cox and Shugart 1991). Most of the literature, however, has focused on proportionality and an array of workable summary measures of it exist (Gallagher 1991; Monroe N.d.). In contrast, measuring big-party bias (especially in multi-party contexts) has proved more difficult (for the state of the art, see Monroe N.d.).

The Number of Seats Per District, Tier and Segment

For a given structure of districts, tiers and segments, the question arises as to how many seats will be at stake at each point in the system. For simple (one-tier, one-segment) electoral systems, the number of seats elected from a given district (known as the district magnitude) is a key parameter, because it determines the minimum vote share that guarantees that a list or candidate will win a seat, hence the minimum viable size of electoral alliances. For example, in a single-member district in the U.S., a candidate must win over 50% of the vote to guarantee a seat, whereas in a 3-seat district in pre-1993 Japan, over 25% sufficed.[5]

In multi-tiered systems, it is harder to define the minimum vote share that guarantees that a party will win a seat. Electoral scholars have come up with approximate formulas, under the rubric of the *effective magnitude* or *effective threshold*, that translate complex systems to their equivalent one-tier systems (Taagepera and Shugart 1989; Lijphart 1994). The effective magnitude, in other words, is an attempt to put all systems on a single metric, reflecting the minimum or threshold size which office-seeking politicians might aim to exceed. In what follows, I denote the effective magnitude of a system by M. The larger the effective magnitude, the lower the threshold an alliance must surpass to guarantee a seat.[6]

The Number of Votes Per Voter

The method of voting in a system regulates the translation of citizens' preferences into votes and can be characterized as enabling them either to reward the best competitor(s) or to punish the worst competitor(s) (Cox 1987). To understand this characterization, note that different systems allow different numbers of votes per voter. Those that give voters only one vote enable each of them to reward the candidate they judge best (by casting their single vote for that candidate). However, voters have no ability to single out for special opprobrium the worst among the candidates not voted for. In contrast, consider systems that give voters M – 1 votes and force them to cast all of them for separate competitors, as used to be the case in many local elections in the U.S. (Cox 1984). Such systems enable each voter to punish the candidate they judge worst (by withholding a vote). However, voters have no ability to single out for special favor the best among those voted for. Yet other voting methods fall along a continuum running from the pure best-rewarding to the pure worst-punishing cases.

A summary measure of the degree to which a system is best-rewarding has been devised by Cox (1987). I shall call a transformation of this measure the *effective number of votes per voter*, denoted V. The logic is that, after one clears away the details of different voting rules, one is left with a simple contrast

---

[5] To clarify the meaning of "guarantee" here, note that it is possible to lose a single-member district with a vote percentage of 49.9% but not with 50.1%.

[6] See Lijphart and Gibberd 1977 for a study of thresholds.

between systems that give few votes (and thus enable voters only to distinguish between the best and the rest) and systems that give many votes (and thus enable voters only to distinguish between the worst and the rest).

Empirically, most national assemblies are elected using one-vote ($V = 1$) best-rewarding methods. A certain number do use methods intermediate between the best-rewarding and worst-punishing extremes, however. For example, Spain's Senate is elected using a limited vote (Lijphart, Lopez Pintor and Sone 1986), as was part of Great Britain's House of Commons in the nineteenth century. There are even fewer who use a pure worst-punishing method—the only one of which I am aware is Mauritius (Cox 1997:146–7).

Another distinction worth noting at this point is that between systems in which votes are cast directly for individual *candidates*; and those in which votes are cast for sets or *lists* of candidates, with each list endorsed by one or more parties. When votes are cast for lists (or aggregate to the list level), it is possible to use various proportional representation formulas in translating votes into seats. When votes aggregate only to the level of the individual candidate, in contrast, it is not possible to use proportional representation formulas (except in a mathematically trivial sense). Thus, the distinction drawn below between more and less proportional formulas is in part a function of the voting options given to voters.

Summary

In summary, electoral systems can be characterized by how many votes voters cast (by extension, the effective number of votes per voter, V), how many seats are awarded in the typical district (by extension, the effective magnitude, M), and how proportionally votes are converted into seats (P). In the sections that follow, I review what we know about how electoral competitors' strategies of coordination, persuasion and mobilization change, in response to changes in V, M and P.

2. Electoral Coordination

Modern representative democracy presents at its core a series of coordination problems that arise as natural consequences of electoral competition for governmental offices. A group with enough votes to elect some number of candidates in a given (legislative or executive) race will in fact elect that number only if it can make its votes count by concentrating them appropriately. One way to avoid spreading votes too thinly is to limit the number of candidates vying for the group's support. But which potential candidates, representing what shades of opinion, will withdraw in favor of which others? If attempts to limit the number of candidates fail, another chance to make votes count arises on polling day, when voters can concentrate their votes on a subset of the available candidates.

But which candidates will bear the brunt of strategic voting and which will be its beneficiaries?

Electoral coordination—whether the coordination of entry, resources or votes—can occur via a variety of processes. These processes can be classified in terms of the main actors involved (voters or elites) and the level at which their interaction is pitched (within individual electoral districts or across districts), yielding four categories. I shall briefly discuss each of these.

Coordination of Votes within Districts

Traditionally, strategic voting (voting so as to secure the best possible outcome rather than to support the most-preferred competitor) has been thought to concentrate votes. Consider, for example, a three-candidate contest for a single seat in which candidates A and B are tied in the polls at 40%, with C trailing at 20%. Those who most prefer the trailing candidate, C, may decide to vote for whichever of the leading candidates they prefer. Such strategic voting would have the consequence of concentrating the actual vote, relative to what would result if every voter simply voted for their most-preferred candidate. Indeed, in the extreme, all C's supporters might vote strategically and what had been a three-way race would reduce to a two-way race.

Does strategic voting have similar vote-concentrating consequences in other electoral contexts? As it turns out, the extent to which strategic voting concentrates votes depends on the electoral system in place, in two main ways (cf. Cox 1997). First, only in best-rewarding systems does strategic voting concentrate votes; in worst-punishing systems, it typically does just the opposite. Second, within the class of best-rewarding systems, smaller effective magnitudes lead to a greater concentration of votes, according to the "$M + 1$ rule." Let's consider this second proposition in greater detail.

The "$M + 1$ rule": Theory

Best-rewarding systems can be thought of as each having a maximum "carrying capacity" of parties, call it C. When the number of parties falls short of C it is theoretically possible that every party in the system can be in serious competition to win a seat—either expected to win one or more seats or to finish as the runner-up for the last-allocated seat. Strategic voting should be minimal in such situations. When the number of parties exceeds C, in contrast, it is increasingly unlikely that all parties can be seriously in contention for a seat. Instrumentally rational voters will avoid voting for parties that are unlikely to contend for a seat, however. Thus, if voters' initial priors concerning the distribution of preferences in the electorate are sufficiently precise, so that the identity of the trailing competitors is clear enough, one expects the vote share of trailing parties to fall short of what their vote share would be were all voters to vote sincerely.[7] That is, weak parties find some of their supporters voting for the best of the candidates still in contention for the last-allocated seat, rather than for them.

For systems using M-seat districts in which each voter has a single vote, cast either for a candidate or a party list, we know that the "carrying capacity" $C = M + 1$ (Cox 1997). That is, in an M-seat district one expects no more than $M + 1$ viable competitors.[8]

The "M + 1 rule": Evidence

Empirical evidence supporting the $M + 1$ rule comes in a variety of forms. Here, I shall briefly discuss evidence from mass surveys documenting the existence of strategic voting; and evidence from cross-national aggregate analyses documenting the relationship between district magnitude (M) and the number of viable parties.

Rather than examine survey evidence from a variety of countries, I focus on the case of Great Britain, for which the largest literature on strategic voting exists. Much of this literature deals with the elections of the 1980s, when the Alliance surged to near-parity in votes with the Labour Party. Estimates of the percentage of voters who voted for their second- or third-preference rather than first-preference candidate range from 5.1% to 17% (see e.g. Johnston and Pattie 1991; Heath *et al.* 1991:54; Lanoue and Bowler 1992; Niemi, Whitten and Franklin 1992; Crewe 1987:55). Estimates of the percentage of voters that would "consider" voting tactically vary from an average Gallup figure in 1986–87 of 15% to an average BBC Newsnight figure of 41% (Catt 1989). Even taking the low estimates both of voters that did cast, and voters that would consider casting, a tactical vote, the impact in terms of seats is potentially significant. Butler and Kavanagh (1988:266), for example, reckon that the Conservatives would have won 16 more seats than they did in 1987, had there been no strategic

---

[7] The models of Palfrey (1989), Myerson and Weber (1993), and Cox (1997) all assume that voters' know the *expected* constituency-wide breakdown of preferences with certainty. Myatt (n.d.), in contrast, assumes that voters have diffuse priors over this expected breakdown of preferences. These two differing formal assumptions correspond to two polar substantive assumptions. To take the case of three-party competition in a single-member district, one might assume that voters know, from previous elections, that the Conservatives generally get between 40–42% of the vote, with Labour at 38–42% and the Liberals at 16–22%. Pushing this substantive idea—that the voters know a lot about the *expected* breakdown of the vote between the three parties—to its logical extreme, one arrives at the models of Palfrey, Myerson and Weber, and Cox. On the other hand, what if the race is between three new parties in a new democracy; or a realignment of forces has made past results a poor guide to the future? Pushing this idea—that voters know little about the expected breakdown of preferences in a constituency—to its logical extreme, one arrives at the model of Myatt.

[8] The results stated in this paragraph follow from the Palfrey/Myerson-Weber/Cox model. In Myatt's model (which is fully developed for the $M = 1$ case), there is a *tendency* to concentrate votes on two competitors, but it stops short of the extreme identified in the earlier models. Thus, the version of the "M + 1 rule" that Myatt's model would support would probably read something like: "When there are more than $M + 1$ competitors, votes will concentrate on $M + 1$ of them (but only to a limited extent)."

voting. Kim and Fording (2001), however, estimate much lower impacts until the 1997 election.

These estimates of the proportion of the British population who vote strategically all use narrow definitions whereby a respondent votes strategically only if they report voting for a candidate who was not their most preferred but who was "in the running" to win the seat. If one looks only at voters who have an opportunity to vote strategically—supporters of trailing candidates—one of course finds very much higher rates of strategic voting (cf. Blais and Nadeau 1996).

This excursion into the literature on strategic voting suffices to demonstrate that part of the causal mechanism underlying the M + 1 rule appears to operate more or less as envisioned by the theory. Another sort of study that bears more directly on the M + 1 rule relates characteristics of electoral systems to the size of the party system. Many works investigate this relationship cross-nationally, including Rae (1971), Taagepera and Shugart (1989), and Lijphart (1994) (for further citations, consult these works). All report a relationship between the number of parties in a country and the average or median district magnitude that is broadly consistent with the M + 1 rule.

For a limited number of systems, there are more direct tests of the M + 1 rule. These can be roughly divided into systems where the M + 1 rule is predictively accurate—such as the U.S., Japan (Reed 1991; Cox 1997; Niemi and Hsieh 2002), Taiwan (Hsieh and Niemi 1999), and India (Chhibber and Kollman 1998)—and systems where it is not—such as Canada (Gaines 1999, Blais 2002) and Papua New Guinea (Cox 1997). For both cases of apparent success and apparent failure, the interesting question is whether the theoretical preconditions of the M + 1 rule (e.g., relatively precise public knowledge of the candidates' likely order of finish, prior to polling day) are met or not. Thus far, none of the exceptions to the rule occur where the theoretical preconditions are met; and none of the successes occur where the preconditions clearly fail. Nonetheless, it remains unclear how much the rule's variable success is driven by variations in strategic voting as opposed to variations in strategic coordination at the elite level.

Summary

To reframe the two results just noted, variations in the voting method (V) affect whether strategic voting leads to a deconcentration of votes (in worst-punishing systems) or to a concentration of votes (in best-rewarding systems). Variations in the effective magnitude (M) affect the carrying capacity of best-rewarding systems, with higher values allowing more competitors in equilibrium.[9]

---

[9] The third feature, P (proportionality), also plays a role—though it is harder to disentangle from that of V and M. For either V > 1 or M > 1, the possibility of significant variation in P arises, and the general rule is this: the more proportional the system, the less coordination is demanded, and the more parties there can be in equilibrium.

3. Coordination of Elites within Districts

There are several species of coordination problem that elites face within electoral districts, of which I consider two. One deals with the provision of campaign finance by contributors. Another concerns optimal nomination.

Strategic Contributions

Suppose that contributors of campaign finance are primarily interested in legislative services that an elected representative can provide once in office (e.g., lobbying party leaders on behalf of the contributor; introducing bills for the contributor). Suppose also that potential entrants seek financing for a campaign by essentially selling access to their future labor (cf. Denzau and Munger 1986). If elected to office, candidates pay off their financial backers. Otherwise, their contributors get nothing. Given these assumptions, there will be a tendency for contributors to coordinate their contributions, because only winning candidates pay off and those with more contributions are more likely to win. At an informal level, what can be conjectured is that no more than $M+1$ competitors in an M-seat district will attract significant financial backing from contributors seeking legislative services (although contributions from ideologically motivated sources are a different story).

Such a conjecture seems to fit the facts in the U.S. congressional case (cf. Jacobson 1980). Often, there is only one well-financed candidate: the incumbent. Occasionally, there are two well-financed candidates, in which case the actual outcome tends to be much closer. Finding three or more well-financed candidates in the general election is extremely rare.

Optimal Nomination

Parties face three recurring problems when nominating candidates for office: overnomination, undernomination, and factional cheating on nomination deals. In this section, I briefly consider each of these problems.

Overnomination means nominating too many candidates, who then split the party's vote too thinly and end up winning fewer seats than would have been possible had the party nominated fewer candidates.[10] Undernomination means nominating fewer candidates than the party has votes to elect. Optimal nomination means fielding a number of nominees that maximizes the party's expected seat share in the district.

---

[10] In single-member districts, overnomination simply means nominating more than one candidate. It is an easy mistake to spot and all parties operating in single-member districts go to considerable (and generally successful) lengths to avoid dual candidacies. In M-seat districts, it is harder to say what constitutes overnomination. Nominating more than M candidates will usually be overnominating—but not necessarily if votes transfer or pool. In systems where votes do not transfer or pool, the party will have beliefs about its likely vote share. If it has votes enough to win M-2 seats, then it should nominate M-2 candidates and no more.

In some systems, figuring out the optimal number of nominees is easy. For example, in the U.S. each major party either runs zero or one candidate in each district. The zeroes typically arise in districts that are so "safe" for the other party that the party decides to save itself the cost of running a candidate there. In most districts, both parties decide to run a candidate, although their commitment of resources is highly sensitive to the closeness of the race.

In systems with larger-magnitude districts, figuring out the optimal number of nominees is not as easy. For example, in a three-seat district in the Japanese election of 1980, some Liberal Democrats might have thought the party had enough votes to sweep the three seats, while others believed that only two seats could be won. If there were currently two Liberal Democratic incumbents in the district, they would naturally not wish to have a third colleague nominated, as this might reduce their probability of winning a seat from essentially 1 to roughly 2/3 (if they are correct that the party will win only two seats and if additionally each of the party's nominees has an equal chance of winning a seat).

Studies of nomination in the Japanese system over the period of Liberal Democratic dominance (1955–1993) find a steady improvement in the party's ability to arbitrate internal disagreements over nominations of the sort described above. In particular, early in the period the party fairly often overnominated, with the consequence that two or more of its candidates "fell down together," as the Japanese put it, in a version of the game of Chicken. Experiences of this sort led fairly quickly to improved deal-making among the factions and fewer overnominations (Reed 1991; Cox and Rosenbluth 1994; Niemi and Hsieh 2002).

Similar coordination problems arise under other systems with multi-member districts, such as the limited vote in Spain (Lijphart, Pintor and Sone 1986), the single non-transferable vote in Taiwan (Cox and Niou 1994), and the cumulative vote system in Illinois (Goldburg 1994). When district magnitudes exceed five, there is an increasing probability that elections will be based on lists, which essentially solve the coordination problem mechanically by forcing candidates to share their votes with one another (or, alternatively, forcing voters to vote for indivisible groups rather than individuals).

4. Coordinating Across Districts

A distinctly different problem of coordination arises at the cross-district level. If there are multiple districts, each with its own population of parties, will those parties cooperate across district lines or not?

One advantage of cross-district coordination—or linkage—can be suggested by considering two districts in which two leftist parties each run a candidate against a single rightist candidate. Let us suppose that the leftists can win both districts, if they combine their votes, but neither, if they split. One solution to their problem is to negotiate cooperation in each district separately. Another, potentially easier, solution is to *trade* withdrawals: party A withdraws in district 1 in exchange for party B withdrawing in district 2. Part of the deal, of course, is that each party's supporters will be encouraged to vote for the other's nominee.[11]

Cross-district trading of nominations and withdrawals can occur at various levels of "intensity." At the low end, there can be a few scattered deals affecting only a small number of districts (e.g., early cooperation between the *Komeito* and other parties in Japan; cf. Christensen 2000). Then there can be comprehensive but nonetheless election-specific deals, in which the whole pattern of nominations is decided centrally (e.g., the alliance between the Social Democrats and Liberals in the U.K.). A set of parties' (or factions') relations can be even further deepened if they *regularly* negotiate nominations centrally—as has occurred, for example, in Chile within the *Concertación*, in post-reform Italy within Berlusconi's group (Di Virgilio 1998), and in pre-reform Japan within the LDP (Cox and Rosenbluth 1996). Finally, the various parties might fuse, formally abandoning their separate labels and organizations.

In addition to trading nominations, parties in some systems have a clear incentive to legally unite for purposes of seat allocations in upper tiers. In Belgium, a party in a given *arrondissement* can participate in the allocation of seats at the provincial level only if it formally affiliates with parties from other *arrondissements* in the province. In Hungary, parties are eligible to run national-level lists only if they field at least seven regional lists. In Japan, a candidate running in one of the single-member districts is eligible to win a seat in the encompassing PR district only if she formally affiliates with a party running such a list. Similar incentives to affiliate with larger electoral forces arise in a number of other multi-tier and multi-segment systems (cf. Shugart and Wattenberg 2001).

A third incentive to form broad national parties arises in presidential systems. The presidential election so greatly dominates the mass media that hanging on to the president's coat-tails is in some systems a natural electoral strategy for legislators. At the same time, cultivating the support of local politicians is a natural strategy for presidential candidates. This may help explain why the resuscitation of real competition for the presidency in the U.S. brought with it the emergence of our second party system (McCormick 1975); why the creation of presidential elections in France led quickly to a bipolarization of legislative elections (Wilson 1980); and why nominations in Uruguay are dominated by the presidential candidates (Morgenstern 2001). The same story can play out in parliamentary systems, to the extent that parliamentary elections revolve around the prospective prime ministers, as in the United Kingdom, Israel or Germany.

The extent of cross-district coordination (in its various forms) depends on what such coordination can win. Two obvious prizes are legislative seats and

---

[11] Yet another solution along the same lines is for party A actually to jointly nominate B's candidate; and vice versa. This is legally permissible in some but not all systems.

executive portfolios. As noted above, each electoral system presents different incentives to coordinate across districts in pursuit of legislative seats—to use votes in primary districts more efficiently; to pool votes in secondary districts; to take advantage of executive coat-tail effects. Each system also presents different incentives to coordinate in pursuit of portfolios, although here the key conditions pertain not so much to the electoral system proper as to various constitutional and legislative features.

Hicken (2002) points out that incentives to coordinate are greater the more concentrated is power in a single post whose election depends on winning a majority in the assembly. From this perspective, federalism can diminish such incentives, as can bicameralism, presidentialism, and the dispersion of executive power among co-equal ministers. Chhibber and Kollman (1998) and Samuels (1998) both explore a more specific version of this hypothesis—that greater fiscal centralization in a state will lead to greater linkage.

Another line of studies looks not at the short-term office benefits of forming larger electoral aggregates but instead at the long-term policy benefits of refusing to coordinate. Studies of third-party movements (e.g., Rosenstone 1996 and Hug 2001) typically find strong policy preferences motivating the formation of separate vehicles, even when going it alone sacrifices seats that could be won with a more pragmatic stance (and the consequent alliance that would then become feasible). A variant on this theme concerns regional parties, especially those based on ethnic identities. Also related are studies of coordination in newly established democracies, where uncertainty about who the players are and who can outlast whom delays coordination (cf. Moser 1999; Zielinski 2002).

5. Electoral Persuasion

One way to win office is, *given* a particular distribution of preferences, to coordinate campaign finance, candidate entry and voters' choices in such a way as to maximize the number of seats the "socialists" or "liberals" or "Christian Democrats" win. The focus is on translating preferences efficiently into seats (via votes).

Another way to win office is to persuade. Rather than take preferences as given, one influences those preferences as best one can.

The models of persuasion that I shall consider in this section all take parties or candidates as the main actors. Some assume that competitors seek only office, while others assume they seek to maximize the rents they can extract from office. Some assume that competitors can promise only public goods, while others assume that they can promise private goods (only or as well).

Office-Seeking Competitors with Credible Promises

Suppose that competitors seek only to win office and can make credible promises during the campaign concerning the policies they will pursue if elected. One possibility is that candidates promise packages of public goods which can be characterized as falling somewhere along the left-right spectrum ("position taking"). Another possibility is that candidates promise packages of transfers ("bribing").

When competitors take positions (i.e., promise only public goods), the consequences of changing electoral rules on their behavior can be stated as follows: higher values of V or M, along with more proportional values of P, lead competitors to disperse across the left-right spectrum (Cox 1987; 1990). The intuition behind the last two results is roughly as follows. When there are many seats to win and they are allocated proportionally, small shares of the vote suffice to win seats. Thus, electoral competitors can carve out narrow ideological niches and still be successful. In contrast, when there is only one seat to win and it is allocated to the plurality winner, electoral competitors can win seats only if they can amass the largest share of votes. This means that appealing to a narrow ideological niche is insufficient to win seats and a broader appeal must be fashioned.[12]

When competitors distribute (only) private goods, similar results obtain. Higher values of V or M, along with more proportional values of P, lead competitors to concentrate their "bribes" on smaller subsets of voters, giving the rest almost nothing (Myerson 1993). The logic is again driven by the minimum share of votes that will suffice to win a seat. In electoral systems where this minimum is lower, more concentrated appeals are more effective. The main difference between the models is simply in the tools that competitors are assumed to have available.

A related theoretical effort is that of Carey and Shugart (1995), who attempt to rank-order a wide range of electoral systems in terms of the incentives they provide politicians to cultivate a personal vote, rather than rely on their party's overall image. As the means by which one might cultivate a personal reputation is usually the distribution of particularistic goods, Carey and Shugart's ranking reflects the insight offered above. In addition, however, Carey and Shugart identify a number of other features of electoral systems that promote personal vote seeking, including a range of provisions that essentially force members of the same party and district to compete against one another (e.g., the single non-transferable vote, open lists, and preference votes). The degree of forced intra-party competition is an important feature of electoral systems that is not captured by the (V, M, P) coding suggested here.

Office-Seeking Competitors without Credible Promises

What if voters do not believe the competitors' promises, because they suspect that, once elected, politicians will have incentives to do the bidding of special

---

[12] The first result is somewhat more subtle. See Cox 1987; 1990.

interests, rather than fulfill campaign pledges?[13] The credibility of competitors' promises is an important analytical issue for some purposes. However, this problem does not appear to affect the main comparative statics result derived above—that increases in V, M or P induce greater niche-seeking by competitors. Thus, I ignore it here.

Rent-Seeking Competitors with Credible Promises

In the office-seeking models discussed above, winning an office confers a fixed amount of utility on the victor. Conceptually, this utility might consist of the salary of the office, its prestige and any other "ego rents" attached thereto.

Another class of models assumes that office-holders can extract a variable amount from their office. In particular, several models envision one or more "predatory parties" whose maximand is their *expected rent*: the probability of their winning control of government, times the fiscal residuum they can extract once in control. Each party promises a certain tax rate; a certain expenditure on public goods; and a certain bundle of transfers to the groups in the electorate. If elected, the party collects taxes, provides the level of public goods and transfers promised, and keeps any residual for itself.

Several comparative static results drawn from this model hinge on electoral rules. I consider just one here: Persson and Tabellini (2000) show that changing from a single nationwide district operating under proportional representation (high M and high P) to a set of single-member districts operating under plurality rule (low M and low P) induces the following changes: parties promise more transfers to swing districts, financing the increased expenditure by reducing both the provision of public goods and their own rents. The logic of this result is as follows. If control of government comes down to who wins in a particular handful of districts, as it can in a district-based electoral system, competition will focus on those districts. But this means that both parties will offer more transfers to the voters in the swing districts, than they would offer to the same voters were there were no districts (just a nationwide PR election).[14] Studies

---

[13] There are several approaches to dealing with this credibility problem. Ferejohn (1986) and Alesina (1988), for example, consider repeated games of various sorts, attempting to identify when credibility will emerge endogenously. Bernhardt and Ingberman (1985) simply assume it is costly to state positions distant from those taken in the past. Osborne and Slivinski (1996) and Besley and Coate (1997) go even further, stipulating that the only credible promise that a candidate can make is to implement his or her ideal point. The Besley-Coate and Osborne-Slivinski models can be construed as replacing one sort of credibility problem with another. There is no longer the problem of voters believing anything the candidates say, because the candidates only state their ideals, which they then have an incentive to implement if elected. However, the models depend heavily on common knowledge of ideal points of all citizens. If a particular citizen's ideal point is not common knowledge, then that citizen faces the issue of how credibly to communicate what his or her ideal really is.

[14] That these increased transfers are financed by reducing *both* public goods *and* private rents simply reflects that neither the level of public goods nor the fiscal residuum were pegged at corner solutions prior to the lower of M and P.

by Lizzeri and Persico (2001) and Milesi-Ferretti, Perotti and Rostagno (2000) also conclude that, because targetable goods are electorally more valuable in district-based systems, the equilibrium level of transfers (pork barrel projects and other geographically targetable benefits) will be higher. As evidence in favor of the idea that district-based electoral systems promote transfers at the expense of general public goods, Persson and Tabellini (2000) show that expenditures on welfare are higher in more proportional systems, controlling for the age structure of the population, per-capita income, trade openness and federalism, inter alia.

6. MOBILIZATION

There are no formal game-theoretic models that consider how electoral mobilization varies with electoral rules. However, the literature has offered decision-theoretic analyses (see Cox 1999b for a review). In terms of the current independent variables, the main results appear to be as follows. Higher levels of mobilization are more likely as V decreases; M increases; or P becomes more proportional. The logic of the first result is simply that, if voters cast lots of votes, then the mobilizing competitor may not internalize the full benefits of mobilizing any particular voter or segment of voters. The argument in favor of the second and third results is that more proportional translations of votes into seats reward mobilizational effort more surely and smoothly. In contrast, mobilizing in a single-member district may simply reduce the margin by which one loses, or increase the margin by which one wins—and neither of these outcomes is worth the effort to an office-seeking competitor. Empirical evidence in favor of these arguments can be found in Blais and Carty (1990), Blais and Dobrzynska (1998), Jackman (1987), Jackman and Miller (1995), and Powell (1980, 1982, 1986).

7. CONCLUSION

The vast majority of models of electoral competition have not been concerned with institutional comparative statics. Only a few take the electoral rules themselves as the primary independent variables. And, thus far, there is almost no work that alters non-institutional features of the model, then considers whether those alterations condition the effect of changing the rules. In this sense, the formal literature analyzing electoral systems is relatively thin.

In this essay, I have characterized the independent variable—the electoral system—in terms of three features: the effective number of votes per voter, the effective number of seats per district, and the proportionality of the votes-to-seats mapping(s). The dependent variables—the strategies adopted by electoral competitors within a given electoral system—have been parsed into strategies of coordination, persuasion and mobilization.

Coordination

Taking voters' preferences and turnout probabilities as fixed, political competitors face problems in coordinating endorsements, entry, campaign finance and votes to maximize their respective seat shares. The severity of the coordination problem(s) that competitors face depends on the electoral rules governing their competition. The most prevalent voting methods give citizens just one vote to cast (either for a candidate or a list) and fall into the "best-rewarding" category. For such voting methods, strategic coordination leads to a concentration of votes upon a subset of viable candidates. The size of this subset is determined by the number of seats available to be won, with the most general rule of thumb encapsulated in the "$M + 1$ rule": the number of viable competitors cannot exceed $M + 1$ in equilibrium (when voters are primarily interested in who wins the current election and have sufficiently precise information concerning the likely order of finish of the competitors).

Persuasion

Rather than taking preferences as fixed, political competitors can also engage in a variety of persuasive activities. They can promise to deliver either broadly targeted goods (in the extreme, Samuelsonian public goods) or narrowly targeted goods (in the extreme, private goods) or something in-between. The results on persuasion I have reviewed here all make essentially the same point: that electoral systems differ in the extent to which they encourage competitors to fashion narrow appeals.

At the within-district level, fewer votes per voter, more seats per district, and greater proportionality lead competitors to cater to narrower clienteles within the electorate. If competitors are constrained to promise only public goods, they "cater to narrower clienteles" by spreading out over the ideological spectrum, rather than bunching at the median (Cox 1987; 1990). If they are constrained to promise only private goods, they "cater to narrower clienteles" by targeting their bribes, rather than diffusing them (Myerson 1993).

At the across-district level, elections based on small-magnitude districts lead competitors to prefer geographically targetable goods, rather than national public goods. The reason is, roughly, that geographically targetable goods can be promised specifically to districts where the competition is close, whereas public goods cannot.

Mobilization

Holding voters' preferences and their estimates of candidates' viability constant, competitors can seek to affect their decisions to vote or abstain. The general findings in the literature are that fewer votes per voter, more seats per district, and greater proportionality increase the mean level of turnout and decrease the variance in turnout. This relationship suggests an alternative causal mechanism to explain the observation (Persson and Tabellini 2000) that more proportional electoral systems foster greater expenditures on welfare: more proportional systems (higher M and P) lead to higher turnout rates among the poorest citizens (those who are the first to "drop out" under more majoritarian systems with their lower turnouts); more consistent turnout among the poorest citizens leads to more consistent policies serving their social insurance desires (cf. Lijphart 1997).

REFERENCES

Alesina, Alberto. 1988. "Credibility and Policy Convergence in a Two-Party System with Rational Voters". *American Economic Review* 78(4): 796–805.

Amorim Neto, Octavio and Gary W. Cox. 1997. "Electoral Institutions, Cleavage Structures, and the Number of Parties". *American Journal of Political Science* 41(1): 149–174.

Besley, Timothy and Stephen Coate. 1997. "An Economic Model of Representative Democracy". *Quarterly Journal of Economics* 112(1): 85–114.

Blais, André. 2002. "Why Is There So Little Strategic Voting in Canadian Plurality Elections?" *Political Studies* 50(3): 445–454.

Blais, André and R. Ken Carty. 1990. "Does Proportional Representation Foster Voter Turnout?" *European Journal of Political Research* 18: 167–182.

Blais, André and Agnieszka Dobrzynska. 1998 "Turnout in Electoral Democracies". *European Journal of Political Research* 33: 239–261.

Blais, André and Richard Nadeau. 1996. "Measuring Strategic Voting: A Two-Step Procedure". *Electoral Studies* 15(1): 39–52.

Butler, David and Dennis Kavanagh. 1988. *The British General Election of 1987*. London: Macmillan.

Carey, John and Matthew S. Shugart. 1995. "Incentives to Cultivate a Personal Vote: A Rank Ordering of Electoral Formulas". *Electoral Studies* 14(4): 417–439.

Catt, Helena. 1989. "Tactical Voting in Britain". *Parliamentary Affairs* 42: 548–559.

Chhibber, Pradeep and Ken Kollman. 1998. "Party Aggregation and the Number of Parties in India and the United States". *American Political Science Review* 92(2): 329–342.

Christensen, Ray. 2000. *Ending the LDP Hegemony: Party Cooperation in Japan*. Honolulu: University of Hawaii Press.

Cox, Gary W. 1984. "Strategic Electoral Choice in Multi-Member Districts: Approval Voting in Practice?" *American Journal of Political Science* 28(4): 722–738.

Cox, Gary W. 1987. "Electoral Equilibrium under Alternative Voting Institutions". *American Journal of Political Science* 31(1): 82–108.

Cox, Gary W. 1990. "Centripetal and Centrifugal Incentives in Electoral Systems". *American Journal of Political Science* 34(4): 903–935.

Cox, Gary W. 1997. *Making Votes Count: Strategic Coordination in the World's Electoral System*. New York: Cambridge University Press.

Cox, Gary W. 1999a. "Electoral Rules and Electoral Coordination". *Annual Review of Political Science* 2: 145–161.

Cox, Gary W. 1999b. "Electoral Rules and the Calculus of Mobilization". *Legislative Studies Quarterly* 24(3): 387–419.

Cox, Gary W. and Mathew D. McCubbins. 2001. "The Institutional Determinants of Economic Policy Outcomes" in Mathew D. McCubbins and Stephan Haggard (eds.), *Presidents, Parliaments and Policy*. New York: Cambridge University Press, pp. 21–63.

Cox, Gary W. and Frances Rosenbluth. 1994. "Reducing Nomination Errors: Factional Competition and Party Strategy in Japan". *Electoral Studies* 13(1): 4–16.

Cox, Gary W. and Frances Rosenbluth. 1996. "Factional Competition for the Party Endorsement: The Case of Japan's Liberal Democratic Party". *British Journal of Political Science* 26(2): 259–297.

Cox, Gary W. and Matthew Shugart. 1991. "Comment on Gallagher's 'Proportionality, Disproportionality and Electoral Systems'". *Electoral Studies* 10(4): 348–352.

Crewe, Ivor. 1987. "What's Left for Labour: An Analysis of Thatcher's Victory". *Public Opinion* 10: 52–56.

Di Virgilio, Aldo. 1998. "Electoral Alliances: Party Identities and Coalition Games". *European Journal of Political Research* 34(1): 5–33.

Downs, Anthony. 1957. *An Economic Theory of Democracy*. New York: Harper and Row.

Erikson, Robert and Thomas Palfrey. 1998. "Campaign Spending and Incumbency: An Alternative Simultaneous Equations Approach". *Journal of Politics* 60(2): 355–373.

Feddersen, Timothy J., Itai Sened, and Stephen G. Wright. 1990. "Rational Voting and Candidate Entry under Plurality Rule". *American Journal of Political Science* 34(4): 1005–1016.

Gaines, Brian. 1999. "Duverger's Law and the Meaning of Canadian Exceptionalism". *Comparative Political Studies* 32(7): 835–861.

Gallagher, Michael. 1991. "Proportionality, Disproportionality, and Electoral Systems". *Electoral Studies* 10(1): 33–51.

Goldburg, Carol. 1994. "The Accuracy of Game Theory Predictions for Political Behavior: Cumulative Voting in Illinois Revisited". *Journal of Politics* 56(4): 885–900.

Heath, Anthony and Roger Jowell (eds.). 1991. *Understanding Political Change: The British Voter 1964–87*. Oxford: Pergamon Press.

Hicken, Allen. 2002. "Party Systems, Political Institutions and Policy: Policymaking in Developing Democracies", Unpublished Ph.D. dissertation. University of California, San Diego.

Hug, Simon. 2001. *Altering Party Systems: Strategic Behavior and the Emergence of New Political Parties in Western Democracies*. Ann Arbor, MI: University of Michigan Press.

Hsieh, John and Richard Niemi. 1999. "Can Duverger's Law be Extended to SNTV? The Case of Taiwan's Legislative Yuan Elections". *Electoral Studies* 18(1): 101–116.

Jackman, Robert W. 1987. "Political Institutions and Voter Turnout in the Industrial Democracies". *American Political Science Review* 81(2): 405–424.

Jackman, Robert W. and Ross A. Miller. 1995. "Voter Turnout in the Industrial Democracies During the 1980s". *Comparative Political Studies* 27(4): 467–492.

Jacobson, Gary C. 1980. *Money in Congressional Elections*. New Haven, CT: Yale University Press.

Johnston, Richard J. and Charles J. Pattie. 1991. "Tactical Voting in Great Britain in 1983 and 1987: An Alternative Approach". *British Journal of Political Science* 21(1): 95–108.

Kim, HeeMin and Richard C. Fording. 2001. "Does Tactical Voting Matter? The Political Impact of Tactical Voting in Recent British Elections". *Comparative Political Studies* 34(3): 294–311.

Lanoue, David J. and Shaun Bowler. 1992. "The Sources of Tactical Voting in British Parliamentary Elections, 1983–1987". *Political Behavior* 14(2): 141–157.

Lijphart, Arend. 1994. *Electoral Systems and Party Systems: A Study of Twenty-Seven Democracies, 1945–1990*. Oxford: Oxford University Press.

Lijphart, Arend. 1997. "Unequal Participation: Democracy's Unresolved Dilemma". *American Political Science Review* 91(1): 1–14.

Lijphart, Arend; Rafael Lopez Pintor, and Yasunori Stone. 1986. "The Limited Vote and the Single Nontransferable Vote: Lessons from the Japanese and Spanish Examples" in Bernard Grofman and Arend Lijphart, (eds.), *Electoral Laws and their Political Consequences*. New York: Agathon Press, pp. 154–169.

Lizzeri, Alessandro and Nicola Persico. 2001. "The Provision of Public Goods Under Alternative Electoral Incentives". *American Economic Review* 91(1): 225–239.

McCormick, Richard P. 1975. "Political Development and the Second American Party System" in William N. Chambers and Walter Dean Burnham, (eds.), *The American Party Systems*, 2nd edn. New York: Oxford University Press, pp. 90–116.

Monroe, Burt. N.d. *Electoral Systems in Theory and Practice*. Unpublished book manuscript, Indiana University.

Morgenstern, Scott. 2001. "Organized Factions and Disorganized Parties: Electoral Incentives in Uruguay". *Party Politics* 7(2): 235–256.

Moser, Robert G. 1999. "Electoral Systems and the Number of Parties in Postcommunist States". *World Politics* 51(3): 359–384.

Myatt, David. N.d. "A New Theory of Strategic Voting". Unpublished typescript. Oxford University.

Myerson, Roger. 1993. "Incentives to Cultivate Favored Minorities Under Alternative Electoral Systems". *American Political Science Review* 87(4): 856–869.

Myerson, Roger. 1995. "Analysis of Democratic Institutions: Structure, Conduct and Performance". *Journal of Economic Perspectives* 9(1): 77–89.

Myerson, Roger. 1999. "Theoretical Comparisons of Electoral Systems". *European Economic Review* 43(4–6): 671–697.

Myerson, Roger and Robert Weber. 1993. "A Theory of Voting Equilibria". *American Political Science Review* 87(1): 102–114.

Niemi, Richard and John Hsieh. 2002. "Counting Candidates: An Alternative to the Effective N (with an Application to the M + 1 Rule in Japan". *Party Politics* 8(1): 75–99.

Niemi, Richard, Guy Whitten, and Mark Franklin. 1992. "Constituency Characteristics, Individual Characteristics and Tactical Voting in the 1987 British General Election". *British Journal of Political Science* 23(4): 549–563.

Osborne, Martin and Al Slivinski. 1996. "A Model of Political Competition with Citizen Candidates". *Quarterly Journal of Economics* 111(1): 65–96.

Palfrey, Thomas. 1989. "A Mathematical Proof of Duverger's Law" in Peter C. Ordeshook, (ed.), *Models of Strategic Choice in Politics*. Ann Arbor, MI: University of Michigan Press, pp. 69–91.

Powell, G. Bingham, Jr. 1980. "Voting Turnout in Thirty Democracies: Partisan, Legal, and Socio-Economic Influences," in Richard Rose, (ed.), *Electoral Participation: A Comparative Analysis*. Beverly Hills, CA: Sage Press, pp. 5–34.

Powell, G. Bingham, Jr. 1982. *Contemporary Democracies: Participation, Stability, and Violence*. Cambridge, MA: Harvard University Press.

Powell, G. Bingham, Jr. 1986. "American Voter Turnout in Comparative Perspective". *American Political Science Review* 80(1): 17–43.

Rae, Douglas. 1971. *The Political Consequences of Electoral Laws*, rev. edn. New Haven, CT: Yale University Press.

Reed, Steven. 1990. "Structure and Behavior: Extending Duverger's Law to the Japanese Case". *British Journal of Political Science* 20(3): 335–356.

Reed, Steven and Michael Thies. 2001. "The Causes of Electoral Reform in Japan" in Mathew S. Shugart and Martin P. Wattenberg, (eds.), *Mixed-Member Electoral Systems: The Best of Both Worlds?* Oxford: Oxford University Press, pp. 152–172.

Rosenstone, Steven J., Roy Behr, and Edward Lazarus. 1996. *Third Parties in America: Citizen Response to Major Party Failure*, 2nd edn. Princeton, NJ: Princeton University Press.

Samuels, David J. 1998. "Careerism and Its Consequences: Federalism, Elections, and Policy-Making in Brazil". Unpublished Ph.D. dissertation, University of California at San Diego.

Samuels, David J. and Richard Snyder. N.d. "The Value of a Vote: Malapportionment in Comparative Perspective". *British Journal of Political Science*, forthcoming.

Shugart, Matthew S. 2001. "'Extreme' Electoral Systems and the Appeal of the Mixed-Member Alternative" in Mathew S. Shugart and Martin P. Wattenberg, (eds.), *Mixed-Member Electoral Systems: The Best of Both Worlds?* Oxford: Oxford University Press, pp. 25–54.

Shugart, Matthew S. and Martin P. Wattenberg, (eds.). 2001. *Mixed-Member Electoral Systems: The Best of Both Worlds?* Oxford: Oxford University Press.
Schumpeter, Joseph. 1942. *Capitalism, Socialism, and Democracy.* New York: Harper.
Taagepera, Rein and Matthew S. Shugart. 1989. *Seats and Votes: The Effects and Determinants of Electoral Systems.* New Haven, CT: Yale University Press.
Tsebelis, George. 2002. *Veto Players: How Political Institutions Work.* Princeton, NJ: Princeton University Press.
Wilson, Frank L. 1980. "Sources of Party Transformation: The Case of France" in Peter H. Merkl, (ed.), *Western European Party Systems.* New York: Free Press, pp. 526–551.
Zielinski, Jakub. 2002. "Translating Social Cleavages into Party Systems: The Significance of New Democracies". *World Politics* 54(2): 184–211.

5. Presidential versus Parliamentary Government

JOHN M. CAREY

1. INTRODUCTION

The last twenty-five years have witnessed dramatic growth in the number of political regimes that meet basic standards of procedural democracy, such as freedom of association and expression, competitive elections that determine who holds political power, and systematic constraints on the exercise of authority (Robert Dahl 1971; Samuel Huntington 1991). What has been called the "third wave of democracy" is driven by the confluence of various trends—the establishment of democracy in countries with no prior democratic experience, its reestablishment in countries that had experienced periods of authoritarian rule, and the expansion in the number of independent states following the demise of European and Soviet communism. A common consequence of these transitions is to focus attention on the constitutional rules that guide competition for and the exercise of political authority under democracy. One of the fundamental aspects of constitutional design is the choice between parliamentary government, presidential government, or a hybrid format that combines some aspects of these two.

The distinctions among regime types at issue here have to do with how the popular branches of government—the assembly and executive—are selected and how they interact to form policy and administer the government. Assemblies—variously known as congresses, parliaments, legislatures, or a host of country-specific names—are popularly elected in all democracies, but executives are not. The general characteristics of parliamentary and presidential regimes are as follows.

Parliamentarism

- the executive is selected by the assembly;
- the executive remains in office subject to legislative confidence.

Presidentialism

- the chief executive is popularly elected;
- the terms of the chief executive and of the assembly are fixed, and not subject to mutual confidence;

- the elected executive names and directs the composition of the government, and has some constitutionally granted lawmaking authority.

The key principles that distinguish parliamentary and presidential government entail the *origin* and the *survival* of the popular branches. Under parliamentarism, only the assembly is elected, so the origin of the executive is derivative to that of the assembly. The requirement of parliamentary confidence means that the executive's survival is similarly tied to approval of an assembly majority. In most parliamentary systems, moreover, this dependence is mutual, and the executive may dissolve the assembly and call new elections prior to the expiration of its maximum constitutional period. Thus, parliamentarism is frequently distinguished from presidentialism on the grounds that powers are fused, rather than separated.

Under presidentialism the origins of the two branches are electorally distinct, with the chief executive (always the president, and sometimes one or more vice-presidents as well) elected separately from the assembly, for a fixed term. The last element in the definition of presidentialism, above, is simply that this elected president wields substantial powers over the executive branch—the ministries—and over the lawmaking process. This distinguishes presidential regimes from those that elect a ceremonial head of state who may be called a president, but who lacks constitutional authority (e.g. Ireland).

If the principles according to which the executive and assembly are founded and operate are distinct under presidentialism and parliamentarism, it is also the case that many constitutional regimes combine elements from both ideal types. Hybrid regimes have the following characteristics.

Hybrid Regimes

- the president is popularly elected, and is endowed with meaningful powers;
- there also exists a prime minister and cabinet, subject to assembly confidence.

Within this broad definition fits a wide range of hybrids in which the specific powers of the elected president, and her relationship to the prime minister and cabinet, vary considerably. Table 1 charts constitutional regime types for 80 political systems characterized by the Freedom House index of civil and political freedom as 'free' or 'partly free.'

In the course of this chapter, I review the debate over the relative advantages and disadvantages of various constitutional frameworks, the characteristics of regimes that have been of particular interest to academics and reformers, and some recent trends in the design and performance of regimes. Most of the focus is on presidentialism and hybrid regimes, for a couple of reasons. First, whereas pure parliamentary democracies are clustered among the relatively prosperous and politically stable OECD countries, presidential and hybrid systems are more common among newer democracies and among countries that have experienced

Table 1. Constitutional regime type among democracies[a], 2002

	Parliamentary	Presidential	Hybrid
Americas	Canada, Jamaica	Brazil, Chile, Colombia, Costa Rica, Dominican Republic, Ecuador, El Salvador, Guatemala, Honduras, Mexico, Nicaragua, Paraguay, United States, Uruguay	Argentina, Bolivia, Peru, Venezuela
Post-communist	Bulgaria, Czech Republic, Estonia, Hungary, Latvia, Slovak Republic	Belarus	Lithuania, Poland, Romania, Russia, Ukraine
Western Europe	Austria, Belgium, Denmark, Germany, Greece, Iceland, Ireland, Italy, Luxembourg, Netherlands, Norway, Spain, Sweden, United Kingdom		Portugal, Finland, France, Switzerland
Asia	Australia, Fiji, Israel, India, Japan, Jordan, Malaysia, Nepal, New Zealand, Papua New Guinea, Singapore, Thailand, Turkey	Bangladesh, Pakistan, Philippines, South Korea	Sri Lanka, Taiwan
Africa	Botswana, Senegal, South Africa	Gambia, Ghana, Malawi, Namibia, Uganda, Zambia, Zimbabwe	

[a] Includes regimes with Freedom House indices of civil and political rights below 5 (scale 1—7, where 1 indicates "free" and 7 "not free"). Presidential and parliamentary regime codes are from dataset for Persson and Tabellini (2002). Hybrid regimes coded by author.

more political and constitutional instability. Thus, most of the empirical action in constitutional design in recent decades has been located among the systems with elected presidencies. Second, pursuant to this empirical trend, academic debate over regime type has focused on the design and performance of systems with presidencies. Among systems with consequential presidencies, I devote more attention to Latin American cases than to presidencies elsewhere, again for a couple of reasons. First, the presidential tradition is oldest in the Americas, so the wealth of empirical material is there. Second, my own research experience is primarily in Latin America.

2. THE ACADEMIC CONSENSUS AGAINST PRESIDENTIALISM

The contemporary debate over regime type was triggered largely by the transitions to democracy in Latin America after the protracted experience of many countries in the region with military authoritarian regimes from the 1960s through the 1980s. The process of reestablishing civilian government raised the question whether faulty institutional design contributed earlier breakdowns of democratic government, and a number of observers argued that Latin America's presidential constitutional tradition contributed to democratic failure. Most influential here was work by Juan Linz (1994), who argued that presidentialism was inherently more prone to democratic breakdown than parliamentarism, and consequently advocated the adoption of parliamentary constitutions in the new Latin American democracies. The central elements of Linz's case against presidentialism are twofold. First, presidentialism lacks parliamentarism's safety valve, the confidence vote, that allows for the removal of a government from office in the event of a crisis without discarding the constitution. Second, presidentialism creates incentives and conditions that encourage such crises in the first place, and particularly that aggravate the relationship between the executive and the legislature.

Linz highlights a number of specific characteristics of presidentialism as pathological. One is the openness of executive elections to political "outsiders"—those lacking in previous parliamentary or ministerial experience—who are inclined to campaign for office by running against the existing political and party system. This problem is reinforced by the single-person nature of the office of president. Whereas parliamentary cabinets can be regarded as collegial executives, often reflecting coalitions in which more than one party is essential, the presidential executive privileges an individual whose election may induce her to claim a popular mandate even when popular support may be more limited. Coupled with this, absent a requirement of parliamentary confidence, legislators under presidentialism—even those within the president's party or coalition—are less inclined than under parliamentarism to support the executive, because intransigence does not (directly) jeopardize the survival of the government (Daniel Diermeier and Timothy Feddersen 1998). Thus, the efficiency of governments in winning legislative endorsement for their proposals that observers as far back as Walter Bagehot (1872) associated with parliamentary government does not necessarily apply under presidentialism.

The combination of all these forces suggests that presidentialism inflames antagonism between the popular branches while proscribing any constitutional mechanism for resolving the most serious conflicts. The separation of survival means presidents lack the option of dissolving intransigent assemblies, and assemblies lack the option of voting no-confidence in the executive. This lack of options can encourage one party or the other to resort to unconstitutional outside options in the event of conflict, threatening the stability of presidential democracy itself.

The breakdown of a number of Latin American democracies in the 1960s and 1970s supported Linz's case for the failure of presidential government. In Brazil in 1964, Peru in 1968, Chile in 1973, Uruguay in 1974, and Argentina in 1976, episodes of legislative-executive conflict had preceded military intervention in politics that displaced civilian leaders, imposing long periods of authoritarian rule. A number of scholars endorsed Linz's arguments as to the mechanics of presidential breakdown with country case studies (Giuseppe DiPalma 1990; Bolivar Lamounier 1993; Arend Lijphart 1990 and 1999; Arturo Valenzuela 1994; GiovanniSartori 1994). And broad cross-national studies based on quantitative data supported the proposition that, even controlling for factors such as economic development and colonial history, presidential regimes are more inclined toward democratic breakdown than are parliamentary ones (Alfred Stepan and Cindy Skach 1993; Adam Przeworski and Fernando Limongi 1997).

3. THE WORLD RESPONDS—MORE PRESIDENTS, MORE HYBRIDS

By the time a near consensus in favor of parliamentarism had formed among scholars of comparative politics, events outside the academy demonstrated that the political world was moving another direction. In Argentina, a presidentially-appointed commission in the 1980s studied the issue of regime type and recommended a move toward parliamentarism, but the proposal did not make headway among politicians (Humberto Nogueira Alcala 1986). Similar proposals were debated, but not adopted, in Chile. In Brazil, politicians put the question before voters in a 1993 referendum that offered not only parliamentarism, but also the option or returning to monarchy, as alternatives to presidentialism. When presidentialism prevailed among Brazilian voters, the prospects for fundamental reforms to convert presidential regimes to parliamentarism appeared dead.[1]

Despite the failure to embrace parliamentarism outright, Latin America witnessed some modest constitutional moves toward the principle of legislative confidence in the 1990s. Indeed, the requirement of assembly confidence for ministers is not unprecedented in the region. Although presidents have never been subject to confidence, cabinets were during Chile's period of "parliamentary republic" in the late 19th and early 20th centuries, as have ministers in Ecuador, Uruguay, and Peru more recently (Matthew Shugart and John Carey 1992). Reforms in the 1990s expanded in this direction. As part of a package of constitutional changes in 1994, Argentina created a new office, called Chief of the Cabinet of Ministers. Venezuela's new 1999 constitution creates a similar position, which it calls Prime Minister; and Peru's 1993 constitution maintains

---

[1] Indeed, redemocratizing Latin America is not exceptional in this regard. In a recent study of the effects of regime type on party systems, David Samuels (2002) finds no historical examples of democracies shifting from presidentialism to parliamentarism or vice-versa, and only two cases of parliamentary regimes shifting toward hybrid systems in which the chief executive would be directly elected: France in 1958, and Israel in 1992. Israel has since retracted this move, eliminating the direct election of the Prime Minister, although as of this writing (June 2002), the government of Ariel Sharon, directly elected in 2001, remains in office.

a Prime Minister, consistent with earlier charters. These chief ministers are constitutionally designated as chairs of the cabinet, and are removable by Congress, although the barriers to confidence votes are higher than the simple majority norm in parliamentary systems. Peru requires an absolute legislative majority (Art. 132), Venezuela a 3/5 supermajority (Art. 246), and Argentina requires concurrent absolute majorities in its bicameral legislature (Art. 101).

Outside Latin America, the trend during the 1990s was toward the creation of powerful presidencies—a pattern reinforced by the sudden proliferation of new, post-communist regimes in central Europe and the former Soviet Union. The greatest concentrations of formal presidential power are found among the post-Soviet systems whose credentials as democracies are most dubious, particularly in the 'Stans of Central Asia. Elected presidents, however, are central to politics in many of the more democratic post-communist systems as well, including Poland, Bulgaria, Romania, Lithuania, Croatia, Serbia, Georgia, Ukraine, Moldova, and of course in Russia itself (Timothy Frye 1997; J.T. Ishiyama and R. Kennedy 2001). Finally, during the late 1980s and 1990s, transitions from authoritarian rule to democracy in South Korea, Taiwan, and the Philippines produced a crop of new, or renewed, regimes with powerful presidencies in East Asia.

The rules governing the relative status of president and the cabinet, and the relationship between cabinet and parliament, vary across these new regimes. The Polish Constitution of 1997 provides the president the opportunity to act as *formateur*, nominating a candidate for prime minister, who in turn names and directs the government; but the constitution reserves to the Sejm the right to ignore the president's recommendation and form a government on its own. Moreover, once the government is installed, it is responsible to the Sejm rather than to the president (Arts. 157–161). The Russian Constitution of 1993 allows the president to name the Prime Minister (Art. 83) and makes the president arbiter of cabinet resignations (Art. 117). It also deters the State Duma from exercising its no-confidence authority by stipulating that if it insists, through multiple votes, on dismissing the government, the president may dissolve the Duma. The effect is to leave the president effectively in control of the government.

All of the post-communist regimes discussed here, as well as the Taiwanese and the Latin American cases that provide for confidence votes, are hybrids, combining elected presidents endowed with substantial constitutional authorities with prime ministers and cabinets that are subject to parliamentary confidence (Christian Lucky 1993; Frye 1997). Such regimes are characterized in some accounts as *semi-presidential*—a term originally coined by Maurice Duverger (1980) to describe the 1958 constitution of the French Fifth Republic. None of the new hybrids, however, as nearly approximates the parliamentary ideal as does France, where the president acts as *formateur*, and retains the authority to dissolve the assembly, but controls neither the composition of the cabinet nor the legislative agenda, nor wields a legislative veto. The new hybrids of the 1990s are constitutionally distinct from the French system in important ways. First, in most cases presidents can name *and* remove the prime minister, rendering this post primarily a creature of the president rather than an agent of assembly majorities. Second, the hybrid regimes of the 1990s endow presidents with formidable legislative powers—including vetoes that require extraordinary assemblies majorities for override, and in many cases the authority to issue decrees with the force of law. These powers make presidents, whose origin and survival in office remain independent from assembly confidence, central players in the lawmaking process in the new hybrid systems.

To sum up, across the various regimes that engaged in constitutional engineering in the latter decades of the 20th Century, there was a strong inclination to create and to retain powerful, elected presidencies. There was, at the same time, a trend toward acknowledging some role for assemblies in exercising confidence authority over at least some part of the executive. I will return to this theme subsequently, with the suggestion that the norm of legislative control over executives is extending beyond the provisions written on constitutional parchment.

4. RESEARCH ON INSTITUTIONAL DESIGN IN PARLIAMENTARY AND PRESIDENTIAL SYSTEMS

Institutions Under Parliamentarism

During the past decade, the academic literature on democratic institutions has expanded enormously. Among scholars focusing primarily on parliamentary systems, electoral systems are the element of institutional design attracting the most scrutiny. Rein Taagepera and Shugart (1989), Lijphart (1994), Gary Cox (1997), and Josep Colomer (2001) all provide landmark investigations of the effects of electoral rules on representation. The main focus within the electoral systems literature, moreover, is on the effects of different rules for selecting multi-member bodies—primarily parliaments—the rules for which exhibit more variance than those for selecting presidents. I discuss the interaction of presidential and legislative electoral rules below, but the electoral systems literature more generally is discussed independently in Cox's contribution to this volume, so I will not pursue those themes here.

Beyond the effects of electoral rules, research on parliamentary systems has focused less than that on presidential systems on matters of institutional design. One reason is that, whereas much of the interest in the institutional configuration of powers in presidentialism seeks to explain regime instability, few parliamentary regimes experienced breakdowns of democracy in the latter half of the 20th Century. The stability of democracy among the OECD countries has generated little concern among scholarship on modern parliamentary systems with understanding the sources of regime stability. Much of the research on parliamentary systems has been motivated by interest in instability of a different sort: that of governing coalitions. The principal theoretical motivation here is the potential for instability of decisions under majority rule identified by social choice theory

(Kenneth Arrow 1951; Richard McKelvey 1976; William Riker 1982). The suspicions raised by social choice theorists about the coherence of majority rule in the presence of multiple issue dimensions apply in a straightforward manner to parliamentary government, particularly where majorities in a single legislative chamber are sovereign over national governments, and where party system fragmentation and multiple social cleavages create the potential for fluid majority coalitions. Much of the initial literature on coalition formation in parliamentary systems motivated by social choice theory is reviewed and in Michael Laver and Norman Schofield (1990). In the ensuing decade, advances in the study of parliamentary government have examined in greater detail the rules and practices that determine how authority within governments is allocated, in an effort to understand not only which governments form, but the implications of this for the policies they produce (Terry Moe and Michael Caldwell 1994; Kathleen Bawn 1999; John Huber 1998).

Many of these advances have drawn on ideas developed in the study of a particular legislature in a presidential system—the United States Congress—testing the extent to which they apply in the parliamentary context. One example is Laver and Kenneth Shepsle's (1994, 1996) work on ministerial portfolio allocation in coalition governments, which is an extension of theories of committee jurisdiction originally developed to explain the stability of policy choices in the U.S. House of Representatives. In the parliamentary setting, the premise that ministerial portfolios endow their occupants with the ability to set policy within particular domains provides a theoretical basis for phenomena that otherwise appear anomalous, including the frequency of minority and surplus majority parliamentary governments, and the prevalence of certain, ideologically centrist parties in key portfolios regardless of shifts in their electoral fortunes.

Another example is work by Huber (1992) who looks beyond the government formation process to the rules on how legislative proposals are offered, amended, and approved, demonstrating that procedures that impose limitations on debate and amendment opportunities are employed under similar conditions in parliamentary systems as in the United States, and that control over such restrictive procedures implies substantial leverage over policy outcomes. George Tsebelis (1995, 1999) provides yet another example of work that erases the conceptual distinction between presidential and parliamentary government by introducing the idea of generic veto players as constraints on the ability of governments to make changes in policy, and demonstrating that the diversity of preferences among veto players can explain policy stability in European parliamentary systems and the European Union, as well as in separation of powers systems.

One of the key themes implicit in much of this work, rooted empirically in the study of parliamentary government, is a blurring of the theoretical distinction between parliamentary and presidential systems. The key innovation in Laver and Shepsle's model of parliamentary government builds directly on the idea, developed with respect to the U.S. Congress, that majority rule equilibrium could result from monopoly control by committees over specific policy dimensions (Shepsle 1979). The effects of restrictive procedures and agenda control emphasized by Huber and Tsebelis, similarly, follow on theoretical work originally developed in the context of U.S. politics (Thomas Romer and Howard Rosenthal 1982). The broader points that follow from this line of research are that (1) the rules by which powers are allocated can be critical to understanding which outcome prevails—and therefore how power is distributed—in environments where majority rule by itself does not provide solid expectations, and (2) in many instances, rules that govern bargaining over policy in parliamentary systems are analogous to those in presidential systems, and once the parallels are recognized it is evident that their effects are comparable.

All that said, it is important not to understate the importance of the inherent differences between parliamentary and presidential regimes. In one important sense, parliamentary constitutions are "thinner" than presidential constitutions with respect to the rules that govern bargaining among legislative actors. Consider Huber's (1996) investigation into the effects of confidence vote procedures, which examines how the agenda control implied by the confidence vote affects the relative bargaining strengths of ministers and legislative majorities when their preferences over policy differ. The model illuminates how the rules of procedure can tilt policy outcomes, but the empirical data presented on the confidence vote rules themselves and their sources illustrate that they are generally the products of informal arrangements rather than parchment institutions (Carey 2000). Of the eighteen European parliamentary systems Huber investigates, provisions governing confidence vote procedures are rooted in convention twice as frequently as they are stipulated in the constitution (p. 271).

The status of the veto, the particulars of which among presidential systems are discussed at some length below, offers another example. Under parliamentarism, where the origin and survival of the legislative and executive branches are bound together, bargaining over legislative proposals can be largely subsumed within the foundational bargain to form a government. Under presidentialism, by contrast, the provisions to govern proposals, counterproposals, and vetoes among independent legislative actors must be articulated more elaborately in formal constitutional rules. In this sense, models that count "veto players" of different institutional sorts as equivalent are potentially misleading (Tsebelis 1995). A party that is member to a minimum winning coalition cabinet may exercise a veto of sorts over government proposals, but if there is another potential coalition partner available, its objections will be ineffectual. In contrast, a president who opposes the proposals of a majority legislative coalition cannot be so easily replaced, and therefore not so easily disregarded. Veto players in parliamentary regimes are more likely to be of the partisan variety, whereas veto players of the constitutional sort are more abundant in presidential systems.

Torsten Persson, Gerald Roland, and Guido Tabellini (1997) underscore the implications for bargaining over policy inherent the mutual independence of legislature and executive. Their argument is that separation of powers systems generate stronger incentives than do parliamentary systems for information revelation by politicians to the electorate regarding the state of the economic world and the prospects for governments to deliver benefits voters care about. The advantage rests on the idea that both legislators and executives are better informed than voters about the connection between policy and outcomes, but that whichever institutional actor holds the weaker bargaining position has an incentive to reveal information in order to avoid the risk of electoral punishment for the actions of the stronger institutional actor. The argument that separation of powers reduces moral hazard through this mechanism is a variant of the broader Madisonian proposition that separation of powers, by pitting the ambitions of officials in different branches against one another, provides protection against predatory behavior by politicians. In support of this position, Persson and Tabellini (2002) present evidence that government spending consumes a larger share of GDP under parliamentary than under presidential systems.

To sum up, research on parliamentary democracy demonstrates that the rules of political competition and bargaining systematically affect representation and policy outcomes. The institutional context of parliamentary democracy, however, is somewhat thinner than that in presidential and hybrid systems, insofar as the separation of powers requires more elaborate and explicit institutional arrangements to govern bargaining over policy. Research on presidential systems devotes relatively more attention to institutional design, and it is to the particulars of this research agenda that I now turn.

Partisan Compatibility of Presidents and Assemblies

Empirical work on presidential and hybrid regimes has focused on the mechanics of relations between the executive and legislative branches largely in an effort to evaluate the case against presidentialism articulated by Linz and the presidentialism critics. Pursuant to that battery of criticisms, much of the research among scholars of presidential systems focused on whether presidentialism inherently undermines bargaining and cooperation between the branches, and if so, to what effect. An initial reaction was to point out that there is tremendous variance among systems with presidents in terms of institutional design, and to examine whether these details could help explain regime performance (Shugart and Carey 1992; Scott Mainwaring and Shugart 1997). One of the central themes in this research is the interaction between presidential and legislative elections, and the implications for party systems. Understanding the sources of divided government in the United States is, of course, a longstanding cottage industry (Morris Fiorina 1996; Walter Mebane and Jasjeet Sekhon 2002). But the diversity of electoral arrangements across presidential systems provides a richer environment for examining institutional explanations for partisan conflict or compatibility across branches. Moreover, one of the central questions raised by presidentialism critics is whether regime crises are encouraged when presidents lack majority support in Congress (Mainwaring 1993; Jose Cheibub 2002). Two key factors associated with the system for electing presidents are central to this research: the formula for electing presidents, and the relative timing of presidential and legislative elections.

Methods of Electing Presidents

The two most common formula for electing presidents are the plurality and the majority run-off systems. Under plurality rule, there is one election, and the candidate with the most votes is elected. Under the majority run-off system, if no candidate wins an outright majority of the vote in the first round, there is a second round pitting the top first-round candidates against each other. One of the central conclusions from research on methods of presidential election is that, relative to plurality elections for president, the majority run-off format contributes to the proliferation of presidential candidates, and the fragmentation of the first-round presidential vote (Shugart and Carey 1992, Mark Jones 1995, Mainwaring and Shugart 1997, Cox 1997).

The rationale rests on both the differing incentives for strategic voting under the two systems (Maurice Duverger 1954), and the opportunities for between-rounds bargaining unique to run-off elections for presidential office. Under plurality elections, where the threshold for success is high, the best strategy for a presidential aspirant who cannot reasonably expect to win the most votes is to enter a pre-election coalition with a viable candidate. Under a run-off system, on the other hand, the initial threshold is lower, as the second-place first-round candidate survives. Moreover, given that electoral coalitions can be renegotiated after the first round in anticipation of the run-off, even nonviable candidates are induced to compete in the first round to establish the value of their second-round endorsement. The more marginal candidates enter in the first round, moreover, the more fragmented the expected vote, and the more unpredictable the results become.

By encouraging fragmentation and unpredictability, majority run-off elections provide a favorable environment for outsider candidates. The advance of Jean Marie Le Pen through a crowded first-round field to the second round of the 2002 French presidential election drove this point home to Europeans, but the effect was visible in Latin America earlier. Prominent cases in which outsider candidates built surprising first-round performances into second-round victories include Fernando Collor in Brazil in 1989, and Jorge Serrano in Guatemala and Alberto Fujimori in Peru in 1990. Each ran against the traditional party system in his country, survived the first round with less than one-third of the vote, and won the presidency in a run-off. Despite their second-round "mandates," moreover, each of these presidents quickly found themselves mired in interbranch conflicts which culminated in the premature deaths of Collor's and Serrano's presidencies, and of Peru's Congress. The rapid rise of Alejandro Toledo against Fujimori himself in the first round of the 2000 Peruvian election, and his victory the next year in the special election to fill the office vacated by Fujimori, reinforces the premise that the run-off format can catapult outsiders into contention, primarily as "anyone-but-X" candidates.

Electoral Cycles

A second key element of institutional design is the relative timing of executive and legislative elections—the electoral cycle—which interacts with the presidential electoral formula to affect the prospects for partisan compatibility between the branches. Where elections are held on dissynchronous schedules, campaigns are conducted independently, and the contours of the legislative party system are not bound to presidential elections. Where elections for the presidency and those for the assembly are concurrent, presidential candidates' electoral coattails can affect fragmentation in assembly elections, and therefore the partisan distribution of seats (Shugart 1995). Whereas plurality elections for the president can reduce fragmentation of legislative party systems, this effect is absent under the two-round format. As a result, the likelihood of divided government—that is, of presidents who lack the support of partisan majorities in the assembly—is higher under non-concurrent than under concurrent electoral cycles, and among systems with concurrent cycles, is higher when presidents are elected by majority run-off than by plurality (Mainwaring and Shugart 1997).

This body of research underscores an irony in the choices of electoral system designers in recent years. Prior to the latest wave of redemocratization in Latin America, and the institutional reforms that accompanied it, the plurality formula was the norm for presidential elections. By the late 1990s, majority run-off systems had been adopted in Chile, Colombia, Brazil, Dominican Republic, Ecuador, El Salvador, Guatemala, Paraguay, Peru, and Uruguay. Argentina and Nicaragua had established first-round victory thresholds of 45% of the popular vote, and Costa Rica 40%, with run-offs to ensue if the winning candidate did not surpass these marks.[2] Among the new post-communist systems, the trend is even more stark—every one of the popularly elected presidencies is chosen by the majority run-off rule. A prominent rationale for adopting the run-off format is that to do so required that the eventual winner be endorsed by a majority of voters (Jones 1995). Yet in guaranteeing such an electoral mandate in the second round, the run-off systems may systematically produce presidents that confront greater opposition among legislators than they would under the old plurality systems.

Policymaking Powers of Presidents

Partisan support in the legislature is critical to the effectiveness of presidents in realizing their agenda. Indeed, dominance over policymaking is frequently attributed to presidents with relatively limited formal authority over standard lawmaking procedures, provided that their party or coalition controls the

---

[2] Costa Rica's system has been in place since 1949, and its first-round threshold is low enough to approximate the effects of a plurality system. Argentina's reform, in 1994, and Nicaragua's, in 1995, were evidently attempts to split the difference between the Costa Rican threshold and the standard majority run-off format.

legislature and that the president is the effective leader of his party (R. Lynn Kelley 1973; Daniel Levine 1973; Jeffrey Weldon 1997). In such cases, it is not the formal authority of the presidency that accounts for executive influence, but rather the coincidence of the presidency with party leadership in the same individual. In other cases, however, formal authorities are enshrined in the office of the presidency, independent of partisan support. The specific nature of these powers varies considerably across presidencies, but here I briefly discuss three common types of presidential power over legislation: decree, agenda-setting, and veto authority.

Decree

Decree is the authority of the executive to establish law in lieu of action by the assembly. This may include executive policy initiatives that eventually require legislative ratification, provided the initiatives go into effect without prior legislative action (Carey and Shugart 1998a and 1998b). Empirically, then, constitutional decree authority of executives varies according to whether the initiatives:

- are effective as policy immediately (yes/no); and
- become permanent law even without legislative action (yes/no).

The four possible combinations form a 2X2 matrix, shown in Table 2, with empirical examples in each box. The formal procedures attached to decree authority determine whether there is an opportunity for assembly debate on a measure before it becomes law, and whether the assembly must take explicit action to rescind the measure.

At the top left of Table 2 is the prototypical decree authority whereby the executive issues a proposal that becomes permanent law immediately and without any legislative action. Executives can effectively present policy initiatives under this format as fait accompli, and only through the passage of new legislation (or a new decree) can the policy be altered. Very few democratic constitutions grant presidents such power, and those that do generally include some constraints on the policy jurisdictions in which executives may exercise decree.

Table 2. Examples of presidential decree authority

		Decree becomes permanent law?	
		YES	NO
Decree in effect immediately?	YES	Russia (Art. 90) Peru (Art. 118(19)) Colombia (Art. 215)	Brazil (Art. 62) Colombia (Art. 213) Argentina (Art. 99.3)
	NO	Ecuador (Art. 65) France (Art. 49.3)*	

*Refers to power vested in the premier, not the president, to make proposals under the *guillotine* procedure.

The Colombian president may use decree to "restore economic order," and the Peruvian "on economic and financial matters, when so required by the national interest." Presidents in both countries have interpreted these powers expansively in setting economic policy—for example, changing tax rates, privatizing public assets, transferring assets to regional governments (Daniel Archer and Shugart 1997; Gregory Schmidt 1998).

The top right box in Table 2 represents *provisional* decree authority in which executive proposals take effect immediately, but lapse after some designated period unless ratified by the legislature.[3] In Brazil, presidential decrees lapse after thirty days; in Colombia decrees other than those "to restore economic order" lapse after a maximum of 180 days. Whether such a provision is effective for initiating long-term changes even against legislative opposition depends in part on whether the decrees may be reissued at the end of the period. The reiteration of decrees was a matter of constitutional controversy in Brazil in the 1980s, where judicial precedent currently holds that the president can reissue decrees on which Congress has not acted, but cannot reissue decrees Congress has explicitly rejected (Timothy Power 1998).

The bottom left of Table 2 describes *delayed* decree, whereby executive proposals do not take effect immediately, but become law *unless* the legislature acts to reject them. In Ecuador, for example, the president can propose legislation, declaring it "urgent," and if Congress fails to act within fifteen days, the proposal becomes law. The format is similar to France's *guillotine* (Art. 49.3), whereby if parliament rejects the executive's proposal, then the government falls; but if parliament takes no action, the proposal becomes law. It is important to note, however, that the authority over the *guillotine* is vested in the French premier, not the president, consistent with France's relatively parliamentary hybrid regime. Delayed decree allows the time for debate and negotiation between the branches, but like the other forms of decree it may encourage legislators to abdicate responsibility for policies by allowing assemblies to accede to executive proposals simply by failing to act.

The use of decree authority has been central to conflicts between legislatures and executives that have generated constitutional crises in a number of countries. In the first years of Fujimori's administration in Peru, the president's increasing reliance on decree in the face of legislative opposition to his policy proposals prompted Congress to pass legislation clarifying and constraining the scope of executive decree authority (Schmidt 1998). Before the bill could be passed over an expected presidential veto, Fujimori called out the tanks and closed Congress (Maxwell Cameron 1997; Philip Mauceri 1997).

Presidential decree authority was a focal point of the conflict in Russia in the early 1990s. The highly fragmented Russian Congress of People's Deputies

---

[3] This type of decree authority is not unique to presidential government. For example, the Italian cabinet can issue decrees with immediate force, but which lapse after 60 days if not ratified by parliament (Art. 77).

initially delegated sweeping decree authority to President Yeltsin during the Soviet constitutional crisis in late 1991. But Yeltsin's use of decree to enact broad economic reforms and abolish the Communist Party immediately prompted challenges from the legislature. Throughout 1992 and 1993, Russia experienced a "war of laws" in which presidential decrees were implemented, then overturned by legislation, which in turn was supplanted by subsequent decrees (Thomas Remington, Stephen Smith, D. Roderick Kiewiet, and Moshe Haspel 1994). As in Peru, the president eventually prevailed in this "war" through the use of military force, rather than negotiation with the other branch, in the process securing a new constitution in 1993 that enshrined presidential decree authority. Decree under Russia's 1993 Constitution is constrained not by policy area, but by the limitation that presidential edicts "cannot contradict the Constitution of the Russian Federation or Federal Law" (Art. 90). Initially, President Yeltsin invoked Article 90 aggressively, both to set national policy and to control the timing of regional elections, which in turn determine the composition of Russia's upper legislative chamber. The broad scope of presidential decree authority in Russia in the mid-1990s, however, was partly a product of the legal vacuum that accompanied the establishment of a new regime and constitution in 1993—a vacuum that has been filled in subsequent years, shrinking the range of presidential discretion under Article 90 (Scott Parrish 1998). Decree authority in Russia can still provide the president leverage in shaping legislative outcomes, principally by establishing a new status quo policy that induces the legislature to act, rather than by setting policies by fiat (Remington, Olga Shvetsova, and Smith 2002).

This is also a critical characteristic of provisional decree authority, as in the Brazilian or Argentine constitutions, which ostensibly prevent unilateral presidential action because permanent policy changes require assembly ratification. Because executive proposals take effect immediately, however, overturning them can entail substantial "clean-up" costs. Once a policy is set, there may be steep economic and/or political transaction costs to backing away from it, thus making it difficult for the legislature to let a decree lapse even if no majority favored it in the first place. The adoption of new currency systems by the successive Brazilian administrations of Jose Sarney (1985–1990) and Fernando Collor (1990–1992) illustrate this point. Twice in the space of four years, Brazilian presidents relied on provisional decree to impose currency and economic reforms, arguing that the element of surprise was necessary to avoid panic in currency markets. Once in place, the decrees could not be overturned by Congress without inducing even greater financial instability, yet lacking prior negotiated support in the legislature, the broader economic reforms packages of both presidents were abandoned quickly once initial waves of popular support ebbed (Power 1998).

In sum, where constitutions provide presidents with decree, the use of this authority to avoid negotiation with legislative opponents has frequently been the subject of conflict between the branches, which in some cases has evolved into regime crisis.

Agenda Powers

Short of outright decree authority, presidents are frequently endowed with the authority to make policy proposals that have privileged procedural status before the legislature, either because

- they must be considered within a limited time period; or
- there are limitations on the manner in which they can be amended; or
- the proposal determines the set of policy alternatives among which the assembly must choose; or
- some combination of these.

In most presidential systems, presidents are endowed with the ability to introduce legislation, and in many cases with the authority to require legislative action on proposals within a limited time. When executive agenda authority includes limitations on amendments or influence over what policy pertains even if the legislature does not support the executive proposal, then executives can wield enormous influence over policy outcomes.

I focus here only on one example that is particularly instructive because it illustrates all the aspects of agenda authority outlined above: presidential budget authority in Chile. The current Chilean constitution was written by the military government of General Augusto Pinochet well before the transition back to civilian government in that country (Genaro Arriagada and Carol Graham 1994; J.S. Valenzuela 1992). In an effort to limit congressional logrolling capacity and guarantee fiscal austerity, the constitution (Art. 64) establishes that:

- the president introduces the annual budget bill;
- Congress is allowed to amend each spending item within the budget downward only, and cannot transfer funds cut from one item to other areas of the budget;
- Congress must pass its version of the budget within 60 days, or else the executive's original proposal becomes law;
- only the executive may introduce legislation on spending or tax matters; thus prohibiting Congress from side-stepping the executive budget by introducing and passing supplementary spending bills.

The overall effects of this procedure, compared with budgetary procedures in regimes where the president's agenda powers are more modest, are to constrain government spending levels and to increase the president's bargaining strength relative to Congress. Spending is constrained because whichever branch prefers less spending on a particular budget item can always secure its ideal level—the president by setting the spending ceiling in his proposal, Congress by amending downward. Logrolling agreements between the two branches are discouraged because the president's proposal is not accepted or rejected as a package, but rather can be disaggregated into its component items and altered. The president's bargaining advantage is rooted in the fact that his initial proposal sets the reversionary policy (Lisa Baldez and Carey 1999, 2001). These effects of executive agenda powers are supported more generally in research showing that more "hierarchical" budget procedures contribute to fiscal discipline across Latin American regimes (Alberto Alesina, Ricardo Hausmann, Rudolf Hommes, and Ernesto Stein 1999).

One critical difference between agenda and decree authority is worth noting. Agenda power entails presidential control over the policy alternatives among which legislatures debate and select, whereas decree allows presidents to implement policies without legislative debate or assent. Democratic theory commonly holds that debate in itself is a valuable political good, even apart from its effects on policy choices (Lijphart 1977, 1999; David Miller 1993). The experience of many presidential systems with decree authority supports this intuition. Agenda powers may provide presidents influence over policy as great decree authority, yet even legislative debate and negotiation constrained by presidential agenda control appear to mitigate conflict between the branches, whereas policymaking by decree can contribute to intractable conflict between the branches.

Vetoes

The most common presidential power over legislation is the veto. The structure of presidential vetoes varies along two critical dimensions. The first is the requirement for the assembly to override a veto, which varies from:

- simple majority (e.g. Venezuela);[4] to
- absolute majority of the assembly's membership (e.g. Nicaragua); to
- absolute majority in joint session in a bicameral system (e.g. Brazil); to
- absolute majorities of both chambers in a bicameral system (e.g. Colombia); to
- 3/5 majority of those voting in joint session of a bicameral system (e.g. Uruguay); to
- 2/3 majorities of those voting in each chamber (e.g. most bicameral systems).

The second dimension is whether the veto may be partial (also known as the item veto) or must apply to an entire piece of legislation (package veto).[5]

The veto is generally considered a reactive authority—one that allows presidents to hold up legislative initiatives, requiring further deliberation and even the construction of supermajorities—rather than a proactive authority such as decree or agenda power, that allows presidents to initiate policy changes. Although this characterization is accurate in the case of the package veto format, however, it is not for the partial veto. The package veto allows legislatures to offer logroll-type proposals to presidents, enticing presidents to accept some

---

[4] This is effectively a presidential request for to reconsider the legislation, given that the same majority that passed legislation initially can override the veto.

[5] For the configurations of veto authorities across presidencies, see Shugart and Carey (1992), Lucky (1993), and Carey, Amorim Neto, and Shugart (1997).

policies the legislature wants in exchange for securing some preferred by the president. Advocates of the partial veto contend it allows presidents to unpack such legislative logrolls, removing wasteful or inefficient programs supported by individual legislators or factions. This account, however, overlooks the strategic impact the partial veto has on bargaining over legislation between the branches. Presidents can unpack logrolls only if such compromise legislation is passed by the legislature, but the very existence of the partial veto discourages compromise by allowing presidents to alter policies approved by the legislature unilaterally before implementation.

Consider two policy initiatives that are not mutually exclusive: policy L, favored by the legislature, and policy P, favored by the president. Assume the following conditions hold:

- the legislature most prefers to pass policy L and least prefer to pass policy P;
- the president prefers the opposite;
- both sides prefer to pass both policies (LP) rather than nothing at all (SQ).

If a package veto exists, the legislature can pass LP, the president should accept it, and both sides consider themselves better off than if the status quo had prevailed. If a partial veto exists, in contrast, legislature knows that if it passes LP, the president can veto L and promulgate P, securing her most preferred outcome. This is also the legislature's *least* preferred outcome, however, so it should send the president no proposal, leaving both sides worse off than when the president is equipped only with the weaker package veto.

The point with regard to veto authority is the same as that made above regarding other legislative powers entrusted to presidents. When executives can alter policy and then proceed to implement those changes without an intervening step of legislative debate and assent, incentives for compromise between the branches are undermined. Thus, arguments on behalf of the partial veto made on the grounds of budgetary efficiency, for example, must be weighed against the extent to which the partial veto weakens the executive's ability to commit to compromise agreements with the legislature.[6]

5. Used Presidents and Government Crises: "Should I Stay or Should I Go Now?"

The presidentialism versus parliamentarism debate coinciding with the Third Wave was initially motivated by the proposition that regime type can affect democratic stability. That subsequent research honed in on increasingly fine distinctions in institutional design and examined their effects on regime performance is, in part, a happy by-product of the fact that breakdowns of democracy,

---

[6] For an analogous discussion of how sequential budget procedures can discourage compromise by undermining the ability of the last mover to commit, see Persson, Roland, and Tabellini (1997).

across all regime types, were rare in the last two decades of the 20th Century.[7] Yet crises of individual governments persist, and in systems where presidents are chief executives, these present the question of presidential survival. Fixed presidential terms, and the absence of a safety valve procedure allowing for the constitutional removal of a feckless president, remain problematic even when government crises do not directly threaten the survival of democracy. Indeed, fixed terms can generate tensions both when presidents face extraordinary opposition, and when they enjoy strong support. This section reviews the constitutional constraints on presidential reelection, and the outcomes of government crises in Latin America that have pitted presidents against intransigent legislative opposition.

Reelection

Parliamentary systems do not place restrictions on the reelection of chief executives. In this sense, there is no constraint other than sustained assembly support (and, indirectly, voter support) to the perpetuation in office of a popular prime minister. Presidential and hybrid systems, by contrast, not only place greater obstacles to the early removal of the president, they almost uniformly place constitutional limitations on presidential reelection.

Table 3 shows the status of constitutional restrictions on presidential reelection in 44 presidential and hybrid democracies, with the cases organized by region.[8] The only cases that place no restrictions on reelection are Indonesia, whose democratic credentials are marginal, and quite recent; and France, where the Constitution of the Fifth Republic provides only limited policymaking authorities to the president.[9] There is no pattern among the East Asian, with some imposing strict prohibitions on reelection and others allowing consecutive terms. Most of the African presidential systems allow for two consecutive terms, although Mali and Senegal impose lifetime limits after one. The starkest distinction is between the post-communist hybrid systems and the presidential regimes

---

[7] Among the presidential systems of Latin America, this is in part due to the fact that Latin American militaries were unable, or unwilling, to intervene in politics for the long haul. The reasons vary from country to country, but one effect is that when presidents and legislatures find themselves at a stand-off, neither necessarily holds the option of knocking on the barracks door to ask for assistance. Another change is at the international level. The rest of the hemisphere is now much less tolerant of non-democratic neighbors. In particular, Latin America's major democracies are willing to act together to isolate, diplomatically and economically, governments that seize or maintain power through breaches in democratic procedure.

[8] Countries are included if their combined political rights and civil liberties scores are above the midpoint (seven or lower, with lower scores more democratic) on the Freedom House scale for 2001–2002 (http://www.freedomhouse.org/ratings/index.htm). I also include four cases with combined scores of eight, because of longstanding traditions of presidential democracy (Colombia, Venezuela), or their prominence among post-communist European regimes (Ukraine, Yugoslavia).

[9] It is worth noting that in 2000, French voters approved a referendum to shorten the length of the presidential term from seven years—then the longest among democratic systems—to five. The motivation was to synchronize the terms of presidents with those of parliament.

Table 3. Rules on reelection in presidential and hybrid democracies

Group	Lifetime limit	One term, then... Eligible after one interim term	One term, then... Eligible after two interim terms	Two terms, then No reelection	Two terms, then ...eligible after one interim term	No limits
Americas	Colombia Costa Rica Guatemala Honduras Mexico Paraguay	Bolivia Chile Dominican Republic Ecuador El Salvador Nicaragua Uruguay	Panama	Brazil United States Venezuela	Argentina Peru	
Post-communist				Bulgaria Croatia Macedonia Poland Romania Yugoslavia	Armenia Georgia Lithuania Moldova Russia Ukraine	
Africa	Mali Senegal			Botswana Central African Republic Congo Ghana Namibia	Cape Verde	
East Asia	South Korea Philippines			Taiwan		Indonesia
Western Europe					Finland Portugal	France

of the Americas. The former allow for two terms, then either prohibit subsequent reelection altogether, or prohibit more than two consecutive terms. Most of the presidential systems of the Americas employ more severe restrictions. Many impose a one-term lifetime limit; others allow non-consecutive reelection only. Consecutive reelection of any sort is the exception rather than the rule.

A decade ago, the commitment to no presidential reelection in Latin America was even more pronounced—a pattern hidden by the cross-national comparison in Table 3. The most conspicuous changes in electoral institutions in Latin America during the 1990s were constitutional amendments to reverse longstanding prohibitions on consecutive presidential reelection in four of the region's largest countries.

Historically, strict no-reelection provisions in Latin America represented reactions to the abuse of power by presidents seeking to ensure their perpetuation in office (Carey 2002). Popular incumbent presidents intent on securing second terms in office advocated relaxation of these provisions during the 1990s, on the grounds that the possibility of consecutive reelection removes constraints on the electoral choices allowed to voters, enhancing the quality of democracy. Voters appeared to ratify this argument by reelecting the incumbents who secured these constitutional reforms: Alberto Fujimori in Peru and Carlos Menem in Argentina in 1995, and Fernando Henrique Cardoso in Brazil in 1998, and Hugo Chavez in Venezuela in 2000. In the wake of these reelectoral successes, however, ensued government crises that forced reevaluation of the case for presidential reelection.

The potential for incumbents eligible for reelection to subvert democracy in order to hold onto the presidency was clearest in the case of Peru's Fujimori, who was reelected in 1995, and then again in 2000, before being removed from office later that year. Fujimori's eligibility for reelection was first established in a new constitution he engineered, and had ratified by plebiscite in 1993. The charter allowed consecutive reelection one time before a president must step down for at least a term. Fujimori's reelection in 1995, therefore, appeared to have placed him at the constitutional limit. By the late 1990s, however, Fujimori expressed his intention to run again in 2000, on the grounds that his *first* term as president (1990–95) did not count, for having begun under the *previous* constitution. When a plurality of Peru's Constitutional Tribunal objected to Fujimori's creative interpretation of his own charter, the president's compliant congressional majority fired the offending judges.[10] During the 2000 campaign itself, Fujimori's supporters systematically intimidated opposition candidates and disrupted their campaign rallies; his administration used state resources to pressure the Peruvian media to slant its campaign coverage; and there were irregularities

---

[10] Fujimori's majority in Congress had ratified language specifically approving two consecutive presidential terms *under the current constitution*. The Constitutional Tribunal voted 3–0—but with the remaining four members abstaining—that the law was inapplicable to Fujimori. The abstentions rendered the status of the decision dubious. The doubts themselves were rendered moot, however, by Congress's ensuing impeachment of the anti-reelection judges.

in the vote count—all of which induced Fujimori's main opponent, Alejandro Toledo, to withdraw from the race before the second round of elections.

The issue of presidential reelection was also central to Venezuela's political turmoil in the late 1990s and first years of the next decade. Hugo Chavez, who was first elected in 1998, set out to overhaul the Venezuelan political system, securing by plebiscite in 1999 a new constitution that extended the presidential term to six years and allowed two consecutive terms. Chavez called new elections for 2000, explicitly establishing the claim that his clock would start anew if he were elected, which he was. His adversaries are motivated by objections to a variety of his policies, but permeating all opposition is the perceived threat that reelection could allow Chavez to hold the presidency for up to fourteen years, and that he had maneuvered to prevent a viable electoral threat to that prospect. This, at least, was part of the justification offered by *anti-Chavistas* who backed the failed military coup in April 2002.

A year before Fujimori's attempt at a third consecutive election and Chavez's second, Argentina's Menem had attempted a similar move, testing the public's willingness to accept a his candidacy in 1999 on the grounds that his first election, in 1989, pre-dated the constitutional reform allowing two consecutive terms. Politicians, both within and outside Menem's Peronist Party, however, supported the Argentine Supreme Court's objection to such a stratagem, and Menem backed away from his plan.

Three of the four Latin American countries that relaxed restrictions on presidential reelection during the 1990s experienced government crises shortly thereafter. Argentina's travails of the early 2000s were not directly connected to the matter of consecutive reelection. Judicial and political opposition to Menem's aspirations averted that scenario. The conflict between Chavez and his opponents in Venezuela is fueled by a wide range of factors, among which the prospect of presidential *continuismo* remains prominent. Fujimori's election in 2000 provides the clearest warning that perpetuation in office by means of intimidation and fraud had not been relegated decisively to the past, and the tide appears to have turned once again against presidential reelection in Peru, where a constitutional reform rendering the incumbent ineligible attracted initial support in 2001. In any case, the experiences of Fujimori, Chavez, and to a lesser extent Menem, may make it more difficult to defend reelection as a democratic asset in presidential systems.

Government Crises and the Parliamentarization of Presidential Systems

Attempts by incumbents to extend their control over the executive are not the only sources of government crises in presidential systems. In Latin America, there have been eleven cases over the past decade of government crises in which one or the other branch has been supplanted before its constitutional term expired.

Table 4 illustrates a pattern that is remarkable, given Latin America's reputation for *caudillismo* (rule by political strongmen) and presidential dominance. In

Table 4. Curtailment of presidential and legislative terms in the past decade

Country	Year	Circumstances	Survivor	Replacement
Peru	1992	*Autogolpe* by President Fujimori, supported by military.	*President*	*New legislative elections, 1993*
Brazil	1992	President Collor, having been impeached by the Chamber for corruption, resigns.	Congress	Vice-President Itamar Franco, for duration of 5-year term
Guatemala	1993	President Serrano attempts an *autogolpe* against Congress, prompting popular protests, repudiation by the Constitutional Court, and the military.	Congress	Congress selects an interim replacement for Serrano, then calls new elections.
Venezuela	1993	Congress removes President Perez from office on charges of misappropriation of funds and embezzlement.	Congress	Congress selects Ramón José Velásquez interim president for duration of Perez's term.
Ecuador	1997	Congress removes President Abdala Bucarám from office for "mental incompetence."	Congress	Congress selects its then-Speaker, Fabio Alarcón as president for duration of Bucarám's term
Paraguay	1999	Facing impeachment for refusing to comply with a Supreme Court decision countermanding a presidential pardon, President Raul Cubas Grau abdicates.	Congress	Vice President (first constitutional successor) had recently been assassinated. Senate Leader Luis Gonzalez Macchi (second constitutional successor) replaces Cubas Grau for duration of term.
Venezuela	1999	Congress objects to usurpation legislative power by a constituent assembly convoked by newly elected President Chavez, but acquiesces in the face of popular opposition.	President	Interim legislative council appointed by president. Elections for a new legislature follow ratification of new constitution in 2000.
Ecuador	2000	Widespread protests against economic policies are supported by junior military officers, who remove President Mahuad from office.	Congress	Consultation between military and Congress leads to installation in presidency of Vice President Jaime Noboa for duration of presidential term.

(*continued*)

Table 4. (*continued*)

Country	Year	Circumstances	Survivor	Replacement
Peru	2000	Revelations of massive corruption in President Fujimori's administration prompt the president to flee the country and a congressional vote to remove him for "moral incompetence."	Congress	Congress selects a legislator, Valentín Paniagua, as interim president until elections are held, six months later.
Argentina	2001	Facing street protests against economic policies, President Fernando de la Rua resigns.	Congress	Congress selects San Luis state Governor Adolfo Rodriguez Saa as interim president, without determining whether he will serve duration of constitutional term or call early elections.*
Argentina	2001	Continued protests, and Rodriguez Saa's failure to establish a legislative coalition, prompt his resignation after one week in office.	Congress	Congress selects former Senator and Buenos Aires state Governor Eduardo Duhalde as interim president, still without resolving question of duration of term.**

* De la Rua's initial replacement, by legislative selection, was Senate Majority Leader Ramon Puerta, but Puerta's appointment was intended to be of only temporary—48 hours—to allow the selection of a longer-term replacement.
** Rodriguez Saa's initial replacement, by legislative selection, was House Majority Leader Eduardo Camano—48 hours), but Camano's appointment was intended to be of only temporary—48 hours—to allow the selection of a longer-term replacement.

all but two of these interbranch showdowns, it was the legislature that survived, and most often the legislature filled the vacated presidency in a manner akin to that following the fall of a government in parliamentary systems.

How to interpret this pattern of outcomes to government crises in Latin America's presidential systems? First, legislatures have proven more durable over the past decade than presidents. Table 4 does not demonstrate that Latin American legislatures are evenly matched with presidents in their influence over policy under conditions of normal politics, but it casts doubt on the longstanding reputation of Latin American legislatures as ineffectual and dominated by executives.

Second, legislative replacement of the president has become the norm when governments fall, but not—or not entirely—as a result of formal constitutional provisions. Argentina's constitutional reforms of 1994 included language empowering Congress to appoint a new president in cases where the office if vacated (Sección 88), thus providing clear constitutional footing for two consecutive legislative replacements of Presidents de la Rua and Rodriguez Saa five years later (Hector Shamis 2002). Yet these replacements in Argentina followed on the voluntary resignations of the incumbent presidents. Neither Argentina nor any other Latin American presidential system has in place a constitutional provision analogous to a no-confidence procedure for the president, by which the chief executive can be removed simply for having lost the political confidence of a legislative majority.[11]

Many of the legislative replacements listed in Table 4 were justified on idiosyncratic constitutional grounds. The 1961 Venezuelan Constitution, in force during Carlos Andres Perez's removal from office in 1993, did not establish explicit provisions for legislative removal of the president, even in the form of impeachment for violations of the law or constitution. The 1996 Ecuadorian Constitution, in place when President Bucarám was replaced, allowed Congress to remove the president for "physical or mental incompetence" (Art. 100) but did not spell out how such a condition would be established—and President Bucarám disagreed with the legislative diagnosis. Moreover, in appointing the legislative leader Fabio Alarcón to replace Bucarám, Congress ignored the line of succession established in Article 101 of that charter. In 2000, the assumption of Ecuadorian Vice President Jaime Noboa complied with the line of succession established in Article 168 of the new, 1998 Constitution, but there was no constitutional foundation for the removal from office of President Jamil Mahuad by military coup, ratified by Congress in its confirmation of Noboa. In Peru, in 2000, Alberto Fujimori's abdication to Japan left the presidency vacant, in accordance with the constitution, but Congress's subsequent declaration of "moral incapacity" was unconnected to any constitutional provision; and while Fujimori's entire administration had been tainted by the breaking corruption scandal, the constitutional line of succession (Art. 115) formally ran through the first and second Vice Presidents before reaching Congress President Valentín Paniagua, who was installed. In short, even while Latin American constitutions remain presidential, formally providing for the separation of origin and survival of the elected branches, the replacement of presidents in practice increasingly displays a more parliamentarized flavor, with a priority on legislative discretion.

Finally, there are signs that the expectations of elected officials, and their associated behaviors, are changing to reflect the practice of legislative replacement. Consider the approach of Argentine President Eduardo Duhalde in April 2002 as he presented controversial banking legislation that caused even legislators in his

---

[11] The Venezuelan Constitution of 1999 establishes a provision for referenda to recall any elected officials, including the president, upon the collection of signatures of ten percent of registered voters (Arts. 72, 74). The threshold required for recall is the number of votes won in the original popular vote, thus rendering presidents elected with broad support relatively secure, but leaving a president elected by a narrow plurality—perhaps in a divided field of candidates—vulnerable to recall. As this essay was being written, in mid-2002, the Bolivian Congress was debating a constitutional reform to allow for an absolute congressional majority in joint session simultaneously to dissolve itself and call for early presidential elections.

own Peronist party to balk. In a press conference, the president suggested that, "If the Parliament is not in agreement, it will have to elect another president" (Larry Rother 2002). In suggesting the bill represented a confidence vote in his presidency, Duhalde was adopting a strategy directly from the parliamentary playbook. He failed in the immediate term. His bill foundered, and he did not back up his threat to resign. That the president would even present the initiative in such a manner, however, represents a fundamental change in the strategic political environment.

Among legislators, too, there is evidence that replacement is regarded as an option in conflicts with intransigent presidents. In the months following the April 2002 aborted coup against Venezuelan President Hugo Chavez, the president's opponents sought to exploit splits within Chavez's legislative coalition to cobble an Assembly majority in favor of his removal, despite the fact that the Venezuelan Constitution of 1999 is unusually explicit on the mechanisms by which the presidency can be vacated, and a legislative vote is not among them (Article 233).

The association of presidentialism with fixed terms of executive office was challenged on a couple of fronts during the 1990s. Presidential terms were extended through the possibility of reelection in four of Latin America's major presidential systems, with mixed results. Voters embraced the opportunity to return incumbents to office, but the experience of these administrations was not uniformly encouraging for the principle of reelection. The terms of nine presidents were also curtailed by legislative action. Latin America's constitutions remain presidential, but the means of resolving government crises in the region has come to resemble parliamentarism.

6. CONCLUSION

Parliamentary government fuses the selection of the executive to the popular vote for the assembly and the survival of the executive to assembly confidence. Academic research on parliamentary systems has focused extensively on how the selection and maintenance of governments drawn from assembly coalitions affects which parties and interests are represented in the executive (Laver and Schofield 1990; Laver and Shepsle 1996; Lanny Martin and Randolph Stevenson 2001), for what duration (Paul Warwick 1994; Arthur Lupia and Kaare Strom 1995; Laver and Shepsle 1998; Diermeier and Stevenson 2000), and with what effects on the distribution of policymaking authority (Laver and Shepsle 1996; Huber 1998). Although there are important differences in institutional design among parliamentary regimes, with consequences for representation and policy (Huber 1996; Huber and Charles Shipan 2002; G. Bingham Powell 2000; Lijphart 1999), the differences with presidential and hybrid regimes, and the institutional variation among the latter, are substantially more dramatic. Moreover, the level of institutional instability and change in presidential and hybrid regimes has outstripped that in parliamentary systems in recent decades, particularly as the newly democratic, and redemocratizing, regimes associated with democracies Third Wave have overwhelmingly adopted directly elected chief executives.

Presidential systems allow voters maximum discretion over the composition of the executive and legislative branches of government. Hybrid regime formats represent efforts to provide a direct vote on the chief executive while retaining some mechanisms to ensure that the politicians administering the day to day operation of government maintain assembly support.

In all systems with consequential presidencies, and thus with parallel elections that determine the shape of government at the national level, the specific rules of competition affect whether those branches will support complimentary objectives. Most directly, concurrent elections for the two branches, and electoral rules that encourage the construction of broad first-round coalitions, maximize the prospects for unified government.

To the extent that the preferences of the branches differ, the rules of legislative procedure affect the manner in which presidents and assemblies resolve policy differences through negotiation and compromise, or whether such conflict leads to government crisis. The specific legislative powers of presidents vary enormously, with some configurations encouraging negotiation with legislative opponents prior to the adoption of policy, and others allowing executive action to implement policies—perhaps provisionally—even in lieu of prior legislative ratification.

Finally, the past decade has witnessed two important trends in the operation of presidential regimes in Latin America: loosening restrictions on reelection, and the rise of legislative replacement of presidents during government crises. Both imply convergence with parliamentary systems in that they relax the fixed nature of presidential terms. In this sense, both phenomena are consistent with broader arguments, particularly prominent among Brazilian scholars, that presidential systems do not necessarily operate as differently from parliamentary regimes as pure institutional analyses often suggest (Cheibub 2002; Argelina Figueiredo and Fernando Limongi 2000; Octavio Amorim Neto 2002), and which focus on the incentives for accommodation even between branches of government whose origins and survival are, constitutionally, separated.

References

Abney G., Lauth T.P. 1997. "The Item Veto and Fiscal Responsibility". *Journal of Poltics* 59(3):882–892.

Alesina, Alberto, Ricardo Hausman, Rudolf Hommes, and Ernesto Stein. 1999. "Budget Institutions and Fiscal Performance in Latin America". *Journal of Development Economics* 59:253–273.

Amorim Neto, Octavio. 2002. "Presidential Cabinets, Electoral Cycles, and Coaltion Discipline in Brazil" in Scott Morgenstern and Benito Nacif (eds.), *Legislative Politics in Latin America*. Cambridge University Press, pp. 48–78.

Archer, Ronald P. and Matthew S. Shugart. 1997. "The Unrealized Potential of Presidential Dominance in Colombia" in Matthew S. Shugart and Scott P. Mainwaring (eds.), *Presidentialism and Democracy in Latin America*. New York: Cambridge University Press, pp. 110–159.

Arriagada, Genaro and Carol Graham. 1994. "Chile: Sustaining Admustment During Democratic Transition" in Stephan Haggard and Steven B. Webb (eds.), *Voting for Reform: Democracy, Liberalization, and Economic Adjustment*. New York: The World Bank.

Arrow, Kenneth. 1951. *Social Choice and Individual Values*. New York: Wiley.

Baldez, Lisa A. and John M. Carey. 1999. "Presidential Agenda Control and Spending Policy: Lessons from General Pinochet's Constitution." Co-authored with Lisa Baldez. *American Jounal of Political Science* 43(1):29–55.

Baldez, Lisa A. and John M. Carey. 2001. "Budget Procedure and Fiscal Restraint in Post-Transition Chile," co-authored with Lisa Baldez, in Mathew D. McCubbins and Stephan Haggard, (eds.), *Presidents, Parliaments, and Policy*. New York: Cambridge University Press, pp. 105–148.

Bagehot, Walter. 1872. *The English Constitution*. Garden City, NY: Doubleday [reprinted 1961].

Bawn, Kathleen. 1999. "Money and Majorities in the Federal Republic of Germany: Evidence for a Veto Players Model of Government Spending". *American Journal of Political Science* 43(3): 707–736.

Cameron, Maxwell A. 1997. "Political and Economic Origins of Regime Change in Peru: The Eighteenth Brumaire of Alberto Fujimori" in Maxwell A. Cameron and Philip Mauceri, (eds.), *The Peruvian Labyrinth: Polity, Society, Economy*. University Park, PA: Penn State Press, pp. 37–69.

Carey, John M. 2000. "Parchment, Equilibria, and Institutions". *Comparative Political Studies* 33(6/7):735–761.

Carey, John M. 2002. "The Reelection Debate in Latin America". *Latin American Politics and Society* (forthcoming).

Carey, John M., Octavio Amorim Neto, and Matthew S. Shugart. 1997. "Appendix: Outlines of Constitutional Powers in Latin America" in Scott P. Mainwaring and Matthew S. Shugart, (eds.), *Presidentialism and Political Parties in Latin America*. New York: Cambridge University Press, pp. 440–460.

Carey, John M. and Matthew S. Shugart. 1998a. "Calling Out the Tanks or Filling Out the Forms?" in John M. Carey and Matthew S. Shugart, (eds.), *Executive Decree Authority*. New York: Cambridge University Press, pp. 1–32.

Carey, John M. and Matthew S. Shugart. 1998b. "Institutional Design and Executive Decree" in John M. Carey and Matthew S. Shugart, (eds.), *Executive Decree Authority*. New York: Cambridge University Press, pp. 274–298.

Cheibub, Jose Antonio. 2002. "Minority governments, deadlock situations, and the survival of presidential democracies." *Comparative Political Studies* 35(3): 284–312.

Cheng, Tun-jen and Stephan Haggard. 2001. "Democracy and Deficits in Taiwan: The Politics of Fiscal Policy, 1986–1996" in Stephan Haggard and Mathew D. McCubbins (eds.), *Presidents, parliaments, and policy*. New York: Cambridge University Press, pp. 183–228.

Colomer, Josep M. 2001. *Political Institutions: Democracy and Social Choice*. New York: Oxford University Press.

Coppedge, Michael J. 1994. *Strong Parties and Lame Ducks: Presidentialism, Partyarchy, and Factionalism in Venezuela*. Stanford: Stanford University Press.

Cox, Gary W. 1997. *Making Votes Count: Strategic Coordination in the World's Electoral Systems*. Cambridge University Press.

Dahl, Robert Alan. 1971. *Polyarchy : Participation and Opposition*. New Haven, CT: Yale University Press.

Diermeier, Daniel and Timothy J. Feddersen. 1998. "Cohesion in Legislatures and the Vote of Confidence Procedure". *American Political Science Review* 92(3):611–621.

Diermeier Daniel and Randolph T. Stevenson. 2000. "Cabinet Terminations and Critical Events". *American Political Science Review* 94(3):627–640.
DiPalma, Giuseppe. 1990. *To Craft Democracies*. Berkeley, CA: University of California Press.
Duverger, Maurice. 1954. *Political Parties*. New York: John Wiley.
Duverger, Maurice. 1980. "A New Political System Model: Semi-Presidential Government". *European Journal of Political Research* 8:165–187.
Figueiredo, Argelina C. and Fernando Limongi. 2000. "Presidential Power, Legislative Organization, and Party Behavior in Brazil". *Comparative Politics* 32(2):151–172.
Fiorina, Morris P. 1996. *Divided Government*. Boston, MA: Allyn and Bacon.
Frye, Timothy. 1997. "A Politics of Institutional Choice: Post-Communist Presidencies". *Comparative Political Studies* 30(5):523–552.
Huber, John D. 1992. "Restrictive Legislative Procedures in France and the United States". *American Political Science Review* 86(3):675–687.
Huber, John D. 1996. "The Vote of Confidence in Parliamentary Democracies". *American Political Science Review* 90:269–82.
Huber, John D. 1998. "How Does Cabinet Instability Affect Political Performance? Portfolio Volatility and Health Care Cost Containment in Parliamentary Democracies". *American Political Science Review* 92(3):577–591.
Huber, John D. and Arthur Lupia. 2001. "Cabinet Instability and Delegation in Parliamentary Democracies". *AJPS* 45(1):18–32.
Huber, John D. and G. Bingham Powell. 1994. "Congruence Between Citizens and Policymakers in Two Visions of Liberal Democracy". *World Politics* 46:291–326.
Huber, John D. and Charles Shipan. 2002. *Laws and Bureaucratic Autonomy in Modern Democracies: Wise and Salutary Neglect*. New York: Cambridge University Press.
Huntington, Samuel P. 1991. *The third Wave: Democratization in the Late Twentieth Century*. Norman, OK: University of Oklahoma Press.
Ishiyama, J.T. and Kennedy, R. 2001. "Superpresidentialism and Political Party Development in Russia, Ukraine, Armenia and Kyrgyzstan". *Europe-Asia Studies* 53(8):1177–1191.
Jones, Mark P. 1995. *Electoral Laws and the Survival of Presidential Democracies*. Notre Dame, IN: University of Notre Dame Press.
Jones, Mark P. 1997. "Evaluating Argentina's Presidential Democracy" in Scott Mainwaring and Matthew Soberg Shugart (eds.), *Presidentialism and Democracy in Latin America*. New York: Cambridge University Press, pp. 259–299.
Kelley, R. Lynn. 1973. "Venezuelan Constitutional Forms and Realities" in John D. Martz and David J. Myers (eds.), *Venezuela: The Democratic Experience*. New York: Praeger Publishers.
Lamounier, Bolivar. 1993. "Institutional Structure and Governability in the 1990s" in Maria D'Alva G. Kinzo (ed.), *Brazil, the Challenges of the 1990s*. New York: St. Martin's Press, pp. 117–137.
Laver, Michael and Norman Schofield. 1990. *Multiparty Government: The Politics of Coalition in Europe*. New York: Cambridge University Press.
Laver, Michael and Kenneth Shepsle (eds.). 1994. *Cabinet Ministers and Parliamentary Government*. New York: Cambridge University Press.
Laver, Michael and Kenneth Shepsle. 1996. *Making and Breaking Governments: Cabinets and Legislatures in Parliamentary Democracies*. New York: Cambridge University Press.
Laver, Michael and Kenneth Shepsle. 1998. "Events, Equilibria, and Government survival". *American Journal of Political Science* 42(1):28–54.
Levine, Daniel. 1973. *Conflict and Political Change in Venezuela*. Princeton, NJ: Princeton University Press.
Lijphart, Arend. 1977. *Democracy in Plural Societies: A Comparative Exploration*. New Haven, CT: Yale University Press.

Lijphart, Arend. 1990. "Presidencialismo y democracia de mayoría" in Oscar Godoy Arcaya, (ed.), *Hacia un democracia moderna: La opción parlamentaria*. Santiago: Ediciones Universidad Católica de Chile, pp. 109–128.

Lijphart, Arend. 1994. *Electoral systems and Party Systems: A Study of 27 Democracies, 1945–1990.* New York: Oxford University Press.

Lijphart, Arend. 1999. *Patterns of Democracy: Government Forms and Performance in Thirty-Six Countries*. New Haven, CT: Yale University Press.

Linz, Juan J. 1994. "Presidentialism or Parliamentarism: Does It Make a Difference?" in Linz, Juan J. and Arturo Valenzuela, (eds.), *The Failure of Presidential Democracy*. Baltimore, MD: Johns Hopkins University Press, pp. 3–90.

Lucky, Christian. 1993. "A Comparative Chart of Presidential Powers in Eastern Europe". *East European Constitutional Review* 2(4):81–94.

Lupia, Arthur and Kaare Strom. 1995. "Coalition Termination and the Strategic Timing of Parliamentary Elections". *American Political Science Review* 89(3):648–665.

Mainwaring, Scott P. 1993. "Presidentialism, Multipartism, and Democracy: The Difficult Combination". *Comparative Political Studies* 26(2):198–228.

Martin, Lanny W. and Randolph T. Stevenson. 2001. "Government Formation in Parliamentary Democracies". *American Journal of Political Science* 45(1):33–50.

Mauceri, Philip. 1997. "The Transition to 'Democracy' and the Failures of Institution Building" in Maxwell A. Cameron and Philip Mauceri, (eds.), *The Peruvian Labyrinth: Polity, Society, Economy*. University Park, PA: Penn State Press, pp. 13–36.

McKelvey, Richard. 1976. "Intransitivities in Multidimensional Voting Models: Some Implications for Agenda Control". *Journal of Economic Theory* 12:472–482.

Mebane, Walter R. and Jasjeet S. Sekhon. 2002. "Coordination and Policy Moderation at Midterm". *American Political Science Review* 96(1):141–157.

Miller, David. 1993. "Deliberative Democracy and Social Choice" in David Held, (ed.), *Prospects for Democracy*, Stanford, CA: Stanford University Press.

Moe, Terry M. and Michael Caldwell. 1994. "The Institutional Foundations of Democratic Government: A Comparison of Presidential and Parliamentary Systems". *Journal of Institutional Theoretical Economics* 150(1):171–195.

Nogueira Alcala, Humberto. 1986. *El régimen semipresidencial: Una neuva forma de gobierno democrático?* Santiago, Chile: Editorial Andante.

Open Media Research Institute. 1996. "Duma Attacks Presidential Administration". *Daily Digest* No. 219(1).

Parrish, Scott. 1998. "Presidential Decree Authority in Russia, 1991–1995" in John M. Carey and Matthew S. Shugart (eds.), *Executive Decree Authority: Calling Out the Tanks or Just Filling Out the Forms?* New York: Cambridge University Press, pp. 62–103.

Persson, Torsten, and Guido Tabellini. 2000. *Political Economics: Explaining Economic Policy.* Cambridge, MA: MIT Press.

Persson, Torsten, and Guido Tabellini. 2002. "Do constitutions Cause Large Governments? Quasi-Experimental Evidence". *European Economic Review* 46:908–918.

Persson, Torsten, Gerard Roland, and Guido Tabellini. 1997. "Separation of Powers and Political Accountability". *Quarterly Journal of Economics* 112:1163–1202.

Powell, G. Bingham. 2000. *Elections as Instruments of Democracy : Majoritarian and Proportional Visions*. New Haven, CT: Yale University Press.

Power, Timothy. 1998. "The Pen is Mightier than the Congress: Presidential Decree Power in Brazil" in John M. Carey and Matthew S. Shugart (eds.), *Executive Decree Authority: Calling Out the Tanks or Just Filling Out the Forms?* New York: Cambridge University Press, pp. 197–232.

Przeworski, Adam and Fernando Limongi. 1997. "Modernization: Theories and Facts". *World Politics* 49(2):155–183.

Rasch, Bjorn E. 2000. "Parliamentary Floor Voting Procedures and Agenda Setting in Europe". *LSQ* 25(1):3–23.

Remington, Thomas, Stephen Smith, D. Roderick Kiewiet, and Moshe Haspel. 1994. "Transitional Institutions and Parliamentary Alignments in Russia, 1991–1993" in Thomas Remington, (ed.), *Parliaments in Transition: The New Legislative Politics in the Former USSR and Eastern Europe.* Boulder, CO: Westview Press.

Remington, Thomas, Olga Shvetsova, and Steven S. Smith. 2002. "Decrees, Laws, and Presidential-Parliamentary Bargaining in Russia". Working paper.

Riker, William H. 1962. *The Theory of Political Coalitions.* New Haven, CT: Yale University Press.

Riker, William H. 1982. *Liberalism Against Populism.* Prospect Heights, IL: Waveland Press.

Romer, Thomas and Howard Rosenthal. 1979. "Elusive Median Voter". *Journal of Public Economics* 12(2):143–170.

Rother, Larry. 2002. "Argentina's President Suffers Double Blow." *New York Times* online. April 24.

Samuels, David J. "Presidentialized Parties: The Separation of Powers and Party Organization and Behavior". *Comparative Political Studies* 35(4):461–483.

Sartori, Giovanni. 1994. *Comparative Constitutional Engineering: An Inquiry into Structures, Incentives and Outcomes.* New York: New York University Press.

Shepsle, Kenneth A. 1979. "Institutional Arrangements and Equilibrium in Multidimensional Voting Models". *American Journal of Political Science* 23(1):27–59.

Schmidt, Gregory. 1996. "Fujimori's 1990 Upset Victory in Peru: Electoral Rules, Contingencies, and Adaptive Strategies". *Comparative Politics* 28(3):321–354.

Schmidt, Gregory. 1998. "Presidential Usurpation or Congressional Preference?: The Evolution of Executive Decree Authority in Peru" in John M. Carey and Matthew S. Shugart (eds.), *Executive Decree Authority: Calling Out the Tanks or Just Filling Out the Forms?* New York: Cambridge University Press:104–141.

Shamis, Hector E. 2002. "Argentina: Crisis and Democratic Consolidation". *Journal of Democracy* 13(2):81–94.

Shugart, Matthew S. 1995. "The Electoral Cycle and Institutional Sources of Divided Government". *American Political Science Review* 89(2):327–343.

Shugart, Matthew S. and John M. Carey. 1992. *Presidents and Assemblies: Constitutional Design and Electoral Dynamics.* New York: Cambridge University Press.

Shugart, Matthew S. and Scott P. Mainwaring. 1997. "Presidentialism and Democracy in Latin America: Rethinking the Terms of the Debate" in Matthew S. Shugart and Scott P. Mainwaring (eds.), *Presidentialism and Democracy in Latin America.* New York: Cambridge University Press, pp. 12–54.

Siavelis, Peter. 2002. "Exaggerated Presidentialism and Moderate Presidents: Executive-Legislative Relations in Chile" in Scott Morgenstern and Benito Nacif, (eds.), *Legislative Politics in Latin America.* Cambridge University, Press pp. 79–113.

Stepan, Alfred and Cindy Skach. 1993. "Constitutional Frameworks and Democratic Consolidation". *World Politics* 46:1–22.

Strom, Kaare. 1990. *Minority Government and Majority Rule.* New York: Cambridge University Press.

Taagepera, Rein and Matthew Sobert Shugart. 1989. *Seats and Votes: The Effects and Determinants of Electoral Systems.* New Haven, CT: Yale University Press.

Tsebelis, George. 1995. "Decision Making in Political Systems: Veto Players in Presidentialism, Parliamentarism, Multicameralism and Multipartyism". *British Journal of Poltical Science* 25:289–325.

Tsebelis, George. 1999. "Veto Players and Law Production in Parliamentary Democracies: An Empirical Analysis". *American Political Science Review* 93(3):591–608.

Valenzuela, Arturo. 1994. "Party Politics and the Crisis of Presidentialism in Chile: A Proposal for a Parliamentary form of Government" in Juan J. Linz and Arturo Valenzuela (eds.), *The Failure of Presidential Democracy: The Case of Latin America,* vol. 2. Baltimore, MD: Johns Hopkins University Press, pp. 91–150.

Valenzuela, J. S. 1992. "Democratic Consolidation in Post-Transitional Settings: Notion, Process, and Facilitating Conditions" in Scott Mainwaring, Guillermo O'Donnell, and J.S. Valenzuela (eds.), *Issues in Democratic Consolidation: The New South American Democracies in Comparative Perspective.* Notre Dame, IN: University of Notre Dame Press.

Warwick, Paul V. 1992. "Rising Hazards: An Underlying Dynamic of Parliamentary Government". *American Journal of Political Science* 36(4):857–876.

Warwick, Paul V. 1994. *Government Survival in Parliamentary Democracies.* New York: Cambridge University Press.

Weldon, Jeffrey. 1997. "Politcal Sources of *Presidencialismo* in Mexico" in Matthew S. Shugart and Scott P. Mainwaring (eds.), *Presidentialism and Democracy in Latin America.* New York: Cambridge University Press, pp. 225–258.

6. Legislative Process and the Mirroring Principle

MATHEW D. McCUBBINS

At the center of all democratic governments are legislatures. In all legislatures, members compete for access to a variety of valuable resources, such as floor time and committee or cabinet positions. The internal distribution of these resources fundamentally shapes the legislative process, and by extension, determines which individuals or coalitions can influence legislative outcomes. In this paper, I argue that, within a given legislature, the distribution of legislative influence tends to mirror the external checks and balances in the polity as a whole. In other words, as Lijphart (1984) has argued, just as polities with little separation of purpose (i.e., with limited diversity of interests and factions) tend to have more unitary governmental institutions than do polities with greater separation of purpose (which tend toward institutions that create separation of powers), so too will internal legislative institutions reflect the separations of purpose and power within a polity.[1] This law of organization is referred to as the *mirroring principle*.[2]

In making my argument, I consider legislatures generally and use examples from a wide range of parliamentary and non-parliamentary bodies. I argue that many elements of legislatures, as well as the ways that we think about them, are common across most (and perhaps all) legislatures. Thus, a goal of this paper is to present a general analytic framework within which many aspects of the world's diverse legislative bodies can be considered.

I proceed as follows: In the next section, I discuss the nature of legislative resources, and briefly review the various arguments about how they are allocated. The section after that deals with control over the legislative agenda. In the third section, I discuss two cases that illustrate the mirroring principle. I end with a brief conclusion.

---

[1] See Cox and McCubbins (2001) on separation of purpose and separation of power.

[2] McCubbins, Noll, and Weingast (1987) coined the term "mirroring principle," arguing that agency structure mirrors the political forces that create, oversee, and fund the agency. The concept is essentially the same as Ferejohn's (1987) "structuring principle."

1. LEGISLATIVE RESOURCES AND THEIR ALLOCATION

Broadly speaking, resources fall into four categories: The first is legislative time, including caucus time in cabinet or committee, time on the floor (i.e., in the legislature as a whole—sometimes called *plenary time*), or time in conference committees (in the cases of some bicameral legislatures, such as the U.S. Congress). The second is institutional positions, such as party and committee (or ministry), leadership spots and membership. The third is staff and funding (for either parties, committees, or ministries). And the fourth is legislative outcomes, including budget and appropriation decisions, tax decisions, and vetoes in presidential systems (i.e., the status quo).

Given the value of these resources, the method by which they are allocated is of obvious importance. In the case of majority-party-dominated parliaments such as the British House of Commons, it is widely accepted that the majority party controls resource allocation. In many other cases, however—and most notably in the U.S. Congress or the Japanese Diet—claims of majority dominance are not as widely accepted (this is also true for U.S. state legislatures). This is also the case for countries in which, due to electoral rules or other factors, legislators have strong incentives to act independently of their parties, or in which presidents possess legislative agenda setting powers (e.g. in Brazil). Accordingly, I spend a good deal of this section reviewing alternative explanations for the allocation of resources. Since these alternative explanations, dubbed the distributive theory of politics, are most fully developed in the literature on the U.S. House of Representatives, I focus primarily on the U.S. case in this section, before returning to a more comparative discussion in subsequent sections. In addition to reviewing these explanations, I outline problems with each of them and then turn to more detailed consideration of the majority-party explanation for resource allocation.

Scholars of the U.S. House have suggested a variety of bases for the allocation of resources, including universalism,[3] logrolls,[4] the regular order,[5] the need for policy information, and partisanship. I consider each of these possibilities in turn, beginning with allocation on the basis of either *universalism*, whereby resources are distributed more-or-less evenly among all members, or by *distributive logrolls* (Shepsle and Weingast 1987; Weingast and Marshall 1988),[6] whereby each gatekeeper[7] (be it a committee, ministry, faction, or coalition)

---

[3] "Universalism" implies that all members of the legislature are beneficiaries of distributive policies (see Weingast 1979).

[4] "Logrolls" involve two or more legislators agreeing to trade their votes on one bill they care little about in exchange for another bill that is personally much more important to them.

[5] "Regular order" refers to the regular rules of procedure in the legislative chamber.

[6] The term "distributive" is used because, according to this model, the primary purpose of the House's internal structure is to make it easy for members to distribute such benefits as government projects, spending, and pork to their constituents.

[7] A "gatekeeper" is someone who has access to or a veto over a particular policy or policy area.

and its members get the outcomes that they want in their area of jurisdiction, in exchange for acquiescing to the wishes of other gatekeepers in other areas of jurisdiction.[8]

For the U.S. Congress, the universalistic and distributive models of allocation are cut from the same theoretical cloth, which views policy making as a logroll among gatekeepers.[9] In this view, (1) members self-select onto committees or ministries with jurisdictions of particular electoral value to them; (2) committees and ministries are therefore not representative of the legislature as a whole; (3) leadership positions are distributed automatically via seniority; (4) committees and ministries show deference to one another in cabinet or on the floor (i.e., within each gate-keeper's jurisdiction, other gate-keepers let them have their way); and (5) members thereby realize gains from exchange by controlling policies that they care about most, while deferring on policies that they care about less. Thus, everyone gets policy outcomes that they want (the universalism claim), and members are able to distribute valuable concentrated benefits to their districts.

There is some evidence that outcomes are at times universalistic (Weingast 1979; Cox and Tutt 1984), and that floor voting in the U.S. House and Senate became more universalistic during the 1960's and 1970's (Collie 1988a). There is also evidence, in U.S. state legislatures, that resources are shared universally: all members receive a committee assignment, travel privileges, resources for mailing their constituents, office space, and staff (in the capitol as well as in their districts). Universal committee representation is not unique to the U.S.; it is found in many legislatures, including most of those in Western Europe (Mattson and Strom 1995).

In addition, there is some evidence of distributive logrolls in a handful of policy areas, such as river and harbor improvements and military construction (Ferejohn 1974; Murphy 1974; Weingast 1979; Wilson 1986; Shepsle and Weingast 1987; Collie 1988b; Evans 1994). For example, telecommunications policy in the 1980's in the Japanese Diet was determined by logrolls between the Liberal Democratic Party's (LDP) Policy Affairs Research Council (PARC) and committees on telecommunications and agriculture (Noll and Rosenbluth 1995, McCubbins and Thies 1997). In the Costa Rican assembly, small local development projects are allocated by similar means (Carey 1996). While important, however, such logrolls are the exception rather than the rule (Stein

---

[8] In the US House, each committee has authority, or "jurisdiction," over bills dealing with particular policy issues. This arrangement is similar to the division of policy into various cabinet portfolios in parliamentary systems (Laver and Shepsle 1990; Thies 2001) and is similar to the division of authority among factions in the Japanese LDP (Rosenbluth 1989; Cox and Rosenbluth 1993) and among committee gate-keepers in the LDP's Policy Affairs Research Council or PARC (Ramseyer and Rosenbluth 1993).

[9] Theoretically, this literature has deep roots in transaction cost economics, which focuses heavily on the role of institutions and organization as means of reducing transaction costs involved in both economic and other interactions that occur repeatedly (Coase 1937; Alchian and Demsetz 1972; Williamson 1975; North 1981, 1990; Barzel 1989; Libecap 1989; Miller 1992; Alston, Eggertsson, and North 1996).

and Bickers 1994), and are not the basis for the allocation of most resources (Browning 1986).[10]

There are other reasons, both theoretical and empirical, to doubt the distributive model. First, it does not explain changes to the committee system in the U.S. House, or changes in committee autonomy over time—both of which occur in the House across U.S. history.[11] It also does not explain a similar evolution of cabinet government in Great Britain (Cox 1987). In addition, members do not freely self-select onto committees, most committees are not composed of preference outliers, seniority is sometimes violated, and committees' ability to act contrary to the wishes of the floor waxes and wanes over time (Gilligan and Krehbiel 1990, 1994; Kiewiet and McCubbins 1991; Krehbiel 1991; Rohde 1991; Cox and McCubbins 1993). I return to these issues when I discuss partisan allocation below.

When a legislature uses *the regular order* to allocate resources, members place bills on the legislative calendar and the bills are called up on the floor in the order they were placed in the queue. Thus, agenda setting is done by something like a random selection mechanism, and resources such as plenary time are distributed haphazardly.[12] The regular order *has* been used to control resources; however, this process *has not* been followed in the House since the late 19th century, nor in the Senate since the early 20th century. The explosive growth in the number of bills introduced in the House, combined with standing rules that allowed minorities to cause endless delays, made the regular order an impractical way of legislating and led to its abandonment in the 1880's (Alexander 1916; Galloway 1976; Cooper and Young 1989; Den Hartog 2001). A similar process unfolded in Britain earlier in the 19th century, as increased suffrage led to increased competition for floor time, triggering the emergence of cabinet control over resources in the House of Commons (Cox 1987).

Another possible basis for the allocation of resources is to facilitate the gathering of information about policy (Gilligan and Krehbiel 1990; Krehbiel

---

[10] Certainly, the allocation of resources in most other countries appears quite partisan. See, for example, Thies (1998) on pork-barreling in Japan. Partisan allocation of pork, moreover, is not limited to polities in which electoral rules create incentives for members to cultivate personal votes. As Denemark (2000) shows, the allocation of pork in Australia has been quite partisan, despite their parliamentary legislature and party-centric electoral rules.

[11] For more on committee power, see Wilson (1885); McConachie (1974) [1898]; Cooper and Brady (1981); Rohde (1991).

[12] Though they do not use the phrase regular order, a number of formal voting models at least implicitly feature a similar agenda-setting mechanism. In many such models, voting occurs on an exogenously-given single dimension, with the implicit assumption that no one strategically selects which dimension is voted on (Black 1958; Downs 1957; Krehbiel 1991, 1998; see Riker and Ordeshook 1968 and Enelow and Hinich 1984 for more general uses of spatial voting). In other models, agenda-setting is explicitly modeled in a manner similar to the regular order (Baron and Ferejohn 1989). Cox and McCubbins (2002) test (and reject) a unidimensional version of this model, which they call the Floor Agenda Model, against a model in which the majority party chooses which bills reach the floor (the Cartel Agenda Model).

1991). According to the informational model, the desire to be re-elected leads legislators to try to make good policy, which in turn drives legislators to seek information about policy. Legislators therefore create committees or ministries and delegate to them the job of information gathering. Committee members' or ministers' actions send signals to other legislators about what positions they should adopt on particular bills. At heart, this model is a variant on the distributive model (already discussed), with each committee or ministry and its members taking advantage of gains from specialization.

Though legislators no doubt want information about possible policy decisions, the informational model is subject to challenge. First, the assumption that an individual's re-election is driven by voters' reactions to the policies adopted by the legislature as a whole is at odds with a large literature showing that U.S. House members' re-election is largely a function of *personal voting* (i.e., voting based on individual candidate characteristics) and *partisan voting* (i.e., voting based on candidate partisanship).[13] In addition, the model depends upon the assumption of a one-dimensional policy space. If in fact policy is multi-dimensional, then the model's conclusions do not hold. Similarly, even if all policy spaces are one-dimensional but floor time is scarce (that is, there is not enough time for the legislature to consider all policy spaces), then there are gains to be realized by controlling which policy spaces get floor time. The informational model does contemplate this possibility, but does not explain the various mechanisms designed to regulate which policy spaces a legislature does or does not consider. Lastly, how much information do members of Congress need to make reasonable decisions, and who in society possesses this information? In casting a vote in Congress, members need only know whether voting yes or voting no is optimal for them; and they can rely on informational cues or signals to inform them whether voting yes or no is optimal on a given vote (Lupia and McCubbins 1998). They need not know detailed information about the bill or issue. Information, moreover, resides in society, not in congressional committees or with committee members—and every member of Congress has connections to informed "fire alarm" interests and parties, who can provide them with trusted cues and signals about bills and motions (McCubbins and Schwartz 1984; Lupia and McCubbins 1994).

The order of business, both in committee or cabinet and on the floor, is tightly controlled in almost all legislatures—and is usually controlled on a *partisan* basis. Typically, it is the majority party, perhaps along with the presiding officer or the cabinet, who allocates these resources to meet their own ends. In essence, the members of the majority party, within both the government and the legislature, form a cartel to monopolize control of the key aspects of law making

---

[13] C.f. Fenno (1978); Mayhew (1974); Cain, Ferejohn, and Fiorina (1987). See Chapter Five of Jacobson (2001) for an overview.

in the legislature (Kiewiet and McCubbins 1991; Cox and McCubbins 1993, 2004).[14]

This finding is consistent with roll call voting patterns both in U.S. House committees and on the floors of all but one legislature (Brazil).[15] Almost all recorded votes in House committees, for example, divide strictly on party lines (Parker and Parker 1985). Many scholars note a comparable pattern on floor voting (c.f. Cooper, Brady, and Hurley 1977). Poole and Rosenthal's (1997) findings, which cover the entire span of congressional history, are typical of this work. They find that, in every Congress, both roll call votes and legislator ideal points tend to divide along party lines (pp. 34–5). Lawrence, Maltzman, and Smith (1999) find, moreover, that majority party members are significantly more likely than minority party members to be on the winning side on floor votes. Similar patterns are noted in Germany (Patzelt 1996), Austria (Muller 2000), Norway, Denmark (Muller and Strom 2000), and Argentina (Morgenstern 2004).

Agenda cartelization, however, entails delegation of authority from party backbenchers to party leaders. This in turn creates the possibility of mischief—i.e., not serving the interests of the party's rank-and-file members—by party leaders. Thus, there is a tradeoff between empowering leaders to allocate resources for the benefit of members of the cartel, and running the risk of agency losses when these leaders diverge from the collective good of the party. Many internal legislative institutions embody this tradeoff; for instance, allowing the Speaker of the House to unilaterally make committee appointments facilitates a coherent appointment strategy, but runs the risk that the Speaker will pursue his or her own personal agenda when making appointments. Thus, changes in legislative rules and practices are often the result of a new tradeoff between these two considerations.

Further, the internal politics of any institution tend to mirror the institution's external political environment (Ferejohn 1987). This mirroring drives the origins of many legislative institutions, and changes in internal organization often mirror changes in the external political environment. The legislature's external environment, in turn, is derived principally from the constitutional separation of powers and purpose. For example, early in the 20th century, electoral rules favored rural areas and the House Agriculture Committee had privileged status and could report its bills directly to the House. As the proportion of representatives from rural areas declined, especially after the "reapportionment revolution" of the 1960's, the House revoked the Agriculture Committee's privileged status. In the wake of these changes, there was a decline in federal spending on agriculture

---

[14] Within the literature on distributive logrolls and pork barrel politics, there is ample incidental evidence that majority party members do better than minority party members, all else constant. Though many such works include party only as a control variable, it repeatedly has a significant positive impact (Goss 1972; Browning 1973; Fiorina 1974; Murphy 1974; Kalt and Zupan 1990; Levitt and Snyder 1995). Majority party membership also has a positive effect on other legislator resources, such as campaign contributions (Cox and Magar 1999; Ansolabehere and Snyder 1999, 2000).

[15] See Amorim Neto, Cox, and McCubbins (2003).

programs that benefited rural residents (McCubbins and Schwartz 1988). The same pattern of rural over-representation that is mirrored in legislative institutions can be seen in the LDP's large and influential Agriculture committee in the PARC and in the extensive agriculture subsidies in Japan (see essays in Cowhey and McCubbins 1995, McCubbins and Thies 1997).

Thus, the two major factors driving legislative organization are the delegation tradeoff and the mirroring of the external environment. Legislative organization in turn has systematic policy consequences.[16] As the majority party or coalition's external environment becomes more heterogeneous (i.e. the parties are more thoroughly divided and are divided on more issues), we expect to see more checks and balances within the legislative process (i.e. the separation of powers will be accompanied by a separation of purpose). This, in turn, makes it more costly to change policy; it also means that policy changes that do occur are likely to be more "private-regarding" (i.e., policy with more concentrated benefits) than "public-regarding" (i.e., policy with fewer concentrated benefits), all else constant, as an increasing number of veto players demand "payoffs" in return for agreeing to policy changes.[17] Similarly, as the majority party or coalition's environment becomes more homogeneous, we expect to see increasing delegation and centralization (that is, parties will be able to demand higher levels of loyalty from members, and backbenchers will delegate increasing control of resources to party leaders). As this shrinks the number of legislative veto actors, we expect to see more public-regarding policy, all else constant, as the majority party's leaders serve to control resources for the benefit of their membership (Sinclair 1983; Rohde 1991; Cox and McCubbins 1993; Aldrich 1995; Aldrich and Rohde 1997, 2000).[18] This pattern has been observed in the U.S. as well as in Mexico—as the PRI waned with the coming of the PAN, new internal legislative checks emerged to mirror the new, more heterogeneous political environment.

Roughly speaking, if the polity is divided along dimensions that are non-partisan, then the legislative process and organization will have a less partisan cast to it. If the polity is divided into numerous small party divisions, then the legislative process will give agenda control to several parties. For example, in Denmark in the 1970's, the government lost control of the agenda on domestic social issues, but continued to control the agenda on foreign and budgetary issues (Damgaard and Svenson 1989). When the polity is represented by two parties that are each internally homogeneous, but who pursue quite different goals, then the party that wins the majority will monopolize control of the agenda, and the legislative process will be centralized and streamlined. This dynamic has played

---

[16] See Cox and McCubbins (2002) for a more thorough discussion of this topic.

[17] Note that "private-regarding" is essentially a normatively neutral term for the same types of policy that are commonly referred to as "pork" (i.e., geographically targeted government appropriations or projects) or "rents" (i.e., graft or government benefits allocated to special interests) (Buchanan, Tollison, and Tullock 1980).

[18] See, however, both Denzau and Munger (1986) and Arnold (1990) on ways that legislatures with private-regarding tendencies can produce public-regarding policy.

out in the U.S. House over the past 200-plus years, in the form of (virtually) constant changes to the standing rules, as well as the behavioral patterns, of the House (Polsby 1968; Polsby, Gallaher, and Rundquist 1969; Cooper 1970; Galloway 1976; Bach and Smith 1988; Cooper and Young 1989; Stewart 1989; Rohde 1991; Katz and Sala 1996; Dion 1997; Binder 1997; Schickler 2001; Cox and McCubbins 2004). When the majority party has been homogeneous, as in the late-19th and early-20th centuries, and again in the late 20th century, party leaders have been strongest. When the majority party has been most divided into regional factions, as in the period leading up to the Civil War and the mid-20th century Conservative Coalition era (where Republicans often allied with southern Democrats on votes), party leaders have been weakest (see Galloway 1976, and Table 1 of Cox and McCubbins 2002, for an overview of various congressional eras).

It is important to bear in mind, however, that even in the eras in which the majority party is thought to have been weak, such as the Conservative Coalition era, the majority party has enjoyed overwhelming advantages relative to the minority party. Cox and McCubbins (1997, p. 1379) argue that the types of rules changes that have occurred in the House over the past hundred years have affected the *marginal* power of the party to allocate resources for its members' benefit, but that the party has *always* enjoyed an overwhelmingly fixed advantage vis-à-vis resource allocation in this period:

> When one considers that, even during the heyday of committee government, no minority party member served as chair of any committee, no minority party member served as Speaker, the majority got the lion's share of staff allocations on all committees, and majority party members got a more than proportional share of seats on the key committees, it seems clear that the deck was stacked. Even if no further party action occurred after the initial allocation of posts and resources, members of the majority party held the best cards.

From this point of view, a partisan cartel model of legislative organization subsumes the distributive committee-government model and the ministerial-portfolio model (Laver and Shepsle 1996), while avoiding the pitfalls of the latter model. The cartel model "... complements the committee government model, by endogenizing its key assumptions ... [and] is consistent with ... earlier work such as Shepsle and Weingast (1987) and Weingast and Marshall (1988)" (Cox and McCubbins 1997, pp. 1378–9).[19] Having discussed the theoretical

---

[19] Cox and McCubbins (1997, p. 1378) elaborate on this point. If one takes committee autonomy as an exogenous given, then the committee government model does not have anything to say about the increased rate of seniority violations in the post-1974 period. To put it another way, the model cannot explain variations over time in seniority violations. If instead one takes committee autonomy as endogenously determined, then one has to specify the (endogenous) processes that generate autonomy. One possibility is that autonomy is protected by generalized norms of reciprocity developed on the floor of the House (as was central to Shepsle and Weingast's 1987 explanation of committee power). Another possibility, emphasized in *Legislative Leviathan*, is that autonomy is protected by stalemate in the majority party caucus. Our story, in other words, can be viewed as one of several ways to endogenize the agenda power of committees.

underpinnings of legislative organization, I now turn to a more general and comparative discussion of the legislative process. Many component parts of the legislative process are common to all legislatures; we can systematically characterize these components, as well as the role of majority parties and coalitions in manipulating them for their own advantage.

2. THE LEGISLATIVE PROCESS

Three elements of procedure are common to all legislatures. First, because each legislature must allocate plenary time, a substantial fraction of each legislature's rules, procedures, and structure are devoted to defining and prescribing the means by which the legislature's agenda is controlled. Second, the rules must also prescribe what happens when no new laws are passed (i.e., what is the "reversionary policy"?). Third, once plenary time is allocated and the reversionary policy is set, the legislature must have rules and procedure that dictate how a collective decision on policy change will be reached. While the just listed features of the legislative process are ubiquitous, of course, there are many additional elements that vary from one legislature to the next. Many of these involve attempts to mitigate the aforementioned problem of agency loss, and have important effects on the flow of legislation.

Controlling the Agenda

Controlling the legislative agenda involves the creation and prescription of two types of powers. One type of power is the authority to get proposed policy changes onto the legislative agenda; I call this authority *positive agenda control*. The alternative type of power is the authority to keep proposed policy changes off of the legislative agenda, and thereby protect the status quo—or reversionary policy—from change; I call this authority *negative agenda control*. Moreover, both negative and positive agenda control can be divided into internal and external categories, referring to agenda control exercised by some actor(s) inside the legislature, or outside the legislature. In what follows, I discuss each.

Positive Agenda Control

Positive agenda control is the power to propose new policies. The issues of who has it or controls access to it, and who does not, may affect the decisions that a legislature can make depending on the various policy makers' preferences. Possessing positive agenda power grants the policy maker the formal right to introduce bills, or at very least, it entails the privilege to bring up for consideration a motion or an amendment before the full legislative body.

In the United States, there are a variety of routes by which bills are considered. While the Constitution grants the President the right to submit proposals to Congress, it does not mandate that Congress consider them. Thus, only the

House of Representatives and Senate possess final authority to decide which proposals are considered in their own chamber. Within the House, some committees and specialized task forces have the power to initiate policy change in their policy area. But simply proposing legislation hardly implies that it will be considered by the full legislative body. With the exception of some bills that are "privileged,"[20] most House scheduling is controlled by the Speaker and the Rules Committee. In the United Kingdom, by contrast, the executive dominates the agenda setting process. While members of Parliament are allowed to submit bills, the Cabinet initiates most successful legislative proposals (Andeweg and Nijzink 1995). Because the legislature can choose and remove the executive, these two branches are interdependent; consequently, they are less likely to be at cross-purposes. The Japanese system presents another variation on positive agenda control. The Diet, Japan's legislature, has a standing committee system; and the LDP, which has been the majority party for most of the postwar period, also has its own committee system, the PARC. It is the PARC system that possesses formal initiation/proposal power, passing its proposals on to the cabinet to be submitted to the Diet (Sato and Matsuzaki 1986; McCubbins and Rosenbluth 1995). Note, however, that there are sometimes opportunities for external agenda control. In many Latin American countries, the president has formal authority to place items on the legislative agenda, or to give them the force of law via decree. And even in the U.S. Congress, each house can sometimes use political leverage to force items onto the agenda of the other house, as can the president.

Negative Agenda Control

An alternative form of agenda control also exists, which essentially is the veto power. The authority to halt or to delay a bill's progress is *negative* agenda control, and it can be exercised either explicitly through vetoes or implicitly through inaction. Veto power is usually held by the legislature, although when the executive possesses a decree power, for example, policy may be changed without legislative assent.

Any person or faction with the power to block, or significantly delay policy, is often referred to as a "veto gate." There exists significant variance across nations in the number of veto gates that inhabit the legislative process, and veto gates can be internal or external to the legislature. The United States' presidential system, with its bicameral and decentralized legislature, represents one end of the spectrum; the United Kingdom's unitary parliamentary system is at the other end of the spectrum. In the House of Representatives alone, the substantive committees, Rules Committee, Speaker, and the Committee of the Whole each constitute internal veto gates through which legislation must pass,

---

[20] For example, in U.S. House of Representatives a handful of committees, such as Appropriations and Budget, have direct access (or "privilege") to bring their bills directly to the floor, bypassing the House calendars, on select legislation.

and the Senate has even more veto gates due to the filibuster (Ripley 1969, Binder and Smith 1997; Krehbiel 1998), which allows any member to hold up legislation with unending "debate" unless three-fifths of Senators call for a vote on the bill. By contrast, in the United Kingdom, the legislative process is much more efficient, since the Cabinet and Prime Minister serve as the main veto gates through which new legislation must pass.[21] Apart from its weak negative agenda control, the Swedish committee system resembles the system found in the U.S. House of Representatives, but represents another important variation. In the Swedish Riksdag, members of the Cabinet or backbenchers alike may submit bills for consideration, but every proposal must go the appropriate committee for consideration. That is, there is no discretion over which committee has jurisdiction; it is pre-determined. The committees, however, cannot kill a bill by failing to act on it. As their rules specify, each committee must submit a report, whether positive or negative, on all policy proposals.

Agenda control, of course, interacts with amendment control to shape legislative outcomes. Legislatures often restrict the number and nature of admissible amendments (Sinclair 1981, Huber 1992, Doring 1995, Bawn 1998, Oleszek 2004) and the government or majority party almost always reserves to itself the final motion on a bill (Kiewiet and McCubbins 1991, Heller 2001, Wolfensberger 2003).

Reversion Control

Whenever legislatures consider passing a law, they must always consider its effects relative to what would occur if no law were passed. Indeed, in virtually every legislature the final vote taken on a proposal is that for final passage, which forces members to directly compare the proposed change in policy with the status quo. Reversion control is the power of setting the default policy outcome that will result if no new legislation is enacted. It is important to note that the reversionary policy is not necessarily the status quo. For example, some laws are crafted with 'sunset provisions,' which mandate that a program be dissolved or an appropriation be terminated by some specified date. Also, in some Latin American legislatures, once it is determined that a policy change is necessary, the final vote is between two versions of the same bill, rather than between the bill (as amended) and the status quo.[22]

To understand law making, it is important to know which actors, if any, can manipulate the reversionary outcome. This requires an understanding of the relationship between the reversionary policy, any new policy proposal, and the various policy makers' preferences. Reversionary policies can be defined

---

[21] The discussion above ignores the role of the House of Lords, just as upper houses are often dismissed in analyses of parliamentary systems. In fact, upper houses typically have some form of dilatory veto, meaning that they can delay, but not ultimately block, bills passed by the lower house. As the upper house veto becomes broader in scope, it gains greater negative agenda control.

[22] See Amorim Neto, Cox, and McCubbins (2003) on Brazil, and Heller and Weldon (2001) on Mexico.

formally by a constitution and/or statutes, or as the result of informal solutions to immediate problems. In Germany and the United States, the constitution defines the reversion for budgetary items, but the reversionary policy for entitlements, such as Social Security, are typically defined by statutes.

In addition, external actors sometimes control the reversionary policy. For instance, presidents with decree authority can change the outcome that will obtain in the absence of new legislation (Shugart and Carey 1992). Similarly, courts sometimes change the reversion, as in the U.S. in the 1960's when the Supreme Court claimed for itself and lower courts the ability to impose requirements for legislative districts (Cox and Katz 2002). In parliamentary systems, the cabinet can dictate that votes on bills are also confidence votes, thereby dramatically altering the reversion (De Winter 1995; Huber 1996; Laver and Shepsle 1996; Baron 1998). Indeed, tying confidence votes to policy votes dramatically increases voting cohesion amongst members of the ruling coalition on votes that might not otherwise garner such agreement (Diermeier and Feddersen 1998).

In fact, the effectiveness of agenda control is sometimes contingent on the reversionary outcome. The ability of those who possess positive agenda control to make take-it-or-leave-it offers that the legislature will accept depends largely on how the legislature values the reversionary outcome (Romer and Rosenthal 1978, Kiewiet and McCubbins 1988).

Procedural Control

Most legislatures possess rules that structure the handling of proposed legislation. Rules define voting procedures, the types of amendments that will be allowed, if any, how amendments will be considered, provisions for debate, the public's access, and so forth. It is possible to draw a distinction between two different forms of procedural rules: standing rules and special rules. Standing rules guide the day-to-day procedure by which the legislature conducts itself and the internal lawmaking processes. Standing rules may continue from a previous legislative session, or they may be redrafted each new legislative session.

By contrast, special rules create exceptions for consideration of a bill, and thereby violate the standing rules. In the House of Representatives, floor debate usually takes place under a special rule restricting debate and amendments, and the Rules Committee possesses the power to write special rules. Successful consideration of nontrivial bills typically entails giving certain members procedural privileges, usually attaching a special rule to the bill (Oleszek 2004).[23] Restrictive rules, such as limiting debate or amendments, is one way for the majority

---

[23] A special rule is a House resolution, drawn up and proposed by the Rules Committee and adopted by a simple majority in the House, that specifies the conditions under which a bill will be considered on the floor. The primary importance of such rules is that they take bills from a calendar and grant them floor consideration. In addition, these rules sometimes restrict debate, amendments, or procedures that are allowed during a bill's floor consideration.

party leadership to eliminate opportunities for defection by their party members (Sinclair 2002).

Interestingly, although Japan has a parliamentary system, its internal legislative procedure resembles that of the United States. The Diet decentralizes its policymaking into the PARC divisions (McCubbins and Noble 1995), but the majority party's leadership holds a veto over their actions through a hierarchy of party-dominated veto gates (in the cabinet) and through its control of the legislative agenda. But, since Japan is parliamentary, the majority party leadership serves at the pleasure of the full membership, and consequently the full membership has a conditional veto over the actions of that "committee system."

The procedure structuring debate, and restrictions on debate, is typically encompassed by a legislature's standing and special rules. In addition to the obvious importance of who gets to participate in the deliberative process and how extensively, control of debate may have serious policy implications. For example, in the United States, judicial interpretation of laws often refers to the *Congressional Record* to ascertain the lawmakers' intent. As a consequence of the ability to participate in debate is a potential opportunity for legislators to have their preferences or understanding of a law incorporated in its interpretation.

In the House of Representatives, unless proposed legislation is governed by a special rule or there is a suspension of the rules,[24] the House's standing rules and precedents limit each member's speaking time to one hour during debate and five minutes when considering amendments. Upon recognition, a member controls his or her allotted time to yield or allocate as she desires, but this rule is circumscribed by the fact that the Speaker of the House possesses recognition power. Hence, given their power to suspend the rules, and to write special rules, and given the Speaker's discretion to recognize members, the majority party leadership is able to structure chamber debate quite effectively.

In the Senate, however, the majority party's control over debate is a bit more tenuous. The Senate's standing rules do not limit debate, and the chamber has developed a notorious reputation for members' ability to frustrate a majority through the filibuster. Over time, the rules have been modified, to allow a three-fifths majority to invoke what is called "cloture," a procedure that ends a filibuster by either limiting debate to one hour per member, or establishing a maximum of thirty hours more for debate.

By comparison, parliamentary debate in the United Kingdom is fairly structured. In the House of Commons, for example, there are two main types of debate: general and adjournment. General debate is used to discuss specific government policies. Adjournment debate includes matters for which the government has no explicit position, such as new or bipartisan issues. Another type is emergency debate, which acts as a safety valve for issues needing immediate attention and lacking another avenue to the floor.

---

[24] Suspension of the rules requires a two-thirds majority and thus typically requires some bipartisan support.

Delegation and the Legislative Process

As discussed earlier, the delegation of authority to the government, to ministers, and to the party or committee leaders creates the potential for mischief, which gives rise to measures designed to limit agency loss. In general, legislatures use both checks and balances to accomplish these tasks. They provide others with a veto over the actions of agenda setters and give these others an opportunity and incentive to act as checks. These checks and balances may be very subtle. In the U.S. House of Representatives, for example, the front-bench and back-bench may check each other through the committee system. During the Conservative Coalition era, roughly from 1937 to 1974, the Southern Democrats, who had greater seniority and safer seats, held the control committees and especially the Rules Committee, and for decades were able to bottle up civil rights legislation from those perches of power. Meanwhile the Northern Democrats held control of the substantive committees, and they used the implicit gate-keeping power that came with that control to pursue a civil rights agenda by creating logrolls that could survive the control committees and would benefit both Northern and Southern Democrats. The two coalition partners of the New Deal effectively checked the actions of one another until the redistrictings of the reapportionment revolution caused the decline of the rural-based Conservative Coalition (Robinson 1963; Bolling 1966; Jones 1968; Manley 1973; Brady and Bullock 1980, 1981; McCubbins and Schwartz 1988; Rohde 1991).

By way of summary, the following figure demonstrates many of the preceding points regarding control of the agenda, reversionary policy, procedure, and checks on delegated authority. Figure 1 is a graphic representation of the

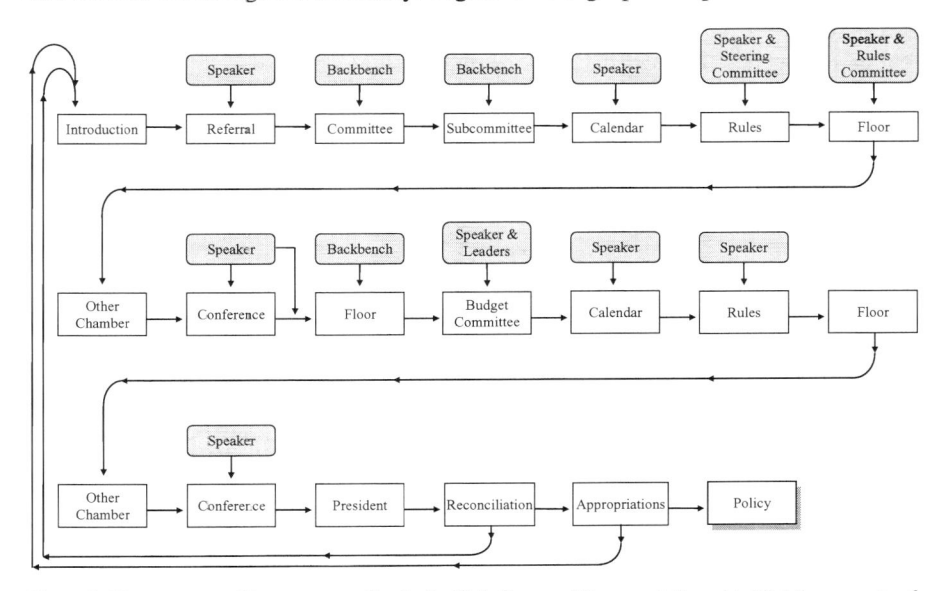

Figure 1. How a proposal becomes a policy in the U.S. House of Representatives, highlighting aspects of party control.

legislative process in the U.S. House of Representatives, demonstrating the path that any piece of legislation must travel in order to become law. It is important to note the numerous places where a proposal may be revised or amended, or halted altogether—i.e., where there are opportunities for negative agenda control. By unraveling who influences the decision at each of these points (control of agenda and procedure)—whether an individual, a faction, or a party—it is possible to assess the degree to which interests are balanced in a nation's legislative process.

In the initial stages of the U.S. policymaking process, the substantive committees in each chamber possess significant agenda control within their jurisdiction. Given members' attraction to committees that are substantively salient to their constituents, legislators who are most concerned with the policy at hand have asymmetric influence at this early stage. As a proposal approaches the floor, however, the party's influence may be felt more and more. The majority party's members delegate to their leadership to represent their interests on a broad variety of matters. The Rules Committee and the Speaker—as well as the Appropriations Committee, if any funding is required to implement the proposal—check committee members' ability to exploit their agenda control, for these two central coordinating bodies control access to plenary time. If a substantive committee's proposal is unrepresentative of the party's collective interests, and it is an issue of importance to the party, then either the Speaker or the Rules Committee are likely to kill the proposal. The shortage of plenary time itself creates incentives for the substantive committees to compete against each other, in something of a tournament, where the reward for satisfying the party's interest is time for floor consideration (Cox and McCubbins 1993). Before the proposal leaves the chamber are the floor amendment and final passage vote stages, which provide ordinary members with the opportunity to form coalitions in order to influence and potentially kill a bill. Throughout this process, the ability to block or push a bill at each veto gate is crucial, as is the ability to control the reversion. Even policies that command majority support may be difficult to take up if the reversionary policy is preferred by a member or members who control a veto gate. In sum, the three elements discussed—agenda, reversion, and procedural control—repeatedly overlap with one another throughout policymaking process to structure the policymaking, provide checks and balances between the various interests, and define the boundaries of which interests will be represented.

Comparatively, we also find that the majority party or coalition retains control over the use of plenary time. This control is strongest in the British (Cox 1987, Cox and Ingram 1992) and Irish parliaments. Across Europe, the majority party or coalition retains substantial control over plenary time in virtually all parliaments (Doring 1995). In coalition governments we find, moreover, that the coalition members use appointments to monitor and check the other coalition members within various ministries.

There is, in effect, a dual process at work (Cox and McCubbins 1993). On one side the rank-and-file's interests, and thus local constituencies' interests, are favored in the substantive committees' efforts to pass legislation. On the other side the party's collective interests are enforced by the Speaker and Majority Leader and by members of the control committees. Before even reaching the floor, then, a piece of legislation must satisfy numerous, potentially diverse, actors.

Mirroring of the Legislative Process

The committee system in the House plays an important role in the mirroring of external separations of powers and purpose in society, at least to the extent that members of the majority party have diverse preferences. Cox and McCubbins (1993) show that the extent that the majority can go to in stacking substantive committees with party loyalists, delegating to a central agent to enforce the party's collective reputation, and reinforcing that delegation with procedural powers, depends heavily on the majority party's homogeneity. Across time, moreover, committees are established and eliminated as the demand for committees with particular jurisdictions waxes and wanes.

We can contrast the U.S. case with the British case, which is at the opposite end of the spectrum with respect to diversity of the external environment. The standing committee system in Britain, established in 1979, theoretically creates the potential for an American-styled power base outside of the cabinet, but in practice the committees have been quite weak relative to the cabinet. The so-called "Westminsterian" form of government constitutes Lijphart's (1984) prototype "majoritarian" system, meaning that legislative majorities can govern virtually at will. For example, the Maastricht rebels could not prosecute their case from an institutional power position, and thus they had to fight (and lose, when Prime Minister John Major turned it into a vote of confidence) their battle over European integration on the floor of the House of Commons. The contrast between this inability of a portion of the British Tory party to halt a policy change, versus the American Southern Democrats' ability to maintain a status quo civil rights policy by using veto gates that precluded floor consideration could not be more clear.[25] While it has been suggested that the cabinet ministries in Britain may function similarly to a committee system (Laver and Shepsle 1990, 1996), I contend that it is highly unlikely that ministers will possess anything like the veto power and conflicting purposes that House and Senate committees have exercised during certain periods in the United States. This, I argue, is due to Britain's electoral institutions. While the British electorate is approximately as diverse as the American electorate, national nomination control and the absence of personal voting in legislative elections lead to a low level of heterogeneity within the legislative parties. Since party brand names are so important (Cox

---

[25] The Maastricht issue was arguably more electorally salient in Britain than was the civil rights issue in the US, and it is possible that this explains the difference in the success with which party factions blocked action on the issues in question. However, it in part precisely *because* of the more convoluted US process that civil rights opponents were able to block bills. They were able to use their control of veto gates *off the floor* to veto civil rights bills in ways that did not draw widespread public attention, and therefore did not put Northern Democrats in electorally uncomfortable positions.

1987), and since parties control access to elections, and can use that access as a means to discipline members, they can behave as a "legislative cartel" (Cox and McCubbins 1993).

Japan, by contrast, has a constitutional structure quite like Britain, in that it is parliamentary, but its policy outcomes more closely resemble those in the United States (Noll and Rosenbluth 1995; Cohen, McCubbins, and Rosenthal 1995; Cowhey 1995; Fukui and Weatherford 1995). A critical difference between the structures of British and Japanese politics is their electoral institutions. Japan's old single non-transferable vote (SNTV) electoral rules required candidates to develop personal votes, thereby creating groups with divergent interests within the ruling LDP.[26] This diversity is reflected in a highly factionalized party structure, so members of the LDP in the Japanese legislature developed a committee system that resembles that of the United States, in which party rank-and-file were given autonomous jurisdictions over policy. Thus, the PARC committees provide the foundation for individual members to develop personal reputations for providing policy benefits to their constituents and thereby gain an advantage in achieving reelection. Similar to the American case, in which the majority party caucus's ability to engage in party politics is conditional on the diversity of its members' preferences, the LDP has recognized both the presence of these electorally-induced internal tensions, and the advisability of allowing its members to pursue reelection through a decentralized legislative process. Thus, in Japan, the intra-legislative institutions mirror the institutionally-created diversity within the party.

Taiwan presents another useful case study. The 1990's were a period of immense change in Taiwan. Early in this decade, the political structure was altered in a fundamental way, which I argue led to the legislature being inhabited by actors with more diverse goals than was previously the case. The most important reform came in the way legislators were selected. Until 1991, the Kuomintang (KMT), Taiwan's ruling party, appointed a majority of legislators as representatives of 'occupied' districts in mainland China. These appointed representatives were responsive solely to the KMT leadership, since reappointment depended on their loyalty to the party. In 1991, however, the Taiwanese government halted this process, reapportioned the legislative districts, and then chose the first popularly-elected legislature in Taiwanese history. They chose an SNTV electoral system, similar to that used in Japan at that time. As mentioned earlier, SNTV creates strong incentives for legislators to cultivate personal votes. This new external pressure triggered new legislative demands (for more private-regarding policy), and thus led to a restructuring of the legislature's internal process.

Prior to 1991, the Taiwanese legislature functioned primarily as a rubber-stamp for the executive. All legislative proposals originated in the executive, were sent to the Rules Committee to be assigned to substantive committees, and then were subject to simple yes-or-no votes on whether to *recommend*

---

[26] See Cox (1994) and Cox and Niou (1994) on SNTV voting. For more on the personal vote, see Mayhew (1974); Fenno (1978); Cain, Ferejohn, and Fiorina (1987); Reed (1994); and Carey and Shugart (1995).

the policy only. Since 1991, there has been substantial decentralization of the legislative process. While most bills continue to be proposed by the executive, the proposals now usually go through committees which actually possess both amendment powers and veto powers (budget proposals are an important exception to this rule).

Also, since 1991 the system of committee appointments in Taiwan has changed from one of self-selection to one which is tightly controlled by the KMT's legislative caucus. The caucus nominates, votes on, and then monitors each committee's members. This latter task is accomplished through the use of party "moles" on each committee, who are responsible solely to the KMT caucus, who report back to the caucus, and who possess the authority to halt committee proceedings if they perceive that the party's collective interests are not being pursued by the committee. The reports of these informants play an important role in determining committees' access to floor consideration, as the Taiwanese legislature has a Rules Committee that is tightly controlled by the KMT leadership and that has some agenda power. The KMT has also formed ten party committees that hold independent reviews of legislation (similar to a "shadow" committee system) within the party caucus, and the caucus has organized a standing committee, the Central Policy Committee (CPC) that determines whether to enforce discipline on floor votes. The CPC is composed of all the highest KMT officials in the legislative and executive branches, and, on controversial issues in particular, balances constituency versus party interests in a manner similar to the Japanese PARC.

These changes again illustrate the mirroring principle: the introduction of direct popular elections for the full legislature led the KMT to lodge much greater authority in the standing committees, and led the caucus to develop procedures similar to those used by the majority party in the United States Congress. The party has established procedures that allow it to enforce discipline on issues that are important for the party's collective reputation, but the presence of relatively autonomous substantive committees establishes the institutional foundations for representatives to pursue policies that favor their constituents (or maintain the status quo against policies that may harm them). Thus, a new system of checks and balances between the backbenchers and the party leaders has been established, and there is substantial evidence that policy has become increasingly private-regarding.

3. Conclusion

I conclude with a brief recapitulation of the main points of this paper. First, there are two driving forces behind legislative organization. One is the need to delegate authority in order to allocate resources in effective and electorally-beneficial ways, which involves the classic tradeoff inherent in delegation of any kind: giving the agent enough power to do what needs to be done, while simultaneously limiting the agent's ability to act in mischievous ways. The other is the need to structure this delegation such that it mirrors external political forces.

Second, the type of policy that follows from internal legislative organization varies systematically: as the number of veto gates in the legislative process increases, policy tends to become more private-regarding and less public-regarding. Thus, we expect to see more particularistic policy in complex, diverse polities, and more public-oriented policy in more homogeneous polities.

In addition, an increase in the number of legislative veto gates makes it more costly to change policy, and therefore makes change less likely than when there are fewer veto gates, all else constant. In other words, more veto gates make a government less *decisive*, but more *resolute*. Such a decrease in the likelihood of change has both positive and negative policy implications. On the one hand, decisions and commitments become more stable and more credible; on the other hand, deadlock and an inability to react to new problems are also more likely. These pros and cons are flipped when there are few veto players, and policy change is therefore less costly and more likely. In such cases, it is easier to respond quickly when there is a need to do so. This flexibility, however, makes decisions less stable and makes commitments less credible.

This tradeoff exactly parallels the tradeoff inherent at the constitutional level, where the number of veto gates and the number of actors holding those gates also systematically affect policy making (Laver and Schofield 1990; North 1990; Cox and McCubbins 1991; Fiorina 1992; Alt and Lowry 1994; Alesina and Rosenthal 1995; Haggard and Kaufman 1995; Tsebelis 1995; Weingast 1995; Druckman 1996; Bawn 1999). When the government features many different veto gates, as in separation-of-powers and federal systems, commitments are more credible—but more difficult to make in the first place. And, when the government is unitary, decision making is more flexible, but more likely to be beset by instability—and is therefore less credible (Cox and McCubbins 2001).

Given the mirroring principle, moreover, we expect heterogeneous polities' governments to feature many veto gates at both the legislative and constitutional levels, and expect homogeneous polities' governments to feature few veto gates at each level. Thus, with regard to both the public vs. private character of policy, and the flexibility vs. credibility of policy, the institutional effects are magnified, not attenuated, by legislative organization.

REFERENCES

Alchian, Armen and Harold Demsetz. 1972. "Production, Information Costs, and Economic Organization". *American Economic Review* 62: 777–795.

Aldrich, John H. 1995. *Why Parties? The Origin and Transformation of Political Parties in America*. Chicago, IL: University of Chicago Press.

Aldrich, John H. and David W. Rohde. 1997. "The Transition to Republican Rule in the House: Implications for Theories of Congressional Politics". *Political Science Quarterly* 112: 541–567.

Aldrich, John H. and David W. Rohde. 2000. "The Republican Revolution and the House Appropriations Committee". *Journal of Politics* 62: 1–33.

Alesina, Alberto and Howard Rosenthal. 1995. *Partisan Politics, Divided Government, and the Economy*. Cambridge: Cambridge University Press.

Alexander, De Alva Stanwood. 1916. *History and Procedure of the House of Representatives*. Boston, MA: Houghton Mifflin.

Alston, Lee J., Thrainn Eggertsson, and Douglass C. North, (eds.), 1996. *Empirical Studies in Institutional Change*. Cambridge: Cambridge University Press.

Alt, James E. and Robert C. Lowry. 1994. "Divided Government, Fiscal Institutions, and Budget Deficits-Evidence from the States". *American Political Science Review* 88: 811–828.

Amorim Neto, Octavio, Gary W. Cox, and Mathew D. McCubbins. 2003. "Agenda Power in Brazil's Camaro". *World Politics* 55: 550–578.

Andeweg, Rudy B. and Lia Nijzink 1995. "Beyond the Two-Body Image: Relations Between Ministers and MPs" in Herbert Doring (ed.), *Parliaments and Majority Rule in Western Europe*. New York: St. Martin's Press.

Ansolabehere, Stephen and James M. Snyder, Jr. 1999. "Money and Institutional Power". *Texas Law Review* 77: 1673–1704.

Ansolabehere, Stephen and James M. Snyder, Jr. 2000. "Soft Money, Hard Money, Strong Parties". *Columbia Law Review* 100: 598–619.

Arnold, R. Douglas. 1990. *The Logic of Congressional Action*. New Haven, CT: Yale University Press.

Bach, Stanley and Steven S. Smith. 1988. *Managing Uncertainty in the House of Representatives: Adaptation and Innovation in Special Rules*. Washington, DC: Brookings.

Baron, David P. 1998. "Comparative Dynamics of Parliamentary Governments". *The American Political Science Review*, 92: 593–609.

Baron, David P. and John A. Ferejohn. 1989. "Bargaining in Legislatures". *American Political Science Review* 83: 1181–1206.

Barzel, Yoram. 1989. *Economic Analysis of Property Rights*. Cambridge: Cambridge University Press.

Bawn, Kathleen. 1998. "Congressional Party Leadership: Utilitarian versus Majoritarian Incentives", *Legislative Studies Quarterly* 23: 219–243.

Bawn, Kathleen. 1999. "Money and Majorities in the Federal Republic of Germany: Evidence for a Veto Players Model of Government Spending". *American Journal of Political Science* 43: 707–736.

Binder, Sarah A. 1997. *Minority Rights, Majority Rule: Partisanship and the Development of Congress*. Cambridge: Cambridge University Press.

Binder, Sarah A. and Steven S. Smith. 1997. *Politics or Principle? Filibustering in the United States Senate*. Washington, DC: Brookings Institution.

Black, Duncan. 1958. *The Theory of Committee and Elections*. Cambridge, UK: Cambridge University Press.

Bolling, Richard. 1966. *House Out of Order*. New York: Dutton.

Brady, David W. and Charles S. Bullock III. 1980. "Is There a Conservative Coalition in the House?" *Journal of Politics* 42: 549–559.

Brady, David W. and Charles S. Bullock III. 1981. "Coalition Politics in the House of Representatives" in Lawrence C. Dodd and Bruce I. Oppenheimer (eds.), *Congress Reconsidered*, 2nd edn. Washington, DC: CQ Press.

Browning, Clyde E. 1973. *The Geography of Federal Outlays*. Studies in Geography No. 4. Chapel Hill, NC: University of North Carolina Department of Geography.

Browning, Robert X. 1986. *Politics and Social Welfare Policy in the United States*. Knoxville, TN: University of Tennessee Press.

Buchanan, James M., Robert D. Tollison, and Gordon Tullock (eds.). 1980. *Toward a Theory of the Rent-Seeking Society*. College Station, TX: Texas A&M University.

Cain, Bruce, John Ferejohn, and Morris P. Fiorina. 1987. *The Personal Vote: Constituency Service and Electoral Independence*. Cambridge: Cambridge University Press.

Carey, John M. 1996. *Term Limits and Legislative Representation*. Cambridge: Cambridge University Press.

Carey, John M. and Matthew S. Shugart. 1995. "Incentives to Cultivate a Personal Vote: A Rank Ordering of Electoral Formulas". *Electoral Studies* 14: 417–439.
Coase, Ronald H. 1937. "The Nature of the Firm". *Economica*, New Series 4: 386–405.
Cohen, Linda, Mathew D. McCubbins, and Frances M. Rosenbluth. 1995. "The Politics of Nuclear Power in Japan and the United States" in Peter Cowhey and Mathew D. McCubbins (eds.), *Structure and Policy in Japan and the United States*. Cambridge: Cambridge University Press.
Collie, Melissa P. 1988a. "Universalism and the Parties in the House of Representatives, 1921–80". *American Journal of Political Science* 32: 865–883.
Collie, Melissa P. 1988b. "The Legislature and Distributive Policy Making in Formal Perspective". *Legislative Studies Quarterly* 13: 427–458.
Cooper, Joseph. 1970. *The Origins of the Standing Committees and the Development of the Modern House*. Houston, TX: William Marsh Rice University.
Cooper, Joseph, and David W. Brady. 1981. "Institutional Context and Leadership Style: The House from Cannon to Rayburn". *American Political Science Review* 75: 411–425.
Cooper, Joseph, David Brady, and Patricia Hurley. 1977. "The Electoral Basis of Party Voting." In Louis Maisel and Joseph. Cooper, (eds.), The Impact of the Electoral Process, Beverly Hills, CA: Sage Publications.
Cooper, Joseph and Cheryl D. Young. 1989. "Bill Introduction in the Nineteenth Century: A Study of Institutional Change". *Legislative Studies Quarterly* 14: 67–105.
Cowhey, Peter. 1995. "The Politics of Foreign Policy in Japan and the United States" in Peter Cowhey and Mathew D. McCubbins (eds.), *Structure and Policy in Japan and the United States*. Cambridge: Cambridge University Press.
Cowhey, Peter and Mathew D. McCubbins (eds.). 1995. *Structure and Policy in Japan and the United States*. Cambridge: Cambridge University Press.
Cox, Gary W. 1987. *The Efficient Secret: The Cabinet and the Development of Political Parties in Victorian England*. Cambridge: Cambridge University Press.
Cox, Gary W. 1994. "Strategic Voting Equilibria under The Single Nontransferable Vote". *American Political Science Review* 88: 608–621.
Cox, Gary W. and Tim Tutt. 1984. "Universalism and Allocative Decision-Making in the Los Angeles County Board of Supervisors". *Journal of Politics* 46: 546–555.
Cox, Gary W. and James W. Ingram. 1992. "Suffrage Expansion and Legislative Behavior in 19th-Century Britain". *Social Science History* 16: 539–560.
Cox, Gary W. and Eric Magar. 1999. "How Much is Majority in the U.S. Congress Worth?" *American Political Science Review* 93: 299–309.
Cox, Gary W. and Mathew D. McCubbins. 1991. " Divided Control of Fiscal Policy" in Cox, Gary W. and Samuel Kernell (eds.), *The Politics of Divided Government*. Boulder, CO: Westview Press.
Cox, Gary W. and Mathew D. McCubbins. 1993. *Legislative Leviathan: Party Government in the House*. Berkeley, CA: University of California Press.
Cox, Gary W. and Frances Rosenbluth. 1993. "The Electoral Fortunes of Legislative Factions in Japan". *The American Political Science Review* 87: 577–589.
Cox, Gary W. and Emerson Niou. 1994. "Seat Bonuses under the Single Nontransferable Vote System: Evidence from Japan and Taiwan". *Comparative Politics* 26: 221–236.
Cox, Gary W. and Mathew D. McCubbins. 1997. "Toward a Theory of Legislative Rules Changes: Assessing Schickler and Rich's Evidence". *American Journal of Political Science* 41: 1376–1386.
Cox, Gary W. and Mathew D. McCubbins. 2001. "The Institutional Determinants of Economic Policy Outcomes" in Stephan Haggard and Mathew D. McCubbins (eds.), *Presidents, Parliaments, and Policy*. Cambridge, UK: Cambridge University Press.
Cox, Gary W. and Jonathan Katz. 2002. *Elbridge Gerry's Salamander: The Electoral Consequences of the Reapportionment Revolution*. Cambridge: Cambridge University Press.

Cox, Gary W. and Mathew D. McCubbins. 2002. "Agenda Power in the U.S. House of Representatives, 1877 to 1986" in David Brady and Mathew D. McCubbins (eds.), *Party, Process, and Political Change in Congress: New Perspectives on the History of Congress*. Palo Alto, CA: Stanford University Press.

Cox, Gary W. and Mathew D. McCubbins. 2004. *Legislative Leviathan Revisited*. Cambridge: Cambridge University Press.

Damgaard, Erik and Palle Svenson. 1989. "Who Governs? Parties and Policies in Denmark", *European Journal of Political Research* 17: 731–745.

De Winter, Lieven. 1995. "The Role of Parliament in Government Formation and Resignation" in Herbert Doring (ed.), *Parliaments and Majority Rule in Western Europe*. New York: St. Martin's Press.

Den Hartog, Chris. 2001. "Gatekeeping and the Majority Party in the Antebellum House". Paper presented at the Annual Meeting of the American Political Science Association, San Francisco, August 30–September 2, 2001.

Denmark, David. 2000. "Partisan Pork Barrel in Parliamentary Systems: Australian Constituency-Level Grants". *Journal of Politics* 62: 896–915

Denzau, Arthur T. and Michael C. Munger. 1986. "Legislators and Interest Groups: How Unorganized Interests Get Represented". *American Political Science Review* 80: 89–106.

Diermeier, Daniel and Timothy J. Feddersen. 1998. "Cohesion in Legislatures and the Vote of Confidence Procedure". *The American Political Science Review* 92: 611–621.

Dion, Douglas. 1997. *Turning the Legislative Thumbscrew: Minority Rights and Procedural Change in Legislative Politics*. Ann Arbor, MI: University of Michigan Press.

Doring, Herbert. 1995. "Time as a Scarce Resource: Government Control of the Agenda" in Herbert Doring (ed.), *Parliaments and Majority Rule in Western Europe*. New York: St. Martin's Press.

Downs, Anthony. 1957. *An Economic Theory of Democracy*. New York: Harper.

Druckman, James N. 1996. "Party Factionalism and Cabinet Durability". *Party Politics* 2: 397–407.

Enelow, James, and Melvin Hinich. 1984. *The Spatial Theory of Voting*. New York: Cambridge University Press.

Evans, Diana. 1994. "Policy and Pork: The Use of Pork Barrel Projects to Build Policy Coalitions in the House Of Representatives." *American Journal of Political Science* 38: 894–917.

Fenno, Richard. 1978. *Home Style: House Members in Their Districts*. Boston, MA: Little, Brown.

Ferejohn, John. 1974. *Pork Barrel Politics: Rivers and Harbors Legislation, 1947–1968*. Stanford: Stanford University Press.

Ferejohn, John. 1987. "The Structure of Agency Decision Processes" in Mathew D. McCubbins and Terry Sullivan (eds.), *Congress: Structure and Policy*. Cambridge; New York: Cambridge University Press.

Fiorina, Morris P. 1974. *Representatives, Roll Calls, and Constituencies*. Lexington, MA: Lexington Books.

Fiorina, Morris P. 1992. *Divided Government*. New York: Macmillan.

Fukui, Haruhiro, and M. Stephen Weatherford. 1995. "Coordinating Economic Policies: A Schematic Model and Some Remarks on Japan–U.S. Exchange-Rate Politics" in Peter Cowhey and Mathew D. McCubbins (eds.), *Structure and Policy in Japan and the United States*. Cambridge: Cambridge University Press.

Galloway, George B. 1976. *History of the House of Representatives*, 2nd edn. New York: Thomas Y. Crowell.

Gilligan, Thomas W. and Keith K. Krehbiel. 1990. "Organization of Informative Committees by a Rational Legislature". *American Journal of Political Science* 34: 531–564.

Gilligan, Thomas W. and Keith K. Krehbiel. 1994. "The Gains from Exchange Hypothesis of Legislative Organization". *Legislative Studies Quarterly* 19: 181–214.

Goss, Carol F. 1972. "Military Committee Membership and Defense-Related Benefits in the House of Representatives". *Western Political Quarterly* 25: 215–233.
Haggard, Stephan and Robert R. Kaufman. 1995. *The Political Economy of Democratic Transitions*. Princeton NJ: Princeton University Press.
Heller, William B. 2001. "Making Policy Stick: Why the Government Gets What it Wants in Multiparty Parliaments". *American Journal of Political Science* 45: 780–798.
Heller, William B. and Jeffrey Weldon. 2001. "Legislative Rules and Voting Stability in the Mexican Chamber of Deputies". Paper presented at the annual meeting of the Midwest Political Science Association.
Huber, John. 1992. "Restrictive Legislative Procedures in France and the United States". *The American Political Science Review* 86: 675–687.
Huber, John. 1996. *Rationalizing Parliament: Legislative Institutions and Party Politics in France*. Cambridge: Cambridge University Press.
Jacobson, Gary C. 2001. *The Politics of Congressional Elections*, 5th edn. New York: Longman.
Jones, Charles O. 1968. "Joseph G. Cannon and Howard W. Smith: An Essay on the Limits of Leadership in the House of Representatives". *Journal of Politics* 30: 617–646.
Kalt, J.P. and Zupan, M.A. 1990. "The Apparent Ideological Behavior of Legislators: Testing for Principal-Agent Slack in Political Institutions". *Journal of Law & Economics* 33: 103–131.
Katz, Jonathan N. and Brian R. Sala. 1996. "Committee Assignments and the Electoral Connection". *American Political Science Review* 90: 21–33.
Kiewiet, D. Roderick and Mathew D. McCubbins. 1988. "Presidential Influence on Congressional Appropriations Decisions". *American Journal of Political Science* 32: 713–736.
Kiewiet, D. Roderick and Mathew D. McCubbins. 1991. *The Logic of Delegation: Congressional Parties and the Appropriations Process*. Chicago, IL: University of Chicago Press.
Krehbiel, Keith. 1991. *Information and Legislative Organization*. Ann Arbor, MI: University of Michigan Press.
Krehbiel, Keith K. 1998. *Pivotal Politics: A Theory of U.S. Lawmaking*. Chicago, IL: University of Chicago Press.
Laver, Michael, and Norman Schofield. 1990. *Multiparty Government: The Politics of Coalition in Europe*. Oxford: Oxford University Press.
Laver, Michael, and Kenneth A. Shepsle. 1990. "Coalitions and Cabinet Government". *American Political Science Review* 84: 873–890.
Laver, Michael, and Kenneth A. Shepsle. 1996. *Making and Breaking Governments: Cabinets and Legislatures in Parliamentary Democracies*. Cambridge: Cambridge University Press.
Lawrence, Eric D., Forrest Maltzman, and Steven S. Smith. 1999. "Who Wins? Party Effects in Legislative Voting". Unpublished typescript. George Washington University.
Levitt, Steven D., and James M. Snyder. 1995. "Political Parties and the Distribution of Federal Outlays". *American Journal of Political Science* 39: 958–80.
Libecap, Gary D. 1989. *Contracting for Property Rights*. Cambridge: Cambridge University Press.
Lijphart, Arend. 1984. *Democracies: Patterns of Majoritarian and Consensus Government in Twenty-one Countries*. New Haven, CT: Yale University Press.
Lupia, Arthur and Mathew D. McCubbins. 1994. "Learning From Oversight: Police Patrols and Fire Alarms Reconsidered". *Journal of Law, Economics and Organization* 10: 96–105.
Lupia, Arthur and Mathew D. McCubbins. 1998. *The Democratic Dilemma: Can Citizens Learn What They Really Need to Know?* Cambridge: Cambridge University Press.
Manley, John F. 1973. "The Conservative Coalition in Congress". *American Behavioral Scientist* 17:223–47.
Mattson, Ingvar and Kaare Strom. 1995. "Parliamentary Committees" in Herbert Doring (ed.), *Parliaments and Majority Rule in Western Europe*. New York: St. Martin's Press.
Mayhew, David. 1974. *The Electoral Connection*. New Haven, CT: Yale University Press.
McConachie, Lauros G. 1974 [1898]. *Congressional Committees*. New York: B. Franklin [reprint].

McCubbins, Mathew D. and Gregory W. Noble. 1995. "Perceptions and Realities of Japanese Budgeting" in Peter Cowhey and Mathew D. McCubbins (eds.), *Structure and Policy in Japan and the United States*. Cambridge: Cambridge University Press.

McCubbins, Mathew D., Roger G. Noll, and Barry R. Weingast. 1987. "Administrative Procedures as an Instrument of Political Control". *Journal of Law, Economics, and Organization* 3: 243–277.

McCubbins, Mathew D. and Frances Rosenbluth. 1995. "Party Provision for Personal Politics: dividing the vote in Japan" in Peter Cowhey and Mathew D. McCubbins (eds.), *Structure and Policy in Japan and the United States*. Cambridge: Cambridge University Press.

McCubbins, Mathew D. and Thomas Schwartz. 1984. "Congressional Oversight Overlooked: Police Patrols versus Fire Alarms". *American Journal of Political Science* 28: 165–179.

McCubbins, Mathew D. and Thomas Schwartz. 1988. "Congress, the Courts, and Public Policy: Consequences of the One Man, One Vote Rule". *American Journal of Political Science* 32: 388–415.

McCubbins, Mathew D. and Michael F. Thies. 1997. "As a Matter of Factions: The Budgetary Implications of Shifting Factional Control in Japan's LDP". *Legislative Studies Quarterly* 22: 293–328.

Miller, Gary J. 1992. *Managerial Dilemmas: The Political Economy of Hierarchy*. Cambridge; New York: Cambridge University Press.

Morgenstern, Scott. 2004. *Patterns of Legislative Politics. Roll call voting in Latin America and the United States*. Cambridge: Cambridge University Press.

Muller, Wolfgang. 2000. "Tight Coalitions and Stable Government" in Wolfgang, Muller and (eds.), Kaare Strom. *Coalition Goverments in Western Europe*. Oxford: Oxford University Press.

Muller, Wolfgang and Kaare Strom. 2000. "Coalition Governance in Western Europe" in Wolfgang, Muller and Kaare Strom (eds.), *Coalition Goverments in Western Europe*. Oxford: Oxford University Press.

Murphy, James T. 1974. "Political Parties and the Porkbarrel: Party Conflict and Cooperation in House Public Works Committee Decision-Making". *American Political Science Review* 68: 169–86.

Noll, Roger G. and Frances M. Rosenbluth. 1995. "Telecommunications Policy: Structure, Process, Outcomes" in Peter Cowhey and Mathew D. McCubbins (eds.), *Structure and Policy in Japan and the United States*. Cambridge: Cambridge University Press.

North, Douglass C. 1981. *Structure and Change in Economic History*. New York: Norton.

North, Douglass C. 1990. *Institutions, Institutional Change, and Economic performance*. New York: Cambridge University Press.

Oleszek, Walter. 2004. *Congressional Procedures and the Policy Process*, 6th edn. Washington, DC: CQ Press.

Parker, Glenn R. and Suzanne L. Parker. 1985. *Factions in House Committees*. Knoxville, TN: University of Tennessee Press.

Patzelt, J Werner. 1996. "German MPs and their Roles," *The Journal of Legislative Studies* (special issue) 3(1).

Poole, Keith T., and Howard Rosenthal. 1997. *Congress: A Political-Economic History of Roll Call Voting*. New York: Oxford University Press.

Polsby, Nelson W. 1968. "The Institutionalization of the U.S. House of Representatives". *American Political Science Review* 62: 144–168.

Polsby, Nelson W., Miriam Gallaher, and Barry S. Rundquist. 1969. "The Growth of the Seniority System in the U. S. House of Representatives". *American Political Science Review* 63: 787–807.

Ramseyer, J. Mark and Frances Rosenbluth. 1993. *Japan's Political Marketplace*. Cambridge: Harvard University Press.

Reed, Steven R. 1994. "Democracy and the Personal Vote: A Cautionary Tale from Japan". *Electoral Studies* 13: 17–28.

Riker, William H. and Peter C. Ordeshook. 1968. "A Theory of the Calculus of Voting". *American Political Science Review* 62: 25–42.
Ripley, Randall B. 1969. *Power in the Senate*. New York: St. Martin's.
Robinson, James A. 1963. *The House Rules Committee*. Indianapolis: Bobbs-Merrill.
Rohde, David. 1991. *Parties and Leaders in the Postreform House*. Chicago, IL: University of Chicago Press.
Romer, Thomas and Howard Rosenthal. 1978. "Political Resource Allocation, Controlled Agendas, and the Status Quo". *Public Choice* 33: 27–44.
Rosenbluth, Frances. 1989. *Financial Politics in Contemporary Japan*. Ithaca, NY: Cornell University Press.
Sato, Seizaburo and Tetsuhisa Matsuzaki. 1986. *Jiminto Seiken* [The LDP Regime]. Tokyo: Chuo Koronsha.
Schickler, Eric, 2001. *Disjointed Pluralism: Institutional Innovation and the Development of the U.S. Congress*. Princeton, NJ: Princeton University Press.
Sinclair, Barbara. 1981. "The Speaker's Task Force in the Post-Reform House of Representatives". *The American Political Science Review* 75: 397–410.
Shepsle, Kenneth A. and Barry R. Weingast. 1987. "The Institutional Foundations of Committee Power". *American Political Science Review* 81: 85–104.
Shugart, Matthew Soberg and John Carey. 1992. *Presidents and Assemblies: Constitutional Design and Electoral Dynamics*. Cambridge: Cambridge University Press.
Sinclair, Barbara. 1983. *Majority Leadership in the U.S. House*. Baltimore, MD: Johns Hopkins University Press.
Sinclair, Barbara. 2002. "Do Parties Matter?" in David Brady and Mathew D. McCubbins (eds.), *Party, Process, and Political Change in Congress: New Perspectives on the History of Congress*. Palo Alto, CA: Stanford University Press.
Stein, Robert M. and Kenneth N. Bickers. 1994. "Universalism and the Electoral Connection: A Test and Some Doubts." *Political Research Quarterly* 47: 295–317.
Stewart, Charles H. III. 1989. *Budget Reform Politics: The Design of the Appropriations Process in the House of Representatives, 1865–1921*. New York: Cambridge University Press.
Thies, Michael F. 1998. "When Will Pork Leave the Farm? Institutional Bias in Japan and the United States". *Legislative Studies Quarterly* 23: 467–492
Thies, Michael F. 2001. "Keeping Tabs on Partners: The Logic of Delegation in Coalition Governments". *American Journal of Political Science* 45: 580–598.
Tsebelis, George. 1995. "Decision Making in Political Systems: Veto Players in Presidentialism, Parliamentarism, Multicameralism and Multipartyism". *British Journal of Political Science* 25: 289–325.
Weingast, Barry R. 1979. "A Rational Choice Perspective on Congressional Norms". *American Journal of Political Science* 23: 245–262.
Weingast, Barry R. 1995. "The Economic Role of Political Institutions: Federalism, Markets, and Economic Development". *Journal of Law, Economics, and Organization* 11: 1–31.
Weingast, Barry and William Marshall. 1988. "The Industrial Organization of Congress". *Journal of Political Economy* 96: 132–63.
Williamson, Oliver. 1975. *Markets and Hierarchies: Analysis and Antitrust Implications*. New York: The Free Press.
Wilson, Rick. 1986. "An Empirical Test of Preferences for Political Pork Barrel: District Level Appropriations for River and Harbor Legislation". *American Journal of Political Science* 30: 729–53.
Wilson, Woodrow. 1885. *Congressional Government*. Boston, MA: Houghton, Mifflin.
Wolfensberger, Don. 2003. "The Motion to Recommit in the House: The Creation, Evisceration, and Restoration of a Minority Right". Paper presented at the 2003 History of Congress Conference at the University of California, San Diego, CA.

7. The Performance and Stability of Federalism: An Institutional Perspective

BARRY R. WEINGAST

1. Introduction

The literatures on the performance of federal systems divide around three central questions. The first concerns the economic performance of federalism; the second, the political performance; and the third, the sources of stability for federal arrangements.

Economists typically focus on the first question, with an emphasis on the normative aspects, such as: How ought federalism to be designed? In answering this question, the economic theory of federalism provides a theory about the optimal organization of the state, addressing issues, such as what powers should be assigned to what levels of government; why should not the central government do everything? This literature has strong positive implications, for it also explains the economic implications of alternative divisions of powers among the various levels of government.

Economists and political scientists have also focused on various political aspects of federalism, such as the degree to which the federal institutions affect the incentives of public officials. A range of results show how performance of a federation depends on these institutional arrangements underpinning the federal system. For example, a series of recent models show how different forms of tax system give subnational governments different incentives to provide public goods and foster economic growth.

Finally, the most recent questions involve how a federal system is sustained. The first two literatures take the structure of federalism as given and study its implications. This third literature treats federal structure as endogenous. To understand this question, we follow Riker (1964) and pose the twin dilemmas of federalism (de Figueiredo and Weingast 2004): Although federations differ on many dimensions, all face the two fundamental dilemmas:

Dilemma 1: What prevents the national government from destroying federalism by over-awing its constituent units?

Dilemma 2: What prevents the constituent units from undermining federalism by free-riding and other forms of failure to cooperate?

To illustrate the first dilemma, for much of the late twentieth century modern Mexico was federal in name only, as the central government centralized political authority from 1940 through the 1980s (though this trend has been modestly reversed in the last decade). To illustrate the second dilemma, consider the United States under the Articles of Confederation where the national government was too weak to provide national public goods, such as defense, policing the common market, or a stable monetary regime. In each policy area, some states had followed their common pool incentives, resulting in a series of welfare losses and disputes among states.

Although these three literatures are complementary, they remain incompletely integrated, precluding a more complete theory of the performance of federal systems. The purpose of this paper is twofold: first, to survey these three sets of works; and second, to draw on aspects of the new institutional economics and political science to suggest aspects of an integration and hence a more complete theory of federal performance.

The economics literature tells us the economic implications of alternative assignment of policies across levels of government, while the political science literature discusses the issue of what divisions are self-enforcing. As Riker (1964) demonstrates, not all types of divisions of powers within federal systems are self-enforcing. Unfortunately, the literatures on these two topics are largely separate.

The economic classics of federalism, identified with Hayek, Tiebout and Musgrave, emphasized the felicitous aspects of federalism generated through inter-jurisdictional competition and through appropriate matching of authority over public goods with different levels of government. Modern economics tends to qualify the positive conclusions of the earlier literature, analyzing incentives problems with lower governments, often emphasizing various common pool problems (race to the bottom; internal trade barriers; soft budget constraints) and intergenerational spillovers.

The underlying conceptual distinction between these two literatures is important: the classical economic works assumed benevolent governments at all levels, so certain types of incentive problems simply did not arise. The modern economics literature takes the first step in relaxing this assumption by looking at the incentive effects of lower governments, assuming that they ignore all external effects of their decisions. This reveals several types of common pool problems where decentralized decisionmaking yields problems.

Although the modern literature takes the first step, two limitations remain. First, scholars in this tradition tend to assume that local governments are benevolent governments with respect to their own citizens, ignoring how this comes about. Second, students in this tradition often retain the assumption that the federal government is benevolent and thus argue that, in the face of common pool problems, the federal government should be responsible for policymaking. Both problems limit the ability of this literature to develop a complete positive model of a federal system, treating each level of government in parallel, with its own interests and incentive problems.

A more complete theory of federalism drops the assumption of benevolent government at all levels, attempting to explain what do governments really do. An alternative assumption, associated with James Buchanan, is the opposite from the benevolent government—that government is Leviathan. In one sense, this position is too extreme—like that of the benevolent government, it fails to explain how the government's maximand arises. Yet this perspective contains an important insight: different institutional arrangements affect the incentives of various levels of government and hence affect their performance (Brennan and Buchanan 1980).

The important lesson of Buchanan for present purposes is to ask how different types of institutional arrangements affect the incentives of different levels of government. In particular, the second substantive section of this paper asks under what conditions will governments find it in their interests to foster markets? And here, federalism organized in the appropriate way has felicitous effects.

Finally, surveying the three separate literatures points toward a more complete theory of federalism, one encompassing both political and economic aspects. This also allows us to consider the structure of federalism—indeed, whether a country can sustain federalism at all—as endogenous.

This essay is organized as follows. Section 2 discusses both the economic classics and the modern economics literature on federalism. Section 3 discusses the literature on how federalism affects the incentives and objectives of subnational government officials. Section 4 turns more generally to the question of the conditions under which federalism is self-enforcing. Section 5 applies the framework to a discussion of the evolution of federalism in the United States since inception.

2. Economic Theories of Federalism

The economic theory divides into two types of analyses, which I call here the classical and the modern. The classic economic contributions to federalism rest on the work of Hayek, Tiebout, and Musgrave and are strongly normative in character based on the assumption of a benevolent government. The modern work extends this tradition to include the study of various incentives problems among the many subnational governments created by federalism itself.

The Economic Classics of Federalism

The classic economics of federalism revolves around Hayek's (1939) emphasis on the role of differential information across levels of government; Tiebout's (1956) emphasis on interjurisdictional competition, and Musgrave's (1959) notions of the assignment of policy and tax authority across jurisdictions. Oates (1972) codified this work into a relatively coherent approach. These are straightforward but powerful ideas. As these works are the most well-known and as many good surveys exist, I will summarize them briefly.[1]

Hayek emphasized the importance of differential information. Subnational governments and their citizens typically have better information than the national government about local conditions and preferences. Thus, for local public goods, local decisionmakers are likely to make more informed and thus better decisions about matching local policy to local conditions than will national policymakers. Moreover, national governments have a tendency to promulgate "one-size-fits-all" policies that are insufficiently variable to adapt to differing local conditions.

National governments typically provide money for various subnational government expenditures. Yet the categories often fail to reflect local priorities. For example, a recent crime bill provided funds for hi-tech squad cars. These cars are quite expensive, and most smaller jurisdictions would not purchase them if they have to pay for the cars from their own funds. The bill offered to pay for 95% of the cost of the cars, so, at 5% of the cost, a large number of jurisdictions will elect to put up their (small) share and buy obtain the cars. Yet for most jurisdictions, this is not the highest priority use of the subsidy. Some need newer electronic communications; others need more policeman, and so on. But the bill did not offer the items most needed by the local governments; so instead the local governments chose what was available. This example could be repeated almost endlessly given the huge range of federal expenditure programs in the United States that foster local public goods provision.[2]

Tiebout (1956) emphasized the critical importance of interjurisdictional competition, which has at least three separate components.[3] In the presence of labor and capital mobility, this competition leads to matching policies to citizens and communities; to citizens and capital owners sorting across jurisdictions to reside in those with policies most favorable to their needs and circumstances; and to provide incentives for city managers, who must anticipate the effects of their decisions for citizens and firm location decisions. Interjurisdictional competition combines with the mobility of citizens and capital to imply that policies at variance with the population or firms means that citizens and capital leave for more hospitable locations, lowering the tax base. City managers, ever worried about their city's tax base, are thus led to provide policies hospitable to those located in their jurisdiction. This last point implies that incentives of governmental officials are endogenous to the structure of federalism, a topic discussed at greater length below.

Economists provide lots of evidence for these propositions. The United States has a very mobile population, and the evidence suggests that the provision of

---

[1] For surveys of federalism, see: Inman and Rubinfeld (1997), Nechyba and Mckinnon (1997), Oates (1972, 2001), and Rubinfeld (1987).

[2] The same holds for other federal governments, such as Mexico where, until recently, expenditures were highly centralized.

[3] In addition to the surveys cited in note 1, supra, Scotchmer (1994) surveys the theoretical literature following Tiebout.

local public services is important in these moves (see e.g., Oates 1969, Gramlich and Rubinfeld 1982, Nechyba and Strauss 1997).

The third idea derives from Musgrave (1959), who studied the assignment problem, which asks for a federal system how should authority over public goods, policy, and taxes be assigned to the different levels of government to maximize citizen welfare? Musgrave observed that public goods differed along several dimensions, including the degree to which they exhibit economies of scale and congestion as the number of people consuming the public good grows. Some public goods, like national defense, a common market, and a stable currency, are truly national in scope in the sense that there are large economies of scale and little congestion. Other public goods, such as parks, schools, sanitation, are more local in scope.

The assignment principle holds that authority over public goods should be assigned to that level of government that can most efficiently produce it. Thus, the national government should provide public goods which exhibit little congestion, such as national defense, while local governments should provide public goods that are more local in scope, such as parks, schools, and sanitation facilities, particularly as jurisdictions can adjust their provision of these goods to suit citizen tastes.

As Oates (1972) emphasized, these ideas combine to provide a powerful normative argument in favor of federalism: federalism enhances citizen welfare through the appropriate assignment of functions across levels of government; through matching and sorting individuals and firms across jurisdictions that provide polices and public goods best suited for their firms and citizenry; and through the appropriate use of information.

Modern Economics of Federalism

The classic economic approach to federalism is relatively pro-decentralization. Modern economic research on federalism has tempered the felicitous conclusions of the classic economic contributions, in part by studying various incentive problems created by virtue that subnational governments face various forms of free-riding and common pool problems.

Externalities provide the paradigmatic example in which a locality fails to bear all the consequences of its decisions. For example, consider environmental regulation in the United States. In many geographic areas, particularly those with prevailing winds, it is possible for one jurisdiction to export its pollution to other jurisdictions. Thus, part of the costs of pollution may be born by others. This externality also implies that some of the benefits of this jurisdiction's addressing this issue accrue to residents outside the jurisdiction.

For example, consider the problem of sulfur dioxide pollution from electric power plants that burn high sulfur coalitional in Ohio. The prevailing winds blow east, carrying much of this pollution 100s and 1000s of miles away from the source. Suppose Ohio were to act alone and impose pollution controls within its jurisdiction. This would raise its firm's costs without affecting these firms' competitors located outside the jurisdiction; and further, much of the benefits would accrue outside the jurisdiction. Reflecting a classic common pool problem, Ohio has incentives to ignore the problem. When all states act this way, the problem remains unaddressed. Under the assumption of benevolent national government, this perspective implies that pollution control should be assigned to the national instead of the state or local governments.

A second and more serious common pool problem concerns internal trade barriers among the federal units, historically in the United States and common in many modern federations, such as Russia. Internal trade barriers were a major problem under the Articles of Confederation, part of the rationale cited by the Federalists for a stronger national government. Under the Constitution, the United States was assiduous in policing state trade barriers. Indeed, examples abound in the nineteenth century of states trying to erect such barriers.

The importance of the common market for the Tiebout mechanism and, more generally, for the process of national specialization and exchange to gain the economies of scale associated with a large country, require that states be prevented from raising internal trade barriers. This is a task that must be assigned the national government.[4]

Another critical mechanism studied extensively in recent years concerns whether subnational governments face a hard or soft budget constraint (Dillinger and Webb 1999, McKinnon 1997, Rodden 2000, Rodden, Eskeland, and Litvack 2001, Roland and Qian 1999, Sanguinetti 1994, Wildasin 1997). A hard budget constraint requires that subnational governments bear the full financial consequences of their decisions: they cannot be bailed out or receive endless forgiveable loans from the central banking system. A subnational government facing a hard budget constraint cannot spend beyond its means without risking bankruptcy. A soft budget constraint allows an subnational government to spend beyond its means. Although a soft budget constraints creates budget deficits, these are financed either through central government bailouts or by access to forgivable loans from a central bank.

Because subnational governments do not bear the full financial consequences of their fiscal decisions under a soft budget constraint, their spending is more profligate. In extreme cases, where subnational governments expect bailouts, spending is rampant on rents, special interest benefits, and corruption. This process is sadly illustrated by the explosive state deficits and consequent national macroeconomic imbalances in late 1990s Brazil and late 1980s Argentina.

The various forms of incentive problems facing subnational governments yield two conclusions. First, these problems qualify the normative argument favoring federalism, as common pool problem hinder a federation's performances. Second, it provides a role for the national government, one of policing these problems. Of course, studies of the national government in this role often find

---

[4] Notice that, here too, the assumption of benevolent government is critical to this normative judgement. The reason is that something must prevent the federal government from abusing its power over the subnational governments to force these governments to adhere to particular policies, such as rent-seeking.

it lacking, as Revesz's (1997) analysis of environmental policy in the United States illustrates.

Market-Preserving Federalism

Market-preserving federalism provides a framework for assessing different forms of federal system.[5] The framework makes explicit a set of axioms implicit in the type of federalism studied by the classical era economists. Specifically, the classic economic approach requires the following assumptions about the political structure of federalism:

(A1): A hierarchy of governments, each with their own sphere's of policy autonomy;
(A2): that subnational governments have substantial regulatory controls over their economies;
(A3) that a common market exists, including the federal government's ability to prevent subnational governments from raising internal trade barriers;
(A4) that subnational governments face a HBC;
(A5) that a set of institutions protect the federal arrangement from encroachment by political officials at the various levels of government.

Each of these axioms is implicit in the classical economic studies noted above. Moreover, making these assumptions explicit emphasizes that the economic approach also contains a comparative theory of federalism. Consider: Axiom A1 is a defining condition of federalism which all federations satisfy. Federal systems delegate very different types of powers to their subnational governments. Axiom A2 emphasizes that, for federalism to have the effects noted by Musgrave, Oates, and Tiebout, subnational governments must have meaningful policy authority over local public goods and other regulatory policy that affects their local economies. The common market (A3) is also essential for interjurisdictional competition. When subnational governments can raise internal trade barriers, they can protect their firms from outside competition, extract rents from constituents and assetholders, and indulge in a higher degree of corruption. These barriers can also hinder the factor mobility necessary for matching and sorting of factors and local public goods emphasized in the Tiebout literature. Problems with the failure of the HBC (A4) are also well-known, as discussed above. When subnational governments do not bear the full financial consequences of their decisions, they are more likely to spend profligately, dispense rents, and engage in corruption. Finally, the failure of A5 compromises federalism. Thus, when the constitution allows the federal government to take over states (India) or fire state governors (Mexico), the federal government can use these tools to control subnational governments.

[5] Weingast (1995), Montinola, Qian, and Weingast (1995), and Parikh and Weingast (1997).

3. POLITICAL INCENTIVES

The classic economic literature makes a heroic assumption—that governmental actors are non-strategic, benevolent maximizers of citizen welfare. This assumption rules out corruption, rent-seeking, service to interest groups, and generally, manipulation of public policy to serve private instead of public ends.

As the Federalist observed more than 200 years ago, "if men were angels" we would not have to worry about structuring incentives through the appropriate design of political institutions; but as they observed, because men are not angels, we must be concerned with creating political institutions that provide government officials with the appropriate incentives.[6]

No theory of federal design is complete without attention to the incentives of public officials. As the Federalists noted, to the extent that governments in some countries are concerned with citizen welfare, it is because their public officials face incentives to do so. The sad fact is that many governments in the twentieth century have been among the worst perpetrators of violence and destruction against their citizens.

In this section, we rely on positive political theory to discuss some insights into the types of mechanisms that help align the interests of governmental officials with those of their citizens. A look around the world demonstrates that most governments on the planet fail on this dimension, so the problem ignored by economists is a non-trivial one.

Once we relax the assumption of benevolent governments and understand that government officials generally face political pressure to use their policy authority to provide rents, private goods, and confiscate wealth to transfer to supporters, we see that federal governments have advantages over unitary states (Persson and Tabellini 2001). When the central government holds a monopoly on violence, its officials often abuse its policymaking authority to serve private ends.

By decentralizing a range of policies to lower governments, federalism affects the ability and incentives of governments to serve private instead of public ends (as Hayek 1939 and Brennan and Buchanan 1980 emphasize). First, decentralization limits the powers of the federal government in a range of areas. Second, decentralization places lower governments in competition with one another (Tiebout 1956), so that those that abuse their citizens' rights are likely to lose mobile factors. Third, appropriately structured federalism forces lower governments to bear the financial consequences of their decisions. In this section, we discuss the consequences of this structure, investigating the finer-grained details of institutions, incentives, and performance. The next investigates how this structure can be maintained given the political pressure to undo it for political ends.

---

[6] In *Federalist* No 51: "If men were angels, no government would be necessary. If angels were to govern men, neither external nor internal controls on government would be necessary. In framing a government which is to be administered by men over men, the great difficulty lies in this: you must first enable the government to control the governed; and in the next place oblige it to control itself. " [337]

The Fiscal Interest Model

Wallis, Sylla, and Legler (1994) provide an important perspective on these problems. They observe that, whatever a government's goals, it must obtain revenue to further them. Governments therefore prefer, ceteris paribus, institutions and policies that relax their budget constraints. This observation implies that the micro-institutional details about the way in which governments tax their citizens affect the government's incentives and hence its performance.

This approach has profound implications for how governments behave. Thus, consider how governments tax banks. Governments that raise revenue through taxing bank charters—effectively taxing numbers of banks—have incentives to maintain a small numbers of banks. By creating monopoly rents through restricting the supply of banks, businesses are willing to pay more for bank charters and hence increase government tax revenue. In contrast, governments that tax bank capital have the opposite incentives—they want to maximize the number of banks and to foster a healthy climate for banks so that the tax base is the largest.

Interjurisdictional competition combines with the fiscal interest in interesting ways. Consider two illustrations. In the early United States, Philadelphia was a major banking center.[7] As with most states, Pennsylvania taxed bank charters, having incentives to restrict the number of banks. Massachusetts, another home to banking, taxed bank capital and found the revenue from this sufficiently high that it could end the property tax, the principal source of revenue for most states. Sometime in the 1820s, however, New York switched to taxing bank capital and, at the same time, greatly relaxed the requirements necessary to become a bank. The result was a fast-growing industry in New York City that took over from Philadelphia as the nation's banking center. In the wake of New York's success, several other states switched to taxing bank capital.

Second, the contrast with the early United States and Mexico is also instructive.[8] Wallis et al. (1994) also show that, to attract capital and labor, every new state had to create a banking industry, both to finance local enterprises and to finance (through bills of exchange) shipments of goods across state lines. Thus, the number of banks in the United States grew enormously. By the early twentieth century, the United States had over 10,000 banks.

Turn of the twentieth century Mexico, in contrast, was a federal system in name only. As with so many dictators, Mexico's used national policymaking to create monopolies as a means of raising revenue and securing power by creating constituents dependent on maintaining the state (see Haber et al. 2004). The result was that each state had its monopoly bank, and the national government had two. In contrast to United States's 10,000 banks, Mexico had less than 50.

This illustration emphasizes the importance of federalism for government incentives. As Haber (2003) shows, governments in both the early United

---

[7] This discussion draws on the work of Wallis, Sylla and Legler (1994).
[8] I draw on Haber (2003) for the contrast of the United States and Mexican banks.

States and in late nineteenth century and twentieth century Mexico had incentives to restrict the number of banks. But the United States' federal structure induced competition among the states, providing some states with an advantage if they removed these restrictions, later forcing others to do so in response.

Careaga and Weingast (2002), Inman (1988), and Inman and Rubinfeld (1997) study variants of the fiscal interest model. Traditional fiscal federalism of revenue sharing emphasizes redistribution (Musgrave 1959, Oates 1972). Although the economics literature on federalism has traditionally ignored the incentives created by revenue sharing, the fiscal interest model has important implications for the behavior of subnational government officials.

These positive models study two different effects of revenue sharing: the incentive of the national government to allocate these funds; and the incentives these funds create for subnational governments. We consider these in turn.

Inman (1988) and Inman and Rubinfeld (1997) study the incentives of national elected officials to allocate national revenue sharing funds to lower jurisdictions to finance public goods. Studying allocation by the legislature, they show that legislators face a form of common pool problem: because expenditures in their own districts yield each the full benefits but taxes are spread over the entire nation, each legislator has an incentive to demand a higher than optimal level of public goods expenditures.[9] When each representative behaves in this way, the total level of such expenditures is too high. Inman (1988) and Poterba and von Hagen (1999) provide evidence for this type of common pool problem in a variety of fiscal contexts.

Revenue sharing also affects subnational government incentives. To see this, suppose that subnational governmental actors are concerned about maintaining their political careers and that may use public policies in two broad categories to further their goals. First, they can provide market enhancing public goods, P; and second, they can provide private rents (corruption, service to interest groups), R, that have deadweight social losses. What determines how they make this tradeoff? Careaga and Weingast show that the type of tax system affects how they make this tradeoff.

Providing rents has a direct benefit — providing individuals and groups with benefits increases their willingness to support governmental actors. Providing market-enhancing public goods has two benefits. First, in parallel with providing rents, providing public goods benefits some individuals and groups and thus increases their willingness to support governmental actors. Second, it also relaxes the government's budget constraint: by increasing the market, these public goods expand the government's tax base and thus allows it to provide more of both types of services.

Next, consider the proportion of revenue of locally generated revenue, α, retained by the subnational government, with the federal government capturing

---
[9] Weingast, Shepsle and Johnsen (1981) provide a model of this process.

the remainder, 1-α. Careaga and Weingast's main comparative static result is that, as the proportion of locally generated revenue, α, that the subnational government captures increases, the amount of market-enhancing public goods they provide also increases. The reason is that higher α raises the increase in revenue captured by the subnational government from increasing the tax base through an increase in P.

This approach has considerable implications for the type of revenue sharing system used by a federal country. Under complete revenue sharing, where the central government collects all revenue and then distributes this to states based on its own political criterion, the amount of revenue received by a given subnational government is only minimally responsive to P. In contrast, in a system where the subnational government raises the lion's share of its own revenue, increases in P enhance the local market, raise the tax base, and increase the tax revenue that the local subnational government captures.

Put simply, the type of revenue sharing system affects the incentives of subnational governments to foster markets. Governments that raise their own revenue are more likely to focus on market-enhancing public goods, while governments that obtain most of their revenue from the central government are more likely to be corrupt.

Consistent with this result is the following pattern among federal systems. During the United States's rise from a small economy on the periphery of the developed world in the late eighteenth century to become the richest nation by early twentieth century, states depended almost exclusively on their own sources of revenue. So too do provinces in modern China (see Jin, Qian, and Weingast 2005, although this has changed somewhat in the late 1990s). Iaryczower, Saiegh, and Tommasi (2000) suggest that this characteristic also held in Argentina during its high growth phase in the latter part of the nineteenth century and early twentieth centuries. In contrast, this condition fails for modern Argentina, India, Mexico, and Russia.

Rodden (2001) provides systematic evidence for a strong effect of own taxes on size of government. Previously Stein (1999), among others, had shown that greater degrees of fiscal decentralization is associated with larger governments. Rodden studying a larger sample, added a variable measuring the degree to which subnational governments fund their spending through their own taxes. He shows that federal systems in which subnational government raise their own taxes tend to have smaller governments.

Finally, Epple and Zelenitz (1981) and Epple and Romer (1991) study how the Tiebout process limits the ability of local jurisdiction to extract tax revenue from constituents. Epple and Zelenitz find that more jurisdictions limit this extraction but do not eliminate it. Epple and Romer show that local jurisdiction can extract rents from landowners because land is a fixed rather than a mobile factor.

In short, economists since Hayek and Buchanan have argued that federalism affects the incentives of state actors. Brennan and Buchanan (1980) studied this in the context of the assumption that governments sought to maximize tax revenue. More recent work applies Wallis et al's (1994) fiscal interest model, showing how federalism affects the policy and fiscal behavior of subnational governments with more diverse goals.

4. ENDOGENOUS FEDERALISM

As the survey thus far indicates, most analyses of federalism take the structure federalism as given, analyzing its effects. This yields an impressive and well-developed theory about the effects of federalism. Nonetheless, this approach neglects the question of what sustains federalism over the long-run. This question is of interest for its own sake; but also because it interacts with the above concerns about performance. To the extent that only certain types of federal structures can be sustained, some normative prescriptions will focus on worlds that cannot exist. The literature on federal stability is sufficiently new that no such conclusions have yet to be derived; but it holds the promise of adding significantly to the theory of federal performance.

The question of federal stability relates to a more general problem. In the United States, we take constitutional stability—and with it, the stability of both American federalism and democracy—for granted. Yet looking around the world, it is clear that most countries have difficulty adhering to constitutional and political rules supporting critical national institutions, such as federalism, democracy, and the market. Moreover, we tend to ignore the significant problems with the stability of American democracy, federalism and the constitution during the first 100 years of the American Republic, as the failure of these institutions in the Civil War amply demonstrates (Weingast 1998). In short, a theory of the performance of federalism requires that we endogenize it; that is, we must understand the forces that produce federal stability and hence explain why some countries can sustain federalism while others not.

In this section, we study some of the principles emerging that help explain how federalism is sustained. In the language of modern rational choice theory, this requires that federalism be self-enforcing in the sense that relevant national and subnational political actors have incentives to adhere to the rules of federalism.

The two fundamental dilemmas of federalism noted in the introduction demonstrate the fragility of federalism: As Riker (1964) observed—and in keeping with the modern economics literature—subnational governments have a tendency to destroy federalism through common pool problems. Similarly, the national government has a tendency to agglomerate power and overawe the subnational governments. The two fundamental dilemmas are especially difficult to solve because institutional mechanisms designed to mitigate one tend to exacerbate the other. To police the subnational governments, the federal government must have the power to punish them. But this power also allows a non-benevolent federal government to abuse the states. In other words, sustaining federalism requires a careful balance between the two dilemmas (de Figueiredo and Weingast 2004). The center must have sufficient power to prevent the states from free-riding; yet not be so powerful as to be able to overawe the states.

How is this balance accomplished? The literature provides only partial answers. To address this question, I draw on the emerging literature on self-enforcing constitutions. I first present three principles of constitutional stability, for the issue of federalism's stability is part of the larger question of how some constitutions are sustained.[10] I then turn to some additional insights provided in the literature.

The first principle concerns the ability of both levels of government to deter each other if the other over-steps the bounds of federalism.[11] Thus, the center must have the ability and incentive to police common pool problems by the subnational governments, while the latter must have the ability to police the center if it abuses its authority and threatens the subnational government's independent authority. The difficulty in this setup is a coordination problem: the subnational governments must somehow have the ability to act in concert against potential abuses by the federal government. In game theoretic terms, the latter requires that they have a common focal point on which to react (de Figueiredo and Weingast 2004). Such focal solutions to the subnational government coordination problem typically arise through pacts and constitutions that make explicit the rules of the federal game that specify readily identifiable bounds on the center. When subnational governments have the ability to act in concert, they can police the center because the center knows it will be punished if it oversteps the agreed upon bounds. As Madison observed in *Federalist* 46, "But ambitious encroachments by the federal government on the authority of the state governments would not excite the oppositive of a single state, or a few states only. They would be general signals of alarm. Every government would espouse the common cause."

Consider two examples. As discussed at greater length in section 5, the American Constitution helped create limits on the new national government through several mechanisms. First, it articulated specific limits on the national government, such as a series of rights accorded to citizens. Second, it specified a series of institutions that defined how national policy was produced. In particular, the separation of powers system limited the types of policies that the national government could pursue. Third, specifying both rights and restrictions on the national government; and procedures by which policy could be made helped create a series of focal solutions so that, per *Federalist 46*, citizens could react in concert against potential abuses. This trigger strategy, in turn, provided the incentives for the national government to adhere to these limits.

As a second example, consider China's fiscal decentralization of the 1980s, granting provinces considerable policy freedom of their economies (notably, to

---

[10] Works in this new literature include: Bednar (1999), deFigueiredo and Weingast (2004), Fearon (2000), Przeworski (1991), and Weingast (1997).

[11] This discussion draws on recent game theoretic approaches to self-enforcing federalism, especially deFigueiredo and Weingast (2004), Bednar (1999), and Weingast (1997).

create a transition from socialism). Provinces were also granted considerable fiscal authority, with a remarkably high degree of tax retention at the margin (Jin, Qian, and Weingast 2005). After the violence in Tiananmen Square in 1989, reactionary forces in the central government sought to undermine many of the reforms by recentralizing. At a critical meeting where this was proposed, the governor of Guangdong argued forcefully against this, with most other governors supporting him. As a consequence, the center had to back down (Shirk 1993, Montinola, Qian, and Weingast 1995).

The second principle of sustaining federalism draws on a general point about constitutional stability. All successful constitutions limit the stakes of politics (Przeworski 1991, ch 2).[12] The reason is that, in the absence of credible limits on the government, circumstances inevitably arise where individuals and groups feel their livelihood and their property threatened. In such circumstances, they are likely to favor extra-constitutional means of protecting themselves, such as supporting a coup. Chile in 1973 and the Second Republic in Spain during the 1930s both illustrate this principle. In both cases, property owners felt their property threatened by the democratically elected regime; in both cases, they supported a military coup, resulting in an immediate transfer of power in Chile and in a bloody Civil War in Spain (1936–39) culminating in the military's success against the regime.

Per the second principle, a critical aspect of federalism is that, by decentralizing authority over a range of important policy issues over which people disagree, federalism lowers the stakes of national politics. When a critical issue over which people disagree is decentralized, citizens avoid both the conflict at the national level of whose view will win and also the risk that the winners impose their will on the losers.

As an illustration consider the issue of slavery in the early United States. Northerners and Southerners strongly disagreed about the appropriate form of rights in slaves. The huge value of slaves in the southern economy was so large as to give Southerners little choice but to support strong rights in slaves. By decentralizing this issue, federalism helped the country survive for three generations. Had the national government sought to deal with this issue for the entire nation, disagreements over this issue imply that the country would likely have been dissolved much earlier than 1860.

The third principle, first proposed by Riker (1964), concerns the role of elections and the party system. The need to win elections is one of the principal incentives that sustains federalism. When local and national politicians do better by coordinating their activities, officials at each level have incentives to respect the power and prerogatives of the other levels. Consider a two party system (though the same logic holds with more parties). Suppose that party officials at one level of government attempt to usurp the power of another level. Then officials at the other level are likely to resist, thus hindering the cooperating necessary to win elections. This lack of coordination, in turn, grants their opponents

---

[12] Weingast (1997) provides a model of this principle.

a competitive advantage in the elections. To avoid losing, therefore, officials at each level have an incentive to respect the federal allocation of authority.

In the United States, parties have long been federal organizations, with the bulk of supporters at the state level. To win national elections, members in many localities had to cooperate, allowing them the ability to protect their prerogatives. In contrast, Ordeshook and Svetsova (1996) show how Russia's electoral institutions imply lack of coordination among subnational and national officials and how this in part underpins Russia's non-cooperative federalism. Garman, Haggard, and Willis (2001) show that this principle underlies much of the differences in federalism across Latin America.

Further Insights

Two recent approaches focus on the national government's policing of subnational governments. Bednar, Eskridge, and Ferejohn (2002) argue that national courts often play this role. Yet such courts by their nature cannot as easily police the national government. They show how this approach helps illuminate the history of federalism in the United States and Canada. Bednar (2001) develops a formal model arguing that the national government must develop a reputation for punishing subnational governments that pursue common pool incentives. In a game theoretic context, she provides conditions for an equilibrium in which the national government's policing efforts succeed. Both these approaches, however, study only the problem of subnational governments, ignoring the problem of policing the national government.

In addition, two approaches endogenize aspects of federal structure. Cremer and Palfrey (2002) are the first to endogenize the assignment problem by considering a polity divided into subnational jurisdictions. Voters in these jurisdictions are to choose a level of public goods. But voters may also decide to nationalize the public good: that is, to provide one level of the public good at the national level. They show that under some configurations of preferences, citizens will nationalize the local public good. Suppose there are three jurisdictions, each with three citizens with the following configuration: two jurisdictions have a majority of two who want a low level of public good and a minority of one who wants a high level. In the third jurisdiction, all citizens want a high level of public goods. Nationally, then, there is a majority of 5 of 9 citizens who (weakly) favor providing a high level of the public good: the three citizens from the jurisdiction who want high public goods are weakly in favor, and the minority in each of the other jurisdictions strictly favor nationalization.

Wibbels (2003) provides an important insight into the problem of how federations maintain a hard budget constraint for subnational governments. He observes that most studies of this problem are exhortations — they advise the federal government to impose hard budgets and not to give in to state demands for deficit relief. But exhortations are not self-implementing. Wibbels observes that if most states run up large debts simultaneously, the pressure on the national government to take over this debt is likely to be impossible to avoid.[13] So where does the pressure not to bail out states arise? The answer is in part the states that have maintained sound finances: they must bear their costs of a bailout without any of the benefits and will thus oppose bailouts. This has two implications. First, the distribution of profligate states matter. Second, constitutional rules governing how national financial decisions affect the likelihood of bailouts. For example, if an upper chamber represents the states, the bias in representation (e.g., in favor of poor, small states) can affect the national bailout. Wibbels (2003) shows that this process was important for preventing the proposed bailout of bankrupt and near-bankrupt American states in 1841 and thus for maintaining hard budget constraints on the states.

Conclusions

To summarize, this section surveys a new, exciting, but incomplete approach to studying the stability of federalism. To survive, federalism must be self-enforcing. Yet the two fundamental dilemmas of federalism make this problematic. The center needs sufficient power to police common pool problems among the states; and yet more power makes it more likely that the center will abuse its power. Three principles of self-enforcing federalism were noted. Although the works discussed here do not yet constitute a coherent theory, they do suggest the difficulties in maintaining a federal system and that the set of federal rules that can be sustained in practice may be far smaller than the set of potential rules discussed in the normative literature.

5. FEDERALISM IN THE UNITED STATES

The history of American federalism illustrates the various principles studied above. Indeed, most of the major turning points in American history reflect changes in federalism, including the formation of the Constitution; the conflict over slavery and the Civil War; the changing relationship of the national government to the economy during the New Deal and during the 1960s.

The theories summarized above provide considerable insight into the structure and performance of the American economy and political institutions in its first century.

The United States under the Articles of Confederation, 1781–88

Per the modern economics literature, the United States under the Articles of Confederation exhibited a range of common pool problems. Three such problems

---

[13] This suggests that maintaining a hard budget constraint is in part a coordination game, so that mechanisms that prevent subnational governments from coordinating are important.

stand out as threatening the economic and political future of the new nation: the inability to defend itself; the lack of a stable, national currency and hence the ability of states to export part of the costs of monetary inflation (and hence SBC); and the rise of internal trade barriers. The Articles represented a loose federation, with the center unable to police common pool problems. Indeed, these problems were central to the Federalists' arguments in favor of their proposed Constitution in 1787. The inability to defend itself was one of the Federalist's major arguments (and the substantive subject raised in the *Federalist Papers*—numbers 2–5 entitled, "Concerning Dangers from Foreign Force and Influence"). The Congress could not raise its own taxes to pay for national defense. Instead, the national government could pass a law authorizing defense expenditures. To finance this authorization, it had to request that each state provide its share of the funds, which required that each state pass laws raising new taxes. This created a classic common pool problem, as each state had an incentive to free ride. Many of the states failed to make their contributions, greatly hindering the ability of the national government to defend the country. Similarly, some states raised internal trade barriers hindering the common market. Other states inflated their own currencies rather than raising taxes, creating monetary problems. Moreover, per the assignment problem, it is clear that the Articles of Confederation failed to provide adequate powers and authority to the national government to address these public goods problems.

Per the market-preserving federalism framework, the United States under the Articles of Confederation failed the common market condition and the hard budget constraint condition. Internal trade barriers allowed states to create local monopolies, keep out products from neighboring states and thus hindered the benefits noted by the classic economic treatment of Tiebout. This political framework had high opportunity costs, as it left considerable gains from cooperation uncaptured.

Federalism under the New Constitution

The debates prior to the Constitution corresponded to the problems identified by the two fundamental dilemmas of federalism. The Federalists emphasized the second dilemma's common pool problems and the dangers for the future of the new republic. To address the national government's inability to provide essential public goods, the Federalists argued to increase the national government's powers. On three occasions prior to the proposed new Constitution, they failed. The reason is that the Antifederalists had the upper hand. In combating the Federalists, the Antifederalists emphasized the first federal dilemma, namely, the dangers that a national government with too much power would overawe the states and destroy the liberty so recently won from Great Britain. To resolve this problem in 1787, the Federalists proposed to grant the national government more powers while, at the same time, embedding that government in a framework that limited its powers and lowered its potential to abuse those powers.

The new Constitution dramatically altered the federal arrangement. Consistent with the classic economic analysis, the Constitution created a federal structure that helped promote economic development and put the United States onto the path of becoming the richest nation in the world. First, it created institutions and powers allowing the national government to provide the three national public goods lacking under the Articles: defense, the common market, and a stable currency. Per modern economic's focus on common pool problems, the Constitution also granted the national government the power to police the common market and allowed the federal government to police the propensity of states to create internal trade barriers and to export their bad monetary behavior. Although states proved quite imaginative in the ways that they invented new means of internal trade barriers, the Supreme Court was equally imaginative at creating new Constitutional doctrine to rule these unconstitutional.[14] The result was one of the largest unregulated common markets in the world, combined with a strong system of private property rights and the enforcement of contracts. Federalism thus helped to underpin the thriving national market, the engine of American economic growth that brought the United States from the periphery to the richest country in the world.

Second, the new Constitution's division of policy authority between national and state governments corresponded to that following Musgrave's assignment logic: the national government retained policy authority over national public goods, such as those noted above, and foreign policy; while the states retained power over nearly all local issues, including the types of property rights system, social regulation, and religious freedom. Per Tiebout, states faced strong competition with one another. This was especially true for new states and territories on the frontier which needed to compete for scarce capital and labor. After 1825, most citizens who moved to the frontier did so to gain land and become participants in a national and international economy; indeed, many grew grain shipped east, often bound for Europe. The evidence suggests that these territory and state governments focused attention on providing market-enhancing public goods.[15]

As North (1961) first argued, this system result in a remarkable degree of regional specialization and exchange that emerged after 1815.[16] By the Civil War the South produced primarily export crops, such as cotton, but also tobacco, indigo, sugar, and rice. The Northeast produced transportation, financial, and marketing services for the South's export economy. By the end of this period, the Northeast was also home of the emerging manufacturing economy, exporting its

---

[14] For example, Supreme Court *Bank of Augusta v. Earle* (1839) used the privileges and immunities clause to prevent the state of Alabama from taxing out of state banks at a higher rate than in state banks. In *Gibbons v Ogden* (1824), the Court used the commerce clause to prevent the state of New York from granting a monopoly to operate steamships in that state.

[15] See Heckleman and Wallis (1997) on railroads; Haber (2003) and Wallis, Sylla, and Legler (1994) on banks; and Wallis (2001) on canal building in Indiana.

[16] See also Calendar (1901).

products west and south. The Northwest, largely self-sufficient at the beginning of the nineteenth century, slowly became specialized producers of food for the rest of the nation, particularly the Northeast.

The theory of self-enforcing federalism also helps explain the stability of the new Constitution. Whereas the Antifederalists had defeated the Federalists' earlier attempts to increase the national government's powers, the Federalists succeeded with the Constitution. The Federalists' failed attempts focused exclusively on addressing the second dilemma. In contrast, the Federalists attended to both dilemmas of federalism, not just the common pool problems, when they devised the new Constitution.

The genius of the new Constitution was to create a new set of institutions that at once provided critically needed national public goods while limiting the national government's powers to these domains. Per the theory of self-enforcing federalism, subnational governments must have a means of coordinating against the national government when it attempts to overstep its bounds. To address this, the Federalists attempted not only to articulate new powers for the national government, but also a series of limits on its powers. First, the national government was to be one of enumerated powers only. Federalism was explicitly recognized, with many of the most important policy domains explicitly reserved for the states. At the same time, the Bill of Rights charged the national government to respect a range of citizen rights.

Second, the national government could act only under a series of well-specified procedures governed by the separation of powers system. This not only ensured supra-majority support before the national government could act, but, as the Federalist articulated, it would pit "ambition against ambition," making rash action less likely.

Third, these provisions were to be enforced in part through trigger strategies that made adhering to these bounds self-enforcing for national political officials. As quoted above in section 4, Federalist 46, states and citizens were to react in concert in the event of an attempt by the national government to overstep the Constitution's bounds. Expectations of this reaction, in turn, provided the critical incentives for national political officials to honor the Constitution's prescriptions. Of course, the fact that the states were to maintain militias while the federal government was likely to have a very limited domestic standing army meant that as a group the states had far more military resources than the national government.

The Failure of American Federalism and Democracy in the Civil War

American democracy and federalism failed in 1860 with the election of Republican Abraham Lincoln. Many Southerners feared that the national government would not adhere to the Constitution's historic bargain. For three generations, rights in slaves had been the domain of the states, although the federal government had from the beginning legislated about slavery in the territories and hence the future states.[17] Many Southerners felt the Republicans antislavery sentiments would lead them, once in power, to break the bargain. Of course, many other factors also underlay the Civil War, but the threat to slavery was one of the most important. The value of slaves in 1860 was phenomenally large — on the order of the entire American GNP (see Atack and Passell 1994, ch 13). This implies that even modest threats against slavery would have large expected effects on Southerners.

A variety of institutions helped protect slavery within the American system, including the Constitution's separation of powers system making national legislation difficult, and federalism that left issues of property to the states. The issue of whether these institutions protecting slavery were self-enforcing was of central concern to Southerners (Weingast 1998). One of the principle institutions protecting slavery was the balance rule, the notion that the United States would be composed of an equal number of slave and free states, maintained (though with occasional difficulties) until 1850. The difficulty in the 1850s was that the North was growing far faster than the South and that slavery had no legal territories within which to expand. The long-run political stability of slavery was therefore in doubt.

Although the reasons for southern secession were complex and hardly preordained, the issue of maintaining self-enforcing federalism that protected rights in slaves within the American system was one of the principal reasons for the Union's breakup. The main point is that, even a well-designed federal system like the United States had problems that caused massive failure.

After the Civil War, federalism reemerged as Southerners' regained power in the nation. In this period, too, federalism helped underpin long-term economic growth. The growing integration of the economy generated a range of new problems that could not be solved by the states, leading to greater national regulation, notably railroad regulation and antitrust in the late nineteenth century. This regulation foreshadowed the question of the relationship of the national government to the economy that would dominate much of the politics and economic policymaking of the twentieth century, but that is another story.

Conclusions

This brief survey of American history illustrates the importance of the various approaches to federalism surveyed above. All aspects were shown to be relevant. Moreover, the fact that the American federal system fell apart in 1860 combines with the fragility of federalism elsewhere (e.g., the large federations in Latin America) reinforces the importance of the question of what conditions provide for the stability of federalism. Nonetheless, American federalism survived the

---

[17] Part of what made this system self-enforcing was the balance rule, the notion that free states and slave states would be admitted in pairs so that the two sections would have equal representation in the Senate. Equal representation, in turn, gave each section a veto over national policy. With its veto, southerners could protect the federal arrangement to leave slavery alone. See Weingast (1998) for details.

Civil War and helped foster American economic growth, creating the richest nation in the world.

6. Conclusions

This paper surveys several literatures on federalism and provides a partial integration. Three categories of works were discussed. First, it considers the economic literature on federalism as an optimal theory of the organization of the state. This includes the classic economic works on federalism of Hayek, Musgrave, Oates, and Tiebout, emphasizing the benefits of federalism through the efficient use of information; the appropriate assignment of policies to levels of government; and the important effects of interjurisdictional competition. More modern economic works have tended to qualify the classic economic literature's conclusions, typically emphasizing various types of common pool problems. The literature on market-preserving federalism was also discussed.

The second literature steps beyond the first by emphasizing the economic literature's assumption of benevolent government. Although this assumption is useful for some questions, it hinders the development of a positive theory of federalism. Thus, I discussed several works studying how federalism affects the incentives of subnational government officials. The traditional economic framework, taking government goals as given, misses an important aspect of federalism emphasized by Buchanan, Hayek, and Tiebout among others, namely, that federalism helps shape preferences of political officials in ways consistent with furthering citizens' welfare. In particular, interjurisdictional competition in the presence of several conditions—an HBC, policy authority, and a common market—helps align subnational government officials' incentives with those of their citizens. A range of recent works also demonstrates the importance of fiscal system for subnational government officials' incentives.

The third literature discussed is the least developed, but opens the possibility of greatly extending the breadth of the literature on federalism. It begins with the observation that both the first two literatures take federalism's structure as given. The third literature makes the structure of federalism endogenous and asks, what makes federalism self-enforcing in the sense that political officials have incentives to abide by federalism's rules.

The common theme among all these works is the role of institutions in economic and political performance. By analyzing the three literatures and suggesting how they fit together, this essay points toward a more complete theory of federalism.

Let me conclude this essay by suggesting some implications for developing countries, where it is now widely recognized that government incentives toward rent-seeking and corruption rather than citizen welfare represents a major hindrance of development (e.g., Easterly 2001). The literature on federalism has long emphasized the importance of federal institutions for aligning the incentives of political actors with citizen welfare. Competition among jurisdictions in combination with factor mobility places limits on the degree to which governments can extract taxes and rents from citizens. This process is not perfect, as the work of Epple and Zelenitz (1981) and Epple and Romer (1991) suggest.

Because security of property rights and protection against government confiscation or rapaciousness is a major problem in the developing world, the institutions of federalism hold significant promise of mitigating these problems. Of course, not just any type of federalism performs this role. As the market-preserving federalism framework suggests, federal systems differ significantly in how they devolve power and authority, and only some types of devolution are likely to improve political and economic performance in the developing context. In particular, appropriately structured federalism requires that subnational governments have real policy authority, face a common market and factor mobility, and face a hard budget constraint. Institutions supporting each of these seem necessary to obtain the beneficial effects of federalism.

Unfortunately, the political reality in most developing countries implies unstable regimes that typically use various forms of rents, subsidies, and market intervention to make political deals necessary to survive. These political forces work against implementing the type of federal system just outlined, in part because it forces political officials to break the deals used to maintain power.

Acknowledgement

The author thanks Rui de Figueiredo, Stephen Haber, Robert Inman, Wallace Oates, Yingyi Qian, Antonio Rangel, John Wallis, and David Wildasin for helpful conversation.

References

Bednar, Jennifer L. 1996. "Federalism: Unstable by Design". MS, University of Michigan.
Bednar, Jennifer L., William Eskridge, and John A. Ferejohn. 2001. "A Political Theory of Federalism" in John Ferejohn, Jack Rakove, and Jonathan Riley (eds.), *Constitutions and Constitutionalism*. New York: Cambridge University Press.
Brennan and Buchanan 1980. *The Power to Tax*. New York: Cambridge University Press.
Callender, Guy S. 1903. "The Early Transportation and Banking Enterprises of the States in Relation to the Growth of the Corporation". *Quarterly Journal of Economics* XVII: 111–62.
Careaga, Maite and Barry R. Weingast. 2002. "Fiscal Federalism, Good Governance, and Economic Growth in Mexico" in Dani Rodrik (ed.), *In Search of Prosperity: Analytic Narratives on Economic Growth*. Princeton, NJ: Princeton University Press, forthcoming.
Cremer, Jacques, and Thomas R. Palfrey. 2002. "Federal Mandates by Popular Demand". *Journal of Political Economy* 108(5): 905–27.
de Figueiredo and Barry R. Weingast. 2005. "Self-Enforcing Federalism". *Journal of Law, Economics, and Organization* (forthcoming).
Dillinger, William and Steven B. Webb. 1999. "Fiscal Management in Federal Democracies: Argentina and Brazil". Working Paper, World Bank.
Easterly, William. 2001. *The Elusive Quest for Growth: Economists' Adventures and Misadventures in the Tropics*. Cambridge, MA: MIT Press.

Epple, Dennis and Thomas Romer. 1991. "Mobility and Redistribution". *Journal of Political Economy* 99: 828–76.

Epple, Dennis and Alan Zelenitz. 1981. "The Implications of Competition among Jurisdictions: Does Tiebout Need Politics?" *Journal of Political Economy* 89: 1197–217.

Fearon, James D. 2000. "Why Use Elections to Allocate Power?" W.P., Department of Political Science, Stanford University.

Garman, Christopher, Stephan Haggard, and Eliza Willis. 2001. "Fiscal Decentralization: A Political Theory with Latin American Cases". *World Politics* 53: 205–236.

Gramlich, Edward and Danile Rubinfeld. 1982. "Micro Estimates of Public Spending Demand Functions and Tests of the Tiebout and Median Voter Hypotheses". *Journal of Political Economy* 90: 536–560.

Haber, Stephen. 2003. "Banks, Financial Markets, and Industrial Development: Lessons from the Economic Histories of Brazil and Mexico" in José Antonio Gonzalez, Vittorio Corbo, Anne O. Krueger, and Aaron Tornell (eds.), *Macroeconomic Reform in Latin America: The Second Stage.* Chicago, IL: University of Chicago Press, forthcoming.

Haber, Stephen, Armando Razo, and Noel Mauer. 2004. *The Politics of Property Rights: Political Instability, Credible Commitments, and Economic Growth in Mexico, 1876–1929.* New York: Cambridge University Press.

Hayek, Friedrich A. 1939. "The Economic Conditions of Interstate Federalism". *New Commonwealth Quarterly* V: 131–149. Reprinted in his *Individualism and Economic Order*. Chicago: University of Chicago Press, 1948.

Heckleman, Jac C. and John Joseph Wallis. 1997. "Railroads and Property Taxes". *Explorations in Economic History* 34: 77–99.

Inman, Robert P. 1988. "Federal Assistance and Local Services in the United States: The Evolution of a New Federalist Fiscal Order" In Harvey S. Rosen (ed.), *Fiscal Federalism: Quantitative Studies*. Chicago, IL: University of Chicago Press.

Inman, Robert P., and Daniel L. Rubinfeld. 1997. "The Political Economy of Federalism" in Dennis C. Mueller (ed.), *Perspectives on Public Choice Theory*. New York: Cambridge University Press.

Jin, Hehui, Yingyi Qian, and Barry R. Weingast, 2005, "Regional Decentralization and Fiscal Incentives: Federalism, Chinese Style". *Journal of Public Economics* (forthcoming).

Jones, Mark P., Pablo Sanguinetti, and Mariano Tommasi. 2000. "Politics, Institutions, and Fiscal Performance in a Federal System: An Analysis of the Argentine Provinces". *Journal of Development Economics.*

McKinnon, Ronald I. 1997. "Market-Preserving Fiscal Federalism in the American Monetary Union" in Mario I. Blejer and Teresa Ter-Minassian (eds.), *Macroeconomic Dimensions of Public Finance*. New York: Routledge, pp. 73–93.

Montinola, Gabriella, Yingyi Qian, and Barry R. Weingast. 1995. "Federalism, Chinese Style: The Political Basis for Economic Success in China". *World Politics* 48: 50–81.

Musgrave, Richard. 1959. *Public Finance.* New York: McGraw Hill.

McKinnon, Ronald and Thomas Nechyba. 1997. "Competition in Federal Systes: The Role of Political and Financial Constraints" in John Ferejohn and Barry R. Weingast (eds.), *The New Federalism: Can the States Be Trusted?* Stanford: Hoover Institution Press.

Nechyba, Thomas and R. Strauss. 1997. "Community Choice and Local Public Services: A Discrete Choice Approach". *Regional Science and Urgan Economics.*

Oates, Wallace. 1969. "The Effect of Property Taxes and Local Public Spending on Property Values: An Empirical Study of Tax Capitalization and the Tiebout Hypothesis". *Journal of Political Economy* 77: 757–71.

Oates, Wallace. 1992. *Fiscal Federalism*. New York: Harcourt Brace Jovanovich.

Oates, Wallace. 2001. "Fiscal Federalism" *Journal of Economic Literature.*

Ordeshook, Peter C. 1996. "Russia's Party System: Is Russian Federalism Viable?" *Post-Soviet Affairs* 12(3): 195–217.

Ordeshook, Peter C. and Olga Shvetsova. 1997. "Federalism and Constitutional Design". *Journal of Democracy* 8(1): 27–42.

Persson, Torsten and Guido Tabellini. 1996. "Federal Fiscal Constitutions: Risk Sharing and Moral Hazard". *Econometrica* 64(3): 623–646.
Persson, Torsten and Guido Tabellini. 1996. "Federal Fiscal Constitutions: Risk Sharing and Redistribution". *Journal of Political Economy* 104(5): 979–1009.
Persson, Torsten and Guido Tabellini. 2001. *Political Economics*. Cambridge, MA: MIT Press.
Poterba, James and Jürgen von Hagen (ed.). 1999. *Fiscal Institutions and Fiscal Performance*. Chicago, IL: University of Chicago Press.
Przeworski, Adam. 1991. *Democracy and the Market*. New York: Cambridge University Press.
Revesz, Richard. 1997. "Federalism and Environmental Policy: A Normative Critique" in John Ferejohn and Barry R. Weingast (eds.), *The New Federalism: Can the States Be Trusted?* Stanford: Hoover Institution Press.
Riker, William H. 1964. *Federalism: Origins, Operations, and Significance*. Boston, MA: Little, Brown.
Riker, William H. 1987. "The Lessons of 1787". *Public Choice* 55: 5–34.
Rodden, Jonathan. 1999. "Strategy and Structure in Decentralized Fiscal Systems: A Comparative Theory of Hard Budget Constraint". Working Paper, Department of Political Science, Yale University.
Rodden, Jonathan. 2000. "The Dilemma of Fiscal Federalism: Hard and Soft Budget Constraints Around the World". Working Paper, Department of Political Science, MIT.
Rodden, Jonathan. 2003. "Reviving Leviathan". *International Organization*.
Rodden, Jonathan, Gunnar Eskeland, and Jennie Litvack (eds.). 2001. *Decentralization and the Challenge of Hard Budget Constraints*. Cambridge: MIT Press. Forthcoming.
Rubinfeld, Daniel. 1987. "Economics of the Local Public Sector". A. UJ. Auerbach and M. Feldstein (eds.), *Handbook of Public Economics*, Vol. II. New York: Elsevier, pp. 571–646.
Sanguinetti, Pablo J. 1994. "Intergovernmental Transfers and Public Sector Expenditures: A Game-Theoretic Approach". *Estudios de Economia* 21(2): 179–212.
Scotchmer, Suzanne. 1994. "Public Goods and the Invisible Hand" In J. Quigley and E. Smolenski (eds.), *Modern Public Finance*. Cambridge, MA: Harvard University Press.
Tiebout, Charles. 1956. "A Pure Theory of Local Expenditures". *Journal of Political Economy* 64:416–24.
Wallis, John Joseph. 2001. "The Property Tax as a Coordinating Device: Financing Indiana's Mammoth Internal Improvement System, 1835–1842". Working Paper, University of Maryland.
Wallis, John Joseph, Richard E. Sylla, and John B. Legler. 1994. The Interaction of Taxation and Regulation in Nineteenth Century U.S. Banking" in Claudia Goldin and Gary D. Libecap (eds.), *The Regulated Economy: A Historical Approach to Political Economy*. Chicago, IL: University of Chicago Press.
Weingast, Barry R. 1995. "The Economic Role of Political Institutions: Market-Preserving Federalism and Economic Development". *Journal of Law, Economics, and Organization* 11: 1–31.
Weingast, Barry R. 1997. "The Political Foundations of Democracy and the Rule of Law" *American Political Science Review* 91: 245–263.
Weingast, Barry R. 1998. "Political Institutions and Civil War: Institutions, Commitment, and American Democracy" in Robert Bates, Avner Greif, Margaret Levi, Jean-Laurent Rosenthal, and Barry R. Weingast (eds.), *Analytic Narratives*. Princeton, NJ: Princeton University Press.
Wildasin, David. 1997. "Externalities and Bailouts: Hard and Soft Budget Constraints in Intergovernmental Fiscal Relations." Typescript. Vanderbilt University.

SECTION III

Legal Institutions of a Market Economy

8. The Many Legal Institutions that Support Contractual Commitments

GILLIAN K. HADFIELD

The problems of achieving third-party enforcement of agreements via an effective judicial system . . . are only imperfectly understood and are a major dilemma in the study of institutional evolution.

North (1990)

1. INTRODUCTION

The problem of enforcing agreements in exchange is at the heart of economic life and has been a central topic for economic theory in the past several decades. As economists have focused more closely on what goes on inside the 'black box' of the firm, especially under conditions of uncertainty and asymmetric information, the role of contractual commitment in economic organization has come to the fore. Much of the theory of incentives that has emerged since the 1970s depends crucially on assumptions about the enforceability of contractual mechanisms designed to align the interests of principal and agent and achieve efficient production and exchange (Laffont and Martimort 2002).

One of the fundamental contributions of transaction cost theory and institutional economics has been to focus attention on opening the 'black box' of contract enforcement, drawing attention to the institutions required to achieve effective and low-cost contract enforcement. Williamson (1985) emphasizes the obstacles to perfect complete contracting in his approach to analyzing the institutions of capitalism. North (1990) places specific emphasis on understanding the costs of third-party enforcement in his analysis of the dynamics of institutional change and the differential performance of economies across time and space. Our understanding of the critical interplay between institutions, the enforcement of contracts and economic development has been substantially advanced by the work of Greif (1989; 1993), Milgrom, North and Weingast (1990), Greif, Milgrom and Weingast (1994) and others on the role of coalitions, the private law merchant and the merchant guilds in securing the commitments necessary to facilitate long-distance trade and the commercial revolution in medieval Europe. Even in cyberspace, focus has shifted to the need to develop institutional mechanisms for secure commitment—notably for the problems of identification, security and verification in electronic transactions that in many ways recapitulate the problems of the legal vacuum facing traders in the 12th century (Hadfield 2004).

The idea that the effectiveness of contract law is critical to the growth of economic activity is widespread in the literature on development and transition economies. Study of the problems of economies making the transition from socialist to market organization has, somewhat belatedly, focused on the role of institutions necessary to support the enforcement of contracts (Greif and Kandel 1995, Hay and Shleifer 1998, Murrell 2001, Johnson, McMillan and Woodruff 2002). Numerous studies are beginning to emerge, attempting to document the strength of formal contract enforcement in different settings. (McMillan and Woodruff 2000; Hendley, Murrell and Ryterman 2001; Lee and Meagher 2001; Pei 2001; World Bank 2003; Johnson, McMillan and Woodruff 2002). Most of the measures of enforcement, however, are based on the confidence in courts or perceptions of court effectiveness reported in surveys of business managers; hard evidence on the relative effectiveness of contract enforcement is largely absent. Johnson, McMillan and Woodruff (2002), for example, asked respondent managers in five transition countries whether (yes or no) courts "can enforce an agreement with a customer or supplier" and whether courts had assisted (yes or no) in a recent payment dispute.

While providing important top-level data about the perceived effectiveness of (contract) law as an institution, this empirical work to date has yet to investigate, with limited exceptions, the institutional features that make contract law effective and low-cost as an enforcement mechanism in a given setting. It is now clearly understood that merely having contract laws on the books is not sufficient; the institution of contract law is much more complex than this. Djankov et al (2003) make an attempt to correlate procedural formalism with the length of time it takes in different countries to collect on a bounced check or evict a tenant for non-payment of rent; their measure of time, however, is a measure of the time estimated by lawyers that it would take to complete the procedural steps necessary to carry a case through to final adjudication and enforcement. They find that the more formal the legal system, the longer it takes to obtain formal enforcement of these simple contracts. Yet by focusing on the theoretical process, they have not captured data on contract enforcement in practice, most importantly, the extent to which formal contract law is in fact relied on in these instances as the exclusive enforcement mechanism.

Other efforts to assess the relative effectiveness of different legal families (German civil law, French civil law, Scandinavian civil law and English common law) in achieving legality (contract enforcement is a particularly important instance of legality) give us a clue that institutional features matter in practice but provide little guidance in identifying which features matter and how and in what combinations. La Porta et al (1998) found a significant relationship between legal family and legality; legality, however, is measured by law on the books and survey reports from business managers and private market risk assessments (largely for foreign investors) on the perceived overall effectiveness of the "efficiency and integrity of the legal environment as it affects business, particularly foreign firms" and the "law and order tradition" of a country.[1]

Berkowitz, Pistor and Richard (2003), emphasizing the legal realist observation that it is law in practice not law on the books that matters (Pound 1911), find (using La Porta et al's 49-country data set) that it is not so much legal family that affects legality but rather whether the local law was transplanted from elsewhere, and if transplanted, whether the law was either adapted to local conditions or introduced into a population already familiar with its basic legal principles. They theorize that in order for law to be effective, the local population has to have "an incentive to use the law and to demand institutions that work to enforce and develop the law" and local legal actors such as judges, lawyers and legislators "must be able to increase the quality of law in a way that is responsive to the demand for legality."

This insight points us to the *complexity* of the operation of law in practice, and the need for a much more detailed appreciation of the multiple legal institutions at work to make contract law effective. Without this greater detail and sophistication in our understanding of these multiple legal institutions, the literature's current effort to identify differences between the economic productivity of "common law" and "civil code" systems runs the risk of being both oversimplified and misleading. Even if it is correct to identify "common law legal systems" as productive of greater economic growth, we still do not know what it is about those systems that produces this growth and in particular how these systems achieve more effective and lower cost contract enforcement. Nor do we know very much about how, in practice, specific "common law" systems differ from specific "civil code" systems. As Messick (1999) has observed, most of our questions—both theoretical and empirical—about what constitutes effective legal design in a given setting remain unanswered. Without a far more detailed appreciation of the institutions that interact to produce "contract law" we cannot hope to be able to investigate the relative cost and efficacy of institutions in different environments and to develop effective policy prescriptions for improving economic development and growth through improved contract enforcement.

This chapter provides a starting point for this research agenda. It explores the many legal institutions that support contractual commitments by structuring an essential environment for basic contract law and by increasing the efficacy and decreasing the cost of formal enforcement of agreements. By way of background, Section 2 sets out the basic problem of contractual commitment and places formal contract law in context as one of a range of enforcement mechanisms available. Section 3 then provides the principal contribution of this chapter, surveying a range of legal institutions necessary to support even simple contract law. Here I examine the many institutional structures at work in the

---

[1] La Porta et al's measure of contract enforcement is specifically limited to the risk of repudiation by government of its contracts.

organization of courts, the judiciary, the legal profession, enforcement services, and the process of lawmaking and legal innovation.

2. The Problem of Contractual Commitment and the Selection of Efficient Enforcement Mechanisms

The problem of contractual commitment refers to the commitment necessary to support agreed-upon exchanges that take place over time. The problem is essentially this: if I act today—invest my resources or give up other opportunities—and you take the actions we agreed on in exchange for my efforts—paying me money or providing a return service—tomorrow, how can I be sure that you will in fact do as you promise and that I will not be left having spent resources I will never recoup? The solutions to this problem can all be understood in terms of how they affect the likelihood that the first-mover in exchange will not be disappointed or exploited by the second-mover. (Of course in any exchange both parties—all parties in a multilateral contract—may be first or second-movers or both.) The second-mover's failure to act as agreed can stem from a number of sources: there may be an obstacle to performance, there may be a lack of information about the conditions of performance having been met, there may be a dispute about what performance was in fact promised. These are not, however, problems of *commitment*. The problem of commitment refers to the incentives on the part of the second-mover: the failure to act stems from the divergence between the second-mover's *ex ante* incentives—the incentives that led to the agreement to act—and his *ex post* incentives—the incentives that determine his behavior after the agreement has been struck and the time for performance has arrived. (Note that a commitment problem in need of an enforcement solution only arises when a gap in incentives arises, that is, when the limits of baseline norms of trust and trustworthiness are reached.)

There are many potential enforcement mechanisms available to support agreements. The list includes: self-enforcement, reputation, organization, technology and contract law. These enforcement mechanisms in one form or another all have a common feature: they seek to bring *ex post* incentives in line with *ex ante* agreements, to produce the outcome that the second-mover promised. They differ only in how they manage this shift.

Self-enforcement mechanisms and *reputation mechanisms* change the incentives of the actors by changing the consequences of actions. Self-enforcement mechanisms include the posting of bonds or exchange of hostages and the termination of valuable trading relationships (particularly those in which quasi-rents are generated by investment in assets specific to a particular relationship) (Williamson 1983; Klein, Crawford and Alchian 1978; Klein and Leffler 1981; Telser 1981). Reputation mechanisms alter the likelihood of future transactions with potential trading partners if an agent defaults on an agreement. Greif, Milgrom and Weingast (1994) demonstrate the potentially complex structures involved in reputation mechanisms at work in medieval Europe. Reputation mechanisms fundamentally rely on institutions that capture and disseminate information about an agent's performance to a set of potential trading partners (such as coalition members) and include such diverse structures as trademark law, trade associations and third-party certification.

Organizational mechanisms change the actors involved in a decision and hence the incentives that are operative *ex post*. The most dramatic organizational mechanism, of course, is horizontal or vertical integration: transforming a transaction across organizational boundaries to one within organizational boundaries (Williamson 1975). Other organizational mechanisms include delegating control over corporate oversight—such as auditing of financial reports or electronic commerce security systems (Hadfield 2004)—to third parties and information channeling to alter the information available to an agent who may be tempted to renege on performance.

Technological mechanisms change the costs of actions and the capacity of an agent to act in various ways. Internet transactions, for example, are increasingly dependent on technological solutions such as encryption to assist e-commerce providers in committing to security procedures to protect private information and the integrity of a transaction. Technology provides a mechanism for customers to verify the use of encryption (by, for example, clicking on a website 'seal' that connects the user to a third-party verification server), making it very costly for a provider to renege on the promise to use encryption (Hadfield 2004).

In its most rudimentary form, *contract law* achieves enforcement by establishing a set of rules administered by a third-party—generally the state—which determines when an agreement or promise is enforceable, establishes the grounds on which a breach of the agreement will be found and sets out the consequences for breach. Contract law backs up agreements with the third party's power to extract penalties or issue injunctions in the event a party to a contract fails to act as promised.

What enforcement mechanisms share in common is their impact on a first-mover's rational beliefs, at the time the bargain is struck, about the likelihood of performance: in the presence of the mechanism the first-mover attaches a higher probability to the occurrence of the event in which he or she receives the value of the promised performance. Formal contract law, in theory, achieves this transformation in beliefs in two ways. First, it alters the payoff associated with reneging on a promise and thus alters the incentives of the second-mover. Second, it provides some guarantee of compensation or court-ordered performance in the event the second-mover fails to fully respond to the risk of legal consequences.

Enforcement mechanisms can vary in their effectiveness at transforming the rational beliefs of contracting parties about the likelihood of performance. Consider a simple agreement to accept deferred payment for goods. One enforcement mechanism could be completely effective, generating a belief in the seller that full future payment will occur with probability one. Another could be incompletely effective, increasing the seller's expectation of payment from a baseline given generalized norms of trust and trustworthiness of, say, 20% to 50%. Moreover, the way in which expectations of payment are increased can vary: a mechanism could increase the probability of full recovery to .5 or it could increase the amount of certain recovery to one-half of the amount owed.

The use of an enforcement mechanism is generally costly. It may require time, information collection and/or dissemination, human capital investments, or the services of others. It may make errors. It may require technology. It may require distortions in incentives or reductions in the liquidity of assets. In order for an enforcement mechanism to be effective for a given agreement, these costs must not outweigh the gains achieved from increased contractual commitment in that agreement. Selecting an *efficient* enforcement mechanism, or combination of mechanisms, involves an assessment of the relative cost and efficacy of the alternatives available for a given contract in a given environment. As the minimum cost of enforcement across the range of available enforcement mechanisms increases, so too do the minimum gains that must be available from contractual commitment. Put differently, in an environment with only high-cost enforcement mechanisms, only high-value contracts and those that are supported effectively by baseline institutions such as trust or family relationships are likely to go forward.

The problem of contractual commitment from an economy-wide perspective is thus not a discrete question of whether contracts can or cannot be enforced. Rather it is a question of the *cost* of various enforcement mechanisms and the *efficacy* with which these mechanisms improve the confidence contracting parties have in the performance of their agreements. This is where attention to the institutional environment in which enforcement mechanisms operate becomes essential to understanding an economy's relative capacity to generate economic activity and growth. A self-enforcing mechanism such as a bond requires an institutional environment that recognizes and enforces the transfer of property rights; a lower cost mechanism is achieved if the institutional environment provides, for example, the organizational and legal elements necessary to establish escrow accounts or liens. Conversely, a higher cost mechanism is produced if, for example, legal rules override or penalize the use of the mechanism. (This is the concern, for example, of the literature criticizing US courts for applying antitrust law in ways that undercut the use of contracts to achieve efficient agency relationships. See, for example, Mathewson and Winter 1984, Masten and Snyder 1993.) A reputation mechanism such as a trademark requires an institutional environment that protects the integrity of the trademark as a reliable indicator of the origin (producer) of a product; this is the function of trademark law and the authority it gives a trademark owner to prevent others from copying the mark and thereby diluting the reputation incentive to provide high quality goods or services. If establishing or protecting trademarks is costly, the reputation mechanism is less effective in generating economic activity.

An understanding of the many institutions that support formal contract law is thus a prerequisite to the even more complex institutional analysis necessary to appreciate the full range of enforcement mechanisms available to contracting parties, particularly those that merge features of different mechanisms (such as relational contracts which rely both on formal contract law and self-enforcement and reputation mechanisms), to assess the relative cost and efficacy of these mechanisms in different institutional settings, and to analyze the interactions between institutions that may either increase or decrease the cost and efficacy of particular enforcement mechanisms. Although I leave the analytical components of this research agenda to future work, in what follows I survey the wide range of institutions and considerations on which such analysis should focus.

3. THE ROLE OF LEGAL INSTITUTIONS IN STRUCTURING AN EFFECTIVE LAW OF CONTRACTS

Basic contract law seems simple enough: contracting parties designate a set of actions that each will perform (deliver goods, pay money, perform work, etc.) and the law establishes a right to marshal the coercive power of the state to extract penalties (damages, injunctions, fines, etc.) in the event the actions are not performed as promised. But in order for even this simple, although critical, enforcement mechanism to be effective and relatively low-cost, a wide array of legal institutions has to be in place. Contract law makes its own promises to contracting parties: it promises to be available to accurately interpret the agreement the contracting parties have made, to impartially judge the performances rendered, and to reliably implement the appropriate remedies. The fulfillment of these promises, and the cost of accessing them, depends on many other legal institutions and the coordination and interaction between them.

A. Courts and Judges

Contract law requires the institutions of courts and judges; this much is plain. What is less obvious are the multiple court- and judge-related legal rules and institutions that are essential to the effective and low-cost operation of courts and the judiciary.

1. The Organization of Courts

Courts must be accessible at relatively low-cost in geographic and linguistic terms to contracting parties. They must also be accessible in legal terms, and this is a function of the legal rules governing personal jurisdiction (who may be required to appear in court and bound by its determinations), subject matter jurisdiction (what contract issues may the court adjudicate—contracts involving the government? Contracts involving foreign entities?) and standing (who has legally-recognized interests in a contract dispute for purposes of invoking the work of the court—the parties to the contract? The competition authority of the government? Third-party beneficiaries of the contract?)

Delay in the resolution of contract disputes is an important impediment to the effectiveness of contract law—not only does the value of payment decrease with time but so too does the probability of recovery diminish as the potential for assets to be dissipated increases and circumstances change to make performance more difficult and/or less valuable. Thus courts must operate effectively as organizations if contract law is to operate effectively. Effective courts require personnel and resources to administer their procedures, and mechanisms by which they can establish effective and low-cost internal rules and procedures.

Most importantly, courts must be able to perform a critical role in the coordination of contract dispute processes. They require effective systems and rules for scheduling and giving notice of hearings, trials and other meetings requiring the coordination of court personnel, court space, parties, lawyers and witnesses. Achieving this coordination requires tools for enforcing a schedule (such as the power to sanction failures to appear with fines or legal consequences such as dismissal or the entry of a default judgment) and for assessing what are legitimate reasons for not appearing (such as inadequate notice or conflicts in obligations.) These coordination functions are distinctively different in Anglo-American systems, in which there is a culmination in a single event—namely a trial—and civil law systems, in which evidence and legal theories are developed and explored in a series of hearings that can address evidence in a piecemeal fashion and which are not governed by a strictly sequenced presentation of plaintiff's and then defendant's case (Merryman 1985).

Coordination also requires effective information systems for tracking cases and reliably storing documents and evidence of the actions taken by the court (such as orders that have been issued) and the parties (such as compliance with filing deadlines and procedural obligations or the submission of motions or other requests for court action). Information systems are also important for implementing procedural and jurisdictional rules coordinating the relationship between courts over time and space: has the matter already been adjudicated in this court? Is it currently being adjudicated in a different court, whether in another region or at another level in the court system? And information systems must also be externally accessible at low cost by those who must use them to assess the validity of legal claims, to convey requests for court action, to monitor court action, and coordinate procedures.

The implementation of court procedures may also implicate a host of auxiliary service providers. Process servers are necessary to ensure that notification of parties and witnesses (through subpoenas for example) takes place as required by court rules. Notaries may be required to verify signatures on contract documents, reducing the cost of procedures of proof in the court; notaries may also play a role in the drafting of specialized contracts such as corporate by-laws. The power of the court to enforce its procedures (such as appearances by subpoenaed witnesses or the production of subpoenaed documents) also depends on the availability of enforcement services from institutions such as the police. Finally, the power of a court's order—to pay damages or deliver goods for example—depends on the institutions available to identify, seize and/or liquidate assets. These are services that may be performed by police, court personnel or private bailiffs. The effectiveness, cost and integrity of these services depends then on the host of institutions that govern these service providers. Private bailiffs in some transition economies, for example, receive law degrees equivalent to those received by lawyers, are subject to the rules established by their professional organization and potentially subject to limits on their numbers and fees set by the government.

Finally, courts must, in fact, follow their rules and procedures in a reliable way. This requires court personnel and auxiliary service providers who possess the necessary human capital—knowledge of the rules and procedures, expertise in making judgments about scheduling and information systems, and so on—and who are motivated to act in accordance with the rules as opposed to shirking or accepting bribes. As I discuss in more detail in the context of judicial corruption below, protecting against the corruption of court personnel and auxiliary services is a function of multiple institutions including civil service compensation systems, monitoring mechanisms (including the court's own information systems for tracking the actions taken by the court), professional organizations (such as those regulating bailiffs in some transition economies) and penalties.

2. Judges

Just as the institution of a court is more than a building, so too is the institution of a 'judge' more than a person or public office. As the heavy emphasis on the problem of corruption in developing and transition market democracies attests (World Bank 2000), the institution of judging supports contractual commitments only when judges are expected to implement contract law accurately and reliably. This requires multiple legal institutions to support and complement the role of the judge.

The fundamental requirement for effective judging in contract law is the accurate and faithful application of the legal rules parties relied on when making their contracts. There are many reasons why judges may fail to apply contract law: they may not know the law, they may lack the human capital necessary to apply the law, they may make mistakes, they make shirk their duties, or they may intentionally act at variance with the law because they will receive private benefits in the form of bribes or other benefits such as political influence, judicial advancement or the satisfaction of their own policy preferences. Many legal institutions play a role in reducing the risk of judicial failure to implement basic contract law.

The human capital of judges depends most obviously on the institutions of legal education and training. Who may become a judge? What are the educational requirements? What is in the curriculum? What resources and requirements are there for ongoing judicial education? What are the requirements for practical experience or training? More subtly, however, judges' human capital depends on the organization of their work. Are courts and case assignments organized in a way such that judges develop specialized knowledge in particular areas of law or are able to transmit specialized knowledge within the court system? What resources—such as law clerks, databases, legislative updates, legal commentaries and libraries—are available to judges to learn legal rules and develop legal reasoning? Are the reasons for decisions reached by other courts and judges recorded and disseminated?

A judge's case-specific knowledge, of both law and facts, is also a function of the organization of legal work, much of which is fundamentally determined by legal rules of procedure and the institutions of legal practice. This is not merely a matter of information transmission but also of the incentives created by these rules and institutions for the discovery and development of information that can be used by the judge.

In Anglo-American legal practice judges are largely passive with respect to the production of case-specific information. Litigants are responsible for obtaining evidence, interviewing witnesses, researching the law and developing legal reasoning about the application of the law to the evidence and then conveying this to the judge. The incentives for litigants to make these investments in developing the judge's human capital are based on the legal rules governing judicial practice and the exercise of judicial power. Judges are generally prohibited, for example, from having *ex parte* independent contacts with witnesses or reviewing documents that are not obtained from the parties according to the rules of evidence. They may dismiss a lawsuit or enter a valid default judgment against a party if the party has failed to present the evidence necessary to support the application of a legal rule.

In civil law systems, in contrast, judges play a more active role in obtaining evidence and, less often, legal principles (Merryman 1985). Although litigants may provide documents in their possession and suggest potential witnesses, German judges, for example, take on significant responsibility for obtaining additional documents and testimony, shaping the development of evidence, questioning witnesses and determining the order in which issues will be investigated (Langbein 1985). The development of case-specific human capital is therefore more heavily dependent on judicial and bureaucratic incentives and resources.

Notice that these differences in the regime governing the production of evidence and legal rules and reasoning have important implications not only for the incentive for the development of the judge's human capital, but also for the allocation of costs between litigants and public legal institutions: litigants may bear these costs in adversarial systems more extensively than litigants in civil law systems. Unfortunately, data on the costs of litigation are very difficult to come by and comparative assessments difficult to undertake. These institutional features however are quite likely to affect the private cost of, and hence the private reliance upon, contract law.

Judicial human capital and the institutions that determine the development of judicial human capital have an impact on the incidence of judicial error. Judicial error is also affected by the legal rules and mechanisms available for auditing or correcting judicial error. Appeal mechanisms are more or less effective, and more or less costly, depending on whether appeals are available as of right or only with permission of the appellate court and the extent to which appellate courts defer to the fact-finding or legal conclusions of trial courts. Moreover, appeal mechanisms depend fundamentally on the assumption of the cost of an appeal by the parties in litigation; this has important implications for the selection of cases in which judicial error may be discovered. Other review mechanisms—such as bureaucratic supervision and auditing—alter the selection of cases for higher review, while also shifting the cost from private litigants to the public civil service.

In developing and transition economies there has been substantial attention paid to the problem of "error" caused by corruption in judging, that is, the risk that judges will decide and manage cases not on the basis of legal rules and evidence but on the basis of personal rewards in the form of bribes (Bardhan 1997, World Bank 2000). Although selection mechanisms for judges are obviously important, corruption is a complex institutional phenomenon, not merely a failure of personal ethics. Compensation systems for judges play a role in determining judicial incentives to accept bribes: judges whose incomes have in the past depended on supplementing official salaries with payments collected directly from litigants and lawyers—whether legal or illegal—may be embedded in economic and social circumstances (where they live, the obligations they have taken on, the standard of living or social status they enjoy) that make for powerful incentives to continue accepting payments.

The incidence of judicial bribery also depends on the institutions that generate the incentives for litigants to offer bribes. Among these are some of the legal institutions we have already discussed, namely the rules and procedures in courts that may result in substantial delays in obtaining court action or significant failures in scheduling, case tracking or information management. Similar failures in other institutions that generate important pieces of evidence in contract disputes—such as title registries or banks—may also contribute to judicial bribery as judges are offered payments to overcome these obstacles. If required documents are unavailable or costly to obtain, litigants will have an incentive to offer bribes to induce judges to accept faulty documents or proceed with inadequate evidence. This is an incentive that can face litigants who seek justified outcomes as well as those who seek unjustified outcomes. The frequency with which bribes are offered, the belief that any outcome—right or wrong—cannot be obtained without them, and the difficulty of distinguishing between those who offer payments to bring outcomes closer to the one contract law would achieve under full information and those who offer payments to distort outcomes—all of these factors contribute to the incidence of judicial bribery and the loss of integrity in contract law.

Corruption, whether in transition or advanced market economies, can also take the form of distortions in judicial decision-making caused by political influence and the pursuit of private policy preferences. The institutions of judicial selection and appointment (are judges elected? selected from those with expertise through a civil service process?) and removal (do judges have life tenure? can they be removed by the electorate? by administrators? politicians?) influences the likelihood that judges act on the basis of the legal rules contracting parties expect.

Finally, efforts to control judicial failures to apply contract law accurately and faithfully—whether due to bribery, political influence, the pursuit of private policy preferences, error or shirking—depend critically on institutions for detecting and sanctioning failures. Legal institutions determine whether legal decisions and reasons are written and to whom they are disseminated. Errors or corruption in written decisions made available only to the parties are less likely to be detected than are errors or corruption in decisions made available more generally. Are other judges aware of how individual judges are determining cases? Are lawyers and litigants in future cases? Are legislators and administrators? The general public? The publication of legal commentary by lawyers, law professors, and other legal experts—made available to judges and those who appoint judges—also serves the function of supporting the accuracy and fidelity of judging to the announced rules and principles of law.

B. Lawyers

Although lawyers are often derided as mere clogs on the operation of legal rules and courts, the institutions organizing the training, selection, governance, compensation and incentives of lawyers in fact are fundamental determinants of the cost and efficacy of contract law. With rare exception (Grajzl and Murrell 2003) the role of these institutions has generally been overlooked in, for example, legal reform efforts in transition economies, where attention has focused instead on the development of contract rules and independent courts (Messick 1999). Lawyers, however, play a critical role in connecting litigants with law and courts and in the process of legal development. The institutions governing the production and allocation of legal services play a crucial role in determining the cost of accessing both contract law and the many other laws (evidence, procedure, judicial selection and conduct, etc.) on which contract law depends and on the substance of law as it develops through precedent, legislation, regulation and practice.

Legal services can be generally thought of as falling into two types: the provision of information and advice about law and legal institutions, and representation before legal bodies such as courts. The cost and quality of legal services—and hence the cost and value of relying on contract law as an enforcement mechanism—is fundamentally dependent on the legal institutions governing who may provide legal services and when legal services must be used in order to make use of law.

At one extreme, we can imagine legal services being treated no differently than any other service in a market economy: supplied by private actors at a price solely determined by market conditions. Under this pure market model there would be no restrictions on who could give legal advice, draft legal documents or appear in court to act on behalf of someone else. At the other extreme would be legal services provided exclusively as a public good: supplied by public actors selected by government officials and paid out of the public purse.

The pure public good model is generally rejected in a democratic regime on the basis of the argument that lawyers who are independent of the government must be available in order to enforce laws that restrict the power of government. The pure market model is rare but not unheard of: in England and Wales, for example, with few exceptions (immigration and asylum advice, conveyancing and probate matters), anyone may give legal advice. Even under a pure market model, however, legal institutions will influence the cost and quality of legal services. Most importantly, the complexity of legal rules and procedures—and hence the necessity of specialized investments in human capital—will affect both the underlying cost of the service and the competitiveness of the market for these services (Hadfield 2000).

In most market democracies the organization of legal services is a mix of market and public good mechanisms and thus there are many legal institutions that influence the cost and quality of legal services.

1. Legal Education

In order for lawyers to play an effective role in reducing the cost and increasing the efficacy of contractual commitments it is in the first instance necessary for lawyers to know the relevant law. The extent of this need is a function of the complexity of law and hence the demand for expertise. Legal rules prohibiting those without a law degree from practicing law serve the goal of ensuring that suppliers of legal advice and representation know the law, but they also restrict the supply of legal services and create a role for degree-granting institutions and their governance structures in determining the conditions of supply. Shepherd and Shepherd (1999), for example, argue that the cost of legal services in the United States is significantly affected by the fact that in most states law schools must be accredited by the American Bar Association. They claim that the ABA exercises monopoly power in establishing accreditation requirements, such as large library holdings and high remuneration for law professors, that are driven not by pure competence considerations but also by rent-seeking. The institutions governing legal education influence curriculum as well, with implications for the cost of human capital and the value of legal services. In transition economies, for example, a law school curriculum that continues to emphasize abstract legal theory relevant to law under socialism and does not effectively teach commercial contract law produces lawyers who must either invest additional years in learning this area of law or who do not provide the services demanded by businesses in an emerging market democracy. Whether or not the law school curriculum effectively trains lawyers to provide services for the new market environment depends on the institutions that govern, fund and create incentives for curriculum development.

2. Professional Organizations

In most advanced market democracies, legal services are organized as a self-governing profession meaning that the state delegates to one or more professional organizations the authority to regulate the conduct of its members. This institutional structure has enormous implications for the cost and quality of legal services relevant to the use of contract law. In this institutional environment, the profession establishes controls over who may practice law by establishing the standards and procedures governing admission to and continued authorization to practice by the profession.

The rationale for professional oversight is rooted in the perceived need to regulate the exercise of expertise on behalf of clients who are, by definition, poorly placed to monitor the competence and loyalty of their lawyer agents. Low quality legal services reduce the value of contract law; so too do legal services that lack fidelity to the client's expectation that contract law (whether in drafting and negotiation or in enforcement and defense) will be implemented on the basis of the relevant facts and principles. Lawyers may corrupt the value of contract law by acting against their client's interest in exchange for a bribe or in collusion with other professionals; they may also corrupt the value of contract law in a longer-term sense when, acting consistently with the interests of their clients, they transmit bribes to court personnel or judges. Corruption of lawyers is only recently coming into view as an important factor in the corruption of the legal system as a whole in developing and transition economies.

Professional control over the supply of lawyers (through both initial admission to practice and suspension of the right to practice in the event of failures of competence, honesty or loyalty) is thus potentially an important institutional instrument for increasing the value of legal services to contracting parties. Professional control, however, also gives rise to the risk of rent-seeking by the profession as a whole (Shaked and Sutton 1981). Historically bar associations have, in the name of quality control, played a tremendous role in structuring the market for lawyers: restricting advertising, establishing minimum fees, requiring that legal services firms be organized as partnerships or sole proprietorships and not limited liability corporations, prohibiting the practice of law in conjunction with the practice of other professions such as accounting or business consulting, outlawing the selling of shares (and thus risk allocation and investment) in legal outcomes, preventing the use of contingency fees, and so on. The institution of the self-governing profession thus plays an essential role in structuring the determinants of the cost and quality of legal services and hence the cost and efficacy of contract law as an enforcement mechanism.

The economics of how the structure of the market for lawyers influences the cost and quality of legal services are only beginning to be studied. Many of the effects of this institutional environment are subtle, going beyond the fairly well-understood mechanisms of monopolistic restrictions on supply or advertising for example. Hadfield (2000) identifies some of the features of the profession in Anglo-American systems that contribute to imperfect competition and hence cost of legal services.

Numerous aspects of the organization of the legal profession have implications for the development of legal human capital and specialization. Professional organizations may promote the development and sharing of legal human capital through continuing legal education requirements, the organization of professional meetings and seminars, and the publication of legal reports, bulletins, newsletters and so on. But they also may inhibit investments in and diffusion of legal human capital through organizational restrictions on the practice of law.

There may be explicit prohibitions on specialization or mandatory representation requirements that penalize a lawyer who is unable to serve a general clientele. More subtly, requirements that lawyers practice in sole proprietorships or partnerships may restrict the size of a law firm. In Slovakia, for example, lawyers are not permitted to be employed by other lawyers; they must have direct client relationships. This limits the size of law firms and the scale of legal practice and thus limits the potential for the accumulation and sharing of human capital acquired through experience and the potential for the provision of lower-cost bundles of legal services, particularly to corporate clients with multi-dimensional legal needs. (Hadfield, in progress) Similarly the continued restriction on multi-disciplinary practices in the United States—preventing lawyers from combining with accountants or business consultants for example—prevents the offering of lower cost contract advice in settings in which contractual design involves not only the goal of securing commitment to the agreed upon exchange but also tax or business considerations affecting the value of the exchange.

These factors take on special significance in the context of contract enforcement. Contracts are essentially products designed by lawyers. As Gilson (1984) emphasizes, lawyers in advanced market economies are "transaction cost engineers": they assist in the development of transaction-cost reducing contractual provisions. They do this in conversation with contract law, establishing the legal meaning for the provisions they invent and their clients implement. Indeed, in common law systems contract law evolves significantly through the ongoing adjudication of contract innovations developed by lawyers. Larger law firms and more diverse law firms (potentially multi-disciplinary firms) are able to specialize more effectively and pool learning on a larger scale and across a broader range; they are also able to share this information at lower cost among members of the firm, minimizing the risks of free-riding by competitors or the need for more costly intellectual property protections for their innovations. The capacity to specialize, share knowledge and capture the returns to human capital investments is an especially important determinant of the extent to which contractual commitment is an effective and low-cost enforcement device for complex transactions and environments.

3. Courts and Judicial Oversight of Lawyers

The potential for rent-seeking by a self-governing legal profession can be limited to some extent in an institutional environment that gives courts and judges a role in overseeing legal practice. In many U. S. jurisdictions (but not in many civil law countries), for example, the authority to admit or suspend a lawyer ultimately rests with the courts. Although judges are also members of the legal profession, they face incentives and constraints on the exercise of their authority over the profession that differ from those facing bar officials and thus may mitigate rent-seeking that increases the cost of legal services.

Perhaps more importantly, courts and judges may play an important role in determining the cost of legal services by establishing the incentives facing lawyers in the day-to-day practice of their profession. An essential determinant of the cost of legal services is the coordination of the activities of lawyers, witnesses, parties, court personnel and judges. Low-cost litigation requires, for example, documents to be exchanged when expected, evidence to be presented when the opportunity for response and cross-examination is also made available, and attendance at hearings by those required to resolve a matter. Courts that possess the authority to sanction lawyers for failure to comply with scheduling orders, appear at hearings or present the evidence necessary to decide a matter are able to control the time and hence expense of litigation more effectively than those that do not. Sanctions can include penalties expressly directed at the lawyer—such as fines or disbarment—and penalties that indirectly penalize the lawyer by imposing a loss on the lawyer's client—the authority to enter a default judgment or dismiss an action to the detriment of a party whose lawyer fails to attend a hearing or to present evidence—are powerful weapons for courts and powerful incentives for lawyers.

Courts may also play a direct role in establishing the legal fees earned by lawyers. Courts may be empowered to award legal fees to litigating parties as a routine matter, such as under the "British" rule awarding legal fees to a prevailing party, either based on an assessment of reasonable rates by the court or based on actual expenditures. Even under the "American" rule, in which parties routinely bear their own legal fees whether they prevail in litigation or not, courts may be involved in assessing legal fees when litigation takes place under a statute or under a contract that provides for fee-shifting. Finally, courts' management and scheduling procedures can have important, and sometimes unexpected, indirect effects on legal fees. Kakalik et al (1996), for example, assessed the impact of novel case management efforts intended to reduce delay through more active judicial management. The study demonstrated that the new court procedures led to substantial *increases* in expenditures on legal fees, a result that is likely explained by the fact that more active judicial management requires litigants to interact with the court more often and creates a wider set of potential disputes between litigants as litigants can argue about the particular management decisions (setting discovery deadlines or requiring efforts to come up with an agreed set of facts, for example) judges make in an adversarial system.

4. Norms and Practices of Judicial Reasoning

Legal practice and the organization of legal services are also significantly affected by the norms and practices of legal and judicial reasoning. Much of what happens in a court depends not on formal legal rules about procedure but the practical way in which a judge manages a case. If a judge relies on adversarial presentation of evidence and legal argument, this requires and induces investments in legal human capital by lawyers, triggering the importance of organizational attributes such as law firm size and form as discussed above. If a judge is attentive to the decisions of other judges, this has significant implications for the cost of what lawyers do and the investments that they make in acquiring information from precedent. It also spurs the development of services to help reduce the cost of these investments, such as case reporters, journals and bulletins.

More subtle informal norms of legal reasoning also influence the cost of legal services. Legal reasoning rewards increasingly sophisticated argument about the contours of legal categories and concepts. A seller who argues, for example, that a contractual promise to accept a price P for goods was not intended to apply in the event that the market for these goods was subject to unexpected government rationing making the market price several times higher than P will have his argument assessed on the basis of an analysis of language and context and contract doctrine. He will not face an argument that he shouldn't be allowed to prevail on such an argument because doing so will lead to an overly complex inquiry not warranted by the marginal gain such inquiry will achieve in terms of efficient contracting: there is no legal norm counterbalancing the scholastic inquiry into the nature of contractual intent, for example, with judicial authority to take into account the impact of an argument on the complexity of law. Such legal reasoning norms value incremental increases in scholastic precision without attention to the marginal payoff in improved contract enforcement or efficiency. And because it is the decisions of courts in the Anglo-American system that generate the legal principles applied in future cases, this approach to legal decisionmaking generates legal complexity and ambiguity.[2] Increased complexity and ambiguity directly raise the human capital investments necessary to provide legal services. Indirectly, more complex law contributes to the imperfect nature of competition in the market for lawyers (Hadfield 2000).

---

[2] In civil law systems norms of legal reasoning are also scholastic in the sense that cases are analyzed on the basis of the meaning of language, particularly the language of legal codes. There is debate, however, about the extent to which legal decisionmaking in civil law systems is influenced by the decisions of judges (Schneider 2003) and thus whether a given instance in which a more refined understanding of a legal term is adopted has ramifications for the complexity of the legal environment facing future litigants.

Legal services are a credence good; complexity and ambiguity increase the information asymmetry between providers and consumers of legal services and thus inhibit the effectiveness of competition. Complexity of law also promotes specialization among lawyers, again reducing the effectiveness of competition. This effect can be particularly pronounced when ambiguity in law increases the role of judicial discretion and thus creates returns to highly localized experience with particular judges and courts—experience that is gained by only a limited number of practitioners.

5. Direct Government Regulation and Service Provision

Finally, the cost and quality of legal services may be influenced by the institutions of direct regulation and service provision by government. As mentioned previously, the pure public good model is generally rejected in market democracies in light of the perceived need for an independent legal profession capable of challenging government action. Still, particularly in the context of contract law where the goals are primarily focused on structuring an effective market system, there are numerous public institutions that may be involved directly or indirectly in the provision of legal services.

Legal services may be provided by government-employed lawyers; this is frequently the case for criminal defense work for example. Legal services in the context of contract law, however, may be more likely to be afforded by government funding of private lawyers through legal aid mechanisms providing assistance to lower income contracting parties, such as consumers, employees or small business operators. Legal services in support of contracting may also be provided directly by government agencies in the form of legal information and/or dispute resolution services: consumer complaint bureaus, labor tribunals, motor vehicle arbitration panels and so on. Government subsidies of legal education also have an impact on the supply of legal services to contracting parties.

Government institutions are also an important alternative source of regulation for private legal service providers, effectively taking back some or conceivably all of the powers traditionally delegated for independence reasons to a self-regulating profession. Government may directly license service providers, as the Office of the Immigration Services Commissioner in the U.K. does with respect to the provision of immigration and asylum legal services by non-lawyer practitioners. Government may regulate legal fees and insurance requirements for lawyers. Government laws and regulation may also establish the conditions for admission to practice and competition among lawyers, and the penalties and procedures for failures of competence or loyalty.

The absence of such policy levers in the government, particularly in transition governments attempting to solidify effective market economies and support the development of contracting relationships, is a serious concern (Hadfield, in progress). The twin goals of democracy and a market economy can create tension over the allocation of power to regulate lawyers between government and the profession: democracy requires the independence of providers of legal services necessary to ensure fidelity to constitutional and legislative constraints on government; a vibrant market economy requires government power to structure a competitive market for legal services necessary to reduce the cost and increase the efficacy of contract law. It is matter of institutional choice, however, whether to structure provision of legal services necessary to enforce democratic controls on government in the same way as legal services necessary to enforce contractual controls on private market actors are structured. The failure to distinguish between democratic concerns and economic concerns in designing the institutional environment for legal services is a fundamental problem for both advanced and developing market economies (Hadfield 2000).

C. Legal Environment

Lawyers like to say that "the law is a seamless web." They mean by this that it is impossible to deal with one legal issue—such as the enforceability of a contract—without coming within the purview of a host of other legal rules: procedural rules, property laws, economic regulations, principles of legal rule development, and so on. In this section I first examine particular sets of collateral legal rules and doctrines that influence the efficacy and cost of particular instances of contract law, and then turn to the longer-term impact of legal rule development and evolution on contract law as a dynamic component of a changing economic environment.

1. Procedural Laws

Consider the basic problem of ensuring that contract law is applied on the basis of accurately determined facts: what was promised, what was performed, what loss was caused by a breach. Ensuring accuracy in factual determinations requires a host of procedural rules to be in place to answer questions such as the following: Who can determine facts: judges, juries, administrators, specially appointed referees, private evaluators? What evidence is admissible? What documents or testimony may be discovered before a hearing or trial by the parties and/or the adjudicator? Are parties obligated to produce documents or witnesses sought by the opposing side or the judge? What penalties are in place to enforce those obligations? What are the penalties for presenting false testimony or fraudulent documents in court? What third parties can be required to present documents and testimony in court? What penalties are available to prevent the abuse or strategic misuse of rights to discover documents and witnesses? What rules are in place to ensure that the process of fact discovery takes place in a reasonable amount of time and is coordinated at low-cost?

Contract law must also be reliably applied: as an institution, it must credibly commit to apply its announced rules and procedures. This commitment depends on legal rules regulating the exercise of judicial powers. In what cases *may* a court apply contract law? In what cases *must* it apply contract law—can parties avoid contract law by pleading their case under some other set of rules such as tort law?

When do particular courts (local courts, specialized courts, etc.) have jurisdiction to decide a particular contract dispute (such as one involving foreign parties)? Does the court have the authority to order particular remedies—to order parties (governments? foreign firms? state-owned enterprises?) to perform a contract? What if a judge simply ignores the law: what recourse of appeal or complaint is available? What if a judge follows the law: will he or she face repercussions such as removal, non-promotion or the dilution of his or her authority by the expansion of the number of judges? How likely is it that *these* legal rules—of appeal or complaint or judicial appointment, removal and promotion—will be implemented as announced?

Procedural and structural rules such as these governing evidence, discovery, jurisdiction and so on have an impact not only on the efficacy of contract law in theory but also, very importantly, in practice. These rules play a fundamental role in determining the transaction costs of using contract law as an enforcement mechanism. Extensive pre-trial discovery processes, while potentially promoting increased accuracy in fact-finding, may also give rise to costly strategic behavior and delays. A major legislative effort to promote the use of pretrial judicial management techniques to overcome delays and reduce costs in U.S. courts, for example, significantly *increased* litigation expenditures (Kakalik 1996). Complexity of the structural rules governing legal decisionmaking—such as norms governing the production and use of precedent within the common law system or norms governing the interpretation of texts in code-based systems—may also raise the cost and reduce the effectiveness of using contract law if they reduce the predictability of legal outcomes and increase the need for specialized human capital (and thus the services of specialized professionals such as lawyers) (Hadfield 2001). The more expensive these processes are and the greater the delay and unpredictability in resolution they create, the less effective contract law is as an enforcement mechanism as the cost of enforcement exceeds the value of commitment gains in an increasing number of agreements.

2. Laws Governing the Contracting Environment

Basic contract law also relies on laws governing the environment in which contracting takes place, laws that regulate information and bargaining conditions. For example, the integrity of contractual exchange relies on fraud law to punish those who have positively misled their contracting partners into a contractual relationship and who are best (from an efficiency point of view) deterred by fines and the threat of criminal punishment. This is particularly the case when contract law is limited to the awarding of damages, a remedy that may be inadequate to deter deliberate fraud and that may be no deterrence at all against those who have no assets. Laws requiring truth in advertising and other consumer protection measures support the creation of contracts that reflect more closely the deals that those exchanging contractual commitments prefer under full information (Hadfield, Howse and Trebilcock 1998).

Legal rules governing the allocation of assets to satisfy contractual obligations (particularly debt obligations) also have an important impact on the efficacy of contract law. Bankruptcy law supports the credibility of commitments by providing a basis for committing to the order in which various creditors (including those who are entitled to collect payments or damages under contracts for goods and services) may lay claim to the assets of an insolvent contracting partner. The laws enabling and governing transactions secured by collateral, deposits, bonds and so on, provide mechanisms for increasing the effectiveness of a contractual promise by reducing the cost of enforcement and/or the risk of unsatisfactory court adjudication and orders. Hansmann and Kraakman (2000), for example, have illuminated the role of corporate law in allowing the owners of a firm to partition assets and make them available only to the firm as an entity (and not the owners themselves) for purposes of securing the contractual commitments of the firm.

The institutional nature of contract law also varies across different types of contract. In many cases particular types of contracts are regulated by statutes addressed to the particular contracting environment. Contract law in civil code systems, for example, tends to separately regulate particular types of contracts: sale contracts, credit contracts, transportation contracts, agency contracts and so on. Even in common law systems, however, with an overarching law of contract applicable in the abstract to any bargained-for exchange, there are numerous laws and regulations specific to particular types of contracts and particular contracting relationships, often with a view to consumer protection and balancing perceived inequalities in bargaining power that may disrupt the efficiency of a bargained-for exchange. Insurance contracts, for example, are often heavily regulated, both with respect to terms and allowed rates, to achieve goals of efficiency and fairness. Franchise contracts may be subject to state regulation—sometimes specifically at the level of industry as is the case in the U.S. with respect to automobile dealerships and gasoline service stations—in response to concerns about defects in the bargaining process or the judicial interpretation of these contracts (Hadfield 1990). Labor law such as the U.S. National Labor Relations Act regulates the process of collective bargaining and contract negotiation between unions and management. Other employment statutes may regulate contracts between non-unionized workers and their employers, guaranteeing minimum notice periods for dismissal for example. Consumer credit contracts are frequently subject to regulations governing required disclosures and terms; in some settings, consumer contracts are voidable to protect against overreaching sales efforts, such as in the door-to-door sales context. Competition laws more generally offer protection against abuse of market power through contracting, and specific contract doctrines such as doctrines of unconscionability (which render unenforceable contracts produced through excessive procedural or substantive inequality), duress and mistake seek to ensure that the contracts that courts do enforce are those that are, in fact, reached under conditions at least approximating efficient information and negotiation.

Laws such as these, which regulate the environment in which specific types of contracts are negotiated, may reduce the costs of contracting by reducing the need for more costly self-protective and enforcement measures, such as costly avoidance, costly negotiation, or costly legal interpretation. They may also increase the costs of contracting, and/or decrease the efficacy of contractual enforcement mechanisms, when they substitute other (public) goals—such as redistribution or political equality—for the efficiency goals of private ordering. They thus constitute an important part of the richer institutional setting in which "simple" contracts are enforced.

More complex contracts are also dependent on the features of a richer institutional environment to achieve effective and low-cost enforcement. The corporation as a "nexus of contracts" is heavily dependent on the law of corporations supplying rules governing, for example, the duties of corporate officers, shareholder rights and the potential to achieve managerial change through takeovers. Contracts for cooperative business endeavors, such as partnerships, agency agreements and joint ventures, are frequently supported by detailed legal rules governing when these relationships are established, what rights and obligations they confer on the participants, what activities they may undertake, how profits will be shared, and how they may be dissolved. Although much of this law is supplied as default rules in Anglo-American systems—meaning contracting parties can substitute their own privately-tailored terms for the statutory terms—the development of specialized legal human capital, regularized interpretations, customized procedures and so on have an important impact on the cost and efficacy of contract law in these settings. In the absence of a developed law of partnership contracts, for example, it is perfectly possible for contracting parties to use basic contract law to create the features of a partnership such as fiduciary obligations, profit-sharing, an agency relationship, a definition of what activities belong to the partnership and so on. The cost of doing so is much reduced if by simply announcing that they are "partners" the parties are able to effectively obtain the same result through reliance on the default law of what the "partnership" contract entails. Moreover, the amount of information available to the parties to assess the likely consequences of various acts is much greater when they are working within an established legal category such as 'partnership' than when they rely on their one-shot effort to demonstrate the content of their contractual relationship to a court in the event of a future dispute.

Similarly, when parties face a setting in which a contract that fully specifies the obligations they wish to create in all contingencies (a complete contract) is not possible—such as when the features of a good or service are too complex to carefully delineate or when conditions are likely to change making it efficient to adapt performance over time or when the value of a contractual relationship depends on the delegation of roles and responsibilities in making future choices and it is difficult to judge ex post whether the choices made were efficient or self-serving—the cost and efficacy of contract enforcement depends on the availability of legal institutions capable of, and willing to, fills gaps and interpret the incomplete contracts the parties write (Goetz & Scott 1981, Williamson

1985, Macneil 1985, Hadfield 1990). Whether and how this happens depends not so much on the contract law on the books as on the norms and practices of legal reasoning as applied to contract interpretation and enforcement.

The cost and efficacy of specific types of contracts is thus heavily dependent on the institutional environment and the resources it provides to contracting parties in designing a particular contractual relationship.

3. Rulemaking and Legal Evolution

The absence of institutional detail in our appreciation of what it takes to operate a low-cost and effective system of contract enforcement also reflects a deeper failure to recognize the importance of the institutions that support the essentially *organic* nature of contract law. In any modern economy, and especially in economies that are struggling to develop or transition to markets, the essence of the productivity of contractual relationships is their fluidity and their capacity to respond to and innovate in the presence of changing conditions, technologies, norms and political, social and legal constraints. Agreed-upon exchange generates economic wealth because it seeks out new opportunities and moves resources in response to changing prices and environments. Berkowitz et al (2003) present evidence that the adaptation of transplanted law to local conditions is an important determinant of the ultimate achievement of legality. Effective contract law must therefore be adaptive and changing. The dynamic nature of contract law, however, depends on many legal institutions.

The evolution of law is fundamentally dependent on the designation of which actors are able to adapt and change law and the sources of information available to those that possess the capacity to adapt law. Much of this is itself subtly determined by norms of judicial reasoning and practice, rather than formal rules. Pure common law systems—in which judges overtly possess the capacity to establish legal rules (albeit under the rubric of 'discovering' the law in custom or prior decisions)—create the potential for ground-level adaptation to changing conditions and this is frequently thought to be a strong virtue of common law. Empirical studies have attempted to bolster this conclusion with evidence that countries that have a common law rather than civil code tradition generate more efficient legal rules (La Porta et al 1998).

Whether adaptation occurs and whether it is an efficient response to the changing needs of contracting parties, however, is a more complex institutional question than these studies let on. A common law/stare decisis system that is not combined with an adversarial process that places primary responsibility for the development of evidence and legal argument on profit-motivated lawyers could well be expected to be unresponsive to changing conditions. Judges who continue to look backwards for legal rules and who are not exposed to the stories of parties' needs and the changing problems of contracting are likely to produce a hidebound and conservative set of legal rules, impervious to the changes outside the courthouse and legal thought. Conversely, "code" systems may be more or less responsive to change depending on judicial practice. Indeed,

Merryman (1985) presents the view that the goal of the civil code of France in particular was precisely to break from the past and to locate the power to change the law not in a backward-looking judiciary but rather a forward-looking legislature.

Moreover, even in common law systems, there are vast quantities of code law. Statutory legal reasoning is heavily influenced by common law legal reasoning in Anglo-American systems. There is as yet no account of why civil code systems, although lacking a historical body of judge-made law, cannot also behave in this way. Schneider (2001), for example, presents evidence that German judges rely extensively on precedent in deciding cases under the civil code; Merryman (1985) suggests that this is generally true in many civil law systems. Institutions such as the practice of publishing and disseminating legal decisions and the subtle norms of judicial behavior and preferences are likely to play a far more important role in the development of a vibrant adaptive contract law than whether or not the formal "source" of law is a civil code.

A comparative institutional analysis of the relative success of common law and civil law systems in generating effective and low cost contract law also has to take into account the impact of these institutions on the quality of information available as law is adapted over time. Precedent-based systems may fall into the problem of bias as they evolve solely on the basis of information culled from existing cases (which are in turn generated by the existing set of rules) rather than information culled (potentially) through the more systematic and representative methods of research available to a legislative process (Hadfield 1992). The bureaucratic and legislative processes involved in drafting legislation, however, may face other distortions in information and incentives arising from interest group politics or organizational failures within the civil service (Bailey and Rubin 1994; Schwartz and Scott 1995).

The evolution of law is also particularly dependent on the subtle interactions between norms of judicial reasoning and legal practice. Law in practice is what judges say it is; if judges resist or do not understand legal rules, then lawyers must respond to what judges perceive and implement rather than what the law says on the books. This can be a particularly important obstacle to the evolution of contract law in economies in transition from socialism to markets. (For examples in Russia, see Hendley 2001.)

Informal judicial norms of legal reasoning will also play an important role in the development of low cost and effective contract law in the face of changing circumstances by making judges more or less receptive to the use of incomplete and relational contracts. These contracts are important devices to provide commitment in settings in which it is difficult *ex ante* to specify precise legal obligations. Judges that are willing to employ relatively expansive approaches to contract interpretation may support contractual commitments in these settings (Goetz & Scott 1981; Hadfield 1990, Shavell 2003); errors in this process may, or may not, undercut contractual commitment (Hadfield 1994; Schwartz and Scott 2003). A judicial approach to interpreting vague and incomplete contracts that attempts to identify the obligation that the parties would have created had they anticipated a particular contingency may promote more efficient contracting; an approach that penalizes parties for failing to divulge information about the contingency in initial contract negotiations may produce lower cost and effective contracting (Ayres and Gertner 1989). The judicial approach to these contracts in turn affects the investment by lawyers and others in the development of contracting innovations.

D. Private Dispute Resolution Mechanisms

Contracting parties, in theory, can contract not only over the substance of their transaction but also over the enforcement mechanism they will use to resolve disputes in the event of a failure of commitment. In theory they can therefore avoid public courts, procedures and judges, even public contract rules—other than the rules enforcing their agreement about dispute resolution. Historically, private contract enforcement has been an important factor in the development of commercial contracting (Benson 1989, Greif 1993). Internationally, private arbitration plays an essential role in trade between countries. In the United States, commercial parties have long relied on arbitration and fought in the early part of the 19th century to have their arbitration agreements enforced in public courts (Stone 1999). Trade associations frequently rely on an agreement among members to bring all contract disputes to arbitration conducted under the 'laws' and procedures established by the trade association (Bernstein 1992).

Private dispute resolution holds out the potential to contracting parties of reducing the cost and increasing the efficacy of contractual commitments, by overcoming failures of the institutions that support the public contract law regime: corruption; inadequate judicial investments in human capital (particularly with respect to the specific details of a trade or industry); slow, disorganized or overburdened courts; high cost pre-trial procedures or evidentiary standards; overly complex or ambiguous contract rules that require high-cost legal services; and so on.

Private dispute resolution of contract disputes, however, is itself dependent on the background institutions of public contract law. Private arbitration outcomes are valuable only if they are enforceable by the state in the same way that court orders are enforceable. Private arbitration arises through contract, and hence is effective only if the arbitration contract is itself enforced by the public courts. Indeed, arbitration agreements have to be enforced with specific performance in order to be effective, a remedy that may or may not be available under ordinary contract law. Moreover, public courts must cooperate with the private agreement to arbitrate by refusing to hear a dispute that the parties have agreed to submit to arbitration.

The importance of these background legal institutions necessary to support private contracting are evident in the history of the pressure in 1925 for passage of a federal statute in the United States, in the form of the Federal Arbitration Act, in order to overcome Anglo-American common law doctrines dating back to the 17th Century enshrining judicial hostility to the enforcement of agreements to arbitrate (Stone 1999). Similar issues face courts today in deciding how to respond to the evolution of efforts to develop alternative methods of resolving contract disputes such as mediation agreements, agreements to negotiate in good faith, agreements to refer issues to third-party evaluators, and so on. In this setting we can see vividly the organic role of legal institutions in supporting not only enforcement of contractual agreements but also the evolution of contractual mechanisms to respond to changing conditions, including the conditions of the institutional environment itself.

4. Conclusion

New institutional economists have understood for some time that there is a need to investigate the institutions that support contractual commitments if we are to understand the determinants of economic growth and prosperity. The complexity and multiplicity of the institutions that support contracting, however, are still underappreciated in the literature. The institutional needs of contracting range from the mundane—court scheduling and case tracking practices—to the sublime—judicial philosophy and the legitimate sources of lawmaking authority. We lack detailed accounts across the entire spectrum. Some (such as La Porta 1998) have suggested that "common law" systems outperform "civil code" systems but these studies are based on highly simplified notions of the legal institutional differences between "common" and "civil" law; moreover, we do not know what particular features of "common law" institutions matter and whether they are in any way essential to "common law." We have some evidence that "formality" in contract law is associated with longer delays in enforcing some simple contracts but we do not know whether formality depresses contract enforcement in practice or whether formality survives because other institutional adaptations make it irrelevant, reducing the pressure on the law to evolve.

In this chapter I have documented a wide range of institutions that play a role in supporting basic contract law, potentially contributing to the cost and efficacy of this method of enforcing agreed-upon exchange. What we most need to know, however, is which of these institutions matter and how in a given environment. The challenging aspect of studying contractual commitment is the fluidity and adaptability of contracting relationships. Contracting parties have available to them a wide array of enforcement mechanisms and an even wider array of mixed mechanisms such as relational contracts that combine features of formal contracting with reputation and self-enforcement. These enforcement mechanisms vary in cost and effectiveness and what we ultimately require in order to explain and predict economic growth in general and contractual activity in particular are data on the cost and effectiveness of different mechanisms in different institutional environments. For this institutional economists need to explore in far greater detail than we have to date the wide variety of specific institutions that support contractual exchange.

REFERENCES

Ayres, Ian and Robert Gertner. 1989. "Filling Gaps in Incomplete Contracts: An Economic Theory of Default Rules". *Yale Law Journal* 99: 87–130.
Bailey, Martin J and Paul H. Rubin. 1994. "A Positive Theory of Legal Change". *International Review of Law and Economics* 14: 467–477.
Bardhan, Pranab. 1997. "Corruption and Development: A Review of Issues". *Journal of Economic Literature* 35: 1320–1346.
Benson, Bruce. L. 1989. "The Spontaneous Evolution of Commercial Law". *Southern Economic Journal* 55: 644–661.
Berkowitz, Daniel, Katharina Pistor, and Jean-Francois Richard. 2003. "The Transplant Effect". *American Journal of Comparative Law* 51: 163–203.
Bernstein, Lisa. 1992. "Opting Out of the Legal System: Extralegal Contractual Relations in the Diamond Industry". *Journal of Legal Studies* 21: 115–157.
Djankov, Simeon, Rafael La Porta, Florencio Lopez-de-Silanes, and Andrei Shleifer. 2003. "Courts: The Lex Mundi Project". *The Quarterly Journal of Economics* 118: 453–517.
Gilson, Ronald J. 1984. "Value Creation by Business Lawyers: Legal Skills and Asset Pricing". *Yale Law Journal* 94: 239–313.
Grajzl, Peter and Peter Murrell. 2003. "Professions, Politicians and Institutional Reforms". University of Maryland Department of Economics Working Paper.
Greif, Avner. 1989. "Reputation and Coalitions in Medieval Trade: Evidence on the Maghribi Traders". *Journal of Economic History* 49: 857–882.
———. 1993. "Contract Enforceability and Economic Institutions in Early Trade: The Maghribi Traders' Coalition". *American Economic Review* 83: 525–548.
Greif, Avner, Paul R. Milgrom, and Barry R. Weingast. 1994. "Coordination, Commitment, and Enforcement: The Case of the Merchant Guild". *Journal of Political Economy* 102: 745–776.
Greif, Avner and Eugene Kandel. 1995. "Contract Enforcement Institutions: Historical Perspective and Current Status in Russia" in Edward P. Lazear (ed.), *Economic Transition in Eastern Europe and Russia: Realities of Reform*. (Stanford, CA: Hoover Institution Press).
Goetz, Charles and Robert Scott. 1981. "Principles of Relational Contracts". *Virginia Law Review* 67: 1089–1151.
Hadfield, Gillian K. 1990. "Problematic Relations: Franchising and the Law of Incomplete Contracts". *Stanford Law Review* 42: 927–992.
———. 1992. "Bias in the Evolution of Legal Rules". *Georgetown Law Journal* 80: 583–616.
———. 1994. "Judicial Competence and the Interpretation of Incomplete Contracts". *Journal of Legal Studies* 29: 159–184.
———. 2001. "Privatizing Commercial Law". *Regulation* 24(1): 40–45. Also reprinted in *New Zealand Business Law Quarterly* 7: 287–295.
———. 2002 "Privatizing Commercial Law: Lessons from ICANN". *Journal of Small and Emerging Business Law* 6: 257–283.
———. 2004. "Delivering Legality on the Internet: Developing Principles for the Private Provision of Commercial Law". *American Law and Economics Review* 6: 154–184.
———. (in progress) "Assessing the Structure and Regulation of the Legal Professions in Slovakia."
———, Robert Howse, and Michael Trebilcock. 1998. "Information-Based Principles for Rethinking Consumer Protection Policy". *Journal of Consumer Policy* 21: 131–169.
Hansmann, Henry and Reinier Kraakman. 2000. "The Essential Role of Organizational Law". *Yale Law Journal* 110: 387–440.
Hay, Jonathan R. and Andrei Shleifer. 1998. "Private Enforcement of Public Laws: A Theory of Legal Reform". *The American Economic Review* 88: 398–403.
Hendley, Kathryn. 2001. "Beyond the Tip of the Iceberg: Business Disputes in Russia" in Peter Murrell (ed.), *Assessing the Value of Law in Transition Economies*, pp. 20–55.

_____, Peter Murrell, and Randi Ryterman. 2001. "Law Works in Russia: The Role of Law in Interenterprise Transactions" in Peter Murrell (ed.), *Assessing the Value of Law in Transition Economies*, pp. 56–93.

Johnson, Simon, John McMillan, and Christopher Woodruff. 2002. "Courts and Relational Contracts". *Journal of Law, Economics and Organization* 18: 221–261.

Kakalik, James S. et al. 1996. *Just, Speedy and Inexpensive? An Evaluation of Judicial Case Management Under the Civil Justice Reform Act.* Santa Monica, CA: RAND Institute for Civil Justice.

Klein, Benjamin, R.A. Crawford, and A.A. Alchian. 1978. "Vertical Integration, appropriable rents, and the competitive contracting process". *Journal of Law and Economics* 21: 297–326.

Klein, Benjamin and K.B. Leffler. 1981. "The role of market forces in assuring contractual performance". *Journal of Political Economy* 89: 615–641.

Laffont, Jean-Jacques and David Martimort. 2002. *The Theory of Incentives.* Princeton, NJ: Princeton University Press.

Langbein, John. H. 1985. "The German Advantage in Civil Procedure". *The University of Chicago Law Review* 52: 823–866.

La Porta, Rafael, Florencio Lopez-de-Silanes, Andrei Shleifer, and Robert Vishny. 1998. "Law and Finance." *Journal of Political Economy* 106: 1113–1155.

Lee, Young and Patrick Meagher. 2001. "Misgovernance or Misperception? Law and Finance in Central Asia" in Peter Murrell (ed.), *Assessing the Value of Law in Transition Economies*, pp. 133–179.

Macneil, Ian R. 1985. "Relational Contract: What We Do and Do Not Know." *Wisconsin Law Review* 3: 482–524.

Mathewson, Frank and Ralph Winter. 1984. "An Economic Theory of Vertical Restraints". *RAND Journal of Economics* 15: 27–38.

Masten, Scott and Edward Snyder. 1993. "*United States Versus United Shoe Machinery Corporation*: On the Merits." *Journal of Law and Economics* 36: 33–70.

McMillan, John and Christopher Woodruff. 2000. "Private Order Under Dysfunctional Public Order." *Michigan Law Review* 98: 2421–2458.

Merryman, John. 1985. *The Civil Law Tradition*, Stanford, CA: Stanford University Press.

Messick, Richard. 1999. "Judicial Reform and Economic Development: A Survey of the Issues." *The World Bank Research Observer* 14: 117–136.

Milgrom, Paul R., Douglass C. North, and Barry R. Weingast. 1990. "The Role of Institutions in the Revival of Trade: The Law Merchant, Private Judges and the Champagne Fairs." *Economics and Politics* 2: 1–23.

Murrell, Peter. 2001. *Assessing the Value of Law in Transition Economies.* Ann Arbor, MI: University of Michigan Press.

North, Douglass C. 1990. *Institutions, Institutional Change and Economic Performance* Cambridge: Cambridge University Press.

Pei, Minxin. 2001. "Does Legal Reform Protect Economic Transactions? Commercial Disputes in China" in Peter Murrell (ed.), *Assessing the Value of Law in Transition Economies*, pp. 180–210.

Pound, Roscoe. 1911. "The Scope and Purpose of Sociological Jurisprudence". *Harvard Law Review* 24: 591–619.

Schneider, Martin J. 2003. "Employment Litigation on the Rise? Comparing British Employment Tribunals and German Labor Courts". *Comparative Labor Law and Policy Journal* 22: 261–280.

Schwartz, Alan and Robert Scott. 1995. "The Political Economy of Private Legislatures". *University of Pennsylvania Law Review* 143: 595–692.

_____. 2003. "Contract Theory and the Limits of Contract Law." *Yale Law Journal* 113: 541–619.

Shaked, A. and J. Sutton. 1981. "The Self-Regulating Profession". *Review of Economic Studies* 11: 217–234.

Shavell, Steven. 2003. "On the Wring and Interpretation of Contracts". Harvard Law and Economics Discussion Paper No. 445.

Shepherd, George B. and William G. Shepherd. 1999. "Scholarly Restraints? ABA Accreditation and Legal Education." *Cardozo Law Review* 19: 2091–2257.

Stone, Katherine Van Wezel. 1999. "Rustic Justice: Community and Coercion under the Federal Arbitration Act." *North Carolina Law Review* 77: 931–1036.

Telser, Lester. 1981. "A theory of self-enforcing agreements." *Journal of Business* 53: 27–44.

Williamson, Oliver E. 1975. *Markets and Hierarchies: Analysis and Antitrust Implications*. New York: Free Press.

―――. 1983. "Credible Commitments: Using Hostages To Support Exchange", *American Economic Review* 73: 519–540.

―――. 1985. *The Economic Institutions of Capitalism*. New York: The Free Press.

World Bank. 2000. *Anti-Corruption in Transition: A Contribution to the Policy Debate*. Washington, DC: The World Bank.

―――. 2003. *Doing Business in 2004: Understanding Regulation*. Washington, DC: World Bank.

9. Legal Systems as Frameworks for Market Exchanges

PAUL H. RUBIN

We have learned about the importance of private property and the rule of law as a basis for economic freedom... It turns out that the rule of law is probably more basic than privatization. Privatization is meaningless if you don't have the rule of law.

Milton Friedman (2002)

1. INTRODUCTION

The quotation from Milton Friedman heading this chapter summarizes the evolution of beliefs of many economists (including myself) following the collapse of the Soviet Union and its satellites. Initially, it was widely believed that creation of markets and the freeing of the economy would be enough to lead to economic growth and prosperity. The lesson of this episode in human history is that removal of restraints and creation of property rights is not sufficient. Rather, an economy needs a legal system in order to thrive and grow, and creation of such a legal system is a difficult task. Indeed, it is not obvious that it is always possible to succeed in this process.

One characteristic of legal institutions that pervades the empirical analysis is their persistence. Many of the papers cited below indicate that legal systems date back some hundreds of years. For example, in the empirical papers, whether the English, the Spanish, or the French colonized a country is quite important in explaining the legal system that exists today. Daron Acemoglu, Simon Johnson and James Robinson (2001a) further distinguish between types of colonies. In areas where weather and other conditions made settlement by residents of the colonizing country dangerous, institutions were developed that made exploitation by the home country of the colony easier, which meant little protection of property rights. Where residents of the home country were able to settle in large numbers, institutions that provided more protection to residents were put in place. They find that difference in mortality rates among colonizers can explain much of the difference in current incomes.

Bernard Black and Anna Tarassova (2003) discuss the tremendous difficulties in creating market-supporting institutions, including legal institutions, from scratch. In particular, legal frameworks are interrelated in numerous dimensions, and so it is necessary to change many laws simultaneously to improve performance. In the case of Russia, Black and Tarassova identify 59 elements in six categories that must be changed to achieve reform. (For example, creation of a "Civil Code" is only one of fourteen elements of the category "Commercial Law Reform.") There are numerous links between each of these elements. (The "Civil Code" element is linked to "Enterprise Privatization and Restructuring" and "Banking Reform.") This difficulty may in part explain the persistence of a given set of institutions.

I first discuss the components of a legal system, so that the reader will have an idea of the sorts of institutions at issue. I then discuss the main economic functions of a legal system: creating, transferring, and protecting property rights, the functions of property, contract, and tort and criminal law. I present s simple transaction as an example of the use of these rules. The following section discusses the "Rule of Law" as a protector of property rights. I discuss the benefits of protecting property rights in terms of incentives for investment. I also discuss the historical and empirical evidence on the value of protection of property rights in order to show that the issue is economically significant and important. I then examine specific types of institutions that protect property rights, so that policy makers will have the basis for choosing efficient institutions. I first consider various forms of private ordering, including arbitration and the multilateral mechanisms available for enforcement of agreements. I then discuss common law and code (civil) law systems, the two main legal systems in the West. There is evidence that common law is more efficient than code law, perhaps because common law provides more independence from government control than does code law. This added protection may be particularly important in countries without a strong rule of law tradition, where predation by government is especially dangerous. This is relevant since much law throughout the world is transplanted from European countries. An important source of legal efficiency is competition between various forms of law. I conclude with a discussion of implications, both for future research and for policy makers. The most important policy implication is that decision makers should allow free choice of law, as in allowing arbitration in contracts. The analysis of legal institutions clearly indicates that they are important for economic growth, but it is perhaps less helpful in indicating how countries can be induced to adopt efficient institutions.

2. Components of a Legal System

A legal system contains numerous institutions. There are mechanisms for the creation of rules and regulations. Some of these are legislatures, government agencies, private entities (such as trade associations), and, particularly in common law jurisdictions, judges and courts. There are entities that enforce rules and regulations, including courts, administrative tribunals, private arbitrators, and also the ultimate enforcers, the armed police. There are the institutions that organize the production and delivery of legal services, including the legal profession, legal education, and government provision of direct and indirect subsidization. There are the institutions—coercive and voluntary—which resolve disputes, including courts, ombudsmen, mediators, arbitrators, and grievance review boards. Moreover, there are extralegal institutions that facilitate the functioning of the legal system, such as the accounting profession, which provides the information used in the legal system; banks, which keep records of transactions; credit agencies, which provide information about consumers; rating agencies providing information about the reliability and soundness of businesses; and title systems which keep records of property ownership. For the system to function optimally, all of these institutions must be honest and non-corrupt, and also competent. Moreover they must work together.

The Transition (from socialism to capitalism) has taught us much about property rights. One important point is that it is not possible to simply graft a set of rules onto an existing society (Paul Rubin, 1994; Andrzej Rapaczynski, 1996). A legal system must grow up with the economy and is in an important sense embedded in the economic system. Rapaczynski (1996, p. 89) discusses the example of property owned by a typical American: "The only significant tangible thing that person is likely to own is a house; the rest of the wealth probably consists in various rights to future income streams, such as a pension, return on shares in a mutual fund, expectations of support from Social Security or Medicare..." The assets defining these streams of wealth and the rules governing them cannot be created independently of the wealth itself; the state cannot create the categories for individuals to fill. Rather, the legal rules and the wealth itself come into being at the same time and are dependent on each other in fundamental ways.

3. Functions of a Legal System

In this section, I briefly discuss the details of a legal system that are necessary for operating a market system. There are private legal rules, governing private transactions, and public rules, controlling externalities. For markets to operate efficiently, the private legal system must perform three functions, all related to property and property rights. (For comprehensive introductions to law and economics, see Richard Posner, 1973/2003 or Robert Cooter and Thomas Ulen, 1999.) First, the system must define property rights; this is the task of property law itself. Second, the system must allow for transfer of property; this is the role of contract law. Finally, the system must protect property rights; this is the function of tort law and criminal law. Public law is mainly aimed at providing public goods and controlling externalities, or third party effects. These exist when private transactions effect other parties to a transaction. Important classes include monopoly issues (controlled in many cases by antitrust laws) and environmental harms.

In general, it is important that a legal system provide clear definitions of property rights. That is, for any asset, it is important that parties be able to determine unambiguously who owns the asset and exactly what set of rights this ownership entails. Ideally, in a dispute, the right should go to the party who values it the most. But if exchanges of rights are allowed, the efficiency of the initial allocation is of secondary importance. The "Coase theorem"—the most fundamental result in the economic study of law—is that if rights are transferable and if transactions costs are not too large, then the exact definition of property rights is not important because parties can trade rights and they will move to their highest valued uses (Ronal Coase, 1960). However, to facilitate bargaining, in some circumstances where asymmetric information is important, rights should be divided so as to encourage parties to reveal true valuations (Jason Johnson, 1995; Ian Ayres and Eric Talley, 1995; Patrick Schmitz, 2001). This may require some uncertainty about the ownership of rights. For experimental evidence on this issue, see Rachel Croson and Jason Johnson, 2000.

Moreover, in most circumstances the actual owners of rights will matter. Transactions costs are never zero, and so if rights are incorrectly allocated at a minimum there will be a transaction needed to correct this misallocation. In some circumstances, if transactions costs are greater than the increase in value from moving the resource to the efficient owner, there will be no corrective mechanism. This can happen in any sort of economy. For an extreme example, in Russia the courts have not been able to provide clear definitions of property rights, and those with control of firms are not necessarily the owners. That is, those with control over the firm cannot sell it and keep the proceeds. This creates incentives for inefficient use of the assets, such as sale of valuable raw materials for below market prices, with the proceeds deposited outside the country. In this set of circumstances the Coase theorem will not operate, and it becomes important to correctly define property rights (Rubin, 1994). Indeed, some rights in Russia are defined in such a way as to greatly hinder both efficient transactions and use—a problem that has been called the "anti-commons" (Michael Heller, 1998). An important function of property rights is to protect property from the state, as discussed below.

Contract law—the law governing exchange—is crucial for a market economy. I do not want to examine fully the economics of efficient contract law; Chapters 8 and Section V in the present volume deal with these issues in detail. I do discuss some aspects briefly below. I also discuss exchange in the absence of contract enforcement.

Tort law and criminal law protect property rights from intentional or unintentional harm. The primary purpose of these laws is to induce potential tortfeasors or criminals to internalize the external costs of their actions, although there are other functions of criminal law as well. Tort law is part of the system of private law, and is enforced through private actions. Traditionally, tort law had been an uninteresting and unimportant branch of law, dealing largely with automobile accidents. But in the U.S. it has in the last 50 years become quite important.

Criminal law is enforced by the state. This is because efficient enforcement requires that only a fraction of criminals be caught (in order to conserve on enforcement resources) and the punishment of this fraction be multiplied to reflect the probability of detection and conviction. However, most criminals do not have sufficient wealth to pay such multiplied fines, and so incarceration or other forms of non-pecuniary punishment must be used. But this in turn means that private enforcement would not be privately profitable for potential enforcers, and so the state provides enforcement. In some circumstances, incarceration serves the additional function of incapacitation of potential wrongdoers.

I spend less time on regulation. Government regulation is an important part of the legal system. It can serve to correct market failures such as monopoly and externalities (caused by incorrectly or imperfectly defined property rights.) Section VI of this volume discusses regulation.

The function of these rules may be illustrated by a standard transaction, the purchase of an automobile on credit. Before the transaction can occur, both parties want information about the other. Thus, the buyer will rely on information services to provide information about the quality of products of the seller. The seller will rely on credit rating agencies to learn of the reliability of the buyer in making payments. Once it has occurred, the transaction requires ongoing commitments by both parties. The buyer must agree to continue to pay for the purchase. The seller will generally provide various warranties that also require behavior over time. Contract law can overcome the commitment problems of performance over time. The car itself may cause harm to third parties or be harmed by third parties, if it is involved in a accident. Tort law governs these harms. Assets such as cars are valuable only if they are protected from theft; this is the function of criminal law. Environmental regulation may control the pollution created by the car. The antitrust laws serve to promote the competitiveness of the market and thus restrain prices, although there are probably enough car manufacturers so that these laws are less important in this context. Fraud law can protect the integrity of informational exchanges, for example by guaranteeing that the seller truly owns the car. The existence of the car itself may be a result of intellectual property law, such as patents to protect incentives for design and trademarks to protect incentives to build reputations for quality. Labor law governs the relationship between the manufacturer and the workers who create the car. The law of finance enables the firm to raise the capital needed for production. Property rights in the profits of the auto seller are important for the support of incentives to invest, perform on contracts, avoid tort liability, and develop reputations

4. Property Rights and the Rule of Law

The economic purpose of a system of law and property rights is to provide incentives for economic agents to undertake productive activity. If there is a high probability that the fruits of one's investments will be taken by others,

210   *Paul H. Rubin*

then there is little or no incentive to undertake the investment in the first place. Predation on investments can come from two sources: government and other individuals.

Predation: Private and State

Humans have never existed in a Hobbesian world with a "war of all against all." (Rubin, 2002). Rather, even in pre-human societies, our ancestors defined and protected property rights against predation by other individuals. Humans in a "state of nature" (a world before formal governments were instituted) defined property rights efficiently (Martin Bailey, 1992). For example, while rights to hunt on certain land were generally available to all, those who had planted crops on the land had the right to harvest these crops. Property rights to land could also change seasonally. This does not say that theft and other forms or predation did not exist, but only that societies then as now tried with varying degrees of success to define and protect property rights from other individuals within society. Additionally, there has always been a danger of predation against humans by other bands or tribes or states, and a value in protecting against this source of predation. Here, a rule of law was not useful, but some sort of government was.

For most of our existence as humans (probably 50,000–100,000 years), our ancestors lived in small bands or groups and the power of dominants was severely limited. It is only relatively recently (perhaps the last 10,000 years, the major period of written history but not of human existence), as human societies became larger, that kings and other rulers obtained power (Rubin, 2002). These powerful individuals provided benefits to members of their group in the form of protection of property rights from other bands or groups (and later, nations) and also from the fruits of predation against other bands. But they were also the source of domestic predation against property rights. Boaz Moselle and Benjamin Polak (2001) show that predatory states may lead to increases in wealth but may also be associated with reduced welfare for citizens, as the rulers may be able to engross all of the wealth increase. Indeed, the purpose of a "rule of law" is to protect members of society from predation by the sovereign. It is only recently in human history that subordinates successfully cooperated to protect themselves from dominants, although in periods preceding written history they were apparently more successful.

If property rights cannot be effectively protected, then there are several detrimental effects on income and wealth. First, people will invest less in creating wealth because returns are uncertain. Second, some people will spend their time in the fundamentally unproductive activity of trying to predate against others as, for example, by becoming thieves, or by becoming corrupt bureaucrats. The potential productivity of these people in producing goods and services is lost to the economy. Third, productive people will spend part of their time and effort in protecting themselves from predators, as by guarding resources from thieves or hiding resources from corrupt tax collectors. The effort spend in these activities is also lost to the economy. Finally, to the extent that people invest in less productive but more easily protected resources, then the economy becomes less productive. For example, if people invest in gold because it is portable and easily concealed, then the possible productivity of houses or businesses that could have been built is lost.

The modern conception of the "rule of law" was defined by Albert Dicey (1914): "In England no man can be made to suffer punishment or to pay damages for any conduct not definitely forbidden by law; every man's legal rights or liabilities are almost invariably determined by the ordinary Courts of the realm... These principles mean that there can be no punishment or taking of property without an explicit law, and all persons (including officers of the government) are subject to the power of the courts." Numerous scholars have documented the importance of a rule of law and protection of property rights for economic growth. This has been done both by examining the historical record (time series analysis) and by comparing countries at a point in time (cross section analysis.)

Time Series Analysis

Consider first time series or historical analysis. In modern times, the first example was probably Douglas North and Robert Thomas (1973). Nathan Rosenberg and L. Birdzell (1986) provided a detailed historical analysis of the economic growth of the West in response to property rights and market facilitating institutions. In a recent paper, Acemoglu, Johnson and Robinson (2002) show that the major impetus for European growth beginning in the 16th century was Atlantic trade. This trade strengthened the power of merchants and enabled them to obtain changes in institutions that strengthened the power of markets and the rule of law. An interesting approach is in Charles Jones (2001) who argues that it was specifically the increase in protection of intellectual property rights that has led to economic growth. Richard Pipes (1999) has also argued for the efficiency of a private property regime from a historical, not economic, perspective. The form of property rights can change over time as costs and benefits change; for example, Henry Smith (2002) shows that in England land went from individually owned to commons fields (albeit with strict usage rules) back to individuals use, as values changed. (The issue of *Journal of Legal Studies* containing this article, a special issue on "The Evolution of Property Rights" has several other interesting articles relevant for this analysis.)

Cross Section Analysis

There are also numerous cross section studies that find that the existence of economic freedom and a rule of law are associated with higher levels of economic growth. Robert Barro (1991) began this line of research, focusing on rates of growth. Gerald Scully (1992) was also an early pioneer. Other important recent contributions include Barro (1997), Robert Hall and Jones (1999), Acemoglu,

Johnson and Robinson (2001a, 2002), and Stephen Knack and Philip Keefer (1997). Dani Rodrik, Arvind Subramanian and Frencesco Trebbi (2002) find that institutions, measured either as a "rule of law" variable or as a measure of low risk of expropriation (following Acemoglu, Johnson and Robinson, 2001a) are much more important than openness or geography in explaining levels of incomes in a sample of eighty countries for 1995. Acemoglu, Johnson and Robinson (2001b) also find that institutions are more important than geography in explaining incomes. Fredrik Carlsson and Susanna Lunström (2001) decompose the effect of indices of economic freedom, and find that, while the overall index is significant in explaining economic growth, some components are not significant. Notably for our purposes, they find that the variable "Legal Structure and Security of Private Ownership" is significant and robust in explaining growth.

The effects are economically as well as statistically significant. Scully (1992, p. 176) finds that politically open societies grew at a compound real per capita annual rate of 2.5 percent per annum, compared to a 1.4 percent growth rate for politically closed societies. Societies that obey the rule of law grew at a 2.8 percent rate, compared to a 1.2 per cent rate in societies where state rights take precedence over individual rights. Societies that subscribe to private property rights and a market allocation of resources grew at a 2.8 percent rate, compared to a 1.1 percent rate in nations where private property rights are circumscribed and the government intervenes in resource allocation. Scully summarizes his results (p. 179): "Thus, societies where freedom is restricted are less than half as efficient in converting resources into gross domestic product as free societies. Alternatively, more that twice the standard of living could be obtained with these same resource endowments in these societies, if liberty prevailed."

The argument is this: There may be differences in incomes between countries because of different amounts of capital per worker, of education, and of technology. But none of these differences are fundamental. Capital is mobile internationally, and it should be profitable for owners of capital to move it to low capital countries by investing in these countries because capital will have higher returns where it is scarcer. Similarly, education should have a higher return in countries with low levels of human capital, and some individuals should find it worthwhile to undertake the investment. Educated persons can also migrate to places where their education is more valuable. Technology is also mobile across countries, through licensing or direct investment. But if institutions differ across countries, and if property rights are not well protected in some countries, then the above results do not hold. For example, capital will not flow into countries where property rights are not secure, even with very high potential returns. Rather, capital may actually flow out of such countries into countries with lower returns but more security. Thus, most scholars studying differences across countries recently have focused on institutions, and particularly the rule of law and the existence of property rights, to explain income differences.

It might appear that less successful countries could adopt institutions from more successful countries and so copy their success. But there are factors limiting this possibility. Powerful individuals or groups would often lose from the adoption of more efficient institutions and are often in a position to block the adoption of these advances (Acemoglu and Robinson, 2002). Moreover, because long-term commitments for compensation from those who would gain from new institutions to those who would lose are unworkable, there is no possibility of paying off these elites to get them to allow more efficient institutions (Acemoglu, 2002). One class of those who benefit are those with monopoly rights to supply some market; it is possible for the existence of such rights to lead to substantial reductions in income (Stephen Parente and Edward Prescott, 1999).

5. Specific Private Institutions to Protect Property Rights

In the previous section, I cited literature showing that a system based on a rule of law and enforced property rights leads to higher incomes and more robust economic growth. Once property rights are enforced, individual can engage in mutually beneficial exchange, even if the courts do not enforce contracts. I discuss private mechanisms available for such exchange. The main benefit of private ordering is protection from opportunism, which I discuss first. I then discuss mechanisms available to prevent opportunism. (This section is based on Rubin, 1994. See also Oliver Williamson, 1985.)

Predation by Individuals: Opportunism

In many transactions, one party will have performed his part of the deal before the other, who will then have an incentive to cheat. Examples of opportunism can be so crude as simply to refuse to make an agreed upon payment. More sophisticated forms of cheating include offering of high quality goods for sale and delivering low quality. A firm may also put a trading partner in a position where the partner is dependent on the firm for some input, and then raise the price, an action called "holdup."

The general form of opportunism is appropriating the "quasi-rents" associated with some transaction (Benjamin Klein, Robert Crawford and Armen Alchian, 1978). (A "quasi-rent" is a return on a fixed investment. Once a fixed investment is made, its return can be expropriated. If it were known in advance that the quasi-rent would be expropriated, then the initial investment would never have been made.) Such quasi-rents are often created by "asset specificity," creations of valuable assets that are specialized to one transaction or trading partner. A famous example is the creation of an auto-body plant by Fisher Body to service a General Motors plant. Once these specific assets are created, an opportunistic trading partner can sometimes appropriate their value. An important function of contract law is to protect transactors from such exploitation.

There are mechanisms traders can use themselves to enforce agreements (Rubin, 1994). For example, someone who cheats on an agreement may lose his reputation and trading partners, knowing this, will place trust in a party who will lose reputation capital if he cheats. But the value of this mechanism is only as great as the value of the reputation, so the ability of this mechanism to enforce agreements with large values at risk is severely limited. Similarly, some trades can occur within religious or ethnic trading groups because such groups can impose extralegal sanctions on cheaters (Janet Landa, 1981). However, if the party who places the highest value on some item is not within the trading group, then the most efficient transaction cannot occur and the item will not move to its highest valued use. For these reasons, additional mechanisms can facilitate efficient exchanges.

The major cost of opportunism when it cannot effectively be prevented is neither the cost of cheating, nor even the cost of precautions taken to avoid being victimized. Rather, it is the lost social value from the otherwise profitable deals that do not transpire. For example, if sellers cannot credibly promise to deliver high quality goods, then consumers will not be willing to pay a higher price for allegedly higher quality and manufacturers will therefore not produce them, even if consumers would have been willing to pay for assured quality.

In general, less formal enforcement mechanisms can work better for shorter-term transactions and for transactions involving smaller amounts of money. As the time horizon of a contract becomes longer or the amount at issue becomes larger, the value of formal enforcement increases. Thus, an additional benefit of enforcement mechanisms is the gain from the long-term investments and the large investments that would be deterred by the lack of enforceability To the extent that mechanisms can be designed and adopted that reduce or eliminate opportunism, then social wealth can be greatly increased. Thus, part of the reason for the increased growth in economies with efficient enforcement mechanisms is the increase in private transactions.

I now discuss mechanisms available to prevent opportunism in the absence of courts. I find it useful to discuss private protection mechanisms in terms of unilateral, bilateral, and multilateral mechanisms.

Unilateral Mechanisms

The major class of unilateral mechanisms is investment in reputation. Advertising is one form of such investment (Klein and Keith Leffler, 1981). Firms can invest in expensive signs or logos that become worthless if the firm cheats. Law firms invest in expensive decor serving the same function. Private firms can create reputations, but such creation may be costly, particularly in a large economy.

Bilateral Mechanisms

These mechanisms involve only two firms, often a buyer and a seller. Three relevant types of bilateral arrangements are self enforcing contracts, vertical relationships between dealers and manufacturers, and the use of "hostages," including collateral. It might appear that contracts including private arbitration clauses would be relevant here, but as we see below, these fit better into the multilateral analysis.

The most important type of bilateral mechanism is the creation of what has been called a "self enforcing agreement" (Lester Telser, 1980). This is an agreement between two firms that contains no external enforcement provisions. The agreement operates as long as it is in the interest of both firms to maintain it. For each firm, the value of the agreement is the value of the expected future business from maintaining the relationship. If a firm cheats, then it gains in the short run but loses the value of the future business.

An interesting class of bilateral transactions is between manufacturers and retailers of the product. There are various policies that manufacturers with brand name capital might want retailers to carry out. Some are: demonstrating and advertising the product; certification of quality; maintaining freshness; promoting the product to marginal consumers; maintenance of complete inventories; and refraining from "switching" customers to alternative product lines when consumers respond to manufacturers' advertisements.

There are numerous mechanisms or private institutions that can achieve these goals. These include: establishment of maximum or minimum prices for sale of goods (resale price maintenance); territorial restrictions, including exclusive territories; requirements that dealers carry only the brand of the manufacturer (exclusive dealing); and requirements of certain methods of retailing (such as shelf space requirements.) Manufacturers may also integrate directly into retailing or may establish franchises for selling their product. It is not my purpose here to discuss the business reasons for these restrictions; such discussions are available elsewhere (Rubin, 1990, Chapter 6). These restrictions can be carried out as self enforcing agreements, with the threat of termination as the only sanction. There is no need for state enforcement of these types of arrangements. However, state hostility (as, for example, through much American antitrust law) can make such agreements non-viable.

One way for a firm to commit to not cheating is to offer a hostage to its trading partner. A simple hostage is collateral, some cash deposit that will be lost if the firm cheats. Such a hostage requires some outside enforcement, but not by the state. For example, the firms could jointly hire an attorney who would be empowered to decide if cheating had occurred and to award the payment to the victim. Of course, there is a problem in trusting the attorney not to expropriate the hostage. However, firms might exist whose with a valuable reputation for enforcing such agreements and who therefore would not have an incentive to cheat in this way as long as their reputations were worth more than any one hostage. Law firms or investment banking firms might be able to perform this function. International firms might be particularly well suited for this role because they have established valuable reputations.

A more natural method is the creation of bilateral hostages. If firm A is dependent on firm B for some input, then firm A would have an incentive to put firm B in a position of being dependent on firm A as well. Moreover, firm B would have an incentive to be put in this position in order to be able to guarantee not to cheat. For example, firms making cardboard boxes commonly trade components with each other across geographic areas, and in this case neither firm can holdup the other without also putting itself at risk.

Multilateral Mechanisms

These are the most interesting class of adaptations. A well-defined multilateral arrangement involving a group of member firms can enforce honest dealing both between members of the group and between members and outsiders. The Law Merchant (the medieval body of commercial law) was exactly this sort of multilateral private legal system that enforced honesty by threats of reputation loss; see, for example, Paul Milgrom, Douglass North and Barry Weingast, 1990; Harold Berman, 1983; Bruce Benson, 1990. The Law Merchant was then adopted into the English Common Law. Similar institutions survive today in advanced countries. The Better Business Bureau, for example, is a reputation guaranteeing device with properties similar to those of the Law Merchant. Many trade associations have codes of ethics with many of the properties of the Law Merchant (Hill, 1976).

Private contracts requiring arbitration of disputes require similar enforcement mechanisms. Much international commercial law is based on arbitration, with loss of reputation as the major sanction for breach (Benson, 1989). I begin with an analysis of private arbitration that demonstrates the value of multilateral enforcement.

Arbitration

There is a substantial literature examining arbitration as a method of dispute resolution; much of this is summarized in Benson (2000), which is the source of much of what follows. In arbitration, parties rely on a non-judicial third party to resolve a dispute, and the parties agree that the decision of the arbitrator will be binding. Although I know of no empirical study of the efficiency of arbitration, it does pass a market test. Benson indicates that about 90 percent of international transactions contain arbitration clauses, and arbitration in the U.S. is used to resolve three times as many commercial disputes as do the common law courts.

There are several benefits to the parties from arbitration relative to use of the formal legal system. First, many arbitrators are experts in the relevant industry, so that the cost of informing the decision maker about the circumstances of the dispute may be much less. Second, since the parties pay for the arbitration, there is much more flexibility in arbitration than in the courts. For example, if a timely resolution is valuable, then the parties can pay more and have the dispute resolved more quickly. If there are benefits to secrecy, then the parties can instruct the arbitrator not to publicly discuss the matter.

Another benefit of arbitration is the freedom of the parties to choose the law that will govern their dispute. Parties in their contracts with each other or with the arbitrator can specify whichever body of law they find most congenial.

For example, in many industries there is a large body of customary law that arbitrators will often use; for an illustration from the diamond industry, see Lisa Bernstein, 1992. If the formal law in place is inefficient or vague, the parties can indicate that they will have their dispute governed by a different body of law, or by the rules of the arbitration association. This allows more flexibility in choice of law and means that it is more likely that an efficient law will govern. If it turns out that one body of law is generally chosen by parties, then this will be evidence that this law might be the most efficient to be used as public law. Arbitrators can sometimes use industry custom as a method of determining liability. Indeed, much common law and most commercial law are ultimately based on custom. This means that arbitration provide an additional choice of law, in the sense discussed by Todd Zywicki (2003).

Even if judges do not have much experience with business disputes and legal precedents may be weak, it should be possible to choose arbitrators who will be more likely to reach efficient decisions. Arbitrators will be paid only if hired, and so will have an incentive to reach correct decisions because this will lead to future business. If there are competing "court" systems, or competing groups of arbitrators, the parties can select the one they desire. Parties to contracts written in good faith will not expect to breach at the time of drafting the agreement. Therefore, *ex ante* the parties will desire to select that forum for dispute resolution in which they expect to obtain the most efficient results, so that *ex ante* competition among arbitrators will favor those with a reputation for providing the most efficient (wealth maximizing) decisions. Moreover, parties can specify the amount to be paid to arbitrators. This means that arbitrators in more important (costly) disputes can be paid more, so that parties will have access to the quality of arbitrator appropriate to the value of the case.

William Landes and Posner (1979) argued that arbitrators would not write opinions explaining their reasoning because clients would not be willing to pay for them. Benson (2000) points out that there are several incentives for writing opinions. Some arbitrators work for an industry or the equivalent of a trade association and this association may be willing to pay for written opinions since these will create a precedent useful to members in planning their affairs. Some arbitrators may write opinions to demonstrate their wisdom and ability, so as to generate future business. To the extent that arbitrators do write opinions, then their decisions can be the basis for additions or modifications to the legal system, as when the common law was modified by incorporating decisions of many competing courts.

There is a limit to purely private arbitration. That limit is that the party who loses in a dispute has an incentive to ignore the decision. In countries with an established body of contract law, the solution is that the courts will often enforce the decree of the arbitrator. In a society where there is no court enforcement of such decrees, the only remedy is a reputation remedy. In small societies where reputation is common knowledge among all parties, then simple publicizing of cheating may work. However, in larger societies, where there are many trading partners, it may be necessary to devise more complex devices for private enforcement of arbitration decrees. This is the topic of the next section.

Multilateral Enforcement Devices

Consider a trade association with the following policies:

1. The association collects dues from all members. These dues are used to subsidize part of the costs of arbitration proceedings in which disputes among members and between members and customers or suppliers are resolved. Disputants also pay part of the costs.
2. Information is made available to all potential customers and suppliers regarding the list of members. Thus, it is possible for a potential customer to ascertain at low cost if a potential seller is a member of the trade association.
3. If the decision of the arbitrator goes against a party and the party ignores the decision (e.g., refuses to pay damages as ordered by the arbitrator) then the party will be expelled from the association.
4. Therefore, if a party has been expelled, then when a new potential trading partner queries the association, he will learn that the seller is not a member, and will accordingly be able to avoid trading with the party, or will trade on different terms.

The structure of this mechanism corresponds to the Law Merchant mechanism. Milgrom et al. (1990) provide a game theoretic analysis of this mechanism and show that the outcome is stable and will lead to efficient trading patterns. This pattern is also followed by many trade associations that engage in self-policing; see Bernstein, 1995, for a partial listing. (It is desirable that whatever antitrust laws exist do not restrict the ability of firms to engage in such self regulation.)

Various Codes of Ethics of trade associations call for expulsion if there is misconduct. This pattern is followed by diamond "bourses" (diamond exchange markets) such as the New York Diamond Dealers Club, and by the World Federation of Diamond Bourses (Bernstein, 1992). Better Business Bureaus (BBBs), private reputation enforcing groups in the U.S., also follow this procedure, although these organizations also provide information about non-member firms. A simple mechanism would be for member firms to display on their doors or in their advertising a logo indicating that they are approved by the BBB. Trade associations and BBBs illustrate the types of organization of reputation guaranteeing associations that might be useful. Trade associations commonly include members of a given business, irrespective of geographic location. Conversely, BBB's include businesses in a particular area, irrespective of the nature of the business. The latter type of organization is more likely to be useful to guarantee reputations of those who sell to consumers; the former, of those who transact with businesses.

While private mechanisms can support some exchange, there are limits to the power of these mechanisms. It is useful to assume that a party will behave opportunistically whenever it pays to do so. Explicit enforceable agreements can mean that opportunism will be prohibitively expensive. A court order or an enforceable arbitration decree can remove any profit from opportunistic behavior. One key purpose of the law of contracts is to discourage such opportunism (Timothy Muris, 1981). Other mechanisms are less reliable. This means that the amount that can be exchanged without an enforceable agreement will be limited. The most that can be put at risk is the value of the reputation that would be lost if cheating occurs.

6. COMMON LAW AND CODE LAW

Compared to private ordering as discussed above, private litigation in independent courts is more able to control predation by private parties, but allows more predation by the state. It is useful to compare two methods of organizing courts: common law and code law. Common law is somewhat less restrictive than code law; that is, it generates less state power. However, there is also evidence that common law is more efficient and more desirable than its alternatives. (There is also a literature discussing the common law and finance; see for example Rafael La Porta, Florencio Lopez-de-Silanes, Andrei Shleifer and Robert Vishny, 1998. However, this is discussed in Chapter 13 of the present volume, and so I will omit it here.)

The two major legal systems in Europe are the common law and code or civil law. Common law is the British legal system, and is now used in former British colonies, including the U.S. It is sometimes referred to a "judge made law" since the law itself is not written down anywhere, but is the product of judicial decisions, and in particular the decision of appellate courts in resolving actual disputes between individuals, or between individuals and the state. Scully (1992) identifies 54 countries as using common law. In contrast, legal codes are passed by legislatures and interpreted by judges. Thus, in code countries judges are said to interpret the law, but not make it. In practice, this distinction between the role of judges is not the major difference between code and common law systems. Rather, as discussed below, the major difference is in the amount of deference given to the state. Scully (1992) identifies 94 countries in his sample as following code law. (The term "civil law" refers to code countries, but also to the non-criminal part of the common law and sometimes to non-ecclesiastical law. To avoid confusion, I refer throughout to "code" law.)

Evolutionary Models of Efficiency

A basic question for law and economics is the efficiency of law. Friedrich Hayek (1960, 1973), argued that common or judge made law was superior to statute law. Hayek's argument was that common law was "bottom up" law, which began with judges and individuals, while code law was "top down" and so paid more attention to the state and gave more power to the state. The common law existed independently of the legislature or the sovereign. In Hayek's view, deference to the state was undesirable. Hayek's argument is that common law provides more protection against predation by the state and leads to more freedom than code or civil law. Others agree with Hayek. La Porta et al. (1999) indicate that one of the purposes of the French code law was to consolidate government power, and they point out that the two major codes in Europe were introduced by Napoleon and Bismarck, two advocates of central state power. Paul Mahoney (2001) makes a similar argument. He indicates that common law judges have more autonomy, and that government officials in code law countries are less subject to legal controls than in common law countries. Common law makes no distinction between private and public law. The same legal principles apply to actions of government officials and private persons. This is not true in code law and in particular in French law.

More recently, Posner (1973/2003) has of course argued often and forcefully that the common law is efficient. His arguments are based on examination of particular legal doctrines. The difficulty of this method is that often the conclusion regarding the efficiency of a particular rule depends on unmeasured transactions costs of various sorts; if Posner's intuition about relative magnitudes of costs is incorrect, then doctrines he claims are efficient may not be so. The first explanation for the putative efficiency of the common law was due to Posner (1973/2003, elaborated in Posner, 1993.) His argument depended on utility maximization by judges. The argument is that judges are so insulated from personal factors and from interest group and other pressures that the only remaining decision factor is efficiency. The only other candidate is income redistribution, and judges lack the tools needed for such redistribution. This explanation was and is not terribly convincing to economists because it ultimately relies on judicial tastes for efficiency and economists prefer not to explain behavior on the basis of arbitrary tastes.

Since this argument was unsatisfactory, scholars turned to evolutionary models to try to explain efficiency. The evolutionary models are attempts to explain the form of legal rules without resort to utility functions. Initially, these models aimed at explaining Posner's observation that the common law was efficient. It is fair to say that the models failed in this endeavor, perhaps because the law is not so efficient as Posner argued. Nonetheless, these models have had an important impact on our understanding of the law because they have called attention to forces other than judicial preferences in explaining the law.

The first paper applying an evolutionary model to the common law was Rubin (1977). Following Landes (1971) Rubin argued that most cases are settled, rather than litigated, and that it is only litigated cases that can lead to legal change. Cases are settled when the expected value to the plaintiff of a case is less than the expected cost to the defendant, which is generally true if stakes are symmetric. However, inefficient laws can sometimes create asymmetric stakes because the inefficiency means that there are deadweight losses than cannot be bargained away in the settlement process. That is, an inefficient rule creates a loss to one party that is greater than the gain to the other because of future stakes in similar type cases. Thus, litigation becomes more likely when rules are inefficient, and so inefficient rules are subject to greater selection pressure, and more likely to be overturned. (Note that this model, like many of its successors, depends on parties having ongoing interests in disputes of a certain sort, rather than merely in the matter at hand.) Following this initial contribution were several extensions and modifications, by George Priest (1977), John Goodman (1979), Avery Katz (1988), and Peter Terreborne (1981).

Other scholars began critically examining these models. These include Landes and Posner (1979), Wes Parsons (1983), Robert Cooter and Lewis Kornhauser (1980), Gordon Tullock (1997) and Gillian Hadfield (1992). Jack Hirshleifer (1982), building on Rubin's discussion of inefficiency when stakes in precedent are asymmetric, provided what may be the most useful and influential criticism of the evolutionary models. Recall that in the original Rubin (1977) model and in some others, including Goodman (1979) and Landes and Posner (1979) evolutionary forces moved the law towards efficiency only if the party with an interest in efficiency had an ongoing interest in the form of the law. Hirshleifer generalized this point to show that the law could come to favor whichever party could most easily organize and mobilize resources for litigation of unfavorable precedents. This movement would be independent of efficiency.

Rubin (1982) uses this point to argue that common law was more like statute law than many want to admit: interest groups could use either common or statute law to achieve their goals. Michael Crew and Charlotte Twight (1990) expanded on this point and found common law less subject to rent seeking than statute law. Charles Rowley and Wayne Brough (1987) find that contract and property might be expected to be efficient, but not tort; Yoram Barzel (2000) presents a similar model. Rubin and Bailey (1994) have shown that plaintiffs' attorneys have been responsible for the shape of modern American tort law, using an evolutionary mechanism to shape the law. Vincy Fon and Francesco Parisi (2003) provide an additional mechanism to explain expansion of tort (mainly product liability) law: since plaintiffs chose courts in which to file, judges who are in favor of expansive law will see more cases and have more influence than more conservative judges. Although shaped by evolutionary forces, this law is socially quite inefficient.

Competition Among Legal Systems

In a recent paper, Zywicki (2003) has added what he calls a "supply side" to the efficiency of law models. He points out that the evolutionary models discussed above are "demand side" models, with litigants demanding efficient rules. Following Berman (1983), Zywicki shows that during the formative period of the common law there was competition between several court systems. There was first competition between civil and ecclesiastical courts. Within the civil system, there were royal law, feudal law, manorial law, urban law and mercantile law courts, all competing for the fees and business of litigants. There were courts of the King's Bench, the Exchequer, and the Court of Common Pleas, and four more obscure royal courts as well. All of these courts competed for business and fees; for example, church courts jurisdiction over testamentary succession could be used to increase the domain of these courts. This created an incentive for each court to provide unbiased, accurate and quick resolution of disputes. This is the supply side: judges and courts competed to supply efficient rules to get the business of disputants. Courts could also borrow remedies and rules from each other, which facilitated the evolution and spread of efficient rules and remedies.

In this competition, the Law Merchant (*Lex mercatoria*) played a major role in commercial law, including contract law (Benson, 1989). Ultimately the common law under Mansfield adopted the law merchant and this is the source of the efficient contract and commercial law rules that many have observed in the common law. It is important to note that in many circumstances (and particularly in business or contractual disputes) the parties would pick the forum ex ante, so that both would have an incentive to choose efficient courts. Thus, in this large class of disputes, there would be no pro-plaintiff bias as might exist when plaintiffs choose courts after a dispute has arisen.

In this view, an important source of efficiency is the existence of competing courts and bodies of law. Where such competition exists, rules will tend towards efficiency; where competition is lacking, there will be weak or non-existent tendencies for efficiency. This explains the actual path of the common law. In its formative stages, there was competition, and the law became efficient. More recently, there has been less competition, and the law has moved towards some inefficiencies. For example in the U.S., federal and state common law originally competed. This competition ended in 1938, as a result of the case *Erie Railroad v. Tompkins* (304 U.S. 64). After that period there was less competition as the federal courts were required to use the relevant state law. Now, arbitrators do compete with the courts for commercial business.

What can we say about the evolutionary models? By focusing on the role of litigants and, with the addition of the important Zywicki analysis on the role of competing courts, the models have a good deal of explanatory power. They do not (as first thought) indicate that the common law will always be efficient. However, they do explain both why common law was efficient in the past and why it is now less efficient. They also provide some guidance for methods of channeling the law towards efficiency, as discussed below.

Common and Code Law

There is less evidence on the efficiency of the common law relative to code law then of the overall efficiency of a rule of law. Nonetheless, what evidence there is is consistent with the arguments made above. Scully (1992) finds a significant relationship between protection of individual liberties and the common law (p. 162): "... the probability of having one's civil liberties protected is 2.5 times greater in common law nations than in countries with a codified legal tradition." He also finds that Marxist-Leninist and Muslim countries have significantly less political and civil freedom than non-Marxist and non-Muslim countries (p. 161). La Porta et al. (1999) examine the relationship between legal systems and "good" government, where good government is defined as "good-for-economic-development" and includes measures of government intervention, public sector efficiency, provision of public goods, size of the public sector, and political freedom. They find that countries with socialist legal systems are more interventionist, in that they provide less protection to property rights, more regulation and higher tax rates. Systems with French origin legal systems are also more interventionist than common law systems. Scandinavian countries are more interventionist than common law, but German law countries are about the same. Mahoney (2001) compares incomes and legal systems. He looks at growth rates for a sample of 102 countries from 1960–1992. He finds that common law countries grew .71 percent faster than did code countries. These results are approximately robust through many alternative specifications. He concludes that common law origin legal systems lead to significantly increased economic growth because they provide more stable property rights and better contract enforcement.

Transplanted Law

Much law is transplanted. (The following discussion is based largely on Simeon Djankov et al., 2003). Europe colonized much of the world, and the basic European legal systems (French and German code law, English common law) have been widely transplanted. The French system was spread by Napoleon and governs in Latin America, much of Europe and Africa and parts of Asia. The German system has influenced much of northern Europe, Japan, and parts of Asia. The English system governs North America, Australia, and parts of Asia, including India. It is quite possible for a system of law to be well adapted to its country of origin but not adapted to places where it is transplanted. Djankov et al. (2003) argue that much law becomes too dictatorial when transplanted to poorer countries; that is, legal systems that might give substantial power to governments may work well is countries where there are powerful institutions protecting against corruption and government exploitation, but may be subverted in countries without such protections. In their view, this is particularly likely with legal systems based on the French system, and this can create serious problems of overregulation. This is of course consistent with the arguments above regarding relative power of the state in code and common law countries. One implication is that, while the system of laws may not matter much in Europe itself, it is important for poorer countries to choose the appropriate legal institutions, where such choice is politically possible. Daniel Berkowitz et al. (2003) find that what they call "legality" (enforcement and effective legal institutions) is the most important factor for economic development, and they also find that transplanted law can lead to great inefficiencies through reduced legality if the receiving country is not suitable for the law. Hernando De Soto's (1989) well-known results regarding the cost and difficulty of starting a new business in Latin America is consistent with an excessively regulatory legal system.

7. IMPLICATIONS

In this section I first discuss implications for further research. I then discuss implications for policy.

Implications for Future Research

The point that legal institutions matter for economic growth is well established, although further confirmation would always be useful. The difference between common law and code regimes is less clearly documented; further research on this issue, and tests of robustness, would clearly be useful. For example, Mahoney (2001) shows that common law countries grow faster than code countries; there is clearly room for examination of levels of income as well as growth. Additionally, it is important to try to determine the particular properties of common law that lead to this benefit. It may not be feasible for code countries to replace their entire legal systems with common law, but it might be possible to impose some principles of common law onto a code system if we fully understood which aspects of the legal system were most beneficial. It is generally believed that the major difference between the systems is the protection of property rights from government in common law systems, but further research on this issue would be very useful. In this regard, Djankov et al. (2003) is an important paper.

Another important line of research is that suggested by Zywicki (2003). This paper attributes the efficiency of the common law to competition between legal systems. This point is clearly worthy of further study. For example, it would be worth examining other situations in which there is such competition. To what extent does commercial arbitration increase efficiency of commercial law? In the U.S., parties engaging in contract have some freedom to choose which state law will govern their contract; does this serve to increase the efficiency of contract law? (Larry Ribstein has written extensively on choice of law; see for example Erin O'Hara and Ribstein, 2000). Because such research will take both knowledge of legal systems and econometric and modeling techniques, it might be a useful area for further collaboration between legal and economic scholars.

Policy Implications

One important lesson of institutional economics is that institutions are difficult to change. Thus, policy suggestions may not be terribly useful, but some may be more feasible than others. It is clear that a rule of law and protection of property rights increase economic well-being. Thus, the first policy suggestion is that those countries that do not have these institutions in place should adopt them. Moreover, if possible, countries should adopt more common law like institutions, rather than systems based on codes. Additionally, where possible, competing legal systems within the same jurisdiction are useful for generating efficient outcomes. One possibility that meets many of these goals is to allow arbitration clauses in contracts, and for the courts to enforce these contracts to the maximum extent feasible. There are numerous benefits from arbitration, including greater choice of law. I have elsewhere suggested that it would be useful for new legal systems to freely allow arbitration and then to adopt the decisions of arbitrators into the law, just as the common law adopted the decisions of the Law Merchant (Rubin, 1994). Similarly, courts should allow and enforce contractual choice of law clauses wherever possible. Federal systems should try to preserve the underlying law of the individual states and allow choice of law.

Acemoglu (2002), Acemoglu and Robinson (2002), and Parente and Prescott (1999) have argued that there are constraints on adopting efficient institutions. These constraints are that powerful individuals or groups may lose from changing institutions, and that it may not be possible to devise enforceable contracts to compensate them. This issue is worth further examination. For example, organizations like the World Bank may be able to devise appropriate compensation mechanisms to induce powerful elites to adopt efficient rules.

The literature demonstrates conclusively that legal institutions matter for economic success, and improved methods of implementation of better legal systems is an important way to increase social wealth. It is less clear in explaining how to adopt such legal systems.

Acknowledgement

The author would like to thank Mary M. Shirley and two anonymous referees for helpful comments.

References

Acemoglu, Daron. 2002. "Why Not a Political Coase Theorem? Social Conflict, Commitment, and Politics," MIT Department of Economics working paper 02–44, available at SSRN, http://papers.ssrn.com/sol3/papers.cfm?abstract_id=355900.

Acemoglu, Daron, Simon H. Johnson, and James A. Robinson. 2001a. "The Colonial Origins of Comparative Development: An Empirical Investigation". *American Economic Review* 91(5): 1369–1401.

Acemoglu, Daron, Simon H. Johnson, and James A. Robinson. 2001b. "Reversal of Fortune: Geography and Institutions in the Making of the Modern World Income Distribution", NBER working paper 8460, available at SSRN, http://papers.ssrn.com/sol3/papers.cfm?abstract_id=281865.

Acemoglu, Daron, Simon H. Johnson, and James A. Robinson. 2002. "The Rise of Europe: Atlantic Trade, Institutional Change and Economic Growth," MIT working paper, available online from SSRN, http://papers.ssrn.com/sol3/papers.cfm?abstract_id=355880.

Acemoglu, Daron and James A. Robinson. 2002. "Economic Backwardness in Political Perspective," MIT Department of Economics working paper 02–13, available from SSRN, http://papers.ssrn.com/sol3/papers.cfm?abstract_id=303188.

Ayres, Ian and Eric Talley. 1995. "Solomonic Bargaining: Dividing a Legal Entitlement to Facilitate Coasean Trade". *Yale Law Journal* 104(5): 1027–1117.

Bailey, Martin J. 1992. "Approximate Optimality of Aboriginal Property Rights". *Journal of Law and Economics* 35(1): 183–198.

Barro, Robert. 1991. "Economic Growth in a Cross Section of Countries". *Quarterly Journal of Economics* 106(2): 407–43.
Barro, Robert J. 1997. *Determinants of Economic Growth: A Cross Country Study*. Cambridge MA: MIT Press.
Barzel, Yoram. 2000. "Dispute and Its Resolution: Delineating the Economic Role of the Common Law". *American Law and Economics Review* 2(2): 238–258.
Benson, Bruce L. 1989. "The Spontaneous Evolution of Commercial Law". *Southern Economic Journal* 55(3): 644–661.
Benson, Bruce L. 1990. *The Enterprise of Law.* San Francisco, LA: Pacific Research Institute.
Benson, Bruce. 2000. "Arbitration" in Boudewijn Bouckaert and Gerrit De Geest (eds.), *Encyclopedia of Law and Economics*, Cheltenham: Edward Elgar, Online at http://encyclo.findlaw.com/tablebib.html, visited December 25, 2002.
Berkowitz, Daniel, Katharina Pistor, and Jean-Francois Richard. 2003. "Economic Development, Legality, and the Transplant Effect". *European Economic Review* 47(1): 165–195.
Berman, Harold J. 1983. *Law and Revolution: The Formation of the Western Legal Tradition*. Cambridge, MA: Harvard University Press.
Bernstein, Lisa. 1992. "Opting Out of the Legal System: Extralegal contractual Relations in the Diamond Industry". *Journal of Legal Studies* 21(1): 115–157.
Bernstein, Lisa (1995), "The Newest Law Merchant: Private Commercial Law in the United States". Paper presented at the American Law and Economics Association Meeting, Berkeley, CA.
Black, Bernard S. and Anna Tarassova. 2003. "Institutional Reform in Transition: A Case Study of Russia". *Supreme Court Economic Review* 10: 211–278.
Carlsson, Fredrik and Susanna Lunström. 2001. "Economic Freedom and Growth: Decomposing the Effects". *Public Choice* 112(3–4): 335–344.
Coase, Ronald H. 1960. "The Problem of Social Cost". *Journal of Law and Economics* 3(1): 1–44.
Cooter, Robert D. and Kornhauser, Lewis A. 1980. "Can Litigation Improve the Law Without the Help of Judges?" *Journal of Legal Studies* 9(1): 139–163.
Cooter, Robert D. and Thomas Ulen. 1999. *Law and Economics*, 3rd ed. New York: Addison-Wesley.
Crew, Michael A. and Charlotte Twight. 1990. "On the Efficiency of Law: A Public Choice Perspective". *Public Choice* 66(1): 15–36.
Croson, Rachel and Johnson, Jason Scott. 2000. " Experimental Results on Bargaining Under Alternative Property Rights Regimes. *Journal of Law, Economics, and Organization* 16(1): 50–73.
de Soto, Hernando. 1989. *The Other Path: The Invisible Revolution in the Third World*, New York: Harper & Row.
Dicey, A. V. (1914). *Introduction To The Study Of The Law Of The Constitution*, 8th edn. Available online at http://www.constitution.org/cmt/avd/law_con.htm.
Djankov, Simeon, Edward L. Glaeser, Rafael La Porta, Florencio Lopez-de-Silanes, and Andre Shleifer. 2003. "The New Comparative Economics," NBER Working Paper 9608, available from SSRN, http://papers.ssrn.com/sol3/papers.cfm?abstract_id=392995.
Fon, Vincy and Francesco Parisi. 2003. "Litigation and the Evolution of Legal Remedies: A Dynamic Model". *Public Choice* 116(3–4): 419–433.
Friedman, Milton. 2002. " 'Privatization' Isn't Enough" in James Gwartney and Robert Lawson, (eds.), *Economic Freedom of the World: 2002 Annual Report.* Vancouver, Canada: Fraser Institute; reprinted in the *Heritage Foundation Insider*, August, 2002, Washington, DC.
Goodman, John C. 1979. "An Economic Theory of the Evolution of the Common Law". *Journal of Legal Studies* 7(2): 393–406.
Hadfield, Gillian K. (1992). "Biases in the Evolution of Legal Rules". *Georgetown Law Journal* 80:583–616.

Hall, Robert E. and Charles I. Jones. 1999. "Why Do Some Countries Produce So Much More Output Per Worker Than Others?" *The Quarterly Journal of Economics* 114(1): 83–116.

Hayek, Friedrich. 1960. *The Constitution of Liberty*. Chicago IL: The University of Chicago Press.

Hayek, Friedrich. 1973. *Law, Legislation and Liberty*. Chicago IL: The University of Chicago Press.

Heller, Michael. 1998. "The Tragedy of the Anticommons". *Harvard Law Review* 111(3): 621–688.

Hirshleifer, Jack. 1982. "Evolutionary Models in Economics and Law". in Paul H. Rubin and Richard Zerbe (eds.), 4 *Research in Law and Economics*.

Johnson, Jason Scott. 1995. "Bargaining Under Rules versus Standards". *Journal of Law, Economics, and Organization* 11(2): 256–281.

Jones, Charles I. 2001. "Was an Industrial Revolution Inevitable? Economic Growth Over the Very Long Run". *Advances in Macroeconomics*, 1(2): 1. Available at http://www.bepress.com/bejm/advances/vol1/iss2/art1.

Katz, Avery. 1988. "Judicial Decisionmaking and Litigation Expenditure". *International Review of Law and Economics* 8(2): 127–143.

Klein, Benjamin, Robert Crawford, and Armen Alchian. 1978. "Vertical Integration, Appropriable Rents, and the Competitive Contracting Process". *Journal of Law and Economics* 21(2): 297–326.

Klein, Benjamin and Keith B. Leffler. 1981. "The Role of Market Forces in Assuring Contractual Performance". *Journal of Political Economy* 89(4): 615–641.

Knack, Stephen and Philip Keefer. 1997. "Does Social Capital Have an Economic Payoff? A Cross-country Investigation," *Quarterly Journal of Economics* 112(4): 1251–1288.

La Porta, Rafael, Florencio López-de-Silanes, Andrei Shleifer, and Robert Vishny., 1998. "Law and Finance". *Journal of Political Economy* 106(6): 1113–1155.

La Porta, Rafael, Florencio López-de-Silanes, Andrei Shleifer, and Robert Vishny. 1999. "The Quality of Government". *Journal of Law, Economics and Organization* 15(1): 222–279.

Landa, Janet T., (1981), "A Theory of The Ethnically Homogenous Middleman Group: An Institutional Alternative to Contract Law". *Journal of Legal Studies* 10(2): 349–362.

Landes, William M. and Posner, Richard A. 1979. "Adjudication as a Private Good". *Journal of Legal Studies* 8(2): 235–284.

Landes, William M. 1971. "An Economic Analysis of the Courts". *Journal of Law and Economics* 14(1): 61–107.

Mahoney, Paul G. 2001. "The Common Law and Economic Growth: Hayek Might be Right". *Journal of Legal Studies* 30(2 Part 1): 503–523.

Milgrom, Paul R., Douglass C. North, and Barry W. Weingast. 1990. "The Role of Institutions in the Revival of Trade: The Law Merchant, Private Judges, and the Champagne Fairs". *Economics and Politics* 2(1): 1–23.

Mozelle, Boaz and Benjamin Polack. 2001. "A Model of a Predatory State". *Journal of Law, Economics, and Organization* 17(1): 1–33.

Muris, Timothy J. 1981. "Opportunistic Behavior and the Law of Contracts". *Minnesota Law Review* 65: 527.

North, Douglass C. and Robert P. Thomas. 1973. *The Rise of the Western World: A New Economic History*. Cambridge: Cambridge University Press.

O'Hara, Erin A. and Larry E. Ribstein. 2000. "From Politics to Efficiency in Choice of Law". *University of Chicago Law Review* 67: 1151–1232.

Parente, Stephen and Edward C. Prescott. 1999. "Monopoly Rights: A Barrier to Riches". *American Economic Review* 89(5): 1216–1233.

Parsons, Wes. 1983. "The Inefficient Common Law". *Yale Law Journal* 92: 863–887.

Pipes, Richard. 1999. *Property and Freedom*, New York: Knopf.

Posner, Richard A. 1973/2003. *Economic Analysis of Law*, 1st edn. Boston, MA: Little, Brown; 5th edition, Aspen Publishers.

Posner, Richard A. 1993. "What Do Judges Maximize? (The Same Thing Everybody Else Does)". *Supreme Court Economic Review* 3(1): 1–41.
Priest, George L. 1977. "The Common Law Process and the Selection of Efficient Rules". *Journal of Legal Studies* 6(1): 65–82.
Rapaczynski, Amdrzej. 1996. "The Roles of the State and the Market in Establishing Property Rights". *Journal of Economic Perspectives* 10(2): 87–103.
Rodrik, Dani, Arvind Subramanian, and Frencesco Treddi. 2002. "Institutions Rule: the Primacy of Institutions Over Geography and Integration in Economic Development," NBER working paper 9305, available from SSRN, http://papers.ssrn.com/sol3/papers.cfm?abstract_id=347077.
Rosenberg, Nathan and L. E. Birdzell. 1986. *How the West Grew Rich: The Economic Transformation of the Western World*. New York: Basic Books.
Rowley, Charles K. and Brough, Wayne. 1987. "The Efficiency of the Common Law: A New Institutional Economics Perspective" in Rudiger Pethig, and Ulrich Schlieper, (eds.), *Efficiency, Institutions, and Economic Policy: Proceedings of a Workshop Held by the Sonderforschungsbereich 5 at the University of Mannheim*, New York. New York: Springer, pp. 103–121.
Rubin, Paul H. 1977. "Why is the Common Law Efficient?" *Journal of Legal Studies* 6(1): 51–63.
Rubin, Paul H. 1982. "Common Law and Statute Law". *Journal of Legal Studies* 11: 205–223.
Rubin, Paul H. 1990. *Managing Business Transactions: Controlling the Costs of Coordinating, Communicating and Decision Making*. New York: Free Press.
Rubin, Paul H. 1994. "Growing a Legal System in the Post-Communist Economies". *Cornell International Law Journal* 27: 1–47.
Rubin, Paul H. 2002. *Darwinian Politics: The Evolutionary Origin of Freedom*. New Brunswick, NJ: Rutgers University Press.
Rubin, Paul H. and Martin J. Bailey. 1994. "The Role of Lawyers in Changing the Law". *Journal of Legal Studies* 23(2): 807–831.
Scully, Gerald W. 1992. *Constitutional Environments and Economic Growth*. Princeton NJ: Princeton University Press.
Schmitz, Patrick W. 2001. "The Coase Theorem, Private Information, and the Benefits of Not Assigning Property Rights". *European Journal of Law and Economics* 11(1): 23–28.
Smith, Henry E. 2002. "Exclusion versus Governance: Two Strategies for Delineating Property Rights". *Journal of Legal Studies* 31(2 part 2): S453–S489.
Telser, Lester. 1980. "A Theory of Self Enforcing Agreements". *Journal of Business* 53(1): 27–44.
Terrebonne, R. Peter. 1981. "A Strictly Evolutionary Model of Common Law". 10 *Journal of Legal Studies* 10(2): 397–408.
Tullock, Gordon. 1997. The *Case Against the Common Law*. Durham, NC: Carolina Academic Press.
Williamson, Oliver E. 1985. *The Economic Institutions of Capitalism*. Free Press, New York.
Zywicki, Todd J. 2003. "The Rise and Fall of Efficiency in the Common Law: A Supply-Side Analysis". *Northwestern Law Review* 97(4): 1551–1633.

10. Market Institutions and Judicial Rulemaking

BENITO ARRUÑADA and VENETA ANDONOVA

1. INTRODUCTION AND SUMMARY

The proper functioning of a market economy requires that freedom of contract be protected effectively. This can be achieved in different ways. A major design decision concerns the rulemaking discretion that the legislator delegates to the courts. When taking this decision, the legislator should take into account the specialization advantages and transaction costs that come with more or less specialized rulemaking. Factors influencing this trade-off explain the different solutions adopted in the two main legal traditions of the West. Common law evolved keeping more rulemaking powers in the judiciary, and thus was characterized by unspecialized rulemaking. The civil law tradition, however, was transformed during the 19th century, reserving greater rulemaking power for the legislative branch and thus reducing the discretion that judges had enjoyed during the Ancient Regime.

By stressing this difference, some recent studies claim that common law legal systems provide superior solutions to those developed in the civil law tradition, in which judges have less rulemaking power. This chapter criticizes these claims by developing and testing an alternative "self-selection" hypothesis, according to which both common and civil law supported a transition to the market economy adapted to local circumstances. In particular, judicial discretion, which is seen here as the main difference between the two legal systems, is introduced in civil law jurisdictions to protect, rather than limit, freedom of contract against a potential judicial backlash. This protection was unnecessary in common law countries, where free-market relations enjoyed safer judicial ground mainly due to their relatively gradual evolution, their reliance on practitioners as judges and the earlier development of institutional checks and balances that supported private property rights.

From this adaptation perspective, we see that much of the discussion on the "efficiency" of both legal traditions (pioneered by Posner, 1973; Priest, 1977; Rubin, 1977, 2000; and further developed by Cooter and Kornhauser, 1980; Terreborne, 1981, and Katz, 1988) focuses on relevant but relatively minor matters. This is compounded in recent comparative studies by the difficulty for such empirical comparisons of distinguishing causalities from correlations and by the fact that performances are observed only for those choices that were effectively taken, while the relevant comparison would be between the chosen option and its unobserved alternative. Such analyses therefore provide shaky grounds for policy recommendations and this may explain the recurrent paradox that, even though these empirical comparisons support the claim that common law is superior to civil law for the development of financial markets (e.g., La Porta *et al.*, 1998: 1148) and economic growth (Mahoney, 2001), both transition and emerging economies opt for statute law for creating the legal basis of such markets, following the regulatory model of developed economies, which for many decades has been based on statutes.[1]

Our discussion therefore broadens the argument by Rubin (1982) that both common law and civil law facilitated freedom of contract and were *efficient* in the 19th century. Without claiming anything regarding "efficiency," however, we argue that both common law and civil law solutions were well adapted to their particular circumstances. Considering that the value of legal systems depends not only on their specific traits but also on good environmental fit, we aim to identify the local circumstances which defined the balance of the institutional trade-off. Further work is needed, however, to develop and test the conjecture that the problem of transition and developing economies resembles the challenge of creating market institutions in 19th century Europe rather than the remote, evolutionary emergence of such institutions in common law countries.

The remainder of the Chapter is organized as follows. In Section 2 we state our hypothesis concerning the evolution of common and civil law. We argue that common law countries featured greater judicial discretion because, given their more gradual evolution away from the Ancient Regime, judges did not threaten the development of a modern market economy. Civil law reformers, in contrast, placed more rulemaking in the hands of the legislature and limited the discretion of judges in an attempt to shelter free-market relations, especially freedom of contract, from a potential judicial backlash. Both of these policies, promulgating systematized default rules and reducing judges' discretion, shared the same goal, that of protecting freedom of contract and promoting market relationships and economic prosperity in areas previously suffering from mandatory rules and judicial regulation of private contracts. We then confirm the consistency of our argument by reviewing the relevant historical evidence, in Section 3, and the alternative explanations provided in recent comparative performance of legal systems, in Section 4. In particular, Section 3 analyzes the historical evidence on the evolution of both legal traditions which seemingly culminated at the end of the 19th century. Then, in Section 4, we compare our argument with those produced in the recent debates on the comparative efficiency and performance

---

[1] This selection of statute law has even been interpreted as a selection of specific legal origins within civil law, as in the first of the annual *Doing Business* reports, which are based on methodologies developed within the "Law and Finance" literature and, specially, La Porta *et al.* (1998) and Djankov *et al.* (2002, 2003). In particular, *Doing Business 2004* classified 19 of the 30 jurisdictions which had formerly been considered of Socialist legal origin within that literature (La Porta *et al.*, 1999) as of either French or German legal origin. At the same time, 11 of these 30 countries remained classified as being of Socialist origin, and none was reclassified as having a common law origin (World Bank, 2004, 115–117).

of common and civil law. We contend that both theoretical and empirical claims on the superiority of common law remain unproven. Legal systems are not efficient in a vacuum, but rather their performance depends on environmental conditions. Section 5 concludes offering some conjectures on viable policies, acknowledging the idea that legal systems must fit their environment.

2. The Allocation of Rulemaking Powers

In modern economies, wealth creation depends substantially on market exchange, which requires a legal environment capable of increasing the capacity of parties to define the wealth-enhancing terms of trade and to enforce their agreements. Two key elements of this legal environment are rules and courts. Rules, given by customs, previous judicial sentences and statutes, provide parties with a detailed default contract and also predetermine the terms of trade when the law so mandates. Courts fill in the gaps in the contract and the received set of rules, define the terms of exchange for all remaining unforeseen contingencies, and also provide last-resort enforcement of contractual agreements. The presence of courts thus saves on contractual and enforcement costs for all parties. They also perform various functions with respect to rules: from merely enforcing statute law to creating and modifying rules.

For our purposes, rules may be made by a central authority, like the legislature, or by courts. In addition, judicial rulemaking becomes more centralized when low-level courts must decide according to jurisprudence exclusively produced by some higher courts. Both of these dimensions of judicial discretion—the rulemaking authority enjoyed by the judicial system versus the legislature and the decentralization of its powers—are usually positively correlated, which allows us to treat judicial discretion as a single organizational variable on which the main difference between legal systems hinges.

The idealized model of common law, as it finally emerged in the 19th century, is characterized by greater discretion for courts because statute law plays a minor role and each court is relatively free to rule, originally even with respect to precedent. Common law developed in England and was imposed on the former British colonies. It creates legal rules in a relatively decentralized and bottom-up manner. Initiatives for new rules start at the local level when a case is decided by a judge who creates a new rule, which remains local until other judges use it in their rulings. Successful rules may eventually become accepted by all courts in the state. Rules therefore result from the interaction between plaintiffs, defendants, lawyers, judges and jurors, as courts are *relatively* free to decide each case by distinguishing from, reconciling with or disapproving an earlier case.

In contrast, the civil law model, as crystallized more or less at the same time, gives priority to legislative rulemaking. Courts are instructed to enforce the received law and, even for filling gaps in rules and contracts, lower-level courts have to comply with the jurisprudence created by higher courts. Civil law is more centralized since the starting point for most new rules is legislation that applies to the whole State territory and not only to the jurisdiction of one court. This legal tradition is based on Roman law and is dominant in Continental Europe, Japan, Turkey, and the former colonies of France, Italy, Portugal and Spain. In civil law, judges are required to apply the rules, defined both by statutes and established case law (jurisprudence). Judges also fill the gaps in contracts and rules in a manner similar to common law judges but with greater centralization, as explicit jurisprudence is only produced by repeated and consistent rulings of certain higher courts. This different scope in the rulemaking capacity of the civil law judge is not substantially affected by the fact that even the ideal civil and common law models of the 19th century share many other features. For instance, in both paradigms, courts form a hierarchy and superior courts can overrule decisions from lower courts, which in any case have substantial freedom for interpretation, as can be seen in the fact that US appellate courts defer broadly to the trial judge's and jury's findings of fact (Posner, 1998: 584–586). The presence of these common characteristics should not, however, obscure the existence of a basic difference in the extent of judges' rulemaking discretion.

Additionally, common and civil law differ in other dimensions, such as the nature of the process, use of juries and justification of judicial decisions (Cooter and Ulen, 1997: 57). In common law, litigation is led by parties' lawyers while judges remain neutral referees who only ensure that the parties follow the rules of procedure and evidence. The idea behind this "adversarial" process is that the truth will emerge in the dispute between the two sides. In civil law, however, judges take a more active, "inquisitorial" role and parties often have to answer judicial questions, on the basis that judges have a direct interest in revealing the truth in private disputes. Common and civil law also differ in their reliance on juries, with civil law making limited use of juries, a feature that ties in with the lesser discretion and the inquisitorial role of the judge. Finally, judge-made law in common law countries is justified by reliance on precedent, social norms, or rationality. Judicial rulings in civil law countries are based more on the meaning of the code, with case law and rationality playing secondary roles. This difference also affects the way that lawyers are trained. Civil law is taught by studying the code and commentaries on it, while common law is learned by analyzing case law.

All kinds of rulemaking systems are likely to fail in achieving the public good because they pursue private interests or, even when pursuing the public good, they fail to ascertain which rules are most suitable, often triggering rent-seeking by parties to private contracts. We will argue that, in the development of Western legal systems, local circumstances like institutional checks and balances and judicial education condition the degree of judicial discretion.

We assume that predispositions towards the market order may develop differently among legislators and judges.[2] Consequently, legislators will allocate

---

[2] See Arruñada and Andonova (2004) for details.

rulemaking discretion to the judiciary considering the specific circumstances in each country. In particular, legislators creating market institutions may restrain judicial rulemaking to avoid judges' opposition to freedom of contract and market exchange. From this perspective, both Western legal systems might therefore be understood as adaptations to specific conditions that allow the development of effective market-supporting institutions in different historical circumstances.

In particular, modern market relations were introduced sooner in England, as many feudal constraints were abrogated earlier and the Industrial Revolution also took hold earlier, as well as more slowly, without such drastic changes in property rights as on the Continent. This creeping evolutionary process, together with a generalized respect of private property, gave time for judges and the public to be cultured in an intellectual tradition more propitious to the free market. In most of Continental Europe, however, modern market relations, suppressing the constraints that the Ancient Regime imposed on trade and movement of land and people, were generalized later and more abruptly, often together with redistribution of property. Most judges were then still the intellectual product of the Ancient Regime, in addition to forming part of the former ruling elite. Their lack of understanding of the market and disrespect for the institution of private property drove defenders of contractual freedom responsible for designing the institutions for continental markets to constraint judicial discretion.[3] From this perspective, we explain the restrictions imposed on judges in the civil law tradition, whereby they had to subject their rulings to contractual terms (whether defined explicitly by the parties or tacitly by default through statute law and jurisprudence) as an institutional control designed to protect market contracting.

3. THE TEST OF HISTORY

We will now examine in more detail the evolution of both legal traditions to corroborate that the above arguments are consistent with their history. In essence, we will confirm that institutional checks and balances and judicial training shaped the common tendency towards market-based relationships in England and on the Continent in very different ways.

The Evolution of Common Law

The commencement of what was to become the English common law system dates back to the 12th century, when Henry II (1154–89) created a professional royal judiciary and enlisted local communities to participate in the administration of justice. The further development of English common law was shaped by

---

[3] It is possible that judicial discretion was to a certain extent already limited in the Roman law tradition from the 12th century but this did not prevent later evolution from *additionally* constraining judges' discretion.

the political struggle and the resulting balance between Crown and Parliament. The English Parliament was one of the few to survive from the Middle Ages, constantly increasing its control over the Crown (North and Thomas, 1988; Pipes, 1999). The result was a creeping shift of power from the Crown to the Parliament, eventually culminating in the Glorious Revolution, which limited further the Crown's right to tax and thus to interfere with private property rights but was only one more step in a relatively continuous process (North and Weingast, 1989). The English Parliament, staffed by merchants and landed gentry, then used its enhanced powers to ignite a series of market-oriented reforms based on the principle of non-interference with private property (North, 1981; North and Weingast, 1989).[4]

The success of the reforms was guaranteed as the common law courts and the English judiciary shared the Parliament's appreciation of property rights and its understanding of market mechanisms. The appointment of English judgeships depended to a much greater extent than elsewhere in Europe on professional practice, as English judges were chosen from among barristers. As such, they had seen the world from the perspective of the parties they had represented and were therefore more familiar and educated on the intricacies of the incipient market economy (Duman, 1982: 29; Abbott and Pendlebury, 1993). The understanding by English judges of the fundamentals of the market economy also benefited from the early checks imposed on royal authority, as these checks limited the ability of the Crown to sell new public offices (Swart, 1980), making judgeships secure investments and converting early common law judges into defenders of private property rights. As a result, the transformation of the feudal economy spurred on by Parliament received an early ally in the English judiciary which, by making incremental changes in long-standing customs, assisted the evolutionary development of common law toward the new market order.

The expansion of market opportunities by the Industrial Revolution demanded more substantial changes in terms of both more developed and uniform rules. Common law satisfied these demands during the 19th century, mainly through the introduction of many Roman law solutions, and the strengthening of the doctrine of binding precedent, by which courts are reluctant to interfere with principles established in previous decisions (*stare decisis*). Despite these changes, however, the development of common law towards more

---

[4] This view has been criticized by some historians for exaggerating the role of the English Parliament in creating a market-friendly institutional environment (for example, Carruthers, 1990; Clark, 1996; Epstein, 2000). These arguments do not question, however, the fundamental point that the English Parliament exerted much greater control over the Crown. In a similar vein, researchers point out that, even in the absence of strong parliaments, there were well-developed markets on the Continent, specifically credit markets (for instance, Hoffman, Postel-Vinay and Rosenthal, 2000). The dominance of agriculture in the economies of the 16th to 18th centuries should be kept in mind, however, when considering these markets as well as that market relations for trade in goods had been well-established in some areas of the Continent, earlier than in England, as shown by the history of Italian cities in the Middle Ages, the Hanseatic League or the Champagne fairs, to give just a few examples. This also applies, in particular, for ascertaining the importance of merchant law. The challenge for those creating the institutions of the modern market was to develop institutions not only for trade but mainly for transactions among non-merchants.

market-oriented institutions remained evolutionary in nature and its courts retained a high degree of discretion, both in England and the USA. This was for two reasons. First, because the introduction of Roman law took place mainly at the level of concepts, as codification attempts did not succeed, arguably because they were less necessary than on the Continent. (This divergence in the success of codification is consistent with the argument that continental codification was driven by the need to constrain judges, more than to systematize the law, which probably was equally unsystematic in England and on the Continent). In addition, common law lawyers did not merely borrow ideas from Continental jurists, but developed and adapted such ideas in their own way. Moreover, the legal development of common law, which supported the huge economic development of the 19th century, remained almost exclusively the work of courts, with few legislative initiatives. Second, the strengthening of the doctrine of binding precedent did not divert common law from its evolutionary path, as precedents could still be overturned with relative ease by distinguishing the case at hand from the one in the precedent. Together with the right of appeal, it was, however, important in ensuring consistency and equality across increasingly wider markets (Manne, 1997: 13-19). In any case, it is consistent with our argument that the doctrine of binding precedent was introduced at this time, as cheaper transportation via canal, rail and steamship, increased the size of the market, requiring faster adoption of legal standards in a wider geographic area.

American common law, to the extent that it was independent of English law, shows remarkable similarities. Until the 20th century, the US had an arrangement similar to the English system of competing courts, with State and federal courts. Court competition, however, was not so intense and judges were not paid on a fee basis. Many judges, however, were elected and this probably served as a substitute incentive mechanism in the absence of a fee for service. American common law judges also enjoyed great discretion which was marginally reduced in the 19th century by the adoption of the doctrine of binding precedent, first for procedural and later for substantive rules (Zywicki, 2003: 22).

Continental Law

Legal history in what are now civil law jurisdictions originally resembled that of English law. The evolution of civil law, however, was influenced by a relatively different balance of powers among the main political actors, as Parliaments in Continental Europe, with a few exceptions, rapidly lost their ability to impose controls on the Crown. Most monarchies became financially independent and a considerable part of their income no longer came from taxes needing previous parliamentary approval. As a result, absolutist Continental kings enjoyed unchecked power and interfered with relative ease with private property rights, thus hampering the development of market relations based on secure private property (North and Thomas, 1988; Pipes, 1999).

These institutional limitations were reinforced by the fact that Continental judges were appointed without previous practice (Doyle, 1996). In addition, their training was based on the university study of *ius commune*, a doctrinal system developed mainly by scholars proficient in Roman and Canon law, and only secondarily affected by statutes and judicial rulemaking. It has been claimed that both the lack of practice and these doctrinal influences made Continental judges more resistant to capitalist wealth accumulation and hindered their understanding of market transactions. Market relationships, with their considerable exposure to risk and striving for profit, were hardly understood by a judiciary which derived most of its income and status from risk-free rents (Taylor, 1967). Judicial respect for property rights also probably suffered because judgeships were often expropriated by kings who were free to sell new judicial offices (Doyle, 1996; Swart, 1980). Thus, the judiciary on the Continent did not gradually erode the constraints of the Ancient Regime. Because of both institutional constraints and judicial training, civil law judges ended up constituting a barrier to the development of new market relationships. An abrupt change in both the law and the administration of justice was therefore necessary.

The Creation of Modern Civil Law

Consequently, the new legal order was mostly implemented in a top-down fashion even if it was essentially a liberal (that is, free-market-enhancing) initiative. Legislators issuing Civil and Commercial Codes in the 19th century aimed at both regulating what we would now call externalities and systematizing custom and case law, mainly through default rules. They did not promulgate mandatory rules unless they were necessary to establish basic political and economic principles of freedom, equality and property, often debasing interventionist legal doctrines (Van Caenegem, 1992). Their reliance on case law led to the codification of well-tried default rules, when available, without precluding parties from adapting contracts freely to their circumstances by writing specific clauses into them. In addition, codification benefited from the substantial convergence of doctrinal criteria that was already highly influential in courts' rulings because of the prevalent regime of judicial personal liability. As a result, 19th century codified law was mainly the distillation of customary law, and codes represented a combination of local customs, local laws and subsidiary Roman law (Sirks, 1998).[5]

In addition, most mandatory rules enacted at the time had a clear function in grounding the market economy. Probably the most important of these mandatory rules are a direct consequence of the political principles of freedom and equality, which have contractual correlates in terms of mandatory freedom of contract and mandatory equality of all contractual parties. (For example, previous law often granted higher probative status to the word of employers than to that of employees.) But this is also applicable to the emphasis of liberal reforms in avoiding the future entail of property, facilitating the emergence of a proper

---

[5] In particular, codifiers of commercial law, from the Code Savary in 1673 to the Uniform Commercial Code of 1970, relied heavily on the *lex mercatoria*, developed by merchant courts (Benson, 1998).

market for land.[6] Property law provides another interesting case in its treatment of a particular kind of externalities, those caused in the Ancient Regime by the proliferation of property rights and their enforcement as rights *in rem* even when they remained hidden to third parties. During the 19th century, land law reform and the creation of land registers led to a stricter policy of *numerus clausus* in most European countries—that is, the legal system started to enforce *in rem* only a limited number of rights, enforcing the rest as mere personal (in other words, contractual) rights. In parallel, publicity was increasingly required to produce rights enforceable *in rem*. Both of these constraints seem to diminish parties' freedom to produce rights *in rem* but in fact are essential for making some of them possible, reducing transaction costs in land and, in particular, making it possible to use land as collateral for credit (Arruñada, 2003), precisely the declared purpose of the reforms in this area.

Furthermore, operationally, civil law bound the judge to the law. This has often been seen only as a tool to enforce state law, disregarding the fact that, when the law set default rules, its main effect was to protect freedom of contract, because it made sure that the judge was constrained by the will of the parties. Therefore, the law protected the private legal order freely created by the parties, whereas under a system of greater judicial discretion this private legal order would have been in danger.[7] This fear drives the efforts of 19th century legislators to purge many dogmatic rules from received law, often rooted in Canon law, that were contrary to freedom of contract. A prominent example is the liberalization of credit transactions, which were still subject to substantial constraints, including the prohibition of interest and foreclosure.[8] Similarly, they often prohibited the judge from reducing the amount of penal clauses contractually established to punish the debtor for default in paying back a loan (Danet, 2002: 218). Most codes also derogated rules that had allowed courts to disregard some "unequal"

---

[6] Notice that, by the 17th century, common law had already developed the Rule Against Perpetuities, which enabled a court to declare void future or postponed interests in property that might possibly vest outside a certain perpetuity period. The goal was also to prevent land being tied up and to protect free markets.

[7] We pay no attention to private legal order solutions (of the type analyzed, for instance in Benson, 1989; Ellickson, 1991; Milgrom, North and Weingast, 1990; Bernstein, 1992, 1996, 2001; Greif, Milgrom and Weingast, 1994; Shavell, 1995), as we think they involve intrinsic difficulties for becoming the legal order for a modern capitalist economy. First, because the reliance of private enforcement on group membership limits its effectiveness to intra-industry trade, often on a personal level. Second, because they are only effective when state judges abstain from acting as appellate courts and they are permanently threatened by this possibility. Otherwise, private enforcement is only based on informal social sanctions, increasing its personal nature. This happened in particular with merchant courts, which, by being subordinated to royal courts in terms of appeals and enforcement, can be seen as mere local courts with an additional functional specialization.

[8] Until the 18th century, for example, French laws against usury outlawed short-term credits that were indispensable for commerce, industry and banking. Borrowers and debtors therefore had to spend substantially on circumventing the prohibition, which hindered the development of the financial market (Taylor, 1967: 480). Understandably, one of the main goals of the Napoleonic Code was to empower contractual parties to act on their own behalf, protecting them from anybody, including judges, who could alter the terms of their agreement (Mattei, 1997).

contractual clauses on the basis of scholastic "just price" arguments, such as the doctrine of "lesion."[9] More importantly, the scope of "cause" as a necessary element of any enforceable contract was considerably reduced (by reversing the burden of proof, for instance), and even fully eliminated in the "abstract" transaction of the German civil code, as well as, more generally, in the laws of mortgages and bills of exchange. This pruning of the concept of cause curtailed notably the possibilities of constraining contractual freedom with moral principles that the canonist interpretation of the original Roman concept had previously offered.

Understandably, legislators also tried to shelter legal reform from any reactionary backlash, including the possibility that judges would exert their discretion to issue sentences on the basis of abstract principles and against the new rules,[10] thus rendering the reform ineffective and hindering development towards the market economy. Legislators therefore subordinated the judiciary to the law and to jurisprudence, and restructured the professional career of judges.

Not only were codes and statutes given priority as a source of law, but the production of binding precedents was allocated to the higher court of appeals, which was conceived, at least originally, more as a court-controlling body than as a proper court. Its function was to supervise the legal interpretations given by lower courts, guaranteeing uniformity, making sentences predictable and enhancing legal security. Furthermore, no court had powers to question the constitutionality of legislation. In the French model, even controlling the legality of governmental action was assigned to a quasi-governmental body, the Conseil d'État.

In parallel, the practice of purchasing judicial offices was abolished and judges were converted into civil servants. They started their judicial career young and inexperienced, by passing specific exams after law school. Even today their promotions and salaries increase with seniority and sometimes with discretionary governmental appointments to the higher courts and other public offices. This meant that judges could lose substantial quasi-rents if they opposed the government or, even worse, were expelled from their positions. Compliance was further constrained in some countries by modifying their liability, making judges personally liable if they issued sentences contrary, not to dominant doctrinal opinion, as before, but to the statute law and formally established jurisprudence.

Summing up, our explanation as to why pro-market reformers in civil law countries reduced the discretion of the judiciary lies in the fact that in such

---

[9] Ascribing the doctrine of lesion to "the civil law," without warning of its removal or reduction by 19th century codifiers (as made, for example, by Cooter and Ulen, 1997: 191, 253), exemplifies the ambiguities that complicate comparisons between legal systems. See, for a detailed analysis, Abril Campoy (2003: 42–70).

[10] For example, Hayek (1960), among many others, emphasizes that the revolutionaries distrusted judges and their desire to control judicial discretion led them both to issue codes and to adopt more formalized legal procedures. This is confirmed by recent empirical evidence showing that civil law countries regulate the judicial process more thoroughly (Djankov *et al.*, 2003).

countries the transition to market economies was more revolutionary than in those under common law. Institutional change in England did not suffer the radical transformations that took place in Continental Europe at the end of the 18th and during most of the 19th century but followed a relatively smooth, evolutionary process, which started much earlier. In contrast, judiciaries in Continental Europe were structured with greater central control with a view to achieving and enforcing an intended change.[11]

4. A CRITIQUE OF ALTERNATIVE EXPLANATIONS

Our interpretation of 19th century civil law as an adaptive top-down introduction of the market has important consequences for the arguments given in debates on the comparative efficiency and performance of common law versus civil law. The first of these debates started when part of the American "law and economics" school argued in favor of the efficiency of the solutions being used in 19th century common law. Later, the quest for institutional explanations of differences in economic performance has led to quantitative comparisons of multiple performance indicators across legal systems. Even though both of these explanations involve evolutionary arguments and path-dependency, they differ in an important way from our hypotheses, as they do not consider the possibility of adaptation to local circumstances as the main force behind divergent legal systems. Moreover, these alternative explanations fail to prove the universal superiority of common law arrangements which many of them more or less explicitly advocate. Consequently, they can lead to flawed policy when they neglect local circumstances which might strongly limit the feasibility of legal reforms.

The Efficiency Debate

The Efficiency of Common Law

The efficiency of common law was first suggested by Posner (1973), based on the metaphor that the decentralized creation of common law mimicked how the market worked, leading judges to unconsciously pursue an efficiency standard. This hypothesis has been successfully used to explain many common law rules, related to negligence, contributory negligence, strict liability, restitution and

---

[11] The evolutionary versus revolutionary nature of the transition was not the only historical accident having an influence on the adaptiveness of legal systems. Technological innovation after common law became entrenched may have also reduced the comparative advantage of judicial discretion. The conjecture is that, in common law jurisdictions, the market economy was established before the emergence of national markets, which mostly waited until the development of railways. Most codification in Europe took place when, thanks to the impact of rail transport, it became clear that markets would become much wider in scope. Understandably, legislatures strove to provide unified legal standards for the whole of the national market, as local rulemaking made less sense after the development of national markets.

collateral source, to name just a few (Posner, 1998). For instance, Landes and Posner (1987) illustrate the argument by examining the application of the Hand Formula, a special type of cost and benefit analysis applied in the field of torts, and conclude that judges do actually, even though not necessarily consciously, use this method when assessing liability and thus take efficiency-enhancing decisions. This kind of argument has been criticized, however, for its lack of verifiability. In particular, there is no evidence that judges consciously perform this calculation. Furthermore, the information needed to apply the rule is not readily available. In addition, even if a rule in common law is shown to be efficient, it does not follow that it is the common law system that has produced such efficiency, as many of these rules were developed in older legal systems (Simpson, 1998) and are also applied in civil law jurisdictions (Faure, 2001) or, when different, differences are functional and fit well into other design features of legal systems (Rubin, 1982).

The efficiency hypothesis has also been grounded in more detailed models of the judicial process. Adapting Harold Demsetz's (1967) seminal argument on property rights, Rubin (1977) argued that inefficient rules tend to be abolished as an unintended by-product of litigation between self-interested parties who share a common interest in changing the rule. To encompass cases in which parties do not share such a common interest, the argument has been extended to model common law as an evolutionary process (Priest, 1977; Terreborne, 1981; Katz, 1988). Litigation, however, is often unable to produce the same legal rules as the ones that the parties would have introduced if they had explicitly agreed ex ante on the issue being litigated ex post, because litigation does not aggregate over all parties' interests and it can therefore aspire to achieve only local instead of global efficiency (Wagner, 1998). Taking this critique into account and extending the argument, Rubin (1982) argues that ingrained, albeit different, mechanisms drive both common law and civil law to efficiency. He claims that this drive to efficiency lasted until well into the 19th century and that the susceptibility to interest group pressure that characterizes the later evolution of rulemaking institutions corrupted both common law and civil law. This idea has been further explored by Crew and Twight (1990), Bailey and Rubin (1994) and Osborne (2002), among others; it remains silent, however, on why the two centuries differed so drastically on the extent of rent-seeking.[12]

Furthermore, common law understood as judge-made law may be imperfect for deeper reasons. Its nature is retrospective and thus unsuitable for creating completely new rules or for making rapid legal changes. As with any design produced in an evolutionary process, it suffers path dependency because innovations are introduced not by designing them from scratch but by tinkering with a received solution. Paraphrasing Tooby and Cosmides, common law then evolves "like the proverbial ship that is always at sea. The ship can never go into dry dock for a major overhaul; whatever improvements are made must be implemented

---

[12] For an extensive review of the literature on the efficiency of judge-made law, see Rubin (2000).

plank by plank, so that the ship does not sink" (Tooby and Cosmides, 1992: 60). Statute law, in contrast, is produced in what can be described as a rational process, benefiting from planning and foresight, and it is less constrained by the previous legal order. It suffers from rent-seeking, but the severity of this varies greatly and the evolutionary processes in common law are not free of their own versions of it as, for example in the case of politically-motivated judges, who implement their own version of morality (Bork, 1990). Even Richard Posner (1973: 569) concedes that "legislative law-making is apt to be more efficient than judicial law-making" because the litigation of cases often fails to raise the pertinent questions for initiation of a legal reform. As argued by Wagner (1998: 315), common law can probably pass the test of local efficiency but is bound to fail the test of global efficiency.

Lastly, the claim that case law is more efficient than statute law remains unproved because most of the discussion has been on the internal consistency of common law and not on its advantages with respect to civil law. Internal consistency, however, is not exclusive to common law, as many rules in civil law also seem to reflect or lead to efficiency (Faure, 2001: 179; Harnay, 2002: 237). Robert Cooter (1994), for example, suggests that the efficiency of common law depends on the enactment of efficient customs by judges. This is as much a characteristic of common law as it is of civil law. According to this argument, judges make common law efficient when they find customary law and raise it to the level of law. However, the selection of social norms is also frequently carried out in the codification process. For example, the most successful US code, The Uniform Commercial Code, was built by identifying and systematizing the best business practices, and most of the rest of the common law of contracts has also been codified in the Restatement of Contracts published by the American Law Institute and state statutes revising the Statute of Frauds (Cooter and Ulen, 1997: 205, 378). This argument leads us to the debate of the efficiency of statute law.

The Efficiency of Civil Law

Work asserting the economic efficiency of common law often suggests, more or less implicitly, that statute law does not achieve the same degree of efficiency. This claim has been opposed, however, by scholars arguing that civil law also strives towards efficiency through both of its sources of rules—legislation and judicial activity.[13]

Legislation may produce superior rules because its centralization provides an advantage in terms of standards and innovation. Industrial organization shows that markets do not always provide universal standards and do not fully guarantee that the surviving standard is the best. A possible solution is an industrial

---

[13] In a survey among members of the American Law and Economics Association, Moorhouse, Morriss and Whaples (1999) find that 84% of respondents believe that common law is generally efficient and 42% consider it more efficient than civil law.

agreement or some kind of coordination mechanism guaranteeing the compatibility of all elements of the network. By analogy, Harnay (2002) sees legal codes as standards within a social network, providing legal coordination in a setting of adoption externalities. Codified law can then avoid the emergence of inefficient legal rules in the process of decentralized litigation that characterizes common law systems. The argument has been applied to explain codification as a conscious effort to systematize and organize previous statutes and customs.[14] Civil law is also thought to have some advantages, perhaps being more innovative than common law. It is grounded on legal rules, which may be easier to create than social norms (Garoupa, 2001). Although this argument obviously begs the question as to whether or when such creativity is desirable, it also indicates that civil law has the potential to be flexible despite often being perceived as rigid.

The concept that civil law is more concerned with distribution than with efficiency has also been opposed by pointing out the extent to which civil law principles rely on a logic of economic efficiency (Faure, 2001). For example, even though French tort law does not use a Learned Hand test to evaluate the standard of care, it does not exclude the use of costs and benefits analysis. Furthermore, it is questionable whether judicial practice strays away from economic efficiency and favors redistribution more in civil than in common law. For example, it has been argued that case civil law tends to apply strict liability when this application is more consistent with compensating victims than with economic efficiency, perhaps reflecting different social priorities (Faure, 2001). However, the scope of strict liability has also been taken in common law to probably inefficient extremes (Priest, 1985).

The capacity of civil law judges to modify and adapt inefficient legal rules is also greater than might be imagined because judges retain some normative capacity (Michelman, 1980). It has been observed on numerous occasions that, when the efficiency of a codified rule is doubtful, civil law courts end up circumventing it, usually by stretching the interpretation of flexible standards such as "good faith," "reasonably," "fairly" and so on. This happened, for instance, in areas as diverse as encroachments, ostensible possession and formal contract requirements. For example, according to the Spanish Civil code, encroached constructions should be demolished if the two neighboring owners do not reach an agreement, which would be inefficient in cases of minor good-faith encroachments; consequently, the jurisprudence came to enforce a liability rule (Paz-Ares, 1995: 2860–65). It is also common for land registration laws to deny property (that is, real or *in rem*) status to mere possession. However, case law often interprets good faith requirements extensively, considering ostensible possession as proof of bad faith on the part of a third party acquiring from a registered owner without possession.[15] As a last example, the requirement of

---

[14] See, for instance, the analysis of the French civil code by Josselin and Marciano (2002).

[15] The judicial proclivity to transform "crystal" property rules into "muddy" liability rules, originally analyzed by Rose (1988) in common law but also present in civil law (Arruñada, 2003).

written form established for debts by the French civil code was rapidly abrogated by judges for business contracting (Danet, 2002).[16]

It therefore seems clear that efficiency and departures from it are not exclusively a common law or a civil law trait (Rubin, 1982) but respond to deeper causes. Mattei (1997) suggests, for instance, that changes in the role of both common and civil law courts have resulted in substituting social organization by contract for what he describes as "government by judges". The result of this shift and the risks involved in it show remarkable similarities across legal traditions. In civil law countries, jurisprudence soon reintroduced moralistic views by interpreting more or less freely the original "intent" of the legislative rulemaker. In a recent example, court rulings on cases of workers' dismissal in Italy have been shown to be influenced by conditions in the local labor market—the probability of a ruling in the worker's favor increases with the unemployment rate in the court's jurisdiction, which is consistent with greater consideration of "fairness" in such rulings (Ichino *et al.*, 2003). Similar events take place, however, in most areas of common law. Even US federal judges have been severely criticized for implementing their own views and disregarding the constitutional and statutory constraints they are supposed to be bound by (Bork, 1990).

The Comparative Performance Discussion

The debate on the efficiency of legal systems, confined for decades to law and economics, has recently reached wider audiences, when some related hypotheses started to be tested empirically by Simeon Djankov, Rafael La Porta, Florencio Lopez-de-Silanes, Paul Mahoney, Andrei Shleifer and Robert Vishny (La Porta *et al.*, 1997, 1998, 1999; Mahoney, 2001; Djankov *et al.*, 2002, 2003). These works classify a sample of countries according to the historical origin of their legal system as common law; French, German and Scandinavian civil law; and former Socialist countries; and then test through statistical regression the explanatory power of these "legal origin" variables on diverse indicators of countries' institutional and economic performance, ranging from stock ownership concentration to economic growth. The first studies explored the relevance that this classification criterion had on the development of financial markets and companies' ownership dispersion (La Porta *et al.*, 1997, 1998). Five-scale indices of investor and shareholder protection were elaborated after inspecting the commercial code and bankruptcy regulation in each country and these were assumed to reflect the degree of legal protection that the law was providing to minority investors. A statistically significant positive correlation was found between the shareholder and investor protection, on the one hand, and the common law tradition, on the other. The analysis was later extended in a series of

---

[16] Even if this judicial overruling of statutes is a powerful force, we are not arguing that it equates the position of civil law judges to their common law counterparts. Furthermore, such overruling is not always efficient, as shown by the judicial treatment of possessory rights.

works that showed significant correlations between belonging to a particular legal system and the measured level of regulation, property rights protection, the efficiency of government, the level of political freedom, economic growth and judicial independence. The punch-line in all these works is that the civil law tradition and, in particular, its French version, shows consistently worse performance than the common law tradition.

This line of research is valuable because it is a pioneer effort in quantifying differences in performance across the legal institutions that sustain modern economies, and this motivates further discussion and allows it to proceed in a more systematic, albeit some would claim distorted, fashion. It suffers substantial weaknesses, however, related to selection bias, measurement difficulties and questionable causation.

First, even if performances were perfectly measured, their comparisons suffer from an intrinsic self-selection problem because actual observed levels of performance result from those choices that were effectively taken in the past, and we lack information on their alternatives. If we recognize that not all legal systems perform well in all contexts, the relevant comparison is between the performance of the chosen option and that of its alternatives, but these alternative performances are by definition never observed. For example, even if someone demonstrates that the economic performance of the US is better than that of France because France has a civil law system, this would not prove that it was a mistake for the French to mold their Ancient Regime legal system in the direction of what is now known as civil law. To show that such a move was a mistake, one would have to compare the actual performance of France with the performance France would have exhibited under common law.[17]

Second, the value of measurement is not greater than its accuracy, and measuring institutions is hampered by methodological difficulties. Thus, most findings are based on indices that capture only a few of many relevant dimensions, such as the index of shareholders' rights in La Porta *et al.* (1998), which does not distinguish between the mandatory or default character of the rules, a major issue if they are to be properly understood. In addition, they measure shareholders' rights along dimensions that do not necessarily capture the real degree of protection. For example, the index considers the fact that German shareholders cannot vote by mail as a shortcoming of German corporate law, disregarding

---

[17] La Porta *et al.* (1998, 1999) claim that their studies do not suffer endogeneity because in most cases the actual origin of the legal system is imposed by conquest. This is doubtful, however, because it is applicable neither to colonizing powers nor to former colonies, which often enacted their codes after independence—in the case of former Spanish colonies, many decades later. In addition, even when introducing new legal institutions, there was a choice of system and the decision was often to delay its introduction in the colonies, thus implicitly opting for temporarily maintaining the older system, which provided greater judicial discretion. Furthermore, as a version of this self-selection problem, the legal origin variables fail to consider the indigenous legal institutions (Berkowitz *et al.*, 2001). The prior strength of indigenous institutions, which made it unnecessary, more costly and less effective to introduce Western law, has also often been disregarded as an explanatory factor. See, however, Acemoglu, Johnson and Robinson (2002) about the potentially negative effect of pre-colonial institutions in long-run economic growth.

the fact that most German shareholders send their instructions by mail to their banks and that banks do vote (Roe, 2002). The problem is even worse, however, as what is lacking is a global measure of institutional performance that takes into account interactions among a number of institutions, determining what we define as present-day common law or civil law jurisdictions.[18]

More generally, advancing causation arguments is dangerous in the absence of theory. For example, concluding from a correlation that concentrated ownership is due to allegedly weak legal protection of investors' rights might look intuitively correct but it is nevertheless superficial. As Roe (2002) shows, a complex mix of economic, social and political conditions affects managerial agency costs and determines the degree of ownership dispersion.

In the same way, legal systems are imbedded in a complex network of political structures and social preferences that cannot be studied in isolation, which apparently La Porta *et al.* (2004) do, when they take as a symptom of inefficiency of the legal procedure their finding that courts in civil law countries are slower to decide a case of eviction of a tenant or collection of a bounced check. Suggested inefficiencies, however, are difficult to substantiate without considering factors such as the incidence of these events, the complementary enforcement mechanisms that are at work and the costs incurred in each system for a comparable level of quality.

Within this literature, the superior economic performance of common law countries has been attributed not only to the statutory protection of property rights but also to the greater judicial independence supposedly enjoyed by common law judges (La Porta *et al.*, 2004). The benefits of greater judicial independence and, as a consequence, the inferred relationship with economic performance, however, have been severely questioned in a period where politically-motivated judges implement their notion of fairness and morality in an institutional setting in which they are not accountable to a considerable degree to anybody (Bork, 1990: 5).

Lastly, causation is also in doubt when superior performance is attributed to common law in legal fields which are everywhere based on statute law. This happens not only in corporate law but also in regulation and administrative law, as well as with some specific indicators, like eviction time. With this in mind, it is unsurprising that these legal origin variables also "explain" such phenomena as sports success,[19] showing once more that correlation does not imply causation.

---

[18] Some steps towards a more detailed analysis have already been taken. See, for example, Beck, Demirgüç-Kunt and Levine (2003), who defend the importance of the legal system's adaptability to evolving economic conditions; Acemoglu, Johnson and Robinson (2002), who defend the primary importance of local conditions for the development of strong property rights institutions; and Acemoglu and Johnson (2003), who show a statistical relationship between growth and protection of property rights against state expropriation but not between growth and the quality of contracting institutions, a variable that other works link to legal origin.

[19] West (2002) finds that FIFA rankings of national soccer teams correlate in a statistically significant manner with countries' legal origins.

The Need for Further Detail

More generally, both the efficiency and performance debates opposing common law and civil law have been formulated at a high level of abstraction that may lead to a focus on ambiguous categories and to mistaken conclusions. This abstraction takes place both vertically and horizontally.

Vertically, because the various "civil law" labels are defined by country and are therefore applied to related but separate and historically variable phenomena, such as statute, codified and systematic law versus case law, mandatory rules versus default rules, judicial dependence versus judicial discretion, and even rigid versus flexible rules of judicial procedure. These dimensions are better seen as variables in institutional design. All legal systems use them as ingredients but mix them in different proportions and manage them differently through history. Comparison among systems should aim to consider the weight of each ingredient and their interdependencies. In doing so, the analyses should ideally incorporate the institutional determinants that lie beyond the legal system and are frequently found in the nature of the political process (Backhaus, 1998; Wagner, 1998, 1992; Andonova, 2003), as well as wider economic factors relevant in specific fields of law, such as, in the field of property, the expected number of transactions, the risk of political opportunism and regulatory consistency (Arruñada, 2003).

Something similar happens horizontally, as legal systems often adopt structures pertaining to foreign traditions. This is also clear in the field of property law, in which legal traditions do not explain the adoption of the most relevant institutions. For example, until recently England had a system of private transactions akin to that of the Romans, but moved in the last century to the German system of registration, the same as Australia and most of Canada. Most of the US, however, introduced early a system of publicity by recording that is typically French (Arruñada, 2003). Similarly, the *numerus clausus* of property, *in rem*, rights is now almost unrelated to the common versus civil law divide. It remains to be documented to what extent this institutional cross-breeding also happens in other fields of law.

5. CONCLUDING REMARKS

It is time now to present some policy considerations, which aim to be pertinent for the unsolved problem of how to build market institutions in transition and developing economies.

In previous sections we argue that the evolution of both common and civil law in the 19th century was instrumental in protecting freedom of contract and developing market economies. We also explain the different degrees of discretion granted to courts in both systems as optimal adaptations to particular circumstances. In this way, greater judicial discretion in classic common law courts emerges more as a historical and perhaps unique exception than as a replicable solution.

This casts an additional doubt on the normative interpretation of some results on the efficiency and performance of legal systems which, asserting the superiority of common law, seemingly recommend applying it. We have sketched above why such superiority is open to question and likely to depend on environmental factors. But, more clearly, even if common law were shown to be superior today, the normative consequences of such superiority might be insignificant. Both common and civil law were probably well adapted to their original circumstances. Those creating the institutions of the market in Continental Europe did not opt for constraining judicial discretion to control the market but to protect it.

In line with this interpretation, our analysis does not advise any specific system for transition and developing economies in general but instead suggests that institutional development and academic research should aim at identifying the contextual circumstances which affect the costs and benefits of the different solutions. The problems of these economies may, in some cases, be more similar to those faced on the Continent at the demise of the Ancient Regime than to those enjoyed by England more or less at the same time. If so, restraining judicial discretion may be now necessary in developing economies in order to guarantee freedom of contract.

Lastly, if we are correct in considering both legal systems as adaptations to local circumstances, our analysis points out the risk that the debates on the relative efficiency and performance of common and civil law may be sterile because the comparison does not take place between viable alternatives.

Acknowledgement

The authors thank Jesús Alfaro Águila-Real, Douglas W. Allen, Marco Casari, John Drobak, Paul S. Edwards, Pierre Garrouste, Fernando Gómez-Pomar, Emily Kadens, Pierre-Cyrille Hautcoeur, Claire Hill, Marta Lorente, Thomas Lundmark, Bertrand du Marais, Armelle Mazé, Claude Ménard, Fernando P. Méndez González, John Nye, Elinor Ostrom, Celestino Pardo Núñez, Cándido Paz-Ares, Mary M. Shirley, Stefan Voigt, Will Wilkinson, several anonymous referees and participants at several workshops and conferences for their comments and criticism. This work has received financial support from the MCYT, an agency of the Spanish Government, through Project SEC2002-04471-C02-02.

References

Abbott, Keith and Norman Pendlebury. 1993. *Business Law*. London: DP Publications Ltd.
Abril Campoy, Juan Manuel. 2003. *La rescisión del contrato por lesión: Enfoque doctrinal y jurisprudencial*. Valencia: Tirant lo Blanch.
Acemoglu, Daron and Simon Johnson. 2003. "Unbundling Institutions," NBER Working Paper 9934, revised version: July, 2003 (http://econ-www.mit.edu/faculty/download_pdf.php?id=660, accessed September, 13, 2003).

Acemoglu, Daron, Simon Johnson, and James A. Robinson. 2002. "Reversal of Fortune: Geography and Institutions in the Making of the Modern World Income Distribution". *Quarterly Journal of Economics* 117: 1231–1294.
Andonova, Veneta. 2003. "Property Rights and the Structure of Political Competition". Universitat Pompeu Fabra, mimeo.
Arruñada, Benito. 2003. "Property Enforcement as Organized Consent". *Journal of Law, Economics, and Organization* 19: 401–444.
Arruñada, Benito and Veneta Andonova. 2004. "Cognition, Judges and Market Order," Universitat Pompeu Fabra, Economics and Business Working Paper Series 768, July (http://www.econ.upf.es/cgi-bin/onepaper?768, accessed September 2, 2004).
Backhaus, Jürgen G. 1998. "Efficient Statute Law" in Peter Newman (ed.), *The New Palgrave Dictionary of Economics and the Law*, Vol. 2. London: Macmillan, pp. 24–28.
Bailey, Martin and Paul H. Rubin. 1994. "A Positive Theory of Legal Change". *International Review of Law and Economics* 14: 467–477.
Beck, Thorsten, Asli Demirgüç-Kunt, and Ross Levine. 2003. "Law and Finance: Why Does Legal Origin Matter?" *Journal of Comparative Economics* 31: 653–675.
Benson, Bruce L. 1989. "The Spontaneous Evolution of Commercial Law". *Southern Economic Journal* 55: 644–661.
Benson, Bruce L. 1998. "Evolution of Commercial Law" in Peter Newman (ed.), *The New Palgrave Dictionary of Economics and the Law*, Vol. 2. London: Macmillan, pp. 88–93.
Berkowitz, Daniel, Katerina Pistor, and Jean-Francois Richard. 2001. "Economic Development, Legality and the Transplant Effect". *European Economic Review* 47: 165–195.
Bernstein, Lisa. 1992. "Opting Out of the Legal System: Extralegal Contractual Relations in the Diamond Industry". *Journal of Legal Studies* 21: 115–157.
Bernstein, Lisa. 1996. "Merchant Law in a Merchant Court: Rethinking the Code's Search for Immanent Business Norms". *University of Pennsylvania Law Review* 144: 1765–1821.
Bernstein, Lisa. 2001. "Private Commercial Law in the Cotton Industry: Creating Cooperation through Rules, Norms, and Institutions". *Michigan Law Review* 99: 1724–1788.
Bork, Robert H. 1990. *The Tempting of America*. New York: The Free Press.
Caenegem, R. C. van. 1992. *An Historical Introduction to Private Law*. Cambridge: Cambridge University Press. (Translator: D. E. L. Johnston).
Carruthers, Bruce G. 1990. "Politics, Popery, and Property: A Comment on North and Weingast". *Journal of Economic History* 50: 693–698.
Clark, Gregory. 1996. "The Political Foundations of Modern Economic Growth: England 1540–1800". *Journal of Interdisciplinary History* 26: 563–588.
Cooter, Robert. 1994. "Structural Adjudication and the New Law Merchant: A Model of Decentralized Law". *International Review of Law and Economics* 14: 215–231.
Cooter, Robert and Lewis Kornhauser. 1980. "Can Litigation Improve the Law without the Help of Judges?" *Journal of Legal Studies* 9: 139–163.
Cooter, Robert and Thomas Ulen. 1997. *Law and Economics*, 2nd edn. Reading, MA: Addison-Wesley.
Crew, Michael and Charlotte Twight. 1990. "On the Efficiency of Law: A Public Choice Perspective". *Public Choice* 66: 15–136.
Danet, Didier. 2002. "Does the Code Civil Matter?". *European Journal of Law and Economics* 14: 215–225.
Demsetz, Harold. 1967. "Towards a Theory of Property Rights". *American Economic Review* 57: 347–359.
Djankov, Simeon, Rafael La Porta, Florencio Lopez-de-Silanes, and Andrei Shleifer. 2002. "The Regulation of Entry". *Quarterly Journal of Economics* 117: 1–37.
Djankov, Simeon, Rafael La Porta, Florencio Lopez-de-Silanes, and Andrei Shleifer. 2003. "Courts". *Quarterly Journal of Economics* 118: 453–517.
Doyle, William. 1996. *Venality: The Sale of Offices in Eighteenth-Century France*. Oxford: Clarendon Press.

Duman, Daniel. 1982. *The Judicial Bench in England 1727–1875: The Reshaping of a Professional Elite*. London: Royal Historical Society.
Ellickson, Robert C. 1991. *Order without Law: How Neighbors Settle Disputes*. Cambridge, MA: Harvard University Press.
Epstein, Stephen R. 2000. *The Rise of States and Markets in Europe, 1300–1750*. London: Routledge.
Faure, Michael. 2001. "Tort Liability in France: An Introductory Economic Analysis" in Bruno Deffains and Thierry Kirat (eds.), *Law and Economics in Civil Law Countries*, The Economics of Legal Relationships Series, Vol. 6. Amsterdam: Elsevier Science, pp. 169–181.
Garoupa, Nuno. 2001. "An Economic Analysis of Criminal Systems in Civil Law Countries" in Bruno Deffains and Thierry Kirat (eds.), *Law and Economics in Civil Law Countries*, The Economics of Legal Relationships Series, Vol. 6. Amsterdam: Elsevier Science, pp. 199–215.
Greif, Avner, Paul Milgrom and Barry R. Weingast. 1994. "Coordination, Commitment and Enforcement: The Case of the Merchant Guild". *Journal of Political Economy* 102: 745–776.
Harnay, Sophie. 2002. "Was Napoleon a Benevolent Dictator? An Economic Justification for Codification". *European Journal of Law and Economics* 14: 237–251.
Hayek, Friedrich A. 1960. *The Constitution of Liberty*. South Bend: Gateway Editions Ltd.
Hoffmann, Philip T., Gilles Postel-Vinay and Jean-Laurent Rosenthal. 2000. *Priceless Markets: The Political Economy of Credit in Paris, 1660–1870*. Chicago, IL: University of Chicago Press.
Ichino, Andrea, Michele Polo and Enrico Rettore. 2003. "Are Judges Biased by Labor Market Conditions?" *European Economic Review* 47: 913–944.
Josselin, Jean-Michel and Alain Marciano. 2002. "The Making of the French Civil Code: An Economic Interpretation". *European Journal of Law and Economics* 14: 193–203.
Katz, Avery. 1988. "Judicial Decisionmaking and Litigation Expenditures". *International Review of Law and Economics* 8: 127–143.
La Porta, Rafael, Florencio Lopez-de-Silanes, Andrei Shleifer and Robert Vishny. 1997. "Legal Determinants of External Finance". *Journal of Finance* 52: 1131–1150.
La Porta, Rafael, Florencio Lopez-de-Silanes, Andrei Shleifer and Robert Vishny. 1998. "Law and Finance". *Journal of Political Economy* 106: 1113–1155.
La Porta, Rafael, Florencio Lopez-de-Silanes, Andrei Shleifer, and Robert Vishny. 1999. "The Quality of Government". *Journal of Law, Economics, and Organization* 15: 222–279.
La Porta, Rafael, Florencio Lopez-de-Silanes, Christian Pop-Elches, and Andrei Shleifer. 2004. "Judicial Checks and Balances". *Journal of Political Economy* 112: 445–470.
Landes, William M. and Richard A. Posner. 1987. *The Economic Structure of Tort Law*. Cambridge, MA: Harvard University Press.
Mahoney, Paul. 2001. "The Common Law and Economic Growth: Hayek Might Be Right". *Journal of Legal Studies* 30: 503–523.
Manne, Henry. 1997. "The Judiciary and Free Markets". *Harvard Journal of Law and Public Policy* 21: 11–37.
Mattei, Ugo. 1997. *Comparative Law and Economics*, Ann Arbor, MI: The University of Michigan Press.
Michelman, Frank I. 1980. "Constitutions, Statutes, and the Theory of Efficient Adjudication". *Journal of Legal Studies* 9: 431–461.
Milgrom, Paul R., Douglas C. North and Barry R. Weingast. 1990. "The Role of Institutions in the Revival of Trade: The Law Merchant, Private Judges, and the Champagne Fairs". *Economics and Politics* 2: 1–23.
Moorhouse, John, Andrew Morriss and Robert Whaples. 1999. "Economics and the Law: Where is There Consensus?" *American Economist* 43: 81–88.
North, Douglass C. 1981. *Structure and Change in Economic History*. New York: Norton.

North, Douglass C. and Barry R. Weingast. 1989. "Constitutions and Commitment: The Evolution of Institutions Governing Public Choice in Seventeenth-Century England". *Journal of Economic History* 49: 803–832.
North, Douglass C. and Robert P. Thomas. 1988. *The Rise of the Western World: A New Economic History.* Cambridge, England: Cambridge University Press.
Osborne, Evan. 2002. "What's Yours is Mine: Rent-Seeking and the Common Law". *Public Choice* 111: 399–415.
Paz-Ares, Cándido. 1995. "Principio de eficiencia y derecho privado" in *Estudios en homenaje a M. Broseta Pont*, Vol. 3. Valencia: Tirant Lo Blanch, pp. 2843–2900.
Pipes, Richard. 1999. *Property and Freedom.* New York: Vintage Books.
Posner, Richard. A. 1998. *Economic Analysis of Law*, 5th edn. (1st ed., 1973). Boston, MA: Little, Brown and Company.
Priest, George L. 1977. "The Common Law Process and the Selection of Efficient Rules". *Journal of Legal Studies* 6: 65–82.
Priest, George L. 1985. "The Invention of Enterprise Liability: A Critical History of the Intellectual Foundations of Modern Tort Law". *Journal of Legal Studies* 14: 461–528.
Roe, Mark J. 2002. "Corporate Law's Limits". *Journal of Legal Studies* 31: 233–271.
Rose, Carol M. 1988. "Crystals and Mud in Property Law". *Stanford Law Review* 40: 577–610.
Rubin, Paul H. 1977. "Why Is the Common Law Efficient". *Journal of Legal Studies* 6: 51–64.
Rubin, Paul H. 1982. "Common Law and Statute Law". *Journal of Legal Studies* 11: 205–223.
Rubin, Paul H. 2000. "Judge-Made Law" in Boudewijn Boukaert and Gerrit de Geest (eds.), *Encyclopedia of Law and Economics, vol. 5: The Economics of Crime and Litigation.* Cheltenham and Northampton: Edward Elgar, pp. 543–558. http://encyclo.findlaw.com/9200book.pdf, accessed May 18, 2003.
Shavell, Steven. 1995. "Alternative Dispute Resolution: An Economic Analysis". *Journal of Legal Studies* 24: 1–28.
Simpson, Brian. 1998. "English Common Law" in Peter Newman (ed.), *The New Palgrave Dictionary of Economics and the Law*, Vol. 2. Macmillan, London, pp. 57–70.
Sirks, Boudewijn. 1998. "Roman Law" in Peter Newman (ed.), *The New Palgrave Dictionary of Economics and the Law*, Vol. 3. London: Macmillan, pp. 356–363.
Swart, Koendraad W. 1980. *Sale of Offices in the Seventeenth Century.* Utrecht: Hes Publishers.
Taylor, George. 1967. "Noncapitalist Wealth and the Origins of the French Revolution". *The American Historical Review* 72: 469–496.
Terrebonne, Peter. 1981. "A Strictly Evolutionary Model of Common Law". *Journal of Legal Studies* 10: 397–407.
Tooby, John and Leda Cosmides. 1992. "The Psychological Foundations of Culture," in Jerome H. Barkow, Leda Cosmides, and John Tooby (eds.), *The Adapted Mind: Evolutionary Psychology and the Generation of Culture.* New York: Oxford University Press, pp. 19–136.
Wagner, Richard E. 1998. "Common Law, Statute Law and Economic Efficiency" in Peter Newman (ed.), *The New Palgrave Dictionary of Economics and the Law*, Vol. 1. London: Macmillan, pp. 313–317.
West, Mark. 2002. "Legal Determinants of World Cup Success". University of Michigan Law School, Working Paper 02–009. http://papers.ssrn.com/sol3/papers.cfm?abstract_id=318940, accessed April 27, 2003.
World Bank. 2004. *Doing Business 2004: Understanding regulation.* Washington DC: World Bank and Oxford University Press.
Zywicki, Todd. 2003. "The Rise and Fall of Efficiency in the Common Law: A Supply-Side Analysis". *Northwestern Law Review* 97: 1551–1633.

11. Legal Institutions and Financial Development

THORSTEN BECK and ROSS LEVINE

1. INTRODUCTION

A burgeoning literature finds that financial development exerts a first-order impact on long-run economic growth. Levine and Zervos (1998) show that banking and stock market development are good predictors of economic growth.[1] At the microeconomic level, Demirguc-Kunt and Maksimovic (1998) and Rajan and Zingales (1998) find that financial institutions are crucial for firm and industrial expansion. While disagreements remain, the bulk of existing evidence points to a strong finance-growth nexus.

The finding that financial development influences economic growth raises critical questions, such as why do some countries have well-developed growth-enhancing financial systems, while others do not? Why have some countries developed the necessary investor protection laws and contract-enforcement mechanisms to support financial institutions and markets, while others have not?

The law and finance theory focuses on the role of legal institutions in explaining international differences in financial development (La Porta, Lopez-de-Silanes, Shleifer, and Vishny, 1997, 1998, 2000a, henceforth LLSV). The first part of the law and finance theory holds that in countries where legal systems enforce private property rights, support private contractual arrangements, and protect the legal right of investors, savers are more willing to finance firms and financial markets flourish. In contrast, legal institutions that neither support private property rights nor facilitate private contracting inhibit corporate finance and stunt financial development.

The second part of the law and finance theory emphasizes that the different legal traditions that emerged in Europe over previous centuries and were spread internationally through conquest, colonization, and imitation help explain cross-country differences in investor protection, the contracting environment,

---

[1] Furthermore, King and Levine (1993a,b) show that bank development predicts economic growth. Panel investigations indicate that the relationship between finance and growth is not due to reverse causality (e.g., Beck, Levine, and Loayza (2000), Levine, Loayza, and Beck (2000), and Beck and Levine (2004). For a review of the literature, see Levine (1997, 2004).

and financial development today. More specifically, legal theories emphasize two inter-related mechanisms through which legal origin influences finance (Hayek, 1960). The "political" mechanism holds that (a) legal traditions differ in terms of the priority they attach to private property vis-à-vis the rights of the State and (b) the protection of private contracting rights forms the basis of financial development (LLSV, 1999). The "adaptability" mechanism stresses that (a) legal traditions differ in their formalism and ability to evolve with changing conditions and (b) legal traditions that adapt efficiently to minimize the gap between the contracting needs of the economy and the legal system's capabilities will more effectively foster financial development than more rigid systems (Merryman, 1985).

Countervailing theories and evidence challenge both parts of the law and finance theory. Many researchers accept that effective investor protection facilitates efficient corporate financing and growth-enhancing financial development, but reject the law and finance's view that legal origin is a central determinant of investor protection laws and financial development (Roe, 1994; Pagano and Volpin, 2001; Rajan and Zingales, 2003). Furthermore, while some scholars accept the importance of legal tradition in shaping the efficiency of financial contracting, there are sharp disagreements about which legal systems work best to promote the efficient evolution of the law (Rubin, 1982). Alternatively, some studies directly question the importance of investor protection laws by arguing that changes in investor protection laws did not drive the evolution of corporate ownership and financial development in the United Kingdom and Italy (Franks, et al., 2003; Aganin and Volpin, 2003).

Given debates about the role of legal institutions in shaping financial development, the remainder of the Chapter is organized as follows. Section 2 describes the law and finance theory along with skeptical and competing views.[2] Section 3 reviews empirical evidence on both parts of the law and finance view. That is, we assess (i) whether legal origins account for cross-country variations in property rights protection, support of private contractual arrangements, investor protection laws, and financial development and (ii) the degree to which cross-country differences in investor protection laws explain differences in corporate finance and financial development. Besides examining supportive and conflicting evidence on these two parts of the law and finance theory, we also summarize recent findings on the mechanisms—the political and adaptability mechanisms—through which law and finance may be related. Section 4 concludes.

---

[2] To qualify our approach, however, we recognize that many participants in the law and finance debate may not agree that the law and finance view is necessarily composed of the two parts mentioned above. This is not crucial for our review. We simply note that many contributors to the debate on the links between legal institutions and financial development examine (i) the impact of legal origin on property rights protection, support for private contractual arrangements, and investor protection laws, (ii) the impact of investor protection laws and their enforcement on financial development, or (iii) both. This review examines these different components.

2. Legal Theories of Financial Development

This section describes the law and finance theory. We devote considerable space to tracing the historical evolution of legal institutions because the law and finance theory stresses that historically determined differences in legal heritage continue to shape private property rights protection, investor protection laws, and financial development today. Furthermore, this section describes two mechanisms through which legal origin may influence the contracting environment: the political and adaptability mechanisms. Finally, we review countervailing views that question the law and finance theory.

Law, Enforcement, and Financial Development

The first part of the law and finance theory stresses that legal institutions influence corporate finance and financial development (LLSV, 1998). As LLSV (2000a) emphasize, the law and finance view follows naturally from the evolution of corporate finance theory during the past half century. Modigliani and Miller (1958) view debt and equity as legal claims on the cash flow of firms. Jensen and Meckling (1976) stress that statutory laws and the degree to which courts enforce those laws shape the types of contracts that are used to address agency problems. Furthermore, as summarized by Hart (1995), financial economists have increasingly focused on (i) the control rights that financial securities bring to their owners and (ii) the impact of different legal rules on corporate control. From this perspective, we may view finance as a set of contracts. Thus, a country's contract, company, bankruptcy, and securities laws, and the enforcement of these laws fundamentally determine the rights of securities holders and the operation of financial systems.

At the firm level, Shleifer and Vishny (1997) note both that inside managers and controlling shareholder are frequently in a position to expropriate minority shareholders and creditors and that legal institutions play a crucial role in determining the degree of expropriation. Expropriation may include theft, as well as transfer pricing, asset stripping, the hiring of family members, and other "perquisites" that benefit insiders at the expense of minority shareholders and creditors (LLSV, 2000a). The law and finance theory emphasizes that cross-country differences in (i) contract, company, bankruptcy, and securities laws, (ii) the legal systems' emphasis on private property rights, and (iii) the efficiency of enforcement influence the degree of expropriation and hence the confidence with which people purchase securities and participate in financial markets.

Within the broad vision that legal institutions influence corporate finance and financial development, there are differing opinions regarding the degree to which the legal system should simply support private contractual arrangements and the degree to which the legal system should have specific laws concerning shareholder and creditor rights. Coasians hold that the legal system should simply enforce private contracts. Effective legal institutions allow knowledgeable and experienced financial market participants to design a vast array of sophisticated private contracts to ameliorate complex agency problems (Coase, 1960; Stigler, 1964; Easterbrook and Fischel, 1991). For this to work effectively, however, courts must enforce private contracts impartially and have both the ability and willingness to read complex contracts and verify technically intricate clauses that trigger specific actions (Glaeser, et al., 2001, p. 853). Given the difficulty in enforcing complex private contracts, there are potential advantages to developing company, bankruptcy, and securities laws that provide a framework for organizing financial transactions and protecting minority shareholders and creditors. While standardization may improve efficiency by lowering the transactions costs associated with many financial market contracts, the imposition of too rigid a framework may curtail customization and thereby hinder efficient contracting.[3] Whether assuming a Coasian reliance on enforcing complex private contracts or an approach that augments the support of private contracts with company, bankruptcy, securities laws, etc., the law and finance view's first part argues that the degree of protection of private investors is a crucial determinant of financial development.

The Historical Development of Europe's Legal Systems

The second part of the law and finance theory stresses that a country's legal heritage shapes its approach to property rights, private contracting, investor protection, and hence financial development. Comparative legal scholars note that the world's major legal families were formed in Europe over many centuries and then spread internationally. Thus, we begin our discussion with Roman law.

Hayek (1960) notes that when Emperor Justinian had the Roman law compiled in the sixth century, he attempted to implement two substantive modifications. First, while Roman law placed the law above all individuals, the Justinian texts placed the emperor above the law. Second, Justinian broke with Roman law by attempting to eliminate jurisprudence. Roman law had developed over centuries on a case-by-case basis, adjusting from the needs of a small farmer community to the needs of a world empire with only a minor role left for formal legislation. Justinian changed this doctrine and "...asserted for himself a monopoly, not only over all law-making power, but over legal interpretations." (Dawson, 1968, p. 22). This "Justinian deviation" did not take root; jurisprudence continued to shape the law.

From the 15th century, France's legal system evolved as a regionally diverse mélange of customary law, law based on the Justinian texts, and case

---

[3] There may exist complex tradeoffs between law-making and enforcement conducted by the courts versus regulation. One difference is that courts enforce the law reactively, while regulators enforce laws proactively. For analyses of the conditions under which these different approaches work best, see Glaeser, Johnson, and Shleifer (2001) and Pistor and Xu (2002).

law (Dawson, 1968, p. 349). Three observations are notable. First France had a very fragmented legal system.[4] Second, although courts must have debated the appropriate application of conflicting Roman and customary law as new circumstances emerged, these deliberations generally occurred in private and without the same public, scholarly debates seen in Germany or England (Dawson, 1968, p. 286–302). Third, by the 18th century, there was a notable deterioration in the integrity and prestige of the judiciary. The Crown sold judgeships to rich families and the judges unabashedly promoted the interests of the elite and impeded progressive reforms.[5]

Unsurprisingly, the French Revolution turned its fury on the judiciary and quickly strove to (a) place the State above the courts and (b) eliminate jurisprudence.[6] Codification under Napoleon supported the unification and strengthening of the State and relegated judges to a minor, bureaucratic role. According to the theory underlying the French Civil Code, the legislature drafts laws without gaps, so judges do not make law by interpreting existing laws. The theory is that the legislature does not draft conflicting laws, so that judges do not make law by choosing between laws. The theory is that the legislature drafts clear laws so that judges do not make law by giving meaning to ambiguous laws. Like Justinian, Napoleon sought a code that was so clear, complete, and coherent that there would be no need for judges to deliberate publicly about which laws, customs, and past experiences apply to new, evolving situations.[7] Furthermore, this approach required a high degree of procedural formalism to reduce the discretion of judges in regulating the presentation of evidence, witnesses, arguments, and appeals (Schlesinger, et al., 1988). Thus, to reduce corruption and enhance the fair application of the law, France adopted both greater procedural formalism and more limited judicial discretion.

There are conflicting views on the success of the Napoleonic Code's goal of eliminating jurisprudence. Merryman (1985, 1996) argues that the Napoleonic doctrine was a temporary, largely theoretical "deviation" from two thousand years of a legal tradition built on jurisprudence. Indeed, the lead draftsman of the Code recognized explicitly that the legislature could not revise the Code sufficiently rapidly to handle efficiently the myriad of changing problems that arise in a dynamic nation. In contrast to theory, the French courts eventually built an entire body of tort law on the basis of Article 1382 of the Code Napoleon that states that one whose act injures another must compensate that person. In contrast to theory, French courts have used case law to recast the law of unjust

---

[4] Voltaire mocked it by writing, "When you travel in this Kingdom, you change legal systems as often as you change horses." (Quoted from Zweigert and Kötz, 1998, p. 80)

[5] See, Dawson (1968, p. 373). Also, while the Crown at times issued progressive reforms, the courts "... refused to apply the new laws, interpreted them contrary to their intent, or hindered the attempts of officials to administer them." (Merryman, 1985, p. 16)

[6] Robespierre even argued that, "the word jurisprudence ... must be effaced from our language." (Quoted from Dawson, 1968, p. 426)

[7] When the first commentary on the Code was published in 1805, Napoleon is said to have exclaimed, "My Code is lost!' (Quoted from Dawson, 1968, p. 387)

enrichment, alter the law on obligations, re-work the law of contracts regarding gifts, and change the system of administrative law (Dawson, 1968, 400–415). From this perspective, while the theory of the Napoleonic code rejected jurisprudence and embraced judicial formalism, practicalities in conjunction with a legal tradition grounded in jurisprudence produced in France a legal system that has increasingly employed judicial discretion over the last two centuries and thereby circumvented inefficient qualities of the Code.

Others disagree and argue that antagonism toward jurisprudence and the exaltation of the role of the state produced a comparatively static, rigid legal tradition.[8] The French situation encouraged the development of easily verifiable "bright-line-rules" that do not rely on the discretion of judges (Glaeser and Shleifer, 2002). While simple and clear, Johnson et al. (2000) argue that bright-line-rules and excessive judicial formalism may not allow judges sufficient discretion to apply laws fairly to changing conditions and therefore not support evolving commercial needs.

Turning to Germany, Bismarck—like Napoleon—unified the country (in 1871) and placed a high priority on unifying the courts through codification. Although Bavaria and Prussia codified parts of the law during the 18th century, it was Bismarck's decision in 1873 to codify and unify the whole of private law in Germany that led to the adoption of the German civil law in 1900.

The parallels between France and Germany's legal history, however, can be exaggerated. Unlike in France, German courts have published (since at least the 16th century) comprehensive deliberations that illustrated how courts weighted conflicting statutes, resolved ambiguities, and addressed changing situations (Dawson, 1968). Law faculties at German universities worked directly with courts and tried to reconcile emerging situations with the logic of the Justinian texts. Through active debate between scholars and practitioners, Germany developed a dynamic, common fund of legal principles that then formed the basis for codification in the 19th century.

Moreover, in contrast to the revolutionary zeal and antagonism toward judges that shaped the Napoleonic Code, German legal history sheds a much more favorable light on jurisprudence and explicitly rejected France's approach.[9] Thus, the German Code "was not intended to abolish prior law and substitute a new legal system; on the contrary, the idea was to codify those principles of German law that would emerge from careful historical study of the German legal system." (Merryman, 1985, p. 31)

Whereas the Napoleonic code was designed to be immutable, the *Bürgerliches Gesetzbuch* was designed to evolve. For instance, France technically denies judicial review of legislative actions, while Germany formally recognizes this power and German courts actively exercise it (Glendon, et al.,

---

[8] See, Posner (1973), Rubin (1977), and Priest (1977).

[9] The German legal scholar Karl von Savigny argued that the law of a people was a product of the history and culture of that people's development (Merryman, 1985, p. 30).

1982, p. 57). Similarly, in terms of adjudicating disputes involving the government, France's administrative courts are within the executive branch itself. In Germany, the judiciary handles these disputes. Further, the Court of Cassation in France was originally viewed as an institution to assist the legislature. It had powers to quash decisions, but not decide cases. This is different from the Bundesgerichtshof in Germany that can reverse, remand, modify, or enter final judgment on cases, and where the judicial decision-making process tends to be more openly debated.[10] Thus, while codification had a similar role in Germany and France in unifying the country and reasserting the power of the central state, Germany had a very different approach toward jurisprudence.

The Scandinavian Civil law developed relatively independently from the other traditions in the 17th and 18th centuries and is less closely linked with Roman Civil law than the French or German traditions (Zweigert and Kötz, 1988, henceforth ZK). Moreover, neither the construction, nor the subsequent evolution, of the Scandinavian Civil law has been used to eliminate jurisprudence and boost the role of the State relative to private investors to the same extent as in the French Civil law (LLSV, 1998).[11] While extensive, active scholarship examines differences between French, German, and British law, comparatively less effort has been devoted to understanding the functioning of the Scandinavian civil law tradition and its influence on the development of financial systems in Scandinavia.

The historical development of the British common law is unique both in terms of (a) the relationship between the State and the Courts and (b) jurisprudence. From 1066, the English law evolved based on the resolution of specific disputes and increasingly stressed the rights of private property. While landholding rights in England were originally based on William I's feudal system, the courts developed legal rules that treated large estate holders as private property owners and not as tenants of the king. Indeed, the common law at the dawn of the 17th century was principally a law of private property (e.g., Littleton, 1481, and Coke, 1628).

The English Common law asserted its independence from the State during the tumultuous 16th and 17th centuries, during the great conflict between Parliament and the English kings. The Crown attempted to reassert feudal prerogatives and sell monopoly rights to cope with budgetary shortfalls. Parliament (composed mostly of landowners and wealthy merchants) along with the courts took the side of the property owners against the Crown. While King James I argued that royal prerogative superseded the common law, the courts asserted that the law is king, *Lex, Rex*. This political struggle culminated in 1688, when the Stuarts were thrown out. This allowed the courts to place the law above the

---

[10] See Zweigert and Kötz (1998, p. 264) and Glendon, et al. (1982, p. 96–100, 123–133).
[11] Coffee (2001) points to the superior performance of the Scandinavian countries relative to other Civil Law countries and even to Common Law countries and explains this with the high level of social cohesion in these countries.

Crown and limit the Crown's power to alter property rights and grant monopoly rights.[12]

Besides the power of the law vis-à-vis the State, the Common law's history is also importantly different from France's in terms of jurisprudence and legal formalism. Unlike in Pre-Revolutionary France, the courts in England were frequently viewed more favorably and sometimes as supporters of progressive reforms, so that judges were afforded greater discretion. In terms of legal formalism, English law typically imposes less rigid and formalistic requirements on the presentation of evidence, witnesses, etc., and instead offers judges greater latitude (Schlesinger, et al., 1988). In terms of jurisprudence, the English common law tradition is almost synonymous with judges having broad interpretation powers and with courts molding and creating law as circumstances change. The common law is obsessed with facts and deciding concrete cases, rather than adhering to the logical principles of codified law. Thus, the popular dictum: "The life of the law has not been logic: it has been experience." (ZK, 1998, p. 181). Unlike the Napoleonic doctrine, judges continually—and as a matter of general practice—shape the law through their decisions.

The Spread of Europe's Legal Systems

The English, French, and German legal traditions spread throughout the world through conquest, colonization, and imitation. Napoleon secured the adoption of the Code in all conquered territories, including Italy, Poland, the Low Countries, and the Habsburg Empire. Also, France extended her legal influence to parts of the Near East, Northern and Sub-Saharan Africa, Indochina, Oceania, French Guyana, and the French Caribbean islands during the colonial era. Furthermore, the French Code heavily influenced the Portuguese and Spanish legal systems, which helped spread the French legal tradition to Central and South America. The English common law spread through colonization and conquest to all corners of the world. The Austrian and Swiss civil codes were developed at the same time as the German civil code and the three influenced each other heavily. In turn, Czechoslovakia, Hungary, Yugoslavia, and Greece relied on German civil law in formulating and modernizing their legal systems in the early part of the 20th century. The German Civil Code was not imposed but exerted a big influence on Japan. At the end of the 19th century, Japan looked toward Europe as it sought to draft a commercial code. While Japan considered the French civil code, Japanese legal scholars were attracted to the systematic theorizing of the German code and its emphasis on fitting the evolution of the law into a country's historical context (ZK, 1998, p. 296–302.) The Japanese commercial

---

[12] There are two additional related issues. First, England was unified during the formative period of the Common law. This reduced political incentives for codification. Second, English courts were a liberalizing force that helped dismantle the feudal system and protected the rights of landowners against the Crown (Hayek, 1960). Whereas the French Revolution sought individual rights through strict prohibitions on the discretion of judges, England found liberty through an independent and influential judiciary.

code of 1899 is squarely based on the German counterpart. Although Japan came under the influence of the Common law during the post World War II occupation period (especially in the area of public law), it is not uncommon to classify Japan as a German civil law country, particularly when focusing on Commercial and Company law. Similarly, the German code influenced the development of commercial law in Korea, especially through the Japanese occupation. During the early decades of the 20th century, China (and hence Taiwan) examined European law in seeking to improve the operation of their commercial law. China introduced civil codes in 1925 and 1935 that, except for family and inheritance law, were shaped by German civil law. Of course, China has its own ancient legal tradition and also experienced Mao and the Cultural Revolution. The Scandinavian legal system was not spread to any country outside Northern Europe.

While the subject of active debate, Merryman (1996) advances four interrelated reasons for why the exportation of the Napoleonic Code had more pernicious effects in French, Belgian, Dutch, Spanish and Portuguese colonies than in France itself. According to this view, the adoption of the French civil code has crippled the judicial systems of many French legal origin colonies and hindered their ability to develop efficiently adaptive legal systems.

First, the French rigidly imposed the Code Civil in its colonies even though there were—and remain—serious conflicts between the Code and local laws (ZK, 1998, p. 109–13).[13] Tensions between local law and the transferred doctrine may impede the efficient development and application of the law with negative implications for financial development (Berkowitz, Pistor, and Richard, 2002).

Second, when the French instilled the Code, they brought the theory of the Napoleonic doctrine with its antagonism toward jurisprudence and its reliance on judicial formalism to minimize the role of judges. The French did not also bring the practical knowledge of how to circumvent some of the negative attributes of the Code and create an efficient role for judges (Merryman, 1996).

Third, given the Napoleonic doctrine, judges frequently "... are at the bottom of the scale of prestige among the legal professions in France and in many nations that adopted the French Revolutionary reforms, and the best people in those nations accordingly seek other legal careers" (Merryman, 1996, p. 116). Consequently, it is more difficult to develop efficiently responsive legal systems if the courts do not attract the best minds. Also, the static theory of the Napoleonic doctrine may become self-fulfilling: the best minds choose other professions, which hinders efficient legal flexibility. As a consequence, the legislature will have a tendency to write "bright line laws" to limit the role of the

---

[13] England did not try to replace Islamic, Hindu, or unwritten African law and the flexibility of the Common law eased its transfer. For instance, the English courts in India were instructed to apply Islamic or Hindu law depending on the faith of the parties in cases of inheritance, marriage, caste, etc. In Africa, judges were to apply the English law only to the extent that local circumstances permitted and matters were to be decided by equity and good conscience as rendered necessary by local circumstances (ZK, 1998, 225–9). While somewhat chaotic, this arguably set the stage for the evolution of an independent, dynamic common law in the post-colonial era.

courts. As argued by Pistor et al. (2002, 2003), once a country adopts the "bright line" approach to law making, it is very difficult to change. Courts will not be challenged to develop legal procedures and methods to deal with emerging conditions. Thus, according to some scholars, these characteristics of the French law have worked to retard the development of efficiently adaptive legal systems that support financial development.

Fourth, France has a long history of avoiding open disputes about legal interpretation (Dawson, 1968). Moreover, Napoleonic doctrine formally inhibits open disputations by judges on how they weigh competing statutes, ambiguous laws, and past court decisions in deciding new cases. The exportation of this characteristic to French legal origin colonies, i.e., the absence of a legal culture of openly discussing the application of the law to evolving conditions, hindered the development of efficient legal systems around the world accordingly. From this perspective, French legal origin colonies imported a restrictive, formalistic legal doctrine under particular conditions that enhanced the probability that their legal systems would be less efficiently adaptable than Common and German civil law countries and even than the legal system in France itself.

From Legal Origin to Finance: Political & Adaptability Mechanisms

We now describe two mechanisms through which legal origin may influence financial development. The political mechanism is based on two premises. First, legal traditions differ in the emphasis they place on protecting the rights of private investors relative to the rights of the State. Second, private property rights protection forms the foundation for financial development. Thus, historically determined differences in legal origin can help explain existing differences in financial development according to this component of the law and finance view (LLSV, 1998).

Some scholars argue that the Civil law has tended to support the rights of the State, relative to private property rights, to a greater degree than the Common law with adverse implications for financial development. Indeed, La Porta, et al. (2003) find that in civil law countries, the State is less likely to grant judges tenure, give courts jurisdiction over cases involving the government, or permit judicial review of the constitutionality of laws. LLSV (1999, p. 231–2) state that a civil legal tradition, then, can be taken as a proxy for the intent to build institutions to further the power of the State. A powerful State with a responsive civil law at its disposal will tend to divert the flow of society's resources toward favored ends, which is antithetical to competitive financial markets. Furthermore, a powerful State will have difficulty credibly committing to not interfere in financial markets, which will also hinder financial development. Thus, the law and finance theory holds that Civil law countries will have weaker property rights protection and lower levels of financial development than countries with other legal traditions.

In contrast, the Common law has historically tended to side with private property owners against the State according to this view. Rather than becoming a tool of the State, the Common law has acted as a powerful counterbalance that promotes private property rights. Rajan and Zingales (2003) note that governments in Civil Law countries were more effective than governments in Common Law countries in expanding the role of government at the cost of financial market development during the Interwar period 1919–1939. They attribute this to the stronger role of the judiciary vis-à-vis the legislature in Common Law countries. Thus, the law and finance theory holds that the British Common law supports financial development to a greater degree than the Civil law systems.

The second mechanism linking legal origin with financial development is the adaptability mechanism, which is built on two premises. First, legal systems differ in their ability to adjust to changing circumstances. Second, if a country's legal system adapts only slowly to changing circumstances, large gaps will open between the financial needs of an economy and the ability of the legal system to support those needs.

An influential, though by no means unanimous, line of inquiry holds that legal systems that embrace case law and judicial discretion tend to adapt more efficiently to changing conditions than legal systems that adhere rigidly to formalistic procedures and that rely more strictly on judgments based narrowly on statutory law (Coase, 1960). Posner (1973) argues that while legislators consider the impact on particular individuals and interest groups when writing statutes, judges are forbidden from considering the deservedness of specific litigants and therefore more likely to render decisions based on objective efficiency criteria (Rubin, 1982, p. 205). Rubin (1977) and Priest (1977) hold that common law systems are more efficient than statutory-based systems because inefficient laws are routinely litigated and re-litigated pushing the law toward more efficient outcome. In contrast, Posner (1973) and Bailey and Rubin (1994) argue that statutory law evolves slowly and is subject to a greater degree of inefficient political pressures than the Common law.[14] If statutes are constantly playing "catch-up" and are constantly pushed in inefficient direction by the legislative process, then this will hinder efficient corporate finance and financial development.

Thus, while subject to countervailing views presented below, the adaptability channel predicts that French legal origin countries, albeit not necessarily France itself, have a lower probability of developing efficiently flexible financial systems than German civil law and especially Common law countries. The adaptability channel holds that the Common law is inherently dynamic as it responds case-by-case to the changing needs of society. This limits the opportunities for

---

[14] For example in the United States, corporate officers and directors have a legal responsibility to maximize firm value for shareholders. Macey and Miller (1993) argue that the efficiency justification for these broad fiduciary responsibilities is to fill in gaps because it is impossible to pre-contract for all contingencies. This gap-filling role of fiduciary duties can lower transactions costs and improve corporate governance by requiring directors to promote the interests of shareholder above their own interests. For example, in a legal system where judges do not got beyond the statutes, "...a corporate insider who finds a way not explicitly forbidden by the statutes to expropriate outside investors can proceed without fear of an adverse judicial ruling" (LLSV, 2000a, p. 9).

large gaps to grow between the demands of society and the law. Indeed, La Porta, et al. (2003) show that common law countries are more likely to admit judicial decisions as a source of law. In addition, Djankov, et al. (2003a) stress that differences in legal formalism also influence the adaptability of the law. They find that common law countries tend to have less legal formalism in terms of regulating the collection and presentation of evidence, requiring elaborate and extensive procedures throughout judicial processes, insisting on written documentation at every stage of the process, and setting rigid procedural requirements on communication between parties. In contrast, the Napoleonic doctrine's distrust of judges induces a reliance on judicial formalism. This hinders the flexibility of the legal system in many French law countries, with adverse implications on financial development. Furthermore, as noted, many legal scholars argue that the German law falls close to the Common law in terms of adaptability since it rejected the Napoleonic doctrine and instead maintained its historical roots in jurisprudence.

While the political and adaptability mechanisms are inter-related parts of the law and finance theory and while they both predict that legal origin shapes financial development, they make conflicting predictions regarding French versus German civil law countries. The political channel holds that the Civil law tradition—both French and German—tends to centralize and intensify state power and therefore takes a more wary stance toward the development of free financial systems than the Common law. In contrast, the adaptability channel stresses that Common law and German civil law countries have notably more adaptable legal traditions than French civil law countries.

The two mechanisms also make different predictions concerning the channels through which legal systems influence the development of financial markets. The political mechanism contends that State control of the judiciary produces a system that focuses more on the power of the State and less on the private contracting rights of individual investors than a legal system characterized by an independent judiciary. Thus, the political channel stresses that cross-country differences in the independence of the judiciary are critical for explaining cross-country differences in financial development. In contrast, the adaptability mechanism stresses that cross-country differences in the flexibility of the law are critical for explaining cross-country differences in financial development.[15]

One can overemphasize the differences between the political and adaptability channels, however. The political channel focuses on the power of the State while the adaptability channel highlights differences in the ability of legal systems to

---

[15] Proponents of the political channel argue that historically Germany had much more efficient institutions than France did. Citing Ertman (1997) and Finer (1997), LLSV (1998, 1999) note that Germany built a professional bureaucracy based on the military and professional civil servants, while France developed a patrimonial bureaucracy with strong links to political elites. Arguably, these differences have also worked to create German courts that are more independent from the State, more efficient at protecting private contracting rights, and less focused on the rights of the State than in France. Proponents of the legal-adaptability channel would counter that this cannot explain why other German legal origin countries, such as Korea and Japan have developed relatively efficient financial markets.

evolve with changing conditions. Jurisprudence, however, may be much less likely in a system where the State controls the judiciary than in a system where the judiciary enjoys greater independence (Damaska, 1986; Glaeser and Shleifer, 2002).

Skeptical Views Regarding the Law and Finance Theory

Many influential legal scholars and economists question each of the premises underlying the law and finance theory. There are disagreements about the comparative flexibility of the Common and Civil law traditions, doubts about the view that the common law places greater emphasis on private property rights protection than the Civil law, skepticism about classifying countries by legal origin, questions about whether legal origin is a fundamental determinant of financial development, and doubts about the central role of investor protection laws in promoting financial development.

Specifically, Backhaus (1997) and Blume and Rubinfeld (1982) argue that precedent can stymie the efficient evolution of the law. Indeed, Epstein (1975) and Rubin (1982) provide a rich set of examples, including the evolution of the law of property during 19th century and the design of private clauses in contracts, when statutory law changes were necessary to produce more efficient outcomes in the United States. As another example, English law has clung with remarkable tenacity to the principle that "only a person who is a party to a contract can sue on it." (ZK. 1998, p. 468) In contrast, the Continental countries granted greater rights to third parties through statutory changes. Furthermore, Lamoreaux and Rosenthal (2002) provide a fascinating comparison of the laws of incorporation and partnerships in the United States and France. They argue that the French civil law system responded more effectively to evolving economic conditions than the U.S common law system. Finally, Bentham (1789) noted that the Common law's lack of coherence hinders its ability to evolve efficiently.

Another line of criticism questions Posner's (1973) argument that the courts have better incentives to select socially efficient outcomes than the legislature. Galanter (1974) and Tullock (1980) argue that rich disputants and well-endowed special interest groups can litigate and re-litigate cases, which blurs Posner's (1973) delineation between the processes of legislation and litigation. Furthermore, the choice of litigation and legislation may be primarily a strategic, decision regarding which avenue offers the greatest probability of success. From this perspective, there is no reason to presume that Common or Civil Law systems will produce more efficient outcomes.

Research also questions whether Common law systems emphasize property rights relative to the rights of the State to a greater degree than Civil law systems. For instance Ekelund and Tollison (1980) and Rubin (1982) argue that while the courts in England sided with Parliament against the Crown's efforts to grant monopolies in 16th and 17th centuries, this should not be viewed as a general characteristic that Common law legal systems favor private property rights and competition more than Civil law systems. Arguing along similar lines,

Coffee (2000) argues that Civil law systems are not inherently against minority shareholder rights, but rather the law has evolved sufficiently in Civil law countries to protect minority shareholder effectively given the patterns of corporate ownership in those countries.

Furthermore, many question whether it is appropriate and analytically useful to categorize countries as simply having British, French, German, or Scandinavian legal origins. As stressed above, Dawson (1960, 1968) and Merryman (1985, 1996) stress than when the French legal system was exported to colonies around the world, it operated less effectively than in France itself. One may further refine the categorization of legal systems. For instance, Franks and Sussman (1999) describe differences in the adaptability of two Common law countries: the United Kingdom and the United States. Also, legal scholars study differences across the French civil law countries of Latin America. Along the same lines, Berkowitz, Pistor, and Richard (2002) stress that the manner in which national legal systems were initially transplanted and received, e.g., through conquest, colonization, or imitation, around the world is very important for economic development. They stress that the transplant process—not just whether countries are classified as having British, French, German, or Scandinavian legal origins—is important for establishing well-functioning legal systems. Thus, many observers question the usefulness of using legal origin to explain property rights protection, the efficient adaptability of legal systems, and hence financial development.

Some researchers question whether legal heritage is a crucial determinant of legal and financial institutions and instead stress that politics determines the degree of investor protection laws, the energy devoted to private contract enforcement, the extent to which legal systems emphasize the rights of property owners relative to the rights of the State, and hence the development of competitive financial markets (Pound, 1991; Roe, 1994; Pagano and Volpin, 2001; Rajan and Zingales, 2003; Haber, et al., 2003). From this perspective, those in power shape policies and institutions—including legal and financial institutions—to stay in power and enrich themselves. The elite may or may not favor financial development, which ultimately influences the operation of legal and financial institutions. This view does not reject the importance of legal institutions in shaping financial systems. Rather, it stresses the political roots of differences in legal and financial institutions.[16]

Skepticism about the central role of legal institutions in shaping financial development also emanates from those highlighting culture. Stulz and Williamson (2003) note that different religions have different attitudes toward the rights of creditors. In particular, the Catholic Church has historically taken a negative

---

[16] Glaeser and Shleifer (2002) model the evolution of legal institutions, while Glaeser and Shleifer (2003) show that legal and regulatory institutions may evolve together and sometimes substitute for each other depending on specific conditions. For broad discussions of the co-evolution of legal, regulatory, and political institutions see Olson (1993), North (1981, 1990), Djankov, Glaeser, LaPorta, Lopez-de-Silanes, and Shleifer (2003b), and Barth, Caprio, and Levine (2003). Easterly and Levine (1997) show that ethnic division may shape the wide range of institutions and policies.

stance toward the charging of interest and creditor rights. Similarly, the Qur'an prohibits the charging of interest, so that some countries still impose this prohibition. In contrast, according to this culture-religion view, the Reformation advanced a different religious attitude towards finance, whereby the payment of interest was considered a normal part of commerce, so that the rights of creditors were more naturally emphasized in countries dominated by Protestant religions. From this perspective, countries with a predominantly Catholic religious heritage would tend to have less developed credit markets and more poorly developed loan issuing financial institutions.

An additional line of attack comes from geography. The endowment view stresses that differences in geography and disease have critically shaped patterns of political, institutional, and economic development (Diamond 1997; Jones 1981; McNeill 1963; Crosby 1989; Engerman and Sokoloff 1997, 2002; Sokoloff and Engerman, 2000; Acemoglu, Johnson, and Robinson, 2001, 2002).

Acemoglu, Johnson, and Robinson (2001, henceforth AJR) base their theory of how endowments influence enduring institutions on three premises. First, AJR note that Europeans adopted different types of colonization strategies. At one end of the spectrum, the Europeans settled and created institutions to support private property and check the power of the State. These "settler colonies" include the United States, Australia, and New Zealand. At the other end of the spectrum, Europeans sought to extract as much from the colony as possible. In these "extractive states," Europeans did not create institutions to support private property rights; rather, they established institutions that empowered the elite to extract gold, silver, etc. (e.g., Congo, Ivory Coast, and much of Latin America). Second, AJR's theory holds that the type of colonization strategy was heavily influenced by the feasibility of settlement. In inhospitable environments, Europeans tended to create extractive states (AJR, 2001). In areas where endowments favored settlement, Europeans tended to form settler colonies. The final piece of the AJR theory of institutional development stresses that the institutions created by European colonizers endured after independence. Settler colonies tended to produce post-colonial governments that were more democratic and more devoted to defending private property rights than extractive colonies. In contrast, since extractive colonies had already constructed institutions for effectively extracting resources, the post-colonial elite frequently assumed power and readily exploited the pre-existing extractive institutions. AJR (2001, 2002), Beck, Demirguc-Kunt, and Levine (2003a, henceforth BDL), and Easterly and Levine (2003) provide empirical support for the view that endowments influence institutions, including financial institutions.

Other work questions the central role of investor protection laws in shaping the efficient flow of capital to corporations and overall financial development. For instance, Dyck and Zingales (2003) find that non-traditional corporate control mechanisms, such as an open, competitive media and a high degree of product market competition, are as important as statutory protection of minority shareholders in explaining the private benefits of controlling a corporation.

Furthermore, Guiso, et al. (2000) hold that "social capital" the informal rules that govern social interactions play a critical role in determining financial development in Italy. Similarly, Franks, et al. (2003) argue that implicit contracts enforced by informal mechanisms fostered small shareholder participation in financial markets in late 19th and early 20th century England. Johnson, McMillan, and Woodruff (2002a), however, note that while informal, relational contracting has been important in post-communist countries and can sustain old relationships, effective formal court systems are crucial in fostering new commercial relationships and boosting the overall level of trust in society.

3. Empirical Evidence on Law and Finance

In this section, we review the empirical evidence on the law and finance view. The first sub-section discusses evidence on the links between legal origin and financial development, investor protection laws, and private property rights protection. Next, we assess whether investor protection laws influence corporate valuations, corporate governance, and the operation of financial markets? The third subsection reviews emerging evidence on the mechanisms—the political and adaptability mechanisms—linking the law to financial development.

Legal Origin and Financial Development

To measure legal origin, many researchers follow LLSV (1998) in classifying a country as having either a British common law, French civil law, German civil law, or Scandinavian civil law based on the source of each country's Company or Commercial code. David and Brierley (1985) argue that commercial legal systems of most countries derive from these four major legal families. Reynolds and Flores (1989) provide information on the origins of national laws for over 100 countries. Using these legal origin dummy variables, researchers have initiated an energetic examination of the relationship between legal and financial institutions.

LLSV (1997, 1998) find that French civil law countries have the lowest levels of financial development even after controlling for the overall level of economic development. French civil law countries have smaller stock markets (as measured by market capitalization divided by GDP), less active initial public offering markets, and lower levels of bank credit as a share of GDP. These results are broadly consistent with the theories of law and finance discussed above.[17]

Empirical work also examines the connection between legal origin and specific laws governing the rights of external investors in firms. To the extent that the legal system protects shareholders and creditors, this may tend to (1) foster

---

[17] Additional work further shows that Common law countries have significantly greater Market Capitalization than the combined group of civil law countries (BDL, 2001).

better functioning stock and debt markets and (2) facilitate the flow of capital to firms.

Consider LLSV's (1998) **Shareholder rights** measure, which is an index aggregates the following six measures. The index is created by adding 1 when (a) the country allows shareholders to mail their proxy vote to the firms, (b) shareholders are not required to deposit their shares prior to the General Shareholders Meeting, (c) cumulative voting or proportional representation of minorities on the board of directors is allowed, (d) an oppressed minorities mechanism is in place, (e) the minimum percentage of share capital that entitles a shareholder to call for an Extraordinary Shareholders Meeting is less than the sample median (10 percent), or (f) shareholders have preemptive rights that can only be waived by a shareholders vote. Higher values indicate greater minority shareholder rights such that majority shareholders have less discretion in exploiting minority shareholders.

LLSV (1998) show that French civil law countries have lower levels of **Shareholder Rights**. LLSV (1997) and Levine (2003) go on to show that low levels of **Shareholder Rights** are associated with poorly developed equity markets. In contrast, Common law countries have high levels of **Shareholder Rights** with correspondingly high levels of equity market development. Furthermore, LLS (2003) find laws and regulations that force information disclosure and that foster private enforcement through strict liability rules enhance market development. Moreover, LLS (2003) show that French legal origin countries tend to have relatively weak liability rules and weak information disclosure requirements, such that the legal and regulatory environment in French civil law countries tends to emphasize private contract enforcement less effectively than in Common law countries.

Next, consider **Creditor Rights**, which is an index that is formed by adding one when (a) the country imposes restrictions, such as creditors consent or minimum dividends, to file for reorganization, (b) secured creditors are able to gain possession of their security once the reorganization petition has been approved (no automatic stay on assets), (c) secured creditors are ranked first in the distribution of the proceeds that result from the disposition of the assets of a bankrupt firm, and (d) the debtor does not retain the administration of its property pending the resolution of the reorganization. Higher values indicate greater creditor rights.

As shown by LLSV (1998), countries with a Common law tradition tend to have greater **Creditor Rights** than French civil law countries. Furthermore, LLSV (1997) and Levine (1998, 1999) show that greater **Creditor Rights** are positively associated with financial intermediary development.

Furthermore, Levine (1998, 1999) and Levine, Loayza, and Beck (2000) empirically trace the chain of connections from legal origin to financial development to economic growth. Specifically, legal origin importantly accounts for cross-country differences in the development of bank and stock markets and these differences in financial development explain international differences in long-run rates of economic growth. Thus, a growing body of work suggests that legal institutions influence the operation of financial institutions with substantial implications for corporate finance and investment decisions, along with the overall rate of economic growth.

Nevertheless, legal origin is certainly not the whole story. Rajan and Zingales (2003) argue that financial development does not always evolve monotonically over time and that cross-country differences in financial development also change materially over time. Thus, time-invariant factors such as legal origin cannot fully explain time-variation in the relative levels of financial development across countries. Rajan and Zingales (2003) stress the important role of political forces in shaping policies toward financial markets and intermediaries and hence the development of financial systems. Pistor, et al. (2002, 2003) disagree with Rajan and Zingales (2003) in the area of corporate law and argue that even acute political changes in Germany, France, and England during the 20th century did not substantively alter the evolution of corporate law.

While recognizing the limitations of the law and finance theory's ability to explain intertemporal changes in relative levels of financial development across countries, recent research has conducted a number of robustness checks regarding the linkages between legal origin and financial development. Levine, (1998, 1999, 2003a), Levine, Loayza, and Beck (2000), and BDL (2003a) use different measures of financial development and also expand the set of countries to over 100. This research confirms that legal origin helps explain cross-country differences in financial development. In particular, French civil law countries, though not France itself, tend to have particularly low levels of equity market development. To the extent that competitive securities markets rely more on legal institutions than banks, these results are very consistent with theories that suggest a strong link between legal institutions and financial development.

Furthermore, BDL (2003a) show that French civil law countries tend to have lower levels of private property rights protection. Again, this is consistent with the view that French legal origin countries place comparatively less emphasis on the rights of private property holders than countries with a Common or German civil law tradition.

While still in its nascent stages, research is also running statistical horse races between theories that stress the role of legal institutions and alternative theories. As noted earlier, an influential body of works stresses the dominating role of political forces in shaping financial development. While it is extraordinarily difficult to measure cross-country differences in political institutions, BDL (2003a) make an initial attempt to control for differences in political systems in assessing the law and finance relationship. They include measures of the degree of competitive and executive elections, measures of the number of influential veto players in legislative process, and an overall index of national openness based on trade openness. BDL (2003a) continue to find that legal origin explains differences in equity market development, banking sector development, and the level of private property rights protection even when controlling for these proxies for characteristics of the political environment.

BDL (2003a) also control for natural resource endowments and religion in examining the robustness of the connection between legal heritage and financial development. To control for religion, BDL (2003a) measure the percentage of the population adhering to different religious faiths. To proxy for natural resource endowments, BDL (2003a) use the AJR measures of settler mortality. As a further check, they use measures of each country's latitude (the absolute value of either the geographic mean of the country or of the country's capital city) as an exogenous proxy for the degree to which the country is in a tropic environment. They find that endowments importantly explain cross-country differences in financial institutions, confirming the AJR and Engerman and Sokoloff (1997) theories of institutional development. Nevertheless, legal origin continues to explain property rights differences and stock market development even when controlling for endowments.

Similarly, Stulz and Williamson (2003) examine the impact of legal origin on financial development while controlling for cross-country differences in culture, as measured by the dominant religion in each country. They find that legal origin is more important than religion in explaining laws protecting equity holders, while religious differences are more closely tied to laws protecting creditors. Thus, while culture matters, legal origin still explains cross-country differences in financial development, especially equity market development, after controlling for differences in religious heritage.

Investor Protection Laws, Corporate Finance, and Financial Development

We now examine the empirical evidence concerned with the relationship between investor protection laws and the corporate financing decisions of firms and the operation of financial markets. This subsection discusses this more microeconomic-based work.

Recent work suggests that legal institutions influence the valuation of firms and banks and hence the cost of capital. Claessens, et al., (2002), LLSV (2002), and Caprio, et al, (2003) find that stronger investor protection laws, as measured by higher values of the **Shareholder Rights** indicator defined above, tend to enhance corporate valuations. Furthermore, LLSV (2000b) show that countries with strong **Shareholder Rights** are able to force firms to disgorge cash and pay higher dividends. This evidence is consistent with the view that investor protection laws influence corporate governance with measurable implications on stock prices and dividend policies. In related work Johnson, McMillan, and Woodruff (2002b) show that countries with strong private property rights protection tend to have firms the reinvest their profits, but where property rights are relatively weakly enforced, entrepreneurs are less inclined to invest retained earnings.

Empirical analyses also find a strong connection between investor protection laws and both ownership concentration and the private benefits of corporate control. The data are consistent with the view that stronger legal protection of investor rights makes minority investors more confident about their investments, which reduces the need for firms (Claessens, et al., 2000; LLS, 1999) and banks (Caprio, et al., 2003) to use concentrated ownership as a mechanism for alleviating corporate governance problems. Furthermore, Dyck and Zingales (2003) and Zingales (1994) show that greater statutory protection of minority shareholder rights and more effective legal enforcement of those rights lowers the private benefits of controlling a corporation.

Legal institutions also influence the ability of firms to raise capital. Thus, laws may influence the degree to which firms operate at financially constrained levels. Kumar, Rajan, and Zingales (2001) and Beck, Demirguc-Kunt and Maksimovic (2002) find that countries with legal institutions that more effectively protect property rights tend to have larger firms. This is consistent with the law and finance theory that in countries with better legal institutions, firms are less constrained by retained earnings and operate at more efficient scales.

Recent work has also drawn a connection between legal institutions and the efficiency of equity markets. Morck, Yeung, and Yu (2000) examine the relationship between legal institutions, the availability and precision of information on firms, and the efficiency of stock prices. They find that the degree to which legal institutions protect private property rights and the rights of minority shareholders help account for cross-country differences in stock market synchronicity. That is, in countries where legal institutions do not protect shareholders effectively, domestic stock prices move together, so there is less information in individual stock prices.

The impact of legal institutions on corporate finance may also play a role in explaining the Asian financial crisis. Johnson, Boone, Breach, and Friedman (2000) show that weak legal institutions—legal institutions that do not effectively support the claims of outside investors—help account for cross-country differences in stock market declines and exchange rate depreciations during the Asian crisis. Specifically, if managers expropriate more firm assets as expected rates of return on firm investment fall, then adverse shocks to the economy will lead to greater expropriation, larger stock declines, and bigger incipient capital outflows in countries with weak legal institutions. Johnson, Boone, Breach, and Friedman (2000) find evidence consistent with this legal institution explanation of exchange rate and stock price declines.

Wurgler (2000) and Beck and Levine (2002) examine whether legal institutions influence the allocation of capital across firms and industries. They show that legal institutions influence the efficiency with which financial systems reallocate capital across industries. Specifically, countries with legal institutions that define and enforce strong rights for small, outside investors more effectively reallocate the flow of finance toward growing firms and away from declining firms. Thus, well-functioning legal systems boost the efficiency with which financial systems allocate capital.

Also, Demirguc-Kunt and Maksimovic (1998) show that countries with legal institutions that protect outside investors tend to create better functioning financial systems that fund faster growing firms. Claessens and Laeven (2003) show that legal rules regarding investor protection influence the types of firms that get financed. Specifically, in countries with strong investor protection laws, firms with less collateral have an easier time getting external finance than similar firms in countries with poorly functioning legal institutions. Furthermore, building on Rajan and Zingales (1998), Beck and Levine (2002) show that the efficiency of legal institutions increases the availability of financing to industries and the creation of new establishments. Along these lines, Demirguc-Kunt and Levine (2001), Beck and Levine (2002), Demirguc-Kunt and Maksimovic (2002), and Levine (2002) provide empirical support for the view advanced by LLSV (2000a) that the legal approach is a more fruitful way to explain corporate performance than the more conventional distinction between bank-based and market-based financial systems. Thus, national legal institutions are critically important in determining the supply of capital available for corporate investment.

Some careful case-studies, however, challenge the importance of investor protection laws. For example, Franks et al. (2003) trace the history of investor protection laws and corporate ownership in the United Kingdom. They note that in a landmark court case, Foss v. Harbottle (1843), the judge found that no individual shareholder could sustain an action against the company, thereby rejecting the notion of minority investor protection. Not until 1948 did Parliament begin to enact limited legislation to protect minority shareholders and Franks, et al. (2003) stress that it was not until 1980 that Parliament enacted strong minority shareholder rights statutes. According to the law and finance view, the U.K. should have had comparatively inactive equity markets and concentrated ownership in the 19th and early 20th centuries and then had more dispersed ownership and greater equity market activity after 1948 and especially after 1980. The evidence, however, is at best mixed. Ownership concentration was similar in 1900 and 1960, which is not consistent with the law and finance prediction, but market liquidity did jump substantially with enactment of stronger shareholder rights legislation.

Similarly, Aganin and Volpin (2003) argue that the history of investor protection laws and corporate ownership in Italy during the twentieth century do not provide strong support for the law and finance view. They hold that investor protection laws were weak at the beginning of the century, did not change much after World War II, but were strengthened after 1974 and especially after 1990. They note that the law and finance theory predicts a fall in corporate ownership concentration after 1974 as stronger investor protection laws make small shareholder more confident about their investments. But, corporate ownership concentration did not fall after 1974; it rose, and ownership concentration was more diffuse at the beginning of the 20th century than at the start of the 21st century. Aganin and Volpin (2003), therefore, question the applicability of the law and finance view in Italy and stress the importance of considering politics in explaining corporate ownership and the evolution of investor protection laws.

Law and Finance Theory's Political and Adaptability Mechanisms

While an exploding body of research examines (a) the links between legal origin and investor protection and financial development and (b) the links between investor protection laws and corporate financing efficiency, researchers are only beginning to examine the mechanisms through which legal origin operates. The political channel postulates that legal traditions differ in terms of the priority they give to private property rights relative to the rights of the state. The adaptability channel stresses that legal traditions differ in terms of their responsiveness to changing socioeconomic conditions.

BDL (2003b,c) study whether legal origin influences financial development primarily through the political or adaptability mechanism by exploiting the data assembled by Djankov et al. (2003a) and La Porta, Lopez-de-Silanes, Pop-Eleches, and Shleifer. (2003). To proxy for the political channel, **Supreme Court Power** is a dummy variable that takes on the value one if Supreme Court Judges have both life-long tenure and power over administrative cases, and zero otherwise. The political channel predicts that (i) Civil law countries are less likely to grant **Supreme Court Power** and (ii) **Supreme Court Power** will be positively associated with private property rights protection and financial development. To proxy for the adaptability channel, **Case Law** is a dummy variable that indicates whether judicial decisions are a source of law. The adaptability channel predicts that (a) Common law and German civil law countries are more likely to admit judicial decisions as a source of law than French law countries and (b) countries in which judicial decisions are a source of law will adapt more efficiently to changing financial conditions.

BDL (2003b) find that, French and German civil law countries have significantly less **Supreme Court Power** than British common law countries. This is consistent with the view that the State grants less independence in a civil law tradition than in a common law system. The results also indicate that French civil law countries have significantly less **Case Law**—i.e., a significantly smaller role for judicial decisions as a source of law—than in German civil law or British common law. This is consistent with the view that German civil and British common legal traditions rely more on jurisprudence than French civil law systems.

BDL (2003b) next examine whether the proxy for the political channel or the proxy for the adaptability channel is better able to account for international differences in stock market, financial intermediary, and private property rights development. They use two-stage least squares, where the instrumental variables are legal origin dummy variables.

The results provide support for the adaptability channel but not the political channel. Specifically, the political channel predicts that **Supreme Court Power** will enter positively: less State control of the courts will translate into greater financial development. In contrast, however, **Supreme Court Power** enters either insignificantly, or negatively. Instead, the data are consistent with the adaptability channel: **Case Law** is positively associated with stock market development, bank development, and private property rights protection.

Research also focuses on judicial formalism, which is related to the adaptability mechanism. Excessive formalism may slow legal processes, increase legal costs, and hinder the ability of courts to arrive at fair judgments due to the rigid adherence to bright-line-rules (Johnson et al., 2000; Djankov et al., 2003a; Glaeser and Shleifer, 2002). Indeed, Djankov, et al. (2003a) construct an index of legal formalism that measures the need for legal professionals, written documents, statutory justification, the statutory codification of evidence, and the formal procedural steps associated with legal processes. They find that legal formalism is lower in common law countries and that less legal formalism is associated with shorter proceedings and less corruption.

In terms of finance, Acemoglu and Johnson (2003) examine the impact of legal formalism on financial development using legal origin as an instrumental variable. Although legal formalism is not linked with banking sector development, they find that the exogenous component of legal formalism is associated with stock market development. Greater legal formalism lowers stock market development, which is consistent with the adaptability mechanism.

4. Conclusions

A rapidly growing body of research examines the role of legal institutions in explaining financial development. The law and finance theory holds that (i) historically determined differences in legal tradition influence national approaches to private property rights protection, the support of private contractual arrangements, and the enactment and enforcement of investor protection laws and (ii) these resultant legal institutions shape the willingness of savers to invest in firms, the effectiveness of corporate governance, and the degree of financial market development. Each of the components of the law and finance theory is being dissected, critiqued, and evaluated from a broad array of perspectives. Many economists, legal scholars, political scientists, and historians are questioning, testing and modifying the law and finance theory. This promises to be an exciting and important area of inquiry in coming years.

Acknowledgements

We have received very helpful guidance from Mary M. Shirley, Andrei Shleifer, and three anonymous referees. All remaining errors and omissions, however, are our responsibility. This chapter's findings, interpretations, and conclusions are entirely those of the authors and do not necessarily represent the views of the World Bank, its Executive Directors, or the countries they represent.

References

Acemoglu, Daron and Simon Johnson. 2003. "Unbundling Institutions: Law versus Politics". Unpublished MIT mimeo.
Acemoglu, Daron, Simon Johnson, and James A. Robinson. 2001. "The Colonial Origins of Comparative Development: An Empirical Investigation". *American Economic Review* 91: 1369–1401.

Acemoglu, Daron, Simon Johnson, and James A. Robinson. 2002. "Reversal of Fortunes: Geography and Institutions in the Making of the Modern World Income Distribution". *Quarterly Journal of Economics* 117: 1133–1192.

Aganin, Alexander and Paolo Volpin. 2003. "History of Corporate Ownership in Italy". London Business School mimeo.

Bailey, Martin J. and Paul H. Rubin. 1994. "A Positive Theory of Legal Change". *International Review of Law and Economics* 14: 467–477.

Backhaus, Jurgen G. 1998. "Efficient Statute Law" in Peter Newman (ed.), *New Palgrave Dictionary of Economics and Law*. London: MacMillan, pp. 24–28.

Barth, James, Gerard Caprio, and Ross Levine. 2004. "Bank Supervision and Regulation: What Works Best?" *Journal of Financial Intermediaries*, forthcoming.

Beck, Thorsten, Asli. Demirgüç-Kunt, and Ross Levine. 2005. "Law and Firms". *Access to Finance American Law and Economic Review*, forthcoming.

Beck, Thorsten, Asli Demirgüç-Kunt, and Ross Levine. 2003b. "Law and Finance. Why Does Legal Origin Matter?" *Journ. of Comp. Econ.* 31: 653–675.

Beck, Thorsten, Asli Demirgüç-Kunt, and Ross Levine. 2003a. "Law, Endowments, and Finance". *Journal of Financial Economics* 70: 137–181.

Beck, Thorsten, Asli Demirgüç-Kunt, and Ross Levine. 2001. "Legal Theories of Financial Development". *Oxford Review of Economic Policy* 17: 483–501.

Beck, Thorsten, Asli Demirgüç-Kunt, and Vojislav Maksimovic. 2002. "Financial and Legal Institutions and Firm Size". World Bank unpublished working paper.

Beck, Thorsten and Ross Levine. 2002. "Industry Growth and Capital Allocation: Does Having a Market- or Bank-based System Matter?" *Journal of Financial Economics* 64: 147–180.

Beck, Thorsten and Ross Levine. 2004. "Stock Markets, Banks, and Growth: Panel Evidence". *Journal of Banking and Finance* 28: 423–442.

Beck, Thorsten. Ross Levine, and Norman Loayza. 2000. "Finance and the Sources of Growth". *Journal of Financial Economics* 58: 261–300.

Bentham, Jeremy. 1789. *An Introduction to the Principles of Morals and Legislation*. London: T. Payne & Sons.

Berkowitz, Daniel, Katharina Pistor, and Jean-Francois Richard. 2002. "Economic Development, Legality, and the Transplant Effect". *European Economic Review* 47: 165–195.

Blume, Lawrence E. and Daniel L. Rubinfeld. 1982. "The Dynamics of the Legal Process". *Journal of Legal Studies* 11: 405–419.

Caprio, Gerard, Luc Laeven, and Ross Levine. 2003. "Governance and Bank Valuation". National Bureau of Economic Research Working Paper, 10158.

Claessens, Stijn and Luc Laeven. 2003. "Financial Development, Property Rights, and Growth". *Journal of Finance* 58: 2401–2436.

Claessens, Stijn., Simeon Djankov, Joseph P.H. Fan, and Larry H.P. Lang. 2002. "Expropriation of Minority Shareholders in East Asia". *Journal of Finance* 57: 2741–2771.

Claessens, Stijn, Simeon Djankov, and Larry H.P. Lang. 2000. "The Separation of Ownership and Control in East Asian Corporations". *Journal of Financial Economics* 58: 81–112.

Coase, Ronald. 1960. "The Problem of Social Cost". *Journal of Law and Economics* 3: 1–44.

Coke, Edward. 1628 [1979 version]. *The First Part of the Institutes of the Laws of England*. New York: Garland Publishing, Inc.

Coffee, John C. 2001. "Do Norms Matter? A Cross-Country Examination of the Private Benefits of Control". Unpublished working paper 183, Columbia Law School, New York.

Coffee, John C. 2000. "Privatization and Corporate Governance: The Lessons from Securities Market Failure". Unpublished working paper 158, Columbia Law School, New York.

Cooter, Robert and Lewis Kornhauser. 1980. "Can Litigation Improve the Law without the Help of Judges?" *Journal of Legal Studies* 9: 139–163.

Cooter, Robert, Lewis Kornhauser, and David Lane. 1979. "Liability Rules, Limited Information and the Role of Precedent". *Bell Journal of Economics* 10: 366–381.

Crosby, Alfred W. 1989. *Ecological Imperialism: The Biological Expansion of Europe, 900–1900*. Cambridge: Cambridge University Press.
Damaska, Mirjan R. 1986. *The Faces of Justice and State Authority: A Comparative Approach to the Legal Process*. New Haven, CT: Yale University Press.
David. Rene and John E.C. Brierley. 1985. *Major Legal Systems in the World Today*. London: Stevens and Sons.
Dawson, John P. 1960. *A History of Lay Judges*. Cambridge, MA: Harvard University Press.
Dawson, John P. 1968. *The Oracles of the Law*. Ann Arbor, MI: University of Michigan Law School (Reprinted in 1986 by William S. Hein & Co., Inc. Buffalo, New York).
Demirgüç-Kunt, Asli and Ross Levine. 2001. *Financial Structure and Economic Growth: A Cross-Country Comparison of Banks, Markets, and Development*. Cambridge, MA: MIT Press.
Demirgüç-Kunt, Asli and Vojislav Maksimovic. 1998. "Law, Finance, and Firm Growth". *Journal of Finance*, 53: 2107–2137.
Demirgüç-Kunt, Asli and Vojislav Maksimovic. 2002. "Funding Growth in Bank-based and Market-based Financial Systems: Evidence from Firm Level Data". *Journal of Financial Economics* 65: 337–363.
Diamond, Jared. 1997. *Guns, Germs, and Steel: The Fates of Human Societies*. New York: W.W. Norton.
Djankov, Simeon, Edward Glaeser, Rafael La Porta, Florencio Lopez-de-Silanes, and Andrei Shleifer. 2003b. "The New Comparative Economics". *Journal of Comparative Economics* 31, forthcoming.
Djankov, Simeon, Rafael La Porta, Florencio Lopez-de-Silanes, and Andrei Shleifer. 2003a. "Courts." *Quarterly Journal of Economics* 118: 453–518.
Dyck, Alexander and Luigi Zingales. 2003. "Private Benefits of Control: An International Comparison." *Journal of Finance*, forthcoming.
Easterbrook, Frank and Daniel R. Fischel. 1991. *The Economic Structure of Corporate Law*. Cambridge, MA: Harvard University Press.
Easterly, William and Ross Levine. 1997. "Africa's Growth Tragedy: Policies and Ethnic Divisions". *Quarterly Journal of Economics* 112: 1203–1250.
Easterly, William and Ross Levine. 2003. "Tropics, Germs, and Crops". *Journal of Monetary Economics* 50: 3–39.
Ekelund, Robert B. and Robert D. Tollison. 1980. "Economic Regulation in Mercantile England: Heckscher Revisited". *Economic Inquiry* 18: 567–599.
Engerman, Stanley L. and Kenneth L. Sokoloff. 1997. "Factor Endowments, Institutions, and Differential Paths of Growth among New World Economies" in Stephen Haber, (ed.), *How Latin America Fell Behind*. Stanford, CA: Stanford University Press, pp. 260–304.
Engerman, Stanley L., and Kenneth L. Sokoloff. 2002. "Factor Endowments, Inequality, and Paths of Development Among New World Economies". National Bureau of Economic Research Working Paper #9259.
Epstein, Richard A. 1975. "Unconscionability: A Critical Reappraisal". *J. Law and Economics* 18: 293–315.
Ertman, Thomas. 1997. *Birth of the Leviathan*. Cambridge: Cambridge University Press.
Finer, Samuel. 1997. *The History of Government. Vol. I–III*. Cambridge: Cambridge University Press.
Franks, Julian, Colin Mayer, and Stefano Rossi. 2003. "The Origination and Evolution of Ownership and Control". Oxford Financial Research Centre Working Paper No. 1003-FE01.
Franks, Julian and Oren Sussman. 1999. "Financial Innovations and Corporate Insolvency". London Business School unpublished working paper.
Galanter, Marc. 1974. "Why the 'Haves' Come Out Ahead: Speculation on the Limits of Legal Change". *Law and Social Review* 9: 95–160.
Glaeser, Edward, Simon Johnson, and Andrei Shleifer. 2001. "Coase versus the Coasians". *Quarterly Journal of Economics* 116: 853–899.

Glaeser, Edward and Andrei Shleifer. 2003. "The Rise of the Regulatory State". *Journal of Economic Literature* 41: 401–425.

Glaeser, Edward and Andrei Shleifer. 2002. "Legal Origins". *Quarterly Journal of Economics* 117: 1193–1230.

Glendon, Mary Ann, Michael W. Gordon, and Christopher Osakwe. 1982. *Comparative Legal Tradition in a Nutshell.* St. Paul, MN: West Publishing Co.

Guiso, Luigi, Paola Sapienza, and Luigi Zingales. 2000. "The Role of Social Capital in Financial Development". National Bureau of Economic Research Working Paper, no. 7563.

Haber, Stephen, Armando Razo, and Noel Maurer. 2003. *The Politics of Property Rights: Political Instability, Credible Commitments, and Economic Growth in Mexico.* Cambridge: Cambridge University Press.

Hart, Oliver. 1995. *Firms, Contracts, and Financial Structure.* London: Oxford University Press.

Hayek, Friedrich A. 1960. *The Constitution of Liberty.* Chicago, IL: The University of Chicago Press.

Jensen, Michael C. and William H. Meckling, W. 1976. "Theory of the Firm: Managerial Behavior, Agency Costs, and Ownership Structure". *Journal of Financial Economics* 3: 305–360.

Johnson, Simon, Peter Boone, Alasdair Breach, and Eric Friedman. 2000. "Corporate Governance in the Asian Financial Crisis". *Journal of Financial Economics* 58: 141–186.

Johnson, Simon, John McMillan, and Chrirtopher Woodruff. 2002a. "Courts and Relational Contracts". *Journal of Law, Economics, and Organization* 18: 221–277.

Johnson, Simon, John McMillan, and Christopher Woodruff. 2002b. "Property Rights and Finance". *Amer. Econ. Rev.* 92: 1335–1356.

Johnson, Simon, Rafael La Porta, Florencio Lopez-de-Silanes, and Andrei Shleifer. 2000. "Tunneling". *Amer. Econ. Rev.* (Papers and Proceedings), 90: 22–27.

Jones, Eric L. 1981. *The European Miracle: Environments, Economies, and Geopolitics in the History of Europe and Asia.* Cambridge: Cambridge University Press.

Kaplow, Louis. 1992. "Rules versus Standards: An Economic Analysis". *Duke Law Journal* 42: 557–629.

King, Robert G. and Ross Levine. 1993a. "Finance and Growth: Schumpeter Might Be Right". *Quarterly Journal of Economics* 108: 717–738.

King, Robert G. and Ross Levine. 1993b. "Finance, Entrepreneurship, and Growth: Theory and Evidence". *Journal of Monetary Economics* 32: 513–542.

Kumar, Krishna B., Raghuram G. Rajan, and Luigi Zingales. 2001. "What Determines Firm Size?" University of Chicago unpublished working paper.

Lamoreaux, Naomi and Jean-Laurent Rosenthal. 2002. "Organizational Choice and Economic Development: A Comparison of France and the United States during the Mid-19th Century". University of California at Los Angeles mimeo.

La Porta, Rafael, Florencio Lopez-de-Silanes, Cristian Pop-Eleches, and Andrei Shleifer. 2003. "Judicial Checks and Balances," National Bureau of Economic Research Working Paper 9775.

La Porta, Rafael, Florencio Lopez-de-Silanes, and Andrei Shleifer. 2005. "What Works in Securities Laws?" *Journal of Finance*, (forthcoming).

La Porta, Rafael, Florencio Lopez-de-Silanes, Andrei Shleifer, and Robert W. Vishny. 2002. "Investor Protection and Corporate Valuation". *Journal of Finance* 57: 1147–1170.

La Porta, Rafael, Florencio Lopez-de-Silanes, Andrei Shleifer, and Robert W Vishny. 2000b. "Agency Problems and Dividend Policies around the World". *Journal of Finance* 55: 1–33.

La Porta, Rafael, Florencio Lopez-de-Silanes, Andrei Shleifer, and Robert W. Vishny. 2000a. "Investor Protection and Corporate Governance". *Journal of Financial Economics* 58: 3–27.

La Porta, Rafael, Florencio Lopez-de-Silanes, Andrei Shleifer, and Robert W. Vishny. 1999. "The Quality of Government". *Journal of Law, Economics, and Organization* 15: 222–279.

La Porta, Rafael, Florencio Lopez-de-Silanes, Andrei Shleifer, and Robert W. Vishny. 1998. "Law and Finance". *Journal of Political Economy* 106: 1113–1155.

La Porta, Rafael, Florencio Lopez-de-Silanes, Andrei Shleifer, and Robert W. Vishny. 1997. "Legal Determinants of External Finance". *Journal of Finance* 52: 1131–1150.

Levine, Ross. 1997. "Financial Development and Economic Growth: Views and Agenda". *Journal of Economic Literature* 35: 688–726.

Levine, Ross. 1998. "The Legal Environment, Banks, and Long-run Economic Growth". *Journal of Money, Credits, and Banking* 30: 596–620.

Levine, Ross. 1999. "Law, Finance, and Economic Growth". *Journ. of Financl. Intermed.* 8: 36–67.

Levine, Ross. 2003. "Bank-Based or Market-Based Financial Systems: Which Is Better?" *Journ. of Financl. Intermed.* 11: 398–428.

Levine, Ross. 2003. "Napoleon, Bourses, and Growth: With a Focus on Latin America" in Azfar Omar and Charles A. Cadwell (eds.), *Market Augmenting Government: Essays in Honor of Mancur Olson*. Ann Arbor, MI: University of Michigan Press.

Levine, Ross. 2004. "Finance and Growth: Theory and Evidence" in Philippe Aghion and Steven Durlauf (eds.), *Handbook of Economic Growth*. Amsterdam: North-Holland Elsevier Publishers, forthcoming.

Levine, Ross, Norman Loayza, and Thorsten Beck. 2000. "Financial Intermediation and Growth: Causality and Causes". *Journal of Monetary Economics* 46: 31–77.

Levine, Ross and Sara Zervos. 1998. "Stock Markets Banks and Economic Growth". *American Economic Review* 88: 537–558.

Littleton, Thomas. 1481 [1903 version]. *Littleton's Tenures in English*. Eugene Wambaugh, ed. Washington, DC: John Bryne & Co.

Macey, Jonathan R. and Geoffrey P. Miller. 1993. "Corporate Stakeholders: A Contractual Perspective". *University of Toronto Law Journal* 43: 401–427.

Mahoney, Paul. 2001. "The Common Law and Economic Growth: Hayek Might Be Right". *Journal of Legal Studies* 30: 503–525.

McNeill, William H. 1963. *The Rise of the West: A History of the Human Community*. Chicago, IL: University of Chicago Press.

Merryman, John H. 1985. *The Civil Law Tradition: An Introduction to the Legal Systems of Western Europe and Latin America*. Stanford, CA: Stanford University Press.

Merryman, John H. 1996. "The French Deviation". *The American Journal of Comparative Law* 44: 109–119.

Modigliani, Franco and Merton Miller. 1958. "The Cost of Capital, Corporation Finance, and the Theory of Investment". *American Economic Review* 48: 261–297.

Morck, Randall, Bernard Yeung, and Wayne Yu. 2000. "The Information Content of Stock Markets: Why Do Emerging Markets Have Synchronous Stock Price Movements?" *Journal of Financial Economics* 58: 215–260.

North, Douglass. 1981. *Structure and Change in Economic History*. Cambridge, MA: W.W. Norton and Company.

North, Douglass. 1990. *Institutions, Institutional Change, and Economic Performance*. Cambridge: Cambridge University Press.

Olson, Mancur. 1993. "Dictatorship, Democracy, and Development". *American Political Science Review* 87: 567–576.

Pagano, Marco and Paolo Volpin. 2001. "The Political Economy of Finance". *Oxford Review of Economic Policy* 17: 502–519.

Pistor, K., Keinan, Y., Kleinheisterkamp, J., and West, M.D., 2002. The evolution of corporate law. *University of Pennsylvania Journal of International Economics and Law* 23: 791–871.

Pistor, Katharina, Yoram Keinan, Jan Kleinheisterkamp, and Mark D. West. 2003. "Innovation in Corporate Law". *Journal of Comparatve Economics* 31: 676–694.

Pistor, Katharina and Chen-Gang Xu. 2002. "Law Enforcement under Incomplete Law: Theory and Evidence from Financial Market Regulation". London School of Economics Working Paper no. TE/02/442.

Priest, George L. 1977. "The Common Law Process and the Selection of Efficient Rules". *Journal of Legal Studies* 6: 65–82.

Posner, Richard A. 1973. *Economic Analysis of the Law*. Boston, MA: Little-Brown.

Pound, John. 1991. "Proxy Voting and the SEC". *Journal of Financial Economics* 29: 241–285.

Rajan, Raghuram G. and Luigi Zingales. 1998. "Financial Dependence and Growth". *American Economics Review* 88: 559–586.

Rajan, Raghuram G. and Luigi Zingales. 2003. "The Great Reversals: The Politics of Financial Development in the 20th Century". *Journal of Financial Economics* 69: 5–50.

Reynolds, Thomas H. and Arturo A. Flores. 1989. *Foreign Law: Current Sources of Basic Legislation in Jurisdictions of the World*. Littleton, CO: Rothman and Co.

Roe, Mark J. 1994. *Strong Managers Weak Owners: The Political Roots of American Corporate Finance*. Princeton, NJ: Princeton University Press.

Rubin, Paul H., 1977. "Why Is the Common Law Efficient?" *Journal of Legal Studies* 6: 51–64.

Rubin, Paul H., 1982. "Common Law and Statute Law". *Journal of Legal Studies* 11: 205–33.

Schlesinger, Rudolph B., Hans W. Baade, Mirjan R. Damaska, and Peter E. Herzog. 1988. *Comparative Law. Case-Text-Materials*. New York: The Foundation Press.

Sokoloff, Kenneth and Stanley L. Engerman. 2000. "Institutions, Factor Endowments, and Paths of Development in the New World". *Journal of Economic Perspectives* 14: 217–232.

Stigler, George J. 1964. "Public Regulation of the Securities Market". *Journal of Business* 37: 117–142.

Stulz, Rene and Rohan Williamson. 2003. "Culture, Openness, and Finance". *Journal of Financial Economy* 70: 313–349.

Tullock, Gordon. 1980. *Trials on Trial*. New York: Columbia University Press.

Weber, Max. 1958. *The Protestant Ethic and the Spirit of Capitalism*. New York: Charles Scribner's Sons.

Wurgler, Jeffrey. 2000. "Financial Markets and the Allocation of Capital". *Journal of Financial Economy* 58: 187–214.

Zingales, Luigi. 1994. "The Value of the Voting Right: A Study of the Milan Stock Exchange". *The Rev. of Financl. Stud.* 7: 125–148.

Zweigert, Konrad and Hein Kötz. 1998. *An Introduction to Comparative Law*. New York: Oxford University Press.

SECTION IV

Modes of Governance

12. A New Institutional Approach to Organization

CLAUDE MENARD

1. Introduction

Modern economic theory has long neglected, even ignored, the analysis of the different modes of organization that characterize a market economy. Notwithstanding the efforts of Alfred Marshall, one of its founding fathers, in identifying the properties of "business organizations" (1920, Book IV, chap. 10 sq.), standard microeconomics relied for decades on the concept of firms as production functions, an umbrella to the technologically determined combination of inputs.

This situation has changed under the influence of the celebrated paper by Coase on "The Nature of the Firm" (1937). There are now several alternative theories of organization in economics[1], with "transaction cost economics", "agency theory", "property rights theory", and a mix of resource-based and evolutionary perspective as the leading approaches.[2] Beyond serious divergences, this diversity of approaches is striking. The development of competing explanations reflects an increasing interest for the nature of organizations. This becomes particularly obvious when looking at the resurgence of the literature on the theory of the firm, but also at the booming number of papers on other modes of organizations, e.g., strategic alliances, joint ventures, etc. However, it also suggests that we still miss an integrated theory.

This chapter reviews what we have learned and some unsolved problems about alternative modes of organization. It does so by focusing almost exclusively on contributions rooted in the new institutional approach, which is

---

[1] The analysis of organization actually developed initially in other disciplines, generating a field of its own (Organization Theory).

[2] The hard core of these theories can be summarized as follows. Transaction cost focuses mostly on explaining the existence and properties of alternative modes of organization and the tradeoffs among them. Agency theory primarily examines incentives, i.e., the way a principal can induce agents to behave according to his interest. The property rights paradigm, "old" or "new", centers on ownership and the related allocation of decision rights as a determinant for understanding relationship-specific investments. The resource-based–evolutionary view explores mainly how organizations develop internal characteristics, such as routines and know-how, in order to deal with their environment. Gibbons (2004) proposes a slightly different typology.

primarily based on transaction cost economics. Notwithstanding significant intersections, I refer to alternative explanations only marginally. My analysis centers on modes of organization understood as institutional arrangements within which a transaction or a set of related transactions are decided upon and then implemented.

Therefore, the perspective adopted is in the continuation of Coase and Williamson. I assume the existence of alternative ways of organizing relationships among economic units in order to take advantage of the division of labor while economizing on bounded rationality and safeguarding parties against contractual hazards. Coase grouped these arrangements under the expression "institutional structure of production", while Williamson speaks of "mechanisms of governance".[3] In what follows, I capture the same ideas under the generic expression "modes of organization". My analysis is grounded in the golden triangle defining New Institutional Economics (NIE): transaction costs, contracts, and property rights. Transaction costs provide an explanation to the existence of alternative modes of organization as well as tools for understanding the characteristics of these arrangements. Contracts represent a focal point in NIE because of their role in relaxing the constraints of bounded rationality, fixing schemes of references for future actions, and checking on opportunistic behavior. Lastly, relatively well-defined property rights, and institutions for implementing them, form a prerequisite for making the transfer of rights possible and the trade-off among arrangements meaningful. Property rights thus affect contractual hazards and embed transactions into specific institutional environments. However, in what follows I focus exclusively on the micro level, with no specific analysis of embedding issues.

More precisely, this chapter reviews different modes of organization, from integrated firms to hybrids and markets. A clarification is needed here. 'Market' is not a simple term and this often creates confusion. On the one hand, it delineates a mode of organizing exchanges, with spot markets as the archetypical example, as opposed to exchanges arranged, say, within a firm. On the other hand, in a market economy 'market' designates the set of institutions that embed all modes of organization since they all have to go through or be confronted to markets at some point. In this chapter I focus mainly on the first and relatively narrow sense.[4]

My presentation is organized as follows. Section 2 summarizes the fundamental story behind the new institutional approach to organization. Section 3 reviews specific characteristics of firms and more generally of integrated organizations in a transaction cost perspective. Section 4 examines characteristics of a variety of arrangements, the hybrid forms, long ignored by economic theory and now at the forefront of a substantial body of research. Section 5 turns to the analysis of markets as a mode of organization and challenges the idea that

---

[3] Referring to John Commons, Williamson defines governance structures as ways to implement order for facing potential conflicts that could threaten opportunities to realize mutual gains (1996, Prologue, p. 12)

[4] More on this in section 5.

markets would be a "black box" in NIE. Section 6 concludes with an overview of some unanswered questions.

2. A Long Story Made Short

The development of a theory that allows identifying and characterizing alternative ways to organize transactions and that provides tools for analyzing the tradeoff among these modes remains a major contribution of NIE. The model emerged through several papers, mostly from the 1970s, in which Williamson played a key role in putting the pieces together.[5]

Some Landmarks

As it is now well-known, we owe to Coase (1937) the initial formulation of the problem, later summarized by Goldberg: "...which imperfect institutions should govern particular sets of transactions"? (1976, p. 46). Almost simultaneously, Chester Barnard published *The Functions of the Executive* (1938), in which he emphasized the role of "authority" as demarcating firms from markets. Simon (1951) modeled this idea in his paper on the employment relationship, while Arrow (1964) developed the role of control in hierarchies.[6]

Several publications built on these preliminaries in the 1970s, shaping the NIE approach to organization. Williamson initiated the movement with his paper from 1971, in which he put at the forefront the role of transaction costs in examining "Vertical Integration" and simultaneously pointed out contracts as a key organizational device.[7] The controversial paper by Alchian and Demsetz (1972) followed almost immediately, re-examining the Coasian approach and interpreting firms as a nexus of contracts. Arrow then pushed organizational issues higher on the agenda of economists with his *Limits of Organization* (1974). However, the publication of *Markets and Hierarchies* (1975) signaled a turning point. In this influential book, Williamson assembled disperse elements (including his previous contributions) into a coherent framework that linked transaction costs, contractual arrangements, and modes of organization, thus providing a model that remains at the core of the micro-analytical branch of NIE. Klein et al. (1978) closed the decade, focusing the attention on the role of specific investments and the risks of hold-up as the explanation to the choice of a mode of organization. A stream of research, and of controversies, was born.

---

[5] North took the leadership in the other branch of NIE, focused on the analysis of institutional environments.

[6] Others could be mentioned, e.g., Commons (1934), Hayek (1945), Malmgren (1961), Macaulay (1963), etc. I do not pretend to develop a historical review here, I only point out major landmarks.

[7] Amazingly, Davis and North published the book that imposed the other branch of NIE the same year.

The Analytical Framework: A Reminder

The heuristic model that summarizes these contributions and that has inspired most institutional analysis derives from Williamson (1975; 1985). Its underlying logic can be decomposed in the following sequence.[8]

The entry to the model is the central problem identified by Coase: how can agents take advantage of the division of labor without loosing the potential advantages of cooperation? The division of labor implies decomposition of tasks, which raises the issue of coordination, its organizational modalities, and their costs. Cooperation has to do with the behavior of agents and relates to incentives, that is, devices that can make agents with diverse goals efficiently complementing each other. The two concepts are distinct; even when cooperation prevails, coordination issues remain.

The argument supporting the model looks for the answer in the organization of transactions: in order to specialize, agents must be able to transfer rights on goods and services that they control. Therefore, economics must analyze and compare the different modes of processing and monitoring transactions. Two important consequences result: (1) there are various ways of organizing transactions, and choosing the right way is a fundamental issue; (2) all forms of organization are costly, and their respective advantages can be assessed only comparatively. In the post-Coasian world of positive transaction costs, all devices for transferring rights consume resources. For example the elaboration, negotiation, monitoring, and enforcement of contracts involve costs (Dahlman, 1979). Sources of these costs are twofold. First, transactions relate agents, so behavior matters. The model assumes agents who have a propensity to behave opportunistically. Opportunism can generate contractual hazards: costly safeguards need to be defined and implemented. Second, transactions develop in environments plagued with uncertainties. Although probabilities can be attached to some so that reallocation of resources can be specified ex-ante in Arrow-Debreu type contracts, Knightian uncertainty cannot be discarded: significant decisions remain noncontractibles. The combination of these two sources of hazards makes all devices (including technology) needed to support transactions flawed. At the micro level, these devices take shapes in different modes of organization. At the macro level, they are embedded in complex institutions required for arranging transfers of rights at acceptable costs (North, 1981; 1990).

In order to compare alternative ways of organizing transactions, the analysis focuses on the attributes of a transaction that determine variations in its

---

[8] This sequence reflects the Coase-Williamson approach to organization and differs from the Alchian-Demsetz story. Demsetz in particular has become increasingly critical to the framework presented here, going as far as considering the coasian approach as misleading (1988a; 2002). In his view, economies of scale, particularly those resulting from managerial knowledge, are the main explanation to why firms may overcome markets. However, he also challenges mainstream economists, arguing that they are wrong in seeing prices as a coordination mechanism: prices do not coordinate, they signal opportunities. The real trade-off would not be between markets and hierarchies, but between firms and households. With high transaction costs or without advantages to specialization, production would be carry on by households. Otherwise, firms organize production.

costs. Following Williamson (1985, chap. 3), most new institutionalists now routinely refer to three major characteristics: the specificity of assets involved, the uncertainties surrounding the transaction at stake, and the frequency of that transaction. *Specificity of assets* has been defined as the value of investments that would be lost in any alternative use. Highly specific assets create mutual dependence that opens the possibility of "hold-up", defined as the detrimental ex-post appropriation of the quasi-rent by one or some partner(s) (Klein et al., 1978; Alchian and Woodward, 1987, p. 114).[9] *Uncertainties* surrounding the organization of a transaction may also involve significant costs, whether it comes out of agents' behavior or organizational deficiencies; or from inadequate institutions or the state of nature. A third attribute, *frequency*, proved to be more difficult to enter into operation. According to Williamson, "The frequency of a transaction matters because the more often it takes place, the mode widely spread are the fixed costs establishing a non-market governance system" (1985, p. 76). However, there is little empirical research about frequency and that research show ambiguous effects on governance. Together, these three attributes determine the following relationship (signs show the predicted impact of a positive variation of each characteristic on transaction costs):

$$TC = f(AS, F, U) \atop + \; - \; + \qquad (1)$$

Of course these three variables are notoriously difficult to measure, and almost all the empirical literature avoids any attempts at measuring transaction costs directly, using instead a reduced-form model in which transaction costs are assumed to be minimized (see Joskow, chap. 13, and Klein, chap. 17 in this book).[10] Note also that all transactions involve the three variables.[10] What differentiates them are the level of each variable and their respective weight in the determination of transaction costs. It also makes the transactions complex, an important point for understanding why contracts are usually incomplete. Indeed, the more complex a transaction is, the more difficult and costly it is to encapsulate all its characteristics (ex-ante) and to predict all adaptations required (ex-post) in a contract; a simple framework may be preferable or even the only possible solution. Moreover, this complexity suggests ways to develop a dynamic approach: attributes combine differently over time, change at different speeds, and overlap with other transactions. Not much has been done in that direction yet.[11]

---

[9] Coase has vigorously challenged the significance of hold-up and it remains a highly controversial issue in NIE (see Klein, 1988; Coase, 1988; Coase, 2000; Klein, 2000; and Klein, 2004). More on this in section 6.

[10] In the continuity of Klein et al. (1978) and under the influence of the property rights approach, numerous studies consider appropriability as an important variable. However, there are few empirical tests available (see Whinston, 2003).

[11] One important dimension of transaction costs that may result from the variables above is the measurement problem emphasized by Barzel (1982). This is discussed in section 5, "The Costs of using market organization".

The next step in the reasoning connects transaction costs with modes of organization. If transaction costs vary with their attributes, how does this affect the choice of a mode of organization, or its comparative performance? Williamson linked the two pieces through what he called the "discrete alignment principle" (1985, Preface; and chap. 3 of this book): calculative agents operating in a competitive environment will adopt the mode of organization that fits comparatively better with the attributes of the transaction at stake. In doing so, Williamson provided a way for empirical studies to go around the difficulty of measuring directly transaction costs, making organizational form the dependent variable. If agents have incentives to reduce transaction costs so that these costs tend to be minimized, the attention then turns to the mode of organization chosen over alternatives in order to allow the development of contractual relationships that economize on bounded rationality while safeguarding transactions against opportunism.

One may also consider going further, using the transaction costs apparatus to better understand characteristics of the alternative modes of organizations and how that could explain the prevalence of one mode over others. For example, what properties of firms can make their administrative costs lower than those of a hybrid arrangement when the assets involved are highly specific? Transaction costs economics clearly overlaps with organization theory here. Not much has been developed in that direction yet, and there is even some debate about whether this is relevant or not.[12] The following sections explore these aspects further.

This short reminder summarizes the central argument of transaction costs analysis on the tradeoffs among modes of organization and their determinants. The underlying model provides the background to the rest of the chapter. In what follows, I assume the transaction cost explanation to the tradeoffs is known (see chap. 13 and 17 of this book), and I focus on the comparative properties of the different modes of organization.

3. FIRMS

The new institutional approach to firms and, more generally, to integrated "formal organizations" (Barnard, 1938) looks at them primarily as governance structures. This demarcates NIE from the neoclassical view, still prevailing in most textbooks, that represents firms as "a unitary profit-maximizing entity defined by a technologically determined production function" (Yarbrough and Yarbrough, 1988, p. 2).[13] NIE does acknowledge the role of technology in delineating the

---

[12] Demsetz (1988a), among others, considers transaction costs as strictly applicable to market exchanges, while internal characteristics of firms, e.g. administrative costs, would require other analytical tools. More generally the problem is that transaction costs may be orthogonal to the internal costs of the firm (hence the tradeoff).

[13] Models built on these premises assume that: (1) monitoring is costless, or can be endogenized at no cost through an adequate contract; (2) shirking can be detected and punished, which requires perfect revelation of information and no enforcement problems; and (3) employees do not accept a job, really, but a fully contingent contract.

set of feasible activities; however, it considers that the restrictive conception of firm-as-production function must be subsumed under the concept of firm-as-governance structure, which understanding is "mainly an exercise in transaction cost economics" (Williamson, 1988c, p. 356). Indeed, firms can better be represented as a complex combination of legal, economic, and social dimensions. As a legal entity, it operates and is liable as one single agent when it comes to the transfer of rights. As an economic device, it relies on a complex set of contractual arrangements coordinated by a hierarchy. And as a social unit, it defines a space in which motivations go far beyond monetary incentives.[14] In what follows, I focus on the economic dimension, emphasizing characteristics that differentiate firms from other arrangements and that provide potential explanations to why they may prevail over markets or hybrids in organizing some transactions.

Is Command the Key Issue?

Coase (1937) raised the fundamental question that launched the NIE research program: why do agents give up the price system in so many circumstances? Why do firms so often supersede the price mechanism? His answer pointed at the role of "person or persons who, in a competitive system, take the place of the price mechanism in the direction of resources." And he added: "A firm, therefore, consists of the system of relationship which comes into existence when the direction of resources is dependent on an entrepreneur" (p. 393). When the cost of using the price system becomes too high, the organization of activities under a central command may become advantageous. This puts hierarchy at the core of the firm, a view challenged by many economists, including several new institutionalists (e.g., Alchian and Demsetz, 1972). It also raises another question: why do people give up part of their freedom, submitting to an authority? "Why should a private property owner voluntarily surrender his rights and be told what to do by a visible hand?"(Cheung, 1983, p. 2). I start with the second question and then come back to the first one.

Preliminaries: Why do Agents Accept to Be Directed by a Visible Hand?

Answer to this question perhaps remains one of the most controversial in NIE, and more generally in economics. The reason may be that it exhibits a tension between the representation of market economies as based on free will and voluntary agreements on the one hand, and the potential role of hierarchy and command on the other hand. Any interpretation is therefore subject to vigorous challenges. My view is that answers provided by new institutionalists go in two different and somewhat conflicting directions. One emphasizes a representation

---

[14] The view of firms as social entities with properties shaping and moderating members' behavior is not as widely acknowledged in economics as it is in economic sociology (see Nee and Swedberg, chap. 29 of this book). For a related interpretation, see Kogut and Zander (1996).

of the firm as a "team" based on a nexus of contracts, pooling specific assets owned by distinct entities, the difficulty being to explain why some entities have more power than others in directing resources. An alternative conception emphasizes the firm as a hierarchical structure grounded in an asymmetric relationship, the difficulty being to explain the source of this asymmetry. However, these diverging views meet in acknowledging the key role of the allocation of property rights.

The first explanation views firms as means for coordinating holders of different assets, the nature of these assets being central to the explanation of what a firm is. Two complementary arguments have been developed here. The "old" property rights approach focuses on the issue of the efficient coordination of assets' holders and interprets an entrepreneur as the agent who holds a specific asset, his or her competence in processing information, which he/she uses for directing resources efficiently, his or her incentives for doing so coming from his or her status as a residual claimant. Therefore, a firm could be properly characterized by "a team use of inputs and a centralized position of some party in the contractual arrangement of all other inputs" (Alchian and Demsetz, 1972, p. 778). Other 'members' of the team-firm accept this visible hand because of the expected gains from this efficient coordination. The "new" property rights approach rather puts the emphasis on incentive to invest as the core of what a firm is, with the type of rights held as the main issue. Indeed, property rights over physical assets would be distinctive because they give holders control over decisions to invest and because they give them leverage over the activity of those who do not own such assets, or who do not own enough rights to have direct leverage over their use. As stated by Holmstrom (1999, p. 76): "... ownership confers contracting rights that allow the firm to decide who should be offered the opportunity to work with particular asset and on what term".

This last expression brings us close to the alternative analysis, viewing firms as hierarchical systems, based on the key role of authority. This approach prevails in organization theory, but also predominates among those who view the employment relationship as distinctive and typical of the firm, from Barnard (1938) and Simon (1951) to Williamson (1975), Beckmann (1988), Radner (1992) and Aoki (2001). The difficulty here lies in explaining what the foundations of this accepted asymmetry are. I see two potential and likely intertwined answers, based on the idea that asymmetries in property rights may play a different role from the one described above.[15] Indeed, the interpretation of the firm as nexus-of-contracts presumes the standard neoclassical assumptions that all participants do have "survival endowments" and that the labor market works perfectly well: in the 'team' approach, all asset holders are symmetrical in that they can always leave the firm at will because they can redeploy at no significant cost and/or because they have endowments that allow them to keep full flexibility in the allocation of their assets. But what happens if it is not so? Constraints

---

[15] Holmstrom (1999) is probably the one who comes closer to this interpretation, although there were already indications in Simon (1951).

on their endowments and high costs of going on the labor market may provide a powerful explanation to why agents accept the direction of a Visible Hand. In doing so, they relax these constraints by securing their income. Plainly, one may need a job or need to keep a job to make a living! This does not preclude the acceptance of authority as a potential source of benefit through entrepreneurial coordination. However, it prioritizes the arguments. Symmetrically, holders of rights on physical assets accept that internal governance prevails because it can "... shield and protect the transaction and insure the full utilization of the specialized assets." (Teece, 1986)[16]

My interpretation clearly leans in this second direction, acknowledging that hierarchy matters. Beyond the convergence between the two explanations that allocation of property rights shapes the nature of the firm, I thereafter endorse the view that agents make the organization called "firm" possible because they surrender significant decision rights to a "central coordinator". As noted by Barnard (1938, chap. 12, p. 184): "Authority is another name for the willingness and capacity of individuals to submit to the necessity of cooperative systems."

What can make Firms more Efficient than Markets?

Although he later mitigated his view on this issue (1991 [1988] chap. 5, p. 64), Coase initially emphasized that the comparative advantage of firms does not result from market failures or externalities, but rather from their capacity to organize transactions through command rather than by using the price system when the latter becomes too costly. "If a workman moves from department Y to department X, he does not so because of a change in relative prices but because he is advised to do so" (1937, p. 387). At about the same time, Barnard defined formal organizations as "... <u>a system of consciously coordinated personal activities or forces</u>" (1938, p. 72; his emphasis), the efficiency of which depends on: (i) communication; (ii) willingness to serve; and (iii) shared purposes. In his view, supervisors in charge of implementing this system form the core of the firm and their role characterizes employment relationship. In other terms command, understood as a relationship in which an agent who performs a job has to report to the person who is in charge and who can be held accountable for the performance of the job thus assigned, forms the distinctive characteristic of hierarchy (Barnard, 1938, chap. 12; Beckmann, 1988, p. 3). With some nuances, Williamson concurs when he emphasizes that what distinguishes commercial and employment contracts is that in the latter employees "must <u>obey first</u>, then seek recourse" (1985, p. 249).[17] The very title of his book from 1975, *Markets and Hierarchies*, already suggested this view. His later emphasis on 'forbearance law' (1996 [1991], pp. 97–100) understood as the reluctance of courts to

---

[16] Therefore, we are far from the risk adverse story, an interpretation not very popular among the new institutional crowd, which is a significant difference with agency theory.

[17] Masten (1988) substantiated this difference through a study of the American jurisprudence on contracts.

intervene in intra-firm disputes, reinforces the concept of hierarchy as distinctive.

What comparative advantages can be expected from that hierarchical relationship? Again, this remains an open question, subject to vigorous controversies. In what follows I develop three sets of arguments. First, the capacity of supervisors to reallocate human resources without negotiation reduces transaction costs and provides a powerful tool for dealing with uncertainty (Simon, 1951; Beckmann, 1988, chap. 1 and 2). Second, internalizing transactions provides means for extending the domain of rationality, thus improving decisions, thanks to "the division of cognitive labor" that hierarchies make possible (Aoki, 2001; chap. 5). Third, the communication system developed and coordinated by the "entrepreneur" is a potential gain when information provided by markets is costly and difficult to process (Alchian and Woodward, 1987, p. 112).

In sum, I remain of the view that command constitutes the central adaptation mode of firms (Williamson, 1996, p. 31). It provides supervisors with the capacity to choose among possibilities delineated by contracts. This capacity relies on many different tools: allocating tasks, pairing human capabilities with physical assets, monitoring agents, checking the adequacy of actions to orders, according rewards, etc. (Radner, 1992; Miller, Chap. 14 of this book).

How Command Works

In order to provide a credible alternative to markets as an adaptation device when tight coordination is needed, command requires a complex combination of control, cooperation, and communication. The potential advantage of formal organizations lies in this combination; however, it also generates "administrative" or "bureaucratic" costs.

Control

Control makes command credible. It provides means for implementing orders, for evaluating the adequacy of actions chosen, and for checking on members tempted to renege their commitments (Williamson 1985, chaps. 9 and 10; Beckmann, 1988, chap. 3; Demsetz, 1995, first and third commentaries). It determines a major function of managers within the firm, and it substantiates the role of corporate governance in finding "ways to govern the manager in the use of assets entrusted to the firm" (Aoki, 2001, chap. 10, section 1). It also provides important indications for understanding why firms have limits, a problem already discussed by Coase (1937, p. 394–395) and developed by Williamson in his pioneering paper on the loss of control (1967).

There is an extensive literature on the issue of control over employees as well as over managers in managerial sciences. However, as noted by Radner (1992, p. 1383), economics seemed little concerned until recently. One set of contributions comes from agency theory (Miller, Chap. 14 of this book). It mostly focuses on incentives issues, trying to find contractual solutions to two problems: How to prevent employees from shirking? and how to keep managers align with the interests of property rights holders? These are relevant questions in a new institutional perspective, although they provide a very restrictive view of the role of managers and of the "[many] control problems [that] plague complex organizations" (Demsetz, 1995, p. 42; also Roe, chap. 15 of this book).

What might distinguish the NIE approach is its emphasis on the advantages control can provide over the use of prices as a device to coordinate and adapt when specificity of assets makes mutual dependence unavoidable. First, control provides some flexibility in giving supervisors the capacity to evaluate the adequacy of action to orders and the right to reallocate tasks accordingly, without renegotiating contracts and using the price system. In that respect, central coordination can be faster than decentralized adaptation (Bolton and Farrell, 1990). Second, control provides powerful tools for constraining opportunism through interactions among levels of management, although this may also give senior managers the possibility to appropriate gains from subgroups (Tirole, 1986). Third, and more positively, some authors have recently suggested that central control may allow performing "controlled experiments" to learn how to organize assets more effectively (Foss et al., 2002). Fourth, control allows settling disputes without the time and costs that arbitration by third parties would require (Williamson, 1975, p. 29; Dow, 1987). Fifth, internal control such as auditing might often be superior to external control (e.g., by courts) with respect to the capacity of collecting and processing the relevant information and to the rapidity in making required adaptations (Williamson, 1975, pp. 146–147).

However, the NIE literature has also emphasized that control is subject to rigidities and costs, which severely limits the efficiency of command. In the continuity of the property rights perspective, Demsetz has analyzed the costs of excluding non-owners from the use of resources as a major limitation to control in large corporations (1988b, 1995, and 2002). Similarly, Hansmann (1988) has emphasized that owners of physical assets are actually as much concerned by controlling the use of their assets as by controlling residual profits.[18] The resulting costs represent a major limitation to the advantages of firms over markets. Another limit to control was pointed out by Williamson (1985, chap. 6, pp. 135–138): it originates in the non-replicativity (the impossibility of "selective intervention" in his terminology) within the firm of market devices that could alleviate control costs. If firms could replicate the powerful incentives provided by markets, the comparative disadvantage of administrative costs with respect to the cost of trading on markets could be overcome. The search for labor contracts that would allow perfect revelation of information represents an illusory effort in that direction. A third limit comes from influence activities among managers (Milgrom and Roberts, 1990, pp. 78 sq.). A last and related limit, discussed later, results from the loss of information along transmission lines that characterizes control in a hierarchical organization.

---

[18] This aspect partially relates to the metering activity of entrepreneurs (Alchian and Demsetz, 1972), although command can hardly be reduced to metering.

Cooperation

However, cooperation might partially relax these limits. Cooperation necessarily complements command in an efficient firm. No formal organization could rely exclusively on command and control (Simon, 1991). New institutional economists go further, emphasizing the important role of cooperation in understanding how firms can subsume markets and in understanding the positive role of managers. Cooperation remains a difficult concept to define if one wants to go beyond purely self-interested behavior (Dow, 1987; Ménard, 1994b). Here I understand cooperation as the willingness of agents to pool resources even when they cannot assess ex-ante the benefits expected or if there are benefits at all to be expected in doing so.

In their 1972 paper, Alchian and Demsetz in defining firm as a team already raised the measurement issue. More recently, Alchian emphasized that a firm is not "an output-generating 'black box' [but] a contractually related collection of resources of various cooperative owners"; and a corporation is "the organization of cooperative joint production" (1987, p. 1031). Williamson went further in analyzing the role of cooperation in formal organizations, noting particularly the importance of "atmosphere" as a source of efficiency. Following Commons' valuation of mutuality (1934, p. 2) and Arrow's emphasis on the economic value of social interactions (1974, chap. 1), *Markets and Hierarchies* (particularly chap. 2, sections 2 and 4; also chap. 3) examined how cooperation can limit the costs of control. "Attitudinal interactions" make formal organizations less prone to conflicts and more apt at settling disputes. Four advantages can result from a cooperative "atmosphere": (1) scale economies in the acquisition of information; (2) risk-bearing among the group when facing unanticipated contingencies; (3) mitigation of adverse selection and moral hazard; and (4) increased productivity due to a more developed "sense of responsibility" (see also Arrow, 1974, chap. 4). However, there are also limits and costs to cooperation, resulting from: (a) free riding strategies through selection of members (ex-ante) and malingering behavior once selected (ex-post); (b) collective decision-making that may hamper the advantages of command; (c) incentives to collude and develop side-payments; and (d) the high cost of processing information and communicating in a team-oriented organization.[19] Williamson did not pursue the analysis of cooperation in subsequent books. Other institutionalists have tried to go further, notably Aoki (1988, chap. 3 and 8; 1990; and 2001, chap. 11).[20]

Information and Communication

The examination of control and cooperation and of their limits, as reported above, systematically exhibits the important role of information. New institutional

---

[19] Puterman (1986) and Dow (1987) criticized Williamson for having based his evaluation of cooperation exclusively on peer groups, thus ignoring other modes of cooperation, while Granovetter (1985) argued that Williamson shares with neo-classicists an under-socialization approach to agents.

[20] See also Ménard (1994a, 1994b, 1997); Vazquez-Vicente (2002).

economists played a pioneering role here (Malmgren, 1961; Williamson, 1967; Alchian and Demsetz, 1972), partly because they had to deal with Hayek's statement about markets as particularly efficient information processors (Hayek, 1945). On the one hand, if firms can overcome markets in organizing certain transactions, there must be some informational advantages to integration. On the other hand, information noises in firms may provide a rationale for defining the boundaries of firms. Both dimensions have been explored.

Formal organizations have ways to gain advantages in processing information. First, they can develop routines that make codification possible, thus reducing internal costs. Second, the development of a common language, e.g., corporate culture, provides efficient supports for sharing knowledge. Third, hierarchies introduce "filters" that reduce the number of messages circulating. Fourth, the combination of human resources extends the capacity of individuals to absorb information while the reallocation of tasks through command provides means for processing information and transforming it into action rapidly. Williamson (1975, chap. 2), Aoki (1986; 2001, chap. 5) and Demsetz (1988a, 1988b, and 1995) have played a particularly important role in exploring these factors and their consequences. These informational advantages also relate to the role of 'entrepreneur' or 'business manager', an aspect already emphasized by early contributors (Coase, 1937; Williamson, 1967; Alchian and Demsetz, 1972) who viewed these figures essentially as efficient information processors. As strongly put by Demsetz (1988a), the fundamental reason that makes management meaningful is their superior capacity to make sense of the signals provided by markets in a world of incomplete knowledge. They may also possess 'decisive information', partially due to their specialization in processing signals. Others have adopted a more structural approach, emphasizing how the internal mode of organization may allow efficiency gains and economies of scale in processing information (Williamson, 1975, chap. 2 and 8; 1985, chap. 10 and 11; Aoki, 1986) and, more generally, in making decisions (Demsetz, 1988a). These aspects open a bridge towards the evolutionary perspective on firms as set of competencies processing information efficiently (Witt, 1998; Jacobides and Winter, 2003).

On the other hand, the complexity of internal coordination generates noises, and therefore uncertainties of its own, making firms prone to loss of control. Williamson (1967) provides a pioneering reference, with the examination of how a small noise in the transmission of signals in a multi-layered hierarchy ends up imposing limits on the size of the firm. Demsetz (1988b, 1995) has explored the "decreasing returns" in the capabilities of business managers to monitor information, while Aoki (1986; 1990) has exhibited the trade-off in processing information between a centralized organization, which accumulates noises along the multiple layers of the hierarchical system; and a decentralized organization that confronts dispersion of information, a challenge to the advantages of integration. In other terms, different internal structures carry distinct administrative costs. Unfortunately we still do not know much about the costs involved, a limit that NIE shares with other approaches.

More generally, the analysis of the internal characteristics of formal organizations and of their related costs remains an underdeveloped area. Since it is so crucial for better understanding the comparative advantages and disadvantages of these arrangements over other modes of organization, particularly the use of markets, one can expect significant developments in this direction in the future. Whether or not the transaction cost apparatus can help in doing internal investigations remains debatable. Some neo-institutionalists argue that transaction costs concern exclusively market exchanges, so that the analysis of the internal costs of firms requires other tools (Demsetz, 1988a; 2002). Others consider that beyond semantics, efforts are needed for better identifying the administrative costs that are involved in the "make-or-buy" trade-off and, more generally, in the trade-off among different organizational arrangements (Masten et al., 1991; Joskow, chap. 13 of this book). In doing so, we can expect more interactions between NIE, evolutionary economics, and some mainstream economists.

4. HYBRID ARRANGEMENTS[21]

Having focused on integration as an alternative to markets, NIE initially paid little attention to other modes of organizations, which were considered unstable and transitory. This situation began to change two decades ago. In 1985 (p. 83), Williamson acknowledged that: "Whereas I was earlier of the view that transactions of the middle kind were very difficult to organize and hence were unstable, [...], I am now persuaded that transactions in the middle range are much more common." However, the expression "middle-range" maintained some ambiguity, suggesting modes of organization with no specific content. Williamson later (1991) called these arrangements "hybrids", a more appropriate although not entirely satisfying term.

This section is about these forms, understood as alternative to firms as well as to markets. Firms integrate property rights, thus subsuming in last resort all transaction costs related to the production of a set of goods and/or services; hybrid arrangements cover only a subset of the transactions in which participating firms are involved. Traders making independent decisions commonly characterize markets; hybrids pool some resources, and share a subset of decisions in their domain of choice. A very preliminary notion of hybrids thus includes all forms of inter-firm collaboration in which property rights remain distinct while joint decisions are made, requiring specific modes of coordination. The emphasis is on the commitment of distinct property rights holders, operating distinct legal entities, but organizing some transactions through governance forms mutually agreed upon.

---

[21] This section borrows from the more extensive analysis developed in Ménard (2004a).

What are Hybrids?

The rapidly expanding literature on these "non-standard" organizational arrangements signals an increasing interest among economists for the issues at stake. Until the mid-eighties only a handful of exploratory papers were available on inter-firm contracts (Klein et al., 1978; Ouchi, 1980; Eccles, 1981; Cheung, 1983), franchising (Rubin, 1978), or "non-standard contracting" (Williamson, 1975; Palay, 1984; Masten, 1984; Joskow, 1985). The real takeoff dates from the 1990s, initially with a majority of contributions in non-economic journals. However, the concepts as well as the vocabulary of these analyses remain approximate. Hybrids, clusters, networks, symbiotic arrangements, and chain systems are used quite indifferently. The forms encapsulated by these fluctuating terms seem also heterogeneous. They include subcontracting, networks, alliances, franchising, collective trademarks, partnership, and even forms of cooperative.[22] However, they are connected by the underlying idea that they participate to the same "family" of agreements among autonomous entities doing business together, mutually adjusting with little help from the price system, and sharing or exchanging technologies, capital, products, and services without a unified ownership.

Beyond the heterogeneity of cases and the fluctuating vocabulary, studies progressively revealed regularities that make hybrids distinctive. The first one is the importance of *pooled resources*. Whatever the form they take, hybrids systematically organize joint activities based on inter-firm coordination. Hybrids develop because markets are perceived as unable to adequately bundle the relevant resources and capabilities (Teece and Pisano, 1994), while integration would reduce flexibility, create irreversibility, and weaken incentives. Sharing some resources and coordinating some decisions in order to generate rents represents the fundamental motivation behind hybrids. However, it may also be a source of conflicts: distributing rents involves discretionary choices that can easily destabilize an agreement. On the other hand, pooling resources does not make sense without some continuity in the relationship, which requires cooperation. Legally distinct entities must accept to loose part of the autonomy that markets would provide without benefiting from the capacity to control that hierarchies have. Hence a first problem for hybrids: how can they secure cooperation in order to achieve coordination without losing the advantages of decentralized decisions?

The existence of *relational contracting* is a second characteristic shared by hybrids. Of course contracts play a role in other modes of organization. But what

---

[22] Some significant references are: (1) on subcontracting: Eccles, 1981; Aoki, 1988, chap. 6; and Bajari and Tadelis, 2001; (2) on networks: Thorelli, 1986; Powell, 1990; Podolny and Page, 1998; (3) on alliances: Oxley, 1999; Baker et al., 2003; (4) on franchising: Rubin, 1978; Williamson, 1985; Lafontaine and Slade, 1997; (5) on collective trademarks: Dwyer and Oh, 1988; Ménard, 1996; Sauvée, 2002; (6) on partnership: Farrell and Scotchmer, 1988; Powell, 1996; and (7) on cooperatives: Cook, 1995; Cook and Iliopoulos, 2000.

distinguishes hybrids is that their contracts link activities and resources among partners who simultaneously operate unconnected transactions. These contracts intend to secure the relationship and, because the identity of partners matters, they create a framework for "transactional reciprocity" (Park, 1996). The relational aspect is grounded in the advantages and risks of sharing resources among independent partners (Goldberg, 1980; Williamson, 1985; Baker et al., 2002). Advantages can be expected from increased market shares, transfer of competencies, and access to scarce resources (e.g., finance). However, risks are also at stake. Partners coordinate only part of their decisions, subject to unforeseeable revisions, particularly when specific investments support highly uncertain process or products, or target volatile demand (e.g., R & D alliances). Typical transaction cost problems result. Contracts tend to be incomplete, providing a simple and uniform framework[23]. Hence the importance of the relational dimension, and the need for modes of governance that can fill blanks left in contracts, monitor partners, and solve conflicts without repeated renegotiation. Thus a second problem: how can hybrids secure relational contracts while minimizing renegotiations?

A third characteristic of hybrids is their relation to *competition*. Of course, competition exists among agents in a firm, e.g., job-promotion tournaments, or among firms on markets. The difference in the case of hybrids lays in the combination of interdependence and autonomy, partners remaining residual claimants in charge of their own decisions in last resort. In that context, competitive pressures have two dimensions. (a) Although they cooperate on some issues, partners also compete against each other. Even bilateral agreements with long-term contracts can be subject to internal competition since strategies of partners remain distinct (Coase, 2000). Moreover, the agreement can be designed to make parties recurrently competing, as in subcontracting (Eccles, 1981; Dyer, 1997). Activities may overlap with partners trying to attract customers from the same subset, notwithstanding restrictive clauses (Raynaud, 1997). Parties may also cooperate on some activities and compete on others, as in joint R & D projects (Baker et al., 2003). (b) Hybrids usually compete with other arrangements, including other hybrids. Indeed, they develop on highly competitive markets in which pooling resource is a way to deal with uncertainties and to survive. However, if investments are moderately specific, partners may be tempted to switch among arrangements, making them highly unstable. Hence a third problem for hybrids: what is the best mechanism for delineating joint decisions, disciplining partners, and solving conflicts while preventing free riding?

Therefore, significant regularities underlie the heterogeneous set of hybrids. Aspects of these regularities exist in markets and hierarchies. What distinguishes (and plagues) hybrids is the grounding of these regularities in a mix of competition and cooperation that subordinate the key role played by prices on markets

---

[23] For example, studies on franchising show that contrarily to what agency theory predicts, contracts are not tailored to suit characteristics of transactors or transactions (Lafontaine and Slade, 1997; Ménard, 2004a).

and by command in hierarchies (Jorde and Teece, 1989; Grandori and Soda, 1995; Ménard, 1997). Because they cannot or can only weakly rely on prices or on hierarchy to discipline partners, hybrids depend on specific mechanisms of governance for their survival.

Why Choose a Hybrid Arrangement?

Considering the difficulties involved, one may wonder why there are hybrid organizations at all. Williamson (1991) provides a convincing explanation, based on the model initially developed for understanding the "make-or-buy" tradeoff. The underlying idea is that when investments among partners are specific enough to generate substantial contractual hazards without justifying integration and its burdens, and when uncertainties are consequential enough to require tighter coordination than what markets can provide, parties have an incentive to choose hybrids. Empirical studies have begun substantiating this approach (Ménard, 2004a, section 3). I develop these two aspects successively.

Investing in Mutual Dependence

A fundamental determinant already noted comes from the incentive for partners to create durable mutual dependence while keeping property and decision rights distinct. Two investment strategies can be adopted, with distinct consequences. Each party may invest in specific assets, creating a network based on complementarities; or partners may pool resources, making joint investments for part of their activities. The first strategy was analyzed early by transaction cost economists, who highlighted the role of the duration of agreements. Most initial studies focused on bilateral contracts of that type (Masten, 1984; Palay, 1985; Joskow, 1985). The second strategy, requiring joint investments, typically develops with agreements for transferring products among organizations with different minimum efficiency scales, or involving technology transfers (Hennart, 1988; Teece, 1992; Gulati, 1998; Oxley, 1999).

These examples refer to investments in physical assets. Indeed, most empirical studies of the impact of specific investments on the choice of inter-firm agreements, particularly econometric tests, took inspiration from the paradigmatic analysis of vertical integration, with its emphasis on physical capital (site specificity, physical specificity, dedicated assets). Without ignoring this aspect, a significant contribution of the literature on hybrids is its concern with human assets (Loasby, 1994). This comes out quite naturally from the centrality of agents in charge of coordinating legally autonomous decision makers while checking their propensity to free ride. In franchising, success depends largely on the capacity of the franchisor to select and monitor adequately franchisees (Dnes, 1996; Raynaud, 1997; Lafontaine and Shaw, 1999). Specific human assets are also crucial in other hybrid forms, e.g., mutual investments in human resources among biotechnology firms (Powell, 1996) or transfer of competencies in networks confronted to rapidly changing technologies (Teece, 1992).

The very existence of interdependent physical assets requires substantial investments in managers that can monitor the arrangement. As already pointed out by Palay (1985), acquiring inter-firm specific knowledge takes time and efforts, so that "go-betweens" are highly regarded as problem-solvers, contributing to the continuity of the relationship.

Another form of specific investments that creates incentives to choose a hybrid arrangement is brand name capital. The abundant managerial literature on distribution channels inspired by transaction cost economics emphasizes the strategic issue of what governance can control partners and maintain reputation (e.g., Brown, 1984; Dwyer and Oh, 1988; John and Weitz, 1988; Fein and Anderson, 1997; Fearne, 1998). Similarly, studies on collective trademarks show the importance of devices designed for guaranteeing quality and preventing opportunistic behavior. When the reputation of a collective brand depends on the quality of products highly correlated to human assets, training and network-specific competences represent a key value (Ménard, 1996; Raynaud, 1997).

Hence, hybrids develop because of the advantages expected from mutual dependence. However, the level and forms of the specific investments required determine the significance of contractual hazards and the nature of safeguards needed for securing the agreement.

Monitoring Uncertainty

This brings in the issue of uncertainty, the second determinant of hybrids forms. Transaction cost theory suggests that the degree of uncertainty surrounding the transactions that hybrids organize also contributes to shaping the form adopted. Uncertainty is secondary to specific investments in that without some mutual dependence in assets, there would be no hybrid; parties would trade through markets. But once investment-specific relationships develop, uncertainty impregnates decisions about the level of resources pooled and their monitoring. Hybrids operate as a "buffer": the more consequential the uncertainty is, the more centralized the coordination tends to be (Ménard, 1996, 1997; Nooteboom, 1999).

Internal as well as external factors of uncertainties among partners are relatively well identified. Internal uncertainty outgrows from problems with inputs, outputs, or the transformation process. Problems with inputs may come from non-observabilities in resources or services traded, as in supply chain systems (Fearne, 1998); from difficulties in the coordination of inputs, as in the construction industry (Eccles, 1981); or from outside suppliers with no specific commitment to the arrangement, as in the food industry (Mazé, 2002). Uncertainties about outputs can result from difficulties in controlling that deliverables meet the standards agreed upon: from maladjustments to consumers' preferences; or from lack of flexibility in adapting to a changing demand. (Anderson and Schmittlein, 1984; John and Weitz, 1988). The transformation process itself may generate uncertainties: hybrids pool resources that may overlap with activities excluded from the agreement thus making control and planning uncertain, and complex technologies and human skills may be involved, as with joint R & D projects. Defining rules for the distribution of rents or for supporting unexpected costs then becomes a potential source of conflicts (Ghosh and John, 1999, p. 131).

The role of the institutional environment as an external source of uncertainty, influencing the choice of one form of hybrid rather than another is often mentioned, although not often analyzed. North (1981, 1990, 1991) has repeatedly insisted on the importance of the rules of the game for understanding how actors play that game. Williamson (1991) went a step further, suggesting how shifts in parameters could explain changes in the modes of governance. Fortunately recent studies on hybrid forms have initiated a more systematic exploration of this issue (e.g., Khanna, 1998; Oxley, 1999).

But what really matters for understanding the choice and the form of hybrids is whether these uncertainties are consequential or not. Confronted to consequential uncertainty, hybrids must combine adaptation, in order to provide flexible adjustments; control, in order to reduce discrepancies among inputs, outputs, or quality in the process itself; and safeguards, in order to prevent opportunistic behavior that uncertainties make difficult to detect. The intensity of adaptation, control, and safeguards needed provides a good predictor of the degree of centralization in the governance of hybrids.

In sum, hybrids develop when specific investments can be spread over partners without losing the advantages of autonomy, while uncertainties are consequential enough to make pooling a valuable alternative to markets. It is the combination of these two dimensions that matters. If only one attribute is present, the governance leans towards contract-based arrangements. When the two attributes combine, the governance becomes more authoritarian. Therefore, it is the combination of opportunism, or the risk of opportunism, and of miscoordination, or the risk of miscoordination, which determines the governance characterizing hybrid organizations.

What Governance for the Hybrids?

There are basically two channels through which monitor hybrids: through contracts and/or through formal governing bodies. Both aspects have been explored by new institutional economists, although the literature on the former is much more abundant so far.

Contractual Safeguards

Indeed, most studies on hybrids in a transaction cost perspective emphasize the role of contracts as safeguards against the high risk of opportunistic behavior that threatens these arrangements, but also show their limits (Masten, 1996; Ménard, 2004b, vol. 3). For example, selecting partners is of utmost importance in hybrids because of what it could cost redeploying mutually dependent assets. However, competition as a selection process, e.g., through bidding, is used sparsely, mostly to "test the market" occasionally (Eccles, 1981; Ménard, 1996) and to discipline partners (Knoeber, 1989; Dyer, 1997). Similarly, provisions for constraining opportunism often remain at a very general level, likely because comprehensive-binding contracts would be far too complex and/or too costly to design and implement. This likely explains the highly relational dimension of contracts in hybrids, a regularity noted above.

Notwithstanding these limits, there are different ways through which contracts help coordinating, and new institutional economists have substantially contributed to the analysis of these aspects. Contracts may specify criteria for selecting partners and even fix their number.[24] Choosing duration of the contract also provides means for testing willingness to commit and for guaranteeing some continuity in the relationship. As a consequence, formal duration of contracts does not necessarily correspond to the actual duration of the relationship (Joskow, 1985; Ménard, 1996; Dyer, 1997). Clauses determining quality standards, often complemented by annexes, also contribute thus making commitments as observable as possible (Ménard, 1996; Gaucher, 2002).[25] Adaptation clauses, e.g., index clauses or clauses delegating adaptation to identifiable managers or arbitrators, can prove a framework that smoothens relationships among partners (Rubin. chap. 9 of this book). Safeguard clauses help to overcome the incompleteness of contracts (Hadfield, 1990), whether safeguards are formal (e.g., financial hostages a la Klein, 1980; mutual commitments guaranteed by specific investments a la Williamson, 1983) or informal, based on relations or reputation (Macaulay, 1963; Garvey, 1995; Baker et al., 2002).

The combination of these characteristics provides tools for governing hybrids. It also generates complexity and costs, which define a central issue: how to economize on the costs of extensive contracting among autonomous partners in order to maintain some advantages in comparison to the cost of administering a broader range of assets within one single firm (Klein et al., 1978)? The answer may well be that contracts provide only a framework, which must be completed by other mechanisms of governance.

Private Order: Forms of Governance

Indeed, empirical studies reveal an array of mechanisms developed by hybrids for economizing on transaction costs while smoothing relations among partners. The issue of rent sharing, not discussed here, is particularly important in that respect (Ménard, 2004a). However, these studies still lack a theoretical framework that could unify the analysis. What follows offers only a partial and provisory view.

---

[24] A difficult tradeoff concerns the choice, when possible, between bilateral or multilateral agreements. The former is easier to monitor but involves higher dependency; the latter makes monitoring more complex but allows comparisons and benchmarking, a powerful tool for constraining opportunism. Most hybrid arrangements are of the second type. One suspects it is because it better captures positive properties of markets.

[25] Studies on contracts, particularly econometric tests, ignore annexes, in which the essence often lies.

Building on indications provided by Klein et al. (1978) and Williamson (1985, chap. 3; 1991), Ménard (1994a, 1996, 1997, 2004a) has developed evidence of the presence of regulating devices (or "authorities", distinct from "hierarchies") as a core element in the architecture of hybrids. These devices all share one common characteristic: they depend on the transfer by partners of subclasses of decisions to entities coordinating their action, while property and decision rights remain distinct. Thus, they rely on *intentionality and mutuality*, maintaining a formal symmetry that distinguishes hybrids from hierarchies.

Available studies mostly based on cases or on sector samples suggest that the degree of centralization adopted depends on the degree of mutual dependence among partners and on the complexity and turbulence of the environment (Dwyer and Oh, 1988; Ménard, 1996; Park, 1996). An illustration is provided in Raynaud (1997), who analyzed a brand name for high quality bread developed by a group of French millers. In order to prevent opportunism, the partners created a distinct legal entity holding the brand name and defining and implementing standards of quality; they also created a private "court" with peers elected as judges, who are in charge of solving conflicts. An amazing element of this arrangement is the power delegated to these judges to penalize and even expel a partner free-riding "excessively". The group has grown successfully for the last 25 years. Sauvée (2002) examined another pattern, implemented by a firm holding a brand name of canned vegetables of high quality. Inputs come from a diversified set of growers operating under contracts. The formal side of the contract is quite standard, in line with characteristics described above. The interesting point though is that the success of the firm rapidly translated in the high transaction costs of monitoring all these contracts. In order to reduce these costs and secure the arrangement, growers have been structured in several groups with delegates for negotiating contracts and adjustments. A joint committee, with four representatives from the producers and two from the firm, is in charge of solving conflicts, deciding changes, and distributing the quasi-rents.

More generally, empirical studies show a highly variable degree of formalism and power embodied in governing entities adopted by hybrids, which likely reflects the significance of contractual hazards and the resulting transaction costs. I have suggested elsewhere that four forms deserve particular attention (Ménard, 2004a; see also Oxley, 1997). At one end of the spectrum, close to market arrangements, hybrids rely primarily on *trust*: decisions are decentralized and coordination relies on mutual "influence" and reciprocity. At the other end, hybrids come close to integration, with tight coordination through quasi-autonomous *governing bodies* or "bureaus" sharing some attributes of a hierarchy (e.g., the millers). Between these polar cases, mild forms of "authority" develop, based on relational networks or on leadership. Relational *networks* have attracted a lot of attention in organization studies (Powell, 1990; Hakansson and Johanson, 1993; Grandori and Soda, 1995). They rely on tighter coordination than trust, with formal rules and conventions based on long-term relationships, on complementary competences, and/or on social "connivance" (Powell et al., 1996). By contrast, hybrids coordinated by a *leader* leave little room for autonomy although some formal symmetry can be maintained (as in the case of the canned vegetables firm). Subcontracting, particularly with long-term contractual relationships, or alliances related to R & D projects are often of that mode (Eccles, 1981; Pisano, 1990; Powell, 1996).

The long ignored hybrid modes of organization have attracted increasing attention. They provide unique opportunities for theoretical investigation on enforcement mechanisms, on diverse forms of authority for coordinating autonomous partners, on decision processes involved in multi-partnership, etc. They also call for studies about what determines the type of arrangement adopted, the contractual provisions implemented, the incentives selected, and the dispute-solving mechanisms developed. NIE is a major contributor to that research program.

5. MARKETS

It has been suggested that markets would be the "black box" of transaction cost economics (Holmstrom and Roberts, 1998, p. 77). The underlying argument seems to be that the benchmark to which NIE refers when discussing market issues is the neoclassical model: supply, demand, and the price mechanism form the hard core of markets, as exemplified by spot markets. In this section I would like to show briefly that the picture offered is definitely more complex.

In order to do so, a preliminary clarification is necessary.[26] As suggested in the introduction of this chapter, considering its extensive use in economic theory as well as in daily life, the very concept of "market" is not as simple as one would think. I have emphasized elsewhere that it is actually quite a protean concept, and its definition, even by the most prominent economists, tends to fluctuate (Ménard, 1995). The main ambiguity with respect to the central goal of this chapter comes from the fact that market can designate: (a) either a mode of organizing transactions, with substitutes such as firms or hybrid arrangements, as when carmakers buy parts from suppliers on competitive markets rather than producing these parts in-house; or (b) the general set of arrangements that characterize a market economy, in which markets represent the central economic institution in last resort in that at some point all modes of organizations intersect with and/or are embedded in markets, e.g. firms and hybrids obtain resources through voluntary exchanges, compete in capital and labor markets, etc. Because this chapter focuses on alternative ways of organizing transactions, I essentially refer to the first meaning. The problem is that there are many areas where the two dimensions intersect. Future research in NIE will surely need to better articulate the study of markets as an alternative way to organize exchange with the analysis of market structures and the regulatory environment within which different modes of organization interact. Plainly, we need better integration between the economics of organization, industrial organization, and institutional analysis. In what follows, I only review elements relevant to the analysis of markets

---

[26] I am particularly indebted to an anonymous referee who raised this issue and provided several insights.

as ways to organize exchange distinct from how firms or hybrids proceed in doing so.

Why are There Markets?

In a certain sense, markets thus understood have been at the center of NIE from the very beginning. The initial question raised by Coase (1937) about the nature of the firm can indeed be rephrased as: Why is it that markets do not do it all, all the time? The answer to this question requires a thorough examination of the cost of using the price mechanism. A substantial part of the literature from new institutionalists is just about that: it either explores the institutions required for markets to exist, to develop, and to be efficient, in the continuation of the research program initiated by North; or it examines why going through markets for trading rights and for enforcing contracts may be so costly that other arrangements are preferred, following the perspective opened by Ronald Coase and Oliver Williamson. My approach here focuses essentially on this second aspect.

As with the analysis of firms and hybrids, the starting point is the assumption that, due to the presence of positive transaction costs, alternative modes of organization do exist. Markets represent a subset of the many institutional arrangements that have developed over time for transferring rights. The fundamental characteristic of this subset is that it specializes in the exchange of property rights through mechanisms that require the mutual consent of parties involved (markets don't give "orders") and that coordinate the decentralized decisions made by agents using the information provided through the price system (Coase, this book, chap. 2). In fully acknowledging the role of prices, new institutional economists do give credit to the contributions of mainstream economists analyzing how the price system works. But they take distance with that literature in four aspects: (1) They consider that markets cannot be fully understood as pure structures but must be analyzed in taking into account the institutional factors that shape them. (2) As emphasized by Demsetz (1988a, 1988b), prices do not coordinate, but rather they send signals to those coordinating. A consequence is that markets and their structures result from the activities of households, firms, and inter-firm relationships. (3) Moreover, prices are not signals to which agents adapt passively. Again, Demsetz among others has exhibited how entrepreneurs and business managers actively affect products and prices, guiding and directing the allocation of resources with strategies of their rivals in mind (see also Anderson and Gatignon, chap. 16 of this book). (4) Therefore, markets need to be studied in relation to the alternative modes of organization with which they interact. Several consequences result from this approach. I examine only a few here, in order to facilitate the comparison with the other arrangements.

Markets as Mode of Organization

One key feature of markets in a transaction costs perspective is that they are organized, a point emphasized by Furubotn and Richter in their synthesis of NIE

(1997, chap. 7, p. 284). This is a non-trivial observation. It means that markets are embedded in institutions that shape them. Hence markets can take a variety of forms depending on the "rules of the game".

First, markets require institutional supports to exist and develop. We know from an already abundant literature that these supports combine complex legal, political, and social factors, with enforcement of agreements among parties as a key issue (North, 1981; 1990; and several chapters of this book; also White, 1981). The evolution of different market arrangements in the past as well as the difficult transition from a planned economy to a market economy provide dramatic examples of the complexity of institutions required.[27] A major contribution of new institutional economists (e.g., Alston, Libecap and Mueller, 1997) and of social scientists endorsing their perspective (e.g., Ensminger, 1992) has been to exhibit the particularly important and complex role of the definition and implementation of property rights. One basic assumption in standard models of market equilibrium is that all goods and services are "owned" by agents at no costs and that transfers of these rights are costless as well. NIE has gone the other way, exhibiting the complexity of the rules of the game needed for organizing these transfers, the economic and social costs of implementing these rules, and the difficulties of establishing adequate prices. Ensminger (1997), for example, has shown the importance of norms and customs in the definition of property rights and in the usage of prices for transferring these rights, while Libecap (1989) and Alston and Mueller (chap. 22 of this book) have analyzed the severe problems encountered in defining adequate supports for property rights (e.g., defining and enforcing land titles) and, above all, in implementing them.

Second, not all markets are alike. Since markets are institutionally embedded and shaped by varying rules of the game, they differ according to the arrangements that support them. The organization of the New York Stock Exchange differs from the Frankfurt Stock Exchange, and even more from the market for diamonds. A perfect illustration of this diversity and its determination by the surrounding institutions is provided by the implementation of markets for the production and distribution of electricity in Europe (Glachant, 2002). This diversity does not mean that markets escape theory and could only be described. Markets do share some common properties that have partially been captured by standard microeconomics through the analytics of supply and demand (Ménard, 1995). However, the point made by new institutionalists is that the varied institutional supports on which they are built have a significant impact on the comparative costs and benefits of using them. The institutional design defining the North Pool of electricity does not have the same costs than the NETA (New Electricity Trade Agreement) covering England and Wales. On some markets, personal relations play a key role in determining what transactions will be possible at what price (Ben Porath, 1980). Other markets remain highly impersonal,

---

[27] Milgrom et al. (1989) and Greif (1993; and chap. 28 of this book) provide good examples on the historical side. Murrell (chap. 26) covers transition issues, while Engerman and Sokoloff (chap. 25) propose a stimulating comparison of the divergent evolution of American countries.

as with auctions monitored through Internet. We still know little about the costs and benefits of these different institutional arrangements.[28]

Third, this diversity in the ways markets are organized reflects in the variety of mechanisms involved in the formation of prices: posted prices, prices determined by auction, the different types of auctions, prices formed through negotiations, etc. These mechanisms repose on distinct processes, requiring different supports, arrangements and rules, and they likely translate in different transaction costs. Here again we do not have a clear picture of the procedures involved, the underlying logic and, above all, the comparative costs that result.

Fourth, market organization critically depends on enforcement mechanisms. New institutionalists have developed an extensive body of research on different enforcement mechanisms, from very informal ones, rooted in the beliefs and shared values of traders (Greif, 1993 and chap. 28 of this book; North, 2004) to more formal mechanisms of enforcement. North has played an important role in that respect, pointing out the crucial role of both formal and informal constraints for shaping markets.[29] Among the formal mechanisms, two dimensions have been particularly explored that partially overlap: the role of legal regimes in establishing property rights (e.g., Alston, Libecap, and Schneider, 1996; Alston, Libecap and Mueller, 1997, pp. 145 sq.); and the role of the State as an enforcer of property rights on markets (Libecap and Wiggins, 1985; Barzel, 1999 and 2000).

The Costs of Using Market Organization

The neoclassical view of markets assumes these mechanisms as given and/or implementable at no costs. For example, notwithstanding their role in designing alternative solutions, which is the source of heated academic debates, mainstream economists have proposed no analysis that I know comparing the costs of the different institutional arrangements chosen for creating electricity markets, or the comparative costs of the different arrangements required by the distinct types of auctions used for selling licenses in the telecommunication sector. As a result, the mainstream approach misses substantial aspects of the importance and significance of the diversity of market organizations and the central role that supporting institutions play in their functioning, development, and success or failure. In the continuation of Coase (1937, 1960), NIE has clearly opened the way to the analysis of these underlying and indispensable mechanisms and to the examination of their costs.[30] Here again the literature is considerable, and I touch only the tip of the iceberg.

---

[28] The tentative evaluation of transaction costs on the NYSE by Demsetz (1968) did not generate the flow of research one would have expected.

[29] For a synthesis of his ideas on this issue, see North, 1990, chaps. 5, 6, and 7.

[30] See for example Levy and Spiller (1994) and Joskow (1991; 1997) Although not always with due recognition of their debt to new institutionalists, mainstream economists are increasingly acknowledging the role of these institutions (e.g., La Porta et al., 1998).

As a mean for organizing transactions, markets serve coordination: agents collect information about the characteristics of goods and services through the price system in order to decide which rights to transfer one way or the other. Dahlman (1979) is among the first to have explored systematically the different costs involved in that activity which is at the core of market transactions. Two dimensions deserve particular attention.

The first one concerns the costs related to the collection of information about goods or services to be traded. Hayek noted in a now famous contribution (1945) the role of prices in carrying that information. However, besides the pioneering paper by Stigler (1961), it took a long time before attention was paid to the problems involved and to the institutional devices that their solution may require. Information became a fashionable issue among neoclassical economists in the late 1970s and the 1980s, but it focused mostly on the problem of asymmetries in the information held by different parties, with almost no attention to the supports needed for carrying information and their impact on the quality and costs of information. In a new institutional perspective, Barzel (1982; 1989) has made a significant contribution in that respect raising a central issue of price systems, which is the measurement of goods or services to be traded. The evaluation of goods apparently as simple as oranges can be tricky and requires complex arrangements. Sellers may develop specific devices for alleviating the burden of buyers and gaining their loyalty. Intermediaries may proliferate as agents specializing in measurement, thus reducing transaction costs for the trading parties. Public rules and institutions for implementing them may be adopted for homogenizing measures and making evaluation less costly. Recent empirical researches support this analysis. For example, Leffler et al. (2000) have shown the complexity of the arrangements implemented by sellers through presale measurement in the timber industry, in order to reduce uncertainties of transactions. One difficult issue that needs to be mentioned here is that in a transaction cost perspective, evaluating the costs of these different arrangements requires a comparative approach, often a comparison between the costs of existing arrangements and potential alternatives. Masten et al. (1991) have discussed nicely a problem of that nature in transaction costs economics, although in a different context.[31]

Beyond the cost of measurement associated to the collection and processing of information that make prices meaningful, a second dimension of particular significance in evaluating what it costs to run markets relates to the devices required for identifying and matching potential buyers and sellers. North raised the issue in the early 1980s (1981, chap. 4; 1984), and illustrated it nicely in a model with Milgrom and Weingast (1989) about the role of private institutions for matching and disciplining parties participating to Champagne fairs in the Middle Age. More generally, parties operating on extensive markets need elaborated systems for identifying whom they want to deal with. Technical supports are required, from the relatively simple organization of local markets to

---

[31] Their discussion is about the difficulties in assessing the comparative advantages of one mode of organization. Joskow (Chap. 13 of this book) provides a useful summary of their contribution.

the complex arrangements associated to Internet. Costly devices allow these markets to exist and develop. Contracts are one of them.

Market contracting: Is There any Specificity?

Indeed, contracts represent an important arrangement for organizing market transactions. Of course, as shown in the previous sections, contracts play also a significant role in other modes of organization. However, their centrality may be specific to markets, besides and in connection with the price system. Firms rely mostly on the role of hierarchy for coordinating, while hybrids use contracts as a framework completed by complex institutional arrangements for planning their joint activities. In market transactions, there is not much besides contracts that parties can rely upon.

The question of whether or not market contracts are of the same nature than that characterizing firms or hybrids has generated controversies, following the provocative paper by Alchian and Demsetz (1972). In simplifying, two polar conceptions have developed. At one end of the spectrum, Benjamin Klein has continuously maintained that all contractual relationships are market relationships. In 1983, he stated: "The question what is the essential characteristic of a firm now appears to be unimportant. Thinking of all organizations as group of explicit and implicit contracts among owners of factors of production represents a fundamental advance" And again, in 2000 (p. 138): "... it is useful to think of all arrangements, including vertical integration, as forms of markets contracts chosen by transactors to supplement self enforcement when transactors have limited reputational capital". In that respect, contracts on spot markets would represent the essence of all modes of organization. Williamson has adopted a distinctively different perspective on this issue. Coming from the Carnegie tradition (Williamson, 1996, chap. 1), for which firms matter, he has consistently emphasized the existence and role of discrete mechanisms of governance, with distinct forms of contracts for the different modes of governance. Referring to Macneil (1978), he has put at the forefront the specificity of the "classical contract law" that would characterize market contracts. "The emphasis [is] on legal rules, formal documents, and self-liquidating transactions" (1985, p. 69). As a result "... the specific identity of the parties is of negligible importance; substantive content is determined by reference to formal terms of the contract, and legal rules apply. Market alternatives are mainly what protect each party against opportunism by his opposite. Litigation is strictly for settling claims; concentrated efforts to sustain the relation are not made, because the relation is not independently valued" (id. p. 74). This characterization contrasts nicely markets contracts with arrangements prevailing in firms or in hybrids, and it is the view I have adopted in this chapter.

One important consequence of market contracts as arrangements in which the identity of parties does not matter, concerns the role of safeguards for protecting parties and of *credible commitments* for markets to operate efficiently. At least two different mechanisms are involved. One is market pressure: the existence of substitutes, which is essential to the existence of markets, disciplines parties. But because markets are not perfect, this is usually not enough to procure adequate safeguards. Hence the role of specific contractual clauses developed for protecting traders. "Hostage" clauses intend to reinforce credibility (Williamson, 1985, chaps. 7 and 8 [1983]). Third parties such as courts (Schwartz, 1992) and arbitrators (Rubin, this book, chap. 9), and informal mechanisms such as reputation or trust contribute to the respect of market contracts, suspending a sword over the head of undisciplined parties.[32] Once more we are back to the necessity of looking at institutions needed for markets to operate.

To summarize, the main lesson learned from the extensive new institutional literature on markets is that they are all but "black boxes". (1) Markets can take many different forms, a neglected issue that requires further investigation. (2) They share fundamental characteristics only partially summarized by the price system.[33] (3) They are costly to use. (4) They require a dense web of institutions in order to develop. In that respect, and like the other modes of organization, they have flaws of their own, which makes them part of the continuous tradeoff among institutional arrangements that characterize a complex market economy.

6. Some Unsolved Problems

The previous sections summarize a fraction of the contributions of NIE to the analysis of the different modes of organization supporting transactions in a market economy. Notwithstanding its limitations, this survey illustrates how substantial these contributions are. Progress made has also exhibited grey areas and domains of divergence that are likely to generate new research. I conclude this chapter by a short review of some of these issues.

The Contractual Divide

The role of contracts in the analysis of organization emerges as a central theme in recent literature, and new institutionalists have played a pioneering role here (Brousseau and Glachant, 2002). However, and without overemphasizing the divergences, several problems persist regarding the nature and status of contracts. First, the question of their importance with respect to other devices remains open. The answer may be partially semantic depending on how extensively one defines contracts.[34] However, it has also a crucial analytical implication: Do contracts tell us the essentials of what we need to know about organizations? Alchian,

---

[32] The role of trust remains controversial. For two opposite views, see Zucker, 1986 and Williamson, 1993.

[33] As firmly stated by Demsetz (1988a, p. 159): "What parades as perfect competition is a model that has much to say about the price system, but little to say about competition or the organization of firms. [...] What is modeled is not competition, but extreme decentralization".

[34] Personally, I endorse the definition provided by Macaulay (1963, p. 31): "Contract,..., involves two distinct elements: (a) rational planning of the transaction with careful provision for as many future contingencies as can be foreseen; and (b) the existence or use of actual or potential sanctions to induce performance of the exchange or to compensate for non-performance."

Demsetz, Klein, among others, argue that contracts provide the fundamental characteristic of all trading activities in a market economy, with firms or hybrids viewed as subsumed markets. The concept of the firm as a nexus-of-contract illustrates, with no role for authority. Williamson has adopted a more nuanced position, more in line with the organization theory perspective: contracts permeate all forms of organizations, but they tell only part of the story. I have clearly endorsed this position here, emphasizing the incompleteness of contracts and the existence of complementary devices. But the question remains open.

Second, there is the problem of determining if contracts differ across modes of organization. This chapter adopted the view that there exist discrete organizational structures, with properties of their own. If so, one expects contracts to exhibit substantial differences according to the type of arrangement in which they are embedded. Several neo-institutionalists (as well as mainstream economists) disagree. Once more, the contrast in the initial positions adopted by Alchian and Demsetz (1972) and Williamson (1979) is illustrative: the former defended the idea that all contracts share the same fundamental properties,[35] while the later endorsed the typology proposed by Macneil (1974), differentiating contracts along modes of organization. Further developments, in theory and in empirical studies, are needed, to make the decision.

Third, the question of the incompleteness of contracts remains controversial. This issue particularly concerns the relationship between new institutionalists and mainstream economists. The former share quite unanimously the view that contracts are "unavoidably incomplete", with non-contractible decisions both ex-ante and ex-post (Williamson, 1993, section 5). This question is crucial. If complete contracts provide the adequate unit of analysis, all relevant actions concentrate in the ex-ante incentive alignment, making ex-post governance largely irrelevant. Therefore, the study of contracts would be what matters while studying the "structural properties" of different modes of organization would at best be a minor issue. In a NIE perspective, the challenge is to model behavioral assumptions in order to provide microfoundations to incompleteness.

The Role of Specific Assets

Another controversial issue concerns the attributes of transactions that determine their costs and the weight of these attributes in the choice and/or fitness of a mode of organization. A series of papers on the paradigmatic case of the relationship between Fisher Body and General Motors in the 1920s recently reignited the debate. I do not intend to summarize this controversy.[36] I simply want to point out its importance for the analysis of organizations.

---

[35] Hence the provocative statement by B. Klein (1983, p. 373): "The question what is the essential characteristic of a firm now appears to be unimportant. Thinking of all organizations as group of explicit and implicit contracts among owners of factors of production represents a fundamental advance."

[36] The main elements of the debate are exposed in the April 2001 issue of the *Journal of Law and Economics*. Several chapters in this Handbook refer to the GM-FB case (e.g., Joskow, chap. 13; Klein, chap. 17).

In his 1937 paper, Coase linked the decision to integrate and the effort to economize on costs that the price system may impose on transactions. When the idea caught up, in the 1970s, two interpretations developed. Williamson (1975; 1979) established the well-known model identifying the three major attributes that would determine transaction costs: asset specificity, uncertainty, and frequency (see my section 2). At about the same time, Klein et al. (1978) argued that the main explanation to vertical integration was the risk of hold up from opportunistic partners once specific investments have been made. They illustrated with the decision of General Motors to integrate Fisher Body in 1926, which ended a long contractual relationship. This example has become a paradigmatic case, referenced in innumerable papers (Bolton and Scharfstein, 1998). The view developed in Klein et al. converged with Williamson's emphasis on the role played by contractual hazards in the tradeoffs among modes of organization, and with the development of empirical studies and econometric tests that largely focused on specific assets as the main source of these hazards.[37] This is what Coase has repeatedly challenged, since 1988 (1991, chap. 5), using the Fisher Body-General Motors case to defend the role of uncertainties and, above all, of human assets (in this case, the Fisher brothers) for explaining the decision to integrate.

This debate raises important issues for the theory of organization. One points the need for more extensive analyses and more sophisticated models of the determinants of transaction costs, and how they affect the choice and performance of different modes of organizations. Uncertainty and the role of human assets deserve particular attention in that respect. Second, we need more empirical studies, identifying and measuring relevant proxies in order to assess the role of these variables and their impact. As noted by Masten et al. (1991) and Joskow (Chap. 13, this book), most tests so far have focused on the role of specific investments, at the sector level. Looking at other variables and digging into data at the firm level or at the level of inter-firm agreements involve difficulties that need to be dealt with.

Digging Deeper in Organizational Arrangements

The initial research program in the micro-analytical branch of NIE focused on the tradeoff between markets and hierarchies. History explains this agenda: in arguing that there are situations in which firms may efficiently prevail over markets in organizing transactions, Coase challenged the conventional wisdom about the superiority of markets. For those convinced by the argument, making it operational and testing it was a legitimate priority. However, it has become increasingly clear that a satisfying explanation of *why* and *under what circumstance* one mode of organization overcomes another one requires investigating the internal characteristics of these arrangements. Some key issues are summarized hereafter.

---

[37] Beside theoretical problems, practical factors explain these developments, e.g., available data, easiness in defining proxies, etc. Joskow (chap. 13) discusses some of these issues.

First, we need more studies on how the internal organization of labor within a firm might affect "administrative costs" in comparison to the costs of taking advantage of specialization through markets. Although Williamson (1975, chap. 4 and 5; 1985, chap. 9) raised the issue, few studies followed that would use transaction costs lenses.[38]

Second, with the exception of Williamson and Demsetz, few new institutionalists have paid attention to the classical problem of the separation of ownership and management.[39] However, the varied institutions of corporate governance likely have an impact on the internal costs of organizing transactions. Demsetz (1995, commentaries 2,3 and 6) suggested that if operating in properly designed institutions, managers may save on transaction costs by their capacity to combine and develop dispersed knowledge. Further studies are needed here.

Third, a transaction cost approach to financial issues within firms and among hybrids remains to be developed. Alchian and Woodward (1987) briefly discussed the trade-off between debt and equity, noting that when risks of hold-up are high, users will have an incentive to own rather than to rent more exposed resources and will rather finance through equity than debt. Williamson (1988a; 1988 b) proposed a similar analysis, linking the choice between debt and equity to the redeployability of assets to be financed. However, few developments have followed these intuitions.

A fourth dimension that requires further exploration involves how transaction costs affect the selection of incentive mechanisms. Empirical evidences suggest that contracts for aligning interests of agents and principals are relatively simple and complemented by other motivational devices. Most new institutionalists share with mainstream economists the view that formal organizations have lower incentives than markets, since on markets agents can cash directly the results of their efforts (Williamson, 1996, p. 105). However, if the replication of market incentives ("selective intervention" in Williamson's terminology) is not possible, what factors allow firms to overcome costs of control and perform better than markets under some circumstances? The answer likely lies in the combination of organizational incentives, e.g., bonuses, job design, work rules, tasks assignments, strategic plans, delegation of power, information channels, corporate culture, and so on (Aoki, 1988, chap. 3 and 8; Holmstrom, 1999). Clearly, an institutional approach can improve our understanding of these issues.

One last problem, which attracted the attention in NIE earlier but has been neglected later on, concerns the emergence of new organizational forms, the evolution of existing ones, and their interaction with institutional changes. As early as 1975 (chap. 8), Williamson reinterpreted Chandler's view on large

---

[38] For example the suggestion (Williamson, 1988; Alchian and Woodward, 1987, p. 120; Aoki, 1988, chap. 5; and Ménard, 1997, pp. 40 sq.) that highly specific human assets are more exposed to contractual hazards so that they are likely to look for safeguards such as representation on the Board presumably have a significant impact on the internal organization and its costs. But we know almost nothing about this.

[39] The classic reference for this problem is Berle and Means (1934). This relative disinterest is particularly surprising if one notes a comment by Demsetz, according to which "... ownership of even the largest U.S. corporations is more concentrated than Berle and Means' discussion of the separation issue would lead one to believe" (1995, p. 63).

corporations with a transactional perspective. The first econometric tests in NIE were on this issue (e.g., Armour and Teece, 1978). Teece later combined transaction costs and evolutionary factors to go further (e.g., Teece et al., 1994), while Aoki (1990) extended the model. But Alchian and Woodward (1988, section 5) rightly noted that efforts to link organizational forms, and more generally organizational innovation, to asset specificity remain in a very preliminary stage.[40] Links with evolutionary economics may be fruitful on these issues.

These unsolved problems pay a tribute to the development of NIE. They suggest that the initial explanations to the existence of alternative modes of organization and the tradeoffs among them have opened the way to new questions. Innumerable empirical studies and econometric tests have substantiated the initial intuitions but also complicated them. It supports the idea that New Institutional Economics remains a progressive research program. New questions require to be investigated and a toolbox exists for exploring them.

ACKNOWLEDGEMENTS

I am particularly grateful to Mary M. Shirley and two anonymous referees for their very helpful comments on previous versions of this chapter. The chapter was finalized while I was visiting MIT. I greatly benefited from discussions with Robert Gibbons, Luis Garicano, Mathias Dewatripont, and participants to MIT workshops, as well as from discussions with Victor Nee and Richard Swedberg at Cornell. The usual disclaimer fully applies.

REFERENCES

Alchian, Armen and Harold Demsetz. 1972. "Production, Information Costs and Economic Organization". *American Economic Review* 62(5): 777–795.

Alchian, Armen, and Woodward. Susan. 1987. "Reflections on the Theory of the Firm". *Journal of Institutional and Theoretical Economics* 143(1): 110–137.

Alchian, Armen and Susan Woodward. 1988. "The Firm is Dead. Long Live the Firm". *Journal of Economic Literature* 26(1): 65–79.

Alston, Lee, Gary Libecap, and Bernardo Mueller. 1997. "Violence and the Development of Property Rights to Land in the Brazilian Amazon" in John Drobak and John Nye (eds.), *The Frontiers of the New Institutional Economics*. San Diego: Academic Press, pp. 145–164.

Alston, Lee J., Gary D. Libecap, and Robert Schneider. 1996. "The Determinants and Impact of Property Rights: Land Titles on the Brazilian Frontier". *Journal of Law Economics and Organization* 12: 25–61.

Anderson, Erin and David C. Schmittlein. 1984. "Integration of the Sales Force: An Empirical Examination". *Rand Journal of Economics* 15(3): 385–395.

Aoki, Masahiko. 1986. "Horizontal versus Vertical Information Structure of the Firm". *American Economic Review* 76:971–983.

Aoki, Masahiko. 1988. *Information, Incentives, and Bargaining in the Japanese Economy*. Cambridge: Cambridge University Press.

---

[40] A preliminary exploration was proposed in Ménard, 1994c.

Aoki, Masahiko. 1990. "Toward an Economic Model of the Japanese Firm". *Journal of Economic Literature* 28(1): 1–27.
Aoki, Masahiko. 2001. *Toward A Comparative Institutional Analysis*. Cambridge: MIT Press.
Armour, Henry O. and David J. Teece. 1978. "Organizational Structure and Economic Performance: A Test of the Multidivisional Hypothesis". *Bell Journal of Economics* 9: 106–122.
Arrow, Kenneth, J. 1964. "Control in Large Organizations". *Management Science* 10(3): 397–408.
Arrow, Kenneth J. 1974. *The Limits of Organization*. New York: Norton and Co.
Bajari, P and Stephen Tadelis. 2001. "Incentives versus Transaction Costs: A Theory of Procurement Contracts". *Rand Journal of Economics* 32(3): 387–407.
Baker, George, Robert Gibbons, and Kevin Murphy 2002. "Relational Contracts and the Theory of the Firm". *Quarterly Journal of Economics* 117(1): 39–84.
Baker, George, Robert Gibbons, and Kevin Murphy. 2003. "Relational Contracts in Strategic Alliances". Unpublished manuscript. Sloan School of Management, MIT, Cambridge.
Barnard, Chester I. 1938. *The Functions of the Executive*. Cambridge, MA: Harvard University Press.
Barzel, Yoram. 1982. "Measurement Costs and the Organization of Markets". *Journal of Law and Economics* 25(2): 27–48.
Barzel, Yoram. 1989. *Economic Analysis of Property Rights*. Cambridge: Cambridge University Press. New edition, 1999.
Barzel, Yoram. 2000. "The state and the diversity of third-party enforcers" in Claude Menard (ed.), *Institutions, Contracts and Organizations. Perspective from New Institutional Economics*. Cheltenham, UK: Edward Elgar, pp. 211–233.
Beckmann, Martin J. 1988. *Tinbergen Lectures on Organizational Theory*. New York: Springer-Verlag.
Ben-Porath, Yoram. 1980. "The F-Connection: Families, Friends, and Firms and the Organization of Exchange". *Population and Development Review* 6: 1–30.
Berle, Adolf E. and Gardiner C. Means. 1932. *The Modern Corporation and Private Property*. New York: Commerce Clearing House.
Bolton, Patrick and Joseph Farrel. 1990. "Decentralization, Duplication, and Delay". *Journal of Political Economy* 98: 803–826.
Bolton, Patrick and David Scharfstein. 1998. "Corporate Finance, the Theory of the Firm, and Organizations". *Journal of Economic Perspectives* 12(4): 95–114.
Brousseau, Eric and Jean-Michel Glachant (eds.). 2002. *The Economics of Contracts. Theory and Applications*. Cambridge: Cambridge University Press.
Cheung, Steven. 1983. "The Contractual Nature of the Firm". *Journal of Law and Economics.* 26(1): 1–22.
Coase, Ronald H. 1937. "The Nature of the Firm". *Economica* 2(1): 386–405.
Coase, Ronald H. 1960. "The Problem of Social Cost". *Journal of Law and Economics* 3: 1–44.
Coase, Ronald H. 1988. "The Nature of the Firm: Origin, Meaning, and Influence". *Journal of Law, Economics, and Organization* 4(1): 3–59.
Coase, Ronald H. 2000. "The Acquisition of Fisher Body by General Motors". *Journal of Law and Economics* 43(1): 15–32.
Commons, John. 1934. *Institutional Economics. Its Place in Political Economy*. New York: Macmillan.
Cook, Michael L. 1995. "The Future of US Agricultural Cooperatives: A Neo-institutional Approach". *American Journal of Agricultural Economics* 77: 1153–1159.
Cook, Michael L. and Constantine Iliopoulos. 2000. "Ill-defined Property Rights in Collective Action: The Case of US Agricultural Cooperatives" in C. Menard (ed.), *Institutions, Contracts and Organizations. Perspectives from New Institutional Economics*. Cheltenham, UK; E. Elgar, pp. 335–348.
Dahlman, Carl J. 1979. "The Problem of Externality". *Journal of Law and Economics* 22(1): 141–162.

Demsetz, Harold. 1968. "The Cost of Transacting". *Quarterly Journal of Economics* 82(1): 33–53.
Demsetz, Harold. 1988a. "The Theory of the Firm Revisited". *Journal of Law, Economics, and Organization* 4(1): 141–161.
Demsetz, Harold. 1988b. *The Organization of Economic Activity*, 2 Vols. Oxford: Basil Blackwell.
Demsetz, Harold. 1995. *The Economics of the Business Firm. Seven Critical Commentaries.* Cambridge: Cambridge University Press.
Demsetz, Harold. 2002. "Theories of the Firm and Externalities: A Critical Evaluation of the Role of Transaction Costs". WP, 20 pages.
Dnes, Anthony. 1996. "The Economic Analysis of Franchise Contracts". *Journal of Institutional and Theoretical Economics* 152(1): 297–324.
Dow, Gregory. 1987. "The Function of Authority in Transaction Costs Economics". *Journal of Economic Behavior and Organization* 8(1): 13–38.
Dwyer, F. Robert and Sejo Oh. 1988. "A Transaction Cost Perspective on Vertical Contractual Structure and Interchannel Competitive Strategies". *Journal of Marketing* 52:21–34.
Dyer, Jeffrey H. 1997. "Effective Interfirm Collaboration: How Firms Minimize Transaction Costs and Maximize Transaction Value" *Strategic Management Journal* 18(7): 535–556.
Eccles, Robert. 1981. "The Quasifirm in the Construction Industry". *Journal of Economic Behavior and Organization* 2(4): 335–357.
Ensminger, Jean. 1992. *Making a Market. The Institutional Transformation of an African Society*. Cambridge: Cambridge University Press.
Ensminger, Jean. 1997. "Changing Property Rights: Reconciling Formal and Informal Rights to Land in Africa" in John Drobak and John Nye (eds.), *The Frontiers of the New Institutional Economics*. San Diergo, CA: Academic Press, pp. 165–196.
Farrell, Joseph and Suzanne Scotchmer. 1988. "Partnerships". *Quarterly Journal of Economics* 103:279–297.
Fearne, Andrew. 1998. "The Evolution of Partnership in the Meat Supply Chain: Insights from the Beef Industry". *Supply Chain Management* 3:214–231.
Fein, Adam J. and Erin Anderson. 1997. "Patterns of Credible Commitments: Territory and Category Selectivity in Industrial Distribution Channels". *Journal of Marketing* 61:19–34.
Foss, Nicolai J., Kirsten Foss, Peter G. Klein, and Sandra K. Klein. 2002. "Heterogeneous Capital, Entrepreneurship, and Economic Organization". *Journal des Economistes et des Etudes Humaines* 12(1): 79–96.
Furubotn, Eirik G. and Rudolf Richter. 1997. *Institutions and Economic Theory. The Contribution of the New Institutional Economics*. Ann Arbor, MI: The University of Michigan Press.
Garvey, Gerald. 1995. "Why Reputation Favors Joint Ventures over Vertical and Horizontal Integration: A Simple Model". *Journal of Economic Behavior and Organization* 38:387.
Gaucher, Severine. 2002. *Organisation de filière et politiques d'approvisionnement. Analyse appliquée au cas des filières agroalimentaires*. Ph.D., Ecole des Mines de Paris, 343 p.
Ghosh, Mrinal and George John. 1999. "Governance Value Analysis and Marketing Strategy". *Journal of Marketing* 63:131–145.
Gibbons, Robert. 2004. "Four Formal(izable) Theories of the Firm". January 30, 2004. Working Paper, MIT and NBER.
Glachant, Jean-Michel and Dominique Finon (eds.). 2002. *Competition in European Electricity Markets. A cross-country Comparison*. Cheltenham, UK: Edward Elgard.
Goldberg, Victor P. 1976 "Toward an Expanded Economic Theory of Contracts". *Journal of Economic Issues* 10(1): 45–61.
Goldberg, Victor P. 1980. "Relational Exchange: Economics and Complex Contracts". *American Behavioral Scientist* 23(3): 337–352.
Grandori, Anna and Giuseppe Soda. 1995. "Inter-firm Networks: Antecedents, Mechanisms and Forms". *Organization Studies* 16(2): 183–214.

Greif, Avner. 1993. "Contract Enforceability and Economic Institutions in Early Trade: The Maghribi Traders". *American Economic Review* 83(3): 525–547.

Gulati, Ranjay. 1998. "Alliances and Networks". *Strategic Management Journal* 19:293–317.

Hadfield, Gillian. 1990. "Problematic Relations: Franchising and the Law of Incomplete Contracts". *Stanford Law Review* 42:927–992.

Hakansson, H. and J. Johanson 1993 "The Network as a Governance Structure: Interfirm Cooperation Beyond Markets and Hierarchies" in G. Grabher (ed.), *The Embedded Firm: On the Socioeconomics of Networks*. London: Routledge, pp. 35–51.

Hansmann, Henry. 1988. "The Ownership of the Firm". *Journal of Law, Economics and Organization* 4(2): 267–304.

Hayek, Friedrich von. 1945. "The Use of Knowledge in Society". *American Economic Review* 35(4): 519–530.

Hennart, Jean Francois. 1988. "Upstream Vertical Integration in the Aluminium and Tin Industries". *Journal of Economic Behavior and Organization* 9(3): 281–299.

Holmstrom, Bengt. 1999. "The Firm as a Subeconomy". *Journal of Law, Economics and Organization* 15(1): 74–102.

Holmstrom, Bengt and John Roberts. 1998. "The Boundaries of the Firm Revisited". *Journal of Economic Perspective* 12(4): 73–94.

Jacobides, Michael G. and Sidney G. Winter. 2003. "Capabilities, Transaction Costs, and Evolution: Understanding the Institutional Structure of Production". Working Paper, the Wharton School of the University of Pennsylvania.

John, George and Barton A.. Weitz. 1988. "Forward Integration into Distribution: An Empirical Test of Transaction Cost Analysis". *Journal of Law, Economics, and Organization* 4(2): 337–355.

Jorde T. and David Teece. 1989. "Competition and Cooperation: Striking the Right Balance". *California Management Review* 27–37.

Joskow, Paul. 1985. "Vertical Integration and Long-Term Contracts: The Case of Coal-Burning Electric Generating Plants". *Journal of Law, Economics, and Organization* 1(1): 33–80.

Joskow, Paul. 1991. "The Role of Transaction Cost Economics in Antitrust and Public Utility Regulatory Policies". *Journal of Law, Economics and Organization* 7: 253–283.

Joskow, Paul. 1997. "Restructuring, Competition and Regulatory Reform in the US Electricity Sector". *Journal of Economic Perspectives* 11(3): 119–138.

Khanna, Tarun. 1998. "The Scope of Alliance". *Organization Science* 9(3): 340–355.

Klein, Benjamin. 1980. "Transaction Costs Determinants of ≪Unfair≫ Contractual Arrangements". *American Economic Review* 70(5): 356–362.

Klein, Benjamin. 1983. "Contracting Costs and Residual Claims: The Separation of Ownership and Control". *Journal of Law and Economics* 26:367–374.

Klein, Benjamin. 1988. "Vertical Integration as Organized Ownership: The Fisher Body-General Motors Relationship Revisited". *Journal of Law, Economics, and Organization* 4:199–233.

Klein, Benjamin. 2000. "Fisher-General Motors and the Nature of the Firm". *Journal of Law and Economics* 43(1): 105–141.

Klein, Benjamin. 2004. "Fisher Body-General Motors Once Again: How Do We Know When a Holdup Occurs?" WP, UCLA. 41 pages.

Klein, Benjamin, Robert G. Crawford, and Armen A. Alchian. 1978. "Vertical Integration, Appropriable Rents, and the Competitive Contracting Process". *Journal of Law and Economics* 21:297–326.

Knoeber, Charles R. 1989. "A Real Game of Chicken: Contracts, Tournaments, and the Production of Broilers". *Journal of Law, Economics and Organization* 5:271–292.

Kogut, Bruce and U. Zander. 1996. "What Firms Do: Coordination, Identity and Learning". *Organization Science* 7:502–518.

Lafontaine, Francine and Kathrin Shaw. 1999. "The Dynamics of Franchise Contracting: Evidence from Panel Data". *Journal of Political Economy* 107:1041–1080.

Lafontaine, Francine and Margaret Slade. 1997. "Retail Contracting: Theory and Practice". *Journal of Industrial Economics* 45:1–25.
La Porta, Rafael, Florencio López-de-Silanes, Andrei Shleifer and Robert Vishny. 1998. "Law and Finance". *Journal of Political Economy* 106(6): 1113–1155.
Leffler, Keith B., Randal P. Rucker, and Jan A. Munn. 2000. "Transaction Costs and the Collection of Information: Presale Measurement on Private Timber Sales". *Journal of Law, Economics and Organization* 16(1): 166–88.
Levy, Brian and Pablo Spiller. 1994. "The Institutional Foundations of Regulatory Commitment". *Journal of Law, Economics and Organization* 9: 201–246.
Libecap, Gary D. 1989. *Contracting for Property Rights*. New York: Cambridge University Press.
Libecap, Gary D. and Steven Wiggins. 1985. "The Influence of Private Contratual Failure on Regulation: The Case of Oil Field Unitization". *Journal of Political Economy* 93:690–714.
Loasby, Brian. 1994. "Organizational Capabilities and Interfirm Relationships". *Metroeconomica* 45:248–265.
Macaulay, Stewart. 1963. "Noncontractual Relations in Business: A Preliminary Study". *American Sociological Review* 28(1): 55–67.
MacNeil, Ian R. 1974. "The Many Futures of Contracts". *Southern California Law Review* 47:691–816.
MacNeil, Ian R. 1978 "Contracts: Adjustments of a Long Term Economic Relation under Classical, Neoclassical, and Relational Contract Law". *Northwestern University Law Review* 72:854–906.
Malmgren, H. 1961. "Information, Expectations, and the Theory of the Firm". *Quarterly Journal of Economics* 75(3): 399–421.
Marshall, Alfred. 1920. *Principles of Economics*, 8th edn. London: MacMillan.
Masten, Scott E. 1984. "The Organization of Production: Evidence from the Aerospace Industry". *Journal of Law and Economics* 27:403–417.
Masten, Scott E. 1988. "A Legal Basis for the Firm". *Journal of Law, Economics and Organization* 4:181–198.
Masten, Scott E. (ed.). 1996. *Case Studies in Contracting and Organization*. Oxford: Oxford University Press.
Masten, Scott, James Meehan, and Edward Snyder. 1991. "The Costs of Organization". *Journal of Law, Economics, and Organization* 7(1): 1–25.
Mazé Armelle. 2002. "Retailer's Branding Strategy: Contract design, organisational Change and Learning". *Journal of Chain and Network Science* 2(1): 33–45.
Ménard, Claude. 1994a. "Organizations as Coordinating Devices". *Metroeconomica* 45(3): 224–247.
Ménard, Claude. 1994b. "Comportement Coopératif et Coopération: Le dilemme organisationnel". *Cahiers d'Economie Politique* 24–25.
Ménard, Claude. 1994c. "La nature de l'innovation organisationnelle. Eléments de réflexion". *Revue d'Economie Industrielle*, no hors-serie: pp. 173–192.
Ménard, Claude. 1995. "Markets as Institutions vs Organizations as Markets: Disentangling Some Fundamental Concepts". *Journal of Economic Behavior and Organizations* 28(3): 161–182.
Ménard, Claude. 1996. "On Clusters, Hybrids and other Strange Forms. The Case of the French Poultry Industry". *Journal of Institutional and Theoretical Economics* 152(1): 154–183.
Ménard, Claude. 1997. "Le Pilotage des Formes Organisationnelles Hybrides". *Revue Economique* 48(2): 741–751. English Translation, "The Governance of Hybrid Organizational Forms", in Ménard (ed.), 2004b, Vol. IV.
Ménard, Claude. 2004a. "The Economics of Hybrid Organizations". *Journal of Institutional and Theoretical Economics* 160(3), forthcoming.
Ménard, Claude (ed.). 2004b. *The International Library of New Institutional Economics*, 7 vols. Cheltenham, UK: Edward Elgar.

Milgrom, Paul, Douglass C. North, and Barry Weingast. 1989. "The Role of Institutions in the Revival of Trade: The Law Merchant, Private Judges, and the Champagne Fairs". *Economics and Politics* 2:1–23.

Milgrom, Paul and John Roberts. 1990. "The Economics of Modern Manufacturing: Technology, Strategy, and Organization". *American Economic Review* 80:511–528.

Nooteboom, Bart. 1999. *Inter-firm Alliances. Analysis and Design*. London: Routledge.

North, Douglass C. 1981. *Structure and Change in Economic History*. New York: Norton and Co.

North, Douglass C. 1984. "Government and the Cost of Exchange in History". *Journal of Economic History* 44:255–264.

North, Douglass C. 1990. *Institutions, Institutional Change, and Economic Performance*. Cambridge: Cambridge University Press.

North, Douglass C. 1991. "Institutions". *Journal of Economic Perspectives* 5:97–112.

North, Douglass C. 2004. *Understanding the Process of Economic Change*, Princeton, NJ: Princeton University Press Forthcoming.

Oxley, Joanne. 1997. "Appropriability of Hazards and Governance in Strategic Alliances: A Transaction Cost Approach". *Journal of Law, Economics and Organization* 13:387–409.

Oxley, Joanne. 1999. "Institutional Environment and the Mechanism of Governance: The Impact of Intellectual Property Protection on the Structure of Inter-firm Alliances". *Journal of Economic Behavior and Organization* 38:283–309.

Palay, Thomas M. 1984. "Comparative Institutional Economics: the Governance of the Rail Freight Contract". *Journal of Legal Studies* 13:265–288.

Palay, Thomas M. 1985. "Avoiding Regulatory Constraints: Contracting Safeguards and the Role of Informal Agreements". *Journal of Law, Economics, and Organization* 1(1): 155–175.

Park, Seung Ho. 1996. "Managing an Interorganizational Network: A Framework of the Institutional Mechanism for Network Control". *Organization Studies* 17(5): 795–824.

Pisano, Garry P. 1990. "The R&D Boundaries of the Firm: An Empirical Analysis". *Administrative Science Quarterly* 35(1): 153–176.

Podolny, Joel and Karen Page. 1998. "Network Forms of Organizations". *Annual Review of Sociology* 24:57–76.

Powell, Water W. 1990. "Neither Market nor Hierarchy: Network Forms of Organization". In L.L. Cummmings and Barry Staw (eds.), *Readings in Organizational Behavior*, Vol. 12, Greenwich, CT: JAI Press, pp. 295–336.

Powell, Walter W. 1996. "Inter-Organizational Collaboration in the Biotechnology Industry". *Journal of Institutional and Theoretical Economics* 152(1): 197–215.

Putterman, Louis (ed.). 1986. *The Economic Nature of the Firm*. Cambridge: Cambridge University Press.

Radner, Roy. 1992. "The Economics of Managing". *Journal of Economic Literature* 30(3): 1382–1415.

Raynaud, Emmanuel. 1997. *Propriété et exploitation partagée d'une marque commerciale: aléas contractuels et ordre privé*. Ph.D. Université de Paris (Panthéon-Sorbonne).

Rubin, Paul H. 1978. "The Theory of the Firm and the Structure of the Franchise Contract". *Journal of Law and Economics* 21(1): 223–233.

Sauvée, Loic. 1997. "Managing a Brand in the Tomato Sector: Authority and Enforcement Mechanisms in a Collective Organization". *Acta Horticulturae* 536:537–554.

Sauvée, Loic. 2002. "Governance in Strategic Networks". WP, ISAB, 19 pages.

Schwartz, Alan. 1992. "Relational Contracts in the Courts: An Analysis of Incomplete Agreements and Judicial Strategies". *Journal of Legal Studies* 21:271–318.

Simon, Herbert A. 1951. "A Formal Theory of the Employment Relationship". *Econometrica* 19(3): 293–305.

Simon, Herbert A. 1991. "Organizations and Markets". *Journal of Economic Perspectives* 5(2): 25–44.
Stigler, George. 1961. "The Economics of Information". *Journal of Political Economy* 69(3): 213–225.
Teece, David J. 1986. "Transaction Cost Economics and the Multinational Entreprise". *Journal of Economic Behavior and Organization* 7(1): 21–45.
Teece, David J. 1992. "Competition, Cooperation and Innovation: Organizational Arrangements for Regimes of Rapid Technological Progress". *Journal of Economic Behavior and Organization* 18(1): 1–25.
Teece, David and Garry P. Pisano. 1994. "The Dynamic Capabilities of Firms: An Introduction". *Journal of Economic Behavior and Organization* 27(3): 537–556.
Teece, David, Richard Rumelt, Giovanni Dosi, and Sidney Winter. 1994. "Understanding Corporate Coherence: Theory and Evidence". *Journal of Economic Behavior and Organization* 23: 1–30.
Thorelli, Hans B. 1986. "Networks: Between Markets and Hierarchies". *Strategic Management Journal* 7(1): 37–51.
Tirole, Jean. 1986. "Hierarchies and Bureaucracies: On the Role of Collusion in Organizations". *Journal of Law, Economics, and Organizations* 2(2): 181–214.
Vazquez-Vicente, Xosé Henrique. 2002. *LAbor Transactions and Governance Structure on the Shop Floor: A Neo-Institutional Approach to the Spanish Food and Electronics Industry*. Vigo: Universidade de Vigo.
Whinston, Michael. 2003. "On the Transaction Costs Determinants of Vertical Integration". *Journal of Law, Economics and Organization* 19(1): 1–23.
White, Harrison C. 1981. "Where Do Markets Come From?" *American Journal of Sociology* 87: 548–577.
Williamson, Oliver E. 1967. "Hierarchical Control and Optimum Firm Size". *Journal of Political Economy* 75(2): 123–138.
Williamson, Oliver E. 1975. *Markets and Hierarchies: Analysis and Antitrust Implications*. New York: Free Press.
Williamson, Oliver E. 1979. "Transaction Cost Economics: The Governance of Contractual Relations". *Journal of Law and Economics* 22(2): 3–61.
Williamson, Oliver E. 1983. "Credible Commitments: Using Hostage to Support Exchange". *American Economic Review* 73(5): 519–540.
Williamson, Oliver E. 1985. *The Economic Institutions of Capitalism*. New York: The Free Press-Macmillan.
Williamson, Oliver E. 1988a. "The Logic of Economic Organization". *Journal of Law, Economics and Organization* 4(1): 65–93.
Williamson, Oliver E. 1988b. "Corporate Finance and Corporate Governance". *Journal of Finance* 43(3): 567–591.
Williamson, Oliver E. 1988c. "Technology and Transaction Costs: A Reply". *Journal of Economic Behavior and Organization* 10(3): 355–363.
Williamson, Oliver E. 1991. "Comparative Economic Organization: The Analysis of Discrete Structural Alternatives". *Administrative Science Quarterly* 36(2): 269–296.
Williamson, Oliver E. 1993. "Transaction Cost Economics and Organization Theory". *Industrial and Corporate Change* 2(2): 107–156.
Williamson, Oliver E. 1996. *The Mechanisms of Governance*. Oxford: Oxford University Press.
Witt, Ulrich. 1998. "Imagination and Leadership: the Neglected Dimension of an Evolutionary Theory of the Firm." *Journal of Economic Behavior and Organization* 35: 161–177.
Yarbrough, B.; Yarbrough, R. 1988. "The Transaction Structure of the Firm: A Comparative Survey". *Journal of Economic Behavior and Organization* 10(1): 1–28.
Zucker, Lynne G. 1986. "Production of Trust: Institutional Sources of Economic Structure, 1840–1920 In B.R. Staw and L.L. Cummings (eds.), *Research in Organizational Behavior*, Vol. 8. Greenwich: JAI Press, pp. 53–111.

13. Vertical Integration

PAUL L. JOSKOW

1. Introduction

Understanding the factors that determine which types of transactions are mediated through markets and which within hierarchical organizations called firms has been an important subject of theoretical and empirical work in microeconomics generally and central to work in New Institutional Economics (NIE) in particular for at least the last 25 years. This essay reviews research that examines the choice between governance of vertical relationships involving suppliers of intermediate goods and services ("upstream") and the purchasers of those goods and services ("downstream") through some form of market-based contractual arrangement versus governance within an organization through vertical integration. My primary emphasis is on the transaction cost economics (TCE) framework for understanding the choice of governance arrangements, though I will briefly discuss several other theories of vertical integration as well.

The essay proceeds in the following way. First, I discuss the general comparative governance framework that is a basic feature of transaction cost economics (TCE) analysis and within which theoretical and empirical analysis of vertical integration associated with the NIE has proceeded. Next, I discuss traditional "neoclassical" theories of vertical integration that rely on market imperfections associated with market power, free riding, uncertainty, and economies of scale as explanations for vertical integration. I then proceed to discuss theories of vertical integration from a TCE perspective, focusing on the role of incomplete contracts and relationship specific investment. This section includes a brief discussion of the "property rights" (PR) approach to vertical integration, emphasizing the similarities and differences between the TCE and PR frameworks. Finally, I provide a brief discussion of the extensive empirical literature on vertical integration that has been stimulated by this theoretical research, focusing on key methodological issues (Peter Klein's chapter in this volume reviews empirical studies of the "make of buy" decision in more detail).

2. COMPARATIVE GOVERNANCE ARRANGEMENTS FROM A TRANSACTION COST ECONOMICS (TCE) PERSPECTIVE: THE BASIC STORY

I want to emphasize at the outset that there is not and will never be one unified theory of vertical integration. While the literature on vertical integration tends to focus on a simple dichotomy between the decision to "make" internally or "buy" through the market, from a TCE or NIE perspective we must be sensitive to the fact that there are a wide array of market-based governance arrangements that represent alternatives to both simple anonymous repeated spot market transactions and vertical integration. These two governance arrangements are polar cases. Theoretical and empirical research in the NIE tradition examines not only the determinants of the boundaries between firms and markets but also the origins of various "hybrid forms" of governance structure that lie between simple anonymous spot market transactions and unified hierarchical organizations with varying expanses of vertical and horizontal control. These hybrid forms include various types of long term contracts, joint ventures, dual sourcing (partial vertical integration), holding companies, and public enterprises. In addition, NIE research examines the attributes of internal organizations with different internal structures, incentive arrangements, vertical, horizontal and multi-product dimensions (Williamson, 1996, 2000). Accordingly, vertical integration is only one of many potential vertical governance arrangements that transacting parties may choose from and represents only one component of broader theories of the governance of contractual relationships and theories of the firm. Indeed, except in cases where there are significant market imperfections "... market mediation is generally to be preferred over internal supply..." (Williamson, 1971, p. 113)

Virtually all theories of vertical integration turn in one way or another on the presence of market imperfections of some type. Traditional approaches to vertical integration have tended to focus (though not exclusively as I discuss further below) on vertical integration as a response to pre-existing market power problems or as a strategic move to create or enhance market power in upstream or downstream markets. While not excluding these rationales for vertical integration, the NIE approach to the analysis of alternative market and internal organizational governance arrangements is much broader. It focuses on a well-defined array of attributes of individual transactions between buyers and sellers of goods or services and how they affect the performance (total cost) of alternative governance arrangements. It recognizes that there is a wide array of governance structures through which transactions can be mediated—from anonymous spot markets to internal administrative procedures within hierarchical organizations. It recognizes further that the task of consummating transactions must confront a variety of potential transaction costs, contractual, and organizational hazards, which are related to the attributes of the transactions at issue and their interplay with the attributes of alternative governance arrangements. These transactions costs involve the direct costs of writing, monitoring and enforcing contingent contracts as well as the costs associated with the <u>ex ante</u> investment <u>and ex post</u>

performance inefficiencies that arise as a consequence of contractual hazards of various types and various bureaucratic costs associated with internal organization. The inefficiencies of particular interest are those that arise as a consequence of <u>ex post</u> bargaining, haggling, pricing and production decisions, especially those that arise as the relationship must adapt to changes in supply and demand conditions over time, though inefficiencies in <u>ex ante</u> investments are also relevant. (Williamson, 1975, 2000) The governance structures that are chosen, whether market or hierarchical, are those that are best adapted to the attributes of the transactions of interest in the sense that they economize on the total costs of the trading relationship. That is, governance mechanisms are chosen in an effort to reduce inefficiencies associated with both <u>ex ante</u> investment and <u>ex post</u> performance of a trading relationship.

Contractual incompleteness, and its interaction with the attributes of different types of transactional attributes including asset specificity, complexity, and uncertainty, plays a central role in the evaluation of the relative costs of governance through market-based bilateral contracts versus governance through internal organization. When transactions are mediated through market-based contracts, circumstances may arise where the buyer and seller have conflicting interests. Consider the situation where transacting parties are locked-in to a bilateral trading relationship, in the sense that the potential aggregate value of continuing the bilateral relationship is higher than terminating it and turning to alternative buyers or sellers. In this situation one or both parties may have the incentive and ability to behave "opportunistically" to serve their own interests. The resulting bargaining over the terms and conditions of trade will affect both the distribution of the rents associated with this particular bilateral trading relationship and potentially the efficiency (quantities and production cost distortions) of the trades that are consummated <u>ex post</u> as well (reducing the rents about which the parties can argue as well as the aggregate value of the trading relationship <u>ex ante</u> and <u>ex post</u>). The potential advantage of internal organization in this case is that internal organizations are likely to better harmonize these conflicting interests and provide for a smoother and less costly adaptation process under these circumstances, facilitating more efficient <u>ex ante</u> investment in the relationship <u>and</u> more efficient adaptation to changing supply and demand conditions over time. As Williamson (1971, pp. 116–117) observed many years ago:

> "...The contractual dilemma is this: On the one hand, it may be prohibitively costly, if not infeasible, to specify contractually the full range of contingencies and stipulate appropriate responses between stages. On the other hand, if the contract is seriously incomplete in these respects but, once the original negotiations are settled, the contracting parties are locked into a bilateral exchange, the divergent interests between the parties will predictably lead to individually opportunistic behavior and joint losses. The advantages of integration thus are not that technological (flow process) economies are unavailable to non-integrated firms, but that integration harmonizes interests (or reconciles differences, often

by fiat) and permits an efficient (adaptive, sequential) decision process to be utilized...."

Accordingly, there do not exist, except perhaps at very high cost, complete contingent contracts that can specify at the time a contractual relationship is being contemplated how each of the parties will perform under all possible contingencies that could arise as the trading relationship proceeds over time. Contracts may be incomplete because of the direct costs of specifying and writing contracts that anticipate all contingencies, because of "bounded rationality" that makes it unlikely that the transacting parties can foresee all possible contingencies, and/or because of high monitoring, verification, and enforcement costs.

Incomplete contracts per se do not necessarily lead to market inefficiencies. It is the interaction between contractual incompleteness and certain attributes of transactions that can lead the parties to a trading relationship to become "locked-in" to the relationship once the relationship is consummated. This in term can lead to adaptation problems that can adversely affect ex ante investment incentives and the ex post efficiency of the trading relationship. These potential problems are especially acute when supply and demand conditions that are uncertain ex ante change over time and the bargaining threat points of the parties to the relationship move outside of a "self-enforcing range" (Klein and Leffler, 1981) or "off the contract curve" (Williamson, 2000) anticipated in the design of the initial market governance arrangements or contracts.

In this regard, as this literature has developed, relationship specific investments of various kinds, when they are required to support an efficient trading relationship, have come to play a central, though not exclusive, role in creating bilateral trading relationships that are susceptible to ex post bargaining and contractual performance problems. As I will discuss in more detail below, relationship-specific investments are investments which, once made, have a value in alternative uses that is less than the value in the use originally intended to support a specific trading relationship. Once specific investments have been made a potential "hold up" or "opportunism" situation is created if the parties can bargain over the appropriable ex post quasi rents (the difference in asset values between the intended and next best use—Klein, Crawford and Alchian, 1978; Williamson 1979, 1996) created by specific investments or must bargain or "haggle" to adapt to changing circumstances as the relationship proceeds over time. If contractual arrangements cannot be fashioned ex ante to mitigate these ex post incentives to bargain opportunistically without full regard for the total surplus produced by the relationship, ex ante incentives to make specific investments in the first place will be adversely affected and ex post performance and adaptation may be inefficient as well. To protect against these potential problems, transacting parties will explore the availability of alternative governance arrangements that reduce the costs of these contractual hazards, stimulating more efficient investment incentives ex ante, more efficient contract execution ex post and, more generally, that reduce the overall cost of the relationship. Vertical integration is favored when the benefits of mitigating opportunism problems by moving the transactions inside the firm, by reducing ex ante investment and ex post performance inefficiencies, are greater than other sources of static and dynamic inefficiency associated with resource allocation within bureaucratic organizations.

3. Traditional Approaches to Explaining Vertical Integration

The explanations of the causes and consequences of vertical integration that emerged in the field of industrial organization during the post-World War II period were heavily influenced by the sharp distinction drawn by neoclassical economics between resource allocation mediated through markets and resource allocation taking place within private firms and related types of hierarchical organizations (e.g public enterprises). Microeconomics in general and applied price theory in particular were concerned with the way anonymous spot markets worked to allocate resources. The factors that determined the boundaries between firms and markets were largely ignored and issues associated with the internal organization of firms and the way firms allocated resources internally were, with a few exceptions (Simon, 1947; Cyert and March 1963; Arrow, 1974), viewed as outside of the domain of economics. Firms were conceptualized as production sets that defined the technologically most efficient opportunities to transform inputs into outputs. They relied on anonymous spot markets to buy and sell inputs and outputs. That is, what firms did and what markets did were *complementary* activities. Coase's (1937, 1972) view that firms and markets were *substitute* governance mechanisms was not an accepted part of received wisdom until relatively recently. Precisely what was in a firm's production set and what was not was, at best, rather vague and there existed no meaningful economic theory to explain where to draw the line between firms and market transactions or to explain the diverse types of "non-standard" contractual arrangements observed in the real world.

Industrial organization theorists like Bain (1956, 1959) viewed the relevant firm production set rather narrowly as encompassing activities that were clearly physically related to one another. Both multi-plant economies and vertical integration downstream and upstream were generally viewed as being unnecessary for a firm to produce at minimum cost in the absence of technological relationships that physically joined production between plants. Instead, the presumption was that vertical integration, and non-standard vertical contractual arrangements, reflected the presence of market power somewhere in the system and/or efforts to create or exploit market power. Vertical integration could be a profitable response to costs of successive monopolies (e.g. double marginalization and related "vertical externalities" Tirole, 1988, Chapter 4), or it could facilitate price discrimination in a variety of different ways (Perry, 1978), or vertical integration (and long term contracts) could be used strategically to soften competition in the short run by raising rivals' costs or in the long run by increasing the costs of entry to foreclose rivals that might otherwise enter the market (Aghion and Bolton, 1987; Ordover, Salop and Saloner, 1990; Hart and Tirole, 1990).

Moreover, vertical integration itself was viewed theoretically as being "costless." That is, no internal organization costs were recognized, but only any costs realized through distortions in market prices, quantities, or the factor proportions used to produce output from a neoclassical production function. "Costless" vertical integration was also used as a benchmark against which alternative "costless" contractual arrangements could be compared. So, for example, distortions arising in one way or another as a consequence of double marginalization can be "solved" through vertical integration as well as with alternative (costless) contractual arrangements—two-part tariffs, maximum retail price maintenance, quantity forcing contracts, requirements contracts, service obligations, etc. (Tirole, 1988, Chapter 4). Absent transactions costs of some type, the alternative instruments are all equally attractive mechanisms for responding to double marginalization. Price discrimination could be accomplished with vertical integration or with contracts that prohibited resale and eliminated the associated arbitrage that could otherwise undermine price discrimination. The potential advantages and disadvantages of alternative contractual responses were discussed primarily in the context of their effects on market prices and quantities and their ability to allocate risk more or less efficiently between parties with different degrees of risk aversion. There was nothing embedded directly in the neoclassical theoretical approach to vertical relationships that allowed for attributes of the contractual and organization arrangements themselves to provide a basis to choose among alternative governance arrangements because there were no transactions costs associated with any of the institutional alternatives identified.

Another potential source of incentives for vertical integration is the free rider problem associated with the provision of pre-sale information and post-sale service by competing downstream retailers (Telser, 1960; Mathewson and Winter, 1986). If retailer's cannot fully appropriate for themselves the benefits of retail service expenditures but instead see some of the benefits accrue to their downstream competitors, this "horizontal externality" (Tirole, 1998, Chapter 4) will lead downstream retailers to under-invest in retail service (at least from the perspective of the manufacturer). Vertical integration is one potential solution to this problem. So too are various combinations of exclusive territorial agreements, resale price maintenance, profit pass-over contracts and other mechanisms. The unanswered question is how to choose among the alternative institutional arrangements in a systematic way?

Dennis Carlton (1979) has shown how the combination of uncertain demand for inputs and the failure of markets to be cleared by spot prices under some contingencies can create a private incentive for downstream firms to integrate backwards partially or fully for "supply security" reasons (See also Malmgren, 1961; Arrow, 1975; Green, 1986; and Bolton and Whinston, 1993 for related theoretical work). And there is abundant support in the business history literature for such a motivation for vertical integration (Chandler, 1964, p. 84). "The strong incentives for vertical integration arise because the vertically integrated firm is able to satisfy high probability demand by itself, and pass on the low probability demand to some other firm" (Carlton, 1979; p. 207). Willliamson (1971, p. 117) points out that "... arguments favorable to vertical integration that turn on 'supply reliability' considerations commonly reduce to the contractual incompleteness issue (footnote omitted)." Moreover, it is not clear that the market imperfections that create the incentive to vertically integrate here could not be equally well (or even better) mitigated by downstream firms by arranging a portfolio of fixed price and spot market contracts.

Finally, George Stigler (1951) proposed a theory of vertical integration based upon Adam Smith's famous theorem that "the division of labor is limited by the extent of the market." Stigler advanced a dynamic or life-cycle theory of vertical integration. He argued that in an infant industry producing a new downstream product vertical integration would be more likely to occur because the demand for specialized inputs would be too small to support independent firms supplying intermediate goods. As the demand for the new product grows, intermediate good suppliers whose production is characterized by increasing returns would be spun off as independent firms supplying inputs to multiple competing downstream suppliers. The empirical prediction is that as industries grow the extent of vertical integration should decline and as industries contract vertical integration should increase. Eberfeld (2002) argues that Stigler's theory is correct as long as there are no barriers to entry. Stigler's theory turns primarily on economies and diseconomies of scale and the implicit assumption that suppliers of new products require specialized inputs. It ignores transactions costs associated with both internal organization and market contracting. The theory has found little empirical support.

There is clearly no shortage of theories identifying potential incentives for vertical integration. This should not be surprising. As long as it is assumed that there are no additional costs associated with internal organization, almost any market imperfection necessarily becomes a candidate for creating private incentives for vertical integration. However, this approach ignores both the costs of internal organization and other costs of more complex contractual alternatives to either simple linear spot market contracts or vertical integration. In principle, the TCE framework should be able to encompass these traditional sources of market failure that have been identified as factors that increase incentives for vertical integration as well, and to do so in a richer and more systematic fashion. However, the emphasis of TCE to date has been on looking for other than traditional vertical and horizontal externality, foreclosure, uncertainty and risk allocation explanations for vertical integration and nonstandard vertical restraints rather than trying to incorporate these considerations into the analysis. This is a deficiency that can be and should be remedied (Joskow, 1991, 2002).

4. INCOMPLETE CONTRACTS AND ASSET SPECIFICITY

As noted earlier, one of the foundations of TCE is the recognition that contracts are incomplete and potentially lead to contractual hazards that adversely affect ex ante investment incentives and the efficiency of ex post performance, especially in response to adaptations required to respond to changing supply and demand conditions. These problems arise when the parties to a contractual relationship find themselves in a bilateral bargaining position ex post as a consequence of lock-in as discussed earlier. While there are several potential sources of lock-in that lead to potential bilateral bargaining and adaptation problems, much of the theoretical and empirical work in the TCE tradition has focused on relationship specific investments (asset specificity) and/or the interaction between asset specificity and other transactional attributes such as uncertainty, product complexity, and information asymmetries. Accordingly, I will focus the discussion here on the role of asset specificity.

Before proceeding, it is useful to outline an idealized set of steps that leads to a well functioning vertical relationship to provide a framework for further analysis. The actual structural attributes of each of these steps and their implications for the costs of the feasible set of alternative governance arrangements then becomes the focus of comparative governance analysis. How would an idealized contractual relationship be structured? First, the responsibilities and authorities of the parties to the transaction (including the appropriate assignment of property rights) would be defined ex ante. Second, contractual provisions would need to be agreed to ex ante that align the parties' incentives so that they have a mutual interest in performing in conformity with the intent of the contractual agreement. These contractual provisions include contractual formulas for adjusting prices and quantities as conditions change, cost and profit sharing provisions, assignment of investment responsibilities, financial guarantees and collateral requirements, etc., (Joskow, 1988b). Under normal conditions these provisions are incentive compatible and self-enforcing. Finally, the parties may agree to a process through which the terms of the contract can be adjusted (a renegotiation process) to facilitate smooth adaptation to changing circumstances that were not fully anticipated in the original terms of the contract. By facilitating realignment the costs of haggling over the consequences of changed circumstances can be reduced. These governance design challenges are confronted in a broader context that includes, among other things, the effects of parties' behavior on the value of reputational capital, and the external financial constraints on their behavior that reputational considerations imply.

What departures from these idealized contractual attributes might emerge in practice and increase the cost of consummating the transactions covered by the contract? The assignment of responsibilities, authorities or property rights may be incorrect or fail to cover all contingencies. The performance incentives may not work as intended under all contingencies and create ex post rent extraction opportunities and bargaining inefficiencies. The terms of the contract may be difficult to adapt to significant changes in economic circumstances leading to further rent extraction opportunities and performance inefficiencies. Imperfections in each step of the institutional design process can lead to distortions in ex ante investment incentives and ex post performance and adaptation inefficiencies. These imperfections in turn will vary based on the attributes of the transactions covered and the relative strengths and weaknesses of alternative governance arrangements in supporting a smooth trading relationship over time. As I will discuss in more detail below, the TCE approach takes into account all aspects of the trading relationship and compares their performance attributes under alternative governance arrangements, including internal organization. It emphasizes ex post adaptation problems, but also recognizes potential inefficiencies in ex ante investment.

Asset Specificity in Detail

As noted earlier, a relationship specific investment is an investment which once made (sunk) by one or both parties to an ongoing trading relationship has a lower value in alternative uses than it has in the intended use supporting this specific bilateral trading relationship. In the extreme, an investment made by a supplier in anticipation of supplying a product to a particular customer could be worthless if used to serve any other customer. More generally, we can think of specific investments as having significantly lower values, or producing lower gains from trade, when employed other than in supporting the intended relationship with a particular customer or supplier. Such investments create a bilateral dependency after they have been sunk defined by the difference between the value of the investment in its intended use and its next best alternative use. The parties to the transaction may then have an incentive to haggle over the distribution of the ex post quasi rents created by the specific investments. It is the problem of economically protecting the aggregate value of the specific investments from being reduced through this potential haggling that drives the choice of governance structure.

Asset specificity that is directly relevant to vertical integration is thought to arise in a number of different contexts (Williamson, 1983; 1996, Chapter 4):[2]

1. *site specificity*: The buyer and the seller are in a "cheek-by-jowl" relationship with one another, reflecting ex ante decisions to minimize inventory and transportation expenses. Once sited the assets in question are highly immobile. A mine mouth coal plant (Joskow, 1985, 1987) or a bauxite processing plant and the associated mines (Stuckey, 1983) are examples of site specificity.

2. *physical asset specificity*: When one or both parties to the transaction make investments in equipment and machinery that involve design characteristics specific to the transaction which have lower values in alternative uses. A boiler that has been designed to burn a particular type of coal (Joskow, 1985) and investments in tools and dies to produce parts that can be used in a specific downstream

---

[2] Masten, Meehan and Snyder (1991) identify "temporal asset specificity" as a sixth category. Williamson (1996, p. 106) argues that this is a form of site specificity and I agree with his assessment.

manufacturer's products (Klein, Crawford and Alchian, 1978; Klein, 1988) have this characteristic.

3. *human asset specificity*: When, as a consequence of learning by doing, workers accumulate relationship specific human capital that makes it possible for them to produce goods and services more efficiently than can otherwise equivalent workers who do not have this firm specific human capital. Such human capital is of particular value to the suppliers and customers that benefit from it, and is of lower value to the workers (or the firms they work for) if not utilized to support the specific relationship within which it accumulated. Design engineers who have developed special skills in designing a particular type of aircraft or automotive components are examples of human asset specificity (Monteverde and Teece, 1982; Masten, Meehan and Snyder, 1989).

4. *dedicated assets*: General investment by a supplier that would not otherwise be made but for the prospect of selling a significant amount of product to a particular customer. If the relationship is terminated prematurely, it would leave the supplier with significant excess capacity and a lower price to support the investment would be realized ex post than had been ancticipated ex ante. The development of a large natural resource deposit in a remote location to supply a large upstream user is an example of dedicated assets (Joskow, 1985).

5. *intangible assets*: Although specific investments are most frequently conceptualized as either physical investments or relationship specific human capital, intangible capital such as brand name loyalty can have relationship specific attributes. For example, McDonalds has significant brand name value which has accumulated over time through investments in product quality, advertising and promotion. The value of these investments is tied completely to the McDonalds brand name. In order to sell its products, however, McDonalds must convey the use of its valuable brand name to its distribution outlets, some of which it owns (vertical integration) and some of which are independent franchisees.

Effects on Ex Ante Investment and Ex Post Adaptation and Performance

The combination of incomplete contracts and relationship specific investments can have adverse effects on both ex ante investment and the efficiency of ex post performance by creating a bilateral trading situation in which the parties' bargaining in their own individual self-interest leads to a reduction in the overall size of the pie. The property rights literature (Grossman and Hart, 1986; Hart and Moore, 1990; Hart 1995) discussed below focuses on ex ante investment incentives and assumes that transactions are consummated efficiently ex post. The only inefficiencies that arise from improper alignment of property rights are reflected in distortions in ex ante investments, and these investment distortions are the primary focus of the analysis. Under these and other assumptions (Maskin and Tirole, 1999) the proper assignment of property rights or decision making authority can mitigate hold-ups over the ex post division of appropriable quasi rents and the associated adverse effects on ex ante investments. On the other hand, TCE is concerned with both ex ante and ex post inefficiencies that arise in bilateral trading relationships, though Williamson has generally placed more emphasis on ex post haggling and associated inefficiencies (Williamson, 1971, 1975, 2001; Klein, 2002) than on ex ante investment distortions. This emphasis, in turn, apparently reflects the view that internal organization is most likely to be superior to market contracting in circumstances where ex post bargaining/haggling costs associated with market contracting are high since what internal organization is good at is harmonizing the otherwise conflicting interest of the parties to the transaction and facilitating a smooth and efficient adaptation to changing supply and demand conditions.

For ease of exposition, I focus first on a simple model in which contractual incompleteness leads to an ex post expropriation of quasi-rents but not to inefficiencies in ex post trade. That is, while there is bargaining over the appropriable ex post quasi rents, and this affects ex ante investment incentives, given a particular level of ex ante investment the efficient quantity is produced and traded ex post. As we shall see, contractual incompleteness plus asset specificity leads to underinvestment ex ante.

Before relationship specific investments are made to support a trading relationship, let us assume buyers and sellers may have numerous potential suppliers and customers among whom they can choose to enter into an ongoing relationship (though there is no reason why there cannot be small numbers bargaining ex ante and "smaller numbers" bargaining ex post to incorporate pre-existing market power considerations as reflected in the traditional vertical externality and foreclosure literatures discussed above). That is, the markets are reasonably competitive ex ante. However, once a relationship is developed and relationship specific investments are made to support it, a competitive bargaining situation ex ante is transformed into a small numbers or bilateral monopoly bargaining position ex post. The small numbers bargaining situation results from the investment in relationship specific assets. Once these investments are made, the fact that they have lower values in alternative uses creates a stream of potentially appropriable quasi rents (the difference between the value in the intended uses and in alternative uses). It is these quasi rents over which buyers and sellers may haggle and bargain in the absence of a complete and easily enforceable contract that defines clearly the rights and obligations of each party when various contingencies arise. The potential for ex post bargaining over these quasi rents in turn affects the expected returns from the initial investment in specific assets and the associated incentives to invest ex ante. Accordingly, the level of investment in relationship specific assets will differ from what would maximize the aggregate gains from trade that potentially could be achieved absent opportunistic behavior. This increases the total costs of providing the goods and services being traded and is a social cost of opportunistic behavior.

The nature of the problem that arises when specific investments must be supported by incomplete contracts can be articulated more precisely with the help of a set of very simple analytical examples which are drawn from Tirole (1988, pp. 25–28). Assume that we have a buyer that is interested in acquiring one unit (for simplicity) of a product with particular characteristics. In order to meet the buyer's requirements efficiently, a supplier must make investments that are specific to the product that the buyer desires. Once these investments are sunk, their value in producing products for other buyers is lower than it is when the investments are employed to produce output for the intended buyer. The buyer and its supplier agree to enter into a supply relationship in period 0, the supplier must make its investment in period 1, and production and trade take place in period 2. (In this sense we have a "long term" relationship.)

Let I be the amount of the supplier's investment and $C(I)$ the ex post costs of producing the product to this specific buyer's satisfaction once the investment has been made, where $C'(I) < 0$ and $C''(I) > 0$. Assume initially that the value of the investment is zero if it is employed in alternative uses. The value of the output to the buyer is $v > C(0)$. Finally, assume that the parties do not enter into a contract prior to the supplier's investment, but instead agree to bargain over the price when the product is finally delivered.

To solve for the transaction price in period 2 and the supplier's expected profit maximizing investment in period 1 we must specify how the transactions price is determined ex post. Assume that the buyer and seller negotiate a price that splits the ex post gains from trade evenly between them once the investment has been made (i.e. Nash bargaining) and that the product is (efficiently) supplied given the level of specific investment that is forthcoming ex ante. Then the ex post price is given by:

$$P(I) - C(I) = v - P(I) \quad or \tag{1}$$
$$P(I) = [C(I) + v]/2$$

and the supplier's profit is given by:

$$max_I[P(I) - C(I) - I] = max[v/2 - C(I)/2 - I] \tag{2}$$

Equation (2) shows that from the supplier's perspective a $1 ex ante investment in cost reduction yields only a $0.5 return to the supplier. The rest of the ex post surplus is captured or "held up" by the buyer. Accordingly, the privately optimal investment in cost reduction is lower than the socially optimal investment in cost reduction. Solving equation (2) yields the result that the supplier invests up to the point where:

$$-C'(I) = 2 \tag{3}$$

while the optimal investment is defined by the maximization of the total surplus $[v - C(I) - I]$, not just the supplier's slice of the surplus. The socially optimal investment is then given by:

$$max[v - C(I) - I] \quad or \tag{4}$$
$$-C'(I) = 1 \tag{5}$$

Since $C(I)$ is convex, the supplier chooses a level of investment in cost reduction (equation (3)) that is too low compared to the level of investment that would maximize the gains from trade (equation (5)). The difference in production costs associated with these different investment levels is the cost of contractual hazards arising from the combination of the need for specific investments to support cost minimizing trade between the buyer and the seller and the absence of a contract that defines what the terms of trade will be ex post. The example's assumption that a specific investment has no value in alternative uses is, of course, extreme. However, the problem continues to emerge as long as the value of the specific investment in alternative uses is less than its value in the intended relationship (Tirole, 1988, p. 25.)

If the investments in specific assets could somehow be protected from this type of ex post hold-up problem, the supplier would be willing to increase investment in specific assets and reduce the overall cost of the trading relationship. The challenge in this case is to find a set of institutional arrangements that mitigate the hold-up problem which leads to underinvestment ex ante without incurring other costs that more than exceed the increased surplus resulting from additional investment in cost reducing specific assets.

Of course, in our example, we assumed that there was no contract negotiated by the parties in period 0, before the specific investments were made, which defined the terms and conditions of trade in period 2. We have assumed the ultimate in incomplete contracts—no ex ante contract at all. The most obvious way to solve the problem that is identified in the example above is to allow the parties to enter into a binding contract prior to the time that the supplier makes its investment decisions. In particular, the contract could specify that the buyer would pay a price $p = P^*$ in period 2 where P^* is any price that lies between v and $C(I) + I$. The critical assumption is that P^* does not depend on I, but is fixed ex ante. For example, P^* could be arrived at in period 0 through competitive bidding by suppliers competing to gain the right to supply the goods required by the buyer in period 2. If such a contract could be written and enforced costlessly, our problem would be solved. There would be no ex post bargaining opportunities and the supplier would have precisely the correct investment incentives since its payoff is given by $(P^* - C(I) - I)$ whose maximum satisfies equation (5) above. This is the ultimate complete contract and eliminates the contractual hazard that was previously identified with no contract.

Ex Post Contractual Adaptation and Performance Problems

The departure of TCE is to recognize that this type of complete contract will be impossible to write in many interesting situations. For example, even in this simple case, let's say that the seller refuses to deliver the product unless a price higher than the agreed price is paid, perhaps reflecting the quasi rents that could be expropriated if there were no contract at all. The buyer could go to court to enforce delivery at the contract price, but court enforcement can be costly, uncertain and time consuming. In addition, if it turns out that the supplier is unable to deliver in a timely way (specific performance), damages must be calculated which gets the courts involved in potentially complicated valuation deliberations with an uncertain outcome. These "haggling costs" both reduce ex post surplus and can affect its division among the parties, reducing both ex ante incentive to invest efficiently and the ex post value of the relationship given any particular level of investment.

The latter observations suggest that the assumption that ex post bargaining is efficient and, as a result, that the only inefficiencies arise with regard to ex ante investments is not a particularly realistic assumption. More generally with uncertainty and asymmetric information (Tirole, 1988, pp. 21–24; Myerson and Satterthwaite, 1983; Williamson, 1975, 2000) in the presence of bilateral monopoly ex post, bargaining will generally be inefficient. These inefficiencies in turn reduce the quasi-rents available to cover investment costs which further distorts ex ante investment incentives. The overall costs of the relationship increase due to the combination of ex ante and ex post inefficiencies. As already noted, Williamson (2000) argues that it is with regard to the ex post bargaining and adaptation inefficiencies where the action lies in terms of the opportunities for internal organization to reduce transactions costs and become a lower cost alternative than even the best available market contracting alternative.

Of course, real world transactions are often more complicated than what is captured in these simple examples, but the basic problems created by ex post lock-in and incomplete contracts are similar. For example, the nature of the technology for producing the goods or services at issue may lead to a situation where cost minimizing exchange requires complementary relationship specific investments by both the buyer and the seller (there may be other effective governance-related reasons, rather than technological reasons, for a contract to require both the buyer and the seller to make specific investments to mitigate incentives to behave opportunistically—Williamson, 1983). This not only changes the attributes of the ex post bargaining space, but also complicates the effects of outside opportunities on ex ante investment decisions. When we introduce uncertainty about future production and investment costs, uncertainty about the buyer's ex post valuation and the quantities of the product required, the need for bilateral investments in specific assets to be made by both parties in order to support an efficient trading relationship, and a product quality dimension, we face a much more significant contracting and enforcement problem than in the simple model presented above. Correspondingly, it becomes more and more likely that it will be extremely costly or even impossible to write credible complete contracts that specify ex ante how the buyer and seller will behave when any contingency arises; or to design an associated enforcement mechanism that will require the performance promised or assess damages for non-performance without distorting behavior and increasing the total costs of the transactions at issue. Moreover, complex long term contracts aimed at tying the hands of the parties so that they cannot behave opportunistically when foreseeable contingencies arise may also embody costly rigidities and have poor adaptive properties when contingencies not specifically provided for in the contract arise (Joskow, 1988, 1990; Williamson 1996, Chapter 4). Accordingly, while complex long term contracts carry potential benefits by better protecting against the opportunistic behavior associated with specific investments than would simpler but more incomplete contracts, they also incur potential adaptation costs when unanticipated contingencies arise. Inefficiencies associated with ex ante investment distortions and ex post contract performance problems will increase and internal organization will become a relatively more attractive governance structure.

On the other hand, there may be other constraints operating to affect ex post bargaining power that may mitigate the hold up problem and the effects of opportunism on ex ante investments. In particular, the presence of reputational capital and the potential erosion of its value by opportunistic behavior may operate to mitigate such behavior (Williamson, 1975, chapter 9; Klein and Leffler, 1981; Klein, 2002) and facilitate efficient relational contracting in the presence of specific investments and incomplete formal contracts.

5. Vertical Integration as an Alternative Governance Structure

These considerations help to explain why we observe a wide array of contractual arrangements in the real world that sometimes look very different from the "standard" anonymous spot market transaction that is featured in elementary and intermediate micro economics textbooks. However, these more complex contractual arrangements are unlikely to protect completely against the opportunistic behavior associated with specific investments and other sources of ex post lock-in, and necessarily incur negotiating, monitoring, enforcement and adaptation costs when changed circumstances push the threat points of the parties outside of the "self-enforcing range." Vertical integration represents an alternative governance structure to bilateral contracts for mediating the supply of a product that requires specific investments to support cost minimizing exchange. Rather than fiddling with contractual protections to mitigate the inherent conflicts of interest that may arise between independent buyers and sellers in the presence of specific investments, and dealing with other distortions and rigidities that such contracts may entail, the buyer may choose instead to integrate backward (or the seller integrate forward) into the supply of the input at issue (or sale of the downstream good). By so doing the parties to the transaction would substitute internal hierarchical governance mechanisms within a firm for governance by market-based bilateral contracts. The vertically integrated firm's managers (arguably) will pursue a common objective to maximize the firm's value. They are not expected to engage in the kinds of opportunistic behavior associated with specific investments and an incomplete contract between an individual buyer and seller each pursuing its individual firm's objectives.

If we were to apply the traditional methodology for analyzing incentives for vertical integration in response to market power and other standard market imperfections as discussed above (e.g. Tirole 1988, Chapter 4), the vertically integrated firm would simply be modeled as a costless entity having the objective function specified in equation (4) above. That is, the vertically integrated firm would have the incentive to maximize the aggregate gains from trade associated with the transactions at issue without any offsetting costs of internal organization. The contractual hazard associated with the specific investment is removed because there is no longer an economic agent in the picture that has the incentive or ability to haggle over the distribution of the ex post quasi rents. This approach assumes that both pieces of the ex post quasi rent pie are internalized into the unified objective function of the vertically integrated firm that can execute the associated transactions costlessly and efficiently.

This analytical approach is not fully satisfactory. As Coase has observed (1937), this approach implies that vertical integration will always either have superior efficiency properties or equivalent efficiency properties to decentralized trade between independent buyers and sellers in a market. Why then doesn't all economic activity take place within vertically integrated hierarchies with a single objective function? The problem is that this basic approach to analyzing vertical integration doesn't tell us what it is about internal organization that makes it a superior governance structure to imperfect market transactions in some circumstances but not in others. The attributes and associated costs of allocating resources within internal organization are missing.

An important difference between internal organization and market contracting is the nature of the delegation of authority to make decisions when contingencies arise which could not otherwise be contracted on effectively through bilateral contracts. The property rights approach focuses on ownership of physical and intangible assets (but not human capital that accrues to individual workers) where ownership carries with it the authority to determine how these assets will be used (Grossman and Hart, 1986; Hart and Moore, 1990; Hart 1995). Ownership of specific investments (e.g. through vertical integration) gives the owner the residual authority to use the assets to further the owner's objective function. While negotiations between managers within a firm may arise, the firm establishes clear lines of authority to resolve them. Ownership and the rights of control that go along with it change the status quo bargaining point within the firm and the ultimate allocation of the rents over which the bargaining takes place. That is, when specific investments are involved, ownership of the specific assets allocates the residual rights of control to the party that makes the specific investment. The owner then has the authority over the ex post trading decision and any internal transfer prices that may be relevant. Hart (1995) shows how various combinations of specific physical and human capital can affect the allocation of resources under alternative ownership arrangements. The residual rights of control that are conveyed by ownership affect the ex post distribution of surplus which in turn affects the ex ante incentives to invest.

The property rights approach strips the firm of most of its organizational features and focuses on how ownership and the associated residual rights of control affect the bargaining power of otherwise self-interested economic agents engaged in bilateral trade. This approach does not allow for any other changes in incentives and behavior of the transacting parties when the relationship is brought from the market inside of the firm (vertical integration). Thus, it largely ignores important differences between market transactions and internal organization other than simply a change in relative bargaining power between self-interested managers (Williamson, 1996, Chapter 4). However, the objective functions possessed by managers and the incentive and payoff structure that they face are different for managers within a firm as compared to managers in separate firms. One of the key tasks of management is to develop monitoring and financial incentive arrangements within the firm that induce the managers and employees to pursue the interests of the firm rather than the interests of a hypothetical independent division of the firm producing for its own account (Williamson, 1985, Chapter 6; Holmstrom and Milgrom 1990; Williamson, Wachter and Harris, 1975). These incentive arrangements include compensation contracts that partially tie compensation to overall firm performance and the effects of employee behavior on promotion opportunities and continued employment. In short, other things equal, the incentive and ability of a manager within a firm to exploit specific investments to hold up another division is different from what it would be if the managers were managing two independent firms.

Monitoring behavior and the costs and distribution of information are also likely to be different within a firm than between independent firms (Williamson, 1975; Arrow, 1975; Hart, 1995, p. 72). Employees within a firm have different incentives and obligations to reveal information to senior management from those of employees of an independent firm and can be subject to swifter and different penalties for hiding information (e.g. termination). Moreover, senior management has authority to use a variety of monitoring and information gathering mechanisms that can be matched quickly to problems as they arise without adhering to formal (incomplete) auditing contracts. The internal auditing departments of large firms have substantial authority to range far and wide in identifying behavior that is inconsistent with the firm's objectives. Accordingly, internal organization is likely to be better at obtaining those types of information that are directly relevant to monitoring, and controlling the opportunistic behavior by the firm's managers that would otherwise arise from the combination of asset specificity and incomplete contracts if the transactions took place between independent firms.

Internal organization can also rely on more informal and less time consuming procedures to resolve conflicts inside the firm than would independent agents bound by formal contracts. As Williamson (1996, Chapter 4) observes, the internal "contract law" within a firm is quite different from the arbitration and litigation procedures to which independent economic agents would have to turn if they could not resolve disputes. The latter can be a costly and time consuming process that typically involves a third party decision maker who must become informed about the issues de novo. The internal decision maker, whether the CEO or the relevant division manager, can utilize simpler and faster internal procedures for resolving conflicts between divisions and also is likely to come to the problem with much more information of relevance than would a third party arbitrator.

If hierarchical organizations have these attractive properties, why don't we see more economic activity taking place within very large organizations rather than through markets? The answer is that internal organization is good at some things, but not at others. Williamson (1996, Chapter 4) observes that when we look at the bigger dynamic picture, internal organization is a last resort that we turn to only in the presence of significant contracting hazards and associated transactions costs. This is because, opportunistic behavior associated with specific investments aside, decentralized market arrangements have superior adaptive properties to internal organization in many other important dimensions. Differences in the information structure between market and hierarchical governance structures which help to mitigate opportunism problems associated with specific investments may lead to inefficiencies in other dimensions (Hart, 1995, pp. 71–72). For example, employees may be less willing to reveal information that adversely affects their promotion possibilities or continuing employment. The kinds of low-powered incentives that characterize internal compensation arrangements may also mute incentives to exert the optimal amount of worker effort (Williamson, 1985, Chapter 6; Holmstrom and Milgrom, 1990). In addition, while internal organization is likely to be better at removing certain kinds of internal information asymmetries in the short run, it may be an inferior structure for obtaining, processing and using external information about prices, costs, quality, and technological change in the long run compared to repeated market transactions. For example, when a firm vertically integrates (or enters into a very long term full requirements contract) it is likely to lose some of the benefits associated with continually examining and accessing outside opportunities through repeated contracting. These opportunities include information about the "least cost" prices of the goods and services that the firm is producing internally and the availability of new technologies and production methods. While there is nothing that prohibits a vertically integrated firm continuing to look to outside opportunities to benchmark its performance, an internal division in competition with outside sources may have strong incentives to hide or misrepresent outside opportunities in order to protect itself from external competition. This type of organizational opportunism is different from the kinds of hold-up problems created by specific investments, but may be even more costly in the long run.

For these reasons, even in the face of significant contractual hazards resulting from specific investments and incomplete contracts, firms may still find it advantageous to continue to rely on arms-length market transactions for all or a fraction of their input or distribution requirements (dual sourcing) involving specific investments rather than turning to complete vertical integration. This choice may be made to provide management with external information that it can use to assess the performance of its internal divisions and to counteract the costs of various types of internal organizational inefficiencies. Competitive market prices convey a tremendous amount of information that is difficult to reproduce using internal accounting cost and auditing information. Moreover, this information is updated very quickly as supply and demand conditions change if a firm is in the market repeatedly. As organizations get larger the volume of auditing information that must be processed by management grows non-linearly with the size and scope of the firm (Williamson, 1975) and becomes more difficult to use to control costs and quality effectively and to adapt to changing market conditions. The potential shirking problems resulting from low power internal compensation incentives are also likely to become more significant as monitoring becomes more difficult in large organizations.

There are other dynamic considerations that may make the relative attractiveness of alternative governance arrangements in a particular industry or transactional setting change over time (Langlois and Robertson, 1989). As revealed by the extensive analysis of the GM-Fisher Body relationship (Klein, Crawford and Alchian, 1978; Klein, 1988, 2000, 2002) a detailed long term contract involving a transaction with significant relationship specific investment may work satisfactorily for some period of time. However, when external circumstances change, the existing contractual arrangements can lead to significant adaptation problems and associated performance inefficiencies. These adaptation problems are less likely to have emerged if the production of car bodies had been governed through internal organization rather than a rigid contract that did not anticipate a big increase in demand and the conflicts that emerged over plant location decisions. Changes in technology or government regulations may also change the relative attractiveness of alternative governance arrangements. For example, with specific reference to my work on coal contracts, changes in environmental laws in the U.S. have independently made it attractive to invest in fuel-flexibility capabilities in coal burning power plants. This flexibility in turn makes coal users less dependent on specific coal suppliers or coal supply locations, reducing the value of long term contracts. Accordingly, one would anticipate seeing a shift to shorter term more flexible contracts as the net costs of fuel-flexibility to mitigate potential hold-up problems declines as a consequence of environmental regulations that increase the value of such flexibility.

The bottom line is that there are benefits and costs of internal organization. Market transactions incur transactions costs associated with writing and enforcing contingent contracts and the inefficiencies ex ante and ex post resulting from opportunistic behavior that exploits specific investments. Internal bureaucratic allocation mechanisms can help to mitigate these types of transactions costs but incur other types of transactions or organization costs. The costs of internal organization are associated with the relatively inferior adaptive properties of bureaucratic hierarchies to rapidly changing outside opportunities over the longer term and the difficulty of designing compensation mechanisms to give managers and employees appropriate incentives to control costs and product quality. No governance structure is free from at least some transactions costs. The decision whether or not to vertically integrate then becomes a tradeoff between the costs of alternative governance arrangements. Governance arrangements are selected which represent the best that can be accomplished from a set of imperfect governance alternatives. Understanding the tradeoffs between governance alternatives and how they are affect by the attributes of products, production processes, inputs, legal, political and regulatory institutions is what the comparative governance approach is all about.

Despite these observations, however, I think that it is fair to say that the TCE literature on vertical integration, especially the empirical literature, has focused much more on the inefficiencies of market transactions than it has on the strengths and weaknesses of internal organization. Indeed, this may be one of the reasons why Gibbons (2003) argues that there is a lot of confusion about the similarities and differences between the TCE approach attributed to Williamson, Klein and others and the property rights or rights of control approach attributed to Grossman and Hart (1986) and Hart and Moore (1990). TCE emphasizes (verbally) ex post adaptation issues and the associated bargaining and performance costs, recognizing that these costs also affect ex ante investment incentives. The property rights literature assumes that ex post bargaining is efficient and emphasizes the effects of ex post rent expropriation on ex ante investment. However, both literatures have emphasized specific investments and, as we shall see, much of the empirical literature relates variations in the costs of governance structure to variables measuring asset specificity of various kinds, rather than on direct measures of ex post adaptation costs (which could be argued would be off the equilibrium path anyway), good proxies for their expected magnitude, or variables measuring variations in the costs of internal organization. The full implementation of a comparative governance framework requires that the costs of alternative market governance arrangements and the costs of internal organizations with different attributes be given equal treatment. The situation has not changed all that much since 1971 when Williamson (1971, p. 113) observed that:

> "A complete treatment of vertical integration requires that the limits as well as the powers of internal organization be assessed. As the frictions associated with the powers of administrative coordination become progressively more severe, recourse to market exchange becomes more attractive, *ceteris paribus* ... it is simply asserted [in this essay] that, mainly on account of bounded rationality and greater confidence in the objectivity of market exchange in comparison with bureaucratic process market intermediation is generally to be preferred over internal supply in circumstances in which markets may be said to 'work well'" (footnote omitted)
>
> "The properties of the firm that commend internal organization as a market substitute ... fall into three categories: incentives, controls, and what may be referred to broadly as 'inherent structural advantages.' In an incentive sense, internal organization attenuates the aggressive advocacy that epitomizes arm's length bargaining. Interests, if not perfectly harmonized, are at least free of representations of narrowly opportunistic sort ... In circumstances ... where protracted bargaining between independent parties to a transaction can be reasonably anticipated, internalization becomes attractive (footnote omitted)."
>
> "... when conflicts develop, the firm possesses a comparatively efficient conflict resolution machinery ... fiat is frequently a more efficient way to settle minor conflicts (say differences in interpretation) than is haggling or litigations."

6. EMPIRICAL EVIDENCE

The choice of governance structure and how this choice is affected by the kinds of transaction cost considerations that have been discussed here have attracted considerable empirical study. This empirical work has focused on decisions to vertically integrate, the design of non-standard contractual arrangements and the performance of both vertical integration and non-standard contractual arrangements over time as supply and demand conditions change. This work has included both detailed case studies of particular firms or types of contractual and organizational arrangements as well as econometric analyses based on large numbers of observations on the governance arrangements chosen for transactions with different attributes. Interestingly, the TCE framework has stimulated much more empirical work than either the traditional theories of vertical integration outlined above or the more recent property rights literature. This is to the credit of the scholars who have done theoretical work in the TCE tradition since they have produced testable hypotheses and endeavored to provide guidance to empirical researchers regarding how to measure relevant attributes of transactions affecting market contracting and internal organization. It also reflects the continuing interaction between theory, empirical analysis and public policy that has characterized developments in TCE over the last 25 years, a productive interaction that is largely absent from many other areas of industrial organization. Moreover, in the case of TCE related research, the empirical results are much more supportive of the relevant theory than is the case with the other theories of vertical integration (see for example Waterman and Weiss, 1996; Chipty, 2001; Mason and Phillips, 2000). Whinston (2003) argues that the empirical work stimulated by TCE does not do a good job distinguishing between TCE-based theories and property rights based theories of vertical integration and provides suggestions for how the predictions of property rights theories might be tested and its distinct predictions, including those that are contrary to the implications of TCE-based theories, tested empirically. Empirical work to date has not focused on trying to distinguish between TCE and property rights theories of vertical integration and there has been little effort to test property rights theories directly. This is probably the case because those who have led the development of property rights theories of vertical integration have made little effort to specify clear testable hypotheses or to relate them to variables that are likely to be measurable and available for empirical analysis. That is, they have not provided adequate guidance to empirical researchers and, as a result, the similarities and differences between TCE-based theories and property rights theories have been of much more interest to theorists than to empiricists. Perhaps the guidance provided by Whinston will lead empirical researchers to focus more attention on property rights theories.

There have been at least 500 papers published that have examined various aspects of comparative institutional choice from a TCE perspective. A significant fraction of these studies have examined the vertical integration or "make or buy" decision. There have also been several survey articles that have reviewed the empirical literature stimulated by TCE theories, including many related to vertical integration and non-standard vertical contracting arrangements (Joskow, 1988; Shelanski and Klein, 1995; Crocker and Masten, 1996; Coeurderoy and Quélin, 1997; Vannoni 2002). In addition, Peter Klein has written a chapter in this volume that reviews the empirical work on the "make or buy" decision. Accordingly, my discussion here will be relatively brief and focus on methodological issues rather than providing a complete catalogue of empirical studies and their results. Masten, Mehan and Snyder (1991) present a very useful empirical model that captures the essence of the comparative governance approach, the associated TCE predictions regarding the choice between governing vertical relationships with market contracts or through vertical integration (internal organization), and the issues raised for empirical analysis. I will use that model here since it helps to organize alternative empirical approaches and to identify important empirical issues. While it is most relevant to econometric studies of the choice between "market" and "organization," it also provides useful guidance for related case study research.

Masten, Mehan and Snyder focus on a model of the choice between market contracting (m) and internal organization—vertical integration—(o). Following the comparative governance arrangements approach they define the costs of the two alternative governance arrangements as:

C_o = cost of organizing transactions inside a firm (e.g. VI)
C_m = cost of organizing transactions through a (least cost) market contracting mechanism

Then the choice between market contracting and vertical integration depends on the relative costs of the too alternative governance arrangements. That is, the theory implies that transacting parties will choose internal organization if $C_o < C_m$ and vice versa. The total costs of transacting associated with the alternative governance arrangements then depend on those attributes of the transactions that affect the costs of market contracting (measured by the elements of a vector Z) and the costs of vertical integration (measured by the elements of a vector X). X and Z may or may not include common elements. Accordingly, the costs of vertical integration or internal organization (o) and of market contracting (m) can be modeled as:

$$C_o = \alpha X + e \qquad (6)$$
$$C_m = \beta Z + u \qquad (7)$$

where α and β are the coefficients that measure the marginal governance cost associated with each relevant transactional attribute for internal organization and market governance structures respectively and e and u are random disturbance terms which may or may not be correlated with one another. It follows immediately that the probability of choosing vertical integration depends on the probability that the costs of internal organization are less than the costs of market transactions.

Probability of choosing internal organization $= Pr(C_o < C_m)$
$$= Pr(e - u < \beta Z - \alpha X) \quad (8)$$

Unfortunately, it is rarely possible to measure the costs of internal organization (C_o) and the costs of market contracting (C_M) directly. As a result, we cannot estimate the parameters of the structural model (1) and (2) directly. Nor do we typically have good cardinal measures of the transactional attributes that enter X and Z. Instead, as we shall see, researchers frequently must rely on ordinal proxy variables to measure variations in the elements of X and Z. So, empirical studies often rely on observations indicating whether or not a relationship is governed by internal organization or market contract, creating a 0,1 limited dependant variable, and various proxies for variations in transaction related variables that are elements of X and/or Z, such as asset specificity, complexity, uncertainty, and frequency of transactions or repeated interaction. Hypotheses regarding organization form can then be based on the estimated coefficients of α and β. These coefficients can be estimated using limited dependent variable techniques like probit or logit (though only up to a proportionality factor without independent information about the variance of $(e - u)$). Moreover, if X and Z share common variables (e.g. asset specificity) then one can test whether $(\beta_k - \alpha_k) > 0$, but not whether both coefficients are non-negative, which weakens the power of the associated hypothesis tests. For example, if one believed that when cost minimizing exchange requires more resources devoted to specific investments the costs of both market contracts <u>and</u> internal organization increased, we would only be able to identify the relative costs (or net costs) of one governance arrangement compared to the other. If it were the case that asset specificity has little effect on market transactions, but reduced the costs of internal organization, then α_k would be negative and $(\beta_k - \alpha_k) > 0$ even though asset specificity has no effect on the costs of transacting through bilateral contracts. These possibilities reduce the power of the reduced form approach to hypothesis testing, though how important this is depends on whether there is good reason to believe that asset specificity affects internal organization costs in any systematic way. I have not been convinced that there is. If X and Z do not share common elements (e.g. variations in asset specificity affect the cost of market transactions but do not affect the costs of internal organization directly), we can identify the signs of the relevant coefficients independently. In many applications, the implicit assumption is that X and Z are orthogonal (e.g. variations in asset specificity affect the costs of market organization but not the costs of internal organization), the focus is on the measurement of the elements of Z (i.e. when $\beta_k > 0$ then $\alpha_k = 0$ and vice versa) and on the signs and magnitudes the estimated coefficients of the "market failure" variables included in Z. If the assumption that X and Z are orthogonal is not correct, not only can we measure only the sign and magnitude of $(\beta_k - \alpha_k)$, but if there are left out variables in X that are correlated with the included elements of Z it may not even be possible to get unbiased estimated of $(\beta_k - \alpha_k)$.

Masten, Meehan and Snyder go on to show that if we can measure C_o or C_m directly, we can measure the individual structural coefficients (not just their difference) and the cost of the other organizational form using switching regression techniques (if X and Z are orthogonal or e and u are uncorrelated). They then apply this technique to measure the costs of governing the production of several components used in naval shipbuilding with varying transactional attributes using either vertical integration or contracting with third parties. I am familiar with only one other study that measures the costs of alternative governance arrangements directly (Kerkvliet 1991).

With this basic empirical model in mind, let us now turn to the methods used in the empirical literature that seeks to test whether variations in transaction attributes such as asset specificity affect the choice between vertical integration and market contracting as TCE theory predicts. These studies tend to follow a similar empirical methodology. They generally focus on a particular good or service that is used as an input to produce or distribute a specific class of products: automobile components, (Klein, Crawford and Alchian, 1978; Klein, 2000, 2002; Monteverde and Teece, 1982; Walker and Weber, 1984; Langois and Robertson, 1989); coal (Joskow, 1985, 1987, 1988b, 1990; Kerkvliet 1991); aerospace systems (Masten, 1984); aluminum (Stukey, 1983); chemicals (Lieberman, 1991); forestry (Globerman and Schwindt, 1986)); carbonated beverages (Muris, Scheffman and Spiller 1992); pulp and paper (Ohanian, 1994); property-liability insurance (Regan, 1997). Other studies focus on a set of products that can be distributed through a similar set of alternative distribution modes (Anderson and Schmittlein (1984)). The sale of these goods and services is mediated by several different governance structures (e.g. vertical integration, franchise agreements, long term contracts, spot market sales) and the governance choices are observable.

The empirical challenge is then to determine whether the incidence of the alternative governance structures observed in practice can be explained by variations in the transactional characteristics of the goods and services whose governance structures are being investigated, in particular by the importance of asset specificity, holding other transactional attributes constant (or assuming that any associated missing variables are uncorrelated with the measures of asset specificity). That is, to measure the coefficients β and α. In light of the empirical model discussed above this challenge is more daunting than might first meet the eye given the limitations on measuring all of the dependent and independent variables that we would measure under ideal conditions.

To respond to this empirical challenge in the absence of direct measures of the costs of transacting under different governance arrangements, empirical work typically relies instead on information about the actual utilization of alternative governance structures to mediate specific groups of transactions within the (narrow) class of products being studied. For example, in my work on coal supply arrangements for electric utilities I identified specific generating stations that relied on coal supplies from affiliated mines as well as generating stations that contracted for coal with unaffiliated suppliers. (My research program involved an examination of the choice between vertical integration and market contracting (1985), the duration of contracts for the bulk of the coal supply relationships that did not involve vertical integration (Joskow, 1987), the adjustment features built into the contracts to allow prices and quantities to adapt over time (Joskow, 1988), and the ex post performance of the contractual arrangements, including the use of the courts to enforce contractual commitments (Joskow, 1990). As another example, Monteverde and Teece identify the proportions of various automobile components utilized by U.S. automobile manufacturers which are produced internally compared to the proportion procured from third parties. In both sets of studies, there is substantial variation across the sample in the reliance on vertical integration. Many other studies take a similar approach.

The next step is to develop measures of the exogenous characteristics of the underlying transactions, with particular attention devoted to measuring the importance of specific investments and other variables that may interact with asset specificity to affect the costs of market contracting and the incidence of opportunistic behavior that could make market contracting more costly in terms of ex ante investment distortions and ex post performance inefficiencies. Measuring variations in the importance of specific investments to support cost-minimizing exchange is difficult. In a number of cases survey data have been used to characterize the importance of specific investments in supporting different groups of transactions within the set that is being studied (Monteverde and Teece, 1982; Anderson and Schmittlein, 1984). In other cases efforts are made to develop ordinal characterizations of the different types of asset specificity associated with specific sets of transactions within the groups (e.g. Joskow, 1985) focuses on mine-mouth plants as classical examples of site specificity).

Ideally, it would be desirable to identify attributes of the firms in the sample that are expected to affect the costs of internal organization as well. Then the comparative costs of alternative governance arrangements could be captured directly. As a practical matter, most of these studies rely on samples of firms that are reasonably assumed to have identical "internal organizational" attributes. The implicit assumption is that the variables that affect the costs of market contracting are orthogonal to the variables that affect the costs of internal organization. For example, in my work on coal contracts, the firms involved all produced electricity (a homogeneous product), were regulated monopolies and where subject to similar types of economic regulation. I had no reason to believe that variations in the importance of asset specificity affected the costs of internal organization significantly, while they were expected to affect the costs of market contracting significantly. Monteverde and Teece (1982) look at transactions involving a small number of automobile firms with widely varying demands for components. They implicitly assumed that some variables (e.g. firm size) affected the costs of internal organization and others affected the costs of market contracting. That is, the implicit assumption again is that X and Z

are orthogonal. If this assumption is not correct it reduces the power of the tests of the TCE theory and may lead to biased estimates of the coefficients being estimated.

With these data in hand, and recognizing the potential problems associated with the measurement issues that I have discussed, the analysis then proceeds to determine whether the variations in the governance structures observed (vertical integration or bilateral contracting, extent of vertical integration, extent of contractual pre-commitment) can be associated with variations in the importance of specific investments and other characteristics of transactions that the theory suggests will lead to opportunistic behavior and related contractual hazards. As noted earlier, in econometric application, the dependent variable is typically a limited dependent variable that indicates whether vertical integration is utilized ($y = 1$) or not ($y = 0$) or the intensity of vertical integration ($y = \%$ of purchases by a buyer from internal sources). For the reasons discussed above, and nicely illuminated by Masten, Mehan and Snyder (1991), the results and power of the tests must be interpreted with great care.

In the end, we become convinced about the validity of a theory based on the accumulation of evidence from many studies examining a wide range of transactions and governance arrangements. The accumulation of results provides the most important power of the hypothesis tests. The empirical studies of vertical integration and how the choice of this governance structure is influenced by the importance of specific investment and other variables that could lead to ex ante and ex post contractual inefficiencies overwhelmingly show that the importance of specific investments is both a statistically and economically important causal factor influencing the decision to vertically integrate. Indeed, it is hard to find many other areas in industrial organization where there is such an abundance of empirical work supporting a theory of firm or market structure. And it is the combination of compelling theoretical analysis combined with a large body of supporting evidence that makes the TCE approach to understand vertical integration and alternative vertical governance arrangements so important.

7. CONCLUSIONS

Let me conclude where I began. There is no single unified theory of vertical integration that exists today or is likely to exist in the future. There are many types of market imperfections that could lead transacting parties to turn to vertical integration as an alternative governance arrangement, recognizing that vertical integration is one of many governance alternatives to relying on anonymous spot market contracting. However, the NIE/TCE approach provides a framework that can encompass and enrich all leading theories of vertical integration. It does so by taking a comparative governance approach, recognizing that there are unique but systematic costs associated with alternative market contracting structures, with vertical integration and with various hybrid forms, and by building on a synergistic relationship between theoretical and empirical analysis.

This being said, there is still much to learn about vertical integration, alternative market contracting structures and various hybrid forms. In my view, we have made more progress in understanding and measuring the hazards and associated costs of market contracting in the presence of alternative transactional attributes than we have about the costs of internal organization and how these costs are affected by different internal organizational and incentive structures. This observation is especially relevant to the state of empirical analysis where measurement issues remain a serious challenge. In addition, I believe that it would be very productive to focus more attention on the dynamic properties of both contractual relationships and internal organization. The "make or buy" decision is not a once and for all decision. Firms may choose to vertically integrate and then decide that it is less costly to rely on market contracting. As in the case of GM-Fisher body, firms may choose to govern a relationship by contract and then decide to take production in house. Better understanding how idiosyncratic contractual relationships adapt to changing supply and demand conditions over time, how organizations respond to changing circumstances and ageing over time, and why governance arrangements change over time will provide deeper insights into both the market imperfection and organizational imperfection considerations that affect the choice of governance arrangements.

Acknowledgement

I have benefited enormously from discussions with my colleague Bob Gibbons and from comments from Claude Menard and two anonymous referees. Portions of this essay are drawn from my paper "Asset Specificity and Vertical Integrations" (1998).

References

Aghion, Philippe and Patrick Bolton. 1987. "Contracts as a Barrier to Entry". *American Economic Review* 77:388–401.
Anderson, Erin and David Schmittlein. 1984. "Integration of the Sales Force: An Empirical Examination". *Rand Journal of Economics* 15:385–395.
Arrow, Kenneth J. 1974. *The Limits of Organization*. New York: W.W. Norton.
Arrow, Kennth, J. 1975. "Vertical Integration and Communication". *The Bell Journal of Economics*, 173–183.
Bain, Joe. 1956. *Barriers to New Competition*. Cambridge, MA: Harvard University Press.
Bain, Joe. 1959. *Industrial Organization*. New York: Wiley.
Bolton, Patrick and Michael Whinston. 1993. "Incomplete Contracts, Vertical Integration, and Supply Assurance". *Review of Economic Studies* 60:121–48.
Carlton, Dennis. 1979. "Vertical Integration in Competitive Markets Under Uncertainty". *Journal of Industrial Economics* 27:189–209.
Chandler, Alfred. 1964. *Strategy and Structure: Chapters in the History of American Industrial Experience*. Cambridge, MA: MIT Press.
Chipty, Tasneem. 2001. "Vertical Integration, Market Foreclosure, and Consumer Welfare in the Cable Television Industry". *American Economic Review* 91:428–453.

Coase, Ronald. 1937. "The Nature of the Firm". *Economica* 4:386–405.
Coase, Ronald. 1972. "Industrial Organization: A Proposal for Research" in. V.R. Fuchs (ed.), *Policy Issues and Research Opportunities in Industrial Organization*. New York: National Bureau of Economics Research, pp. 59–73.
Coeurderoy, Régis and Bertrand Quélin. 1997. "Transaction Cost Theory: A Survey on Empirical Studies on Vertical Integration". *Revue Economie Politique* 107:146–181 [in French].
Crocker, Keith and Scott Masten. 1996. "Regulation and Administered Contracts Revisited: Lessons Fram Transaction-Cost Economics for Public Utility Regulation". *Journal of Regulatory Economics* 9:5–40.
Cyert, Richard and James March. 1963. *A Behavioral Theory of the Firm*. Englewood Cliffs, NJ: Prentice Hall.
Elberfeld, Walter. 2002. "Market Size and Vertical Integration: Stigler's Hypothesis Reconsidered". *Journal of Industrial Economics* 50:23–43.
Gibbons, Robert. 2003. "Four Formal(izable) Theories of the Firm?" preliminary and incomplete draft, August 6, 2003.
Globerman, Steven and Richard Schwindt. 1986. "The Organization of Vertically Integrated Transactions in the Canadian Forest Products Industry". *Journal of Economic Behavior and Organization* 7:199–212.
Green, Jerry. 1986. "Vertical Integration and Assurance of Markets". in F.G. Mathewson and J.E. Stiglitz (eds.), *New Developments in the Analysis of Market Structure*. Cambridge, MA: MIT Press.
Grossman Sanford and Oliver Hart. 1986. "The Costs and Benefits of Ownership: A Theory of Vertical and Lateral Integration". *Journal of Political Economy* 94:691–719.
Hart, Oliver. 1995. *Firms Contracts and Financial Structure*. Oxford: Clarendon Press.
Hart, Oliver and John Moore. 1990. "Property Rights and the Nature of the Firm". *Journal of Political Economy* 98:1119–1158.
Hart, Oliver and Jean Tirole. 1990. "Vertical Integration and Market Foreclosure". *Brookings Papers on Economic Activity*, (special issue:), 205–276.
Holmstrom, Bengt and Paul Milgrom. 1990. "Regulating Trade Among Agents". *Journal of Theoretical and Institutional Economics* 146:85–105.
Joskow, Paul L. 1985. "Vertical Integration and Long Term Contracts: The Case of Coal-burning Electric Generating Stations". *Journal of Law, Economics and Organization* 1:33–80.
Joskow, Paul L. 1987. "Contract Duration and Relationship Specific Investments". *American Economic Review* 77:168–175.
Joskow, Paul L. 1988a. "Asset Specificity and the Structure of Vertical Relationships: Empirical Evidence". *Journal of Law, Economics and Organization* 4:95–117.
Joskow, Paul L. 1988b. "Price Adjustment in Long Term Contracts: The Case of Coal". *Journal of Law and Economics* 31:47–83.
Joskow, Paul L. 1990. "Price Adjustment in Long Term Contracts: Further Evidence from Coal Markets". *Rand Journal of Economics* 21:251–274.
Joskow, Paul L. 1991. "The Role of Transactions Cost Economics in Antitrust and Public Utility Regulatory Policies". *Journal of Law, Economics and Organization* 7:497–540.
Joskow, Paul L. 1998. "Asset Specificity and Vertical Integration". Peter Neuman, (ed.), *The New Palgrave Dictionary of Economics and Law* London: MacMillan, pp. 1998.
Joskow, Paul L. 2002. "Transaction Cost Economics, Antitrust Rules and Remedies". *Journal of Law, Economics and Organization* 18:95–116
Kerkvliet, Joe. 1991. "Efficiency and Vertical Integration: The Case of Mine-mouth Electric Generating Plants". *The Journal of Industrial Economics* 39:467–482.
Klein, Benjamin. 1988. "Vertical Integration as Organized Ownership: The Fisher Body-General Motors Relationship Revisited". *Journal of Law, Economics and Organization* 4:199–213.
Klein, Benjamin. 2000. "Fisher-General Motors and the Nature of the Firm". *Journal of Law and Economics* 43:105–141.

Klein, Benjamin. 2002. "Fisher Body-General Motors Once Again: How do We Know When A Holdup Occurs?" Mimeo.
Klein, Benjamin, Robert Crawford, and Armen Alchian. "Vertical Integration, Appropriable Rents, and the Competitive Contracting Process". *Journal of Law and Economics* 21:297–326.
Klein, Benjamin and Kieth Leffler. 1981. "The Role of Market Forces in Assuring Contractual Performance". *Journal of Political Economy* 89:615–641.
Langlois, Richard and Paul L. Robertson. 1989. "Explaining Vertical Integration: Lessons from the American Automobile Industry". *The Journal of Economic History* 69:361–375.
Levy, D.T. 1984. "Testing Stigler's Interpretation of 'Division of Labor is Limited by the Extent of the Market'". *Journal of Industrial Economics* 32:377–389.
Lieberman, Marvin. 1991. "Determinants of Vertical Integration: An Empirical Test". *Journal of Industrial Economics* 39:451–466.
Malmgren, H.B. 1961. "Information, Expectations and the Theory of the Firm". *Quarterly Joutnal of Economics* 75:399–421.
Maskin, Eric and Jean Tirole. 1999. "Two Remarks on the Property-Rights Literature". *Review of Economic Studies* 66:139–149.
Masten, Scott. 1984. "The Organization of Production: Evidence From the Aerospace Industry". *Journal of Law and Economics* 27:403–417.
Masten, Scott, James Meehan, and Keith Crocker. 1989. "Vertical Integration in the U.S. Auto Industry: A Note on Specific Assets". *Journal of Economic Behavior and Organization* 12:265–273.
Masten, Scott, James Meehan and Edward Snyder. 1991. " The Costs or Organization". *Journal of Law, Economics and Organization* 7:1–25.
Mason, Charles F and Owen R. Phullips. 2000. "Vertical Integration and Collusive Incentives: An Experimental Analysis". *International Journal of Industrial Organization.* 18:471–493.
Mathewson, Frank and Ralph Winter. 1986. "The Economics of Vertical Restraints in Distribution" in Frank Mathewson and Joseph Stiglitz (eds.), *New Developments in the Analysis of Market Structures.* Cambridge, MA: MIT Press.
Monteverde Kirk and David Teece. 1982. "Supplier Switching Costs and Vertical Integration in the Automobile Industry". *Bell Journal of Economics* 13:206–213.
Muris, Timothy, J. David Scheffman, and Pablo Spiller. 1992. "Strategy and Transactions Costs: The Organization of Distribution in the Carbonated Soft Drink Industry". *Journal of Economics and Management Strategy* 1:83–128.
Myerson, Roger and M. Satterthwaite. 1983. "Efficient Mechanisms for Bilateral Trading". *Journal of Economic Theory* 28:265–281.
Ohanian, Nancy Kane. 1994. "Vertical Integration in the U.S. Pulp and Paper Industry, 1900–1940". *Review of Economics and Statistics* 76:202–207.
Ordover, Janusz, Steven Salop and Garth Saloner. 1990. "Equilibrium Vertical Foreclosure". *American Economic Review* 80:127–142.
Perry, Martin. 1978. "Price Discrimination and Vertical Integration". *Bell Journal of Economics* 9:209–217.
Regan, Laureen. 1997. "Vertical Integration in the Property-Liability Insurance Industry: A Transaction Cost Approach". *Journal of Risk and Insurance* 64:41–62.
Shelanski, Howard and Peter Klein. 1995. "Empirical Research in Transaction Cost Economics: A Review and Assessment". *Journal of Law, Economics and Organization* 11:335–361.
Simon, Herbert A. 1947. *Administrative Behavior.* New York: Macmillan.
Stigler, George. 1951. "The Division of Labor is Limited by the Extent of the Market". *Journal of Political Economy* 59:185–193.
Stukey, John. 1983. *Vertical Integration and Joint Ventures in the Aluminum Industry.* Cambridge, MA: Harvard University Press.
Tirole, Jean. 1988. *The Theory of Industrial Organization.* Cambridge, MA: MIT Press.
Vannoni, Davide. 2002., "Empirical Studies of Vertical Integration: The Transaction Cost Othodoxy". *International Review of Economics and Business* 49:113–141.

Vita, Michael. 2000. "Regulatory Restrictions on Vertical Integration and Control: The Competitive Impact of Gasoline Divorcement Policies". *Journal of Regulatory Economics* 18:217–233.

Walker, Gordon and David Weber. 1984. "A Transactions Cost Approach to Make or Buy Decisions". *Administrative Science Quarterly* 29:373–391.

Waterman, David and Andrew Weiss. 1996. "The Effects of Vertical Integration Between Cable Television Systems and Pay Cable Networks". *Journal of Econometrics* 72:357–395.

Whinston, Michael. 2003. "On the Transaction Cost Determinants of Vertical Integration". *Journal of Law, Economics and Organization* 19:1–23.

Williamson, Oliver. 1971. "The Vertical Integration of Production: Market Failure Considerations". *American Economic Review* 61:112–123.

Williamson, Oliver. 1975. *Markets and Hierarchies: Analysis and Antitrust Implications*. New York: Free Press.

Williamson, Oliver. 1983. "Credible Commitments: Using Hostages to Support Exchange". *American Economic Review* 73:519–540.

Williamson, Oliver. 1985. *The Economic Institutions of Capitalism*. New York: Free Press.

Williamson, Oliver. 1996. *The Mechanisms of Governance*. New York: Oxford University Press.

Williamson, Oliver. 2000. "The New Institutional Economics: Taking Stock, Looking Ahead". *Journal of Economic Literature* 38:595–613.

Williamson, Oliver, Michael Wachter, and Jeffrey Harris. 1975. "Understanding the Employment Relation: The Analysis of Idiosyncratic Exchange". *Bell Journal of Economics* 6:250–280.

14. Solutions to Principal-Agent Problems in Firms

GARY J. MILLER

There are many settings in which one economic actor (the principal) delegates authority to an agent to act on her behalf. The primary reason for doing so is that the agent has an advantage in terms of expertise or information. This informational advantage, or information asymmetry, poses a problem for the principal—how can the principal be sure that the agent has in fact acted in her best interests? Can a contract be written defining incentives in such a way that the principal can be assured that the agent is taking just the action that she would take, had she the information available to the agent?

Solving this problem is a matter of some concern for patients dealing with their doctors, clients dealing with their lawyers, or celebrities dealing with their publicists. It is also a crucial concern for business firms dealing with their employees. Especially in the twenty-first century, employees are often hired precisely because they have information available that is unavailable to the managers of a firm. Making sure that employee expertise is put to work in the interest of the firm can make the difference between success and bankruptcy—as illustrated by the relative performance of Southwest Airlines compared to much of the rest of the airlines industry.

This paper examines the large principal-agency literature as it relates to management patterns in the firm. A powerful conclusion emerges, not from any one segment of the literature as much as from a bird's-eye view of the literature as a whole, that there is no unique "solution" to the principal-agent problems in a firm. Instead, a Coasean "contingency" theory can be constructed in which different conditions inside the firm (characterized by production technology, severity of information asymmetry, and relative risk-preferences of principals and agents) call for different "solutions" to the principal-agent problems.

While the first significant papers in principal-agency theory were developed independently of Coasian theory, this chapter of the Handbook will try to establish that there is a natural connection between the two. Coase (1937) hypothesized that transactions may be structured in different ways—in particular, some can be better managed via hierarchy *within* a firm rather than by the market *between* firms. This insight has led, in recent years, to a large and successful literature on the "boundaries of the firm"—examining when transactions are best organized within the firm, and when they should be organized between firms. (See the articles by Joskow and Klein in this Handbook.)

But the same Coasean logic can be applied to those transactions that occur strictly *within* the firm—notably, those hierarchical transactions between employer and employee. In particular, *incentives*, *monitoring*, and *cooperation* can and do play different roles in the infinite variety of contractual forms that can govern transactions within the firms. Which kinds of within-firm transactions are best governed by powerful incentives? In which transactions should the firm invest in high levels of monitoring capacity? In which should a long-term, cooperative relationship be encouraged among employees, or between firm and employees? In a Coasian manner, I argue that different intra-organizational transactions can best be structured by different kinds of employment contracts. I also suggest that the literature on principal-agency theory can help to explain *why* particular contracts are best applied to particular transactions. Fundamentally, principal-agency theory is about trade-offs; it is not surprising that the nature of the tradeoffs shifts subtly as conditions change, resulting in different kinds of solutions in different setting.

Furthermore, different solutions create very different types of firms. Some firms that rely heavily on incentives, like marketing powerhouse Pepsico, are known for a free-wheeling, risk-taking, entrepreneurial style of decision-making. Others that use monitoring more, like manufacturing giant General Motors, are often characterized as "bureaucratic"—implying that employees tend to avoid risk-taking by looking to hierarchical superiors and standard operating procedures for justification of their actions. In still other firms, like Southwest Airlines, the observer sees high levels of cooperation and teamwork within the firm. These behavioral characteristics may be thought of as derivative of the different kinds of contracts and transactions that emerge in response to different types of principal-agent relationships.

While there are multiple solutions, no one solution is perfect. Or rather, there are multiple solutions *because* no one solution is perfect. Except in "ideal" conditions (with zero risk-aversion and no information asymmetry), agency costs persist with each style of attempted solution. However, there are certain indicators that suggest those situations in which one type of solution may be systematically better than others. One of the tricks of good management is therefore to be sensitive to trade-offs between different kinds of costs associated with different transactional arrangements—within as well as between firms.

The purpose of this paper is to show how principal-agency theory has evolved to help explicate differences in within-firm managerial styles. Section I discusses those firms that tend to rely on high levels of risky financial incentives, thereby mimicking the market. Section II discusses why some firms cannot efficiently use outcome-based financial incentives, and turn to bureaucratic oversight, thereby mimicking the state. And Sections III and IV demonstrate that, for some firms, both incentives and monitoring can be improved on by long-term cooperation, between supervisors and subordinates, and among teams of subordinates. The paper concludes with a re-affirmation of the Coasean claim that efficiency in transactions calls for variety of contracts, even within the general structure we call "the firm".

1. SOLUTIONS BASED ON INCENTIVES LINKED TO AGENT OUTCOMES

Principal-agency theory is grounded in the study of information asymmetries. The agent takes actions that determine (in combination with a random component) an outcome of interest to the principal. Probably the first influential paper to develop these themes was Spence and Zeckhauser (1971) on insurance. A risk-averse homeowner, facing a ten percent chance of a $100,000 loss, would be willing to pay *more* than $10,000 to be insured against the loss. A risk-neutral insurance company would be willing to accept any premium larger than $10,000 to cover the loss. Both sides could be made better off by shifting the risk to the insurance company for the appropriate premium; failure to make the trade would be a manifestation of inefficient risk-bearing.

However, as Spence and Zeckhauser demonstrate, there *are* potential obstacles to this efficient trade. When the individual is insured, the individual has no reason to avoid actions that may actually *increase* the probability of the loss. This notion of *moral hazard* became crucial for both the insurance literature and the subsequent principal-agency literature. The insurance company would like to be able to monitor whether or not the homeowner engages in moral hazard; when this is impossible or too costly, then the insurance company may have to refrain from fully insuring the homeowner, thereby forcing the homeowner to face the loss as an incentive to discourage moral hazard. That is, the insurance company will have to turn down a full insurance contract that would make both it and the homeowner better off! This is an example of market failure in the market for risk.

> "Given [the insurer's] limited information-monitoring capability, his selection of the optimal insurance payoff function is a second-best exercise. Neither complete risk spreading nor appropriate incentives for individual action will be achieved. To find the optimal mixture of these two competing objectives is a difficult problem, here as in the real world." (1973:387)

The problem of balancing incentives and efficient risk-bearing transfers neatly and quickly to employment relationships. The sales agent (for example) is more risk averse than the employer, just as the homeowner is more risk-averse than the insurance company. The variation in auto sales is in part due to economic conditions beyond the control of either the sales agent or her employer. The agent would prefer a smaller, fixed wage over a risky commission with a higher average payoff—and the employer would prefer the smaller fixed wage as well. Efficient risk-bearing would require that the employer insure the employee against the risk by paying the flat wage. The match to the insurance problem is nearly perfect.

But as in the insurance industry, the problem is moral hazard: the flat wage leaves the agent with no incentive to avoid behaviors (shirking) that increase the risk of a "bad month" for auto sales. Nor can anyone work backward from the outcome to deduce the agent's effort level. When a month with low car sales occurs, the sales agent can blame those external conditions that are known to impact sales. Efficiency in incentives must be traded off against efficiency in risk-bearing. The flat wage contract has insufficient incentives for effort, but contracts that provide incentives for agent effort are more costly to the employer.

This problem of balancing efficiency in risk-bearing against incentives, when effort levels are costly to discover, became the defining problem for principal-agent theory. Harris and Raviv (1978) assume that an agent's costly effort, combined with an exogenous random variable (e.g., the state of the economy), determine some outcome of interest to the principal. Assuming that the outcome (but not the agent's effort) is public information, Harris and Raviv are interested in discovering if and when information about the agent's effort level is valuable. That is, should the employer spend money to monitor whether the agent is shirking? They conclude: "There are *no* gains to be derived from monitoring the agent's action when the agent is risk neutral." (1979: 233) This is the case because an outcome-based incentive contract can be written that will induce optimal effort, consistent with efficient risk-sharing. In particular, the optimal contract is one in which the risk-neutral agent bears all the risk, making a fixed payment to the principal.

However, there *are* potential gains from monitoring when the agent is both effort-averse *and* risk-averse (Harris and Raviv 1978). In that case, the absence of information about effort means that the principal must motivate effort by outcome-contingent incentives. But these incentives imply that the risk-averse agent must bear some of the risk, since the outcome is in part dependent on an exogenous random variable. Therefore, efficient risk-sharing is sacrificed for the second-best incentive contract.

Shavell (1979) and Holmstrom (1979) elaborate on this basic result—that efficiency losses result from a situation in which the principal is ignorant of the action taken by a risk-averse and effort-averse agent. Shavell reiterates that, just as in the insurance problem, suboptimal risk-sharing is necessary to induce effort; equivalently, optimal risk-sharing undermines the incentives for efficient levels of effort. Shavell also shows that if the agent is risk averse, the most efficient possible contract is one that nevertheless forces the agent to bear some of the risk—i.e., his fee *always depends to some extent on the risky outcome*.

Furthermore, "the achievable level of welfare approaches the first-best level" as the agent's effectiveness (i.e., the impact of the agent's efforts compared to Nature's impact) approaches either zero or one (1979:56). If the agent's impact is zero, the outcome is not affected by the agent's effort, and optimal risk-sharing (a flat wage) is first-best . If the agent's effort swamps the effect of the random variable with nearly zero cost, then a relatively small (infinitesimal) imposition of risk on the risk-averse agent will produce a nearly-best solution. It is in the intermediate levels, when the agent has a significant but not overwhelming impact, that efficiency losses are greatest.

Holmstrom (1979) provides a significant paper that rounds out our understanding of the principal-agent problem. He agrees with Shavell that when the agent is risk-averse and effort-averse, "Pareto-optimal risk sharing is generally precluded, because it will not induce proper incentives" (1987:74). Given this constraint, Holmstrom demonstrates that the second-best compensation scheme will be one in which the agent's share of the output is always increasing in output. The shape of that relationship may be steep or flat, convex or concave, depending on the agent's risk preferences. The more risk-averse agents will, in general, have flatter payoff functions in output (more like a flat wage).

For firm settings in which agent action is costly to monitor, the best solution is one in which agents are paid based on an outcome-based commission, and allowed to go their own way without much hierarchical supervision. The employee-employer relation resembles a market transaction. The difference between such an employee and the outside contractor may, therefore, be a fuzzy one.

Incentives for Sales Agents

The literature on principal-agency theory found a ready application to the subject of sales force compensation. In an early paper, Basu et al. (1985) note that, within the firm, sales is a particularly appropriate setting for applying principal-agency theory. Normally, they point out, "it is very difficult to monitor the actual efforts of each salesperson" (1985: 268); and a low or high level of sales in a given month may be due either to the agent's efforts or to sales conditions.

A firm has available a variety of different compensation contracts for sales personnel, from straight commission, to variable commissions (based on sales), to straight salary, to various combinations of salary and commissions. Basu et al. (1985:277–79) show how this variation in compensation schemes can be understood in terms of different parameters in the solution to the principal-agency problem. In particular, they apply and extend Holmstrom's second-best sharing (compensation) scheme. The best compensation will be monotonic in sales, but the compensation function can be many shapes. The more risk averse the sales agent, the flatter the compensation plan in sales: a decrease or increase in sales should result in less impact on the sales agent's compensation. The more risk tolerant, the more the firm should rely on intense incentives in the form of higher commissions and lower flat wages. If the agent becomes more risk acceptant with income, then the commission rate should increase with sales. If the agent's risk tolerance is constant with income, then the agent's compensation function will be a straight line against sales revenue. The more uncertainty in the environment, the less control the sales agent has over sales; this implies that the sales agent will receive a higher fixed salary parameter and a lower commission rate—and a lower expected total compensation (Basu et al. 1985:282).

Empirical research on sales has supported many of these results. Eisenhart (1988) found that routine sales jobs like operating a cash register were paid with fixed salaries, while sales positions that involved establishing a close relationship with the customer were paid with a commission. This is consistent with principal-agency theory in that employers bore the risk for those positions in which employees could be cheaply and easily monitored, but risk was shifted to those employees where monitoring was more expensive. Presumably, agents with the most risk-aversion were more likely to stick with lower-paid but safer fixed wages, operating the cash register, while agents who had the least risk-aversion were those who accepted the commission pay for the less easily monitored personal sales positions.

Experiments provide further support for the empirical applicability of principal-agency theory. McLean Parks and Conlon (1995) provide a controlled laboratory study with owner/employee dyads that produced solutions to a mathematical problem. The employee's contribution was to spend money for computer-generated solutions that stochastically increased in accuracy with the agent's expenditures. The pairs negotiated compensation contracts composed in part of a flat wage and in part of an outcome-based bonus. Each dyad participated in twenty trials, negotiating a contract and completing the exercise in each trial. In half of the dyads, the agent's expenditure could be monitored by the owner in the next period, and in half, the agent's expenditure could never be made public. Another, independent treatment was the profitability to the owner.

In profitable environments, dyads agreed to an increased use of outcome-contingent bonuses when monitoring was not possible. This result is entirely analogous to Eisenhardt's observation that commissions are used more frequently for difficult-to-monitor sales assignments. However, in unprofitable environments, dyads used contingent bonuses *less* frequently. Most interestingly, employees tended to *over-produce* in all settings. In the profitable environments, employees spent on average 2.6 times the rational amount on information, regardless of monitoring. In the unprofitable treatments, the ratio was 1.7 or 5.6, depending on whether monitoring was or was not possible (McLean Parks and Conlon 1995: 826). The striking over-investment in information indicates that some other motivation (e.g., competition with other subjects or an inner desire to solve the math problem) was driving the experimental subjects to provide the overly large expenditures that they did.

Like sales agents, CEOs have outcome measures which are impacted by individual effort and exogenous random variables. Jensen and Murphy (1990: 227) use regression (of CEO wealth on corporate performance) to find that a typical CEO's wealth increases by only $3.25 for every $1000 in the corporation's value. They believe that this regression coefficient is so low that it must be "inconsistent with the implications of formal agency models of optimal contracting.

Garen (1994) believes that Jensen and Murphy exaggerate the importance of their finding. While Jensen and Murphy find an *average* pay-performance sensitivity coefficient b of CEO compensation on organizational performance,

Garen estimates a different such *b* term for different industries, and examines determinants of this coefficient. In his view, principal-agency theory implies that "As the output the agent produces becomes inherently riskier, the insurance component of pay is increased and the incentive component is reduced." This hypothesis is consistent with his finding that the CEO pay-performance sensitivity coefficient is lower in firms with a higher variability in return. In industries where exogenous variables have more impact on outcomes than does the CEO's own effort, the compensation is less fixed to those outcomes.

An outcome-based contract, in which monitoring is minimal, will almost certainly *attract* certain kinds of employees—in particular, those who are least risk-averse, and most appreciative of the absence of close scrutiny by hierarchical supervisors. The more risk-neutral are the employees who are attracted to such an employment opportunity, the more intensely incentivized is the optimal contract. Some production jobs are compensated by piece-rates, which rely on outcome-based compensation rather than supervision to motivate effort.

For example, Lazear (1996) examined the effect of a change from fixed wages to piece rates in a firm that installed auto windshields. Lazear argued that productivity rose by approximately a third in this case, and wages by 12 percent. He also found evidence for a selection effect—those who were less willing to have their compensation linked to outcome (due to either risk- or effort-aversion) left the firm and were replaced by employees who preferred the new compensation package. One can readily imagine that the recruitment process and compensation practice reinforce each other, and result in an entrepreneurial, market-like environment *within the firm*.

Tournaments

In general, information about an individual's effort is economically valuable—especially if that information can be gathered with little expense. One form of information that can often be cheaply collected is that regarding *relative performance:* how well do agents do compared to each other? Can that information be helpful to firms trying to solve principal-agent problems?

The assumption is that, if all agents are facing similar risks, then relative performance provides information about relative effort. Even a hard-working agent may not produce much in the way of sales when some event, such as a recession, reduces overall demand. Considering that the best possible outcome-based compensation is upward sloping (and steeply upward sloping for some agents), then a recession such as this would produce low compensation for all—and presumably poor motivation and morale as well, considering that everyone would be aware that the sales force was not responsible for the recession.

A tournament among sales agents may be implemented by paying the top-selling agent a bonus or prize, paying the second-ranked agent a smaller bonus, and so on. The motivation to do as well as possible would persist—even in the face of a recession that would discourage an agent based on a commission only.

The prize may be a promotion—with opportunities to continue promotion up the line. For any such prize, competition may lead to increased effort by all agents (Lazear and Rosen 1981).

The effort required to win a tournament depends on how hard other agents work—so a tournament implies the existence of a game between agents. Nalebuff and Stiglitz (1983) show that, as in a non-competitive output-based compensation scheme, the first-best solution is available with tournaments among *risk-neutral* agents. With *risk-averse* agents, a tournament can induce a "better" second-best compensation scheme than can an outcome-based non-competitive scheme. It can induce risk-averse agents to supply more effort, and to take "riskier" and more profitable actions (1983:23)

The competitive tournament is more desirable when agents face common risks, such as the risk of a recession. It is less useful when agents faces *different* risks, because a comparatively low or high outcome may be due to the agent's unique risk factors, not the agent's effort. Each agent's chances of winning the tournament depend on the particular risk factors that affect each *other* agent's performance. In the limit, when all agents face *no* common risk, the best possible compensation scheme is a non-competitive outcome-based contract. (1983:25); with enough agents facing a *common* risk, a competitive tournament can approach the first-best solution.

Eriksson (1999) finds consistent results in executive compensation. He notes that tournament theory predicts a convex relationship between compensation and rank, as each promotional "prize" needs to be greater than the last. This result—convexity—is affirmed in his data on Danish executives.

As Nalebuff and Stiglitz point out, tournaments do have a downside. A big disadvantage seems to stem from differential abilities: "the presence of a sure loser destroys everyone's incentive to work hard." (1983:40). So does the presence of a sure winner. Tournaments work best among agents of equal abilities. A system of "handicapping" by abilities requires shared, public knowledge of each person's abilities. Considering that most people regard themselves in the upper half of any ability measure, there is likely to be little possibility of mutual agreement on abilities.

Another limitation is that a tournament can eliminate any cooperation between agents. In some settings, such as sales, cooperation is not desirable; but in others, such as designing a new computer, it may be essential to the production process. As Lazear (1989) notes, "It is not sensible to create rivalry by setting up implicit promotion contests.

Up to this point, the focus has been on contracts in which the agent's compensation is pegged to observed (individual or relative) outcomes. The presence of "high-powered" incentives creates a non-hierarchical, market-like atmosphere that encourages entrepreneurialism, competition, and risk-taking. But Holmstrom showed (1979) that contracts based on direct observation of the agent's actions (e.g. shirking) are better as long as the cost of monitoring is sufficiently low. The following section suggests that most firms find monitoring preferable most of the time—and the result is a very different kind of firm.

2. SOLUTIONS BASED ON DIRECT MONITORING OF AGENT ACTIONS

The assumption for the previous section was that information about agent actions is costly to obtain, forcing compensation based on risky outcomes. Holmstrom also observes that since the source of the problem is information asymmetry, a "natural remedy is to invest resources into monitoring of actions" (1978:74). Of course, monitoring may be prohibitively expensive, or it may be inaccurate, and therefore just as risky as outcome-based incentive contracts. But Holmstrom (1979) shows that even "noisy" monitoring—where the information about agent performance is subject to random error—can lead to a Pareto improvement. A partial reliance on even a faulty, subjective measure of agent effort can allow the use of a smaller, less risky compensation scheme, making both the principal and agent better off. As long as the noise in the monitoring signal is not perfectly correlated with the noisy outcome of the production process, then the combination serves (like an investor's portfolio) to decrease risk. As a result, we would expect to see performance-based contracting solely in those principal-agent relationships where monitoring is very noisy or very costly, or agents are relatively risk-acceptant. Otherwise, we would expect to see principals invest in monitoring.

In the sales context, Joseph and Thevaranjan (1998) show that monitoring permits a less intense incentive system. This allows the firm to pay risk-averse sales staff a smaller and flatter wage, making both happier; it also allows the firm to hire more risk-averse sales staff. If the monitor cannot observe all aspects of the agent's productive behavior equally well, then the agent has an incentive to try to please the monitor by emphasizing the more observable behaviors (and spending less effort on the less observable aspects of productive behavior).

But monitoring changes the nature of the employment relationship drastically. Monitoring, I will argue, is filled with hazards, and results inevitably in a much more hierarchical and bureaucratic organizational culture.

Hierarchical Monitoring

Clearly, monitoring is not a trivial task, and there is no special reason to believe that the principal will be the best person to supply the monitoring services. Someone else, a specialist whom we may call a "supervisor", may be able to provide the monitoring services more cheaply and/or more expertly than the principal herself. The result will be a three-level (at least) hierarchy, in which the principal attempts to induce a supervisor to act in the principal's own best interests, as the supervisor is monitoring the agent.

Tirole (1986) shows that, ideally, the principal will pay the supervisor a flat wage for learning about the agent's efforts; this will result in a decrease in agency costs as the risk-averse agent is in turn paid a (smaller) flat wage that makes both principal and agent better off than would be possible without monitoring.

However, this ideal solution is not immune to a problem that Tirole identifies: collusion between the supervisor and the agent. The supervisor and agent can make themselves better off (with appropriate side-payments) when the supervisor acts to protect the agent from the sanctions that should result from inadequate performance. In Tirole's analysis, this makes hierarchies less efficient, and, frequently, more rigid, as a result of bureaucratic rules that the principal may impose to protect herself from this collusion. Tirole also allows that, outside of his model, there are situations in which collusion (more properly termed "cooperation") may be helpful. This possibility will be discussed later in this essay.

Even if the supervisor has no special technological advantage, there will be good reasons for the principal to hire a supervisor to supply the principal with monitoring services for the agent. One important reason is that the principal's profit-maximizing offer will be a higher compensation if the principal observes a high effort; however, the principal may not be able to credibly commit to this "carrot", leading the agent to doubt that the principal will ever hand it out (Strausz 1997: 341).[1] Delegating control of the carrot to the supervisor may make it credible as an inducement, creating appropriate incentives for the agent to supply high effort, and making everyone (including the principal) better off. Strausz is able to prove (1997: 351) that the principal can achieve a strictly higher payoff by hiring a monitor than by monitoring herself.

Creating Authority: Efficiency Wage

Solutions based on monitoring agent behavior are necessarily more intrusive, and potentially resented, than contracting for outcomes. Agents may dislike having their actions observed and sanctioned by supervisors. While outcome-based incentives resembles a normal market relationship—with all that that implies in the way of agent autonomy—contracts requiring monitoring may create an atmosphere of subservience, antagonism, and covert resistance.

The sanction for non-performance may be getting fired—but as long as employment markets clear, there is no excess supply of employees in the marketplace, and consequently little wait before finding an equivalent job. The anonymity of the large labor market guarantees that the cost of getting fired is small, and provides little disincentive for shirking as long as unemployment rates are low. The result will be that the scope of the supervisor's authority to monitor and direct employee behavior is sharply constrained.

In order to give greater scope to supervisorial monitoring and direction, one answer is to contract at a wage level *higher* than the market-clearing wage. At this wage, called an "efficiency wage", the quantity of labor supplied increases, meaning that the market no longer clears (Akerlof and Yellen 1986). Agents queue up seeking relatively scarce jobs, and the prospect of quitting and finding a replacement job looks more costly. The net result is that the agent's willingness to accept a broad scope of direction and monitoring increases substantially. This

---

[1] In Strausz's model, the agent is risk-neutral, but neither the effort nor outcome are directly observable. The agent provides a service (like car maintenance or termite inspection) that the principal cannot tell for sure she received.

is precisely what Henry Ford was seeking when he began paying a $5 day at Ford Motor Company. (Raff 1988).

Solutions Relying on Programmed Behavior: Bureaucracy

Each "solution" to principal-agent problems seems to initiate another set of problems. A "monitoring" solution creates the necessity of additional authority. But once the problem of creating authority in a firm is created, then comes yet another problem: agent attempts to *influence* authority.

Milgrom (1988) points out that one of the last things the principal wants an agent to do is to spend his time and energy in attempts to lobby the supervisor in order to influence task assignments and distribution of rewards. These "influence activities", at a minimum, detract from the effort being put into the job. And at the worst, influence activities can generate the kind of collusive coalition between agent and supervisor that Tirole (1986) warns us against.

Consequently, principals will try to restrict the degrees of freedom of supervisors by binding their actions with rules. The supervisor will be judged by his willingness to abide by those rules. The more rules, and the more inflexibly they are enforced by supervisors and monitored by principals, the more the firm begins to look like a Weberian bureaucracy. A firm that designs a rule-bound hierarchy for itself will inevitably lose the capacity to respond quickly to a change in its operating environment. The fluidity and spontaneity of the market may be approximated in firms based on performance-incentive contracts, but will be scarce indeed in effort-monitoring organizations.

Contingency Theory

The net result is that organizations which rely on monitoring solutions to principal-agent problems tend to look a great deal different than those based on outcome incentives. They are more hierarchical, more rule-bound, and more intrusive of agent autonomy. In a very interesting analysis, Holmstrom and Milgrom (1994) show that worker freedom and worker ownership of assets should theoretically co-vary with intensity of performance incentives: the three are complementary organizational characteristics, characterizing a more market-like organizational setting.

Furthermore, Holmstrom and Milgrom (1994) argue that each bundle of characteristics is more appropriate in a particular organizational setting. In some sales settings, for example, the agent will be asked to engage in multiple tasks, some of which will be hard to measure. In such a setting, incentivizing one easy-to-measure task may result in the employee spending too much effort on that task at the expense of other, equally important but less measurable, tasks:

> when the cost of measuring sales performance is high (e.g., because it involves team selling) or when hard-to-measure nonselling activities are important, it is more likely that the agent's optimal incentives will conform with the attributes of

employment: modest commissions, firm ownership of customers, and no right for the agent to sell the products of other manufacturers. (Holmstrom and Milgrom 1994:974)

In other cases, multi-tasking and joint production may not be a problem; then the firm should loosen the rules, allow the agent to "own" access to customers, and intensify incentives. In this agents (whether formally considered inside employees or outside contractors) may more closely resemble autonomous market agents than employees of a hierarchy.

3. SOLUTIONS BASED ON COOPERATION BETWEEN PRINCIPAL AND AGENT

All of the contracting solutions discussed so far fall short of a first-best solution, as long as agents are risk-averse, effort-averse, and monitoring is costly. It is possible to minimize agency costs by selecting output-based incentive contracts when agents are efficacious or not very risk-averse, or monitoring contracts when monitoring is relatively inexpensive. But in each of these games, the Coasean prospect of negotiating to a first-best solution is an attractive solution. Managers who can somehow negotiate cooperative solutions on the Pareto possibility frontier have a skill that is worth a great deal on the market for managerial talent.

Solutions Based on Gift Exchange

In the case of either output-based or monitoring solutions, it is clear what cooperation would look like. In output-based contracts, cooperation would consist of a trade of optimal risk sharing (flat wages) for effort; in monitoring contracts, cooperation would consist of a trade of increased agent autonomy (decreased monitoring) for extra effort. Akerlof (1982), in his article on "Gift Exchange", proposes that such outcomes may well be negotiated in organizational settings.

Akerlof used Homans' (1954) classic study of "cash posters" to motivate his model. The "cash posters" registered payments to a utility company against customer ledgers. The firm set a standard of performance, and employees were paid a flat wage for satisfactory performance of this repetitive, even monotonous work. Since there was no compensation for work beyond the standard, Akerlof notes that "the standard economic model of contract would predict that workers set their work habits to meet the company's minimum standards of performance" (1982:547). Surprisingly, however, cash posters exceeded the minimum by an average 17.7%, with a range from 2% to 46%.

Akerlof interprets this extra effort as a "gift" to the firm. The firm reciprocated the employees' extra effort with what Akerlof calls "leniency". Leniency may be valued by employees both instrumentally and for its own right. Instrumentally, it is valued because it means a reduction in the possibility of punishment. Leniency is also directly valued as "freedom" or "autonomy". Employees experience a utility cost from "having someone breath down their neck". A "good" (i.e., lenient) employer is one that will allow the employees the flexibility to arrive late occasionally when the children are ill, will allow changes in work rates to correspond to varying energy levels during the day, and will turn a blind eye to minor rule violations, like conversing on the job, that relieve tedium.

The fact is that cash posting was a hard and dull job. A number of girls who were offered it had turned it down. The supervisors realized that "a group of young girls like this one" would have resented a managerial style of "bearing down" on them, meaning that the supervisors would have a still harder time getting recruits and maintaining production (Homans1954, 726). As a result, a variety of work "rules" were simply not enforced—notably the work rule forbidding conversation among the employees.

> They were convinced they could do their work without concentrating on it—they could work and talk at the same time. In theory, talking was discouraged. In practice, the supervisors made little effort to stop it... (Homans 1952: 727)

Homans notes that there was a time in the not-too-distant past in which relations between employees and supervisor were much more hostile. Supervisors "cracked down" on a variety of work rules that were intended to boost performance but had little real impact, and employees gave only the minimum effort, grudgingly. Greater effort by employees, and greater leniency from supervisors, emerged as a negotiated solution over time. The negotiated "gift exchange" was one in which supervisors got what they really wanted most (high output) and the employees got what they wanted most (a relaxed and lenient work environment).

Repeated Game Solutions to Principal-Agency Problems

The problematic principal-agency relationships we have looked at resemble a prisoners' dilemma game in that, in each, the Nash equilibrium is Pareto dominated by some outcome that is not a Nash equilibrium. For example, when monitoring is impossible and the agent is risk-averse, the Pareto preferred outcome is one in which the principal pays a low flat wage and the agent provides the optimal effort level. (Miller and Whitford 2002) This is not a Nash equilibrium because the flat wage induces moral hazard in the agent.

Radner (1985) points out that, like a repeated prisoners' dilemma game, the repeated principal-agent game could recapture these agency losses (and approach the first-best solution). The obvious way to re-capture some of the losses associated with agency problems is to play a repeated game. Radner shows that, with a sufficiently high discount factor, cooperative outcomes may be supported as Nash equilibria in a (non-cooperative) supergame.

This result, a manifestation of the Folk Theorem to principal-agent problems, occurs with no incentive other than self-interest on the part of principal and agent; both are induced to play cooperatively by contingent strategies in which non-cooperative play by either side is met with punishment by the other. In the case of Homans' cash posters, envisioning the outcome as a repeated game means that the employees' "gift" of extra effort was in fact in equilibrium because it was enforced by the threat of reduced leniency; similarly, the supervisors' leniency was enforced by the threat of reduced effort.

In these cooperative solutions, optimal risk-sharing and effective incentives are reconciled in an interesting an important way. In the efficient equilibrium, the principal pays a flat wage, *contingent on a long-term pattern of outcomes that is consistent with high effort by* the agent. While the agent still has a short-term incentive to shirk, the agent knows that shirking in the short-run will result in an imposition of unwanted risk in the long run. As long as the agent and the principal both value the long run enough, the threat of a risky compensation scheme will serve to avert moral hazard as effectively as the reality—and without the efficiency loss.

4. Solutions Based on Cooperation within Teams

Holmstrom (1982) discuss a particular aspect of principal-agent problems: team production. In many technologies, each member's productivity depends on the effort levels of other agents in the team. As an example, consider a computer programming team that is trying to develop a new computer game. The output of the team may be readily observable, even though the efforts of each individual member of the team may be completely obscure, at least to someone outside the team.

As Holmstrom argues, this creates a special form of moral hazard. There is no risk in the formal sense, because the output may be completely determined by the actions of the members of the team (with no random exogenous variable entering the production function). But even without risk, there is a similar problem of tracing backward from the observed output to the effort levels of individual members. Each agent would prefer to cut back effort while hoping that the other team members pick up the slack. The efficient outcome is not a Nash equilibrium because each would prefer to cut back when the other members of the team are working at the efficient level.

> In contrast to the single-agent case, moral hazard problems may occur even when there is no uncertainty in output. The reason is that agents who cheat cannot be identified if joint output is the only observable indicator of inputs." (Holmstrom 1982:325)

Monitoring individual team members is always a possibility, but this implies an efficiency loss due to supervision, as long as supervision does not have zero cost. It is tempting, then, to ask if there isn't an incentive solution–some way of allocating the team's joint product so that moral hazard is eliminated. Holmstrom looks for a sharing rule that induces a Pareto optimal Nash equilibrium. He would also like for such a solution to *budget-balancing*, requiring that the team's output exactly equal the sum of all the payoffs to the productive team members. An allocation is budget-balanced if there is no "deficit" financing agent shares and no surplus left over.

Holmstrom shows that these requirements are logically inconsistent. There is *no budget-balanced allocation of the team's revenue product that eliminates moral hazard in teams.* As long as the sharing rule is budget-balanced, some team member will have an incentive to shirk: budget-balancing implies moral hazard.

Dealing with team-induced moral hazard can be manifest within the team members, or at the level of the principal herself. Each of these possibilities, and some of the solutions attempted by the firm, are addressed in what follows.

Moral Hazard in a Team of Agents

Moral hazard in the team should be especially salient whenever the compensation for the team members is dependent on team, rather than individual, production levels. With a team piece-rate, each individual will be experiencing the full cost of his own efforts, but will experience only 1/N of the benefits—what Prendergast (1999: 39) calls "the 1/N problem." In medical partnerships (Gaynor and Pauly 1990) and law partnerships (Leibowitz and Tollison 1980), cost containment and productivity figures decrease as larger proportions of revenue are shared among partners.

However, the empirical evidence suggests that when teams are compensated as teams, social processes can be developed to address the moral hazard problem. This does not mean the moral hazard problem disappears. Rather, group-based compensation makes moral hazard such a salient issue for the group that solving the problem becomes an essential first order of business (Miller 1992: 188–195). Firms delegate the problem of monitoring effort within the group to the group itself, and implicitly at least encourage the group social norms that include mutual assistance and sanctions for free-riding.

This strategy for addressing moral hazard has been called "high commitment" or "high involvement" management (Lawler 1986). Explicit tests of team-based incentives are relatively few, but a recent careful examination shows striking results. Hamilton et al. (2003) analyze data from a garment manufacturing facility that undertook a well-documented transition from individual piece-rates to team-based compensation as the demand for just-in-time put a premium on more flexibility in production methods. Team-based production increased productivity by about 21 percent (Hamilton et al. 2003: 481). More heterogeneous teams, in terms of individual ability, were more productive than teams of uniform quality. Most workers received more hourly compensation after moving to teams, with the exception of high ability workers who actually received an average 8 percent reduction in wage; they were nevertheless no more likely to leave than low quality workers. The authors note that this result suggest that "nonpecuniary benefits of team membership, such as more control over the work environment and less repetition, appear to be important for many workers." (2000, 487).

The Principal's Moral Hazard

Holmstrom (1982), together with related studies (Eswaran and Kotwal 1984), is able to show that moral hazard can be eliminated among team members by the appropriate incentives as long as budget-balancing is sacrificed. That is, residual profits must be allocated to a budget-breaker who is removed from the team production process. However, then moral hazard is necessarily relocated in the owner of the budget residual. This poses its own principal-agent problems for firms.

Holmstrom shows that *group forcing contracts* eliminate moral hazard within the team, while necessarily violating budget-balancing. The group forcing-contract rewards everyone in the team if the efficient outcome is observed—without trying to monitor any individual's effort. *No* team member is paid if the efficient outcome is not observed. Among the team, this creates a Nash equilibrium at the optimal outcome, because any one shirker would deprive herself (and everyone else) of the payment. The budget-breaker absorbs the surplus revenues after the efficient outcome is observed and individual team members are paid.

Holmstrom points out that a standard solution in firms to this particular principal-agent problem, the separation of ownership and control, is a common feature of firms. The shareholders of the modern firm do not, and should not, provide any contribution to the production process. Their role in the firm should be limited simply to absorbing the surpluses and deficits generated by the productive members of the firm.

As Eswaran and Kotwal (1984) demonstrate, the budget-breaking principal is endowed with perverse incentives; moral hazard has been removed from the team but deposited with her. Consider the joint-forcing contract. The productive team members, together with the residual owner, constitute a budget-balanced whole that *must* include at least one actor with moral hazard. But by construction, moral hazard has been eliminated among the productive team members. Therefore, the residual owner must be endowed with moral hazard. As shown by Eswaran and Kotwal, the residual owner would be better off by bribing one team member to shirk, thereby relieving her of any contractual obligation to pay any of the team members. This thought experiment demonstrates that the ownership of the residual does not in general guarantee incentives that are aligned with efficiency.

Because of this, the principal must not only be passive, she must be *credibly constrained* from altering the incentive schemes, because the incentive systems that maximize her residuals are inconsistent with the incentive schemes that encourage Pareto optimal levels of team effort (Falaschetti and Miller 2001).

Consequently, one fundamental aspect of any solution to principal-agent problems is a delicate constitutional balancing act, in which the principal is credibly constrained from acting on her moral hazard. Without this constraint, an efficient incentive scheme could not be effective in inducing the efficient Nash equilibrium, because the team members would expect that the principal would act on her moral hazard and ultimately deprive them of their compensation.

As an example, Prendergast (1999: 29) notes that principal moral hazard is especially threatening with subjective performance evaluations; "even though an agent exerts effort and performs well, the supervisor may claim otherwise" because the bonus comes from the pocket of the residual claimant. As evidence of this, she notes the tendency of film companies to manipulate book profits in order to keep down contractual obligations to film stars and others. James Garner sued Universal Studies when his promised 37.5 percent of net profits proved to be worthless in the wake of zero reported profits.

Kahn and Huberman (1988) point out that firm-specific human capital provides another setting for moral hazard by the residual claimant. A firm may have reason to offer a bonus to an employee for investing in firm-specific human capital—then wish to renege after the employee has made the investment. One solution that Kahn and Huberman point to is a kind of credible commitment device—an enforceable "up or out" contract that would require the firm to either give the bonus or fire the employee—and the latter would be prohibitively costly to the firm. The up-or-out contracts at law partnerships, for example, are thus understandable as a way of constraining moral hazard by firms and thereby inducing the immense commitment in human capital that is required by its employees.

Another potential object of moral hazard is the deferred compensation plans studied by Lazear (1981). In many firms and industries, employees are often paid less than their marginal products early in their careers, and then paid more than their marginal product later in their careers. One interpretation is that employees are in effect bonding themselves as diligent workers: they accept the low wage early for a long enough time that their true effort can be discerned and rewarded by the firm. This pattern also has the benefit of rewarding investments in firm-specific human capital. As a reward scheme, it therefore has efficiency benefits with regard to both adverse selection and moral hazard by agents. However, it is vulnerable to moral hazard by owners. Owners have every reason to renege on the higher compensation schemes the employees come to expect late in their careers.

Shleifer and Summers (1988) argue that these deferred compensation schemes offer a temptation to owners: they can let employees work at low wages early in their careers, invest in firm-specific capital, and then either fire them or refuse to pay the career-ending bonuses. The downsizing accompanying a takeover has the same profit-maximizing effect. A downsizing takeover therefore represents a one-time appropriation of employees' investments—which have the effect of destroying future credible commitment. Later employees and managers are unlikely to negotiated deferred compensation plans, and employees are less likely to make firm-specific human capital investments.

To the extent that managers earn only a tiny fraction of increased profits, their incentive to renege on such long-term arrangements is much less than that of shareholders. The credible constraint of budget-breakers often relies, then, on effective delegation from shareholders to managers. Falaschetti (2002) finds evidence of the use of "golden parachutes" as a mechanism for insulating managers, and therefore credibly constraining shareholders. He argues that if golden parachutes were simply a manifestation of managerial shirking, then they would be more in evidence in those firms in with lower concentration of ownership. However, he finds that golden parachutes are in fact *more common* in those firms with high concentration, where the owner's moral hazard is more likely to be acted on. Thus, in his perspective, diffusion of ownership and golden parachutes are alternative mechanisms of credible constraint of owners' moral hazard; both mechanisms allow managers to make contractual commitments in such a way that employees, suppliers, and other stakeholders need not worry about shareholder reneging.

Credible Commitment and Group Incentives

Credible commitment may also explain some of the variability in the effectiveness of group incentive plans. In a large firm, group incentives by themselves do little to encourage effort by any individual team member; the reason is that each person has such a tiny impact on the probability or size of the bonus that it motivates little extra effort. This is similar to the argument that there is little to no reason for any citizen in large democracy to go to the trouble of voting, no matter how much the citizen may care about the outcome. However, just as has been argued in the literature on voting, one obstacle to free-riding is the mutual monitoring and sanctioning within groups which support voting as a group norm.

Similarly, Knez and Simester (2001) analyze "mutual monitoring" among employees of Continental Airline. In 1995, Continental had had the worst record among the top ten airlines in on-time arrival, baggage handling, and customer complaints, and was in danger of bankruptcy (2001: 747). Management created a group incentive scheme paying a monthly bonus, contingent on firm-wide on-time performance. In the succeeding months, Continental moved to the top half of on-time performance, and made sizable profits for the first time in recent years (2001:748). Knez and Simester were able to compare Continental's performance at airports where Continental employees were subject to the bonus plan with airports where services had been outsourced to firms without such a bonus; their statistical analysis indicated that the outsourced airports did not experience the same boost in performance. Managers and employees both felt that the incentive system had been effective in changing group norms. They reported that employee work groups began initiating their own performance reviews when flights were delayed; they increasingly chastised team members who seemed to be shirking, even calling colleagues from break rooms; gate employees would enter aircraft to identify the source of delays. (2001:767)

If Continental's incentives were in fact instrumental, then the case stands in contrast with other firms where such bonus plans were ineffectual and abandoned. One such was at Dupont fibers division, where group work norms seemed to be little affected by the group bonus plan (Hays 1988). One difference seems to be the credibility of the firm's commitment to the plan (Miller 1992). At Dupont, employees openly suspected management of reneging. Firm managers could avoid paying the bonus by manipulating tax write-offs or other accounting procedures. Said one union representative: "There are so many loopholes for management.... How do we know if we've reached our goal?" (Hays 1988)

On the other hand, the more successful Continental program seemed to have satisfied its employees that the firm could not renege on the bonus plan. They did this by making the bonuses contingent, not on the firm's own accounting figures, but publicly announced Department of Transportation on-time arrival figures (2001:747). The transparency of the plan made the effort of changing group norms a more rational investment.

It is worth emphasizing that the problem of the principal's moral hazard, as revealed in the analysis of Holmstrom (1982) and in Eswaran and Kotwal (1984), drastically redefines the nature of the principal-agent problem. Rather than simply being an incentive design problem in which the principal constrains the agent, what emerges is a constitutional problem in which the principal must first be constrained *not* to act in her own self-interest. This credible commitment allows for the negotiation of contracts such as deferred compensation schemes that provide incentives for efficient long-term investment in human capital and cooperative work group norms.

Piece-rates are notorious for failing to have the desired productivity-enhancing benefits when employers have the power to reduce piece-rates when productivity goes up or to fire employees when inventories grow (Miller 1992). Black and Lynch (2001) note that unionized firms that allow for employee participation in decision-making generate more efficiency benefits from incentive-based compensation plans than nonunionized plants; presumably this is because unionization is one means by which management can credibly commit to the incentive scheme.

When management is credibly constrained, combined with the emphasis on autonomy and production flexibility within the work teams, this creates a much less hierarchical and bureaucratic style than the monitoring-intensive organizations discussed in Section 2. Furthermore, the emphasis on cooperation and socialization within work teams results in a culture that is less competitive than the entrepreneurial teams discussed in Section 1. The result is sometimes called a "clan" (Ouchi 1981) or "community" style of culture.

5. Conclusion

Coase (1937: 388) observed, "The main reason why it is profitable to establish a firm would seem to be that there is a cost of using the price mechanism."

However, the firms that are established for this common reason are not themselves uniform. While the price mechanism enforces certain basic similarities among markets for a variety of different goods and services (the wheat market looks a lot like the bond market), the absence of the price mechanism allows for a great diversity of transactional forms (a wheat farm is fundamentally different from bond-trading firm). Ouchi noted as long ago as 1980, some firms don't look so very different from markets, while others resemble hierarchical bureaucracies or cooperative clans. The theme of this essay has been that the development of principal-agency theory since 1980 can aid our understanding of this diversity of form and behavior across firms.

In some cases, the price mechanism must be modified very little in order to serve the firm's purposes: the individual agent's output is easily verified; the agent's impact on that output is neither too low nor too high (Shavell 1979); the agent's degree of risk aversion does not require an exorbitant risk premium. In these cases, the firm may use commissions or piece-rates—which create market-like incentives for the agent. The result is what organizational behavioralists observe as a "market culture" within the firm (Kerr and Slocum 1987), with little socialization needed among employees, limited supervision from relatively distant supervisors, an emphasis on individual initiative, and a sense of autonomy and ownership by the agent in the work setting. The firm's managers will have more authority than that of a client over a contractor, but only marginally so.

In other settings, the price mechanism must be wholly replaced by what Coase calls "direction" (1937: 4) or authority. If monitoring agent activities is both informative and sufficiently inexpensive, contracting on that information makes both risk-averse agent and owner better off. The appropriate form of the contract is a flat wage contingent on satisfactory response to direction, as reported by the monitor (Harris and Raviv 1979). This employment relationship is characterized, in general, by strong hierarchical authority and programmed behavior by agents. The authority of the monitor is supplemented by bureaucratic rules that limit the incentive for the agent and the monitor to collude. The result is a firm culture that is more bureaucratic than market-like.

If the production process is sufficiently inter-dependent, then it may be impossible either to contract on the individual agent's output, or to monitor cheaply the actions of individual agents. As Holmstrom suggested, the best-possible response may be team-based incentives. The cost of implementing team-based incentive systems may nevertheless be significant: group socialization and training sessions in order to coordinate expectations on a high performance equilibrium; and cross-training in technical skills (Lawler 1986). A more subtle requirement is a credibly constrained budget-breaker (Eswaran and Kotwal 1984). The result, when the requirements are met, is a "clan" culture as seen at Hewlett-Packard or Southwest Airlines (Miller 1992).

Coase is correct that "the distinguishing mark of the firm is the supersession of the price mechanism" (1937:389); however, the price mechanism may be replaced in a variety of ways. The development of a rigorous theory of principal-agent contracts in recent decades has allowed us to be much more precise about the essential reasons for the myriad variations in the organization we call the "firm".

REFERENCES

Akerlof, George A. 1982. "Labor Contracts as a Partial Gift Exchange". *Quarterly Journal of Economics* 96(4): 543–569.

Akerlof, George A. and Janet L. Yellen. 1986. *Efficiency Wage Models of the Labor Market*. Cambridge: Cambridge University Press.

Basu, Amiya, Rajiv Lal, V. Srinivasan, and Richard Staelin. 1985. "Salesforce Compensation Plans: An Agency Theoretic Perspective". *Marketing Science* 4: 267–291.

Black, Sandra E. and Lisa M. Lynch. "How to Compete: The Impact of Workplace Practices and Information Technology on Productivity". *Review in Economics and Statistics* 83: 434–445.

Coase, Ronald. 1937. "The Nature of the Firm". *Economica* 4: 386–405.

Conlon, Edward J. and Judi McLean Parks. 1990. "Effects of Monitoring and Tradition on Compensation Arrangements: An Experiment with Principal-Agent Dyads". *The Acadamy of Management Journal* 33: 603–622.

Eisenhart, Kathleen. 1988. "Agency and Institutional-Theory Explanations: The Case of Retail Sales Compensation". *Academy of Management Journal* 31: 488–511.

Eriksson, Tor. 1999. "Executive Compensation and Tournament Theory: Empirical Tests on Danish Data". *Journal of Labor Economics* 17: 262–280.

Eswaran, Mukesh and Ashok Kotwal. 1984. "The Moral Hazard of Budget Breaking". *Rand Journal of Economics* 15(4): 578–581.

Falaschetti, Dino. 2002. "Golden Parachutes, Credible Commitments or Evidence of Shirking?" *Journal of Corporate Finance* 8: 161–180.

Falaschetti, Dino and Gary Miller. 2001. "Constraining Leviathan: Moral Hazard and Credible Commitment in Constitutional Design". *Journal of Theoretical Politics* 13(4): 389–411.

Garen, John. 1994. "Executive Compensation and Principal-Agency Theory". *Journal of Political Economy* 102: 1175–1199.

Gaynor, Martin and M. Pauly. 1990. "Compensation and Productive Efficiency in Partnerhsips: Evidence from Medical Group Practice". *Journal of Political Economy* 98: 544–574.

Harris, Milton and Artur Raviv. 1979. "Optimal Incentive Contracts with Imperfect Information". *Journal of Economic Theory* 20: 231–259.

Hamilton, Barton H., Jack Nickerson, and Hideo Owan. 2003. "Team Incentives and Worker Heterogeneity". *Journal of Political Economy* 111: 465–497.

Hays, L. 1988. "All Eyes on Du Pont's Incentive-Pay Plan". *Wall Street Journal* 1: p. A1.

Holmstrom, Bengt. 1979. "Moral Hazard and Observability". *Bell Journal of Economics* 10: 74–91.

Holmstrom, Bengt. 1982. "Moral Hazard in Teams". *Bell Journal of Economics* 13: 324–340.

Holmstrom, Bengt and Paul Milgrom. 1994. "The Firm as an Incentive System". *American Economic Review* 84: 972–991.

Homans, G.C. 1954. "The Cash Posters". *American Sociological Review* 19: 724–33.

Jensen, Michael and Kevin Murphy. 1990. "Performance Pay and Top Management Incentives". *Journal of Political Economy* 98(2): 225–264.

Joseph, Kissan and Alex Thevaranjan. 1998. "Monitoring and Incentives in Sales Organizations: An Agency-Theoretic Perspective". *Marketing Science* 7: 107–123.

Kahn, Charles and Gur Huberman. 1988. "Two-Sided Uncertainty and Up-or-Out Contracts". *Journal of Labor Economics* 6: 423–444.

Kerr, Jeffrey and John W. Slocum. 1987. "Managing Corporate Culture Through Reward Systems". *Academy of Management Executive* 1: 99–108.

Knez, Marc and Duncan Simester. 2001. "Firm Wide Incentives and Mutual Monitoring at Continental Airlines". *Journal of Labor Economics* 19: 743–772.
Lawler, Edward E. 1986. *High-Involvement Management*. New York: McGraw-Hill.
Lazear, Edward. 1981. "Agency, Earnings Profiles, Productivity, and Hours Restrictions". *American Economic Review* 71(4): 606–620.
Lazear, Edward. 1989. "Pay Equality and Industrial Politics". *Journal of Political Economy* 97: 561–580.
Lazear, Edward. 1996. "Performance Pay and Productivity". NBER Working Paper 5672.
Lazear, Edward and Shewin Rosen. 1981. "Rank-Order Tournaments as Optimal Labor Contracts". *Journal of Political Economy* 89: 841–864.
Leibowitz, Aleen and Robert Tollison. 1980. "Free Riding, Shirking and Team Production in Legal Partnerships". *Economic Inquiry* 18: 380–394.
Milgrom, Paul. 1988. "Employment Contracts, Influence Activities, and Efficient Organizational Design". *Journal of Political Economy* 96: 42–60.
Miller, Gary J. 1992. *Managerial Dilemmas: The Political Economy of Hierarchy*. Cambridge: Cambridge University Press.
Miller, Gary J. and Andrew B. Whitford. 2002. "Trust and Incentives in Principal-Agent Negotiations". *Journal of Theoretical Politics* 14: 231–267.
Nalebuff, Barry and Joseph Stiglitz. 1983. "Prizes and Incentives: Towards a General Theory of Compensation and Contracts". *Bell Journal of Economics* 14: 21–43.
Ouchi, W.G. 1980. "Markets, Bureaucracies, and Clans". *Administrative Science Quarterly* 25: 124–141.
Prendergast. Canice. 1999. "The Provision of Incentives in Firms". *Journal of Economic Literature* 37: 7–63.
Radner, Roy. 1985. "Repeated Principal-Agent Games with Discounting". *Econometrica* 53: 1173–1198.
Raff, Daniel. 1988. "Wage Determination and the Five-Dollar Day at Ford". *Journal of Economic History* 48: 389–399.
Sappington, David E.M. 1991. "Incentives in Principal-Agent Relationships". *Journal of Economic Perspectives* 5: 45–66.
Shavell, Steven. 1979. "Risk Sharing and Incentives in the Principal and Agent Relationship". *Bell Journal of Economics* 10: 55–73.
Shleifer, Andre and Lawrence Summers. 1988. "Hostile Takeovers as Breaches of Trust" in Alan Auerbach (ed.). *Corporate Takeovers: Causes and Consequences*. Chicago, IL: University of Chicago Press.
Spence, Michael and Richard Zeckhauser. 1971. "Insurance, Information, and Individual Action". *American Economic Review* (Papers and Proceedings) 61: 380–387.
Stiglitz, Joseph. 1974. "Risk Sharing and Incentives in Sharecropping". *Review of Economic Studies* 61: 219–256.
Strausz, Roland. 1997. "Delegation of Monitoring in a Principal-Agent Relationship". *Review of Economic Studies* 64: 337–357.
Tirole, Jean. 1986. "Hierarchies and Bureaucracies: On the Role of Collusion in Organizations". *Journal of Law, Economics, and Organisation* 2: 181–214.

15. The Institutions of Corporate Governance

MARK J. ROE

INTRODUCTION AND SCOPE: THE ORGANIZATION AT THE TOP
OF THE LARGE BUSINESS FIRM

I outline here the institutions of decision-making in the large public firm in the wealthy West, emphasizing those that try to thwart decision-making from going awry.

By corporate governance, I mean the relationships at the top of the firm—the board of directors, the senior managers, and the stockholders. By institutions I mean those repeated mechanisms that allocate authority among the three and that affect, modulate and control the decisions made at the top of the firm.

By taking governance to mean the relationships among the triumvirate at the top—and not taking it to mean their relations with, say, the firm's employees or its labor unions—I right away give the analysis an American cast, not a European one. Although my primary focus here is on American corporate governance institutions, I look at other nations' corporate governance institutions primarily by way of contrast (as opposed to, say, finding the deep functions that all corporate systems must have). Thus, I focus on the division of authority between the board and the CEO on one hand, and the shareholders on the other, with the primary task of the institutions of corporate governance being to make managers inside the firm run that firm well and to make them loyal to shareholders. At the end of this paper, I look at how these relationships relate to basic institutions of contract and political organization in Europe and the United States.

I focus on features that are at the heart of recent academic legal inquiry. Others could, and would, emphasize other governance features: an organizational theorist might look to how a leader motivates the people in a large organization. A psychologist or a sociologist might emphasize how discussion in the boardroom is vibrant, supportive, and inquiring, instead of being stale, formal, and useless. A technology theorist might emphasize the mechanisms by which the firm innovates. Another might emphasize how ideas are transformed into products. One type of economist might relentlessly analyze what goes on inside the firm (and thereby is "governed" within) and what goes on outside it (and is thereby "governed" by contract). These are all worthwhile modes of inquiry. But they are not mine, at least not here.

In Part 1, I sort out the central problems of corporate governance. In Part 2, I catalog the basic institutions of corporate governance, from markets to organization to contract. In Part 3, I consider contract law as corporate law's "primitive" building-block. In Part 4, I briefly examine issues of corporate legitimacy that could, and do, affect corporate governance. The institutions of corporate governance are usually seen as separated from the institutions of political organization. But they should not be. In Part 5, I re-examine corporate governance in terms of economies of scale, contract, markets, and property rights. And then I summarize and conclude.

1. THE CORE PROBLEMS OF CORPORATE GOVERNANCE

The corporate governance triumvirate—the board, the managers, and the stockholders—has a vertical and a horizontal dimension. The vertical dimension is between senior managers and distant shareholders (see Figure 1). The focus there is on keeping the CEO and the top people (the board and the senior officers) loyal to shareholders, and competent for the task of managing the firm. It's this vertical dimension that's especially relevant in the United States.

The horizontal dimension is between dominant stockholders and dispersed stockholders (see Figure 2). The horizontal focus is on preventing or minimizing the shifts in value from dispersed outsiders to controlling inside stockholders. That dimension of inquiry is paler in the United States than it is in Europe, perhaps because controller machinations are resolved well in the United States, or because other forces keep more American firms with dispersed ownership. Lacking a single shareholder-controller, the typical American firm has fewer horizontal problems, but more vertical problems: dispersed ownership fades the horizontal dimension but brings to the forefront the firm's vertical weaknesses. Foreign nations also have legitimacy as a core problem of corporate governance, a muted issue in the United States.

These two corporate governance problems are similar in one dimension—in each a controller extracts rents or private benefits—but less so in other, perhaps more critical dimensions. First, the centrality of each differs around the world—horizontal issues dominate in most of the world, vertical issues in the United States. Second, the means by which the controller extracts benefits differ between the two. And, third, the means to mitigate the costs of each differ. These distinctions are not always made, but should be.

A. Vertical Corporate Governance: Managerial Agency Costs

Public firms with full ownership separation have no dominant shareholder. With shareholders dispersed, the task of keeping managers working primarily in shareholders' interests becomes critical. And ownership in the largest American firms is dispersed: Bill Gates' ownership of Microsoft is an exception; General Motors', without a dominant stockholder, is the norm. This diffused

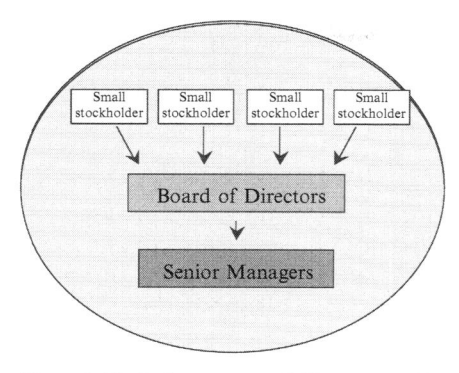

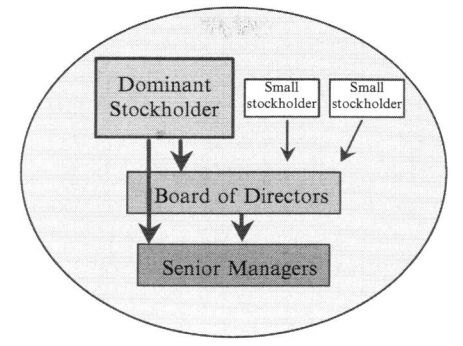

Figure 1. Vertical governance: Diffuse ownership.

Figure 2. Horizontal governance: Controlling vs. minority stockholders in the public firm.

ownership is, in the classical analysis, layered over a basic principal-agent problem: the stockholders' agenda—typically maximizing shareholder value—can be at odds with managers' agendas. In that setting, aligning their interests becomes the typical problem of corporate governance. And the institutions of corporate governance are those repeated mechanisms that tie, or fail to tie, managers to stockholders.

This "agency cost," principal-agent, stockholder-manager alignment problem comes in two main varieties. One variety is of diversion, while the other is of competence, "stealing and shirking" in its alliterative form. Managers could divert value from the firm into their own hands: they could have the firm transfer funds to their own bank accounts (or a relative's), or more surreptitiously have the firm sell goods at low prices to (or buy at high prices from) entities that the managers control, or more transparently pay themselves (excessively) high salaries.

Agency costs come in a second variety. Managers might not be up to running the firm, either because one or another manager never was up to the task (their selection was a mistake) or more plausibly because changed circumstances made the incumbent manager no longer right for this company. Well-functioning corporate governance institutions put the right manager in the right place and give that manager the right set of incentives and constraints.

The alliterative "stealing and shirking" hides a couple of issues. The first is that each specific corporate governance institution does not uniformly reduce both. Some affect one, some affect the other. "Stealing and shirking" are both costs to shareholders and so it is correct to lump them together as costs, but they cannot be lumped together when evaluating the institutions of corporate governance because the institutions affect the two differently. For example, corporate lawsuits are geared to handling observed "stealing," but less good at "shirking" or managerial error. (In fact, via the "business judgment rule," the American corporate judge won't listen to complaints about managerial error.) Corporate disclosure rules, in contrast, are probably better at affecting "shirking"—distant stockholders can see the bottom line results that managers produce, but less good at handling "stealing" (because for very large firms, lots of personal wealth could be obtained from a large firm without destroying the corporate bottom line).

The second submerged element is that "shirking" doesn't convey the subtlety of the vertical problem. Much of the power of an organization comes from routines and embedded information. These give the organization great power and efficiency. Bureaucracy often has a pejorative connotation, but bureaucracies exist for good reason: they are effective at routinizing action to make for powerful output. But when markets or technologies change, the routines and embedded information can weaken the organization. The old routines repeat and the organization works via its embedded information, despite that neither the old routines nor the embedded information correspond to the demands of the market or the new technologies. Henderson & Clark (1990). Organizational change is necessary, but insiders often cannot refashion the firm, because they are subject to its old routines and its embedded information. In a sense, it's not so much that the managers "shirk" in the primary sense of the word—they desperately *want* to work—but they don't know what to do. Their efforts may be intense, but misdirected.

So, the vertical corporate governance problem is one of vertical agency costs. That problem interacts with a shareholder free-rider problem, due to the large firm's ownership by small, distant shareholders. Some corporate governance institutions seek to overcome the free-rider problem, so that large shareholders can focus their ownership and thereby deal better with managerial agency costs. These focusing institutions include a more responsive board of directors (as a focal point for shareholders' impact on managers), takeovers, blockholders capable of reining in some managerial agency costs, proxy voting, and so on. And this possibility of focused shareholder action, especially large blockholder action to mitigate the vertical agency cost problem, leads us into the second core corporate problem: horizontal governance.

B. Horizontal Corporate Governance: Taming Dominant Shareholders

Large firms with a dominant stockholder have a different core problem, one between stockholders, with a focus on a dominant stockholder's potential to shift value from the minority stockholders to itself. Horizontal corporate relationships tend to be the focus of corporate governance in continental Europe, Asia, and Latin America. Again, the alliterative "stealing and shirking" fits, but for these types of firms, the emphasis is less on the "shirking" by managers than on the "stealing" by the dominant stockholders. The recent literature sees the inability to stop controllers' self-dealing as central to developing securities markets and the means to finance large firms. See especially the La Porta et al. series of articles, and the literature summarized in Denis & McConnell (2003). A consensus has arisen that in the transition nations, especially Russia, failure to develop institutions that would stop dominant stockholders' self-dealing fundamentally flawed the transition. See, e.g., Black, Kraakman & Tarassova (2000).

C. External Corporate Governance: Corporate Legitimacy

Corporate governance can have another dimension. Neither necessarily horizontal nor vertical, nor necessarily governing the relationships among owners and managers, this dimension is of governing the firm so that it is legitimate in its society. One could see it as purely defensive: the inside players act, or build institutions, that they would not otherwise have done or built, to deflect outside incursions into the firm. Or one could see this legitimacy dimension as determined by the outsiders: the polity demands that the firm structure its governing institutions in this way or that way, to implement some public policy.

This dimension is shallow for modern corporate governance in the United States (at least as I write), but has not been completely absent: mechanisms to detect and prevent foreign bribery in the 1970s and 1980s could be seen as having been one such governance goal in the United States. One might see anti-takeover laws as resulting in part from the antagonism they attracted from the polity. Romano (1988).

This dimension is deeper in many other nations. For example, in the United States corporate governance vis-à-vis employees is absent from the governance institutions at the top. Employees are typically seen in the academic literature as inputs (like suppliers, capital, etc.), ones that managers transform into sales and profits. Williamson (1985). Employees have to be paid well and think well of their work environment, but this is not usually seen as a corporate governance issue, at least not in terms of vertical or horizontal corporate governance at the "top" of the firm. Not so in other countries, where social considerations and the role of employees have much more impact. Sometimes the impact is formal: German-style codetermination, in which employees end up inside the boardroom, is one such example. Sometimes the impact is indirect: owners might seek to structure the firm so that the outside incursions, or their impact, are minimized. Some of this may be a function of the labor market and general mobility. If people can readily "walk with their feet"—move from, say, Indiana to California if they become disgruntled—they may demand less influence inside the local firm than if they and their ancestors have always lived in the Ruhr Valley and expect to spend their lives working for one big local firm.

These issues of legitimacy also tie into modes of production. By defining the corporate governance inquiry in such stark terms—vertical, horizontal, and legitimacy—I have excluded other perspectives, as I noted in the Introduction. For example, one might view the problem of corporate governance in organizational terms, as how to motivate a team, how to keep it flexible but effective, etc. That kind of an inquiry focuses less on relationships between shareholders and managers or among shareholders. It could have a "legitimacy" angle, and it could have an "efficiency" angle, as such a focus might yield greater productivity and more utility for those inside the organization. (On the idea of legal institutions as reflecting some organization of managers, employees, and capital, see Blair & Stout (1999). On the idea of national systems revolving around varying organizational modes, see Hall & Soskice (2001).)

***

This issue of corporate governance and legitimacy can be seen more abstractly: how, normatively can one organize a business entity that survives politically and socially? And, how as a positive matter have corporate institutions adapted to be legitimate in society?

This kind of inquiry gets little attention in the academic literature, although comments are sometimes made that some institutions gain strength from their political stability: E.g., the wide distribution of American stock (among the upper middle class) helps support American stock market institutions. This issue of legitimacy may well be an important force, equal to the imperatives of economic organization and the horizontal and vertical issues of corporate governance. One might frame the issue thus: What if there are fewer basic ways to organize and own the large firm that are politically/socially stable than are economically/organizationally/competitively possible? If there were, then the choice of which institutions survive might be a choice of which institutions are legitimate, which ones don't attract negative attention from the polity, or which ones manage to deflect outside incursions better than others (even if they turned out to be less effective in another dimension).

D. Enduring or Ephemeral?

What seems important in corporate governance is not enduring, but tends to arise from the problems and issues of the moment. "Core" may more mean "current" and "transitory" than permanent and enduring.

In the 1980s in the United States, the vertical corporate governance issues of agency costs from managers misdirecting the firm's operations were center stage. By the late 1990s and the early 21st century, these seemed less central and the focus was on scandals of (a few?) managers' frauds, not on widespread misdirected operations, perhaps because corporate governance institutions attract most attention when economic performance is weak.

In the late 1990s in Europe and the transition nations, the horizontal corporate governance issues of minimizing controlling shareholders' abuses have been at center stage. Especially in the transition nations, and particularly in Russia, the inability to control insider machinations seems to be a primary gap, La Porta et al. (1999), Black, Kraakman & Tarassova (2000), although it has come to be over-applied to the restricted sample of rich nations for reasons we'll briefly see.

And, during the politicized 1970s in the United States, developing the means to control corporate misconduct, often misconduct just short of violation of law, seemed central. Too many corporate actions seemed to damage society: environmental dumping, or sensitive payments (i.e., bribes) to foreign governments, etc. So regulatory forces sought means to reduce these corporate transgressions.

2. THE BASIC INSTITUTIONS OF CORPORATE GOVERNANCE

We now have some texture to the notion of corporate governance. Some of it is vertical: whether managers stay loyal to shareholders. Some of it is horizontal: whether dominant stockholders shift firm value into their own pockets. And some of it is external, based on issues of legitimacy: what does the rest of society force the firm to do, or how do players inside the firm react to outside pressures?

Which institutions align the players? In particular, given my American focus here, which institutions align American managers with their shareholders? We have about ten such institutions: markets, boards, compensation, gate-keeping transparency, coalescing shareholders (via takeovers and otherwise), information distribution, lawsuits, capital structure, and bankruptcy.

A. Markets

Markets are often the most important institution of corporate governance. Three markets are central: the firm's product market, its capital market, and the managerial labor market. If the firm cannot sell its product, in time it disappears. If the firm cannot raise capital, it cannot grow. If the firm cannot get and retain good managers (and employees), it will fritter away its resources.

This sometimes leads commentators to belittle the importance of other corporate governance institutions, because one or all of the three markets punish deviant firms and reward well-performing firms. This criticism is surely correct as a response to a view that failure in a non-market corporate governance institution would, say, necessarily destroy all firms. But using the market to belittle institutional analysis can go too far, as we see next.

1. Markets vs. institutions? Even if markets roughly aligned the players, a markets-are-everything idea would still face three substantial defects. First, each market is imperfect, sometimes substantially so. Corporate governance institutions might pick up the slack where markets cannot reach. Markets can sometimes deal with extremely gross deviations, while the institutions of corporate governance then deal with middle-sized deviations. Markets often draw an outer limit, but not a tight constraint.

Second, the corporate governance institutions can "prime" or charge-up each one of the market institutions. Good internal decision-making can make the firm react well to product market changes, economize on capital, or make sure good managers come, stay, and perform. Good governance institutions can feed back and become one of the bases for marketplace competition in all three markets. They can facilitate, or retard, the firm's adaptation to the three markets' pressures.

Third, markets may be good for some governance tasks, weak for others. Markets may be good at limiting the most egregious types of "shirking," but be less good at limiting "stealing," especially if the stealing represents a small part of the firm's total value. (If a low percentage of a firm's assets is stolen in relation to forgone market opportunities, the market may not deter the manager.

The manager may never get another job, but that manager will leave rich.) Law and other institutions are probably more important here than markets. That is, sometimes the non-market institutions are better, cheaper, and faster at governing the firm than any of the market constraints.

2. What markets cannot do. So, each market-based institution is incomplete in optimizing the firm's organizational structure. Let us take them each in turn, glancing at their strengths and limits.

Product markets can discipline managers. If there is no marketable product, there will shortly be no firm. But product markets have two serious limits in disciplining managers. Oligopolistic and monopolistic product markets leave slack. The product market doesn't punish managers severely until the product cannot be sold profitably. That means that managers in non-competitive markets can "lose" for shareholders some of the monopoly profit, but as long as customers don't flee and new entry isn't triggered, managers will only be mildly affected. Profits come from finding a way to free the firm from the chains of atomistic competition: a better product, a market niche, some monopoly power. By freeing itself from atomistic competitive constraints, the firm acquires a value, an asset, something, which corporate governance institutions can affect: good corporate governance institutions keep that value for shareholders; bad corporate governance institutions lose it for shareholders. (Or, on the other hand, good corporate governance propels the firm to find that niche; bad corporate governance lets it fall into lassitude.) The public interest and the interest of the firm's shareholders are not coterminous: monopoly profits may or may not be good for society (depending on whether they're a return for innovation or just the profits that come from restricting output). But the point is that the product market constrains managers incompletely.

Product markets have a second serious limit in disciplining managers. Many firms have deep invested capital. Once that capital is invested, the managers need "only" recover the firm's variable costs to survive for the life of that capital (which may be longer than their own working lives). When costs are sunk and long-lived—distinctive features of the "old" economy of steel mills and factories—the constraints on managers weaken. Eventually the badly governed firm would wither and disappear, but that eventuality could be a long time in coming; in the meanwhile, good corporate governance could maximize the value obtained from that firm with heavy invested capital.

Capital markets constraints are also incomplete. The importance of the constraint is simple: firms must raise capital for new projects. Firms with debt must return to capital markets and must pump cash out of operations to pay off that debt. Jensen (1986). And firms and their managers that perform poorly cannot return easily to capital markets: poor performers will face a higher cost of capital. Extremely poor performers cannot get new capital. They wither and disappear, with the strong performers getting more capital, more cheaply, and thereby expanding.

The limit here is that of retained earnings and, again, sunk costs. For some firms, capital once invested, if invested badly, means they cannot eventually return easily to capital markets. But, again, that eventuality could be a very long run if the sunk capital is substantial, if the retained earnings are adequate, or if monopoly profits give them slack. This scenario is especially relevant for the firm that has large fixed investments that cannot be used in other businesses. I.e., once the automotive plant is built, the machinery has no obvious alternative use. True, such badly-governed firms will wither in the long run, but improved corporate governance institutions—given the market's limits here—can make managers better stewards of the resources they control in the medium run. Moreover, given the depth of invested capital, governance institutions can be seen as the constraints on ex post bargaining and maneuvering over the quasi-rents created. When governance institutions are good, they facilitate the ex ante investment. Cf. Williamson (1985); Zingales (1997). When they're bad, an economy may have to forgo a key class of investments.

Managerial labor markets also have their limits. True, directors usually want to be on boards and managers want to be compensated and promoted. If they do badly, they'll jeopardize their compensation and their future career prospects. But many senior managers are at the end of their careers. They aren't usually moving anywhere except into retirement. Labor markets may be important in selecting the "right" people for these final positions, in the competition to get the prized jobs, but thereafter, once "selected" for their final jobs, managers face labor market constraints that are weak.[1] And, although the following idea is not boldly highlighted in the academic analyses, most of these senior managers at large firms are already very rich. While they would surely welcome yet more money, more money may only motivate these people weakly.

3. *Limits vs. irrelevance?* The point here is *not* that these markets utterly fail to constrain managers, but that they are not tight, perfect constraints. Each leaves lots of "play at the joints." Eventually if the firm gets seriously out of line, it will hit a limit in one or another of these markets. But it can, depending on its market setting, waste major corporate resources before hitting that market-imposed limit. In a sense, corporate governance institutions fill in the gaps and detail of these three primary colors of the markets of corporate governance.

B. The Board of Directors

The board is the quintessential vertical corporate governance institution. It's the board that hires and fires the CEO, makes key business decisions, and reviews the work of the firm's senior managers. (Because a dominant stockholder typically controls the board, the board is less important as an institution of horizontal

---

[1] Employee labor markets can be important to labor-management relations, a dimension of governance that's not my focus here. And, again, labor markets, despite their strengths, have their limits: True, a firm that treats employees badly or fails to motivate them or doesn't induce them to be productive, will usually face labor market problems: good ambitious employees will leave, less productive employees will stay. But this labor market has its limits, in that in many nations external labor markets are much less fluid than they've been in the United States. And this lack of fluidity could have contributed to the greater demand for labor input into corporate governance in these nations. E.g., Gilson & Roe (1999).

governance.) Indeed, one could see the other institutions as primarily interacting with the board. (I.e., the means that coalesce shareholders are means to select a new board. Or, law, in the form of rules regulating proxy contests and takeovers, affect the composition of the board of directors. Or, information distribution and transparency allow outside stockholders to see what's happening inside the board. Or, designing CEO incentive compensation is a tool to align managers with shareholders, but it's a tool that can only be as good as the board makes it.)

In the abstract, it's simple: shareholders elect the board. Distant shareholders lack information and focus; they can neither run the company, nor understand its business in any deep sense, nor select or motivate the CEO. So the board manages the company in general, hiring managers to do the job day-to-day. In practice though the board's role has been in flux for decades. It was often seen as captive to senior managers, who "suggested" people for vacancies and, through their control of information, were thought to dominate the board. Davis (1993); Lorsch & MacIver (1989). In recent years, this situation has changed, with many boards bringing on more independent directors, with many getting active audit committees, and with some having membership committees that took the nomination function away from the CEO (or at least shared it). Useem (1992). Evidence of the effectiveness of independent directors is mixed. Franks, Mayer & Renneboog (2001); Hermalin & Weisbach (1998); Bhagat & Black (1999). But the trend is clear: Independent directors have increased as a proportion of the board and dominate important committees, although the level of independence falls short of professional director proposals that would have the directors see themselves as primarily shareholders' agents, not managers' advisors. Gilson & Kraakman (1991). The board, board committees, and reporting systems to the board, are central to the Sarbanes-Oxley Act of 2002, a corporate governance measure responding to the Enron and WorldCom scandals in the United States.

There are enduring understandings: Organizations are thought to improve their decision-making when the people who make proposals are separated from those who approve them. Fama & Jensen (1983), at 303–04, 308. And there is an understanding of the value of committees in making decisions.[2] But beyond that there's empirical uncertainty about the significance of board size, the degree of independence, and other board characteristics, despite that independence, size, and related issues have been "planks" in corporate governance reforms. Eisenberg, Sundgren & Wells (1998); Yermack (1996).

C. Information Distribution and Gate-Keeping

Distant shareholders need information about their companies. They (not all of them, of course) need information so that they can price their securities (and, via

---

[2] Alan B. Krueger, *Economic Scene: A study shows committees can be more than the sum of their members*, N.Y. TIMES, Dec. 7, 2000, at C2, citing Alan Blinder & John Morgan, Are Two Heads Better Than One (available at www.princeton.edu/rjmorgan/working.htm).

that pricing, *other* corporate governance institutions like incentive compensation or board action, which can be triggered by bad pricing results, come into play). They need information so that they can decide whether a corporate control transaction (ousting the board, taking over the company, engaging in a proxy fight) makes sense. And they need information so that they can decide whether legal action makes sense. If the managers engage in a related party transaction but the shareholders know nothing about it, legal remedy might not arise, because no shareholder would know to sue. More generally, they need information so that they can help capital markets to function properly in corporate governance (by denying or rewarding firms with new capital).[3]

The institutions here are the securities law mandates of periodic disclosure (and the penalties for non-compliance). The gate-keepers are those not deeply embedded inside the firm who verify or sometimes warrant the information about the firm. They are the lawyers, accountants, securities analysts, underwriters, and outside directors.

D. Coalescing Shareholders: Takeovers, Proxy Fights, and Shareholder Voice

If the core problems in American vertical corporate governance arise from the dispersion of stockholders, then a core solution could be to coalesce stockholders. Building big blocks has its costs in owner liquidity and diversification, but one would expect coalesced interests to arise when the costs from dispersion are so high that they overcame the costs of coalescing shareholders.

The obvious American mode of coalescing stockholders, overcoming free-rider issues, and then directing and controlling managers has been the takeover. An outsider, or another firm, offers to buy up the stock of the target firm. If the target firm was badly run, then its stock price should have sagged. The offering company can buy up the stock, run the firm better, and profit from the transaction.

Takeovers are not the only means of coalescing shareholders. Proxy fights have one team seeking the votes of other shareholders with a view (usually) to gaining control of the board. Leveraged buyouts are another: a management team (or a group of outsiders) borrows heavily to buy out a division of a conglomerate (or an entire firm). Ownership concentrates.

Institutional investor voice is another means of coalescing shareholders. Institutional investors complain to boards, make lists of badly managed firms, and send around proposals on better governance, such as an improved committee structure for boards. Managers and boards then react, presumably for two reasons: one, many want to do a better job, and if institutional investors have gathered good information, boards can economize by relying on the institutional investors' recommendations of good practice; two, campaigns by institutional investors could indicate incipient disquiet among the firm's shareholder base. The targeted boards and managers might react because they don't

---

[3] Allocative efficiency may be the more important economic task facilitated by good information distribution. Accurate information flow helps both allocative efficiency and corporate governance.

want to activate another corporate governance institution, such as a takeover, a proxy fight, or a melt-down of the company's stock price.

Blockholding also coalesces shareholder interests. A large investor takes a big block of stock, then often sits in the boardroom, and either way has the means and the motivation to make managers work better and smarter for shareholders. Bethel, Liebeskind & Opler (1998). Blockholding would then raise the issues of horizontal governance: it would be most efficacious if the system minimized the horizontal problems so that the blockholders could then act on the vertical issues. For very large firms, only very rich people or very large financial institutions could play this role. In the United States, the "supply" of very rich people is relatively small against the number of firms that could have blocks (surprisingly). Cf. Kafka & Newcomb (2001) (Forbes list of richest Americans). The richest Americans *already* have blocks (think of Gates, the Waltons, Dell). But there are *many* other diffusely-owned firms available for blockholding. Among the largest 10 firms, only a few Americans could take big blocks, but the few who could are *already* occupied with their own blocks at their own firms. Peculiar as it is to think so, there's a relative "shortage" of very rich potential individual blockholders relative the number of very large American firms.

For financial institutions, historical, political, and social considerations took them off the table as American blockholders. At the time of the rise of the large American firm, at the end of the 19th century and the beginning of the 20th, the financial institutions in play were the banks and the large life insurance companies. But American populism stopped this form of blockholding (common in modern Germany and Japan), by denying these institutions national scope (such as via cross-state branching restrictions), restricting their panoply of products (such as the 19th National Bank Act and the more famous Glass-Steagall confirmation of stock trading restrictions), and by barring their basic authority to own stock (such as via the laws resulting from the 1906 Armstrong investigation for life insurers, and via the banking regulatory statutes generally). See Roe (1994).

Other means to coalesce stockholders have arisen, and in the 1980s the takeover was a primary American institution in constraining managers who strayed too far in producing shareholder value. But takeovers also have their limits. The first limit is how much they can do. The typical American premium is about 50%, suggesting takeovers set an outer limit for vertical governance, not a tight one.

Second, the efficacy and purpose of takeovers is uncertain. Two common features are not positive: Takeovers might reflect the *offering* company's empire-building or market-power gains (i.e., violations of perfect antitrust policy). And one positive feature—pure synergy gains—does not implicate corporate governance directly. The gains from takeovers are not always corporate governance gains. And although ex ante event studies suggest shareholder gain, ex post results are less clear in doing so. Post-merger firms display too many operational and financial failures for us to be unconstrained admirers of takeovers as the perfect corporate governance remedy. Caves (1989); Ravenscraft & Scherer (1987).

And third, it's possible that widespread blockholders would raise legitimacy problems. Indeed it's plausible that takeovers are not as widespread as they otherwise would be in the United States because of such legitimacy issues. See Romano (1988); Roe (1994). Other nations would probably face, and probably have faced, more severe legitimacy restrictions on takeovers, making them less efficacious as a tool of vertical governance (and thereby demeaning widespread incidence of diffusely-owned firms). And for the United States it's plausible that one path to coalesce shareholders—that of financial institutional blockholding—wasn't taken because of such legitimacy considerations. In nations where it is taken (as it was in Germany and Japan), it might well bring other governance issues into play, such as an enhanced demand for governmental oversight and stakeholder voice to counteract the very audible financial voice and very visible financial control. The institutions of corporate governance cannot easily be kept in separate domains.

E. Executive Compensation

Compensation, especially stock-based compensation, would seem a quite promising way to align senior mangers with shareholders, and thereby reduce the vertical corporate governance problem.

The theory is simple: managers get, say, options to buy the company's stock. If their management of the firm induces stock price to rise, the managers cash in valuable options and make money. If their management of the firm doesn't induce its stock price to rise, then the managers' options are without value. (Note the interplay with the institutions of information disclosure and gate-keeping: for incentive compensation to be effective, stock analysts must have good information so that the stock on which the options are written is accurately priced. Or: for it to work well, the board must be sufficiently functional to make incentive-compatible compensation deals and then monitor performance.)

This is the theory, and incentive compensation certainly is an important institution of corporate governance. But it too has its limits. First, with shareholders scattered and not themselves writing the incentive contract, the options may not fully motivate managers but may successfully enrich them. Since the common options contracts seem to fall short of an ideal contract, there's good reason to think that the options actually used don't resolve the vertical governance problem as well as they could. (They have typically been based on a general rise in the company's stock price and not its performance compared to that of other firms.) Bebchuk, Fried & Walker (2002); Jensen & Murphy (1990). True, others conclude that incentive compensation is best seen over the long run, and does better in that time-span. Over approximately a decade, managers at strongly performing companies do indeed earn much more than managers at weakly performing companies. Hall & Liebman (1998); Murphy (2002). On the general issues, see Aggarwal & Samwick (1999); Murphy (1999); and Core, Guay & Larcker (2003).

A second problem with the incentive compensation institution is not noted in the literature but ought to be. Even if the compensation is nicely attuned to performance, senior managers quickly become rich. But the successful managers do not, once they become multi-millionaires, turn the firm over to a new crew of hungry but impoverished managers. They instead continue, while wealthy, running the firm. For these people surely more money remains better than less money, but one can question how strongly incentive compensation motivates truly wealthy people. (Its role might then be more to motivate managers *seeking* to be truly wealthy—those lower down in the firm's hierarchy—*not* those already there.)

F. Professionalism and Norms

Managers do not act solely for remuneration, but also for the satisfaction of doing a good job. And "doing a good job" is defined by circumstance, psychology, and culture. Professionals want the firm to do well. They are often acculturated to work for shareholders, and often do so even when the other institutional constraints are not tight. Or, managers who get a new product out, who succeed, who innovate, who turn a division around feel good about themselves, and in turn shareholders profit. Or, organizations depend on managers' capacity for collaboration, cooperation, and trust. These notions of norms and professionalism are softer and less well understood than the other institutions, but that doesn't mean that they're absent, or that they're unimportant.

G. Corporate Lawsuits

Directors can be sued. In the United States there are two broad bases for stockholders to sue directors and managers: breach of state law fiduciary duties and breach of federal securities law obligations. The latter relate most basically to the company's quality of information disclosure, and can involve SEC enforcement actions as well as private lawsuits. Significant resources in the United States are spent on *private* lawsuits, a feature not matched even in nations like Britain that are usually seen to have similar legal structures. Many directors dread the aggressive adversarial questioning of a long deposition in a securities lawsuit.

In the United States, lawsuits arising from state corporate law largely grow from fiduciary duties. Controllers who steal from the firm have typically violated one of those duties. Controllers who divert business opportunities from the firm to themselves will typically violate one of those duties. Controllers who force the firm to sell a product at a low price to the controller's (or the controller's relative's) wholly-owned private firm will typically violate one of those duties.

It's here that market restraints are not likely to strongly reduce insiders' misbehavior, because the value moved might not be large in relation to the size of the firm, or because the value even if large is a one-shot deal that the market will not adequately punish. Moreover, markets cannot work well if they don't know about the wrong-doing, and law-based institutions typically force the information to be disseminated. In the United States, these disclosure-forcing rules primarily come from federal securities law, not state law.

State lawsuits don't go much further though. Managers may make poor decisions on behalf of shareholders, but judges won't hear their complaints. The American business judgment rule precludes shareholder actions against directors for mistakes. Since managers can lose much money for shareholders by mistakes, corporate lawsuits here are less important than the other institutions of corporate governance. Thus key aspects of vertical corporate governance—"shirking"—aren't governed by shareholder lawsuits.

One might see the institutions here, especially markets and lawsuits, as specializing. Lawsuits are more effective in controlling conflicts of interest than are markets; market institutions, coalescing institutions, and the incentive institutions are better primed to channel managers toward pro-shareholder decision-making. The first problem American fiduciary duties seek to control; the latter it typically ignores. Thus the domain of the burgeoning "law and finance" literature (e.g., La Porta et al. (1999)) may be more limited than generally seen in the finance literature, as basic corporate law deals with one core problem of corporate governance—that of diversions, or "stealing"—but only indirectly (and sometimes not at all) with "shirking" and bad business decisions, or with managers who lose sight of shareholder interests. Other institutions beyond corporate law must be key in reducing "shirking."

H. Capital Structure

Capital structure—especially the amount and terms of the company's debt—can affect the way managers work. The theory is simple: An all-common-stock structure, especially one with diffuse ownership, gives managers slack. Earnings can be low, and if they don't need new external capital, the constraints on them are weak. But if the company were capitalized with debt having massive payout obligations, then managerial incentives would change. If they fail to earn enough to pay off the creditors, then their working lives are made miserable, as creditors breathe down their necks, pursue covenant defaults, and, at the limit, force the firm into bankruptcy. If much of the firm's expected cash flow is dedicated to repaying creditors, managers' discretion declines. Moreover, with a thinner equity, managers who become equity owners have a greater upside potential (than when they own a smaller fraction of a wider equity base); their upside motivation increases as well. Carrots as well as sticks.

This kind of capital structure constraint would seem particularly important in firms that have high cash flow that cannot be utilized well, such as oil firms in the 1980s who had huge inventory profits, but few profitable drilling opportunities. Jensen (1986). By binding themselves not to explore for oil (Wall Street then saw exploration as a money-loser), the firm's total value increased. See also Jensen & Meckling (1976); Grossman & Hart (1982).

Capital structure is not the same institution as the capital market prong of our market triumvirate. It's not so much that getting access to capital motivates managers or denies them resources here, but that the incentives of the ongoing structure—and the repeated pressures to come up with lots of cash—motivate managers and owners.

Like the other corporate governance institutions, capital structure has its limits. It's best attuned to firms with predictable cash flow. Volatile firms would need to repeatedly restructure their financings. And lots of debt can distort equity owners' incentives, pushing them toward unwarranted high risks; limiting financing of future projects, due to the debt-overhang effect (Myers (1977)); or inducing other bankruptcy and recapitalization costs.

Moreover, it might work best in corporate governance structures in which the creditors have an institutional role, perhaps directly inside the boardroom, one in which they could, apart from their contract, control managers, mitigate the stockholders' excessive risk-taking incentive, and gather better information. This though is not the American model. Roe (1994).

Once more, we have a useful but imperfect corporate governance institution, one that limits the incidence and magnitude of error for a class of firms.

I. Bankruptcy

Bankruptcy aligns incentives, although in its pure, theoretical form, it doesn't so much align managers with equity, as it has the firm restructure its liabilities to match its reduced operational capabilities. When bankruptcy works well, it can align managerial incentives with creditors' goals, reduce the debt overhang problem by allowing new financing (although it's possible that American bankruptcy goes too far in this direction), and remove managers incapable of engineering a turnaround.

Focus on this last feature. It may not be bankruptcy's most important institutional characteristic, but it's probably the bankruptcy characteristic most important for the core of corporate governance. Consider the firm that's failing. As it slouches toward bankruptcy, its debt is risky, with a significant chance of not being paid off. This "debt overhang" impedes new financing, as potential new creditors don't want to "subsidize" the old debt, knowing that if they—the new guys—lent, they'd have to share the firm's cash flow and bankruptcy division with the old creditors. The "overhang" can stymie new lending. This much is well known.

Less well known is that overhang can stymie the *other* institutions of corporate governance as well. Takeovers and proxy fights might be mounted to oust the incumbent managers, but the "overhang" means that creditors not the offerors would profit first from ousting the failed managers. Potential offerors may desist, realizing that they cannot reap profits from the takeover: if they fail, they fail; if they succeed, the creditors and not they are the winners. Roe (2000, at 451–57; 1983).

Bankruptcy of the large public firm has the potential to reduce this problem, by being the institution that replaces managers. But criticism has been made that American bankruptcy is lax here, in that it favors incumbent managers.

And indeed the remedy of court-ordered replacement (via Bankruptcy Code § 1104) has been viewed as an extraordinary judicial remedy. This and chapter 11's other features led some analysts to explain American bankruptcy as a pro-managerial protection against ouster, one similar to the antitakeover laws and decisions of the 1980s. Bradley & Rosenzweig (1992). But some indicators suggest that managerial turnover around the time of a chapter 11 filing is, despite the managerial-friendly formal structure, quite high, Gilson (1990), and anecdotally seems to be rising.

J. Complements and Substitutes

Are these imperfect corporate governance institutions complements or substitutes? Or both?

Clearly each can independently affect the quality of management. True, some primarily affect insider diversions of value, and others align managers with shareholders. But of those institutions that induce managers to produce the goods for shareholders each can operate independently and substitute for one another. Substitution effects influence institutional arrangements: if one institution is demeaned in a nation, or becomes too costly for ancillary reasons, then the demand for the other corporate governance institutions should rise.

Consider product markets. Product markets confine managerial discretion, and in that sense product markets and the other governance institutions are substitutes. But better product market competition can enhance the other institutions: fierce competition can sharply lower corporate profitability if the managers misstep. Lower profits should lower the firm's stock price, make the incentive compensation less remunerative, and signal takeover entrepreneurs that an opportunity is brewing. Thus, in the United States, which historically has been seen as having had fairly strong product market competition (at least as compared to pre-EU Europe), some large firms could prosper without really strong constraints on managers because product market competition kept managers working effectively.

Or, take the opposite causal direction. Markets might be structured competitively, but *all* incumbent managers could be lackadaisical. Charge up one institution or another of corporate governance in *one* of the competitors—say, incentive compensation or a more dynamic board—and then one group of managers in one firm ramps up production and innovation, grabbing market share away from other firms. To survive, the other competing firms must react. They react by innovating as well, and some of that innovation is, say, better R&D, but some of it is also to improve *their* own internal corporate governance systems, with better boards, better compensation, and so on.

Or take the complementarity of information disclosure. Better information leads investors to price securities more accurately than if they had inferior information. Better information could then "prime" the pump of other institutions. Managers who are professionals would be chagrined to see their stock price decline. Managers who are looking at the value of their stock options would be motivated to make the value of those options rise. Boards who got the feedback of declining stock prices would be on notice that action might be needed. Takeover entrepreneurs might also be primed to act.

Or: better boards could design better compensation plans. Better boards could foster the professionalism of managers. Better boards could induce a capital structure geared toward the firm's product markets and management.

And so on.

3. Contract Law as the Corporate Law "Primitive"?

In a handbook on institutions, one ought to inquire whether corporate law institutions can be broken down further toward a "primitive"—a basic institution on which the corporate governance institutions rest, like chemists looking inside the gas to find the molecule, then inside the molecule to find the atom. Are there more basic building-blocks upon which corporate governance institutions, and, since I am a law professor, upon which corporate law institutions, are built?

A. Corporate Law as Standardized Corporate Contract

Consider contract. It's a basic exercise in teaching corporate law to analyze how most of the corporate charter—the document governing relations among shareholders and between the board and its shareholders—could be created out of contract law, without a separate corporate law. The rules governing, say, meeting frequency, voting rights, the mechanism of vote solicitation, the question of who pays for the proxy solicitation, and so on could all be created via contract. And, indeed the contractarian view of corporate law is an important theoretical strain here: in its normative form, contractarians maintain that corporate law should be a pure contract. Corporate law should be the contract that the shareholders and managers would have come to naturally if bargaining and transaction costs were cheap. Or, it should be the charter that the parties would find easiest to bargain around. Easterbrook & Fischel (1991).

Moreover, the institutions that minimize the opportunism in the corporate charter could be seen as contract-based institutions. Fiduciary duties, in this view, are the terms that the parties, had they anticipated the questionable transaction, would have negotiated toward. Easterbrook & Fischel (1991); but cf. Brudney (1985).

Hence, if contract law is good, then a) much that is useful can be done by contract and b) the primitive institution that could make for good corporate law is in place.

B. Contract Law's Limits

But contract law has its limits in making the corporation work here. Corporate law has its criminal component. Insider trading can destabilize share ownership.

It can also land the perpetrator in jail. A contract against insider trading cannot send a violator to jail.

And corporate contracting entails multi-party contracts that the players cannot immediately standardize. Corporate contract could, one supposes, lead to audit firms and audit firm liability. But building a system up from the two-party contract would not immediately lead to standardized financial information. Even here though, standardized formats may eventually arise without more than contract law. Private associations, such as stock exchanges in the United States, can standardize rules and formats. There's evidence that stock exchanges and other organizations came first, followed by corporate (securities) laws later. Cheffins (2001); Coffee (2001); Macey & Kanda (1990); Mahoney (1997); Miwa and Ramseyer (2002); Roe (2000).

4. INSTITUTIONAL LEGITIMACY

Thus far we have focused on the "internal" effects and purposes of corporate governance institutions, principally those that align managerial and shareholder interests, and secondarily those that prevent massive diversions of value from dispersed shareholders to the insiders. These institutions are needed to stabilize the corporation.

Corporate governance institutions have another role. Players outside the corporation can affect the corporation: if corporate arrangements appear unfair, then the outsiders can intervene through political institutions. They can ban some arrangements, raise the costs of others, and subsidize yet others. They can, and they do, everywhere in the world. When they do so, they can deeply affect the institutions of corporate governance, as illustrated in Figure 3.

And players inside the corporation who cannot get what they want via internal arrangements might appeal to the outsiders, making external political alliances that then press the firm internally. They can sometimes leverage their position inside the firm by calling on institutions outside the firm.

The institutions of corporate governance are not just organizational and technical. They are, or they are affected by, political institutions as well. Three examples follow.

A. American Legitimacy Light: Populism and Anti-Takeover Laws

Takeovers constrain managers. But managers can call on political allies—labor at target firms, or by-standers who sympathize with targets and continuity over offerors and rapid change, and politicians who see more votes in opposing takeovers than in promoting them. Roe (1993, 1994); Romano (1988).

More fundamentally, American populism made visibly powerful financial institutions such as J.P. Morgan's end-of-the-nineteenth century investment bank or a Japanese-style main bank or a German-style universal bank incompatible with American political culture (of an earlier era). Roe (1994). The

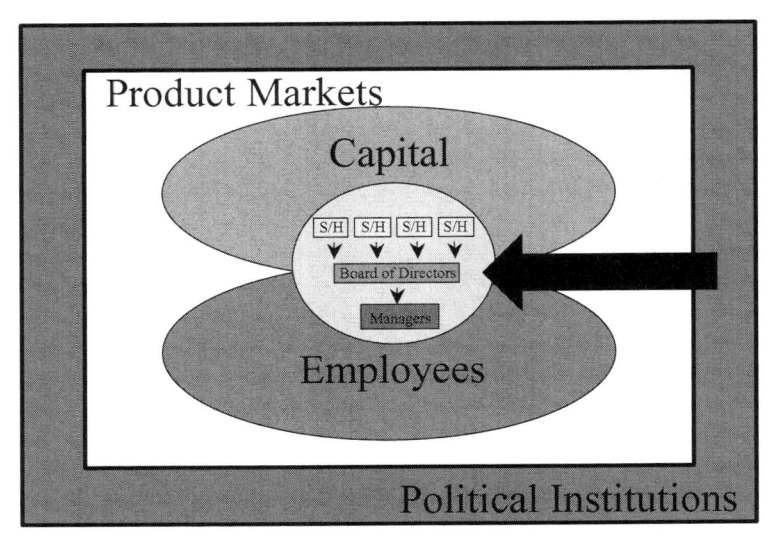

Figure 3. The corporate governance environment.

consequence was that one form of concentrated ownership—that of financial institutions—was largely removed from the menu by American politics. This made the diffusely-owned firm inevitable in the United States.

B. Legitimacy Heavy: European Left-Right Politics

Left-right political orientation affects corporate governance institutions. Ownership by diffuse, dispersed shareholders calls for tools that keep managers loyal to those distant shareholders. (Or at least shareholders do better if they get some of these tools.) Incentive compensation, shareholder primacy norms, and other shareholder-enhancing mechanisms need to be efficacious. But if a nation was lodged toward the left of the modern political spectrum, political institutions tended not to provide these supports.

Nations lodged toward the left would tend to disrupt managerial-shareholder alliances, and promote activities that favor employees with existing jobs. Firms would be encouraged to expand without regard to profitability, delay downsizing when their production is misaligned with the product market, and go slow in taking profitable but disruptive risks. These pressures, and the denigration of some pro-shareholder tools, would lead firms to have more concentrated ownership than otherwise, so that managers could be more directly controlled. Roe (2003). Moreover, these are the kinds of managerial actions that cannot readily be contained by corporate law, which focuses on diversions of value more than pro-shareholder operating decisions. Roe (2002, 2003). These kinds of political pressures—to expand, to avoid down-sizing, and to avoid profitable risks—map exactly onto the kinds of agency costs that are thought to be managers' natural tendencies unless otherwise checked. Jensen (1986).

In nations where labor institutions—whether via social democracy or corporatist power-sharing or other cooperative arrangements—are strong, one would expect managerial agency costs to shareholders to often be higher for firms that had ownership and control divided than in nations where such labor institutions were weaker.

Two channels would be in play, one through the firm and the other through institution-building: First, through the firm, the polity would encourage the firm to expand, irrespective of profitability, and would impede it from downsizing when its capabilities are misaligned with markets. And, there'd be more bargaining over the surplus, with some of that bargaining at the national political level and some inside the firm. Concentrated ownership would be relatively more profitable for shareholders than in other polities, because the concentrated owner could bargain more effectively and resist some of the political pressures.

Second, nations where labor held significant political power could be unwilling to build the institutions that facilitate distant shareholding, such as building good securities regulation, promoting profit-building institutions, facilitating shareholder control over (or influence on) managers, and enhancing shareholder primacy norms that induce managers to align themselves with stockholders, even those stockholders that cannot control the managers day-to-day.

If one or both of these channels is strong, then one could hypothesize a basic model with testable implications. Greater labor protection should predict weaker ownership separation. Consider these results from OECD data indexing the level of job protection in the OECD.

Substantial evidence exists for the strong pressure of politics on corporate governance institutions. Look at the world's richest nations and compare the degree of ownership separation with the strength of labor protection. The correlation is powerful. And even when controlling for the quality of legal institutions and the size of the firms involved, the correlation is quite robust.

In Figure 4, I show the relationship between national employment protection laws in the wealthy West in 1995 and the degree of ownership separation in a sample of similarly-sized firms from each nation. The figure shows the strength of employment protection laws—a rough measure of the left-right shift described earlier in this sub-section—in predicting ownership separation. Similar left-right measures—the GINI index, the ratio of government spending to GDP, and political scientists' ratings of leftness—all similarly predict ownership separation and a separate measure of the size of a nation's stock market (the ratio of stock market capitalization to GDP). See Roe (2003, 2000).

Table 1 controls this result for the quality of corporate law. True, when we run corporate law against ownership separation, it predicts ownership separation. (I use two measures of corporate law. The first is an index developed by financial economists, which is in widespread use among financial economists, despite some legal academics' doubts about its strength, see Vagts (2002). The second is a measure of the premium a controller gets over the trading price of diffuse stock when the controller sells its block of stock.) But when we run the regression with

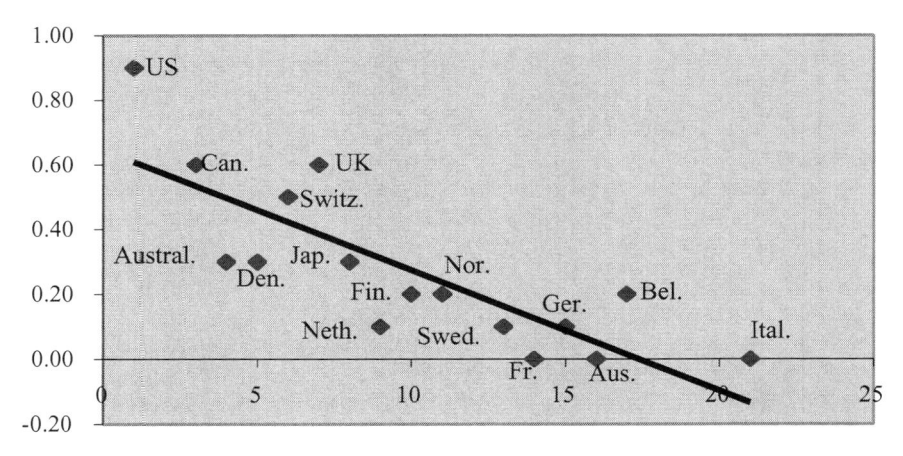

Figure 4. Employment protection vs. ownership dispersion.
Y-axis is dispersion; X-axis is employment protection.

Technical data: med20 v. employment protection	
Regression	$y = -0.04x + 0.65$
Adj R-S q	0.64
t-stat	-5.24^{***}

*** Significant at the .0005 level. Sources: OECD (1994) (employment protection); La Porta (1999) (ownership dispersion of mid-sized firms: percentage of sample of medium-sized firms without a dominant, 20%+ stockholder).

both a legal index and the political index as predictors of ownership dispersion, the political index always survives and often surpasses the legal measure in importance.

These results strongly suggest that political institutions are deeply related to, and often determinative of corporate institutions, opening up a new and not

Table 1. Law and politics as predicting ownership separation

Dependent variable: ownership separation in mid-cap companies					
Corp. law: La Porta	.14			−.03	
	(3.69***)			(.57)	
Corp. law: control		−1.07			.43
premium		(−1.94*)			(.87)
Employment protection			−.04	−.03	−.05
			(−5.24***)	(−2.62**)	(−4.39***)
R^2	.53	.18	.64	.71	.72

Sources: ownership separation and employment protection are the same as for Figure 4 (which graphs the relationship in the third numerical column; the La Porta measure of corporate law quality is from La Porta (1999) and the control premium is from Dyck & Zingales (2003).

yet deeply investigated field for important research. For efforts to link political and corporate institutions, see Roe (1994, 2003); Pagano & Volpin (2002); Perotti & von Thadden (2003); Rajan & Zingales (2003).

The political shift rightward in Europe in the past 10 years may thus be one of the most important of the recent corporate governance changes there, perhaps even more important than changes in any particular corporate governance institution. The shift *allows* corporate governance institutions to strengthen, and makes those that already exist more useful to shareholders. The rightward, pro-market (or less anti-market) move is not always via electing conservative parties; sometimes it's via a left-wing party abandoning its wariness of markets. That movement makes it easier to develop shareholder-oriented institutions.

Table 2. Europe's social democratic parties move to the right

Country	1984	1995
Austria	3.00	4.80
Belgium	2.50	4.20
Denmark	3.80	4.20
Finland	3.00	4.40
France	2.60	4.10
Germany	3.30	3.80
Italy	3.10	3.50
Netherlands	2.60	4.20
Sweden	2.90	4.10
United Kingdom	2.30	4.40

Source: Lipset & Marks (2000), at 275, who array Europe's social democratic parties on a left-right scale, using political scientists' assessments. Lower scores are more left, higher more right.

5. CORPORATE INSTITUTIONS IN THEIR SETTING

A. Contract

1. Firm size. Corporate governance institutions have technological predicates. Corporate governance institutions govern the interface between the capital-providers and the firm's management (at least as we've defined the essential corporate governance problem). For there to be a problem to be governed, especially for vertical corporate governance between shareholders and distant managers, there must be a demand for firms where not all capital-providers are inside the firm. For that condition to arise, there must be heavy demand for capital inside the firm and there must be technologies that demand a size of operation beyond that which managers would ordinarily be able to control directly with their own capital.

In its simple form, there thus must be economies of scale. But in addition those economies of scale must induce capital needs greater than that which a single investor, or a very small group of investors could provide.

The historical story usually told is that advances in communication, production, and transportation technologies facilitated the growth of the large, vertically-integrated firm. Chandler (1990). These new organizations had capital demands that led to the large public firm and its concomitant corporate governance problems, raising the 20th century demand for better standard corporate governance institutions. In its theoretical form, one would cite Coase's *Nature of the Firm* article: Economic activity can be organized inside the firm or across firms. When the transaction costs of bringing the next transaction or the next operation inside the firm exceed the costs of contracting through the market, the firm stops growing. Coase (1937); Williamson (1985).

2. Decentralization vs. centralization. This story can be turned around. If new technologies *reduce* the costs of transacting in the market *across* firms— new internet and information technologies come to mind—then the demand for large integrated organizations would decline. If they declined enough, the needed capital might be within reach of a handful of managers, making the separation problem less acute. One would still have institutional issues—those say of relations among a network, cf. Piore & Sabel (1984), perhaps of a contractual dimension—but they wouldn't be the classic vertical and horizontal problems of corporate governance. One might see the computer's advance in the past half-century as having corporate governance implications. In the age of the mainframe, information was best processed at the central headquarters. The M-form corporation, with centralized strategic decision-making, fit that technology well. In the age of the personal computer and the internet, information is better distributed, and decentralized decision-making becomes relatively favored. Firms decompose, spinning off unrelated operations, as each operation can process its own information well, without the need of a centralized mainframe. Or management's ability to get good information fast facilitates more centralized management. Technology, if it strongly tilted one way or the other, could determine whether and which corporate governance issues are important.

3. The quality of contract. And one could see another role for law here. If the institutions of contract improve greatly relative to the institutions of corporate governance, then one would expect to see pressure on the size of firms. Corporate governance rises in importance when the transactions to be governed cannot be handled well informally, or via contract.[4]

If production needs to be brought inside a single firm (think: the vertical integration that was central to the mid-20th-century American economy), because

---

[4] Consider this small contract riddle: Part of the technology that favors decentralized production is better contract law. If contract law (and related contract institutions) improved, while holding the quality of corporate law constant, that improvement would favor operational decentralization. But better contract law is the corporate law primitive, and corporate law is one of the institutions that facilitates large organizations. Hence, the two should move in tandem, not separately. And if both improve simultaneously, the improvement's effects on relative decentralization are unpredictable.

of the Fisher Bodies problem, see Klein, Crawford & Alchian (1978), then the economy puts pressure on the institutions of corporate governance. But if contractual capacity improves (because of, say, better judges, better information on contractual performance, better third-party verifiers, and so on), then the units of production can be kept in separate firms. When they're in separate firms the problems of horizontal and vertical corporate governance (to the extent those problems arise from large-sized firms) diminish; contract takes over from the institutions of corporate governance.

4. *Markets again.* This trade-off between firm and contract as the mode of governance sets us up for another market-oriented perspective. Markets constrain corporate governance failures. Firms must operate within product, capital, and managerial labor markets, each of which we have seen prods the firm toward efficiency and toward using the best corporate governance institutions.

The market can constrain corporate governance failures in another way. The firm's *internal* governance system brings activities into the firm that could have been transacted *across* the market. The firm is not just competing in the product market with other firms that have brought a similar quantity and scope of activities inside the organization (an organization which hence needs governance institutions to make it work well).

The firm *also* competes with disaggregated units that make the same product. If the disaggregated units can produce the same quality product cheaper, etc., then more resources will go to the disaggregated units, fewer resources to the integrated units, until the integrated units learn—presumably via better corporate governance institutions—how to reduce their governance costs, improve their organization, etc. This mechanism is the Coasean theory of the firm, applied to corporate governance institutions.

B. Property Rights

Ownership separation has two related underlying property rights problems. The first is simple: for firms to get capital, there must be enough savings somewhere in the system to invest. But if property rights are fragile, savers will be unwilling to save, fearing confiscation. Cf. North & Weingast (1989); Mahoney (2001); Williamson (1985): "the suppliers of finance [face the risk that t]he whole of their investment in the firm is potentially placed at hazard. By contrast, the productive assets (plant and equipment; human capital) of suppliers of raw material, labor, intermediate product, electric power, and the like normally remain[] in the suppliers' possession." Some other mechanism of gathering capital would be needed, such as the State, and what now passes for corporate governance problems in the wealthy West would focus on the relationship between the State as capital-provider and large enterprises.

The second property rights problem is more nuanced, but similar: Separation of ownership from control exposes capital-providers. They provide their capital to the firm, but might not get it back. Managers can take it for themselves. Other shareholders might maneuver to grab it. These two risks to investors are the usual focus for corporate governance. But we shouldn't stop there. The State, or employees, might figure out how and why that capital really belongs, or should belong, in their own pockets. When investors feel unprotected in this dimension, they are likely to adopt institutional arrangements that would minimize their losses to the State, or to arrangements favored by the State.

Thus, one can find correlations between, say, weak corporate law and weak ownership separation. And while it's logically possible that it's the weakness in *corporate* law that directly weakens separation, because investors fear dominant stockholders, it's equally logically possible that *it's a more basic weakness in property rights in that society that deters such investment. Investors could fear that others, such as the State or its patrons, will grab the investment.* There must be property rights institutions that make savers relatively comfortable with saving and with visibly investing in distant enterprise. If they fear expropriation, they won't put their savings into public view even if they trust the firm's controllers not to steal from them. In much of the world, such property rights are not in place. In some parts of the wealthy West, putting the money out there in some corporate forms is riskier than in other forms. Hence, there is less reason in such nations to develop strong institutions of corporate governance, because even if developed they wouldn't be widely used.

One might go further. Once basic property rights institutions are in place, corporate law institutions can adapt, usually easily. In this sense, corporate law institutions are not central to social and business organization—to the chagrin perhaps of the corporate law professor—but basic property rights are. If property rights are secure, and if the society has the "primitive" foundation on the ground of good basic contract law, then the institutions of corporate governance become (relatively) easy to build. Corporate governance institutions here are derivative and secondary to the more basic institutions of property and contract.

Summary

We have reviewed the institutions of corporate governance. The institutions in general respond to two distinct problems, one of vertical governance (between distant shareholders and managers) and another of horizontal governance (between a close, controlling shareholder and distant shareholders).

The principal institutions are about ten: the market, the board, gate-keeping, transparency, coalescing (via takeovers, proxy fights, and shareholder voice), incentive compensation, professionalism, lawsuits, capital structure, and bankruptcy. Some institutions deal well with vertical corporate governance but do less well with horizontal governance. The institutions interact as complements and substitutes, and many can be seen as developing out of a "primitive" of contract law. Arguably a system must get contract enforcement, as well as basic property rights, satisfactory before it embarks on more sophisticated corporate governance institutions.

Institutional legitimacy affects the institutions of corporate governance. In the United States, intervention inside large firms from powerful financial institutions was seen as politically illegitimate and was largely banned or made more costly. In modern Europe, the institutions of shareholder value have been denigrated. Each legitimacy issue affects corporate institutions, as firms seek substitutes defensively, for example. The interaction between political institutions and corporate governance institutions is an inquiry still in its infancy but promises large returns. Even simple regressions suggest that political institutions may strongly influence the construction and survival of corporate governance institutions.

References

Aggarwal, Rajesh and Andrew Samwick. 1999. "Executive Compensation, Strategic Competition, and Relative Performance Evaluation: Theory and Evidence". *Journal of Finance* 54: 1999–2043.
Bankruptcy Code § 1104.
Bebchuk, Lucian A. 1999. "A Rent-Protection Theory of Corporate Ownership and Control". Harvard Law and Economics, Cambridge, MA: Working Paper (Discussion Paper no. 260).
———, Jesse M. Fried, and David I. Walker. 2002. "Executive Compensation in America: Optimal Contracting or Extraction of Rents?" *University of Chicago Law Review* 69: 751.
Bethel, Jennifer E., Julia P. Liebeskind and Tim Opler. 1998. Block share purchases and corporate performance. *Journal of Finance* 53: 605–634.
Bhagat, Sanjai and Bernard S. Black. 1999. "The Uncertain Relationship Between Board Composition and Firm Performance." *Business Lawyer* 54: 921.
Black, Bernard, Reinier Kraakman, and Anna Tarassova. 2000. "Russian Privatization and Corporate Governance: What Went Wrong". *Stanford Law Review* 52: 1731.
Blair, Margaret M. and Lynn Stout. 1999. "A Team Production Theory of Corporate Law". *Virginia Law Review* 85: 247.
Bradley, Michael and Michael Rosenzweig. 1992. "The Untenable Case for Chapter 11". *The Yale Law Journal* 101: 1043.
Brudney, Victor. 1985. "Corporate Governance, Agency Costs, and the Rhetoric of Contract". *Columbia Law Review* 85: 1403–1444.
Caves, Richard E. 1989. "Mergers, Takeovers, and Economic Efficiency: Foresight vs. Hindsight". *International Journal of Industrial Organization* 7: 151–174.
Chandler, Alfred P. 1990. *Scale and Scope: The Dynamics of Industrial Capitalism.* Cambridge, MA: Belknap.
Cheffins, Brian R. 2001. "Law, Economics and the UK's System of Corporate Governance: Lessons from History". *Journal of Corporate Law Studies* 1: 71.
Clark, Robert C. 1986. Corporate Law. Boston, MA: Little, Brown.
Coase, R.H. 1937. The Nature of the Firm. *Economica* 4: 386.
Coffee, John C. 2001. "The Rise of Dispersed Ownership: Theories of Law and the State in the Separation of Ownership and Control". *Yale Law Journal* 111: 1–82.
Core, John E., Wayne R. Guay, and David F. Larcker. 2003. "Executive Equity Compensation and Incentives: A Survey". *FRBNY Economic Policy Review* April: 27.
Davis, Gerald F. 1993. "Who Gets Ahead in the Market for Corporate Directors: The Political Economy of Multiple Board Memberships. *Academy of Management Best Papers Proceedings* 1993: 202–211.
Denis, Diane K. and John J. McConnell. 2003. "International Corporate Governance". *Journal of Financial and Quantitative Analysis* 38: 1–36.

Dyck, Alexander and Luigi Zingales. 2003. "Private Benefits of Control: An International Comparison". *Journal of Finance* (forthcoming).
Easterbrook, Frank H. and Daniel R. Fischel. 1991. *The Economic Structure of Corporate Law.* Cambridge, CA: Harvard University Press.
Eisenberg, Theodore, Stefan Sundgren, and Martin T. Wells. 1998. "Larger board size and decreasing firm value". *Journal of Financial Economics* 48: 35–54.
Faccio, Mara and Larry H.P. Lang. 2002. "The Ultimate Ownership of Western European Corporations". *Journal of Financial Economics* 65: 365–396.
Fama, Eugene F. and Michael C. Jensen. 1983. "Separation of Ownership and Control". *Journal of Law and Economics* 26: 301–325.
Franks, Julian, Colin Mayer and Luc Renneboog. 2001. "Who Disciplines Management in Poorly Performing Company?" *Journal of Financial Intermediation* 10: 209–248.
Gilson, Ronald and Mark J. Roe. 1999. "The Political Economy of Japanese Lifetime Employment" in Margaret Blair and Mark Roe (eds.), *Employees and Corporate Governance.* Washington, DC: Brookings.
─── and Reinier Kraakman. 1991. Reinventing the Outside Director: An Agenda for Institutional Investors. *Stanford Law Review* 43: 863.
Gilson, Stuart C. 1990. "Bankruptcy, Boards, Banks, and Blockholders: Evidence on Changes in Corporate Ownership and Control When Firms Default". *Journal of Financial Economics* 27: 355–387.
Grossman, Sanford and Oliver Hart. 1986. "The Costs and Benefits of Ownership: A Theory of Vertical and Lateral Integration". *Journal of Political Economy* 94: 691–719.
───. 1982. "Corporate Financial Structure and Managerial Incentives" in John J. McCall (ed.), *The Economics of Information and Uncertainty.* Chicago, IL: University of Chicago Press, pp. 107–737.
Hall, Brian J. and Jeffrey B. Liebman. 1998. "Are CEOs Really Paid Like Bureaucrats?" *The Quarterly Journal of Economics* 63: 653.
Hall, Peter A. and David Soskice (eds.). 2001. *Varieties of Capitalism: The Institutional Foundations of Comparative Advantage.* Oxford: Oxford University Press.
Henderson, Rebecca H. and Kim B. Clark. 1990. "Architectural Innovation: The Reconfiguration of Existing Product Technologies and the Failure of Established Firms". *Administrative Science Quarterly* 35: 9–30.
Hermalin, Benjamin E. and Michael S. Weisbach. 1998. "Endogenously Chosen Boards of Directors and Their Monitoring of the CEO". *American Economic Review* 88: 96–118.
Jensen, Michael C. 1986. Agency Costs of Free Cash Flow, Corporate Finance, and Takeovers". *American Economic Review Papers and Proceedings.* 76: 323.
─── and William H. Meckling. 1976. "Theory of the Firm: Managerial Behavior, Agency Costs and Ownership Structure". *Journal of Financial Economics* 3: 305–360.
─── and Kevin J. Murphy. 1990. "Performance Pay and Top-Management Incentives". *Journal of Political Economy* 98: 225–264.
Kafka, Peter and Peter Newcomb (eds.). 2001. The Forbes 400. *Forbes.* Oct. 8: 127–270.
Klein, Benjamin, Robert Crawford, and Armen Alchian. 1978. "Vertical Integration, Appropriable Rents, and the Competitive Contracting Process". *Journal of Law and Economics* 21: 297–326.
La Porta, Rafael, Florencio Lopez-de-Silanes and Andrei Shleifer. 1999. "Corporate Ownership Around the World". *Journal of Finance* 54: 471–517.
─── and Robert Vishny. 1998. "Law and Finance". *Journal of Political Economy* 106: 1113–1150.
───. 1997. "Legal Determinants of External Finance". *Journal of Finance* 52: 1131–1155.
Lipset, Seymour Martin and Gary Marks. 2000. "*It Didn't Happen Here—Why Socialism Failed in the United States.* New York: W.W. Norton.
Lorsch, Jay and Elizabeth MacIver. 1989. *Pawns or Potentates: The Reality of America's Corporate Boards.* Boston, MA: Harvard Business School Press.

Macey, Jonathan and Hideki Kanda. 1990. "The Stock Exchange as a Firm: The Emergence of Close Substitutes for the New York and Tokyo Stock Exchanges". *Cornell Law Review* 75: 1007–1052.
Mahoney, Paul G. 2001. "The Common Law and Economic Growth: Hayek Might be Right". *Journal of Legal Studies* 30: 503–525.
———. 1997. The Exchange as Regulator. *Virginia Law Review* 83: 1453–1500.
Miwa, Yoshiro and Mark Ramseyer. 2002. "The Value of Prominent Directors: Corporate Governance and Bank Access in Transitional Japan". *Journal of Legal Studies* 31: 273.
Murphy, Kevin J. 2002. "Explaining Executive Compensation: Managerial Power vs. the Perceived Cost of Stock Options". *University of Chicago Law Review* 69: 847.
———. 1999. "Executive Compensation" in Ashenfelter & Card (eds.), *Handbook of Labor Economics*, Vol. 3. Amsterdam: North Holland.
Myers, Stewart C. 1977. "Determinants of Corporate Borrowing". *Journal of Financial Economics* 5: 147–175.
North, Douglass C. and Barry R. Weingast. 1989. "Constitutions and Commitment: The Evolution of Institutions Governing Public Choice in Seventeenth-Century England". *Journal of Economic History* 49: 803–832.
OECD. 1994. "The OECD *Jobs Study: Evidence and Explanations*, Part II: The Adjustment Potential of the Labour Market. Paris: OECD.
Pagano, Marco and Paolo F. Volpin. 2002. "The Political Economy of Finance". *Oxford Review of Economic Policy* 17: 502.
Perotti, Enrico C. and Ernst-Ludwig von Thadden. 2003. "The Political Economy of Bank and Market Dominance". SSRN working paper.
Piore, Michael J. and Charles F. Sabel. 1984. *The Second Industrial Divide: Possibilities for Prosperity*. New York: Basic.
Rajan, Raghuram G. and Luigi Zingales. 2003. "The Great Reversals: The Politics of Financial Development in the Twentieth Century". *Journal of Financial Economics* 69: 5.
Ravenscraft, David J. and F.M. Scherer. 1987. *Mergers, Sell-Offs, and Economic Efficiency*. Washington, DC: Brookings.
Roe, Mark J. 2003. *Political Determinants of Corporate Governance: Political Conflict, Corporate Impact*. New York: Oxford University Press.
———. 2002. "Corporate Law's Limits". *Journal of Legal Studies* 31: 233.
———. 2000. *Corporate Reorganization and Bankruptcy: Legal and Financial Materials*. New York: Foundation Press.
———. 1994. *Strong Managers, Weak Owners: The Political Roots of American Corporate Finance*. Princeton, NJ: Princeton University Press.
———. 1993. "Takeover Politics", in Margaret Blair (ed.), *The Deal Decade*. Washington, DC: Brookings.
———. 1983. "A New Model for Corporate Reorganization". *Columbia Law Review* 83: 527.
Romano, Roberta. 1988. "The Future of Hostile Takeovers: Legislation and Public Opinion". University of Cincinnati Law Review 57: 457.
Useem, Michael. 1992. *Executive Defense: Shareholder Power and Corporate Reorganization*. Cambridge (MA): Harvard University Press.
Vagts, Detlev. 2002. "Comparative Corporate Law—The New Wave" in Rainer Schweitzer and Urs Gasser (eds.), *Festschrift for Jean-Nicolas Druey*. Basel: Schulthess.
Williamson, Oliver. 1985. *The Economic Institutions of Capitalism*. New York: The Free Press.
Yermack, David. 1996. "Higher Market Valuation of Companies with A Small Board of Directors". *Journal of Financial Economics* 40: 185–211.
Zingales, Luigi. 1997. "Corporate Governance" in Peter Newman (ed.), *The New Palgrave Dictionary of Economics and the Law*. Oxford: Oxford University Press.

16. Firms and the Creation of New Markets

ERIN ANDERSON and HUBERT GATIGNON

1. INTRODUCTION

New markets do not emerge, nor do they appear. They are *made* by the activities of firms. New markets are created when firms correctly sense (by accident or by design) a latent need and communicate their solution to that need: markets spring into being when economic actors shift resources to that firm's solution. The most visible way to create a new market is to offer a product/service that is novel, thereby addressing needs that were not met (and perhaps not even sensed). Much of this chapter focuses on firms' efforts to develop and commercialize new offerings, and on how buyers respond, thereby creating new markets. However, new markets are also created when firms cultivate an underserved clientele with established products. Much of marketing is about how to bring new customers into a developed industry (as opposed to rearranging market shares among existing customers). This chapter will also highlight these market-creation activities.[1]

Capitalist systems exhibit an astonishing ability to create new markets (and, typically, destroy existing ones) based on developing and commercializing innovations. Schumpeter (1943) argued that large firms innovate so well that they raise a society's general standard of living. In the same vein, Schmookler (1966) argues that long-term economic growth is primarily the result of better knowledge of what goods would be useful and how to make them, i.e. invention. There is little argument that innovation, on the whole, increases public welfare: new markets are thought to arise because buyers recognize they will be better off. Breshnahan and Gordon (1996) document why, with a series of innovations that clearly increase buyers' utility. It should be noted, however, that many innovations are not radical but merely incremental, and that their utility is in the eye of the beholder. Although this chapter emphasizes more radical innovation, it will address new products in general.

---
[1] We define a market as the set of all actual and potential buyers of a product or service. Following Williamson (1996), we define a firm as a governance structure, an organizational construction. We treat an industry as a group of sellers (firms) serving a market. In the standard economic perspective, the market is the main central institution, and the firms' black-box actions derive from markets. Here, we treat the firm (which is not a black box) as the central institution. And we view markets as an outcome of corporate activities. This reversal of the standard set up follows from New Institutional Economics.

It is less clear how much firms actually benefit from attempting to create new markets via new products. Firms develop and launch new products with the intention of increasing profitability. Schmookler (1966) shows that invention is not primarily a response to intellectual stimuli but is instead an effort to exploit a profit opportunity. But the payoff to the investing firm is highly uncertain. Frequently, developing firms reap heavy costs, but other firms capture the projected benefits—if indeed, these are not competed away in a ruinous race to build new markets and establish dominance. This may explain why Griliches, Hall, and Pakes (1991) find no relationship between a firm's patent counts and its financial performance. Bayus, Erickson, and Jacobson (2003) note that it is an article of faith among businesspeople that new product development (hereafter NPD) is essential to firm performance, but that the evidence is mixed as to why this is true, and how strong and long-lasting is the effect.

In short, NPD is inherently uncertain: new markets frequently do not materialize, nor do anticipated profits. We contend that the creation of new markets via the creation of new products is best understood through the lens of New Institutional Economics (NIE), leaning on the twin pillars of evolutionary reasoning and Transaction Cost Economics (hereafter TCE). From TCE, we adopt the premise that firms intend to be rational but are bounded in their abilities: in particular, critical information is impacted, and decision makers cannot write complex contingent claims contracts that steer toward optimal outcomes. Instead, executives compare concrete, visible alternatives and attempt to foresee which one does the best job of reducing the total of production and transaction costs long term. Further, opportunism is possible, and given a sufficient scale of operation, worth reducing by employing costly governance mechanisms. Coming sections rely on the TCE mechanisms of asset specificity, environmental uncertainty, and internal uncertainty (difficulty of assessing performance using output measures). The control/commitment continuum from arm's-length market contracting to relational governance through to vertical integration will be invoked frequently to explain how firms develop new products in the hope of creating new markets, and how they form relations with economic actors (such as distributors) that are vital to the product's success.

From evolutionary economics (Nelson 1995, Dosi 1997)), we borrow the premise that markets seldom reach equilibrium, and that if they do so, the equilibrium reached is path dependent at the industry level. Further, firms react to uncertainty by developing routines that are difficult to change, routines that reflect the path of their (unique) history. Learning and imitating feature heavily in our analysis.

Strands of these frameworks also appear in a major part of this chapter that reviews how prospects become converted into customers, thereby calling new markets into existence. We rely here on the study of consumer behavior through the combined lenses of sociology, psychology, and economics. We discard the classical economic assumptions that consumers are well informed, rational maximizers of their own utility, capable of reducing multiple attributes of a product to the lowest common denominator of net utility. We accept that buyers have complex motives, many of them socially determined, and that utility is subjective and individual (including, for example, Veblen effects that could hardly be considered rational). At the same time, we do not portray buyers as capricious, random, or wholly ignorant. We accept that buyers seek to improve their subjective utility, subject to bounds on their rationality, and that they do so by comparing observable outcomes and attempting to foresee which best fits their subjective preferences.

NIE has a number of core approaches, including property rights, the contractual nature of the firm, the tragedy of the commons, and allocation among claimants to common resource pools. While we focus primarily on TCE and on evolutionary reasoning, we acknowledge that other NIE elements can be brought to bear to understand how firms create markets.

This chapter is organized as follows. We begin with the mundane: how do firms create new markets from established products? We then turn to the far more perilous task of creating new markets via new products. We first revisit the problem of why firms bother to try, given that the payoffs of NPD are so uncertain. Three ways to develop new products are then considered in turn: internal development of the sort favored by Schumpeter (1943), third-party development via market contracts of the sort criticized by Williamson (1996), and today's vogue of merely acquiring or appropriating new products developed elsewhere. New product development is a vast topic. We focus on those aspects that determine what sorts of new markets a firm can hope to create, and offer references to other NPD issues.

Given the new product, how do prospects convert to buyers? A large literature, following the tradition of Griliches (1957), empirically summarizes how innovations diffuse through a target population. We examine this literature, focusing on how the firm's marketing strategy opens (or sometimes forecloses) new markets.

2. How Firms Create New Markets without New Products

If one accepts bounded rationality and opportunism, it follows that economic actors benefit from sheer information and stimulation, and that firms can convert prospects into buyers by offering credible reassurance against both adverse selection and moral hazard. Therefore, *mere marketing activity creates new markets*, and does so even with established products. Pawakapan (2000) shows how firms created a market in a remote Thai village merely by sending salespeople with branded merchandise, a pricing schedule, promotional materials, and the authority to book and fulfill orders. The salesforce came from the cities and spoke the national language, not the local dialect. Their novel proposition was so appealing, however, that the villagers undertook to learn the national language. Indeed, Pawakapan (2000) judges salespeople more effective than any other means, including schools and political pressures, in teaching villagers the national language (from which follows national culture). These firms quickly created a market for categories of merchandise the villagers had never seen, let alone considered. Given choice, villagers changed their buying habits. Formerly, they bought essentially on price and exhibited loyalty to selected local traders selling strictly local unbranded products. Rapidly, villagers added variety, convenience, and selected brand preferences to their utility function and took to spreading their business across multiple salespeople. Thus, mere marketing activity not only created new markets but altered how markets function.

Spulber (1999) generalizes this idea to any market, even the most sophisticated. He conceives of firms as intermediaries standing between consumers and the providers of inputs (components, assembly, finance, delivery, and so forth). In Spulber's conception, problems of information are paramount, transaction costs are high, and markets are uncertain. The mere existence of firms motivates prospects to become buyers: firms are the engine of commerce (money being the oil). Firms do so by standing ready to buy and sell (providing liquidity and immediacy to markets), simplifying exchange, devising pricing and contract information to induce parties to reveal demand and cost information, creating commercial routines (e.g. for getting credit), and making credible commitments backed by a firm's longer life and greater volume of transactions. In Spulber's (1999) conception, managers are important players, and mundane marketing and management activities (such as holding inventory) are essential to bring markets into being—even markets for well-understood products.

The Role of Sales and Distribution Activity

In short, marketing activities (product design, branding, promotion, pricing, sales and distribution) and management activities (product manufacture, inventory, and the like) create markets. One of the most important means of creating a market is simply to offer sales and distribution to it in a credible manner. A major justification for vertical restraints (of which the franchising system is the ultimate expression) is precisely to insure that sales and distribution activities represent and support a brand properly. This alone is thought to open new markets, by overcoming objections to purchase. One justification of selective distribution is that resellers, in return for protection from intra-brand competition, will exert themselves more vigorously on behalf of the brand (Williamson 1979). For example, they may open outlets in disadvantaged neighborhoods, unquestionably creating new markets.

Chandler (1977) takes this argument to the level of American industry, tracing how large-scale manufacturers in the nineteenth century developed aggressive new methods of marketing their goods, even reaching into isolated rural areas. Many of these distribution methods involved granting territorial protection to dealers in return for brand support and an unusual degree of cooperation with the manufacturer (e.g. McCormick harvesters). Today, we recognize these innovations in distribution as a form of relational governance. It arises when dealers and suppliers make specific investments in each other: dealers need protection against supplier opportunism (e.g. capricious pricing or contrived termination), and suppliers need assurance that dealers will not degrade the brand name or shirk. At the limit of asset specificity, vertical integration into distribution is appropriate (e.g. Singer sewing machines, originally sold in company-owned stores).

In short, a firm's activities, and particularly its marketing efforts, create new markets, even for familiar products. They do so principally by reducing transaction costs (incurred when using the price mechanism). These capabilities are even more useful when the product itself is new. We now turn to new product development (NPD).

3. How Firms Develop New Products

The Firm's Returns to New Products

As noted earlier, business executives believe that NPD is critical. Indeed, aggregate evidence suggests that profitable firms do innovate (Capon, Farley and Hoenig 1990). However, this does not mean that innovative firms are profitable: as noted, other firms often reap the benefits of NPD. How could the developing firm profit from its own activities? Bayus, Erickson, and Jacobson (2003) lay out four mechanisms. First, new products have new features that could attract buyers. However, this revenue advantage is frequently offset by additional costs of supporting new products. Second, new products might enable the firm to find new markets (or segments) that are price inelastic. Both these arguments involve creating new markets. Third, the firm may be able to move its existing customers to new products that are cheaper to support (for example, might require less after-sales service). Fourth, the firm might develop new capabilities that are difficult to imitate. Without new products, firms eventually fail to adapt to changing market needs and find themselves unable to meet mounting competitive pressures, an argument congenial to evolutionary reasoning. New product launches galvanize firms, giving them impetus to renew and recombine their competences. In this view, new products are a firm's way to overcome inertia, a force to develop new routines and retire old ones. Viewed this way, the gauge of NPD success is not so much whether new products create new markets as it is how much the firm changes.

Nonetheless, firms do develop new products for the primary purpose of capturing some part of the value they add to society by creating new markets (Schmookler 1966). How and why does such innovation occur? Classic economic analysis says little about this issue, tending instead to take innovation by the firm as exogenous. Teece (1996) examines why this is so, arguing that innovation has seven properties that defy the conventions of economic analysis (see Table 1).

Table 1. Seven properties of innovation that contradict standard economic analysis adapted from Teece (1996)

Seven fundamental characteristics of technological development make it difficult to explain innovation using the standard economic lens. The lens of NIE is more appropriate. These characteristics are:

1. Uncertainty: innovation is a quest into the unknown. Therefore, serendipity and luck play an important role.
2. Path Dependence: technology often evolves in path dependent ways, contoured by a technological paradigm. Within a paradigm, research efforts become channeled along certain trajectories. New product and process developments for a particular organization are likely to lie in the technological neighborhood of previous successes.
3. Cumulative nature: technology development, particularly inside a particular paradigm, proceeds cumulatively along the path defined by the paradigm.
4. Irreversibilities: technology progress exhibits strong irreversibilities. The evolution of technologies along certain trajectories eliminates the possibility of competition from older technologies, even if their relative prices change significantly.
5. Technological interrelatedness: it is infeasible to separate out a technology and specialize exclusively in it. Seemingly unrelated technologies share underlying points of commonality.
6. Tacitness: knowledge is difficult to codify, archive, and transmit.
7. Inappropriability: firms face serious hurdles to insuring they, and not a rival firm or a customer, will receive a fair share of the value the firm creates via innovation.

We focus on the governance issues that beset NPD. Below, we examine three ways the firm tries to develop innovations, beginning with vertical integration of new product development activities.

Processes of Internal Development

A very substantial body of descriptive research looks into the "black box" of new product development. Krishnan and Ulrich (2001) review this sprawling literature, seeking to unify it inductively around the literally dozens of decisions firms make to develop and commercialise a new product or service. In the picture that emerges, firms look ahead in a deliberate, goal-directed manner, seeking to develop new products with a minimum of waste and a maximum of market impact. Economic exigencies impose discipline on the process, focusing management on the pursuit of internal process outcomes (such as fast development and roll-out) and external market outcomes (such as market share, revenue growth, and profitability) rather than on organizational politics or pursuit of private sub-goals. In this respect, the picture looks more like economics than sociology or psychology: as Dosi (1997) puts it, abandoning perfect rationality does *not* imply "anything goes."[2]

---

[2] Dosi (1997) reviews a growing body of economic work outside the conventions of rational, identical agents seeking an equilibrium outcome. He argues that an evolutionary lens is particularly well suited to explain technological change. Dosi (1997) concludes that linear models of innovation do not fit the evidence. A more accurate picture is one of feedback loops between innovation, diffusion, and generation of new opportunities.

However, complexity, information impactedness, and bounded rationality massively influence how the firm goes about the task. The myriad decisions that must be made (even if "decided" by the default path of inaction) exhibit important interdependencies, not the least of which is that each development project must fit the firm's competences and strategy: the identity of the players matters. Each project is part of a constellation of other projects, which need to be coordinated. Further, each project team must coordinate across the various functional areas of the organization (R&D, production, marketing, and so forth). Coordination involves friction, which imposes transaction costs. A major finding of this literature is that the transaction costs entailed in new product development *even under unified governance* are high. (This does not contradict TCE, which suggests that firms cannot eliminate transaction costs but can contain them better than do markets.)

The Bounded Rationality of Potential Buyers

Why are transaction costs high? Developing new products demands a great deal of information, which is not readily available and not equally available to everyone involved in the development effort (information impactedness). Much of the information is tacit: Van den Bulte and Moenaert (1998) demonstrate that sheer physical proximity has much to do with whether tacit information will be shared effectively. Krishnan and Ulrich (2001) conclude that developers must combine many types of information from multiple sources, sifting, weighing, interpreting, and combining in a complex and inherently subjective manner. Combining information strains the cognitive abilities of decision makers (bounded rationality at individual and group levels). Numerous market research techniques have been developed to assist here (for a review, see Kaul and Rao 1995), but their usefulness has limits, particularly when developing truly new products and services. One reason is that subjective, holistic aspects of the product (e.g. aesthetic appeal) are difficult to represent and examine, yet are important determinants of success. More fundamentally, the prospect's first response to an innovation is "What is it?" Not surprisingly, potential buyers are usually unable to imagine and report accurately what utility they might derive from an innovation, nor how likely they are to buy it.

A classic example (Nayak and Ketteringham 1986), is the videocassette player: market research undertaken by Sony led management to assume that buyers would use it primarily to record short television programs to play back later. Accordingly, Sony developed a proprietary machine (the Betamax standard) to play a one-hour tape. Rival developer JVC made no assumptions about how people would use the machine and therefore maximized flexibility (which meant longer tapes). As the market developed, the principal utility that emerged was in playing pre-recorded movies. JVC won the subsequent standards race based largely on what turned out to be the superior utility of a long tape. To do so, JVC licensed its VHS standard to competitors, thereby giving away profits from its invention. Sony attempted to do the same with Betamax but could not enlist many other firms—because their managers realized that a short tape would limit the creation of a new market. This is a good example of a firm's efforts to be farsighted: a sociological analysis would have awarded more allies to Sony than to lesser-known JVC.

Disparity of Goals

Complicating the development task is disparity of goals. Krishnan and Ulrich (2001) note that the performance of a product development project team is typically indexed by time taken (lead time to market), or by the manufacturing cost, quality, or market attractiveness of the team's output. These goals involve tradeoffs (e.g. short lead times frequently drive up manufacturing costs). Further, it is not clear how well such internal project development goals map onto external performance goals, such as revenue growth or incremental profit. For example, a review of research on organizational processes (Brown and Eisenhardt 1995) concludes that cross-functional communication improves project development outcomes (e.g. speed, productivity). However, Henard and Szymanski (2001), in a review of over 40 empirical studies, find that cross-functional integration has little impact on the next step of market or firm performance outcomes (e.g. market share, profit margin). Apparently, the advantage of superior project development outcomes can be readily offset by inferior commercialization, a theme we develop in section IV of this review.

Development Routines

Firms develop routines to cope with such challenges, routines that have an important influence on the firm's competences (Nelson 1995, Dosi 1997). A common routine ("sequential development") is to split development efforts into phases, assign each phase to a functional group, and set deadlines for each group to complete its input and hand the project off to the next group (for example, R&D might hand off to Production, which hands off to Marketing). Sequential development addresses the problem of bounded rationality by separating tasks and responsibilities, confining them to groups with similar viewpoints. Sequential development reduces internal friction, but at the price of longer lead times and, more importantly, new products that are poorly suited to fast-changing environments. The voice of the potential customer is usually lost as the project moves through internal groups, awaiting its turn for attention in each group. The solution is to overlap the stages ("concurrent development"). Concurrent development requires managing the information flow so as to insure that each stage not only has more information *but understands the information in the same way*. This raises transaction costs, but give firms the flexibility they need to make major changes quickly to adapt to turbulent environments (Krishnan and Ulrich 2001).

The sequential development issue underscores four points that fit well in the NIE paradigm. First, routines are critical and are costly to alter. Second, bounded rationality means that players will not use information in the same way, even in the unlikely event that all information is available to all players. Third, the uncertainty inherent in a firm's environment has an important impact on the appropriate way of organizing its activities. Fourth, unified governance does not banish transaction costs. Therefore, how a firm structures its internal processes is of importance: firms should not be treated as black boxes, nor as interchangeable production functions.

Internal Team Processes

Brown and Eisenhardt (1995) review a large body of micro-level research examining the workings of project teams. A central challenge here is overcoming the information impactedness that is endemic to innovation development processes. A major obstacle is that functional groups operate in their own "thought worlds," which condition how they obtain, share, and process information. *Even though they work for the same organization*, individuals do not readily cooperate, share information, or reach agreement, especially across functions. Conflicts and information hoarding abound. Traditional internal incentives alone are not sufficiently high-powered to bring forth best efforts from all employees (Teece 1996). Thus, group composition matters because internal cohesion creates better project development outcomes. Moorman (1995) extends this finding from project outcomes to market outcomes: new products are better received 12 months after launch when developed in firms with a strong culture of interpersonal support. In these firms, employees feel a personal loyalty to (and trust in) their employer. Such "clan" structures work by supplementing traditional employment incentives, motivating people to collect, pool, and utilize information candidly. Clan mechanisms, which TCE labels "the economics of atmosphere," are important to the understanding of economic organization: however, they are difficult to unravel (Williamson 1996, p. 270). So doing is a promising research direction in the study of in-house NPD.

The speed and productivity of the project development team increase in teams that rely on "gatekeepers," individuals who go to great lengths to scan for information, bring it into the team and make sure it is dispersed (Brown and Eisenhardt 1995). Three findings are striking. First, effective teams engage in external communication, bringing fresh information and viewpoints into the organizations. Information from suppliers is particularly useful: it appears to substantially improve the development team's results. Second, attempting to reduce friction by burying conflict is counterproductive: better performance comes when team members, who inevitably see the situation differently, discuss freely. Such teams negotiate their way to a solution that mitigates bounded rationality at the individual level: internal cohesion facilitates by keeping the conflict manageable and task focused. Third, the classic approach is for the team to develop one best new project, for which it then garners organizational support. This minimizes transaction costs, and is effective in stable, relatively mature environments. But in rapidly changing environments, planning one's way to a single best project outcome is a counterproductive exercise because such environments strain rationality. Project development teams perform better by engaging in seemingly wasteful trial-and-error processes, such as experimenting, moving quickly without thorough analysis, and testing competing designs simultaneously. Trial and error, in turn, requires a risk-tolerant, improvisational management style that goes against the routines embedded in many firms.

Purposefully Designing Creative Products with High Market Appeal

How can teams set about purposefully to design something highly creative that will attract buyers, thereby creating new markets? The evidence is that they often cannot, and frequently, they do not. Many successful innovations are not the deliberate output of a creative process. They are by-products, often accidental, of efforts to create a variation of something known (for example, the weak, unconventional glue on Post-It Notes was a failed by-product of 3M's efforts to make conventional glue stronger). Efforts to distinguish what purposeful processes do lead to successful innovative products have not found a dominant answer. However, some generalizations emerge. For example, at a very microlevel, Dahl, Chattopadhyay, and Gorn (1999) uncover thought processes that help designers imagine products that meet the dual (and somewhat conflicting) criteria of being creative, yet acceptable to buyers. Urban and Von Hippel (1988) show that, in business-to-business markets, certain customer profiles correspond to "lead users" who are excellent forecasters of overall market reaction. Enlisting such customers to cooperate with designers early in the development process raises the probability that an innovation will find buyers after launch.

Brown and Eisenhardt (1995) extend the idea: in many markets, project teams that seek information from potential customers tend to develop products that are better accepted in the marketplace. This is particularly the case in uncertain (complex, fast-changing) markets, where, by nature, it is difficult to understand customers. In uncertain markets, an overriding customer orientation improves new product performance by guiding managers to devote resources to decoding customers' needs and options, in spite of the difficulty in so doing (Gatignon and Xuereb 1997). The difficulty of this challenge is underscored by Moorman (1995), who finds that in turbulent markets, firms tend to introduce new products that are less creative than those in more stable markets. A likely explanation is that such markets strain the decision makers' ability to discern customer reaction, making it more risky to introduce something novel. Hence, more conventional new products can be seen as a means of coping with bounded rationality in the face of market uncertainty.

When Is Experience an Asset?

Firms invest in a market, acquiring experience, much of which is idiosyncratic to the firm. Experience should serve useful purposes for some time, which would make it an asset. Indeed, there is a tendency in TCE to equate idiosyncratic investments and idiosyncratic assets, as though all investments generate durable utility. But an investment is a commitment of resources. This does not always create an asset. Indeed, it could create a lasting disadvantage.

Is a firm's market experience truly an asset in developing new products, particularly innovations? In general, the answer is yes (Moorman and Miner 1997): organizations that gather experience and are capable of dispersing it to multiple decision makers create new products that are more successful (though not more creative). However, there are important qualifications here. Experience can be a drawback, particularly in the context of innovations. Experienced, successful firms often fail to recognize shifts in technologies or markets because they are biased towards existing markets (Krishnan and Ulrich 2001). This focus leads them to overlook or distort information that threatens the status quo.[3] Moorman and Miner (1997) show that in experienced firms in which project team members have a strong consensus about what they know, rapid changes in the technological environment overwhelm team members. Rather than update, they develop *less* creative products than do competitors that have less experience and consensus. Brown and Eisenhardt (1995) show that project teams can become too cohesive by being together too long. After five years of working together, team members lose speed and productivity, apparently because they are less likely to cultivate and use external information.

Net, it appears that not all idiosyncratic investments that build up over time can really be considered assets. Experience, in particular, can become a liability, or a "core rigidity" (Leonard-Barton 1992) because the experience is *too* specific. The routines acquired by experience often do not generalize to other circumstances. By attempting to preserve and apply overly specific knowledge, the firm creates path dependence, which in turn makes it difficult to be flexible and creative. Experience prevents the firm from moving to a new,superior path.

If so, a transaction-specific investment is one thing and a transaction-specific asset is another. An asset generates value, and an idiosyncratic asset does so in a manner uniquely suited to a usage or user. In changing environments, idiosyncratic investments may become idiosyncratic liabilities. Afuah (2001) demonstrates this effect in the computing industry. A massive, competence-destroying technological change (the move to RISC technology, Reduced Instruction Set Computing) threatened all competitors—but not equally. Those whose performance suffered the most were vertically integrated into the old technology and used suppliers to learn the new technology. Via vertical integration, these firms had maximized idiosyncratic assets that were rendered useless, even a liability, by the advent of RISC (which required a great deal of unlearning, then relearning). Further, the firms had no routines for dealing in a relational manner

---

[3] Two examples, once considered plausible, are ludicrous in hindsight. "It is an ideal dream to imagine that auto trucks and automobiles will take the place of railways in the long-distance movement of freight and passengers," proclaimed a railway trade association in 1913. And in 1977, the president of Digital Equipment Corporation, Ken Olsen, opined that "There is no reason for any individual to have a computer in their home." DEC's product line rested on the mainframe computer: the company ultimately was put out of business by personal computers. See Cerf and Navasky (1984).

with suppliers. They were unable to transition effectively using arm's-length market contracting because the newness of RISC required developing new idiosyncratic assets, which in turn demand safeguarding by vertical integration or by relational governance. In contrast, the best performers were not vertically integrated in the old technology but did vertically integrate to acquire RISC capabilities. Thus, they could more easily shed their old capabilities and could more readily develop idiosyncratic new ones.

Afuah (2001) is a first step in a valuable research direction: when is a transaction-specific investment truly an asset, rather than merely being idiosyncratic *per se*—or worse yet, a liability? TCE has tended to take the decision to create an idiosyncratic asset as given, or exogenous. But TCE has developed to the point that it is useful to endogenize asset specificity, that is, to explain the decision to invest in specific assets. When should firms undertake the transaction costs of customization? When they settle instead for generic investments—or walk away from a transaction altogether? Testing predictions about walking away is an empirical challenge: although TCE predicts circumstances that will not support transactions, it is difficult to find traces of transactions that were considered without being executed.

Development Relying on Third Parties

The last two decades have seen a strong trend towards outsourcing even sensitive functions once considered too central to confide to outsiders, such as new product development. A significant percentage of the sample of firms surveyed in Robertson and Gatignon (1998) reports using partners to develop new products. Shared development invokes the TCE prediction that outsourcing innovating activity creates high exposure to small-numbers bargaining, hence opportunism. The contractual hazards that arise challenge firms to refine ways to safeguard these transactions, including relational governance, or alliances (see Gulati and Singh 1998 for a review). By TCE reasoning, *the move to outsource NPD will fail unless firms dramatically increase their capacity to ally by such means as the exchange of credible commitments.*

Credible Commitments

The automobile industry is a leading example. Automakers are in the forefront of efforts to delegate new product development upstream. Contractual hazards arise because suppliers are expected to invent components that work with each particular brand and model, which are highly idiosyncratic. Thus, suppliers must invest in idiosyncratic learning to develop highly specific components. This puts suppliers squarely into a position of small-numbers bargaining, exposing them to the buyer's opportunism. Transaction Cost Economics (TCE) predicts that suppliers will hesitate, and will demand concrete assurances in order to proceed: promises of good faith will not suffice. The single best assurance is when a buyer creates a reciprocal exposure by itself making investments that are idiosyncratic *to the supplier.* In so doing, the buyer creates a vulnerability to a supplier: mutual vulnerability creates incentives to eschew opportunism, thereby protecting the relationship.

Bensaou and Anderson (1999) examine when buyers take the risk of investing idiosyncratically in a supplier. They find firms trade off between production costs motives to invest and transaction cost disincentives to invest. On the production side, the more technically challenging the necessary invention, the more buyers make idiosyncratic investments in their supplier. Buyers do so because they cannot simply put out a contract to motivate the supplier to make such investments, but must offer safeguards. Offering safeguards to the supplier is particularly necessary under fast technological change: buyers must absorb some of the risk for their suppliers if they are to obtain the close cooperation needed. Notably, the institutional environment matters: Japanese automakers are able to induce considerably more cooperation from their suppliers for a given level of investment, consistent with findings by Sako and Helper (1998).

More generally, Oxley (1999) compares governance choices made by U.S. firms in their collaborations with firms from 110 countries, collaborations intended to develop and commercialize intellectual property. She finds U.S. firms to be sensitive to both the transaction and the environment. Specifically, firms structure their relationships to approximate hierarchies (by using equity joint ventures, vs. market contracts) when idiosyncratic assets need safeguarding, when performance is difficult to monitor by observing outputs, and when countries provide weak protection of intellectual property.

TCE argues that idiosyncratic investments serve to generate better performance. In support, Jap (1999) shows that close buyer-supplier relationships built on idiosyncratic investments outperform rivals over time, generating significant competitive advantage. Dyer (1995) finds that automakers which build tightly integrated supplier networks based on high levels of mutual asset specificity reap performance benefits: their new products enjoy higher quality and take less time to develop. These studies affirm TCE reasoning that offering credible commitments is necessary to forestall opportunism. However, other solutions to the specificity problem exist: for example, Dutta and John (1995) show that buyers are more willing to make supplier-specific investments if the supplier licenses the innovation. Thus, buyers know they can use a second source to safeguard against opportunism.

How the Downstream Protects Itself Against Upstream Opportunism

Firms also go downstream to develop innovations, and find many ideas among members of their channel of distribution. These are not end customers: channel members move product or service along the path to the end user. Resellers and sales agencies are prime channel members for purposes of developing new products. Typically, they sell complements, and frequently substitutes, giving them a broad perspective on the market. As noted earlier, project teams perform better when they bring this expertise into their deliberations. Some producers develop close relationships with channel members in order to secure their cooperation in the development effort. Anderson and Weitz (1992) show that they do so by exchanging mutual idiosyncratic investments and investing heavily in communication over time. However, relationship building exhibits considerable path dependence: reseller-producer dyads find it difficult to set aside a contentious history in their efforts to achieve coordination. Sako and Helper (1998) reach the same conclusion upstream, for customer-supplier dyads.

An emerging issue is how franchising systems (for a review, see Coughlan et al. 2001) generate new product ideas. Franchising is a form of relational governance, a hybrid balancing properties of both markets and hierarchies. The institution of franchising is particularly well suited to generating, refining, then transmitting and commercializing, new product ideas. Darr, Argote, and Epple (1995) analyze how they do so, showing that new ideas (e.g. process innovations) spread by interpersonal communication within a social system, facilitated by geographical proximity. Thus, new ideas tend not to spread beyond the inventive franchisee and his/her immediate circle. The franchisor is an institution that collects, culls, refines, and then spreads innovations across franchisees. Schmookler (1966) notes that much of the energy that goes into invention is really diverted into reproducing inventions that have "depreciated" (been forgotten). Darr, Argote, and Epple (1995) show this effect is particularly powerful when personnel turnover is high and production processes are simple: the relevant knowledge is difficult to embed in anything other than an individual's mind. Getting individuals to share information with each other is therefore critical. Bradach (1997) analyzes how some franchisors do this. He focuses on "plural governance," which is frequent, structured interaction between company-owned and independently owned outlets. Plural governance facilitates remembering and transmitting innovations. This is a new rationale for a poorly understood phenomenon, the simultaneous use of market *and* hierarchy (dual distribution). Explaining dual distribution, a seemingly wasteful duplication of resources, deserves research priority.

Observations on the Hazards of Cooperation

It is highly risky to engage in mutual building of idiosyncratic investments. Giving and taking hostages (exchanging credible commitments) is a difficult affair to calibrate and to execute in practice (Williamson 1996, Wathne and Heide 2000). Teece (1992) uses TCE reasoning to build the argument that vertical integration is appropriate for assets that are "co-specialized," i.e. both complementary and specialized to the innovation. Teece argues that hazards are pronounced with human assets: integration is vital to impede people from leaking knowledge or switching to a competitor. Indeed, Brown and Eisenhardt (1995) underscore that project team gatekeepers enhance performance by performing a "guard" function to protect proprietary information.

There has been a trend (reviewed by Osborn and Hagedoorn 1997) toward increasing cooperation among producers, particularly producers of potentially complementary goods or services. Cooperation among producers is a new way to outsource the development of innovation. One purpose of these programs is what may broadly be termed co-promotion or co-marketing of each other's brands, including new products. A promising research area is how firms manage the transactional hazards of cooperation. For example, Terpstra and Yu (1990) examine carrier-rider relationships ("piggybacking"), in which firm A (the carrier) uses its sales force to promote the (complementary) new products of firm B (the rider). The obvious danger is that A will behave opportunistically to appropriate B's innovation, (reverse engineering, misleading B about the product's market position, and so forth). How do firms govern such relationships, and which methods are more effective? For example, there is some evidence that in the pharmaceutical industry, firms exchange hostages: piggybacking is reciprocal, with A and B exchanging carrier-rider roles in multiple markets. Such issues deserve research.

Develop by Acquisition or Appropriation

Given the difficulties of successfully developing innovations, including new products, it is not surprising that many producers don't bother to do so. Instead, they watch the activities of other firms, waiting for a "winner" to emerge, which they then acquire—or appropriate. Kogut and Kulatilaka (2001) point out that where firms can merely observe, they will do so. Frequently, mere observation is inadequate: the firm must have some involvement so as to discern the emerging trends and be able to adapt readily. Many seemingly wasteful or indecisive actions, such as investing in multiple (potentially competing) channels of distribution or multiple technologies, or spending inordinately on sales forces or market research, can be interpreted as investments in "real options" that enable the firm to act as soon as uncertainty falls.

Teece (1996) questions the practicality of buying technology elsewhere (e.g. licensing another firm's innovation). Teece concludes that, in spite of the myriad obstacles to developing new products internally, vertical integration is usually the most attractive of the feasible alternatives. Our earlier discussion of the transactions costs inherent in new product development supports this approach by suggesting that complex contingent claims contracting, based on a high level of rationality and information, is simply not practicable. However, management practice indicates that many firms do effectively outsource innovation.

Re truly innovative new products (not mere extensions of the firm's existing products), a common strategy is to merely purchase rights to innovations developed elsewhere. For example, as developing new pharmaceuticals has become slower, more expensive, and more prone to failure, more producers let others invest, then buy licenses to market the results (Tapon 1989). While promising, this approach is fraught with transaction cost perils. To evaluate an innovation developed elsewhere, the firm needs more information than the seller would be wise to reveal. Even if the firm manages to buy the innovation, it may find that idiosyncratic assets are difficult to uproot and relocate, especially if they involve tacit knowledge or go counter to the firm's established routines.

An example is the biotechnology industry. Start-up firms regularly emerge with innovations, but lack the co-specialized assets (such as sales forces) to commercialize them. Therefore, large, established players, facing internal barriers to developing innovation themselves, often invest in purchasing start-ups, rather than in R&D.[4] However, a considerable body of research on acquisition (for reviews, see Capron 1999, Haspeslagh and Jemison 1991) concludes that many of the same obstacles to licensing examined by Teece (1996) persist, notably difficulties in valuing the acquisition and in meshing the acquiring and acquired firm. Thus, Pisano (1990) finds even for biotechnology innovations, firms integrate R&D to mitigate hazards of opportunism. Argyres and Liebeskind (2002) examine the tradeoff between acquisition and integration, incorporating path dependence in their analysis.

A promising research direction here is to connect models of what firms do (which is the bulk of this literature) to the performance outcomes they achieve. Such an approach fits squarely within the NIE paradigm, in which it is accepted that, although there is a selection mechanism, uncertainty, bounded rationality, heterogeneous agents, and path dependence conspire to permit some firms to "get it wrong," yet survive alongside firms that "get it right" (Dosi 1997).

4. How Firms Create New Markets by Commercializing New Products

To this point, we have focused on how firms attempt to create new markets by inventing novel products. As noted earlier, developing a promising concept is one step, creating a market is another step, and deriving profits from the exercise is still another step. Here, we focus on step two: how do prospects become buyers, thereby calling new markets into existence? Following Griliches (1957), we focus on the adoption (i.e. *first-time purchase*) of the innovation. Markets are born when prospects adopt. But markets grow and become established only when adopters make repeat purchases (replacements, upgrades, multiple units, gifts). As a general rule, if a new product is widely adopted, it has sufficient utility that repeat purchases will occur. Therefore, the creation of new markets rests heavily on the diffusion of the innovation, i.e. the spread of first-time purchases among members of a target population.

Typically, for successful innovations, diffusion starts slowly, then accelerates, then tapers off to a saturation level that is less than 100% of all the potential buying units in a population. Such a process produces a capped S-shaped curve

---

[4] This is an interesting twist on Schumpeter (1943), who feared that large firms would eventually stifle the entrepreneurial spirit necessary to drive successful internal R&D. Schumpeter did not foresee the solution of buying the entrepreneur's firm, in part because today's institution of venture capital to fund entrepreneurs was not well developed in the 1940's.

Firms and the Creation of New Markets 417

when cumulative first-time sales are plotted over time. Griliches (1957) pioneered the study of such curves: he examined farmers' adoption of hybrid corn, noting that the same innovation diffused in a different way among different groups of seemingly identical farmers.

Why does one innovation penetrate the market more thoroughly (closer to 100% adoption) than another? Why do some innovations reach their potential more quickly than others? These are central questions. Subsequent to Griliches (1957), a huge literature on diffusion theory has developed in parallel in the fields of psychology, sociology, economics and marketing. Most of it rests on the S curve. Zvi Griliches offered this observation:

> The basic notion was that here was a technical change that was going on, and it was not just happening entirely out of the air, but it was being affected by economics, and to some extent, being created by the economic situation, as well as being affected by it... The funny thing is that diffusion, as such, has never taken off on a large scale in economics. It's a major topic for people in marketing, and they do that. But not very much in mainstream economics, partly because of the way, possibly, I formulated the problem—there is a fundamental disequilibrium... knowledge matters, and the spread of knowledge matters. It's interesting to model how the knowledge spreads. (Krueger and Taylor (2000, p. 180))

Nerlove (2001) also concludes that Griliches' ideas about diffusion have had their greatest influence outside mainstream economics. In this section, we review briefly the diffusion theory and modeling literatures. We first focus on why some innovations diffuse successfully, a necessary condition for new markets to come into being. Then we discuss the strategic commercialization decisions taken at the time of the introduction of the new product or service, focusing on how these decisions help to create (or foreclose) new markets.

Diffusion Theory and Models

New products are outside a buyer's routines. Radical innovations go further: they are outside a buyer's cognitive space: their attributes are difficult to understand, let alone to value. Therefore, innovations arouse a buyer's sense of risk. If they displace the buyer's current routines (for example, new software replacing software the buyer has mastered), innovations also arouse resistance. And innovations can create suspicion. If I become locked in to this brand, will the supplier subsequently exploit my dependence, say by raising price or by failing to deliver on service promises? Uncertainty, fear of small-numbers bargaining, disruption of routines—this scenario fits comfortably in evolutionary economics and in TCE.

Cognitive and Social Processes of Adoption of Innovations

Diffusion theory has focused on fundamental cognitive and social processes as an explanation of adoption decisions by individual consumers or by organizational customers (Rogers 1983). Until recently, this process has typically ignored the marketing of the innovation by the firm commercializing the product or service and the competitive forces at play (Gatignon and Robertson, 1989, 1991, Robertson and Gatignon 1986) with the exception of studies of mass communication (Katz 1957) and inter-personal influence through word-of-mouth (Brown and Reingen 1987, Herr, Kardes, and Kim 1991). We shall return to these influences.

The basic adoption process that underlies most diffusion models considers that individual buyers (who are potential users of the new product or service) can receive information about this new product or service from two sources: inside and outside the "social system" (i.e. the set of individuals whom they can observe and with whom they interact). Sources outside the social system include mass media (buyers can be exposed to these without mediation by the influence of other people). Sources within the social system are a function of the number of prior adopters of the innovation (creating network externalities). Diffusion theory designates two categories of adopters. *Innovators* are those who adopt early because they learn about the innovation from sources independent of prior adopters (as these do not exist early on in the product life cycle). Innovators have a profile (see Rogers 1983, Gatignon and Robertson 1985) that suggests Veblen effects are powerful: innovators seek social status by being among the first to own something new, and often pay high prices to do so. Fortunately for the firm, innovators like to be seen with their acquisition. Their display spurs *imitators*, who tend to be more risk averse and/or more bound to their habits. Imitators adopt later than the innovators, after they gather information (proactively or passively) from those buyers who have already experienced the innovation (have already adopted). The innovator-imitator process implies that, rather than making broad efforts to gain acceptance, firms need to target potential innovators (e.g. by mass media) and win them over first, so that the imitation process can get underway and gather momentum. Diffusion models represent this dynamic in an as-if fashion, for both consumers (individuals) and businesses.

Typically, it is in the firm's interest to spur diffusion as much as possible. However, markets are differentiated institutions. Not all of them depend on widespread adoption. Some rest on a very selective approach, in which exclusivity is considered a positive and widespread diffusion is viewed as a negative. Luxury items, such as certain cars, jewelry, and clothing are examples. Their makers search for terms to differentiate them from their widely-diffused mass-market counterparts. For example, "*haute couture,*" "designer clothes," and "ready-to-wear" are terms used to designate three levels of exclusivity in the clothing category, which generates a wave of new products every season. Makers of *haute couture* seek media mention that they design clothes for specific individuals and occasions (a named actress at the Academy Awards ceremony, for example). Their customers don't want to see other people wearing a similar outfit: diffusion is a negative and exclusivity is a positive. In contrast, makers of designer clothes seek somewhat wider diffusion: they advertise that their wares are derived from *haute couture* and are sold only in selected stores. Seeking maximal diffusion, makers of ready-to-wear advertise that their clothes are readily available and are appropriate for almost anyone on any occasion.

Some Generalizations from Empirical Models

Bass (1969) proposed a robust, generalizable, readily estimable model that integrates both a propensity to innovate (through a coefficient of external influence) and a propensity to imitate (through a coefficient of internal influence). Based on the Bass model, a large number of empirical studies have been conducted over the last thirty years, permitting us to reach generalizable conclusions regarding diffusion research (Mahajan, Muller, and Bass 1993, Mahajan, Muller, and Wind 2000, Sultan, Farley, and Lehmann 1990). Chief among these is that imitation forces are much more powerful than innovation forces. In other words, a firm's efforts amount to little until there is a solid base of visible users: factors such as word of mouth matter more than the inherent innovative tendencies of buyers. Further, as noted by Griliches (1957), there are many ways to draw an S curve: variation in diffusion patterns is considerable, even for the same innovation in different populations. Finally, diffusion models are robust: they provide a good overall representation of a very large range of situations, including both process and product innovations, and organizations as well as individuals, across a broad range of environments.

A major contribution of the marketing field to diffusion modeling concerns the incorporation of marketing activities into diffusion models. Based on these observed generalizations of the patterns of diffusion, it is clear that *what firms do (or fail to do) matters*. The addition of factors controlled by the firm that is marketing the innovation enables management to influence the adoption and diffusion by consumers. This issue is developed in a later discussion of marketing decisions.

International Diffusion

One particularly recent development in this stream of research concerns the role of multi-market marketing, especially the international introduction of new products and services in multiple countries. It is rare for a firm to enter multiple markets simultaneously. Typically, firms follow a sequence, conquering first one market, then another. To some extent, this is explained by resource constraints.

One of the major ways management affects the creation of new markets is in deciding which countries to enter. The question of knowing which countries to select for entry to commercialize a new product or service, and in which order to enter target countries, has received much attention in international business. However, the focus has been in identifying segments of countries sharing similarities. The idea is to find submarkets that make some groups of countries more attractive and less risky to enter than others. This segmentation by clustering of countries is typically based on macro-political, demographic, geographic or economic variables (Sethi 1971) and is usually rather atheoretical.

Gatignon, Eliashberg, and Robertson (1989) brought a new theoretical focus to this issue by comparing countries in terms of their diffusion parameters and searching for explanations of similar parameters. They explain similarity and differences in patterns of diffusion by invoking sociological explanations concerning the cosmopolitanism of the culture in a country, the mobility of its population, and the role played by working women. Helsen, Jedidi, and DeSarbo (1993) develop clusters of countries based on these similarities.

This segmentation, however, ignores the fact that some countries adopt earlier than others. In fact, the decision to enter one country is not independent of knowing if and when entries in other countries will occur. Usually, the innovation is marketed first in the country that is the home of the firm that developed the innovation (the lead country). Then, other countries are attacked with a lag of different durations. Understanding the reasons for these lags is important: see Dekimpe, Parker, and Sarvary (2000), who investigate the reasons for initial sales and for the diffusion speed across a large group of countries.

Another aspect of the multinational diffusion of an innovation concerns cross-country effects, that is the role that diffusion in one country plays in determining diffusion in another one. Putsis et al. (1997) show that it is possible to analyze the leading role of some countries in explaining the speed of diffusion in other countries. For example, they find that within European countries, Germany, France, Italy and Spain demonstrate a high level of influence on the diffusion of several innovations in the other countries. These findings suggest which countries should be entered first, as the (later) diffusion in the lag countries will require smaller investments on the part of the firm. Therefore, this research demonstrates the inter-relationships that exist between countries that lead to the necessity of taking a global management approach to world markets.

In short, the creation of one market is not independent of the creation of another. Decisions taken earlier as to which countries to enter first can have a very substantial influence on how successfully the firm creates a later market. In other words, there is path dependence in the creation of new markets.

Industry Effects

Initially, the diffusion process was viewed as a monolithic centralized process focused on the innovation itself and on innate features of the adopter. A more recent research thrust focuses on how technological innovations diffuse among firms, as opposed to individuals (Robertson and Gatignon (1986). This stream considers characteristics of the *industry in which the innovation occurs* (e.g. overall competitiveness, reputation, marketing intensity), as well as characteristics of the *target industry* (e.g. demand uncertainty, professionalization). Gatignon and Robertson (1989) and Parker and Gatignon (1994) offer empirical evidence that such factors significantly impact the diffusion pattern.

Taking into account features of the industry of the innovator and the adopter follows naturally from evolutionary economics (which presumes that actors are not homogeneous) and from TCE (which stresses differences in a firm's stock of idiosyncratic assets). This stream of research directly addresses the issue that motivated Griliches (1957): why do seemingly identical farmers react differently to the same innovation? This research stream unpacks the "seemingly identical" aspect of the target population, as well as differences among the brands competing to be the most successful prototype.

Marketing Entry Strategy Effects

Kuester, Gatignon, and Robertson (2000) identify five strategic actions of the firm at the time of entry that affects the speed of diffusion of an innovation: (1) the choice of the market segment(s) targeted, (2) the order of the firm's entry into the market, (3) pre-announcing activities, (4) market-entry commitment and (5) the distribution strategy. We cover these areas below. In addition, the mode of entry into foreign markets has been a favorite subject of research in the international business field and will be reviewed.

Choice of the Market Segment(s) Targeted

It follows from diffusion theory that the innovators (who adopt without expecting or awaiting information from prior adopters) should be the first group of consumers to be targeted. Characteristics of innovators have been studied extensively, and generalizations emerge (reviewed in Gatignon and Robertson 1985). For example, innovators spread information about the innovations more than do others, and tend to be more exposed to, and more receptive to, mass media communications. Innovators have also been shown to tend to be younger, richer, and less price sensitive than late adopters.

Becker (1970) argues that this profile of innovators may not be the same for all products. For innovations that are inconsistent with the norms in place in the social system, marginal individuals (i.e. noncomformists at the margin of their community) can actually have more influence on other prospective adopters. In contrast, usual groups of innovators typically include individuals who are very well socially integrated with the majority in their community.

Order of Entry

That there is an advantage to being the first entrant in what becomes a product category has been demonstrated in a significant number of empirical studies (Bowman and Gatignon 1996, Kalyanaram and Urban 1992, Mascarenhas 1992, Urban et al. 1984). Gielens and Dekimpe (2000) find that order of entry is the most critical factor of those they study in analyzing the entries of retail firms in foreign markets. However, this first-mover advantage is not always maintained, depending on the later entrants and on the marketing decisions of the first entrant, especially its reactions to the subsequent entries (Bowman and Gatignon 1995, Gatignon, Robertson, and Fein 1997, Shankar, Carpenter, and Krishnamurthi 1998).

There are many explanations for the first-mover advantage. One is switching costs: early buyers become locked in, for example, by investments in learning how to use the innovative brand. Other explanations for the first-mover advantage include becoming the reference brand for preferences in the consumers' cognitions, distributional advantage, and cost advantages through economies of scale. Regardless of the source of the advantage, first-mover benefits tend to last beyond the entry period and throughout the diffusion process in terms of market potential (saturation or cumulative penetration) and market share (Kalyanaram and Urban 1992). However, late movers tend to exhibit a faster speed of diffusion than the pioneers, who must face resistance to trial, due to the complexity of innovations as well as the new patterns of behaviors characteristic of discontinuous innovations (Robertson 1971).

Pre-Announcements

The marketing of a product may actually precede its availability in the market. This is certainly the case with the distribution system: distribution channel members face routine requests that they pre-commit to carry products and services that are said to be under development and are promised at a future date. Pre-announcements (vigorous promotion of nonexistent products) has become common, even the prevailing practice in some industries (such as the software industry—vaporware—or the movie industry—the endlessly forthcoming latest film from director X or star Y). Eliashberg and Robertson (1988) discuss two reasons for the practice, one being to gain an advantage with the consumer (who will hopefully wait for the product) and the other as a preemptive move vis-a-vis the competitors (in hopes they will withdraw resources from the market). While the benefits of pre-announcements are clear in theory, empirical evidence of the extent of their effects is limited. In addition, there are also clear risks associated with the firm's potential inability to bring the new product to market on time (or at all). The firms may be suspected of incompetence—or worse yet, opportunism.

Entry Commitment

The commitment of the firm to a new product in a given market is demonstrated by different actions. Commitment is important: it reassures buyers worried about the firm's potential opportunism (sell, then leave) and discourages competition. Three actions to signal commitment are covered below.

Scale Scale is a classical deterrent to entry. Earlier work has concentrated on barriers that form naturally (Bain 1956, Scherer and Ross 1990). The more recent focus has been on decisions that have the express intent to deter entry, especially decisions on manufacturing capacity (Spence 1977, Dixit 1979, Demsetz 1982). Gielens and Dekimpe (2001) provide empirical support for the long-term impact of the scale of entry in the analysis of retail entries into foreign markets.

Product Adaptation This factor concerns the adaptation of the product to the local environment (as opposed to product standardization—the same item in all markets). While standardization creates economies of scale, adaptation exhibits sensitivity to local market needs. The positive impact of adaptation on the long-term sales of an entry is studied by Gielens and Dekimpe (2001). While adaptation may be beneficial (as it raises demand), some standardization may also be necessary. Standardization is particularly appropriate when externalities are involved. In this case, compatibility is a critical factor in the innovation's development of the market. As global externalities become prevalent, the global standardization of products may be inevitable. Path dependence looms here: the standard is likely to be decided in a country quite different from the one entered—and may be rather poorly suited to countries entered after the standard has been set.

Price Achieving a high level of market penetration through low prices at initial stages of the introduction of a product serves to achieve rapid diffusion, as buyers outside the innovator segment are price sensitive. Further, low initial prices show both consumers and competitors that the firm is committed to the market. The opposite strategy (initial high prices, or skimming) leads to slow, shallow diffusion and implies the firm may readily leave the market as prices drop.

Promotion A penetration strategy is also obtained through intensive advertising and communication expenditures. These fuel the rate of diffusion and enlarge the market, in part by converting early prospects (innovators) into adopters. Heavy promotion may also be interpreted as a sign of the firm's commitment to the innovation, and hence may function like a hostage: prospects may reason that a firm would not knowingly invest heavily in a dubious innovation. In this respect, promotion reinforces a firm's reputation, which in turn reassures potential adopters about the (unknown) quality of the innovation (Kirmani and Rao 2000).

Sales Force The firm's sales force is a critical factor in gaining acceptance among business buyers. In pharmaceuticals, Aitken et al. (2000) argue that the key to obtaining good licenses to new products (a crucial factor in this industry) is to have a strong sales force. McGrath (1997) notes that high technology firms field extremely expensive sales forces. The logic is that salespeople build relationships with prospects, and redeploy these relationships over successive innovations to reduce a prospect's uncertainty over the latest generation of product. Given the high rate of change in these industries, the salesforce's ability to speed up adoption justifies its high cost.

Here, too, transaction costs arise. Salespeople frequently resist selling new products, particularly innovative ones. Overcoming this resistance is not easily done, and requires resources and active management intervention (Anderson and Robertson 1995). Being vertically integrated forward into sales is a major advantage in so doing. Anderson and Schmittlein (1984) compare producers that have their own sales forces to those that contract with third-party sales organizations (a classic choice between market and hierarchy).[5] As per TCE predictions, in-house sales forces possessed significantly higher levels of transaction-specific assets, in more volatile environments, and operated under conditions of greater performance ambiguity. These are precisely the circumstances surrounding the introduction of new products.

A distinguishing feature of personal selling is that the salespeople are better informed about their customers than are their superiors. This information impactedness underlies why independent insurance agents thrive, in the face of myriad institutional and transaction cost factors that suggest they should not (Regan and Tennyson 1996). Accordingly, a major role of salespeople is not to sell anything. Instead, they act as market researchers and as partners to marketers in new product development. Such non-sales behavior is essential for an innovation, which invariably has difficulty finding its markets/applications.

Distribution

The firm's *channels of distribution* have substantial influence on how well the innovation connects with buyers. Resellers and agents cultivate a reputation among their clientele and put this reputation behind what they sell. Producers effectively rent the selling firm's reputation, and find it particularly valuable to overcome resistance to new products.

As noted earlier, producers may seek to build close, committed relationships with resellers and agents, and exchange credible commitments to do so. One object of such relational governance is to secure quality of effort: producers want their channels to present the innovation a certain way to a targeted segment. Selective distribution is important to this effort. Fein and Anderson (1996) show that resellers and producers employ selectivity in an elaborate exchange of hostages: producers concede market exclusivity in return for category exclusivity (non-representation of competing brands), as well as other safeguards. One reason selective distribution is effective for selling innovations, particularly in final goods markets, is that representation by the "right" channels sends a quality signal to consumers (Wathne and Heide (2000).

An issue resellers and agents face is how to cope with opportunism by suppliers. For example, suppliers have an incentive to be opportunistic by telling

---

[5] The difference between these two institutions—employee sales force and third-party sales force—is not always understood. In particular, independent sales forces are sometimes confused with franchisees. They are also sometimes assimilated to employee salespeople who are paid on commission. This is incorrect. The third party organization is paid on commission, but it is a company, and therefore makes its own decisions how to pay its salespeople. Frequently, the organization pays its salespeople on salary, not commission. An independent sales force is akin to an independent advertising agency, law firm, accounting firm, or consulting firm. For each function—selling, advertising, legal advice, accounting, consulting—the firm's choice is whether to perform the function with its own employees or contract with another organization. How the individual's compensation is determined is a separate issue.

resellers that all their new products are highly saleable, including those they know to be otherwise. Channel members need to safeguard: one way to do so is to screen out such false information. Here, Chu (1992) offers a novel interpretation of what has become an institution in grocery retailing. Slotting allowances are fixed fees producers pay to "rent" shelf space to introduce new products, and are in addition to margins. Resellers can use them to oblige producers to signal which new products they truly consider to be most likely to sell. Slotting fees can be viewed as a means of negating supplier opportunism (self interest seeking with guile) concerning its new products. This is particularly important in fast moving consumer goods, in which literally thousands of supposedly "new" products come out each year.

More generally, channel members need to safeguard against supplier opportunism whenever they sell new products. By the time channel members discover the product's shortcomings, they have already invested. Further, the producer may fail to live up to its promises, including the promise of a fair return to commercialization efforts. Not surprisingly, Heide and John (1988) show that agents who safeguard their idiosyncratic investments are more profitable than those who do not.

Modes of Entry

How a firm enters a market impacts how well its new products perform there. *Modes of entry* are institutional arrangements (e.g. minority joint ventures) that firms use to govern their activities when launching operations in foreign markets. There are many entry modes: these arrangements can be understood by arraying them along Williamson's (1996) market-to-hierarchy continuum. Gatignon and Anderson (1988) study over a thousand entry mode decisions and show that they tend to follow transaction cost reasoning about the tradeoff between the benefits of control and the costs of risk taking. In particular, when firms invest heavily in R&D or in advertising (and for innovations, they tend to do both), they safeguard these investments by such high-control entry modes as owning their entry vehicle outright or holding enough equity to dominate their partners.

In short, the diffusion of an innovation rests heavily on the governance structure the firm uses to enter a new market, and on the marketing strategy the firm employs. These are decisions made by managers operating under bounded rationality in uncertain markets. The identity of the firm matters because new products are sufficiently unique that they cannot be readily compared to existing products. Traditional economic analysis is difficult to apply in its entirety to these situations.

5. REPRISE

How do firms create new markets? We have learned a good deal by positive study of what firms do and how well it works, especially in the marketplaces that arise in response to market offerings. These patterns fit well in the paradigm of New Institutional Economics, particularly with TCE and evolutionary reasoning. The patterns do not fit an optimizing logic, nor an equilibrium logic, nor a logic of full rationality. Instead, they fit a comparative logic, in which only concrete alternatives are considered by boundedly rational actors, and equilibrium may never be achieved.

The processes uncovered in this research reflect several critical themes. Firms strive to follow an economic logic, and exercise their capacity for conscious foresight to the fullest. But the nature of innovation strains this capacity severely. Bounded rationality, information impactedness, and the tacit nature of knowledge shape what firms do and how well their practices work. Forecasting abilities are highly limited. Calculations are problematic, valuation is error-prone, and risks and uncertainty are irreducibly high. Opportunities for self-interest seeking with guile abound: the institutional environment cannot offer enough protection of property rights to make market contracting the best approach in many circumstances. Thus, many patterns of business practice are motivated heavily by the need to erect governance mechanisms that safeguard innovation activities and their outputs against opportunism. Opportunism cuts multiple ways. Suppliers fear being shortchanged by owners of co-specialized assets. Business partners fear being drawn into small-numbers bargaining, then exploited by their suppliers. Prospective buyers fear being misled by firms that oversell their innovations or exit the market, leaving the buyer with an obsolete or unsupported product. Short of outright vertical integration, hostages appear to be effective safeguards. Mechanisms for creating markets merit a broader analysis than any single perspective provides: in particular, a transaction cost approach needs to be informed by considerations of path dependency. Research directions here are offered by Argyres and Liebeskind (1999) and Williamson (1999).

For the most part, contracts are an unsatisfactory way to safeguard, leading to high levels of vertical integration (or failing that, posting of mutual credible commitments). *Ex post* adaptation to unfolding events is the order of the day, aided by the low-powered nature of incentives in firms: because employees are *not* rewarded as entrepreneurs, it is easier to coordinate the massive efforts needed to develop and commercialize innovations. The identity of the players matters. In particular, the internal structure, culture, and routines of organizations are critical. Path dependence also plays a substantial role because firms cannot easily acquire what they have failed to build painstakingly over time.

Patterns on the buyer side reflect that prospects are not perfectly informed about how well an innovation meets their needs. Indeed, they may not even sense their needs unless the innovation emerges as a solution. Fearful of making an error and unable to resolve their uncertainty, most prospects wait to adopt the innovation until they see others do so or know the product has been successful in another country. Hence, the firm must find, target, and convince a small set of innovative souls in a lead country. This requires intensive marketing effort and opens the possibility that a superb innovation will not create a market because the firm mishandled its introduction. Conversely, a relatively mediocre innovation may be skillfully commercialized, create a market, and even become a standard because the firm astutely priced, promoted, distributed, and targeted the innovation. Further, the diffusion of innovations exhibits path dependence. How the S curve unfolds depends on the firm's order of entry into a given market, order of entry into serial markets, and early success (or lack thereof) with the innovators.

A key theme of this work is that organizations matter, not only in the development of an innovation but in the creation of new markets. Buyers are not homogeneous in their needs. They do not simply emerge, because they do not easily appreciate the utility an innovation offers to them. How a firm takes its innovation to market has a great deal to do with whether markets come into existence and how those markets function. These patterns merit further study. The paradigm of NIE is a fruitful way to frame them.

References

Afuah, Allan. 2001. "Dynamic Boundaries of the Firm: Are Firms Better off Being Vertically Integrated in the Face of a Technological Change?" *Academy of Management Journal* 44(6): 1211–128.
Aitken, Murray, Sunitha Baskaran, Eric Lamarre, Michael Silber, and Susan Walters. 2000. "A License to Cure". *McKinsey Quarterly* 10(1): 80–89.
Anderson, Erin and David C. Schmittlein. 1984. "Integration of the Sales Force : An Empirical Examination". *Rand Journal of Economics* 15(3): 385–395.
Anderson, Erin and Thomas S. Robertson. 1995. "Inducing Multi-Line Salespeople to Adopt House Brands". *Journal of Marketing* 59: 16–31.
Anderson, Erin and Barton Weitz. 1992. "The Use of Pledges to Build and Sustain Commitment in Distribution Channels". *Journal of Marketing Research* 24: 18–34.
Argyres, Nicholas S. and Julia Porter Liebeskind. 2002. "Governance Inseparability and the Evolution of the US Biotechnology Industry". *Journal of Economic Behavior and Organization* 47(2): 197–219.
Argyres, Nicholas S. and Julia Porter Liebeskind. 1999. "Contractual Commitments, Bargaining Power, and Governance Inseparability: Incorporating History Into Transaction Cost Theory". *Academy of Marketing Review* 24(1): 49–63.
Bain, Joseph. 1956. *Barriers to Competition*. Cambridge: MA: Harvard University Press.
Bass, Frank M. 1969. "A New Product Growth for Model Consumer Durables". *Management Science* 15(5): 215–227.
Bayus, Barry L., Gary Erickson, and Robert Jacobson. 2003. "The Financial Rewards of New Product Introductions in the Personal Computer Industry". *Management Science* 49(2): 197–210.
Becker, Marshall H. 1970. "Sociometric Location and Innovativeness: Reformulation and Extension of the Diffusion Model". *American Sociological Review* April: 267–282.
Bensaou, Ben. M. and Erin Anderson. 1999. "Buyer-Supplier Relations in Industrial Markets: When Do Buyers Enter the Trap of Making Idiosyncratic Investments?" *Organization Science* 10: 460–481.
Bowman, Douglas and Hubert Gatignon. 1995. "Determinants of Competitor Response Time to a New Product Introduction". *Journal of Marketing Research* 32(1): 42.
Bowman, Douglas and Hubert Gatignon. 1996. "Order of Entry as a Moderator of the Effect of the Marketing Mix on Market Share". *Marketing Science* 15(3): 222–242.
Bradach, Jeffrey L. 1997. "Using the Plural Form in the Management of Restaurant Chains". *Administrative Science Quarterly* 42(2): 276–303.

Breshnahan, Timothy F. and Robert J. Gordon. 1996. *The Economics of New Goods*. Chicago, IL: University of Chicago Press.

Brown, Jacqueline and Peter H. Reingen. 1987. "Social Ties and Word-of-Mouth Referral Behavior". *Journal of Consumer Research* 14: 350–362.

Brown, Shona L. and Kathleen M. Eisenhardt. 1995. "Product Development: Past Research, Present Findings, and Future Directions". *Academy of Management Review* 20(2) 343–378.

Capon, Noel, John U. Farley, and Scott Hoenig. 1990. "Determinants of Financial Performance: A Meta-Analysis". *Management Science* 36(10): 1143–1159.

Capron, Laurence. 1999. "The Long Term Performance of Horizontal Acquisitions". *Strategic Management Journal* 20(11): 987–1018.

Cerf, Christopher and Victor Navasky. 1984. *The Experts Speak*. New York: Pantheon Books.

Chandler, Alfred D. 1977. *The Visible Hand: The Managerial Revolution in American Business*. Cambridge, MA: Belknap Press.

Chu, Wujin. 1992. "Demand Signalling and Screening in Channels of Distribution". *Marketing Science* 11(3): 327–347.

Coughlan, Anne T., Erin Anderson, Louis W. Stern, and Adel I. El-Ansary. 2001. *Marketing Channels*, 6th Edn. Englewood Cliffs, NJ: Prentice-Hall.

Dahl, Darren W., Amitiva Chattopadhyay, and Gerald J. Gorn. 1999. "The Use of Visual Mental Imagery in New Product Design". *Journal of Marketing rq* 36(1): 18–28.

Darr, Eric D., Linda Argote, and Dennis Epple. 1995. "The Acquisition, Transfer, and Depreciation of Knowledge in Service Organizations: Productivity in Franchises". *Management Science* 41(11): 1750–1762.

Dekimpe, Marnik G, Philip M Parker, and Miklos Sarvary. 2000. "Global Diffusion of Technological Innovations: A Coupled-Hazard Approach". *Journal of Marketing Research* 37(1): 47–59.

Demsetz, Harold. 1982. "Barriers to Entry". *American Economic Review* 72(1): 47–57.

Dixit, Avinash 1979. "A Model of Duopoly Suggesting a Theory of Entry Barriers". *Bell Journal of Economics* 10(1): 20–32.

Dosi, Giovanni. 1997. "Opportunities, Incentives and the Collective Patterns of Technological Change". *The Economic Journal* 107(3): 1530–1547.

Dutta, Shantanu and George John. 1995. "Combining Lab Experiments and Industry Data in Transaction Cost Analysis: The Case of Competition as a Safeguard". *Journal of Law, Economics, and Organization* 11: 87–111.

Dyer, Jeffrey H. 1995. "Specialized Supplier Networks as a Source of Competitive Advantage: Evidence from the Auto Industry". *Strategic Management Journal* 11(3): 42–55.

Eliashberg, Jehoshua and Thomas S. Robertson. 1988. "New Product Preannouncing Behavior: A Market Signaling Study". *Journal of Marketing Research* 25(3): 282–292.

Fein, Adam J. and Erin Anderson. 1997. "Patterns of Credible Commitments: Territory and Category Selectivity in Industrial Distribution Channels". *Journal of Marketing* 61: 19–34.

Gatignon, Hubert and Erin Anderson. 1988. "The Multinational Corporation's Degree of Control over Foreign Subsidiaries: An Empirical Test of a Transaction Cost Explanation". *Journal of Law, Economics, and Organization* 4(2): 305–336.

Gatignon, Hubert, Jehoshua Eliashberg, and Thomas S. Robertson. 1989. "Modeling Multinational Diffusion Patterns: An Efficient Methodology". *Marketing Science* 8(3): 231.

Gatignon, Hubert and Thomas S. Robertson. 1985. "A Propositional Inventory for New Diffusion Research". *Journal of Consumer Research* 11(4): 859–867.

Gatignon, Hubert and Thomas S. Robertson. 1989. "Technology Diffusion: An Empirical Test of Competitive Effects". *Journal of Marketing* 53(1): 35–49.

Gatignon, Hubert and Thomas S. Robertson. 1991. "Innovative Decision Processes" in Harold Kassarjian and Thomas S. Robertson (eds.), *Handbook of Consumer Behavior Theory and Research*. Englewood Cliffs, NJ: Prentice-Hall, pp. 316–348.

Gatignon, Hubert, Thomas S Robertson, and Adam J. Fein. 1997. "Incumbent Defense Strategies Against New Product Entry". *International Journal of Research in Marketing* 14(2): 163–176.

Gatignon, Hubert and Jean-Marc Xuereb. 1997. "Strategic Orientation of the Firm and New Product Performance". *Journal of Marketing Research* 34(1): 77–90.

Gielens, Katrijn and Marnik G. Dekimpe. 2001. "Do International Entry Decisions of Retail Chains Matter in the Long Run?" *International Journal of Research in Marketing* 18(3): 235–259.

Griliches, Zvi. 1957. "Hybrid Corn: An Exploration in the Economics of Technical Change". *Econometrica* 25(4): 501–522.

Griliches, Zvi, Bronwyn Hall, and Ariel Pakes. 1991. "R&D, Patents, and Market Value Revisited: Is There A Second (Technological Opportunity) Factor?" *Economic Innovation and New Technology* 1(1): 183–201.

Gulati, Ranjay and Harbir Singh. 1998. "The Architecture of Cooperation: Managing Coordination Costs and Appropriation Concerns in Strategic Alliances". *Administrative Science Quarterly* 43(4): 781–814.

Haspeslagh, Philippe and David Jemison. 1991. *Managing Acquisitions*. New York: Free Press.

Heide, Jan B. and George John. 1988. "The Role of Dependence Balancing in Safeguarding Transaction-Specific Assets in Conventional Channels". *Journal of Marketing* 52(1): 20–35.

Helsen, Kristiaan, Kamel Jedidi, and Wayne S. DeSarbo. 1993. "A New Approach to Country Segmentation Utilizing Multinational Diffusion Patterns". *Journal of Marketing* 57: 60–71.

Henard, David H. and David M Szymanski. 2001. "Why Some New Products Are More Successful Than Others". *Journal of Marketing Research* 38(3): 362–375.

Herr, Paul M., Frank R. Kardes, and John Kim. 1991. "Effects of Word-of-Mouth and Product-Attribute Information on Persuasion: An Accessibility-Diagnosticity Perspective". *Journal of Consumer Research* 17: 454–462.

Jap, Sandy D. 1999. "'Pie-Expansion' Efforts: Collaboration Processes in Buyer-Supplier Relationships". *Journal of Marketing Research* 36: 461–475.

Kalyanaram, Gurumurthy and Glen L. Urban. 1992. "Dynamic Effects of the Order of Entry on Market Share, Trial Penetration, and Repeat Purchases for Frequently Purchased Consumer Goods". *Marketing Science* 11: 235–250.

Katz, Elihu 1957. "The Two-Step Flow of Communication: An Up-To-Date Report on an Hypothesis". *Public Opinion Quarterly* 21: 61–78.

Kaul, Anil and Vithala R. Rao. 1995. "Research for Product Positioning and Design Decisions: An Integrative Review". *International Journal of Research in Marketing* 12(4): 293–320.

Kirmani, Amna and Akshay R. Rao. 2000. "No Pain, No Gain: A Critical Review of the Literature on Signaling Unobservable Quality". *Journal of Marketing* 64: 66–79.

Kogut, Bruce and Nalin Kulatilaka. 2001. "Capabilities as Real Options". *Organization Science* 12(6): 744–758.

Krishnan, V. and Karl T. Ulrich. 2001. "Product Development Decisions: A Review of the Literature". *Management Science* 47(1): 1–21.

Krueger, Alan B. and Timothy Taylor. 2000. "An Interview With Zvi Griliches". *Journal of Economic Perspectives* 14(2): 171–189.

Kuester, Sabine, Hubert Gatignon, and Thomas S. Robertson. 2000. "Firm Strategy and Speed of Diffusion". in Vijay Mahajan, Eitan Muller and Yoram Wind (eds.), *New-Product Diffusion Models*. Boston, MA: Kluwer Academic Publishers.

Leonard-Barton, Dorothy. 1992. "Core Capabilities and Core Rigidities: A Paradox in Managing New Products". *Strategic Management Journal* 13(1): 11–125.

Mahajan, Vijay, Eitan Muller, and Frank Bass. 1993. "New Product Diffusion Models," in Jehoshua Eliashberg and Gary L. Lilien (eds.), *Handbooks in Operations Research and Management Science*. Amsterdam: Elsevier Science, pp. 349–408.

Mahajan, Vijay, Eitan Muller, and Yoram Wind (eds.). 2000. *New-Product Diffusion Models*. Boston, MA: Kluwer Academic Publishers.

Mascarenhas, Briance 1992. "Order of Entry and Performance in International Markets". *Strategic Management Journal* 13: 499–510.

McGrath, Rita Gunther. 1997. "A Real Options Logic for Initiating Technology Positioning Investments". *Academy of Management Review* 22(4): 974–996.

Moorman, Christine. 1995. "Organizational Market Information Processes: Cultural Antecedents and New Product Outcomes". *Journal of Marketing Research* 32(3): 318–335.

Moorman, Christine and Anne S. Miner. 1997. "The Impact of Organizational Memory on New Product Performance and Creativity". *Journal of Marketing Research* 34(1): 91–106.

Nayak, P. Ranganath and John M. Ketteringham. 1986. *Breakthroughs!* New York: Rawson Associates.

Nelson, Richard R. 1995. "Recent Evolutionary Theorizing About Economic Change". *Journal of Economic Literature* 32: 48–90.

Nerlove, Marc. 2001. "Zvi Griliches, 1930–1999: A Critical Appreciation". *The Economic Journal* 111(3): F422-F448.

Osborn, Richard N. and John Hageboorn. 1997. "The Institutionalization and Evolutionary Dynamics of Interorganizational Alliances and Networks". *Academy of Management Journal* 40(2): 261–278.

Oxley, Joanne E. 1999. "Institutional Environment and the Mechanisms of Governance: the Impact of Intellectual Property Protection on the Structure of Inter-Firm Alliances". *Journal of Economic Behavior and Organization* 38: 283–309.

Parker, Philip and Hubert Gatignon. 1994. "Specifying Competitive Effects in Diffusion Models: An Empirical Analysis". *International Journal of Research in Marketing* 11(1): 17–23.

Pawakapan, Niti. 2000. "Trade and Traders: Local Becomes National". *Journal of Southeast Asian Studies* 31(2): 374–389.

Pisano, Gary P. 1990. "The R&D Boundaries of the Firm: An Empirical Analysis". *Administrative Science Quarterly* 35(3): 153–176.

Putsis, William P., Sridhar Balasubramanian, Edward H. Kaplan, and Subrata K. Sen. 1997. "Mixing Behavior in Cross-Country Diffusion". *Marketing Science* 16(4): 354–369.

Regan, Laureen and Sharon Tennyson. 1996. "Agent Discretion and the Choice of Insurance Marketing Systems". *Journal of Law and Economics* 39: 637–666.

Robertson, Thomas S. 1971. *Innovative Behavior and Communication.* New York: The Free Press.

Robertson, Thomas S. and Hubert Gatignon. 1986. "Competitive Effects on Technology Diffusion". *Journal of Marketing* 50(3): 1.

Robertson, Thomas S and Hubert Gatignon. 1998. "Technology Development Mode: A Transaction Cost Conceptualization". *Strategic Management Journal* 19(6): 515–531.

Rogers, Everett M. 1983. *Diffusion of Innovations*: New York: The Free Press.

Sethi, S. Prakash. 1971. "Comparative Cluster Analysis for World Markets". *Journal of Marketing Research* 8(3): 348–354.

Sako, Mari and Susan Helper. 1998. "Determinants of Trust in Supplier Relations: Evidence From the Automotive Industry in Japan and the United States". *Journal of Economic Behavior and Organization* 34(3): 387–417.

Scherer, F. M. and David Ross. 1990. *Industrial Market Structure and Economic Performance*, 3rd edn. Dallas: TX: Houghton Mifflin.

Schmookler, Jacob. 1966. *Invention and Economic Growth.* Cambridge, MA: Harvard University Press.

Schumpeter, Joseph A. 1943. *Capitalism, Socialism, and Democracy.* London: George Allen & Unwin.

Shankar, Venkatesh, Gregory S. Carpenter, and Lakshman Krishnamurthi. 1998. "Late Mover Advantage: How Innovative Late Entrants Outsell Pioneers". *Journal of Marketing Research* 35(1): 54–70.

Spence, A. Michael 1977. "Entry, Capacity, Investment and Oligopolistic Pricing". *Bell Journal of Economics* 8(2): 534–544.

Spulber, Daniel F. 1999. *Market Microstructure: Intermediaries and the Theory of the Firm.* Cambridge: Cambridge University Press.

Sultan, Fareena, John U. Farley, and Donald R. Lehmann. 1990. "A Meta-Analysis of Applications of Diffusion Models". *Journal of Marketing Research* 27(1): 70–77.

Tapon, Francis. 1989. "A Transaction Costs Analysis of Innovations in the Organization of Pharmaceutical R & D". *Journal of Economic Behavior & Organization Oct* 12(2): 197–213.

Teece, David. 1996. "Firm Organization, Industrial Structure, and Technological Innovation". *Journal of Economic Behavior and Organization* 31: 193–224.

Teece, David J. 1992. "Competition, Cooperation, and Innovation". *Journal of Economic Behavior and Organization* 18: 1–25.

Terpstra, Vern and Chwo-Ming J. Yu. "Piggybacking: A Quick Road to Internatlisation1990". *International Marketing Review* 7(4): 52–63.

Urban, Glen L., Theresa Carter, Steven Gaskin, and Zofia Mucha. 1984. "Market Share Rewards to Pioneering Brands: An Empirical Analysis and Strategic Implications". *Management Science* 32(6): 645–659.

Urban, Glen L. and Eric Von Hippel. 1988. "Lead User Analyses for the Development of New Industrial Products". *Management Science* 34(5): 569–582.

Van den Bulte, Christophe and Rudy K. Moenaert. 1998. "The Effects of R&D Team Co-location on Communication Patterns among R&D, Marketing, and Manufacturing". *Management Science* 44(11): S1–S18.

Wathne, Kenneth H. and Jan B. Heide. 2000. "Opportunism in Interfirm Relationships: Forms, Outcomes, and Solutions". *Journal of Marketing* 64(4): 36–51.

Williamson, Oliver E. 1979, "Assessing Vertical Market Restrictions". *University of Pennsylvania Law Review* 127: 953–993.

Williamson, Oliver E. 1996. *The Mechanisms of Governance*. New York: Oxford University Press.

Williamson, Oliver E. 1999. "Strategy Research: Governance and Competence Perspectives". *Strategic Management Journal* 20(3): 1087–1108.

SECTION V

Contractual Arrangements

17. The Make-or-Buy Decision: Lessons from Empirical Studies

PETER G. KLEIN

1. Introduction

The "transaction cost" theory of the firm introduced by Coase (1937) has become a standard framework for the study of institutional arrangements. The Coasian framework helps explain not only the existence of the firm, but also its size and scope. Why, in Coase's (1937, pp. 393–94) words, "does the entrepreneur not organize one less transaction or one more?" Some firms are highly integrated: IBM, for example, produces many of its components and software and maintains its own sales force for mainframe computers. Others are much more specialized: Dell Computer outsources virtually all its hardware and software components, selling directly to end users through its catalog and website, while the shoe company Reebok owns no manufacturing plants, relying on outside suppliers to make its products. U.S. manufacturing and service companies are increasingly contracting with specialized information technology firms for their computing and data warehousing needs, spending $7.2 billion on outsourced computer operations in 1990. Standard and Poor's estimates total worldwide outsourcing for 2003 at $170 billion.[1]

Why do some firms choose a vertically integrated structure, while others specialize in one stage of production and outsource the remaining stages to other firms? In other words, should a firm make its own inputs, should it buy them on the spot market, or should it maintain an ongoing relationship with a particular supplier? Traditionally, economists viewed vertical integration or vertical control as an attempt to earn monopoly rents by gaining control of input markets or distribution channels. The transaction cost approach, by contrast, emphasizes that vertical coordination can be an efficient means of protecting relationship-specific investments or mitigating other potential conflicts under incomplete contracting. As transaction cost economics was developed in the 1970s and 1980s, a stream of empirical literature emerged explaining the "make-or-buy decision" using transaction cost reasoning. (The traditional approach has generated relatively few empirical applications beyond analyses of particular antitrust cases.) This chapter surveys the empirical literature

---

[1] These and other examples are provided by Brickley, Smith, and Zimmerman (2004, p. 515).

on vertical boundaries, focusing on the transaction cost approach and emphasizing the most important results, while highlighting the challenges that remain.[2]

2. THE THEORY OF VERTICAL BOUNDARIES

Coase was the first to explain that the boundaries of the organization depend not only on the productive technology, but also on the costs of transacting business. In the Coasian framework, the decision to organize transactions within the firm as opposed to on the open market—the "make or buy decision"—depends on the relative costs of internal versus external exchange. The market mechanism entails certain costs: discovering the relevant prices, negotiating and enforcing contracts, and so on. Within the firm, the entrepreneur may be able to reduce these "transaction costs" by coordinating these activities himself. However, internal organization brings other kinds of transaction costs, namely problems of information flow, incentives, monitoring, and performance evaluation. The boundary of the firm, then, is determined by the tradeoff, at the margin, between the relative transaction costs of external and internal exchange. In this sense, firm boundaries depend not only on technology, but also on organizational considerations; that is, on the costs and benefits of various contracting alternatives.

This is explained in detail in Paul Joskow's chapter in this volume. A few highlights are worth mentioning here to guide the reader through the empirical literature. First, economic organization, both internal and external, imposes costs because complex contracts are usually incomplete—they provide remedies for only some possible future contingencies. This obviously applies to written contracts for all but the simplest forms of trade. It also applies to relational contracts, agreements that describe shared goals and a set of general principles that govern the relationship (Goldberg, 1980; Baker, Gibbons, and Murphy, 2001), and to implicit contracts, agreements that while unstated, are assumed to be understood by all sides. Second, contractual incompleteness exposes the contracting parties to certain risks. Primarily, if circumstances change unexpectedly, the original governing agreement may no longer be effective. The need to adapt to unforeseen contingencies constitutes an additional cost of contracting; failure to adapt imposes what Williamson (1991a) calls "maladaptation costs."

The most-often-discussed example of maladaptation is the "holdup" problem associated with relationship-specific investments.[3] The holdup problem figures

---

[2] Earlier surveys of this literature, from a variety of perspectives, include Joskow (1988a), Shelanski and Klein (1995), Rindfleisch and Heide (1997), Masten and Saussier (2000), Vannoni (2002), Boerner and Macher (2002), and David and Han (2004). Masten (1996) collects many of the important earlier articles.

[3] More generally, contractual difficulties can arise from several sources: "(1) bilateral dependence; (2) weak property rights; (3) measurement difficulties and/or oversearching; (4) intertemporal issues that

prominently Williamson's (1975, 1985, 1996b), Klein, Crawford, and Alchian's (1978), and Grossman and Hart's (1986) interpretations of the transaction cost theory. Investment in such assets exposes agents to a potential hazard: If circumstances change, their trading partners may try to expropriate the rents accruing to the specific assets. Rents can be safeguarded through vertical integration, where a merger eliminates any adversarial interests. Less extreme options include long-term contracts, partial ownership, or agreements for both parties to invest in offsetting relationship-specific investments. Overall, several governance structures may be employed. According to transaction cost theory, parties tend to choose the governance structure that best controls the underinvestment problem, given the particulars of the relationship.

In this sense, transaction cost economics may be considered the study of *alternative institutions of governance.* Its working hypothesis, as expressed by Williamson (1991b, p. 79), is that economic organization is mainly an effort to "align transactions, which differ in their attributes, with governance structures, which differ in their costs and competencies, in a discriminating (mainly, transaction cost economizing) way." Simply put, the contractual approach tries to explain how trading partners choose, from the set of feasible institutional alternatives, the arrangement that best mitigates the relevant contractual hazards at least cost.

The theory is fleshed out by specifying which governance structures go with which transactions. Transactions differ in the degree to which relationship-specific assets are involved, the amount of uncertainty about the future and about other parties' actions, the frequency with which the transaction occurs, and so on. Each matters for the preferred institution of governance, although the first—asset specificity—is particularly important. Williamson (1985, p. 55) defines asset specificity as "durable investments that are undertaken in support of particular transactions, the opportunity cost of which investments is much lower in best alternative uses or by alternative users should the original transaction be prematurely terminated."[4] This could describe a variety of relationship-specific investments, including both specialized physical and human capital, along with intangibles such as R&D and firm-specific knowledge or capabilities.

Governance structures include markets, hierarchies, and hybrids. The pure anonymous spot market suffices for simple transactions such as basic commodity sales. Market prices provide powerful incentives for exploiting profit

---

can take the form of disequilibrium contracting, real time responsiveness, long latency and strategic abuse; and (5) weaknesses in the institutional environment" (Williamson, 1996b, p. 14). Each of these has the potential to impose maladaptation costs. Foreseeing this possibility, agents seek to reduce the potential costs of maladaptation by matching the appropriate governance structure with the particular characteristics of the transaction.

[4] Klein, Crawford, and Alchian's (1978) definition is similar, though they omit the qualifier "much." Essentially they define a relationship-specific asset ("specialized asset") as any asset that generates appropriable quasi-rents; i.e., any asset whose value to its current renter exceeds its value to another renter.

opportunities and market participants are quick to adapt to changing circumstances as information is revealed through prices. When relationship-specific assets are at stake, however and when product or input markets are thin, bilateral coordination of investment decisions may be desirable and combined ownership of these assets may be efficient. Ownership is completely combined in the fully integrated firm. The transaction cost approach maintains that such hierarchies offer greater protection for specific investments and provide relatively efficient mechanisms for responding to change where coordinated adaptation is necessary. Compared with decentralized structures, however, hierarchies provide managers with weaker incentives to maximize profits and normally incur additional bureaucratic costs.

Alternatively, partial alignment may be achieved within an intermediate or hybrid form such as long-term contracts, partial ownership agreements, franchises, networks, alliances, and firms with highly decentralized assignments of decision rights. Hybrids attempt to achieve some level of central coordination and protection for specific investments while retaining the high-powered incentives of market relations.

3. STRATEGIES FOR EMPIRICAL RESEARCH

Most of the empirical work on the make-or-buy decision adopts the transaction cost framework and follows the same basic model. The efficient form of organization for a given economic relationship—and, therefore, the likelihood of observing a particular organizational form or governance structure—is seen as a function of certain properties of the underlying transaction or transactions: asset specificity, uncertainty, frequency, and so on. Organizational form is the dependent variable, while asset specificity, uncertainty, complexity, and frequency are independent variables. Specifically, the probability of observing a more integrated governance structure depends positively on the amount or value of the relationship-specific assets involved and, for significant levels of asset specificity, on the degree of uncertainty about the future of the relationship, on the complexity of the transaction, on the frequency of trade, and possibly on some aspects of the institutional environment.

Organizational form is often modeled as a discrete variable—"make," "buy," or "hybrid," for example—though it can sometimes be represented by a continuous variable. Of the independent variables, asset specificity has received the most attention, presumably because of the central role it plays in the transaction cost approach to vertical integration. Williamson (1991a) distinguishes among six types of asset specificity. The first is site specificity, in which parties are in a "cheek-by-jowl" relationship to reduce transportation and inventory costs and assets are highly immobile. The second, physical asset specificity, refers to relationship-specific equipment and machinery. The third is human asset specificity, describing transaction-specific knowledge or human capital, achieved through specialized training or learning-by-doing. The fourth is brand-name capital, reflected in intangible assets reflected in consumer perceptions. The fifth is "dedicated assets," referring to substantial, general-purpose investments that would not have been made outside a particular transaction, the commitment of which is necessary to serve a large customer. The sixth is temporal specificity, describing assets that must be used in a particular sequence.

Data and Methods

Among the common empirical proxies for asset specificity are technical specifications like product complexity, qualitatively coded from survey data or quantitatively assigned by inspection, as a proxy for physical asset specificity (Masten, 1984; Bigelow, 2001); worker-specific knowledge, again coded from survey data, as a proxy for human asset specificity (Monteverde and Teece, 1982a, 1982b; Masters and Miles, 2002); physical proximity of contracting firms, as a proxy for site specificity (Joskow, 1985, 1987, 1988b, 1990; Spiller, 1985; González,-Diaz, Arruñada, and Fernández, 2000); and spatial and temporal proximity (Masten, Meehan, and Snyder, 1991; Pirrong, 1993; Hubbard, 1999). Other proxies, such as fixed costs or "capital intensity," have more obvious limitations and are rarely used. Where asset specificity cannot be easily measured, concentration has been used in single-industry studies to capture situations where small-numbers bargaining situations are likely to appear (Ohanian, 1994). Common proxies for uncertainty include sales variance (Levy, 1985; Anderson and Schmittlein, 1984) and some measure of technological uncertainty, such as the frequency of changes in product specification and the probability of technological change (Walker and Weber, 1984; Crocker and Reynolds, 1993).

The empirical literature includes qualitative case studies, quantitative case studies focusing on a single firm or industry, and econometric analysis of cross-sectional or panel data from multiple firms or industries. Williamson's (1976) study of cable TV franchising in Oakland, California and Coase's (2000) reinterpretation of the G.M.–Fisher Body case are examples of the first category, while Masten's (1984) investigation of contracting practices in a large aerospace corporation and Saussier's (2000) study of electricity contracts are examples of the second.[5] Cross-industry analyses include Levy's (1985) study of manufacturing and John and Weitz's (1988) paper on forward integration into distribution.

---

[5] Other case studies on vertical integration include Stuckey (1983) on the aluminum industry, Palay (1984) on rail shipping, Gallick (1984) on tuna processing, Joskow (1985) on coal-burning electric plants, Goldberg and Erickson (1987) on petroleum coke, Masten and Snyder (1993) on shoes, Pirrong (1993) on ocean shipping, Ohanian (1994) on pulp and paper, Ménard (1996) on poultry, and Martinez (2002) on poultry, egg, and pork.

Case studies comprise the bulk of the studies on the make-or-buy decision, primarily because the main variables of interest—asset specificity, uncertainty, frequency—are difficult to measure consistently across firms and industries. In many of the early studies these characteristics were estimated based on surveys or interviews: for example, a manager might be asked to rate the degree to which an investment has value in outside uses, on a Likert-type 1 to 7 scale. Such data are of course subject to the general limits of survey data; namely, that they are based on the respondents' stated beliefs, rather than on their beliefs or valuations as revealed through choice. More important, since these measurements are based on ordinal rankings, it is hard to compare them from industry to industry. What is ranked as a relatively specialized asset in one firm may be rated differently in another firm or industry. Similarly, what one firm considers a comparatively uncertain production process may be the standard operating environment in another. Multi-industry studies may therefore contain variables that are labeled the same thing but are really incommensurable, or, conversely, may contain variables that are identical but labeled differently.

While avoiding the problem of inconsistent measurement across industries, case studies have their own problems. The classification of discrete variables like "make-or-buy," for example, may require more discretion by the researcher than economists are comfortable with. And, of course, the evidence from individual cases may not apply to other cases. Still, the cumulative evidence from different studies and industries is remarkably consistent with the basic transaction cost argument, though naturally there remain outstanding puzzles, challenges, and controversies.[6]

Are All Organizations "Efficient"?

A more general problem with the empirical literature on vertical integration—or, for that matter, any aspect of organizational form—is that we usually observe only the business arrangements actually chosen. If these arrangements are presumed to be efficient, then we can draw inferences about the appropriate alignment between transactional characteristics and organizational form simply by observing what firms do. Indeed, the early empirical work on the transaction cost approach implicitly assumed that market forces work to cause an "efficient sort" between transactions and governance structures. Williamson (1988, p. 174) acknowledges this assumption, while recognizing that the process of transaction cost economizing is not automatic:

---

[6] Moreover, a case study is often better than the alternative: no study. In Simon's (1992, p. 1504) words, "Although case studies are only samples of one, such samples are infinitely more informative than samples of none... [V]alid hypotheses are much more likely to emerge from direct, intimate encounter with organizations than from speculation."

The [transaction cost] argument relies in a general, background way on the efficacy of competition to perform a sort between more and less efficient modes and to shift resources in favor of the former. This seems plausible, especially if the relevant outcomes are those that appear over intervals of five and ten years rather than in the very near term. This intuition would nevertheless benefit from a more fully developed theory of the selection process. Transaction cost arguments are thus open to some of the same objections that evolutionary economists have made of orthodoxy.

Still, he maintains that the efficiency presumption is reasonable, offering the argument—analogous to Friedman's famous (1953) statement on the selection process—that inefficient governance arrangements will tend to be discovered and undone. Concerning vertical integration, for example, Williamson (1985, pp. 119–20) writes that "backward integration that lacks a transaction cost rationale or serves no strategic purposes will presumably be recognized and will be undone," adding that mistakes will be corrected more quickly "if the firm is confronted with an active rivalry."

Recently, researchers have begun to examine this conjecture more closely, looking to see if appropriately organized firms—that is, firms that match transactional characteristics to governance structures as the theory says they should—really do outperform the feasible alternatives. Several papers use a two-step procedure in which organizational form (in particular, the relationship between transactional characteristics and governance structure) is endogenously chosen in the first stage, then used to explain performance in the second stage. By endogenizing both organizational form and performance this approach also mitigates the selection bias associated with OLS regressions of performance on firm characteristics.[7]

One important performance measure, in light of Williamson's conjecture regarding the selection process, is firm survival. Silverman, Nickerson and Freeman (1997), for example, show that transaction cost efficiency is positively correlated with firm survival in the for-hire trucking industry, while Bigelow (2001) examines outsourcing arrangements in the U.S. automobile industry and finds that transactions that are appropriately aligned tend to last longer than inappropriately organized ones.

This evolutionary approach sheds considerable light on the processes by which organizations adapt and change, along with the costs of misalignment or maladaptation. However, reliance on evolutionary models introduces additional problems. In many cases, survival may not be the best measure of performance, compared with profitability or market value. Poorly performing firms may survive due to inefficient competitors, regulatory protection, or legal barriers to exit such anti-takeover amendments or an overprotective bankruptcy code. In short, efficient alignment between transactions and governance should be expected

---

[7] Papers using a two-stage approach (such as Heckman's selection model) in this fashion include Masten, Meehan, and Snyder (1991), Poppo and Zenger (1998), Saussier (2000), Nickerson, Hamilton, and Wada (2001), Sampson (2001), Macher (2001), and Yvrande-Billon (2004).

only if the selection environment is strong. Moreover, when market conditions change rapidly and unexpectedly, ex post survival may not be a good measure of ex ante efficiency; a particular organizational form may be right for the times, but the times change. Indeed, the optimal organizational forms may be those that adapt most readily to new circumstances (Boger, Hobbs, and Kerr, 2001).[8]

4. Evidence on the Make-or-Buy Decision: A Sampler

Component Procurement

The decision to make components internally or procure them on the open market was the first topic studied extensively within the transaction cost framework. Early efforts by Monteverde and Teece (1982b) and Masten (1984) use samples of components, coded as either made or bought, along with proxies for asset specificity such as worker-specific knowledge and component complexity as rated by industrial engineers. Each paper uses a probit model to test the relationship between in-house production and asset specificity, along with uncertainty and other control variables, and each finds that asset specificity is a statistically significant predictor of vertical integration.

Refinements to this basic approach include distinguishing among types of uncertainty and among types of asset specificity. Walker and Weber (1984) study automobile component procurement and find that uncertainty about production volume raises the probability that a component is made in-house, but "technological uncertainty," measured as the frequency of changes in product specification and the probability of technological improvements, has little effect. Masten, Meehan, and Snyder (1989) compare relative importance of relationship-specific human and physical capital. Also studying automobile production, they find that engineering effort, as a proxy for human asset specificity, appears to affect the integration decision more than physical or site specificity. Klein (1988), in a discussion of the G.M.–Fisher Body case, also suggests that specific human capital in the form of technical knowledge was a major determinant of G.M.'s decision to buy out Fisher.

Indeed, the relationship between G.M. and Fisher Body in the 1920s is the most commonly cited example of a holdup problem solved by vertical integration. Both Klein, Crawford, and Alchian (1978) and Williamson (1985, pp. 114–15) explain G.M.'s buyout of Fisher in terms of the specific physical assets that accompanied the switch from wooden- to metal-bodied cars. The account in Klein (1988) is somewhat different, emphasizing specific human capital. Langlois and Robertson (1989) also criticize the earlier account of the G.M.–Fisher relationship, arguing that systemic uncertainty, rather than asset specificity, was the motive for vertical integration. Helper, MacDuffie and Sabel

---

[8] An emerging literature on firms as experiments makes the case that organizational change—even the reversal or "undoing" of previous actions—can be consistent with efficient behavior (Mosakowski, 1997; Boot, Milbourn, and Thakor, 1999; Matsusaka, 2001; Klein and Klein, 2002).

(2000) suggest that vertical integration promoted collaborative learning, while Casadesus-Masanell and Spulber (2000) argue it improved the coordination of production and inventories. Interestingly, as Gibbons (2000) points out, few studies investigate the relationship between Fisher and G.M. after the acquisition. An exception is Freeland (2000), who maintains that the Fisher brothers successfully held up G.M. after they became employees. (See below for more on the continuing controversy over this case.)

Other papers document a similar link between integration and R&D, which usually involves specific human capital (Armour and Teece, 1980; Joskow, 1985; Pisano, 1990). Asset specificity is associated with tighter vertical coordination in many industries, including electricity generation (Joskow, 1985; Saussier, 2000), aerospace (Masten, 1984), aluminum (Stuckey, 1983; Hennart, 1988), forestry (Globerman and Schindt, 1986), chemicals (Lieberman, 1991), engineering (Lyons, 1995), trucking (Nickerson and Silverman, 2003), offshore oil gathering (Hallwood, 1991), information technology (Ulset, 1996), electronic components (Weiss and Kurland, 1997), construction (González-Diaz, Arruñada, and Fernández, 2000), and even stock exchanges (Bindseil, 1997).

Many of these studies include controls for other possible determinants of vertical structure such as market structure, scale and scope economies, and other industry characteristics, and the impact of asset specificity usually remains statistically (and economically) significant. As discussed above, the latest papers also try to minimize selection bias and the effects of unobserved heterogeneity though improved econometric procedures.

Nearly all the studies cited above are focused, single-industry case studies. A few studies have used cross-sectional or panel data to estimate the effects of transactional characteristics on vertical integration using multi-industry data. An early effort by Levy (1985) uses the ratio of value-added to sales as a cross-industry measure of vertical integration[9]; the number of firms and amount of R&D spending as measures of asset specificity; and the variance of sales as a measure of uncertainty. Using data from 69 firms representing 37 industries, he finds each of the independent variables to have a statistically significant effect on the likelihood of vertical integration. Macmillan, Hambrick, and Pennings (1986) obtain very similar results with a larger sample. Harrigan (1986), by contrast, finds sales variability to result in a lower chance of vertical integration, although she does not include a measure for asset specificity.

Accounting constructs like the ratio of value-added to sales, however, are problematic as measures of vertical integration. Value-added figures are reported inconsistently across firms and industries, and there are several accepted methods for computing value-added ratios.[10] Caves and Bradburd (1988) construct a more complicated cross-industry measure of integration based on an

---

[9] A fully vertical integrated firm will have a value-added-to-sales ratio of one, while a firm that procures components externally will have a smaller ratio.

[10] See the discussion in Bender (2002).

input–output matrix of distribution shipments across several industries. They use this metric to compare asset specificity, small-numbers bargaining conditions, and risk as determinants of vertical integration. They find asset specificity and small-numbers situations, but not risk, to be significant. Hypotheses based on contractual hazards thus do well in their study as compared to competing approaches. Unfortunately, their procedures are exceptionally data-intensive and may not be feasible in many cases. Other potentially fruitful approaches use financial data on merging firms' pre- and post-merger performance, either to study the gains from merger as a function of asset specificity (Spiller, 1985) or to examine the likelihood of merger as a function of pre-merger bilateral relationships (Weiss, 1992).

A problem with these cross-sectional studies is that they cannot control for time and for unobserved firm-specific characteristics. Using panel data can overcome this limitation. González-Diaz, Arruñada, and Fernández (2000) assemble a panel of Spanish construction firms over a six-year period and study the use of independent subcontractors. They regress the percentage of subcontracting on a distance-based measure of asset specificity, a measure of uncertainty, time- and firm-fixed effects, and other control variables. They find that asset specificity, but not uncertainty, explains most of the outsourcing decision, even when controlling for unobserved heterogeneity. Other studies using panel data, such as Ohanian's (1994) investigation of vertical integration in the U.S. pulp and paper industry and Lafontaine and Shaw's (1999) study of franchise contracting, also support transaction cost explanations even when fixed effects are included. These studies suggest that the generally recognized relationship between asset specificity and vertical control is probably not driven by unobservable firm-specific factors.

Forward Integration into Marketing and Distribution

While economists typically think of vertical integration as backward integration into components, materials or R&D, forward integration into marketing and distribution may be just as important. As Anderson and Gatignon discuss in their chapter in this volume, several studies of integration of marketing channels have used transaction cost reasoning. Anderson and Schmittlein (1984) consider two marketing alternatives for an electronics component producer: the use of employees as a direct sales force (a form of vertical integration), or reliance on independent manufacturers' representatives. This choice is regressed on managers' perceptions of the importance of specific human capital, sales volume uncertainty, and measurement uncertainty (all based on survey data), each of which is predicted to increase the likelihood of a direct sales force. Both specific human capital and measurement uncertainty are statistically significant, though sales uncertainty is not. Another study by Anderson (1985), also on the electronics industry, finds the same basic results, as does work by John and Weitz (1988) using data from a variety of industrial-product industries. Regan (1997) looks at the insurance business and finds that independent sales agencies are more common when relationship-specific investment data processing and communications systems are less important. Fein and Anderson (1997) use transaction cost reasoning to show that geographic and brand restrictions serve to protect manufacturers' and distributors' specific reputational capital.

As Holmström and Milgrom (1994) point out, however, the evidence from many of these studies is consistent not only with the transaction cost model, but also with a multitask principal–agent model in which certain clusters of attributes (here, high-performance incentives, worker ownership of assets, and worker freedom from direct controls) go together. Still, the fact that the evidence in marketing and distribution is so similar to the evidence from backward integration into manufacturing and supplies suggests that the transaction cost interpretation should not be easily dismissed.

Marketing and distribution depend on other factors as well, of course. Muris, Scheffman, and Spiller's (1992) study of the carbonated beverage industry finds that the shift from independent bottlers to captive subsidiaries during the late twentieth century can be explained without reference to changes in physical asset specificity or site specificity. Instead, they account for the shift in terms of the emergence of national cola markets, which required greater coordination of advertising and promotional activities. Along with changing technologies in cola production and distribution (namely, falling transportation and communication costs), it was this need for more centralized decision-making—for given levels of asset specificity—that explains the change toward a more vertically integrated industry.

Contracts and Contractual Design

The earliest literature on the make-or-buy decision—starting with Coase (1937)—treated external sourcing and in-house procurement as polar opposites. Firms were modeled as choosing, as expressed by the title of Williamson's influential (1975) book, between "markets and hierarchies." And yet, we observe firms choosing a variety of intermediate or hybrid forms of organization, such as long-term contracts, partial ownership agreements, franchises, networks, alliances, and other combinations. A good theory of the make-or-buy decision must also explain under what circumstances firms choose one of these intermediate forms.

In the transaction cost approach, a hybrid such as a long-term contract represents a blend, or compromise, between the benefits of centralized coordination and control and the incentive and informational advantages of decentralized decision-making (Williamson, 1991a; Ménard, 2004). For certain types of transactions an intermediate form of governance is appropriate. For instance, under conditions of asset specificity but negligible uncertainty, long-term contracts may be an effective means of mitigating opportunism. When asset specificity and uncertainty are both high, however, contracts may be insufficiently flexible, leading to vertical integration instead.

Some key issues related to the choice between market, hierarchy, and contracts (or other hybrids) are presented below. For a more detailed treatment of the relevant econometric issues see Saussier's chapter in this volume.

Why Contract?

Surprisingly, while there is an extensive empirical literature explaining contractual form—duration, completeness, complexity, and other attributes—in terms of transaction costs (see Saussier, this volume, for a survey), the choice between contract and vertical integration or spot-market procurement has received less attention. An exception is the continuing controversy surrounding the purchase of Fisher Body by G.M. in 1926. Klein, Crawford, and Alchian (1978) and Klein (1988) cite the case as a classic example of vertical integration designed to mitigate holdup in the presence of asset specificity. Fisher refused to locate its plants near G.M. assembly plants and to change its production technology in the face of an unanticipated increase in the demand for car bodies, leading G.M. to terminate its existing ten-year supply contract with Fisher and acquire full ownership. Coase (2000), revisiting the original documents, argues instead that the contract performed well, and was gradually replaced with full ownership only to get Fisher's top managers (the Fisher brothers) more closely involved in G.M.'s other operation.

Coase (2000) reveals that the original ten-year supply contract included provisions that G.M. would acquire 60 percent of Fisher's stock and that three of the five members of Fisher's finance committee would be appointed by G.M. Moreover, in 1921 one of the Fisher brothers became a director of G.M., with two other brothers joining him in 1924, one of whom became president of G.M.'s Cadillac division. A fourth brother was added to the board in 1926 when G.M. acquired the remainder of Fisher's stock. As Coase points out, the interests of the two companies were sufficiently aligned during the period covered by the original contract that it is unlikely that Fisher would have used the contract to extract rents from G.M. Also, contrary to the conventional understanding of the case, Fisher did in fact build eight new body plants between 1922 and 1925 that were close to G.M. facilities and had incentives to use the most efficient technology available. In short, G.M. did not acquire the remaining 40 percent of Fisher's stock in response to an inappropriate alignment between transactional attributes and an existing governance structure. Rather, the long-term contract signed in 1919 was adequate for mitigating holdup in the face of asset specificity and uncertainty, and was replaced by vertical integration for secondary reasons.

A few papers study the choice between contracts and other hybrids such as partial ownership agreements or "equity linkages" for conducting R&D. Pisano (1990) argues that partial ownership dominates contracts under certain combinations of asset specificity, uncertainty, the number of trading partners, and other variables. Equity linkages are more likely when R&D is to be done during collaboration and when collaboration encompasses multiple projects and less likely when there are more potential collaborators. Oxley (1997, 1999) shows that the choice between contractual and equity-based vertical alliances is largely explained by the costs of contracting.

Contractual Design

Given that contracts are used, what provisions should they contain, how long and how complete should they be, and so on? An influential series of papers by Joskow (1985, 1987, 1988b, 1990) focuses on duration and price-adjustment provisions in agreements between coal suppliers and coal-burning electrical plants. He examined a large sample of coal contracts and found that contracts tended to be longer, all else equal, when relationship-specific investments (here, site specificity and dedicated assets) are at stake. Crocker and Masten (1988) find the same result for the natural gas industry. More generally, they argue that efficient contract duration depends on the costs of contracting; contract terms become shorter, for example, as uncertainty increases.[11]

Another important contractual dimension is incompleteness. As discussed above, the transaction cost approach holds that all complex contracts are necessarily incomplete; otherwise, why would specialized governance arrangements be necessary? But the degree of incompleteness—for instance, the extent to which renegotiation procedures are specified—is endogenous. Crocker and Reynolds (1993) test the relationship between contractual incompleteness and the likelihood of opportunistic behavior in a study of Air Force engine procurement. Using a sample of procurement agreements from the 1970s and 1980s they find that contracts are more complete when the contractor has a history of disputes with purchasers and less complete when there are increases in associated intertemporal or technological uncertainty (increasing the cost of writing more complete contracts).

As Saussier (2000) points out, however, both this study and Crocker and Masten's (1991) analysis of incompleteness in natural-gas contracting rely on highly indirect measures of asset specificity. Saussier's (2000) study of French electricity contracts uses more direct measures for both physical asset specificity and site specificity, based on interviews, and finds that these are positively related to completeness, ceteris paribus. Saussier also attempts to endogenize asset specificity by employing a two-stage estimation procedure in which asset specificity is regressed on exogenous predictors in a first stage, and the fitted values used in the second-stage regression of incompleteness on asset specificity. (Correcting for endogeneity has little effect on the results).

Besides duration, price-adjustment provisions, and completeness, other contractual practices such as "take-or-pay" and exclusive-dealing provisions have been analyzed with transaction cost reasoning. An example is DeCanio and Frech's (1993) study of take-or-pay contracts in the natural gas industry. These contracts, which require the buyer to pay for some minimum quantity even if

---

[11] On natural gas contracts see also Crocker and Masten (1991), Hubbard and Weiner (1991), and Dahl and Matson (1998).

delivery is not taken, are used to safeguard against buyer (pipeline) opportunism. In 1987, the Federal Energy Regulatory Commission (FERC) outlawed take-or-pay contracts. The authors used data from before and after the FERC order to test its effect on spot gas prices and prices at the wellhead. They found that FERC's interference with parties' ability to craft long-term governance mechanisms raised natural gas prices between 21 percent and 31 percent in the year following FERC's order. The results support the theory that long-term contracts add substantial value where asset specificity is high, while representing an effort to quantify that efficiency gain.[12]

Exclusive dealing—long regarded by economists and antitrust authorities as an anticompetitive practice—can also be explained using transaction cost reasoning. Gallick's (1984) study of the U.S. tuna industry argues that exclusive dealing is an efficient means of discouraging ex-post opportunism by fishing boat captains. Because most tuna sold in the U.S. is canned, buying a boat's output at a price reflecting average quality is cheaper for tuna processors than paying for the inspection, sorting, and grading usually found in fresh-fish markets. Exclusive dealing arrangements prevent the boat captains from selling the higher-quality tuna, ex post, to rival processors at higher prices. Exclusive dealing can enhance the efficiency of trade in other settings as well (Heide, Dutta, and Bergen, 1998).

Other Hybrids

Other hybrid forms of organization include sharing arrangements such as franchising or agricultural cropsharing; groups of firms organized as networks, clusters, or alliances; and reciprocal investments or reciprocal-trading arrangements (see Ménard, 2004, for an overview of the literature on hybrids).[13] Franchising and cropsharing have each received substantial attention, both within the transaction cost and agency literatures. Under franchising, the franchisor's brand-name capital is a valuable asset (though it may or may not be specific to particular franchisees). Franchise contracts allow the franchisor to leverage this asset while retaining the high-powered incentives the franchisee would lose under vertical integration. An extensive empirical literature has tried to explain pricing arrangements such as license fees and royalty rates (Lafontaine, 1992; Bercovitz, 1999), along with specific franchising provisions such as formal procedural rules, standardization of inputs and outputs, and centralization of core functions like training and information technology (Dnes, 1996; Lafontaine and Slade, 1997; Lafontaine and Raynaud, 2002), using transaction cost and agency theory. Still, important puzzles remain; one is the coexistence of franchised and company-owned stores within the same brand.[14]

---

[12] Mulherin (1986) and Masten and Crocker (1985) also examine "take-or-pay" contracts.

[13] A firm in which decision rights are highly decentralized, as described by Jensen and Meckling (1992), may also be considered a hybrid.

[14] On sharing arrangements in food and agriculture see Allen and Lueck (1993) and Arruñada, González-Diaz, and Lopez (1996). On hybrids in agriculture more generally see the discussion in Ménard and Klein (2004).

Firms may also organize themselves into networks, groups that pool resources but often rely on relational contracts, rather than formal written agreements, to coordinate their behavior. Networks are particularly important in agriculture, where an increasing emphasis on quality control necessitates tight coordination among members of the vertical production process (Ménard, 1996). Formal ties can also help firms realize the agglomeration economies that result from knowledge and other geographic spillovers (Porter, 2000). Transaction cost reasoning helps explain the observed variety of network structures (Ménard, 1996) as well as the specific contractual arrangements used by network (or formal alliance) partners to protect specific investments (Oxley, 1997). Still, we know relatively little about the efficiency of networks and alliances relative to integrated firms and the rules network members use to govern the returns to shared resources. Another important question is whether networks are a stable mode of organization, or a transitional form, eventually giving way to more consolidated (or fragmented) structures (Ménard and Klein, 2004).

Another way for parties to protect their relationship-specific investments is by making other, "offsetting" investments. Heide and John (1988) provide an example from marketing. To service a particular manufacturer, sales agencies typically make investments specific to that manufacturer—most often, a human-capital investment in developing a sales territory for the manufacturer's product. Because agencies are small compared with manufacturers, they cannot safeguard their investments by backwards integration into manufacturing. Similarly, they lack the bargaining power to demand long-term contracts with manufacturers. Instead, they protect their relationship-specific assets by making *other* specific investments, namely in routines or procedures that tie or "bond" them with a manufacturer's customers. These might involve establishing personal relationships with the customers, developing an identity separate from the manufacturer's particular product, or creating specialized procedures for ordering, shipping, and servicing the product. In this way they "balance their dependence" on the manufacturer with the customers' dependence on them.[15]

Informal Agreements

As mentioned above, contractual relations need not be fully formal and explicit; trading arrangements are often governed by less formal, relational norms. Palay (1984, 1985) studies the role of informal, legally unenforceable agreements between rail-freight carriers and shippers. Shipment of items like automobile parts and chemicals, for example, requires specially designed rail cars and equipment that cannot be easily redeployed for other uses. Because vertical integration was prohibited by regulation, informal agreements emerged to protect these relationship-specific investments. Wilson (1980) shows how the New England fresh-fish market works through mutual dependence created by the particular trade arrangements there, governed by reputation. Acheson's (1985) study of

---

[15] "Countertrade" agreements appear to perform a similar function (Hennart, 1989).

the Maine lobster market reaches similar conclusions, finding the lobster market to be characterized by long-term, informal relationships between fishermen and lobster-pound operators.[16]

Baker, Gibbons, and Murphy (2001) show, more generally, how relational contracting—both between and within firms—differs from formal contracting. Relational contracts have the advantage that outcomes need not be verifiable to third parties, such as courts, to limit parties' incentives to behave opportunistically. On the other hand, the absence of third-party participation means that such agreements must be self-enforcing.[17] Heide and John's (1992) study of buyer–supplier relations finds that relational norms often substitute for vertical integration as a means of protecting specific assets; Anderson and Weitz (1992) and Brown, Dev, and Lee (2000) show that such norms are also important in marketing.

Other Examples

Other examples of vertical relations studied within the transaction cost framework include tie-ins and "block booking" (Kenney and Klein, 1983), multinational corporations (Hennart, 1989; Yarbrough and Yarbrough, 1987b; Gatignon and Anderson, 1988; Klein, Frazer, and Roth, 1990; Hu and Chen, 1993; Henisz, 2000), company towns and company stores (Fishback, 1986, 1992), the rise of medieval marketplaces and towns (Bindseil and Pfeil, 1999), and even marriage (Hamilton, 1999). These and other "non-standard" contracting practices, when viewed through a transaction cost lens, often turn out to have efficiency properties, particularly in offering safeguards for specific investments.

5. CHALLENGES AND DIRECTIONS FOR FURTHER RESEARCH

The vast empirical literature on the make-or-buy decision, including the structure of long-term contracts and hybrid forms of organization, is largely consistent with the transaction cost theory of the firm: vertical arrangements are usually best understood as attempts to protect trading partners from the hazards of exchange under incomplete contracting. As Joskow (1991, p. 47) observes, the literature on the make-or-buy decision is in many ways in "much better shape than much of the empirical work in industrial organization generally."[18] However, important challenges, puzzles, and opportunities remain. First, the

---

[16] Informal agreements and norms in eighteenth- and nineteenth-century whaling have been studied similarly by Ellickson (1989) and Gifford (1993).

[17] Self-enforcing agreements can be interpreted as noncooperative Nash equilibria in a set of repeated games; such agreements have been called "norms" (Ullman-Margalit, 1977), "conventions" (Sugden, 1986), and "social institutions" (Schotter, 1981). Ellickson's (1991) study of relationships between cattle ranchers and farmers in Shasta County, California shows that social norms (what he calls "customary law") can be superior to administrative or judicial dispute resolution among people with close social ties.

[18] Williamson (1996a, p. 55) puts it bluntly: "Transaction cost economics is an empirical success story."

The Make-or-Buy Decision: Lessons from Empirical Studies 451

measurement and definition of asset specificity, uncertainty, and other variables remains inconsistent. Second, many studies do not explicitly compare rival explanations for vertical relationships. Third, correlation between transactional attributes and governance structures is often mistaken for causality. Fourth, the legal and regulatory environments do not always get sufficient attention.

Measurement and Definition

As mentioned above, empirical research on make-or-buy decisions is often hampered by confusion about the definitions of, and therefore the empirical proxies for, key variables such as asset specificity and uncertainty. Asset specificity is difficult to measure consistently across industries, partially explaining why there are far more single-industry studies of vertical boundaries than cross-industry studies. Uncertainty is hard to define, let alone measure.[19] Moreover, empirical studies sometimes treat uncertainty as an independent variable, regressing the choice of organizational form on the variance of sales or another variable, but without including any measure of asset specificity in the model. Absent fixed investments, however, transaction cost economics does not predict that uncertainty would itself lead to hierarchical governance. Changes in circumstances only allow for expropriation where there are quasi-rents at risk; that is, where one side's investment is exposed. Where there are no relationship-specific investments at stake, it may be less costly for a firm to contract on the market for goods and services in an uncertain environment than to assume the risk of producing them internally. In this way, the effect of uncertainty depends on competitive conditions. If there is no asset specificity and thus there are many potential suppliers of a component for which future demand is uncertain, it may be cheaper to buy the component than to make it internally.[20]

Asset specificity has been more successfully treated in the empirical literature; relationship-specific physical, site and human capital investments have all been studied, both independently and comparatively. However, further refinement and analysis needs to be done here, particularly concerning measurement. Proxies such as capital intensity or fixed costs are very imperfect and may not capture

---

[19] As discussed above, the empirical literature on vertical integration tends to use fairly crude measures of uncertainty (such as the variation of sales). Distinctions between systemic and idiosyncratic risk, between demand and supply (or technological) risk, and between risk and Knightian uncertainty have rarely been addressed.

[20] In some situations uncertainty is so great that efficient governance structures cannot be crafted at all, in which case trade may fail to materialize. While there is a considerable stream of theoretical literature, following Akerlof (1970), on the possibility that markets might break down due to private information, there is relatively little theoretical or empirical work on non-market exchange under these conditions. An exception is Wiggins and Libecap's (1985) study of unitization agreements in oil production. Under such an agreement producers designate a single firm to develop a given field, with the net returns shared among all producers. This reduces recovery costs and improves oil yields by eliminating the negative externalities associated with concurrent independent development of a single field. Yet very few oil fields are unitized. Wiggins and Libecap argue that asymmetric information encourages opportunistic holdout strategies that have usually prevented the agreements from being signed.

whether the investment has value outside the transaction for which it was initially made.[21] Another concern is that asset-specificity effects may be confused with market power. While specific investment may lead to bilateral monopoly, a small-numbers bargaining situation is not by itself evidence of relationship-specific investment.

The Role of Asset Specificity

While the early transaction cost literature emphasized asset specificity as the key to an efficiency explanation for vertical integration, several studies use transaction cost and incomplete-contracting theory to explain vertical integration in the absence of asset specificity. Pirrong (1993) argues that long-term contracts (and sometimes vertical integration) can be efficient in the presence of smaller contracting hazards—even when physical, human, and site asset specificities are absent. In a study of bulk shipping, he finds that more integrated governance structures can dominate spot trading in the presence of what Masten, Meehan, and Snyder (1991) call "temporal specificities." When a processing or refinery plant contracts with a particular bulk carrier, for example, both plant and carrier capacities suddenly become specific assets. Small delays in delivery can then result in large losses of quasi-rents for the plant, just as the plant's refusal to take full delivery can impose substantial losses on the carrier. To avoid costly strategic bargaining, then, these parties will choose a complex, long-term agreement. Martinez (2002) shows how temporal specificities lead to tight vertical coordination in poultry and egg production.

Three recent studies of the U.S. trucking market also find long-term contracts in the absence of asset specificity. Both Williamson (1985, p. 54) and Klein, Crawford, and Alchian (1978, p. 244) cite trucks as clear examples of durable, but nonspecific, assets. Yet, as shown by Hubbard (1999) and Nickerson and Silverman (2003), trucking continues to be characterized by tight vertical coordination between hired drivers and shippers, rather than market-based coordination between independent owner-operators and shippers, even after the industry was deregulated in the 1970s. Hubbard (1999) uses this evidence to challenge the scope of holdup theories more generally. Nickerson and Silverman (2003) show that the need for temporal coordination among hauls, and the shipper's desire to protect its brand-name capital, leads to tight vertical control, explaining why many shippers continue to use company-owned trucks. Lafontaine and Masten (2002) argue that the observed variation in contractual arrangements in trucking can best be explained by driver and truck heterogeneity, not asset specificity or marginal incentive considerations.

None of these studies denies that physical asset specificity and site specificity are important determinants of vertical relations, only that some cases of vertical

---

[21] The same applies to measures of human asset specificity, such as training, used to explain labor outsourcing (see, for example, Masters and Miles, 2002).

control can be explained without reference to them, or to holdup problems at all. At present, these results appear as exceptions to a more general rule. Still, an accumulation of such anomalies could challenge the key underlying structure of the transaction cost approach.

Comparing Rival Explanations

Besides these difficulties of measurement and definition, and the role of key independent variables, empirical research on vertical boundaries is also subject to the problem found in empirical work generally: alternate hypotheses that could also fit the data are rarely stated and compared. Usually, the data are found only consistent or inconsistent with the hypothesis at hand. Undoubtedly, studies that explicitly compare competing, observationally distinct hypotheses about contractual relationships are needed, because rival theories commonly posit mutually exclusive outcomes.

One example is Spiller's (1985) comparison of asset-specificity and market-power explanations for vertical mergers, explanations that have rival predictions about the size of the gains from mergers under various competitive conditions. While transaction cost theory predicts that the gains from merger should be increasing in the degree of asset specificity, market-power considerations suggest that the gains will be increasing in the degree of supplier-market concentration. Using site specificity, defined as the proximity of the merging firms, to represent asset specificity, Spiller studies the gains from merger according to unexpected changes in the firms' stock prices at the announcement of the merger. He finds the total gain from merger to be smaller where the distance between the merging firms is greater (i.e., where site specificity is lower). He also finds no significant relationship between industry concentration and the distance between merging firms. These findings appear to support the asset-specificity explanation over the market-power explanation.

Poppo and Zenger's (1995) investigation of transaction cost and resourced-based explanations for information-technology (IT) outsourcing represents another comparative study. They use a survey of corporate IT managers to measure perceived satisfaction with both outsourced and in-house IT services. Consistent with transaction cost reasoning, they find that asset specificity is negatively related to the performance of market transactions. Contrary to the resource-based view (and specific predictions offered by Ghoshal and Moran, 1996, for example), they find that asset specificity does not improve the performance of in-house transactions. (Some findings are consistent with both theories.) Other studies that assess both transaction cost and rival theories include Poppo and Zenger (1998), Silverman (1999), and Nickerson, Hamilton, and Wada (2001). Most of these comparative studies appear in the strategic management literature, where theories of the firm based on capabilities, power, and trust are important rivals to the transaction cost view. In industrial organization, by contrast, theories of vertical boundaries built on market power or technological foundations have not inspired much empirical research.

Moreover, while the evidence presented in this chapter is often interpreted as supportive of both (a) the transaction cost theory as explicated by Williamson and Klein, Crawford, and Alchian and (b) the more formal version (the "property rights approach") associated with Grossman, Hart, and Moore, there are important differences between these two sets of explanations for firm boundaries. (See Williamson, 2000, pp. 605–07 for a detailed discussion of these differences.) For example, property-rights models focus exclusively on ex ante underinvestment in relationship-specific human capital brought about by inefficient ownership arrangements, while transaction cost theories look more at the ex post contract-execution stage. Partly because ex post contractual problems are easier to observe than ex ante human capital underinvestment—How, for instance, is optimal investment to be measured?—there have been relatively few empirical studies explicitly in the property-rights tradition.[22] Whinston (2000) argues that the empirical evidence described above is not necessarily consistent with the property-rights approach. As he points out, in property-rights models the *level* of appropriable quasi-rents is not relevant for the integration decision; only *marginal* quasi-rents matter. Few empirical studies make this distinction. Furthermore, property-rights models offer specific predictions on the direction of integration (whether buyer acquires seller or seller acquires buyer), a distinction that is also generally ignored in the empirical literature.

Causality

A more general concern is that most of the empirical studies discussed here establish correlations, not causal relations, between asset specificity and internal governance. These studies typically test a reduced-form model where the probability of observing a more hierarchical form of governance increases with the degree of relationship-specific investments. Plausibly, if the presence of such investments reduces the costs of internal organization, then asset specificity could lead to integration, independent of the holdup problem or other maladaptation costs (Masten, 1994, p. 10). Masten, Meehan and Snyder (1991) attempt to distinguish these two effects in the context of human capital. They find that specific human capital investments appear to reduce internal governance costs more than they increase market governance costs. Further studies of this type would be valuable in assessing the implications of the evidence for the reduced-form version of the basic theory. However, we do not yet have a general theory of how relationship-specific assets might reduce the costs of internal organization. By contrast, the underinvestment problem associated with specific assets and market governance is fairly well understood.

---

[22] Hart (1995, p. 49) remarks that there has been "no formal testing of the property rights approach." (By "formal testing" he presumably excludes case studies.)

The Regulatory and Legal Environment

Contracting takes place "in the shadow of the law" (Cooter, Marks and Mnookin, 1982), and the empirical work on vertical boundaries could be improved by greater attention to the effects of the regulatory and legal environments. With notable exceptions (like the work on contracting among public utilities and their suppliers), the literature has generally focused on relatively unregulated industries operating under a relatively stable legal regime. However, differences in regulatory structures, or how judges interpret contractual clauses, can have substantial effects on the performance of alternative vertical arrangements. Neglecting such differences leads to biased estimates of the effects of other factors, such as asset specificity and uncertainty, on the decision to vertically integrate or to use long-term contracts.

Recent papers by Henisz (2000), Delios and Henisz (2000), and Henisz and Zelner (2001) have begun looking more closely at the relationship between contractual hazards and political hazards. Henisz's (2000) study of foreign investment finds that firms tend to prefer joint ventures with foreign partners rather than majority owned plants where political hazards are high, even though majority ownership may better mitigate the contractual hazards associated with asset specificity. The available contracting options may also be limited by regulation. Moreover, as discussed above, Palay (1984, 1985) shows that informal agreements can substitute for regulation when vertical integration is prohibited. Loredo and Suárez (2000) study the coal-burning electricity plants in Spain and find that the opportunism was mitigated by the regulatory compact between firms and the state, instead of the long-term contracts used by U.S. plants. Ménard and Klein (2004) compare vertical relations in U.S. and European agriculture and suggest that the variation is partly explained by differences in the institutional environment.

The evolution of contractual relations in rapidly changing environments, such as transition economies, is another important area (see Boger, Hobbs, and Kerr, 2001, for one example). These settings not only allow for comparative analysis, but also provide insight into the ability of various contractual arrangements to adapt to changing circumstances.

6. CONCLUSION

Despite the ongoing challenges described above, the transaction cost theory of the firm has had remarkable success in explaining the vertical structure of the enterprise. Indeed, the empirical literature on the make-or-buy decision is generally considered one of the best-developed parts of the new institutional economics. The recent survey by Boerner and Macher (2002) estimates the number of empirical papers in transaction cost economics at over 600, and a large share of these focus on vertical integration. As Williamson (2000, p. 607) remarks, "Those who have done this modest, slow, molecular, definitive work deserve enormous credit."

What lessons have we learned from this literature? First, asset specificity is an important determinant of vertical contractual relations. It is not the sole determinant, however; even in the face of uncertainty, arms-length contracting may effectively protect parties' relationship-specific investments. Tight vertical coordination or control may also generate efficiencies unrelated to the protection of specific assets.

Indeed, paradigmatic cases like the acquisition of Fisher Body by G.M. continue to generate controversy about the role of asset specificity compared to other contractual or organizational considerations. Still, the transaction cost approach remains the dominant framework within which such debates take place. No rival theory has produced a body of evidence remotely rivaling the transaction cost explanation for vertical integration. Market power theories continue to be relevant, particularly in the antitrust literature, but are substantially less influential today than two or three decades ago. The resource-based or capabilities view of firm boundaries is important, perhaps even dominant, within the strategic-management literature, but it has not generated a substantial body of empirical work. This is not to deny that some of the evidence usually taken to support the transaction cost approach may also be consistent with these or other alternative approaches. Indeed, as discussed above, relatively few studies attempt to distinguish among rival explanations. Much more comparative work is needed to address this concern.

A related issue is that most new theoretical work in economics on firm boundaries builds on the incomplete-contracting framework of Grossman, Hart, and Moore, not the closely related—but not identical—transaction cost framework of Williamson and Klein, Crawford, and Alchian. As explained above, the former does not lend itself to empirical testing as easily as the latter. However, the formal language in which the Grossman-Hart-Moore theory is expressed is more in tune with contemporary economic theorizing than the mostly informal language of the transaction cost approach. If the Grossman-Hart-Moore framework comes to displace the transaction cost framework, the relevance of the empirical evidence highlighted in this chapter may be called into question. On the other hand, the difficulty in finding empirical support for incomplete-contracting models may ultimately limit their popularity. Moreover, new formalizations of transaction cost economics are beginning to emerge (for example, Bajari and Tadelis, 2001).

A second lesson is that vertical relations are often subtle and complex. While early empirical work on transaction cost determinations of vertical integration tended to focus on black-and-white distinctions between "make" or "buy," researchers increasingly recognize that a wide variety of contractual and organizational options are available; there are many shades of gray. The literature on hybrids has grown dramatically in the last ten years, while there are fewer studies of mundane issues such as outsourcing versus in-house production per se.

Third, while we know much about the transaction cost determinants of vertical relations, we know relatively little about the relation between the costs of contracting and organization and the wider legal, political, and social environments. The progression from single-industry case studies to cross-industry, within-country analyses, to cross-country investigations is a natural one (we see it in empirical corporate finance, for example; see the chapter by Roe in this volume). Comparisons of institutional arrangements across institutional environments may become the next growth area in the transaction cost literature.

ACKNOWLEDGEMENT

I am grateful to Tom Gibel, Claude Ménard, Mary M. Shirley, Mike Sykuta, and three anonymous referees for helpful suggestions.

REFERENCES

Akerlof, George A. 1970. "The Market for 'Lemons': Qualitative Uncertainty and the Market Mechanism". *Quarterly Journal of Economics* 84: 488–500.
Alchian, Armen A. and Harold Demsetz. 1972. "Production, Information Costs, and Economic Organization". *American Economic Review* 62: 777–795.
Anderson, Erin. 1985. "The Salesperson as Outside Agent or Employee: A Transaction Cost Analysis". *Marketing Science* 4: 234–254.
Anderson, Erin and David C. Schmittlein. 1984. "Integration of the Sales Force: An Empirical Examination". *Rand Journal of Economics* 15: 385–395.
Anderson, Erin and A.T. Coughlan. 1987. "International Market Entry and Expansion via Independent or Integrated Channels of Distribution". *Journal of Marketing* 51: 71–82.
Armour, Henry O. and David J. Teece. 1980. "Vertical Integration and Technological Innovation". *Review of Economics and Statistics* 62: 470–474.
Arruñada, Benito, Manuel Gonzalez-Diaz, and Begona Lopez. 1996. "The Role of Competition in Controlling Team Production: The Case of Fishing Industry". Working Paper, University Pompeu Fabra.
Bajari, Patrick and Steven Tadelis. 2001. "Incentives versus Transactions Costs: A Theory of Procurement Contracts". *Rand Journal of Economics* 32: 387–407.
Baye, Michael and Richard Beil. 1994. *Managerial Economics and Business Strategy*. Burr Ridge, IL.: Irwin.
Bercovitz, Janet E. L. 1999. "Having It Their Way? The Franchising Decision and the Structure of Franchise Contracts". Ph.D. dissertation, Haas School of Business, University of California, Berkeley, CA.
Bender, Christian. 2002. "The Theory of the Firm Revisited: Changing Firm Boundaries in a New Information and Communication Environment". Working Paper, Department of International Business, University of Muenster.
Bigelow, Lyda. 2001. "Efficient Alignment and Survival in the U.S. Automobile Industry". Working Paper, Olin School of Business, Washington University, St. Louis.
Bindseil, Ulrich. 1997. "Vertical Integration in the Long Run: The Provision of Physical Assets to the London and New York Stock Exchanges". *Journal of Institutional and Theoretical Economics* 153: 641–656.
Bindseil, Ulrich and Christian Pfeil. 1999. "Specialization as a Specific Investment into the Market: A Transaction Cost Approach to the Rise of Markets and Towns in Medieval Germany, 800–1200". *Journal of Institutional and Theoretical Economics* 155: 738–754.
Boger, Silke, Jill E. Hobbs, and William A. Kerr. 2001. "Supply Chain Relationships in the Polish Pork Sector". *Supply Chain Management* 6: 74–82.

Boot, Arnoud W. A., Todd T. Milbourn, and Anjan V. Thakor. 1999. "Megamergers and Expanded Scope: Theories of Bank Size and Activity Diversity". *Journal of Banking and Finance* 23: 195–214.
Brickley, James A. 1999. "Incentives, Conflicts and Contractual Restraints: Evidence from Franchising". *Journal of Law and Economics* 42: 745–774.
Brickley, James A., Clifford W. Smith Jr., and Jerrold L. Zimmerman. 2004. *Managerial Economics and Organizational Architecture*, 3rd edn. New York: McGraw Hill–Irwin.
Brown, James R., C. S. Dev, and D. J. Lee. 2000. "Managing Marketing Channel Opportunism: The Efficacy of Alternative Governance Mechanisms". *Journal of Marketing* 64: 51–65.
Casadesus-Masanell, Ramon and Daniel F. Spulber. 2000. "The Fable of Fisher Body". *Journal of Law and Economics* 43: 67–104.
Caves, Richard E. and Ralph E. Bradburd. 1988. "The Empirical Determinants of Vertical Integration". *Journal of Economic Behavior and Organization* 9: 265–279.
Coase, Ronald H. 1937. "The Nature of the Firm" in idem. *The Firm, the Market and the Law*. Chicago, IL: University of Chicago Press.
Coase, Ronald H. 2000. "The Acquisition of Fisher Body by General Motors". *Journal of Law and Economics* 43: 15–31.
Cooter, Robert, Stephen Marks, and Robert Mnookin. 1982. "Bargaining in the Shadow of the Law: A Testable Model of Strategic Behavior". *Journal of Legal Studies* 11: 225–251.
Crocker, Keith J. and Scott E. Masten. 1988. "Mitigating Contractual Hazards: Unilateral Options and Contract Length". *Rand Journal of Economics* 19: 327–343.
Crocker, Keith J. and Scott E. Masten. 1991. "Pretia Ex Machina? Prices and Process in Long-Term Contracts". *Journal of Law and Economics* 24: 69–99.
Crocker, Keith J. and Kenneth J. Reynolds. 1993. "The Efficiency of Incomplete Contracts: An Empirical Analysis of Air Force Engine Procurement". *Rand Journal of Economics* 24: 126–146.
Dahl, Carol A. and Thomas K. Matson. 1998. "Evolution of the U.S. Natural Gas Industry in Response to Changes in Transaction Costs". *Land Economics* 74: 390–408.
David, Robert J. and Shin-Kap Han. 2004. "A Systematic Assessment of the Empirical Support for Transaction Cost Economics". *Strategic Management Journal* 25: 39–58.
DeCanio, Stephen J. and H. E. Frech. 1993. "Vertical Contracts: A Natural Experiment in Natural Gas Pipeline Regulation". *Journal of Institutional and Theoretical Economics* 149: 370–392.
Delios, Andrew and Witold J. Henisz. 2000. "Japanese Firms' Investment Strategies in Emerging Economies". *Academy of Management Journal* 43: 305–323.
Dnes, Anthony. 1996. "The Economic Analysis of Franchise Contracts". *Journal of Institutional and Theoretical Economics* 152: 297–324.
Ellickson, Robert C. 1991. *Order Without Law: How Neighbors Settle Disputes*. Cambridge, MA: Harvard University Press.
Fein, A. J. and Erin Anderson. 1997. "Patterns of Credible Commitments: Territory and Brand Selectivity in Industrial Distribution Channels". *Journal of Marketing* 61: 19–34.
Fishback, Price V. 1985. "Did Coal Miners 'Owe Their Souls to the Company Store'? Theory and Evidence from the early 1900s". *Journal of Economic History* 46: 1011–1029.
Fishback, Price V. 1992. "The Economics of Company Housing: Historical Perspectives from the Coal Fields". *Journal of Law, Economics, and Organization* 8: 346–365.
Freeland, Robert F. 2000. "Creating Holdup Through Vertical Integration: Fisher Body Revisited". *Journal of Law and Economics* 43: 33–66.
Friedman, Milton. 1953. "The Methodology of Positive Economics" in idem. *Essays in Positive Economics* Chicago, IL: University of Chicago Press, pp. 3–43.
Gallick, Edward C. 1984. *Exclusive Dealing and Vertical Integration: The Efficiency of Contracts in the Tuna Industry*. Federal Trade Commission Bureau of Economics Staff Report. Washington, DC: Federal Trade Commission.
Gatignon, Hubert and Erin Anderson. 1988. "The Multinational Corporation's Degree of Control over Foreign Subsidiaries: An Empirical Test of a Transaction Cost Explanation". *Journal of Law, Economics and Organization* 4: 305–336.

Ghoshal, Sumantra, and Peter Moran. 1996. "Bad for Practice: A Critique of the Transaction Cost Theory". *Academy of Management Review* 21: 13–47.
Gibbons, Robert. 2000. "Firms and Other Relationships". Working Paper, MIT Department of Economics.
Gifford, Adam, Jr. 1993. "The Economic Organization of 17th- through mid 19th-Century Whaling and Shipping. *Journal of Economic Behavior and Organization* 20: 137–150.
Globerman, Steven and Richard Schwindt. 1986. "The Organization of Vertically Related Transactions in the Canadian Forest Products Industries". *Journal of Economic Behavior and Organization* 7: 199–212.
Goldberg, Victor. 1980. "Relational Exchange: Economics and Complex Contracts". *American Behavioral Scientist* 23: 337–352.
Goldberg, Victor and John R. Erickson. 1987. "Quantity and Price Adjustment in Long-Term Contracts: A Case Study of Petroleum Coke". *Journal of Law and Economics* 30: 369–398.
González,-Diaz, Manuel, Benito Arruñada, and Alberto Fernández. 2000. "Causes of Subcontracting: Evidence from Panel Data on Construction Firms". *Journal of Economic Behavior and Organization* 42: 167–187.
Grossman, Sanford J. and Oliver D. Hart. 1986. "The Costs and Benefits of Ownership: A Theory of Vertical and Lateral Integration". *Journal of Political Economy* 94: 691–719.
Hallwood, Paul C. 1991. "On Choosing Organizational Arrangements: The Example of Offshore Oil Gathering". *Scottish Journal of Political Economy* 38: 227–241.
Hamilton, Gillian. 1999. "Property Rights and Transaction Costs in Marriage: Evidence from Prenuptial Contracts". *Journal of Economic History* 59: 68–103.
Harrigan, Kathryn Rudie. 1986. "Matching Vertical Integration Strategies to Competitive Conditions". *Strategic Management Journal* 7: 535–555.
Hart, Oliver D. 1995. *Firms, Contracts, and Financial Structure.* New York: Oxford University Press.
Hart, Oliver D. and John Moore. 1990. "Property Rights and the Nature of the Firm". *Journal of Political Economy* 98: 1119–1158.
Heide, J. B. and G. John. 1988. "The Role of Dependence Balancing in Safeguarding Transaction-Specific Assets". *Journal of Marketing* 52: 20–35.
Heide, J. B., S. Dutta, and M. Bergen. 1998. "Exclusive Dealing and Business Efficiency: Evidence from Industry Practice". *Journal of Law and Economics* 41: 387–407.
Helper, Susan, John Paul MacDuffie, and Charles F. Sabel. 2000. "Pragmatic Collaborations: Advancing Knowledge While Controlling Opportunism". *Industrial and Corporate Change* 9: 443–483.
Henisz, Witold J. 2000. "The Institutional Environment for Multinational Investment". *Journal of Law, Economics, and Organization* 16: 334–364.
Henisz, Witold J. and Bennett A. Zelner. 2001. "The Institutional Environment for Telecommunications Investment". *Journal of Economics and Management Strategy* 10.
Hennart, Jean-Francois. 1988. "Upstream Vertical Integration in the Aluminum and Tin Industries". *Journal of Economic Behavior and Organization* 9: 281–299.
Hennart, Jean-Francois. 1989. "The Transaction Cost Rationale for Countertrade". *Journal of Law, Economics and Organization* 5: 127–153.
Holmström, Bengt and Paul Milgrom. 1994. "The Firm as an Incentive System". *American Economic Review* 84: 972–991.
Hu, M., and H. Chen. 1993. "Foreign Ownership in Chinese Joint Ventures". *Journal of Business Research* 26: 500–513.
Hubbard, R. Glenn, and Robert J. Weiner. 1991. "Efficient Contracting and Market Power: Evidence from the U.S. Natural Gas Industry". *Journal of Law and Economics* 34: 25–67.
Hubbard, Thomas N. 1999. "How Wide is the Scope of Hold-Up Based Theories of Governance? Shipper–Carrier Relations in Trucking". Working Paper, Department of Economics, UCLA.
Jensen, Michael C. and William H. Meckling. 1992. "General and Specific Knowledge, and Organizational Structure" in Lars Werin and Hans Wijkander (eds.), *Contract Economics.* Oxford: Blackwell.

John, George and Barton A. Weitz. 1988. "Forward Integration into Distribution: An Empirical Test of Transaction Cost Analysis". *Journal of Law, Economics and Organization* 4: 337–355.

Joskow, Paul L. 1985. "Vertical Integration and Long Term Contracts: The Case of Coal-Burning Electric Generating Plants". *Journal of Law, Economics and Organization* 1: 33–80.

Joskow, Paul L. 1987. "Contract Duration and Relationship-Specific Investments: Empirical Evidence from Coal Markets". *American Economic Review* 77: 168–185.

Joskow, Paul L. 1988a. "Asset Specificity and the Structure of Vertical Relationships: Empirical Evidence". *Journal of Law, Economics, and Organization* 4: 95–117.

Joskow, Paul L. 1988b. "Price Adjustment in Long-Term Contracts: The Case of Coal". *Journal of Law and Economics* 31: 47–83.

Joskow, Paul L. 1990. "The Performance of Long-Term Contracts: Further Evidence from the Coal Markets". *Rand Journal of Economics* 21: 251–274.

Kenney, Roy W. and Benjamin Klein. 1983. "The Economics of Block Booking". *Journal of Law and Economics* 26: 497–540.

Klein, Benjamin. 1988. "Vertical Integration as Organized Ownership: The Fisher Body–General Motors Relationship Revisited". *Journal of Law, Economics and Organization* 4: 199–213.

Klein, Benjamin. 2000. "Fisher–General Motors and the Nature of the Firm". *Journal of Law and Economics* 43: 105–141.

Klein, Benjamin, Robert A. Crawford, and Armen A. Alchian. 1978. "Vertical Integration, Appropriable Rents, and the Competitive Contracting Process". *Journal of Law and Economics* 21: 297–326.

Klein, Peter G. and Sandra K. Klein. 2002. "Do Entrepreneurs Make Predictable Mistakes? Evidence from Corporate Divestitures". in Nicolai J. Foss and Peter G. Klein (eds.), *Entrepreneurship and the Firm*. Aldershott, UK: Edward Elgar.

Klein, Saul, Gary L. Frazier, and Victor J. Roth. 1990. "A Transaction Cost Analysis Model of Channel Integration in International Markets". *Journal of Marketing Research* 27: 196–208.

Lafontaine, Francine. 1992. "Agency Theory and Franchising: Some Empirical Results". *Rand Journal of Economics* 23: 263–283.

Lafontaine, Francine and Kathrin Shaw. 1999. "The Dynamics of Franchise Contracting: Evidence from Panel Data". *Journal of Political Economy* 107: 1041–1080.

Lafontaine, Francine and Margaret Slade. 1997. "Retail Contracting: Theory and Practice". *Journal of Industrial Economics* 45: 1–25.

Lafontaine, Francine and Emmanuel Raynaud. 2002. "The Role of Residual Claims and Self-Enforcement in Franchise Contracting". NBER Working Paper 8868.

Lafontaine, Francine and Scott E. Masten. 2002. "Contracting in the Absence of Specific Investments and Moral Hazard: Understanding Carrier-Driver Relations in U.S. Trucking". Working Paper, University of Michigan Business School.

Langlois, Richard N. and Paul L. Robertson. 1989. "Explaining Vertical Integration: Lessons from the American Automobile Industry". *Journal of Economic History* 49: 361–375.

Levy, David. 1985. "The Transaction Cost Approach to Vertical Integration: An Empirical Examination". *Review of Economics and Statistics* 67: 438–445.

Lieberman, Marvin B. 1991. "Determinants of Vertical Integration: An Empirical Test". *Journal of Industrial Economics* 39: 451–466.

Loredo, Enrique and Eugenia Suárez. 2000. "The Governance of Transactions: Joskow's Coal-Burning Generating Plants Example Revisited". *Energy Policy* 28: 107–114.

Lyons, Bruce R. 1995. "Specific Investment, Economies of Scale, and the Make-or-Buy Decision: A Test of Transaction Cost Theory". *Journal of Economic Behavior and Organization* 26: 431–443.

MacDonald, James M. 1985. "Market Exchange or Vertical Integration: An Empirical Analysis". *Review of Economics and Statistics* 67: 327–331.
Macher, Jeffrey T. 2001. "Vertical Disintegration and Process Innovation in Semiconductor Manufacturing: Foundries vs. Integrated Device Manufacturers". Working Paper, McDonough School of Business, Georgetown University.
MacMillan, Ian C. Donald C. Hambrick, and Johannes M. Pennings. 1986. "Uncertainty Reduction and the Threat of Supplier Retaliation: Two Views of the Backward Integration Decision". *Organization Studies* 7: 263–278.
Martinez, Steve. W. 2002. "A Comparison of Vertical Coordination in the U.S. Poultry, Egg, and Pork Industries". *Current Issues in Economics of Food Markets*, Agriculture Information Bulletin No. 747-05, U.S. Department of Agriculture, Economic Research Service.
Masten, Scott E. 1984. "The Organization of Production: Evidence from the Aerospace Industry". *Journal of Law and Economics* 27: 403–417.
Masten, Scott E. 1994. "Empirical Research in Transaction-cost Economics: Challenges, Progress, Directions". Mimeo, University of Michigan Business School.
Masten, Scott E. (ed.). 1996. *Case Studies in Contracting and Organization*. New York: Oxford University Press.
Masten, Scott E. and Keith J. Crocker. 1985. "Efficient Adaptation in Long-Term Contracts: Take-or-Pay Provisions for Natural Gas". *American Economic Review* 75: 1083–1093.
Masten, Scott E., James W. Meehan, and Edward A. Snyder. 1989. "Vertical Integration in the U.S. Auto Industry: A Note on the Influence of Specific Assets". *Journal of Economic Behavior and Organization* 12: 265–273.
Masten, Scott E., James W. Meehan, and Edward A. Snyder. 1991. "The Costs of Organization". *Journal of Law, Economics and Organization* 7: 1–25.
Masten, Scott E. and Edward A. Snyder. 1993. "United States versus United Shoe Machinery Corporation: On the Merits". *Journal of Law and Economics* 36: 33–70.
Masten, Scott E. and Stéphane Saussier. 2000. "Econometrics of Contracts: An Assessment of Developments in the Empirical Literature on Contracting". *Revue d'Economie Industrielle* 215–236.
Masters, John K. and Grant Miles. 2002. "Predicting the Use of External Labor Arrangements: A Test of the Transaction Cost Perspective". *Academy of Management Journal* 45: 431–442.
Matsusaka, John G. 2001. "Corporate Diversification, Value Maximization, and Organizational Capabilities". *Journal of Business* 74: 409–431.
Ménard, Claude. 1996. "On Clusters, Hybrids and other Strange Forms. The Case of the French Poultry Industry". *Journal of Institutional and Theoretical Economics* 152: 154–183.
Ménard, Claude. 2004. "The Economics of Hybrid Organizations". *Journal of Institutional and Theoretical Economics* 160: 1–32.
Ménard, Claude and Peter G. Klein. 2004. "Organizational Issues in the Agri-Food Sector: Toward a Comparative Approach". *American Journal of Agricultural Economics* 86: 746–751.
Milgrom, Paul A. and John Roberts. 1990. "Bargaining Costs, Influence Costs, and the Organization of Economic Activity" in James E. Alt and Kenneth A. Shepsle (eds.), *Perspectives on Positive Political Economy*. Cambridge: Cambridge University Press.
Monteverde, Kirk and David J. Teece. 1982a. "Appropriable Rents and Quasi-Vertical Integration". *Journal of Law and Economics* 25: 321–328.
Monteverde, Kirk and David J. Teece. 1982b. "Supplier Switching Costs and Vertical Integration in the Automobile Industry". *Bell Journal of Economics* 13: 206–213.
Mosakowski, Elaine. 1997. "Strategy Making Under Causal Ambiguity: Conceptual Issues and Empirical Evidence". *Organization Science* 8: 414–442.

Mulherin, J. Harold. 1986. "Complexity in Long-Term Contracts: An Analysis of Natural Gas Contractual Provisions". *Journal of Law, Economics, and Organization* 2: 105–117.

Muris, Timothy J., David Scheffman, and Pablo T. Spiller. 1992. "Strategy and Transaction Costs: The Organization of Distribution in the Carbonated Soft Drink Industry". *Journal of Economics and Management Strategy* 1: 83–128.

Murtha, Thomas P. 1993. "Credible Enticements: Can Host Governments Tailor Multinational Firms' Organizations to Suit National Objectives?" *Journal of Economic Behavior and Organization* 20: 171–186.

Nelson, Richard R., and Sidney G. Winter. 1982. *An Evolutionary Theory of Economic Change*. Cambridge. MA: Harvard University Press.

Nickerson, Jackson A., Barton H. Hamilton, and Tetsuo Wada. 2001. "Market Position, Resource Profile, and Governance: Linking Porter and Williamson in the Context of International courier and Small Package Services in Japan". *Strategic Management Journal* 22: 251–273.

Nickerson, Jackson A. and Brian S. Silverman. 2003. "Why Aren't All Truck Drivers Owner Operators? Asset Ownership and the Employment Relation in Interstate For-Hire Trucking *Journal of Economics and Management Strategy* 12: 91–118.

Ohanian, Nancy Kane. 1994. "Vertical Integration in the U.S. Pulp and Paper Industry, 1900–1940". *Review of Economics and Statistics* 74: 202–207.

Oxley, Joanne E. 1997. "Appropriability Hazards and Governance in Strategic Alliances: A Transaction Cost Approach". *Journal of Law, Economics, and Organization* 13: 387–409.

Oxley, Joanne E. 1999. "Institutional Environment and the Mechanisms of Governance: The Impact of Intellectual Property Protection on the Structure of Inter-firm Alliances". *Journal of Economic Behavior and Organization* 38: 283–309.

Palay, Thomas M. 1984. "Comparative Institutional Economics: The Governance of Rail Freight Contracting". *Journal of Legal Studies* 13: 265–287.

Palay, Thomas M. 1985. "Avoiding Regulatory Constraints: Contracting Safeguards and the Role of Informal Agreements". *Journal of Law, Economics, and Organization* 1: 155–176.

Pirrong, Stephen Craig. 1993. "Contracting Practices in Bulk Shipping Markets: A Transactions Cost Explanation". *Journal of Law and Economics* 36: 937–976.

Pisano, Gary P. 1990. "Using Equity Participation to Support Exchange: Evidence from the Biotechnology Industry". *Journal of Law, Economics and Organization* 5: 109–126.

Poppo, Laura and Todd Zenger. 1995. "Opportunism, Routines, and Boundary Choices: A Comparative Test of Transaction Cost and Resource-based Explanations for Make-or-Buy Decisions". *Academy of Management Journal, Best Papers Proceedings*, pp. 42–46.

Poppo, Laura and Todd Zenger. 1998. "Testing Alternative Theories of the Firm: Transaction Cost, Knowledge-Based, and Measurement Explanations for Make-or-Buy Decisions in Information Services". *Strategic Management Journal* 19: 853–877.

Porter, Michael E. 2000. "Location, Competition and Economic Development: Local Clusters in a Global Economy". *Economic Development Quarterly* 14: 15–34.

Regan, Laureen. 1997. "Vertical Integration in the Property-Liability Insurance Industry: A Transaction Cost Approach". *Journal of Risk and Insurance* 64: 41–62.

Rindfleisch, A. and J. B. Heide. 1997. "Transaction Cost Analysis: Past, Present, and Future Applications". *Journal of Marketing* 61: 30–54.

Sampson, Rachelle C. 2001. "The Cost of Inappropriate Governance in R&D Alliances". Working Paper, Stern School of Business, New York University.

Saussier, Stéphane. 2000. "Transaction Costs and Contractual Incompleteness: The Case of Electricitie de France". *Journal of Economic Behavior and Organization* 42: 189–206.

Schotter, Andrew. 1981. *The Economic Theory of Social Institutions*. Cambridge: Cambridge University Press.

Shelanski, Howard A. and Peter G. Klein. 1995. "Empirical Research in Transaction Cost Economics: A Review and Assessment". *Journal of Law, Economics and Organization* 11: 335–361.

Silverman, Brian S. 1999. "Technological Resources and the Direction of Corporate Diversification: Toward an Integration of the Resource-Based View and Transaction Cost Economics". *Management Science* 45: 1109–1124.

Silverman, Brian S., Jackson A. Nickerson, and John B. Freeman. 1997. "Profitability, Transactional Alignment, and Organizational Mortality in the U.S. Trucking Industry". *Strategic Management Journal* (Special Issue) 18: 31–52.

Simon, Herbert A. 1992. Review of "Organization Theory: From Chester Barnard to the Present and Beyond". *Journal of Economic Literature* 30: 1503–1505. Oliver E. Williamson, ed.

Spiller, Pablo. 1985. "On Vertical Mergers". *Journal of Law, Economics and Organization* 1: 285–312.

Stuckey, John. 1983. *Vertical Integration and Joint Ventures in the Aluminum Industry.* Cambridge, MA: Harvard University Press.

Sugden, Robert. 1986. *The Economics of Rights, Cooperation, and Welfare.* Oxford: Blackwell.

Ullman-Margalit, Edna. 1977. *The Emergence of Norms.* Oxford: Clarendon Press.

Ulset, Svein. 1996. "R&D Outsourcing and Contractual Governance: An Empirical Study of Commercial R&D Projects". *Journal of Economic Behavior and Organization* 30: 63–82.

Vannoni, Davide. 2002. "Empirical Studies of Vertical Integration: The Transaction Cost Orthodoxy". *International Review of Economics and Business* 49: 113–141.

Walker, Gordon and David Weber. 1984. "A Transaction Cost Approach to Make-or-Buy Decisions". *Administrative Science Quarterly* 29: 373–391.

Weiss, Allen M. and Nancy Kurland. 1997. "Holding Distribution Channel Relationships Together: The Role of Transaction-Specific Assets and Length of Prior Relationships". *Organization Science* 8(6): 612–623.

Weiss, Avi. 1992. "The Role of Firm-Specific Capital in Vertical Mergers". *Journal of Law and Economics* 35: 71–88.

Wiggins, Steven N., and Gary D. Libecap. 1985. "Oil Field Unitization: Commercial Failure in the Presence of Imperfect Information". *American Economic Review* 75: 368–385.

Whinston, Michael D. 2000. "On the Transaction Cost Determinants of Vertical Integration". Working Paper, Department of Economics, Northwestern University.

Williamson, Oliver E. 1975. *Markets and Hierarchies: Analysis and Antitrust Implications.* New York: Free Press.

Williamson, Oliver E. 1976. "Franchise Bidding for Natural Monopolies—In General and with Respect to CATV". *Bell Journal of Economics* 7: 73–104.

Williamson, Oliver E. 1985. *The Economic Institutions of Capitalism.* New York: Free Press.

Williamson, Oliver E. 1988. "The Economics and Sociology of Organizatiton: Promoting a Dialogue" in George Farkas and Paula England (eds.), *Industries, Firms, and Jobs: Sociological and Economic Approaches.* New York: Plenum Press.

Williamson, Oliver E. 1991a. "Comparative Economic Organization: The Analysis of Discrete Structural Alternatives". *Administrative Science Quarterly* 36: 269–296.

Williamson, Oliver E. 1991b. "Strategizing, Economizing, and Economic Organization". *Strategic Management Journal* 23: 75–94.

Williamson, Oliver E. 1993. "Opportunism and its Critics". *Managerial and Decision Economics* 14: 97–107.

Williamson, Oliver E. 1996a. "Economic Organization: The Case for Candor". *Academy of Management Review* 21: 48–57.

Williamson, Oliver E. 1996b. *The Mechanisms of Governance.* New York: Oxford University Press.

Williamson, Oliver E. 2000. "The New Institutional Economics: Taking Stock, Looking Ahead". *Journal of Economic Literature* 38: 595–613.

Wilson, James A. 1980. "Adaptation to Uncertainty and Small Numbers Exchange: The New England Fresh Fish Market". *Bell Journal of Economics* 4: 491–504.

Yarbrough, Beth V. and Robert M. Yarbrough. 1987a. "Cooperation in the Liberalization of International Trade: After Hegemony, What?" *International Organization* 41: 1–26.

Yarbrough, Beth V. and Robert M. Yarbrough. 1987b. "Institutions for the Governance of Opportunism in International Trade". *Journal of Law, Economics and Organization* 3: 129–139.

Yvrande-Billon, Anne. 2004. "Contractual Choices and Performances: Evidence from the British Railways" in George Hendrikse, Josef Windsperger, Gérard Cliquet, and Mika Tuunanen (eds.), *Economics and Management of Franchising Networks*. Heidelberg: Physica/Springer, forthcoming.

18. Agricultural Contracts

DOUGLAS W. ALLEN and DEAN LUECK

1. Introduction

It is somewhat surprising that academic economists are interested in agricultural contracts given their otherwise urban affiliations. No doubt this interest arises because farming has historically been the fundamental economic enterprise of mankind. Its omnipresent place in our culture makes it a familiar context to couch otherwise abstract theoretical models. Thus we find casual reference to landowners and tenant farmers in economic theory (e.g., Sappington 1991) and, indeed, the modern theory of contracts developed in this context.[1] There is also a seemingly disproportionate amount of attention paid to agricultural contracts in literatures dealing with economic institutions. Again, this partly stems from agriculture having always been with us. Adam Smith could hardly have written about restaurant franchise contracts, but he, John Stuart Mill, and other classical economists concerned themselves with the contracting and organization of farming.

Agriculture, says Webster's Dictionary, is "the science and art of farming" and the term typically refers to a sequence of biological production stages, which in the broadest interpretation, could run from breaking land to restaurant services.[2] More typically, agriculture is thought of as a narrower set of stages than these, usually from land preparation to food processing. Still others consider agriculture to span only those production stages controlled by the "farm". Figure 1 presents various stages of production for a generic crop—animal or plant—and draws attention to the arbitrariness of what is meant by "agriculture," since drawing a firm boundary at any given stage seems almost *ad hoc*. Figure 1 also shows that the range of farm production activities has narrowed over time. In 1800 the typical North American farm would have broken the land, produced its own seeds, and carried production through to some form of crude processing and, in many cases, to marketing as well. Today, what we normally think of as "the farm" is a firm that essentially controls just the narrowest growth-based biological stages of production. For example, a wheat farmer plants the seed,

---

[1] In fact, the theory of contracts really begins with Cheung (1968) and Stiglitz (1974) and their analyses of cropshare contracts.
[2] See Webster's *New World College Dictionary*, 3rd. Edition, 1997

Typical Farm Sequence in 1800

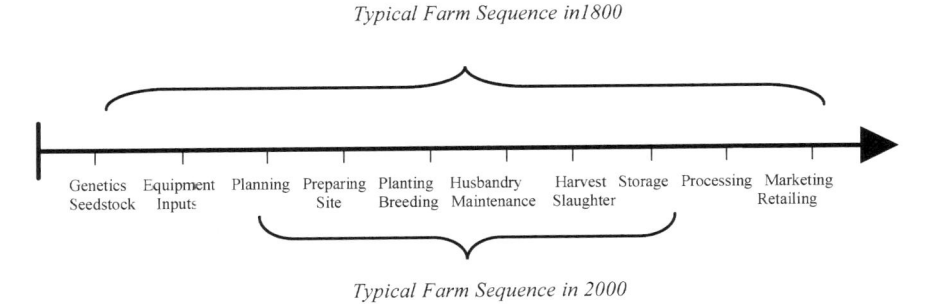

| Genetics | Equipment | Planning | Preparing | Planting | Husbandry | Harvest | Storage | Processing | Marketing |
| Seedstock | Inputs | | Site | Breeding | Maintenance | Slaughter | | | Retailing |

Typical Farm Sequence in 2000

Figure 1. The extent of agricultural production.

controls pests, and harvests the wheat. Seed development, storage, and milling into flour are routinely undertaken by separate enterprises.

The distinction between the growth-based biological stages and the other manufacturing stages is important. In this chapter, we focus on the contracts that exist over these particular growth-based biological stages. We do this for several reasons. First, our expertise lies in these stages of agriculture. Second, our data are concentrated here. And finally, for reasons that will become apparent, the contracts that exist outside of these stages generally have more in common with contracts found elsewhere in the economy, and are less unique to farming. Although we make some effort to discuss agricultural contracts over a broad number of stages, and some attention is given to international contracts, there remains a focus on the farming contracts found in North America. Still there is reason to believe the issues we examine will have application elsewhere and agriculture and other sectors of the economy.

Agriculture within the biological range, to a greater extent than most other forms of modern production, is heavily linked to Nature, and this linkage importantly affects the institution of agricultural contracts. Here 'Nature' refers to the aggregate of natural forces that can influence the outcome of agricultural production and includes the forces of climate and weather, pests, seasons, geology, and hydrology. In the aggregate, Nature not only generates random havoc and blessings on crops and livestock, but Nature also restricts the ability of farmers to specialize and exploit the gains from specialization.

In many cases the constraints of Nature, coupled with social and economic forces, lead to rather simple contracts.[3] For example, contracts between farmers and landowners tend to be enforced through the use of reputation. When agriculture includes the non-biological or non-growing stages of production, or when production is designed in such a way that Nature's role during the growing stage is minimized, contracts tend to become more complex and the organizational structure of the farm tends to move from simple family farms

---

[3] What is not explored here is the possibility that Nature's incentives are the root cause of the social and economic structures of farm communities, which in turn, influence contract structure.

Table 1. Features of typical agricultural contracts

Type	Features (parties, payment, duties)	Examples
Equipment	Farmer rents equipment on a time basis (day, month, year) or on a hourly rate of use.	Field implements, tractors.
Labor	Farmer hires labor for skilled and unskilled work. Payment can be hourly, monthly, or based on piece rates.	Equipment operation, harvesting, field work.
Land	Farmer rents land in return for cash or share of the crop. Input costs are sometimes shared.	Small grains, pasture, hay, row crops.
Marketing	Farmer agrees to deliver crops of a specific quantity and quality to a processor. Farmer and marketing firm share the revenues. Farmer controls overall production and owns the crop.	Apples and other fruit, dairy, sugar, cattle, vegetables.
Production	Farmer ('grower') agrees to produce a crop under the direction of another firm. Farmer will be required to use certain inputs and techniques and may share costs. The contracting firm will generally control production and own the crop.	Seed, vegetables, poultry, swine.
Service	Farmer hires firm to perform specific tasks. Typically, the firm provides both the labor and the specialized equipment required.	Harvesting, pest control, cattle feeding.

with simple contracts between farmers and landowners, to larger corporate firms with complicated contracts between relatively small, often family-based growers and the larger firms. For example, the introduction of antibiotics, which allowed for the intensive indoor raising of cattle, hogs, and poultry, dramatically limited major natural inputs (e.g., disease) in the production process. This allowed for corporate governance and complicated incentive contracts for the local growers.[4]

Contracting in agriculture is not, of course, limited exclusively to agreements between farmers and landowners. There are contracts for equipment, labor, marketing, production, and services. These contracts use various methods of payment (e.g., hours for tractors, revenue share for marketing) and impose various duties on both farmers and other contracting parties. These duties include sharing input costs, using specified techniques, and performing tasks at specified times. The contracts can be simple and short-term, or they can be complicated and long-term. Table 1 summarizes some the features of these contracts and shows where they are most commonly found.[5] For example, marketing contracts for fruits, dairy, sugar, and many vegetables are often established between

---

[4] For examples of complex agricultural production see Frank and Henderson (1992), Fulton (1995), Knoeber (1989), Kleibenstein and Lawrence (1995), Knoeber and Thurman (1994), Lazzarini et al (2001), Martinez and Reed (1996), Menard (1996), and Sauvee (2002).

[5] Roy (1963) gives an early account of contracting practices in agriculture. See Perry et al. (1997) for a more recent account, which finds that such contracts cover almost one-third of the value of farm production in the United States.

the farmer and a processor. In these contracts, although the farmer (or "grower") typically controls production, he is partly integrated with the processing firm and agrees to deliver a specific quantity and quality of crop, usually at a specific time. For poultry, swine, and some vegetables, farmers enter into production contracts where the farmer agrees to produce a crop under the direction of another firm. In these contracts the farmer is often required to use certain inputs and techniques, and may share costs with the firm.

In this chapter, our focus is contracts for land, equipment, and labor; and not contracts for marketing, production and services. We begin by describing the structure and extent of contracts for land, equipment, and labor. We do this in non-theoretical manner in order to lay out the unique features of agricultural contracts we believe need explaining. In Section 3 we develop the transaction cost framework for examining such contracts and contrast this approach to more traditional principle-agent models. Once this theoretical base is developed we apply it in the last section, which examines the empirical evidence that explains the variance in these contracts discussed in Section 2.

2. DESCRIPTION OF CONTRACTS

We rely on several key data sources for our understanding of agricultural contracts. Two data sets contain information on more than 3,000 contracts from Nebraska and South Dakota for the 1986 crop year. Two additional data sets contain information on more than 1,000 farms and nearly 2,500 plots of land (both owned and leased) from British Columbia and Louisiana during the 1992 crop year.[6] Although our detailed data do not represent all the different types of agriculture practiced in North America, they are representative of large and important sectors, especially those involving small grains and row crops. We make use of other data and studies when they are available. In addition to information on land contracts, these data include information on the ownership of land, buildings, and equipment. We also use publicly available data from the censuses of agriculture in both Canada and the United States. Along with these statistical datasets we use historical data on industries and case studies as well as the findings from studies of other economists. We do not discuss data related to Europe or LDC's, except for a few historical cases. There is, however, a growing literature that examines agricultural contracts in these regions.

---

[6] These data are described in Allen and Lueck (2002) but a few more details can be offered here. The data from Nebraska and South Dakota come from the *1986 Nebraska and South Dakota Leasing Survey*, which has 1,615 observations for Nebraska and 1,155 for South Dakota, in which each observation represents a single farmer or landowner for the 1986 crop season. The main data for British Columbia and Louisiana come from two surveys we conducted in January 1993, for the 1992 crop year. There were 460 usable responses for British Columbia and 530 for Louisiana. Unlike the Nebraska/South Dakota data, these data do not have detailed information on landowners who lease to farmers, or information on input sharing within cropshare contracts. They do, however, have information on ownership of land and other assets.

Land Leases

Farmland leases take two basic forms: cropshare and cash rent. A *cropshare* contract is an agreement between a landowner and a farmer for the use of farmland.[7] The contracts are called "crop" shares because the two parties share the physical output, as opposed to the revenue generated by the crop. Cropshare contracts typically require the farmer to compensate the landowner only in terms of the harvested crop, and tend not to have additional cash payments. Although the cropshares vary—from as low as 20% for the farmer to as high as 90%—the overwhelming majority of observed shares are between 50% to 75% and tend to be simple fractions (e.g., 1/2, 2/3, 3/5, and 3/4). Worldwide, 50% appears to be the most common output share, although in North America the three most common shares (the share kept by the farmer) are 50%, 60%, and 67%, which are often called "halves", "fifths", and "thirds" by farmers.[8] The source of these dominant fractions is not clear, although Young and Burke (2001) attempt to explain this custom using a model of evolutionary focal points.

The farmer may pay for all of the inputs (e.g., seed, fertilizer, harvesting) or share these input costs with the landowner. Sharing input costs is almost always done in a dichotomous fashion, with the input share either equaling the output share, or equaling 100% for the farmer. This means that if the farmer and landowner are sharing output 50/50, then when inputs are being shared, they are also shared 50/50. If inputs are not shared, then the farmer almost always pays for them. When inputs are not shared, then the share of output to the farmer is always higher.[9]

The primary alternative form of land contract in agriculture is a *cash rent* contract. In a cash rent contract, the farmer pays the landowner a fixed monetary sum for the exclusive use of the land for a specific period. Usually the payment is made before the crop is harvested, but sometimes a series of payments is spread out over the year. The cash rent prices (usually delineated in dollars per acre) tend to vary more than do the shares paid by a farmer in a cropshare contract. Also, unlike cropshare contracts, in cash rent contracts farmers typically do not share input costs with the landowner. Occasionally cash rent contracts will have an "adjustment" clause in them, increasing the rent if there is an exceptionally good or "bumper" crop. The 1986 Nebraska—South Dakota data show that about ten percent of the cash contracts have such clauses. Finally, cash rent contracts are more sensitive than cropshare contracts to differences in economic fundamentals, such as land quality, input prices, and tract size.

To see the distinction between these two types of contracts, let the farmer's payment for a plot of land be $\alpha + (1-s)Q$ where Q is farm output, s is the

---

[7] In the law of property, a temporary agreement for the exclusive and possessory use of land is called a 'lease,' thus we use the terms contract and lease synonymously for farmland.

[8] For example, in our Nebraska-South Dakota sample (from 1986) these values account for 23.7%, 36%, and 32.3% of the contracts, or 92% of the total.

[9] See chapter 5 in Allen and Lueck (2002). Young and Burke (2001) also find this pattern in their analysis of cropshare contracts in Illinois.

Table 2. Some features of modern farmland contracts

	United States	Canada	British Columbia	Louisiana	Nebraska	South Dakota
General Information, 1996–1997						
Acres leased (%)	41	37	19	54	43	38
Average lease size (acres)	494	553	282	397	680	906
Average land value ($/acre)	$933	$848	$2,274	$1,206	$645	$348
Cash Leases, 1999						
All leases (%)	57	NA	71	47	42	57
Leased acreage (%)	59	NA	72	45	52	55
Share Leases, 1999						
All leases (%)	21	NA	29	35	42	29
Leased acreage (%)	24	NA	28	43	30	27

Source: Allen and Lueck (2002, Table 2.4). NA = 4 no data available.

farmer's share and α is a fixed payment. In a cropshare contract, $\alpha = 0$ and $0 > s > 1$, but in a cash rent contract $\alpha > 0$ and $s = 1$. In a cash rent contract with an adjustment clause the farmer pays $\alpha + sQ^*$ where Q^* is a specified output level beyond which $0 > s > 1$ and below which $s = 1$. What the data show is that for cropshare contracts the actual values of s are quite discrete (0.5, 0.6, 0.75) and are usually no higher than $s = .75$ or $s = .8$. For cash rent contracts, however, α varies almost continuously when $s = 1$. In this respect it is not correct to think of a cash rent contract as just an extreme cropshare contract with a share of one since a smooth continuum of share contracts does not exist.

In many non-agricultural settings, exchanges are governed by rather complicated contracts that explicitly denote dates, individuals, locations, prices, products, qualities, quantities, and contingencies for changing conditions.[10] Contracts often extend for many years and may have complicated procedures in case of breach, dissolution, or changing economic conditions. In agriculture, however, cropshare and cash rent contracts are surprisingly simple, often just oral agreements lasting only a year or two. If the contracts are written, they tend to be less than one full page. Written contracts contain minimal information, such as plot location, names of parties, and dates of tenure. Most interesting is that these contracts tend not to contain detailed descriptions regarding duties, techniques, or other farming practices.[11]

Both cash rent and cropshare leases are very common in North America.[12] Table 2 shows some basic features of modern farmland contracts. The table shows that farmland leasing accounts for about 40% of all acres farmed in both

---

[10] There are also simple contracts outside of agriculture, as Macauley (1963) first pointed out.

[11] Agricultural land leases are often between family members. In our Nebraska and South Dakota data, 44.3% of land contracts are between family members. In our British Columbia and Louisiana data, 25.8% of the contracts are between family members. Although we cannot distinguish "neighbors" in the data, our casual observation is that this group would account for most of the remaining contracts.

[12] Gray et al. (1924) note that leasing was widespread in early twentieth century America and that cash rent and cropshare contracts were the dominant forms.

Canada and the United States. Depending on whether they are measured by the number of leases or by the acreage, just under 60% of these leases are cash rent and between 20 and 25% are cropshares.[13] It is also clear from the table that the distribution of type of contract varies across different regions. In 1999 Nebraska cropshare leases accounted for 42% of the land leases, while they accounted for 29% of all leases in South Dakota. Despite the commonly held view that cropsharing is a phenomena only found in developing countries, it is clear that cropshare contracts do not evaporate in modern economies. North America is arguably the most developed economy in the world, yet cropshare contracts still dominate cash rent contracts in important farming regions.

Equipment Contracts

Although farmland leases are the most common agricultural contract analyzed by economists, farmers also contract for the use of equipment—both general (e.g., tractors) and specialized (e.g., swathers). The value of a major piece of equipment relative to a typical plot of land on a farm varies by location and type of farming. In some situations, farmers might have more wealth tied to their farm equipment than to other assets. For example, a half section (320 acres) of dry wheat land may be worth $128,000 at $400 per acre. A large modern combine or tractor would easily be worth more than $100,000. Thus equipment contracts are often as important as land contracts in terms of the value of the contracted assets.

Although the data are limited, equipment is much more likely to be owned than rented, and is much more likely to be owned compared to farmland. Farmers often hold large inventories of infrequently used equipment like combines, cultivators, harvesters, and sprayers. In this sense it is common to casually state that farmers own too much capital. Many of these expensive assets are used for surprisingly short periods and are simply held in inventory the remainder of the year. Table 3 shows this pattern quite dramatically for British Columbia and Louisiana (our two data sets with this information) where equipment and building ownership accounts for 98–100 percent of the assets examined.[14] For example, of the tractors used by the farmers, in British Columbia 99% were owned and in Louisiana 96% were owned.

When farmers rent equipment such as combines and tractors they are typically charged by the hour or some other unit of time (e.g., day, week, month).[15] The

---

[13] The remainder are divided between cash leases with adjustment clauses (just 5.6% of the cash contracts), cash-share combination leases (about 10.5% of all leases), and 'other' leases (about 10.5% of all leases). See *1999 Agricultural Economics and Landownership Survey*, Table 98.

[14] Irwin and Smith (1972) note that relatively little equipment is leased in agriculture compared to non-agricultural industries where leasing of automobiles, trucks, and large-scale equipment is routine. In recent years, however, year-long leasing of tractors has become more common. Our data are unlikely to represent combine ownership rates for the wheat producing regions of the Great Plains, where it is common for a farmer to own one combine but hire many others during the prime harvest season.

[15] Tractors prices vary with horsepower, so rates are often discussed in terms of "horsepower hours." See Edwards and Meyer (1986) and Pflueger (1994) for some details on modern farm equipment leasing.

Table 3. Fraction of farmer owned assets: British Columbia and Louisiana, 1992

Asset	British Columbia	Louisiana
Land	82%	38%
Equipment		
Tractors	99%	96%
Harvestors	99%	96%
Cultivators	100%	97%
Planters	100%	98%
Trucks	99%	98%
Sprayers	100%	98%
Other	99%	92%
Buildings		
House	99%	92%
Shop	97%	78%
Barn	99%	85%
Storage	98%	78%
Other	99%	94%

Source: Allen and Lueck (2002, Table 2.9).

firms that lease out equipment tend to be local farm implement dealers that deal primarily in the sale of farm equipment. Equipment leases are usually written and usually last less than a year.[16] In fact, equipment is seldom rented for an entire season and is often rented for only a particular stage of production. This means that for certain kinds of equipment, during crucial stages, farmers in a locale demand the equipment at the same time.

Even though farmers have under-utilized equipment, they often use multiple pieces of the same or similar machines as well (e.g., combines, tractors, trucks). Farmers who use more than one machine are much more likely to rent the secondary machines than own them. Farmers often attempt to lower capital costs by sharing equipment with neighbors. However, since farmers in a locale often need the equipment at the same time the types of shared equipment are limited to those machines for which timeliness costs are small.[17] Equipment that is specialized to a crop (e.g., cotton gin) or to a specific stage (e.g., planting, harvesting) is seldom shared or contracted for.

Of particular interest among equipment contracts, and a subject that has escaped the attention of most economists, is that of custom contracting. In agriculture, the term "custom" refers to the practice of contracting for equipment and an operator (often the owner) at the same time. In a typical case, a farmer may contract for a plane to do crop spraying and hire the pilot as well. Farmers also hire custom firms for baling, cultivating, fertilizer and pesticide application, feed grinding, fencing, hauling, land clearing, planting, plowing, and seed

---

[16] Most long-term (greater than one year) equipment leases have options to buy (Pflueger 1994).

[17] The contractual implications of timing are discussed in Section 3 below.

cleaning (Strikler, Smith and Walker 1966). By far, the most important custom contracting is for grain harvesting. And by far the most important custom grain harvesting is the 1,000-mile south-to-north migration of harvesters that takes place in the wheat belt of the Great Plains. A 1971 study by the USDA showed that nearly 3,500 custom combiners or "cutters" harvested 35% of the wheat on the Great Plains (Lagrone and Gavett 1975). In 1997, roughly 2,000 custom cutters harvested one-half of the United State's wheat crop (DuBow 1999). Overall, however, all custom work comprises just two percent of all U.S. farm expenses.[18] Although some cutters work only locally, more than 90% make the long interstate journeys.

Contracts between custom combiners and farmers have a structure that dates back to the 1940s when the industry had its first major expansion. Since that time cutters have been paid according to a three-part formula that includes a per-acre fee for cutting, a per-bushel fee for hauling grain to a local storage site, and a per-bushel fee for high yield crops (usually over 20 bushels per acre). Today the typical contract is "13/13/13" which means: $13 per acre of harvested wheat, 13 cents per bushel hauled, and 13 cents per bushel added to the per-acre charge for high yields.[19] In unusual cases—drought, hail, long hauls, or wind—special harvest rates would be developed to suit both parties.

As with agricultural contracts in general, farmers and cutters rely heavily on verbal agreements, enforced with handshakes and the possibility of renewal.[20] As Isern (1981, p. 92) notes:

> The unwritten code of custom combining was a flexible one, but the person who stretched it beyond reason suffered the consequences. The custom cutter who failed to live up to his obligations to a farmer found it hard to obtain work in the locality the next year. Likewise, if a farmer reneged on an agreement, the word spread among custom cutters working the area, and the farmer might be left with no harvesters at all.

Labor Contracts

Of all contracts related to agriculture, labor contracts seem to resemble contracts outside agriculture the most. For land contracts, sharing is important; and for equipment contracts, under-utilization is obvious; yet nothing particularly striking or unusual is apparent in agricultural labor contracts. No doubt, this results from the limited role that hired labor plays in most farming contexts.

---

[18] This shows how distinctive the custom grain harvest is. See *1997 Census of Agriculture*, Table 3 "Farm Production Expenses." The census does not collect data on specific custom services.

[19] According to Isern (1981), this formula was typically 3/3/3 when it first emerged in the early 1940s. The high yield payment compensates the cutter for slower progress (in terms of acres) with higher yields and greater wear and tear on the machines.

[20] Our information on this is limited but contracts for equipment rental from farm implement dealers are more formal, written agreements, much like those used when renting a car.

Table 4. Farm labor contracts

Duties	Wage	Salary	Piece
General farming	1,016	210	5
Supervisory	43	128	0
Harvest	157	5	169

Source: Allen and Lueck, *British Columbia and Louisiana Farmland Ownership and Leasing Survey* (1993).

Farming is dominated by family farms where the farmer (or members of his family) provides most of the labor services.[21]

Table 4 provides a breakdown of the types of tasks performed on farms and the types of labor contracts offered, according to our data on labor contracts. The table shows a pattern familiar to most labor contracts. When laborers engage in general farm duties, such as cleaning barns, mending fences, and operating basic equipment, wages are the dominant form of compensation. When workers are take on supervisory or management roles, such as foreman, office worker, or manager, they are often paid by monthly salary. Finally, when workers are hired for harvest, both wage and piece rate contracts are used.

3. TRANSACTION COSTS AND THE NEW INSTITUTIONAL ECONOMICS

The New Institutional Economics (NIE) is based on the premise that positive transaction costs lead to incomplete property rights. When transaction costs are zero, it does not matter how ownership of inputs and outputs is distributed by the terms of a contract. Farmers can control land through cash leases, share contracts, or ownership; farmers can own or rent their equipment in any proportion; and labor produces an equal amount of output under any compensation scheme. These applications of Coase (1960), of course, apply to other aspects of agricultural organization. If transaction costs are zero, then a farm could be a family-run sole proprietorship or a large scale corporation. Farms could be integrated completely—from breaking ground to baking the bread—or disintegrated to the point of owning a wheat field for one day.

Differences in how contracts assign property rights are thus explained by differences in transaction costs. This focus on transaction costs will allow us to explain the variation in contract types across and within the various assets described in the last section. In the broadest sense, the NIE extends beyond the transaction cost focus in this chapter to customs, norms, politics, and other institutions. Studies of agriculture by Anderson and Lueck (1992), Alston, Libecap, and Mueller (2000), and Deininger and Feder (2001) fit into this category, though our focus is primarily on the private incentives in various types of contracts.

---

[21] The main exception to this would be migrant farm labor for the harvesting of fruits and vegetables, especially along the Pacific Coast.

Transaction Costs and Property Rights

In this chapter transaction costs are defined as the costs of enforcing and maintaining property rights—regardless of whether a market exchange takes place or not, and include the deadweight losses that result from enforcing property rights (Allen 2000, Barzel 1997). As a result, transaction costs are more than the costs of a market exchange. That is, property rights may be required to be enforced in a private contract, through courts or other third party agencies, against thieves, or across market transactions. Thus, the transaction cost approach subsumes traditional moral hazard incentives but also includes the monitoring and enforcement of shared assets.[22]

Farm contracts ultimately depend on transaction costs as the parties attempt to police their interactions with each other. Although farmers enter into contracts with various parties (e.g., custom combiners, laborers, landowners, pesticide applicators, storage firms), these contracts are never complete, and problems arise in their enforcement due to Nature's uncertainty and the complexity of the assets involved in production. Farmers can hide bales of hay that were intended to be shared with landowners; harvest crews can arrive late, causing a reduction in crop value; and of course, workers can generally shirk their duties. The efforts to engage in these activities and the efforts to prevent them, along with any lost gains from trade that result, are transaction costs. In this context contracts are designed to mitigate transaction costs, given the constraints imposed by the particular farming technology, the role of Nature, and the potential gains from specialization.

Transaction Costs Versus Principal-Agent Approaches

The transaction cost approach to contracts assumes that everyone is risk neutral, and relies on a trade-off between different incentive margins to explain contractual terms. This approach contrasts with the dominant economic approach to contracting—the traditional Principal-Agent (P-A) model—which assumes contracts are designed to balance risk against moral hazard incentives. Despite the prominence of the risk-sharing paradigm (Newberry and Stiglitz 1979, Hayami and Otsuka 1993), the empirical evidence to support its implications is scarce, especially for agriculture.[23] In one of the early studies to confront risk-sharing and contract choice, Rao (1971) found that crops with high yield and profit variability were less likely to be sharecropped than crops with low yield and profit variability—a refutation of the P-A model. Using data from several thousand farmland leases, Allen and Lueck (1999, 2002) present a series

---

[22] This approach is broader than that of Hart (1995), who stresses investments in specific assets.
[23] See Allen and Lueck (2002), Masten and Saussier (2000), and Prendergast (1999, 2000) for summaries of the evidence. Salanie (1997) is a good summary of the modern P-A approach. Salanie (p. 5) also describes the Principal-Agent model as "allocating all bargaining power to one of the parties;" it is "therefore a Stackelberg game" in which the Principal gets the entire surplus.

of empirical tests that find virtually no support for the risk-sharing approach. In a variety of empirical tests, they find no support for the general hypothesis that share contracts are more likely to be chosen over cash rent contracts when crop riskiness increases. In fact, there is evidence the relationship is the opposite; that is, as crop riskiness increases, cash rent contracts are often more likely (Allen and Lueck 1995, 2002, and Prendergast 2000, 2002). This result holds across all crops and regions examined in Allen and Lueck (2002).[24]

Compared to the basic P-A model, the transaction cost approach does not explicitly distinguish between principals and agents, nor does it make differential assumption about the risk preferences of the contracting parties. In modern farming it is especially difficult to establish such a dichotomy because farmers and landowners have nearly identical demographic characteristics. Both farmers and landowners make decisions, so formal models more in line with double moral hazard are more appropriate (e.g., Eswaran and Kotwal 1985, Prendergast 2002).[25] More importantly, by diverting attention away from risk-sharing—which is hard to test and has thus far generated little empirical support—the approach opens the door to a wider array of pure incentive effects that shape organization.

Transaction Costs and Agriculture

There are four facets of the transaction cost approach that are important for the study of agricultural contracts. First, *all agricultural inputs and outputs are complex, in the sense that they are composed of many attributes*. When goods are complex they create an opportunity for transaction costs to arise for every attribute. This subsequently allows for ownership to be divided over the various attributes because multi-dimension goods are costly to measure. This means that property rights to all assets—buildings, equipment, human capital, and land—are imperfect. Land, for example, is comprised of features that include terrain, nutrients, moisture, and soil type, but contracts for land typically only specify the amount of land in terms of surface area. Many, if not most, of the attributes of the land are not explicitly specified. Different ownership and contract types affect the various attributes in different ways, creating trade-offs. These trade-offs allow us to explain the choice of contract or related organization.

---

[24] Outside the area of agriculture a series of papers have found similar results. See, for instance, Hallagan (1978), Martin (1988), Lafontaine (1992), Leffler and Rucker (1991), Lyon and Hackett (1993) and the summary in Prendergast (2002). Ackerberg and Botticini (2002), however, argue that risk sharing might still be important in contract choice if one takes into account the endogenous matching of farmers with different risk preferences and lands suitable to crops of varying risk. Nearly all of this literature can be criticized though for data that does not reliably measure exogenous risk.

[25] Even here the distinction between transaction cost approaches and recent advances in agency theory or contract theory is not clear. The work of Holmström and Milgrom (1991), Lazear (1995) and Prendergast (2002), for example, is clearly a departure from the traditional P-A approach, though none of these authors would likely consider their work part of the transaction cost literature.

Second, *uncertainty is a necessary input into production*. The presence of Nature's uncertainty is the source of moral hazard, on both sides of the contract. Nature allows one party to exploit an exchange at the expense of the other party because it masks their actual effort. This factor is important in agriculture because weather, pests, and other natural phenomenon contribute so much to the final output. In a land lease, for example, uncertainty from weather and other natural forces means that the farmer has the opportunity to "exploit" the landowner in several ways: under-supplying effort; over using soil quality attributes; and under-reporting the shared crop, to name a few.

Third, Nature also has a *systematic factor we call seasonality*. Seasonality refers to crop cycles, the number and length of stages, and timeliness costs. For any given crop or livestock, there is a natural order of production: planting comes before cultivation, which is always followed by harvest. For winter wheat in Texas this means planting in the fall and harvesting in late spring or early summer. The predictable aspect of Nature—its seasonality—limits the degree to which farmers can specialize in production (Allen and Lueck 1998, 2002). Seldom is a farmer able to specialize in one task, due to seasonality. A farmer who only plowed or only planted, would be unemployed for most of the year. Most types of farm output are greatly restricted by Nature in terms of how they can be produced. Both plant and animal crops have "growing seasons" that restrict the nature of farm production. As a result, farmers are seldom able to realize potential forms of economies of size. And since individuals are engaged in many tasks, monitoring costs are high. Thus, the force of the seasons often limits farm organization to seemingly small family-based firms, which forgo gains from specialization in return for a nearly complete reduction in moral hazard. Seasonality also influences the use and type of contracts because its presence makes the net gain from ownership and integration larger than it would be, otherwise. In cases where seasonality is less important we expect contracting for farm assets to be more prevalent. *Timeliness costs* are the forgone values from lower crop yields or quality that result from not completing tasks (e.g., planting, cultivating, spraying, harvesting) at the optimal time (Short and Gitu 1991). In many types of agriculture these costs are substantial; waiting a day to harvest wheat might mean a complete crop loss from a hail or wind storm. The structure of contracts and farm organization is thus expected to create incentives to minimize these costs.[26]

Fourth, contracts are chosen to *maximize the expected value of the relationship*, given the characteristics of the contracting parties, the desired output, and the attributes of assets such as land and equipment. This method assumes that natural selection has resulted in the most valuable contract or organization being chosen (Alchian 1950 and Coase 1960). The contracts observed are not the result of inert culture or custom, nor are they the result of one-sided bargaining. In the transaction cost approach, competition is assumed to extend to the nature of the contract. Thus, only those contracts which maximize the gains from trade

---

[26] Allen and Lueck (2002) discuss the implications of timeliness costs.

will survive. By focusing on joint wealth maximization, we ignore issues of bargaining and surplus division. We now use this transaction cost approach to explain the contracting details discussed above.

4. EXPLAINING AGRICULTURAL CONTRACTS

The implications of the theoretical literature on contracts, including agricultural contracts, has been tested against data using econometric methods, often with limited dependent variables, and case study and historical data. A typical empirical specification of contract choice has been as in equations 1.1 and 1.2, where for any contract i the complete model is:

$$C_i^* = X_i \beta_i + \varepsilon_i \quad i = 1, \ldots, n; \tag{1}$$

and

$$C_i = \begin{cases} 1, & \text{if } C_i^* > 0 \\ 0, & \text{if } C_i^* \leq 0 \end{cases} \tag{2}$$

where C_i^* is an unobserved farmland contract response variable; C_i is the observed dichotomous choice of contract structure for contract i (be it a plot of land or a piece of equipment); X_i is a row vector of exogenous variables including the constant; β_i is a column vector of unknown coefficients; and ε_i is a contract-specific error term.

Using this basic specification, for example, a logit or probit model is used to estimate the determinants of the choice between a cropshare and cash rent land lease.[27] In the traditional P-A model, measures of risk or risk preferences are used as explanatory variables (e.g., Garen 1994, Gaynor and Gertler 1995). In the transaction cost framework, explanatory variables include measures of differential costs of measuring shared inputs and outputs, the degree of asset specificity, and the differential costs of moral hazard. In an agricultural setting, this requires contract-level data on the characteristics of the land, the relevant crops, and the contracting parties.[28] We report some of the basic findings below and add case study and historical data as well. In the process, we document the history of economic thought on the various contract questions.

---

[27] Outside of agriculture, empirical studies in this tradition include Crocker and Masten (1988), Laffontaine (1991), and Leffler and Rucker (1990). Shelanski and Klein (1995) and Chiappori and Salanie (2000) summarize this literature. Knoeber (2000) is a survey that focuses on agriculture.

[28] The standard econometric pitfalls are present but perhaps the most important one for this kind of work is the possible unavailability of truly exogenous explanatory variables. The possibility of endogenous matching (Ackerberg and Botticinni 2002) of contracting parties raises new questions about the appropriateness of the general specification used above. The most important endogeneity problem is likely to be that associated with measures of 'risk.' Indeed, most empirical studies that test the P-A model use data that does not address the problem of endogenous risk. In the analysis here, given the biological stages we are concerned with, many variables (e.g., crop choice) are often determined by the exogenous conditions of nature.

Simple Contracts for Land

As noted in Section 2, farmland leases are strikingly simple and often oral contracts. Allen and Lueck (2002) report that 58 percent of the Nebraska-South Dakota leases (from 1986) were oral and 54 percent of the British Columbia leases (from 1992) were oral.[29] Farmland contracts also tend not to stipulate in detail how the land will be farmed; rather, they require the farmer use the land in a "good and husband-like" manner, a term used by lawyers and judges. Not only are these contracts typically oral and simple, they are most often annual agreements, subject to automatic renewal, unless one party makes an early commitment not to renew. In our Nebraska - South Dakota data, 65 percent of the contracts are annual, while for our Louisiana - British Columbia data, 59 percent are annual. Sometimes the agreements are for several years, but rarely are they longer than five years. They are, however, typically renewed for extended periods, even up to 30 years.

Why are these farmland contracts so simple, even though the value of the assets at stake is quite large? Several transaction costs features of agricultural contracts explain the seemingly naive contracts. First, specific assets (Klein, Crawford and Alchian 1978, Williamson 1979) are often relatively minor, so that long-term contracts are not needed to prevent holdup problems.[30] Second, in close-knit farming communities, market enforcement of contracts via reputation (Klein and Leffler 1981) serves to reduce the need to use detailed written contracts.[31] Third, in areas where farming has been long practiced, the common law has developed default rules that define the behavior of farmers and landowners, again rendering detailed contracts superfluous.[32]

Empirical estimates from Allen and Lueck (1992b, 2002), using the data described above, show that contracts are longer when there are specific assets present (e.g., irrigation systems) and that older farmers (with well developed reputations) use oral contracts more often. These findings come from logit regression estimates of the choice between oral and written contracts and the choice between annual and multi-year contracts. In situations where specific

---

[29] Recent studies from Illinois, Kansas, and Oklahoma all show that a majority of farmland leases are oral. See Sotomayer, Ellinger and Barry (2000), Tsoodle and Wilson (2000), and Burkhart (1991).

[30] In cases where specific assets are important, long term contracts and even vertical integration dominate (Joskow 1987). In farming specific investments are often made with irrigation. An important special case of specificity relates to "time specificity," particularly in the harvest and delivery of perishable products. Specific investments may be more important with industrial farming methods, and in these contexts we do not expect simple contracts. Again, these issues arise more in stages outside the biological stages we focus on. One area where specific assets might be important is for orchards in rather uneven terrain (e.g., Columbia River region in the Pacific Northwest). Here the subtleties of aspect, elevation and slope can generate specific knowledge about a plot of land that only a long term farmer might have.

[31] Ellickson (1991) is a detailed study of enforcement in the shadow of the law among members of homogeneous groups.

[32] Burkhart (1991) notes that farm leases contain an implied covenant to work the farm in a "farmer-like manner"—meaning that if the tenant does not use good farming practices, the covenant is breached and the landlord can recover damages. What constitutes a 'farmer-like manner' can be shown by custom, practices of area farmers, or county extension agents.

assets are important, where repeated interaction is limited and where the common law is not well developed, we expect more detailed written contracts to dominate, both inside and outside of agriculture. Our data on the complexity of agricultural contracts is thin beyond farmland leases but we have some anecdotal information that is consistent with the findings above. First, contracts for short term or part time labor are simple, oral agreements (compared to complex, contingent-ridden contracts for professional baseball players or corporate CEOs). Contracts for equipment are more complicated and written, and contracts for marketing and processing are quite detailed. Although many agricultural settings have parameters that make simple contracts the value maximizing choice, there is no reason this needs to be unique to agriculture.[33]

Even farmland contracts can be quite detailed, when the conditions for simple contracts are not met. Consider the case of land leases on the Great Plains during the late 1800's and early 1900's. During this time large so-called Bonanza farms arose on the plains along the Minnesota—North Dakota border and their owners often leased out land in relatively small plots (e.g., 100–200 acres). In sharp contrast to the simple (annual and oral) contracts that dominate modern farmland leases, these leases were remarkably detailed and always seem to have been written. Typically these contracts were several single-spaced typed pages detailing the often complicated terms of payment; the method, depth, and time of plowing; the amount of fallow land; and the time and type of seeding (Allen and Lueck 2002). The relative complexity of these contracts is consistent with the discussion above. In this region, the common law was simply undeveloped and settlements were still being established, so a stable community did not yet exist. There were no common law default rules, so contracting parties needed to specify, in detail, the sorts of things that would now simply fall under the category of good husbandry. Also, because communities had not yet developed, market enforcement via reputation was unlikely to have been important.

Cropshare vs. Cash Rent

Perhaps the oldest contractual issue dealt with by economists has been the question: Under which conditions would a farmer and landowner contract for land with a cash rent as opposed to a cropshare contract? Adam Smith (1776) argued that the cropshare acted as an inefficient tax on effort. In contrast to Smith, John Stuart Mill (1871) offered a much more balanced and surprisingly modern approach to cropsharing and cash renting.[34] Writing roughly a century later than Smith, Mill agreed that France and Italy had a great deal of cropsharing and that this did act as a tax on effort. Mill, however, surveyed several contemporary writers at the time, noting that cropshare contracts had been in existence a long

---

[33] For example, in small towns it is common for homes and apartments to be rented with simple oral agreements.

[34] Cheung (1968) discusses the evolution of thought on this topic among Smith, Mill and the neoclassical economists who followed. See also Allen and Lueck (2002, chapter 4).

time, that the level of cultivation was not overtly suffering, and that there was a great deal of variation in the contracts across the region. Mill, in great contrast to Smith, concluded that at the very least, the subject required more study.

Smith's tax analogy, however, influenced Alfred Marshall and other neoclassical economists who later analyzed the problem, and the dominant view came to be that cropshare contracts were an inefficient choice compared to cash rent. Johnson (1950) raised the same question that Mill had made a hundred years earlier: if cropsharing is so inefficient, then why are so many Iowa farmers and landowners using it? Not until Cheung (1968) extended the Coase Theorem (1960) into share cropping did the modern analysis begin. Cheung demonstrates that if transaction costs were zero, then all contracts must be equivalent, and that, therefore, contract choice must depend on transaction costs. Still, Cheung developed a single margin model of farmer effort and, like Stiglitz (1974), traded off farmer effort moral hazard against farmer risk avoidance. In this P-A framework cropshare contracts create farmer moral hazard but they also allow the farmer to avoid risk.

During the 1970's and 1980's dozens of articles were written on the choice between cropshare and cash rent contracts, with an overwhelming reliance on the traditional P-A model. A major shift came when Eswaran and Kotwal (1985) introduced multiple margins of moral hazard in a model with risk neutral contracting parties. Holmström and Milgrom (1991) used a similar approach in the context of a standard P-A model. Allen and Lueck (1992), using the notions of multiple margins for moral hazard, identified the important margins for contract choice in agriculture. All of these studies, and recent work by Luporini and Parigi (1996) and Prendergast (2002) represent a shift away from the traditional P-A model.

Within this risk neutral, multiple margins framework, the choice between cash rent and cropshare contracts can be explained by focusing on a simple tradeoff. Cash rent contracts provide perfect incentives for farmer effort, but because the farmer's rent is based on the amount of land farmed and not the amount of soil exploited, the cash rent contract provides an incentive to overuse the land. In particular, farmers have an incentive to exploit the valuable water and nutrient attributes, which will enhance their crops. Cropshare contracts, on the other hand, generate moral hazard costs for farmer effort, but this implies that the farmer has less incentive to overwork the land. This reduction in soil exploitation is the benefit of the cropshare contract. Cropshare contracts do not always dominate cash rent contracts because they also contain an incentive for the farmer to under-report the crop. For example, when a farmer has to pay the landowner every other bale of hay in a 50–50 contract, every bale he under reports is an implicit increase in his share.

Allen and Lueck (2002) find support for this tradeoff using data from North America and evidence from around the world. They show that cropshare contracts are more likely when crop division costs are low and where the ability of farmers to adversely affect the soil is high, and that cash rent contracts often contain clauses that discourage exploitation of the soil. For example, hay crops are more susceptible to under-reporting, since they are used on the premises and found to be more often cash rented. Land used for row crops is more susceptible to overuse than is land used for grains, and the data show that row crops are more likely to be cropshared.

This basic framework also explains much of the contract choice found in other parts of the world. For example, a recent study of historical vineyard contracts in Spain (Carmona and Simpson 1999) shows that share contracts dominate because of the incentives they provide for proper long term care of the vines.[35] Dubois (2002) finds that in the Philippines, corn—a crop that is hard on the land—is more likely to be cropshared than are the main alternatives of rice and sugar. Indeed, this view explains Adam Smith's long-standing observation that sharing was more common in France and southern Europe than in England. In northern Europe, the most common type of farming would have been of small grains and grass crops. In Southern France, Italy, and Spain, grapes, olives, and fruit were much more important. With fruit trees, the share contract prevents the farmer from exploiting the tree or vine asset over the short term. With grapes and fruit, pruning can be done in certain ways to increase the short-run volume of fruit, but which, over time, kill the tree or drastically reduce the long-term productivity of the tree. Sharing lowers the incentive of the farmer to do this in the same manner that it lowers the incentive to exploit soil attributes. The observations about European land leasing, first made by Adam Smith and John Stuart Mill, thus suggest that land contracts were chosen in response to the costs of enforcing contracts over assets with many attributes. The dominance of cash rent contracts in England and northern Europe can be explained as the result of the relative dominance of small grain and grass farming. Similarly, the dominance of cropsharing in the Romance countries can be explained as the result of the relative dominance of orchard crops.[36]

Input Sharing in Share Contracts

Economists have given little attention to the details of cropshare contracts, and in particular, one of the most important aspects of any cropshare contract is whether or not the inputs are shared. Producing a crop obviously requires more than land and labor. Seed, fertilizer, tractors and other machines, water, pesticides, and a host of other inputs are also required. Although the cost of the farmer's labor and the cost of the land's attributes cannot be shared, these other inputs are often shared. Thus, some cropshare contracts include the provision that some or all of the inputs be shared, while others contain no such provision.

---

[35] Galassi (1992) and Hoffman (1984) are studies of historical European contracts that are also part of this literature.

[36] As we note in Section 2, just over 10% of all farmland leases in the U.S. are a cash-share combination. Our data are not detailed enough to examine these contracts and we are not aware of any study that attempts to explain the use and structure of such contracts. It thus remains an important open area for study.

In one of the few studies of input sharing, Heady (1947) pointed out that sharing input costs in the same proportion as the output share offsets the moral hazard effect of the share on that input.[37] Recall that a share on output lowers the marginal product of every input, which is the "tax" effect introduced by Adam Smith. When an input cost is shared, this lowers the cost of the input and acts as an input subsidy. When the two shares are the same, the tax and the subsidy completely offset each other, and the input is used at its correct level. Heady's model predicts that all inputs should be shared in the same proportion as the output. Yet, as seen in Section 2, input sharing is done one of two ways: inputs are either shared in the same proportion as the output, or they are not shared at all.[38]

When the costs of monitoring shared inputs are incorporated into the analysis, a model of share contracting explains this dichotomy. Whenever inputs are shared, there is an incentive for the farmer to over-report the actual cost of the inputs. Thus input sharing requires monitoring effort on the part of the landowner. When these monitoring costs are high, the landowner simply opts to have the farmer pay for all input costs, and the share of output to the farmer is adjusted upwards. When these monitoring costs are low, the inputs are shared in the same proportion as the output. This input sharing dichotomy (Allen and Lueck 2002, chapter 5) is clear in the Nebraska-South Dakota data. Those inputs that are difficult to measure tend not to be shared at all. In fact, 50–80% of inputs tend to be shared in cropshare contracts, and virtually all inputs are either shared in the same proportion as the output or not shared at all. Empirical estimates (Allen and Lueck 1993; 2002, chapter 5) support the argument that input and output monitoring costs are crucial in determining input sharing in cropshare contracts. For example, when a farmer has more than one plot of land his cropshare contracts tend not to share input costs, so the landowner can avoid the potential for input cost shifting away from the leased plot.

Equipment Contracting and Custom Operation

Farmers also contract for equipment, but much less so than for land (see Section 2). For economists, the main question is not contract choice but, rather, the choice between ownership and contracting for the use of equipment. Both ownership and contracting have costs: ownership costs include the foregone gains from specialization and the costs of borrowing if there are wealth constraints; contracting costs include moral hazard and timeliness—that is, the reduction in output when tasks are not undertaken at the optimal time.[39] Since equipment is often

---

[37] Other studies include Bardhan and Singh (1987), Berry (1962), and Braverman and Stiglitz (1986).
[38] Braverman and Stiglitz (1982, 1986) reach similar conclusions in a P-A framework.
[39] Timeliness costs, though not often given much attention by economists (an exception is Masten, Meehan, and Snyder, 1991), are considered very important in the agricultural literature. See Edwards (1980), Hopkin (1971), or Short and Gitu (1991).

specialized and used for specific stages of production, it is extremely costly to use rental markets. As a result, the farmer often owns even seldom-used equipment.

Empirical estimates of the choice of ownership versus contracting (Allen and Lueck 2002, chapter 8) show that asset moral hazard, capital constraints, and timeliness costs, are important determinants of whether or not farmers will own or contract for control of equipment.[40] For example, trucks and tractors, used for many general farming tasks, are more likely to be contracted than owned, whereas specialized equipment, such as a combines, are more likely to be owned than rented. Farmers who use more than one piece of a particular type of equipment are more likely to contract for one piece than farmers who use just one piece. Both of these bits of evidence are consistent with the importance of timeliness costs in determining the ratio of contracted to owned assets. Allen and Lueck (2002) also find that wealthier farmers are more likely to own equipment.

Custom combining provides a nice example of the tradeoffs between specialization gains, moral hazard costs, and timeliness costs. The benefit from contracting for custom combining is, of course, derived from the intensive use of highly-specialized equipment with skilled operators. Typical wheat farmers may use their own combines for just twenty days each year. A custom cutter could, however, by moving north with the ripening wheat, use his combines for 100 to 150 days each year. Williams (1953, p. 53) notes these tremendous gains to specialized equipment:

> The economic keynote of the cutters' activities is the ability to get maximum utilization of their expensive and complicated specialized machinery, as they follow the progressive ripening pattern of the south-to-north contour of the wheat belt.

The gains from specialized labor are also important. Combine operators and truck drivers repeatedly working long seasons are more specialized than any farmer and his short-term help. These specialized operators are extremely knowledgeable in the use and maintenance of this expensive equipment.

The gains from specialized machines and labor would seem to imply that contracting for harvesting would dominate wheat and grain farming. Timeliness costs for a wheat harvest, however, are severe and limiting. For any given wheat farmer, the window for optimal harvest is just a few weeks and standing grain is extremely vulnerable to hail, rain, and wind. How do migratory custom cutters and the farmers who hire them reduce these timeliness costs enough to sustain a viable industry? The answer is found in the geographic and climatic contiguousness of the Great Plains. Custom cutters know they can reliably follow the ripening wheat north in order to make intensive use of their expensive equipment. The exceptional circumstances of the contiguous wheat harvest of the U.S. point to how rare year long custom contracting is. For instance, wheat is also an important crop in California and Washington, but the lack of a long and continuous harvest prevents the emergence of large custom harvest industry.

---

[40] Recent studies of ownership and contracting in trucking show similar empirical findings (Baker and Hubbard 2003, Nickerson and Silverman 2002).

Labor Contracts

The basic distribution of payments and job types laid out in Table 4 are relatively easy to explain with the transaction cost approach.[41] Most types of farming have outputs that are relatively easy to measure, and in such cases (e.g., berries, grapes, and other fruits) workers are often hired under piece rate contracts. These contracts induce workers to work quickly, and when speed causes little damage to the output (e.g., fruit) or capital (e.g., trees, land), there is little cost in using this type of payment. When the value of the crop increases, or when the farmer wants his workers to slow down in order to harvest more thoroughly, then wage contracts are used for harvest. For example, piece rate contracts are used for workers picking fruit that is hard to damage, while wage contracts are used for workers picking fruit that must be handled more carefully. In addition, when effort and time are tied closely, or when farm hands are expected to do multiple tasks, wages tend to be used. Wages provide low-powered but equal incentives across tasks and are inexpensive to administer (Holmström and Milgrom 1991). Again, many farm tasks like cleaning barns, spreading manure, and cultivating fields are relatively easy to monitor and wage contracts are an efficient form of payment.

Though the distinction between piece rate and wage contracts for hired labor is important, the major question for agricultural labor contracts is: Why are farmers so often both the major capitalists of the firm and its major source of labor? The family farmer can be thought of a residual claim laborer and capitalist. This labor "contract" exists on farms that control the narrow growth-dominated biological stages of production where Nature plays a large role. In confined livestock operations, where the role of Nature is greatly reduced, the farm capitalist is not the major source of farm labor. Even a family farmer will hire hands to help with chores, routine tasks, and the harvest, but it is not possible to find someone on the farm making all decisions regarding planting, breeding, cultivating, and the like, and being paid a wage.[42]

The reason for the dominance of the family farm or residual claim labor contract lies in the impact Nature has on production and incentives. When Nature plays a large role, it creates enormous moral hazard costs when a non-residual claimant makes major decisions affecting the profitability of the farm. Even in family operations, key inputs (like the timing and application of planting) are usually done by the farmer and not his children, since a careless application of a critical input could easily reduce output at harvest time. The farmer not only has the precise information about optimal timing, but also has the optimal incentive to take advantage of this knowledge. When Nature plays a large role, low quality and quantity of effort which lead to poor outcomes, are hidden by Nature's role. At the same time that Nature creates large moral hazard problems for hired labor, Nature also tends to minimize the gains from hiring specialized

---

[41] The incentive issues examined in Lazear (1986, 1995) are similar to those discussed here.

[42] There seems to really be no such thing as a wage contract farmer, if one takes farmer to mean the crop-livestock decision-maker. There are however, farm managers who make such decisions. They tend to be paid salaries, often with bonuses. The extent of these labor contracts is not well known.

labor. The more seasonal a production process is, the fewer gains there are to specializing in a single task. Thus, the low gains from specialization and the high moral hazard costs of hired labor work in favor of the family farmer supplying most of the capital and labor to production.

5. CONCLUSION

The transaction cost approach is a key component of the New Institutional Economics. The transaction cost approach has an empirical focus on real contracts; it emphasizes testable hypotheses; and it recognizes the complexity of assets in the market and within the firm. When this approach is brought to bear in the study of agricultural contracts, it yields robust and empirically supported explanations for the structure of contracts, in both historical and modern agriculture. The transaction cost approach abstracts from risk aversion and risk avoidance and, instead, focuses on pure incentive tradeoffs. As we have mentioned, the inclusion of risk sharing adds analytical complications without adding empirical tractability.

We have argued the transaction cost approach explains the basic facts regarding agricultural contracts. Without repeating the empirical details, there are several dominant findings. First, when farmers and landowners contract for land, the contracts are simple in the sense that they are mostly oral and short term. They tend to be enforced through the market via reputation and through the common law via its default rules that simplify the structure of contracts. Second, contract structures are used to police behavior that is difficult to verify by a third party. This costly to observe behavior is present when individuals are not full residual claimants, and this behavior is strongly influenced by enforcement and measurement costs. For example, the choice between cash rent and cropshare is a tradeoff between soil exploitation and crop under-reporting incentives. Third, the classic tradeoff between risk and incentives does not explain the choice of contracts or organizations in agriculture, nor elsewhere, as the recent agency literature has shown. Fourth, farming is dominated by family production when the random and systematic effects of Nature cannot be controlled. Nature not only provides an opportunity for moral hazard, but it limits the possibilities of specialization. Generally speaking, farm production provides many opportunities for moral hazard, and few for exploiting economies of size. Thus the dominant labor contract in agriculture is the residual claim farmer.

REFERENCES

Ackerberg, Daniel and Maristella Botticini. 2002. "Endogenous Matching and the Empirical eterminants of Contract Form". *Journal of Political Economy* 110.

Alchian, Armen A. 1950. "Uncertainty, Evolution and Economic Theory". *Journal of Political Economy* 58: 211–221.

Allen, Douglas W. 2000. "Transaction Costs" in Bouckaert, Boudewijn, and DeGeest (eds.), *Encyclopedia of Law and Economics*, Vol. 1. Cheltenham, UK: Edward Elgar Press, pp. 893–926.

Allen, Douglas W. and Dean Lueck. 1992a. "Contract Choice in Modern Agriculture: Cash Rent vs. Cropshare". *Journal of Law and Economics* 35: 397–426.
Allen, Douglas W. and Dean Lueck. 1992b. "The Back-Forty on a Handshake: Specific Assets, Reputation, and the Structure of Farmland Contracts". *Journal of Law, Economics and Organization* 8: 366–377.
Allen, Douglas W. and Dean Lueck. 1993. "Transaction Costs and the Design of Cropshare Contracts". *RAND Journal of Economics* 24: 78–100.
Allen, Douglas W. and Dean Lueck. 1995. "Risk Preferences and the Economics of Contracts". *American Economic Review* 85: 447–451.
Allen, Douglas W. and Dean Lueck. 1998. "The Nature of the Farm". *Journal of Law and Economics* 41: 343–386.
Allen, Douglas W. and Dean Lueck. 1999a. "The Role of Risk in Contract Choice". *Journal of Law, Economics, and Organization* 15: 704–736.
Allen, Douglas W. and Dean Lueck. 2002. *The Nature of the Farm: Contracts, Risk, and Organization in Agriculture.* Cambridge, MA: The MIT Press.
Alston Lee J., Gary D. Libecap, and Bernardo Mueller. 2000. *Title, Conflict and Land Use* Ann Arbor, MI: University of Michigan Press.
Anderson, Terry L. and Dean Lueck. 1992. "Land Tenure and Agricultural Productivity on Indian Reservations". *Journal of Law and Economics* 35: 427–454.
Baker, George P. and Thomas N. Hubbard. 2003. "Make versus Buy in Trucking: Asset Ownership, Job Design and Information". *American Economic Review*, in press.
Bardhan, P. and Singh, N. 1987. "On Moral Hazard and Cost Sharing Under Sharecropping". *American Journal of Agricultural Economics* 69: 382–383.
Barzel, Yoram. 1997. *Economic Analysis of Property Rights*, 2nd edn. Cambridge: Cambridge University Press.
Berry, Russell L. 1962. "Cost Sharing as a Means of Improving the Share Rent Lease". *Journal of Farm Economics* 44: 796–807.
Braverman, Avishay and Stiglitz, Joseph E. 1982. "Sharecropping and the Interlinking of Agrarian Markets". *American Economic Review* 72: 695–715.
Braverman, Avishay and Stiglitz, Joseph E. 1986. "Cost-Sharing Arrangements Under Sharecropping: Moral Hazard, Incentive Flexibility, and Risk". *American Journal of Agricultural Economics* 68: 642–652.
Burkhart, Barry G. 1991. "Leases: Farmland Lease Provisions in Oklahoma". *Oklahoma Law Review* 44: 461–491.
Carmona, Juan and James Simpson. 1999. "'Rabassa Morta in Catalan Viticulture: The Rise and Decline of a Long-Term Sharecropping Contract, 1670s–1920s". *Journal of Economic History* 59: 290–315.
Chiappori, Pierre Andre and Bernard Salanie. 2000. "Testing Contract Theory: A Survey of Some Recent Work". Invited Lecture, World Congress of the Econometric Society, Seattle.
Cheung, Steven N. S. 1969. *The Theory of Share Tenancy.* Chicago, IL: University of Chicago Press.
Coase, Ronald H. 1960. "The Problem of Social Cost". *Journal of Law and Economics* 3: 1–41.
Crocker, Keith J. and Masten, Scott E. 1988. "Mitigating Contractual Hazards: Unilateral Options and Contract Length". *RAND Journal of Economics* 19: 327–343.
Deininger, Klaus and Gershon Feder. 2001. "Land Institution and Land Markets" in B.L. Gardner and G.C. Rausser, (eds.), *Handbook of Agricultural Economics,* Vol. 1B. Amsterdam: Elsevier Science.
Drache, Hiram. 1964. *The Day of the Bonanza.* Fargo: North Dakota Institute for Regional Studies.
Dubois, Pierre. 2002. "Moral Hazard, Land Fertility and Sharecropping in a Rural Area of the Phillipines". *Journal of Development Economics,* 68: 35–64.
DuBow, Shane. 1999. "Wheaties: Chasing the Ripening Harvest Across America's Great Plains". *Harper's Magazine* August. 33–44.

Edwards, William and V. Meyer. 1986. "Acquiring Farm Machinery Services: Ownership, Custom Hire, Rental, Lease". Ames: Cooperative Extension Service of Iowa State University.
Edwards, William and Michael Boehle. 1980. "Machinery Selection Considering Timeliness Losses". Transactions of the American Society of Agricultural Engineers 810–821.
Ellickson, Robert C. 1991. *Order Without Law*. Cambridge, MA: Harvard University Press.
Eswaran, M. and A. Kotwal. 1985. "A Theory of Contractual Structure in Agriculture". *American Economic Review* 75: 352–367.
Frank, S. D. and D. R. Henderson. 1992. "Transaction Cost as Determinants of Vertical Coordination in the U.S. Food Industries". *American Journal of Agricultural Economics*, November.
Fulton, Murray. 1995. "The Future of Canadian Agriculture Cooperatives: A Property Rights Approach". *American Journal of Agricultural Economics* 77.
Galassi, Francesco. 1992. "Tuscans and Their Farms: The Economics of Share Tenancy in Fifteenth Century Florence". *Rivista di Storia Economica* 9: 77–94.
Garen, John E. 1994. "Executive Compensation and Principal-Agent Theory". *Journal of Political Economy* 102: 1175–1199.
Gaynor, Martin and Paul J. Gertler. 1995. "Moral Hazard and Risk Spreading in Partnership". *RAND Journal of Economics* 26: 591–613.
Gray, L.C., Charles Stewart, Howard Turner, J.T. Sanders, and W. J. Spillman, 1924. "Farm Ownership and Tenancy". *Yearbook of the Department of Agriculture, 1923*. Washington: U.S. Printing Office.
Hallagan, William. 1978. "Self-Selection by Contractual Choice and the Theory of Sharecropping". *Bell Journal of Economics* 9: 344–354.
Hart, O.D. 1995. *Firms, Contracts and Financial Structure*. Oxford: Clarendon Press.
Hayami, Yuruiro and Keijiro Otsuka. 1993. *The Economics of Contract Choice: An Agrarian Perspective*. Oxford: Oxford University Press.
Heady, E.O. 1947. "Economics of Farm Leasing Systems". *Journal of Farm Economics* 29: 659–678.
Hoffman, Phillip T. 1984. "The Economic Theory of Sharecropping in Early Modern France". *Journal of Economic History* 44: 309–319.
Holmström, Bengt. and Paul Milgrom. 1991. "Multi-Task Principal-Agent Analyses: Incentive Contracts, Asset Ownership, and Job Design". *Journal of Law, Economics, and Organization* 7: 24–25.
Hopkin, J. 1971. "Leasing versus Buying of Machinery". *Journal of American Society of Farm Managers and Rural Appraisers* 17–23.
Irwin, George D. and Lawrence N. Smith. 1972. "Machinery Leasing: Perspectives and Prospects". *Agricultural Finance Review* 33: 42–47.
Isern, Thomas D. 1981. *Custom Combining on the Great Plains*. Norman, OK: University of Oklahoma Press.
Johnson, D. Gale. 1950. "Resource Allocation Under Share Contracts". *Journal of Political Economy* 58: 111–123.
Joskow, Paul L. 1987. "Contract Duration and Relationship-Specific Investments: Empirical Evidence from Coal Markets". *American Economic Review* 77: 168–185.
Klein, Benjamin, Crawford, Robert G. and Armen A. Alchian. 1978. "Vertical Integration, Appropriable Rents, and the Competitive Contracting Process". *Journal of Law and Economics* 21: 297–326.
Klein, Benjamin and Keith B. Leffler. 1981. "The Role of Market Forces in Assuring Contractual Performance". *Journal of Political Economy* 89: 615–641.
Kliebenstein, James B. and John D. Lawrence. 1995. "Contracting and Vertical Coordination in the United States Pork Industry". *American Journal of Agricultural Economics* 77: 1213–1218.
Knoeber, Charles R. 1989. "A Real Game of Chicken: Contracts, Tournaments, and the Production of Broilers". *Journal of Law, Economics, and Organization* 5: 271–292.

Knoeber, Charles R. 2000. "Land and Livestock Contracting in Agriculture: A Principal-Agent Perspective" in Vol. III, Boudewijn Bouckaert and Gerrit De Geest (eds.), *The Encyclopedia of Law and Economics*. Cheltenham UK: Edward Elgar, pp. 1133–1153.

Knoeber, Charles R. and Walter N. Thurman. 1994. "Testing the Theory of Tournaments: An Empirical Analysis of Broiler Production". *Journal of Labor Economics* 12: 155–179.

Lagrone, William F. and Earle E. Gavett. 1975. *Interstate Custom Combining in the Great Plains in 1971*. Economic Research Service Paper no. 563. Washington, DC: U.S. Department of Agriculture.

Laffontaine, Francine. 1992. "Agency Theory and Franchising: Some Empirical Results". *RAND Journal of Economics* 26: 263–283.

Lazzarini, S.G., F.R. Chaddad, and M.L. Cook. 2001. "Integrating Supply Chain and Network Analysis: The Study of Netchains". *Journal of Chain and Network Science* 1.

Lazear, Edward P. 1986. "Salaries and Piece Rates". *Journal of Business* 59: 405–431.

Lazear, Edward P. 1995. *Personnel Economics*. Cambridge, MA: MIT Press.

Leffler Keith and Randall Rucker. 1991. "Transactions Costs and the Efficient Organization of Production: A Study of Timber-Harvesting Contracts". *Journal of Political Economy* 99: 1060–1087.

Luporini, Annalisa, and Bruno Parigi. 1996. "Multi-Task Sharecropping Contracts: The Italian Mezzadria". *Economica* 63: 445–457.

Lyon, Thomas P. and Steven C. Hackett. 1993. "Bottlenecks and Governance Structures: Open-Access and Long-Term Contracting in Natural Gas". *Journal of Law, Economics, and Organization* 9: 380–398.

Macauley, Stewart. 1963. "Non-Contractual Relations in Business: A Preliminary Study". *American Sociological Review* 28: 55–67.

Masten, Scott E. and Stephane Saussier. 2000. "Econometrics of Contracts: An Assessment of Developments in the Empirical Literature on Contracting". *Revue-d'Economie Industrielle* 92: (2nd–3rd Trimesters) 215–236.

Masten, Scott E., James Meehan, and Edward Snyder. 1991. "The Costs of Organization". *Journal of Law, Economics, and Organization* 7: 1–26.

Martin, Robert. 1988. "Risk Sharing and Franchising". *American Economic Review* 78: 954–968.

Martinez, S.W. and Reed. 1996. "From Farmers to Consumers: Vertical Coordination in the Food Industry". USDA Report 720.

Ménard, Claude. 1996. "On Clusters, Hybrids, and other Strange Forms: The Case of the French Poultry Industry". *Journal of Institutional and Theoretical Economics* 152: 154–183.

Mill, John S. [1871] 1965. *Principles of Political Economy* Ashley (ed.). New York: Kelley.

Newberry, David and Joseph Stiglitz. 1979. "Sharecropping, risk-sharing, and the Importance of Imperfect Information" in James Roumasset, Jean-Marc Boussard, and Inderjit Singh (eds.), *Risk, Uncertainty and Agricultural Development*. Berkeley, CA: University of California Press.

Nickerson, Jack A. and Brian S. Silverman. 2002. "Why Aren't All Truck Drivers Owner-Operators?" *Journal of Economics, Management and Strategy*.

Perry, Janet, Mitch Morehart, David Banker, and Jim Johnson. 1997. "Contracting: A Business Option for Many Farmers" 1997. *Agricultural Outlook* May: 2–5.

Pflueger, Burton W. 1994. "Farm Machinery Costs: Own, Lease, or Custom Hire". Cooperative Extension Service of South Dakota State University.

Prendergast, Canice. 1999. "The Provision of Incentives in Firms". *Journal of Economic Literature* 37: 7–63.

Prendergast, Canice. 2000. "What Trade-Off of Risk and Incentives?" *American Economic Review* 90: 421–425.

Prendergast, Canice. 2002. "The Tenuous Trade-Off Between Risk and Incentives". *Journal of Political Economy* 110: 1071–1102.

Rao, C.H. Hanamutha. 1971. "Uncertainty, Entrepreneurship, and Sharecropping in India". *Journal of Political Economy* 79: 578–595.

Roy, Ewell Paul. 1963. *Contract Farming, U.S.A.* Danville, IL: Interstate Printers and Publishers.

Salanie, Bernard. 1997. *The Economics of Contracts.* Cambridge, MA: MIT Press.

Sappington, David E.M. 1991. "Incentives in Principal-Agent Relationships". *Journal of Economic Perspectives* 5: 45–66.

Sauvee, L. "Efficiency, Effectiveness and the Design of Network Governance" 5th *Conference on Chain Management in Agribusiness and the Food Industry*, The Netherlands.

Shelanski, Howard A. and Peter G. Klein. 1995. "Empirical Research in Transaction Cost Economics: A Review and Assessment". *Journal of Law, Economics, and Organization* 11: 335–361.

Short, Cameron and Kangethe W. Gitu. 1991. "Timeliness Costs for Machinery Selection". *Canadian Journal of Agricultural Economics* 39: 457–462.

Smith, Adam. [1776] 1992. *The Wealth of Nations*, Kathryn Sutherland. (ed.), Oxford: Oxford University Press.

Sotomayer, Narda L., Paul N. Ellinger, and Peter J. Barry. 2000. "Choice Among Leasing Contracts in Farm Real Estate". *Agricultural Finance Review* 60: 71–84.

Stiglitz, Joseph. 1974. "Incentives and Risk-Sharing in Sharecropping". *Review of Economic Studies* 41: 219–255.

Tsoodle, Leah J. and Christine A. Wilson. 2000. "Nonirrigated Crop-Share Leasing Arrangements in Kansas" Staff Paper No. 01–02 Kansas State University Department of Agricultural Economics (Manhattan, KS).

Williams, Charles M. 1953. "Enterprise on the Prairies". *Harvard Business Review* 31: 97–102.

Williamson, Oliver. E. 1979. "Transaction-Cost Economics: The Governance of Contractual Relations" *Journal of Law and Economics* 22: 233–261.

Young, H. Peyton and Mary A. Burke. 2001. "Competition and Custom in Economic Contracts: A Case Study of Illinois Agriculture". *American Economic Review* 559–573.

19. The Enforcement of Contracts and Private Ordering

VICTOR P. GOLDBERG

The primary purpose of contract law is, most would concede, to facilitate private ordering. The parties are the best judges of their interests and the law should, as much as possible, stay out of the way. There are exceptions–there might turn out to be good reasons to discourage, or prohibit, certain classes of promises (for example, disclaimers or promises to commit illegal acts) or to be suspicious of the manner in which agreements have been reached (for example, the battle of the forms or duress). Still, the facilitation of voluntary exchange remains the primary goal of contract law. Voluntary exchange is not a zero-sum game; it allows parties to achieve gains from trade. The parties enter into their agreement because they each expect to be better off. They might, of course, turn out to be wrong. It might have seemed a good idea at the time, but conditions might have changed so that one party now regretted having entered into the agreement. Or, one party might simply have misperceived the possible outcome. Had it known more (or been a more intelligent processor of available information), it would not have entered into the deal. Regardless, the basic presumption that there are gains from trade is the economic foundation for a facilitative law of contract.

Even if all agree on the economic virtues of private ordering, it does not follow that economic analysis would be of use in designing, evaluating, or operating the system of contract law. In a recent paper Eric Posner [2003] asked whether, after three decades, the economic analysis of contract law had been a success or failure. His answer, somewhat qualified, was the latter. About the best that he could say is that it seems to have failed less than other approaches. He is probably right in claiming that economic scholarship has had little impact on American courts (and presumably on courts throughout the world as well). Economic concepts like efficiency or the Coase Theorem virtually never make their way into contract opinions. Indeed, it could be argued that since the birth of the economic analysis of contract law, the doctrinal evolution has been away from economics.

Posner's assessment, however well it characterizes the present situation, is too pessimistic. Lawyers are transactional engineers, designing structures to cope with problems such as information asymmetry, moral hazard, costly enforcement and the like. I perceive a significant disjunction between the intellectual frameworks of the transactional lawyers structuring deals and the litigators and judges interpreting those transactional structures after problems had arisen. The theoretical framework of the transaction-cost engineer, I will argue, is appropriate for analyzing contract disputes and for developing contract doctrine—at least for business to business transactions. The central questions of a transactionally sensitive contract law are: Why might reasonable, profit-seeking actors structure their relationship in a particular way? How does the answer to that question affect the interpretation of a contract or suggest the appropriate contract law rule?

Application of this approach has led me to be much more optimistic than Posner. It works. Rather than present a superficial overview, I will illustrate by concentrating on a few examples. First, I want to consider a basic puzzle of contract law: why enforce a contract even when there has been no reliance? The answer to that question, developed in Part II, suggests how, ideally, the contract should be enforced. The breacher should pay the market-contract price differential. In practice, that might be too difficult to administer, but it should remain the guiding principal. I illustrate how the rule might be applied by discussing a few American cases in which ascertaining the contract-market differential becomes progressively more difficult.

The argument for this damage rule is derived from the economics of imperfect information. The other two illustrations also revolve around imperfect information. First, there is a standard "lemons" problem when a deal involves sale of an asset of uncertain value. How can the seller convince the buyer that he is not buying a lemon? I illustrate this by analyzing *Bloor v. Falstaff*, discussed in Part III. This case is the standard casebook illustration of the judicial interpretation of a "best efforts" clause. Remarkably, despite the fact that the essence of the transaction was a sale of most of a corporation's assets, the court (and the litigators) ignored the fact entirely. Instead, they attempted to interpret the "best efforts" clause without any analytical framework and, not surprisingly, botched it. Once the problem is properly framed, the role of the "best efforts" clause is clear: it was ancillary to that sale and was meant to cope with the lemons problem. So framed, the outcome should have been straightforward. The court asked the wrong question and gave the wrong answer. The only problem with *Bloor* as an illustration of the power of the analysis is that the case doesn't generalize. It is a one-shot clean kill.

The other theme concerns the sequential nature of decision-making and the allocation of discretion. The particular focus is long-term contracts with variable quantity (requirements or full output contracts) giving one party the discretion to determine the quantity. Parties enter into such arrangements in order to facilitate adaptation to changing circumstances, particularly adapting to new information as it comes in. The contracts typically provide rather nuanced boundaries on the discretion to protect the reliance of the party without the discretion. The Uniform Commercial Code, provides a blunter instrument: "good faith" and courts will in some instances override the balancing chosen by the parties. In Part IV, I will analyze two cases, *Feld v. Levy,* the leading New York decision, and *Amerada Hess v. Orange & Rockland Utilities, Inc.,* in which the court used good faith to trump a perfectly sensible balancing by the parties.

The analysis, whether right or wrong, will not be of much use in deciding cases if its application requires training and skills beyond those of judge and jury. In some instances, the framework simply helps pose the proper question. Litigation is story-telling and if the parties use the right framework, the answer becomes obvious. Perhaps the most useful role of the analysis is in providing a rationale for classes of contract clauses in order to shield them from judicial modification or nullification with interpretative tools like "good faith." To the extent that the moral of such analyses is "don't meddle," this framework makes the court's task easier. Ironically, to the extent that the analysis succeeds in this negative role, the economic analysis will not appear in the decided cases.

Notably absent in my cataloging of the transactional engineer's concerns is attitudes toward risk. Contracts allocate risk, and the first response of many economists and lawyers is to invoke risk aversion to explain behavior or analyze doctrine. I argue that what matters is not *attitudes* toward risk, but, rather, the *management* of risk. In Part I, I explain why I regard risk aversion as the explanation of last resort.

1. AVERSION TO RISK AVERSION

When explaining contracting behavior or contract doctrine, it seems natural to look to attitudes toward risk. Much of its intuitive appeal, especially to law professors, derives from a misunderstanding. Most people are averse to downside risk—they don't like bad outcomes. But risk aversion means something quite different: given the choice between two outcomes with the same mean and a different variance, people will prefer the one with the smaller variance. Perhaps they will. But even if that were true, would it help much in understanding why contracting parties structure a transaction as they do? If a particular contract is only one element in a firm's portfolio of contracts, there would be no reason to believe that its features should reflect the firm's risk preferences. Indeed, even if all people are risk averse, there is no reason to believe that when they act collectively in business firms, that the firms would display risk aversion. My objection is not an empirical one regarding individual psychology. It is a methodological one: we can make more progress in understanding contracting behavior and contract law by ignoring attitudes toward risk. As a research strategy I propose that we tie our hands and agree not to invoke risk aversion. My claim is that it is a more fruitful strategy to ignore *attitudes* toward risk and to focus instead on risk *management*.

As an illustration, consider the purchase of liability insurance by public corporations. Risk aversion cannot explain this; the corporations are, after all, owned by shareholders who have the ability to diversify their portfolio. Are corporations or their officers risk averse? Are they more risk averse than other corporations, which choose instead to self-insure? Those explanations are implausible. If we constrain ourselves to explanations which do not depend on relative risk aversion, a number of plausible explanations emerge. Insurance companies provide risk management services including inspection, litigation, and administration of compensation. An insurance policy can act like a guarantee or a security interest, providing some assurance to lenders that the firm will be able to make payments even if certain unfortunate contingencies arise. Buying insurance means that the corporation can carry a smaller inventory of liquid assets. Insurance can be viewed as part of the firm's capital structure. It is a substitute for maintaining a line of credit. (Indeed, it is also a complement since line of credit contracts typically require that the buyer carry insurance.)

The corporation's purchase of liability insurance depends on the firm's decision as to whether certain services it needs should be met by firms characterized as insurance companies, other firms producing substitutes (guarantees, inspection services), or by vertical integration. This is a standard make-versus-buy problem, analytically no different than questions like: should an aluminum ingot producer buy fabrication services from outsiders or fabricate its own products; should a manufacturer own retail outlets, franchise, or sell to independent firms? Thus, we can ask whether lenders will give credence to firms that self-insure against certain casualty risks; or would the purchase of insurance result in a lower net cost of borrowing?

Price adjustment provides a good example of an instance in which risk aversion is superficially plausible but ultimately unhelpful. Contracts, one might argue, are indexed because the parties worry about inflation. But that doesn't get us very far. Why shift the risk of inflation to the buyer? Is there any reason to believe that buyers as a class are more risk averse than sellers? A better answer starts by recognizing that firms do not enter into long-term contractual relations in order to insure themselves against future price changes. Rather, they enter into long-term relations for good economic reasons, for example, to encourage one party to make a specific investment the value of which is contingent upon the continued existence of the contractual relationship. Having decided to do so, the parties have to say something about the future prices even if it is only to fix a single price (or schedule of prices) for the entire contract duration. They have a rich array of alternatives to the one-shot solution. These alternatives allow for adjustment of prices as new information comes in. Indexing is one such device, but there are many others. The parties could agree to renegotiate under specified circumstances (when an index has gone up by more than a certain percentage, on specified anniversaries, or even when one party requests renegotiation). The right of first refusal can be viewed as an indexing device which ties the contract price to current market conditions. Parties could leave price determination in the hands of third parties (arbitrators or courts) with "gross inequity" or "hardship" clauses. For a more complete cataloging of methods of price adjustment, see Goldberg [1985], Goldberg & Erickson [1987], and Goldberg [1991].

Given the existence of a large number of tools for achieving price adjustment, the question is why sophisticated commercial entities would want to use them. Why might it matter to the parties if the contract price is out of line with present conditions? I will suggest three reasons, two of which involve reducing the variance of outcomes but do not require differential risk aversion. The first is that unadjusted contract prices can give the wrong signals. If the contract price is too low, the buyer will not have sufficient incentive to economize. However, this point is subject to two significant qualifications. If the buyer is free to resell, then the buyer's incentive problem disappears; the opportunity cost of its internal use of, say, natural gas, is the net price it could receive from reselling; even if resale is not practical (perhaps the contract forbade it), the parties have an incentive to reset the contract price to reflect current conditions, with one party making a lump sum payment to the other. That is, even if the contract were silent on the matter, the parties could renegotiate and reset the price to reflect current conditions. Of course, renegotiation is itself costly, a point to which I return in the following paragraph.

Price adjustment can reduce the variance of outcomes, a reduction which might be desirable regardless of attitudes toward risk. It can reduce joint costs by influencing both pre-contract search and post-contract incentives. Suppose that parties could improve their private information on the future course of prices by spending more money today. They might both be better off if they could structure their deal so that the incentives to seek out this information are weakened. Spending less in their hunt for an informational advantage could leave the parties with a bigger pie to split. If the price adjustment mechanism shrinks the variance of future outcomes, then the parties will waste fewer resources in pursuit of a bargaining advantage. Similarly, if after the parties have entered into a long-term contract, the contract price is well out of line, the loser has an incentive to renegotiate the deal by engaging in behavior which is technically not a breach, but which reduces the value of the deal to both parties. To the extent that a price adjustment mechanism keeps the contract price from getting too far out of line, this unproductive behavior is discouraged.

There are, to be sure, many instances in which contract prices become substantially out of line despite the fact that the contracts were indexed. Most of the cases arising from the dramatic changes in energy prices in the last thirty years included price adjustment mechanisms that had failed. (See, for example, *Alcoa v. Essex, Nipsco v Carbon County,* and Joskow's [1977] discussion of the Westinghouse uranium contracts). Nonetheless, other things equal, incorporating a price adjustment mechanism can reduce the potential profitability of uncooperative behavior. And, to bring the argument full circle, the reasons have nothing to do with attitudes toward risk.

2. A Property Right in Price and the Measurement of Damages

Suppose that on April 1, Able enters into a contract to sell a commodity to Baker at a price of $2.00 per bushel for delivery at Baker's plant on June 1. Five days later, Able changes his mind and says he wants to withdraw the promise. Baker, in the meanwhile, has done nothing in reliance upon the existence of this particular contract. What functions are served by enforcing this purely executory agreement in the absence of any evidence that Baker has relied upon the existence of the contract? This is the question posed by Fuller and Perdue [1936]. The answers to this question can be divided into two categories: practical and conceptual.

Three practical reasons for not requiring evidence that the promisee relied in any way on the contract are: (a) it would complicate the litigation with a messy fact question of whether the promisee had indeed relied; (b) the promisee might be encouraged to act in a manner that established his reliance to lock in a good deal–even if this action would be inefficient; for example, it might enter into a resale contract specifying delivery of the goods associated with this particular contract rather than promising to sell goods that meet certain specifications; (c) requiring reliance might induce the promisor to expend resources to determine whether or not particular promisees have relied, an inquiry that would serve no useful purpose.

With an executory commodity contract, the promisee can avoid the costs arising from untimely contracting. Entering into a contract too close to the performance date can raise costs. Thus, if a buyer of wheat in Buffalo waits until he needs the wheat before entering into the contract, he might find that there is little wheat of the proper quality on hand at that time. Timely contracting avoids the costs associated with last-minute search. Whether this constitutes a "reliance" justification is, I suppose, a semantic problem. In any event, if the seller's breach were early enough so that the buyer could cover without incurring these additional costs, this argument would not provide a reason for compensating the buyer for a rise in the commodity price. But that still leaves the question of why the parties would find it worthwhile to enter into the executory contract in the first place. Why contract on April 1 to fix the price for a June 1 delivery?

To simplify the following discussion assume that the commodity is traded in a thick market (ex ante and ex post) so that the promisee could always cover by buying (or selling) at the current market price. The answer to the puzzle lies in the fact that the production of information on the future course of prices is costly and by early contracting the parties can economize on those costs. A commodity's future price is uncertain and there exist potential rewards to people for obtaining information as to what the prices will be. The closer we are to the performance date, the more information will exist about factors that might affect the price. The traders will have an incentive to expend resources to evaluate that information. By making their contract early, the parties reduce the incentive to expend resources on this activity, thereby economizing on their joint search costs. Early contracting enables them to avoid excessive searching for price information.

Analytically, this is a rent-seeking problem. The contracting parties expend resources to improve their information about the future course of prices. If one party has better information, it will get the better of the bargain. Knowing this, the parties' incentive is to spend until the marginal benefit just equals the marginal cost (given their assumption about the level of their counterparty's spending). The higher the level of spending by the two, the less sensitive the result to one party's outspending the other. Varying the time between contract formation and contract performance has two offsetting effects. On the one hand, the longer the period between contract formation and the date of execution, the greater the dispersion of price estimates. Hence, the reward to acquiring information should be higher; the earlier the contract date the greater the incentive to spend resources in pursuit of information. On the other hand, the earlier the contract date, the less likely an incremental investment in pursuit of information will be valuable. Expenditures on weather patterns two months from now might prove very useful in projecting future prices, but attempts to produce two-year projections would be fruitless. This factor would lead to a reduction of expenditures on information gathering as the length of time between the contract date and performance date increases.

Thus, there are both benefits and costs from increasing the length of time between the performance date of the contract and the time at which the parties enter into the contract. The problem the parties face is determining the optimal lead time. Absent enforceable contracts they would be unable to attain that lead time since the party disadvantaged by a price change in the interval between contract execution and performance would have no reason to honor the original agreement. If the law does enforce these executory contracts, parties will be able to contract in a timely fashion, thereby enabling them to avoid the wastes inherent in the search for price information. I do not mean to imply that businessmen make calculations about the optimal time for entering into a contract or even that they pose the problem in this way. It is reasonable to presume, however, that market forces would sort this out, penalizing those who contract too early or too late and rewarding those who contract in a timely manner. Enforceable contracts enable the market to perform that function. In effect, enforcement allows the parties to assert a "property right" in the price just as a patent allows the patentee to assert a property right in an idea.[1]

The notion that enforcement of the executory contract enables people to economize on price search costs goes a long way towards illuminating some of the problems arising in the area of contract damages. In particular, the idea that the parties were attempting to establish a property right in the price suggests that damage measures should be designed to protect that interest. Returning to the hypothetical transaction between Able and Baker, the damages should be the market price contract price differential, but which market price? Suppose that on April 5, the spot price for the commodity was $3 per pound and on June 1 it had fallen to $2.50 per pound. Should either of these be taken as the market price? In the ideal case, the answer is No. The relevant price is the price on April 5 for goods to be delivered on June 1 to Baker's plant. That is the market price at the time of breach for what had been promised: delivery at a particular time and place. That damage remedy preserves Baker's property in the price. Damages measurement, at least for this component of damages, is an asset

---

[1] Note that this argument is a variant on the discussion in the preceding section regarding the effect of price adjustment mechanisms on pre-contract search.

valuation problem. We ask what would the seller have to pay at the time of breach to get a new contract to provide the same quantities at the same time and location at the same price? For some commodities there is a sufficiently thick market so that the value of the contract is easily determined. Futures contracts are an example. The contract is for wheat meeting certain specifications to be delivered at a certain location and certain date. Most real-world situations fall short of this, and compromises will have to be made. But these should be guided by the basic principle: the price we are trying to replicate is the price at the time of breach for performance at the relevant time and place.

To illustrate this, we can consider a few examples where the measurement problem gets progressively harder. In the ideal situation, post-breach price movements should be irrelevant, but in less-than-ideal conditions they might have to be taken into account. If the buyer in a long-term contract covered by entering into a similar contract for the remainder of the contracting period, then the price differential would be the remedy. That is what the court should have found, but didn't, in the venerable case of *Missouri Furnace Co. v. Cochrane*. The seller was to deliver a fixed quantity of coke at a price of $1.20 per ton every day for a year. After the first month the spot price soared to over $4 per ton and the seller breached. The buyer covered by entering into a contract for the remainder of the year at a price of $4. By May the spot price began to fall and it remained relatively low for the rest of the year. Missouri Furnace sued for the difference between the contract price and the price of its cover transaction—a little more than $80,000. The defendant countered, arguing that the relevant damages were the spot price of coal at each delivery date, roughly $22,000. The court held for the defendant. The time of breach, the court held, was the moment at which the defendant failed to perform; each day was a new failure and a new time of breach.

This case long stood for the proposition that cover was not a remedy for a contract breach. Even today cover is treated as an alternative remedy to the contract-market differential rather than as evidence of that differential. Tom Jackson [1978, pp. 76–78] did an excellent job debunking *Missouri Furnace*. If Missouri Furnace had known that the court would impose this remedy, covering as it did would have been an unprofitable strategy. Covering with a forward contract at a fixed price would mean that if spot prices had risen in the interim Missouri Furnace's damages would be limited to the difference between the initial contract price and the single cover contract. That damage remedy would "make the plaintiff whole." If the spot prices fell, however, all the benefit would accrue to Cochrane. The asymmetric payoffs make covering in this manner a negative value proposition.

The symmetry would be restored if the cover contract were for daily deliveries of the same quantity, but with the price being the spot price on the date of delivery. Contracts in which the price will be a market price or posted price at time of delivery are not uncommon. But that is not the contract the parties entered into. Theirs was a contract for delivery throughout the year at a price determined at the beginning of the year. Had they wanted to enter into a variable price contract, they could have chosen to enter into such an agreement in the first place. In effect, the court's remedy transformed the contract into something completely different. In some contexts, the transformation could be justified on the ground of convenience. That factor cut the other way in *Missouri Furnace*. The replacement contract was available and using it to cover was more convenient than daily purchases on the spot market.

A slightly more complicated case arose in *Compania Naviera Asiatic v. The Burmah Oil Co.*, which concerned a seven-year charter on a ship. Before performance of the charter began, the Yom Kippur War disrupted the international shipping market; the market price of shipping doubled and the owner breached, chartering the ship to someone else for one year. In subsequent years a glut developed in the ship charter market so that the annual price of a charter fell considerably below the initial charter rate. The breaching owner attempted to introduce evidence on the subsequent course of prices. However, testimony on the value of a seven-year charter at the time of breach would provide a better picture of the damages than would annual charter rates in the remaining period. In such circumstances the court should refuse to allow the breacher to introduce evidence on the subsequent decline in price. The determination of when it is appropriate to take subsequent events into account will not always be easy, but it will be easier if the courts have a theoretical framework to guide them.

In *Laredo Hides Co. Inc. v. H & H Meat Products Co., Inc.*, convenience trumped. The seller breached in the third month of a ten-month full-output contract to provide hides. The ideal damage measure would be the amount that would be paid at the time of the breach in an arm's length transaction for the right to receive the producer's output at the contractually specified price for the remaining seven months. However, you can't just look that up in the papers. If the buyer covered by purchasing in the spot market for the remainder of the contract period, the comparisons between those prices (weighted by the monthly output) and the contract prices would be the damages as reckoned under the UCC §2-712. If the spot market price had changed substantially after the breach in a way not anticipated at the time of the breach, these cover prices would not reflect accurately the true contract-market differential at the time of the breach. However, they are likely the best that a court could do. The variable quantity and odd remaining term make it very difficult for a finder of fact to approximate the "true price."

The preceding discussion started with a simple commodity contract in which the parties set a single price and their task was to minimize information costs by varying the timing of their contracting. If we start at the opposite extreme, a long term supply contract in which there is considerable relation-specific investment and great uncertainty about future supply and demand conditions, then the analysis looks quite different. The contract most likely will not entail a single price; rather it will include a price adjustment mechanism. And the remedy will look quite different. But those differences should not obscure the fact that the parties (and the law) are trying to resolve the same problems; the context dictates different solutions.

What would happen if one party were dissatisfied with the price in the twelfth year of a thirty-year, variable price, take-or-pay contract for delivery of coal from a particular mine? If it breached, the ideal remedy would be the value at the time of the breach of the remaining 18 years. Given that price and quantity for the duration are both uncertain and given that there likely are no quoted prices for this rather unique asset, it would be extremely difficult to ascertain that value. Rather than having the finder of fact put a value on the remainder, courts will often resort to the specific performance remedy. The court doesn't have to engage in the futile exercise of valuing the contract today. Nor does it have to wait eighteen years to look at the actual trajectory of prices and quantity. Specific performance does not, of course, mean that the parties would be bound together for the duration. The breaching party could buy its way out. The remedy, in effect, gives the nonbreaching party the option to terminate, with the price to be determined by negotiation away from the status quo.

3. BLOOR V. FALSTAFF[2]

Consider a firm that is selling one of its divisions. There is likely to be a significant information asymmetry. The buyer, concerned that it might be buying a lemon, is apt to undervalue the property. The seller has a number of tools at its disposal to convey positive information that would enhance the sale price. It could make extensive representations and warranties; it could give the potential buyer liberal access to "kick the tires;" it could solicit assurance from reputable third parties (lawyers, accountants, insurers); or it could make some of its payment contingent upon the future success of the division. When Falstaff bought most of the assets of Ballantine Beer, it chose to rely on the last of these. When the future turned out to be disappointing the seller (more precisely, the seller's trustee in bankruptcy) sued because its contingent compensation turned out to be less than it had anticipated. The decision hinged on the court's interpretation of a "best efforts" clause.

Bloor v. Falstaff is the standard casebook illustration of how to interpret a "best efforts" clause. The court found that Falstaff's behavior amounted to less than best efforts. The opinion has been well-received, with commentators generally agreeing that Falstaff's breach was so egregious as to not provide much of a test of the boundaries of "best efforts." Farnsworth (1984, p. 10), for example, says: "Unfortunately, its decision did relatively little to add precision to the meaning of 'best efforts,' since Kalmanovitz [of Falstaff] fell so far short of the mark." Had the court framed the issue properly, it would have reached the opposite conclusion.

The owners of Ballantine beer (IFC) sold Ballantine's brand name and distribution network (but not the brewery) to Falstaff, another brewer, for $4 million plus a 50¢ per barrel royalty for beer sold with the Ballantine brand name for a

---
[2] This section is based on Goldberg [2000].

six year period. Ballantine's primary market had been the New York metropolitan area, a market that Falstaff had not penetrated. Had Falstaff maintained Ballantine's sales volume the royalty payment would have been over $1,000,000 per year. Falstaff agreed to use "best efforts" to promote and maintain a high volume of sales and further agreed to pay liquidated damages in the event of a substantial discontinuance of distribution under the Ballantine brand name, a complication we can ignore. The Ballantine sales fell well short of the 2 million barrel level; Falstaff, after a change of ownership, changed its marketing strategy for Ballantine, slashing its advertising budget. The seller subsequently went bankrupt and the bankruptcy trustee sued Falstaff under the contract claiming that Falstaff had not used "best efforts" in promoting Ballantine.

Judge Friendly held that the "best efforts" clause required Falstaff to generate sales of Ballantine beer even if that came at the expense of Falstaff's profits.

> While [the best efforts] clause clearly required Falstaff to treat the Ballantine brands as well as its own, it does not follow that it required no more. With respect to its own brands, management was entirely free to exercise its business judgment as to how to maximize profit even if this meant serious loss in volume. Because of the obligation it had assumed under the sales contract, its situation with respect to the Ballantine brands was quite different.... Clause 8 imposed an added obligation to use "best efforts to promote and maintain a high volume of sales...." Although we agree that even this did not require Falstaff to spend itself into bankruptcy to promote the sales of Ballantine products, it did prevent the application to them of Kalmanovitz' philosophy of emphasizing profit über alles without fair consideration of the effect on Ballantine volume. Plaintiff was not obliged to show just what steps Falstaff could reasonably have taken to maintain a high volume for Ballantine products. It was sufficient to show that Falstaff simply didn't care about Ballantine's volume and was content to allow this to plummet so long as that course was best for Falstaff's overall profit picture, an inference which the judge permissibly drew. The burden then shifted to Falstaff to prove there was nothing significant it could have done to promote Ballantine sales that would not have been financially disastrous. (pp. 614–615)

The evidence was sufficient to convince the court that Falstaff had not tried hard enough to generate sales of Ballantine beer.

Judge Friendly takes it as axiomatic that the contract required Falstaff to trade off its profits for Ballantine's sales. Conspicuous by its absence in his decision is any analysis of why the contract included the royalty arrangement and the best efforts covenant. That is not entirely his fault, as the record was completely silent on this point. So, we are left with the somewhat peculiar spectacle of a court giving meaning to a context-sensitive phrase with no guidance as to the context. Had the court recognized that the royalty was, in effect, an "earnout," ancillary to the one-shot sale of some of Ballantine's assets to Falstaff, the outcome would have (or, at least, should have) been different.

IFC was, essentially, selling two assets—Ballantine's brand name and its distribution network. Its purpose was simple. It wanted to sell at the highest price.

Other things equal, the fewer post-sale restrictions on a buyer's exploitation of the assets, the more the buyer would be willing to pay. That should be obvious, but the court's failure to recognize this basic point is the core of the problem. Falstaff's pursuit of "profit über alles," *ex post*, redounds to IFC's benefit, *ex ante*. So, any restriction, like the best efforts clause, immediately raises a red flag: how might the particular restriction raise the value of the Ballantine assets, ex ante?

The earnout was a response to the problem of asymmetric information. In some earnouts, the managers of the seller are expected to provide managerial services to the buyer for a transition period. The seller's compensation would depend in part on the quality of the work performed by the sellers during the transition. That was not the case here, as the IFC managers were real estate people with no useful knowledge about the beer industry and no intent to stay in the business. IFC was certifying the quality of the Ballantine assets. In sales of complex assets the seller typically has more information than the prospective buyer. If buyers cannot distinguish good assets from bad, then they are likely to be suspicious of any particular asset and to reduce their offer price accordingly. Sellers can get a better price if they can convince buyers of the quality of the asset. There are myriad ways of providing assurance. (See Gilson [1984, 262–4].) The seller could provide extensive representations and warranties; the buyer could engage in extensive due diligence investigation. By accepting some of its compensation in a contingent form, the seller provides some assurance to the buyer of the quality of the asset.

The parties want an arrangement which maximizes the value to the buyer ex ante. But producing information and assurance is not costless. The process of maximizing the value of the asset can reduce the size of the joint pie. That would obviously be true if the parties had spent months negotiating elaborate representations and warranties and/or engaging in a due diligence investigation. In this instance the parties avoided all these costs using the royalty payment instead. It, too, is not costless. Earnouts in general have a number of value-reducing features. They do not track value perfectly; they can distort incentives; and they are not strategy-proof–that is, the buyer can operate the business in a way that exploits the mechanism. For example, if an earnout were based on profits in the first three years, the buyer could make investment decisions which shift profits from the third to the fourth year. Anticipation of these costs would influence the final price of the asset.

The Ballantine royalty had the potential to alter Falstaff's incentives in two ways. First, the royalty acts as a tax (roughly 2%) on sales, which could induce Falstaff to market a somewhat smaller amount of Ballantine product than it would have, but for the royalty. So "best efforts" might possibly mean that Falstaff should push its sales effort a bit beyond the point that would otherwise be optimal, ex post. The distortion of incentives (which in this instance is quite minor) is a common problem in contingent compensation arrangements (franchise fees, percentage leases, oil and gas royalties, and so forth) and "best efforts" is just one of the devices for dealing with the problem.

The relatively low "tax" suggests that this was not the concern of the parties. The more likely concern was diversion: there were two assets being sold and the earnout only tracked one of them. If Falstaff could use the distribution network to sell Falstaff rather than Ballantine, the royalty would not track the value of the asset. The "best efforts" requirement would be one contractual device for protecting against this sort of diversion. But the context suggests how the clause should be read. "Best efforts" in this context means that Falstaff agreed that in its pursuit of "profit über alles" it would not opportunistically divert sales from Ballantine (the sales of which were to track asset quality) to Falstaff. And that poses the central question: Did Falstaff use the network to divert more sales than the parties should reasonably have expected? That might be a difficult question to answer for some fact patterns, but for the facts of this case the answer is easy and negative. When Kalmanovitz took charge he dismantled the distribution system. Falstaff did not divert resources to the more profitable brand, it simply terminated (or at least drastically pared) a project that did not work.

So, we are left with two plausible meanings of "best efforts" in the context of this transaction. First, it could be aimed at correcting Falstaff's incentives, which were a bit distorted by the royalty "tax." Second, and more plausible, it could have been an attempt to limit diversion of revenue away from the device chosen to provide assurance of that value. Neither of these provides a basis for concluding that Falstaff's pursuit of profit über alles, by revising its Ballantine marketing strategy and dismantling much of the Ballantine distribution network, violated its obligation to Ballantine.

What did the lawyers drafting the Ballantine contract mean by "best efforts"? We'll never know, and, I suspect, they probably didn't either. Their casualness in using the phrase—they used it in six other places in the agreement—suggests that they gave it little thought. My point is that the context of the transactions should constrain the court in interpreting what reasonable parties could (and should) have meant. An interpretation of a contract which begins with the presumption that the seller intended to restrict the buyer's subsequent use of the asset is bound to fail unless there is an understanding of the possible gains from tying the buyer's hands. Had Judge Friendly understood that—and I must emphasize that the litigators gave him no help whatsoever—then Falstaff would have been an easy case, but for the other side.

4. Discretion in Long-Term Contracts[3]

Long-term contracts cannot completely specify in advance all the obligations of both parties over the life of the agreement. In order to adapt their relationship to changing circumstances they will find it necessary to give one, or both, parties the discretion to respond as new information becomes available. In particular, they might find that shifting supply and demand conditions would be better met

---

[3] This section is based on Goldberg [2002].

by giving one party the discretion to vary quantity. Suppose that the party with discretion is the buyer, as in a requirements contract. The seller would have two concerns. First, the buyer could use its discretion opportunistically to rewrite the contract. Second, if the seller intended to make decisions in reliance on the continued performance of the buyer, it would want a means of conveying the extent of that reliance, perhaps by setting a minimum quantity or establishing a multi-part pricing regime.

The common law and the Uniform Commercial Code §2-306(1) limited that discretion by invoking good faith: "A term which measures the quantity by the output of the seller or the requirements of the buyer means such actual output or requirements as may occur in good faith, except that no quantity unreasonably disproportionate to any stated estimate or in the absence of a stated estimate to any normal or otherwise comparable prior output or requirements, may be tendered or demanded." My thesis is that the courts have used good faith as a blunt instrument for providing protection to one party's reliance without asking whether that party would have been willing to pay for such protection in the first place. In effect, the seller wants to confront the buyer with a price reflecting the extent of its reliance. If that price is set too high, both parties lose. It is in their joint interest to fine-tune the protection of the reliance.

Commentators have converged on the implications of the good faith standard for open quantity contracts. According to Silkworth [1990, p. 236], "[c]ourts consider two related factors in deciding these cases. First, courts will uphold quantity variations if they find a valid business reason that justifies the variation. Second, courts will disallow a quantity variation and award damages where they find that the quantity determining party has attempted to manipulate the contract in light of a contract price and market price disparity." Similarly, Burton and Andersen [1995, p. 127] state: "Most cases involving the obligation to perform in good faith can be synthesized using the following principle: a party performs in bad faith by using discretion in performance for reasons outside the justified expectations of the parties arising from their agreement." The problem with both formulations is that they do not provide a framework for inferring the valid business reasons (Silkworth) and reasonable expectations (Burton & Andersen) that would define the contours of good faith. Indeed, once the analytical framework is understood, it is clear that "good faith" does no work.

To facilitate adaptation to changed circumstances, long-term contracts typically allow one party some discretion regarding quantity, requirements and output contracts being extreme forms. Even in these, that discretion will rarely be unbounded. One limitation on discretion is physical. A contract, for example, would not typically require the seller to provide whatever quantity of widgets the buyer desires. Rather, the seller would commit to providing widgets the buyer needs for a particular purpose or to supply a particular plant. The capacity of the buyer's plant would place an outer limit on the buyer's discretion. There are numerous devices for constraining discretion. The contract could set up a mechanism, requiring, for example, that changes be ratified by both parties. Or it could give one party the power to determine output, confronting that party with a cost if it were to change the quantity in a way that would affect adversely the counterparty. If Y is the party with discretion, other things equal, the greater X's reliance, the greater the price Y must pay for quantity adjustments adversely affecting X.

The law, as currently embodied in §2-306(1), provides a set of default rules and barriers to surmounting them. The Code exhibits a lack of faith in the ability of the contracting parties to fine-tune the protection of the reliance. In fact, their ability to fine-tune ex ante is quite impressive, much better, I would assert, than that of courts invoking good faith ex post. I will illustrate this with an analysis of two decisions. In the first, a seller under an output contract reduced its output to zero; in the second, a buyer in a requirements contract significantly increased its requirements following an increase in the market-contract price difference. In both instances the court invoked good faith to reject the defendant's exercise of discretion.

Feld v. Henry S. Levy & Sons, Inc., the leading New York case, illustrates the confused legal response to the seller's decision to reduce its output (or a buyer its requirements) to zero. Levy & Sons operated a wholesale bread baking business. As part of its operations it generated considerable waste product in the form of stale or imperfectly appearing loaves. One option for disposing of this material was to convert it into "bread crumbs" by removing the labels, processing the loaves through two grinders, toasting the product in an oven and bagging it. It purchased the oven and entered into a one year evergreen (automatically renewed) contract with the Crushed Toast Company which agreed to purchase "all bread crumbs produced by the Seller in its factory at 115 Thames Street, Brooklyn, New York" (p. 468) at a price of 6 ¢ a pound. Either party could cancel on six months notice. The Crushed Toast Company was required to deliver a "faithful performance bond," presumably to provide assurance to Levy of timely removal of the waste. In the first eleven months, Levy delivered about $30,000 worth of bread crumbs. Apparently the operation was not profitable for Levy. It attempted to renegotiate the contract price up to 7 ¢, but was rebuffed. One month before the end of the first year Levy dismantled the toasting oven and ceased production of bread crumbs. The waste was then sold to animal food manufacturers. Feld sued for breach.

The New York Court of Appeals held that good faith constrained how the seller was required to conduct his business. The seller was not free to decide whether he should produce any bread crumbs. "The seller's duty to remain in crumb production is a matter calling for close scrutiny of its motives." (p. 471) That scrutiny would require data on "the actual cost of the finished bread crumbs to defendant, statements as to the profits derived or the losses sustained, or data specifying the net or gross return realized from the animal food transactions." (p. 471) Moreover, "[s]ince bread crumbs were but a part of defendant's enterprise and since there was a contractual right of cancellation, good faith requires continued production until cancellation, even if there be no profit. In circumstances such as these and without more, defendant would be justified, in good faith, in ceasing production of the single item prior to cancellation only if its losses from continuance would be more than trivial, which, overall, is a question of fact." (p. 472)

The court failed to recognize that, in its own statement of the facts, it had already provided the relevant economic data. The contract price was six cents per pound and Levy's actions (dismantling the oven) indicate that this amount would not even cover the variable costs; it was cheaper to shut the project down. However, Levy indicated that a price of seven cents per pound would have been sufficient to warrant its continued operation of the toaster oven. So, the fight is over one penny. The court gives no hint as to how that information would help answer the question it has posed. Further, it glosses over the question of why Levy's termination of an operation that does not cover variable costs would be in bad faith. Given the incoherence of the question, the elusiveness of the answer is hardly surprising.

That this was an output contract rather than a requirements contract matters not. It can be viewed as a requirements contract for a service—waste removal. The deformed loaves and day old bread were waste products that happened, by chance, to have a positive market value for various uses. Suppose, instead that they were of no value and that Levy had entered into a contract to have all its trash hauled away at a price of, say, 3 ¢ a pound. The only difference is that the net flow of cash now would be from Levy to Feld. Can one seriously argue that Levy has a duty to stay in business to produce garbage for Feld to haul away? Yet that is precisely what the court has done.

It is conceivable that a producer would under certain circumstances promise to produce a specific level of a waste product. There are circumstances in which the parties might want to give substantial protection to the trash remover's reliance interest. But, in general, the reverse would be true. Those conditions are certainly not met in *Feld v. Levy*. The Crushed Toast Company was in existence prior to the formation of this contract and had other suppliers; toasted bread crumbs could be held in inventory at less expense and for a greater period of time than unsold loaves of bread. Hence its willingness ex ante to both subject itself to Levy's discretion in determining the bread crumb production and to post a faithful performance bond. The fact that Levy, the party that had carefully protected its reliance because it had purchased an oven for making bread crumbs and had a clear need to assure the removal of unsold loaves, dismantled the oven should have been sufficient to end the inquiry. Instead the court, under the banner of good faith, encouraged a fruitless inquiry into the costs and revenues associated with the two alternative ways of disposing of the waste.

In *Feld v. Levy* the issue was the seller's cutting its output to zero. In *Amerada Hess* the court held that the buyer had unreasonably expanded its requirements in response to an increase in the market price. The parties entered into a ten-year contract in December 1969 in which Amerada Hess agreed to supply O&R's requirements for fuel oil No. 6 for its Lovett generating plant in Tompkin's Cove, New York The facts can be pieced together from this decision and a prior dispute between the parties in which Hess was enjoined from terminating the contract, *Orange and Rockland Utilities, Inc. v. Amerada Hess Corporation*. The contract required that Hess lease a parcel of land from O&R and erect storage facilities to which it would deliver the fuel oil. The price for the first five years was $2.14 per barrel, subject to escalation for cost-related factors. The price for the second term would be renegotiated; if the parties failed to reach agreement, the contract would terminate. The quantity clause specified estimated annual sales for the five years. It was expected that the primary fuel at the plant would be gas; projections were for gas to account for about 60% of the BTU's generated by the plant. However, the contract stated: "[nothing] herein shall preclude the use by Buyer of ... natural gas in such quantities as may be or become available." (p. 112)

Five months after the contract was signed, the market price of fuel oil began to rise. By March of 1971 it had more than doubled. O&R increased its fuel oil requirements by over 60% in 1970 and continued to order quantities that were more than double the contractual estimates. In April, 1971, Hess unilaterally attempted to raise the price by 97.7 cents per barrel and threatened to terminate deliveries if O&R declined. O&R purchased additional fuel oil at the market price and sued Hess for the difference for fuel oil purchased through September 1973. Hess' obligation terminated prematurely because of an environmental regulation that went into effect in October 1973. Ironically, the huge run up in oil prices began almost exactly when the contract terminated. O&R's complaint was dismissed because, said the court, its requirements were not incurred in good faith. They were, as a matter of law, unreasonably disproportionate.

O&R could not (and did not) take oil under the contract and resell it at the higher market price. It could only demand fuel oil to supply the needs of the Lovett plant. Its requirements increased over the estimated needs for two reasons. First, it increased its sales to the New York Power Pool, in effect sharing with other utilities the benefits of its below-market price. Second, it substituted oil for gas at the Lovett plant.

> The former factor is tantamount to making the other utilities in the state silent partners to the contract, ... while the latter factor amounts to a unilateral and arbitrary change in the conditions prevailing at the time of the contract so as to take advantage of market conditions at the seller's expense.... Hess was therefore justified in 1970 in refusing to meet plaintiff's demands, by reason of the fact that plaintiff's "requirements" were not incurred in good faith. (pp. 117–118)

The court used "good faith" to impose a quantity ceiling short of the plant's capacity. The contract placed a clear limit on O&R's maximum demand—the capacity of the Lovett generating plant. It should surprise no one in the industry that if the relative prices of oil and gas change, the buyer would react in the appropriate manner. Nor was the existence of the New York Power Pool a deep secret. O&R's requirements depended only in part on the electricity demand of their direct customers. The contract gave O&R flexibility both in its choice of fuel and its dealings with the power pool. If Hess wanted to place tighter limits on O&R's discretion it would have been easy to do so. It could have included a quantity maximum short of the plant's capacity or tied its supply obligation to the market price. Or it could have constrained O&R's ability to take advantage of changes in the relative price of fuels by placing constraints on interfuel substitutability. To be sure, Hess did not anticipate the price increase in 1970 (let alone the much larger increase after October 1973), but that risk was allocated to Hess in the contract. By interposing the "unreasonably disproportionate" standard, the courts deprived O&R of the flexibility it had bargained for, converting the contract into a (nearly) fixed quantity contract. The court implicitly ruled that the buyer had promised to run its plant at less than full capacity for the life of the agreement, never asking why on earth a party would make such an odd promise.

The buyer in *Amerada Hess* did not increase its requirements by expanding its plant. Nor, under the contracts, could it. The physical limits of the plant were the only constraints on their discretion. The contracts could have imposed further limits on interfuel substitution, sales to non-end users (the New York Power Pool), or on total sales. Or they could have set the price as a function of annual power sales (perhaps allowing for renegotiation of the price for all sales above a certain level.) Apparently, the parties felt these additional constraints unnecessary; the court rewrote the contract placing additional constraints on the seller's discretion.

Had the seller wanted to more tightly constrain O&R's discretion it could have included such constraints in the contract. How sharply the buyer's flexibility should be constrained is a decision variable—Hess would have to give up something in exchange. There are many mechanisms for constraining the buyer's discretion, and these are commonly used in long-term contracts between sophisticated players. For one, by incorporating flexible pricing, the contracts could decrease the rewards to opportunistic behavior by the quantity-determining party. Two-part pricing is another example. If the per unit price for small quantities is high, then, so long as the buyer is likely to require an amount above that minimum, the seller will have some assurance that it will receive enough compensation to make its initial investment worth while. Two-part pricing would mean that if the buyer's demand fell off dramatically, the seller could end up bearing all the risk. Alternatively, the buyer could be required to make a fixed payment. The seller might insist upon more assurance, so that even if the buyer took nothing, the seller would still receive some compensation. There are numerous devices for reaching this outcome: take-or-pay, minimum quantity, standby charges, or liquidated damages (and variations on these) all set the marginal price at zero for low quantities.

The backdrop against which both of these contracts were written included "good faith." If the parties drafted their agreements against that backdrop, then, it could be argued, they had incorporated the present understanding of the law into the contract. If the parties expected courts to apply the Code's good faith standard, then a failure to do so would amount to a rewriting of the agreement. Putting a "rational expectations" spin on things, when they entered into the agreement, the parties could have anticipated what the courts ultimately did.

The implied limitation, the argument goes, was part of the deal. Without a theoretical framework there is no particular reason to prefer one interpretation to another. The theoretical framework proposed here allows us to break the circle and to reject the notion that the parties intended to incorporate the Code's good faith standard.

5. Concluding Remarks

One source of Posner's pessimism is his ambition. The economics of contracts has failed because it has failed to produce a Grand Theory. In particular, the malleability of the default rules should be endogenous. If drafting around the rules were easy, then the precise content of the rules would be of little consequence, and the economic analysis might be of value for transactional lawyers, but less so for judges and litigators. Not everything, however, is negotiable. At the extreme, some rules are mandatory. More generally, default rules can be sticky either because the law imposes hurdles of varying heights to drafting around the defaults or because of non-legal factors (for example, the costs of negotiating). The stickiness of the defaults (which includes the uncertainty that any particular deviation will survive in litigation) then becomes a critical factor in analyzing contracts. Characterizing or modeling that stickiness is extremely difficult, especially if one wants to make bold generalizations.

My more optimistic conclusion is based in part on my less ambitious reach. I am content to develop a framework for analyzing contract questions and to put aside the quest for a Grand Theory. A second source of my relative optimism is my focus. Absent from the preceding discussion is any reference to efficient breach, an organizing concept of much of the economics of contract law. Much economic analysis has gone to determining how various remedies might induce parties to choose not to perform their contractual obligation and whether nonperformance would be the right outcome (an efficient breach). The initial result—expectation damages would lead to efficient breach—was, as Posner observes, swamped by a plethora of complications. Those included encouraging reliance, the costs of the initial negotiation, renegotiation, and litigation.

In this paper, I have broken out one piece of expectation damages—the contract-market differential and proposed a rationale for enforcement, a rationale that has implications for how the differential ought to be measured in some complicated settings. I did not deal with other elements of expectation damages: consequential damages and lost profits. A strong case can be made, I believe, for the notion that reasonable parties would choose not to compensate for these. Contrary to the usual claim that contract damages are undercompensatory, I would suggest that it is more likely that allowing compensation for these categories is likely to result in remedies that are too generous. That argument I will save for a later day.

Under the court's interpretation of both *Bloor* and *Levy*, the outcome hinged on how much the promisor would have to lose. Falstaff's best efforts obligation did not require that its Ballantine promotion be "financially disastrous." Good faith required that Levy incur losses unless those losses "would be more than trivial." In neither case should it have been necessary to engage in such an inquiry. To be sure, courts regularly confront the question of how much is too much. That they do it often does not mean that they do it well. Other things equal, a framework that enables courts to avoid such inquiries is likely to provide a sounder basis for resolving contract disputes. And in those two cases other things were not equal—the economic framework led to posing the problem in a more sensible way.

REFERENCES

Burton, Steven and Eric G. Andersen. 1995. *Contractual Good Faith*. New York: Little Brown.
Farnsworth, E. Allan. 1984. "On Trying to Keep One's Promises: The Duty of Best Efforts in Contract Law". *University of Pittsburg Law Review* 46: 1–20.
Fuller, Lon and William Perdue. 1936. "The Reliance Interest in Contract Damages". *Yale Law Journal* 46: 52–96, 373–420.
Gilson, Ronald J. 1984. "Value Creation by Business Lawyers: Legal Skills and Asset Pricing". *Yale Law Journal* 94: 239–313.
Goldberg, Victor P. 1985. "Price Adjustment in Long-Term Contracts". *Wisconsin Law Review* 1985: 527–543.
Goldberg, Victor P. 1991. "The International Salt Puzzle". *Research in Law and Economics* 14: 31–49.
Goldberg, Victor P. 2000. "In Search of Best Efforts: Reinterpreting *Bloor v. Falstaff*". *St. Louis University Law Journal* 44: 1465–1485.
Goldberg, Victor P. 2002. "Discretion in Long-Term Open Quantity Contracts: Reining in Good Faith". *UC Davis Law Review* 35: 319–385.
Goldberg, Victor P. and John Erickson. 1987. "Quantity and Price Adjustment in Long-Term Contracts: A Case Study of Petroleum Coke". *Journal of Law and Economics* 30: 369–398.
Jackson, Thomas H. 1978. "'Anticipatory Repudiation' and the Temporal Element of Contract Law: An Economic Inquiry into Contract Damages in Cases of Prospective Nonperformance". *Stanford Law Review* 31: 69–119.
Joskow, Paul. 1977. Commercial Impossibility, the Uranium Market and the Westinghouse Case. *Journal of Legal Studies* 6: 119–176.
Posner, Eric. 2003. "Economic Analysis of Contract Law after Three Decades: Success or Failure?" *Yale Law Journal* 112: 829–880.
Silkworth, Stacy A. 1990. "Quantity Variation in Open Quantity Contracts". *University of Pittsburg Law Review* 51: 235–279.

Cases

Aluminum Company of America v. Essex Group, Inc., 499 F. Supp. 53 (W.D.Pa. 1980).
Amerada Hess v. Orange & Rockland Utilities, Inc. 59 A.D.2d 110; 397 N.Y.S.2d 814; 96 A.L.R.3d 1263; 22 U.C.C. Rep. Serv. (Callaghan) 310 (1977).
Bloor v. Falstaff 601 F. 2d 609 (2d Cir. 1979).
Compania Naviera Asiatic v. The Burmah Oil Co. Findings of Fact and Conclusions of Law in No. 74-2025 (S. D. N. Y. Apr. 27, 1977) (Frankel, J.)

Feld v. Levy 37 N.Y.2d 466, 373 N.Y.S.2d 102, 335 N.E.2d 320 (N.Y. 1975).
Laredo Hides Co. Inc. v. H & H Meat Products Co., Inc. 513 S. W. 2d 210 (1974).
Missouri Furnace Co. v. Cochrane. 8 F. 463 (C. C. W. D. Pa. 1881).
Northern Indiana Public Service Company v Carbon County Coal Co., 799 F. 2d 265 (7th Cir., 1986).
Orange and Rockland Utilities, Inc. v. Amerada Hess Corporation, 67 Misc.2d 560, 324 N.Y.S.2d 494 (1971).

SECTION VI

Regulation

20. The Institutions of Regulation: An Application to Public Utilities

PABLO T. SPILLER and MARIANO TOMMASI

1. Introduction

Regulation is part of the complex web of a nation's public policy. To understand regulatory design, then, it is imperative to understand the general determinants of public policy. The purpose of this essay is to highlight the usefulness of a transactional approach to public policy determination in understanding the origins, nature and the evolution of the institutions of regulation. As it merits an essay in a volume on the New Institutional Economics, we approach public policy as a (complex and often intertemporal) transaction among policy makers.[1] As such, the nature and features of public policies are impacted by the type of contracts facilitated by the institutions—i.e., the rules of the political game—of the country in question.[2] Here, then, we analyze the institutional determinants of regulatory policy making by looking at regulation as the outcome of complex intertemporal exchanges among policy makers. As in normal economic transactions, efficient intertemporal exchanges require safeguarding institutions. In their absence, we will observe the development of non-cooperative and short-term behavior, inflexible rules to avoid political opportunism, and in general low quality regulatory policies.

There are three basic types of regulatory equilibrium outcomes: public ownership, flexible regulation or rigid regulation. The type of regulatory outcome observed in a jurisdiction, then, is a direct result of the polity's ability to undertake complex intertemporal exchanges.

This approach, with strong intellectual underpinnings in the transaction costs approach as developed by Oliver Williamson,[3] places the emphasis on what Levy and Spiller (1994) calls regulatory governance, and less on regulatory incentives. They see regulatory governance as the mechanisms that societies use to constrain regulatory discretion, and to resolve conflicts that arise in

---

[1] This approach traces its roots to the path breaking contributions of the McNollGast team. See McCubbins, et al (1987, 1989).

[2] North (1990) separates institutions from organizations. Institutions are "the rules of the game" of a society, while organizations (such as firms, or legislatures) are formal structures with certain objectives, constrained by society's institutions.

[3] See, in particular, Williamson (1975), (1979), (1985), (1996).

relation to these constraints.[4] On the other hand, regulatory incentives are the rules governing utility pricing, cross- or direct-subsidies, entry, interconnection, etc. While regulatory incentives may affect performance, a main insight from Levy and Spiller (1994) is that the impact of regulatory incentives (whether positive or negative) comes to the forefront only if regulatory governance has successfully been put into place. We go, however, one step further, and suggest that to understand regulatory performance we need to understand the institutional determinants of regulatory governance. In this sense, our neo-institutional approach to regulatory institutions differs from the two main strands of the economics of regulation literature of the last twenty years: the Chicago school and the incentives theory of regulation.

We differ from the Chicago School, as exemplified in the path breaking work by Stigler (1971), Peltzman (1976) and Posner (1971), in that, although rent seeking and distributional effects are important to understand public policy outcomes, we emphasize the institutional aspects that impact on the nature of regulatory institutions, and thus of regulation and sectoral performance. In other words, we believe it is important to open the black box of regulation. We differ also from the incentives theory of regulation, as developed following the path breaking work of, among others, Loeb and Magat (1979), Baron and Myerson (1982), and Laffont and Tirole,[5] in two main respects. First, we emphasize that the contracting schemes that are required to provide second best incentives are dependent on the institutional environment in which the firms operate. By developing the link between the institutional environment and the type of regulatory institutions that are feasible, we can, implicitly, develop the institutional conditions under which incentive regulation becomes feasible. Second, since the incentive theory of regulation shares the "black box" approach to politics of the Chicago School,[6] our emphasis on institutional determinants rather than pure efficiency incentives separates us also from the incentive theory of regulation.

Our emphasis in moving one step (or even two steps) higher in the hierarchy of issues not only makes us shift the object from regulatory policy itself (are prices closer to long run marginal cost, are mark-ups sensitive to cost changes),[7] to regulatory governance (are regulatory processes and rules to uphold those policies well established and stable?) and its link to the institutional environment that implements it, but also shifts the performance metric of analysis. Levy and Spiller (1994) emphasize that there are multiple regulatory regimes that are consistent with good performance. What is important, though, is that regulatory policy be stable, coherent, consistent across areas, predictable. In other words,

---

[4] Williamson would call such constraints on regulatory decision making "contractual governance institutions." See Williamson (1985, p. 35).

[5] See the summary of their work in Laffont and Tirole (1993).

[6] Observe that in most of the incentive theory of regulation literature, the regulatory process is described by a regulator's utility function. Interesting extensions into hierarchical or more dynamic models of regulation have brought some institutional flavors to this literature. See, for example, Demski and Sappington (1987), Baron and Besanko (1987) and Laffont and Tirole (1991).

[7] These are the object of analysis of the Chicago school and the incentive regulation literature.

what public administration scholars would call "good quality."[8] One could ask why not all regulatory outcomes are of high quality. Some may emphasize issue complexity, or administrative capabilities, or distributional features, or bureaucratic discretion. Here we propose to explore the implications of looking at regulation as a political transaction for the resulting features of regulatory policy. Thus, we suggest we move the discussion of regulation as an implicit contract between a regulator, or the government, and a firm, as is implicitly done in the literature on incentive regulation, to one among policy makers, where the result of that exchange, the nature of regulation, has direct implications to sector performance. This approach, then, places more emphasis on structure and process than necessarily on outcomes, and in that way it has important predecessors. Among those, Joskow (1974) and Williamson (1976) were some of the first to introduce process in the positive analysis of regulation. More directly related is the fundamental work of McCubbins, et al (1987 and 1989) who, as applied to United States regulatory issues, were the first to link political structure to regulatory process.

The approach presented here, then, combines two of the pillars of the New Institutional Economics—transaction costs economics and positive political economy. Transaction costs economics provides the underlying framework to understand the contracting issues among legislatures. Positive political economy provides the framework to understand the connection between institutions and politicians' incentives.

In this chapter we analyze the implications of this approach to the rise and evolution of regulatory institutions. Exclusively for the purpose of keeping the focus, we apply this essay to the regulation of public services, or as it is called in the United States, public utilities. The reader, however, should be able to extrapolate the implications of this analysis to other regulatory issues, like financial regulation, fiscal federalism, and so on and so forth. Finally, the analysis is applied to developed and developing nations as well. The structure of the chapter is as follows. In Section 2 we introduce what we see is the basic problem of utilities. We use this section to highlight the issues that regulatory institutions must deal with. Section 3 introduces a framework that we use to highlight some key issues in the design of regulatory institutions: in particular the delegation to agencies and courts. Section 4 deals with regulatory governance in detail, by looking at its theoretical underpinnings and actual practice, and we provide some final comments in Section 5.

2. THE PROBLEM OF UTILITIES

In this section we contend that the overarching problem driving the regulation of utilities, whether public or private, and thus the issues politicians have to deal with, is how to limit governmental opportunism, understood as the incentives

---

[8] These features are what Spiller and Tommasi (2003) call the "outer features" of policies.

politicians have to expropriate –once the investments are made- the utilities' quasi rents, whether under private or public ownership, so as to garner political support. Institutional environments that are successful in generating regulatory institutions that limit governmental opportunism will be able to also provide successful sector performance. This, by no means, implies that other issues like the exercise of market power, the main topic in the incentives regulation literature, or interest group politics, the main topic in the Chicago School of regulation, are irrelevant or of no interest. Instead, our thrust is that what drives institutional design in public utility regulation is limiting governmental opportunism, not allocative efficiency. What drives the implementation of regulatory incentives, on the other hand, is the trade-off between allocative efficiency and distributional issues, given the constraints given by regulatory governance. Our focus, however, is on regulatory governance. Thus, in what follows we focus on its main determinants, and less on the implications of restraining the exercise of market power by utilities.[9]

What Defines Utilities

Three features characterize utilities: first, their technologies are characterized by large specific, sunk, investments;[10] second, their technologies are characterized by important economies of scale and scope; and third, their products are massively consumed. Consider, for example, an electricity distribution company. Its assets have very little value in alternative uses (it is very expensive to bring down cables and posts, to dig out trenches, etc);[11] network externalities and economies of density imply that it may not be economical to have multiple wires deployed on the same street; and finally, its product is consumed by a large proportion of the city's population. Compare this situation to that of another industry characterized by large sunk investments: steel. While steel mills have very little value in alternative uses, the economies of scale and scope are trivial compared to the size of the market,[12] and furthermore, while everybody indirectly consume steel products, very few individuals in society pay any attention to the price of steel. Thus, it is not simply specific investments that characterize utilities. Nor is it simply economies of scale. Nor is it widespread consumption. What separates the utility sector from the rest of the economy is the combination of the three features: specific investments, economies of

---

[9] Almost all of the incentives regulation literature deals with restraining market power, while neglecting, except for some remarkable exceptions (e.g. Baron and Besanko 1987), the implications of governmental opportunism.

[10] Specific or sunk investments are those that once undertaken their value in alternative uses is substantially below their investment cost.

[11] Although the development of fiber optics has increased the value in alternative uses of their electricity poles.

[12] In some developing countries that protect the production of steel, that may not be so, as there may be just a few steel mills producing for the relatively small local market.

scale and widespread domestic consumption. These features are at the core of contracting problems that have traditionally raised the need for governmental regulation of utilities.[13] In turn, they make the pricing of utilities inherently political.

The reason for the politicization of infrastructure pricing is threefold. First, the fact that a large component of infrastructure investments is sunk, implies that once the investment is undertaken the operator will be willing to continue operating as long as operating revenues exceed operating costs. Since operating costs do not include a return on sunk investments (but only on the alternative value of these assets), the operating company will be willing to operate even if prices are below total average costs.[14] Second, economies of scale imply that in most utility services, there will be few suppliers in each locality. Thus, the whiff of monopoly will always surround utility operations. Finally, the fact that utility services tend to be massively consumed, and thus that the set of consumers closely approximates the set of voters, implies that politicians and interest groups will care about the level of utility pricing. Thus, massive consumption, economies of scale and sunk investments provide governments (either national or local) with the opportunity to behave opportunistically vis-à-vis the investing company.[15] For example, after the investment is sunk, the government may try to restrict the operating company's pricing flexibility, may require the company to undertake special investments, purchasing or employment patterns or may try to restrict the movement of capital. All these are attempts to expropriate the company's sunk costs by administrative measures. Thus, expropriation may be indirect and undertaken by subtle means.

Expropriation of the firm's sunk assets, however, does not mean that the government takes over the operation of the company, but rather that it sets operating conditions that just compensate for the firm's operating costs and the return on its non-specific assets. Such returns will provide sufficient ex-post incentives for the firm to operate, but not to invest.[16] Indeed, sunk assets expropriation has been more prevalent in the developing world than direct utility takeovers or

---

[13] See, among others, North (1990), Williamson (1988), Goldberg (1976), Levy and Spiller (1994) and Spiller (1993).

[14] Observe that the source of financing does not change this computation. For example, if the company is completely leveraged, a price below average cost will bring the company to bankruptcy, eliminating the part of the debt associated with the sunk investments. Only the part of the debt that is associated with the value of the non-sunk investments would be able to be subsequently serviced.

[15] Observe that this incentive is as strong vis-à-vis private *and* public companies. See Savedoff and Spiller (1999).

[16] The company will be willing to continue operating because its return from operating will exceed its return from shutting down and deploying its assets elsewhere. On the other hand, the firm will have very little incentive to invest new capital as it will not be able to obtain a return. While it is feasible to conceive loan financing for new investments, as non-repayment would bring the company to bankruptcy, that will not however be the case. Bankruptcy does not mean that the company shuts down. Since the assets are specific, bankruptcy implies a change of ownership from stockholders to creditors. Now creditors' incentives to operate will be the same as the firm, and they would be willing to operate even if quasi-rents are expropriated. Thus, loan financing will not be feasible either.

expropriation without compensation.[17] While the government may uphold and protect traditionally conceived property rights, it may still capture the utilities' quasi-rents via regulatory decision-making, what is commonly called "indirect expropriation" in international law. By setting prices, investment or quality requirements, taxes and the like, the state may limit the ability of the utility to recover its sunk investments, while still granting it enough cash flow to cover its variable operating costs. The government, in this way, obtain political support from relatively low prices *and* the maintenance of service, albeit with diminished incentives to invest and expand and in continuous conflicts with the utility.

Governmental Opportunism

Sunk assets' expropriation may be profitable for a government if the direct costs (reputation loss vis-à-vis other utilities, lack of future investments by utilities) are small compared to the (short term) benefits of such action (achieving re-election by reducing utilities' prices, by attacking the monopoly, etc), and if the indirect institutional costs (e.g., disregarding the judiciary, not following the proper, or traditional, administrative procedures, etc) are not too large.

Thus, incentives for expropriation of sunk assets should be expected to be largest in environments where indirect institutional costs are low,[18] direct costs are also small,[19] and, perhaps, more importantly, the government's horizon is relatively short.[20] Forecasting such expropriation, private utilities will not undertake investments in the first place. Thus, government direct intervention may become the default mode of operation.

The Performance Implications of Government Opportunism

If, in the presence of such incentives a government wants to motivate investment in utilities, then, it will have to design institutional arrangements that will

---

[17] Consider, for example, the case of Azurix Buenos Aires S.A. Azurix purchased the right to operate a large water concession in the Province of Buenos Aires in early 1999, paying almost $440 million. Right after taking possession, Azurix encountered multiple unexepected breaches by the Provincial government of prior written commitments (e.g., inability to adjust old property records to new information; lack of investment by the government in various water works needed to provide service; lack of tariff adjustments based on producer price index, imposition of subsidy requirement without compensation) to the point that in two years the company found it impossible to continue, and decided to return the concession and file for international arbitration under a claim of indirect expropriation. This case is an example of expropriating without taking ownership. According to Azurix, the Provincial Government simply reneged on its revenue promises, not allowing Azurix to obtain a return commensurate with its original investment. See La Nación, October 10, 2001, "Azurix anunció formalmente que en 90 días deja de operar."

[18] Indirect institutional costs are low when, for example, there are no formal or informal governmental procedures -checks and balances- required for regulatory decision making; regulatory policy is centralized in the administration; the judiciary does not have a tradition of, or the power to, reviewing administrative decisions, and in general, the executive expects little in terms of political downfall or retaliation from other branches of government.

[19] E.g., the utilities in general do not require massive investment programs, nor technological change is an important factor in the sector.

[20] I.e., highly contested elections, need to satisfy key constituencies, etc.

limit its own ability to behave opportunistically once the utility undertook its investment program. Such institutional arrangements are nothing but the design of regulatory governance. Regulatory governance, if credible, solves a key contracting problem between the government and the utilities—whether public or private—[21] by restraining the government from opportunistically expropriating the utilities' sunk investments.[22] This, however, does not mean that the utility has to receive assurances of a rate of return nature, or that it has to receive exclusive licenses. In some countries, however, where the incentives for governmental opportunism are high, exclusive licenses and well-specified assurances on rates of return may be the only way to grant investors sufficient incentives to invest.

Unless regulatory governance is credible, then, investments will not be undertaken, or if undertaken will not be efficient. Investment inefficiencies may arise in several fronts. A first order effect is underinvestment. Although the utility may invest, it will do so exclusively in areas whose market return is very high and where the payback period is relatively short.[23] Second, maintenance expenditures may be kept to the minimum, thus degrading quality. Third, investment may be undertaken with technologies that have a lower degree of specificity, even at the cost of, again, degrading quality.[24] Fourth, up-front rents may be achieved by very high prices which although may provide incentives for some investment, may be politically unsustainable.[25]

Regulatory governance schemes that do not limit the potential for governmental opportunism, then, create strong inefficiencies and poor sector

---

[21] Savedoff and Spiller (1999).

[22] See, Goldberg (1976) for one of the first treatments of this problem. See also Williamson (1976). See also Troesken (1996) and (1997) for a seminal treatment of the origins of state regulation of utilities in the United States.

[23] An alternative way of reducing the specificity of the investment is by customers undertaking the financing of the sunk assets. For example, SAGUAPAC, the water public service cooperative of Santa Cruz, Bolivia, requires commitment of customer financing prior to undertaking an expansion plan. For a discussion of Saguapac's strategy, see Walton (2003). Similarly, Chile's Electricity Services General Law of 1982 allows the utilities to require that customers requesting service finance, via a reimbursable charge, any required expansion cost, or that they undertake the investment directly. See Arts. 75 and 76. (http://www.sec.cl/OpenDocs/data/13/DFL%201%20Electricidad.doc)

[24] In this sense it is not surprising that private telecommunications operators that rushed to develop the telecommunications sector in Easter European countries, moved first and foremost into cellular rather than fixed link networks. While cellular has a higher long run cost than fixed link, and on some quality dimensions is also an inferior product, the magnitude of investment in specific assets is much smaller than in fixed link networks. Furthermore, a large portion of the specific investments in cellular telephony are undertaken by the customers themselves (who purchase the handsets). See also, Noll and Shirley (2002) for an analysis of telecommunications development in Africa.

[25] The privatization of Argentina's telecommunications companies is particularly illuminating. Prior to the privatization, telephone prices were raised well beyond international levels. It is not surprising, that following the privatization the government reneged on aspects of the license, like its price indexation as ways to limit the quasi-rents of the investors. The initial high prices, though, allowed the companies to remain profitable, even following government's deviation from the license provisions. See Levy and Spiller (1996).

performance. Poor quality, lack of investments and high prices lead, eventually, to the conflicts between operators and the government. Unless those are resolved by a new regulatory governance scheme, popular support for efficient pricing will fade, as higher prices will not translate into improved service. In those environments, government ownership may be the only feasible mode.[27]

Contrasting Firm with Governmental Opportunism

At the core of both the Chicago School and the Incentives approach is a normative or passive view of the regulatory process. In the Chicago School, regulation can be perceived as an arena where conflicting private interests are accommodated, while in the incentives regulation literature, regulatory rules are optimally designed to placate the firm's profit motive. The former approaches political actors as essentially passive, while the latter approaches political actors as benevolent. We see political actors differently. They are neither passive nor benevolent. They are not different than any of us. They are opportunistic—willing to lie and deceive and to pursue "self-interest with guile."[28]

There is, though, a fundamental difference between governmental opportunism and the opportunism or exercise of market power that is perceived to be at the root of the regulatory problem by most neoclassical economists. If what drove the design of regulatory policy-making is the potential for private firm opportunism or exercise of market power, then that could be undertaken by the application of general antitrust (and common law) provisions.[29] There would be no need for industry specific regulation. Indeed granting the power to limit the exercise of market power by regulatory fiat—say by setting maximum prices, conducting cost reviews, requiring specific investments, and the like, grants the political and administrative power that is behind governmental opportunism.[30] Troesken (1996 and 1997) has convincingly argued that the early 1900 movement away from municipal regulation towards state regulation was a way to reduce the incentives to behave opportunistically by the municipal regulators. Although some will argue that the complexities of modern regulatory issues (e.g., interconnection, prices and standards) tilts the balance towards regulatory

---

[26] While the link between aggregate institutional features of a country and general economic growth is by now a growth industry (see, for example, Knack and Keefer 1995 and Haggard and Kaufman 1995), few have taken the step of linking actual country's general and regulatory institutions and explored the impact on sector performance. For such examples, see Henisz and Zelner (2001) for an application to investment in telecommunications, Henisz and Zelner (2002) for an application to electricity investment, and Henisz (2002) for an application to railways, telecommunications and electricity generation across 129 countries over the period 1815–1998.

[27] For an analysis to the water sector, see Savedoff and Spiller (1999).

[28] See Williamson (1975, p. 26).

[29] This light-handed regulation approach was implemented in New Zealand following the reforms of the mid 1980s. See Evans et al. (1996).

[30] Indeed, Barry Weingast's (1995, p. 1) opening paragraph perfectly exemplifies this point. He says: "A government strong enough to protect property rights and enforce contracts is also strong enough to confiscate the wealth of its citizens."

agencies, regulatory agencies were created more than 100 years ago, at times when the pressing regulatory issues were less interconnection and other complex regulatory issues, and more investment incentives in the presence of strong pressure to limit prices.[31] Thus, although on a day-to-day regulators' main concerns are indeed firm opportunism and the restrain of market power, rather than thinking how to restrain themselves from expropriating the firms' quasirents, the origins of regulatory governance is rooted in restraining governmental opportunism.

Although in some environments regulatory governance may have been designed to facilitate private capture, such design exposes the regulatory process to *political capture* following a turn of the political wheel.[32] Private investors fearing such event will be cautious on long-term investments, and more interested in short term gains. Thus, regulatory design that limits the potential for governmental opportunism not only facilitates investment, but also serves to credibly enhance the political restrain over operators' opportunism.

3. A Transactions Approach to Regulatory Governance

In this section we develop a framework that we use to relate the design of regulatory governance to the nature of the country's institutional environment. The main thrust is that in environments in which intertemporal political exchanges are difficult to make, the type of regulatory institutions chosen will become extremely important in determining the extent of commitment the polity can provide to private (and public) enterprises, and thus, the potential for sector performance. In particular, in "difficult contracting" political environments, the equilibrium regulatory governance may not provide for sufficient regulatory flexibility to implement complex regulatory schemes as required in the incentives regulation literature. Instead, under some conditions regulation will be stable but inflexible, providing thus little in the sense of high power incentives. In other words, it will be "third best." Under other circumstances, however, the regulatory governance itself will be ill defined. Policy, as a consequence, will be erratic, not providing strong incentives for private investment and sector performance.

We develop this framework in two stages. First, we explore an abstract game among policy makers, where the outcome of the game may consist on institutional restrains on policy making. We then implement the insights of this game to the real world, by analyzing the features of the political environment that help determine the nature of these institutional restraints.

---

[31] See for example Troesken and Geddes (2003) analysis of the municipalization of water works in the late 1800s early 1900s in the US.
[32] See, Esfahani (1996) for a fascinating description of the regulatory process in the Philippines, where political alignment between the utilities' shareholders and the government seems to have been determinative of the shareholders' incentives to invest.

A Framework to Understand Regulatory Institutions

We approach public policy as a game among politicians with conflicting interests reflecting basic ideological or constituency differences. Thus, some may take a long term view of promoting investments, while others may feel the need for achieving short term distributive gains.

Institutions, and for that matter, regulatory institutions, are (contractual) outcomes to that game, whose purpose is to provide some limits on future political behavior. Since all contracts are incomplete, the limitation in the power of the political agent cannot be fully contingent. Thus, in an environment in which political actors take (random) turns at the helm of the political machine, limiting the ability of the political actor in power has a cost. The more this power is limited, the less policy can be adjusted to unexpected economic and technological shocks, even when, under full information, all political actors would be *ex-post* better off with such an adaptation. On the other hand, such limits also have benefits. By limiting policy drifts associated with random political outcomes, policy becomes more predictable, and economic agents may undertake more long-term investments.

Politicians, however, may not find it necessary to put institutional limits to their own discretion. Such limits may arise endogenously as behavioral norms from the repeated nature of the game they play. In such circumstances, political opportunism will not be an issue, as the threat of retaliation from breaking the norm will keep politicians from deviating from efficient policies, thus maximizing the common (political) good.[33] In those circumstances, policies will adapt to technological and economic shocks, while will be insensitive to the randomness of politics.

It is easy to show that if political actors are infinitely lived and patient enough (a characterization, though, that one does not normally assign to political agents), their repeated interaction could sustain such first-best policies as a Nash equilibrium in an infinitely repeated game.[34] If their discount rate is high enough, though, (full) cooperation will not be sustainable in equilibrium. In such a case, policies will depend on the realization of political uncertainty. Policies will alternate with the identity of the ruling politician. We can describe this regulatory policy as unstable, not providing safeguards for investors.

It is in these environments, more closely associated with the real world, that policy-makers may consider entering into some type of *ex-ante* agreements that would limit their *ex-post* power. The set of feasible (enforceable) agreements will depend on the issue under consideration, as well as on the available enforcement technologies. Suppose, for instance, that *ex-ante* regulatory compacts can be enforced by third parties,[35] but that the realization of economic shocks is not verifiable. In that case, it will not be feasible to enforce agreements that prescribe

---

[33] See Spiller and Tommasi (2003) and Saporiti et al (2002) for further developments of this idea.

[34] More generally, the possibility of sustaining cooperation will depend on a number of factors beyond the discount rate, including the number of players, and the parameters that characterize the details of the intra-period decision procedure.

[35] Third parties could constitute the domestic courts, or even international arbitration courts.

regulatory rules contingent on the state of technology or costs. Simple rules, though, can be agreed upon. These simple rules will then be highly inflexible regulatory policies or procedures. They will set regulatory policy or processes independent of technological or economic shocks.[36]

Such "best feasible" policies come, though, at a cost. Thus, if repeated play among policy-makers delivers cooperation, a rigid rule will not be utilized. But when the parties have a limited capacity to self-enforce cooperative agreements (whether because of impatience or lack of enforcement technologies), policy makers must make a choice between rigid policy rules and procedures (not responsive to the economic environment) or erratic (i.e., alternating) policies, subject to the outcome of the political wheel. Spiller and Tommasi (2003) show that a condition for rigid rules to arise in equilibrium is that the divergence in politicians' interests concerning the issue at hand be more extreme than the volatility of the underlying economic and technological shocks. Utility regulation, particularly in the early years, seems to be more characterized by distributional aspects than by the importance of adaptation to technological shocks. It is in those environments, then, that policy and procedural rigidities may arise to move away from the costs of political randomness.

Thus, when intertemporal political exchanges are hard to enforce, we may observe highly inflexible institutionally designed policies, with policies not adjusting well neither to politics nor to economic shocks, or highly erratic policies, reflecting not just economic shocks, but also electoral politics.

This discussion can be interpreted in standard transaction costs arguments. If the institutional environment facilitates political cooperation, then relatively efficient and adaptable policies can be implemented without many (and costly) safeguards. When the environment does not facilitate cooperation, but the costs of implementing safeguards are relatively low, then the policy will be implemented with the support of associated safeguards (*ex-ante* rigid –institutionally driven- rules). When, on the other hand, the costs of implementing safeguards are very high, then policies will respond to political shocks.[37]

The Determinants of Political Cooperation

The previous section, then, provides an abstract characterization of the political environment by exploring the ability of the polity to reach intertemporal cooperation, thus relating the nature of the political environment to the nature of

---

[36] Thus, for example, the regulatory regime will not allow the return on assets to be adjusted to changes in interest rates. For example, Chile's Electric Services Law (DFL #1 of 1982) sets, in its Art 106, at 10% the real rate of return on assets to use in setting retail tariffs.

[37] This basic idea can be extended in multiple ways. For example, there may be intertemporal links to regulatory issues. Those linkages arise in the regulatory environment because of the impact of policies on investment. In other policy domains they could arise from technical reasons (i.e., policies that have intertemporal effects), legal reasons (a law is in placed until it is changed), or economic reasons (present fiscal actions have future effects through intertemporal budget constraints). Saporiti et al (2002) explore such linkages, and show that in bad transactions environments, some welfare improving policies (or reforms) are not undertaken, and there is also under-investment in policymaking capabilities.

regulatory rules and policies. In this section we start discussing the features of the political environment that make for a more or less cooperative environment. In the next section we develop the type of regulatory and procedural rigidities that societies may find necessary to provide long term regulatory credibility. In moving the abstract discussion of the previous section to the real world, we now discuss six features of political environments that impact of the ability of political actors to engage in long term cooperation:

1. *Number of political actors with power over a given decision.* Theory predicts that the larger the number of relevant policy-makers players, the smaller the set of other parameters for which cooperation obtains. This result obtains in general games under some reasonable conditions on the set of feasible payoffs.[38] Electoral rules have also important effects on the "effective number of parties"— or legislative players—that will tend to result from elections, and thus, the extent of governmental control over the legislative process. It is widely perceived, for example, that proportional representation tends to generate a large number of parties, while first-past-the-post with relatively small district elections tends to create bipolar party configurations.[39]

2. *Intertemporal linkages among key political actors.* The intertemporal pattern of interactions among individuals in formal political positions (such as legislators, president, bureaucrats) matters for developing cooperative outcomes. It is not the same to have a legislature in which the same individuals interact over extended periods of time, as to have a legislature where individuals are drawn at random from given populations (parties, provinces, etc) with frequent replacement. Non-simultaneous elections for the different branches of government, for example, tend to enhance political continuity and thus electoral checks and balances.[40]

3. *Timing and observability of moves.* Cooperation is harder to sustain if unilateral moves are hard to observe or hard to verify (Green and Porter 1984,

---

[38] In some simple games, such as common-pool ones, the result is fairly straight-forward and general. See Fudenberg and Tirole (1991) for the result that, holding constant the dimension of the set of feasible payoffs, increasing the number of players reduces the set of equilibria towards less cooperative ones. Holding constant the number of players, the theory has predictions in terms of the parameters of the stochastic recognition process. For instance, tacit cooperation is more likely the more uncertain are election results over time; i.e., the more evenly divided are the chances of being in power at each point in time (as in Dixit et al 2000, de Figueiredo 2001, and Alesina 1988). Separation of powers dampens here the volatility of politics as restrains changes in the set of implementable politics. On this see Cox and McCubbins (2001), Shugart and Haggard (2001), Tsebelis (2002), Cooter (2000) and Epstein and O'Halloran (1999). For earlier treatments of the topic, see also Gely and Spiller (1990) and McCubbins, et al (1987, 1989).

[39] This result has been coined Duverger's Law in political science. See Duverger (1954). More generally, see Taagepera and Shugart (1993). For analyses of how the structure of political parties depends on the nature of electoral rules (with applications to the UK) see Cain, et al (1987) and Cox (1987). See also Cox (1997) linking electoral systems to political behavior more generally, and Haggard and McCubbins (2001) for more references. Federalist structures create another dimension to the "number of players." On the role of federalism in limiting discretion see Weingast (1995). On possible "complications" once you enter into the details of the way federalism is structured in each county, see Tommasi (2002) and Careaga and Weingast (2002).

[40] See Jacobson (1990). See also Shugart and Carey (1992).

"d *Exchange arenas*"

Lehrer 1989). The ability of the executive to legislate is one such feature. While parliamentary systems grant such powers in principle, whether they do so in practice depends upon the nature of electoral rules and the political party system. Parliamentary systems whose electoral rules bring about fragmented legislatures would not provide the executive—usually headed by a minority party with a coalition built on a very narrow set of specific common interests—with much scope for legislative initiative. By contrast, electoral rules that create strong two-party parliamentary systems—as well as some other kinds of non-parliamentary political institutions—would grant the executive large legislative powers.[41]

4. *Availability of enforcement technologies.* Other than self-enforcement through repeated play, certain forms of cooperation may be achieved by alternative institutional means. One alternative consists on fixing policy rules of the type analyzed above, which limit future opportunistic behavior. Another alternative is to delegate policy to an independent bureaucracy. Although bureaucratic delegation is a choice (Moe 1990, Epstein and O'Halloran 1994, 1996 and 1999, Huber and Shipan 2002), it is partly constrained by some general properties of civil service in the country, like its professionalism. These generic features of the bureaucracy are themselves endogenous to more fundamental constitutional, electoral, and historical factors, but can be taken as given when considering a specific policy deal. It can be shown, though, that delegating policy forever to an individual with preferences in between those of the two parties, leads to the first best. Delegation, as we discuss later in this essay, has its problems, but there will be cases in which the cost of those problems is smaller than the cost of "partisan" policymaking. A somewhat similar reasoning applies to the presence and characteristics of an impartial umpire and enforcer of political agreements, such as an independent Judiciary. This has traditionally been the way administrative discretion is restrained in the US, as regulatory statutes have tended to be quite vague, thus delegating to the courts the enforcement of explicit or implicit contracts among politicians.[42]

5. *Characteristics of the arenas where key political actors undertake their exchanges.* The complex intertemporal exchanges required for the implementation of effective public policies would be facilitated by the existence of exchange arenas organized in ways that make cooperation easier to enforce. Weingast and Marshall (1988), for example, claim that the organization of the US Congress is designed to facilitate intertemporal cooperation in political exchanges.[43] Their main thrust is that in the United States the legislature is the arena where the key political transactions take place. As a consequence, legislators designed the institutional framework of the legislature in ways to increase the predictability

---

[41] See, among others, Cox and McCubbins (2001), Moe and Caldwell (1994), Persson, et al (1997), Persson and Tabellini (2002 and 2003), and Tsebelis (1995 and 2002).

[42] For an analysis of the choice of specificity of statutes, see Schwartz, Spiller and Urbiztondo (1993). Observe, however, that administrative law may not develop in a system where the executive has strong control over the legislative process, and thus may not serve as an effective enforcement entity. See, for example, Iaryczower, et al (2002).

[43] See also Shepsle and Bonchek (1997) and the collection in Shepsle and Weingast (1996).

of its functioning and to protect the interests of its members—including their re-election chances. In general, though, whether the legislature, as the arena where these transactions take place, is adequately institutionalized or not, depends on several factors including legislators' incentives and capabilities. In environments with weak legislatures,[44] and many developed and developing nations have such legislatures, political exchanges will take place in alternative settings that will tend to be less formal, more uncertain, and harder to monitor, observe and enforce. These "arenas," however, need not be the edifice of Congress or of the regulatory agency. In most parliamentary systems these transactions are carried out outside the legislature, most often within parliamentary parties or the cabinet. Nonetheless, the degree of institutionalization of the key exchange arena is important. For example, while Japan's LDP developed complex decision making processes with Diet members and committees playing a secondary role, the decision making itself provided for participation by various interested parties so as to develop an internal party consensus. Thus, in Japan under the LDP, the key decision making arenas were the LDP committees and the cabinet (Baron 2003).[45]

6. *Intra-period payoff structure.* The sensitivity of per-period payoff to alternative spot actions is an important determinant of whether cooperation is sustainable in equilibrium. As in models of collusion, if the payoff from deviating today is very high, *ceteris paribus,* full cooperation is less likely.[46] For example, in environments where fiscal accountability has not been implemented, long term cooperation will be hard to achieve, as deviations will have a high short term payoff.[47]

To sum up, political cooperation leading to a stable and flexible (i.e., effective) regulatory policy is more likely if: (1) the number of key political actors is small; (2) those actors have strong intertemporal linkages; (3) policy and political moves are widely observable; (4) good enforcement technologies (a strong bureaucracy to delegate, or a strong Court to arbitrate) are available, (5) the key political exchanges take place in arenas where properties (1)–(4) tend to be satisfied, and (6) the short-run payoffs from non-cooperation are not too high.

In this section, then, we showed that regulatory policy is highly dependent on the nature of the institutional environment. Although "formal" policies may, on paper, look efficient, in fact the workings of institutions imply that under some conditions regulatory policy and procedures will be erratic, under other

---

[44] Weak legislatures are those that, because of electoral or constitutional rules, or just because of the evolution of history, have little control over the legislative agenda. For an in-depth analysis of the institutional determinants of the relative powers of the executive vis-à-vis legislatures, see Shugart and Carey (1992).

[45] See, also Cowhey and McCubbins (1995).

[46] In oligopoly games, this is the case with the incentives to discount: if a firm stands to gain very large short-term profits by lowering its price (for instance because there are a large number of competitors from where to steal customers, related to point 1 above), collusive oligopoly is harder to sustain.

[47] Tommasi (2002) develops this issue for explaining the rigid fiscal arrangements in Argentina.

conditions it will be highly inflexible, while under other conditions it will be highly adaptable and effective. Thus, to explain the real characteristics of regulatory policy and policy-making in specific political systems and periods, we need to look at the workings of political institutions and their determinants in specific countries/time periods. Identifying these variables is a difficult task. It requires immersion in the "micro-detail" of politics (and policies) in each case.

The abstract listing we provided would correspond to characteristics of the policy making environment, which in turn will be (in many cases) endogenous (in interrelated ways) to some deeper determinants.[48] The type of variables to analyze include: key political actors, determinants of their payoffs, institutional veto points, variables determining who holds those institutional veto points at each point in time (related to parameters of stochastic description of the political process), horizons of key political actors and their determinants, institutional features (constitution, budget procedures, informal practices) that facilitate unchecked moves by some actors, independence and strength of Supreme Court or equivalent, characteristics of the bureaucracy. These are all institutional characteristics that serve as sources of regulatory commitment. In the next section we move beyond the abstract nature of these features to discuss how they arise and have been implemented through time.

4. REGULATORY GOVERNANCE IN THEORY AND PRACTICE

Political and social institutions not only affect the ability to restrain political and administrative action, but also have an independent impact on the type of regulation that can be implemented, and hence on the appropriate balance between commitment and flexibility. For example, relatively efficient regulatory rules (e.g., price caps, incentive schemes, use of yardstick competition) usually require substantial regulatory flexibility and granting discretion to the regulators. Thus, unless the country's institutions allow for the separation of arbitrariness from useful regulatory discretion, systems that grant too much administrative discretion may not generate the high levels of investment and welfare expected from private sector participation. Conversely, some countries might have regulatory regimes that drastically limit the scope of regulatory flexibility. Although such regulatory regimes may look inefficient, they may in fact fit the institutional endowments of the countries in question, and may provide reasonable incentives for investment. Regulatory governance is a choice, although a constrained one. In that sense, the institutional endowment of the country limits and conditions the menu of regulatory governance available.

Regulatory governance may take very different forms. In the United States, for example, regulatory governance consists of a complex set of formal administrative procedures. In the UK, however, regulatory governance is based on

---

[48] A somewhat similar logic is presented in Cohwey and McCubbins (1995), where they speak of political institutions (structure), politics (conduct) and policy (performance), using an apt industrial organization metaphor.

the use of contract law. In democracies with weaker institutional environments, regulatory governance consists of highly inflexible regulatory structures.

In this section we will try to show that the difference between these regulatory styles can be traced back to the difference in institutional environments (Spiller 1997). The UK has a parliamentary system that has systematically brought about unified governments without the need for coalition building. On the other hand, the US electoral system assures the development of divided governments, with the President seldom having full control over the legislative process (Jacobson 1990). As a consequence, legislators in the US have been reluctant to delegate to the executive too much regulatory discretion, and instead they have tended to impose on the executive branch much stronger procedural burdens as a way to limit the executive's ability to deviate from legislators' interests. Thus, the use in the United States of formal administrative procedures. On the other hand, in the UK, as in other countries with British style parliamentary systems, the government controls the legislative process (Shugart and Carey 1992). Procedural restrictions on regulatory decision-making, then, will seldom be introduced as not only they may be unnecessary to assure consistency between legislative interests and executive action (Spiller and Vogelsang 1997), but may also not bind future governments, as these, via their control of both the executive and the legislature, will be able to adapt the rules and procedures to their current needs. Similarly, in less developed democracies, procedural restrictions may not provide guarantees of appropriate regulatory decision-making, if they can be disregarded with little political cost. In the utilities' case, however, companies will not invest in highly specific sunk assets without either very high up-front rents, or assurances that once invested, regulatory rules will not be changed to expropriate those assets via the administrative process. Thus, the use of more rigid regulatory governance schemes. Licenses used as regulatory mechanisms, based essentially on contract law, may provide such credibility, as contracts (in this case, the license and thus the regulatory regime) cannot be changed unilaterally. The UK has introduced some flexibility in this highly inflexible scheme by regulating the license amendment process (Spiller and Vogelsang 1997).

In the remaining of this section we discuss how countries have actually dealt with—or failed to—facilitating long-term political cooperation. We focus on three key issues that common wisdom suggests are fundamental for providing a safe investment environment: delegation to the bureaucracy, delegation to the judiciary, and regulatory transparency. We show, though, that these features cannot be exogenously implemented, and that their relative effectiveness will depend on the nature of the institutional environment in which they operate.

Regulatory Governance I: Why Delegation to Independent Agencies?

In Section III we discuss that delegation to a third party for policy implementation could bring improvements upon the one shot Nash equilibrium. Such delegation, however, requires that there be such an independent agency. Thus, before we can answer whether delegation to an agency is done so as to achieve a substantive policy improvement over centralization of decision-making, we need to ask whether there is such a thing as independent agencies. Only then can we examine, why legislatures may delegate to independent agencies.

Spiller and Urbiztondo (1994) answered the independence question in the following way: the probability of observing independent agencies is higher in systems characterized by divided government. In systems characterized by unified governments (where the preferences of the legislature and the executive are systematically aligned, as in a two party parliamentary system) with relatively stable polities, control over the bureaucracy will be stronger, with a much smaller proportion of political appointees than in systems characterized by divided government (what we call here true division of power systems). The use of political appointees (including independent agencies), then, arises from the fact that in systems characterized by divided government the executive has less control over the professional bureaucracy, as the latter will naturally tend to be aligned with the legislature, a political institution that tends to be longer lasting than the executive. They find that such characterization of divided and unified governments holds both across countries and across cities in the United States.

In an important article, Weingast and Moran (1983) raised the Congressional Dominance Hypothesis. This hypothesis suggests that independent agencies are not truly independent, as they are subject to continuous congressional oversight. In a system of division of powers, however, Congressional Dominance is a corner solution. Spiller (1990) shows that Congressional budgetary decisions of agencies reflect an internal rather than a corner solution. Thus, agencies do not fully respond to Congressional desires. If this is the case, then, a basic question is why does Congress delegate to agencies that are not fully aligned with it, and what are the implications of such delegation for regulatory commitment?

Our analysis of Section 3 brings delegation as an *ex-ante* commitment device in an environment in which complex intertemporal transactions among policymakers are hard to implement. Delegation, however, can also be seen as an equilibrium way to commit future polities to a particular policy if the probability of regime change is high (de Figueiredo 2001). Delegation, though, requires that the right incentives be given to the bureaucracy to undertake legislative intents. Civil service provisions have been thought as providing such incentives (Spiller and Urbiztondo 1994). Bambaci et al (2002), however, consider circumstances where the legislature is weak and the executive has a high level of rotation (as is the case in Argentina). In those environments, they claim, traditional bureaucracies will be very difficult to motivate, thus triggering the politicization of the bureaucracy.[49]

In sum, delegation to independent agencies requires a system of division of powers. In this environment, legislative specificity will most probably not be the norm, as legislative costs will be high and preference homogeneity among

---

[49] Bambaci et al (2002) provide evidence that the extent of politicization of Argentine's bureaucracy is very high. With some secretaries having more the 70% of its personnel outside the normal civil service.

the members of the legislature will most probably be low, increasing the costs of reversing agencies and courts. It is under those circumstances where we can expect agency independence. But, it is also here where we should expect judicial independence that, to some extent, counterbalances and limits the independence of agencies. This does not imply that in unified governments we may not see delegation to administrative agencies. Indeed, most advanced democracies have developed strong administrative agencies, including such unified governments as Canada, New Zealand and the U.K. These agencies, however, while seemingly independent, would not be able to stand in opposition to the executive, as by an act of parliament the executive could change their term, their nature or even eliminate them.[50]

Regulatory Governance II: The Design of Administrative Processes

The discussion of Section 3 highlights the potential role of the Courts as an enforcement device. The Court plays such a role in the McCubbins, et al (1987, 1989) world. Indeed, in the United States, administrative law stipulates that Federal Courts can review all administrative agencies' decisions.[51] In the framework of Section 3, then, the US Congress has delegated to the Courts a major role in limiting the ability of the Executive to take unilateral action. The most far reaching procedural limitation is the Administrative Procedures Act. These standards, however, are quite vague.[52] The courts are not restricted to review agency decisions exclusively by interpreting the APA. They can also use the due process clauses of the Constitution. While in principle courts decide questions of law and not of facts, providing deference to the agencies on the latter, the difference between a question of law and a question of fact is also vague.[53]

The vagueness of the criteria under which Courts can review administrative decisions is not a legislative mistake. The APA was passed precisely with the dual intention of providing the Courts with the ability to monitor the agencies, and of increasing transparency in agency decision making, by allowing interest groups to participate in the regulatory process. Both aspects of the APA foster participation by interested parties, and provide members of Congress with the ability to preempt the implementation of administrative decisions they may

---

[50] Consider, for example, the relative ease with which the UK Labor Government combined the electricity (Offer) and gas (Ofgas) regulators into a single energy regulatory agency (Ofgem). Such smooth adaptation—which was opposed by the incumbent electricity regulator—would be difficult to implement in a political environment in which the Executive does not have a tight control over the legislature and over the bureaucracy.

[51] Except for the Social Security Administration disability decisions which are heard at the Federal District Courts, most decisions of administrative agencies are reviewed directly by Federal Courts of Appeals.

[52] See, for example, Section 706 of the Administrative Procedure Act.

[53] See, e.g., NLRB v. Hearst Publications, 322 U.S. 111, where the Supreme Court held that newsboys are employees under the NLRA, reversing a previous Court of Appeals decision, thus making a statement of fact, based, however, on the interpretation of the statute.

dislike, as agencies may have an incentive to deviate from their original mandate, whether explicit or implicit.[54]

Regulatory Governance III: The Independent Judiciary Question

Judicial review, however, does not assure objective adherence to the initial legislative mandate. In particular, the strategic approach to judicial decision making[55,56] emphasizes that Courts are ideologically motivated bodies with well defined political preferences, making decisions based not on the traditional legal rules of precedent, but on the constraints imposed by the other political institutions (i.e. Congress and the Presidency).[57] In such a framework the main constraint on the Courts' power and independence is the potential for legislative reversal,[58] not the original legislative intent.[59] Indeed, as the power of the executive increases, either because of a stronger control over the legislature, or an increased ability to undertake unilateral moves, the Court's ability to undertake independent action falls. Thus, the court will, in general, tend to have more freedom of action under divided rather than unified governments. In unified governments, not only Courts may fear legislative reversals, but also stronger punishing acts.[60] The central idea is that in environments where political

---

[54] See McCubbins and Schwartz (1984) for the original analysis of regulatory process as a "fire-alarm." See de Figueiredo, Spiller and Urbiztondo (1999) for an analysis of logic of APA's requirement of multiple interest group participation. Shepsle (1992) and Macey (1992) develop three reasons for bureaucratic drift. First, interest groups will attempt to move the agency towards their own directions, separate from the original mandate. Second, the agency may attempt to implement its own view of the world. And finally, legislators will attempt to move the agency towards their own view of the world. To limit the extent of agency discretion, legislators will strategically design the agency's structure and organization (Gilligan, et al 1989), its administrative procedures for decision-making (McCubbins, et al 1989, Spiller and Tiller 1997), its budgetary allocation (Spiller and Tiller 1997) and the nature of judicial review.

[55] The modern version of the strategic approach to judicial decision making emerged from the non-strategic approach developed in Marks (1988). See Gely and Spiller (1990); Ferejohn and Shipan (1990), Eskridge (1991), Eskridge and Ferejohn (1992a) and (1992b), Ferejohn and Weingast (1992), Schwartz (1992), Epstein and Walker (1995), Epstein and Knight (1997). Previous "strategic" approaches to judicial decision making can be found in Murphy's (1964) book on judicial strategy and in Dahl's (1957) suggestion that the selection process of Supreme Court justices caused judicial decisions to reflect the public's policy preferences since voters elected the judge-appointing politicians. See also Funston's (1975) analysis of the disagreements between the judicial and legislative branches during "change-over" periods of the Court.

[56] This approach is often called "the division of powers game." For a critical review of this literature see Segal (1997), and for a reply, see, Bergara et al (2003).

[57] Spiller and Spitzer (1995) analyze in detail the theoretical implications of assuming that courts are not strategic players. They show that such assumption has empirical implications not consistent with current evidence.

[58] If the decision touches on a constitutional issue, reversal has to be undertaken by a constitutional amendment. See Gely and Spiller (1992) and Spiller and Spitzer (1992).

[59] For a strategic approach to legislative intent, see Schwartz, et al (1994)

[60] A series of papers (in particular, Cooter and Ginsburg (1996), Ramseyer (1994), and Salzberg, 1991) suggest that the power of the judiciary is limited in parliamentary systems like those in Japan or Europe, where cabinet's control over the legislature limits the ability of the court to innovate (Cooter and Ginsburg 1996).

fragmentation is the norm, the Judiciary is able, over time, to create a doctrine of judicial independence without fear of political reprisals, whether as a constitutional amendment limiting its review power, dismissal from the Court or increases in its size. Similar attempts in a more unified political environment would generate political clashes, eventually limiting the Judiciary's power.[61] This theory suggests that courts would tend to be more subjugated to political power in the presence of unified governments, like strong parliamentary systems, and more aggressive in the presence of divided governments, like presidential systems or fragmented parliamentary systems where governments are formed from multi-party coalitions, and where the potential for coalition break-up is substantially bigger.[62]

Thus, it is not surprising that in countries with traditionally unified governments such as the UK, Japan, or Mexico (pre-Fox), Courts have not developed a strong tradition of judicial review of administrative actions, developing a rudimentary administrative law.[63,64] On the other hand, less unified (often presidential systems), like France have developed substantial bodies of administrative law, giving also raise to important doctrines of regulatory protection of investments.[65]

Regulatory Governance IV: Regulatory Transparency, or Arranging Interest Group Participation in the Regulatory Process

Policy making transparency is a much touted regulatory recipe. In this section we discuss the implications of transparency for agency performance, and we show that as a long-term policy, effective transparency requires the existence of a set of institutions that cannot be exogenously created.

Policy making transparency involves regulating and formalizing the participation of interest groups in the administrative process.[66] Interest groups play a particularly important role in the administrative process in the US (McCubbins

---

[61] See Epstein and Knight (2000) and Helmke (1999).

[62] See, for example, Steunenberg (1995) for an analysis of judicial intervention in the euthanasia debate arising from the fragmentation of the government coalition.

[63] On UK's administrative law see Baldwin and McCrudden (1987).

[64] This, however, does not imply that in unified countries judicial review does not develop. For example, Iaryczower et al (2002) find that the Argentine Court is much more likely to reverse a decision of a provincial government than of the central government.

[65] The evolution of water regulation in France is a fascinating example. The *General Code of Territorial Communities* (Code général des collectivités territoriales) regulates, among many other issues, the ways municipalities must handle its water and sewerage works and concessions. A fundamental issue of the Code is that water services must be in financial equilibrium. Water service prices must cover their costs, with municipalities (except for very small communities) not being able to cover water services deficits from their general budgets, nor can they transfer operating surplus to their own budgets. See Cour de Comptes, "La Gestion Des Services Publics Locaux D'eau Et D'assainissement" January 1997, available (in summary form) at http://www.ccomptes.fr/Cour-des-comptes/publications/rapports/eau/cdc72.htm. This feature substantially limits the potential for opportunistic behavior from the municipalities vis-à-vis the water operators, whether private *or* public.

[66] We refer here to interest groups in a very generic form, including regulated firms, consumer groups, unions, environmental groups, and so on and so forth.

and Schwartz 1984). Indeed, the Administrative Procedure Act, as well as most of the enabling legislation of regulatory agencies, sets a series of procedural requirements that provides for ample participation of interest groups in the regulatory process. Regulatory agencies must provide notice, must inform about proposed rule makings, must make their decisions taking into account the submissions of interested parties, and cannot rush nor make decisions in the dark. Transparency, in this setting, has two important effects: first, it allows the agency to receive information about the state of the world in an open and organized fashion, and second, it allows the manifestation of particularistic interests. Both are important for the agency. On the one hand, agencies are resource constrained and hence information about the state of the world is always beneficial. On the other hand, information about interest groups' preferences is important as it allows the agency to forecast potential political problems they may encounter at the legislature. Procedural restrictions on decision making also provide the opportunity to affected interests to attempt to block agency decision making through lobbying their politicians. In a particularly important article, McCubbins and Schwartz (1984) claim that the participation by interest groups makes the regulatory process work like a "fire alarm."

Transparency, then, allows legislators to supervise the agency without having to be actively involved in the regulatory process, and hence limiting the time that legislators have to expend in regulating regulators. Interested parties, however, are seldom unbiased (de Figueiredo, et al 1999, Lupia and McCubbins 1994). Interest groups will not reveal information that will bring about a regulatory outcome that makes them worse off than if they hadn't revealed the information. As a consequence, politicians that base their decisions exclusively on the information provided by a single interest group, even if that group is a natural ally, will find the legislative outcome to be biased. Thus, the incentive for politicians to increase transparency allowing for the participation of multiple interest groups, preferably with conflicting interests as ways to limit the information power of interest groups, even of those supporting them.[67]

As we discuss in Section 3, however, transparency comes at a cost. It delays decision-making, and it may also block regulatory adaptation to important shocks. Furthermore, for regulatory transparency to develop, judicial review must arise in equilibrium.

Regulatory Governance in Unified Government Systems: Contract Law

The previous discussion suggests that purely administrative procedures with judicial review may not provide substantial regulatory commitment in systems characterized by unified government, unless there is substantial polity stability. The main deterrent to stable policies is that government controls both the administrative and the legislative processes. Thus, political changes that bring about a

---

[67] de Figueiredo et al (1999) show that by increasing participation politicians reduce their informational dependency on their own aligned interest groups, and thus, in equilibrium, limit the rents these groups will extract from policy-making, increasing, thus, the politicians' welfare.

change in government can also bring about legislative changes. By having few institutional checks and balances, such systems have an inherent instability that raises questions about their ability to provide regulatory commitment. Nevertheless several countries that can be characterized as having a unified form of government have developed private ownership of utilities (e.g., Japan, the UK, Jamaica, Mexico). Such countries have developed alternative institutional ways to provide regulatory commitment based on the idea of rigid regulatory rules discussed at the beginning of Section 4.

Indeed, some, like the UK, Jamaica and other Caribbean countries, have based their regulatory governance structures on contract law.[68] Japan, prior to the collapse of the LDP, developed internal party structures that provided for substantial regulatory commitment.[69] Other countries, e.g., Mexico telecommunications,[70] developed private ownership of utilities by providing for substantial up-front rents.

A main purpose of the regulatory and institutional schemes in countries like Japan, Jamaica and the UK is to provide the regulated companies with some amount of veto power over regulatory decisions. Consider the case of British utilities. British utilities are regulated by different price caps methods. The distinguishing feature of these price cap methods, however, is that they are embedded in the companies' license rather than in an agency decision or piece of legislation.[71] The advantage of regulatory frameworks instituted through licenses is that since the latter usually have the power of contracts between governments and the firms, any amendment to the license will usually require the agreement of the company.[72] This feature, however, provides credibility at the cost of inflexibility. For example, if a technological breakthrough substantially erodes economies of scale in a segment of the market where the company has—by virtue of the license—an exclusive operating right, the regulator may have to "bribe" the company into accepting to relinquish its legal exclusive rights over that segment. In a more flexible regulatory governance choice, such decision could be taken administratively.[73] Thus, while contracts may be useful in providing

---

[68] See Spiller and Sampson (1995) and Spiller and Vogelsang (1997) for analyses of the regulatory structures in Jamaica and the UK respectively.

[69] See, in particular, the volume by Cowhey and McCubbins (1995) for an analysis of the organization of the LDP and its implications for policy determination.

[70] There are those, though, who would claim that Mexico's privatization of telecommunications was nothing but the capture of social wealth by politically connected individuals.

[71] Indeed, the enabling laws in the UK are silent about pricing schemes.

[72] In the British case, the law stipulates that in the case that the company does not agree to a license amendment proposed by the regulator, there is a process involving the Competition Commission that the regulator may use to amend the license against the will of the company. This, however, requires the Competition Commission to agree with the regulator against the company. See Spiller and Vogelsang (1997).

[73] This was the case with Cable & Wireless in Jamaica, where it had a concession granting it a monopoly over telecommunications services since 1988 (Spiller and Sampson 1996). Eventually, and after much negotiations, an agreement was reached in 1999, that included the opening by 2001 of the cellular market. In 2001 Digicel became the first cellular competitor to C&W. By 2003 there were a total of four cellular operators in the island.

assurances to the companies, they do so only by introducing rigidities in the regulatory system.

For contracts as a governance structure to provide regulatory stability, then, they must be very specific and clearly limit what the regulator can do. A license that does not specify the regulatory mechanism in any detail, but leaves the administration free to make all regulatory decisions will fail the first criteria for regulatory stability.[74] Operating licenses in the US, for example, do not serve as a governance structure, as they deal mostly with eminent domain and geographic operation boundaries. Whether specific licenses will provide regulatory credibility depends on whether the courts will see licenses as binding contracts. In particular, it must be the case that courts will be willing to uphold contracts against the wish of the administration. If courts do not treat licenses as contracts, or grant the administration substantial leeway in interpreting those contracts, then, license-based regulatory contracts will fail as a source of regulatory stability.[75] Observe, then, that contracts can be implemented in nations with very strong or very weak executives, with parliamentary or Presidential systems. Indeed, a basic requirement is the judiciary will treat licenses as contracts.

Contract based regulation, however, are particularly appealing to polities with few veto players and with high rates of turnover, environments in which our model of Section 3 predicts highly unstable or highly rigid polices. In such cases, changes in political preferences would either bring about a new piece of legislation if the current regulatory regime is based on specific legislation, or a modification of the agency's interpretation of the statute if the current regulatory regime is based on general administrative procedures. On the other hand, if regulatory policy was initially hard-wired through a license, then the desire to change regulatory policy will be constrained by *ex-ante* agreements. These agreements, when regulation is based on contract law, require the acquiescence of the company. Thus, by introducing the regulatory process in the license an additional veto point is introduced, namely the company itself. Thus, the relevant set of parties required to change the status quo now includes also the company. Thus, it is not surprising that countries like Jamaica, the UK and many of the other Caribbean countries have adopted license based regulatory systems.[76]

---

[74] Comparing the licenses issued in Jamaica under the Jamaican Public Utilities Act of 1966 to those issued prior to 1966 or after the privatization of 1988 shows the total failure of licenses to restrain the regulators based on the 1966 Act. See Spiller and Sampson (1993).

[75] Breaching a contract may, however, be an expensive proposition for a government if the private counterpart is a foreign company protected by a Bilateral Investment Treaty (BIT). BITs developed after the Second World War as ways to provide assurances to foreign investors. See www.worldbank.org/icsid/.

[76] Bolivia has had the longest lasting private electricity company in South America. COBEE, founded in the late 1910s, has provided electricity to La Paz and its environs. Its regulatory structure, although set by a Presidential Decree was enshrined in its license. Thus, future Presidential Decrees will not be able to amend the terms of the license (Spiller 1995). Argentina privatization process in the 1990s was also based on contracts as regulatory instruments, and it worked reasonably well until the havoc created by the mega devaluation of 2002.

5. CONCLUSIONS

The institutions of regulation arise to deal with basic transaction problems among policy-makers, and thus to guarantee investors that their investments will be protected against opportunistic behavior by current or future governments. In this chapter we provide a general transaction framework to analyze the rise and evolution of regulatory institutions. Regulatory structures work very different as credible regulatory governance depending on the nature of the institutional environment, and the way it affects policy-makers' capacity to enter into complex intertemporal agreements among themselves. Thus, this chapter emphasizes the shift away from exploring regulation as a pure government/firm game, to understanding the institutions of regulation as facilitating entering into complex intertemporal agreements among policy-makers, agreements that have direct consequences for firms' investment incentives and performance.

This chapter also points to the intrinsically inter-disciplinary nature of the research on regulatory institutions. Neoclassical economics has contributed greatly to our understandings of incentives and the potential for market failures. As it relates to the real performance of regulatory institutions, though, we must branch out of the narrow confines of economics, and add to it deeper understandings of the institutional environments in which regulatory issues are at stake, to which political sciences and the law provide fundamental insights. In particular, this chapter has emphasized the need for more "nitty-gritty" work on regulatory institutions and their origins. Williamson (1976) path-breaking work on the way Cable TV regulation actually worked in the US of the 1970s is the type of work that, at the level of institutions, needs to be undertaken to unravel the key details of the institutional environment in which policy making is made. Only equipped with that knowledge will we be able to grasp the complexities of the workings of regulatory institutions.

REFERENCES

Alesina, A. 1988. "Credibility and Policy Convergence in a Two-Party System with Rational Voters". *American Economic Review* 78(4): 796–805.

Bambaci, J., P.T. Spiller, and M. Tommasi. 2001. "Bureaucracy and Public Policy in Argentina". Mimeo, CEDI.

Baldwin, R, and C. McCrudden. 1987. *Regulation and Public Law*, London: Weidenfeld & Nicholson.

Baron, D., 2003. *Business and its Environment*, Englewood Cliffs, NJ: Prentice Hall, 4th edn.

_____, and D. Besanko, 1987. "Commitment and Fairness in a Continuing Regulatory Relationship". *Review of Economic Studies* 413–436.

_____, and R. Myerson. 1982. "Regulating a Monopolist with Unknown Costs". 50, *Econometrica* 911–930.

Bergara, M., B. Richman, and P.T. Spiller. 2003. "Modeling Supreme Court Preferences in a Strategic Context". *Legislative Studies Quarterly* 247–280.

Cain, B., J. Ferejohn and M. Fiorina. 1987. *The Personal Vote*. Cambridge, MA: Harvard University Press.

Careaga, M. and B. Weingast 2002. "Fiscal Federalism, Good Governance, and Economic Growth in Mexico" in D. Rodrik (ed.), *In Search of Prosperity: Analytic Narratives on Economic Growth.* Princeton, NJ: Princeton University Press.

Cowhey, P., and M. McCubbins. 1995. *Structure and Policy in Japan and the United States.* Cambridge: Cambridge University Press.

Cooter, R. 1997. "The Rule of State Law and the Rule-of-Law State: Economic Analysis of the Legal Foundations of Development" in Buscaglia, E., R. Cooter, and W. Ratliff (eds.), *Law and Economics of Development.* Greenwich, CT: JAI Press.

_____, 2000. *The Strategic Constitution.* Princeton, NJ: Princeton University Press.

Cooter R. and T.B. Ginsburg. 1996. "Comparing Judicial Discretion: An Empirical Test of Economic Models". 16 *International Review of Law And Economics* 295.

Cox, G.. 1987. *The Efficient Secret.* New York: Cambridge University Press.

_____ 1997. *Making Votes Count: Strategic Coordination in the World's Electoral Systems.* Cambridge: Cambridge University Press.

_____ and M. McCubbins 2001. "The Institutional Determinants of Economic Policy Outcomes" in Haggard and McCubbins (eds.), *Presidents, Parliaments and Policy.* Cambridge University Press.

Dahl, R. 1957. "Decision-Making in a Democracy: The Supreme Court as a National Policy-Maker". *Journal of Public Law* 6: 179–295.

de Figueiredo, R. 2001. "Electoral Competition, Political Uncertainty and Policy Insulation". Mimeo, UC-Berkeley.

De Figueiredo, R. P.T. Spiller, and S. Urbiztondo. 1999. "An Informational Perspective on Administrative Procedures". *Journal of Law, Economics & Organization* 15(1): 283–305.

Demski, J. and D. Sappington. 1987. "Hierarchical Regulatory Control". *The Rand Journal of Economics* 18(3): 369–383.

Dixit, A., G. Grossman, and F. Gul 2000. "The Dynamics of Political Compromise". *Journal of Political Economy* 108(3): 531–568.

Duverger, M. 1954. *Political Parties: Their Organization and Activity in the Modern State.* New York: Wiley.

Epstein, L. and Knight, J. 1997. *The Choices Justices Make.* Washington, DC: Congressional Quarterly Press.

_____ and _____ 2000. "The Role of Constitutional Courts in the Establishment and Maintenance of Democratic Systems of Government." Paper presented at the 2000 American Political Science Association Meetings.

_____ and Walker, T.G. 1995. "The Role of the Supreme Court on American Society: Playing the Reconstruction Game" in L. Epstein (ed.), *Contemplating Courts.* Washington, DC: CQ Press.

Epstein, D. and S. O'Halloran. 1994. "Administrative Procedures, Information, and Agency Discretion". *American Journal of Political Science* 38: 697–722.

Epstein, D. and S. O'Halloran. 1996. "Divided Government and the Design of Administrative Procedures: A Formal Model and Empirical Test". *The Journal of Politics* 58: 373–397.

Epstein, D. and S. O'Halloran, 1999. *Delegating Powers: A Transaction Politics Approach to Policy Making under Separate Powers.* Cambridge University Press.

Esfahani, H. (1996). "The Political Economy of the Philippines' Telecommunications Sector" in Levy, B. and P.T. Spiller (eds.), *Regulations, Institutions and Commitment: The Case of Telecommunication.* Cambridge University Press, pp. 145–201.

Eskridge, W.N., Jr. 1991. "Overriding Supreme Court Statutory Interpretation Decisions". *Yale Law Journal* 101: 825–841.

Eskridge, W., Jr. and J. Ferejohn. 1992a. "The Article I, Section 7 Game". *Georgetown Law Journal* 80(3).

_____ and _____ 1992b. "Making the Deal Stick". *Journal of Law, Economics and Organization* 8(1).

Evans, L., A. Grimes, D.J. Teece, and B. Wilkinson. (1996), "Economic Reform in New Zealand 1984–95: The Pursuit of Efficiency". *Journal of Economic Literature* 34: 1856–1902.
Ferejohn, J. and C. Shipan (1990). "Congressional Influence on Bureaucracy". *Journal of Law, Economics and Organization* 6: 1990.
Fudenberg, D. and J. Tirole 1991. *Game Theory*. Cambridge, MA: MIT Press.
Funston, R. "The Supreme Court and Critical Elections". *American Political Science Review* 69: 795–811.
Gely, R. and Spiller, P.T. 1990. "A Rational Choice Theory of Supreme Court Statutory Decisions, with Applications to the *State Farm* and *Grove City* Cases". *Journal of Law, Economics and Organization* 6: 263–301.
_____. 1992, "The Political Economy of Supreme Court Constitutional Decisions: The Case of Roosevelt's Court Packing Plan". 12 *International Review of Law and Economics*, pp. 45–67.
Gilligan, M., W. Marshall, and B. Weingast. 1989. "Regulation and the Theory of Legislative Choice: The Interstate Commerce Act of 1887". *Journal of Law and Economics* 32: 35–61.
Goldberg, V. 1976. "Regulation and Administered Contracts". *Bell Journal of Economics* 426–452.
Green, E. and R. Porter. 1984. "Noncooperative Collusion Under Imperfect Price Information". *Econometrica* 52: 87–100.
Haggard S. and R. Kaufman, 1995. *The Political Economy of Democratic Transitions*. Princeton NJ: Princeton University Press.
_____. and M. McCubbins, 2001, *Presidents, Parliaments and Policy*. New York: Cambridge University Press.
Helmke, G.. 1999. "Judicial Decision Making and Strategic Defection: Court-Executive Relations in Argentina, 1976–1995". Paper presented at the Annual Meeting of the Conference Group on the Scientific Study of Judicial Politics, College Station, TX.
Henisz, V. (2002). "The Institutional Environment for Infrastructure Investment". *Industrial and Corporate Change* 11(2): 355–389.
_____, and B. Zelner, 2001. "The Institutional Environment for Telecommunications Investment". *Journal of Economics, Management and Strategy* 10(1): 123–147.
_____, and _____. 2002. "Interest Groups, Political Institutions and Electricity Investment". mimeo.
Iaryczower, M., P. Spiller, and M. Tommasi. 2002. "Judicial Decision-Making in Unstable Environments: The Argentine Supreme Court, 1936–1998". *American Journal of Political Science* 46(4): 699–716.
Jacobson, G.C. 1990. *The Electoral Origins of Divided Government: Competition in the U.S. House Elections, 1946–1988*. Boulder, CO: Westview Press.
Joskow, P. L. 1974. "Inflation and Environmental Concern: Structural Change in the Process of Public Utility Price Regulation". *Journal of Law and Economics*.
Knack, S. and P. Keefer. 1995. "Institutions and Economic Performance: Cross Country Tests Using Alternative Institutional Measures". *Economics and Politics* 207–227.
Laffont, J.J. and J. Tirole. 1991. "The Politics of Government Decision-Making; A Theory of Regulatory Capture". *Quarterly Journal of Economics* 106: 1089–1127.
_____, and _____. 1993. *A Theory of Incentives in Procurement and Regulation*. Cambridge, MA: MIT Press.
Lehrer, Ehud. 1989. "Lower Equilibrium Payoffs in Two-Player Repeated Games with Non-Observable Actions". 18 *International Journal of Game Theory* 57–89.
Levy, B. and Spiller, P.T. 1994. "The Institutional Foundations of Regulatory Commitment: A Comparative Analysis of Telecommunications Regulation". *Journal of Law, Economics, and Organization* 10: 201–246.
_____. 1996. *Regulations, Institutions and Commitment: Comparative Studies of Telecommunications*. Cambridge University Press.

Loeb, M. and W.A. Magat. 1979. "A Decentralized Method of Utility Regulation". *Journal of Law and Economics* 399–404.

Lupia, S. and McCubbins, M.D. 1994. "Learning from Oversight: Fire Alarms and Police Patrols Reconstructed". *Journal of Law, Economics, and Organization* 10: 96–125.

Macey, J. 1992. "Organizational Design and Political Control of Administrative Agencies". *Journal of Law, Economics, and Organization* 8: 93–110.

Marks, B. 1988. "A Model of Judicial Influence on Congressional Policymaking: Grove City College v. Bell". Working Paper in Political Science P-88-7, Hoover Institution.

McCubbins, M.D., Noll, R.G., and Weingast, B.R.1987. "Administrative Procedures as Instruments of Political Control". *Journal of Law, Economics, and Organization* 3: 243–277.

———, ———, and ———, 1989. "Structure and Process, Politics and Policy: Administrative Arrangements and the Political Control of Agencies". *Virginia Law Review* 75: 431–482.

———, and Shwartz, T. 1984. "Congressional Oversight Overlooked: Police Patrol vs Fire Alarms". *American Journal of Political Sciences* 28: 165.179.

Moe, T. 1990. "The Politics of Structural Choice: Toward a Theory of Public Bureaucracy", in O. Williamson (ed.), *Organization Theory: From Chester Barnard to the Present and Beyond*. New York: Oxford University Press.

———, and M. Caldwell. 1994. "The Institutional Foundations of Democratic Government: A Comparison of Presidential and Parliamentary Systems". *Journal of Institutional and Theoretical Economics* 150(1): 171–195.

Murphy, W.F. 1964. *Elements of Judicial Strategy*. Chicago, IL: University of Chicago Press.

North, D.C. 1990. *Institutions, Institutional Change, and Economic Performance*. Cambridge, MA: Cambridge University Press.

Peltzman, S. 1976. "Toward a More General Theory of Regulation". *Journal of Law and Economics* 19(2): 211–240.

Persson, T., G. Roland y G. Tabellini 1997. "Separation of Powers and Political Accountability". *Quarterly Journal of Economics* November: 1163–1202.

———, and G. Tabellini. 2002. "Political Institutions and Economic Policy Outcomes: What Are the Stylized Facts?" Mimeo, Institute for International Economic Studies.

———, and G. Tabellini. 2003. *The Economic Effect of Constitutions. What Do the Data Say?* Cambridge, MA: MIT Press, forthcoming.

Posner, R. 1971. "Taxation by Regulation". *Bell Journal of Economics* 2(1): 22–50.

Ramseyer, M. 1994, "The Puzzling (In)Dependence of Courts: A Comparative Approach". *Journal of Legal Studies*, 721–748.

Salzberg, E.M. 1991. "The Delegation of Legislative Powers to the Courts and the Independence of the Judiciary". Mimeo.

Saporiti, A., Spiller, P. and M. Tommasi 2002. "Institutions, Intertemporal Political Agreements, and Public Policy". Mimeo.

Schwartz, E.P. 1992. "Policy, Precedent and Power: A Positive Theory of Supreme Court Decision-making". *Journal of Law, Economics and Organization* 8: 219–52.

———, Spiller, P.T., and Urbiztondo, S. 1993. "A Positive Theory of Legislative Intent". *Law and Contemporary Problems* 57: 51–74.

Segal, J.A. 1997. "Separation-of-Powers Games in the Positive Theory of Congress and Courts". *American Political Science Review* 91: 28–44.

Shepsle, KA., 1992. "Bureaucratic Drift, Coalitional Drift, and Time Inconsistency—A Comment". *Journal of Law, Economics and Organization* 8: 111–118.

Shugart, M.S. and Carey, J.M. 1992. *Presidents and Assemblies*. New York: Cambridge University Press.

———, and S. Haggard 2001. "Institutions and Public Policy in Presidential Systems" in Haggard S. and M. McCubbins (eds.), *Presidents, Parliaments and Policy*.

Spiller, P.T. 1990. "Politicians, Interest Groups and Regulators: A Multiple Principals Agency Theory of Regulation, (or Let Them Be Bribed)". *Journal of Law and Economics* 33: 65–101.

_____, 1992. "Agency Discretion under Judicial Review" in *Formal Theory of Politics II: Mathematical Modelling in Political Science, Mathematical and Computer Modelling*, Vol. 16, pp. 185–200.

_____. 1995. "A Positive Political Theory of Regulatory Instruments: Contracts, Administrative Law or Regulatory Specificity". *Southern California Law Review* 69: 477–515.

_____. 1997. "Institutions and Commitment". *Industrial and Corporate Change* 5: 421–452.

_____ and C.I. Sampson. 1996. "Regulation, Institutions and Commitment: The Jamaican Telecommunications Sector" in Levy B. and P.T. Spiller (eds.), *1993 Regulation, Institutions and Commitment: Comparative Studies in Telecommunications*. Cambridge MA: Cambridge University Press.

_____ and M. Spitzer, 1992. "Judicial Choice of Legal Doctrines". *Journal of Law, Economics and Organization* 8(1): 8–46.

_____ and _____. 1995. "Where is the Sin in Sincere: Sophisticated Voting in the Courts". *Journal of Law Economics and Organization* 11: 32–63.

_____ and E. Tiller. 1997. "Decision Costs and the Strategic Design of Administrative Process and Judicial Review". *Journal of Legal Studies* XXVI(2): 347–370.

_____ and M. Tommasi, 2003. "The Institutional Foundations of Public Policy: Theory and an Application to Argentina". *Journal of Law, Economics and Organization.*

_____ and S. Urbiztondo, 1994. "Political Appointees vs. Career Civil Servants: A Multiple-Principals Theory of Political Institutions". *European Journal of Political Economy* 10: 465–497.

_____ and I. Vogelsang. 1997. "The Institutional Foundations of Regulatory Commitment in the UK, (with special emphasis on telecommunications)". *Journal of Institutional and Theoretical Economics*.

Steunenberg, B. 1995. "Courts, Cabinet and Coalition Parties: The Politics of Euthanasia in a Parliamentary Setting". University of Twente, The Netherlands.

Stigler, G.J., 1971. "The Theory of Economics Regulation". *Bell Journal of Economics and Management Science* 2: 3–21.

Taagepera, R. and M. Shugart, 1993. "Predicting the Number of Parties: A Quantitative Model of Duverger Mechanical Effect". 87, *American Political Science Review*, 455–464.

Tommasi M. (2002) "Federalism in Argentina and the Reforms of the 1990s" Working Paper 147, Center for Research on Economic Development and Policy Reform, Stanford University.

Troesken, W. 1996. *Why Regulate Utilities? The New Institutional Economics and the Chicago Gas Industry, 1849–1924*. Ann Arbor, MI: University of Michigan Press.

_____. 1997. "The Sources of Public Ownership: Historical Evidence from the Gas Industry". *Journal of Law, Economics and Organization* 13(1): 1–25.

_____ and R. Geddes, 2002. "Municipalizing American Waterworks: 1897–1915". *Journal of Law, Economics and Organization* 19(2): 373–400.

Tsebelis, G. 1995. "Decision Making in Political Systems: Veto Players in Presidentialism, Parliamentarism, Multicameralism and Multipartyism". *British Journal of Political Science* 25.

_____. 2002. *Veto Players. How Political Institutions Work*. Princeton, NJ: Princeton University Press.

Walton, B. 2003. "Bolivia—A Perspective on Water Supply and Sewerage". WEDC, Loughborough University.

Weingast, B.R. 1995. "The Economic Role of Institutions: Market Preserving Federalism and Economic Development". *Journal of Law, Economics and Organization* 11(1): 1–31.

_____ and Moran, M.J. 1983. "Bureaucratic Discretion or Congressional Control? Regulatory Policymaking by the Federal Trade Commission". *Journal of Political Economy* 91: 765–800.

_____ and W. Marshall. 1988. "The Industrial Organization of Congress". 96 *Journal of Political Economy*, pp. 132–163.

Williamson, O.E. 1975. *Markets and Hierarchies: Analysis and Antitrust Implications*. New York: Free Press.
_____. 1976. "Franchise Bidding for Natural Monopolies: In General and With Respect to CATV". *Bell Journal of Economics* 73–104.
_____. 1979. "Transaction-Cost Economics: The Governance of Contractual Relations". *Journal of Law and Economics* 3–61.
_____. 1985. *The Economic Institutions of Capitalism*. New York: Free Press.
_____. 1988. "The Logic of Economic Organization". *Journal of Law, Economics and Organization* 65–93.
_____. 1996. *The Mechanisms of Governance*. Oxford: Oxford University Press.

21. State Regulation of Open-Access, Common-Pool Resources

GARY D. LIBECAP

"But still another inquiry remains; one often agitated by the more recondite Nantucketers. Whether, owning to the almost omniscient look-outs at the mast-heads of the whaleships, now penetrating even Behring's straits, and into the remotest secret drawers and lockers of the world; and the thousand harpoons and lances darted along all continental coasts, and so remorseless a havoc; whether he must at last be exterminated from the waters, and the last whale, like the last man, smoke his last pipe and then himself evaporate in the final puff." (Melville, Moby Dick, 1922, 425).[1]

1. INTRODUCTION

The Problem At Hand

Open-access, common-pool resources, such as many fisheries, aquifers, oil pools, and the atmosphere, often require some type of regulation of private access and use to avoid wasteful exploitation.[2] In the absence of constraints on users, such as those provided by informal community norms, more formal property rights, or other types of state regulation, individuals competitively exploit the resource rapidly and wastefully. Short-term horizons dominate, with little investment or trade to channel the resource across time or across users to higher-valued applications. This excessive extraction, which amounts to private plunder, continues so long as it is in the interests of the individual parties, even if society would be better off with less intensive and extensive use. Without some limits on individual behavior to better reflect broader, social benefits and costs, only private net benefit calculations govern resource use decisions.

The historical and contemporary record of open-access resources is not a happy one. The depletion of valuable fisheries, the overdrawing of critical

---

[1] I am grateful to Jim Smith who brought this passage to my attention. In this chapter, I cite selections from the literature on regulation of the common pool. The literature is a large one, and the list referenced here is only suggestive, not exclusive.

[2] I benefited from comments and suggestions provided by the editor and referees, Joe Bial, Ryan Johnson, Dean Lueck, Steve Salant, and Jim Smith. The International Center for Economic Research (ICER) Turin, Italy provided research support.

aquifers, the stranding of rich oil deposits following excessive, competitive extraction, and the dumping of smoke and other pollutants into the air are examples of the common pool. Unfortunately, many of these open-access problems persist, and the discussion here suggests why that is the case. Throughout this chapter, the terms common pool, commons, and open access are used interchangeably. They do not refer to common property, which is a type of solution to the open-access, common pool, as described below.

The Costs of Reducing the Losses of the Commons

Despite the documented losses of the commons, it is not always in society's interest to completely confront the problem. Too many resources may be required, relative to the benefits achieved. In some cases, for example, where very large geographic scales or highly mobile resources are encountered, the transaction costs of defining and enforcing even loose constraints can be prohibitive, at least compared to the value of the resource at stake. In other cases, where there are large numbers of heterogeneous parties competing for the asset, the transaction costs of reaching agreement among the competitors on access and use restrictions also can be very high, relative to the anticipated gains. Or, in a third case, information may be so limited or controversial regarding the benefits of controlling entry and use that no consensus is achieved on the need to take action. Such information problems arise from high transaction costs of collecting and conveying data regarding the status of the resource being exploited.

In all of these situations, the "commons" persists because of transaction costs. It is too costly to place boundaries around the resource; it is too costly to secure agreement to limit individual actions; and it is too costly to obtain enough information to determine the proper course of action to protect the resource. In these cases of high transaction costs, continuation of the commons is efficient, as Coase (1960, 39) has taught us.

By contrast, in other situations where information is clearer about the costs of the common pool and where monitoring entry and agreeing on acceptable uses can take place with relatively lower transaction costs, then community rules can reduce open-access losses. Indeed, if a common resource is accessed locally by a comparatively small number of parties with similar or generally homogeneous objectives and production costs, then the problem of overuse often can be effectively addressed through informal rules or norms that constrain individual actions.

Under these circumstances it can be relatively easier for a small group of similar people who have a history of interaction with one another to gather and interpret information about the resource's status and to agree upon the types of uses and constraints necessary to conserve it. They also can accept the distribution of the costs and benefits (and ultimately, of wealth and political power) within the community that is inherent in any definition and assignment of use privileges, even under informal arrangements. Community management of regional agricultural irrigation water, pastures, or inshore fisheries provides examples of successful mitigation of the losses of the commons. These solutions to open access are termed, "common property."[3]

When transaction costs rise due to larger numbers of heterogeneous competitors, perhaps attracted by exogenous forces, such as price increases or technological changes, that raise the value of the asset or that lower the costs of entry, then local, informal arrangements, such as community norms may no longer be effective in combating the wastes of open access. The demands of new entrants who have not been part of the previous arrangement now have to be addressed. The previous allocation of costs and benefits of resource use must be reassigned among a larger group of claimants. Old claimants receive less as more of the resource is diverted to the new parties. It will be difficult for both parties to agree to the required new division. They have had either limited or no past interaction and share no common, verifiable information about the state of the resource. They are unlikely to have common norms regarding resource use or income and cost distribution, and they likely have very different time constraints that govern harvest practices. All of these factors, together with the shear increase in the number of competing parties, raise the transaction costs of agreeing to and abiding by informal community rules (Olson, 1965).

Transactions Costs and Government Remedies for the Losses of the Commons

When community rules break down, more formal state intervention may be required, if open-access losses are to be avoided.[4] The coercive power of the state transcends or at least mediates the claims of any one group. Through the political process summarized below the state can define and enforce new access and use arrangements and provide more formal mechanisms for arbitrating disputes. Indeed, there are a variety of possibilities for state involvement to reduce the wastes of the common pool.

One response is the assignment and enforcement of more definite property rights to the resource, whereby only owners are granted access. If completely defined, a system of private property rights equates private incentives with social benefits and costs. The owner becomes the residual claimant of the resulting benefits and costs from resource use decisions. Property owners have the right to sell or otherwise exchange the asset or to pass it along to their heirs.

Under these circumstances, socially-optimal resource use decisions result, even though the actions are made by private parties. Reliance on private property

---

[3] Ostrom (1990) provides a theory and empirical evidence regarding successful local collective action to address common-pool resource (CPR) problems. Experiments and more field studies are included in Ostrom, Gardner and Walker (1994). Other case studies and conceptual arguments are in the readings included in McCay and Acheson (1987); Ellickson (1991); Hess (1996); Burger, Ostrom, Norgaard, Policansky, and Goldstein (2001); and Ostrom, Dietz, Dolsak, Stern, Stonich, and Weber (2002). Useful summaries of the uses of NIE in examining commons problems are found in the readings included in Acheson (1994).

[4] For discussion of the development of property rights in the Amazon frontier, see Alston, Libecap, and Schneider (1996); Alston, Libecap, and Mueller (1999, 2000). Deacon (1999) examines the relationship between deforestation of the common forest and property rights arrangements.

rights reduces the role of state regulation to one of enforcing ownership, arbitrating disputes, and refining rights through the judiciary or legislative process as relative prices or technologies change.[5]

Another response to the common pool is state ownership, whereby the state retains formal property rights and controls individual access and use through a variety of entry and production restrictions. Under state ownership, resource use decisions will be made by government officials, either politicians or bureaucrats, who technically are not residual claimants. They are not "owners," but authorized agents or managers. Because they are not to be guided by private pecuniary objectives in their decisions, production, investment, and exchange decisions involving state-owned assets are determined by political factors as described below. Under these circumstances, there may or may not be a close blending of private and social considerations when the agents make resource use decisions. Accordingly, distortions may result, but they may be socially acceptable if private rights either are not possible or are not politically feasible for reasons to be examined shortly.

A third response to the problem of open access is a hybrid of private ownership and state regulation, whereby individuals hold property rights, but the range of resource options is heavily constrained by regulatory restrictions and taxes. The regulations define how much of the resource can be extracted at any point in time, when it can be accessed, the types of investment that can be made, and the nature of allowable exchange. Receipts from sales are taxed to reduce private returns from harvesting or otherwise using the resource in order to better preserve the stock. A related hybrid arrangement retains government ownership but delegates use privileges to private parties. Again, the private use privileges are sharply limited by regulation and fees to close the margins through which resource rents would otherwise be dissipated.

The type of state response selected depends upon a number of factors. One is the physical nature of the resource and whether private property rights to it can be assigned and monitored at reasonable cost. As noted earlier, broadly-spread resources, such as the atmosphere, or mobile resources, such as ocean fisheries, are examples where private property rights may not be feasible. The higher the cost of assigning and enforcing private property rights, the more likely is reliance upon government ownership and regulation of private use. Indeed, some ubiquitous resources often are viewed by the population as "common" or public resources precisely because restricted access historically had not been possible. Distributional objections can impede government actions to limit access and use of what had been viewed as a "public" resource. Sustained resistance to the charging of fees to public beaches or parklands to ration use is an example of this problem.

Another factor affecting the nature of state response to open-access losses is resource value. More valuable resources attract greater competition for control

---

[5] See the development of property rights and the limited role of the state as enforcer in Anderson and Hill (1975); Libecap (1978, 1989); and Barzel (1989).

and potentially, greater rental losses as the parties compete to appropriate the asset. Under these circumstances, government ownership and regulation of private access and use is unlikely to be as effective in maximizing resource values as is a system of private property rights. Private property rights better align incentives for effective resource use because, as noted earlier, "owners" are residual claimants, unless there are critical externalities involved. By contrast, under state ownership there is no clear residual claimant.

If there are important third-party effects associated with private ownership and use, however, private property rights may not be socially-optimal, even when resource values are high. It is often asserted, for example, that very special or unique national assets with high amenity values be retained and managed under public ownership. National parks for the management of important natural regions or phenomena are an example.

A third, and related factor that influences the nature of the state response to the commons is equity. Equity issues dominate politics and political action. The assignment of more precise private property rights to avoid rent dissipation implicitly involves an assignment of wealth and political power. Exclusion is required if property rights are to have any meaning, and exclusion means that some parties will not be able to use or earn a living from a resource that previously been available to them. This situation may raise equity concerns, especially if the new rights arrangement importantly changes *status quo* economic and political rankings.[6] The new rights assignment may lead to a more skewed wealth distribution than has previously been acceptable. Politicians may respond to these equity concerns by adopting tax schemes to reduce the wealth gains of rights holders. Although such actions might address equity concerns, they can have efficiency consequences, allowing some of the losses of the commons to continue. For example, taxation reduces the expected private returns from otherwise desirable long-term investment, and as a result, it is neglected.

This chapter focuses on government responses to the common pool, the private and political negotiations underlying them, and the information and transaction costs that influence the design of property rights and regulatory policies. Understanding the type of institution that emerges and its effects on the commons depends upon identifying the key parties involved, their objectives, and their political influence.[7] Further, it requires detailed analysis of the bargaining that occurs within and across groups. The analytical problem is compounded if the common resource crosses political boundaries or if citizens of multiple jurisdictions or nations are involved. In these cases, intergovernmental regulations are required, so that political bargaining within and across jurisdictions must be examined as well.

Among the transaction costs involved in addressing the commons, information problems play an especially important role. There may be limited or controversial data regarding the magnitude of the open-access problem. If this

---

[6] Demsetz (1967) notes the role of social norms in influencing the type of property system selected.

[7] For analysis of bureaucratic incentives, see Johnson and Libecap (1994).

is the case, it will be difficult for the parties to predict how they will be affected by any institutional change to address the commons. If there is no consensus on the size of waste or risk to the stock associated with the commons, then it will be even more difficult to agree to a distribution of the rewards and costs as part of any proposed regulation or property rights arrangement. Disagreements over the seriousness of the losses of the common pool increase if the problem cannot be readily observed and verified by generally-available information. Similarly, disputes are likely if the scientific or engineering evidence on the problem is obscure, inconclusive, or asymmetrically held. Since these conflicts increase the transaction costs of taking action, they delay responses to open-access situations.

Resolving information disputes not only requires additional data, but agreement on their interpretation and implications for the distribution of the aggregate benefits and costs of controlling the commons. Reaching agreement on all fronts may not be easy if the data remain controversial and if the negotiating parties are very different in how they access and react to the data. How these bargaining or negotiation problems are resolved and the time that it takes to do so, influences the nature of the institutions adopted, when they are implemented, and their ultimate impact on common-pool externalities.

Disputes over solutions to the commons are not merely academic. Successful policies require that some parties be denied access and that others have their use practices significantly constrained. This may curtail access and use that has spanned generations with important distributional consequences. The more severe the open-access problem, the greater the needed restrictions on individual behavior. More and more parties must be expelled or have their access sharply constrained and regulated. Current income from resource use for many parties will fall dramatically. Others who are granted property rights or regulated, controlled-access, may find their wealth position sharply improved. As a result, the costs and benefits of resolving the commons are unlikely to be uniformly spread.

Some parties see themselves made worse off from institutional change, absent compensation, even in the face of potentially large aggregate gains. Others see clear improvements, unless their gains are taxed away. Accordingly, the seriousness of the problem, the nature of the solution, the identities of who gains and loses, the compensation to be paid, and its form are the issues that dominate both private and political debate over state regulation of the common pool. Even though intervention might reduce losses in the aggregate, politics determines the nature of the outcome, the distribution of the benefits and costs, and the resulting institutional response may bear little resemblance to what an ideal solution might be.

The Contributions of the New Institutional Economics for Understanding the Losses of the Commons and Reactions to Them

With its attention to the transaction costs associated with the bargaining that must take place among heterogeneous parties, private, politicians, bureaucrats, and judges, all of whom will act with limited and/or asymmetric information, the New Institutional Economics (NIE) provides a useful way of analyzing state regulation of the common pool.[8] The NIE helps explain why regulation is often delayed, takes different forms across jurisdictions and countries, and why the suggested approach using a strict, neo-classical framework, which routinely abstracts from transaction costs, most likely will not be the observed solution to open access.[9] Consideration of transaction costs helps to make clear why property rights or regulation take the forms that they do. As such, the NIE makes possible a better understanding of actual human behavior, institutions, and resource outcomes.

Section 2 briefly reviews the common-pool problem, and Section 3 describes some of the transaction costs associated with assigning more complete property rights or devising alternative regulatory solutions. Sections 4 through 6 examine common-pool fisheries, oil reservoirs, and the atmosphere. The final section summarizes the general themes and the advantages of the NIE approach.

2. THE COMMON POOL

The Tragedy of the Commons

Frank Knight (1924), H. Scott Gordon (1954), Anthony Scott (1955) and Steven N.S. Cheung (1970) describe the problem of the commons in their classic articles.[10] Using open-access fisheries to define the issue, Gordon discusses the motivation and effects of infinite entry by homogeneous fishers, operating under the rule of capture. According to Gordon, entry occurs so long as the private marginal costs of access and harvest are less than or equal to the average returns for all fishers. Continued entry and the associated fishing pressure eventually dissipate all economic rent. He identifies the institutional conditions underlying this dismal outcome (Gordon, 1954, 124): "There appears then, to be some truth in the conservative dictum that everybody's property is nobody's property. Wealth that is free for all is valued by no one because he who is foolhardy enough to wait for its proper time of use will only find that it has been taken by another... The fish in the sea are valueless to the fisherman, because there is no assurance that they will be there for him tomorrow if they are left behind today."

---

[8] For summaries of the approaches of the NIE, see Williamson (1975, 1979), Eggertsson (1990), Furubotn and Richter (1997). Allen (1991) discusses transaction costs.

[9] Similarly, see North's (1990) observation that property rights institutions that promote efficient resource use are the exception rather than the norm.

[10] The wastes of the common pool also are outlined in Libecap (1998a). Heller (1998) and Buchanan and Yoon (2000) describe the counter problem of under utilization of a resource when the right to exclude is held by multiple parties. Brooks, Murray, Salant, and Weise (1999) model common property extraction using two approaches. Bial (1998) examines interstate arrangements in the Ohio River valley to control water pollution prior to federal intervention. Early discussion of open access and private roads is in Frank Knight's classic article on social costs (1924).

Transaction Costs and Solutions to the Commons

As noted in the Introduction, open-access conditions usually arise when the costs of defining and enforcing restrictive boundaries are high relative to potential benefits. Hence, low-valued resources that are migratory or otherwise difficult to delineate often exist as a common pool. Other resources may lie within the commons due to cultural, legal, or political precedents that mandate free and open access, at least to particular parties. In either case, individuals who use the resource do not bear the full social costs of their actions, and because of this, they exploit it too intensively and do not invest in the long term. The benefits of individual actions are narrowly focused, but the costs are spread among all parties.

With the resulting relentless pressure to extract the commons, total output or use exceeds the social wealth-maximization point, where total social costs and benefits are equated. The rush to produce and accompanying ownership uncertainty leads to waste as competing claimants divert labor and capital inputs to predation and defense.[11] Violence is characteristic, particularly if external factors lead to a rise in resource values or lower access and use costs.

For example, Alston, Libecap, and Mueller (2000) describe violent conflict over land in the Brazilian Amazon frontier. As access roads are provided, lowering transportation costs, competition for open agricultural land increases, and land values rise. Yet, property rights on the frontier are unclear and enforcement of claims uncertain. Accordingly, infringement of holdings and occupancy of land claimed by others results in disputes, sometimes with deadly outcomes.

The problem of the commons also is outlined by Garrett Hardin in his 1968 *Science* article, "The Tragedy of the Commons." In discussing incentives among competitive herders to overgraze a common pasture, he concludes (1968, 1244): "Therein is the tragedy. Each man is locked into a system that compels him to increase his herd without limit—in a world that is limited. Ruin is the destination toward which all men rush, each pursuing his own best interest..."

Johnson and Libecap (1980) describe the empirical case of Navajo herders in the American southwest that illustrates the problem raised by Hardin. Since rights to rangeland are not formally defined or enforced on the Navajo Reservation, each herder is motivated to have his sheep occupy and graze the land completely. Individual control of a particular part of the range is respected only so long as the sheep occupy the land. If they are withdrawn, other herders move their animals onto the range. Any grass that is left by one herder for the future by reducing harvest, only invites entry from neighboring herders. The incentives to overgraze open-access pastures are clear, and over time the land gradually erodes and loses its productive capacity.

Hardin's solution (1968, 1247) to the tragedy of the commons is coercive regulation of individual behavior—"mutual coercion, mutually agreed upon" to

---

[11] Bohn and Deacon (2000) argue that insecure ownership can reduce investment and use of natural resources when capital costs for extraction are relative high. This result counters the usual case of higher extraction rates when rights are poorly defined.

escape the "horror of the commons." And he notes, but does not develop, the critical problem of regulating the commons–distributional outcomes that are not acceptable to key parties. He asserts, however, that "injustice is preferable to total ruin." But total ruin is not so obvious to all parties in many common-pool settings. As mentioned above, the parties often disagree with the timing and appropriate form of intervention, and they object to the allocation of the costs and benefits associated with addressing the commons. These concerns raise the transaction costs of reaching agreement on the commons problem, affecting both the timing and nature of the action taken.

3. REGULATION OF OPEN ACCESS

Institutional Change to Mitigate the Losses of the Commons

The losses of the common pool often seem so apparent that difficulties in devising effective regulation come as a surprise. In fact, unfortunately, by the time the wastes associated with open access become very visible, much of the damage already has been done.[12] Avoiding these losses motivates collective action to define more exclusive property rights or to assemble regulatory policies for controlling access and use. Historical and contemporary experiences with large commons problems, however, reveal that the process of institutional change is neither very smooth nor complete.[13] Indeed, state intervention typically occurs late in resource use and depletion, when there is finally a political consensus among the parties regarding the extent of the common-pool losses and the distribution of the benefits and costs of taking action.

This pattern of late responses is repeated in the examples provided below for fisheries and oil. Without considering the costs of gathering, interpreting, and conveying information about the resource stock as well as the costs of negotiating among the relevant parties for institutional change, it is not possible to understand the timing and form of state intervention.

Aggregate Gains from Institutional Change

The larger the expected aggregate gains from controlling open access, the more likely some institutional change in the form of regulation and/or the assignment of property rights will take place. As Garrett Hardin (1968, 1248) argues, the commons can be tolerated so long as the magnitudes of the waste are low, but as they rise, the social benefits of resolving it increase. Still as noted, broad agreement on the wastes of open access and the means to resolve it may take considerable time.[14]

---

[12] See the summary in Brown (2000) regarding the timing of management efforts.
[13] Libecap (1989); North (1990).
[14] For examples in the case of oil fields and global warming, see Wiggins and Libecap (1985), and Bial, Houser, and Libecap (2002).

In general consensus that common-pool losses are large is not always sufficient to bring about a successful institutional response due to conflicts over the distribution of benefits and costs among the various constituencies involved. These include competing private parties, politicians, and regulators, and in the design of regulation each attempts to maximize their private net gains. Lobby groups are formed to advance the objectives of particular groups, and interest groups in turn, negotiate to build larger coalitions in favor of desired arrangements. When state action is required, politicians are lobbied to implement the proposed regulation or property rights. Logrolling exchanges and other compromises are necessary within the political arena in order to devise a solution that has sufficient support to be enacted. Each of these layers of negotiation involves different transaction costs that mold the institutions that eventually result.[15]

Number and Heterogeneity of the Parties Involved

Negotiations within and across groups of resource users are more difficult the greater the number and heterogeneity of the parties involved. With larger numbers, more claims to the resource must be resolved and more must be excluded (Olson, 1965). With greater heterogeneity in terms of objectives, production costs, and access to information, it is more difficult to reach a policy consensus, and to enforce agreement. This is a standard outcome in cartels and other collective action settings (Schmalensee, 1987), and it plagues negotiations over institutional change and the common pool.

Parties who anticipate that new regulation or assignment of property rights will make them worse off relative to the *status quo* will see few benefits from the new regime and will attempt to block it, unless compensation is forthcoming.[16] Conversely, proponent constituencies anticipating improved access to the resource will, along with their political representatives and administrative agencies, seek either enhanced regulatory authority or preferential property rights.

Information and Measurement Problems

Information and measurement problems, however, raise uncertainty about the actual nature and distribution of the benefits and costs of regulating the commons. For instance, a resource's response to reduced harvest pressure may be understood very imperfectly. This is a common problem, for example, in fisheries where fishing pressure is only one of many factors influencing the health of the stock. Similarly, good information about the precarious nature of the resource often is held asymmetrically by advocates, but their claims are viewed with skepticism by opponents who view the claims as self-serving. In cases, such as the oil example provided below, the status of the resource cannot not be conveyed credibly by proponents because data interpretation typically is *ad hoc*

---

[15] Libecap (1989, 10–28).
[16] Johnson and Libecap (1982); Lueck (1995).

and not easily replicated. Some parties, as we will see below, take advantage of these information and measurement problems to opportunistically advance their own interests that are only tangentially related to the commons problem.[17] With limited data it can be very costly for using parties to sort through the claims that are made regarding the need for regulation.

As noted above, measurement costs are lower for observable, stationary resources, and conversely are higher for larger, mobile, unobservable resources. Compliance must be verified in order to maintain an effective coalition for reducing the losses of the commons. The aggregate benefits of any institutional response to open access, as well as individual shares of those benefits, depend upon general adherence. Otherwise, harvest pressure will be not reduced and the commons not addressed. Cheating by some reduces incentives of all parties to adhere to the arrangement.

The Feasibility of Side Payments

Within political negotiations to address the common pool, side payments in the form of preferential regulation, subsidies, or property rights to the resource often are proposed to mitigate opposition from those who otherwise expect to be harmed by any new constraint on general access. As illustrated below, this practice occurred when small oil producers in Texas in the 1940s and 1950s were offered beneficial production quotas within a proposed regulatory framework to control output. Small producers had opposed regulation because they had taken advantage of open-access conditions to drain their larger neighbors. Larger producers, however, were willing to agree to these preferential quotas as a means to secure political support for regulation.

When side payments like these are offered to mitigate potential losses from restricting the commons, there must be agreement on which parties will be affected; the magnitude of the harms involved; whether compensation is warranted; and its size, source, and form. Measurement problems raise the costs of assessing competing claims in negotiations over transfer payments. Compensation requires some agreement on the value of current and proposed uses of the open-access resource so that an acceptable level of taxation can be determined to fund the transfers. Valuation is controversial if there are information asymmetries among the parties, which impedes consensus on the value of resource use with or without regulation. Further, there may be political opposition to the form of compensation to be paid. Cash transfers typically involve the fewest economic distortions because real resources are not involved, but if the political visibility of cash payments makes them unacceptable, less efficient alternatives must be devised.

This situation, for example, explains why small oil producers in Texas received preferential production quotas, even though they led to wasteful extra drilling and output. The alternative of cash payments to certain producers to

---

[17] Williamson (1975, 1979) discusses opportunism.

retire their production was too transparent to be politically acceptable and too difficult to calculate effectively. The granting of special production quotas, in contrast, was simpler and less obvious to general taxpayers.

Compensating side payments to broaden support for regulation or a change in property rights may not be possible for some key parties. They may not have legal standing for such transfers and measurement of claims may be very difficult. One important group affected are politicians, who might lose constituents if the closing of the commons dramatically reduces the population of communities that previously had exploited the open resource. Another group is regulatory officials whose mandates are reduced if a system of private property rights replaces a regulated commons. A third group are those parties who supply inputs or otherwise provide services to those who use the commons. Successful regulation of open access resources, however, reduces their customers by lowering both production and the number of accessing parties. Absent compensation, these groups can be expected to strongly oppose institutional change, and politicians, especially, may be in an excellent position to block or mold any response to the commons.

The Role of Precedent

Finally, precedents affect the range of feasible options for addressing the common pool. A legacy of past informal or formal property rights can give some parties a vested interest in the commons. They will oppose institutional changes, even ones that promise aggregate benefits, unless they can be made better off under the proposed arrangement. It may not be possible, however, to improve their welfare and still maintain the advantages of the institutional change, especially if they must be denied access to the resource and full compensation is not provided. Groups with vested interests may have advantages in political bargaining relative to other groups through lower costs of collective action. Their current position in the system binds them together to make them a relatively cohesive bargaining group. They also have beneficial ties to established political processes and leaders. These advantages make vested interests effective political lobbyists, biasing institutional change toward maintenance of the commons and limiting successful resolution of common-property problems. This situation is illustrated in the examples that follow, and it suggested that institutional change generally will involve only incremental adjustments from open access.

These information and bargaining issues complicate accord on political side payments to draw in recalcitrant parties and they raise the transaction costs of reaching agreement on new property rights arrangements or regulations to reduce the losses of open access. By contrast, if transaction costs were zero or very low, then action could be taken quickly. Indeed, if transaction costs were zero, there would be no open-access problem to begin with. It would be possible to costlessly devise restrictions on access and use (Coase, 1960). But in practice, transaction costs are high, allowing commons problems to develop and persist, and solutions in some cases may only be slow in developing.[18]

4. REGULATION OF A CLASSIC COMMON-POOL RESOURCE: WILD OCEAN FISHERIES

The Open-Access Problem

Wild ocean fisheries are characterized by open access and competing fishers who have no ownership in the stock. Except for relatively stationary inshore shellfish fisheries, private property rights to fish stocks are not feasible due to high definition and enforcement costs. Rights to migratory species that cover wide expanses of the ocean also require coordination across multiple political jurisdictions. Inshore species that remain within more limited spaces, such as in a bay or restricted coastal region, can have more clearly defined ownership institutions. Examples include private leases for oyster beds and territorial rights in U.S. coastal lobster fisheries. In Japan, fishers' associations manage local inshore stocks.[19] In some cases, however, even where potentially feasible, private ownership of fish stocks have met with opposition by those who object to such broad grants of property rights to wild species.[20] In the 1950s the U.S. Department of Justice rejected, as violations of the Sherman Act, attempts by fishery unions to control access to inshore bay fisheries.[21] The result of these actions, which were prompted by excluded fishers, was to return the fishery to a common pool.

Transaction Costs and the History of Regulation

Historically, addressing commons problems in fisheries has started with denying some groups access to a fishery. Usually these arrangements involve giving preference to well-defined political constituencies, such as a country's citizens relative to non citizens, sports relative to commercial fishers, inshore relative to offshore fishers, or large boat owners relative to small boat owners. This approach temporarily, at least, reduces entry and total fishing pressure while avoiding politically-controversial distributional issues in regulating the catch of

---

[18] Yoram Barzel (1989) emphasizes transaction costs and measurement problems in implementing property rights regimes.

[19] For territorial rules and their enforcement in U.S. oyster beds, see Agnello and Donnelley (1975). For the U.S. Northeast lobster fishery, see Acheson (1975, 1988) who provides details on the institutions that lobster fishers have developed. Berkes (1986) describes local management of inshore fisheries in Turkey. For Japan, see, Asada, Hirasawa, and Nagasaki (1983) and Yamamoto (1995).

[20] See discussion by Lund (1980) and Lueck (1989, 1991).

[21] See discussion of court cases in Johnson and Libecap (1982).

those allowed to remain.[22] Limited-access controls without accompanying harvest restrictions, however, increase individual returns and eventually, encourage new entry and rent depletion by group members. When this occurs, other regulations must be added, such as reductions in the allowable number of fishing days, as well as boat size and gear restrictions that raise fishing costs. Monitoring and enforcement problems reduce the effectiveness of these controls, and fishers compete on unregulated dimensions, dissipating the economic value of the fishery. The underlying problem is that the regulatory structure does not make fishers residual claimants in the stock.

One effort aimed at forestalling the depletion of large, coastal fisheries was the adoption of 200-mile exclusive economic zones, beginning in 1976 by the U.S and other countries.[23] The exclusive zones at least meant that foreign fishers could be denied access, thereby reducing harvest pressure. Domestic fishers, however, increased their intensity in response. In the U.S., for instance, a frenzy of investment in new boats and equipment soon replaced the excluded foreign fishers. Fisheries outside the 200-mile limit remained under open-access, and international efforts have had no power to exclude and no jurisdiction for enforcement. Within the 200-mile zones, attempts at regulation to maintain fish stocks have mostly been unsuccessful due to opportunistic maneuvering by fishers, processors, regulators, and politicians representing depressed fishing communities. In addition, the effects of harvest cannot always be convincingly separated from natural factors, such as fluctuations in ocean currents and temperature, and as a result, fishers have not accepted arguments for stricter rules.

In cases where agreement can be reached on the condition of the stock and appropriate total allowable catch (TAC), it must be divided among eligible fishers. Here, however, there are critical distributional effects with important political ramifications. The tighter the limits, the more fishers who must exit and the greater the political outcry, especially from politicians from fishing communities where there are few alternative economic opportunities. Additionally, Johnson and Libecap's (1982) examination of fishery regulation points out how restrictions can have differential impacts on fishers who vary according to ability, capital equipment, and size.

In particular, very productive fishers, who have adapted well to the common pool, will be harmed if regulations involve the assignment of politically-popular

---

[22] For example, Higgs (1982) describes the rise of sport fishers as an effective interest group in lobbying for regulations that constrained commercial fishers in the Pacific Northwest salmon fishery. Similarly, in the Gulf of Mexico shrimp fishery analyzed by Johnson and Libecap (1982) inshore, bay shrimpers and offshore Gulf shrimpers competed to place differential constraints on one another, rather than to find more comprehensive management arrangements. General fishery regulation problems are described in Johnson and Libecap (1982); Karpoff (1987); Wilen (1985, 1988, 2002); Anderson and Leal (1993); Homans and Wilen (1997); De Alessi (1998); Arnason, Hannesson, and Schrank (2000); and Hannesson (2002).

[23] The Law of the Sea Convention of 1982 authorized 200-mile exclusive economic zones. For discussion see Hollick and Cooper (1997, 148–9) and Sebenius (1984).

uniform catch quotas.[24] Uniform catch quotas are popular among many fishers, politicians, and regulators because they are comparatively easy to define, at least compared to quotas that vary across fishers; they do not require the information necessary to verify past catch, which is often the alternative basis for assigning quotas; and they do not explicitly provide differential rights and wealth assignments to what had previously been an open or "common" resource. For all of these reasons, uniform catch quotas involve lower transaction costs of definition and assignment. But they obviously can make better fishers who had been successful under open access, worse off under the new regulatory regime.

The Problem of Heterogeneity Once Again

Accordingly, with differential histories of productivity among fishers, some may have a stake in maintaining the commons and resisting regulations that could redistribute income. When the fishery is virtually depleted these distributional concerns can become less important, allowing for agreement on tighter controls. Many fishers have left the fishery, and those that remain are more homogeneous with regard to expected future prospects and are more likely to see themselves made better off from new arrangements. Under such conditions, regulation is more likely to be adopted and to be more successful, but by this time, the stock may be critically damaged.

In the meantime, regulations that do not explicitly redistribute income, such as fixed fishing seasons, can be adopted without much controversy. These general regulations, however, allow fishers to compete in other ways, usually through increased capitalization–larger boats with more costly search and harvest gear. These investments increase catch and deplete the stock, forcing even shorter seasons, which in turn, lead to a new round of wasteful competitive capitalization.

The Pacific Northwest Halibut Fishery

The Pacific Northwest halibut fishery is an example. A limited entry regime was put into place in 1979 in British Columbia with the maximum number of vessel licenses set at 435, gear restrictions, total allowable catch within the fishing season, and minimum fish size rules. A fishing derby ensued as fishers competed by adding vessels, crews, and times spent fishing. The number of vessels rose quickly from 333 in 1980 to the limit of 435 by 1988, when total harvest peaked at 12,859,562 pounds, up 128 percent from 1980. The halibut stock declined, forcing regulators to reduce the allowable season to ensure the TAC was not exceeded. By 1990 the season had shrunk to 6 days from 65 days

---

[24] Uniform rules are popular with regulators because the ease of design and enforcement, and they are attractive to politicians because they do not appear to grant preferential privileges to the fishery. Similarly, Lueck (1995) has argued that very productive parties within a common-pool setting may seek to maintain *status quo* first-possession rules, even though broad social costs might be involved.

in 1980. With a very short fishing season, the catch had to be stored frozen for the rest of the year, denying consumers higher-valued fresh fish.[25] This unsatisfactory situation led to a new regulatory approach, the introduction of Individual Transferable Quotas in British Columbia in 1991 and in Alaska in 1995. Through quota exchanges, gradually the number of vessels declined, the stock rebounded, and the season was extended, reaching 245 days by 1993.[26]

Individual Transferable Quotas (ITQs)

Under a ITQ regime, a total allowable catch is determined by the regulatory authority, based on evaluation of the stock and ocean conditions and then divided among fishers as harvest quotas.[27] These quotas are valuable use rights that are exchanged among fishers and gradually accumulated by those who are most productive and have lowest fishing costs. In this manner, fishing effort is adjusted to maximize returns. Although there are enforcement problems and incentives to discard less valuable fish under ITQs, they represent a more effective method of regulating the fishery commons. Nevertheless, ITQs are controversial.

The issue hinges on who will get them and the wealth they represent. There must be some limits on the quotas in order for them to have value and for the fishery to be protected. One method is to assign quotas to those who have a history of fishing in the industry, but this arrangement disadvantages potential new entrants, and they mobilize in opposition.[28] Uniform allocations harm "highliners," those captains who consistently outperform other fishers. There are other objections to granting certain fishers ownership windfalls to a common resource. Windfall-profit taxes and the distribution of quotas through auctions would allow the state to capture more fishery rents, but are naturally opposed by fishers.

ITQs were adopted in New Zealand in 1986, and in 1991 in Iceland, two nations that depend critically on their fisheries and conservation of the stock. In other countries, ITQs have had more limited experiences. Political opposition in the U.S. resulted in them being placed on hold in 1996. In Norway ITQs have been resisted by regulatory officials, politicians from small fishing villages, and

---

[25] Gaudet, Moreaux, and Salant (2002) argue that the ability to privately store a common-pool resource can accelerate extraction and increase waste. Further, if there are both common-pool and privately-owned resources, the race to extract and store can shift the of exploitation to the common resource.

[26] Discussion of regulation of the Halibut fishery is provided in Grafton, Squires, and Fox (2000); Wilen and Homans (1998); and Wilen (2002). Edwards (1994) discusses the political economy of usufructuary rights such as ITQs.

[27] Even so, ITQs do not grant property rights to the stock. Such rights could allow for the adding of fertilizer to increase the growth of plankton and other food sources for fish. For additional discussion of ITQs, see Johnson, (1995) and the readings included in Arnason and Gissurarson (1999). The readings included in the two volumes edited by Shotton (1999) provide a very complete discussion of property rights issues and regulation in fisheries, including why ITQs are often resisted, despite their many beneficial attributes. The volumes also include histories of management efforts across a variety of fisheries and countries.

[28] See Lueck (1995) for discussion of the right of first possession.

some processors. Even where they have been adopted, small fishing boats have been exempted.[29]

As a result of the slow and fitful movement of regulation, most wild ocean fish stocks are at precariously low levels due to heavy fishing pressure. Myers and Worm (2003) estimate that that the large predatory fish biomass in the world's oceans is only about 10 percent of pre-industrial levels. These include some of the most commercially valuable species. Hence, despite a large and (in some cases) old literature in economics and biology on fishery management and equally large and expensive fishery management regimes, many of the world's leading fisheries remain under some variant of open access.

The high costs of controlling entry; the information problems associated with determining fish stocks and the usefulness of various regulatory policies; the equity concerns raised in denying entry to some fishers; and the related transaction costs of forming and implementing effective property rights and regulatory programs help explain why the record of closing the commons in major fisheries is such a disappointing one.

5. REGULATION OF A COMMON RESOURCE: OIL

The Open-Access Problem

As with wild ocean fisheries, subsurface oil and gas reservoirs can be a common-pool resource. The condition arises when multiple parties competitively extract hydrocarbons from a subsurface reservoir. Under the rule of capture, ownership of the oil is obtained only upon extraction. In the U.S. the problem occurs because ownership of the mineral rights to a single reservoir often is fragmented, with many firms seeking the same migratory oil. The problem also occurs to a lesser degree in places like the North Sea and Caspian Sea where reservoirs are partitioned by international boundaries with separate production concessions within each partition.[30] Because fragmentation is less severe in the North Sea, competitive extraction is less of a problem, but it still occurs along concession boundary lines.

In either case, producing firms have incentives to maximize the economic value of their holdings, rather than that of the reservoir as a whole. They competitively drill and drain, including the oil of their neighbors to increase their private returns, even though these actions reduce the overall value of the reservoir. Capital costs are driven up with excessive investment in wells, pipelines, and surface storage, and production costs rise with too-rapid extraction. This practice leads to the premature venting of natural gas or other fluids that help drive the oil to the surface. Total oil recovery is reduced. As in fisheries, the

---

[29] For discussion of the political economy of Icelandic regulation, see Gissurarson (2000); for New Zealand, see Clark, Major, and Mollett (1989) and Sharp (2002); and for Norway, see Hannesson (1985). Regulation in these and other fisheries also is discussed in the readings included in Shotton (1999).

[30] Libecap (1998, 643).

commons problem in oil production has been recognized for a very long time, and the property rights/regulatory responses have been similarly complex and controversial.

The number of firms involved in competing for oil provides a sense of the scope of the problem. On the Yates, Hendrick, and Seminole fields of Texas and Oklahoma, all discovered in the 1920s, there were respectively, 16, 18, and 40 different firms with extraction leases, and on the huge East Texas field discovered in 1932, over 1,000 firms were pumping its oil by 1933.[31] A possible solution was early consolidation of production rights, at least in domestic U.S. oil fields. Empirically, however, buy-outs to internalize externalities were not the solution to the common pool. The early or 'gusher' stage of field development with its fury of production and waste, was the time of least information about the value of individual holdings, limiting the possibilities for exchange.[32] The conflicting strategic bargaining positions of so many independent agents, compounded by the problem of holdouts, posed insurmountable difficulties in consolidating production leases or in privately coordinating production programs.

Transaction Costs and the History of Regulation

As a result in the U.S., state regulations were implemented in the 1930s to limit the drilling of wells, control their spacing, and constrain the extraction of oil and gas through assignment of production quotas. These regulations were supported by some producers, resisted by others, and the policies that emerged were molded by political factors. The compromises necessary to build a political consensus for regulation ultimately weakened its ability to address the common-pool externality, although it was still an improvement over open access. In Texas, the Railroad Commission set monthly statewide production levels and allocated the total among regulated wells. The production rules were applied uniformly to all fields, even though each oil field had a unique physical configuration and optimum production potential. This approach raised production costs relative to what might have occurred with alternative regulatory designs.

Further, as noted earlier the numerous and politically-influential owners of high-cost wells were exempted from production controls altogether.[33] Small, high-cost producers (often called "independents") were located in almost every Texas county and they had close ties to local politicians. Further, they were serviced by local oil-field supply firms and they hired local labor. These firms were comparatively homogeneous and effectively organized for political action as the Texas Independent Producers Organization (TIPRO). Larger producers (the so-called, "majors") often were headquartered out-of-state and hence, viewed as "foreign." Moreover, they were located on the largest, most productive fields,

---

[31] Libecap and Wiggins (1984, 89–94).

[32] Some of the problems of asymmetric information in valuing leases are addressed in Wiggins and Libecap (1985).

[33] See Libecap and Smith (forthcoming).

which were in fewer parts of the state. They often had internal oil-field supply support and brought in their own labor. For all of these reasons, despite their wealth and size, the major oil firms were less politically effective in designing oil production regulation in Texas than were the independents.

Unitization

Unitization, which placed the management of the reservoir under a single firm, while granting other producers shares in the net revenues, became an increasingly popular alternative response to the common pool by the 1940s.[34] Although it offered an effective remedy to production externalities, its progress was limited. The key issue was conflict over a share formula to divide the net proceeds of unit production among the various parties. Agreements often were not forthcoming until late in a reservoir's productive life, when enough common information had emerged about the nature and value of both the reservoir and individual leases. If unit contracts were to succeed, they had to award each party a fixed share of production and costs, making them residual claimants to reservoir-wide rents. If such uniform shares could not be agreed to, then either no unit was formed or less effective contracts were concluded.

In their analysis of unitization negotiations on seven fields in the United States, Wiggins and Libecap (1985, 377–83) found that on average it took six years for agreements to be reached. During the process, many parties became discouraged and dropped out of unitization efforts. The bargaining problem was so widespread that even as late as 1975 only 38 percent of Oklahoma and 20 percent of Texas production came from unitized fields.[35] Similarly, because the parties on the immense Prudhoe Bay field of Alaska could not reach agreement on the value of their respective leases so as to assign cost and revenue shares to a complete unit, the reservoir was partitioned in 1977 into an "oil rim" and "gas cap." Two unit operators were selected for each partition, and there were separate allocations of production costs and benefits among the parties in each partition, even though they covered the same reservoir. Conflicting motivations for production developed, resulting in serious waste until 1999 when company mergers and consolidation of holdings finally (after 22 years) completely unitized the reservoir.[36]

In face of these problems, state governments adopted legislation to force unitization through majority rules. Compulsory unitization laws were adopted in most states, but in Texas political resistance by small firm owners blocked enactment. Small firm owners sought to protect the production advantages they held under existing regulation.[37] Compulsory unitization laws facilitated the adoption

---

[34] For more on unitization, see James L. Smith (1987); Libecap (1998b); Libecap and Smith (1999, 2001).
[35] Libecap and Wiggins (1985, 702).
[36] Libecap and Smith (2003).
[37] Libecap and Wiggins (1985).

of units, and where the problem was due to holdouts by those seeking a greater share of reservoir rents and the reservoir contained only oil, the effect was to improve welfare. But in cases where the reservoir contained both oil and natural gas, the impact of compulsory unitization was not so straightforward.[38]

Because future relative oil and gas prices were uncertain, the respective owners often held disparate expectations about lease values, making it impossible to agree on the terms of trade necessary to assign overall unit shares.[39] When the coercive power of the state was used to force trades and unitization, the resisting parties could be made worse off because they were forced into an exchange that was no longer voluntary. The terms of trade under these conditions is conceived by reluctant parties as offering less than what they require for full compensation for resource. Hence, what otherwise appeared to be an obvious government solution to a breakdown in private bargaining may not have improved welfare.

6. STATE REGULATION OF THE COMMON POOL: AIR POLLUTION

The Open-Access Problem

Air pollution also is a common-pool resource problem. Because there historically has been no effective means of assigning property rights to the atmosphere to control private access and use, the air has been a convenient, low-cost medium for disposing of the byproducts of production. The emissions from one plant are carried into the atmosphere, spreading the costs of pollution and diluting any negative effects on the polluter. In the same manner, however, the benefits of controlling emissions are distributed across multiple parties and regions, whereas the costs of regulation are directly born by the owners of the plant. This setting creates collective action problems for combating polluting, while plant owners have incentives to resist or minimize the effects of regulation.

Transaction Costs and Solutions

If pollution is localized, then it may be possible for private negotiations to take place among those emitting the pollutants and those seeking cleaner air.[40] Similarly, where large industrial plants are involved, firms have incentive to recognize the effects of emissions on their workers and equipment because they internalize at least some of the pollution costs and because only one or two parties are involved in negotiating and implementing controls. Where pollution problems are more broadly spread, however, the transaction costs of private collective action

---

[38] Such situations have been frequent since 63 percent of the largest U.S. oil fields have contained significant volumes of natural gas along with oil. See Libecap and Smith (forthcoming).

[39] Libecap and Smith (2001).

[40] Similarly, see James Buchanan's (1972) interpretation of the possibilities for private negotiation to resolve conflicts between owners of red cedar trees and owners of apple trees.

are much higher. The number of parties involved is greater as are the incentives to free ride. Monitoring compliance is more difficult. The fundamental theorem regarding such transaction costs in dealing with externalities was developed by Ronald Coase. He made clear that consideration of the costs and benefits was essential and that in some cases "... it would cost too much to put the matter right" (Coase, 1960, 39).

Some form of state regulation, then, may be the only reasonable means of controlling air pollution.[41] Traditionally, emission regulation has relied upon "cap-and-control" rules issued from regulators regarding setting overall pollution targets, defining allowable discharges from particular sites, and requiring installation of scrubbing technology and filter equipment. Much of the attention has been directed to electric utilities as major sources of pollution. Since plants vary as to their age, technology used, and fuel source—natural gas, high-sulfur coal, low-sulfur coal–the costs of compliance vary sharply. Accordingly, the way in which regulation is administered affects both the overall cost of achieving air quality standards and the competitive positions of utilities, their customers, and fuel suppliers. There is opportunity for molding regulation to the advantage of the politically influential in ways that do not necessarily assist in meeting air quality objectives.

For instance, the first significant federal air pollution legislation in the U.S. was the 1970 Clean Air Act. It established national maximum standards for ambient concentrations of SO_2 and created new source performance standards (NSPS) for new or refurbished power plants and factories. The NSPS required upgrades of pollution controls whenever plants were constructed or improved. Further, the 1977 Clean Air Act Amendments required that all new coal-powered plants adopt scrubbers even if they burned low-sulfur coal. This rule weakened the competitive advantage of low-sulfur western coal and those utilities that used it relative to high-sulfur eastern coal. The "new source bias" of regulation raised the costs of shifting to new, less polluting plants and extended the economic lives of older, dirty plants that were not burdened by new control costs. Although overall SO_2 emissions declined after enactment of the 1970 Clean Air Act, by 1990 over two-thirds of remaining discharges came from the less-regulated older plants constructed before 1970.[42] This example, as in the case of oil regulation, demonstrates how bargaining positions and political influence mold the design of regulatory policies to address open access. The resulting design may bear little resemblance to an idealized solution and may be comparatively less effective in reducing the wastes of the commons.

Another example of political manipulation of the design of regulation to address the commons is the Prevention of Significant Deterioration (PSD) requirement of the Clean Air Act of 1970. This provision of the law prohibited deterioration of air quality in any region where it exceeded national standards.[43]

---

[41] Kolstad (1999, 135-54) outlines some of the major issues in environmental regulation.
[42] Joskow and Schmalensee (1998, 45) examine the complex political economy of air pollution regulation.
[43] Pashigian (1985).

The PSD, inserted by congressional representatives from the Northeast, was designed to limit plant migration to the South and West, where industrial pollution was less severe and where regulation compliance would be less costly. The PSD, however, did not improve overall air quality since the closing of old, polluting plants in the Northeast and the construction of new cleaner ones elsewhere could have reduced pollution.[44]

The potential for political opportunism increases if policy evaluation requires scientific information that generally is not available to citizens. For example, extension of the ethanol subsidy of over $10 billion since 1979, in part, depends upon the manipulation of information by proponents, chief of which are representatives of Midwestern corn farmers. Although, ethanol is alleged to improve air quality, its effects are mixed. Adding ethanol to gasoline can reduce carbon monoxide emissions from automobiles, but it increases discharge of nitrogen oxide and other pollutants into the atmosphere.[45] Taxpayers have little easy access to the kind of information necessary to evaluate the claims of ethanol producers. With the costs of the subsidy and the pollution broadly spread across the population and the benefits narrowly focused on a few constituencies, there has been no strong incentive for lobby groups to form to challenge ethanol with the relevant information.[46]

Tradable Pollution Permits

More effective regulatory tools are tradable pollution permits, which were first authorized by Title IV of the Clean Air Act Amendments of 1990 to reduce SO_2 emissions. Tradable permits are alternatives to centralized regulation of pollution sources. They are property rights to pollute, and because they can be exchanged, they allow for flexibility and efficiency in meeting pollution standards. As such, they are similar to ITQs in fisheries and unit shares in oil and gas reservoirs in more effectively addressing common-pool problems. Plant owners who can comply with regulation at lower cost sell their emission allowances to those who have higher compliance costs, allowing pollution to be reduced at lower total cost.

Joskow, Schmalensee, and Bailey (1998) found that the emissions rights market in the U.S. had become reasonably efficient by 1994, lowering the costs of compliance with clean air rules. Aggregate annual targeted SO_2 emissions are prorated among plants, determining their individual emission allowances. If a plant is to discharge more than it is authorized and not face penalties, its

---

[44] The PSD rule was the result of successful political action by representatives of northeastern states. On the other hand, Joskow and Schmalensee (1998) find mixed results for political lobbying. Representatives of polluting states, which had been successful in obtaining preferential rules under Phase I of the Clean Air Act Amendments, did not do as well with Phase II regulations.

[45] Johnson and Libecap (2001, 123).

[46] MTBE producers who were competitors for ethanol did have some incentive to challenge the claims made by ethanol producers. MTBE, however, had problems of its own—contamination of ground water and has been banned in many areas.

owners must secure allowances from another plant that will pollute less than allowed. Brokers also purchase unused allowances and are a source of tradable permits.[47] Accordingly through this process, permits are transferred from newer, "clean" plants to older, "dirty" ones where it would be very costly to meet SO_2 caps.

The success of emission permits in SO_2 regulation has led to proposals to expand their use to regulate other air pollutants, such as nitrogen-oxygen compounds and mercury nationally and CO_2 internationally. The rising value of clean air and associated controls on open access, the comparative ease in which emission permits have been defined and traded, and the fact that these exchanges have been generally between larger, more homogeneous firms, assisted by brokers, explain why "air rights" have emerged in these cases.

Air pollution often crosses political boundaries, and thereby involves international negotiations. These raise special bargaining problems for developing effective state policies as illustrated by international efforts to control greenhouse gas (GHG) emissions in order to slow or reverse possible global warming.[48] There is a great deal of uncertainty about the magnitude of the overall global warming problem, how to address it, and the distribution of benefits and costs across countries and constituencies within them. The scientific information remains controversial, and there are concerns about treaty compliance by sovereign countries. Abatement by any country benefits others as a public good, but if abatement is costly to a country's citizens, its politicians have incentive to invest less in reduction efforts than would be globally optimal. Moreover, representatives of developing countries have demanded concessions to reduce the costs of any treaty. They base their demands on equity grounds, arguing that developed countries were the source of much of past GHG emissions and that developing countries should not be saddled with the costs of regulation.

These information problems, compliance issues, and differential demands made by representatives of both developed and developing countries have raised the transaction costs of designing comprehensive GHG regulation. Further, the expansive scope of the problem involves many constituencies, some that might be harmed by the imposition of taxes or other regulations to control emissions and others that might be benefited.

---

[47] There are also some allowances issued through EPA auctions. See Joskow, Schmalensee, and Bailey (1998) for details on the emission permit markets. See also Joskow and Schmalensee (1998). A thorough discussion of the history and operation of U.S. acid rain regulation is provided in Ellerman et al. (2000). Hahn (1984) outlines some implications for market power resulting from how transferable rights are allocated.

[48] These include the United Nations Framework Convention on Climate Change (FCCC) signed at Rio de Janeiro in 1992 where countries pledged to voluntarily reduce carbon emissions to 1990 levels by 2000; a meeting in 1995 in Berlin of the Conference of Parties (COP), created at the Rio conference, to define a structure for further action; and the Kyoto Protocol on Global Warming of December 1997 For analysis of the political bargaining issues involved, see Bial, Houser, and Libecap (2002). Rose (2002) examines tradable environmental allowances that could be used in global warming regulation.

Heterogeneous constituencies and the uncertainty confronting each party in calculating the net effects of the GHG regulation create political problems for country politicians in formulating bargaining positions in international negotiations. These problems and the transaction costs noted above explain why GHG regulation has been so controversial and is unlikely to be effective for some time. As more information is generated in the future regarding the seriousness of the problem and the distribution of the costs and benefits of regulation, agreement on global warming policies may be more likely, just as it has been in fisheries and in oil pools.

7. STATE REGULATION OF THE COMMON POOL: CONCLUDING REMARKS

Theory and research regarding collective action to regulate common-pool problems comes when: a). there is broad consensus or agreement on the aggregate benefits to be gained, b).the parties perceive positive net gains from agreement, and c). they are homogeneous with respect to bargaining objectives and in the distribution of the costs and benefits to be incurred. Agreements reached under these conditions tend to be self-enforcing because it is in the interest of all parties to insure success. Collective action may also achieve its objectives if the parties are heterogeneous with respect to the net gains from cooperation if: a). the spread is not too great, b). there is little uncertainty as to the consequences of agreement, and c). there are bases for constructing side payments to compensate those parties that may bear more costs or receive fewer gains. The side payments must be long term and predictable, and there must be enforcement arrangements. When these conditions are not met, then responding to the commons will be less straightforward.

In the cases examined in this chapter, the political processes of designing regulation and property rights have been complex, influenced by the positions of the bargaining parties involved and the transaction costs of reaching and enforcing agreements. Even so, there is a gradual trend from centralized, "command-and-control" regulation to greater reliance on individual property rights. In oil and gas, the focus is on promoting unitization; in fisheries, ITQs; and in air quality regulation, tradable emission permits. Property rights are more flexible, and they better link individual incentives with socially-efficient outcomes.[49] As a result, they can lower the costs of addressing the commons. This pattern is consistent with the predictions made by Harold Demsetz (1967) who argued that property rights would emerge gradually as it became cost-effective to do so.

Understanding the process of regulatory change, the institutions that emerge, and the observed effects of regulation requires attention to bargaining among the affected parties and the transaction costs involved. This approach is a hallmark of the NIE, and it provides valuable insights into the nature and results of state regulation of the common pool.

---

[49] Hahn and Hird (1990) and Hopkins (1996) examine costs of regulation.

REFERENCES

Acheson, James M. 1975. "The Lobster Fiefs: Economic and Ecological Effects of Territoriality in the Maine Lobster Industry". *Human Ecology* 3: 183–207.
———. 1988. *The Lobster Gangs of Maine*. Hanover, N.H.: University Press of New England.
——— (ed.), 1994. *Anthropology and Institutional Economics*, Monographs in Economic Anthropology, No. 12, Lanham, MD: University Press of America.
Agnello, Richard J. and Lawrence P. Donnelley. 1975. "Property Rights and Efficiency in the Oyster Industry". *Journal of Law and Economics* 18: 621–634.
Allen, Douglas W. 1991. "What Are Transaction Costs?". *Research in Law and Economics* 14: 1–18.
Alston, Lee J., Gary D. Libecap, and Robert Schneider. 1996. "The Determinants and Impact of Property Rights: Land Titles on the Brazilian Frontier". *The Journal of Law, Economics and Organization* 12(1): 25–61.
Alston, Lee J., Gary D. Libecap, and Bernardo Mueller. 1999. *Titles, Conflict, and Land Use: The Development of Property Rights and Land Reform on the Brazilian Amazon Frontier.* Ann Arbor, MI: University of Michigan Press.
———. 2000. "Land Reform Policies, The Sources of Violent Conflict and Implications for Deforestation in the Brazilian Amazon". *Journal of Environmental Economics and Management* 39: 162–188.
Anderson, Terry L. and P.J. Hill. 1975. "The Evolution of Property Rights: A Study of the American West". *Journal of Law and Economics* 18(1): 163–179.
Anderson, Terry L. and Don R. Leal. 1993. "Fishing for Property Rights to Fish" in Roger E. Meiners and Bruce Yandle (eds.), *Taking the Environment Seriously*. Lanham, MD: Rowman & Littlefield, pp. 161–83.
Arnason, Ragnar, Rognvaldur Hannesson, and William E. Schrank. 2000. "Management Costs in Fisheries". *Marine Policy* 24: 233–243.
Arnason, Ragnar and Hannes H. Gissurarson (eds.). 1999. *Individual Transferable Quotas in Theory and Practice*. Reykjavik: University of Iceland Press.
Asada, Y., Y. Hirasawa and F. Nagasaki. 1983. "Fishery Management in Japan". FAO Fisheries Technical Paper 238, Rome: FAO.
Barzel, Yoram, 1989, *Economic Analysis of Property Rights*. New York: Cambridge University Press.
Brooks, Robin, Michael Murray, Stephen Salant, and Jill C. Weise. "When is the Standard Analysis of Common Property Extraction Under Free Access Correct? A Game-Theoretic Justification for Non-Game Theoretic Analyses". *Journal of Political Economy* 107(4): 843–858.
Brown, Gardner M. 2000. "Renewable Natural Resource Management and Use without Markets". *Journal of Economic Literature* 38(4): 875–915.
Berkes, Fikret. 1986. "Local-Level Management and the Commons Problem: A Comparative Study of Turkish Coastal Fisheries". *Marine Policy* 10: 215–229.
Bial, Joseph J. 1989. "Theoretical and Empirical Examination of Decentralized Environmental Regulation". Ph.D. dissertation, Department of Economics, University of Arizona, Tucson AZ.
Bial, Joseph J., Daniel Houser, and Gary D. Libecap, 2002, "Public Choice Issues in International Collective Action: Global Warming Regulation". Working Paper, Karl Eller Center, University of Arizona, Tucson.
Bohn, Henning and Robert T. Deacon. 2000. "Ownership Risk, Investment, and the Use of Natural Resources". *American Economic Review* 90(3): 526–549.
Buchanan, James M. 1972. "Politics, Property, and the Law: An Alternative Interpretation of *Miller et al. v. Schoene*". *Journal of Law and Economics* XV(2): 439–52.
Buchanan, James M. and Yong J. Yoon. 2000. "Symmetric Tragedies: Commons and Anticommons". *Journal of Law and Economics* 43: 1–13.

Burger, Joanna, Elinor, Richard B. Norgaard, David Policansky, and Bernard D. Goldstein. 2001. *Protecting the Commons: A Framework for Resource Management in the Americas*. Washington, DC: Island Press.

Cheung, Steven N.S. 1970. "The Structure of a Contract and the Theory of a Non-Exclusive Resource". *Journal of Law and Economics* 13(1): 49–70.

Clark, Ian N., Phillip J. Major, and Nina Mollett. 1989. "The Development and Implementation of the New Zealand ITQ Management System" in Phillip Neher, Ragnar Arnason, and Nina Mollett (eds.), *Rights Based Fishing*, NATO ASI Series, Series E: Applied Science, Vol. 169. Dordrecht: Kluwer Academic, pp. 117–151.

Coase, Ronald H. 1960. "The Problem of Social Cost". *Journal of Law and Economics* 3: 1–44.

Deacon, Robert T. 1999. "Deforestation and Ownership: Evidence from Historical Accounts and Contemporary Data". *Land Economics* 75(3): 341–359.

De Alessi, Michael. 1998. *Fishing for Solutions*, IEA Studies on the Environment no. 11. London.

Demsetz, Harold. 1967. "Towards a Theory of Property Rights". *American Economic Review* 57(2): 347–359.

Eggertsson, Thrainn. 1990. *Economic Behavior and Institutions*. New York: Cambridge University Press.

Edwards, Steven F. 1994. "Ownership of Renewable Ocean Resources". *Marine Resource Economics* 9: 253–273.

Ellerman, A. Denny, Paul L. Joskow, Richard Schmalensee, Elizabeth Bailey, and Juan-Pablo Montero. 2000. *Markets for Clean Air: The U.S. Acid Rain Program*. New York: Cambridge University Press.

Ellickson, Robert C. 1991. *Order Without Law: How Neighbors Settle Disputes*. Cambridge: Harvard University Press.

Furubotn, Eirik G. and Rudolf Richter. 1997. *Institutions and Economic Theory: The Contribution of the New Institutional Economics*. Ann Arbor, MI: University of Michigan Press.

Gaudet, Gerard, Michel Moreaux, and Stephen W. Salant. 2002. "Private Storage of Common Property". *Journal of Environmental Economics and Management* 43: 280–302.

Gissurarson, Hannes H. 2000. *Overfishing: The Icelandic Solution*. London: IEA Studies on the Environment No. 17.

Gordon, H. Scott. 1954. "The Economic Theory of a Common Property Resource: The Fishery". *Journal of Political Economy* 62(2): 124–142.

Grafton, R. Quentin, Dale Squires, and Kevin J. Fox. 2000. "Private Property and Economic Efficiency: A Study of a Common-Pool Resource". *Journal of Law and Economics* 43: 679–713.

Hahn, Robert W. 1984. "Market Power and Transferable Property Rights". *Quarterly Journal of Economics* 99(4): 753–765.

Hahn, Robert W. and John A. Hird. 1990. "The Costs and Benefits of Regulation: Review and Synthesis". *Yale Journal on Regulation* 8: 233–278.

Hannesson, Rognvaldur. 1985. "Inefficiency Through Government Regulation: The Case of Norway's Fishery Policy". *Marine Resource Economics* 2: 115–141.

———. 2002. "The Privatization of the Oceans" in Donald R. Leal (ed.), *Evolving Property Rights in Marine Fisheries*. Bozeman, MT: Political Economy Research Center, pp. 1–44.

Hardin, Garrett. 1968. "The Tragedy of the Commons". *Science* 162: 1243–1248.

Heller, Michael. 1998. "The Tragedy of the Anti-Commons: Property in the Transition from Marx to Markets". *Harvard Law Review* 111: 621–706.

Hess, Charlotte. 1996. *Common Pool Resources and Collective Action: A Bibliography*, Vol. 3. Workshop in Political Theory and Policy Analysis, Bloomington, IN: Indiana University.

Higgs, Robert. 1982. "Legally Induced Technical Regress in the Washington Salmon Fishery". *Research in Economic History* 7: 55–86.

Hollick, Ann L. and Richard N. Cooper. 1997. "Global Commons: Can They Be Managed?" in Partha Dasgupta, Karl-Göran Mäler, and Alessandro Vercelli (eds.), *The Economics of Transnational Commons*. Oxford: Clarendon Press, pp. 141–71.

Homans, Frances R. and James E. Wilen. 1997. "A Model of Regulated Open Access Resource Use". *Journal of Environmental Economics and Management* 32(1): 1–21.

Hopkins, Thomas D. 1996. "Regulatory Costs in Profile". Policy Study No. 132, St. Louis: Center for the Study of American Business, Washington University, St. Louis.

Johnson, Ronald N. 1995. "Implications of Taxing Quota Value in an Individual Transferable Quota Fishery". *Marine Resource Economics* 10: 327–340.

Johnson, Ronald N. and Gary D. Libecap. 1980. "Legislating Commons: The Navajo Tribal Council and the Navajo Range". *Economic Enquiry* 17(1): 69–86.

———. 1982. "Contracting Problems and Regulation: The Case of the Fishery". *American Economic Review* 72(5): 1005–1022.

———. 1994. *The Federal Civil Service System and the problem of Bureaucracy: The Economics and Politics of Institutional Change*. Chicago, IL: University of Chicago Press.

———. 2001. "Information Distortion and Competitive Remedies in Government Transfer Programs: The Case of Ethanol". *Economics of Governance* 2: 101–134.

Joskow, Paul L. and Richard Schmalensee. 1998. "The Political Economy of Market-Based Environmental Policy: The U.S. Acid Rain Program". *Journal of Law and Economics* 41(1): 37–84.

Joskow, Paul L., Richard Schmalensee, and Elizabeth M. Bailey. 1998. "The Market for Sulfur Dioxide Emissions". *American Economic Review* 88(4): 669–685.

Karpoff, John M. 1987. "Suboptimal Controls in Common Resource Management: The Case of the Fishery". *Journal of Political Economy* 95: 179–194.

Knight, Frank H. 1924. "Some Fallacies in the Interpretation of Social Costs". *Quarterly Journal of Economics* 38: 582–606.

Kolstad, Charles D. 1999. *Environmental Economics*. New York: Oxford University Press.

Libecap, Gary D. 1978. "Economic Variables and The Development of the Law: The Case of Western Mineral Rights". *Journal of Economic History* 38(2): 338–362.

———. 1989. *Contracting for Property Rights*. New York: Cambridge University Press.

———. 1998a. "Common Property" in Peter Newman (ed.), *The New Palgrave Dictionary of Economics and The Law*, Vol. 1. New York: Macmillan, pp. 317–24.

———. 1998b. Unitization, in Peter Newman (ed.), *The New Palgrave Dictionary of Economics and The Law*, Vol. 3. New York: Macmillan, pp. 641–643.

Libecap, Gary D. and James L. Smith. 1999. "The Self-Enforcing Provisions of Oil and Gas Unit Operating Agreements: Theory and Evidence". *Journal of Law, Economics, and Organization* 15(2): 526–548.

———. 2001. "Regulatory Remedies to the Common Pool: The Limits to Oil Field Unitization". *Energy Journal* 22(1): 1–26.

———. 2003. "The Economic Evolution of Petroleum Property Rights in the United States". *Journal of Legal Studies* 31(2, pt. 2): S589–S608.

Libecap, Gary D. and Steven N. Wiggins. 1984. "Contractual Responses to the Common Pool: Prorationing of Crude Oil Production". *American Economic Review* 74(1): 87–98.

———. 1985. "The Influence of Private Contractual Failure on Regulation: The Case of Oil Field Unitization". *Journal of Political Economy* 93: 690–714.

Lueck, Dean. 1989. "The Economic Nature of Wildlife Law". *Journal of Legal Studies* 18(2): 291–324.

———. 1991. "Ownership and the Regulation of Wildlife". *Economic Inquiry* 29(2): 249–260.

———. 1995. "The Rule of First Possession and the Design of the Law". *Journal of Law and Economics* 38: 393–436.

Lund, Thomas Alan. 1980. *American Wildlife Law*. Berkele, CA: University of California Press.

McCay, Bonnie J. and James M. Acheson (eds.). 1987. *The Question of the Commons: Culture and Ecology of Communal Resources*, Tucson: University of Arizona Press.

Melville, Herman. 1922. *Moby Dick or the White Whale*. New York: Dodd, Mead and Company.
Myers, Ransom and Boris Worm. 2003. "Rapid Worldwide Depletion of Predatory Fish Communities". *Nature* 423: 280–283.
North, Douglass C. 1990. *Institutions, Institutional Change and Economic Performance*. New York: Cambridge University Press.
Olson, Mancur. 1965. *The Logic of Collective Action*. Cambridge, MA: Harvard University Press.
Ostrom, Elinor. 1990. *Governing the Commons: The Evolution of Institutions for Collective Action*. New York: Cambridge University Press.
Ostrom, Elinor, Roy Gardner, and James Walker. 1994. *Rules, Games, and Common-Pool Resources*. Ann Arbor, MI: University of Michigan Press.
Ostrom, Elinor, Thomas Dietz, Nives Dolsak, Paul C. Stern, Susan Stonich, and Elke U. Weber (eds.). 2002. *The Drama of the Commons*. Washington, DC: National Academy Press.
Pashigian, B. Peter. 1985. "Environmental Regulation: Whose Self-Interests are Being Protected". *Economic Inquiry* 23(4): 551–584.
Rose, Carol M. 2002. "Common Property, Regulatory Property, and Environmental Protection: Comparing Community-Based Management to Tradable Environmental Allowances" in Elinor Ostrom, Thomas Dietz, Nives Dolsak, Paul C. Stern, Susan Stonich, and Elke U. Weber (eds.), *The Drama of the Commons*. Washington, DC: National Academy Press.
Schmalensee, Richard. 1987. Competitive Advantage and Collusive Optima. *International Journal of Industrial Organization* 5: 351–367.
Scott, Anthony, D. 1955. "The Fishery: The Objectives of Sole Ownership". *Journal of Political Economy* 63: 116–124.
Sebenius, James K. 1984. *Negotiating the Law of the Sea*. Cambridge: Harvard University Press.
Sharp, Basil. 2002. "New Zealand Fisheries Management" in Donald R. Leal (ed.), *Evolving Property Rights in Marine Fisheries*. Bozeman, MT: Political Economy Research Center, pp. 143–178.
Shotton, Ross (ed.). 1999. *Use of Property Rights in Fisheries Management*, Proceedings of the FishRights99 Conference, Fremantle, Western Australia, 11–19 November. Rome: FAO. Fisheries Technical Paper, 404/1&2.
Smith, James L. 1987. "The Common Pool, Bargaining, and the Rule of Capture". *Economic Inquiry* 25(4): 631–644.
Wiggins, Steven N. and Gary D. Libecap. 1985. "Oil Field Unitization: Contractual Failure in the Presence of Imperfect Information". *American Economic Review* 75(3): 368–385.
Wilen, James E. 1985. "Towards a Theory of the Regulated Fishery". *Marine Resources Economics* 1: 369–388.
_____. 1988. "Limited Entry Licensing: A Retrospective Assessment". *Journal of Marine Resource Economics* 5(4): 313–324.
_____. 2002. "Property Rights and the Texture of Rents in the Fishery" in Donald R. Leal, (ed.), *Evolving Property Rights in Marine Fisheries*. Bozeman, MT: Political Economy Research Center, pp. 45–75.
Wilen, James E. and Frances R. Homans. 1998. "What Do Regulators Do? Dynamic Behavior of Resource Managers in the North Pacific Halibut Fishery 1935–1978". *Ecological Economics* 24(2–3): 289–298.
Williamson, Oliver, E. 1975. *Markets and Hierarchies: Analysis and Antitrust Implications*. New York: Free Press.
_____. 1979. "Transaction-Cost Economics: The Governance of Contractual Relations". *Journal of Law and Economics* 22(2): 233–261.
Yamamoto, Tadashi. 1995. "Development of a Community-Based Fishery Management System in Japan". *Marine Resource Economics* 10(1): 21–34.

22. Property Rights and the State

LEE J. ALSTON and BERNARDO MUELLER

1. INTRODUCTION

Property rights determine the incentives for resource use. Property rights consist of the set of formal and informal rights to use and transfer resources. Property rights range from open access to a fully specified set of private rights. By open access we mean that anyone can use the asset regardless of how their use affects the use of others. A full set of private rights consists of the following: 1) the right to use the asset in any manner that the user wishes, generally with the *caveat* that such use does not interfere with someone else's property right; 2) the right to exclude others from the use of the same asset; 3) the right to derive income from the asset; 4) the right to sell the asset; and 5) the right to bequeath the asset to someone of your choice. In between open access and private property rights are a host of commons arrangements. Commons arrangements differ from open access in several respects. Under a commons arrangement only a select group is allowed access to the asset and the use rights of individuals using the asset may be circumscribed. For example, a societal group, e.g., a village, tribe or homeowner's association, may allow its members to place cattle in a common pasture but limit the number of cattle that any member may put on the commons.

One role of the state is to define, interpret and enforce property rights. Definintion of property rights is a legislative function of the state. Interpretation of property rights is a judicial function of the state. Enforcement of property rights is a police function of the state. All three functions entail costs and for this reason some rights may be left by the state as open access. Moreover, many assets have multiple dimensions and it is costly for the state to define property rights over all valuable dimensions and costly for the state to enforce property rights over all dimensions. As such, some attributes may be either *de jure* or *de facto* left as open access. Individuals and groups have incentives to expropriate the use rights over attributes that the state leaves as open access.

In many situations individuals or groups use violence as a strategy to capture property rights. From the vantage point of societies, violence is wasteful and can be a motivating force for the state to enforce property rights. Violence or threats of violence may also result when the state attempts to redistribute property rights.

In Sections 2 and 3 we briefly discuss the role that property rights play in resource use and provide some background on the determinants of property rights. In Sections 4 and 5 we develop an analytical framework for understanding the evolution of property rights, with special emphasis on the difficulties in changing property rights. In Section 6 we explore the development of property rights in the Brazilian Amazon through the lens of our analytical framework. In Section 7 we present some concluding remarks.

2. The Role of Property Rights

Property rights matter because they determine resource use. The more exclusive are property rights to the individual or group the greater the incentive to maintain the value of the asset. Furthermore, more exclusive rights increase the incentive to improve the value of the asset by investment, e.g. in the case of land this may entail the removal of rocks and stumps or using fertilizers. Having the incentive to invest may not be sufficient to induce investment if individuals or groups are "cash poor." In this situation, the ability to invest is aided if assets can be used as collateral to secure a loan. In developed countries land has served as collateral for centuries. Unfortunately, in many parts of the world mortgage markets are not well-developed and investment suffers.

Allowing sales as a property right may improve resource allocation in two ways: 1) allowing sales help signal scarcity value; and 2) markets enable those who value the asset most the ability to purchase the asset. Of course we need to be careful to note that by value economists include the ability to pay which historically and today is limited by the degree of development of mortgage markets.

To be meaningful, property rights need to be enforced. One of the critical roles of the state is to enforce property rights. Enforcement by the state typically lowers self-enforcement costs which raises the value of the asset directly but also via the incentive for increased investment. A further impact of state enforcement is that asset holders can reallocate their labor from defending their asset to household or market production.[1]

3. The Determinants of Property Rights: Some Background

So far we have discussed the role of property rights in a static world. But, over time several factors affect the scarcity of resources. Scholars studying property rights have typically looked at cases where changes in technology, population, or preferences alter scarcity value. When resources become more or less scarce, the current property rights regime may entail dissipation of the rental stream

---

[1] Field (2003) found that the largest gains from titling projects in urban Peru came from increased labor force participation.

from the asset. The losses that ensue create incentives for those involved to change the property rights to a form more suited to the new reality. The abilities of individuals, groups and states to alter property rights in response to changes in scarcity go a long way towards explaining the economic growth and decline of nations. This is what Douglass North would describe as "adaptive efficiency."

By examining how property rights change in response to the exogenous factors of technology, population and preferences scholars have derived insights for a theory of the emergence of property rights and, more broadly, institutional change and economic growth. The literature is voluminous and we can at best present some illustrative cases. Demsetz (1967) pioneered the empirical study of endogenous property rights development with his work on the introduction of property rights among Native Americans in eastern Canada. Demsetz argued that greater specificity and enforcement of property rights emerge in response to greater scarcity. Anderson and Hill (1975); Dennen (1976); Umbeck (1981) and Libecap (1978) followed in the wake of Demsetz with studies on the emergence of property rights to resource use in the U.S. West.[2]

Scholars have also analyzed contemporary cases of the evolution of property rights. Alston, Libecap and Mueller (1997, 1999a, 1999b, 2000) analyzed the evolution and effects of property rights in the Brazilian Amazon; Ensiminger (1995) examined property rights arrangements in Kenya; Besley (1995) looked at the impact of property rights on land use in Ghana; Feder and Feeny, (1991) examined property rights to land in Thailand and Migot-Adholla et.al. (1991) studied the impact of property rights in Sub-Saharan Africa. The property rights approach has also been used to understand markets besides those for land and natural resources, e.g. Coase (1959) examined the broadcast spectrum and Mueller (2002) analyzed the property rights arrangements over Internet domain names.

Heuristically, we can use the demand and supply framework to structure the analysis of the variation in property rights (Alston, Eggertsson, and North, 1996).[3] Demand forces include the various winners and losers associated with either the status quo set of property rights or some potential set of property rights. Supply forces include the incentives that political actors face given the political institutions in place, e.g. the institutional outcome may vary by whether the political system in place is Presidential, Parliamentary or Dictatorial. In some cases the change in property rights will be endogenous to the system but exogenous to individual actors on either the demand or supply side. For example, under certain situations, the heads of governments may be forced to "do something" in response to a certain natural disaster such as a flood or hurricane. If any conceivable head of state would act in the same manner we maintain that the change was exogenous to them. Alternatively, there are situations when either or both the demanders and the suppliers will be able to

---

[2] For more recent contributions to the literature on property rights see Anderson and McChesney (2003) in a special issue of the *Journal of Legal Studies* (June 2002).

[3] We say "heuristically" because the set of property rights may have multiple equilibria.

directly affect the change. For example, if a President has strong veto power, he may be in a position to maintain the status quo.

In this essay we present a framework for the determinants of the emergence and evolution of property rights. We start with the proposition that some actors must perceive that they can benefit from a change in the status quo set of property rights. Or as put by Demsetz (1967) "property rights arise when it becomes economic for those affected by externalities to internalize benefits and costs." The Demsetz view of property rights has been termed by Eggertsson (1990) as the naïve view of property rights.[4]

We stress that to understand the evolution of property rights it is necessary to carefully examine the interplay between "demanders" and "suppliers." History is replete with examples of conditions where the potential net gains from a change in property rights is not sufficient to prompt change because the costs of making all the appropriate side payments to parties with veto power dissipate the potential gains. The ubiquities of poor economic performances of economies throughout history and in the present suggest that such outcomes are common.

Our purpose is to analyze how a country's institutions determine how property rights evolve and whether this outcome will come about through cooperation, conflict or intermediation by the State. Together with non-institutional factors such as the homogeneity of the population and relative endowments, institutions determine which groups have the ability to block change and whether it is possible to "buy out" the political gatekeepers through side-payments. In the same manner institutions can facilitate cooperation by providing low cost means to make credible commitments.

4. THE DEMAND FOR PROPERTY RIGHTS

In this section we present a framework for analyzing how the demand for property rights arises and may lead to the evolution of property rights. Alston, Libecap and Schneider (1996) developed this general framework to analyze the demand for property rights security over land in the Brazilian Amazon. Underlying the analysis is the notion that the potential rent generation from more secure property rights increases as the resource becomes scarcer. The difference between the rental streams from an asset with more as compared to less secure property rights generates a "demand" for secure property rights. In Figure 1 the horizontal axis measures the relative scarcity of a given resource (from right to left) and the vertical axis measures the net present value that accrues to the owner of that resource. Line AH shows that the net present value of the resource increases as it becomes scarcer. In the case of land the measure of scarcity could be the distance of a plot of land to a market center, as transportation costs are often the main determinant of land value.

---

[4] Eggertsson (1990:250) called this view the "naïve" theory of property rights because it ignores social and political institutions through which demands are filtered.

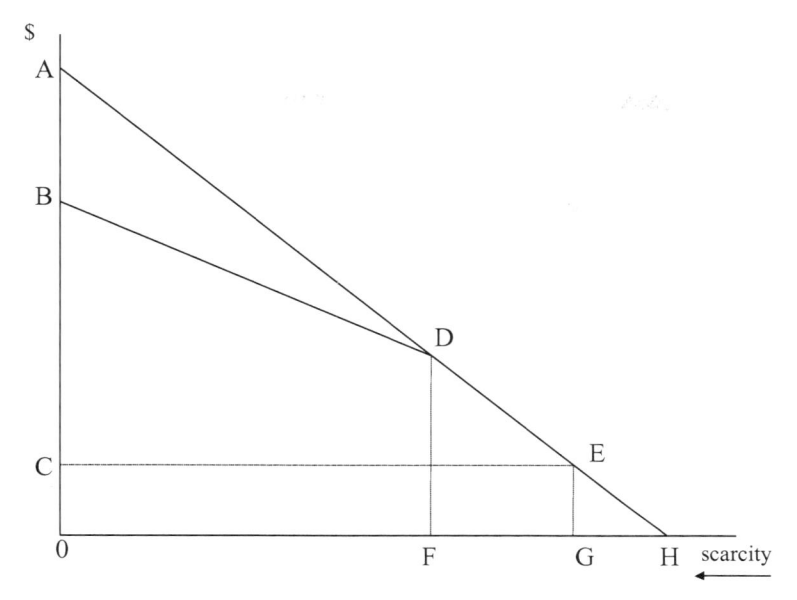

Figure 1. The demand for and evolution of property rights.

At point H land is so far from the market center that the economic return given the transportation costs to market is zero. The segment BDEH represents the net present value of land under a commons arrangement.[5] OC represents the opportunity cost of the marginal laborer. As such, point G represents the economic frontier where, provided costs of migration are low, it becomes worthwhile for labor to migrate to the frontier. In our model distance is the frontier but it could be technological, for example broadcasting on previously unused frequencies at the spectrum frontier.

At points between G and F property rights are not formally defined or enforced, but this does not affect the return to the resource given that it is still abundant relative to the competition for it. As the net present value increases new users arrive yet they are able to get access to the resource without detracting much from the use of those who were already there. At this stage resource users will tend to be relatively homogenous and informal property rights arise that are sufficient to arbitrate the existing competition. Any potential disputes are easily defused as accommodation yields higher expected returns than confrontation. Squatting prevails yet absence of government-enforced private property rights does not pose significant costs.[6] Note that the emergence of informal property rights at this point is already a case of institutional change.

---

[5] We could further segment line DE into the return from a commons versus open access arrangement. The losses from an open access arrangement would increase as one moves towards greater scarcity.

[6] An example of informal arrangements includes Cattlemen's associations in the 19th century U.S. West (Dennen, 1976). See Anderson and Hill (2002); Eggertsson (1990); Ostrom (1990) and Umbeck (1981) for accounts of local groups allocating resources under "common" arrangements. See Smith (2000) for an analysis of "semi-commons" arrangements.

At points to the left of F the returns to the resource have risen and start attracting an ever-growing number of individuals. This new migration typically brings heterogeneous individuals with differing amounts of wealth or human capital, nationalities, cultures, or objectives. The informal institutions that developed can no longer cope with the increased competition for the resource. It becomes necessary to expend effort, time and money to assure continued possession of the resource and the income derived from it. This may involve incurring costs to exclude others or the cost from sub-optimal uses. It may also include the costs to lobbying for changes from informal to formal property rights. At some point it becomes beneficial in the aggregate to have officially defined and enforced property rights. The pie-shaped area ABD represents the increased value of land with secure formal property rights versus the next best commons arrangement for property rights. ABD is the potential rent that forms the basis for the demand for property rights.

In our exposition we used distance as the proxy for scarcity but we could also use fertility of the soil or population density as alternative measures of scarcity.[7] The framework is flexible to allow for changes in technology, preferences or new market opportunities. For example, if the demand for the output of the land increases the divergence between the rental streams may emerge at E, corresponding to the distance OG from the market center.

The increase in net present value of the resource may not rise in a smooth and continuous manner as depicted in Figure 1, but rather in discrete jumps. Nevertheless the same logic holds. The shape of the present value curve will depend on the nature and characteristics of the change that affects the resource's relative scarcity. The main sources of change are technological innovations, changes in relative factor and product prices, and changes in the size of the market. An example of technological change affecting the returns to a resource is the invention of barbed wire that allowed 19th century cattlemen in the US west to confine their cattle, thereby increasing the return to selective breeding as well as better stocking practices (Anderson and Hill, 1975).[8] The effect of the opening of new markets to land is illustrated by the shift in comparative advantage to sugar production in 19th century Hawaii that made it profitable to privatize land (La Croix and Roumasset, 1990). Libecap (1978) examines the legislative response by Nevada from 1858–1895 to secure the rights of claimholders to the potentially lucrative silver deposits in the Comstock Lode. To extract ore from the Comstock mine required considerable investments which in the absence of secure property rights would not be forthcoming.

Many of the early studies on the evolution of property rights simply assumed that as the area ABD became sufficiently large property rights would emerge. This notion has been termed the naïve theory of property rights, as it does not analyze the collective action problems or the politics that determine the supply

---

[7] The framework accomodates any force that either increases (or decreases) demand or supply.

[8] In the Anderson and Hill account local groups allocated exclusivity without formal intervention by the government.

of formal property rights (Eggertsson, 1990:250). We will turn to the supply side in the next section, but here we want to delve in more depth into the determinants of ABD—the differential value of the asset from formal secure property rights versus the next best alternative informal set of property rights

There are at least four incentives which lead to the dissipation of rents if formal property rights are not supplied at the optimal time: incentives to usurp property rights from the existing holder, incentives to defend, incentives to lobby for formal property rights and incentives for sub-optimal use of the resource. Efforts to usurp take place when individuals or groups perceive an expected gain from taking the asset away from the current holder. Efforts include time, money and violence. The more insecure the property rights of the current holder the greater the likelihood that the redistribution transpires.[9] Although the new holder may increase the value of the asset, the efforts to gain the asset are wasteful relative to a world where formal property rights were already assigned or relative to the potential costs of formal assignment through the political marketplace.

Insecure property rights may also lead to dissipation through efforts by the current claimant to defend his asset against potential claimants. In the case of land, this may include fencing the plot, patrolling it or hiring security guards. It may also include an otherwise non-optimal allocation in labor supply: the claimant may spend more time on her plot and less labor in the market in order to maintain property rights. The efforts to defend, together with the efforts by others to usurp, often lead to conflicts, which is one of the most wasteful forms of rent dissipation as the resource itself and human life may be destroyed in the process. Alston, Libecap, and Mueller (1999a, 2000), argue that the current problem of land conflicts in Brazil results from conflicting legislation that creates uncertainty over property rights to land. While the Constitution contains a beneficial use requirement for all land, which provides legal justification for squatters to occupy unproductive properties, the Civil Code allows the titleholder to request an eviction of squatters. The uncertainty over the outcome leads to strategic actions by squatters and titleholders with physical violence and deforestation contributing to dissipation.

Sub-optimal use of the asset likely constitutes the greatest form of dissipation. For example, to the extent that deforestation represents beneficial use, claimants may deforest prematurely which not only increases their private costs but may also entail social costs in terms of global warming or reduction in bio-diversity.[10] Claimants may also alter their cropping decisions as a result of tenure uncertainty. Without a secure claim, farmers are more likely to plant annual crops rather than permanent crops [(Alston, Libecap and Mueller, 1999b), (Besley, 1995), (Feeder and Feeney, 1991), (Place and Hazell, 1993), (Migot-Adholla

---

[9] Insecure property rights may also reduce the value of the resource to the usurper; however one would expect this effect to be smaller than the effect on the probability of successful appropriation.

[10] Allen (2003) argues that owners may purposively reduce the value of their asset to lower enforcement costs.

et al., 1991)]. Because investment is central to economic growth property rights insecurity can be a major impediment to a country's prosperity.

When property rights are insecure, claimants may also invest too much or invest prematurely in hopes of strengthening their claim to the asset. For example, Anderson and Hill (1990) argue that homesteaders in 19th century US effectively paid for land, which was granted for free but required beneficial use, by bearing the costs of premature development. Alston, Libecap and Mueller (1999b) found evidence of the same kind of behavior in the Amazon, as did Besley (1995) in Ghana.

Insecure tenure may also limit the ability of the claimant to invest, by preventing the holder from using the resource as collateral to secure a loan from a formal creditor. In addition insecure property rights decreases the extent of the market thereby reducing the likelihood that the asset will be in the hands of the person who values it the most. In short with insecure property rights society may not exploit all of the gains from trade.

So far we have examined some of the "demand" side determinants of property rights and indicated the impact of property rights on resource use. What is missing is a better understanding of how the demand side determinants of property rights get filtered through a country's political institutions. We turn to this issue in the next section.

5. THE ROLE OF THE STATE: SUPPLY OF PROPERTY RIGHTS[11]

The early literature on property rights focused on cases where changes in the scarcity of a resource lead to more precision in property rights at the optimal time—point D in Figure 1. Though we have no way to truly gauge optimality at a given time, the rich countries of the world stand out in their protection of property rights. Somehow, they have been able to solve a coordination problem in which the political actors refrain, particularly during crises, from acting in their short-run interests.[12] More broadly the issue can be couched in respect for the rule of law. We have some institutional proxies for the rule of law, such as independence of the judiciary or a constitutional court but fundamentally the backbone of the rule of law is a belief mechanism by the citizens and political elites that they will abide by the judgement of an independent third party arbitrator. A set of universally shared beliefs in a system of checks and balances is what separates populist democracies from democracies with respect for the rule of law. Beliefs are at the heart of why some constitutions are a constraint on behavior while others are flagrantly ignored.

---

[11] The literature on the state is vast. We refer the reader to Barzel (2002) and the essays and bibliography in Anderson and McChesney (2002).

[12] Weingast (1997) highlights difficulties in establishing the rule of law, which is a broader set of rights than property rights. Nevertheless, the state with the support of the major political actors has to solve the "time inconsistency problem" in which there will always be times when the people in power have an incentive to abridge property right or erode the rule of law.

The protection of an existing set of property rights is easier than changing property rights. History is replete with examples of societies failing to change property rights at the optimal times in response to changing scarcity. The reasons for such institutional failures lie in the difficulties of compensating actors who are in a position to veto changes to property rights. Most changes in status quo formal property rights harm some people in society. In a world of homogenous participants, e.g. squatters in the Amazonian frontier or cattlemen in the 19th U.S. it is relatively easy to establish informal property rights because all parties see themselves benefiting with more exclusivity. But, when the parties involved are more heterogeneous some will see themselves losing from a change in the status quo set of informal property rights and will expend efforts to resist change to more precise formal property rights. Yet, as scarcity increases there is still pressure to establish more exclusivity. In the absence of third party specification and enforcement violence may be the least cost method for reducing the dissipation that would otherwise result.

We need a better understanding of the political and economic transaction costs associated with the state establishing or changing formal property rights that are more conducive to better economic performance, especially when it becomes obvious that the existing laws and regulations are not fostering economic growth. In many scenarios special interests are in a position to either enact property rights legislation or block legislation so that they reap the gains. Yet society is worse off by such activity. The question is: why can't "we," the citizens or consumers, buy out the special interests?[13] There are several possible explanations for why the state does not change formal property rights in lockstep with scarcity. Here we focus on three aspects.

1. Informational problems abound such that citizens are unaware of the optimal policy moves that would improve on the status quo.
2. Even when aware, there are serious collective action problems.
3. Insecurity in "political" property rights prevents society at large from making the necessary side-payments in the political arena that would change property rights.

We will explore each in turn.

Given rational ignorance it may be that many citizens are simply unaware of property rights arrangements that would improve societal welfare. For example, under the Homestead Act in the U.S. settlers could acquire property rights to 160 acres of unoccupied federal land by residing and "improving" the land. These homestead plots turned out to be economically too small and promoted externalities associated with wind erosion. Even after the great dust bowl of the 1930s, plots remained small through subsidies by the federal government. Why did the federal government not move to reallocate land or at least not interfere with consolidation through markets? It appears that the answer rests

---

[13] For many societies, the poor economic performance is explained by corrupt governments, who are more or less stealing from their own citizens. Here we focus on issues besides corruption.

with the information available to citizens and their beliefs in the virtues of small landholdings. This is coupled with the efforts of local politicians to maintain a population base [Libecap and Hansen (2003)].[14]

Alternatively, people may be aware of the dissipation associated with the status quo arrangement of property rights, but it is in no one's self-interest to mount an organizational campaign to change the existing regulations. This is the classic collective action problem developed independently but almost simultaneously by Buchanan and Tullock (1965) and Olsen (1965). The collective action problems are particularly acute in situations entailing multiple governments across international boundaries, e.g., overfishing in international waters or global warming. The difficulties for international property rights are twofold: specification and enforcement. Specification is difficult because of knowledge or beliefs about the state of world differ (e.g. global warming) but even if beliefs are the same preferences can vary across countries because of incomes (e.g., the U.S. vs Mexico) or simply tastes (e.g., the U.S. versus Germany on green issues). Collective action problems occur in both representative democracies as well as in dictatorial regimes. We have instances of both types of regimes not specifying and enforcing property rights at what would appear to be optimal times. For example, the U.S. squandered considerable oil reserves in the early twentieth century and Indonesia mowed through a large stock of their tropical hardwoods in the latter part of the twentieth century.

A third factor affecting the lack of the emergence of formal property rights to assets is what we will term insecurity in political property rights. It may be that individuals are aware and willing to organize but there is no "market" for the emergence of property rights. Suppose that the winners from a status quo policy have the political power to veto or allow policy changes. Given their power, they would be foolish to acquiesce to policy moves that made them worse off, even if it was wealth enhancing. But, they would allow such a policy move if they were compensated. The actions of the Landless Peasants' Movement (MST) in Brazil are consistent with this argument. The MST is very effective at swaying public opinion and thereby prompting politicians, to expropriate land and transfer it to peasants. But, they do not support deeding the land to peasants. The MST prefers to keep the peasants dependent on the MST as a collective because it is easier for them to extract payments from the group than individual farmers [Alston, Libecap and Mueller (2002)].

Why is it that we generally do not allow such side-payments? One answer is that transparent side-payments would undermine the legitimacy of the organization, whether the organization is the MST, a union or a government. If the current property rights arrangement is viewed as inferior to an alternative, people "believe" that they should not pay to move to a better property rights arrangement. The result is institutional lock-in. Yet, there have been examples of improving

---

[14] In the latter part of the 19th century Major John Wesley Powell recognized the potential problems of settlements in the arid or sub-humid regions of the country but his Reports to Congress were ignored in favor of boosterism [Stegner (1954)].

the status quo for all parties involved. A case involving the sale of water in the 1990s illustrates the difficulties in changing the status quo. The Imperial Valley Irrigation District, which is a governmental unit that has jurisdiction over water, entered into a contract to sell some of their water to the city of San Diego.[15] The Imperial Valley Water District has property rights to water that are subsidized by U.S. taxpayers. As such they can sell water at prices higher than they pay. Interestingly, the members of the Imperial Water District imposed upon themselves that they would only sell water that they have conserved through better irrigation technologies. The interesting question is: why didn't they fallow all of their land and sell their entire water allocation. We speculate that they were concerned about the political fall-out that could have resulted in the district losing their current subsidy. In short, it appears as if they have secure property rights to the rental stream of water but not the clear "political" property right to the stock.

Another factor promoting the insecurity of political property rights falls under the rubric of credible commitment. In representative democracies politicians face the demands of constituents who may be harmed or benefited from a rearrangement of property rights. The demands of the majority of voters may not coincide with the optimal arrangements of property rights, and politicians can not commit to making side-payments over time to compensate the losers. Authoritarian regimes are subject to similar problems associated with catering to populist demands. A good example of this was the infringement in property rights by Peron in Argentina in the late 1940s. Peron imposed rent and price controls in the Pampas, the most fertile and productive agricultural producing area in Argentina. The punitive arrangement in property rights lead to a decline in investment which, along with political instability, affected growth in the long-run [Alston and Gallo 2003)].

A more cynical view of political behavior suggests that we do not want to encourage paying for changes in property rights because it would promote the creation and maintenance of non-optimal property rights in order to be paid to move to a more optimal situation. Campaign finance and corruption around the globe may be testimony to special interests trying to "bribe" politicians to maintain or change property rights. In some instance politicians may use part of the contributions to make side-payments [Norlin (2003)].

6. THE EVOLUTION OF PROPERTY RIGHTS IN THE BRAZILIAN AMAZON: AN ILLUSTRATIVE CASE OF THE DEMAND AND SUPPLY OF PROPERTY RIGHTS[16]

The evolution of property rights in the Amazon since the early 1960s illustrates the demand and supply forces at play in the development of property rights.

---

[15] For information about the sale, we thank Clay Landry of the Political Economy Research Center, Bozeman, Montana.

[16] This section draws on Alston, Libecap and Mueller 1999b and Alston, Libecap and Schneider 1996.

During the 1960s the military governed Brazil. Driven by concerns over national security and an effort to shift some of the burgeoning rural-urban migration to the Amazon, Brazil embarked on several programs to develop and populate the Amazon. The initial effort was known as "Operation Amazonia."

During the 1960s and 1970s Brazil launched several programs to develop the Amazon. They established colonization projects and recruited settlers from Southern Brazil, who were displaced by mechanization. Sponsored colonization projects also induced spontaneous migration from nearby northern and northeastern states. Typically, the settlers from the Northeast had less human and physical capital than the settlers from the South of Brazil.

To encourage migration and establish settlement Brazil undertook the construction of several major highways which made the Amazon more accessible. Examples include the Transamazon highway and the Belém-Brasília highway. In addition to people, the government encouraged capital investment through fiscal incentives, which meant that corporations establishing ranches in the Amazon could reduce their tax burden.

In the early years there was little conflict over land. On the frontier, settlers typically did not have title but established informal property rights of about 150 hectares. Settlers respected the informal property rights to land and when land was exchanged a receipt served as testimony to the transaction. Informal property rights proved sufficient to induce settlement without conflict but we note that the settlers were relatively homogeneous. Over time many informal claims became titled either through efforts of the settlers themselves or politicians who wanted their votes. This was a process of both demand forces—settlers demanding titles because of the anticipated benefits—and supply forces—for political reasons the state of Para titled more expeditiously than the federal government.

Titles mattered. Amongst smallholders having a title increased the value of land by about 20%, holding investment and distance to market constant. This result is consistent with titles lowering defense costs and broadening the market. As expected titles increased investment in fencing and permanent crops—in our survey by about 40%. The process described here of settlement with informal claims eventually leading to formal titles fits the model developed in Sections 2 and 3.

In colonization projects sponsored by the government, there was little conflict over property rights because the government provided titles to those settlers who they recruited. Even in spontaneous settlements near colonization projects there was little conflict because the colonization projects tended to be built on relatively low-valued land so squatters could occupy an alternative plot of land rather than fight over an existing informal claim.

Some squatters occupied unused private claims but here too there was initially little violence. Squatters had the legal right to occupy private land and **if not contested** had the right to a title after 5 years. If contested the squatter had the legal right (though *de facto* at the discretion of the landowner) to be paid for improvements and could be evicted. There was little violence because the squatters knew that the local courts and police sided with the landowner. When asked to leave, the squatters left.

Over time as the density of settlement increased both squatters and landowners placed a higher value on land. As such there was more at stake when squatters invaded and occupied private land. Nevertheless, squatters faced a collective action problem and land owners still had the courts, police and hired gunmen on their side. The status quo might well have continued had it not been for some priests who undertook to organize the squatters into large groups to resist when asked to leave. Conflicts and associated violence escalated in the late 1970s and throughout the 1980s because the outcome became less certain.

In response to a concern by the public over the increase in land conflicts, the federal government put more emphasis on land reform programs. As institutional background it is important to note the roles played by the civil code and the constitution. The civil code gives strong protection to property owners. In short, if squatters occupy private land the landowner has the right to ask the state to evict the squatters. Simultaneously, the most recent constitution in Brazil (though similar to clauses in previous constitutions) stipulates that land should be used in the "social interest," which typically means productive use, i.e., not in forest. If land is not in productive use the federal government has the power to expropriate it. The compensation should equal the market value of the land, however the government accomplishes the expropriations through 20 year government bonds that sell on the secondary market at a discount. The proponents of land reform in the government used the social use clause in the constitution as the basis for expropriations that they then turned over to squatters.

The ideal agenda that the government had in mind was one where the government would select unused land prior to any invasion by squatters, expropriate the land and then give the land to deserving landless farmers. The agenda of the government was short-lived. Squatters learned individually and collectively that the way to get land faster was to invade private land in order to prompt the government to intervene. The government could not intervene everywhere because of its limited resources so getting the government's attention was crucial to the squatters successfully getting land expropriated in their favor. The evidence indicates that it was easier to get the government involved if there was an existing settlement in the county. The irony is that land conflicts increased in counties where the government had expropriated land in the past and transferred it to squatters. Put another way, the government's land reform efforts increased land conflicts.

The government's agenda was further hijacked through the entrepreneurial efforts of the Landless Peasants' Movement (MST). The MST originated in the South but shifted some of their efforts to the North. The MST knew that violence associated with land conflicts was harmful to the domestic and international reputation of politicians. The MST organized large groups of squatters to invade an unused plot of land while simultaneously announcing the time and place of the invasion to the media and the government. The intent of the announcement was to induce the federal government to intervene so as to prevent bloodshed. It took time for the intent to be realized but by the late 1990s violence over land had diminished.[17]

Despite the publicity received by land conflicts and land reform, it has not lead to a dramatic change in the percentage of farms operated by squatters. The major reason is that there are millions of landless peasants and the federal government is income-constrained, i.e., the expropriations must be compensated. Even on the expropriated land, titles have not risen as much as expected. Partially this is due to the MST who prefers the landless peasants to remain dependent and consequently eligible to receive subsidized credit from the government, of which the MST gets a 2 to 3% cut.

The conflict over property rights has had some unintended effects on forests. Recall that the federal government has the authority to expropriate land not used in the social interest. Social interest is a vague criterion but in the Amazon it means that land held in forest is not in beneficial use. As a result some landholders deforest as a means to better secure their land. How much deforestation occurs as a result of land conflicts or efforts to secure land remains an unanswered research question.

Part of the difficulty in maintaining forests intact in the Amazon is that the government has an incentive incompatibility in its land reform and forest policies. As an example, in 1965 Brazil passed a law requiring landowners to keep at least 50% of their property in forest. In 2001 President Cardoso increased the reserve to 80% through an executive decree. But, because enforcement of property rights on private forest land is difficult, due to the enticement of squatters and the possibility of expropriation, landowners chose to ignore the law for the most part. Further encouraging disregard of the law was the difficulty of enforcement by the government because of high transportation costs.

Nevertheless, the law must have imposed some costs on landowners because they spearheaded a bill in Congress to rescind the law. Representatives of landowners in Congress introduced a bill in 2002 that reduced the required forest reserve from 80% to 50% as well as providing compensation to landowners who held more than 50% of their land in forest. The bill sailed through the committee in charge but Congress dropped it on the floor, following an announced veto by President Cardoso who was responding to public opinion [Nepstad et. al (2002); Sato and Silva (2001)]. Though landowners lost this legislative battle, they won in the field where they ensured that the bureaucracy in charge was understaffed or bribed. As a result the 80% requirement in forest is routinely violated with no consequences. For example, in 1996 the average

---

[17] This was not the only reason for the decline in conflicts. By the late 1990s the MST had shifted part of their focus to securing more credit for existing settlements. In addition the fiscal situation of the federal government worsened so that all parties realized that the federal government had fewer resources to expend on land reform.

area in forest cover in six states in the Amazon (weighted by area) was only 47.5%.

What lessons do we learn from this example of the evolution of property rights to land in the Amazon? The short answer is that the assignment and enforcement of property rights to land is not a purely demand driven story: the supply side also matters. This should come as no surprise to economists and certainly will come as no surprise to political scientists. Though there is recognition of the importance of political factors as determinants of property rights, there is no corresponding supply-side theory to match the demand side theory of property rights. Our goal in presenting the example of the Amazon is to encourage other scholars to undertake similar case studies of the development of property rights in other times and places so that we can advance from the framework presented here to ultimately a theory of property rights development. A more comprehensive theory of property rights to land will enable us to design better land polices throughout the world that are not only more efficient and equitable but also less prone to conflict.

7. Concluding Remarks

In this essay we presented a framework for analyzing the determinants of property rights. We can conceptualize the forces for changing property rights as the lost rent from a different set of property rights. In relatively homogeneous societies the supply of property rights may come from the participants themselves. Examples include the codes established in mining camps or the rules established by Cattlemen's association or the norms accepted by squatters. The supply of formal property rights typically emerges from an increase in the heterogeneity of the participants or an increase in the inherent rent of the asset causing a "race for property rights." The state generally has a comparative advantage in violence and hence better capabilities than private actors for the specification and enforcement of formal property rights. Enforcement by the state is never complete because it would be prohibitively costly in money and intrusion was it to attempt to do so. We illustrate the framework by presenting a brief case study of the development of property rights in the Brazilian Amazon.

The comparative advantage of the state in protecting property rights begs the question: if the state can protect citizens from stealing from one another, what protects the state from stealing from its citizens? A short answer is very little; over time and across space many states have plundered their constituents to satisfy their self-interest. But, this has not been the case in the wealthy countries in the world. In the essay we suggest that the answer ultimately rests in the development of a set of beliefs by the citizens and political elites that they all will be better off in the long-run by abiding by the rule of law. Day to day this may not be difficult; the stress comes during times of crises. A more definitive answer to this question is beyond the scope of this essay but it is surely the holy grail of many political scientists and economists.

REFERENCES

Allen, Douglas W. 2002. "The Rhino's Horn: Incomplete Property Rights and the Optimal Value of an Asset". *Journal of Legal Studies* 31: S359–S358.

Alston, Lee J., Thráinn Eggertsson, and Douglass C. North (eds.). 1996. *Empirical Studies in Institutional Change*. Cambridge University Press.

Alston, Lee J. and Andres Gallo. 2003. "The Erosion of Rule of Law in Argentina, 1930–1947: An Explanation of Argentina's Economic Slide from the Top 10". Institute of Behavioral Sciences, Working Paper in the Program on Poltical and Economic Change.

Alston, Lee J., Gary. D. Libecap, and Bernardo Mueller. 1997. "Violence and the Development of Property Rights to Land in the Brazilian Amazon" in J.V.C. Nye, and J.N. Drobak (eds.), *Frontiers of the New Institutional Economics*. San Diego, Academic Press, pp. 145–163.

Alston, Lee J., Gary. D. Libecap, and Bernardo Mueller. 1999a. "A Model of Rural Conflict: Violence and Land Reform Policy in Brazil". *Environment and Development Economics* 4: 135–160.

Alston, Lee J., Gary. D. Libecap, and Bernardo Mueller. 1999b. *Titles, Conflict, and Land Use: The Development of Property Rights and Land Reform on the Brazilian Amazon Frontier*. Ann Arbor, MI: The University of Michigan Press.

Alston, Lee J., Gary. D. Libecap, and Bernardo Mueller. 2000. "Land Reform Policies: The Sources of Violent Conflict, and Implications for Deforestation in the Brazilian Amazon". *Journal of Environmental Economics and Management* 39(2): 162–188.

Alston, Lee J., Gary D. Libecap, and Robert Schnieder. 1996. "The Determinants and Impact of Property Rights: Land Titles on the Brazilian Frontier". *Journal of Law Economics and Organization* 12: 25–61.

Anderson, Terry L., and Peter J. Hill. 1975. "The Evolution of Property Rights: A Study of the American West". *Journal of Law and Economics* 18(1): 163–179.

Anderson, Terry L. and Peter J. Hill. 1990. "The Race for Property Rights". *Journal of Law and Economics* 33: 177–197.

Anderson, Terry L. and Peter J. Hill. 2002. "Cowboys and Contracts". *Journal of Legal Studies* 31: S489–S514.

Anderson, Terry L. and Fred S. McChesney. 1994. "Raid or Trade? An Economic Model of Indian-White Relations". *Journal of Law and Economics* 37(1): 39–74.

Anderson, Terry L. and Fred S. McChesney (eds.). 2003. *Property Rights: Cooperation, Conflict and Law*. Princeton, NJ: Princeton University Press.

Bailey, M. 1992. "Approximate Optimality of Aboriginal Property Rights". *Journal of Law and Economics* 35: 183–198.

Barzel, Yoram. *Economic Analysis of Property Rights*. New York: Cambridge University Press.

Barzel, Yoram. 2002. *A Theory of the State: Economic Rights, Legal Rights and the Scope of the State*. New York: Cambridge University Press.

Besley, Timothy. 1995. "Property Rights and Investment Incentives: Theory and Evidence from Ghana". *Journal of Political Economy* 103: 903–937.

Buchanan, James. M. and Gordon Tullock. 1965. *The Calculus of Consent: Logical Foundations of Constitutional Democracy*. Ann Arbor, MI: University of Michigan Press.

Coase, Ronald. 1959. "The Federal Communications Commission". *The Journal of Law and Economics* 2(1): 1–40.

Coase, Ronald. 1960. "The Problem of Social Cost". *The Journal of Law and Economics* 3: 1–44.

De Soto, Hernando. 2000. *Mystery of Capital: Why Capitalism is Failing Outside the West & Why the Key to Its Success is Right under Our Noses.* New York: Basic Books.

Demsetz, Harold. 1967. "Towards a Theory of Property Rights". *American Economic Review* 57(2): 347–359.

Dennen, R.T. 1976. "Cattlemen's Associations and Property Rights in the American West". *Explorations in Economic History* 13: 423–436.

Ellickson, Robert C. 1991. *Order Without Law: How Neighbors Settle Disputes.* Cambridge, MA: Harvard University Press.

Eggertsson, Thráinn. 1990. *Economic Behavior and Instituions.* New York: Cambridge University Press.

Field, Erica. 2002. "Entitled to Work: Urban Property Rights and Labor Supply in Peru". Working Paper, Princeton University.

Ensminger, Jean. 1995. "Changing Property Rights: Reconciling Formal and Informal Rights to Land in Africa". 1997, *The Frontiers of the New Institutional Economics.* New York: Academic Press.

Feder, Gershon and David Feeny. 1991. "Land Tenure and Property Rights: Theory and Implications for Development Policy". *World Bank Economic Review* 3: 135–153.

Haddock, David D. 2003. "Force, Threat, Negotiation: The Private Enforcement of Rights" in Anderson, Terry L. and Fred S. McChesney (eds.), *Property Rights: Cooperation, Conflict and Law.* Princeton, NJ: Princeton University Press.

La Croix, Sumner J. and James Roumasset. 1990. "The Evolution of Property Rights in Nineteenth-Century Hawaii". *The Journal of Economic History* 50(4): 829–852.

Libecap, Gary D. 1978. "Economic Variables and the Development of the Law: The Case of Western Mineral Rights". *Journal of Economic History* 38(2): 399–458.

Libecap, Gary D. 1989. *Contracting for Property Rights.* New York: Cambridge University Press.

Libecap, Gary D. and Zeynep K. Hansen. 2003. "Small Farms, Externalities, and the Dust Bowl of the 1930s". Working Paper, University of Arizona.

McChesney, Fred S. 2003. "Government as Definer of Property Rights: Tragedy Exiting the Commons" in Anderson, Terry L. and Fred S. McChesney (eds.), *Property Rights: Cooperation, Conflict and Law.* Princeton, NJ: Princeton University Press.

Mendelsohn, Robert. 1994. "Property Rights and Tropical Deforestation". *Oxford Economic Papers* 46: 750–756.

Migot-Adholla, Shem, Peter Hazell, Benoit Blarel, and Frank Place. 1991. "Indigenous Land Rights System in Sub-Saharan Africa: A Constraint on Productivity?" *World Bank Economic Review* 5: 155–175.

Mueller, Milton. 2002. *Ruling the Root: Internet Governance and the Timing of Cyberspace.* Cambridge, MA: MIT Press.

Nepstad, Daniel. 2002. "Frontier Governance in Amazonia". *Science* 295: 629–631.

Norlin, Kara. 2003. "Political Corruption: Theory and Evidence from the Brazilian Experience". PhD dissertation. University of Illinois.

North, Douglass C. and Robert P. Thomas. 1970. "An Economic Theory of the Growth of the Western World". *The Economic History Review*, Second series, XXIII(1): 1–17.

North, Douglass C. and Robert P. Thomas. 1977. "The First Economic Revolution". *The Economic History Review*, Second Series 30(2): 229–241.

North, Douglass C. 1981. *Structure and Change in Economic History.* New York: Norton.

Olson, Mancur. 1965. *The Logic of Collective Action.* Cambridge, MA: Harvard University Press.

Ostrom, Elinor. 1990. *Governing the Commons: The Evolution of Institutions for Collective Action.* New York: Cambridge University Press.

Place, Frank and Peter Hazell. 1993. "Productivity Effects of Indigenous Land Tenure Systems in Sub-Saharan Africa". *American Journal of Agricultural Economics* 75: 10–19.

Sato, S. and S.C. Silva. 2001. "Codigo Floretstal: Projeto Só Passa na Comissão". *Estado de São Paulo*. São Paulo, 8.

Smith, Henry E. 2000. "Semicommon Property Rights and Scattering in the Open Fields". *Journal of Legal Studies* XXIX(1): 131–170.

Stegner, Wallace E. 1954. *Beyond the Hundredth Meridian: John Wesley Powell and the Second Opening of the West.* New York: Penguin Press.

Umbeck, John. 1981. "Might Makes Right: A Theory of the Formation and Initial Distribution of Property Rights". *Economic Inquiry* XIX: 38–59.

Weingast, Barry. 1997. "The Political Foundations of Democracy and the Rule of Law". *The American Political Science Review* 91(2): 245–263.

23. Licit and Illicit Responses to Regulation

LEE BENHAM

1. INTRODUCTION

New regulation can elicit a great variety of responses from individuals, firms, interest groups, and bureaucracies. This chapter examines a range of common legal and illegal behaviors that arise as responses to new regulations. It also compares the approaches that new institutional economics and neoclassical economics use to study these responses. The motivation for introducing new regulation is generally to influence behavior: to promote or restrict competition, to redistribute income, to increase or reduce barriers to entry, to increase or reduce spillovers, and so on. However, regulation often influences behavior in ways that differ from the initially stated rationale. This chapter focuses on the consequences of regulation, on this wide range of responses, rather than on the rationale offered for introducing the regulation.

In economics, the standard literature on regulation emphasizes two dimensions of response—money price and quantity—and neglects other dimensions. This limited focus reflects the small number of variables emphasized in the standard theory, a desire for parsimony, and limited data. However, responses across many dimensions are possible. There is no *a priori* ground for believing that the standard price-and-quantity responses or the income effects are always the most significant ones. We need to discover which consequences are big and which are small, to learn how various effects play out over time, and to understand the conditions under which a particular type of response is likely to occur. On occasion, a single small regulation may cascade into a large regulatory system. At other times, an apparently Draconian regulation may be greatly weakened in its effects by inventive adaptations along various margins.

The range of possible licit and illicit responses to regulation shown in Table 1 illustrates some of the approaches taken by new institutional economics to the study of regulation. Although far from exhaustive, this set is much greater than the set usually examined in the standard literature on regulation.

Table 1. Categories of responses to regulation

Licit responses	
Substitute	*for*
Other goods	Regulated good
Other attributes of good	Regulated attributes
Amenities	Profits in excess of regulated maximum
Barter and other arrangements	Money
Vertical integration	Market exchange
Household production	Market production
Personalized exchange	Impersonal exchange

Alter
Governance and contractual relationships
Organization of the market
Interest groups and their goals
Other formal regulations
Informal norms

Illicit Responses

Vary the extent of
Underground economy
Private coercion and extralegal organizations
Discrimination
Corruption

2. LICIT RESPONSES TO REGULATION

Substitution of Other Goods

If a regulation raises the price of a given good, consumers will tend to consume less of that good and to substitute other goods. The standard neoclassical model focuses principally on this effect.

At a given time and place, the set of goods available in the marketplace is merely a subset of all goods that are potentially available. The set existing in the marketplace is established as the outcome of an equilibrium process that depends on competition, production possibilities, income, and the formal and informal rules of the game. Changes in regulation can affect these factors and hence change the available set of goods. This can alter the range of substitutes available to consumers.

Substitution of Attributes of Goods

Regulation also affects the equilibrium attributes of goods. Even "simple" goods have many attributes beyond their money price, such as size, color, quality, reliability, warranty, availability of credit, associated service, location, and waiting time.[1] All of these can vary with market conditions and regulations. The standard economic model assumes that money price and quantity are the two dimensions along which adjustments take place between buyers and sellers, and that these adjustments continue until net gains are zero for the marginal unit exchanged. By these adjustments, sellers and buyers minimize the deadweight loss. As Yoram Barzel (1997) has discussed, the same logic applies to the non-money attributes of goods: buyers and sellers jointly adjust these other attributes until the net gains are zero for marginal changes there. When a regulation alters one attribute (or a few—it can never control all of them),[2] it is in the mutual interest of buyers and sellers to minimize the deadweight loss by varying other attributes.

Depending on the substitution possibilities, therefore, regulation of money prices can lead not only to shortages or surpluses and welfare losses, but also to changes in other attributes. As an example, consider the price ceilings on gasoline in the U.S. in effect from 1971 to 1974. Faced with regulated prices set below the market-clearing level, service stations reduced their hours of business to the minimum needed to sell their allocation, lowered their quality of service, and offered lower-octane fuel. Customers waited longer in line to obtain gasoline and purchased new vehicles designed with larger gas tanks. Buyers and sellers jointly sought the lowest cost adaptation to the regulation.

Hong Kong rent controls provide another illustration. The first regulations, imposed in 1921, prevented landlords from raising rents except when they demolished an existing building and replaced it with a new one. In such cases, existing tenants received no compensation. A building craze ensued. By 1923, some landlords were even replacing buildings that were only two years old, and many former tenants were sleeping in the streets.[3] The building owners captured some of the returns from attribute substitution (a building just constructed versus a building in use), but many potential gains were dissipated by excessive construction. Eventually, in 1955, under another rent control regulatory system, the government introduced an enforced-compensation scheme

---

[1] Economic theory generally treats goods as purely homogeneous: if two items differ in their attributes, they are treated as being different goods. By this view, a liter of gasoline that requires 30 minutes of waiting time to obtain is a different good from a liter of gasoline that requires zero minutes of waiting time. This is analytically useful, but in empirical analysis this problem is not so easily addressed.

[2] Price controls typically involve attributes that are relatively straightforward for the regulators to measure and monitor—number of units, weight, and money price, rather than aspects that are more costly to measure—like quality, reliability, and associated service. Similarly, empirical work tends to focus on attributes that can be measured at low cost to the investigator. Studies of gasoline regulation typically focus on money price, volume, and octane rating (for which data are readily available) and not on quality of service and waiting time. However, real world responses to regulation may also involve attributes that are very costly for regulators and scholars to measure.

[3] Steven Cheung (1975). Even when rent controls carried over into new buildings, the new tenants would give the owners "key money" for access to the apartments. These side payments could not easily be regulated because they could be disguised as the sale of other items such as old chairs. In principle, key money could be paid on a continuing basis to keep a landlord from tearing down a building, but this was illegal, and it also involved high costs of collective action, since most building had multiple tenants.

for displaced tenants. This new scheme clarified ownership rights and greatly reduced the transaction costs of negotiations between landlords and tenants. It better aligned incentives for recognizing costs borne by displaced tenants and costs for new construction. Steven Cheung argues that the Hong Kong rent control system at that time was highly efficient compared to rent control systems elsewhere in the world. He argues further that Hong Kong's continuing growth through the twentieth century would not have been possible without relatively low transaction costs between tenants and landlords.[4]

Substitution of Amenities

Certain regulations, such as ceilings on money profits in firms, lower the cost to the firms' decision-makers of consuming amenities. Whenever the money profits of a regulated firm are potentially greater than the maximum permitted, this reduces the opportunity cost to the firm of having elegant company dining rooms, chauffeured cars, congenial colleagues, good relations with the unions, nepotism, and the quiet life (Armen Alchian and Reuben Kessel 1962). During the years when U. S. banking regulations severely constrained competition among banks, imposing fixed interest rates, restricted entry, and limited branch banking, the top executives in that industry should have led less stressful lives than their counterparts in more competitive industries. A study of executives' life expectancy during that time period found that bankers indeed had a longer average life expectancy than did executives in other industries. This greater longevity is consistent with the view that these regulations reduce the costs to decision-makers of choosing a desirable lifestyle. (Gili Yen and Lee Benham 1986)

Substitution of Barter and other Means

When regulation lowers the transaction costs of using barter instead of money, barter will increase. Trade restrictions and foreign exchange controls can have a major impact. In recent years, approximately 10% of world trade has been conducted through barter.[5] Historically, barter on a wide scale has been a common occurrence. Consider the case of Germany in the period around World War II. In 1936, before the war, the German government froze prices. At the end of the war, the occupying military governments retained these controls. In 1947 the money in circulation was ten times as great as in 1936, and real income had fallen by half. Official prices did not reflect existing scarcity, and the black

---

[4] Cheung (1979). Over time the tenant-landlord problem also diminished because builders increasingly sold apartments as condominiums rather than rent them out. This movement toward owner-occupants rather than tenants is a form of vertical integration which addresses some problems of incentive alignment. It depends on the existence of capital markets with low transaction costs for prospective condominium owners.

[5] Even in open market conditions, barter is still sometimes the lowest-cost way to trade. Barter exchange among U.S. corporations is growing, partly because computers allow low-cost measurement and tracking of barter arrangements. See Akbar Marvasti and David Smyth (1998).

market was confined to a narrow range of consumer goods. Barter was illegal, but in order to obtain raw materials, firms developed a complicated chain of barter arrangements. Even under the direct control of the British military government, Volkswagen utilized 5% of its production for barter arrangements. Legal wage levels were set too low to secure a regular supply of employees, so employers compensated employees with goods in kind, which could then be used to barter for food (Wendy Carlin 1989). Against the devastation of the war and the harsh regulations of the period, barter and other adaptations kept real income and output from falling further.

In addition to barter, many other substitutes for money arise where they are cost-effective. Radford gives an instructive example in his study of the economics of a prisoner-of-war camp (R. A. Radford 1945). Money was very limited in the camp, and barter began. This was then superseded by the use of a money substitute as the medium of exchange—cigarettes, which were reasonably homogeneous, divisible, and durable.

Substitution of Vertical Integration

Regulations such as price controls and cartel pricing can alter the relative advantages of vertical integration versus market exchange. This was strikingly illustrated in the U.S. during and immediately after World War II, when the imposition of price controls led to a substantial increase in vertical mergers. In the late nineteenth century, the Rhenish-Westphalian Coal Cartel increased coal prices substantially. Many electricity and gas utilities, railroads, and even municipalities then acquired their own coal mines (Archibald H. Stockder 1932).

Regulations that affect the existence or costs of particular markets, such as futures markets, also affect the incentives for vertical integration. A futures market, among many roles, serves as a synthetic storage mechanism and an alternative to vertical integration into storage. When the futures market in oil began in 1983 in the U.S., this lowered the cost to firms of using the market to obtain oil in the future as compared with storing the oil themselves. This was followed by a reduction in vertical integration in the oil industry and by changes in the terms of contracting (Michael Sykuta 1994 and 1996).[6]

Substitution of Household Production

Households produce goods and services both for their own consumption and for trade with the external market (Yoram Ben-Porath 1980). As Robert Pollak describes it (1985, pp. 605–606),

> "The transaction cost approach views marriage as a 'governance structure,' emphasizes the role of 'bargaining' within families, and draws attention to the advantages and disadvantages of family organization in terms of incentives and monitoring,

---

[6] The literature in economics and finance traditionally viewed futures markets as hedging mechanisms, not as substitutes for vertical integration. See Marshall (1920) and Keynes (1930).

and to the special roles of 'altruism' and 'family loyalty'. It also recognizes the disadvantages of family governance: conflict spillover, the toleration of inefficient personnel, inappropriate ability match, and inability to realize economics of scale. If activities are assigned to institutions in an efficient or cost-minimizing fashion, the balance of these advantages and disadvantages plays a major role in determining which activities are carried out within families and which are performed by firms, nonprofit institutions, or the state."

Levels of transaction costs within the family and within the external market will affect the extent and type of household production. Regulations that increase the costs of impersonal exchange in the market will increase the importance of household production and other forms of personalized exchange. In the Soviet Union, when the market system was severely repressed, families vertically integrated into food production for themselves by working on their small garden plots in the countryside. In many settings, land regulations limit individuals' ability to obtain property rights that are clear and protected. This leads to difficulties of finance and contracting. Houses built in such settings are often constructed by the hands of the household members, with bricks purchased when cash is available (Hernando de Soto 1989).

Substitution of Personalized Exchange

One way to characterize regulatory regimes is the extent to which there is impersonal exchange, personalized exchange, or little exchange at all. The extent of impersonal exchange affects the size of the market and the degree of specialization, as Adam Smith (1776) observed. Indeed, Douglass North (1991) has described the process of economic development as a movement from personal to impersonal exchange.

Impersonal exchange requires low costs of measurement and enforcement. Adam Smith's invisible hand depends upon a regulatory regime that encourages impersonal exchange by keeping transaction costs low. By altering such costs, regulation affects the extent of impersonal exchange. Some regulations like standardization of weights and measures can lower measurement and enforcement costs and thus promote impersonal exchange. Many other kinds of regulations raise transaction costs and thereby promote more personalized exchange. When regulatory regimes are arbitrary,[7] impose excessive entry costs, establish price controls, or generally cause high transaction costs, then personalized exchange is likely to be widespread. For example, in late twentieth-century Egypt, markets for many goods were heavily regulated. Shortages arose and it was often difficult to find goods in the impersonal market. Egyptians adapted in part by developing their own reciprocity networks of personalized exchange. These informal personalized networks created more opportunities to locate rationed goods or to find jobs (Diane Singerman 1995).

---

[7] Trade that involves political favors usually involves personalized exchange.

Changes in Governance and Contractual Relationships

Firms and households shape their governance structure—the forms of contracting, ownership, and decision-making—in part by efforts to economize on transaction costs. Since regulations affect transaction costs, changes in regulations can affect governance structures. This argument holds a central place in the work of Oliver Williamson (1985, Williamson and Masten 1995) and in the associated literature on transaction cost economics.

To illustrate, consider the impact of unit banking regulations in the U.S. Historically some U.S. states prohibited bank takeovers by other banks, while other states did not. In states that prohibited takeovers, the banks were less efficient and had lower profits. Why? A competitive constraint on inefficiency had been removed. Where takeovers were not possible, managers were subject to less outside scrutiny, so more inefficient practices could and did arise. This was somewhat mitigated, however, by changes in bank ownership structure. If bank ownership is more concentrated, some individual shareholders are more likely to monitor the managers. This is because the benefits from monitoring, being divided among a smaller, concentrated set of shareholders, are more likely to offset monitoring costs for at least some shareholders. In the U.S. case, in the states that prohibited takeovers, ownership concentration and management ownership were indeed higher. These mechanisms reduced the inefficiencies associated with the restrictions on takeovers, but they were not perfect substitutes for a takeover market (Mary Schranz 1993).

Changes in Organization of the Market

In many markets, regulatory standards exist for advertising, disclosure, and measurement. These regulations affect the types of information and goods produced and can give rise to dramatically different configurations of economic organization—sometimes improving efficiency and sometimes not. In the case of the market for eyeglasses, regulations in many U.S. states historically restricted severely the types of advertising that could be provided to consumers. This greatly limited the ability of the large firms, which were the low-cost providers, to compete. These regulations were also associated with higher prices of eyeglasses to consumers, lower frequency of purchase, and more adverse effects for those with less education (Lee Benham 1972, Lee Benham and Alexandra Benham 1975).

Regulations that lower the costs of measurement, such as standardization of weights and measures, can increase enforceability and credibility, thereby enhancing the efficiency of markets. Regulations of quality standards for food can increase the credibility of brand names. Together these appear to have assisted the development of the market for manufactured foods. Food-manufacturing firms in the U.S. at the beginning of the twentieth century recognized this, and they themselves supported the introduction of quality-control regulations (Marc Law 2003a and 2003b).

Note that even if a regulatory environment lowers the costs of measurement and enforcement, this does not mean that the total resources in the economy devoted to transaction costs will necessarily decline. The transaction costs per transaction may fall, but the total number of transactions may increase dramatically, so that total transaction costs rise. John Wallis and Douglass North (1986) have evidence that bear on this issue. Between 1870 and 1970 in the United States, specialization and per capita income grew enormously. Simultaneously, the transaction sector—those activities such as accounting and law which involve measurement and enforcement—increased from 25% to 45% of GNP.

3. Illicit Responses to Regulation

Development of Underground Economic Activity

The underground economy, the "informal economy," includes (a) legal activities conducted outside the formal legal system (manufacture of legal goods without a permit, providing services like house repairs without reporting income to tax authorities) and (b) illegal activities (illegal drugs, stolen goods, prostitution, gambling). Informal economies play a significant role throughout the world; their relative importance varies by country.[8] Available evidence suggests that variation in regulatory climate is a major reason for variation in the size of the underground economy.

Of particular relevance here are barriers to entry, perhaps the most intensively studied form of all regulation. Adam Smith gave them a central place in *The Wealth of Nations* (1776). Hernando de Soto (1989) documented startlingly high regulatory barriers to small-business entry in Peru in the 1980's.[9] A great proportion of business in Peru was transacted informally. Djankov et al. (2002) studied of regulations governing business entry in 85 countries and found high official costs of entry in most countries. Djankov (2003) also found that where regulation of entry is more extreme, the unofficial economy is larger, corruption is higher, and the quality of public service is not better.

Development of Discrimination

Regulations can alter the incentives to discriminate and thereby influence the extent of discrimination. Through rewards and sanctions they can directly alter the price of discriminating. They can also work indirectly. For example, if the money profits of a regulated firm are restricted below the level achievable, this

---

[8] In the year 2000, the share of the economy that was informal averaged 41% in developing countries, 38% in transition countries, and 18% in OECD countries. Differences within regions were substantial: Bolivia 67% vs. Chile 20%; Zimbabwe 59% vs. South Africa 28%; Thailand 53% vs. Japan 11%; Greece 29% vs. Switzerland 9%. See Friedrich Schneider (2002).

[9] In an experiment, de Soto demonstrated that a person seeking legal permission to open a small clothing factory on the outskirts of Lima in 1983 needed to spend 289 days of full-time effort and pay an irreducible minimum of two bribes to obtain the necessary permits from the bureaucracy.

will lower the cost to the firm of employing workers who are less productive but who have preferred characteristics along other dimensions. In other words, it will lower the cost to the firm of engaging in discrimination.

The regulation of U. S. physicians in the early part of the twentieth century provides an illustration. At that time, medical licensure came under the monopoly control of state medical associations. This strengthened the medical associations' position as an interest group, and they achieved a dramatic reduction in the number of medical schools. As a result, physicians' earnings increased, and applications to surviving medical schools increased. The relative numbers of women and blacks admitted to medical schools then declined sharply, as regulatory-induced entry barriers, waiting lines of applicants, and property rights and organization within medical schools lowered the cost of discrimination to those making the admission decisions (Kessel 1970).

Development of Private Coercion

Regulations that raise the cost of engaging in voluntary exchange will affect the extent to which private coercion is used, individually and through illegal organizations. Regulations such as prohibitions on alcohol, drugs, and gambling increase the potential gains to dealing in these arenas and thereby facilitate the rise of illegal organizations like the Mafia.

Regulations that increase uncertainty concerning ownership of property rights can lead to environmental problems like land invasions, violence, and deforestation. In Brazil, the conflicted regulatory environment concerning property rights has led to all of these (Lee Alston 1999; Alston et al. 2000). In Italy in the nineteenth century, given the weakness of the relevant formal institutions, changes in property rights to land were followed by a great increase in the strength of the Mafia, which had a comparative advantage in contract enforcement (Diego Gambetta 1993).

Development of Corruption

Corruption is the use of public office for private gains in carrying out a public task. Regulations can significantly affect the benefits and costs of engaging in corrupt practices. In settings where regulations are excessive or arbitrary, where civil servants are poorly paid, where the level of political competition is low, where transparency is lacking, where civil servants have discretion over enforcement, where discretionary permits are highly valuable, and/or where the likelihood of exposure is low—in these settings corruption is likely to be extensive.

The number of possible corrupt practices is very large. The organization of corruption and the property rights to associated payoffs vary considerably by country (Andrei Shleifer and Robert Vishny 1993). Where the property rights to bribes are clearly held and enforced, a given level of corruption may produce less inefficiency. If the highest-ranking politicians and political parties are disciplined enough to refrain from seeking additional payoffs after initial lump sums have been paid, corruption on the margin may be circumscribed. In South Korea, for example, political parties are highly disciplined, and bribery has been highly centralized. Many payoffs are lump-sum contributions by major business leaders to presidential campaigns. This arrangement does not tax economic activity at the margin. If the government is weak and fragmented, however, local government regulators often engage in decentralized looting. This undermines credible commitments in both public and private sectors and can be particularly damaging to economic performance (Pranab Bardhan 1997).

Regulators are often active in this process. They may intentionally introduce regulations to create further opportunities for corrupt exchanges. If corruption becomes common in one sector (say, because of high import duties or restrictions on gambling), the cost of spreading corruption to other sectors falls. This in turn lowers the returns to normal entrepreneurial activity, which further slows down economically productive activity, which induces more people to engage in corrupt practices, and so on (Kevin Murphy et al. 1993). Furthermore, it may be easier to introduce corrupt practices than to reduce them: long periods of time may be needed to move from a corrupt to a non-corrupt equilibrium.

4. History, Path Dependence, and Interest Groups

The discussion so far has focused on the responses to regulation made primarily by individual actors, acting on considerations of supply and demand. Let us turn now to the role of history and path dependence. In most of the standard literature on regulation, these have been ignored. However, historical experience is fundamental to the formation and evolution of formal and informal rules, as well as to the consequences of any new formal regulation. Furthermore, one regulation often leads to others, and the historical reach can be long. There is path dependence in regulation, substantially rooted in the political process and in historical experience.

Oliver Williamson's classification of the different levels of institutional constraints, shown in Table 2, provides a perspective on the different time frames involved. Neoclassical economics has focused almost entirely on the bottom level, resource allocation and employment, where adaptation to regulation is restricted to changes in prices and quantities and where adaptation is continuous. However, countries have differing historical experiences, norms and traditions. In Williamson's terminology, "embeddedness" differs. The specifics of Table 2 can be disputed; for example, norms and religions may change more frequently than every 100–1000 years, but this perspective is valuable in emphasizing the varying time spans over which institutional changes can take place. At any point in time, the formal rules, informal norms, and their enforcement characteristics vary substantially across countries. The impact of any new formal regulation—and responses to it—will be affected by these elements and by their historical patterns within a country.

Depending on context and time period, therefore, a particular type of regulation can give rise to very different responses in different settings. The direct

Table 2. Williamson: economics of institutions[10]

Level of Embeddedness Informal institutions,traditions, norms, religion Frequency of change: 100–1000 years
Level of Institutional Environment Formal rules of the game—especially property (polity, judiciary, bureaucracy) Frequency of change: 10–100 years
Level of Governance Play of the game—especially contract (aligning governance structures with transactions) Frequency of change: 1–10 years
Level of Resource Allocation and Employment Prices and quantities, incentive alignment Frequency of change: continuous

allocative effects of a regulation—measured at Williamson's levels of resource allocation and governance—are often only a small part of its total impact. Small and seemingly unimportant details of regulations can lead to large downstream effects.[11] Or apparently far-reaching regulations may turn out to be inconsequential because of innovative adaptations over time. While standard microeconomic analysis of regulation invokes the notion of the long run to some extent, in the perspective of new institutional economics the long run is usually longer, more varied, and more significant. The following case studies illustrate how regulations, constrained by path dependence, can generate long-run responses by interest groups with further policy consequences.[12]

Broadcasting in Britain

Small initial regulatory choices can lead to large downstream effects. Ronald Coase found this in his detailed investigation of the origins of radio broadcasting in Britain (Coase 1947). Initially, the transmission of sound by radio was regarded as a new means for sending telephone messages. Because of this, regulation of broadcasting was assigned to the organization that had jurisdiction over telephones: the Post Office. To avoid the problem of broadcast interference and to avoid having to select from among the many firms who would seek the

---

[10] Table from Oliver Williamson (1999), p. 11.

[11] The impact of any regulatory change will depend in part on the informal rules. If a regulatory change is greatly at variance with the preferences and interests of a particular group, their informal norms can evolve into "opposition norms." These opposition norms can have highly negative consequences for performance. See Victor Nee (1998).

[12] Three major interest group theories of the regulatory process are:

a. The public interest paradigm: government is a benevolent guardian.
b. The special interest "capture" theory: regulations come from the demanders of regulation and not from the suppliers or the government. At the limit, this view holds that special interests are responsible for the origins of the regulation.
c. The public choice view: special interest groups are the demanders of regulation, and politicians and bureaucrats are the suppliers, all working in their own self-interest.

valuable radio spectrum, the Post Office favored having a single broadcasting company.[13] Strategies that could have been used to allocate the radio spectrum, including assigning property rights to the spectrum and selling them off, were not seriously considered.[14] The main advocates for radio broadcasting at that time were the radio manufacturers, who sought their revenues from the sale of radios rather than from broadcasting. Newspapers did not want competition for their advertising revenue and therefore opposed commercial forms of radio broadcasting. There was thus little opposition to the Post Office's proposal to create only one broadcasting company and to finance its programming and transmission from taxes on radio sales. There followed a broadcast monopoly that limited British citizens to BBC programming for many decades. Non-BBC programming could not even be transmitted by wire (although that involved no problem of externalities). When television was eventually introduced, the BBC monopoly was extended to cover television.

In the years just before World War II, the BBC gave the major political parties control over access to the airwaves for political speeches. The political parties then allocated their shares of airtime to politicians who endorsed their standard party positions. When Winston Churchill sought to criticize the government's appeasement policy towards Hitler, he was unable to get permission to speak on the BBC. Given the rules of the game, this result is not surprising. An apparently small regulatory choice driven by specific historic circumstances had these profoundly important later consequences.

U. S. Sugar Production

Sugar production in the U. S. offers another example of the downstream impact of initial regulatory decisions. Sugar is the only U.S. agricultural good now excluded from global free trade. In 2002 raw sugar prices in the U.S. were three times as high as the world spot price. All 11,800 U.S. sugar farmers receive subsidies. As a result of these subsidies, the Everglades region in Florida has been planted with sugar cane, creating significant ecological problems. Sugar-processing and sugar-using industries have moved out of the U.S. because of the high domestic sugar prices. The total costs of this program are vast. How did all this happen?

Anne Krueger's classic study (1990) shows how the complexity and the cost of current sugar regulation can be understood only by an appreciation of past policies. Through most of the nineteenth century, 90% of the sugar consumed in the

---

[13] C. A. Lewis, deputy director of the British Broadcasting Company, stated in 1923, "The chaotic state of affairs in America, where a large number of stations are transmitting on a narrow band of wavelengths and no form of control exists, was an object lesson in what *not* to do, and consequently the control was put into one company's hands." Lewis (1924), quoted in Coase (1947), p. 208, ftn. 2.

[14] "Only many decades later were regulations introduced to define some rights to some spectrum such that sales could take place. The common view at the time among experts was that the regulation came as a necessary result of reckless competition among broadcasters, which retarded the orderly development of radio and subjected the listeners to intolerable strain." Coase (1959), p. 13.

U.S. was imported. Tariffs on sugar were originally imposed as a revenue source. Then in the late 1800's the U. S. Department of Agriculture took initiatives to encourage domestic sugar growing and processing. The sugar industry developed because of this government-initiated program, rather than the reverse.[15]

Several historical accidents appear to have had a major impact on the subsequent evolution of the program, including idiosyncratic committee assignments in Congress and a focus on foreign relations issues. Once the very complex sugar program was in place, a network of program specialists arose in government and industry and became independently influential. Various interest groups were involved over time. A long-standing—and unlikely—coalition of sugar producers, processors, and users persisted until 1978. At that time a new corn-based substitute for sugar began to take market share. Corn producers benefited from having high prices for sugar and they therefore supported a sugar quota system, opposing plans that would have permitted the U.S. sugar price to fall to the world level.

The high domestic price of sugar has led to many market responses: the use of sugar substitutes, the importing of products such as cake mixes with high sugar content, and the subsequent ban on imported cake mixes. Diplomatic complications have been associated with the allocation of sugar import quotas across countries. Although this program has been very costly to consumers and to sugar-using industries, there appear to be few long-term rents earned by domestic sugar producers and processors. Most of the subsidies are dissipated in inducing production where it would not otherwise take place.

Examples from many other industries could be provided. The regulation and deregulation of natural gas, standards for automobile emissions, pharmaceutical regulation, medical licensure, and airline regulation all show a history of interest group politics in which new regulations frequently create new interest groups.[16]

The Old Believers in Russia

The previous examples have shown that small initial regulations can lead step by step to major downstream consequences. On the other hand, Draconian regulations are sometimes followed by surprisingly resilient responses over long time periods. Consider the case of the Old Believers in Russia.

Starting in the seventeenth century, the Old Believers were heavily persecuted for refusing to conform to the new religious doctrines of the Russian Orthodox Church. During the period of most intense persecution, the Old Believers endured removal of all their legal rights, forced exile, no standing in court, and even mass executions. Although the intensity of persecution diminished over time, they remained for centuries without full legal status. However, they survived and

---

[15] In 1934, a quota system that in fact benefited the sugar producers was imposed *over their objections*. They learned from experience, and three years later they began to support the quota system.

[16] Roger Noll and Bruce Owen (1983). Most studies of collective action have emphasized the opposite direction of analysis: interest groups' efforts to create regulations serving their interest. See Mancur Olson (1982). Mary M. Shirley (2002) has examined interest group issues concerning regulation of public water supplies.

eventually prospered by developing strong informal norms of trust, honesty, sobriety, and cooperation within their own community. These norms lowered their internal transaction costs substantially, permitting them to trade over space and through time in ways that outsiders in the broader Russian society could not. By the mid nineteenth century, in relatively unregulated sectors like the textile industry, they were the leading entrepreneurs in Russia. When the government's direct regulatory role increased in the late nineteenth century, their role in this sector then diminished (Danila Raskov 2002).

In the Russian economic system, informal norms evolving over long periods of time had fundamental consequences for who did what, and how efficiently. Excluded from formal state contract enforcement, the Old Believers developed their own informal system of transacting and enforcement. Later state regulations that elevated the importance of political connections, such as state licensing for entry, put them at a disadvantage.

These three historical examples illustrate the broad range of responses to regulation that arise from interest groups rather than from individual action. New regulations create new interests and destroy old interests. The rise and demise of shared interests can change the original politics irreversibly. The overall response to a regulation depends only partially on responses at the level of resource allocation. How the various interest groups respond to the regulation, and which ones seize the regulatory mechanisms over time—these are very significant issues. At this stage in our knowledge, these outcomes are extremely difficult to predict.

5. THE PERSPECTIVE OF NEW INSTITUTIONAL ECONOMICS

The standard neoclassical model in economics assumes that all transaction costs are zero. As Ronald Coase has established (1960), in such a world, if a nonequilibrium money price were set by regulation, the parties to an exchange could simply contract around the regulation. They could use vertical integration, other media of exchange, barter, long-term contracts, or alteration in product attributes. Even with money prices assigned randomly or set to zero, the system could work efficiently. The parties could price-discriminate perfectly, and no mutually advantageous trades would go unexercised (Barzel 1997). In that world, monopolies would not lead to deadweight losses, and there would be no externalities.

Stigler (1971) has commented that the zero-transaction-cost world is a strange world. Coase views the world of zero transaction costs as a useful first step in analysis, but he encourages us to limit the time we spend studying that world. He encourages us instead to focus more on the world of positive transaction costs, the world in which we live.

The standard literature on regulation typically modifies the neoclassical model slightly by assuming that positive (sometimes infinite) transaction costs exist along one or two specified margins, for example, "imperfect capital" or "imperfect information," while along all other margins they remain zero. These regulatory models pay lip service to utility maximization and opportunity costs—as opposed to purely pecuniary maximization and money prices—but usually ignore them in empirical work.

New institutional economics modifies the standard neoclassical model significantly by taking the view that transaction costs are positive and finite along all margins. This perspective draws on the fundamental tenet of economics: the relevant prices facing an individual are the full opportunity costs associated with the various choices. For a given good, these full opportunity costs include the money price of the good itself plus the transaction costs of obtaining the good.[17]

This perspective also emphasizes the possibility of substitution along many margins. Markets typically adjust through a mixture of changes in money prices and changes in other characteristics of the goods traded in that market, including location, waiting time, durability, warranty, freshness, and associated services. Indeed, in many markets, waiting time and quality are highly variable while money prices are relatively sticky.[18] Inside households, firms, and even some markets, money prices may not be used at all.

This has many implications for measuring the full range of responses to regulation. The metric typically used—the money price—is an incomplete measure of the full range of responses possible. Attributes of the goods and also attributes of associated property rights, contractual forms, organizational structures, the medium of exchange, and informal networks—all of these can vary in response to new regulations. These responses can reduce or increase the deadweight losses traditionally associated with formal regulations.

The passage of time introduces additional considerations. A single snapshot of the regulatory process is not sufficient. The long-term impact of a regulation depends upon historical constraints and the nature of the evolving political and bureaucratic responses, including competition among interest groups. Over time, responses to regulations may alter the formation of political interest groups, political processes, and political outcomes. A regulation's greatest impact may lie in its downstream consequences for political interest groups and for subsequent regulations. Inefficiencies created through these political and bureaucratic processes over time can easily be larger than the welfare losses measured by standard calculations.

As Coase (2002) and Krueger (1990) urge, we need many more careful case studies that are comparative in nature. These will eventually permit us to examine the multiple constraints facing decision-makers, to sort out general causal factors from historically specific factors, and to understand better the historical evolution of regulation and responses to it.

---

[17] The opportunity costs an individual faces are likely to be influenced by the specific characteristics of the individual, the type of exchange, and the institutional setting within which the individual is operating. See Benham and Benham (2001).

[18] Facing short- and long-term variations in market conditions, many restaurants deliberately alter waiting time and quality of service as well as money price.

A major objective in studying regulation is to understand its impact, the range of likely responses, and how these play out over time. The perspective of new institutional economics recognizes the role of history, path dependence, and the variability of experience across individuals, firms, and countries. A long-run task is to articulate a general approach that covers both economic and political actors, and both individual and collective action. A prudent scholar would examine policies with a keen eye on the process of creation and destruction of interests.[19] If we can understand the potential consequences of regulators' actions in this broader sense, supplemented by detailed studies of specific regulations in many countries, we may do a better job of understanding the impact of regulation, responses to it, and the regulatory process itself.

ACKNOWLEDGEMENT

I thank Alexandra Benham for many discussions of these ideas and for her generous work in editing and re-editing this manuscript. Kurt Annen, Krishna Ladha, Marc Law, John Nye, Mary M. Shirley, Gili Yen, and two anonymous referees have provided helpful comments. Any errors remaining are mine.

REFERENCES

Alchian, Armen and Reuben Kessel. 1962. "Competition, Monopoly, and the Pursuit of Pecuniary Gain" in *Aspects of Labor Economics*. National Bureau of Economic Research, Princeton, NJ: Princeton University Press, pp. 157–175.

Alston, Lee, Gary Libecap, and Bernardo Mueller. 1999. *Titles, Conflict, and Land Use: The Development of Property Rights and Land Reform on the Brazilian Amazon Frontier*. Ann Arbor, MI: University of Michigan Press.

Alston, Lee, Gary Libecap, and Bernardo Mueller. 2000. "Land Reform Policies, the Sources of Violent Conflict, and the Implications for Deforestation in the Brazilian Amazon". *Journal of Environmental Economics and Management* 39(2): 162–188.

Bardhan, Pranab. 1997. "Corruption and Development: A Review of Issues". *Journal of Economic Literature* 35(3): 1320–1346.

Barzel, Yoram. 1997. *Economic Analysis of Property Rights*, second edition. Cambridge: Cambridge University Press.

Ben-Porath, Yoram. 1980. "The F-Connection: Families, Friends, and Firms and the Organization of Exchange". *Population Development Review* 6(1): 1–30.

Benham, Lee. 1972. "The Effect of Advertising on the Price of Eyeglasses". *Journal of Law and Economics* 15(2): 337–352.

Benham, Alexandra and Lee Benham. 1975. "Regulating Through the Professions: A Perspective on Information Control". *Journal of Law and Economics* 18(2): 421–448.

Benham, Alexandra and Lee Benham. 2000. "Measuring the Costs of Exchange" in Claude Ménard (ed.), *Institutions, Contracts and Organizations: Perspectives from New Institutional Economics*. Cheltenham, UK: Edward Elgar, pp. 367–375.

---

[19] Krishna Ladha (2002) has provided edification on this topic.

Benham, Alexandra and Lee Benham. 2001. "Costs of Exchange". Accessed October 16, 2003 at http://coase.org/w-benham2001thecostsofexchange.pdf.

Carlin, Wendy. 1989. "Economic Reconstruction in Western Germany, 1945: The Displacement of 'Vegetative Control" in Ian D. Turner (ed.), *Reconstruction in Post-War Germany, British Occupation Policy and the Western Zones, 1945–55*, Oxford: Berg, pp. 37–65.

Cheung, Steven N.S. 1975. "Roofs or Stars: The Stated Intents and Actual Effects of a Rents Ordinance". *Economic Inquiry* 13(1): 1–21. Also in Lee J. Alston, Thrainn Eggertsson, and Douglass C. North (eds.), *Empirical Studies in Institutional Change*, Cambridge: Cambridge University Press, pp. 224–243.

Cheung, Steven N.S. 1979. "Rent Control and Housing Reconstruction: The Postwar Experience of Prewar Premises in Hong Kong". *Journal of Law and Economics* 22(1): 27–54.

Coase, Ronald. 1947. "The Origin of the Monopoly of Broadcasting in Great Britain". *Economica* 14: 189–210.

Coase, Ronald. 1959. "The Federal Communications Commission". *Journal of Law and Economics* 2: 1–40. Also in the *Yearbook of Broadcasting Articles*, anthology edition. 1980. Washington DC: Federal Publication.

Coase, Ronald. 1960. "The Problem of Social Cost". *Journal of Law and Economics* 3: 1–44.

Coase, Ronald. 2002. Personal communication. October 23, 2002.

de Soto, Hernando. 1989. *The Other Path.* New York: Harper & Row.

Djankov, Simeon, Rafael La Porta, Florencio Lopez-De-Silanes, and Andrei Shleifer. 2002. "The Regulation of Entry". *The Quarterly Journal of Economics* 117: 1–37.

Djankov, Simeon. 2003. "The Informal Economy: Large and Growing in Most Developing Countries". World Bank Hot Topic Discussion Board. Accessed October 16, 2003 at http://rru.worldbank.org/hottopics/Hot_Topics_djankov_2.asp.

Gambetta, Diego. 1993. *The Sicilian Mafia: The Business of Private Protection.* Cambridge, MA: Harvard University Press.

Kessel, Reuben. 1970. "The AMA and the Supply of Physicians". *Law and Contemporary Problems* 35(2): 267–283.

Krueger, Anne O. 1990. "The Political Economy of Controls: American Sugar" in Maurice Scott and Deepak Lal (eds.), *Public Policy and Development: Essays in Honour of Ian Little*. Reprinted in Lee J. Alston, Thrainn Eggertsson, and Douglass C. North (eds.), *Empirical Studies in Institutional Change*, 1996. Cambridge: Cambridge University Press, pp. 169–218.

Keynes, John Maynard. 1930. *A Treatise on Money, Volume 2: The Applied Theory of Money.* London: Macmillan.

Ladha, Krishna. 2002. Personal communication, August 2002.

Law, Marc. 2003a. *Specialization, Information, and Regulation in American Economic History.* Ph.D. dissertation, Washington University, St. Louis.

Law, Marc. 2003b. "The Origins of State Pure Food Regulation". *Journal of Economic History* 63: 1103–1130.

Lewis, C.A. 1924. *Broadcasting from Within.* London: George Nennes Limited.

Marshall, Alfred. 1920. *Industry and Trade,* 3rd edn. London: Macmillan.

Marvasti, Akbar and David Smyth. 1998. "Barter in the US economy: A Macroeconomic Analysis". *Applied Economics* 30: 1077–1088.

Murphy, Kevin, Andrei Shleifer, and Robert Vishny. 1993. "Why Is Rent-Seeking So Costly to Growth?" *American Economic Review* 83(2): 409–414.

Nee, Victor. 1998. "Norms and Networks in Economic and Organizational Performance". *The American Economic Review,* Papers and Proceedings 88(2): 85–89.

Noll, Roger, and Bruce Owen. 1983. *The Political Economy of Deregulation: Interest Groups in the Regulatory Process.* American Enterprise Institute for Public Policy Research.

North, Douglass. 1991. "Institutions". *Journal of Economic Perspectives* 5(1): 97–112.

Olson, Mancur. 1982. *The Rise and Decline of Nations.* New Haven, CT: Yale University Press.

Pollak, Robert A. 1985. "A Transaction Cost Approach to Families and Households". *Journal of Economic Literature* 23(2): 581–608.

Radford, R.A. 1945. "The Economics of the P.O.W. Camp". *Economica* 12: 189–210.

Raskov, Danila E. 2002. "Norms in the Economic Evolution: Old Believers in the Russian Nineteenth-century Textile Industry". Paper presented at the 2002 Conference of the International Society for New Institutional Economics, Cambridge, MA.

Schneider, Friedrich. 2002. "Size and Measurement of the Informal Economy in 110 Countries Around the World". Paper presented at a Workshop of the Australian National Tax Centre, Canberra, Australia, July 17, 2002. Accessed October 16, 2003 at http://rru.worldbank.org/documents/informal_economy.pdf.

Schranz, Mary. 1993. "Takeovers Improve Firm Performance: Evidence from the Banking Industry". *Journal of Political Economy* 101(2): 299–326.

Shirley, Mary M. (ed.). 2002. *Thirsting for Efficiency: Experiences in Reforming Urban Water Systems*. London: Elsevier.

Shleifer, Andrei and Robert Vishny. 1993. "Corruption". *Quarterly Journal of Economics* 108(3): 599–617.

Singerman, Diane. 1995. *Avenues of Participation: Family, Politics, and Networks in Urban Quarters of Cairo*. Princeton.

Smith, Adam. 1776. *The Wealth of Nations*. Chicago, IL: University of Chicago Press, 1976 edition.

Stigler, George. 1951. "The Division of Labor Is Limited by the Extent of the Market". *The Journal of Political Economy* 59(3): 185–193.

Stockder, Archibald H. 1932. *Regulating an Industry: The Rhenish-Westphalian Coal Syndicate 1893–1929*. New York: Columbia University Press.

Sykuta, Michael. 1994. "Real Effects of Futures Markets on Firm and Industry Behavior: A Study of Institutions and Contracting in the Crude Oil Industry". Ph.D. dissertation, Washington University, St. Louis.

Sykuta, Michael. 1996. "Futures Trading and Supply Contracting in the Oil Refining Industry". *Journal of Corporate Finance: Contracting, Governance and Organization* 2(4): 317–334.

Wallis, John J. and Douglass C. North. 1986. "Measuring the Transaction Sector in the American Economy" in S.L. Engerman and R.E. Gallman (eds.), *Long Term Factors in American Economic Growth*, Chicago, IL: University of Chicago Press.

Williamson, Oliver. 1985. *The Institutions of Capitalism*. New York: The Free Press.

Williamson, Oliver and Scott Masten (eds.). 1995. *The Economics of Transaction Costs*. Northampton, MA: Edward Elgar.

Williamson, Oliver. 1999. "The New Institutional Economics: Taking Stock/Looking Ahead". *Newsletter of the International Society for New Institutional Economics* 2:2.

Yen, Gili and Lee Benham. 1986. "The Best of All Monopoly Profits is a Quiet Life". *Journal of Health Economics* 5(4): 347–353.

SECTION VII

Institutional Change

24. Institutions and Development

MARY M. SHIRLEY

1. THE CHALLENGE OF DEVELOPMENT

Developed countries are the exception, not the rule. Billions of dollars of aid and countless hours of advice notwithstanding, most countries have not been able to foster sustained growth and social progress. Increasingly research has shown that weak, missing or perverse institutions are the roots of underdevelopment. Other explanations for development, such as investment, technological innovation, or years of schooling are not correlated with higher rates of economic growth (Easterly 2002). Instead, cross-country regressions persistently demonstrate large and statistically significant correlations between institutional variables and growth, and in horse races between variables, an index of institutional quality "trumps" geography or trade as an explanation for growth (Rodrik, et al. 2002).

To meet the challenge of development countries need an institutional framework that supports a market economy, which includes two distinct and not necessarily complementary sets of institutions: (i) those that foster exchange by lowering transaction costs and encouraging trust, and (ii) those that influence the state and other powerful actors to protect private property and persons rather than expropriate and subjugate them.[1] The first set of institutions includes contracts and contract enforcement mechanisms, commercial norms and rules, and habits and beliefs favoring shared values and the accumulation of human capital. Among the second set of institutions are constitutions, electoral rules, laws governing speech and education, and norms that motivate people to abide by laws and cooperate in monitoring government. Where property rights are insecure and transaction costs are high, investment will be channeled into activities with rapid returns and resources will be siphoned off as bribes or security. In such societies, individuals are likely to reap higher returns by rent seeking or war lording than by investing in production, innovation, or learning. Today's underdeveloped countries must acquire market-supporting institutions under particularly difficult conditions—in a global market competing with already

---

[1] I use the term development to mean countries which have achieved a level of per capita income that puts them in the World Bank's high income category (above $9,266 in 2000), as well as high scores on selected social indicators (life expectancy at birth of over 70 years, infant mortality rate of less than 10 per 1000, adult literacy rates of 100%).

developed countries (North 2004 forthcoming). Globalization also aggravates the difficulties of building strong institutions by making capital flight and brain drain easier. Although there may be some advantages to being a latecomer—witness Africa's leapfrogging into cellular technology—the disadvantages usually dominate.

The vast majority of humans today live in countries that have failed to create or sustain strong institutions to foster exchange and protect persons and property.[2] Individuals in these countries enforce most bargains using informal mechanisms—private armies; threats to reputation; ostracism—and they have little trust in or trade with people not subject to these mechanisms. The state is either too weak to prevent theft of property by private actors, or so strong that the state itself threatens property rights and personal independence. In either case, individuals and organizations face a high risk that they will not be able to realize a return if they invest in specific knowledge, skills, or physical assets, so they refrain from investment; production, innovation, and productivity are low; and the economy stagnates. Despite countless reform attempts, many countries have not been able to break out of their low level equilibrium, in part because powerful economic and political actors have a stake in preserving the current institutions and in part because society's beliefs and habits support and sustain the status quo. Although learning from new experiences is key to institutional change, education will not necessarily provide a way out of this low level trap. As Easterly points out, the quality of education is different in economies that provide incentives to invest in the future. In such an economy, "students will apply themselves to their studies, parents will monitor the quality of education, and teachers will face pressure to teach" (Easterly 2002, p. 82). Where incentives to invest in the future are low, educational quality will be poor and there will be under-investment in learning and out-migration of high potential individuals.

Why have so few countries been able to create and sustain the rules and norms that foster growth and social progress? Which institutions must function effectively if countries are to develop? How can poorer countries attain well functioning institutions? Can outsiders promote institutional development? The New Institutional Economics (NIE) has made some progress towards answering

---

[2] Throughout this chapter I use North's definition of institutions as the "humanly devised constraints that structure human interaction" including formal constraints such as constitutions and laws and informal constraints, such as norms, conventions and self-imposed codes of conduct (North 1990, p. 3). Organizations differ from institutions; "they are groups of individuals bound together by some common purpose to achieve certain objectives," and include legislatures, firms, trade unions, churches, clubs, schools, etc. (Ibid.) Institutions are the "rules of the game in a society" while organizations are the players (Ibid.). As for markets, Menard defines them as non-cooperative arrangements governed by the price mechanism that permit the voluntary transfer of property rights on a regular basis (Menard 1995). Although North's definition is widely used in the scholarly literature, it is worth reiterating here because some in the aid community use the term in a different way. Definitions may be tedious, but they are not trivial. The failure to employ a standard concept of institutions creates problems in establishing the impact of institutions on development, and affects how aid agencies view their role.

these four questions, but much remains unknown. In what follows I take stock of how the NIE has answered these questions and propose research to fill the gaps in our understanding. Before considering underdeveloped institutions I summarize theory on how modern market institutions evolved.

2. How Do Institutions Evolve and Economies Develop?

Institutions that Foster Exchange

The current literature on the importance of institutions to exchange is rooted in Ronald Coase's theory of transaction costs.[3] As Coase pointed out, the effects of high transaction costs "are pervasive in the economy. Businessmen, in deciding on their ways of doing business and on what to produce, have to take into account transaction costs. " If the costs of making an exchange are greater than the gains which that exchange would bring, that exchange would not take place..." (Coase 1992, p. 197). When information is costly and property rights are poorly protected, contracts become hard to specify and enforce and transaction costs are high. Societies with persistently higher transaction costs have less trade, fewer firms, less specialization, less investment, and lower productivity.

The evolution of institutions that support a modern market economy can be described in the following way (drawing largely on North 1990, 2004). Small communities producing at low levels of specialization rely largely on face-to-face barter trade between individuals who know one another and who typically share kinship, ethnic, religious, or similar ties. Bargains are enforced by informal mechanisms such as family loyalties, ostracism, or coercion by private groups.[4] Over time the group engaging in exchange tends to grow through natural population growth, urbanization, and migration and as more and more people begin to see advantages in trade. Improvements in agricultural and industrial technology, medicine, and education combine to increase human control over their environment, improve nutrition, and reduce disease, contributing to population growth, urbanization and the rise of markets. With the expansion in the size and geographic area of the trading group and the rise of urban centers, traders envision lucrative opportunities to do business with people who live even further away and do not belong to their networks. Merchants and investors seek more information about these unknown trading partners and better enforcement of bargains between strangers.

---

[3] Transaction costs include what Dahlman described as "search and information costs, bargaining and decision costs, policing and enforcement costs." (Dahlman 1979, p. 148) They are the costs of finding a trading partner, deciding on the terms of the trade, drawing up a contract, monitoring and enforcing a contract, and the like.

[4] Private coercion can increase as well as decrease uncertainty. Bates (2001) describes how clashes between private security forces among kinship groups can lead to retaliation and a cycle of violence that spans generations.

Up to a point, parties to contracts may be able to rely largely on norms and networks to enforce agreements between strangers. Greif describes how the Maghribi traders used an extensive network of communication, social ties, a common language, and a common religion (Judaism), to share information on the behavior of their agents and to assure that dishonest agents were collectively punished (Greif 1993). This framework motivated agents to develop a reputation for honest dealing, allowing the Maghribi to safely rely on agents who were not part of their family or community. Enforcing bargains through networks and norms is still important today, but it has drawbacks. Since it is rooted in one group's history and culture it is not easily transferred, and if enforcement requires group membership, opportunities for lucrative trades between those not able to use the enforcement mechanism are lost.[5]

To take advantage of these opportunities for profits and to respond to increased competition in home markets, some merchants look for new ways to trade safely with strangers. Trading parties begin to devise contractual safeguards; for example, one party might pledge an asset as a "hostage" that is forfeit if they renege on the agreement, much as people once enforced treaties by sending a family member to act as a hostage in a show of good faith (Williamson 1985, 1996). Merchants increasingly use written contracts, codes of conduct, standardized weights and measures, disclosure agreements, and enforcement through arbitration and courts.

Traders even today rely principally on private means to enforce contracts (Williamson 1985). And norms of trust and cooperation are still important in reducing transaction costs and fostering exchange (see for example Knack and Keefer 1997 and the chapter by Keefer and Knack in this Handbook). But for increasingly impersonal exchange, private ordering and norms of conduct need to be strengthened with the support of third party rules and enforcement, as happened in Europe, for example, when the codes of conduct of guild merchants evolved into merchant law and was gradually integrated into the body of laws enforced by states (Milgrom, et al. 1990). Written contracts and rules with third party enforcement were important to expanding trade in Western Europe during the Middle Ages, even though they do not always reduce transaction costs. Litigation and legalism can be a hindrance to trade as well as a help.

In places where institutions increase the certainty that contracts will be honored and property protected, individuals will be more willing to specialize, invest in sunk assets, undertake complex transactions and accumulate and share knowledge (North 1990, p. 34). Contract enforcement and property rights protection are not enough, however. Where most citizens lack access to education or health services, literacy, and surplus time and income to invest—as they do in most underdeveloped countries today—specialization is unlikely. Where specialization does occur, knowledge becomes more widely

---

[5] The pros and cons of informal versus formal institutions are reviewed in Keefer (2000).

distributed (Hayek 1979). Ever more complex institutions and organizations—scientific rules, professional networks, universities—are needed to integrate productive knowledge. Without these integrative institutions, the returns to any one individual's investment in human capital will be lower because of the loss of externalities from the knowledge that other members of society have acquired.

Institutions that Protect Property and Persons

Economic and political order accelerates the expansion of exchange, while expanding trade in turn provides a payoff to centralizing power in the hands of a ruler who can assure order. The continual warfare in Europe following the collapse of the Roman Empire, for example, hampered trade in the Middle Ages, but where order permitted, towns become centers of expanding trade and rapid political change, as happened in North and Central Italy or the Low Countries in the tenth century (North 2004). The economic returns to order contributed to the gradual rise of nation states and the establishment of order over larger areas. The increase in the size of political units combined with changes in military technology to raise the cost of warfare and increase the revenue that states needed to survive (Ibid.). The efforts by rulers to raise more revenues from elites led to conflicts and in some instances compromises that increased the power of more representative institutions and helped develop stronger financial markets (North 2004, Rosenthal 1998).

These changes are supported by changes in societies' dominant beliefs and norms. Institutions are the product of intentional human efforts to give structure to an uncertain world, and are congruent with a society's dominant belief system on how the world operates (North 2004). Enduring changes in institutions only occur when this underlying belief system also changes congruently. Changes in beliefs do not drive institutional changes, rather some beliefs allow a learning process that permits beliefs to evolve as institutions change. For example, North argues that Christian dogma was able to evolve in ways that supported economic growth and technological innovation in Western Europe during the Middle Ages. The Christian view that nature should serve mankind supported technological improvements in agriculture. The Protestant Revolution changed beliefs in support of greater individual freedom and economic expansion in the Netherlands and England.

With trade and specialization society's wealth increases and elite demand for protection of rights also increases, including rights to control and protect real property, intellectual property and one's person. In exchange for protection of these rights and the establishment of order, elites accept an expanded government role, pay levies and taxes to cover policing expenses, and give the state a monopoly over the use of force by demilitarizing private armies (Bates 2001, p. 65–66). Where the government is too weak to support contracts, establish order, and protect people and property, exchange, specialization, investment in physical and human capital—and therefore growth—will be limited. Extreme examples of this can be seen currently in some African states that are too weak to curb rival warlords. But as state power grows a dilemma emerges: any state strong enough to protect property and people is also strong enough to expropriate and subjugate them (North and Weingast 1989, Weingast 1993). Unless the state can credibly commit not to expropriate elite rights, risks under a strong state will be higher, lowering the incentive to invest. Accordingly, "... the development of free markets must be accompanied by some credible restrictions on the state's ability to manipulate economic rules to the advantage of itself and its constituents" (North and Weingast 1989, p. 808).

The most developed countries today are those that endowed the state with the power to enforce contracts, protect property rights, and assure stability and peace, yet also developed mechanisms to limit state power, such as independent parliaments and judiciaries, or federalism. These same countries evolved contractual mechanisms and cooperative norms to support expanding exchange among strangers, bargains among competing interest groups, and growing investment in ever more specialized skills and assets. These institutions helped keep down transaction costs and curbed the ascendancy of any single interest group, which created widespread opportunities for employment and consumption and encouraged investment in human capital. Increasing returns reinforced incentives in these societies to refine and strengthen the institutions that made these developments possible, except where "unanticipated consequences of choices, external effects, and sometimes [exogenous] forces" altered the path (North 1990).[6]

Only a few countries exhibit the beneficial institutions described above; most others have institutions inimical to growth. And past economic success is no guarantee of wealth today; consider the currently underdeveloped economies of formally wealthy countries such as Egypt or China. The next section surveys the literature that tries to explain why underdevelopment is so widespread.

3. Why Have So Few Countries Been Able to Create the Rules and Norms that Foster Growth and Social Progress?

New Institutional Economics has made some progress in identifying plausible explanations for underdevelopment, but does not yet boast a satisfactory general explanation. Below I group the extensive literature on this subject into four categories:[7]

---

[6] England and the Low Countries were early examples of these developments in Western Europe, for example.

[7] A large literature explains growth without reference to institutions; Easterly provides an excellent critique of that literature (Easterly 2002).

(i) Colonial heritage—countries inherited poor institutions from their colonial masters;
(ii) Colonial heritage plus—countries had valuable resources, people that could be enslaved, or land suitable to plantation agriculture, enticing colonizers to design institutions to exploit these endowments;
(iii) Political conflict—countries had too little political competition over their borders or between their elites so their rulers were less motivated to appeal to the wider population for support in their battles and faced little effective opposition when they built institutions to serve their selfish interests; and,
(iv) Beliefs and norms—countries had beliefs and norms that were inhospitable to markets or engendered mistrust, preventing them from building institutions that encourage trade and investment.

Table one gives an overview of the studies in these categories.[8]

Colonial Heritage

Sometime during the last 600 years most of the countries that we call underdeveloped today were colonies, prompting some institutional economists to conclude that poor institutions are a colonial legacy. Since some richer countries were also colonized, a stint as a colony is not in itself inimical to institutional development. What features of colonial heritage might cause institutional failings?

North (1990) has suggested that colonial powers created institutions that mirrored their own. Spain transplanted its centralized government, large and interventionist bureaucracy, and hegemonic property rights of favored nobility to Latin America, while England brought its decentralized, limited government to its colonies in the New World. As a result the United States and Canada were better positioned to curb state power, create more competitive markets, and industrialize faster than Latin America. But this explanation fails to explain why the English heritage failed to benefit countries in Africa, the Caribbean or South Asia or why Spain and England converged over time to a greater extent than their former colonies.[9]

---

[8] These explanations focus on what Douglass North has termed the institutional environment, which includes beliefs such as religions; norms such trust or lawfulness; constitutionally determined government structures such as bicameral or unicameral legislatures; and legal systems, such as one based on law and modified by the legislature or one based on precedent plus law and modified by the judiciary plus the legislature. They pay less attention to presumable more malleable micro-institutions, such as commercial codes, standards of weights and measures, electoral laws, political party rules, and legislative and bureaucratic regulations. And, with some exceptions, they emphasize the institutions that direct and curb government power rather than those that directly enable exchange.

[9] Location may be the reason for convergence. Stimulus from the rest of Europe played a key role in the development of England and the Netherlands in the Middle Ages (North 2004), and benefited Spain in the 20th century.

Table 1. Summary of explanations for underdeveloped institutions

Explanations	Summary	Authors	Drawbacks
Colonial Heritage	Countries inherited poor institutions from colonial masters.	North (1990)	Countries with same colonial master but different outcomes.
	Common or civil law origins affect contemporary institutions.	La Porta, Lopez-de-Silanes, Shleifer, & Vishny (1997, 1998, 1999)	Common law has no growth effect. Historical anomalies. Large differences in enforcement.
Colonial Heritage Plus	Countries had valuable resources/people and colonizers designed institutions to exploit them.	Acemoglu, Johnson, & Robinson (2001a&b)	Ignores differences among colonial powers. No test of casual effects of institutions. Africa?
	Interaction institutions & initial conditions created persistent inequality.	Engermann & Sokoloff (2002)	Better description of Americas than Africa or Asia.
Political Conflict	Countries had too little political competition over borders or between elites; allowed rulers to build institutions to serve selfish interests	Bates (2001), Herbst (2000) Nugent & Robinson (2002)	Border or elite conflicts not only factors in institutional development. Case specific arguments hard to generalize.
Beliefs & Norms	Countries had beliefs & norms inhospitable to markets or trust; prevented them from building institutions to encourage trade & investment	North (1994, 2004) Greif (1994) Knack & Keefer(1997)	Hard to falsify. Leaves little room for reform.

La Porta and his coauthors argue that a specific aspect of colonial heritage—a common or civil law system—has a profound effect on a country's current institutions (La Porta, et al. 1997, 1998, 1999). In their view countries that inherited common law systems from the England developed institutions that were better at limiting the state's power, enforcing contracts, and protecting property rights, especially the rights of minority investors. Countries with civil law origins, particularly French civil law, developed a state more prone to threatening property rights, establishing monopolies and squelching innovation, and provided less protection for minority shareholders.[10] Beck and Levine argue in this Handbook that civil law legal origins are also correlated with underdeveloped

---

[10] Not all civil law traditions are the same: French civil law supports a larger bureaucracy and fewer constraints than German or Scandinavian civil law (La Porta, et al. 1999, p. 231). Socialist law is more interventionist than civil law. In their empirical tests French civil law, along with Socialist law, is associated with more government interventionism, greater bureaucratic inefficiency and less democracy than common law or German civil law.

financial systems, and financial system development is highly correlated with growth.

No one has found a direct effect of legal origins on growth, however, and history belies some of the advantages claimed for common law.[11] By many measures France and other civil law countries of continental Europe were more financially developed than the United States in 1913 (Rajan and Zingales 2003). Contrary to the legal origins argument that common law protects minority property rights better than code law, the US created the SEC and other regulatory structures precisely because the common law rules protecting investors were seen as weak (Roe 2002). Also puzzling is how distant legal origins matter so much when current commercial laws and enforcement in countries with similar legal traditions vary so widely (Pistor, et al. 2000). And why were the villains in this story, the colonial powers that brought civil laws to their colonies, able to overcome their own legal origins and develop when many of their former colonies could not? Berkowitz et al. (2002) suggest that how a legal system was initially received—whether through conquest, colonization, or imitation—may have more influence on how it functions today than whether it is French, German, British or Scandinavian.[12]

Colonial Heritage Plus

Some authors try to improve on the colonial heritage explanation by adding other factors. Acemoglu and co-authors argue that the kinds of institutions Europeans imposed in their colonies depended on the conditions they found there. In richer areas that had a large population that could be enslaved or a climate that supported plantation agriculture or mining, such as Mexico, India or Indochina, they created or adapted oppressive production methods and tax and tribute systems designed to "concentrate political power in the hands of a few who used their power to extract resources from the rest of the population." (Acemoglu, et al. 2001a, p. 14). In safer places where the population was relatively sparse and the land less suited for plantations, such as the Northern US, Canada or Hong Kong, Europeans settled in larger numbers bringing beneficial institutions that supported private property and wider participation. When industrialization began in the 19th century, their reasoning goes, formerly rich colonies burdened with "extractive institutions" lacked secure property rights and provided few opportunities for technological and entrepreneurial innovation. The

---

[11] Nor do the originators of the legal traditions idea claim a growth effect (Shleifer, comments at the Annual Meeting of the International Society for New Institutional Economics in Cambridge, MA on September 27, 2002). Beck and Levine's chapter in this Handbook, however, cites studies showing that financial development "exerts a first order impact on long-run economic growth" and conclude that legal origins are a determinant of growth through their effects on financial institutions.

[12] Although the authors of La Porta et al. (1998, 1999) are critical of imported institutions that are imposed without regard for local norms (Djankov, et al. 2002), they still view civil law as a more damaging import than common law.

better institutions inherited by formerly poor colonies allowed them to industrialize and grow more rapidly.[13]

Acemoglu, et al.'s explanation ignores the differences in institutional success among the colonial powers that North describes. In their story, the US would have developed equally well had it been colonized by Spain.[14] Also the authors explain underdevelopment as the result of "extractive colonial institutions," but they do not directly test the causal relationship between growth and colonial institutions. Nor do they detail which "extractive colonial institutions" so cripple societies that they stay poor for centuries. Most of Africa, for example, shares a low level of institutional and economic development despite differences in factor endowments, generally low population density, and other variations in colonial legacy. Dangerous diseases that curbed European settlement are the reason Acemoglu and co-authors give for Africa's general state of underdevelopment. They point to the differences between the rest of Africa and those safer colonies where more Europeans settled because the risk of diseases was less: Rhodesia, South Africa, Kenya. But Europeans intensively settled some places such as the West Indies despite high mortality rates from dangerous diseases (Engerman and Sokoloff 2002). Also Kenya has not done as well as the US or much of East Asia, and there have been recent economic declines in Rhodesia and South Africa despite their presumably superior institutional heritage.

Sokoloff and Engerman (2002) also argue that factor endowments explain why there are large differences in contemporary institutions between countries settled by the same colonial power: the United States and Jamaica or the northern and southern United States, for example. In their view, institutions are endogenous to the conditions the colonists found when they arrived. Where soils, climate, and size or density of the native population encouraged plantation agriculture with slaves, elites were able to establish institutions that insured their ascendancy, contributing to persistence over time of the high degree of inequality (Sokoloff and Engerman 2002). The pernicious influence of slavery—slaves from Africa made up 60 percent of the more than 6 million people who migrated to the New World from 1500 to the end of the 18th century—contributed to persistent disparities in wealth, human capital, and political power. Engerman and Sokoloff (2002) specify the institutions that evolve where initial conditions favored equality and homogeneity, including rules that encouraged immigration, expanded the franchise, promoted secure and cheap land acquisition, and increased access to schooling and banking.

---

[13] Among former colonies, a 10 percent higher population density in 1500 is associated with a 4 percent lower per capita income today (Acemoglu, et al. 2001a). Countries which were never colonized by Western Europe didn't experience this "reversal of fortune" according to Acemoglu and co-authors (2001a). Rodrik, et al. (2002), however, find that institutional quality today among never colonized countries is as widely dispersed as among former colonies.

[14] Adding the identity of the colonial power to the estimate has little effect on the results, perhaps because their instrument (mortality rates of colonial settlers) captures the exogenous sources of variation in institutional quality.

Engerman and Sokoloff's explanation also seems, superficially at least, to be contradicted by experience outside the Americas, especially the relatively higher income equality in some underdeveloped former colonies in Asia, and African countries' similar institutional failures across different factor endowments. These examples may not be counterfactuals but the results of differences in factor endowments, native institutions and imported institutions that can only be uncovered by assembling the same amount of highly detailed historical information that Engerman and Sokoloff amassed for the Americas. The application of their model to at least one other region would be an important area for future research.

Political Conflict

Some scholars argue that it is not colonialism that is responsible for weak institutions but too little political conflict of the sort that led elites in Western Europe to make compromises and build institutions to win supporters, raise revenues, and defeat foreign enemies. In particular the need to raise revenues to fight territorial wars contributed to England's Glorious Revolution in 1688 when merchants and nobles forced the King to offer concessions to the nobles and merchants in exchange for their credible promises to provide the funds and fighters the Crown needed to fight foreign wars (North and Weingast 1989). For example, the King accepted a permanent role for Parliament, which previously met at the Sovereign's whim, greater independence for the judiciary, and prohibitions against the Crown's arbitrary violation of personal liberties. According to Bates, the absence of this form of conflict with outside enemies over territory in the modern history of most poor countries, especially African countries, is an important reason for their underdeveloped state institutions today. Instead of wars to establish territorial boundaries as part of nation building, African countries engaged in extensive conflicts over slaves, mineral wealth, or ethnic rivalries. More recently foreign aid added to state weaknesses in his view. Countries that became independent after the Second World War "faced fewer incentives to forge liberal political institutions," because the international environment did not require them "to seek ways to get their citizens to pay for defense and other costs of government" (Bates 2001, p. 83).

Herbst (2000) similarly suggests that because land was so ample in Africa, precolonial African states did not fight to defend their boundaries, so they did not have to build effective bureaucracies to raise funds or make political concessions to their citizens to persuade them to support the war effort.[15] Instead, African states simply never bothered to consolidate control over their outlying areas. Later, the colonial powers made matters worse. They did little to build state institutions, except where there was a large European presence. They drew

---

[15] Herbst argues that external threats in South Korea and Taiwan enabled their states to extract more resources from their citizens and develop more efficient mechanism to collect resources and control dissident groups (2000, p. 115).

national borders that left opposing ethnic groups concentrated in urban areas separated by vast stretches of largely empty territory that could shelter dissident armies, setting the stage for continual civil war. Much like Bates, Herbst argues that Western nations contributed to the stagnation of Africa's institutions after independence by preventing border disputes, which did not serve their Cold War interests, and propping up the region's weak, even venal, governments with aid.

Robinson (2002) disputes this view; he finds slavery and disease are more likely explanations for Africa's underdevelopment. Pre-colonial African states may have organized themselves for slave raiding and predation rather than for providing public goods, while dangerous diseases kept Europeans from settling in great numbers and building less exploitive, more participatory institutions (Robinson 2002).

It's not obvious that territorial conflicts in Africa or other underdeveloped countries would have forced rulers to limit their power and create institutions similar to those that emerged in advanced Western European nations. According to North and Weingast, England's Glorious Revolution was not prompted solely by border wars. Christian beliefs made competition and the accumulation of wealth respectable at a time when a commercial class was emerging and trade and competition were becoming more important (North 2004). England's king had to make concessions to wage war because he did not have a monopoly on power; the elites had twice deposed the king before striking a bargain with William and Mary in 1688. Nor are territorial conflicts a necessary condition for limited or representative government; less involvement in border wars does not seem to have harmed progress towards democracy in Switzerland or the US. Border wars are not always beneficial for institutions; wars had damaging effects on institutional development for centuries in the Middle Ages, for example.

Nugent and Robinson (2002) emphasize a different kind of political conflict, conflict between elites, as a driving force for institutional development. They argue that Colombia and Costa Rica are richer than El Salvador and Guatemala because the elites in Colombia and Costa Rica were competing merchants rather than cooperating landowners. Colombia's and Costa Rica's merchant elites granted property rights and the franchise to smallholder farmers to mobilize their support in their struggles for political power. Since smallholders are more productive in coffee growing, Colombia's and Costa Rica's coffee economies were more efficient.[16] This story is intriguing but hard to generalize. Merchant elites don't always compete or give concessions to win allies—Africa

---

[16] They argue that there are no scale economies in coffee growing and tending and picking is labor intensive and requires great care. Nugent and Robinson (2002) suggest that smallholders have better incentives to accumulate human capital necessary to improve their productivity further because they can capture part of the rent. The dominance of small holders could be due to the sparse populations in Colombia and Costa Rica compared to Guatemala and El Salvador. The authors cite the case of Nicaragua, which had similar population density to Colombia and Costa Rica, but developed large coffee plantations and expropriated the property of smallholders.

comes to mind—and the authors' explanations for why elites were competitive merchants in one locale and collaborating landowners in another are highly case specific. Nor are competing elites necessarily beneficial to growth: they sometimes engage in protracted wars that deter investment and specialization.

Beliefs and Norms

In other studies beliefs, habits, or what we might call cultures explain why some countries developed better institutions than others.[17] For example, Landes follows Max Weber in stressing the importance of culture in general and the Protestant Reformation in particular for spurring industrialization in Northern Europe.[18] As we saw earlier, North also stresses beliefs, but in a different role, as an important influence on how people learn and the sorts of institutional changes which can be accepted.

Avner Greif shows how beliefs affect institutional development by contrasting the individualistic cultural beliefs of the Christian Genoese and the collectivist cultural beliefs of the Jewish Maghribi traders mentioned earlier.[19] As we have seen the Maghribis' horizontal social structure relied on partnerships, community ties, and "formal friendships" among cooperating traders to enforce bargains. Genoa, however, had a vertical social structure, and its merchants evolved bills of lading, written contracts, laws, and permanent courts to support bargains among traders. The Maghribis did not need written documents and courts to enforce bargains; fears of losing reputation and ostracism worked just as well within their collectivist system. Ultimately, however, the Maghribis' failure to develop formal contracts and laws enforced by courts confined their trade to their network, where their collectivist enforcement was effective, while the Genoese grew rich through extensive and expanding trade.[20]

Not all norms or networks are harmful to the development of market-supportive institutions. Norms that encourage people to cooperate even with those with whom they have no family, business or other relational ties have economic payoffs in a number of studies surveyed by Keefer and Knack in their

---

[17] North (1994, p. 384) defines culture as "the intergenerational transfer of norms, values and ideas."

[18] In his view, Protestantism generalized the virtues of "a new kind of man—rational, ordered, diligent, productive"; it promoted literacy, an appreciation of time, and tolerance and openness to new ideas (Landes 1998, p. 177–78). Landes asserts that Catholic and Muslim religions have often been detrimental to institutional development, despite little empirical support for this claim. One study finds that a predominantly Catholic or Muslim population is associated with poorer government performance, but this effect becomes insignificant when controls for per capita income and latitude are included (La Porta, et al. 1999).

[19] He terms cultural beliefs the ideas and thoughts common to a group of individuals that "govern interaction between these people, and between them, their god and other groups" (994, p. 915).

[20] Similarly, Raskov (2002) shows how the community-based norms of the Old Believers, a traditionalist religious group in Russia, initially fostered but eventually choked development of their textile industry. In these stories strong informal bounds supporting collective action stunted the formal institutions that underpin a modern market economy, even thought they may have supported economic growth for centuries in the past.

chapter in this Handbook.[21] Putnam (1993) argues that the quality of local governments in Italy today can be traced back to the historical development of what he terms social capital, a network of associations that promote a culture of trust between strangers and help overcome collective action problems. Social capital has mixed effects on trust in cross-country regressions, however, perhaps because of external costs imposed on non-members as Keefer and Knack describe in their Handbook chapter. For example, Indian villages with well organized associations were more successful in bribing public officials to increase their allotment of water at the expense of other villages (Wade, 1988 cited in Keefer and Knack's chapter in this Handbook).

Norms, beliefs and similar informal institutions seem to be deeply engrained and the product of intractable factors, such as a society's history or its ethnic, religious, or linguistic heterogeneity. What can a society do if its culture is inhospitable? Keefer and Knack suggest two factors that increase development-promoting norms: income equality and education (see Keefer and Knack's chapter in this Handbook). Studies of East Asia suggest that the relatively high levels of education and income equality help explain why East Asian countries have grown faster and produced better social welfare measures than other less developed regions. If North is correct that beliefs filter the information that people derive from experience then it will be hard for schooling alone to change beliefs. Some of the more effective schools in developing countries are those structured to inculcate current dogma (for example, religious schools that teach fanaticism). Public schools are themselves captives of their institutional environments and are as effective or ineffective as the institutional environment would lead you to expect. For example, on any given day a third of all teachers in Uttar Pradesh, India are absent; 70 percent of students who completed grade 5 in Bangladesh were not minimally competent in writing; and the 1994 Tanzania Primary School Leavers Examination found that four-fifths of students scored less than 13 percent correct in language or mathematics after seven years of schooling (World Bank 2004, p. 112). When and how education and income distribution interact to alter beliefs and cultures in ways that foster development is not well understood and deserves further study.

All of the Above

The institutions that protect property rights and support strong market economies in Western Europe emerged gradually from a long and disorderly process of adaptation and experimentation spurred by competition and wars (see for example, North and Thomas 1973). Perhaps this organic progress toward efficiency would have happened more widely but was interrupted by colonialism's transplants of institutions that were less well adapted to

---

[21] Trust, a specific form of social capital, correlates strongly with growth and development (Fukuyama 1995, Knack 1997). Knack (1997) shows that trust is also correlated with private investment, perhaps because it reduces the transaction costs of securing agreements.

local norms, beliefs and environments (Djankov, et al. 2002). Or it could be that the fortuitous circumstances that produced a supportive institutional environment in today's developed countries were simply missing in many other places. Additional research will be needed to sort out the effects of different determinants.

The explanations converge, by and large, on two points. Despite disagreement on the ultimate determinants of institutional development, they broadly agree on the proximate causes: (i) greater equality combined with (ii) sufficient political competition to limit the ability of rulers to expropriate. Authoritarian regimes where a consolidated, wealthy and despotic ruling group exploited a poor or enslaved workforce might have been successful in the past, when organizing plantation agriculture or mining was key to economic success, but their oppressive institutions were inimical to competition, specialization, and industrialization. Where ruling elites had to bargain with one another or seek support from ordinary citizens, they created institutions to secure those bargains that curbed their power to expropriate. If the payoff to the ruler from abiding by these constraints was larger than the payoff from reneging, the institutions became self-enforcing and endured. In some cases this trend was reinforced where circumstances spread wealth more broadly, allowed greater access to education, and encouraged the development of human capital. What created these fortuitous circumstances? More research is needed to sort out the role of factor endowments, knowledge, historical accidents, and the evolution of supportive norms and beliefs.

Several of the explanations summarized above assume that fundamental institutions endure for centuries. Countries have weak institutions for reasons deep in their past: colonial heritage can date back as far as 1500; norms may have even more distant origins. This invites pessimism. What is the chance for countries to develop today if underdeveloped institutions are produced by distant history; especially if, as Bates and Herbst suggest, foreign assistance has usually locked weak institutions in place? Persistent inequality amongst the world's economies seems to support this pessimism (Pritchett 1997). But optimists counter with evidence that rapid growth in China, and to a lesser extent India, is reducing inequality and poverty among the world's populations (Sala-I-Martin 2002).[22] Rapid transformation of institutions in transitional economies also gives grounds for hope (see Peter Murrell's chapter).

Thanks to the literature surveyed above, we are closer to understanding underdevelopment than ever before. Studies that look for distant determinants of institutional quality, however, tell us little about which specific institutions are necessary for a country to develop today. For that I turn to comparative studies of institutions and growth.

---

[22] Sala-I-Martin (2002) finds convergence, not divergence, when inequality is measured in terms of purchasing power and weighted by population because of the large proportion of people living in China who saw their incomes rise over the last decade. The disturbing stagnation of African economies explains why these countries account for over 95% of the world's poor (Sala-I-Martin 2002, p. 39).

4. WHICH INSTITUTIONS MATTER FOR DEVELOPMENT?

The persistent significance of institutions in cross-country growth regressions has spawned a mushrooming literature and converted a number of former skeptics. Pinpointing which institutions are fundamentally responsible for development has been tough, however. A host of variables turn out to be statistically significant. One survey found measures of development are significantly positively correlated with: protection of property rights and enforcement (seven studies), civil liberties (ten studies); political rights and democracy (ten studies); and institutions supporting cooperation, including trust, religion, and the extent of social clubs and associations (four studies); and negatively with political instability (15 studies) (Aron 2000).[23] Roll and Talbott (2001) conduct a horse race between 14 institutional variables, eliminating those that don't hold up in multiple regressions, and still end up with nine winners—variables that are highly significant in explaining levels of gross national income per capita from 1995 through 1999.[24]

These studies suffer from several major problems. First, many of the explanatory variables are not institutions.[25] Secure property rights, for example, are not institutions but outcomes, the result of norms of conduct, religious precepts, historical traditions, laws and courts, and rules that check the state's ability to expropriate (Keefer and Shirley 2000).[26] Others are socio-economic conditions, such as ethnic fragmentation, or the results of economic policies, such as inflation, trade barriers, and black market premiums.[27] These conditions and policies are often treated as proxies for institutions in cross country regressions, but the studies seldom provide evidence that these variables should be seen as proxies rather than direct determinants of growth.[28]

---

[23] Aron also includes a number of studies that don't measure the effects of institutions, but of socio-economic conditions such as ethnilinguistic diversity, social mobility, fertility rates, and the size of the indigenous middle class. These factors are viewed as proxies for weak institutions in some studies.

[24] The winning explanatory variables are: trade barriers, government expenditures, monetary policy (inflation), property rights, regulation, black market activity, political rights, civil liberties, and freedom of the press.

[25] In addition there are a number of methodological criticisms of cross country regressions in general, as well of those that use growth rates in per capita income (summarized in Hall and Jones 1999, and Roll and Talbott 2001) or levels of per capita income. (See for example, Temple 1999). The most serious problem is reverse causality: do stronger institutions lead to economic growth or do wealthier countries create stronger institutions? Because of data limitations, the institutional variables are usually measured at the end rather than at the beginning of the period under investigation, and as a result, reverse causality is hard to rule out. The study by Roll and Talbott attempts to overcome problem of reverse causality by identifying major democratic events (such as the introduction of elections) and undemocratic events (such as military coups or the suspension of elections) in individual countries, then tracking the growth in GNI per capita for ten years before and 20 years after the event. After a democratic event, countries began to grow more rapidly and growth continued to accelerate, while growth stagnated after a non-democratic event.

[26] See also Rodrik et al. (2002).

[27] Rodrik et al. (2002) raise another objection to the use of policy and institutional variables in growth regressions. In their view measures of institutional quality already contain all the relevant information about policies.

[28] For example, trade barriers are treated as a proxy for poor government policies that might result from weak institutions to curb corrupt deals struck to protect cronies (Roll and Talbott 2001).

Even when the explanatory variable could arguably be described as an institution, another dilemma arises: typically the institutional variable is a broad aggregate. Many specific institutions are encompassed in a variable such as civil liberties: rules governing franchise, association, speech, information, privacy, property, and crime; as well as norms of trust and civic mindedness. Institutional quality measures usually aggregate subjective ratings of, among other things, rule of law, efficiency and honesty of the bureaucracy, and rules and motivation of government to protect property rights, which are themselves outcomes of a host of different specific institutions.

Cross-country regressions are poor tools to determine which particular institutions are necessary for a country to develop: we lack good aggregate measures of complex institutions or an understanding of how these institutions interact with specific country characteristics. Growth regressions have, nevertheless, suggested some important empirical regularities. First, whatever these institutional variables are measuring, they typically explain a sizeable fraction of economic growth. Second, institutions that increase political competition and civil liberties and promote cooperation have a statistically significant and positive association with per capita growth rates and income levels. This fits nicely with the finding of some of the historical studies reviewed earlier that high quality institutions today are rooted in greater equality, political competition and cooperative norms in the distant past.

Given the problems in finding good estimates of institutions for cross-country studies, case studies seem a logical interim approach. But case studies tend to be sui generis. Jütting (2003) reviews cases studying the impact of institutions on natural resource management (6 case studies), conflict resolution (3), and market development (8). Although institutions are more precisely defined than in the cross sectional studies, they are still not always clear or carefully measured. A common finding in these cases is that norms and customs play a critical role, but one highly particular to local circumstance. For example, norms of behavior backed by community sanctions helped enforce contracts in Vietnam, but failed to protect the customary rights of women in Uganda (see Jütting 2003).

Rodrik (2000) argues that since scholars cannot determine which institutions matter, democracy is the most effective way to mobilize local knowledge of how to develop better institutions. A large literature finds only an ambiguous relationship between democracy and growth, however.[29] Democracies do grow at least as well as autocracies and some do significantly better, but on average they don't outperform them.[30] This ambiguity may arise because representative

---

[29] See for example: DeHann and Siermann (1995), Brunetti (1997), Barro (1996), and Minier (1998). This may be because of the obvious problems of classifying a political system as democratic or autocratic, especially when some developing countries show high variability in their democracy ratings over time. Alemida and Ferreira (2002) argue that the variance in findings is caused by the greater volatility in the economic performance of autocracies compared to democracies. More autocratic regimes tend to be outliers, showing much better and much worse growth performance than more democratic regimes, largely because of much better or much worse policy choices.

[30] Democracies do better on other measures. Democracy reduces the volatility of economic performance (Alemida and Ferreira 2002, Rodrik 2000), and protects citizens from extreme abuses by the polity (Sen 1981).

democracy can take many forms; how democracy functions is affected by whether it is parliamentary or presidential, has a unicameral or bicameral legislature, delineates large or small districts that endow some interest groups with more or less disproportionate power, has strong or weak political parties, uses proportional representation or winner-takes-all, or puts a short or long time limit on terms of presidents and legislators. These complexities are hard to measure in a way that lends itself to cross country comparisons. Measurement is further complicated when laws don't reflect practice, which is more likely in countries with underdeveloped institutions.

Informal institutions also influence the functioning of democracy in ways that are seldom studied. Keefer (2002) finds that young democracies are prone to clientelism. Rather than take positions on policy issues or provision of public goods, politicians act as patrons and provide services to their clients (voters) to get reelected. By solidifying a support base of clients, they avoid being thrown out of office despite poor government performance. Over time clientelism tends to be replaced by more representative institutions, but the current flock of clientelist states may, temporarily, be sullying democracy's reputation.

Lack of a culture of trust or civic mindedness also undermines democratic rules. Mistrust may keep citizens from cooperating to monitor politicians and bureaucrats, reduce the ruling party's willingness to turn over power to the opposition for fear the new rules will abuse their power, and impede reform because government's commitments to compensate the losers are not credible. Bardhan (2000, p. 228) maintains that India is a prime example of a highly democratic country whose citizens have not been able to overcome collective action problems to ban together and require government to function more effectively.[31]

Democracy requires supportive beliefs, norms, and constitutional institutions that are usually absent in non-democratic countries. How to install these beneficial preconditions is not well understood. Exhorting poor countries to adopt democracy is about as helpful as exhorting them to adopt other desirable traits, such as rule of law or property rights. Moreover, even in a country with a strong representative democracy, growth may not be assured. Democracy acts as a check on government predation only if the government's policies are at odds with the majority's perception of how to enhance its welfare. Representative democracies may pursue policies that are popular but economically disastrous without any opposition from representative institutions (Rosenthal 1998). India, for example, prices water and electricity below operating cost, leaving utilities with inadequate resources to maintain the services or provide access to the poor. The political opposition to reducing these subsidies has proved insurmountable thus far, even though everyone loses from frequent disruptions in service.

---

[31] Indian society is "heterogeneous and conflict-ridden," and because no individual group is "powerful enough to hijack the state by itself," groups use the democratic process to build an elaborate system of checks and balances and "meticulous rules of equity in sharing the spoils..." (Ibid.).

Representative democracy is not the only institution that can allow choice of institutions and limit government; federalism can also have this effect.[32] Weingast (1995) suggests that China's federalist system placed checks on the elites and permitted experimentation among provinces that produced its successful innovations. Federalism is not always beneficial; it produced large budget deficits that slowed or reversed growth in Mexico and Argentina, for example (Careaga and Weingast 2000, Spiller and Tommasi 2000). Argentina's slide from a developed country at the end of the 19th century to an underdeveloped one today has been attributed in part to its federal system. Federalist institutions fashioned by the government of Juan Peron motivated provinces to free ride on the federal budget and politicians to focus on short term, sectarian interests (Spiller and Tommasi 2000).

Cross-country growth regressions have demonstrated that institutions are a—if not the—determinant of development, but they are ultimately unsatisfying to those seeking specifics. Successful institutional innovations—democracy, federalism—have been transferred from one context to another in some cases but not others, which leaves open the question of how to foster institutional change.

5. How Can Developing Countries Change Their Institutions?

The NIE has had less to say about institutional change, except that it is hard to accomplish. North's work suggests that a great deal of change occurs constantly at the margin, but the institutional framework is typically stable, except when change is imposed by force or revolution. This stability is the product of path dependency—those who make policy and design institutions have a stake in the framework they created and resist changes that may rob them of power or property. Even without this active opposition to change, societies evolve norms, networks and beliefs congruent with their formal institutions that resist dramatic change under many circumstance (North 1990). Formal institutions may be suddenly altered by revolution, invasion or crisis, but unless beliefs and norms also change the new status quo will be overturned after the revolution ends, the invaders leave, or the crisis subsides. Changes in beliefs and norms usually require a period of gradual learning, although education, research, and communication may speed adaptation in ways that are not well studied.

Path dependency and the stickiness of beliefs and norms explain why underdevelopment cannot be overcome by simply importing institutions that were successful in other countries. There are numerous examples of failure. Latin American countries copied the U.S. constitution, transitional countries emulated U.S. or European bankruptcy laws and commercial codes, former French

---

[32] Informal rules may also curb the abuses of autocracies in ways that have not been well researched. The decision of the Pinochet dictatorship to hold a plebiscite on its rule and to restore democracy after losing is a case in point.

colonies in Africa adopted the French educational and bureaucratic system—all with very different and generally disappointing results.

Levy and Spiller (1994) argue that successful micro institutional reforms require what they term "goodness of fit" between the specific innovation and the country's broader, macro institutional environment, including its norms and beliefs.[33] A "good fitting" institutional innovation would be one that does not depend on absent or weak institutions and is insulated from or adapted to perverse institutions as far as possible. In their analysis an imported institution such as complex rules for regulating a privatized utility is not a good fit in a country that lacks essential supportive institutions such as checks on government's capacity to change the laws, strong bureaucratic rules and capability, and an independent judiciary able to hold the government to its contractual obligations.

China's "market preserving federalism" and township and village enterprises have been cited as good fits (Weingast 1995, Murrell's chapter in this Handbook, Djankov 2002). China's federal system allowed provinces and local governments to experiment with different economic rules that could be tested through competition between localities as long as the dominance of the Communist Party went unchallenged (Weingast 1995). Some townships and villages experimented with rules that encouraged private investors to run government-owned enterprises. Formal and informal rules gave these investors—mainly overseas Chinese with kinship ties to the locality—considerable control over the staffing, management and survival of the enterprise in exchange for regular payments to the local government that "owned" the firm, allowing capitalistic incentives to flourish within an officially socialist system (Keefer and Shirley 2000).

These adaptations may be good fits but they have disadvantages. They are poor substitutes for more efficient financial and legal systems. China's government-owned but privately-operated township and village enterprises stimulated markets, but were rife with corruption; China's "market preserving federalism" left large parts of the country behind.

A good fitting institution meets Williamson's "remediableness criterion": "... an extant mode of organization for which no superior feasible alternative can be described and implemented with expected net gains..." (Williamson 2002, p. 12, underlined in original). But the remediableness criterion, as Williamson points out, risks being "too deferential to the status quo" (Ibid). Reforms could be so tailored to initial conditions that they leave countries locked into inefficient institutions when superior improvements were indeed possible. How can we judge an apparently good fit? The appropriate counterfactual is not the status quo or some comparator country, and certainly not a fully developed, Western system of property rights, finance and law. Ideally, we should assess goodness of fit as part of a process of institutional change, and decide whether the direction

---

[33] For example Chile required its SOEs to operate as if they were private firms. Its rules worked to improve efficiency in Chile but failed to improve efficiency when introduced in other countries. The explanations for why these rules worked in Chile seems to be the supportive norms of its civil service. (See for example the chapter on Santiago's municipal water in Shirley 2002)

of change is towards institutions that are more supportive of an efficient market economy and improved social development.[34] This is exceptionally tough to do.

Learning plays an important role in changing norms and beliefs and thus supporting institutional changes in North's view (North 2004). Education and new ideas can play a powerful role when the setting is receptive, as in the impact of the Enlightenment in Western Europe. There are more recent examples as well: the emergence of a critical mass of well-trained economists working in universities and think tanks played an important role in structural changes in Latin America, particularly in Chile (Corbo, 2000), and the education of a number of Chinese in universities abroad had an important effect on the design of reforms there. But there are counter examples (India, perhaps), and the link between knowledge, learning, beliefs and educational reform is not well specified yet.

The specifics of institutional change fall through a gap in the literature; few studies attempt to grapple with the messy details of real institutional change. Given how quickly NIE has evolved from a time when institutions were not even included in most development models, the gap is not surprising. Foreign assistance agencies have entered this gap under the assumption that institutions can be changed by outside advice and funds (see World Bank 2002, 2003).

6. Can Outsiders Promote Institutional Development?

Outsiders have changed deeply rooted institutions, usually by fomenting revolutions or invading, sometimes in consort with a powerful local reformer.[35] For example, Napoleon brought enduring changes to Europe's legal, educational, health, and other institutions in a relatively short period of occupation. Force alone cannot explain Napoleon's enduring impact. Some intellectuals and merchants were receptive to Napoleon's innovations; dissatisfied with domestic institutions and inspired by the Enlightenment they saw his reforms as progressive, the heritage of the French revolution. Outsiders have also contributed to enduring institutional change in countries where powerful elites welcomed foreign ideas, such as Tsar Peter in Russia or Mustafa Kemal Attaturk in Turkey. Absent a powerful local supporter, however, there are few insistences where aid or advice alone has made enduring improvements in another country's embedded institutions. Some observers cited earlier believe that aid may even have slowed institutional change by preventing political competition and preserving the power of local elites who might otherwise have been removed.

---

[34] Early evidence on China's privatization of the township and village enterprises suggests that they have been supportive of further moves towards markets and development (Sonobe and Otsuka 2003).

[35] This section addresses whether outsiders have been able to promote sustainable improvements in the institutional environment by changing constitutions, norms of honesty or cooperation, enforcement mechanisms for laws and contracts, etc. It does not address the more successful record outsiders may have had of influencing changes in less embedded formal rules, such as the regulations governing electricity or water firms.

By promoting rent seeking and shirking aid can actually undermine the sustainability of the reforms it is designed to support. Buchanan termed this problem the Samaritan's dilemma (Buchanan 1977). The payoff is highest to the Samaritan if the Samaritan provides aid and the beneficiary responds by exerting high effort. But the payoff is highest to the beneficiary if s/he can receive the aid without increasing effort. The weaker a country's institutional framework, the more likely it is that this is the game being played. "When the recipient country is governed by officials who are primarily interested in seeking out opportunities for private gain, and few institutions are in place to keep these motivations in check, moral hazard problems can become substantial" (Ostrom, et al. 2002, p. 11). Moral hazard problems are exacerbated when the goal is institutional change because projects directed at changing institutions lack tangible outputs, making impact "more diffuse and hard to verify" (Martens, et al. 2002, p. 17).

Aid projects try to reform institutions through conditionality: a list of specific changes that the country must enact before funds will be disbursed. But conditionality does not fit well with what is known about institutional change. As we have seen, the NIE suggests that institutions usually change as the result of a long and often painful process of competition and adaptation, changes that are only sustained if belief systems and norms change as well. Ruling elites often prefer pro forma changes so they can obtain funds without politically costly changes in deep-seated constitutional rules, norms and beliefs—the Samaritan's dilemma.

Aid as presently constructed is a poor tool to change the deep-seated beliefs and norms that underlie many institutions. Sustained improvements in education, for example depend on curriculum choice; rules governing teacher selection, salaries and accountability; beliefs and norms about schooling (of girls, for example); and the like. These often politically sensitive and culturally bound elements are not likely to change because of conditionality and advice directed at central government ministries or incentives tied to financing for construction of schools, purchase of textbooks or technical assistance.

Over time, the disappointing performance of many aid recipients has led aid agencies to discover institutions. A number of recent reports have stressed institutions, but most have failed to consider seriously the implications of institutions for foreign aid.[36] The World Bank's World Development Reports redefine institutions in an elastic way to include not only formal and informal rules, but also organizations (World Bank 2002) and policies such as interest rates (World Bank 2002). These definitions make a mockery of efforts to measure the impact of institutions on markets or policies or the interactions between institutions and organizations; they also allow aid agencies to characterize virtually any reform activity as institutional reform without radically changing their approach.

The foreign aid community generally assumes that institutions are malleable and can be changed through aid within the three to five year life span of a development project, or at most the 15 to 20 year span of several projects. Another premise is that well-intentioned outsiders can discover needed institutional

---

[36] See, for example: World Bank (1998, 2002); Payne (2002); Quibria (2002).

changes and persuade governments to implement reforms and sustain them. The NIE literature described above suggests that these assumptions are wrong: (i) much institutional change is well beyond the time frame of even a series of aid projects; (ii) institutional change requires alterations in beliefs that cannot be easily pushed or purchased by outsiders; (iii) successful institutional adaptations have been engineered by insiders and sometimes work quite contrary to the conventional wisdom or best practice touted by the aid community; and, (iv) aid in the absence of a supportive institutional framework can create perverse incentives and prop up rulers who are opponents, not catalysts, of reform.

7. WHAT NEXT?

New Institutional Economics has not answered the four questions I posed at the outset: Why have so few countries been able to create and sustain the rules and norms that foster growth and social progress? Which institutions must function effectively if countries are to develop? How can poorer countries attain well functioning institutions? Can outsiders promote institutional development? Historical analyses have produced a number of intriguing explanations, but no single argument is fully satisfactory; there are glaring gaps and some face major counterfactuals. Cross-country studies have put institutional variables into mainstream models and produced some consistent regularities, but the devil is in the details and the details can be numerous.[37] While much is known about how institutions developed in Western Europe, there needs to be more research on institutional development in Third World countries including research on what causes changes in norms and beliefs that underlie successful institutional reforms.

What can be done to fill the gaps in our understanding? Thanks to a new generation of cross-country studies coupled with increasingly detailed databases, we are progressing in understanding how specific institutions affect specific behavior. A good example is Keefer's study of how governments' decisions to bail out banks during financial crises are determined by voter information, proximity of competitive elections, and checks or limits on government (Keefer 2001). Institutional variables in these analyses are still aggregated but far more sophisticated and complex.[38]

It may be possible to fill the gap in our understanding with a pincer movement. Statistical analyses are already moving from aggregation to specificity;

---

[37] Ostrom (1999), for example, found 27 different boundary rules for managing common pool resources in different locations. Shirley (2002) found that the privatization of a city's water supply system is not a single policy option, but an array of choices about regulations and contracts that played out quite differently in different environments.

[38] For example, Keefer measures checks as the number of veto players– the number of organizations dominated by politicians with the motivation and power to veto policy choices. This is complex; for presidential systems, for example, he assigns one point to each house of the legislature, but zero if the president's party has a majority and voters must vote for a partly list, not a candidate. Initially these studies will be messier, with smaller samples and lower significance than the usual well honed but unsatisfying cross-country growth regressions.

case studies will need to move from sui generis to comparative. Case studies can be powerful tools when they are analytical narratives, cases that test hypotheses with methodological rigor and also describe historical context, norms and beliefs and institutional adaptations, all the rich nuances of the institutional setting (see Bates, et al. 1998). Comparative analytical narratives—cases using a common methodology and common conceptual framework to assess a larger sample—would allow us to identify regularities with greater confidence. Although the task seems daunting, there have been examples (see Ostrom 1990, Shirley 2002). Shirley (2002) used a comparative approach to analyze six case studies: it employed the same conceptual framework; applied the same questionnaire to individuals in the same positions in the same types of organizations; defined and measured the same variables in the same ways; and used the same methodology to measure welfare and other effects. Six cases are hardly enough to be sure of robust conclusions, but in combination with broader statistical analyses they can help us begin to sort out true causal variables from among the large array of statistically significant candidates. As the number of cases mount it may be possible to combine them and do a meta-analysis. There are difficulties: comparative case studies can be time consuming and expensive and selection bias continues to be a problem even with comparative case studies, since few researchers choose to study countries that are not reforming.

Deeper analysis of institutions **within** developing countries also holds promise. The Spiller and Tommasi study of Argentina is a good example of the analytical power of tools normally only used in developed countries for studying institutions in a developing context. Lack of reliable information can be a stumbling block to applying these tools in poorer countries, but lack of local researchers is often the more serious obstacle. In many developing countries, low pay, inadequate resources and a sense of isolation drive the best scholars away from research or out of the country. Those who remain face an uphill battle getting funding to build databases, undertake serious research and publish controversial findings.

A critical mass of local researchers is a prerequisite for understanding institutions fully, stimulating an informed debate, and fostering changes in belief systems, the first step to enduring institutional change. Since improvements in formal institutions hinge on changes in long held beliefs, the most important role for outsiders is to support this learning by helping build local knowledge and educational institutions while avoiding actions that fortify the defenders of the old order. Only when this minimum mass of human capital is in place will citizens of poorer countries begin to discover how to meet the challenge of development.

ACKNOWLEDGEMENT

This chapter has benefited greatly from comments by Philip Keefer, Bertin Martens, Claude Ménard, Douglass North, Charles Oman, an anonymous reviewer, participants in seminars at George Mason University, Stanford

University, the University of Sao Paulo, and a panel at the annual meeting of the International Society for New Institutional Economics in Budapest.

REFERENCES

Acemoglu, Daron, Simon Johnson, and James A. Robinson. 2001a. "Reversal of Fortune: Geography and Institutions in the Making of the Modern World Income Distribution". MIT Working Paper #01–38.

Acemoglu, Daron, Simon Johnson, and James A. Robinson. 2001b. "The Colonial Origins of Comparative Development: An Empirical Investigation". *American Economic Review* 91(5): 1369–1401.

Alemida, Heitor and Daniel Ferreira. 2002. "Democracy and the Variability of Economic Performance". *Economics and Politics* 14(3): 225–257.

Aron, Janine. 2000. "Growth and Institutions, a Review of the Evidence". *The World Bank Research Observer* 15(1): 465–490.

Bardhan, Pranab K. 2000. "Understanding Underdevelopment: Challenges for Institutional Economics from the Point of View of Poor Countries". *Journal of Institutional and Theoretical Economics (JITE)* 156(1): 216–235.

Barro, Robert J. 1996. "Democracy and Growth". *Journal of Economic Growth* 1: 1–27.

Bates, Robert H. 2001. *Prosperity and Violence: The Political Economy of Development*. New York: W.W. Norton & Company.

Bates, Robert H., Avner Greif, Margaret Levi, Jean-Laurent Rosenthal, and Barry R. Weingast. 1998. *Analytic Narratives*. Princeton, NJ: Princeton University Press.

Berkowitz, Daniel, Katharina Pistor, and Jean Francois Richard. 2002. "Economic Development, Legality, and the Transplant Effect". *European Economic Review* 47: 165–195.

Brunetti, A. 1997. "Political Variables in Cross-Country Growth Analysis". *Journal of Economic Surveys* 11: 163–190.

Buchanan, James M. 1977. "The Samaritan's Dilemma" in James M. Buchanan (ed.), *Freedom in Constitutional Contract*. College Station, TX: Texas A&M University Press.

Careaga, Maite and Barry R. Weingast. 2000. "The Fiscal Pack with the Devil: A Positive Approach to Fiscal Federalism, Revenue Sharing, and Good Governance in Developing Countries". Hoover Institute Working Paper.

Coase, Ronald H. 1992. "The Economic Structure of Production". *American Economic Review* 82(3): 713–719.

Corbo, Vittorio. 2000. "Economic Policy Reform in Latin America" in Anne O. Krueger (ed.), *Economic Policy Reform: The Second Stage*. Chicago, IL: The University of Chicago Press.

Dahlman, Carl J. 1979. "The Problem of Externality". *The Journal of Law and Economics* 22:1.

DeHaan, J. and C.L.J. Siermann. 1995. "New Evidence on the Relationship between Democracy and Economic Growth". *Public Choice* 86: 175–198.

Djankov, Simeon, Rafael La Porta, Florencio Lopez-de-Silanes, and Andrei Shleifer. 2002. "Appropriate Institutions". Paper presented at the World Bank Conference on Appropriate Institutions for Growth, Washington, September 13, 2002.

Easterly, William. 2002. *The Elusive Quest for Growth. Economists' Adventures and Misadventures in the Tropics*. Cambridge, MA: MIT Press.

Engerman, Stanley L. and Kenneth L. Sokoloff. 2002. "Factor Endowments, Inequality, and Paths of Development among New World Economies". *Economia* 3: 41–109.

Fukuyama, Francis. 1995. *Trust: The Social Virtues and the Creation of Prosperity*. New York: Free Press.

Greif, Avner. 1993. "Contract Enforceability and Economic Institutions in Early Trade: The Maghribi Traders' Coalition". *American Economic Review* 83(3): 525–548.

_____. 1994. "Cultural Beliefs and the Organization of Society: A Historical and Theoretical Reflection on Collectivist and Individualist Societies". *Journal of Political Economy* 102(5): 912–950.

Hall, Robert E. and Charles I. Jones. 1999. "Why Do Some Countries Produce So Much More Output Per Worker Than Others?" *The Quarterly Journal of Economics* 114(1): 83–116.

Hayek, Friedrich August von. 1979. *Law, Legislation and Liberty*, Vol. 3. London: Routledge and Kegan.

Herbst, Jeffrey I. 2000. *States and Power in Africa*. Princeton, NJ: Princeton University Press.

Jütting, Johannes. 2003. "Institutions and Development: A Critical Review". OECD Development Centre Technical Papers No. 210.

Keefer, Philip. 2001. "When Do Special Interests Run Rampant? Disentangling the Role of Elections, Incomplete Information, and Checks and Balances in Banking Crises". World Bank Policy Research Working Paper #2543.

_____. 2002. "Clientelism and Credibility". Paper Presented to the International Society for New Institutional Economics, Cambridge, MA.

Keefer, Philip and Mary M. Shirley. 2000. "Formal Versus Informal Institutions in Economic Development" in Claude Menard (ed.), *Institutions, Contracts, and Organizations: Perspectives from New Institutional Economics*. Cheltenham, UK: Edward Elgar, pp. 88–107.

Knack, Stephen and Philip Keefer. 1997. "Does Social Capital Have an Economic Payoff? A Cross-Country Investigation". *Quarterly Journal of Economics* 112(4): 1251–1288.

La Porta, Rafael, Florencio Lopez-de-Silanes, Andrei Shleifer, and Robert Vishny. 1997. "Legal Determinants of External Finance". *Journal of Finance* 52: 1131–1150.

_____. 1998. "Law and Finance". *Journal of Political Economy* 106: 1113–1155.

_____. 1999. "The Quality of Government". *Journal of Law, Economics and Organization* 15(1): 222–282.

Landes, David S. 1998. *The Wealth and Poverty of Nations: Why Some Are So Rich and Others Are So Poor*. New York: W.W. Norton & Co.

Levy, Brian and Pablo T. Spiller. 1994. *Regulations, Institutions, and Commitment : Comparative Studies of Telecommunications*. New York: Cambridge University Press.

Martens, Bertin, Uwe Mummert, Peter Murrell, and Paul Seabright. 2002. *The Institutional Economics of Foreign Aid*. Cambridge, U.K.: Cambridge University Press.

Menard, Claude. 1995. "Markets as Institutions Versus Organizations as Markets? Disentangling Some Fundamental Concepts". *Journal of Economic Behavior and Organization* 28: 161–182.

Milgrom, Paul, Douglass North, and Barry R. Weingast. 1990. "The Role of Institutions in the Revival of Trade: The Law Merchant, Private Judges, and the Champagne Fairs". *Economics and Politics* 2: 1–24.

Minier, J.A. 1998. "Democracy and Growth: Alternative Approaches". *Journal of Economic Growth* 3: 241–266.

North, Douglass C. 1990. *Institutions, Institutional Change, and Economic Performance*. New York: Cambridge University Press.

_____. 1994. "The Historical Evolution of Polities". *International Review of Law and Economics* 14: 381–391.

_____. 2004. "Understanding the Process of Economic Change," Unpublished Manuscript.

North, Douglass C. and Robert Paul Thomas. 1973. *The Rise of the Western World: A New Economic History*. Cambridge, UK: Cambridge University Press.

North, Douglass C. and Barry R. Weingast. 1989. "Constitutions and Commitment: The Evolution of Institutions Governing Public Choice in Seventeenth-Century England". *The Journal of Economic History* 49(4): 803–832.

Nugent, Jeffrey B. and James A. Robinson. 2002. "Are Endowments Fate?" Centre for Economic Policy Research Discussion Paper No. 3206.

Ostrom, Elinor. 1990. *Governing the Commons: The Evolution of Institutions for Collective Action*. New York: Cambridge University Press.
_____. 1999. "Coping with Tragedies of the Commons". *Annual Review of Political Science* 2: 493–535.
Ostrom, Elinor, Clark Gibson, Sujai Shivakumar, and Krister Andersson. 2002. *Aid, Incentives, and Sustainability: An Institutional Analysis of Development Cooperation*. Stockholm, Sweden: Swedish International Development Cooperation Agency.
Payne, J. Mark, Daniel Zovatto G., Fernando Carillo Flores, and Andrés Allamand Zavala. 2002. *Democracies in Development: Politics and Reform in Latin America*. Washington, DC: The Inter-American Development Bank.
Pistor, Katharina, Martin Raiser, and Stanislaw Gelfer. 2000. "Law and Finance in Transition Economies". *Economics of Transition* 8(2): 325–368.
Pritchett, Lance. 1997. "Divergence Big Time". *Journal of Economic Perspectives* 11(3): 3–17.
Putnam, Robert. 1993. *Making Democracy Work: Civil Traditions in Modern Italy*. Princeton, NJ: Princeton University Press.
Quibria, M.G. 2002. *Growth and Poverty: Lessons from the East Asian Miracle Revisited*. Tokyo: Asian Development Bank Institute.
Rajan, Raghuram G. and Luigi Zingales. 2003. "The Great Reversals: The Politics of Financial Development in the Twentieth Century". *Journal of Financial Economics* 69(1): 5–50.
Raskov, Danila. 2002. "Norms in the Economic Evolution: Old Believers in the Russian Nineteenth-Century Textile Industry". Unpublished Working Paper, St. Petersburg, Russia.
Robinson, James A. 2002. *"States and Power in Africa* by Jeffrey I. Herbst: A Review Essay". *Journal of Economic Literature* 60(2): 510–519.
Rodrik, Dani. 2000. "Institutions for High-Quality Growth: What They Are and How to Acquire Them". National Bureau of Economic Resarch Working Paper 7540.
Rodrik, Dani, Arvind Subramanian, and Francesco Trebbi. 2002. "Institutions Rule: The Primacy of Institutions over Geography and Integration in Economic Development". Centre for Economic Policy Research Discussion Paper Series #3643.
Roe, Mark J. 2002. "Institutional Foundations for Securities Markets in the West". Draft Prepared for the ASSA meetings, January 3–5, 2003.
Roll, Richard and John Talbott. 2001. "Why Many Developing Countries Just Aren't". Unpublished Working Paper.
Rosenthal, Jean-Laurent. 1998. "The Political Economy of Absolutism Reconsidered" in Robert H. Bates, Avner Greif, Margaret Levi, Jean-Laurent Rosenthal and Barry R. Weingast (eds.), *Analytical Narratives*. Princeton, NJ: Princeton University Press, pp. 64–108.
Sala-I-Martin, Xavier. 2002. "The Disturbing "Rise" of Global Income Inequality". National Bureau of Economic Research Working Paper No. 8904.
Sen, Amartya Kumar. 1981. *Poverty and Famines: An Essay on Entitlement and Deprivation*. New York: Oxford University Press.
Shirley, Mary M. (ed.). 2002. *Thirsting for Efficiency: The Economics and Politics of Urban Water System Reform*. Oxford: Elsevier Science.
Sokoloff, Kenneth L. and Stanley L. Engerman. 2000. "Institutions, Factor Endowments, and Paths of Development in the New World". *Journal of Economic Perspectives* 14(3): 217–232.
Sonobe, Tetsushi and Keijiro Otsuka. 2003. "Productivity Effects of Tve Privatization: The Case Study of Garment and Metal Casting Enterprises in the Greater Yangtze River Region". National Bureau of Economic Research Working Paper No. W9621.
Spiller, Pablo T. and Mariano Tommasi. 2000. "The Institutional Foundations of Public Policy: A Transactions Approach with Application to Argentina". Working Paper presented to the Annual Meetings of the International Society for New Institutional Economics, 2000, Tubingen, Germany.

Temple, Jonathan. 1999. "The New Growth Evidence". *Journal of Economic Literature* 37(1): 112–156.

Wade, Robert. 1988. *Village Republics: Economic Conditions for Collective Action in South India*. New York: Cambridge University Press.

Weingast, Barry R. 1993. "Constitutions as Governance Structures: The Political Foundations of Secure Markets". *Journal of Institutional and Theoretical Economics (JITE)* 149(1): 286–311.

———. 1995. "The Economic Role of Political Institutions: Market-Preserving Federalism and Economic Development". *Journal of Law, Economics and Organization* 96: 132–163.

Williamson, Oliver E. 1985. *The Economic Institutions of Capitalism*. New York: The Free Press.

———. 1996. *The Mechanisms of Governance*. New York: Oxford University Press.

———. 2002. "The Lens of Contract Applications to Economic Development and Reform" in *The Institutional Economics Approach to Aid Effectiveness*. The IRIS Center: Washington, D.C.

World Bank. 1998. *Assessing Aid. A World Bank Policy Research Report*. New York: Oxford University Press.

———. 2002. *World Development Report 2002: Building Institutions for Markets*. Washington, DC: The World Bank and Oxford University Press.

———. 2003. *World Development Report 2003: Sustainable Development in a Dynamic World*. Washington, DC: The World Bank and Oxford University Press.

———. 2004. *World Development Report 2004: Making Services Work for Poor People*. Washington, DC: The World Bank and Oxford University Press.

25. Institutional and Non-Institutional Explanations of Economic Differences

STANLEY L. ENGERMAN and KENNETH L. SOKOLOFF

1

Economists have long been concerned with the explanation of differences across countries in levels of national income, population, and per capita incomes, as well as in their rates of growth. Because many of the processes of economic development operate over long periods of time, those studying the sources of these differences have quite naturally turned to the historical record for relevant evidence. Their concern with economic history thus comes not only from a desire to achieve a better understanding of the past, but also from a belief that such knowledge can serve as a guide for policymakers striving to improve the economic and social conditions of currently less developed nations. Many scholars have set about making contributions to knowledge through detailed investigations of the processes of growth in individual countries. Others have sought to discern what factors were crucial through comparative studies, focusing on issues such as why nations differed with regard to the timing of the onset of growth or how and why their records of achieved rates of growth varied over a long period of time.

Recently considerable attention has been given to the question of why European nations and some of their overseas offshoots expanded more rapidly than did the economies of Asia, Africa, and Latin America after the eighteenth century, either generating new gaps in levels of income and rates of growth, or else greatly widening whatever differentials may have previously existed (see Table 1).[1] Previously the principal focus of historians examining the basis for differences in long-term economic performance had been with what led Great Britain to accomplish an Industrial Revolution sometime after the middle of the eighteenth century, and ahead of its European rivals (see Table 2).[2] Given the greater similarity of economic, political, and social structures among the

---

[1] Among a vast literature, see North and Thomas 1973; North 1981; Rosenberg and Birdzell 1986; Jones 1987; Landes 1998; Engerman and Sokoloff 1997 and 2002; Pomeranz 2000; Acemoglu, Johnson, and Robinson 2001 and 2002; and Easterly and Levine 2003. For even earlier discussions, see Weber 1958 and 1961; and Sombart 1969.

[2] See, for example, Hartwell 1971.

Table 1. Levels of Per capita GDP and interregional differences, 1500–1998.
(1990 dollars)

	1500	1820	1870	1913	1950	1973	1998
Western Europe	774	1232	1974	3473	4594	11534	17921
Western Offshoots	400	1201	2431	5257	9288	16172	26146
Japan	500	669	737	1387	1926	11439	20413
Asia (excl. Japan)	572	575	543	640	635	1231	2936
Latin America	416	665	698	1511	2554	4531	5795
Eastern Europe	483	667	917	1501	2601	5729	4354
Africa	400	418	444	585	852	1365	1368
World	565	667	867	1510	2114	4104	5709
Interregional Spreads	2:1	3:1	5:1	9:1	15:1	13:1	19:1

Source: As calculated in Maddison 2001.

Table 2. Per capita GDP in Western Europe, 1500–1998.
(1990 dollars)

	1500	1600	1700	1820	1870	1913	1998
Austria	707	837	993	1218	1863	3465	18905
Belgium	875	976	1144	1319	2697	4220	19442
Denmark	738	875	1039	1274	2003	3912	22123
Finland	453	538	638	781	1140	2111	18324
France	727	841	986	1230	1876	3485	19558
Germany	676	777	894	1058	1821	3648	17799
Italy	1100	1100	1100	1117	1499	2564	17759
Netherlands	754	1368	2110	1821	2753	4049	20224
Norway	640	760	900	1104	1432	2501	23660
Portugal	632	773	854	963	997	1244	12929
Spain	698	900	900	1063	1376	2255	14227
Sweden	695	824	977	1198	1664	3096	18685
Switzerland	742	880	1044	1280	2202	4266	21367
United Kingdom	714	974	1250	1707	3191	4921	18714
Total Western Europe	774	894	1024	1232	1974	3473	17921
World	565	593	615	667	867	1510	5709

Source: As calculated in Maddison 2001.

European nations than those between Europe and the rest of the world, the factors highlighted in the discussions of the development of the Industrial Revolution are rather different from those generally featured in the broader geographic comparisons. In both cases, however, what the economists and economic historians are seeking to explain is why some nations in today's world remain poor, relatively and absolutely, and what conditions can be changed in order to achieve success in spurring growth and improving the welfare of the respective populations. It is this problem that the recent study of institutions has sought to help resolve and that probably represents its most significant contribution.

It is not necessary here to attempt to catalogue the full set of explanations that have been given for differences in economic development, since many books and articles, published and forthcoming, have already done that. For present purposes, however, we highlight a transition over the last few decades from a concentration on the role of narrowly defined economic factors to a focus on the significance of various social structures and culture in providing the conditions conducive to economic development.[3] Arguments based on conditions such as favorable natural resources (including accessible coal and iron, in the case of Britain), high rates of capital formation, and extensive markets or other circumstances that encourage a faster pace of technological change, which had long been central to our understanding of why some economies enjoyed better performance, have been replaced (or supplemented) by arguments concerned with how differences across societies in political and cultural institutions arose, and how they influence the processes of growth.[4] Although we cannot conceive of processes of economic growth that do not involve institutional change, in this essay we outline some reasons why one should be cautious about grounding a theory of growth on institutions. We emphasize how very different institutional structures have often been found to be reasonable substitutes for each other, both in dissimilar as well as similar contexts. The historical record, therefore, does not seem to support the notion that any particular institution, narrowly defined, is indispensable for growth. Moreover, we discuss how the evidence that there are systematic patterns to the ways institutions evolve undercuts the idea that exogenous change in institutions is what powers growth. Institutions matter, but our thinking of how they matter should recognize that they are profoundly influenced by the political and economic environment, and that if any aspect of institutions is crucial for growth, it is that institutions change over time as circumstances change.

2

A basic categorization of explanations for economic growth would include economic, cultural, political, and institutional factors. The import of economic factors was much discussed in the ancient world, and amongst the numerous economic factors that have been considered since that time are: natural resources, such as the supplies of coal and iron; the opportunity to trade at low cost with

---

[3] Early 20th century scholars, such as Weber (1958 and 1961), emphasized the role of culture, but the focus turned to real economic factors by the second half of the century. For a more extensive discussion of how thinking changed over time, see Arndt 1978 and 1987.

[4] On the role of coal, see Kindleberger 1961, and the discussion by Parker in the same volume. Although attention to the significance of coal waned, it has recently revived with Wrigley 1988 and Pomeranz 2000. For discussion of the relative importance of changes in savings rates, or in investment opportunities, see Postan 1935. For discussions of how the pace of technological change was responsive to economic factors, such as the extent of, or access to, markets see Landes 1969 and Sokoloff 1988.

other regions or nations, which provides markets that encourage specialization in producing goods in which the economy has a comparative advantage (and perhaps stimulating more rapid technical progress) as well as serves as a source of imports that a nation may be incapable of producing; climate, which can influence productivity through a variety of mechanisms; colonial empire, which might be associated with especially high private or social returns to investment; and the role of population change. Some contend, for example, that rapid population growth has sometimes proved beneficial, fostering lower labor costs or the advantages in scale effects that come from higher total demand; others argue for the benefits of relatively slow growth in population, on the grounds that lower population density encourages higher per capita incomes and higher rates of capital formation. These, and other so-called economic explanations, say little explicitly about non-economic factors and institutions, although this does not mean that the latter are not implicit in the analysis.

Discussions of the role of non-economic factors (encompassing the cultural, political, and institutional) in accounting for differences across societies in economic development can also be traced back many centuries. Several of the classic theories for the rise of European capitalism and the onset of modern economic growth are based on conditions that clearly fall outside of the conventional economic sphere, such as the spread of particular religious beliefs, be it the Protestantism pointed to by Max Weber, the Judaism highlighted by Werner Sombart, or shifts in the orientation of dominant religions.[5] Other arguments stress the important contributions of the advance of scientific and rational thought, or the impact of changing tastes for consumer goods and the effects on choices between work and leisure on the supply and intensity of labor during early industrialization.[6] Changes in legal systems, in degrees of trust and the extent of social capital, and in the nature of political organization and the extent of democracy, have more recently been advocated as critical factors explaining differentials in economic performances.[7] Although changes in these kinds of circumstances, such as in religion, are generally treated as exogenous to the economy, the nature of the interaction between economic and so-called "non-economic" factors may be complex. The contrast in views between Weber and R.H. Tawney on the relationship between religious changes and the rise of capitalism in Britain, and in northern Europe more generally, for example, corresponds to similar debates over the sources of change in many other purportedly non-economic conditions relevant to economic growth.[8] Moreover, the implications of the very slow diffusion of cultural change (and of institutional change more generally) and economic growth around the world represent a puzzle for those who believe that introducing exogenous changes in these facets

---

[5] See the discussion of non-conformists in Britain in Weber 1958; Sombart 1969; McClelland 1961; and Fogel 2000.

[6] See Steuart 1767; Gilboy 1932; Nef 1958; deVries 1994; and Jacob 1997.

[7] See, the discussions of different views in Berman 1983; Putnam 2002; and O'Brien 1988.

[8] Whereas Weber is well known for his theory of how the content of Protestant thought may have encouraged believers to behave in ways we associate with capitalism, Tawney highlighted how economic change supported change in religious beliefs. See Weber 1958 and Tawney 1926.

Institutional and Non-Institutional Explanations of Economic Differences 643

should have significant, favorable effects and constitute a viable instrument of economic policy.[9]

Quite a wide range of non-economic conditions relevant for growth have featured in the debates over why Britain was the first industrial nation. Many can be subsumed in the blanket category of culture, where cultural factors are understood to include: religion, particularly the impact of non-conformists in the development of technology and entrepreneurship; the scientific spirit and the expansion of knowledge, including a willingness to search out new methods and technologies; and the emergence of an educational system that permitted a wide diffusion of information and skills among the population. Culture has also been defined to include family and kinship patterns; tastes and preferences regarding work versus leisure; time preferences determining the levels of savings and consumption; and the development of a wide-spread desire to financially profit-maximize or pursue material gain more generally. Proponents of the view that cultural change was responsible for economic change generally point to their coincidence in 18th century Britain, and presume that culture consists of behaviors and values that are determined independently of economic factors. This may, however, be an artificial distinction, because the economic effects of cultural factors, if not the cultural beliefs themselves, are often greatly influenced by the relative costs of different patterns of behavior and the amounts of income that people are willing to forgo to obtain chosen ends.[10]

The recent work on the significance of institutions for understanding why Britain industrialized first, and for understanding differences in economic performance more generally, gives relatively little attention to the role of culture per se. In emphasizing property rights and other aspects of the British legal framework, it breaks sharply from the previous stream of work on institutions by economists who emphasized culture in treating the evolution of economies, as part of a critique of classical economic theory.[11] Current thinking about institutions instead follows the pioneering approach of Douglass North in grounding the analysis of the causes and consequences of institutions and institutional change on theory.[12] This perspective defines institutions, though difficult to do with precision, as encompassing the specific organizations or rules that constrain and influence human behavior. A key aspect of these humanly devised rules is that they structure human actions by providing incentives that shape economic and political organization. Formal rules, plus the informal constraints that develop, influence the costs of production and of transaction within society. Among the institutions that are most important for economic performance are those involving the definition and enforcement of property rights, between the

---

[9] For a recent restatement of how the immutability of culture can explain continued backwardness, see Landes 1998.

[10] For the linkage between morality and economics, see the discussion of Quakers and slavery in Smith 1979. Also see Fogel 1989.

[11] See the discussion of institutions, and the approaches of the British and Germans, in Cunningham 1890–1892.

[12] See North 1981, 1988, and 1990; North and Thomas 1973; North and Weingast 1989; and Davis and North 1971.

government and private parties and between the individuals within a society. The link between appropriate institutions and economic growth is that well adapted institutions reduce the costs of production and distribution, allowing private agents more scope to benefit from specialization, investment, and trade. Institutions, as human-imposed constraints, are not the only constraints that society or private actors confront, since there are others due to the state of technological knowledge, demographic forces, nature (including climate and topography), as well as other features of the environment that may also have implications for the patterns of economic activity.[13]

Institutions, as described, play several roles in the economy. They influence the beliefs and behaviors of individuals and groups, and thus the preferences and priorities expressed through both private and public decisions. Another important role of institutions is providing for efficient property rights, trust, and effective incentives, and thus facilitating the organization and conduct of appropriate and constructive transactions and interactions among individuals and firms. Indeed it is claimed, by North and others, that it was sound property rights and incentive schemes made possible by its distinctive institutions that were key to Britain industrializing first.[14] No economic development is possible without secure property rights. The specification of formal rights is only one part of society's problem however. The nature of the enforcement of institutional provisions, both as to accepted legitimacy and effectiveness, is critical to the success of whatever institutions exist. Similarly, legislative decisions and judicial rulings can also influence outcomes, whether or not they seem consistent with the circumstances under which the respective institutions were originally adopted. Enforcement is sometimes bilateral, between individuals, with no government role to ensure compliance, but in other cases enforcement requires governmental participation and action.

Although those who stress the importance of the institutional framework have somewhat different concerns than those who highlight the significance of culture, the two perspectives share an emphasis on the extent to which "non-economic" variables evolve independently of the processes of economic growth. Indeed, proponents of both views champion how the appreciation of this pattern, as well as of the impacts of those variables on the economy, constitute a salient intellectual advance over the earlier (circa 1950s through 1970s) literature on economic development, which focused primarily on economic variables, such as natural resources, physical capital, human capital (mainly education), exchange rates, and technical change. That generation of economists certainly accepted the importance of institutions, culture, or political stability, but presumed either

---

[13] For a classic treatment of how factor endowments can help to shape culture and institutions, see Tocqueville 1835. For interesting discussions of the influences of factor endowments and political forces, see Brenner 1985; Engerman and Sokoloff 1997 and 2002; North 1981 and 1990; and North, Weingast, and Summerhill 2000.

[14] A major concern of the property rights literature is with private agents being secure from expropriation by the state. See North 1981; North and Weingast 1989; Knack and Keefer 1997; Acemoglu and Robinson 2000; and Haber, Razo, and Maurer 2003.

that the appropriate institutions and beliefs existed already, or else that they would evolve in constructive directions relatively easily as the economic factors that could generate economic growth were in place. Since economic forces obviously do not operate in a vacuum, it may have been difficult for them to conceive of a non-institutional interpretation of economic growth.

Even as a purely logical construct, a wholly non-institutional (or anti-institutional) explanation of economic growth seems implausible (as would an explanation that takes no account of real economic factors), but as discussed below, debate on the relative importance of institutional and non-institutional forces has continued.[15] The essential questions, thus, seem to us to be empirical. How much of the variation in economic performance over country and time can be attributed to differences in institutions, with pure economic factors constant or endogenous with respect to institutions, and how much is due to differences in the economic variables, with institutions constant or endogenous? What are the processes that govern the ways specific institutions evolve, and under what circumstances can the introduction of exogenous institutional changes be considered viable economic policies?

3

Although in principle these questions can be framed as empirical issues, it is far from easy to clearly distinguish between, or gauge the relative power of, the institutional and non-institutional explanations of economic differences. No one would claim that there is a general answer, and indeed few, if any, individual cases seem not to allow some role for each type of explanation. There has been considerable interest in recent years, however, in a manner of posing the problem that might appear to make the empirical work more tractable: are the key elements in determining institutions exogenous or endogenous? This distinction has been with us a long time, as in the debates over the superiority of British institutions, but has figured prominently in the study of how the various economies established as colonies by Europeans (or others) developed over time. Even in the absence of a substantial indigenous population in the area of settlement, the presence of one group in the colony, arriving from the metropolis, and another remaining in the metropolis, means that there were different circumstances for institutional development. In principle, therefore, a researcher could evaluate just how much of an impact the different circumstances had on the ways the institutions evolved. That many of the European countries established multiple colonies, in very different environments, further enhances the quality of the information arising from the natural experiment.

If the institutions in the colonies were, or remained, the same as those of the metropolitan nation (or perhaps the same as those of the indigenous societies

---

[15] Even Weber's discussion of the role of Calvinism points out that the relation "was true only when some possibility of capitalistic development in the areas in question was present." See Weber 1958, p. 190.

that predated the arrival of the Europeans), they might be regarded as exogenous. In such a case, the institutions could be reasonably interpreted as evolving independently of the conditions in the respective colonial economies, and systematic patterns in subsequent differences in economic performance across the economies could, after controlling for the purely economic factors, be attributed to institutions. If, however, the institutions in the colony diverged in ways that could be explained as adaptations by the respective population to the different environment, natural or human, then it would support the view that institutions were endogenous with respect to circumstances. Because institutions are human-fashioned structures that presumably reflect the efforts of populations trying to make the best of the opportunities and problems they face, most observers would be surprised if they were not at least partially endogenous. Indeed, most scholars feel that the institutions that emerged across the colonies established by the Europeans do seem to have varied systematically with aspects of the environment such as climate, land type, and natural resources. Some would go even further and suggest that the direction of institutional change is often endogenous to the growth process, as changes in technology and in incomes generate changes in tastes, changes in the returns to organizing production and transactions in various ways, and changes in patterns of behavior more generally.

To acknowledge that there is some endogeneity to institutions does not imply that institutions are unimportant, or that they have only a limited impact on economic performance. Endogenous institutions, once in place, can prove as crucial as if they were exogenous, and they might persist for as long or even longer. The key difference between those who contend that institutions are exogenous and those who argue they are endogenous is not with their impact and influence, but instead with where institutions come from and with the extent to which they are – or might be expected to be – revised over time.

It is widely recognized that it is sometimes useful to fix some types of institutions over time. Credible commitment to property rights is perhaps the classic example of the value of certainty about policy action.[16] More generally, however, allowing some flexibility in institutions, such that they can be altered to make it easier for private or public agents to take fuller advantage of the new opportunities that arise as technology or the environment changes, would normally be expected to foster better economic performance and more rapid growth. Among the many such innovations in institutions that could be cited to illustrate the utility of institutions changing as conditions change are: those that created the modern patent system; those that extended suffrage to a broad range of the population; those that provided tax-supported primary and secondary schools that were free to those who chose to attend; the introduction of taxes on income; and those that had profound impacts on the structure of financial markets and institutions (such as the introduction of limited liability for shareholders in corporations, the establishment and evolution of public agencies to regulate the issuance and trading of securities, and the establishment of central or quasi-central banks such as the Federal Reserve or the Bank of England).

[16] North and Weingast 1989.

Determining the optimum degree of flexibility, and designing mechanisms well suited to respond constructively to ever-changing circumstances with institutional change, are complex issues. While some see the role of constitutional provisions as a means of ensuring stability in the decision-making process and institutions more generally, most constitutions do have provisions for amendments, and allow some degree of legislative and governmental flexibility in setting the legal structure. Allowance for modifications to the laws need not harm the potential for growth, nor even yield instability, particularly given that the voting and other costs of implementing changes are typically high.[17] Indeed, there are likely more cases of how nations and economies suffered from inflexible institutions than from excessive flexibility.[18]

Perhaps the most important elements of institutional structures are those that ensure an ability to adapt to different conditions and to adjust to new circumstances as seems necessary, rather than those that entail the retention and maintenance of any specific set of policies. The capability for adaptation may ultimately be more significant for economic growth than the continuation of any particular set of beliefs, rules, or behavior. Among the characteristics of a society that might be expected to enhance institutional flexibility are a population's level of education, their political liberties, the degree of decentralization in political or economic structures, and the extent of competition within and across polities. Some of these conditions may be relevant in considering the case of European expansion, where colonies were established in a wide range of environments, and settlers had to grapple with new sorts of climates, soil types, natural resources, and economic problems. As shall be discussed below, although there were surely some specific cultural carryovers from Europe early in the settlement process, it is not clear that these factors were immutable or remained unchanged for long periods. The confrontation with new environments led to many adaptations, adjustments, and innovations in institutions, as colonial populations sought to make the most out of opportunities for economic improvement in circumstances that were unfamiliar, or at least different from those that had shaped the evolution of institutions in the Old World.

Another issue that is central to understanding how institutions matter for growth concerns the likelihood that no one particular narrowly-specified institution is required, as there are often alternative institutional forms or structures that are reasonable substitutes for each other and may achieve similar economic performance. Those who hold this view that non-optimal institutions may still be consistent with high rates of economic growth, though perhaps not the highest rate that was possible, often point to the stark contrasts across industrialized countries in the importance of banks relative to securities markets in financial intermediation, in the reliance on common or civil law, in how bankruptcy laws

---

[17] In some cases of change there may be required compensation to be paid to those whose condition is weakened, requiring increased taxation of other members of the population. Nearly all serf and slavery systems that ended during the 19th century did so with compensation paid to property holders, not laborers, but there was no compensation of losers when the slave trade was ended.

[18] See the discussions in Elbaum and Lazonick 1986.

balance the rights of creditors and debtors, in systems and levels of taxation, and in the division of power between the executive, the legislature, and political party structures. These and many other examples, historical and contemporary, suggest the usefulness of institutions generally in helping societies take advantage of the opportunities the environment offers them, but support the idea that no single institutional solution is crucial. In this way, the role of institutions might be considered analogous to the role of technology, in that the processes of change are important but no single method of accomplishing a goal is indispensable.[19]

A perhaps more serious issue is that among the feasible set of institutional solutions to a general problem, different approaches may have different implications for different segments of the population. Depending upon the manner in which institutions evolve, or are designed, in a society, they may develop to favor the interests of more powerful groups at the expense of others, or even of the population at large. For example, elites might prefer policies that raise their share of national income, even if they reduce long-run rates of growth. The nature of the political power structure in society is critical in determining which institutions are adopted. The suffrage, or the distribution of political influence more generally, may be rather broad and inclusive, with a relatively large share of the population able to vote.[20] Or, alternatively, the franchise may be limited, by requirements of literacy, wealth, nationality, age, and gender, with only a small minority of the population able to vote and to directly influence policy. When the suffrage is restricted, many members of society have only very limited political influence and no direct voice in establishing the institutional framework. Even a very small segment of the population, but one with highly disproportionate political power, would be able to establish institutions, legal codes, and property rights regimes that serve their own interests, and be able to exclude other members of society from benefits.[21] Thus, there could well be a well-defined and enforced set of property rights, but one coincident with a large component of the population being outsiders to decision-making in society.[22]

---

[19] Thus, as suggested by Lance Davis and North, evaluating institutional change may be subject to the same type of benefit-cost analysis as are other economic factors. See Davis and North 1971.

[20] See the discussions of the evolution of restrictions on suffrage in Engerman and Sokoloff 2001; and Keyssar 2000.

[21] Of course, other conditions matter as well. Where there is extreme economic inequality, for example, an elite might be able to leverage its wealth into disproportionate political influence through informal channels. Another example of context mattering is where labor is scarce, such as on a frontier. The desire of an elite, even one with a monopoly on political voice, to attract migrants might lead to policies that groups that have no formal representation value. For a discussion of how this might have operated on the U.S. frontier, see Engerman and Sokoloff 2001.

[22] In most cases, we would expect that groups with no formal political influence would have quite circumscribed access to scarce resources. This limited access might be due to the laws explicitly favoring the dominant groups, even if the property rights allowed the "outsiders" were enforceable. A de facto limited access might, however, arise if the outside group lacked the financial or other resources necessary to take advantage of an opportunity they had a de jure legal right too. Thus, even though all citizens might be entitled to bring civil suits to enforce contracts, the poor may find themselves less able to act on this

Slave societies in the Americas often had well-defined institutions and property rights, and were capable of rapid economic growth, but part of their population had no rights and no means to obtain any. They provide a powerful example, albeit an extreme one, of how the determination of the size and nature of the elite groups, by political, economic, and/or military means, is critical to the establishment of institutions. Being excluded from voting does not necessarily mean a failure to benefit from economic change, nor that there will not be subsequent improvements in the rights to suffrage, but the limited nature of the decision-making group still raises important issues for our understanding of the distribution of rewards from economic activity. More generally, the observation that societies vary in how much influence different segments of the population can exert in shaping institutions implies that there may be systematic patterns in how flexible they are in adapting (or innovating) their institutions to enhance the ability of their populations to take advantage of new opportunities created by changes in the environment.

4

It is no doubt easier to isolate the effect of institutions if we believe that they are exogenously determined by the forces of past history or by forces outside of the current economy. Among the factors that have sometimes been suggested as playing this role are: externally generated changes in mentalité due to change in religious belief or secular attitudes; the outcome of a military conflict, either due to externally generated changes in the power structure or of internal revolutionary actions that altered the balance of political power; the non-military introduction of new foreign influence and contacts, reflecting, in part, improvements in transportation and communication; and, as shall be discussed in more detail below, the settling of new areas by people from a distant metropolis, whose institutions could be regarded as exogenous to the new area of settlement. In this context we consider non-institutional explanations to be not an absence of institutions (since that is not possible), but the presence of institutions regarded as endogenous to the socio-economic process, even when the circumstances giving rise to the institutions are themselves exogenous to the economy (as, e.g., climate and natural resources).

In evaluating whether institutions are endogenous, there are several approaches that could be taken. One concerns the impact of resources and natural and human endowments upon institutions. A number of scholars have recently argued that there were systematic patterns in the types of institutions that evolved as settlers in European colonies adjusted to conditions that differed

right. The case of married women is an interesting one to consider in this regard, as in the United States (and many other countries) the law allowed them only very limited rights as to owning property or entering into contracts as compared to those allowed men or single women, until the second half of the 19th century. See Khan 1996.

from those of the metropolis in terms of disease environments and economic opportunities.[23] Subjecting this notion to empirical testing is complicated by the enormous range of institutions that attention could be directed at, some of which reflect metropolitan carryovers, others of which developed very differently in the colonies than they did in the metropolis. Metropolitan institutions did not necessarily disappear in the process of settlement, but many were modified depending on the conditions of the particular settlement. Thus British New World colonies may have employed British law, and French colonies continued French legal institutions, but British and French temperate zone colonies differed in many important regards from the respective Caribbean colonies. French and British Caribbean colonies had greater similarities than they did with either their mainland counterparts or the metropolis. And, while the initial controls over free white labor may have been much the same in all of the colonies, only some British colonies and only some French colonies came to rely on free, rather than slave, labor.[24] Climate and resources were the most powerful determinants of the geographic incidence of slave labor, irrespective of the metropolitan institutional structure. Slavery was legal in all the British colonies until the Revolutionary War, and differences in legal circumstances did not account for the major differences in its prevalence across them, such as between New England and the British West Indies.[25]

Another approach to the question of whether institutions are endogenous is to consider whether economic growth itself influences people's attitudes, and the nature of the economy's institutions. Does the economy itself contain the seeds of its own limitations, whether due to its failure or its successes? Karl Marx is certainly the most prominent of historical economists that have posited a sequence of self-generated endogenous changes in society, from feudalism to capitalism to socialism, with each of the first two stages being successful at first but then failing due to internal contradictions. Joseph Schumpeter claimed that the declining belief in the value of capitalism, which developed with economic growth, weakened capitalism's survival power, and he expected the "march into socialism" to occur based upon the economy's success. Mancur Olson argued that as economies develop over time, vested interests operating in their own self-interest emerge and cause a reduction in the future growth of the economy through their success at rent seeking. Other notions of how self-generated changes in the economy stimulate institutional change highlight the impact of technological change on the scale of enterprise and the development of bureaucracies in business and government.

Scholars interested in how institutions evolve have recently devoted much attention to the contrasts between colonial and metropolitan influences on

---

[23] See Engerman and Sokoloff 1997 and 2002; Acemoglu, Johnson, and Robinson 2001 and 2002; and Easterly and Levine 2003.

[24] For an interesting analysis of adjustments to the laws governing slavery, see Cottrell 2001.

[25] For a discussion of the fascinating case of how a colony established with a prohibition on slavery came to have it lifted, see Wood 1984.

institutions in newly settled areas. A long-standing disagreement, tracing back centuries, regarding the thirteen colonies that became the United States has been the causes of North-South differences in economic and demographic structures, including the explanation of the differences in the relative importance of slavery. Did those settling in different parts of the mainland arrive with rather different cultural patterns from Britain, differences that persisted after settlement, or did the various colonists from Britain arrive with basically similar cultural beliefs, but then adjusted their institutions once established in the New World and confronted with a rather different set of conditions?[26] The evidence to date seems to favor the latter view. Not only has recent work demonstrated that even the Puritans were deeply influenced by the environment in selecting institutions for their two New World colonies, but studies of those Englishmen who came to populate the various settlements in the Americas emphasize how they were drawn from roughly the same social classes.[27] In the words of Edward Channing:

> "Historical writers have been altogether too prone to draw a hard and fast line of demarcation between the settlers of the Southern colonies and those who founded colonies north of the fortieth parallel... It is sometimes said that the Northern colonist came to the New World for conscience sake and the Southern planters sought wealth alone; but no such generalization can truthfully be made. Moreover, it is oftentimes the custom to point out some mysterious differences between the Virginian and the New Englander, which can be expressed by the words 'cavalier' and 'Puritan'... No such characterization is possible."[28]

This perspective receives strong support from the record of slavery in the Americas. The basis for the success (to the owners) of slave labor in one area, and its failure in another, depended less on the initial attitudes of most settlers than upon the influence of climate and soil resources on the nature of those crops which could be grown and the technology and scales of efficient crop production. Wherever the soils and climates were suitable for growing sugar, the most valuable commodity in world trade during the 17th and 18th centuries and a crop that could be produced at lowest cost on large slave plantations (under the gang labor system, which allowed owners to achieve very high labor intensity), slavery became the dominant institution of labor (and those of African descent a dominant share of the population). Elsewhere, where soils and climates favored agricultural products (such as grains and hays) where the gang labor system and slave labor offered no particular advantages, landowners had to rely more on free (often their own) labor, as the productivity of slaves in such settings would not warrant the high prices for slaves that prevailed on world markets. The populations of these settlements accordingly came to be much more homogeneous in wealth, human capital, ethnicity, and other dimensions. Thus, the factor endowments in the various colonies had a major impact on

---

[26] See, for example, Greene 1988, 1993, and 2002; and Fischer 1989.
[27] Kupperman 1993.
[28] Channing 1926, pp. 145–146.

determining which labor institutions were dominant, the distribution of rewards between laborers and landowners, and on the nature of political participation and decision-making. Because slavery was legal in all of the European colonies in the Americas, it is evident that not only did these natural forces lead to differences in institutions, but they also led to different outcomes from similar institutions. Although the Old World background was surely important, it is difficult to explain the extreme differences among the various areas within each colonial empire without reference to the effects of the New World circumstances.

The early history of the New World colonies established by the European nations permits one to examine some of the implications of focusing on exogenous factors in institutional development, as opposed to viewing institutions as largely endogenous. The locations of settlements were themselves subject to some choice, based on the demographic and economic characteristics of different locations. Moreover, the pattern of initial settlement was modified over time, as settlers learned more about prospects in different areas. In the settlement of the Caribbean by the British and the French, for example, the adjustments in terms of crops and labor institutions that took place over the first half-century of settlement were rather different from those that were to emerge in subsequent years. The problems that arise from selection by the colonizing powers notwithstanding, the natural experiment arising from the variety of settling metropolises – including Spain, Portugal, Britain, France, and Holland – and the extreme diversity of environments found among the colonies makes for a wonderful laboratory in which to study the relationships between factor endowments, institutions, and economic growth. It should not be surprising that many scholars have been attracted to work in this laboratory. Their work, of course, does not amount to a comparison of institutional and non-institutional factors in economic growth, since everyone agrees on the importance of institutions. Rather the work has sought to determine whether institutions can be understood as exogenous to the circumstances or economic system, or whether the environment or circumstances more broadly exert a powerful influence on how institutions emerge and evolve over time. Put simply, where do institutions come from?

A key economic question is the explanation for the post-1900 differences in levels of per capita income between the countries of mainland North America and those of Latin America (Table 3), differences that were much smaller during the colonial period. A closely related issue is why Latin America is the region of the world today with the most extreme inequality in income. Since the nations of South and Central America were settled mainly by the Spanish (the Portuguese settled Brazil), and the United States and Canada mainly by the British (pre-1763 Canada by the French and pre-1664 New York by the Dutch, among the relatively less dominant settling nations), the traditional, and still popular, explanation holds that the different cultures, religions, and institutions of Britain and Spain could alone explain the divergent paths of economic development. Since there were sharp contrasts between the home countries of Britain and Spain in terms of economic and political structures, it is argued that the transfer of Old

Table 3. Per capita GDP in selected new world economies, 1700–1997.

Country	GDP per capita relative to the United States			
	1700	1800	1900	1997
Argentina	—	102	52	35
Barbados	150	—	—	51
Brazil	—	50	10	22
Chile	—	46	38	42
Cuba	167	112	—	—
Mexico	89	50	35	28
Peru	—	41	20	15
Canada	—	—	67	76
United States[a]	550	807	3,859	20,230

Source: Sokoloff and Engerman 2000.
[a] U.S. per capita GDP is measured in 1985 dollars.

World institutions established the behavior of the economies and societies of the colonies in the New World, as differences in property rights determination and enforcement, legal frameworks more generally, economic goals, and in religious beliefs were carried over, with little or no modification, into the new areas of settlement. The institutions that failed to generate sustained economic growth on the Iberian Peninsula likewise failed to do so in the New World, whereas the institutions that had evolved over centuries in Britain worked on both sides of the Atlantic. The logic is that either the political elites of the metropolis were carried over into the colonies, providing the political and legal framework for the successful carryover of institutions, or that the elites in the New World, though different from those of the metropolis, were able to use the same institutional structures to achieve similar ends by similar means.[29]

An alternative explanation, one that has gained an increasing number of adherents of late, focuses on the economic and geographic circumstances in the area of settlement, and their influence on the determination of institutions in the new areas. As with the previous argument, there is a long literature on the role of climate and resources in influencing institutions and economic development. While a most detailed examination was provided by Montesquieu in the 1740's, a similar argument was made considerably earlier by Plato.[30] The links include the nature of the effects of climate upon the willingness to work, the desire to emigrate or immigrate, the role played by slavery in society, and related economic concerns. Whether seen as the basic cause of the specific set

---

[29] It may be, however, that the distance between colony and homeland weakens the ability of the metropolis to control the settlers, weakening the nature of any transfer of political structure. See Greene 1988 and 2002. For the argument that the institutional heritage that British colonies drew on was more conducive to long-run growth than that the Spanish colonies worked from, see North 1988.

[30] See Montesquieu 1949; and Plato 1980, book five, section nine.

of institutions, or as a reason to modify some pre-existing set of exogenous institutions, settlement societies can be argued to have been significantly influenced by factors other than some unchanged metropolitan institutions. Indeed most settlements made dramatic changes in their institutions after they were first established, in the search for ways to enhance their profitability and survivability. The impact of climate and resources can also help to explain why the different areas settled by the same metropolitan power had rather different economic structures and performances (as, e.g., New England and the British West Indies), and why geographically contiguous and resource-similar areas settled by different metropolitan powers (as the British and French in the West Indies, as well as the Spanish, Danish, and Dutch there) came to resemble each other in many important ways. Indeed, recent scholarship has found strong evidence of the systematic effects of initial factor endowments on the types of institutions (including institutions involving suffrage and the conduct of elections, schooling, finance, the disposition of public lands, property rights, and intellectual property) that evolved in different colonies (and on long-term economic performance in these colonies), both in the Americas and elsewhere, and highlighted how limited is the explanatory power of national heritage.[31]

A specific example of how institutions can be altered to fit changing circumstances, and of how the distribution of power (both political and economic) as well as the environment influence outcomes, is provided by the adjustments in the societies of the Americas to the abolition of slavery.[32] This most dramatic institutional change of the 19th century was, almost everywhere, imposed on a resistant slaveholding class in the aftermath of armed conflict or by a government elected by a population dominated by non-slaveholders (including European parliaments). All New World societies ended slavery between 1777 and 1888, and the nature of the abolitions were similar with most providing

---

[31] There is some question of what the comparison of institutions would indicate if some different dates were used for the evaluation. Spain arrived in America earlier than the British, went to areas with greater wealth and resources, and it took about another hundred years before the British arrived and were forced to go to areas that they regarded as clearly less promising for economic growth. For a comparison based on the year 1700 we would find the Spanish position seemingly more favorable that that of the British, reflecting the early economic advantages of the areas of Spanish settlement, and, as pointed out by John TePaske, the Spanish had three successful centuries in the Americas, and the British only two. See TePaske 2002. Also see Engerman and Sokoloff 1997 and 2002; Acemoglu, Johnson and Robinson 2002; and Easterly and Levine 2003.

[32] The recent literature on the role of institutions in economic growth has raised important questions as to the extent to which political power is independent of economic power, and to the relative significance of political inequality and economic inequality for how institutions evolve. A full discussion of these issues is beyond the scope of this essay, but we would argue that although they are clearly related, and there is certainly an association across societies (or over time) between political power and economic power, the correlation is far from perfect and it is not all that uncommon for them to diverge. Their relative weight in the processes of institutional development likely varies with context. Moreover, some institutions may be more sensitive to political inequality, while others depend more on the extent of economic inequality. For example, the distribution of political influence would generally be expected to have a greater impact on public institutions, such as laws, and the distribution of wealth matter relatively more for the kinds of private institutions – such as financial institutions – that evolve.

Institutional and Non-Institutional Explanations of Economic Differences   655

Table 4. Land/Labor ratios, changes in sugar production in the British slaves colonies prior to and after emancipation, and contract labor immigration.

	Land/Labor Ratio[1]	% Change in Annual Sugar Prod. 1824–33 to 1839–46	Ratio of Sugar Production in 1887–96 to 1839–46	Contract Labor Immigration 1834–1918 (gross inflow)
Antigua	3.1	+8.7%	1.5	2,600
Barbados	1.7	+5.5	3.5	—
St. Kitts[2]	2.9	+3.8	2.7	2,900
Nevis	5.0	−43.1	(2)	(2)
Trinidad	47.7	+21.7[4]	3.0	157,700
British Guiana	832.4	−43.0	3.4	301,000
Mauritius	8.0	+54.3	3.1	451,800
Dominica	16.3	−6.4	0.7	6,000
St. Lucia	15.5	−21.8	1.7	5,200
Montserrat	4.6	−43.7	2.5	—
St. Vincent	5.7	−47.5	0.7	5,600
Tobago	8.8	−47.5	(4)	(4)
Jamaica	12.2	−51.2	0.6	53,900
Grenada	6.3	−55.9	0.0	6,200

Source: Engerman 1996.
[1] Square Miles per thousand total population, just prior to abolition.
[2] Nevis data merged with St. Kitts after 1882.
[4] Trinidad output did decline slightly after abolition, and it was not until 1845 that the 1834 level of output was regained. Tobago data merged with Trinidad after 1891. The 1877–86 level of sugar production in Tobago was about one-third less than it was in 1824–33.

some form of compensation, in cash, bonds, or labor time to the slaveowners, with very little or nothing going to the former slaves.[33] Nevertheless there were some striking differences in the range of post-emancipation responses. In the British West Indies, for example, slavery was abolished by 1834 and all colonial governments had the same basic goal of inducing labor to work on plantations and imposed legislation to try to accomplish this end. Different environments led to different outcomes, however, as evident in the corresponding variation with the ratio of land to labor (see Table 4).[34] Areas of high population density such as Barbados maintained plantation systems and high sugar output, while those with low population density, with abundant frontier land, initially saw the end of the plantation system and a decline in sugar output. In those cases where the islands had been relatively unproductive, sugar output continued to decline and the plantation system was never re-introduced. However, in those

---

[33] The United States, in 1865, was the one nation to free its slaves without any form of compensation provided in the form of cash, apprenticeship, or a "law of the free womb", which required the free-born offspring of slaves to labor for the mother's master into their late teens or twenties. Even Haiti agreed to pay compensation to the French after 1825, as a condition for the right to engage in trade with France.

[34] See Engerman 1982 and 1996. For a classic treatment of the relationship between the land to labor ratio and institutions, see Domar 1970.

areas where land was highly productive and which had been growing rapidly before emancipation (such as Trinidad and British Guiana), plantation systems returned in several decades, but ones based on indentured labor drawn mainly from India, and not on ex-slaves. Thus the elite's ability to achieve their desired end, extracting the returns to the land they owned, was influenced by various other conditions, including resource endowments, and their efforts to achieve their goals, subject to the dissimilar constraints they faced, led to differences in institutional development.

Another example of how the evolution of institutions across New World societies reflected adjustments to different or changed circumstances is provided by the history of how broadly the franchise was extended over time and what fractions of respective populations actually voted in elections. Since most of the societies in the Americas had achieved independence from their colonial masters, and were at least nominal democracies, by the middle of the 19th century, suffrage institutions had a direct bearing on the extent to which elites based largely on wealth, human capital, and gender held disproportionate political power in their respective countries, and on their ability to shape government policies. The ability and inclination of the elites to maintain disproportionate political influence through the formal rules associated with the electoral process varied with a variety of circumstances. Among these circumstances was the extent of inequality in wealth, human capital, and political influence that existed at the time of independence, when there were generally conventions held to draw up constitutions for the new nations. One simple or straightforward explanation of this pattern is that the greater the disparity in resources (which we have argued in other work was due to factor endowments during initial colonization), the greater was the ability of an elite to frame the rules in such a way as to preserve their relative political power.[35] Among the other factors that appear to have had significant effects on the way institutions evolved, however, was the relative scarcity of labor. Although elites were generally reluctant to share their access to political influence and economic opportunity with other segments of the population, they were more likely to do so in settings where they would benefit from attracting or retaining a scarce resource – labor.

The evidence on the evolution of suffrage institutions in the New World is quite consistent with this view. Summary information on how the right to vote was restricted across New World societies in the 19th and early 20th centuries is reported in Table 5. The estimates reveal that the United States and Canada were the clear leaders in doing away with restrictions based on wealth and literacy and introducing the secret ballot, and much higher fractions of the populations voted in these countries than anywhere else in the Americas. These societies were distinguished for their relative equality, population homogeneity, and scarcity of labor, and it is notable that others of British heritage, such as Barbados, generally retained stringent restrictions on the franchise well into the 20th century.

---

[35] For discussions of how factor endowments are the principal source of the differences in inequality, see Engerman and Sokoloff 1997 and 2002.

Table 5. Laws Governing the Franchise and the Extent of Voting in Selected New World Countries, 1840–1940.

Period and country	Year	Lack of secrecy in balloting	Wealth requirement	Literacy requirement	Percent of the population voting
1840–80					—
Chile	1869	No	Yes	Yes	1.6
	1878	No	No	No[a]	—
Costa Rica	1890	Yes	Yes	Yes	—
Ecuador	1848	Yes	Yes	Yes	0.0
	1856	Yes	Yes	Yes	0.1
Mexico	1840	Yes	Yes	Yes	—
Peru	1875	Yes	Yes	Yes	—
Uruguay	1840	Yes	Yes	Yes	—
	1880	Yes	Yes	Yes	—
Venezuela	1840	Yes	Yes	Yes	—
	1880	Yes	Yes	Yes	—
Canada	1867	Yes	Yes	No	7.7
	1878	No	Yes	No	12.9
United States	1850	No	No	No	12.9
	1880	No	No	No	18.3
1881–1920					
Argentina	1896	Yes	Yes	Yes	1.8[b]
	1916	No	No	No	9.0
Brazil	1894	Yes	Yes	Yes	2.2
	1914	Yes	Yes	Yes	2.4
Chile	1881	No	No	No	3.1
	1920	No	No	Yes	4.4
Colombia	1918[c]	No	No	No	6.9
Costa Rica	1912	Yes	Yes	Yes	—
	1919	Yes	No	No	10.6
Ecuador	1888	No	Yes	Yes	2.8
	1894	No	No	Yes	3.3
Mexico	1920	No	No	No	8.6
Peru	1920	Yes	Yes	Yes	—
Uruguay	1900	Yes	Yes	Yes	—
	1920	No	No	No	13.8
Venezuela	1920	Yes	Yes	Yes	—
Canada	1911	No	No	No	18.1
	1917	No	No	No	20.5
United States	1900	No	No	Yes[d]	18.4
	1920	No	No	Yes	25.1
1921–40					
Argentina	1928	No	No	No	12.8
	1937	No	No	No	15.0
Bolivia	1951	—	Yes	Yes	4.1
Brazil	1930	Yes	Yes	Yes	5.7
Colombia	1930	No	No	No	11.1
	1936	No	No	No	5.9

(*Continued*)

Table 5. (Continued)

Period and country	Year	Lack of secrecy in balloting	Wealth requirement	Literacy requirement	Percent of the population voting
Chile	1920	No	No	Yes	4.4
	1931	No	No	Yes	6.5
	1938	No	No	Yes	9.4
Costa Rica	1940	No	No	No	17.6
Ecuador	1940	No	No	Yes	3.3
Mexico	1940	No	No	No	11.8
Peru	1940	No	No	Yes	—
Uruguay	1940	No	No	No	19.7
Venezuela	1940	No	Yes	Yes	—
Canada	1940	No	No	No	41.1
United States	1940	No	No	Yes	37.8

Source: Engerman, Haber, and Sokoloff 2000.

[a] After having eliminated wealth and education requirements in 1878, Chile instituted a literacy requirement in 1885, which seems to have been responsible for a sharp decline in the proportion of the population that was registered to vote.

[b] This figure is for the city of Buenos Aires, and it likely overstates the proportion who voted at the national level.

[c] The information on restrictions refers to national laws. The 1863 Constitution empowered provincial state governments to regulate electoral affairs. Afterwards, elections became restricted (in terms of the franchise for adult males) and indirect in some states. It was not until 1948 that a national law established universal adult male suffrage throughout the country. This pattern was followed in other Latin American countries, as it was in the United States and Canada to a lesser extent.

[d] Connecticut and Massachusetts introduced literacy requirements during the 1850s. Sixteen other states, seven southern and eleven non-southern, introduced literacy requirements between 1889 and 1926.

Moreover, it is striking that the leaders in extending the suffrage in South and Central America, such as Uruguay, Argentina, and Costa Rica, are generally regarded as having been historically the most egalitarian of Latin American societies, and having initial factor endowments most closely resembling those of the United States and Canada.

The contrast between North and South America in the application of binding restrictions on the franchise was not so evident at the outset. Despite the sentiments popularly attributed to the Founding Fathers, voting in the United States was largely a privilege reserved for white men with significant amounts of property until early in the nineteenth century. By 1815, only four states had adopted universal white male suffrage, but as the movement to do away with political inequality gained strength, the rest of the country followed suit: virtually all new entrants to the Union extended voting rights to all white men (with explicit racial restrictions generally introduced in the same state constitutions that did away with economic requirements), and older states revised their laws in the wake of protracted political debates (see Table 6). The key states of New York and Massachusetts made the break with wealth restrictions in the 1820s, and the shift to full white adult male suffrage was largely complete by the late 1850s (with Rhode Island, Virginia, and North Carolina being the laggards).

Table 6. Summary of economic-based qualifications for suffrage across the United States, 1787–1860.

	Qualification in 1787 or Year of Entry	Year Economic Qualifications Ended, or Qualif. in 1860
Original Thirteen		
New Hampshire	Tax	1792
Massachusetts	Property	1821 (prop), tax req. in 1860
Rhode Island	Property	1842 (prop), tax req. in 1860
Connecticut	Property	1818 (prop), 1845 (tax)
New York	Property	1821 (prop), 1826 (tax)
New Jersey	Property	1807 (prop), 1844 (tax)
Pennsylvania	Tax	tax req. in 1860
Delaware	Property	1792 (prop), tax req. in 1860
Maryland	Property	1802
Virginia	Property	1850
North Carolina	Property	1856 (prop), tax req. in 1860
South Carolina	Tax	1810 (tax)
Georgia	Property	1789 (prop), 1798 (tax)
New States		
Vermont	none (1791)	
Kentucky	none (1792)	
Tennessee	none (1796)	
Ohio	Tax (1803)	1851 (tax)
Louisiana	Tax (1812)	1845 (tax)
Indiana	none (1816)	
Mississippi	Tax (1817)	1832 (tax)
Illinois	none (1818)	
Maine	none (1819)	
Alabama	none (1819)	
Missouri	none (1820)	

Source: Engerman and Sokoloff 2001.

The relatively more egalitarian populations of the western states, which were anxious to increase their populations, were the clear leaders in the movement. The rapid extension of access to the franchise in these areas not coincidentally paralleled liberal policies toward public schools and access to land, as well as other policies that were expected to be attractive to potential migrants. The frontier states in the West continued to be labor scarce, with low female to male ratios, and it is perhaps not surprising that late in the 19th century they were the leaders in extending suffrage to women, as well as in greatly strengthening the property rights available to married women.

Similar political movements with similar outcomes followed with a short lag in the various Canadian provinces, but the analogous developments did not occur in Latin America until the twentieth century. As a result, through 1940 the United States and Canada routinely had proportions voting that were 50 to 100 percent higher than their most progressive neighbors to the South, three times higher than Mexico, and up to five to ten times higher than countries such as Brazil, Bolivia, Ecuador, and even Chile. It is remarkable that as late as 1900, none of the countries in Latin America had the secret ballot or more than a miniscule fraction of the population casting votes. The great majority of European nations, as well as the United States and Canada, achieved secrecy in balloting and universal adult male suffrage long before other countries in the western hemisphere, and the proportions of the populations voting in the former were always higher, often four to five times higher, than those in the latter. Although many factors may have contributed to the low levels of participation in South America and the Caribbean, wealth and literacy requirements were serious binding constraints well into the 20th century.

What accounts for this pattern of diffusion of universal male suffrage across New World societies? One obvious explanation, noted above, is that differences in the degrees of inequality in wealth, human capital, and political influence were related to the likelihood of adopting such an institutional change. The cross-sectional patterns, as well as the histories indicating that the attainment of universal male suffrage and of the secret ballot was often the product of a long series of hard fought political battles, with the elites more likely to be opposed to liberalizing the franchise, are certainly consistent with this view.[36] Another important factor, however, was the desire to attract immigrants. It is striking that pioneers in extending suffrage, such as new (those after the original thirteen) states in the United States, Argentina, and Uruguay, did so during periods in which they hoped to attract migrants, such that the rights to suffrage formed part of a package of policies thought to be potentially attractive to those contemplating relocation. When elites – such as large holders of land or other assets – desire common men to locate in the polity, they thus may choose to extend access to privileges and opportunities without threat of civil disorder; indeed, a polity (or one set of elites) may find itself competing with another to attract the labor or whatever else is desired. Alternative explanations, such as the importance of national heritage, are not very useful in identifying why Argentina, Uruguay, and Costa Rica pulled so far ahead of their Latin American neighbors, or why other British colonies in the New World lagged behind Canada.[37]

How broadly a society chooses to extend the franchise is a fundamental political arrangement. Many scholars, including us, have noted that differences across polities in suffrage institutions, as well as changes over time, can often be related to decisions about government policies, such as what to do about public lands, what types of schooling and other public services and investments to support (and how to raise the revenue for them), and how to regulate financial

---

[36] The achievements of a broadening of the formal requirements for suffrage, as well as of the more administrative procedures governing the conduct of elections, tend to overstate the reduction in the extent of political inequality. Economic elites always enjoy disproportionate informal political influence, and there is likely more scope for them to bypass formal procedures and channels in contexts where there is extreme inequality. Hence, it may not be so surprising that the outcomes did not improve more than they did after the extension of the suffrage in many of the Latin American societies.

[37] For a fuller discussion of the issues involved in the evolution of suffrage institutions in the New World, see Engerman and Sokoloff 2001. Also see Acemoglu and Robinson 2000, for treatment of the somewhat different pattern in Europe.

institutions. As important as it is, however, the breadth of the franchise, or even the rate of participation in elections, is far from the only feature of political systems that matters. Many authoritarian governments stage elections, and voting is often as irrelevant in these contexts as it was in the Soviet Union. Hence, although we have highlighted the uneven evolution of suffrage institutions across the Americas, we do not find it at all surprising that the attainment of something approximating universal adult suffrage throughout the hemisphere has thus far failed to dramatically reduce the disparities in the structure of institutions or in economic performance across countries. Not only is much more involved in determining political outcomes, but there are many factors other than the distribution of political influence that shape the development of institutions.

This brief excursion into specific historical examples of the evolution of key institutions illustrates several key points. The first obvious implication is that important changes in institutions, such as the adaptations to the plantation system after the abolition of slavery in the British West Indies and the expansion of the fraction of the population eligible to vote, do occur, and in different directions in different countries and contexts. A second observation is that there appears to be a substantial systematic component to the variation in how these institutions evolved, with significant explanatory power coming from circumstances that were likely largely exogenous to previously existing institutions.

5

There are always institutions present, and we cannot conceive of a framework for making sense of the processes of economic development that does not include a role for them. There is, moreover, no doubt that for any given society some institutions may limit the extent to which it realizes its potential economic output, while alternatives might do better. That being said, however, it is unclear how firmly theories of economic growth can be grounded on institutions. Economists do not have a very good understanding of where institutions come from, or why some societies have institutions that seem conducive to growth, while others are burdened by institutions less favorable for economic performance. Until they do, it will be quite difficult to specify the precise role of institutions in processes of growth.

As we have sought to highlight in this essay, what little we presently know about the evolution of institutions suggests caution about making strong claims about their relationship to growth. First, it is clear that very different institutional structures often seem to be reasonable substitutes in being conducive to growth, both in dissimilar as well as in similar contexts. Narrow definitions of institutional requirements for growth do not, accordingly, seem appropriate. Second, the case for attributing growth to institutions is weaker if institutions are endogenous rather than exogenous, and the evidence that there are systematic patterns to the ways institutions evolve makes the latter view problematic. The recent studies of the natural experiment in institutional development provided by the European colonization of the Americas (and of many other parts of the globe), for example, imply that the broad environment (reflecting factor endowments, social arrangements, or technology) had powerful effects on the sorts of institutions that evolved in respective colonies. Institutions obviously matter for growth, but the way we understand how they matter will be somewhat different if the agents and other forces shaping institutions are responsive to the conditions they face than if institutions develop independently of (or could be imposed in any) context.

The recognitions that the institutional structure appropriate for one environment may not be appropriate for another, and that the history of institutions in high-performing societies is one of change over time in response to changing circumstances, suggest a different perspective on the relation between institutions and growth. Although we all understand that there are favorable aspects to governments making credible commitments to various obligations or arrangements they enter into, such as enforcement of property rights, it is also clear that in theory one would want institutions to vary over time and place with the environment, technology, and values. One might, therefore, think of societies with institutions conducive for growth as being those that have exhibited greater institutional flexibility – where by institutional flexibility we mean the ease with which institutional adaptations that respond constructively to changes in circumstances are innovated and/or diffused. Societies with good institutions would, therefore, have institutions well adapted for economic performance in their specific settings because they had implemented a series of institutional modifications or innovations (public and private) that cumulatively generated improvements in welfare. Societies with bad institutions are those with institutional inflexibility, whose institutions did not respond constructively to take advantage of the opportunities created by their environment and state of knowledge. Such a framework would encourage scholars interested in the relation between institutions and growth to devote more attention to the factors influencing the rate and direction of institutional change, and rather less attention to the quest for a set of institutional structures that would be universally effective at promoting growth.

ACKNOWLEDGEMENTS

We would like to express deep appreciation for the research assistance of Elisa Mariscal, Patricia Juarez, and Luis Zegarra. We have also benefited from discussions with Daron Acemoglu, Lance Davis, David Dollar, David Eltis, Jeff Frieden, Avner Greif, Stephen Haber, Karla Hoff, Daniel Kaufmann, Zorina Khan, Naomi Lamoreaux, Frank Lewis, Peter Lindert, John Majewski, Douglass North, James Robinson, Jean-Laurent Rosenthal, Mary M. Shirley, Joel Slemrod, Peter Temin, John Wallis, and Jeffrey Williamson. We gratefully acknowledge the financial support we have received from the National Science

Foundation, as well as from the Academic Senate at the University of California, Los Angeles.

REFERENCES

Acemoglu, Daron and James A. Robinson. 2000. "Why Did Western Europe Extend the Franchise?" *Quarterly Journal of Economics* 115: 1167–1199.

Acemoglu, Daron and Simon Johnson, and James A. Robinson. 2001. "The Colonial Origins of Comparative Development: An Empirical Investigation". *American Economic Review* 91: 1369–1401.

―――. 2002. "Reversal of Fortune: Geography and Institutions in the Making of the Modern World Income Distribution". *Quarterly Journal of Economics* 117: 1231–1294.

Arndt, H. W. 1978. *The Rise and Fall of Economic Growth: A Study in Contemporary Thought*. Melbourne: Longman Cheshire.

―――. 1987. *Economic Development: The History of an Idea*. Chicago, IL: University of Chicago Press.

Berman, Harold J. 1983. *Law and Revolution: The Formulation of the Western Legal Tradition*. Cambridge, MA: Harvard University Press.

Brenner, Robert. 1985. "Agrarian Class Structure and Economic Development in Pre-Industrial Europe" in T. H. Aston and C. H. E. Philpin (eds.), *The Brenner Debate: Agrarian Class Structure and Economic Development in Pre-Industrial Europe*. Cambridge: Cambridge University Press.

Channing, Edward. 1926. *A History of the United States: Volume I*. New York: Macmillan.

Cottrell, Robert J. 2001. "The Long Lingering Shadow: Law, Liberalism, and Cultures of Racial Hierarchy and Identity in the Americas". *Tulane Law Review* 76: 11–79.

Cunningham, William. 1890–1892 [1882]. *The Growth of English Industry and Commerce*. 2 vols, 2nd edn. Cambridge: Cambridge University Press.

Davis, Lance E. and Douglass C. North. 1971. *Institutional Change and American Economic Growth*. Cambridge: Cambridge University Press.

De Vries, Jan. 1994. "The Industrial Revolution and the Industrious Revolution". *Journal of Economic History* 54: 249–270.

Domar, Evsey D. 1970. "The Causes of Slavery or Serfdom: A Hypothesis". *Journal of Economic History* 30: 18–32.

Easterly, William and Ross Levine. 2003. "Tropics, Germs, and Crops: The Role of Endowments in Economic Development". *Journal of Monetary Economics* 50: 3–39.

Elbaum, Bernard and William Lazonick. 1986. *The Decline of the British Economy*. Oxford: Clarendon Press.

Engerman, Stanley L. 1982. "Economic Adjustments to Emancipation in the United States and the British West Indies". *Journal of Interdisciplinary History* 12: 191–220.

―――. 1996. "The Land and Labour Problem at the Time of the Legal Emancipation of the West Indian Slaves" in Roderick A. McDonald (ed.), *West Indies Accounts: Essays in the History of the British Caribbean and the Atlantic Economy in Honor of Richard Sheridan*. Kingston: University of West Indies Press.

Engerman, Stanley L., Stephen Haber, and Kenneth L. Sokoloff. 2000. "Inequality, Institutions, and Differential Paths of Growth Among New World Economies" in Claude Menard (ed.), *Institutions, Contracts, and Organizations*. Cheltenham, UK: Edward Elgar.

Engerman, Stanley L. and Kenneth L. Sokoloff. 1997. "Factor Endowments, Institutions, and Differential Paths of Growth Among New World Economies: A View from Economic

Historians of the United States" in Stephen Haber (ed.), *How Latin America Fell Behind.* Stanford, CA: Stanford University Press.
———. 2001. "The Evolution of Suffrage Institutions in the Americas". Working Paper 8512. Cambridge, MA: National Bureau of Economic Research.
———. 2002. "Factor Endowments, Inequality and Paths of Development Among New World Economies". *Economia* 3: 41–109.
Fischer, David Hacket. 1989. *Albion's Seed: Four British Folkways in America.* New York: Oxford University Press.
Fogel, Robert William. 1989. *Without Consent or Contract.* New York: W. W. Norton.
———. 2000. *The Fourth Great Awakening & The Future of Egalitarianism.* Chicago, IL: University of Chicago Press.
Gilboy, Elizabeth. 1932. "Demand As a Factor in the Industrial Revolution" in *Facts and Factors in Economic History: Articles by Former Students of Edwin Francis Gay.* Cambridge, MA: Harvard University Press.
Greene, Jack P. 1988. *Pursuits of Happiness.* Chapel Hill: University of North Carolina Press.
———. 1993. *The Intellectual Construction of America: Exceptionalism and Identity from 1492 to 1800.* Chapel Hill, NC: University of North Carolina Press.
———. 2002. "Transatlantic Colonization and the Redefinition of Empire in the Early Modern Era: The British-America Experience" in Christine Daniels and Michael V. Kennedy (eds.), *Negotiated Empires: Centers and Peripheries in the Americas, 1500–1820.* New York: Routledge.
Haber, Stephen, Armando Razo, and Noel Maurer. 2003. *The Politics of Property Rights.* Cambridge: Cambridge University Press.
Hartwell, R. M. 1971. *The Industrial Revolution and Economic Growth.* London: Methuen.
Jacob, Margaret C. 1997. *Scientific Culture and the Making of the Industrial West.* New York: Oxford University Press.
Jones, E. L. 1987. *The European Miracle: Environments, Economics, and Geopolitics in the History of Europe and Asia.* Cambridge: Cambridge University Press.
Keyssar, Alexander. 2000. *The Right To Vote: The Contested History of Democracy in the United States.* New York: Basic Books.
Khan, B. Zorina. 1996. "Married Women's Property Laws and Female Commercial Activity". *Journal of Economic History* 56: 356–388.
Kindleberger, Charles P. 1961. "International Trade and Investment and Resource Use in Economic Growth" and William N. Parker, "Comment" in Joseph J. Spengler (ed.), *National Resources and Economic Growth.* Washington, DC: Resources for the Future.
Knack, Stephen and Philip Keefer. 1997. "Does Social Capital Have an Economic Payoff". *Quarterly Journal of Economics* 112: 1251–1288.
Kupperman, Karen Ordahl. 1993. *Providence Island. 1630–1641: The Other Puritan Colony.* Cambridge.
Landes, David S. 1969. *The Unbound Prometheus.* Cambridge: Cambridge University Press.
———. 1998. *The Wealth and Poverty of Nations: Why Some Are So Rich and Others So Poor.* New York: W.W. Norton.
McClelland, David C. 1961. *The Achieving Society.* Princeton, NJ: Van Nostrand.
Maddison, Angus. 2001. *The World Economy: A Millennial Perspective.* Paris: OECD.
Merton, Robert K. 1970 [1938]. *Science, Technology and Society in Seventeenth Century England.* New York: Harper & Row.
Montesquieu, Charles de Secondat, baron de. 1949 [1748]. *The Spirit of the Laws.* New York: Hafner Press.
Nef, John U. 1958. *Cultural Foundations of Industrial Civilization.* Cambridge: Cambridge University Press.
North, Douglass C. 1981. *Structure and Change in Economic History.* New York.
———. 1988. "Institutions, Economic Growth and Freedom: An Historical Introduction" in Michael Walker (ed.), *Freedom, Democracy, and Economic Welfare.* Vancouver: Fraser Institute.

———. 1990. *Institutions, Institutional Change and Economic Performance*. Cambridge: Cambridge University Press.
North, Douglass C. and Robert P. Thomas. 1973. *The Rise of the Western World: A New Economic History*. Cambridge: Cambridge University Press.
North, Douglass C. and Barry Weingast. 1989. "Constitutions and Commitment: The Evolution of Institutions Governing Public Choice in Seventeenth-Century England". *Journal of Economic History* 49: 803–832.
North, Douglass C., William Summerhill, and Barry Weingast. 2000. "Order, Disorder, and Economic Change: Latin America Versus North America" in Bruce Bueno de Mesquita and Hilton L. Root (eds.), *Governing for Prosperity*. New Haven, CT: Yale University Press.
O'Brien, Patrick K. 1988. "The Political Economy of British Taxation, 1660–1815". *Economic History Review* 41: 1–32.
Plato. 1980. *Laws*. New York: Basic Books.
Pomeranz, Kenneth. 2000. *The Great Divergence: Europe, China, and the Making of the Modern World Economy*. Princeton, NJ: Princeton University Press.
Postan, M. M. 1935. "Recent Trends in the Accumulation of Capital". *Economic History Review* 6: 1–12.
Putnam, Robert D. (ed.). 2002. *Democracies in Flux: The Evolution of Social Capital in Contemporary Society*. Oxford: Oxford University Press.
Rosenberg, Nathan and L. E. Birdzell, Jr. 1986. *How the West Grew Rich: The Economic Transformation of the Industrial World*. New York: Basic Books.
Smith, Adam. 1979 [1776]. *Inquiry into the Nature and Causes of the Wealth of Nations*. Oxford: Clarendon Press.
Sokoloff, Kenneth L. 1988. "Inventive Activity in Early Industrial America: Evidence from Patent Records, 1790–1846". *Journal of Economic History* 48: 813–850.
Sokoloff, Kenneth L. and Stanley L. Engerman. 2000. "Institutions, Factor Endowments, and Paths of Development in the New World". *Journal of Economic Perspectives* 14: 217–232.
Sombart, Werner. 1969 [1913]. *The Jews and Modern Capitalism*. New York: Burt Franklin.
Steuart, James Sir. 1767. *An Inquiry Into the Principles of Political Economy*. London: A. Millar and T. Cadell.
Tawney, R. H. 1926. *Religion and the Rise of Capitalism: A Historical Study*. New York: Harcourt, Brace and World.
TePaske, John Jay. 2002. "The Vital Peripheries of Colonial South America" in Christine Daniels and Michael V. Kennedy (eds.), *Negotiated Empires: Centers and Peripheries in the Americas, 1500–1820*. New York: Routledge.
Tocqueville, Alexis de. 1969 [1835]. *Democracy in America*. Translated by George Lawrence and edited by J. P. Mayer. Garden City: Doubleday.
Weber, Max. 1958 [1905–6]. *The Protestant Ethic and the Spirit of Capitalism*. New York: Scribner's.
———. 1961 [1927]. *General Economic History*. New York: Collier Books.
Wood, Betty. 1984. *Slavery in Colonial Georgia, 1730–1775*. Athens.
Wrigley, E. A. 1988. *Continuity, Chance, and Change*. Cambridge: Cambridge University Press.

26. Institutions and Firms in Transition Economies

PETER MURRELL

1. THE TRANSITION AND THE NIE

In 1989, the Soviet bloc in Eastern Europe disintegrated. In mid-1991, the old Yugoslavia began its painful, protracted breakup. Later that year, an abortive communist coup led quickly to the FSU (former Soviet Union). Twenty-eight countries were free to choose their own economic and political institutions. Public and elite opinion was set on a large move away from the old socialist system, towards some form of market capitalism. In most countries, there was an accompanying shift toward greater political freedom and democracy. All countries undergoing this transition have now experienced more than eleven years of post-communist change.

Several features of transition contribute to its particular pertinence to the NIE. The reforming countries ended the 1980s with a set of formal institutions far different from those of market capitalism. The predicament was not simply one of underdevelopment, with poorly working, incomplete market-capitalist institutions. Rather, under central planning, most essential economic activities were governed by powerful institutions that were antithetical to market capitalism. Mammoth institutional destruction and construction was on the agenda, whatever strategy drove that agenda.

Consistently, the internal organization of enterprises, the mechanisms of enterprise governance, and the governance of transactional relations were all a product of the institutions of central planning and communist politics. But since planning and communism were the two elements of the old systems that were most roundly rejected, firms faced a truly revolutionary situation. In contrast to normal processes of development, where expanding firms adapt to an evolving institutional environment, transition began with large production units facing an institutional earthquake.

This chapter focuses on how the NIE has been used to understand transition processes and how the experience of transition can help inform the NIE.[1] As the

---
[1] There are three earlier papers that have related goals, although all three focus on the first objective of this paper rather than the second. Lichtenstein (1996) constructs, and critiques, an NIE model of the decline of central planning and the process of transition. Smyth (1998) provides a broad-ranging review of the literature that lies at the intersection of transition and the NIE. Voigt and Engerer

above clearly attests, transition inherently involves phenomena that are of central interest to students of the NIE. However, simply discussing these phenomena is not the same as using the NIE: related branches of economics study many of the same general issues. Therefore, to delineate this chapter's scope, it is necessary to draw the dividing line between specific application of the NIE and more general economic analyses of the phenomena on which the NIE focuses. The next two paragraphs do this by listing the analytical concepts that constitute the central core of the NIE. These paragraphs simply distill the essence of the *Handbook* essays by North, Williamson, and Shirley. They serve as a guide as to what is emphasized in the remaining sections of this chapter.

At a macro level, an analysis driven by the NIE would focus on institutions as the rules of the game. These are the prime determinants of the size and distribution of transaction costs. Institutional change is driven by the demands of organizations seeking to reduce transaction costs. Since the set of organizations present at any moment is determined by the inherited structure of institutions, the process of change is mainly incremental and path dependent: institutions tend to be long-lived and difficult to reform. Although institutional change is driven by the rational actions of organizations, there is bounded rationality and the mental models of actors are a prime ingredient in path dependence.

NIE microeconomic analysis takes the transaction as the basic unit of study and focuses on transaction costs, using contractual reasoning. Such analysis involves an examination of the allocation of economic activity across alternative modes of organization, with the governance structure of firms and of transactions being a central concern. A key focus is on whether there is a discriminating alignment between the attributes of transactions and the properties of governance structures.

This chapter's content reflects the intersection of the features of transition and the characteristics of the NIE that are delineated above. The first task is to assess the role played by the NIE in shaping the way economists analyzed the transition process. Section 2 examines the use of the NIE as an analytical tool, particularly focusing on the early phases of transition when there were vigorous debates on the strategy of transition. The overall conclusion from the section is straightforward: in the early transition, the NIE hardly played any role at all, but now the issues stressed by the NIE are a central focus of the transition literature.

Section 3 considers events in the early years of transition, which provide a concrete example of how strategies of transition might have been very different had they more directly embodied the lessons of the NIE. In the very beginning of transition, the political underpinnings of a set of powerful formal economic institutions were removed overnight. In most cases, the new politicians were either not willing or not able to slow the resultant institutional collapse. Since replacement institutions were not available immediately, firms were left to struggle in an immensely chaotic environment. The effect of this chaos on firm behavior,

---

(2002) consider policy implications of the NIE, reviewing elements of transition experience in the process.

and consequently macroeconomic performance, is a subject of much importance and controversy. The institutional collapse and the reactions of firms are examined in Section 3.

Perhaps one reason why the existing institutions collapsed so rapidly was that there was substantial political consensus on the outlines of institutional construction, which therefore moved forward quickly in virtually all countries.[2] But how long would such construction take and how successful would it be? Which institutions would be built most quickly and which would take more time? These questions bear on ideas that are central to the NIE. Armed with a greater sensitivity to institutions than ever before, economists could watch the construction process in real time and gain new information pertinent to these ideas. The relevant evidence is presented in Sections 4 and 5, which respectively examine the aggregate amount and the structure of institutional development.

At the micro level, firms faced a new institutional environment, which was changing at unprecedented speed. Governance structures, for enterprises and for their transactions, had to be built on new foundations. Which institutions would most influence firm behavior? Which new rules would affect behavior most quickly? How would variations across countries in the new regulatory frameworks and laws be reflected in variations in the behavior of firms across transitional economies? These issues are examined in Section 6 for Eastern Europe and the former Soviet Union. Section 7 ventures further afield by examining the case of China, whose process of institutional construction was largely unique. The conjecture is that China's transition process has elements that correspond quite closely to those that might have been fashioned by an advocate of the NIE.

Transition and the NIE offer lessons for each other, and this chapter considers lessons flowing in both directions. It considers how the immensely productive tools of the NIE have been applied to the study of the remarkable phenomenon of transition. Conversely, it examines how the unique historical experience of transition offers lessons of importance for the NIE, strengthening, or perhaps reshaping, existing knowledge. There are a large number of these lessons and they appear throughout this chapter. Section 8, the conclusion, returns to the most important lessons, ones that seem especially likely to challenge, or to qualify, the existing tenets of the NIE, drawing them together in an attempt to provide an analytical synthesis. This synthesis is left for the conclusion because it is the most conjectural element of the chapter, attempting to tie together the disparate pieces of evidence that are available on institutions and firms in transition.

This introduction concludes with two notes to aid the reader in interpreting what follows. First, much of the discussion focuses on empirical evidence. Nevertheless, readers must be cautioned that the pertinent evidence is often thin: empirical studies that focus directly on institutions in transition have not

---

[2] This consensus was especially the case for the countries that had the goal of entry into the European Union.

been commonplace and the quality of the empirical work has not been at the highest standards of the profession. Quite often it is necessary to infer results from studies that did not have institutions as their first order of business. Thus, the reader must be warned at the outset that at some points this chapter is forced to rely on evidence that is quite weak. That characteristic is a product of how little the NIE has been applied directly to the process of transition and how little we still know about institutions and transition.

Second, the discussion is only on those aspects of transition most germane to the NIE. There has recently been a flood of review papers that cover other aspects of the transition experience. The most informative as complements to this chapter are Djankov and Murrell (2002) on the determinants of enterprise restructuring, Estrin (2002) on competition and corporate governance, Campos and Coricelli (2002) on growth, Boeri and Terrell (2002) on the institutional determinants of labor reallocation, and Berglof and Bolton (2002) on finance. For those unfamiliar with the transition environment, comprehensive surveys are available at successive stages in the *Journal of Economic Perspectives* (Murrell, 1991; Murrell, 1996; Svejnar 2002).

2. THE NIE AND THE EARLY LITERATURE ON TRANSITION

One of the more curious aspects of the economics of transition is that the NIE, used consciously as an analytical tool, played virtually no role during the first few years of the 1990s.[3] Despite the great mutual relevance of transition and the NIE, described in the introduction, it is difficult to find analyses produced in early transition that follow the NIE at all closely.[4] This can be documented using a simple analysis of the subject matter of articles produced during the time period.

The *EconLit* database was used to search for documents (books, journal articles, working papers, and dissertations) that used 'transition' as a keyword.[5] The new institutional economics did not appear as a keyword within these documents until 1995. Transaction costs did not appear until 1992. In the first complete year of transition, 1990, only 3.3% of documents had institutions as

---

[3] The most common and most influential analyses during early transition did not use the NIE (Smyth, 1998, Voigt and Engerer, 2002). Benham and Benham (1997) document in great detail the degree to which the considerations emphasized by the NIE were missing from the debate at the beginning of transition.

[4] Grosfeld (1990), Ickes (1990), and Murrell (1990) present analyses of changes within the old systems using elements of the NIE, but these pieces were written before the political changes. Aoki and Kim (1995) is based on the notion that comparative institutional analysis can be productive in deliberations on institutional reform. Lichtenstein (1996) presents an NIE analysis of the fall of the centrally planned economy and optimal transition policy, but mainly from perspective of a critic of the NIE.

[5] The reader who is, justifiably, skeptical of this type of quantitative summary can be reassured that the conclusions have been verified by a reading of the literature that has been exhaustive (in both senses of the word).

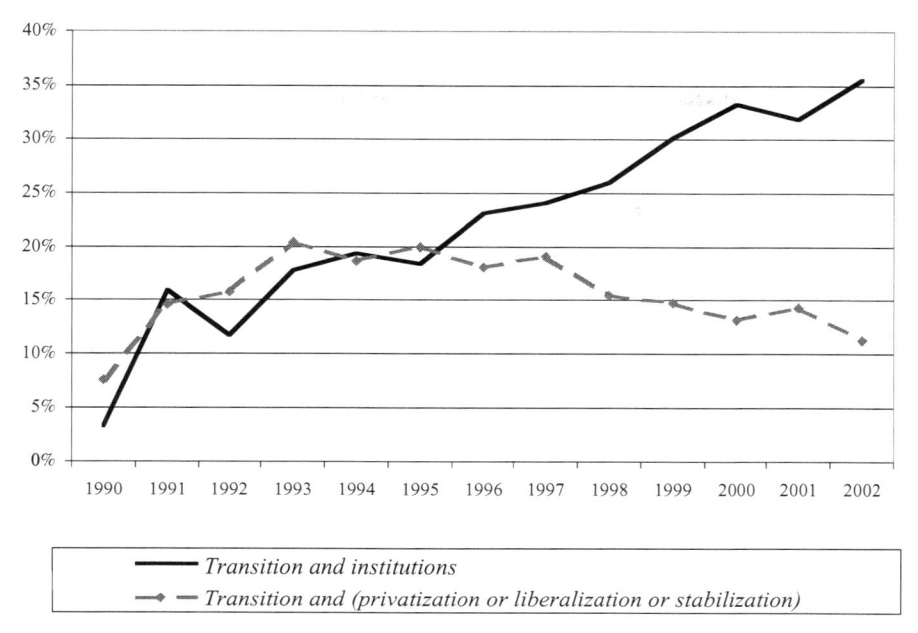

[Figure: line chart showing two series from 1990 to 2002. Solid line "Transition and institutions" rises from about 3% in 1990 to about 35% in 2002. Dashed line "Transition and (privatization or liberalization or stabilization)" rises from about 7% in 1990 to about 20% by 1993-1995 and declines to about 11% in 2002.]

Figure 1. Percentage of those documents in the *EconLit* database having transition as a keyword that also use institutions or Washington consensus policies as keywords.

a keyword and in the first three years only 11.6% did. This can be compared to the Washington Consensus triumvirate of privatization, liberalization, and stabilization, at least one of which appeared in 7.6% of articles in 1990 and in 14% in the first three years of transition.

The simple quantitative story is told in the accompanying Figure.[6] This Figure shows in capsule form how institutional issues were underplayed in the early transition, relative to Washington Consensus issues, and how as time passes they have been ascribed an ever greater emphasis.[7] Even as early as 1991, the increase in attention paid to institutions was a reflection of the events in the preceding two years (Williamson, 1992, p. 69). The steep incline of the 'institutions' time-line and the fact that over 35% of articles on transition now involve discussion of institutions are surely signs that the process of transition has spurred interest in the NIE and that the NIE had something to offer at the beginning of transition that was not fully exploited by economists or policy-makers.

The fact that the NIE was not being used consciously as a primary analytical tool in the early transition is backed up by an examination of those items in the early transition literature that have had a significant impact over time

---

[6] One could tell exactly the same story by looking at the evolution of the subject matter of the EBRD's transition indicators.

[7] The work of the World Bank shows similar changes in emphases over time (Landell-Mills, 2003).

and which reflect on issues closely related to the concerns of the NIE. Where core concerns of the NIE were invoked, the NIE did not seem to provide the stimulus. Kornai (1990) was obviously concerned about governance issues in privatized enterprises but Hayek is much more influential than Williamson in his analysis. Path dependence was especially central for Stark (1992), but this reflected the general interest in this phenomenon among social scientists. McKinnon (1991) emphasized the importance of institutional structure for financial and monetary policy, but his analysis did not reflect an NIE viewpoint. Murrell's (1992) concern with institutions came as much from Schumpeter as from North or Williamson. Dewatripont and Roland (1997) viewed transition as a process of large scale institutional change, but mainly from the perspective of political economy and principal-agent analyses of managerial incentives.

In sum, the NIE was a surprising spectator in the early transition debates. There were analyses that were highly compatible with those of the NIE, but none seemed to be explicitly driven by NIE. In Europe, with the greater prominence of more heterodox modes of analysis, there was probably a greater emphasis on institutions than in the U.S., where neoclassical analysis was relatively more popular.[8] However, these complementary analyses, with their focus on institution-related issues, did not represent the mainstream of the early transition literature.

Had the NIE been more prominent at the start of transition, there would surely have been more focus on institutions as providing the necessary rules of the game. As Coase (1992, p. 714) commented in his Nobel address:

> "The value of including ... institutional factors in the corpus of mainstream economics is made clear by recent events in Eastern Europe. These ex-communist countries are advised to move to a market economy, and their leaders wish to do so, but without the appropriate institutions no market economy of any significance is possible."

This lack of focus on institutions in reform measures is generally credited as important ingredient in determining events in the first years of transition, events that proved to be an important stimulus to the increasing interest in institutions.

Gradually the mainstream view changed, as the Figure shows. Many factors contributed, the continuing recessions in the CIS countries after stabilization, the beginning of growth in some countries that had not fully stabilized, the

---

[8] At least, the greater emphasis on institutions in the European literature is a common assumption. After an extensive search of the literature, I am not entirely persuaded of this point. For example, in 2002, thirty European scholars replied to questions from the Hungarian journal, *Acta Oeconomica*, on what the main roadblocks to transition were. A reading of these papers leaves one with the surprising impression that the emphasis on institutions in Europe was not that much greater than in the U.S. at this time. Only one set of comments of these thirty seems to be influenced by the NIE (Dallago, 1992). Another two (Wagener, 1992, Hanson 1992) stress the importance of institutions. Interestingly, what seems common to these three scholars and those mentioned in the previous paragraph of the text is not the NIE, but rather the old comparative economic systems.

smaller GDP declines in some less-reformed countries, accumulating evidence on widespread corruption, an epidemic of broken agreements and lawsuits, and increasingly common ad hoc observations that firm governance left much to be desired. Roland (2000 p. xix) has described how the transition process has helped to change the very mode of analysis within economics:

> "The [events of transition] have further contributed to a change in focus in thinking about economics and have very much reinforced the institutionalist perspective, emphasizing the importance of the various institutions underpinning a successful capitalist economy... Thus, there is a shift of emphasis from markets and price theory to contracting and the legal, social, and political environment of contracting... transition has forced us to think about institutions not in a static way but in a dynamic way... how institutions can evolve... and how one can get stuck in inefficient institutions."

These sentences resonate closely with the summary of the core NIE issues presented in the introduction to this chapter.

3. THE FIRST FEW YEARS

The transition countries experienced recessions of unprecedented depths. Svejnar (2002) places the declines in GDP at 13–25% in Eastern Europe, 40% in the Baltics, and 45–65% in the Commonwealth of Independent States (CIS).[9] Not surprisingly, there were also large declines in the productivity of existing enterprises. Anderson et al. (2000), for example, estimate a 78% drop in value added per employee within four years in Mongolian firms.

As detailed above, the NIE did not play a role in the most influential analyses during early transition. Fears of hyperinflation rather than recession dominated; macroeconomics governed microeconomics. The extent to which macroeconomics dominated was most clearly exemplified by the IMF's short-term focus on raising taxes in Russia, while largely ignoring sensible tax reforms (Black, Kraakman, and Tarassova, 2000). Rapid liberalization was advocated without consideration of its effects on the governance of contractual relations. Transaction costs during and after the process of privatization were rarely discussed. A simple political economy, which emphasized the destruction of the old institutions, trumped the NIE, which emphasized the dangers of an institution-free environment.[10]

These analyses turned out to be uniformly overoptimistic, as judged for example by IMF forecasts for GDP growth. When production declines proved to be larger than expected, the earliest diagnoses followed the earlier analyses:

---

[9] The CIS comprises the twelve non-Baltic countries that emanated from the Soviet Union.

[10] Early in the transition there were the beginnings of a more refined political economy, as exemplified in the work of Gérard Roland (see Roland 2000). The influence of this political economy grew as transition proceeded.

strong, but necessary, stabilization programs had led to recessions, which were exacerbated by the dilatoriness of politicians in pursuing reforms. For example, Berg and Blanchard (1994) concluded that Poland's fall in output was due to a drop in aggregate demand, not to dislocations of the economic system.[11] That is, in the early 1990's, the most influential analyses did not associate the transitional recessions with institutional problems. Such analyses led to the conclusion that liberalization, privatization, and stabilization should move even faster in Russia in 1992 than they had in Eastern Europe two years earlier. Early 1992 therefore provided an unfortunate conjunction of a momentous economic policy decision with the zenith in the popularity of a theory of economic policy that gave little acknowledgement to institutions.

What would have surfaced if the NIE had played a larger role in the debate at the start of transition? Murrell (1992) and Murrell and Wang (1993) provide some indication, even though these analyses are no more than suggestive and do not use the NIE as fully as seems appropriate in retrospect.[12] These papers stress the dependence of existing organizations on the current institutional framework, concluding that there can be much poorer firm performance in the short-term when old institutions are destroyed and new ones are not yet effective. The view of the market economy as simply decentralization of decision-making is rejected, with emphasis instead placed on the casting of decentralization within an appropriate institutional structure. The latter paper analyzes the interaction between the development of institutions and the implementation of other elements of reform, suggesting that fast privatization could slow the pace of institutional development. The paper argues that the emphasis should be on the growth of the new private sector and on the institutions supporting that growth.

As Section 2 clearly shows, gradually the economics of transition came to focus much more on institutions and transactions. Events on the ground were obviously responsible for stimulating this change. However, one paper that was undoubtedly influential in changing the mainstream focus was that by Blanchard and Kremer (1997), which formalized some of the existing inchoate analyses in a simple, but powerful model. While not cast in the NIE tradition at all, this paper embodies some key elements of the NIE, the focus on transactions rather than production and the need for an effective governance mechanism. The model highlights the incentives to break agreements in the absence of effective governance. Firms start the transition process with highly specific production relations, where large firms must buy inputs from a particular set

---

[11] Murrell (1995) uses simple transactions-cost reasoning to show that the evidence used in support of this conclusion could just as easily be used to support the opposite conclusion. The interpretation of evidence depends on the theoretical lens.

[12] These papers are used because they show what the NIE might have offered at the time reforms were being formulated. (Lichtenstein (1996) and Smyth (1998) interpret Murrell (1992) as being cast in the framework of the NIE.) Now, with the benefit of hindsight, many of the ideas of the NIE are absorbed into a mainstream consensus. McKinnon (1991), Dewatripont and Roland (1992), and Kornai (1990) also differed from the mainstream perspective at the start of transition, but their analyses are even more removed from the NIE.

of suppliers. Previously, supply was ensured by the planning system. But then institutional collapse occurs and alternative outlets appear for the suppliers. Once a single supplier defects, production in the large old firm is impossible. Defection occurs when a supplier receives a good counter-offer, even if the other suppliers do not. There is a loss of production and social welfare, which is greater the more complex are the old production relations.[13] If the outside opportunities for suppliers improve over time, the model generates a U-shaped growth path.

There is weak empirical support for this model, but precise testing is difficult, meaning that the pertinent empirical work is not as convincing as in many other areas. The most important problem in constructing tests lies in measuring the complexity of inherited production relations and the size of the institutional decline. For example, Konings (1998) measures complexity by the number of firms in the enterprise's sector, while Konings and Walsh (1999) use number of products produced by an enterprise. They obtain evidence that is generally supportive of the Blanchard-Kremer model for Bulgaria, Estonia, and Ukraine. Relatedly, Cungu and Swinnen (2003) find that hold-up problems do lead to lower investment levels in Hungarian firms.

Recanatini and Ryterman (2000) provide an empirical examination of the Blanchard-Kremer model that generates insights particularly pertinent to the NIE. Although, they do not find direct support for the specific prediction on complexity, they do find that growth was lower in those firms that formerly received the strongest institutional support from central planning. One interpretation of this result is that these firms have the greatest need for institutional support. Interestingly, some firms do find imperfect, informal substitutes for the moribund old and the embryonic new institutions. The firms suffering most from the absence of supportive institutions have the greatest tendency to join business associations, membership in which ameliorates the decline in production. This is consistent with the results of Perotti and Gelfer (2001), who present evidence that financial-industrial groups in Russia provide an informal substitute for capital markets.

Although the last few years have seen significant advances in the understanding of the relationship between institutional change and production decline in transition, there is much yet to learn. It is now well accepted that socialist economic institutions provided services that contributed to enterprise productivity (albeit contributing much less than many alternatives available in the longer run).[14] These institutions offered credibility that reduced the transaction costs of negotiating agreements, contract enforcement to reduce transaction costs during the implementation stage, specification of control rights over assets (both

---

[13] The loss occurs because the expected value of the first-order statistic of a sample of alternative offers (or social values) is higher than the expected value of the mean of the sample. In the model, complexity is captured by the number of suppliers, which equals sample size. The expected value of the first order statistic minus the mean is positively related to sample size.

[14] Joskow and Schmalansee (1997) make this point strongly in an analysis that uses the NIE.

within enterprises, and between enterprises), mechanisms for the allocation of working and investment capital, and a host of other services. When the communist systems fell apart and market institutions were still waiting in the wings, these crucial services were no longer supplied. Moreover, at the beginning of transition, institutional support was particularly critical because socialist firms were large, implying a need for sophisticated governance mechanisms, and because inter-firm relationships were highly particularized, implying great potential for hold-up. Hence, productivity declined with the decline of the old systems.

On all of this, there is much agreement. On what should have been done had economists pursued this line of thinking more strongly in early transition, there is little agreement. The idea of retaining some of the old institutions (e.g., Murrell, 1992) was rejected as not politically desirable because of the putative danger of the return of communism. The experience of East Germany indicates that immediate implementation of first-best institutions is not a panacea. The success of China, to be examined in Section 8, suggests that transitional institutions, produced by incremental change, can be productive.

4. THE DEVELOPMENT OF INSTITUTIONS: AGGREGATE EVIDENCE[15]

One reason why institutions were not emphasized in early transition was the widely-held assumption that institutional development would be slow and could not contribute much in the short-run.[16] Existing work within the NIE certainly contributed to this general assumption, despite the fact that it is also acknowledged that revolutionary times lead to revolutionary institutional changes (Williamson 2000, North 1990). This pessimism has continued. According to the EBRD (2000, p. 23–5), institutional reform has lagged other reforms. Svejnar (2002, p. 7) concludes that:

> "Virtually no transition country succeeded in rapidly developing a legal system and institutions that would be highly conducive to the preservation of private property and the functioning of a market economy ... This lack of a market-oriented legal structure appears to have been the Achilles' heel of the first dozen years of transition."

This section assesses these conclusions by reviewing evidence on the development of institutions in transition economies. Fortunately, the 1990's saw a proliferation of information that calibrates institutional levels across countries. Using surveys of economic actors, opinions of country experts, and objective information on laws and implementing organizations, many authors have constructed data sets that give a rough quantitative guide to comparative institutional

---

[15] This section and the next draw on Murrell (2003a).
[16] See Fischer and Gelb (1991) for this standard view. This assumption was not universal. Sachs (1991, p. 236) claimed that the economic, legal, and institutional basis for a market economy could be established in one year.

performance. Moreover, most of this data measures institutional effectiveness in some way, so the picture described here is not simply one of formal institutional development, but rather of real progress of institutions in achieving their fundamental objectives.

Campos (2000) generated a data set that covers both general political and economic institutions for 25 transition countries from 1989–1997. For all four of his measures (the quality of the bureaucracy, the rule of law, transparency of policy-making plus accountability of the executive, and the strength of civil society) the data give a very strong impression of profound increases over time, which occur in all time periods for all measures.[17]

The measures produced as part of the International Country Risk Guide (Coplin, O'Leary, and Sealy, 1996) focus more narrowly on economic issues and have been the most popular general measures of the strength of economic institutions (Knack and Keefer, 1995). There are five different series that are most pertinent for economic issues: law and order, corruption within the political system, the institutional strength of the civil service, the risk of repudiation of contracts, and the risk of expropriation of investment. According to these data, there have been widespread, large, continuing improvements in institutional quality. The one exception is in levels of corruption, which, after improvements, rose to back to the 1989 level.

These dramatic increases in measured institutional quality suggest an investigation into just how good institutions are now in transition countries. But what is a reasonable expectation? We know that the level of institutional quality is highly correlated with level of economic development. Therefore, it seems appropriate to examine how the transition countries fare when matched against countries at a comparable level of economic development (Murrell 2003a). This requires institutional measures for a rather large set of countries. For this purpose, the measures produced by Kaufmann, Kraay and Zoido-Lobaton (1999, 2002) are probably the most suitable. Their six measures are voice and accountability, political instability and violence, government effectiveness, regulatory burden, rule of law, and graft.

A crude statistical exercise analysis shows that institutions in Eastern Europe are better than would be expected on the basis of level of economic development (Murrell, 2003a).[18] Institutions in the former Soviet Union are worse than would be expected. Transition countries as a whole are about where they might be expected to be in 2000–1 based on level of economic development. On voice and accountability and political instability, transition countries are better than comparable countries; on rule of law and corruption they are where expected given levels of economic development; and on government effectiveness and regulatory burden they are worse. The regressions also indicate that there is improvement from 1997–8 to 2000–1 for the transition countries as a whole and for Eastern Europe and the former Soviet Union separately. A majority of

---

[17] Except for strength of civil society in the CIS.
[18] It must be emphasized that the statistical analysis is a simple descriptive one, not driven by a precise model of the relationship between institutions and levels of development.

countries is improving, measured either by the number of improving indicators or by the aggregate score. There is improvement on a majority of the indicators.

In sum, although institutional levels were low at the start of transition, there were remarkable improvements over the 1990s. And these were real improvements, not simply the setting up of formal institutions. By the beginning of the present century, the quality of institutions in transition countries was roughly as expected given levels of economic development. Moreover, there are strong signs of continuing improvement in many countries. These results suggest a reevaluation of the usual assumption that institutional development is a glacial process. The transition countries began the 1990s with many powerful institutions that were inimical to the functioning of capitalism and democracy. Most essential market institutions were absent, with dire consequences for economic performance. Yet, a decade later, institutional lacunae are no longer the defining feature of the transition economies.

The generation of this conclusion was based on rough empirical information, more like a hypothesis generated by the data than a test based on the data. To the extent that new independent information supports it, then one can place much more confidence in this conclusion. Such information was generated after the first version of this essay was written. The EBRD has conducted a follow up of its 1999 business environment survey and sees dramatic improvements between 1999 and 2002. One summary of the data examines changes in 7 institutional indicators for 24 countries (EBRD 2002, pp. 42–43). Of the resultant 168 institutional indicators, fully 87.5% show signs of improvement. For example, the quality of the judiciary has improved in 18 of the 24 countries and become worse in only 3. Corruption has declined in 15 countries and become worse in 8. To the extent that the conclusions of this section are conjecture, that conjecture has been ably supported by this later, independent source of information.

5. THE DEVELOPMENT OF INSTITUTIONS: STRUCTURE

How were these aggregate institutional developments produced? There are two ways to interpret this question. First, one can examine proximate cause: which types of institution-producing organizations have mattered most? Second, what factors within the politics and economics of transition economies led to a faster-than-expected development of institutions? Evidence on the latter question is unfortunately very scarce and only brief comments appear at the end of this section. The answer to the first question can take advantage of accumulating evidence on different institutions. However, it must be emphasized that this evidence is still quite thin and all conclusions must be conjectural.

At a very basic level, the following types of institutions can be identified:

1. Those produced by private bodies with a formal role promoted or facilitated by the state, e.g., self-regulation of stock markets; arbitration courts; accounting standards boards.

2. Political institutions, e.g., legislatures, electoral processes, etc.
3. Institution-like behavior by state administrative bodies, e.g., criminal law enforcement by justice departments; product safety and health standards by ministries; patent registration by a patent office.
4. The effects of the actions of independent quasi-governmental bodies, e.g., central banks issuing money and regulating banks; stock-market regulators protecting investors; bureaus licensing prescription medicines.
5. The legal system, e.g., contract law for transactions; systems of definition and enforcement of property rights; corporate governance law and enforcement; the courts and bailiffs.

The evidence on the effectiveness of each of these institutional types is scattered, staccato, and imprecise. It is hard to make definitive conclusions. Nevertheless, one can begin by examining on which of the Kaufmann, Kraay and Zoido-Lobaton measures the transition countries perform best. In order of success (relative to levels of development), the measures are voice and accountability, political instability and violence, rule of law, graft, government effectiveness, and, last, regulatory burden. It therefore seems safe to conclude that political institutions are making a large contribution to the relative overall institutional performance of the transition countries, while state administration (which is largely responsible for the regulatory burden) is a very poor performer.

There is considerable evidence from empirical work that the performance of legal systems in transition countries is much better than initially expected. Some examples are given here and more follow in Section 6.[19] Djankov et al. (2002) collect data on highly specific aspects of the functioning of legal systems in a variety of countries, such as collecting on a bad check. Their data reflect expert assessments of how things actually happen, as well as formal law. They find that the ex-socialist countries fare reasonably well compared to those countries whose legal systems have either French or German origins. The results for the socialist countries are clearly better than those for French-origin countries and slightly better than those for German-origin countries.[20]

Pistor, Raiser, and Gelfer (2000) provide an alternative method, looking at inputs, the quality of laws. They examine the strength of shareholder and creditor rights that have been enacted in transition countries. Formal shareholder rights in transition countries surpass those achieved by countries whose legal systems derive from French, German, or Scandinavian origins and are now midway between those of common law countries and those of French or German origin.[21] On formal creditor rights, the progress is even more remarkable. Creditor rights in transition countries score higher than rights in all other sub-groups

---

[19] There is substantially more evidence than this on legal systems, some of which is presented in later sections of this paper. A comprehensive discussion appears in Murrell (2003a).
[20] The regressions control for level of economic development.
[21] These results occur even though these comparisons match the transition countries against a group of countries in which OECD members are the majority.

of countries, when the groups are defined in terms of legal origins. This performance was essentially achieved in a matter of six years.

Of course, the Pistor et al. (2000) evidence is on formal law, not on its effectiveness, and it is not unusual for formal law to outpace its implementation. Successful reforms are marked by law in practice eventually catching up with the law on the books. Indeed, that is what might be happening in transition countries. For the year 2000, the EBRD (2000, p. 34) rated sixteen transition countries as having commercial law that was rated higher on extensiveness (i.e., formal quality) than effectiveness (i.e., practical effect) while the relative ranking was the opposite in two countries. By 2002, the situation was reversed, with four countries scoring higher on extensiveness than effectiveness and eight countries having the reverse relative ranking EBRD (2002, p. 38). This suggests that implementation might be better than is commonly supposed. Consistently, Ramasastry, Slavova, and Bernstein (1999, p. 39) comment on survey results indicating that court systems are viewed fairly favorably in terms of protection of shareholder rights:

> "At first glance, these results may seem counter-intuitive given the generally negative view of courts in the region. Criticism of the courts and judges ranges from allegations of corruption or bias towards the government or powerful commercial interests, to a general lack of understanding of newer commercial laws and complex commercial transactions. However, the survey results reveal that respondents do feel that the court system can provide an effective means of redress and protection for shareholders' rights."

There is also evidence that independent governmental bodies have contributed to institutional development. For example, Pistor (2001) documents how the success of equity markets in Central Europe depended critically on independent state agencies that supervised stock markets and implemented investor protection rules. Similarly, Johnson (2001) lays out a fascinating story of how great strides have been made in independent central banks. In contrast, there is little evidence that state-facilitated private bodies, e.g., domestic arbitration courts, are making a large contribution to institutional performance.

In sum, returning to the categorization of different types of institutions appearing at the beginning of this section, political institutions seemed to have developed fastest. The legal system and independent governmental bodies have made important contributions. State administration, that is the core governmental bureaucracy, has been very slow to change and offers a compelling example of relative failure of institutional adjustment.

As to the ultimate causes of these developments, only speculation is possible given the absence of empirical studies on the determinants of institutional construction during transition. One question that has been central in the literature is the relative importance of supply or demand. How much will be done by a reforming government that is not being pushed for specific measures by economic interests? The strategy of fast privatization in Russia was determined in part by an answer to this question: "Economic institutions cannot possibly precede the reallocation of property from the government, because people do not care about these institutions until, as property owners, they have an economic interest." (Boycko, Shleifer, and Vishny, 1995, p. 126). But the pertinent empirical evidence has not yet been produced. One of the most fascinating intellectual exercises in the future will be to test this proposition, and other ones that predict the sources of institutional development. Certainly there is much evidence being generated by the transition countries on this score.

6. CHANGING RULES AND CHANGING BEHAVIOR OF FIRMS[22]

The Reaction to Changing Policies in the Short-Term

Section 3 examined the reaction of firms to the decline of the old institutions. This section focuses on the reaction of firms to the new environment created by reforms. Certain aspects of the new environment could be implemented quite quickly, for example, liberalization, privatization, and the removal of soft budgets. The effects of these policy measures have been intensively examined in a large number of empirical studies.[23] Although these measures are all outgrowths, in part, of the institutional framework, they are not extensively examined here, for two reasons. First, the connection between these policies and institutions is indirect and therefore the relevance to the NIE is less obvious. Second, there is an extensive survey on these issues, on competition (primarily induced by liberalization), privatization, and the effects of hardening of budgets (Djankov and Murrell, 2002). The results of pertinence here are:

1. Privatization is strongly associated with better enterprise performance in Eastern Europe, but not in the CIS. Differences in the effectiveness of corporate governance quite possibly explain the differences between the regions.[24]
2. State ownership within traditional state firms is less effective than all other ownership types, except for worker owners. Investment funds, foreigners, and other blockholders produce much more improvement in enterprise performance than diffuse individual ownership. The importance of these types of owners, which concentrate shares in large blocks, suggests a deficiency in corporate governance, which seems to be more pronounced in the CIS than in Eastern Europe.
3. State ownership within partially-privatized firms is surprisingly effective, producing better enterprise performance than that produced by insider-owners and non-blockholder outsiders. Independent state organizations might therefore perform better than some types of fully private actors, when the

---

[22] This section does not aim to be comprehensive, but rather focuses on issues where there is pertinent evidence.
[23] The overwhelming majority of these studies do not use the NIE. Shastitko and Tambovtsev (2001) is an interesting exception, viewing soft budgets as relational contracts.
[24] Section 5.1.d below examines the difficult question of whether it is the institutions of corporate governance or some other factor that has led to the deficiencies in corporate governance.

requisite institutions are lacking. This result resonates with the conclusion in the previous section on the apparent success of institutions produced by independent state bodies, and also with the later discussion of transitional institutions.
4. Product market competition has a large effect on enterprise performance. Institutions might have played a role in producing this effect. Dutz and Vagliasindi (2000) find that the quality of competition policy has a positive and significant effect on the expansion of more efficient firms and Vagliasindi (2001) finds that competition policy has a strong and robust effect on levels of competition.

While there are transparent lessons for the NIE in the above, this chapter turns instead to those areas of research that involve the NIE more centrally, either in methods used or in the direct relevance of the conclusions.

Boundaries of the Firm

The paradigmatic problem of the NIE is the determination of the boundaries of the firm. At the start of transition, firm boundaries reflected the demands of the socialist system, not the transaction costs of a market environment. This was recognized generally, and most explicitly stated by Earle, Estrin, and Leshchenko (1996, p. 7): "A principal task of transition is therefore the reorganization of the groups of productive units which comprised the enterprise sector in the formerly socialist economies through vertical and horizontal disintegration and reintegration to form an industrial structure in which the boundaries of the firm are set to ensure the costs within the new structures are at a minimum." Similarly, Joskow and Schmalansee (1997, pp. 122–3) in an analysis explicitly using elements of the NIE predicted that "Over the next few years, we are likely to see major industrial restructuring take place in Russia as privatized enterprises merge, diversify their product lines, spin off unrelated business activities, and are liquidated or restructured following bankruptcy."

In contrast to these expectations, reported results on changing firm boundaries are surprisingly few and they point to only small movements.[25] For Russia, Earle et al. (1996, p. 86) find that only 14% of firms had major asset sales or transfers over a two and half year period at the start of the transition. Only 3% of employees were in subsidiary firms. Miniscule amounts of work were being contracted out and only tiny amounts of labor were employed in units sold or units acquired. This is in contrast to a 20% drop in employment, a gross hiring rate of 41%, and a separation rate of 51%. In Georgia, Djankov and Kreacic (1998) finds that few directors resort to assets sales. In six CIS countries, Djankov (1999, p. 86) finds only 24% of enterprises engaging in asset sales, however small. For a sample of 300 firms in four East European countries, Earle, Pagano, and Lesi (2002)

---

[25] There are more results on such changes as the production of new goods. But, these can occur without redrawing the boundaries of the firm, as when a car company simply produces a new model with the same production process as before.

find that even though the number of split-ups and mergers is quite high, the resultant effects on employment are quite small. It seems necessary to conclude that market-induced restructuring of firm boundaries is proceeding very slowly.

In contrast, Lizal, Singer, and Svejnar (2001) study a political process at the start of reforms in Czechoslovakia. Divisions of state-owned enterprises could apply for a split, and these occurred in large numbers. These spin-offs turned out to be beneficial in all but large spin-offs, both for the parent enterprise and the subsidiary. This is substantial evidence that the enterprise boundaries inherited from socialism are far from those that would appear under market-determined transaction costs considerations, making the conclusion of the previous paragraph even more surprising.

There is something of a mystery here. There was much interest in this issue, and scholars did pursue it, especially using survey methods to obtain qualitative information on changes in boundaries. Why has so little evidence been produced? This is surely a case of a dog that did not bark in the night. The paucity of published results, and the small effects in those that have been published, suggests that systematic results cannot be found, either because firm boundaries are not changing much (especially relative to changes in output and employment) or because the process of change is dominated by chance rather than choice.

The application of transaction cost calculations in a rapidly changing environment is surely a task that any management team would find daunting, subject to huge error. Perhaps, such calculations are near impossible. Then, the reconstruction of firm boundaries on transaction costs considerations requires natural selection and creative destruction over an extended period. But this is only conjecture, based on the evidence to date, and particularly its paucity. It is certainly a possibility worth considering, and transition countries are producing immense amounts of pertinent evidence.[26]

Transactions in Goods and Services

Another central topic of the NIE is the governance of the firm's external transactions. Under the old socialist system, the central authorities were the overwhelmingly dominant governance mechanism, even to the extent of constructing agreements between firms, as well as enforcing them. With the collapse of central planning, firms were forced to find new mechanisms to support their relationships with trading partners. This was a process fraught with difficulty. Agreements were often not fulfilled and an epidemic of non-payments occurred. The consequences have already been examined in Section 3.

In the early years of transition, there was the almost universal assumption that the legal system, particularly the courts, would be of no service for firms

---

[26] This conjecture is consistent with the fact there is one set of firm boundaries that does seem to be changing very fast indeed: those of the enterprises that have been taken over by foreign corporations. Large experienced multinational corporations surely have far less tight bounds to their rationality than do the enterprises that emanated from the centrally planned economies.

looking to solve their new transactional problems.[27] The characteristics of the old systems led to this assumption. Pessimism was thoroughly justified given the instrumental use of law, the laws ignored and the laws flouted, the telephone justice, the settling of economic disputes through an administrative process (gosarbitrazh) and myriad procedural irregularities (Hendley 1996). Commentators, particularly on Russia, turned these assumptions into a description of interenterprise relations that included a larger role for the gun and the mafia than for contract and the courts. This is a truly interesting case where popular assumption and theoretical logic dominated, when empirical work would have shown a much different picture.

An important contribution to such empirical work, and to the methodology of the NIE itself, was that of McMillan and Woodruff (1999) on Vietnam. Their survey of private firms examines the bases of trust in contracting, using the amount of trade credit as a measure of trust in the partner. The paper identifies several ways in which agreements are secured, through the absence of competition, which reduces the incentive to renege, through the confidence generated by past information on behavior, and through the pressures resultant from membership in a network of firms. This type of relational contracting is highly productive, especially for new small firms. But there are costs in terms of efficiency. Continuing a relationship might mean forgoing new opportunities, especially if these opportunities lie beyond familiar territory. The empirical results in McMillan and Woodruff (1999) clearly show the importance of relational contracting, while at the same time identifying the costs of the absence of a viable court system that can enforce arms-length contracting.

However, Vietnam was quite unlike European and Eurasian transition countries. Vietnamese small private firms had no access to courts. In contrast in Eastern Europe and the former Soviet Union, courts of some substance were refashioned from the institutional legacies of the old planning systems or from pre-communist institutions that had outlasted communism. Contrary to popular assumption, firms used these courts and found them useful. On the basis of survey results, Hendley, Murrell, and Ryterman (2000) concluded that Russian enterprises do not reject the use of law and legal institutions. Many enterprises use the courts, while few resort to private law enforcement. In an econometric analysis of success in the implementation of agreements, Hendley, Murrell, and Ryterman (2001) find that the institutional environment rewards enterprises that pay attention to the legal side of their operations. Better transactional performance occurs when the legal staff works extensively on contractual matters, when enterprise personnel possess larger amounts of legal human capital, when old legal practices have been forsaken, and when new ones have been adopted.

Johnson, McMillan, and Woodruff (2002) come to similar conclusions using survey data from enterprises in five transition countries. In Poland, 72.9% of firms say the courts can enforce contracts, with corresponding figures of 67.9% in Slovakia, 86.9% in Romania, 55.8% in Russia, and 54.6% for Ukraine. Johnson

---

[27] See Hendley, Murrell, and Ryterman (2000) for citations to the pertinent literature.

et al. (2002) conclude that: "The courts...significantly affect contracting. Entrepreneurs who say the courts work behave differently from those who say they do not work." Several other papers with rather similar conclusions can be found in Murrell (2001).

These are somewhat startling results. The courts, burdened by the legacies of communism and often starved of funds, have played a significant role in the governance of transactions in transition countries. But just how significant? This question engages one of the central issues in the economics of institutions, the relative roles of trust and law in promoting cooperation between trading partners. Hendley and Murrell (2003) directly focus on this question when surveying Romanian firms. They asked Romanian company directors about the relative usefulness of six different alternative mechanisms of facilitating cooperation in transactions. The responses suggest that bilateral mechanisms, (i.e., either personal relationships or the shadow of the future) account for 55% of the production of the intermediate output that might be called the support of agreements, while the legal system accounts for 21%. Third-party networks, private enforcement, and the bureaucracy are much less important.

The results reported in this section in some ways diverge from prevailing views on the role of the legal system.[28] The legal system has never been identified as playing a strong role in developing countries, and certainly the transition environment was not conducive to the effectiveness of those institutions. Yet, significant effects have been identified here.

Corporate Governance

It is one thing for the legal system to be able to help enforce simple agreements; it is quite another to ensure that owners can reap the full benefits of complex property rights. It is even more difficult to create an institutional structure that leads to effective property rights when mass privatization has produced owners more dispersed than those in any developed capitalist economy. Thus, there is a general consensus that corporate governance has been a problem in transition and that the retrading of shares after privatization has been slower than hoped (Estrin 2002, p. 110–112). There is less of consensus on why this has been the case. Some see a failure to develop those institutions specifically pertinent to corporate governance (e.g., Zinnes, Eilat, and Sachs, 2001); some see a more general failure of institutional development (e.g., Black et al., 2000), while others have argued that mass privatization created principal-agent problems of such enormity that it would have been impossible for any conceivable set of institutions to straighten out the mess, in less than the long-term.[29]

---

[28] Ramasastry et al. (1999) report a similar inconsistency in the views on court decisions on corporate governance issues. Survey results report a much more positive view of the role of the court system in protecting shareholders' rights than prevails in the conventional wisdom.

[29] This view of the effects of mass privatization is foreshadowed in a very early paper by David Ellerman (1993), and then was developed in Stiglitz (2001a, b), when Ellerman was Stiglitz' advisor/speechwriter at the World Bank.

However, there is only a limited amount of hard evidence on these matters. Even some of the core facts are not known: for example, it is uncertain whether the decline in insider ownership in Russia is due to insider-owners leaving firms (and becoming outsiders) or due to real outsider-owners becoming more important. There is only a sparse empirical literature systematically relating the performance of the corporate sector of different countries to the character of the pertinent institutions. There is an absence of econometric studies relating particular corporate governance rules to the performance of firms.

Nevertheless, some conclusions can be made. The reliance on internally generated funds is so great (Berglof and Bolton 2002, EBRD 1998) as to suggest strongly that financial and corporate governance institutions have not succeeded in their most basic function, facilitating the flow of finance. The retrading of shares after privatization, to concentrate ownership, has been generally slow, except in the advanced reforming countries, suggesting problems with investor protection rules. Djankov and Murrell (2002) offer indirect evidence on the importance of corporate governance institutions. They show that performance after privatization is worse in those enterprises with owners who are more dependent on institutional support, such as diffuse individual owners. This effect is more pronounced in the CIS than in Eastern Europe, suggesting that corporate governance institutions have functioned less well in the CIS. Similarly, Poland and Hungary are often cited as providing examples of better corporate governance within Eastern Europe, while the Czech Republic has been cited as providing an example of what can go wrong (Pistor 2001; Cull, Matesova, and Shirley, 2002).

Pistor (2001) offers a fascinating analysis that interprets some of these differences. She examines the full set of rules that might affect corporate governance, not only the formal shareholder rights that come from corporate law but also investor protection rules that come from a broader set of institutions. The enforcement of shareholder rights usually requires that shareholders pursue their own interests through the courts. The state plays a more proactive role in enforcing investor protection rules, usually with some form of autonomous agency such as a securities commission. While Hungary and Poland established an independent securities commission as early as 1991, it took the Czech Republic until April 1998 to do so. Until then, Czech shareholders had to protect themselves using the courts, a difficult exercise anywhere. Shareholder property rights were weak in all these countries, while differences were more pronounced in investor protection rules, with the Czech Republic having the weakest stance.

Pistor argues that there were significant consequences of these different institutional structures. The Polish and Hungarian stock markets were more important than the Czech one as a source of new capital for firms. There was a stronger perception of stability of financial institutions in the former two countries. The general integrity of large firms and financial markets was questioned much more in the Czech Republic than in the other two countries. This could be a powerful lesson in the comparative performance of different institutional structures.[30]

---

[30] See Glaeser, Johnson, and Shleifer (2001) for a similar analysis.

However, there was a confounding variable that might also be relevant. Poland and Hungary did not have mass privatization, in contrast to the Czech Republic, and also to Russia.

Russia provides a sobering contrast to Poland and Hungary.[31] There is much evidence, albeit not systematic, that corporate practices in Russia are inimical to the development of a healthy economy. Using a small sample of large Russian enterprises, Black (2001) estimates that a 600-fold increase in stock-market valuation would follow from implementing best-practice, rather than worst-practice, corporate governance. These estimates are suggestive of the improvements that might be stimulated by more effective institutions.

There is a lively and continuing debate on the causes of the failures in Russian corporate governance. Black et al. (2000) provide the most detailed overview, suggesting several reasons for the problems in the post-privatization corporate sector in Russia. There was no effective infrastructure for controlling self-dealing by managers when they took control of companies before privatization. Control was given to those had an incentive to steal the assets. Incentives to restructure instead of looting were swamped by many aspects of the business environment, such as the tax system, corruption, crime, bureaucracy, and a business culture that encouraged illegal acts. Stock markets were illiquid, meaning that problems could not be solved by the concentration of outside ownership in powerful blocks.

Black et al. (2000) ultimately conclude, however, that no conceivable institutional development could have led to effective corporate governance immediately after mass privatization. The institutions would not have been strong enough to stop the asset-strippers, and politico-economic power was placed in the hands of those who were not enthusiastic about institutional development. This is consistent with the views of Stiglitz (2001a,b) emphasizing the enormous task of monitoring long agency chains, Heller (2001) arguing that no conceivable corporate governance regime can untangle Byzantine property rights, and Roland (2001) stressing that mass privatization creates a set of owners who are not interested in institutional development.

Viewed in this way, an important observation derived from transition experience on corporate governance is that narrowly targeted institutional reforms cannot quickly negate the effects of tangled and inefficient ownership structures created by mass privatization. The information that does exist on comparative corporate governance performance across transition countries is consistent with this observation.[32] That information is also consistent with the conventional wisdom that corporate governance mechanisms work well in the most advanced

---

[31] Foreign ownership could also explain many differences between these countries, with FDI being much more important in Eastern Europe than in the CIS.

[32] One way to check this point is to examine institutional effectiveness as a function of methods of privatization. Some very simple regressions using data from EBRD (2002) are consistent with the hypothesis that privatization by direct sales is positively related with the later effectiveness of corporate governance law and of financial regulations. Details available from the author on request.

countries but are much less effective elsewhere.[33] Indeed, the highly significant role of group and family ownership in the developing world suggests that the transition countries are not alone in exhibiting corporate governance problems (Burkart, Panunzi, and Shleifer, 2002; Yafeh and Khanna 2000). In this light, the success of the advanced reformers seems even more notable and their experience might point to important lessons about how to produce more effective corporate governance.

Perhaps another lesson is that the types of corporate governance institutions usually implemented in developed countries do not provide appropriate technology to transfer to developing countries when mass privatization has left highly dispersed ownership. Perhaps, transitional institutions are needed, ones that are more suited to the peculiarities of the ownership environment in which they are situated (Roland, 2000). The idea of transitional institutions leads directly to consideration of the Chinese transition.

7. CHINESE INSTITUTIONAL DEVELOPMENT[34]

China began the transition, not with system collapse, but rather with a powerful government desperate to shore up its legitimacy after a decade of turbulence. There was a willingness to adopt new measures to improve the economic situation, but within the requirement of not moving too far from the existing system.[35] This put a constraint on institutional change, which meant new institutions would not be best-practice, but rather incremental variations on existing ones. The puzzle that China presents is the combination of a very non-standard path of institutional development and amazing economic success. The lessons to be derived from the Chinese reform are not on the specific details of the institutional reforms themselves, since these details were partially a product of circumstances specific to China. Rather, the lessons are on the process of institutional reform. The NIE is very helpful in isolating the elements of that process.[36]

One way to interpret the Chinese approach to reform is through the NIE concept of remediableness, a criterion that places the burden on the policy-maker to show that the proposed alternative to the present arrangements will actually result in improvements (Williamson, 2000). The Chinese path of institutional

---

[33] But even in developed economies corporate governance laws can give wide latitude for majority shareholders to plunder the minority. See Johnson et al. (2000).

[34] This section draws heavily on the work of Yingyi Qian, particularly Qian (2003).

[35] Of course, the limits of acceptable change advance as the previous changes generated success.

[36] This way of understanding matters contains an implicit riposte to those who make the observation that Chinese-type reform policies were not applicable in the circumstances of Eastern Europe and the former Soviet Union. I regard this observation as wholly uncontroversial. It is the process of Chinese reform that is pertinent to other countries, not the detailed characteristics of the transitional institutions.

development matched this criterion in several ways. First, the leadership often simply endorsed the results of experiments that had already shown some success at a local level. Second, the effects of incremental changes could be more readily understood than those resultant from large scale changes. This made the decision problem easier for leaders when they chose institutions. It also meant that economic organizations could more readily understand how to react productively to the new institutions. Third, as Qian (2003) emphasizes, China's transitional institutions worked because they transparently protected all important economic actors from significant declines in economic welfare, while providing impetus for improved economic efficiency.

Qian (2003) describes four crucial, successful, transitional institutions. First, the dual-track approach to liberalization kept quotas and controlled prices on production up to those levels planned before the reforms, while freeing above-plan production. This measure promoted efficiency at the margin, while endorsing the existing set of informal rights to infra-marginal production, thus protecting the welfare of those who otherwise might lose heavily from reforms (Lau, Qian, and Roland, 2000). The dual-track was also a very crude contract enforcement mechanism on infra-marginal production. Of course, it slowed reallocation, but in the absence of other mechanisms this might have been exactly what was needed to prevent the types of transactional problems highlighted in Section 3. It is clear that the dual-track satisfied the criterion of remediableness, at least in the short-term, much better than any other process of liberalization implemented in any other transition country.

Second, a highly distinctive ownership form appeared, the township-village enterprises (TVEs), which blossomed in the countryside and were responsible for a large part of China's growth in the 1980's. Che and Qian (1998) interpret the TVE as a mechanism for protecting decentralized property-rights when the state is unable to guarantee more formal ones. Because the local politicians and the managers of TVEs have complementary incentives to produce, the central government finds that surrendering property rights to the local authorities is better than keeping these rights centralized. In the Che-Qian model, remittances to the central government can increase when the center surrenders its property rights. A government unconstrained by law must seek ways other than formal property rights to bind itself.

The third important transitional institution also worked through the mechanisms of governmental decentralization. Fiscal contracts between the central and local governments had high fixed remittances to the center and high marginal retention rates for the localities. These served the dual purposes of ensuring a steady stream of payments to the central government, while aligning the interests of local governments with local producers. Fourth, anonymous banking served as a commitment device, limiting government predation by reducing information flows. This arrangement, going against notions of best practice, can be understood as a crude substitute for the protection of financial property rights, where the independence of the legal system is not a real possibility in the short-term.

The progress of Chinese state-owned enterprises (SOEs) provides some evidence of the effect of transitional institutions, and the fact they eventually become outdated. In the first decade of the Chinese reforms, the SOEs performed at very creditable levels, producing rates of increase of total factor productivity growth that would have been judged as reasonably satisfactory in many contexts (Jefferson et al. 2000). Certainly, this performance contrasted with that in the first decade of transition for the enterprises that began the 1990s in the state sectors of Eastern Europe and the former Soviet Union. Empirical evidence suggests that managerial incentive schemes had an important effect on state enterprise performance in China, but not elsewhere.[37] In the Chinese context, managerial incentive schemes seemed to work well as a transitional institution. However, in the 1990s the incentive schemes were less effective (Shirley and Xu, 2001).

China's transitional institutions complemented managerial incentives in the 1980s. First, a powerful government was willing to impose harsh penalties for enterprise managers who abused their power. Second, the alternatives to focusing on improving efficiency within enterprises were not particularly attractive: moving enterprise assets into the private sector was not an easy alternative. In an environment where negligent or fraudulent behavior by managers is punished, as in China in the 1980s, and where the payoff from transferring assets to the private sector is less than attractive, managers have the choice of working hard and getting bonuses or slacking off and living off their salary alone. In contrast where punishment for bad behavior is not important nor immediate, as in most other transition countries and increasingly in China in the 1990s, managers have the choice of stripping enterprise assets and getting a huge windfall now or working hard through the years and receiving better compensation through bonuses. It is clear which choice is attractive in each instance.

Thus, the general lesson is rather similar to the one drawn at the end of the previous section, that many institutions require complements, and therefore identical institutions might work in one environment but not in another. Transitional institutions are, of necessity, institutions that must be designed to work in the environment in which they are to be implemented. But these transitional institutions outlive their usefulness, as seems to have been the case of managerial incentives in China.

8. Lessons Learned from the Transition for the NIE

One central lesson of transition reinforces a core proposition of the NIE, the importance of institutions. The experience of transition has contributed to the remarkable recent increase in the role attributed to institutions in processes of

---

[37] Djankov and Murrell (2002). This conclusion is based on an aggregation of the evidence in a number of studies.

economic development and economic change.[38] Transition has also reinforced the increasing popularity of research on issues deemed of central importance by the NIE. It has moved NIE methods, such as transaction-cost thinking, further into the mainstream of economics.

Paradoxically, however, this was not because NIE approaches were important at the beginning of transition. They were not. Neither was it because there was an early emphasis on institution-building in reforms. There was not. Rather, the reason for the present emphasis on institutions in transition is the relative failure of reform packages that were developed largely without a focus on institutions. An increasing amount of mainly anecdotal evidence from the formerly socialist countries points toward the crucial role of institutions in promoting the functioning of market capitalist society. However, this evidence is still thin. It is not as abundant as it might have been, since the NIE was not nearly so popular in analyzing transition in 1990 as it is now. NIE researchers still have much to accomplish in laying bare the fundamentals of the transition process.

This chapter contains many other lessons that reinforce propositions of the NIE. Rather than repeating them here, the remainder of this conclusion will focus on a more controversial topic: lessons learned from transition that might challenge existing assumptions of the NIE.

North (1991) characterizes economic history as predominantly a saga of the failure to produce institutions that induce sustained economic growth. The success of the western world is a very special story, one of demand-induced slow accumulation of productive institutions. Yet, Section 4 of this chapter describes a remarkable record of very quick institutional accumulation, especially in Eastern Europe, accompanied by very respectable growth performance.

If one takes the perspective of a decade, there are a number of countries in which success in institutional development is striking. Poland, Hungary, and Slovenia are obvious examples, and their progress is indeed remarkable. However, some observers might discount the importance of these examples because of favorable starting conditions and settled politics. But consider the case of Slovakia. The starting conditions were unfortunate. Slovakia inherited the least useful part of Czechoslovakia's industry. It could only begin building its own national institutions in 1993, after the split with the Czechs. The political situation was even worse. The country teetered on the verge of authoritarianism in the mid-1990's. Yet now institutions in Slovakia are judged better than would be predicted on the basis of its level of economic development, and there are continuing improvements (Murrell, 2003a, EBRD 2002, Kaufmann, Kraay, and Mastruzzi 2003). Such developments, in less than one decade, suggest reevaluation of the conventional story of slow accumulation of institutions.

---

[38] Using the EconLit database as in Section 2, one finds that institutions and development occur together in less than 5% of documents in the early 1990s and in more than 17% in the opening years of the present decade.

There might also be a necessity to reconsider the emphasis placed on the role of the demand side in the politics of institutional development. Although there is no reason to doubt that overall voter and business sentiment provided an important stimulus leading to rapid change, it seems clear that many of the details of the transformation in economic institutions were settled in a process that was rather divorced from politics, removed from specific pressures coming from the demand side. Supply factors were critical, with individual politicians, influential academics, and high-level state officials believing that institution-building was essential for the long-term success of their counties. Foreign actors played crucial roles, especially in the countries hoping to enter the European Union.

These speedy institutional developments contrast with the slower reactions of firms to the new institutions.[39] As Section 6 suggests, movement has been especially ponderous in the recasting of the boundaries of the firm.[40] In his survey of the NIE, Williamson (2000) contrasts the process of institutional development, which takes decades, with adjustments in the governance structures of firms, which occur within a decade. Perhaps, this contrast is true of change, per se, even if chaotic, but it does not characterize processes of successful change in transition. Transition evidence suggests that successful change in institutions can occur in a decade, while change within existing firms requires longer. Indeed, this raises the possibility that processes of entry and exit and natural selection are necessary to align governance structures with institutions. Perhaps, the application of cognitive processes within existing firms is not enough to produce such alignment.

This characterization resonates with the reflections on transitional institutions that appear briefly in Section 6 and that are the focus of Section 7's discussion of China. Perhaps, actors in the Chinese economy were able to react so quickly and so productively to the new set of institutions because the new arrangements were quite close to the old ones. The new institutions presented a simpler cognitive task to economic agents in China than in Eastern Europe and the former Soviet Union. This suggests that normative theories of institutional development must take into account limits on the processing capacities of economic agents. It would be extremely difficult to find a conclusion that is more consistent with the NIE.

So far the discussion has not addressed the mutual consistency of the somewhat disparate observations made above. Certainly, this chapter is not the place to present an extensive conjectural theory to produce that consistency. But adumbration of a general argument will be useful to tie some loose ends. First, it is useful to recap the principal observations. It is now assumed that institutional lacunae were the main source of the problems in early transition. Institutional

---

[39] At least for those firms that were part of the old system.

[40] Murrell (2003b) shows that firms have been slow in matching modes of transactional governance to the new institutions.

construction is happening very quickly, in a process whose detailed character is as much determined by the push of supply as by the pull of demand. Firm-level adjustments to the new institutions are lagging behind institutional construction: transitional institutions might have worked better (in the short-run) than best-practice institutions. The remaining paragraphs tie these conclusions together, highlighting their mutual consistency.

When there is a basic consensus on far-reaching reforms, economic institutions that might be functional in the short-run are demolished with the hated old institutions. Transition has shown that an institutional vacuum can be worse, in the short-run, than an economy with highly substandard institutions. Hence, a consensus on the overall direction of reforms and on the quick destruction of the old institutions can create both short-term economic dislocation and fertile ground for the rapid growth of new institutions. The impediments to change are fewer and the political need to act is very high. Thus, there is no contradiction in attributing the immense problems of early transition to poor institutions and observing that institutions are improving very quickly. Indeed, they are two sides of the same coin.

When the old institutions have lost all credibility and there is a basic consensus on far-reaching reforms, political agents find themselves with much latitude to press for change, with strong incentives to become institutional entrepreneurs. Such agents naturally seek existing models for the institutions to be created, and the ones that are most prominent are those of the developed countries. During transition, this tendency to use existing models was complemented by the pressing attentions of the developed countries, which provided human capital, financial resources, and more than a little political push. This supply-side process was apparently very successful, judged in terms of the institutions that were created. The ultimate reasons for the success are still not clear, but perhaps a role was played by the rather high levels of human capital in the transition countries.

Nevertheless, high quality institutions do not necessarily lead immediately to economic success, for at least three reasons. First, such institutions cannot immediately counter the consequences of past policies, such as jumbled ownership from mass privatization. Second, institutions that are not calibrated to local circumstances can easily be counterproductive in the short-run, even if they are best-practice for the long-run.[41] Third, economic agents need time to learn to use institutions effectively.

The last two reasons are especially important now because of the way in which institutions were built. In transition, capitalist firms, especially the new smaller and medium-size ones that would be the backbone of the reformed economies,

---

[41] To establish this point, consider the following thought experiment. Imagine the consequences of instantaneously and effectively implementing US financial institutions and Delaware corporate governance in Russia in 1997. The early-transition Hungarian bankruptcy law episode provides a further example (Bonin and Schaffer, 2002).

played less of a role in shaping these new institutions than did the institutional entrepreneurs.[42] The new institutions reflected the concerns of these firms far less than might have been appropriate. Moreover, the owners and managers of these firms were far removed from intimate knowledge of how the institutions of developed economies worked. Consequently, an extensive period of learning would be necessary before the adoption of the types of behavior that would be optimal in reaction to these new institutions. Perhaps, therefore, the real effect of the new institutions lies in the future. Perhaps, these businesses could have reacted more quickly to institutions that had changed more slowly and were closer in spirit to those with which the economic entrepreneurs were more familiar. Perhaps China was lucky in not feeling the strong drawing power of Western best practice models. Perhaps future generations in transition countries will thank their predecessors for forgoing the benefits of transitional institutions.[43]

But these last paragraphs are highly conjectural, based on cursory empirical information.[44] Their main purpose is to show the internal consistency of the observations that have been made in the preceding sections of this chapter. Much more empirical work needs to be done to investigate whether these preliminary observations can be established as hard empirical facts. As the above pages have emphasized, the empirical work on transition that has been directly driven by the NIE has been very limited to date. Thus, transition still presents fertile ground for application of the NIE.

ACKNOWLEDGEMENTS

I would like to thank Peter Grajzl, Yingyi Qian, Thomas Rawski, Mary M. Shirley, Oliver Williamson, and three anonymous referees for helpful comments, Gaston Gohou for research assistance, and Simeon Djankov for stimulating several of the ideas in this chapter during discussions on related work. I gratefully acknowledge the support of the U.S. Agency for International Development (USAID) through the Center on Institutional Reform and the Informal Sector (IRIS) at the University of Maryland. The findings, interpretations, and conclusions expressed in this chapter are entirely those of the authors and do not necessarily represent the views of IRIS or USAID.

---

[42] This comment might seem, at first blush, inconsistent with the state capture hypotheses of Hellman, Jones, and Kaufmann (2000), but it is not. The notion of state capture focuses on the sale of micro decisions to firms, rather than the formation of broad institutions in response to the demands of firms. State capture is inversely correlated with institutional development across transition countries, suggesting that the processes of state capture do not lead to institutional development. Moreover, EBRD (2002, p. 30) states, rather cryptically, that "The experiences of recent years suggest that the degree of state capture was not as stable as earlier analyses indicated."

[43] This is the central trade-off raised by Roland (2000, p. xx) "Nevertheless, the question is raised whether 'transitional institutions' represent stepping-stones toward better institutions or whether they create vested interests that block further institutional transition."

[44] And on the author's personal observations on transition economies.

REFERENCES

Anderson, James H. Young Lee, and Peter Murrell. 2000. "Competition and Privatization amidst Weak Institutions: Evidence from Mongolia". *Econ. Inquiry* 38(4): 527–549.
Aoki, Masahiko and Hyung-Ki Kim (eds.). 1995. *Corporate Governance in Transitional Economies: Insider Control and the Role of the Banks.* Washington, DC: The World Bank.
Benham, Alexandra and Lee Benham. 1997. "Property Rights in Transition Economies: A Commentary on What Economists Know" in Joan M. Nelson, Charles Tilly, and Lee Walker (eds.), *Transforming Post-Communist Political Economies.* Washington DC: National Academy Press.
Berg, Andrew and Olivier Blanchard. 1994. "Stabilization and Transition: Poland, 1990–1991" in Olivier Blanchard, Kenneth Froot, and Jeffrey Sachs (eds.), *The Transition in Eastern Europe, Volume 1: Country Studies.* Chicago, IL: The University of Chicago Press.
Berglof, Erik and Patrick Bolton. 2002. "The Great Divide and Beyond: Financial Architecture in Transition". *Journal of Economics Perspectives* 16(1): 77–100.
Black, Bernard. 2001. "Does Corporate Governance Matter? A Crude Test Using Russian Data". *University of Pennsylvania. Law Review* 149: 2131–2150.
Black, Bernard, Reinier Kraakman, and Anna Tarassova. 2000. "Russian Privatization and Corporate Governance: What Went Wrong?" *Stanford Law Review* 52: 1731–1808.
Blanchard, Olivier and Michael Kremer. 1997. "Disorganization". *Quarterly Journal of Economics* 112(4): 1091–1126.
Boeri, Tito and Katherine Terrell. 2002. "Institutional Determinants of Labor Reallocation in Transition". *Journal of Economics Perspectives* 16(1): 51–76.
Bonin, John and Mark Schaffer. 2002. "Revisiting Hungary's Bankruptcy Episode" in Anna Meyendorff and Anjan Thakor (eds.), *Designing Financial Systems in Transition Economies: Strategies for Reform in Central and Eastern Europe.* Cambridge, MA: MIT Press.
Boycko, Maxim; Andrei Shleifer, and Robert Vishny. 1995. *Privatizing Russia*, Cambridge, MA: MIT Press.
Burkart, Mike; Fausto Panunzi, and Andrei Shleifer. 2002. "Family Firms". NBER Working Paper no. 8776.
Campos, Nauro. 2000. "Context is Everything: Measuring Institutional Change in Transition Economies". World Bank Policy Research Working Paper no. 2269.
Campos, Nauro and Fabrizio Coricelli. 2002. "Growth in Transition: What We Know, What We Don't, and What We Should". *Journal of Economic Literature* 40(3): 793–836.
Che, Jiahua and Yingyi Qian. 1998. "Insecure Property Rights and Government Ownership of Firms". *Quarterly Journal of Economics* 113(2): 467–496.
Coase, Ronald. 1992. "The Institutional Structure of Production". *American Economic Review* 82(4): 713–719.
Coplin, William, Michael O'Leary, and Tom Sealy. 1996. *A Business Guide to Political Risk for International Decisions.* Syracuse, NY: Political Risk Services.
Cull, Robert, Jana Matesova, and Mary M. Shirley. 2002. "Ownership and the Temptation to Loot: Evidence from Privatized Firms in the Czech Republic". *Journal of Comparative Economics* 30(1): 1–25.
Cungu, Azeta and Johan Swinnen. 2003. "Investment and Contract Enforcement in Transition: Evidence from Hungary". LICOS Discussion Paper 127/2003, Katholieke Universiteit Leuven.
Dallago, Bruno. 1992. "Debate on the Transition of Post-Communist Economies to a Market Economy". *Acta Oeconomica* 44(3–4): 267–277.
Dewatripont, Mathias and Gérard Roland. 1992. "The Virtues of Gradualism and Legitimacy in the Transition to a Market Economy". *Econ. J.* 102(411): 291–300.
Dewatripont, Mathias and Gérard Roland. 1997. "Transition as a Process of Large Scale Institutional Change" in David Kreps and Kenneth Wallis (eds.), *Advances in Economic Theory*, Vol. 2. Cambridge University Press, pp. 240–78.

Djankov, Simeon. 1999. "Ownership Structure and Enterprise Restructuring in Six Newly Independent States". *Comparative Economic Studies* 41(1): 75–95.

Djankov, Simeon and Vladimir-Goran Kreacic. 1998. "Restructuring of Manufacturing Firms in Georgia: Four Case Studies and a Survey". ECSPF Occasional Papers Series no. 1.

Djankov, Simeon; Rafael La Porta, Florencio Lopez-de-Silanes, and Andrei Shleifer. 2002. "Courts: the Lex Mundi project". NBER Working Paper no. 8890.

Djankov, Simeon and Peter Murrell. 2002. "Enterprise Restructuring in Transition: A Quantitative Survey". *Journal of Economic Literature* 40(3): 739–792.

Dutz, Mark and Maria Vagliasindi. 2000. "Competition Policy Implementation in Transition Economies: An Empirical Assessment". *European Economic Review* 44(4–6): 762–772.

Earle, John, Saul Estrin, and Larisa Leshchenko. 1996. "Ownership Structures, Patterns of Control, and Enterprise Behavior in Russia" in Simon Commander, Qimiao Fan, and Mark Schaffer (eds.), *Enterprise Restructuring and Economic Policy in Russia*. Washington, DC: Economic Development Institute (EDI) Development Studies, The World Bank.

Earle, John, Ugo Pagano, and Maria Lesi. 2002. "Information Technology, Organizational Form, and Transition to the Market". Upjohn Institute Staff Working Paper no. 02–82.

EBRD *Transition Report—1998*. London: EBRD.

EBRD *Transition Report—2000*. London: EBRD.

EBRD *Transition Report—2002*. London: EBRD.

Ellerman, David. 1993. "Management and Employee Buy-Outs in Central and Eastern Europe: Introduction" in David Ellerman (ed.), *Management and Employee Buy-Outs as a Technique of Privatization*. Ljubljana: Central and Eastern European Privatization Network, pp. 13–30.

Estrin, Saul. 2002. "Competition and Corporate Governance in Transition". *Journal of Economics Perspectives* 16(1): 101–124.

Fischer, Stanley and Alan Gelb. 1991. "The Process of Socialist Economic Transformation". *Journal of Economics Perspectives* 5(4): 91–105.

Glaeser, Edward, Simon Johnson, and Andrei Shleifer. 2001. "Coase versus the Coasians". *Quarterly Journal of Economics* 116(3): 853–899.

Grosfeld, Irena. 1990. "Reform Economics and Western Economic Theory: Unexploited Opportunities". *Economic Planning* 23(1): 1–19.

Hanson, Philip. 1992. "Debate on the Transition of Post-Communist Economies to a Market Economy". *Acta Oecon.* 44(3–4): 282–284.

Heller, Michael. 2001. "A Property Theory Perspective on Russian Enterprise Reform" in Peter Murrell (ed.), *Assessing the Value of Law in Transition Economies*. Ann Arbor, MI: University of Michigan Press.

Hellman, Joel, Geraint Jones, and Daniel Kaufmann. 2000. "Seize the State, Seize the Day: State Capture, Corruption, and Influence in Transition Economies". World Bank Policy Research Working Paper no. 2444.

Hendley, Kathryn. 1996. *Trying to Make Law Matter: Legal Reform and Labor Law in the Soviet Union*. Ann Arbor, MI: University of Michigan Press.

Hendley Kathryn and Peter Murrell. 2003. "Which Mechanisms Support the Fulfillment of Sales Agreements? Asking Decision-Makers in Firms". *Economics Letters* 78(1): 49–54.

Hendley, Kathryn; Peter Murrell, and Randi Ryterman. 2000. "Law, Relationships, and Private Enforcement: Transactional Strategies of Russian Enterprises". *Europe-Asia Studies* 52(4): 627–656.

Hendley, Kathryn, Peter Murrell, and Randi Ryterman. 2001. "Law Works in Russia: The Role of Law in Interenterprise Transactions" in Peter Murrell (ed.), *Assessing the Value of Law in Transition Economies*. Ann Arbor, MI: University of Michigan Press.

Ickes, Barry W. 1990. "Obstacles to Economic Reform of Socialism: An Institutional-Choice Approach". *Annals of the American Academy of Political and Social Science* 507: 53–64.

Jefferson, Gary H. Thomas G. Rawski, Wang Li, and Zheng Yuxin. 2000. "Ownership, Productivity Change, and Financial Performance in Chinese Industry". *Journal of Comparative Economics* 28(4): 786–813.
Johnson, Juliet. 2001. "Agents of Transformation: The Role of the West in Post-Communist Central Bank Development". National Council on Eurasian and East European Research (NCEEER) Working Paper.
Johnson, Simon; Florencio López-de-Silanes, Andrei Shleifer, and Robert Vishny. 2000. "Tunnelling," *American Economic Review* (Papers and Proceedings), 90(2): 22–27.
Johnson, Simon, John McMillan, and Christopher Woodruff. 2002. "Courts and Relational Contracts". *Journal of Law, Economics, and Organization* 18(1): 221–277.
Joskow, Paul and Richard Schmalansee. 1997. "Privatization in Russia: What Should Be a Firm?" in Claude Menard (ed.), *Transaction Cost Economics: Recent Developments*. Cheltenham, UK: Edward Elgar.
Kaufmann, Daniel, Aart Kraay, and Massimo Mastruzzi. 2003. "Governance Matters III: Governance Indicators for 1996–2002". World Bank Policy Research Working Paper no. 3106.
Kaufmann, Daniel, Aart Kraay, and Pablo Zoido-Lobaton. 1999. "Governance Matters". World Bank Policy Research Working Paper no. 2196.
Kaufmann, Daniel, Aart Kraay, and Pablo Zoido-Lobaton. 2002. "Governance Matters II: Updated Indicators for 2000/01". World Bank Policy Research Working Paper no. 2772.
Knack, Stephen and Philip Keefer. 1995. "Institutions and Economic Performance: Cross-Country Tests Using Alternative Institutional Measures". *Economics and Politics* 7(3): 207–227.
Konings, Jozef. 1998. "Firm Performance in Bulgaria and Estonia: The Effects of Competitive Pressure, Financial Pressure and Disorganization". William Davison Institute Working Paper no. 185.
Konings, Jozef and Patrick Paul Walsh. 1999. "Disorganization in the Transition Process: Firm-level Evidence from Ukraine". *Economics of Transition* 7(1): 29–46.
Kornai, Janos. 1990. *The Road to a Free Economy*. New York: Norton.
Landell-Mills, Pierre. 2003. "An Evaluation of World Bank Assistance for Governance, Public Sector Management and Institution Building in the Transition Economies 1990–2002". OED, World Bank.
Lau, Lawrence, Yingyi Qian, and Gérard Roland. 2000. "Reform without Losers: An Interpretation of China's Dual-Track Approach to Transition". *Journal of Political Economy* 108(1): 120–143.
Lichtenstein, Peter M. 1996. "A New Institutionalist Story About the Transformation of Former Socialist Economies: A Recounting and an Assessment". *Journal of Economic Issues* 30(1): 243–265.
Lizal, Lubomir; Miroslav Singer, and Jan Svejnar. 2001. "Enterprise Breakups and Performance During the Transition from Plan to Market". *Review of Economics and Statistics* 83(1): 92–99.
McKinnon, Ronald. 1991. *The Order of Economic Liberalization: Financial Control in the Transition to a Market Economy*. Baltimore, MD: Johns Hopkins University Press.
McMillan, John and Christopher Woodruff. 1999. "Interfirm Relationships and Informal Credit in Vietnam". *Quarterly Journal of Economics* 114(6): 1285–1320.
Murrell, Peter. 1990. *The Nature of Socialist Economies: Lessons from Eastern European Foreign Trade*. Princeton, NJ: Princeton University Press.
Murrell, Peter. 1991. "Symposium on Economic Transition in the Soviet Union and Eastern Europe". *Journal of Economics Perspectives* 5(4): 3–10.
Murrell, Peter. 1992. "Evolution in Economics and in the Economic Reform of the Centrally Planned Economies" in Christopher Clague and Gordon Rausser (eds.), *Emergence of Market Economies in Eastern Europe*. London: Blackwell.
Murrell, Peter. 1995. "The Transition According to Cambridge, Mass". *Journal of Economic Literature* 33(1): 164–178.

Murrell, Peter. 1996. "How Far Has the Transition Progressed?" *Journal of Economics Perspectives* 10(2): 25–44.

Murrell, Peter (ed.). 2001. *Assessing the Value of Law in Transition Economies*. Ann Arbor, MI: University of Michigan Press.

Murrell, Peter. 2003a. "The Relative Levels and the Character of Institutional Development in Transition Economies" in Nauro Campos and Jan Fidrmuc (eds.), *Political Economy of Transition and Development: Institutions, Politics and Policies*. Boston, MA: Kluwer Academic Publishers.

Murrell, Peter. 2003b. "Firms Facing New Institutions: Transactional Governance in Romania". *Journal of Comparative Economics* 31(4): 695–714.

Murrell, Peter and Yijiang Wang. 1993. "When Privatization Should Be Delayed: The Effects of Communist Legacies on Organizational and Institutional Development". *Journal of Comparative Economics* 17(2): 385–406.

North, Douglass. 1990. *Institutions, Institutional Change, and Economic Performance*. Cambridge: Cambridge University Press.

North, Douglass. 1991. "Institutions". *Journal of Economics Perspectives* 5(1): 97–112.

Perotti, Enrico and Stanislav Gelfer. 2001. "Red Barons or Robber Barons? Governance and Financing in Russian FIGs". *European Economic Review* 45(9): 1601–1617.

Pistor, Katharina. 2001. "Law as a Determinant for Equity Market Development: The Experience of Transition Economies" in Peter Murrell (ed.), *Assessing the Value of Law in Transition Economies*. Ann Arbor, MI: University of Michigan Press.

Pistor, Katharina, Martin Raiser, and Stanislaw Gelfer. 2000. "Law and Finance in Transition Economies". *Economics of Transition* 8(2): 325–868.

Qian, Yingyi. 2003. "How Reform Worked in China" in Dani Rodrik (ed.), *In Search of Prosperity: Analytic Narratives on Economic Growth*. Princeton, NJ: Princeton University Press, pp. 297–333.

Ramasastry, Anita, Stefka Slavova, and David Bernstein. 1999. "Market Perceptions of Corporate Governance—EBRD Survey Results". *Law in Transition* 24–33.

Recanatini, Francesca and Randi Ryterman. 2000. "Disorganization or Self-Organization? The Emergence of Business Associations in a Transition Economy". World Bank Working Paper no. 2539.

Roland, Gérard. 2000. *Transition and Economics: Politics, Markets, and Firms*. Cambridge, MA: MIT Press.

Roland, Gérard. 2001. "Corporate Governance Systems and Restructuring: The Lessons from the Transition Experience" in *Annual Bank Conference on Development Economics 2000*. Washington, DC: The World Bank, pp. 331–352.

Sachs, Jeffrey. 1991. "Poland and Eastern Europe: What Is To Be Done?" in Andras Koves and Paul Marer (eds.), *Foreign Economic Liberalization: Transformation in Socialist and Market Economies*. Boulder, CO: Westview Press, pp. 235–246.

Shastitko, Andrei and Vitali Tambovtsev. 2001. "Soft Budget Constraints: Contract Approach". Lomonosov Moscow State University.

Shirley, Mary M. and Lixin Colin Xu. 2001. "Empirical Evidence of Performance Contracts: Evidence from China". *Journal of Law, Economics, and Organization* 17(1): 168–200.

Smyth, Russell. 1998. "New Institutional Economics in the Post-Socialist Transformation Debate". *Journal of Economic Surveys* 12(4): 361–398.

Stark, David. 1992. "Path Dependence and Privatization Strategies in East Central Europe". *East European Politics and Societies* 6(1): 17–54.

Stiglitz, Joseph. 2001a. "Whither Reform? Ten Years of the Transition," in Ha-Joon Chang (ed.), *Joseph Stiglitz and the World Bank: The Rebel Within*. London: Anthem Press, pp. 127–171.

Stiglitz, Joseph. 2001b. "*Quis Custodiet Ipsos Custodes?* Corporate Governance Failures in Transition," in Joseph Stiglitz and Pierre-Alain Muet (eds.), *Governance, Equity, and Global*

Markets—*The Annual Bank Conference on Development Economics—Europe*. Oxford: The World Bank.
Svejnar, Jan. 2002. "Transition Economies: Performance and Challenges". *Journal of Economics Perspectives* 16(1): 3–28.
Vagliasindi, Maria. 2001. "Competition Across Transition Economies: An Enterprise-level Analysis of the Main Policy and Structural Determinants". EBRD Working Paper no. 68.
Voigt, Stefan and Hella Engerer. 2002. "Institutions and Transformation—Possible Policy Implications of the New Institutional Economics," in Klaus Zimmermann (ed.), *Frontiers in Economics*. Berlin: Springer-Verlag, pp. 149–215.
Wagener, Hans-Jurgen. 1992. "Debate on the Transition of Post-Communist Economies to a Market Economy". *Acta Oecon.* 44(3–4): 363–370.
Williamson, Oliver. 1992. "Some Issues in the Transformation of Ownership Institutions in Poland: Comment". *Journal of Institutional Theoretical Economics* 148: 69–71.
Williamson, Oliver. 2000. "The New Institutional Economics: Taking Stock, Looking Ahead". *Journal of Economics Literature* 38(3): 595–613.
Yafeh, Yishay and Tarun Khanna. 2000. "Business Groups and Risk Sharing Around the World". Harvard Business School Competition & Strategy Working Paper no. 01–041.
Zinnes, Clifford, Yair Eilat, and Jeffrey Sachs. 2001. "The Gains from Privatization in Transition Economies: Is 'Change of Ownership' Enough?" IMF Staff Paper 48, pp. 146–170.

27. Social Capital, Social Norms and the New Institutional Economics

PHILIP KEEFER and STEPHEN KNACK

Douglass North (1990) describes institutions as the rules of the game that set limits on human behavior, now a universally-accepted definition. North and others especially underline the crucial role of informal social norms. They predict that, like all rules of the game, social norms should affect the economic prosperity enjoyed by individuals and countries—that they should have a crucial impact, for example, on economic and political development. In fact, substantial evidence demonstrates that social norms prescribing cooperative or trustworthy behavior have a significant impact on whether societies can overcome obstacles to contracting and collective action that would otherwise hinder their development. Much of this evidence comes from outside the new institutional economics, emerging instead from scholarly research in the field of "social capital." A review of this evidence, and its implications for our understanding of the role of social norms and institutions, is therefore the focus of this chapter.

The definition of social capital is contentious, but Woolcock's encompasses most of the literature when he defines it as the norms and networks that facilitate collective action (Woolcock 1998).[1] This distinction between norms and networks corresponds roughly to Uphoff's (1990) distinction between "cognitive" and "structural" manifestations of social capital. This chapter emphasizes work related to the first half of the definition, norms, but we also discuss research more firmly rooted in the second half, networks. In particular, we review social

---

[1] Putnam (1993: 167) defines social capital as "features of social organization, such as trust, norms, and networks, that can improve the efficiency of society by facilitating coordinated actions." Most uses of the term in the literature, however, do not limit it to those norms and networks that improve social efficiency. Coleman (1990, ch. 12) defines social capital in terms of the quantity of obligations or informal "credit slips" between parties that are likely to be repaid, thus implicating both networks (extent of obligations) and norms (which affect likelihood of repayment). Social capital that is productive for some purposes may be useless or destructive for others (Coleman, 1990: 302). For discussions of the definition and history of the term "social capital," see Woolcock (1998) and Sobel (2002), who respectively provide a sociologist's and economist's perspective. Durlauf (2002) and Portes (1998) criticize the use of vague and inconsistent definitions of social capital in the literature; Sobel (2002) agrees but argues that "a vague keyword is not sufficient reason to condemn a promising line of research."

701

C. Ménard and M. M. Shirley (eds.), *Handbook of New Institutional Economics*, 701–725.
© 2005 *Springer. Printed in the Netherlands.*

capital research examining the role of trust and trustworthiness in economic and political development; the effect of social norms on the financing of public goods; the role of voluntary association in building socially beneficial norms; and the role of social heterogeneity in undermining them. The importance of networks, including the voluntary associations stressed by Putnam (1993), is considered primarily in the context of the emergence and impact of norms, and we do not address the literature focusing on the informational advantages of networks.

Social norms "specify what actions are regarded by a set of persons as proper or correct, or improper and incorrect" (Coleman, 1990: 243). Norms and their accompanying potential rewards (for compliance) or punishments (for noncompliance) are not the *sole* determinants of decisions by rational actors, but they "affect the costs and benefits which individuals taken into account when exercising choice" (Coleman, 1987: 135). Norms have no legal or other formal basis, and may sometimes even be in conflict with laws (Coleman, 1990: 243). Norms defined in this way can apply to various social settings with a range of payoff structures. For example, norms can take the form of conventions, resolving coordination problems, such as prescribing that one should drive on the right hand side of the road. As used in this chapter, however, "norms" will be used more restrictively to apply to collective action problems with risks of opportunism, specifically the two prisoner's dilemma variants with the most frequent real-world applications, voluntary provision of public goods and principal-agent games (sometimes called one-sided prisoner's dilemma or trust games). Trust and trustworthiness are therefore central themes in the literature discussed here.

Three conclusions emerge from a survey of this work. First, levels of trust and trustworthiness vary significantly across countries. Second, they have a significant effect on economic outcomes and development. Third, trust and trustworthiness are not simply the product of repeated games and formal institutions, which are the subject of enormous investigation in the new institutional economics and in the social sciences more generally. In order to explain the emergence and sustainability of trustworthy or cooperative behavior in principal-agent or voluntary public goods provision settings, one needs to examine as well such phenomena as the dynamics of social ostracism or participation in "dense horizontal networks."

In the first part of this chapter, we document wide variation in trust and trustworthiness across countries and individuals. This variation potentially explains why only some individuals or countries can undertake or sustain exchanges that require credible commitment in the economic, political or social realms. Subsequently we review the connections among trust, trustworthiness and credible commitment. The final section of the chapter concerns the large literature on the sources of trust and trustworthiness; we conclude that these attitudes do indeed have a significant normative aspect and cannot be viewed only as emerging from reputational forces or from formal, third party institutions.

1. VARIATIONS IN TRUST AND TRUSTWORTHINESS ACROSS COUNTRIES AND INDIVIDUALS

There are large differences in the extent to which people express either trust or trustworthiness, the focus of this chapter. A standard measure of trust used in cross-country comparisons is the answer that people give to the World Values Survey question, "Generally speaking, would you say that most people can be trusted, or that you can't be too careful in dealing with people?" Fewer than 10 percent of Brazilians, Peruvians and Filipinos in the World Values Surveys respond that most people can be trusted when asked this question. At the other extreme, more than 50 percent of Nordic respondents (Norwegians, Finns, Swedes and Danes) agree that most people can be trusted (Knack and Keefer 1997; Zak and Knack 2001).[2]

There is no similar standard measure of trustworthiness for a large sample of countries, but substantial evidence nevertheless suggests that societies differ on this dimension, as well. In an experiment conducted by *Reader's Digest*, twenty wallets containing $50 worth of cash and the addresses and phone numbers of their putative owners were "accidentally" dropped in each of 20 cities, selected from 14 different western European countries. Ten wallets were similarly "lost" in each of 12 U.S. cities. The number of wallets returned with their contents intact was recorded for each city. Country-level proportions of the number of returned wallets are then calculated and exhibited a wide variation, from 30 percent of wallets returned in Italy, 45 percent in Portugal, 60 to 75 percent in different cities of the US, up to 100 percent in Norway and Denmark.

Knack and Keefer (1997) develop a measure of trustworthiness from the World Values Survey data that they call "civic cooperation". It is based on survey respondents' beliefs about whether or not the following actions can ever be justified: claiming government benefits to which respondents were not entitled, avoiding a fare on public transport, cheating on taxes if they had the chance, keeping money that they had found, or failing to report damage they had accidentally done to a parked vehicle. Although we sympathize with Fukuyama's (1995) claim that it is meaningful to label societies as high trust or low trust, trust and trustworthiness are in fact the product of individual behavior and decisions, and substantial individual-level deviations from societal averages are a regularity in the data. For example, there is wide individual-level variation within countries in the 50-point civic cooperation index.

Experimental evidence is consistent with this variation in the survey data. Glaeser et al. (2000) conduct an experiment in which they pair individuals; each pair meets and is then separated. One member of the pair, the sender, is given 15 dollars, and has the opportunity to send up to 15 dollars to the other member, the recipient. For each dollar sent, the "experimenter" gives an additional dollar to the recipient. The recipient then can return money to the sender. All rules of

---

[2] Of 79 countries in which this trust question has been asked in recent national surveys, the mean trusting percentage is 27.8, with a standard deviation of 13.7.

the game are known to all players. The amount of money sent is an indication of trusting behavior; the amount of money returned is an indication of trustworthy behavior. The amount sent averaged $12.41 in the experiment, but the standard deviation was quite high ($4.54), indicating that many participants sent much different amounts. Similarly, of the amount they received, senders on average returned 45.5 percent, but the standard deviation was 26.7 percentage points.[3]

Experimental evidence has led some to question how accurate and meaningful are survey measures of trust and trustworthiness. Glaeser et al. (2000), for example, use their experiment to ask whether the survey question on trust ("can most people be trusted") predicts *trusting* or *trustworthy* behavior by participants. Participant responses to this survey question turn out to predict trusting behavior only weakly. They do, however, predict trustworthy behavior, i.e. the willingness of recipients to return money to senders.

Despite those results, there are strong reasons to think that survey results capture aggregate levels of trust in a society. First, we would not expect trusting attitudes to survive for long in a society with few trustworthy people. Second, there is substantial direct evidence of aggregate-level correlations between trust and trustworthiness. Barr (2003) conducted experiments similar to those of Glaeser et al. (2000) in 24 Zimbabwean villages with 141 pairs of players, but did not allow the subjects to know the identity of their partners prior to or during the experiment, unlike Glaeser, et al. The Zimbabwe data indicate a high level of correlation between trusting and trustworthy behavior across villages. Measures of trust and trustworthiness from the World Values survey are also highly correlated: the civic cooperation index designed by Knack and Keefer (1997), reflecting socially trustworthy behavior, is significantly correlated (at .39) with the trust measure at the country level, again controlling for per capita income. Finally, the percentage of wallets returned in the *Readers Digest* experiment, certainly an objective and behavioral measure of trustworthiness, is correlated at .44 with responses to the "found" money question in the World Values Survey, and more generally with standard measures of trust and honesty derived from the Survey, even controlling for per capita income (Knack 2001). Figure 1 depicts the simple correlation between returned wallets and trust survey responses across countries.

The variation across individuals, within countries, in social norms of trust and trustworthiness has important implications. Fukuyama (2000) points out that norms of trust and trustworthiness may have either a narrow or wide "radius". Norms that overcome collective action problems and build trust within but not between families, social classes or ethnic groups often impose negative externalities on non-members of these groups. These narrow-radius norms can have adverse implications for welfare at the societal level, much as clientelism, as viewed by Keefer (2002), may leave clients better off than they would be in a society lacking either formal institutions or the informal institutions of

---

[3] In the original version of this experiment (Berg, Dickhaut and McCabe, 1995), players did not meet each other, and the amounts sent and returned were somewhat lower than in Glaeser et al. (2000).

Trusting survey responses (percent)

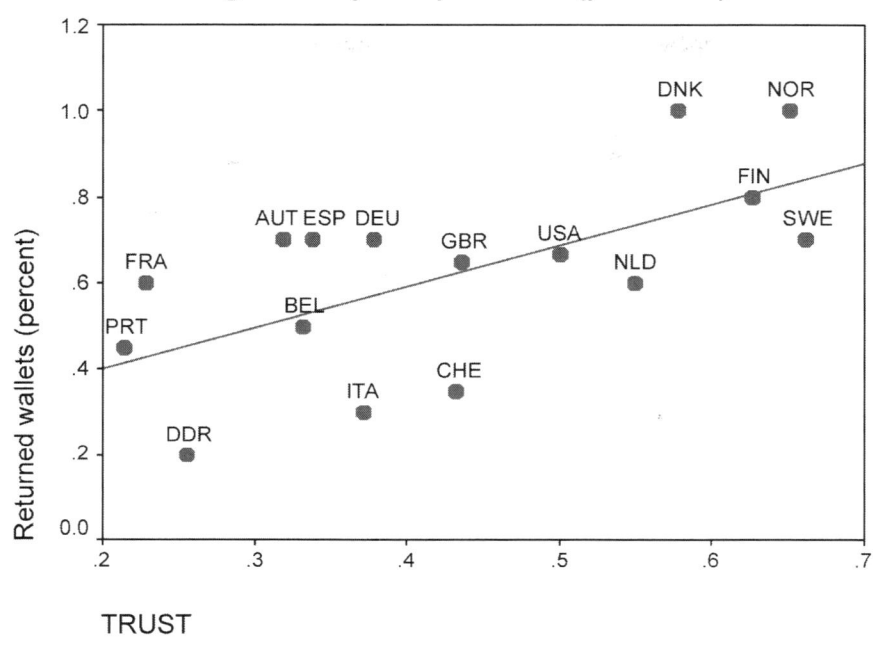

Figure 1. Returned wallets and trust across countries.

clientelism, but likely has negative effects on non-clients.[4] Strong intra-ethnic trust in an ethnically heterogeneous society may restrict the scope for transacting and lead to segmented markets, reducing gains from specialization and economies of scale (Greif 1994). The same strong ties that help members of a group can be used to exclude other (often disadvantaged) community members from the benefits of collective action (e.g. Pantoja 2002).

On the other hand, if a larger fraction of society, due to social norms, can be relied upon to fulfill contracts and fulfill their obligations under the social compact, trustworthiness can be said to be of wide radius.[5] In societies characterized by wide radius trustworthiness, individuals are not only reliable partners in contractual exchange, whether political or economic, but can also be relied upon to act in the interest of others at some expense to oneself by, for example,

---

[4] Even within an extended family, norms of sharing resources can reduce the incentive for a family member to start a business (Portes, 1998). Banfield (1958) attributed incompetent government and poverty in a poor Italian village to "amoral familism" preventing cooperation among citizens.

[5] Knack and Keefer (1997) refer to norms that overcome large-numbers collective action problems and build trust at the level of communities or societies (as opposed to between pairs of traders or other small-numbers settings) as norms of "civic cooperation," or "civic norms." These are simply norms of trustworthiness operating at the level of the social compact.

2. Trust and Trustworthiness and the Problem of Credible Commitment

As many of the contributions to this volume make clear, a central issue in the new institutional economics is the disruption to human interaction caused by the inability to make credible commitments. The absence of credible commitment disrupts three types of human interaction: economic exchange; relationships among voters and politicians; and the "social compact". Social norms that produce trust and trustworthiness can solve the problem of credible commitment in each of these spheres.

Problems of Credible Commitment in Economic, Political and Social Interaction

The ability of one party to an exchange to make credible promises to another party opens up a whole range of economic possibilities that would otherwise be unattainable. Absent the credibility of promises, risks of opportunistic behavior by contracting parties force them to turn to spot market transactions rather than to rely on contracts across time and space. Spot markets are sufficient to allow some gains from trade, but do not capture many or most of the potential benefits from specialization. They are incompatible with, for example, financial contracts, where creditors loan money to debtors on the promise of future repayment; employment contracts, where managers hire employees to accomplish tasks that are difficult to monitor or measure; and fixed investments, where investors rely on assurances by firms and governments that their assets will not be expropriated. Trust is obviously important in this context. Where the parties inherently trust each other, transactions that require credible promises are easier to consummate.

The policy outcomes driven by political competition crucially depend on credibility. Persson and Tabellini (2000) show that the effects of institutional change are dramatically different in societies where political promises prior to elections are credible and in societies where they are not. For example, the shift from majoritarian to proportional electoral rules increases the rents that politicians can extract for themselves when political competitors cannot make credible pre-election promises to voters, but reduces rents when they can.[6] Keefer (2002) shows that young democracies perform substantially worse on many margins than older democracies, controlling for income per capita and other characteristics. He argues that this is due to the peculiarities of political promises in young democracies. Where trust in politicians is narrowly confined to a few

---

[6] Majoritarian electoral rules are those where the number of seats per electoral district is small and citizens vote for candidates rather than parties; proportional representation rules are those where electoral districts are larger and citizens vote for party lists.

voters who have personally interacted with the politicians, one definition of clientelism, political competition need not improve public policy.

The credibility of political commitments also influences the ability of politicians to undertake reforms or respond to crisis, the theme of a large literature (e.g., Acemoglu and Robinson 2001). Socially beneficial reforms would always occur if the winners could compensate the losers. However, spot markets for reform, where compensation is paid at the moment that reform is approved, are notoriously difficult to construct. On the one hand, for numerous reasons, not the least of which are tight budget constraints, governments can rarely offer losers the cash value of the present value of their losses. The government can circumvent this problem by offering future compensation. Non-credible governments do not have this option, however. For example, power sector subsidies are a crippling burden on Indian states. The majority of farmers who benefit from power subsidies are poor and receive collectively a small fraction of the total subsidies. Their support for reform should be easy to buy, and sufficient. Still, even in one of the most progressive Indian states, Andhra Pradesh, reforms of the power sector have proven to be intractable.[7] One reason for this is that poor farmers do not believe government promises to compensate them in exchange for eliminating the subsidies.[8]

Human interaction obviously extends far beyond interactions in the economic and political spheres. Smoothly running societies also benefit from a well-developed and credible "social compact"—the unwritten commitments that citizens have made to each other. In many societies, the extent of these commitments is highly circumscribed because everyone believes that most individuals will shirk on their responsibilities under the compact, even though all would be better off if no one shirked. Societies in which such beliefs are widespread are limited in their ability to collect taxes, enforce laws, even to maintain clean streets.[9] Societies in which decisions of individuals are influenced by social norms are likely to exhibit less shirking on the social compact—i.e. to be more trustworthy—and hence able to govern themselves at substantially lower cost.

Evidence on the Influence of Social Norms on the Problem of Credible Commitment

The larger the fraction of people in a society who share norms prescribing co-operative or trustworthy behavior in collective action settings, the more likely is

---

[7] See, for example, "Power Politics–Process of Power Sector Reform in India," by Navroz Dubash and Sudhir Rajan, in *Economic and Political Weekly*, Sept 1, 2001.

[8] Wealthier farmers are at the center of efforts to organize farmers collectively in support of continued price ceilings on power. If they are excluded from attempts to buy off opponents of power sector reform, they have little interest in continuing to organize farmers—but it is only collective action by farmers that guarantees farmers that they can act against governments that renege on their promises. If wealthier farmers are included in the buy out attempts, the cost of reform goes up substantially.

[9] See Levi (1988) and Scholz and Lubell (1998) for the importance of informal norms and trust in revenue collection.

the society to have overcome problems of credible commitment in the economic, political and social spheres. That is, in the language of Fukuyama (2000), where wide-radius trust and trustworthiness are prevalent, contracting parties can dispense with costly monitoring of performance. Individuals in these societies can spend less to protect themselves from being exploited in economic and political transactions. Written contracts are less likely to be needed and they do not have to specify every possible contingency. Individuals have more resources available for innovation and investment, as they can devote fewer resources to protecting themselves—through tax payments, bribes, or private security services and equipment—from unlawful (criminal) violations of their property rights. Norms of civic cooperation reduce enforcement costs by leading individuals to internalize the value of laws and regulations even when the probability of detection for violation is negligible.

Substantial evidence suggests that trust and trustworthiness matter for interactions that rely on credible commitment. At the individual level, there is ample experimental evidence along the lines of the experiment conducted by Glaeser et al. (2000), showing that recipients who expressed trusting attitudes (the belief that most people can be trusted) returned 10 percent more money to senders than did other recipients (i.e., they were more trustworthy) controlling for other recipient characteristics.[10]

Individual level evidence does not lend itself easily to understanding the broader problems of credible commitment in the context of economic and political development. Nevertheless, a wide range of cross-country evidence also demonstrates the importance of trust and trustworthiness. Fukuyama (1995) attributes cross-national differences in economic performance to variations in trust and "spontaneous sociability."[11] Among the nations he discusses in detail, he classifies the U.S., Japan and Germany as high-trust societies, and France, Italy, China, Korea, Hong Kong and Taiwan as low-trust societies. In statistical cross-country tests, Knack and Keefer (1997) find that a ten percentage point increase in the number of citizens who express trusting attitudes is associated with an increase in per capita economic growth of almost one percentage point per year. The effects of trust on growth turn out to rival those of the fraction of children enrolled in primary education. Using a broader sample and different specifications, Zak and Knack (2001) report similar results.

These results could be affected by reverse causation: the trust coefficient could be biased upward if growth increases trust (for example, by making people more optimistic), or downward if growth decreases trust (for example, by disrupting traditional social and community ties as in Olson 1963 or Miguel, Gertler and Levine 2002). However, Zak and Knack (2001), following La Porta et al. (1997),

---

[10] The controls were the amount originally transferred by the sender to the recipient, whether the pair of participants were of different genders, the gender and race of recipient, and whether recipients were in their first year of college (the participants were all Harvard undergraduates).

[11] "The ability to associate depends, in turn, on the degree to which communities share norms and values and are able to subordinate individual interests to those of larger groups" (Fukuyama, 1995: 10).

use religious composition variables as instruments and find that the exogenous component of trust remains significantly related to growth.

Trust and other manifestations of social capital may also matter fundamentally to the survival of democratic government. Paxton (1999) and Inglehart (1999) argue that a culture of trust is necessary for governments to be willing to surrender power to the opposition, and therefore for the survival of democracy. Inglehart (1999) finds a strong correlation between trust and stability of democratic institutions, using cross-country data. In a classic comparative study of the U.S., U.K., Germany, Italy, and Mexico, Almond and Verba (1963) argue that a stable democratic political system depends on a strong "civic culture" with high interpersonal trust and active involvement in voluntary associations.

Studies linking trust and broad outcomes, such as growth and regime survival, have been complemented by work that looks at specific channels through which informal norms underlying trust and trustworthiness might affect these broad outcomes. Using survey data, Knack and Keefer (1997) report that citizens' confidence in government—the credibility of government—is significantly greater in higher-trust nations.[12] La Porta et al. (1997) and Knack and Keefer (1997) demonstrate that countries with more trusting citizens exhibit higher ratings in foreign investor risk assessments on subjective measures of governmental efficiency, corruption, and infrastructure quality.[13] Knack (2002) reports similar results for the American states, using more "technocratic" measures of governmental quality.

These results suggest that norms prescribing cooperation and trustworthiness enhance governmental effectiveness. Boix and Posner (1998) and Knack (2002) argue that they do this by helping voters overcome the collective action problem in monitoring and sanctioning public officials. Key to citizens' oversight of government officials is their willingness to collect and assess information about government performance and their willingness to take action (such as voting, writing letters, signing petitions, demonstrating etc.) to convey their preferences to officials and to expel poor performers. The purely self-interested citizen would neglect both tasks, and free-ride on the efforts of others. The citizen motivated by a norm of civic cooperation (one manifestation of trustworthiness) becomes more informed about politics and public affairs, and more willing to vote or in other ways exercise "voice" options, creating checks on the ability of politicians and bureaucrats to enrich themselves or narrow interests with which politicians might be allied.

As with trust and economic performance, there is a potential for endogeneity bias in tests linking trust to government performance. For example, high-trust societies may be better at keeping their governments honest, but the honesty

---

[12] This test controlled for income per capita and primary and secondary educational enrollment. The dependent variable was a composite of citizens' confidence in the civil service, legal system, police, and education system.

[13] La Porta et al. control for per capita income, include all countries with available data, and use trust values from the early 1990s. Knack and Keefer control for income and education, exclude formerly-communist nations, and use the earliest-available observation on trust (typically, the early 1980s).

and efficiency of government officials can in turn affect trust. "If government leaders, judges and bureaucrats are corrupt, market participants can more easily justify and rationalize their own dishonest behavior" (Drobak 1998, 103; also see Gambetta 1988, 158–63). If a government provides services effectively, communities may run more smoothly, with less crime and social strife, generating more trust and civic cooperation. However, studies using religious composition variables as instruments have found that the exogenous component of trust remains significantly related to government performance (Knack, 2002; La Porta et al., 1997).

The findings linking trust and trustworthiness in societies with government effectiveness and performance echo the findings of Putnam's (1993) pathbreaking work on the Italian regions. Putnam, however, relied primarily on measures more closely linked to the "network" aspects of social capital than the "norms" aspect from which the trust and trustworthiness discussion springs. Social capital researchers focusing on the "network" aspect, in an empirical context, ask whether people in a community or society are linked in dense horizontal relationships such as those that emerge from participation in civic activities, sports clubs, neighborhood associations and singing societies. Roughly speaking, the more dense are these horizontal relationships and the larger the fraction of the population that participates in them, the more social capital exists.

A growing literature has followed Putnam in examining the effects of horizontal networks or associational activity on economic and political outcomes in a society. Although the discussion in this chapter is focused on the normative aspects of social capital, the network approach to social capital is relevant for two reasons. First, the examination of associational activity in societies may allow investigators to skirt the difficulties raised by the potential endogeneity of measures of trust and trustworthiness. Costa and Kahn (2003a), starting from the premise that trust and trustworthiness are endogenous, consciously focus on horizontal networks rather than social norms directly. Second, the causal path from associational activity through to economic or political outcomes may pass through trust and trustworthiness.

Narayan and Pritchett (1999) find for a sample of Tanzanian villages that higher levels of associational membership are associated with higher household incomes. Isham and Kähkönen (2002) show that in villages in Sri Lanka and India with more active community groups and associations, household participation in design of community-based water projects is higher, and monitoring mechanisms are more likely to be in place. Participation and monitoring in water projects, in turn, were associated with improved health and reduced time devoted to collecting water.

Not all studies yield results consistent with Putnam's earlier findings, however. In their study of neighborhoods in Bangladesh, Pargal, Gilligan, and Huq (2002) found that associational activity in a community at best weakly predicted whether that community was successful in organizing collective action. The presence of associations that provided "private" goods or services (sports clubs and women's organizations) in the neighborhood were associated with a reduced likelihood of success in organizing voluntary waste management services, while associations providing "public" goods or services (neighborhood watch groups, and welfare, library and religious groups) had effects that were significantly positive only for some model specifications.[14]

In addition, the effects of associational activity may break down at higher levels of aggregation. Membership in groups is unrelated to measures of government performance across the American states (Knack, 2002) and across countries (Knack and Keefer, 1997), controlling for income, education and other variables.[15] This pattern is consistent with the possibility that the activities of some groups impose negative externalities on non-members, which are not captured in household-level or even community-level analyses. Knack and Keefer (1997) and Knack (2003) also find little difference in the effects of group activity, even after controlling for the type of group. They distinguish groups that might act as redistributional coalitions, with adverse economic impacts (Olson, 1982), from those that do not. However, when group memberships are divided into "Olson" groups (mainly professional associations and unions) and "Putnam" groups (social or other groups that engage in little or no lobbying on economic issues), neither type tends to be significantly associated with economic performance.

3. THE SOURCES OF TRUST: WHAT DO SOCIAL NORMS CONTRIBUTE THAT REPUTATION AND FORMAL INSTITUTIONS DO NOT?

Although a review of the literature yields substantial evidence suggesting that social norms often make commitments more credible, a far larger literature argues for the importance of two other mechanisms through which individuals and societies lay the foundation of credible commitment: reputation and formal institutions. The role of reputation and its genesis in repeated exchange are the subject of an immense game-theoretic literature. The study of how formal institutions such as courts, industry associations, credit bureaus and political institutions such as checks and balances can solve commitment problems is a key element of the new institutional economics. Unfortunately, it is often difficult to distinguish whether trusting and trustworthy behavior emerges as the consequence of an informal social norm, or because of the presence of reputational and institutional conditions that also give rise to such behavior.

Social norms are especially interesting as a focus of inquiry to the extent that they are a new and different source of trusting and trustworthy behavior. Behavior commonly called "trust" that is grounded in reputation and formal institutions is considered to be so well understood that many authors employ different

---

[14] Number of associations was measured prior to the formation of any voluntary waste management services, to eliminate endogeneity concerns.

[15] These results do not directly contradict those of Putnam (1993, 2000), because his indexes of social capital mix measures of associational activity with other dimensions of social capital.

terminology to describe it, such as "assurance" (Yamagishi and Yamagishi, 1994) or "calculative trust" (Williamson, 1993).

The study of the "network" half of the social capital equation confronts similar ambiguities concerning how they produce trust and cooperation. One well-documented way in which networks operate to improve outcomes is precisely because of their reputational function. Showing the game theoretic (reputational) roots of successful networks is a key element in the influential analysis of Greif (1993), for example. To the extent that networks succeed because of their reputational effects, however, they do not justify the study of social norms, or social capital more broadly, as a separate line of scholarly inquiry into economic and political behavior. Further research is needed to distinguish the role of networks above and beyond their reputational role.

Nevertheless, at least with respect to normative social capital, there are several reasons to think that the role of reputation and formal institutions cannot be the whole story. Neither reputational nor institutional sanctions for non-trusting or non-trustworthy behavior exist in anonymous, single play trust and public goods experiments. However, most participants in these experiments exhibit at least some degree of trust and trustworthiness (Ostrom, 2000; Berg, Dickhaut, and McCabe, 1995). Intuitively, as well, the role of guilt feelings, fear of eternal damnation, or shame—consequences that are intrinsic to an individual's utility function and are linked distantly, if at all, to reputation or formal institutions—should have a significant role in motivating trusting and trustworthy behavior. Even social ostracism, a well-documented deterrent to cheating, is sufficiently removed from the standard reputational story as to constitute a substantially different phenomenon, and one worthy of independent investigation as a "second-order" norm enforcing social norms to contribute to public goods or to behave in a trustworthy manner (e.g. Coleman, 1990: ch. 11; Elster, 1989; Hardin, 1982: 172–9).The remainder of the chapter reviews evidence on the different determinants of trusting and trustworthy behavior. This evidence suggests that such behavior is less likely when institutions and reputation impose weak constraints on human interaction. Nevertheless, numerous other factors, much more difficult to explain within an institutional or reputational framework, also matter significantly.

Formal Institutions

Hobbes in *Leviathan* (1651) viewed government as the sole source of trust between strangers. Certainly, there is ample evidence of the role of formal institutions in lending credibility to exchanges that otherwise would not occur. In countries where legal codes, enforcement agencies and courts are sufficiently well-developed, the prospect of legal sanctions reduces incentives to cheat. Regulatory agencies (such as the Securities and Exchange Commission), stock exchange memberships and professional associations restrain cheating by instituting financial disclosure rules or licensing requirements (e.g. for accountants or realtors), or by promulgating formal ethical codes (e.g. bar and medical associations). Credit bureaus protect lenders from opportunistic debtors, and protect sellers from buyers paying on credit.[16] The Better Business Bureaus (formal or third-party institutions) of the United States permit reputational constraints on firms to flourish, since they facilitate the dissemination of information about firms' compliance with contractual commitments. Finally, formal institutions have more direct effects: by tying the hands of state actors and making it difficult for them to renege on their commitments, formal political institutions can strengthen trusting attitudes among individuals in a society. In societies with strong formal institutions, one would therefore expect individuals to act in more trusting ways, and at the same time to express greater confidence in the trustworthiness of others, even if such trustworthiness were simply the product of a cost-benefit calculation driven by formal institutions.

It is worth emphasizing that although a formal institution can sometimes make an informal norm unnecessary, the decline in informal norms can as well provide an impetus to the development of formal institutions. Zucker (1986) argues that in the United States, between 1840 and 1920, the increasing cultural heterogeneity of immigrants and, to a lesser degree, increasing internal migration, weakened informal institutions and disrupted social ties. "In a heterogeneous social system, a proportionately smaller number of transactions occurred between similar others" (Zucker 1986, 78). However, she further argues that formal institutions emerged to offset the effects of these exogenous demographic shocks on the informal bases for credible commitment.[17] There is nothing inevitable about the emergence of formal institutions to take the place of fading informal institutions, and Zucker attributes greater inevitability to their emergence as a result of immigration and the breakdown in social ties than is warranted. However, the associations she documents are striking and important, and the ambiguities that they inject into any discussion about the determinants of social norms need to be borne in mind.

Regardless of whether formal institutions "cause" informal institutions to disappear, or vice versa, many pieces of evidence suggest that trust and trustworthiness emerge for reasons other than the formal institutional environment. Knack and Keefer (1997) find that the extent to which the executive branch of government is constrained from acting arbitrarily and the extent to which courts are regarded as independent are both significant predictors of trust. However,

---

[16] In the U.S., employers often use credit bureaus to investigate job applicants. Bad credit is viewed as a predictor of shirking and thievery.

[17] At the same time that immigration was undermining informal modes of contract enforcement, letters of credit and later, credit ratings were introduced (Zucker 1986, 87); requirements of financial soundness for listing on stock exchanges became more stringent; banks devoted more resources to investigating borrowers, and increased collateral requirements (Zucker 1986, 88–89); the ratio of managers to workers in manufacturing rose, as monitoring worker effort and output became a greater concern (Zucker 1986, 91–92); the proportion of transactions occurring within hierarchies, as opposed to within markets, increased (Zucker 1986, 93); licensing standards (e.g. certification of accountants) emerged and professional associations were created (Zucker 1986, 94); and third party enforcement increased, as with the increased use of escrow accounts.

the impact of these formal institutions does not overshadow the effects of other influences on trust, such as education and income, and they leave much of the variation in trust and trustworthiness unexplained. Differences in formal institutions also do not explain the large variations in trust and trustworthiness across the U.S. states (Knack, 2002) and among individuals within countries, nor the strong downward trend from about 1965 to 1990 for the U.S. overall (Putnam, 2000; Knack, 1992). While not conclusive, the evidence is at least highly suggestive that norms that exist independently of the formal institutional characteristics of society are a key source of trust and trustworthiness.

Reputation

Reputational considerations are among the most frequently studied sources of trust. The basic reputation story is straightforward: exchange partners that expect to do business or interact in the future are less likely to renege on commitments than partners who have no such expectations. The evidence suggests that this direct reputational constraint explains trusting behavior, as we would expect, but only partially. Glaeser et al. (2000) find that the length of time that paired participants had known each other prior to the experiment had a modest impact on the willingness of senders to transfer money to recipients and a somewhat greater effect on the willingness of recipients to return money (see their Table 4). Other factors, more closely linked to the social capital literature than to the reputational literature, had a much stronger effect: the hours that senders spent studying alone—like bowling alone, a possible indicator of thin social networks which may be associated with weaker norms—had a strongly negative impact on the amounts they transferred (Glaeser et al., Table 7).[18] In situations where one did not anticipate exchanges with a particular partner to continue into the future, one's contractual behavior could still become known by and affect transactions with other potential exchange partners. Reputation with others is an important and well-documented mechanism of contractual enforcement, but not one that has been examined in the context of social norms. In one approximation to this issue, Glaeser et al. (2000, Table 4) find that the number of friends that paired participants have in common has an insignificant positive effect on both the amount sent by the sender to the recipient (trusting behavior) and on the amount returned to the sender by the recipient.[19] This result suggests that the broader reputational story is even less important than the bilateral reputational effect.

---

[18] The Glaeser et al. (2000) experiments provide other positive evidence that non-reputational/non-institutional factors influence the willingness of experiment participants to entrust or to return money. Respondents with siblings were much more trustworthy than respondents without siblings: the former returned more than twice as much money to senders (98 percent of what the senders originally transferred) as the latter (only 46 percent). The participant responses to trust and trustworthiness survey questions also had a significant impact on the willingness of recipients to return funds, controlling for many other participant characteristics.

[19] The regressions with common friends do not control for months that the paired participants have known each other, and vice versa.

The Threat of Social Ostracism

Even if internal sanctions (guilt, shame, fear of afterlife sanctions) from violation of norms prescribing cooperation and trustworthiness have limited force for some individuals, trust and trustworthiness may result from the threat of social ostracism of the untrusting and untrustworthy. Evidence for the importance of ostracism comes from a variety of sources. Experimental evidence indicates that many people are willing to bear sizeable costs in order to punish free-riding behavior by others, even in one-shot games where there are no future rewards for the punisher (Fehr and Gachter, 2000). Survey evidence also suggests social disapproval is a significant deterrent to voter abstention in American elections (Knack, 1992). Wherever people have voluntarily organized themselves to manage common-pool natural resources effectively over a long period of time, a key reason for success is that participants invest in monitoring and sanctioning free riding behavior (Ostrom, 1990).

The work of Henrich et al. (2001) shows that trusting and trustworthy behavior motivated by social ostracism can eventually evolve into social norms. They report the results of public goods experiments on 15 tribes or other small-scale simple societies. The tribes or communities that exhibit the most cooperation in the experimental settings are also those where the payoffs to cooperation in their main economic activities (foraging, herding, slash and burn agriculture, whaling, etc.) are highest. That is, in communities where the payoffs to norms of social ostracism are highest, trusting and trustworthy behavior are most prevalent. Since the threat of ostracism could not have played a role in the experiments—which were anonymous—it is reasonable to conclude that the trust and trustworthiness exhibited by participants had themselves evolved into social norms.

One might argue that social ostracism is simply a reputational game in which members of a society agree to punish those who exhibit destructive behavior. If this were the case, trust and trustworthiness generated by the threat of ostracism could not be seen as independent of reputation. In fact, social ostracism can emerge as the equilibrium of an infinitely repeated game. However, as Sethi and Somanathan (1996) point out, so can countless other equilibria. The difficulty with explaining social ostracism as the simple outcome of a reputational game is easy to see. Ostracism itself imposes costs on the individuals who, on behalf of society, ostracize. A problem of backward regress ensues: who will ostracize those who fail to ostracize? Treating the obligation to ostracize the untrustworthy as a norm—as indeed it seems to be—resolves this problem.[20]

Social Heterogeneity

Numerous sociological explanations of why people might trust or behave in a trustworthy fashion have been advanced. One such explanation is based on

---

[20] See Sethi and Somanathan (1996) for a rigorous statement of how such a norm could emerge and the conditions under which it would be stable over time. Posner and Rasmusen (1989) discuss the difficulties confronting the emergence of norms of ostracism, in the context of a broader discussion of social norms.

social distance: the more numerous the dimensions along which individuals differ and the greater are those differences, the less they interact (Akerlof 1997) and the less able they are to trust each other (Zak and Knack 2001). These dimensions might include blood and ethnic ties, language, culture, education, income, wealth, occupation, social status, political and economic rights, and geographic distance. According to Zucker (1986, 63):

> Just as ethnicity, sex, or age may be used as an index of job skills by employers, they can be used as an index of trust in a transaction. They serve as indicators of membership in a common cultural system, of shared background expectations. In general, the greater the number of social similarities (dissimilarities), the more interactants assume that common background expectations do (do not) exist, hence trust can (cannot) be relied upon.

There are at least four reasons why socially dissimilar people may be less trusting or trustworthy. Similarity may imply greater risk of social opprobrium or ostracism in the event of improper behavior towards another. In smaller or close-knit communities, the strong likelihood of social interaction between agents and principals can enhance trust in their contractual agreements, as cheating may prompt ostracism. If the agent values the principal's respect, shame is another potential cost of cheating, even (or especially) when the principal does not ostracize the cheating agent.[21] John Stuart Mill (1848, 135–136, 444) wrote that "...much of the security of person and property in modern nations is the effect of manners and opinion" and of "the fear of exposure". As the earlier discussion repeatedly notes, a norm enforced by ostracism is similar to, but in substantial ways different from, the usual reputational story.

The quote from Zucker (1986) suggests a second possibility, however. People believe themselves to be inherently trustworthy and are prepared to act that way when they find other people whom they believe to be inherently trustworthy, as well. However, when social distance grows, their confidence in the inherent trustworthiness of others weakens. In this view, convergent expectations and similarity in preferences for public goods (broadly defined) are an important basis for trust, and the divergent experiences and values implied by greater social distance undermine trust formation.

A third possibility relates to the role of fairness in determining the exact content of norms prescribing cooperation, for example how much one should contribute voluntarily to a public good and under what circumstances. Collective action theorists have long posited that much conformity to social norms prescribing cooperation is motivated by a sense of fairness or reciprocity (e.g., Hardin, 1982), and experimentalists are beginning to accumulate empirical evidence supporting this view (Fehr and Gachter, 2000). While a minority may believe they have a moral obligation (based on religious belief for example) to cooperate even if no one else does, most people appear to be "contractarians" or "conditional cooperators" who feel bound by norms to cooperate only

---

[21] Shame differs from guilt in that it is activated only when others learn that one has cheated.

if a sufficient number of others cooperate. Social heterogeneity can reduce the likelihood that a consensus will emerge on what constitutes a fair set of contributions toward the public good. For example, within a group of people with similar incomes and tastes for a public good, equal voluntary contributions to the public good is a prominent solution. Where incomes or tastes vary markedly, however, the rich and poor are likely to disagree on what constitutes fairness, and the sense of obligation to contribute will suffer (Hardin, 1982: 92).[22]

Finally, and most simply, altruism may be greater in more homogeneous groups. Where an individual's utility function takes into account the costs her decisions impose on others, she is more likely to contribute voluntarily to public goods and to refrain from cheating in principal-agent games.

All of these four cases predict that the more homogeneous a society, the more trust a (randomly selected) principal will place in a (randomly selected) agent. Consistent with these arguments, cross-country studies have found that ethnic and linguistic homogeneity increase trust, while income inequality decreases it (Knack and Keefer 1997; Zak and Knack 2001; Alesina and Ferrara 2002, 2000). Experimental evidence is mixed, but not inconsistent with these results. Glaeser et al. (2000, Table 4) present results in which differences in nationality and race have an insignificant negative effect on trusting behavior (the willingness of senders to transfer funds), but a significant and negative effect on trustworthy behavior (recipients returning funds to senders).

There is considerable evidence, as well, that social heterogeneity undermines civic cooperation or social trustworthiness in the sense defined by Knack and Keefer (1997). Cooperation with the census and participation in groups are lower where ethnic heterogeneity and income inequality are higher (Alesina and La Ferrara, 2002, 2000; Vigdor, 2004; Costa and Kahn, 2003a). Desertion in the Union Army in the U.S. Civil War was higher in companies with greater diversity in age and occupation (Costa and Kahn, 2003b). If one equates, as is reasonable, desertion and non-cooperation with the census as evidence of civic non-cooperation or non-trustworthiness, then this work presents strong evidence that social heterogeneity undermines potentially important social norms.

The documented relationship between trust and government performance suggests that to the extent that social heterogeneity influences trust it should also influence government performance. Easterly and Levine (1997) find that ethnic heterogeneity in countries is correlated with a range of indicators of inefficient policies, including a high black market currency premium, high corruption levels, low schooling rates, a lack of financial development, and poor infrastructure. Using cross-city and cross-county data for the U.S., Alesina, Baqir, and Easterly (1999) find lower levels of public good provision in more ethnically-divided areas. Miguel and Gugerty (2002) show similar results across Kenyan communities. Keefer and Knack (2002) conclude that property rights are more uncertain in highly-polarized societies, as measured not only by ethnic tensions

---

[22] Prospects for a high-trust equilibrium would then depend critically on the number of Kantians or unconditional cooperators available to catalyze cooperative behavior by the conditional cooperators.

and heterogeneity but also by income and land inequality. Berg and Sachs (1988) test the effects of income inequality on indebtedness, concluding that polarized countries are more likely to default on sovereign debt, as indicated by discounts on country debt in secondary markets.

At a much lower level of aggregation, Karlan (2003) finds that more culturally homogeneous rotating credit associations have lower default rates on loans.[23] Similarly, Kähkönen (1999) shows that collective action for water supply increases with homogeneity of caste, kinship and ethnicity. Grootaert (1999) finds more frequent participation in collective action by members of homogenous than of heterogeneous associations among Indonesian villagers, with kin group and religious dimensions particularly important.[24] To the extent that co-operation in the pursuit of socially desirable public policies is one indicator of norms of civic cooperation, all of this evidence is consistent with the thesis that social heterogeneity undermines social norms on which trust and trustworthiness heavily rely. Two other possible explanations cannot be easily excluded, however.

First, as Alesina, Baqir and Easterly argue, people may prefer to finance public goods that benefit other people like themselves. Second, as Keefer and Knack (2002) argue, where individuals in a collective are simply more different in their preferences, collective decision making is naturally also more difficult and less likely to yield jointly optimal outcomes, independent of any norms of cooperation or mutual dislike.

Group Membership and Trust

An additional possible determinant of trust and trustworthiness emerges from the "network" or "associational" definition of social capital. Coleman argues that the number, intensity and structure of "horizontal" interactions among individuals in a community facilitate the emergence of desirable norms and trust (1990, 318–319).[25] Putnam argues that voluntary associations, in particular, "instill in their members habits of cooperation, solidarity, and public-spiritedness" with positive spillovers for trust and cooperative behavior in the larger social arena (Putnam 1993: 89–90). The underlying rationale for these conclusions is three-fold. First, common membership may reflect and nurture common interests. Second, greater

---

[23] Homogeneity of credit associations, whether measured by kinship, location, gender, landholding or income levels, is not associated with higher repayment rates in some studies, at least in part because income shocks are likely to covary more in homogeneous groups (van Bastelaer, 2000).

[24] However, he finds household expenditures, asset ownership, and access to credit are positively associated with membership in heterogeneous associations. Diversity of education, occupation and economic status are particularly beneficial, indicating greater gains from exchange when knowledge and skills are more specialized.

[25] However, less dense but more extensive networks may provide access to more valued information (Granovetter, 1973). These "weak ties" may also be less costly to maintain. Research on business firms has found that project teams with the most numerous direct ties with other units took longer to complete their tasks than those with fewer ties (Hansen, 2002). Reviewing the vast literature on informational implications of networks is beyond the scope of this chapter.

and more intense contact with other people may increase the value of social ostracism as a punishment for untrustworthy behavior, operating in the same way as reputation. Finally, this intense contact may increase information about and confidence in the inherent trustworthiness of others.

Other scholars have subsequently argued that whether or not group memberships and other social ties have beneficial effects on norms of reciprocity and generalized trust, or on outcomes such as the performance of governments and economies, depends on the purpose of the group, the diversity and inclusiveness of its membership, and the intensity and nature of the group's activities (e.g., Stolle and Rochon 1998 and Varshney 2002). Groups segregated by class, occupation, or ethnicity may build cooperation and trust only among group members, perhaps even encouraging distrust between members and nonmembers.[26] In Weimar Germany, civil society organizations were organized along existing cleavages, and "socialists, Catholics, and bourgeois Protestants each joined their own choral societies and bird-watching clubs[.]" (Berman, 1997: 425). Under those circumstances, active associational life worked to reinforce rather than overcome narrow particularistic interests.

Not surprisingly, in light of these arguments, the evidence linking group membership and trust is mixed. Brehm and Rahn (1997) find that membership in groups and trust are strongly related in U.S. survey data, and that causation runs in both directions. Using survey data for the U.S., Sweden and Germany, Stolle and Rochon (1998) conclude that membership in all types of associations is conducive to generalized trust, but do not correct for the possibility that more trusting individuals are more likely to be active in groups. Using data from the Michigan Socialization Studies from 1965–82, Claibourn and Martin (2000) find that lagged trust levels are unrelated to contemporaneous group memberships, and that lagged memberships are only weakly related to contemporaneous levels of trust.

All of these studies are conducted at the individual-level, however, and do not capture any external effects—whether positive or negative—of group memberships on non-members. Cross-country analysis, which would capture any such external effects, shows that group memberships are significantly associated with trust (Knack, 2003). This link is particularly strong for groups that have primarily social goals, in contrast to unions and professional or trade associations, which tend to have more redistributional objectives.[27] Pargal, Gilligan and Huq (2002), looking at 65 neighborhoods in Dhaka, Bangladesh, found that the neighborhood average of trust in one's neighbors was unrelated to each neighborhood's average membership in civic associations.

---

[26] In later work, Putnam (2000: 22) is more careful to note that some social networks facilitating cooperation among their members can have detrimental effects for the wider community. Also see Olson (1965, 1982) for discussion of the role of social ties and social sanctions in generating collective action on behalf of narrow interests.

[27] Earlier work (Knack and Keefer, 1997) relying on a smaller sample of countries had surprisingly found trust was linked more closely with membership in redistributional groups than with membership in social groups.

The evidence that group membership does not correlate systematically with measures of trust bears upon only one of the several arguments that Putnam has advanced. For example, group participation—controlling for social heterogeneity and other factors that undermine the effectiveness of group participation—may also stimulate broader elements of civic cooperation, such as choosing to vote and in other ways supervise politicians. These issues have just begun to be addressed (see Varshney 2002). As with trust, however, there can be external costs imposed on non-members. Alatas, Pritchett, and Wetterberg (2002) found that households participating in village organizations sponsored by the Indonesian government reported higher levels of "voice," participation and information. However, a large "crowding-out" effect on other villagers actually led to a net decline in participation. Some of the effects of community-level collective action can be zero-sum. Wade's (1988) study of irrigation and collective action in south India found that well-organized villages were more successful in bribing public officials to increase their water allocations at the expense of other villages.

4. Conclusion

Intense research effort into social capital has yielded important contributions to the new institutional economics. First, levels of trust and trustworthiness are widely divergent across societies. Second, these differences are partly attributable to differences in formal institutions and reputational mechanisms that are of great concern in other literatures. Third, however, the strength of social norms underlying trust and trustworthiness also appears to vary dramatically, with important implications for government effectiveness, growth in incomes, and other development outcomes. A concern for policy implications is an important characteristic of the New Institutional Economics, and is present as well in the literature on social capital. Research into the origins of formal institutions conducive to development (to credible commitment, for example) suggests that such institutions are difficult to develop *de novo*. This research has shown that political institutions matter tremendously for whether political promises are credible and whether public policy is less or more divergent from the socially optimal. However, the research is equally clear that progress in the development of formal institutions is difficult to accelerate and far from guaranteed.

In the same way, the evidence suggests that social norms that prescribe cooperation at the level of entire societies are also difficult to instill.[28] Such broad and intractable features of a society as its social heterogeneity can stand in the way of the development of trust and civic cooperation. Woolcock (1998:186) writes that

---

[28] Questions of how social norms emerge and evolve over time in response to changes in technology, population, the political environment, etc., and the extent to which internalization of norms is individually rational (Coleman, 1990; Elster, 1989), are beyond the scope of this chapter.

"The challenge for development theorists and policy-makers alike is to identify the mechanisms that will create, nurture, and sustain the types and combinations of social relationships conducive to building dynamic participatory societies, sustainable equitable economies, and accountable developmental states".

However, as Keefer and Shirley (2000) argue, in societies where formal and informal institutions of wide "radius" are missing it may be possible in the short and medium-term to improve just the reach and functioning of informal norms that operate only within family, religious or ethnic groups, despite the risks that this poses for inter-group transactions and cohabitation.

At the same time, the evidence is fairly clear that income equality and education are linked to trust and other development-promoting norms; education and income distribution are two characteristics of countries that are much more amenable to intervention. Similarly, the importance of trust and trustworthiness are sufficiently well-documented, and ways to measure them are sufficiently well-developed, that efforts to assess them are amply justified. Such assessments are particularly necessary prior to undertaking activities that appear to be development-promoting, but have a clear potential to disrupt the bases for social norms. The assessments actually could provide an additional rationale for certain projects; for example, a land tax or the construction of rural roads could disrupt feudal social relations that discourage the development of more socially-efficient norms and networks. On the other hand, dislocation due to dam-building or other massive infrastructure development is almost surely destructive of social norms and networks on which trust and trustworthiness depend; the costs of that destruction would need to be weighed against the benefits of the infrastructure project itself.

Even at the community level, it may be difficult to foster social norms or networks. For example, to the extent that voluntary associations may be a dimension of social capital with favorable effects on trust, provision of public services, or economic outcomes, a natural question is whether and how activity in groups can be encouraged by governments or donors. Even among social capital enthusiasts, the consensus is to proceed with great caution on this front. Gugerty and Kremer (2002) examined the impact of a donor-funded program to strengthen rural women's groups in Kenya. They find that groups randomly chosen to receive donor funding experienced larger turnover in membership, and changes in leadership in favor of men or more educated women.

The difficulties of formulating robust policy recommendations are directly related to inadequacies in our knowledge base regarding the sources of social capital, whether norms, networks or trust. Opportunities for future research immediately suggest themselves, however, and do so with some urgency. High priorities for future research include documenting institutional mechanisms for defusing tensions among groups with few common norms or networks to unite them; describing the conditions under which the distrust associated with ethnic heterogeneity can be alleviated; and identifying ways in which governments or donors can support bottom-up production of norms and networks in non-distorting ways. Such research would have been premature ten years ago; now, however, the wealth of evidence showing the pervasive and significant effects of social norms provides a strong impetus to such work.

The authors are grateful to Mary M. Shirley, Thierry van Bastelaer and anonymous reviewers for valuable comments and suggestions. The conclusions of this chapter are not intended to represent the views of the World Bank, its Executive Directors, or the countries they represent.

REFERENCES

Acemoglu, Daron and James A. Robinson. 2001. "Inefficient Redistribution". *American Political Science Review* 95(3): 649–661.
Akerlof, George. 1997. "Social Distance and Social Decisions". *Econometrica* 65(5): 1005–1027.
Alatas, Vivi, Lant Pritchett, and Anna Wetterberg. 2002. "Voice Lessons: Evidence on Social Organizations, Government Mandated Organizations, and Governance from Indonesia's Local Level Institutions Study". Unpublished manuscript.
Alesina, Alberto, Reza Baqir, and William Easterly. 1999. "Public Goods and Ethnic Divisions". *Quarterly Journal of Economics* 114(4): 1243–1284.
Alesina, Alberto and Eliana La Ferrara. 2002. "Who Trusts Others?" *Journal of Public Economics* 85(2): 207–234.
Alesina, Alberto and Eliana La Ferrara. 2000. "Participation in Heterogeneous Communities". *Quarterly Journal of Economics* 115(3): 847–904.
Almond, Gabriel. A. and Sidney Verba. 1963. *The Civic Culture: Political Attitudes and Democracy in Five Nations*. Princeton, NJ: Princeton University Press.
Banfield, Edward C. 1958. *The Moral Basis of a Backward Society*. Chicago, IL: The Free Press.
Barr, Abigail. 2003. "Trust and Expected Trustworthiness: Experimental Evidence from Zimbabwean Villages". *Economic Journal* 113(6): 14–30.
Berg, Andrew and Jeffrey Sachs. 1988. "The Debt Crisis: Structural Explanations of Country Performance". *Journal of Development Economics* 29: 271–306.
Berg, Joyce, John Dickhaut, and Kevin McCabe. 1995. "Trust, Reciprocity, and Social History". *Games and Economic Behavior* 10: 122–142.
Berman, Sheri. 1997. "Civil Society and the Collapse of the Weimar Republic". *World Politics* 49(3): 401–429.
Boix, Carles and Daniel N. Posner. 1998. "Social Capital: Explaining its Origins and Effects on Government Performance". *British Journal of Political Science* 28: 686–693.
Brehm, John and Wendy Rahn. 1997. "Individual-Level Evidence for the Causes and Consequences of Social Capital". *American Journal of Political Science* 41(3): 999–1023.
Claibourn, Michele P. and Paul S. Martin. 2000. "Trusting and Joining? An Empirical Test of the Reciprocal Nature of Social Capital". *Political Behavior* 22(4): 267–291.
Coleman, James. 1990. *Foundations of Social Theory*. Cambridge, MA: Harvard University Press.
Coleman, James. 1987. "Norms as Social Capital" in G. Radnitzky and P. Bernholz (eds.), *Economic Imperialism*. New York: Paragon.
Costa, Dora L. and Matthew E. Kahn. 2003a. "Understanding the Decline in Social Capital, 1952–1998". *Kyklos* 56(1): 17–46.
―――― 2003b. "Cowards and Heroes: Group Loyalty in the American Civil War". *Quarterly Journal of Economics* 118(2): 519–548.

Drobak, John N. 1998. "Law Matters". *Washington University Law Quarterly* 76(1): 97–104.
Durlauf, Steven. 2002. "Bowling Alone: A Review Essay". *Journal of Economic Behavior and Organization* 47: 259–273.
Easterly, William and Ross Levine. 1997. "Africa's Growth Tragedy: Policies and Ethnic Divisions". *Quarterly Journal of Economics* 112(4): 1203–1250.
Elster, Jon. 1989. "Social Norms and Economic Theory". *Journal of Economic Perspectives* 3(4): 99–117.
Fehr, Ernst and Simon Gachter. 2000. "Fairness and Retaliation: The Economics of Reciprocity". *Journal of Economic Perspectives* 14(3): 159–181.
Fukuyama, Francis. 1995. *Trust: The Social Virtues and the Creation of Prosperity*. New York. The Free Press.
Fukuyama, Francis. 2000. *The Great Disruption: Human Nature and the Reconstitution of Social Order*. New York. Simon and Schuster.
Gambetta, Diego. 1988. *Trust: Making and Breaking Cooperative Relations*. Oxford. Blackwell.
Glaeser, Edward L., David Laibson, Jose A. Scheinkman, and Christine L. Soutter. 2000. "Measuring Trust". *Quarterly Journal of Economics* 115(3): 811–846.
Granovetter, Mark. 1973. "The Strength of Weak Ties". *American Journal of Sociology* 78: 1360–1380.
Greif, Avner. 1993. "Contract Enforceability and Economic Institutions in Early Trade: The Maghribi Traders' Coalition". *The American Economic Review* 83(3): 525–548.
_____ 1994. "Cultural Beliefs and the Organization of Society: A Historical and Theoretical Reflection on Collectivist and Individualist Societies". *Journal of Political Economy* 102(5): 912–950.
Grootaert, Christiaan. 1999. "Social Capital, Household Welfare and Poverty in Indonesia". Local Level Institutions. Working Paper no. 6. Washington, DC: The World Bank.
Grootaert, Christiaan and Thierry van Bastelaer (eds.). 2002. *The Role of Social Capital in Development: An Empirical Assessment*. New York: Cambridge University Press.
_____ 2002. *Understanding and Measuring Social Capital: A Multi-Disciplinary Tool for Practitioners*. Washington, DC: The World Bank.
Gugerty, Mary Kay and Michael Kremer. 2002. "The Impact of Development Assistance on Social Capital: Evidence From Kenya" in C. Grootaert and T. van Bastelaer (eds.), *The Role of Social Capital in Development*. New York: Cambridge University Press, Chapter 7, pp. 213–233.
Hansen, Morton T. 2002. "Realizing Opportunities: A Social Capital Model of Knowledge Sharing in Multi-unit Companies". *Organization Science*.
Hardin, Russell. 1982. *Collective Action*. Baltimore, MD: Resources for the Future.
Henrich, Joseph et al. 2001. "In Search of Homo Economicus : Behavioral Experiments in 15 Small-Scale Societies". *American Economic Review Papers and Proceeding* 91(2): 73–78.
Inglehart, Ronald. 1999. "Trust, Well-Being and Democracy" in M. Warren (ed.), *Democracy and Trust*. Cambridge: Cambridge University Press.
Isham, Jon and Satu Kähkönen. 2002. "Institutional Determinants of the Impact of Community-Based Water Services: Evidence from Sri Lanka and India". *Economic Development and Cultural Change* 50(3): 667–691.
Kähkönen, Satu. 1999. "Does Social Capital Matter in Water and Sanitation Delivery? A Review of Literature". Social Capital Initiative Working Paper no. 9. Washington, DC: The World Bank.
Karlan, Dean. 2003. "Social Capital and Group Banking". Dissertation chapter, Massachusetts Institute of Technology.
Keefer, Philip. 2002. "Clientelism and Credibility". Presented at the 2002 Conference of the International Society of New Institutional Economics, Boston, MA.

_____ and Stephen Knack. 2002. "Polarization, Property Rights, and the Links Between Inequality and Growth". *Public Choice* 111: 127–154.

_____ and Mary M. Shirley. 2000. "Formal versus informal institutions in economic development" in Claude Menard (ed.), *Institutions, Contracts and Organizations*. Cheltenham, UK: Edward Elgar.

Knack, Stephen. 1992. "Civic Norms, Social Sanctions, and Voter Turnout". *Rationality and Society* 4: 133–156.

_____ 2001. "Trust, Associational Life, and Economic Performance" in J. Helliwell (ed.), *The Contribution of Human and Social Capital to Sustained Economic Growth and Well-Being*. Quebec: Human Resources Development Canada.

_____ 2002. "Social Capital and the Quality of Government: Evidence From the U.S. States". *American Journal of Political Science* 46(4): 772–785.

_____ 2003. "Groups, Growth and Trust: Cross-Country Evidence on the Olson and Putnam Hypotheses". *Public Choice* 117: 341–355.

_____ and Philip Keefer. 1997. "Does Social Capital Have an Economic Payoff? A Cross-Country Investigation". *Quarterly Journal of Economics* 112(4): 1251–1288.

La Porta, Rafael, Florencio Lopez-de-Silanes, Andrei Shleifer, and Robert W. Vishny. 1997. "Trust in Large Organizations". *American Economic Review Papers and Proceedings* 87: 333–338.

Levi, Margaret. 1988. *Of Rule and Revenue*. Berkeley, CA: University of California Press.

Miguel, Edward and Mary Kay Gugerty. 2002. "Ethnic Diversity, Social Sanctions, and Public Goods in Kenya". Unpublished Working Paper, University of California, Berkeley, CA.

Miguel, Edward, Paul Gertler, and David I. Levine. 2002. "Did Industrialization Destroy Social Capital in Indonesia?" Unpublished Working Paper, University of California, Berkeley, CA.

Mill, John Stuart. 1848. *Principles of Political Economy*. London: John W. Parker.

Narayan, Deepa and Lant Pritchett. 1999. "Cents and Sociability: Household Income and Social Capital in Rural Tanzania". *Economic Development and Cultural Change* 47(4): 871–897.

North, Douglass C. 1990. *Institutions, Institutional Change and Economic Performance*. New York: Cambridge University Press.

Olson, Mancur. 1963. "Rapid Growth as a Destabilizing Force". *Journal of Economic History* 23: 529–552.

_____ 1965. *The Logic of Collective Action: Public Goods and the Theory of Groups*. Cambridge, MA: Harvard University Press.

Olson, Mancur. 1982. *The Rise and Decline of Nations: Economic Growth, Stagflation, and Social Rigidities*. New Haven, CT: Yale University Press.

Ostrom, Elinor. 1990. *Governing the Commons: The Evolution of Institutions for Collective Action*. New York: Cambridge University Press.

Ostrom, Elinor. 2000. "Collective Action and the Evolution of Social Norms". *Journal of Economic Perspectives* 14(3): 137–158.

Pantoja, Enrique. 2002. "Qualitative Analysis of Social Capital: The Case of Coal-mining Areas in Orissa, India" in C. Grootaert and T. van Bastelaer (eds.), *Understanding and Measuring Social Capital*. Ch. 5, pp. 108–151.

Pargal, Sheoli, Daniel Gilligan, and Mainul Huq. 2002. "Social Capital in Solid Waste Management: Evidence from Dhaka, Bangladesh" in C. Grootaert and T. van Bastelaer (eds.), *The Role of Social Capital in Development*. Ch. 6, pp. 188–212.

Paxton, Pamela. 1999. "Is Social Capital Declining in the United States? A Multiple Indicator Assessment". *American Journal of Sociology* 105(1): 88–127.

Persson, Torsten and Guido Tabellini. 2000. *Political Economics: Explaining Public Policy*. Cambridge, MA: The MIT Press.

Portes, Alejandro. 1998. "Social Capital: Its Origins and Applications in Modern Sociology". *Annual Review of Sociology* 24: 1–24.

Posner, Richard and Eric Rasmusen. 1989. "Creating and enforcing norms, with special reference to sanctions". *International Review of Law and Economics* 19: 369–382.

Putnam, Robert. 2000. *Bowling Alone: Collapse and Revival of American Community*. New York: Simon & Schuster.
Putnam, Robert with Robert Leonardi and Raffaella Y. Nanetti. 1993. *Making Democracy Work: Civic Traditions in Modern Italy*. Princeton, NJ: Princeton University Press.
Scholz, John T. and Mark Lubell. 1998. "Trust and Taxpaying: Testing the Heuristic Approach to Collective Action". *American Journal of Political Science* 42(2): 398–417.
Sethi, Rajiv and E. Somanathan. 1996. "The Evolution of Social Norms in Common Property Resource Use". *American Economic Review* 8(4): 766–788.
Sobel, Joel. 2002. "Can We Trust Social Capital?" *Journal of Economic Literature* 55: 139–154.
Stolle, Dietlind and Thomas Rochon. 1998. "Are All Associations Alike? Member Diversity, Associational Type and the Creation of Social Capital". *American Behavioral Scientist* 42(1): 47–65.
Van Bastelaer, Thierry. 2000. "Does Social Capital Facilitate the Poor's Access to Credit? A Review of the Microeconomic Literature". Social Capital Initiative Working Paper no. 8. Washington, DC: The World Bank.
Varshney, Ashutosh. 2002. *Ethnic Conflict and Civic Life: Hindus and Muslims in India*. New Haven, CT: Yale University Press.
Vigdor, Jacob L. 2004. "Community Composition and Collective Action: Analyzing Initial Mail Response to the 2000 Census". *Review of Economics and Statistics* 82(1): 251–271.
Wade, Robert. 1988. *Village Republics: Economic Conditions for Collective Action in South India*. New York: Cambridge University Press.
Williamson, Oliver E. 1993. "Calculativeness, Trust and Economic Organization". *Journal of Law and Economics* 36: 453–486.
Yamagishi, Toshio and Midori Yamagishi. 1994. "Trust and Commitment in the United States and Japan". *Motivation and Emotion* 18(2): 129–166.
Woolcock, Michael. 1998. "Social Capital and Economic Development: Toward a Theoretical Synthesis and Policy Framework". *Theory and Society* 27: 151–208.
Zak, Paul and Stephen Knack. 2001. "Trust and Growth". *Economic Journal* 111: 295–321.
Zucker, Lynne G. 1986. "Production of Trust: Institutional Sources of Economic Structure, 1840–1920". *Research in Organizational Behavior* 8: 53–111.

WEF.

Global Compact + ISO 26000 represent a new development beyond designed, private order contract enforcing institutions

1. "Thin" private participation
2. Non-existent or few inter-party negotiations or contracts serving as basis for rules
3. Thin substantive law, not generated by private participants but by experts

Compare: AICPA; trade associations

28. Commitment, Coercion, and Markets: The Nature and Dynamics of Institutions Supporting Exchange

AVNER GREIF

Markets rest upon institutions. The development of market-based exchange relies on the support of two institutional pillars that are, in turn, shaped by the development of markets. Research in the field of new institutional economics has largely focused upon one such institutional pillar—'contract-enforcement institutions'—that determine the range of transactions in which individuals can commit to keep their contractual obligations. Yet, markets also require institutions that constrain those with coercive power from abusing others' property rights. These 'coercion-constraining' institutions influence whether individuals will bring their goods to the market in the first place.

This chapter's discussion of market-supporting institutions is geared toward the issues we know the least about. First, the dynamics of market-supporting institutions and the implied dynamics of markets; second, the inter-relationships between the dynamics of market-supporting and political institutions where the latter comprise the rules for collective decision-making, political rights, and the legitimate use of coercive power. It argues, in particular, that neither the assertion that liberal political institutions lead to markets nor that markets lead to liberal governance are supported by theory or history. Markets and political institutions co-evolve through a dynamic inter-play between contract-enforcement and coercion-constraining institutions.

Many successful market economies have prevailed in the past; there were adequate market-supporting institutions. Early successes, such as those in the Islamic world or China, were not indicators of later development. It was the commercial expansion that began in Europe during the late medieval period that led to the development of markets that support the complex, dynamic modern economy with its wide-scale reliance on impersonal exchange. Why didn't early success lead to subsequent market expansion? More generally, what does determine the dynamics of market expansion? Addressing these questions is a key to understanding the 'Rise of the West,' the operation of market economies, and the factors that still hinder market development.

The argument advanced here is that markets can rest on different combinations of contract-enforcement and coercion-constraining institutions. Different combinations, in turn, can support distinct sets of exchange relationships, implying that their relative efficiency depends on the details of the related economy. In particular, under conditions elaborated upon below, markets can prosper even in the absence of limited government and the rule of law. Equally important, different initial combinations of contract-enforcement and coercion-constraining institutions lead, in a non-deterministic way, to distinct dynamics of markets and political institutions.

The core idea developed here regarding this dynamic is the following. Contract-enforcement institutions *organically* (spontaneously) emerge in the initial stages of market development as unintended and unforeseeable results from the pursuit of individual interests. Yet, even in the same economic situation, different institutions can emerge as their details are influenced by various factors, including those that are cultural and social (e.g., Greif 1994a; McMillan 2002). The details of these initial contract-enforcement institutions influence which additional institutions the economic agents will find it profitable to use if made available and establish if possible. *Ceteris paribus*, initial contract-enforcement institutions influence what additional, *designed* (intentionally created) institutions the economic agents will 'demand.'

The ability to effectively supply designed—private- or public-order—contract-enforcement institutions, depends on the prevailing coercion-constraining institutions, which are those that influence decisions regarding the acquisition and use of coercive power. This is the case because many designed institutions reveal information about wealth to those with coercive power. Wealth-revealing, designed, contract-enforcement institutions will be utilized only if coercion-constraining institutions are such that this information does not undermine the security of property rights.

Consider, for example, public-order, contract-enforcement institutions. When appealing to the court, using a land registry, applying for a business licence, or submitting to a regulatory agency information regarding one's wealth is generated. This information can be used by those with coercive power to identify and capture this wealth. Wealth-revealing public-order institutions can be *effectively* supplied only if the generation of this type of information does not lead to wealth confiscation. If this is not the case, even if public-order, contract-enforcement institutions are established, they will be underutilized. Distinct coercion-constraining institutions imply distinct abilities for *effectively* supplying various, designed, contract-enforcement institutions that further extend the market.

Interestingly, the coercion-constraining institutions conducive to the growth of the market also likely to lead to the endogenous emergence of political institutions associated with liberal societies in which market participants (the 'commercial sector') have political representation and influence. Political institutions—rules for collective decision-making, political rights, and the legitimate use of coercive power—that are actually followed are self-enforcing in the sense that following them is each political actor's best response. (E.g.,

Barzel 2002; Greif 1994b, 1998; Hardin 1989; Weingast 1997.) An important determinant of a political actor's decision to follow a political rule depends on his relative coercive power. (E.g., Acemoglu and Robinson 2001; Bates 2001; Bates et al. 2002; Downing 1992; Greif 1994b, 1998). Because coercion-constraining institutions influence decisions regarding the acquisition and use of coercive power, they impact the set of self-enforcing political institutions.

In particular, the coercion-constraining institutions conducive to the effective supply of designed, wealth-revealing, contract-enforcement institutions are those in which the commercial sector has coercive (and economic) power that countervails the coercive power of others, such as rulers. Under certain conditions, the fear of risking a costly retaliation by the commercial sector would induce those with coercive power to prefer consulting it rather than taking unilateral actions effecting property rights. The commercial sector's power induces other political actors to provide it with a political voice through such means as political representation. Political voice precedes the establishment of, in particular, designed public-order institutions because it is required for the commercial sector to communicate the need for particular public-order institutions.

The views that market development requires appropriate political institutions (e.g., North 1990; Weingast 1997) or that political development follows the expansion of markets (e.g., Lipset 1959) are too simplistic. Markets and political institutions co-evolve, reflecting the dynamic interplay between coercion-constraining and contract-enforcement institutions. It is no coincidence that the modern market economy and the liberal state jointly emerged.

The above analysis builds on and integrates elements of Old and New Institutionalism. Old Institutionalism (e.g., Menger 1963 [1883]), emphasizes the distinctions and inter-relationships between organic (spontaneous) and designed (pragmatic) institutions; new Institutionalism emphasizes studying the microfoundation of contract-enforcement institutions (e.g., Wiliamson 1985; Greif 1989, 1993) and the inter-relationships between the polity and the economy (e.g., North and Thomas 1973). Finally, the discussion here highlights the importance of understanding coercion-constraining institutions which influence the development of both markets and polities. It thus builds on, and contributes to, the emerging literature on the institutional foundations of social order. (E.g., Bates 2001; Bates et. al. 2002; Greif 1994, 1998, forthcoming.)

This chapter is organized as follows. Section 1 reviews the literature on contract-enforcement institutions while Section 2 defines and elaborates on coercion-constraining institutions. Once the nature of these two types of institutions is clarified, Section 3 provides a tentative theory of the dynamics of market-supporting and political institutions. Section 4 draws on history, particularly that of China and Europe, to illustrate the merits of this conjecture.

The theoretical conjecture and historical analysis presented in Sections 3 and 4 are very rudimentary. Many aspects of the theory have yet to be worked out and additional important issues—such as agency problems within the polity—have yet to be integrated. Yet, this analysis makes an explicit conjecture regarding market expansion that links the institutional foundations of the market and the polity and is derived from history.

1. Contract-Enforcement Institutions

The extent of the market—the degree of voluntary exchange—is determined by its supporting contract-enforcement institutions (CEIs). CEIs determine the transactions in which one can credibly commit to fulfill contractual obligations and therefore the exchange relationships into which economic agents will enter. CEIs determine who can exchange with whom and in what goods. A market extends when the available set of CEIs increases, allowing a greater number of people to enter into more exchange relationships in more situations. Studying the relative efficiency of markets and their dynamics requires examining their CEIs and their development.

CEIs are required to support markets because exchange is almost always sequential. Some time elapses between the *quid* and the *quo,* providing one with the ability to renege.[1] This sequentiality implies the fundamental problem of exchange: A necessary condition for exchange is for all sides to credibly commit to adhere to their contractual obligations, to the extent that each expects to be better off than refusing to exchange. One will not enter into an otherwise profitable exchange relationship unless the other party can commit *ex-ante* (when a decision is made whether or not to exchange) to fulfill his contractual obligation *ex-post* (when he can renege).

Institutionalists have so far concentrated on contract-enforcement institutions that link conduct in current exchange with future payoffs in a way that makes it known *ex-ante* that the best one can do *ex-post* is not to renege.[2] To illustrate the mechanism, suppose it is commonly known that failure to pay a debt implies future inability to borrow, and that a borrower values the gains from future credit more than those from reneging on his debt contract. Because the best a borrower can do *ex-post* is to pay his debt, he can *ex-ante* commit to doing so. The value of future economic exchange is placed as a bond to be lost in case of breach. One can similarly commit when it is known *ex-ante* that failure to pay a debt implies sufficiently large legal sanctions.

---

[1] E.g., Greif 1997, 2000; Aoki 2001; Dixit 2004. Williamson (1985) stressed that sunk, relationships specific investment are important in generating sequentiality. But, as discussed in Greif 2000 exchange is sequential, for example, in financial transactions, in labor relationships, in agency relationships, and in the exchange of experience, goods whose attributes are revealed only with use. Indeed, even in spot exchange it is usually technologically impossible for the quid and the quo to be laterally exchanged simultaneously. The only exception is exchange in which goods with objectively known attributes are exchanged simultaneously.

[2] This is common in works focusing on the law (e.g., Williamson 1985) or reputation mechanisms (e.g., Greif 1989, 1993) to the exclusion of institutions based on internalized norms and intrinsic motivation.

Although various CEIs differ in their details, their effectiveness depends on mitigating the same problems of making the threat of sanctions (or rewards) credible. Those who are to apply the sanctions should have the appropriate information regarding past conduct and the incentives to neither shirk their duty nor abuse their power. The offender should be precluded from fleeing to avoid sanctions and the sanctions should be sufficiently high to deter breach. The parties should also share expectations regarding what behavior constitutes a breach and that should be commonly known that the above conditions are met. The details of CEIs make a difference, however, as they determine who will be able to credibly commit in what exchange relationships. An objective and impartial court is effective only in exchanges in which it can *ex-post* verify conduct.

In considering the relative merits of various CEIs, it is useful to group CEIs according to whether they are 'organic' or 'designed' and whether they are 'private-order' or 'public-order.'[3] According to Carl Menger (1883), organic (spontaneous) institutions emerge as an unintended and unforeseeable results of the pursuit of individual interests. Designed (pragmatic) institutions reflect intentional and conscious design and possibly the coordinated responses of many individuals. The former roughly corresponds to what North (e.g., 1990) defines as informal institutions and the latter, formal institutions. Private-order institutions, the importance of which has been emphasized by Williamson (1985), rely mainly on economic and social sanctions imposed by economic agents, while public-order institutions rely mainly on sanctions imposed by the state. In either of these cases, we can either study institutions as self-enforcing or not.[4] In studying self-enforcing institutions we attempt to study as endogenous the behavior of all relevant agents, including, such as judges, priests, or policemen.

In studying CEIs, the economics of information, contract theory and mechanism design have been extensively employed. (Furubotn and Richter 1997 provide a useful survey.) Game theory, however, has been found particularly useful because it exposes the conditions necessary for threats and promises to be credible. It is common to model the contracting environment as some version

---

[3] More generally, institutions differ according to the associated sanctions: whether they are economic, social, or coercive (in the form of legal sanctions or physical assaults); or by who imposes the sanctions: the interacting economic agents or a third party (either another economic agent such as a trade association or a non-economic agent, such as a legal agency). Actual institutions, as discussed below, often transcend these simple dichotomies. Some combine economic and coercive sanctions imposed by various agents. Organic institutions often evolve to acquire designed components while customs are often codified as laws.

[4] Self-enforcing institutions have been studied under various headings. Relational contracting (in which one's conduct in a particular situation reflects considerations regarding its implications on the entirety of the relationship over time and situations; e.g, McMillan and Woodruff 2000). Social norms (which are rules of behavior that are regularly adhered to although they are not legally enforced; e.g., Kandori 1992). Self-governance (in the sense that the responsibility for contract enforcement is placed in the hands of the interacting individuals; e.g., Dixit 2003) and reputation-based institutions (in which one's current conduct is motivated by fear of losing one's reputation and hence future gains; e.g., Greif 1989, 1997, forthcoming.)

of either a One-Sided Prisoners' Dilemma game or Prisoner's Dilemma.[5] But the flexibility of game theory permits the introduction of various assumptions, regarding, for example, the matching process among the potential parties to exchange or the information available to them, and whether the division of the surplus from exchange should be taken as given or not.[6]

In interpreting these theoretical analyses, however, it is important to recognize that they only expose the conditions required for particular behavior to be an equilibrium outcome and its implications. Empirical analysis, however, is needed to evaluate whether and how these conditions were fulfilled in a particular episode and how this situation became commonly known. This implies considering how the game (or, more generally, the environment) that was assumed in the theoretical analysis was generated.

Organic, Private-Order Institutions

In organic, private-order CEIs the credible threat by the economic agent(s) to impose sanctions deters breach. (Henceforth I will refer to 'organic, private-order CEIs' as 'organic CEIs.) Organic CEIs are likely to emerge when economic agents face the prospect of beneficial, ongoing exchange while breaching a contract is (actually or statistically) observable. The credibility of one's threat to terminate a relationship following a breach is not much of an issue. People are willing to spend resources to punish cheaters (e.g., Fehr and Gächter 2000) and people often expect that past cheaters will cheat again. In either case, the effectiveness of reputation-based deterrence—the range of situations in which it can support exchange—increases as the value of future relationships become higher. It therefore increases, *ceteris paribus*, with the per-period gains from exchange, and the economic agents' patience, and decreases in their alternative income outside the relationship. Organic CEIs are therefore more likely to emerge when the parties are locked into their relationships: the market is thin and it is costly to find a new partner with whom to exchange. McMillan and Woodruff (1999)

---

[5] One-Sided Prisoners' Dilemma game (OSPD) (Greif 1989, 2000) is known as the Game of Trust (Kreps 1990). One player can initiate the relationship and if he has done so, the second player gets to decide whether to cheat or not. Cheating is more profitable to the second player but expecting cheating the first player is better off by not initiating the relationship. Greif (2000) argues that the commitment problem associated with exchange is well captured by this game. In the Prisoners' Dilemma game (PD) both players move sequentially, each can choose to either cooperate (be honest) or defect (cheat). Defecting is a dominant strategy (it is the best action for each player whether the other cooperates or cheats). If both cooperate, they are better off than if they both defect. (E.g., Kandori 1992; Ellison 1994.) Hodgson 1998 reviews the use of evolutionary game theory to study CEIs.

[6] Greif (1989, 1993), for example, considers the implications of transferable utility (where the payoff distributions are endogenous to the interacting parties) and non-random matching. Milgrom, North, and Weingast (1990) and Dixit (2003) examined the implications of asymmetric games in which the players are not symmetric in their actions sets). Kranton (1996a) Ghosh and Ray (1996) and Kali (1999), Dixit (2003) considered adverse selection situations in which players are of different types in the sense that some are less likely to cheat. Clay (1997) examined the incomplete monitoring situation in which one can mistakenly believe that the other cheated.

tested this proposition in contemporary Vietnam and indeed found that where the closest alternative trader is far away, more credit was granted.

The cost of terminating relationships can endogenously emerge as a part of the institutions. Suppose that exchange is supported only by the above bilateral reputation in which one is punished only by the person whom he cheated. Suppose that the one who cheated has to wait until another relationship is naturally dissolved before he establishes a new relationship. If the implied cost of waiting is sufficiently high, a bilateral reputation mechanism can support exchange.[7]

The above discussion assumes a moral hazard situation. All agents are identical and each faces the choice of whether to breach his contract or not. In reality, however, the economic agents have different unobservable characteristics that determine how likely they are to breach a contract. Some may be more patient than others or have better unobserved outside opportunities. In such adverse selection situations, where some agents are of a 'bad' type and hence more likely to cheat, bilateral reputation can operate even if it is technologically costless to immediately find an alternative partner to an exchange. Because some agents are bad types, each agent is motivated to 'test' new partners in exchange to discover their types. One 'builds' a relationship by initially trading small and gradually increasing the stakes or one demands that his partner bear a sunk cost (e.g., giving gifts or wasting time) at the beginning of their relationship. Such initial sunk cost increases the cost of breach. (Watson 2002; Kranton 1996a; Ghosh and Ray 1996.) In contemporary Africa, suppliers of input and credit were indeed found to initiate exchange in small amounts and gradually increase them (Fafchamps 2004.)

Bilateral relationships provide only limited and often costly contract enforcement. They require market imperfections to insure that the value of the exchange is higher than can be achieved by exchanging elsewhere. Each bilateral exchange may require the costs of building relationships or other sunk costs required to establish trust. Organic institutions based on bilateral reputation mechanisms require that one is able to directly monitor the performance of the other. Hence, these institutions are effective in exchanges such as that of goods where quality is easy to verify, or in credit relations. They are ineffective, however, in an exchange where outcomes are uncertain and not directly observable. (E.g., in agency relations.)

Organic, multilateral reputation institutions can support exchange in a wider range of situations than is possible under a bilateral reputation mechanism. More behavior can be monitored, better information circulated, and higher sanctions would be imposed on those who cheat. These institutions are based on information flows regarding past conduct among many economic agents and on economic sanctions imposed by those who were not cheated. Each individual

---

[7] MacLeod and Malcomson 1989 present a comprehensive analysis. In equilibrium, the unemployed agent cannot establish a new relationship by offering to, say, sell his product for less than the market price because at such lower prices it is not credible that one will not cheat.

is willing to exchange information with others, expecting to get information in return. Because economic agents have more to lose by revealing valuable information to competitors, the incentive to share information is higher if this is not the case.

The literature identifies three reasons why an individual might find it optimal to participate in a multilateral punishment against someone who did not cheat him. First, in moral hazard situations, the expectation that others will sanction an individual can be enough to motivate punishment, because punishment by others reduces the ability to perform and reduce loss due to breach (Greif 1989, 1993; Fafchamps 2004.) Second, in adverse selection situations, past cheating reveals bad types who will cheat again (e.g., Kranton 1996a; Ghosh and Ray 1996).[8] Third, individuals participate in multilateral punishment according to an internalized sense of fairness among members of a social structure. (Fehr and Fischbacher 2004.)

Because organic CEIs based on multilateral punishment are not designed, they often have symbiotic relationships with social structures, norms, and cultural beliefs (e.g., Greif 1994a). These social features provide the initial conditions for the rise of the economic institution which, in turn, reproduced these social features. Information flows, personal familiarity within such social structures as networks, communities, business groups, and religious groups, make multilateral (community or collective) punishment possible. Shared norms and beliefs and their representation in customs and merchants' laws coordinates on the actions that constitute cheating is provided by.

Individualistic searching for reliable business partners can also lead to the formation of a social structure in the form of a business network or an 'old boys' network. (Kali 1999; Fafchamps 2004.) In either case, the gains implied by the economic institution to each of the members of the social structure motivate retaining affiliation with the social structure and hence, reproduce it. An economy can therefore end up segregated in the sense that exchange, beyond spot exchange, is conducted among members of groups based on non-economic attributes such as religious sects, lineages, etc. In this case, the overlay of an economic institution on a social structure also implies that social sanctions and social, cultural, racial, or religious exclusion supplement, or even replace, the disciplinary impact of economic sanctions.

To illustrate institutions based on a multilateral reputation mechanism, consider the one that governed agency relationships among the 11th century (Jewish) Maghribi traders who were engaged in long-distance trade all over the Muslim Mediterranean. (Greif 1989, 1993.) Among them, it was efficient—ignoring contractual problems—to operate through overseas agents rather than

---

[8] Kandori (1992) and Ellison (1994) pointed out the possibility that in random matching PD games, a multilateral punishment can be supported by having the one who is being punished play cooperate when the other punishes him by playing cheat. Punishing is thus profitable to the one who punishes. One cooperates in his own punishment, in turn, because doing so implies that the punishment will cease after a finite number of periods.

having each merchant travel abroad with his goods. But because agents could cheat while handling a merchant's capital abroad, to be employed they had to be able to *ex-ante* commit to be honest *ex-post*, after the goods were sent to them. Among the Maghribis, as arguably among others in similar situations, this commitment was achieved based on a multilateral reputation mechanism within a business network by an institution that can be referred to as a coalition.

The Maghribis employed each other as agents, shared the expectations that Maghribi merchants would hire only Maghribis agents, and that all of them would cease employing an agent who had cheated. Information flows within their commercial and social network enabled detection and circulation of information about cheating. Coordination on multilateral punishment was facilitated by a set of cultural rules of behavior—a Merchants' Law—that specified how an agent should act to be considered honest in circumstances not mentioned in a merchant's instructions.[9] False accusations of cheating were curtailed by the extensive use of witnesses to testify to one's honesty. Multilateral punishment was self-enforcing because each merchant, expecting others to punish, found it in his best interest to punish as well.

Multilateral punishment enhanced efficiency and profitability relative to bilateral punishment (in which only the trader who was cheated retaliated), since it enabled the employment of agents even when the relationship between a specific merchant and agent pair was not expected to recur. The resulting additional gains from cooperation, the value of the information flows, and the expectations concerning future hiring ensured the 'closedness' of the coalition. Merchants were motivated to employ only member agents while agents were motivated not to seek employment elsewhere because being a coalition member was profitable. Although wages were lower than under a bilateral punishment, employment was more certain. Finally, agents were motivated not to cheat in their old age fearing that their children's reputations would suffer.

Social and economic sanctions often inter-relate in organic institutions and this interrelationship can reflect strategic manipulation by individuals pursuing their own interests. This complexity is well illustrated in the study of contract enforcement institutions in Mexican California conducted by Clay (1997a, 1997b).[10] This analysis touches upon two neglected issues in institutional economics: the interplay between social and economic sanctions and multi-tier institutions (although see Dixit 2003a; Greif 2004).

Social relationships were central to a contract enforcement institution in the Mexican communities but there was no institution that enabled their members to commit to buy goods for credit from long-distance American traders. Among these traders, contract enforcement was achieved based on a coalition-like

---

[9] Rules that make the meanings of various actions common knowledge are central to any institution based on multilateral or third-party punishment. See Greif 1993 for a discussion of economic institutions and Hardin 1989 and Weingast 1997 for political institutions.

[10] For empirical analyses of the interplay between social sanctions and economic institutions, see Ellickson 1991; Landa, 1994; Bernstein 1992; and Rauch 2001.

institution and economic sanctions. The two institutions were linked, however, to create a composite—two tiers—institution that enabled Mexicans to commit to pay their debts. This institution emerged when individual American traders created a link between the Mexican intra-community institution and the American traders' coalition. These individuals integrated into the communities by marrying local girls, converting to Catholicism, and settling in the villages. Hence, they gained access to the intra-community contract enforcement institution. These American traders also retained their membership in the American traders' coalition. An American who settled in a community used the intra-community, social-based institution to collect debt from locals and he could also commit to not to breach a contract with the American trader who provided the loan by the threat of being excluded from the American traders' coalition.

Efficiency-enhancing organic CEIs are not necessarily optimal given the existing monitoring, information, and enforcement technology as lack of coordination hinders adjustments. Each individual behaves optimally given the constraints and opportunities offered by others' behavior and expected behavior, but whenever the environment changes in a way that makes different behavior optimal, there is no mechanism to adjust expectations regarding others' behavior. This expected behavior therefore continues to influence choices thereby hindering adjustments. The efficiency of organic CEIs is therefore higher in a static economy when rules governing exchange and punishments do not have to adjust frequently.

Similarly, the efficiency of organic CEIs is higher when it is less important to adjust the number of interacting individuals. The optimal size of an organic CEI with multilateral punishment is theoretically linked to the speed of information transmission. The optimal size balances the benefit of greater participation with the cost implied by the delay in punishment due to the additional time required to transmit information. But the actual number of individuals governed by the institution reflects either the original social group around which the institution emerged, or individualistic search for worthy partners. In either case, the size may not be optimal. In the presence of adverse selection, organic CEIs based on multilateral punishment can be welfare-reducing as they lower the incentives among non-members to search for worthy partners. (Greif 1993; Kali 1999; Annen 2003.)

Moreover, organic CEIs based on multilateral punishment reduce incentives to create institutions that would foster impersonal exchange and support the needs of a dynamic economy. (Greif 1994a; Kranton 1996.) More generally, the relative efficiency of organic CEIs declines as populations and markets grow. These institutions are relation-based and hence entail low fixed costs (they do not require special organization or other systemwide special investment) but high and rising marginal costs. The expansion of a business entails exchange where one has successively weaker relational links with the other party to the exchange. Expansion thus requires investment in building relationships and carries a greater risk of collapse. (Li 1999.)

Public-Order CEIs: The Legal and Regulatory Systems

Designed CEIs can support exchange that organic CEIs cannot and often reflect a social or private response to gains from providing additional contract-enforcement. They reflect intentional and conscious design and possibly the coordinated responses of many individuals and therefore are characterized by explicit rules that regulate and coordinate membership, behavior, processes for changing rules, and intentionally created organizations, such as guilds, courts, credit rating companies, escrow companies, and business associations.

A social response to the needs for additional contract enforcement manifests itself in public-order CEIs, the legal and regulatory systems. Public-order CEIs coordinate behavior through laws and regulations, collect and process information using various formal procedures and bureaucratic organizations, and deter contractual breaches by threatening legal and regulatory sanctions. They can be particularly effective in influencing behavior because they rely on the authority of the state. They can, for example, employ coercive power to punish violators, impose various auditing and supervisory requirements, and one to appear in court and reveal information.

The legal system constitutes a third party that alters the costs of a contractual breach, enabling parties to commit to a contractual performance in cases in which contracts will not be self-enforcing based on the value of future relationships.[11] In addition, the law can foster the operation of organic CEIs. Boot et. al. (1993) argued that legal contractual incompleteness can be used to signal reputation while Johnston et. al. (2002) empirically found that in post-communist countries the law is used to reduce the cost and time required to build new relationships that are later sustained by reputation.

Compared to the costs associated with organic CEIs, the public-order institutions that support modern markets require high fixed costs. Large legislative, judicial, administrative, and coordination costs are required to establish the system and render it effective and credible in the context of a highly mobile, non-agrarian economy. Once established, the marginal cost of enforcement—and hence exchange relationships—is low and constant. (E.g., Li 1999.) Indeed, until recently economists studied market economies assuming that public-order CEIs provide costless, perfect, objective, and impartial contract enforcement.

In reality, however, the legal system rarely provides costless, perfect, objective, and impartial contract enforcement. (E.g., Williamson 1985; Ellickson 1991; Greif and Kandel 1995.) Public-order institutions that best approximate this situation operate in a few advanced contemporary countries and only in recent times. We know surprisingly little, however, regarding the institutional

---

[11] Public-order institutions have also been successful in creating markets by compiling and making public the necessary information. Formal land titling and land registrars, for example, underpin mortgage markets in developed economies (Arruñada 2003). Approval by the FDA is central to the trade in drugs.

development that led to these modern successes.[12] But even in these cases, the operation of the law as a contract enforcer is restricted by various factors. For a court to enforce contracts, for example, it should be able to *ex-post* verify actions taken by the litigants and their impact on observed outcomes.[13] Verification of past actions is often costly, particularly in labor relationships and in complex business transactions and production processes.

Apart from the need for verifiable information, other factors lessen the effectiveness of the legal system. States have a limited geographical scope while laws and regulations may be designed to achieve various policy objectives other than securing rights. Budget constraints and administrative capacity imply that legal proceedings may be time consuming. Direct legal costs, such as legal fees, and indirect costs, such as the opportunity cost of time, are often high. Economic agents' strategic responses to the incentives implied by laws and regulations can limit their effectiveness. (E.g., Townsend 1979.) Polinsky and Shavell (2000) surveyed the literature considering how legal rules can be designed to maximize social welfare subject to these constraints. In the models they surveyed, it was implicitly assumed that the prevailing legal tradition is the European tradition of man-made, explicit law. In societies with other, religious and customary legal traditions, different models may be needed.

Further limiting the operation of public-order institutions is the need to mitigate the associated agency problem. Decision-makers within public institutions, such as judges, policemen, and regulators, have to be provided with the incentive to use their power to protect rather than abuse property rights or otherwise reduce property-rights security. Judges can be bribed or take advantage of the fact that it is difficult to measure the quality of their services. The prevalence of corruption in much of the world testifies to the magnitude of this problem. (Rose-Ackerman 1999; Shleifer and Vishny 1993).

The difficulty of providing appropriate incentives to judges and regulators often reflects their concern about their personal safety following an unfavorable judgment. Powerful members of a society can use coercive power and other means to obstruct justice and circumvent regulations. (Glaeser and Shleifer 2003.) Making judges and regulators free of political control and relying relatively more on regulations rather than laws are ways of mitigating this problem. Yet, relaxing the ability to discipline judges can lead to more corruption. Similarly, regulatory agencies can be established to propagate the policy of legislators beyond these legislators' term rather than promoting welfare (e.g., Weingast 1996).

---

[12] See Greif 2001, 2004 regarding endogenously providing incentives for a partial law to provide impartial justice. Klerman 2003 summarizes various theses and emphasizes competition among courts of law; Klerman and Mahoney 2004 elaborate on the importance of freeing the legal system from political intervention.

[13] In general, modern legal systems do not collect information in commercial cases. This has not always been the case. In late medieval Venice, the authorities *ex-ante* collected the information required to verify the conduct of agents in long-distance trade ventures. (Gonzalez de Lara, 2002.) I am not familiar with an analysis of the optimal scope of *ex-ante* or *ex-post* information collection by the legal system.

These limitations of public-order institutions imply, in particular, that organic CEIs are more efficient when information is known but not verifiable, when the speed of resolving contractual disputes is important, and when the issues are too complex for the court to grasp at a low cost or when the issues require particular knowledge that the court lacks. Indeed, Macaulay's (1963) seminal work reveals the large extent to which organic CEIs govern contractual relationships in the contemporary USA. (See also Bernstein 1992.) Where and when public-order institutions are ineffective due to corruption or budgetary constraints, the relative profitability of private-order institutions increases. Indeed, the informal sector is disproportionally larger in developing economies and countries in transition (Portes 1994: 438; De Soto 1989: 12, 131; Fafchamps et. al. 1993; Greif and Kandel 1995).

When effective public-order institutions exist, economic agents can respond to their limitations for fostering contract enforcement by appropriately structuring their contractual relationships, property-rights distribution, and organizational forms. Williamson (1985) has emphasized the importance of private-order institutions operating in the shadow of the law. Hostage-taking, vertical integration, and corporate governance are examples of such structuring. (See Williamson 1985; Hart and Moore 1999; Maskin and Tirole 1999; Tirole 2001. Dixit (forthcoming) also explores the implications of bargaining in the shadow of the law.)

Townsend (1979) initiates the analysis of situations in which one economic agent can, at a cost, falsify or verify information while the court can enforce contracts given the endogenous information structure. Theoretical and empirical analyses examined the structures of optimal contracts in such situations of costly falsification and verification. (E.g., Lacher and Weinberg 1989; Williamson, D. 2002.) Recognizing the contractual and efficiency implications of costly state falsification and verification opens the way for considering the implied motivation to alter the institutions that influence these costs. Gonzalez de Lara (2002) presented such an analysis, when she considered how late medieval Venice structured its legal system to reduce these costs, thereby enabling progressively more efficient contracts and more savings to be invested in profitable long-distance trade.

Designed, Private-Order Institutions

A private response to the needs for additional contract enforcement—beyond that provided by existing organic and public-order CEIs—manifests itself in designed, private-order CEIs. (Henceforth, I will refer to these institutions as 'designed CEIs' although public-order institutions are also designed.) These are intentionally established by economic agents in response to profit opportunities entailed by improving contract enforcement beyond what is possible otherwise.

Designed CEIs, like organic ones, are based on the expected responses of economic agents. They are established either by the interacting parties (e.g., business associations) or by a third party (e.g., the stock exchange and credit rating companies). Institutionalists examined mainly designed CEIs that foster contract enforcement by the credible threat of imposing economic sanctions by the economic agents. Similar to public-order institutions, designed CEIs are intentionally planned and have explicit rules and intentionally created organizations. Because designed CEIs rely on sanctions by the economic agents, they are analytically similar to organic ones. But because designed CEI's are intentional, they often have features similar to those of public-order institutions, such as formal procedures to resolve disputes and impose fines.

The organizations and rules central to designed CEIs increase the disciplinary impact of economic sanctions by changing the information structure, providing coordination, and more generally by altering the strategic interaction among the economic agents. The organizations central to designed CEIs—or the people who control them—are often directly motivated by their economic interests and would not abuse their power seeking profit.[14] This mechanism, as elaborated below, often has to be supplemented by legal means.

Information intermediaries are pervasive in the modern economy, taking such diverse forms as auditing firms, credit reporting firms, the Better Business Bureau, credit rating firms, the Consumer Report, and business associations.[15] They reduce the cost of acquiring information regarding an economic agent's past conduct, ability to perform, and professional credentials. They improve information quality, increase the speed of its circulation, and even certify one's identity in cyberspace. Information intermediaries improve monitoring, aggregate and track information regarding past conduct, and enable one to signal his reputation by paying fines, providing arbitration, and checking the quality of goods and services upon delivery or because of a complaint. Organizations, such as business associations, coordinate responses to contractual breaches, thereby fostering the certainty that a multilateral punishment will be imposed but reducing the risk of being improperly punished.

Other organizations foster contract enforcement by altering the structure of the interactions among the economic agents, particularly by replacing infrequent interactions among any two economic agents with frequent interaction with the organization. This changes the set of self-enforcing beliefs regarding conduct. A prominent example is a credit card company. When one pays with a credit card, the (possibly) infrequent transactions between the seller and the buyer are replaced by the frequent transactions between the buyer and the credit card

---

[14] For a formal analysis, see Milgrom, et. al 1990; Dixit 2003; Greif 2004.

[15] In 1985, for example, a credit reporting firm, currently called 'Seafax', began selling information regarding the past conduct of buyers in the fresh fish industry via the internet. It responded to the profit opportunity presented by the fact that sellers of perishable goods need to quickly market their product. They have little time to verify the creditworthiness of a new customer. Indeed, during the 1980s, the US fresh fish industry was characterized by repeated interactions (lock-in relationships) in which those selling fish were in a weak bargaining position. Seafax capitalized on this situation by becoming an information intermediary. It now provides information regarding companies in all segments of the perishable food industry in North America and its business news is updated every half hour. For analysis of such intermediaries, see Bernstein 1996; Klein 1997.

company. Failing to pay a debt to a credit card company, unlike to a one-time seller, entails losing the gains from future purchases using the card.[16] Exchanges, such as the London Exchange or the NYSE, operate on the same principle. The infrequent interaction between two particular sellers and buyers of securities is replaced by frequent ones between each seller and buyer and the exchange itself. Escrow companies, large retailers, and hotel chains foster contract enforcement in a similar fashion.

Hotels and other chains illustrate how organizations also foster contract enforcement by aggregating reputation. The organization is structured in a way that reputational consideration makes it credible that it will monitor and discipline its constituting members. A hotel chain is motivated to maintain the same level of service quality in its individual hotels, expecting that once disappointed, a customer will shun its other hotels. (Ingram 1996.) A chain enables more commitment than is possible by individually owned hotels. Stock exchanges are similarly motivated by reputational considerations to discipline their member traders.

The credible threat by an organization to discipline its members, increases the value of membership, as each member can attract more trade. This higher value, in turn, provides the organization with an effective disciplinary device in the form of exclusion. Indeed, reputation considerations motivate the NYSE to examine and certify the creditworthiness of its traders, judge disputes among members, suspend members who are at fault, and screen listed firms for their quality (Banner 1998). Arguably, similar considerations motivated craft guilds and credit cooperatives (Guinnane 1994) in the pre-modern economy and large producers, and business associations in modern times.

Because formal organizations are central to designed CEIs, these institutions' cost structure is similar to that of public-order CEIs. There is a high fixed cost in initially setting up an institution, as it requires the acquisition of organizational capacity (such as storing information), specifying and making common knowledge rules and processes (regarding membership, filing a complaint, and sanctions), generating awareness of the new organization, and creating the belief that it can support contract enforcement in a way that is beneficial to its customers. Once established, however, designed CEIs exhibit low marginal cost of expanding the number of individuals covered by the system or the number of transactions each is engaged in.

This assertion regarding the nature of the marginal cost, however, is too simplistic. It considers only the technological determinants of costs. But strategic considerations of these costs muddy the water. The organization (or the individuals who control it) can gain from abusing the information and power at their disposal. A credit rating company can gain by extorting money for good reports or charge customers for unjustifiably improving their rating. A business association can let its members go unpunished for selling defective goods and keeping the gain or sharing it among themselves. Ignoring possible legal

---

[16] A credit card company is also more likely to seek legal sanctions, given that its reputation is on the line and that credit card's debt aggregates the monetary value of many purchases.

sanctions, such behavior is likely to be punished eventually by customers who take their business elsewhere. The threat of losing future business to discipline the organization, however, means that its profits need to be sufficiently high. The costs of the institution also include the mark up—beyond the technological marginal costs—required for providing the organization with the appropriate incentives. The cost of designed private and public CEI's can also be higher than technologically warranted because they are often a natural monopoly and hence, ignoring other factors, would not change marginal cost for their services.

The high fixed costs associated with designed institutions imply that organic ones would be more efficient when there is little to gain from expanding the number of exchanging individuals or when the loss due to bilateral repeated relationships is relatively small. There is rationale behind the observation that the largest (in terms of coverage) designed CEIs seem to be located in the consumer and retail sectors. The credit card companies and stock exchanges are but two examples. In any case, designed CEIs can substitute for organic ones and, due to their lower marginal costs and designed features, may be more efficient in providing contract enforcement in impersonal, complex exchange and in a dynamic environment.

We do not have a systematic body of knowledge regarding either the relative efficiency of public-order and designed, private-order CEIs or the factors influencing their relative efficiency. Public-order CEIs entail the potential benefits of impartial third party enforcer but also entail the various costs elaborated above. The organizations or individuals central to designed CEIs would enforce contracts only to the extent that they can directly profit from doing so. Competition among designed CEIs would therefore not necessarily be beneficial as it is the expectation of future profits that motivates the CEIs not to abuse their enforcement ability. Yet, without competition, the CEIs would charge the price for its service that maximizes its profit rather than gains from exchange. Relative to public-order institutions, designed ones are likely to be better able to learn from the market's feedback, diversify their products, rely on tacit knowledge and statistical measures of performance, provide faster service and be more cost effective than a legal system.

Irrespective of their relative costs or other implications, designed CEIs can often substitute public-order institutions. The Bourse of Amsterdam was the most important and best organized in Europe during the 17th century. Yet, many of the financial instruments traded in it, such as short sales, forward contracts, options, and hypothecation of shares as collateral, were either in legal limbo or actually illegal. Reputation sustained trade until the time when these instruments became legal.[17] The threat of economic sanctions can achieve the same deterrence as the equivalent legal sanctions.[18] Even today, where legal

---

[17] Stringham 2003. Quinn 1997 and Neal and Quinn 2001 report similar findings regarding goldsmith-bankers in London around the same time.

[18] But legal sanctions can be imposed when economic sanctions cannot due to, for example, budget constraints, outside economic opportunity, etc.

systems are relatively ineffective, as for example, in contemporary Mexico, economic sanctions replace legal ones. (E.g., Woodruff 1998.) Even where the legal system is well developed, as in the USA, similar sanctions are important in commercial transactions. (E.g., Bernstein 1992, 1996.)

Arguably, designed CEIs substituted for the public-order CEIs in past economies to a larger extent than in modern ones as the latter were relatively undeveloped and the state had limited administrative capacity. (Although historically the distinction between private and public was less sharp than in modern time). Furthermore, there is evidence to support the claim that designed CEIs were central to the historical process through which various market economies grew and led to the conditions favorable to the establishment of public-order CEIs. Markets did not wait for public-order institutions provided by a centralized, territorial state. Rather, they developed based on designed CEIs.[19]

Consider the case of impersonal exchange characterized by separation between the *quid* and the *quo* over time and space. Despite the lack of impartial legal enforcement provided by the state, such exchange prevailed in late medieval Europe based on an institution that can be referred to as the Community Responsibility System (CRS). This was a designed system (although perhaps with organic roots dating back to the 6th century) with explicit rules and an organization that built on the fact that merchants were members of particular communes that had intra-commune contract-enforcement institutions. These intra-community institutions provided the foundation for an institution that provided contract enforcement in inter-community impersonal exchange despite the absence of a state with effective public-order institutions. (Greif 2002; 2004.)

Under the CRS, communities established organizations in trading centers that enabled merchants to learn the communal and personal identities of their (otherwise unknown) partners in an exchange. If a member of community A, for example, had cheated a member of community B each and every member of community A was held responsible by community B for the damage. Hence, community A had the choice of either ceasing to trade with community B or compensating for the damage and seeking retribution from the individual who cheated. This joint-liability—which was neither contractual nor voluntary for an individual merchant—implied that each community was endogenously motivated to utilize its community enforcement institutions to discipline a merchant member who cheated in inter-community exchange. Anticipating compensation, merchants were motivated to learn the communal and personal identities of their partners to an exchange and could credibly commit to complain in a case of default despite the cost involved. Hence, communal courts provided impartial justice in inter-communal disputes although a community's courts were partial. Indeed, they provided impartial justice because they represented the interests of their merchants and cared about their reputations.

---

[19] See Greif 2000 regarding Europe, and Schaede 1989; Ramseyer 1991; Ryser 1997; Okazaki 2002; and Kambayashi 2002 regarding Japan.

Institutions such as the CRS, that fall in between the way we model private and public-order institutions, probably constituted an important step in the development of market economies. Indeed, if exchange historically began based on organic CEIs founded on personal relationships within relatively small groups, the emergence of the impartial legal system to facilitate impersonal exchange requires an explanation. Why was a high, fixed-cost, legal system for impersonal exchange established if the volume of impersonal exchange was low? We know that contracting efficiency alone does not lead to a transition from one system of contract enforcement to another. (Greif 1994a and Kranton 1996b.) Private-order institutions, such as the CRS, generated the initial volume of impersonal exchange required to justify the high sunk cost of the public-order institutions. Indeed, these institutions were established following a decline in the economic efficiency and political viability the CRS. (Although, as discussed below, the success or failure of this transition depended on the existence of complementing institutions.)

Designed CEIs seem to be equally prominent in modern market economies. They are such an integral part of these economies that it is easy to lose sight of their importance. They manifest themselves in organizations such as banks, credit cooperatives, credit card companies, consumer groups, escrow companies, trading companies, wholesalers, chain stores, hotel chains, banks, trade associations, unions, trading companies, trade and industry associations, stock exchanges, clearinghouses, credit rating agencies, credit bureaus, and better business bureaus. Their operation is reflected in brand names, copyrights, audits, guarantees, accreditations, etc.[20] Although the associated institutions have many other functions, such as reducing search costs, matching savers with investors, and smoothing consumption, contract enforcement seems to be an integral and important part of their operation.

Indeed, although we lack a systematic analysis of the relative importance of different types of institutions in various economies, designed CEIs seem to be the hallmark of advanced market economies. Fafchamps (2004) examined the institutional foundations of markets in contemporary Africa. He found that all have organic institutions and some have effective public-order institutions. Where they uniformly fall behind is in their designed CEIs. Similarly, the engine of growth in modern economies has been the rise of their service and consumers' goods sectors. One can conjecture that this rise is due to their designed CEIs. Such CEIs have a relative advantage in these sectors due to the difficulties of measuring quality, the relatively small sums, and the many instances of infrequent interactions.

We similarly lack a systematic analysis of the relationships among and designed and public-order CEIs. Designed institutions are often established in response to their details and to circumvent the need and reduce the cost of using

---

[20] Separating the identity of a business owner and that of the business itself fosters contract enforcement. The option of selling the business and its reputation increases the cost of a breach. (Kreps 1990 and Tadelis 2002.)

public-order institutions. Title insurance companies and escrow companies are examples. Public-order institutions are often required to prevent designed CEIs from using their economic power to curtail rather than expand exchange and efficiency. A drastic example is that of the Hanseatic League. This was an inter-city alliance that initially secured the property rights of German merchants abroad, and thereby promoted Baltic and Atlantic trade during the late medieval period. The same economic power that enabled the Hanseatic League to check the coercive power of rulers abroad, enabled it also to acquire exclusive trading rights. It eventually turned into a welfare-reducing monopoly that restricted the entry of more efficient traders (Greif 1992).

Although many designed institutions are completely private-order, others critically depend on complementary public-order institutions. Indeed, many designed institutions are what can be referred to as 'quasi-private.' Contract enforcement between the interacting economic agents in the main exchange relationships does not depend, or does so only marginally, on the law. The threat of economic sanctions provides the appropriate motivation. Yet, the law is critical to the operation of these institutions by creating the various conditions necessary for them to function and mitigating auxiliary contractual relationships.

The ability of credit rating agencies to secure property rights in exchange, for example, critically depends on public-order institutions that increase the cost of falsifying one's identity. Hotel chains, large producers, wholesalers, and banks commit by placing their reputations and hence future business as bonds. Yet, the value of this reputation critically depends on public-order institutions that protect their brand names. Accreditation and seals-of-approval provided by business-associations or the Better Business Bureau motivate their holders to adhere to their contractual obligations. This motivation, however, benefits from the increase in the cost of forgery that public-order institutions create. Public-order contributes to maintain the value of organizations' reputations by increasing the cost for copy cats to enter, assume the organization's identity and cheat its customers.

Similarly, the designed CEIs in the modern economy imply separation between ownership and control. The corporate governance literature explores the contractual implication of the associated agency problems, concentrating, in particular, on inducing agents to exert the level of effort most beneficial to the firm in the presence of asymmetric information and contract incompleteness. Yet, an additional first-order problem is preventing these agents from directly taking actions that benefit themselves but harm the company. The corporate governance literature usually ignores such possibilities. Managers are assumed to be able to supply inefficient levels of effort but are unable to take the money and fly to Bermuda. More generally, those in control can, for example, transfer assets to their private accounts, get kickbacks from suppliers, provide their customers with defective products or false information, raise their salaries, and give themselves bonuses, and extort money using their ability to inflict sanctions. The firm or organization and its owners may care about the implied reputational or other losses, but those in control may not care about either their own reputations or the organization's. (E.g., Johnson et. al. 2000).

Very little systematic analytical and empirical attention has been devoted to the importance of quasi-private institutions. Even less attention has been devoted to hybrid institutions that combine elements of private and public-order and/or combine economic, social, and coercion sanctions. The CRS discussed above represents such a hybrid, as the concern of a community's reputation motivated it to use its coercive power against a community member who defaulted in inter-community relationships. Medieval guilds often motivated their members by economic, social, legal and even religious sanctions. (E.g., Richardson 2002; Olds and Liu 2000.) The famous Grameen Bank lends to an individual through a formal contract but conditions its lending to others on repayment, thereby soliciting social pressure to motivate repayment. (E.g., Ghatak and Guinnane 1999.) Several works examined the role of private coercion—organized crime—in providing contract enforcement. (E.g., Gambetta 1993; Greif and Kandel 1995, and Dixit 2003.)

Many other aspects of designed CEIs are still waiting for a rigorous analysis. We don't have a theory for the internal organization of business associations and similarly designed CEIs, or the conditions under which reputation considerations prevent abuse of information and organizational power. The organizations central to many designed CEIs are often natural monopolies implying that despite their low (technical) marginal cost, their prices may be high, diminishing their usefulness. Even in this case, competition may be beneficial for reducing prices and ensuring quality of service. Yet, too much competition can erode the reputational incentives that provide motivation to these organizations not to abuse their information and power. Conversely, firms strategically respond to the information regarding their reputations that is produced, for example, by credit rating companies.

The dynamic process of the emergence of designed CEIs or how exactly they acquire the information critical to their operation has not been rigorously studied either. Empirical studies (e.g., Hoffman et. al. 2000) suggest the importance of initially having sufficiently valuable information which enables the organization to both gain from its distribution and use it to acquire additional information. The implications of increases in market scale (e.g., through globalization) on designed CEIs, has also not been studied. Conversely, the implications of international trade on desiged CEIs have barely been considered. (Although see Greif 1992; Yarbrough and Yarbrough 2003.)

Various contract enforcement institutions—private and public, organic and designed—have their distinct advantages and disadvantages and each complements and substitutes for the other. More reliance on organic CEIs, however, is optimal in relatively small and static economies and when there is less to gain from impersonal exchange. More reliance on public-order and designed CEIs is optimal in relatively large, dynamics economies with much to gain from impersonal exchange. Arguably, public-order institutions are more important in industrial economies in which complexity is relatively low and transactions relatively large. In this case, the court can relatively easily verify past actions and the threat of a law suit is credible given the sums involved. Designed CEIs are relatively more important in complex, consumer- and service-oriented economies in which actions are difficult to verify *ex-post* and the sums are relatively small.

2. COERCION-CONSTRAINING INSTITUTIONS

As noted by John Locke, among many others, the feasible extent of markets depends on protection from coercive power. For one thing, displaying one's goods in the market facilitate their confiscation by those with coercive power. In small social units, such as tribes, communities, and clans, the use of coercive power to capture another's property is likely to be effectively curtailed by the density of personal, social, and economic ties and the relatively even distribution of coercive power. In larger social units, this is not the case leading many, such as Hobbes, to argue that a state is required to protect rights and foster markets. This implies a dilemma: a state strong enough to protect rights is also strong enough to abuse them.

It has been suggested that this dilemma can be resolved by political institutions limiting rulers' power: limiting their prerogatives and placing political decision-making rights in the hands of asset holders. (E.g., North and Weingast 1989; Weingast 1997.) Yet, as was noted in the chapter by Mary M. Shirley, this answer is unsatisfactory. Market economies often prosper despite the lack of such political development. China had an extensive market economy during its Imperial past in the absence of such political rules. More generally, from 1950 to 1990, the rate of growth in national income of democracies and dictatorships was almost the same. (Przeworski et. al. 2000.) Conversely, the political rules of modern developed economies were often adopted in developing economies without disciplining rulers or fostering markets. The political rules of the modern state are neither necessary nor sufficient for markets. Understanding the prevalence of markets and the co-evolution of markets and political rules requires examining deeper factors.

Accordingly, the following concentrates on coercion-constraining institutions (henceforth, CCIs.) CCIs influence decisions at the social level regarding the acquisition and use of coercive power. Effective CCIs make violence economically productive as it is used to protect property rights from abuses, such as expropriation by the state, the ravages of a civil war, and large-scale military raids. They secure property rights by discouraging those who can acquire coercive power to abuse rights from doing so, and by motivating those who have coercive power—rulers, the elite, states (and I henceforth use these terms interchangeably)—to protect rights. These CCIs rely on balancing one's coercive power with either the coercive power of others or their ability to inflict economic sanctions on one who abuses rights. CCIs deter abuse of rights by creating the shared beliefs that attempting to do so will lead to a costly retaliation.

There is no one-to-one correspondence between states and CCIs. There can be effective CCIs in the absence of a state while in predatory states there are no effective CCIs. Yet, the common denominator of CCIs can be illustrated by considering the argument that a state strong enough to protect property rights is also strong enough to abuse them. Two assumptions are implicit in this statement. The first is that only the state has coercive power. But the existence of a state does not preclude social units within it—including those composed of economic agents—from having actual or potential coercive power. Countervailing coercive power can constrain the state. Indeed, states' coercive power has historically often been no more than the aggregation of the coercive power of its composing social units. A balance of coercive powers within a polity—among such social units as towns, clans, tribes, and classes—can limit the abuse of rights.

The second assumption implicit in the above statement is that having coercive power implies an unconstrained ability to gain from abusing rights. This, however is not the case. The costs and benefits to a ruler from abusing rights depend on the state's administration's capacity to gain information regarding assets that can be captured, capturing them, and transforming the proceedings into goods and services beneficial to the ruler. A ruler's costs and benefits from abusing rights depends on administrative capacity and who controls the administration. Furthermore, administration is required for effective ruling. The court and the army need to be provided for and resources have to be mobilized to advance the ruler's policies. Those controlling the administration are therefore in a position to take actions that are costly to the ruler. In particular, if the state's administration is controlled by the asset holders, abusing their rights can undermine, rather than foster a ruler's welfare. The capacity of, and control over the state's administration can be structured in a way that the ruler can either credibly commit not to abuse rights or is deterred from doing so.

Furthermore, various technological and institutional factors limit a ruler's grabbing hand. These factors influence a ruler's benefits from abusing a particular asset and the extent to which economic agents can respond to expropriation by economically sanctioning the ruler. For example, a ruler gains little from capturing an asset whose value is lost without the original owner's complementary human capital, and abusing alien merchants' assets can drive the merchants away, depriving a ruler of trade benefits. Hence, even a ruler with a monopoly over coercive power can be deterred from abusing rights by countervailing economic powers reflecting either administrative structure or institutions taking advantage of limits to a ruler's grabbing hand.

CCIs that are based on either countervailing coercive or economic powers reflect the same principle. The expected responses of those with coercive and economic powers influence one's decision regarding abusing their assets. Protection is afforded, however, only to those who can retaliate. This section presents the principles on which various CCIs rest (although a CCI often rests on several principles), their origin, dynamics, and relationships with political development.

Balancing Coercive Powers

In CCIs based on balancing coercive powers, the expected violent response of the asset holders deters one from abusing these assets. Bates et. al. (2002) provided a general framework to study the nature and costs of various such CCIs in polities with and without a ruler.[21] The analysis considers the strategic decisions regarding acquiring and using coercive powers focusing on equilibria in which no abuse occurs. By imbedding this problem in a resources allocation problem, it is possible to measure the cost of securing rights under various CCIs. It is the difference between the equilibrium and the first-best allocation of resources.

Consider an infinitely repeated interaction among agents (e.g., clans, tribes, and towns). In each period, each agent simultaneously chooses how to allocate a finite amount of effort among production, investment in coercive power, or leisure (which cannot be expropriated). After observing the choice of the other, each can sequentially decide whether to raid the other—at some cost—or not. The amount gained from raiding increases in one's relative coercive strength, the superiority of defense over offence, the amount produced by the other, and the share of the products lost due to a raid.

No Ruler: Mutual Deterrence Among Social Units   When there is no ruler, there are equilibria in which each agent sufficiently invests in coercive power to deter the other from raiding him. Theoretically, such a 'mutual deterrence' equilibrium is more likely to exist the more the agents value the future; the higher the cost of raiding; the more the military technology favors defense; the higher is the share of the products lost due to a raid; and when the agents also gain from economic cooperation (e.g., trading or joint production that they can lose following a raid). Furthermore, the higher the value of these parameters, the lower is the cost of securing property rights as the equilibrium allocation of effort is closer to first-best. Yet, such a mutual deterrence equilibrium generically entails a socially wasteful allocation of effort to acquire coercive power. Furthermore, it reduces the incentives to make productive investments because wealth requires resources to protect it. Finally, mutual deterrence equilibria are unstable in the sense that even transitory changes in relative might or wealth lead to military conflicts.

Tribal societies provide the classic example of polities without a ruler but such polities even exist in urban settings. The commune of Genoa was a polity in which security of property rights was based on mutual deterrence. By the end of the 11th century, the decline in the Muslim and Byzantine naval powers provided maritime cities, such as Genoa, with an opportunity to gain from expanding its overseas trade.[22] The Genoese responded by establishing a commune in which mutual deterrence among Genoa's heavily armed clans

---

[21] See also Greif 1994b, 1998; Muthoo 2000; and Bates 2001. For works considering the relationships between military technology and security of rights, see, e.g., Skaperdas 1992; Skaperdas and Syropoulos 1996; Konrad and Skaperdas 1996, Grossman 1997; Grossman and Kim 1995; Moselle and Polak 2001.

[22] See Epstein 1996 for Genoa's history. For analysis, see Greif 1994b, 1996 1998, forthcoming.

secured property rights. Clans jointly mobilized their resources to equip the navy and the military force required to expand Genoa's commerce. The extent of inter-clan cooperation was limited, however. Consistent with the claim regarding the disincentive for wealth expansion under mutual deterrence, the clan who gained most from the previous expansion ceased cooperating in further expansion. A richer Genoa would have required increasing its military investment to deter others from attacking it.

Wide-scale commercial expansion did not occur until 1155 when the constraint implied by mutual deterrence was relaxed by an external military threat from the German Emperor. Inter-clan military conflict would have made the city more vulnerable to attacks by the Emperor. As each clan had to devote fewer resources to deter the other, each was willing to cooperate by advancing commerce. Yet, as Genoa grew in wealth and the external threat unexpectedly subsided (due to a civil war in Germany) in 1164, a prolonged period of civil war ensued.

Make me a King Extending the model to include a ruler with coercive power enables examining the conditions under which he would better secure rights. Assume that a ruler can use his coercive ability, after paying a fixed cost, to capture assets. He will capture the assets with some positive probability (which can depend on the agent's coercive power). Apart from the actions discussed above, each agent can now also either pay a tax or not.

Consider the equilibria in which property rights are secured. Each economic agent is deterred from raiding by the military ability of the others, but in addition, he is also deterred by the threat of the ruler retaliating against one who raided. The ruler is motivated to retaliate by the expectation that as long as he does so and refrains from abusing rights, the agents will pay him taxes. If he fails to retaliate or abuse rights, the agents will revert to playing another equilibrium strategy in which they invest more in military ability and consume more leisure. In this case, the ruler loses tax revenues. In such equilibria, the coercive power of each player—the ruler and the economic agents—is constrained by the coercive power of the two other players.

Distortions are caused by two factors. If the relative coercive power of the ruler is not sufficiently high, in and of itself, to deter the economic agents from raiding each other, each of them will invest in acquiring coercive ability. Effort allocation is therefore distorted. As the ruler's coercive power increases, however, and his expected retaliation is sufficient to deter raiding, this distortion approaches zero. A second distorting factor is taxation. Although taxation is socially beneficial as it motivates the ruler not to abuse rights, it causes the economic agents to consume more leisure than in the first-best allocation. The per-period equilibrium taxation (on-the-equilibrium-path), and hence distortion, is lower the lower a ruler's per-period payoff after he abused rights (that is, off-the-equilibrium path). Intuitively, if his continuation value is lower, a lower per-period tax (on-the-equilibrium-path) is sufficient to deter the ruler from abusing rights. (The distortion declines in the ruler's discount factor. Olson (1993) presents a non-strategic analysis of this important consideration.)

The extent to which an equilibrium with a ruler can approximate a world with perfectly secured property rights and a first-best allocation of effort thus depends on two factors. The higher a ruler's coercive power, the less effort each agent has to allocate to deter raiding; the lower the ruler's continuation value after he abuses rights, the lower the per-period tax required to deter abuse, and hence the lower is the access consumption of leisure due to taxation. At the limit, the allocation of resources approaches the first-best as the ruler's coercive power increases but his continuation value decreases. The ruler's coercive power constrains the economic agents' coercive power while their ability to acquire coercive power and consume leisure constrains the ruler's coercive power.

Central to the economic efficiency of the CCIs with a ruler is his coercive power on- and off-the-equilibrium path. The CCIs are more efficient the higher is the ruler's coercive power on-the-equilibrium-path (that is, as long as he did not abuse rights or reneged on punishing those who did) and the lower is his coercive power off-the-equilibrium-path (that is, after he abused rights or failed to punish those who did). The following discussion presents historical CCIs in which this condition has been satisfied to various degrees. It highlights the efficiency of CCIs in which there is no ruler with an independent military power.

A Ruler with an Independent Coercive Power

Motivated by a severe external military threat, the Genoese altered their political system in 1194 by introducing a *podestà* (literally, a 'power') to create a balance of coercive power among their clans. The *podestà* was a specialist in violence, a non-Genoese hired by the city for a year to be its military leader, judge, and administrator. He was supported by the soldiers and judges he brought with him. The *podestà's* military strength was such that the threat of him possibly joining forces with a clan that was attacked deterred each of Genoa's main clans from instigating an attack. Yet, the *podestà* was too weak to become a dictator and abuse rights given the strength of Genoa's clans and its population. A set of pre-specified rules defined which actions by the *podestà* constituted an abuse.

Central to the *podesteria* system, however, was the way that the "threat" of the *podestà* retaliating against a transgressor by joining forces with another clan was made credible. The *podestà* was promised a high wage at the end of his term, but because he was weaker than each clan, if one clan took control of the city, there would be no reason to reward the *podestà*. Hence he was motivated to act against a transgressor because otherwise his payoff would be lower. Furthermore, this reward scheme made it in the *podestà*'s interest to not fundamentally alter the balance of power between the clans. Hence, he could credibly be impartial and retaliate against those who broke the law rather than turn against an entire clan.

For this incentive scheme to be effective, however, it was imperative to insure that no clan would be able to credibly commit—using such means as marriage— to rewarding the *podestà* if he assisted that clan against another. More generally, it was imperative that the *podestà* could not acquire a power base within Genoa. This was accomplished through a series of regulations, supervised by a committee, that restricted his actions. E.g., the incoming *podestà* was selected by a council, whose members were chosen to prevent control by any specific clan, and the selection process for the new *podestà* was governed by the outgoing *podestà*. The *podestà*—as well as his relatives to the third degree—was restricted from socializing with Genoese, buying property, marrying a local woman, or managing any commercial transactions for himself or others. Furthermore, the *podestà*, as well as the soldiers who came with him, had to leave the city at the end of his term and not return for several years. A *podestà*'s son could not replace him in office.

The Genoese promise to reward a *podestà* at the end of his term if no clan had initiated and won an inter-clan war was credible because reneging would have impeded Genoa's ability to hire a high quality *podestà* in the future. Indeed, Genoese *podestà*s were recruited from a handful of Italian cities, in particular from Milan, and the contract between Genoa and its *podestà* was read in front of the "parliament" of the city from which the *podestà* was recruited. This does not imply that a *podestà* was given a free hand to mismanage the city's affairs. After the end of his term he had to remain in the city for fifteen days while his conduct was assessed by auditors. Deviations from pre-specified rules were punished by fines that were subtracted from his payment.

Historically, other polities, similar to Genoa, contracted with an external ruler to govern them to mitigate internal conflicts over leadership. Indeed, the prevalence of this practice into the modern period seems to have facilitated colonization (Henley 2004). As colonialism illustrates, rulers with independent coercive power were sometimes able to capture the polity. But even in this case, a balance of coercive powers often secured rights. Consider the Manchurian Qing Dynasty (1644–1911) which gained control over China after the Manchurians were invited to intervene in a civil war in China. The relative size of China and that period's military technology implied a high cost of subduing a revolt by the masses. The Emperors recognized "the people as a persistent potential threat to the Chinese state" (Wong 1997: 93) while a Chinese tradition conferred legitimacy on a dynasty if it was able to foster economic prosperity. Emperors were therefore motivated to commit to protect property rights and foster prosperity.

An elaborate system of rules, organizations, and precedents was used to generate the correct beliefs that rights would not be abused by, ironically, making the threat of revolt credible. The Qing imposed a relatively low tax, coordinated expectations regarding taxation by fixing its amount and making it common knowledge at the village level. Additional customary taxes were collected by the bureaucrats to finance local public goods and to remunerate them. Yet, bureaucrats were disciplined not to tax the peasants beyond the official and customary level. A bureaucrat who increased taxation faced riots by the peasants, which subsequently triggered an investigation and possibly punishment by the central authority. (Yang 2002.)

A Ruler with a Conditional Coercive Power

In the competition among the Italian maritime city-states, it was Venice which overtook Genoa. Interestingly, it had CCIs with a ruler without an independent coercive power but with a conditional power: he was strong on-the-equilibrium-path (that is, as long as he did not abuse rights or failed to punish those who did) but was weak off-the-equilibrium-path (that is, after he abused rights or reneged on punishing those who did). Hence, Venice's CCIs entailed a low-cost protection of property rights.

Initially, however, Venice's polity was characterized by the absence of an effective rule. The Venetians were left to govern themselves from the 8th century due to the decline of the Byzantine Empire.[23] The city's main families and clans became engaged in lengthy and bloody competition over the position of the Doge (who previously was a Byzantine governor sent from Constantinople). Of the twenty-nine Dogi that governed between 742 and 1032, about three-quarters were either assassinated, blinded, resigned, or expelled due to internal conflict.

A stable polity was established, however, during the 11th century, probably in response to the increasing gains from jointly mobilizing resources to promote long-distance trade. The Doge was made a magistrate, elected for life and responsible for establishing social order and providing public goods. Coercive power remained highly diffused among the prominent clans and families of Venice which were represented in a general council. The Doge himself was supervised by an elected council, was not allowed to go against its advice, and was subject to the law. Without a standing army, a Doge could be punished for breaking the law and abusing rights. Yet, the Doge was strong on-the-equilibrium-path as each clan was motivated to support the Doge if any other clan attempted to capture the position of the Dogeship or abuse others' rights.

Motivation for the clans to lend the Doge their coercive power, was based on the way that Venice's institutions distributed gains from the city's wealth. Lucrative economic and political posts were distributed independently of a clan's relative coercive power. Posts, including that of the Doge, were allocated to members of the political elite through a mixture of deliberation and random selection. The random component implied that one's clan relative military power and patronage system had little influence on the outcome. Explicit rules and historical experience coordinated the clans' beliefs on the above behavior.

Balancing Coercive Power with Economic Power

The prospect of losing future economic gains following an abuse can constrain coercive power even in the absence of countervailing coercive power. In considering CCIs based on balancing coercive power with economic power it is useful to differentiate between two groups of institutions. First, institutions based on

---

[23] See Lane 1973; Norwich 1977. The analysis here builds on Greif 1995; forthcoming.

an inherent limit in the ability to gain economically from one's coercive power; second, institutions based on the need for administrative capacity to gain from abusing rights and effectively rule. The following discussion reflects that these institutions have not been extensively studied.

CCIs Based on the Limited Reach of the Ruler's Grabbing Hand Confiscation of an asset can reduce its value due to complementarities between it and other assets, human capital, and expertise. If this reduction is high enough, providing a stream of rent to those with coercive power would be more profitable to them than capturing the asset. Rent can be provided, for example, by paying taxes or providing economically lucrative jobs. The cost of security is the distortions implied by mixing politics and economics in the absence of the rule of law. These costs will decrease the more value is lost from confiscation, which is the case when production requires high human capital, inventiveness, and complementary assets that are difficult to expropriate. Indeed, Mexico has failed for a long time to de facto nationalize its oil industry because the foreign oil companies had the expertise, organizational capacity, and the complementary assets required to render oil production profitable. (Haber, et. al. 2003.)

Abuses can also be deterred by the expectation that the economic agents will shift their activities following an abuse in a manner that would be costly to the abuser. Agents can shift their activities abroad or turn to produce or consume goods, such as leisure, that are more difficult to expropriate. Deterrence is enhanced by the mobility of assets, complementarities with other assets that cannot be captured, and the ability of the economic agents to overcome the collective action and free-rider problems associated with collectively responding to abuses. The following example highlights the general principles underpinning such institutions.

Specifically, consider the case of the medieval merchant guild. (Greif, et. al. 1994.) Long-distance trade in late medieval Europe was based upon exchanging goods in geographically favorable places. Medieval rulers who controlled these areas faced the temptation to abuse merchants' property rights using their coercive power. Furthermore, a ruler could abuse the rights of some merchants but not others implying that, when there are many merchants, the threat of one whose rights were abused to never trade again following an abuse was insufficient to enable a ruler to credibly commit to secure rights. Hence, without an institution making the ruler's pledge to provide protection credible, alien merchants were unlikely to frequent that trading center, a costly outcome for both ruler and merchants.

Theoretically, to surmount the ruler's commitment problem at the efficient level of trade, an organization with two abilities was needed: first, the ability to coordinate the responses of all (or enough) merchants if the rights of any merchant were abused; second, it had to have the ability to enforce its embargo decision on the merchants despite the fact that if an embargo was in force, an individual merchant had a lot to gain from trading. Indeed, the value of his trade to the ruler would be so high, that the ruler could credibly commit to respect that merchant's rights. The late medieval period witnessed the rise of merchants' territorial associations with coordination and internal enforcement capacities that governed the relations between their members and rulers of other territorial areas. These organizations took many forms, such as the German Hansa, merchant guilds, and autonomous cities. Yet, all of them had the capacity to coordinate action and discipline their members. Together with the shared beliefs associated with the above multilateral reputation mechanism that they made possible, these organizations constituted the merchant guild institution.

CCIs Based on the State's Administrative Structure Sending soldiers on a rampage is a costly way for a ruler to materially benefit from his coercive power. In contrast, state-controlled administration with the appropriate information, organizational capacity, and incentive reduces the cost and increases the benefits from confiscating wealth. It has information regarding who has wealth, where it is located, the capacity to take control of it, and the ability to dispose of or employ it in a way that benefits the ruler. Furthermore, administration is required for the state to function: the ruler and the court must be supplied, soldiers have to be recruited, trained, equipped and paid, and the public-order benefitting the ruler has to be maintained. The size, capacity, and control over the administration thus influence the costs and benefits of abusing rights to a ruler.

The (limitedly) **absent state**: By not creating an effective administration to govern a particular economic sphere, a ruler can commit not to abuse rights in that sphere because limited administration increases his cost of confiscation. When a ruler stands to gain less from abuse, property is more secure. Security increases with the cost and time it takes to establish an administration with the capacity to abuse rights at low cost. Similarly, security increases the more the agents are able to consume, transfer, or hide their assets after observing the initial stages of establishing a more effective administration. The initial absence of an effective administration, in turn, fosters their ability to do this. By being absent from a particular economic sphere—in the sense of not having an effective administration—a state can better commit to respect rights. Note that a state committing to rights in this way can be and usually will be absent only to a limited extent. To survive it has to be able to raise revenues, have an effective military force, and be able to provide public goods. These must be supported by an administration confined to these tasks.

Because assets' mobility increases security in the presence of an absent state, CCIs based on such absence were particularly important historically in securing traders' rights. Indeed, a common feature of many past market economies was the small extent to which movable assets were taxed apart from customs and payment for services within the market area itself. This was the case in the medieval Muslim world whose market economy was perhaps second-to-none. Traders were not subject to wealth or income tax and were taxed only when they voluntarily brought their goods to a particular locality such as market places and ports. (Goitein 1971; Udovitch 1988.) The same situation prevailed in the prosperous market economy of Imperial China (Wong 1997; Pomeranz 2000; Yang 2002.) In both cases, however, the state was not absent from other spheres of economic activity. It provided public goods, including social order, personal security, and agricultural and commercial infrastructures.

Delegation of state administration to asset holders: Commitment to not abuse the rights of asset holders can also be achieved by delegating state administration to these asset holders. Instead of having an administration controlled by the state, public goods and services to the state are provided directly by the asset holders. Similar to an absent state, commitment to property rights is achieved by depriving the ruler of the information and organizational capacity required for low-cost abuse of rights. More commitment is possible, however, because the asset holders can respond to abuse of their rights by cutting off the flow of services to the state. When the state depends on financing or tax collection provided by the asset holders to sustain its courts or maintain its army, the cost of withdrawing services can be high. The factors determining the extent of security through delegation are similar to those in the case of the absent state.[24]

The large extent to which delegation can secure rights is reflected in its ability to constrain the most powerful rulers of 16th century Europe: the Hapsburg Kings of Spain. The kings borrowed heavily from Genoese financiers who had an international monopoly over paying the royal army outside Spain. The Genoese could therefore respond by withdrawing these services if the king refused to pay his debt. The famous bankruptcies of the Spanish kings were indeed periods of debt reorganization rather than abuse of rights per-se. (Conklin 1998.)

The experience of the Genoese in Spain also illustrates how delegation fosters security by influencing the information structure and thus the cost of various actions. The Genoese collected the taxes used to pay Spaniards who held the Crown's domestic loans, each of which was linked to a particular tax revenue source. Because the king did not have information about who held the various loans, he could not repudiate them without possibly hurting those—such as his military elite—who could retaliate against him. Abuse risked hurting those upon whom the ruler depended to maintain his control.

Self-governance: Property rights are even more secure when delegation is done in the context of giving the asset holders an autonomy. As before, delegating the administration of the state renders it vulnerable to economic sanctions. But self-governance further fosters the asset holders' ability to commit to retaliating following an abuse of their rights. Self-governance entails having bodies of collective decision-making, mechanisms, such as judicial processes and police forces, to overcome the free-rider problem and motivate and induce

---

[24] Delegation is different from farming out of state administration under which agents (who are not necessarily the asset holders) compete for the right to e.g. collect taxes. Property rights security thus depends on the state's interest and ability to prevent over-taxation. Ottoman history illustrates the fragility of such systems.

Commitment, Coercion, and Markets   757

members to participate in sanctions. (The above discussion of the merchant guild is relevant here.)

Hapsburg Spain illustrates the effectiveness of self-governance. During the sixteenth and seventeenth centuries, towns had administrative autonomy (Nader 1990) that balanced the Crown's coercive power with their economic power. In 1571 the Crown decided to substantially increase the sales taxes collected in the towns. The administration of sales tax collection, however, was in the hands of the towns themselves. They informed the Crown that they would not farm out this higher tax, leaving the king with little option but to look for additional revenue elsewhere.

The Origin and Dynamics of CCIs and Political Institutions

Many factors that are exogenous to CCIs influence whether a particular CCI can be an equilibrium outcome in a given situation. Furthermore, generically, many CCIs can be equilibrium outcomes in a given situation. So while exogenous factors determine the set of feasible institutions, initial, possibly even transitory, historical factors influence which CCI will prevail.

CCIs based on either balance of coercive or economic powers are more likely to be an equilibrium the more those with coercive power value the future. CCIs based on a balance of coercive powers are also more likely to be an equilibrium as the production and military technologies reduce the per-period gain from abuse and increase the asset holders' potential military strength. E.g., the lower is the portion of the product that can be expropriated, the less mobile and more perishable is the product, the more defense is superior to offense, the easier it is to convert civilian production controlled by the asset holders to military production. CCIs based on balancing coercive power with economic power are more likely to be an equilibrium as the geography, production, monitoring, and information technologies increase the costs and reduce the benefits of expropriation. E.g., those with coercive power have limited independent economic resources, it is less costly to move assets away from their reach, and establishing a new administration is time-consuming and costly. The distortions and hence costs entailed by the need to secure rights declines in the above parameters.

For a particular CCI to prevail the relevant actors should share the beliefs that the related strategies will be followed. They should share beliefs regarding what action constitutes an abuse and what the consequences of doing so will be. Which set of shared beliefs, out of the many that are generically possible as an equilibrium outcome, will prevail reflects initial conditions, such as the initial distribution of wealth, military might, and coordinating mechanisms. Non-economic and potentially temporary factors, such as cultural heritage, the legitimacy and interest of coordinating organizations, and charismatic leaders, therefore play a role in institutional selection. Initial conditions, spontaneous evolution, learning, and intentional design influence institutional selection.

The CCIs of Genoa and Venice illustrate this argument. The Genoese and Venetians had similar military technology and similar initial endowments in the form of little arable land and locations favorable to trade. But they differed in their initial social structures, distributions of wealth and military ability, and tradition of centralized endogenous rule. The less concentrated social structure and more even and wide spread distribution of wealth and military might in Venice and the coordinating effect of the tradition of a Doge led to different institutional development.

Once a particular CCI establishes itself as an equilibrium outcome each actor's unilateral ability to change it is limited. An attempt to unilaterally change the CCI by taking such actions as raising a standing army or expanding the administration, entails military or economic retaliation. CCIs imply deterrence; one is prevented from taking an action that he would find beneficial in the absence of the institution. Each actor acts optimally given the constraints on his behavior implied by the institution, but he would have preferred, *ex-ante* or *ex-post*, not to be constrained. This is so even in the case when the CCI is Pareto-improving, enabling one to credibly commit not to abuse rights. E.g., a CCI can enable a ruler to *ex-ante* commit not to confiscate wealth *ex-post*, thereby promoting growth. *Ex-post*, however, the ruler would prefer to be able to confiscate it.

But CCIs do not last forever. They cease being effective, are changed unilaterally or multilaterally, intentionally or spontaneously, in response to exogenous changes in factors rending them equilibria, unexpected consequences, strategic innovations, external threats, and mutual gains. Unilateral institutional changes occurred in Europe, for example, following the 15th century Military Revolution which tilted the balance of coercive power in favor of the Crown and landed nobility and against peasants. Less able to constrain abuse, peasants throughout Europe were subject to increasing serfdom and taxation. This increase, however, was gradual, reflecting a learning process of the implied new balance of power. (Pettengill 1970.)

Gain from cooperation and external threats are a main source of mutually agreed upon institutional change as the histories of Genoa and Venice illustrate. The cities' histories also illustrate that the heritage of previous CCIs influence the set of CCIs that can be established as a new equilibrium outcome. The distribution of military and economic resources, shared beliefs, social structures, cognitive structures, and organizations that were part of the previous CCIs constitute part of the initial conditions in processes of institutional change. Hence new CCIs include institutional elements inherited from previous ones. (Greif, forthcoming.) Before and after the Genoese podesteria, a high concentration of military power and wealth and beliefs regarding the objectives and behavior of clans implied CCIs based on inter-clan mutual deterrence.

The set of feasible, consensual, institutional changes is also limited by the need to insure that each actor who can *ex-ante* block the change will not do so. This requires that those who will, *ex-post*, have more coercive or economic power and commit not to use this power to make others worse off. Changes that otherwise would be Pareto-improving would not feasible without such commitment. For these changes to be agreed upon, those who will have less power should nevertheless expect to be better off by having a smaller share in a larger pie or by *ex-ante* devising *ex-post* safeguards, which take into account the *ex-post* new distribution of powers.[25]

Strategic innovations motivated by the constraints implied by existing CCIs facilitated establishing new CCIs. The introduction of the *podestà* in Genoa represents an innovation leading to a Pareto-improving CCI. The innovation constitutes a response to the needs of the Genoese but it reflects the introduction of a *podestà* in Italian cities that were controlled by the Emperor decades earlier and a learning process through which Italian cities experimented in various CCIs and administrative structures. Strategic innovations aimed at advancing one's relative power often take advantage of the ambiguity over which actions constitute a deviation. E.g., the rights of monopolies were ill defined under feudalism and European kings later attempted to take advantage of this by creating monopolies to gain resources and might.

Gradual and unanticipated consequences implied by existing institutions lead to institutional change. They alter such factors as wealth, military power, and information that constitute the necessary conditions for the existing CCI to remain an equilibrium. The absolutist French kings of the late 16th century who were above the law had to pay a high interest rate for their loans. Aspiring to be able to better commit to pay their debts, they allowed the financiers to establish corporations. These were better able to balance the Crown's coercive power with an economic power. The long-run unexpected consequence was that these financiers became so economically powerful that they blocked institutional reforms that would have hurt them financially but might have saved the monarchy. (Root 1989.)

Such unanticipated consequences imply that those who benefit from the existing CCIs would be wary of organizational, economic, and political changes that can undermine these CCIs. Rulers, in particular, would be wary of delegation, self-governance, and independent military organizations. The threat to rulers from allowing self-governance is well reflected in the history of Genoa where a large scale, designed private-order institution altered CCIs by aligning the incentives of many economic agents and increasing their organizational capacity. The Genoese Bank of San Giorgio was established, according to Niccolo Machiavelli (1532), when the republic conceded control over various revenue sources to its creditors after a military defeat. These creditors organized themselves as a self-governed entity, the Bank of San Giorgio. As Genoa's debts continued to accumulate, the Bank gained the administration of most of the towns and cities in the Genoese dominion. It became so powerful, according to Machiavelli, that whoever gained political control over Genoa, had to respect the rights of the Bank "as it possesses arms, money, and

---

[25] E.g., Greif 1998 and forthcoming (Genoa); Greif 2001 (contemporary Middle Eastern dictators fearing that fostering development will create a countervailing economic power). Acemoglu and Robinson 2000 and Acemoglu 2003 (the limits on political transitions due to the need to commit to *ex-post* compensate a ruler). Fearon 1997(bargaining over distribution when it determines ex-post coercive power and hence further bargaining power). Galor and Moav 2003 (inter-state conflicts motivate capitalists to increase workers' human capital although this leads to their demise).

influence," and abusing its rights entailed "the certainty of a dangerous rebellion" (p. 352).

Although delegation, self-governance, independent military organizations, and large-scale, private-order institutions endanger rulers, they nevertheless will establish or tolerate them when their benefits are high relative to the risk they imply. This is more likely to be the case when the ruler's budget constraint is binding; when the ruler's legitimacy is high and hence the risk of revolt is low; when the organization can be abolished at will (as was true regarding the Merchant Guild); and when the institution provides services that are important for the ruler's control, such as feeding the capital city. Greif (2000), for example, argued that because the legitimacy of European rulers was high relative to that of Muslim rulers in the late medieval period, the former allowed more designed CEIs than the latter. Okazaki (2002) noted that despite initial resistance, the Tokugawa Shogunate (1603–1868) allowed food merchants to organize themselves, fearing that otherwise volatility in food prices would lead to riots that would undermine their control.

CCIs influence political development, particularly whether representative bodies would emerge or be established by rulers as means for collective, political, decision-making. Such bodies have been common in a variety of political systems, ranging from monarchies (e.g., the English Great Council), constitutional monarchies (e.g., the English parliament), and tribal societies (e.g., the Afghani Loya Jirga). Seemingly diverse, these representative bodies reflect the constraint implied by CCIs. CCIs imply that, fearing retaliation, each actor will be deterred from taking unilateral actions that can be considered abusing rights or attempting to undermine the existing CCIs in a manner that would leave them worse off. Hence, an actor wishing to take such an action without invoking retaliation, would seek the consent of those who can retaliate.

This account provides a rationale for a puzzling observation: why do rulers, as was common in pre-modern Europe, allow for representative organizations whose members are not hand-picked by them although such bodies provide an arena for revealing and coordinating opposition to the ruler? The French revolution transpired after the Crown summoned the Estates-General for the first time since 1614. But when a ruler faces effective CCIs, he also stands to gain from representative bodies. They enable him to take actions with lower risk of costly retaliation. Representative bodies are a means to design explicit rules increasing—temporarily or permanently—the range of acceptable actions. Representative bodies are therefore more likely to be established when the ruler's budget constraint is binding and he is unable to provide the public goods he and his subjects desire.

We have no models of bargaining in the context of various CCIs. It is intuitive, however, that those who provide a ruler their consent, will demand and receive concessions for doing so. As noted above, these concessions are likely to take the form of safeguards against future abuses. Providing the ruler with additional resources risks shifting the balance of power in his favor, implying that those who are in a position to authorize this transfer, given the existing CCIs, will seek to safeguard their position. They will demand various concessions—such as freedom from taxes, administrative control, military resources, legal rights, the right to supervise or authorize various actions—to increase their ability to constrain the ruler *ex-post*.

Ironically, representative bodies also facilitate the abuse of property rights. Representative bodies are populated by those who balance each other's coercive and economic powers, providing them with a means to coordinate the abuse of rights for those who are not represented. In Poland, after the European Military Revolution that began in the 15th century, the balance of military power shifted in favor of the landed, lower nobility. They gained dominance in the kingdom's national assembly and used expropriated rights. The Polish serfs lost many rights during that time. Their tax obligations, for example, increased several times.

Conversely, if the economic and coercive power of groups represented in the representative body no longer constrains the ruler's actions, these groups will become, at most, a rubber stamp, a mechanism for a ruler to coordinate collective actions he finds useful. Alternatively, when the risk to the ruler of coordinating opposition through these bodies outweighs their benefits, he will not summon them. When absolutism reached its peak in France during the 17th century, the Estates-General was not summoned.

3. THE DYNAMICS OF MARKET-SUPPORTING INSTITUTION AND THE IMPLIED DYNAMICS OF MARKETS AND POLITICAL INSTITUTIONS

The dynamics of CEIs reflect preceding initial institutions. Initial organic, private-order CEIs influence the extent to which economic agents will find it profitable to use public-order and designed CEIs if available and establish them if possible. Initial CCIs influence the extent to which these CEIs can be effectively provided or established. Public-order and designed CEIs that reveal wealth to those with coercive power will only be utilized if the CCIs are such that revelation of wealth does not undermine property rights security. Conversely, rulers will permit designed, large-scale CEIs only if the CCIs are such that they either cannot prevent their establishment or these institutions do not undermine their control.

Initial institutions can lead market economies along distinct institutional trajectories. Furthermore, the same CCIs that are conducive to the emergence of wealth-revealing public and designed CEIs, and hence to market expansion, are also conducive to the emergence of political institutions in which the commercial sector will be represented and have influence. Members of the commercial sector need not fear revealing their wealth if the CCIs imply that a costly retaliation can be imposed if their rights are abused. These same CCIs imply that a ruler will find it beneficial to get permission from the commercial elite prior to taking action, particularly any action related to their property (e.g., taxation), to reduce the likelihood of costly retaliation. When market expansion and the development of political institutions reflect these kinds of CCIs, market expansion will further strengthen them and enhance their influence.

The Demand for Public-Order and Designed CEIs

Organic, private-order CEIs are universal, reflecting responses to gains from exchange. Although these organic CEIs reflect the need of trade they also reflect social and cultural factors. Initial social structures demarcate and verify membership and provide networks for information transmission. Cultural beliefs and behavioral norms coordinate expectations and provide a shared understanding of the meaning of various actions.*Ceteris paribus,* initial social structures and cultural features therefore influence which, among the many possible organic CEIs, will emerge, become an integral part of these institutions, and be reproduced by them. (Greif 1994a, 1996.)

Empirical and theoretical work indicates the relevance of the extent to which a society is more 'communalist' or more 'individualist.'[26] In the former case, larger, innate social structures that are based on kin, place of birth, or religion (e.g., lineage, tribes, or religious sects) are prominent and members of those societies feel involved in the lives of other members of their group. In more individualist societies, the individual and family, rather than the larger, innate social structure, are prominent and individuals expect that others will interfere relatively little in their affairs. The more communalist a society is in the initial stages of market development, the more, *ceteris paribus*, its organic CEIs will be based on each intra-group's economic and social sanctions among its members. The society will be more 'segregated:' each individual will interact socially and economically mainly with members of his group. The more individualistic a society is in the initial stages of market development, the more its organic CEIs will be based, *ceteris paribus,* on bilateral economic and social sanctions among individuals and families. The society will be more 'integrated:' economic transactions will be conducted among people from different groups. In either case, as discussed above, the symbiotic relationship between organic CEIs and their underlying cultural and social foundations, will lead to their mutual reinforcement.

Organic CEIs that reflect communalism and imply segregation generate relatively weak demand for public-order and designed CEIs. The ability of each social group to punish its members reduces the relative cost of intra-group economic exchange while the thinness of intergroup exchange reduces the benefits to each individual from leaving his group and pursue outside exchange. Even if economic efficiency calls for institutional development, it may nevertheless not

---

[26] This discussion is based on Greif (1994a) in which I used the term 'collectivism' instead of 'communalism.' 'Communalism' was suggested by Timur Kuran and Joel Mokyr. For works indicating the importance social and cultural factors see Granovetter 1985; Clay 1997a, 1997b; McMillan and Woodruff. 2000; Moriguchi 2003; Stulz and Williamson 2003; Biggs et. al. 2002; Fafchamps 2004; Olds and Liu 2000.

be rational for each individual agent to pursue the change. In contrast, organic CEIs that reflect individualism and imply integration, imply relatively weak ability of each group to discipline its members. Such CEIs therefore generate a relatively strong demand for public-order and designed CEIs. (Greif 1994a; Kranton 1996b.)

Initial CEIs thus influence the extent to which the economic agents find it profitable to use, if available and establish, if possible, public-order and designed CEIs. The 'demand' for these CEIs reflects more than non-institutional, environmental and technological conditions.

The Supply of Public-Order and Designed, Private-Order CEIs

Demand for public and designed CEIs will not necessarily be met, however. Using public-order CEIs reveals wealth to those with coercive power. Appealing to the court, using a land registry, applying for a business licence, or submitting to a regulatory agency generates valuable information that can be used to identify and capture a person's wealth. Public-order institutions can be *effectively* supplied only if revealing wealth to those with coercive power does not undermine the effectiveness of the CCIs and hence the security of property rights. If this is not the case, even if public-order CEIs are established, they will be underutilized. Distinct CCIs imply different extents to which public-order CEIs can be *effectively* supplied.

Although the relationships between various CCIs and effectively supplying public-order CEIs have not been systematically studied, tentative conjectures can nevertheless be advanced. Consider first CCIs based on the state's administrative structure. An absent state has a limited ability to provide wealth-revealing, public-order CEIs without undermining property rights' security. It can provide weak public-order institutions which do not increase its ability to abuse rights supporting social order and personal safety. Delegating the state's administration to those in need for wealth-revealing, public-order CEIs entails a greater ability to effectively supply them. The property rights of the administrators are secured and, if they either make a living from providing these administrative services or benefit from commercial expansion, they can better commit than the ruler to respect others' property rights. For similar reasons, self-governance by those in need for wealth-revealing, public-order CEIs entails an even greater ability to provide such institutions, particularly on the local level.

Consider now coercion-constraining institutions based on balancing coercive power. When a balance of coercive power among social units constrains its use, there is no third party with coercive power to back the operation of the public-order institution.[27] A ruler with independent coercive power is able to more effectively provide public-order institutions although his ability is limited because revealing wealth increases the ruler's ability to gain from abusing rights.

---

[27] On the demand side, the expectation that a business dispute among members of different social units can lead to a military conflict among them undermines incentives to enter into such transactions.

764   Avner Greif

This increased ability to gain from abusing rights undermines the previous balance of coercive powers. A ruler whose conditional coercive power is provided by those in need for wealth-revealing public-order CEIs is able to even more effectively provide these institutions. Unlike a ruler with independent coercive power, one with conditional coercive power can be punished by the asset holders following an abuse.

Table 1 summarizes the interrelationships between various organic CEIs and CCIs and the demand for and ability to effectively supply public-order CEIs.

Table 1. Supply and demand for public-order CEIs

Coercion-constraining institutions as determinants of ability to effectively **supply** public-order CEIs:			Organic, private-order CEIs (technological factors) as determinants of **demand** for public-order CEIs:	
			Low	High
			Communalism/ Segregation (Lower demand if small, static economies and low gains from impersonal exchange.)	**Individualism/ Integration** (Higher demand if large, dynamic economies and higher gains from impersonal exchange.)
Low	**Absent state:** Thin administration controlled by the state.	**Mutual deterrence:** No ruler. Asset holders coercive power mutually deters abuse.	Low demand, low ability to effectively supply. *E.g., China under the Qian and the First Muslim Empire. Communalism and an absent state.*	High demand, low ability to effectively supply.
Medium	**Delegation:** The state's administration is controlled by the asset holders.	**A ruler with independent coercive power:** Balanced by the asset holders coercive power.	Low demand, medium ability to effectively supply.	High demand, medium ability to effectively supply.
High	**Self-governance:** Administration provided by autonomous units controlled by the asset holders.	**A ruler with conditional coercive power:** Asset holders provide the ruler with coercive power.	Low demand, high ability to effectively supply.	High demand, high ability to effectively supply. *E.g., England: individualism. Autonomy with economic and coercive powers. A ruler with conditional coercive power.*

Different initial combinations of organic CEIs and CCIs therefore imply distinct institutional dynamics. In particular, organic CEIs reflecting and entailing communalism and segregation combined with an absent state or a balance of coercive power among social units imply low demand and low ability to effectively supply wealth-revealing public-order CEIs. On the other hand, organic CEIs reflecting and entailing individualism and integration imply a high demand for public-order CEIs. These can be particularly effectively supplied if the CCIs are based on self-governance by those who stand to gain from public-order CEIs who also have a coercive power that balances the ruler's.

Similar analysis applies to designed CEIs. Demand for them reflects initial organic CEIs. Many designed CEIs reveal wealth to those with coercive power. The wealth of the guild, the lists of stock holders, the records of transactions in the stock exchange, and the information stored by the credit card companies or credit bureaus, reveal who has wealth and in what form. Furthermore, many designed CEIs operate in the shadow of the law or are quasi-private, as discussed above, and hence their operation depends on public-order CEIs. The ability to effectively supply wealth-revealing designed CEIs is a function of CCIs. Such CEIs will be established and used only by those with the countervailing economic or coercive power required to protect their assets. Others will only use CEIs that neither reveal wealth nor rely on public-order.

Table 1 doesn't reflect two more considerations. First, the demand for public-order and designed CEIs can be more effectively met, *ceteris paribus*, the more a ruler's coercive power is checked by the limited reach of his grabbing hand. E.g., the ability of the asset holders to move their assets elsewhere following an abuse, enhances their ability to reveal wealth without fearing losing it. Second, those with coercive power will permit designed CEIs to be established only if their benefits outweigh the countervailing economic or coercive power that these CEIs entail.

The above discussion emphasizes that institutional dynamics reflect initial—organic, private-order and coercion-constraining—institutions. But technological and other non-institutional factors also influence these dynamics particularly by influencing the relative efficiency of various CEIs and hence their demand. This demand would be, for example, higher in dynamic economies (where there is more to gain from an increased ability to quickly respond to changing needs) and when there is more to gain from impersonal exchange characterized by separation between the *quid* and the *quo* over time and space. We don't have good empirical evidence or theoretical understanding regarding the relative importance of institutional and non-institutional factors in determining demand for various CEIs.

Market Expansion and Political Development

For the reasons discussed above, the CCIs fostering the supply of wealth-revealing, designed and public-order CEIs also aid the development of political institutions in which the commercial sector has voice and influence. These political institutions, in turn, play an important independent role in market expansion by providing information and knowledge required to bring such CEIs about. In markets, discrepancies between demand and supply are filled as individuals respond to the information conveyed and the motivation provided by prices. In the absence of a price system, however, the demand for institutions has to be directly communicated to those with the ability to respond to it. Market development is thus fostered by a polity in which the commercial sector has a voice and influence on the function, policy, and organization of the state. This influence is a reflection of CCIs. The commercial sector will have political representation if it has the coercive and economic powers to balance that of the ruler. Also, as discussed above, these CCIs are also likely to make possible the exchange between the commercial sector and a ruler required to motivate him to provide such public-order CEIs.

Furthermore, when these CCIs exist, market expansion will lead, *ceteris paribus*, to further strengthening the economic and coercive power of the commercial sector, and the development of political institutions in which the commercial sector has voice and influence. When they do not exist, though, commercial expansion is not likely to lead to such political development. Indeed, as further discussed below, in societies such as the medieval Islamic empire or pre-modern China and Spain, the commercial expansion that occurred failed to lead to liberal governance. The opposite occurred, however, in England.

4. Reflections on the Historical Development of Markets and Political Institutions

A comparative analysis of the institutions that supported markets in various historical episodes, their extent, and dynamics has yet to be conducted. Yet, our current state of knowledge suggests the merit of the above conjecture. For example, it postulates that a market can thrive under a state that is absent from the commercial sphere, a ruler with independent coercive power constrained by the coercive power of the masses and coordinated by observing abuse, and communalist and segregated organic CEIs. Such a market, however, would only have a limited ability to extend as there is weak demand and ability to effectively supply public-order and designed CEIs. This may very well have been true of Imperial China.

Indeed, pre-modern Chinese markets—at least as measured by market integration in grain—were no less developed than Europe's as late as the 19th century (Shiue and Keller 2003) and standards of living in various areas within China were comparable to Europe's (Pomeranz 2000). The Chinese state was active in providing public goods, such as defense, famine relief, commercial infrastructure, and distribution of knowledge regarding better agricultural techniques. (E.g., Pomeranz 2002.) The Empire had an effective administration and a long tradition, dating back at least to the Zhou dynasty (1122–256 BC) of the legal enforcement of contracts, particularly those regarding assets relevant to the state's revenues like land. (E.g., Zelin, et. al. 2004.)

At the same time, many students of China's institutions have provided evidence suggesting that its organic CEIs reflect communalism and lead to segregation, and its CCIs were based on a state absent from the commercial sphere that provided only weak public-order CEIs. The administration of the state was heavily centralized yet thin, and did not extend below the roughly 1300 county magistrates. Beneath each of these magistrates "were several towns and hundreds of villages and a population ranging from several tens of thousands to hundreds of thousands" (Wong 1997: 108). In the commercial sector, property rights were secured by an absent state and commercial taxation was low. In the agrarian sector, property rights were secured by balancing the state's coercive power with that of the numerous peasants (Yang 2002), and balancing the power of the local elite by that of the state (Wong 1997; Yang 2002). The state fostered the creation of shared beliefs regarding appropriate taxation by announcing that it would never be raised and distributing information regarding its level in the villages.

Even during most of the last dynasty, the Qing, there was no commercial code of law and it was administered by magistrates, persons of literary and philosophical learning with multiple duties unrelated to the law. These magistrates were subject to heavy penalties if they made mistakes and hence they sought compromises rather than legal rulings. Organic CEIs were central to the operation of the market. In comparing them to the European CEIs, Hamilton (1991) noted the large extent to which they reflected communalism, and that historically "the Chinese society consiste[d] of networks of people whose actions are oriented by normative social relationships" (Hamilton 1994: 199). In particular, lineage was the social structure around which business organizations were formed.

As the economy grew, lineages responded to changing needs and opportunities by becoming more designed. Their economic organization was often based on contractual relationships, had centralized bureaucracies, and drew on outsiders' resources and talents (e.g., Herrmann-Pillath 1999; Redding 1991). In summarizing the related vast literature regarding late Imperial China, however, Herrmann-Pillath (1999) noted that it was the relative absence of the state from the commercial sphere that hindered further development and led to an institutional evolution that was different from Europe's. Similarly, although Pomeranz (2000) highlighted the role of distinct natural endowments in enabling Europe to economically overtake China, he noted that the Chinese state interfered much less than the European states in the operation of the market.

The Qing's responses to the military and economic conflict with the West during the 19th century lends support to the conjecture regarding the institutional foundations of its markets. Constrained from increasing the land tax, the Qing resorted to taxing goods in transit because merchants along the road, being few in number, did not pose a threat, promoting a 'top down' industrialization, and providing public-order CEIs. Departure from an absent state without creating a countervailing economic or coercive power, was counter-productive. Corruption prevailed, trade suffered, and designed CEIs, such as the stock exchange, were not established (Yang 2002; Goetzmann and Köll 2003). The state resorted to expanding the role of guilds, delegating to them such functions as commercial tax collection and provision of local public goods. Top-down industrialization and monopolistic guilds, however, hindered industrialization and commerce. (Goetzmann and Köll 2003; Ma 2004.) Even the famous Chinese silk industry fell behind Japan's.

Political development in China is consistent with the above theoretical conjecture. At least under the Qian (1644–1911), prior to the Opium War (1840), the state's budget constraint was not binding and there were no CCIs empowering the commercial sector. Indeed, representative bodies were not established in China. Furthermore, consistent with the argument that rulers fear large-scale economic organizations, economic corporations were not legal entities, and guilds, although known, were few and relatively weak until the late 19th century when the state delegated various functions to them in response to the fiscal pressure from the conflict with the West.

On the other end of the spectrum, the above conjecture implies that individualism and integration create demand for public-order and designed CEIs. These can be effectively supplied if there is a ruler constrained by a commercial sector with self-governance which, in addition, has coercive power to render the ruler one with a conditional coercive power. In this case, if the ruler's budget constraint is binding and his need for resources fluctuates, he would establish a representative body that includes the commercial sector. Arguably, this has been the case in pre-modern England. Its most distinguishing features were individualism, the autonomy—self-governance and military ability—of its commercial sector, and its rulers' weak independent administrative capacity and lack of sufficient revenues.

While I return to the case of England below, it should be noted that its market economy was arguably not a match for China's circa 1,000 AD. By the 19th century, however, it was the forerunner and symbol of the emergence of the modern market economy. England is well known to have been individualist at least from the late medieval period. (Macfarlane 1978.) The autonomy of its cities and parishes, which were controlled by either the commercial or landed sectors, implied both self-governance and a military ability to check the coercive power of rulers. At the same time, a ruler with conditional coercive power constrained the autonomous cities to compete with each other economically, but not militarily, while coordinating common policies. The budget constraint implied by these CCIs and the inter-state European competition fostered the creation of an effective parliament that facilitated resolving collective action problems associated with providing public-order institutions and other public goods. Public-order CEIs were established, used, and expanded. Markets expanded increasing the relative power of the commercial elite and hence fostering institutional trade. But prior to the rise of democracy, consistent with the argument advanced here, property rights' protection was not universal. Even after the Glorious Revolution of 1688, protection was afforded to the landed, commercial, and financial elite. Only those who had economic and military power received protection.

The rise of the modern market economy, however, was a European (or Western) phenomena. It neither began in pre-modern England nor was it stopped from relatively quickly expanding in the rest of Europe. This observation is consistent with the claim regarding European individualism, which arguably fostered organic CEIs that generated demand for public-order and designed CEIs. Furthermore, the re-emergence of polities in Europe following the collapse of the Roman and the Carolinian Empires transpired in the context of rulers with binding budget constraints (due to inter-state competition) and self-governed units controlled by asset holders with coercive and economic powers. By the late medieval period representative bodies, constitutional and limited monarchies were the rule in Europe alongside republican polities.

Although every society has individualistic and communalist elements, and categorization is a matter of their relative importance, a long line of research has emphasized the relative pervasiveness of European individualism.[28] Individualism is considered a heritage of ancient Greece (e.g., Hsu 1983, Gurevich 1995) and early Christianity encouraged it by placing the individual rather than his social group at the center of its theology. It advanced the creation of "a new society, based not on the family but on the individual, whose salvation, like his original loss of innocence, was personal and private" (Hughes 1974: 61). From as early as the 4th century, the Church was also systematically engaged in weakening kin-based organization of society by prohibiting marriages among kin (sometimes up to 7th degree!). (Goody 1983). By the late medieval period, Western individualism manifested itself in such diverse ways as war tactics, the emergence of confession, nicknames, and landholding. (E.g, Morris 1972; Macfarlane 1978.)

It is important to emphasize that no society is composed of "atomistic" individuals and even in such individualistic contemporary societies like the USA, social and business networks are important. Similarly, European history provides many examples of institutions based on multilateral punishment among neighbors and business associates. (E.g., Muldrew 1998.) By and large, however, these did not reflect innate, kin-based social structures. They either reflected economically motivated processes through which such organic CEIs emerge, as discussed above, or were designed CEIs.

Late medieval, European coercion-constraining institutions reflect a dispersed distribution of coercive and economic powers and states' meager administrative capacities. After the disintegration of the Roman and Carolinian Empires the rulers of the emerging polities had relatively weak coercive power and administrative capacities. The size of European armies was small in absolute and relative terms. Frederic Barbarossa (d. 1190), the Emperor of the Holy Roman Empire, the King of Germany, and the King of Italy sailed to the third Crusade with several hundred knights. As late as the early 15th century, European armies were only a few thousand strong, the largest one (France), numbering circa 40,000 in 1470. (Downing 1992: 69.) Balance of coercive power

---

[28] Various studies, however, used the term individualism differently. For communalism in China see Hamilton 1991. For segregation in the Islamic world, see Lapidus 1984 and Hodgson 1974. Goitein 1955 noted that the organic CEIs among the Maghribis represent those of the Muslim world.

between rulers, great lords, and cities, and administrations based on delegation and self-governance—particularly in the form of autonomy—was the rule.

Indeed, the polity under the European Feudal system was one in which a ruler was a coordinator of coercive power, who was further constrained by the self-governance of its subordinated units, feudal lords and cities alike. These subordinated units had the wealth, technology, organization, and manpower required to sustain military strength in a period in which, for a long time, defense was superior to offense. No wonder that the period's ideology considered the ruler's job to be merely the maintenance of social order—providing the balance of power among his vassals and coordinating their joint protection and other endeavors. As noted by the historian of Frederic Barbarossa, his "duty was merely to protect all the subjective rights everybody had. It was not his business to issue laws of his own ... he was supposed to play a purely passive role as law protector." (Munz 1969: 100.) Indeed, Barbarossa had little independent military might. He had to stop his military campaign against the Normans of southern Italy in 1155, for example, because his vassals declared that they served their time for that year.

Medieval England similarly reflects the essence of the feudal king as a coordinator of power but also the need for constantly refining the associated institution to maintain a balance of power. As noted by Tilly (1990: 154):

> "in the process of making war and intervening in dynastic rivalries, the barons on whom the English king relied for their wars acquired enough power to fight the king as well as each other, exacting chartered concessions—most dramatically the Magna Carta—from the monarch. The Great Charter of 1215 committed the king to cease squeezing feudal obligations for the wherewithal to conduct wars, to stop hiring mercenaries when barons would not fight, and to impose the major taxes only with the consent of the great council, representative of the magnates."

The importance of the underlying balance of coercive power is reflected in a clause in the charter delivering several castles to the barons and the prohibition on a mercenary army.

Increasing peace brought about by the feudal order,[29] population growth, lords' desires to gain from trade, and attempts of kings and lords to strengthen their positions vis-à-vis each other, fostered urban growth. Changes in military technology, particularly after the 11th century, shifted the balance of coercive power to the masses and urban dwellers and away from the armored knights. Among these changes were the reintroduction of stone walls, the invention of the crossbow, the introduction of the longbow and the pike-based, heavy infantries. Once cities grew in population and wealth, they were able to gain military might comparable to that of lords and hence retain autonomy and gain rights.

These changes and the emergence of a new balance of coercive power are well reflected in the rise of representative bodies and republican movements throughout Europe by the 12th century. By then republican movements

---

[29] The 'Peace of God' movement also played a role in bringing peace by coordinating the countervailing coercive power of economic agents. E.g., Head and Landes 1992.

swept European cities, particularly in Northern Italy, whose ruler, the Emperor, was weakened due to its military conflict against the Pope that was a part of the Investiture Controversy. But even the Pope had to confront a militant republican movement in Rome itself. Representative bodies were established throughout Europe, in England, Spain, France, and Flanders among other states. Even the Emperor of the Holy Roman Empire, Charles IV, had to issue a Golden Bull (1356) detailing the rules governing the empire as a constitutional monarchy.

Various rulers' relative military weakness during this time (prior to the 15th century Military Revolution) is well reflected in cases in which they overestimated their ability to extract taxes from their subjects. After the Empire attempted to tax the cities of Northern Italy, they broke away from it militarily gaining de facto independence and de jura freedom in the Peace of Constance (1181). The Swiss Confederation was established in 1291 in response to what residents of several cantons of the Holy Roman Empire considered inappropriate taxation.

In this context of self-governance, rulers with conditional coercive power provided by the economic agents, and economic agents with political representation, the necessary conditions for providing public-order and designed CEIs were met. Indeed, the late medieval period witnessed legal revival, the establishment of public-order and designed CEIs, and market expansion. This legal renewal also reflects other pan-European processes such as the conflict between the secular authorities and the Church (Berman 1983); its details may have been shaped by the need to protect judges from intimidation (Glaeser and Shleifer 2002); and it has been facilitated by the Roman legal tradition and the associated concept of designed, man-made laws.

Yet, the function—serving the economy—and implications—creating public-order and designed CEIs—of this legal revival are illustrated by the fact that the legal foundations of the modern business corporation were laid in this period. The modern corporation was created through the fusion of the late medieval joint-stock company, which was in fact a partnership, and the traditional legal form of the corporation as it was developed during the medieval period. More broadly, the contemporary European laws and practices regarding commerce, bankruptcy, insurance, apprenticeship, patents, and banking originated then. Designed CEIs, as well as hybrids between private and public ones, were established throughout Europe, taking such forms as guilds, municipalities, monasteries, universities, insurance fraternities, banks, and large-scale partnerships and family firms. This led to further innovations and practices, such as trading in shares, limited liability, auditing, and various accounting procedures. The invention of public debt that served Europeans well for centuries to come also attests to the existence of effective CCIs. A necessary condition for public debt is that the state can commit to repay the wealth that was placed in its custody.

Northern Italy, free from any ruler, emerged as Europe's leader in institutional, organizational, and legal innovations that fostered commercial expansion. This freedom, reflected the coercive power they were able to obtain based on their intra cities CCIs, the Investiture Controversy between the Emperor and the Pope that weakened both, and the commercial opportunities in the Mediterranean sea. In the long run, however, Northern Italy declined not least because most cities, like Genoa, failed to establish institutions that were able to constrain violence for long. Internal violence plagued these cities and whoever gained control attempted to make the most of it through profitable but inefficient policies, such as providing guilds with monopoly rights and forestalling technological advances. Later, the Italian city-republics fell prey to the mercenaries they brought in to fight their inter-city wars and to the feudal agrarian lords which the cities never fully defeated.

By the 15th century, the Military Revolution had led to external domination over northern Italy. Cannons, introduced to the Italian battlefields during the 1494 French invasion, made the thin and tall medieval city walls a frail defense. Firearms enabled equipping and training larger armies than had been possible before, providing an advantage to larger and richer states. The Italian city-states failed to coordinate responses against such invasions, arguably due to the rapidity of the Military Revolution and the history of military confrontations among themselves. In the absence of effective CCIs, markets and economic vitality subsided.

This was not true in Flanders, which, together with northern Italy, experienced large-scale urban growth and autonomy during the late medieval period. It began with the fortifications of towns against the Norman invasion and gained momentum when these cities began to process wool exported from England. Several times during this period, the prosperous cities of this area conflicted with their feudal overlords to gain and retain independence, but achieved only self-governance. CCIs based on self-governance and a ruler with independent coercive power prevailed. Unlike northern Italy, therefore, these cities were protected from an external invasion during the initial stages of the Military Revolution. Within Flanders itself, however, the prosperity of cities shifted the balance of coercive power from the ruler to their favor. In 1463 Philip the Good created a representative body, the States General, which enacted laws and had the authority to vote on taxation. European commerce shifted to Flanders which became the center of innovations in public-order and designed CEIs such as the first European bourse in Bruges) the stock market in Amsterdam, and increasing transferability of bills.

When Charles V, the King of Spain and the Holy Roman Emperor, inherited Flanders in the early 16th century, its administration was based on autonomous and well-coordinated cities. The military revolution implied that wealth could buy military might more than before while developments in fortification techniques restored the balance between defense and offense. The growth of the cities therefore shifted the balance of coercive power in their favor. As noted by the prominent historian of Flanders, Israel (1995), the very success of the economy of Flanders posed a danger to the Hapsburg regime. Yet, given the CCIs that limited the ability of the Habsburgs to tax their German possessions (which were, as noted above a constitutional monarchy), the King gambled on pressing

Flanders to pay more to finance his religious and other wars. The resulting tax revolt (1579) turned into a war of independence in which northern Flanders became the Dutch Republic and the center of European commerce during the 17th century.

The internal organization of this republic, however, was such that it was ill-suited to mobilizing resources to wage effective wars elsewhere. In 1651 England passed the first of the Navigation Acts that were directed at undermining Dutch commercial dominance by shifting trade and freight to England and its shipping industry. The chief provisions were that no goods grown or manufactured in Asia, Africa, or America could be transported to England except in English vessels, and that the goods of any European country imported into England must be brought in British vessels, or in those of the country producing them. In the subsequent wars, the Dutch Republic failed to reverse these acts.

While the institutional history of England was not a linear progression toward institutions favorable to market extension, it nevertheless can be characterized as having a ruler who was a coordinator of others' coercive power and an administration provided by autonomous, particularly commercial units controlled by economic agents who had actual or potential military power. Strong feudal lords, autonomous cities, a ruler without a standing army, and a parliament that both approved taxation and coordinated political actions are the manifestations of these coercion-constraining institutions.

Initially, William the Conqueror and his immediate successors faced the challenge of restraining the coercive power of the lords. The military weakness of the Crown is reflected in the Magna Carta (1215) as noted above and the king's obligation not to have a standing royal army, not to recruit mercenaries, and not to tax without consent by the Great Council. That Council, in which the nobles were represented, reflected the prevailing CCIs: a balance of military power between the Crown and the lords.

In the context of the conflict between the Crown and the lords, particularly during the 13th century, the former gave charters to numerous English cities. By the end of the 13th century, there were about 500 such autonomous, self-governed, towns (boroughs) that became an integral part of the kingdom's administration. Furthermore, they had the wealth, manpower, organizational infrastructure, and production capacity to have potential and actual military power. Alongside the self-governed parishes, these towns changed England's CCIs. Indeed, chartering cities had arguably been a strategic response by the Crown, aimed at diverting tax revenues away from the lords and creating a countervailing power.

That these towns became part of England's CCIs is well reflected in the events surrounding the transformation of the Great Council into a Parliament in which the towns' dwellers were represented. In 1265 the King Henry III dissolved the Great Council and levied unapproved taxes. The effectiveness of the CCIs balancing the Crown's power with that of the lords was challenged. Earl Simon de Montfort responded with a revolt, during which he called a meeting in which the nobles, the clergy and representatives of the counties and towns were present.

Although de Montfort and his army were eventually defeated, the event reflects the increasing importance of the counties and towns' support in national conflicts. Recognizing that they were part of the CCIs he was facing, King Edward I summoned the so-called 'model parliament' (1295), which included, for the first time the representation of the commercial sector: two burgesses from each borough and two citizens from each city. It was during this parliament that the Crown issued a charter seceding the right of approving new taxes to the parliament. In 1297 Edward I confirmed the Magna Carta, asserting that it should be observed as common law, and declared that on no account were aids and taxes to be taken without the common assent of the whole kingdom and for the common benefit. Yet, during that period the Crown abused the rights of Italians traders. Only the rights of those with a countervailing power were respected.

CCIs that constrain the power of the state based on the administrative and military power of the commercial sector enable effective provision of public-order CEIs and establish designed CEIs. Indeed, the latter half of the 13th century was a period of reform and expansion of English law and the legal system. Edward I is known as the 'lawyer-king' (Hogue 1996: 69) and his legislation directly influenced the extent of the markets.

Recall, for example, that by the 13th century, the Community Responsibility System (CRS), based on the legal autonomy of the English towns, enabled impersonal exchange characterized by separation between the *quid* and the *quo*. During that century, the CRS began to decline due to the commercial expansion and the growth in the size, number, and economic and social heterogeneity of towns. The CCIs that restricted the Crown's power, at that time, however, were such that it was possible to replace the CRS with a state wide legal process for placing collateral and its collection. This, however, was not the case in other parts of Europe. In Germany, for example, CCIs that balanced the central authority and local lords were no longer an equilibrium due to the Investiture Controversy. Although the CRS declined, a suitable alternative was not provided. (Greif 2004; Volckart 2001.)

The development of the Common Law courts further constrained the Crown with these courts perceived rights for independence in areas where they acquired customary jurisdiction. Infringing on the jurisdiction of these courts was considered an abuse of rights.[30] By the 15th century the ability to effectively provide public-order CEIs was fostered by these semi-independent courts. This situation and its implications regarding the provision of partial public-order CEIs is illustrated in the first known court case in England regarding negotiable credit instruments (1436). The London Mayor's court at Guildhall had customary rights in cases involving merchants, but one of the parties approached the King's Bench to transfer the case to its jurisdiction. The Mayor of London, however refused to consent to the Bench's demand, arguing that "according to the Law Merchant and the ancient liberties and free customs of the city itself... the

---

[30] Exactly how corruption was prevented in these courts is not clear. Arguably, internalization of values, social pressure, compensation by the litigants, and competition among courts over cases played a role.

mayor... have the power and use of hearing" such cases. (Munro 1990: 74.) The king withdrew his demand and the negotiated credit instrument became legal. By the 16th and 17th centuries such public-order CEIs enabled the expansion of credit and bonds beyond that possible based on reputation alone. (Muldrew 1998.)

Subsequent events further reduced the power of the lords and increased the relative ability of the commercial sector to constrain the king's power. The increasing financial needs of the Crown due to the Military Revolution compelled it to sell its landed properties making it more dependent on tax contributions. The War of the Roses (1455–85) decimated the ranks of the great lords making the Crown more dependent than ever on the administrative capacity and other resources of its autonomous towns and the local unpaid Justices of Peace. The Crown confiscated the Church's large land holdings in the 16th century in the context of establishing the Church of England but its coercive power was sufficiently constrained at this point that it was unable to use this resource to undermine the existing CCIs. On the contrary, the Crown's binding budget constraint compelled it to sell this land to the gentry, thereby further strengthening them. Moreover, the greater efficiency in which the gentry utilized the land probably further constrained abuse by the larger implied loss of value. (Rajan and Zingales 2003.) The flow of wealth from the emerging Atlantic trade may have had a similar impact (Acemoglu, et. al. 2002).

The Civil War of the 17th century was another step in this process of institutional evolution. The war made it evident that the crown neither had the independent military ability nor the administrative capacity required to rule without the consent of the economic elite which was also the military elite. The Crown was a ruler with conditional coercive power and the supremacy of the Parliament was firmly established. The zenith of formalizing this situation occurred during the Glorious Revolution (1688). New rules coordinating on appropriate behavior by the Crown, such as the Bill of Rights, a better separation between the judiciary and the executive, and new organizations, such as the Bank of England, formalized and fostered this situation. (North and Weingast 1989.) This essence of the Glorious Revolution—that reflected a de facto prior situation—accounts for the puzzling observation that the historical evidence does not indicate that the Glorious Revolution altered the security of property rights.[31]

Indeed, once the parliament gained supremacy, it was not in the business of protecting property rights per-se. Its policy reflected the interests of those who controlled it, namely, the landed, commercial, and financially elite. The subsequent history is thus marked by gross abuses of property rights through the radical increase in taxation, monopolies, parliamentary enclosures of the open fields, and colonial expansion.[32] Yet, a state controlled by its landed,

---

[31] Clark 1996; O'Brien 2001; Quinn 2001; Sussman and Yafeh 2000, 2004; Harris 2004.

[32] Harris 2004. For economic analyses of the great English trading companies which were monopolies, see Irwin 1988; Carlos and Nicholas 1996; Carlos 1992.

commercial, and financially elite and later empowered by the Industrial Revolution was a boon for the extension of markets. The evolution of the modern market reached its zenith.

Other European states began, under feudalism, with initial conditions similar to England's. Their subsequent institutional evolution, however, differed due to such factors as the greater risk of invasions (France), discoveries that provided resources for the Crown (Spain), and feudal lords too strong for the Crown to constrain in the absence of autonomous cities to do so (Germany). These distinct experiences illustrate how precarious England's institutional evolution was. But Europeans shared a common heritage of individualism, self-governance, a broad distribution of coercive powers, and man-made laws. Reversing their institutional developments and enabling market extension was relatively easy.

Concluding Comments

Contract-enforcement institutions provide the foundations of markets, and their details, expansion, or contraction determine the market's extent and dynamics. Contract-enforcement institutions changed due to environmental changes that influenced various institutions' relative economic efficiency and profitability. In addition, however, as this chapter has argued theoretically and demonstrated historically, the dynamics of contract-enforcement institutions are also a function of initial, organic, contract-enforcement institutions and coercion-constraining institutions. New institutions emerge or are established in the context of existing ones.

Distinct, initial, organic, contract-enforcement institutions generate different demands for additional, public-order and designed, private-order, contract-enforcement institutions that can further extend the market. Distinct, initial, organic institutions can emerge in the initial stages of market formation due to different economic conditions and social and cultural factors, such as individualism and communalism.

Hence, efficiency-promoting, contract-enforcement institutions will not be utilized or have the expected impact even if they are introduced, because they are not compatible with existing, organic, private-order institutions. These institutions create a wedge between the institutions that, if utilized by everyone, will extend the market, and the institutions that each individual, given the existing organic institutions, will find optimal to utilize. Initial, organic, contract-enforcement institutions generate different demands for additional institutions by influencing the extent to which economic agents will find these institutions profitable to use if available, and establish if possible.

But even if there is a demand for public-order and designed, contract-enforcement institutions, their effective supply will not necessarily be forthcoming. Utilizing these institutions implies revealing wealth to those with coercive power, implying an increase in the risk that it will be expropriated. The extent of this increased risk however, depends on the existing coercion-constraining institutions. For markets to function, property has to be protected from those with coercive power. When this is not the case and economic agents are subject to predation, markets are confined to the exchanges that are possible based on private-order, contract-enforcement institutions that are more successful in mitigating the threat posed by coercive power.

More generally, public-order and pragmatic, private-order, contract-enforcement institutions can be supplied only if particular coercion-constraining institutions already prevail—specifically, those whose effectiveness is not undermined by revealing wealth. In particular, coercion-constraining institutions based on the absence of the state from the commercial sphere have a limited ability to effectively supply public-order and pragmatic, public-order institutions. Furthermore, when a ruler's legitimacy is weak and his budget constraints are not binding, he is likely to consider large-scale, private-order institutions more as a threat than a benefit.

In contrast, coercion-constraining institutions based on self-governance by the market participants, and a ruler with conditional coercive power provided by these participants are favorable for effectively supplying public-order institutions and establishing pragmatic, private-order institutions. Where such coercion-constraining institutions prevail, and the ruler's budget constraint is binding, political development associated with the rise of a liberal state will transpire. A state effectively constrained by the commercial sector will have to provide it with political representation, will respect property rights, and will pursue market-enhancing policies.

Historical evidence suggests the merits of this analysis. The pre-modern market leaders—China and the Muslim world—had organic, contract-enforcement institution and coercion-constraining institutions that were neither conducive to the rise of public-order and designed, private-order, contract-enforcement institutions, nor giving political representation to the commercial sector. In contrast, England, considered by many as the initial role model for the modern market, had organic, contract-enforcement institutions and coercion-constraining institutions conducive to the rise of public-order and designed, private-order institutions, as well as representative bodies and a constitutional monarchy. This observation regarding the co-evolution of economic and political institutions is consistent with the argument that at least the security of property initially reflected 'might rather than right.' England was no stranger to abusing rights through, for example, Parliamentary enclosures and the exploitation of colonies.

The public-order and designed contract-enforcement institutions that were initially developed in Europe are considered necessary for market development. It is also perceived that markets follow the creation of a constitutional state with effective administration and public-order institutions. Markets are assumed to follow the creation of public-order. Historically, however, it seems that limited government, representative bodies, and modern markets co-evolved in a process reflecting deeper institutional variables. These variables included particular, organic, contract-enforcement institutions and coercion-constraining institutions that revealed and embodied different cultural and social factors, and the particularities of pre-modern production, communication, transportation, and military technology.

If this is the case, development strategies need to be reconsidered. The same factors, such as communalism and segregation that led developing economies on distinct institutional trajectories may still prevail, implying that their institutional needs are distinct from those that were developed in the West. Indeed, contemporary social psychologists have found that most of the developing countries are communalist, whereas the developed West is individualist. (E.g., Bellah et al. 1985; Reynolds and Norman 1988; and Triandis 1990.)

The details of the optimal contract-enforcement institutions in a communalist/segregated society, however, are arguably distinct from those developed in an individualist/integrated society and some empirical work suggests this is the case. (Ensminger 1997; Goldstein and Udry 2002.) Furthermore, market expansion, economic growth and the development of more costly contract-enforcement institutions in the West has been a process rather than an event. The attempt to duplicate these costly institutions in poor economies may very well be like placing the wagon in front of the horses. Indeed, past European public-order institutions were very distinct from contemporary ones. The experience of the Community Responsibility System suggests, for example, that the optimal unit of non-contractual legal liability is not necessarily the individual. Levinson (2003) has advocated changing legal concepts accordingly.

Similarly, development policy has been predicated on the assumption that growth requires creating a western-style state with extensive administrative capacity. In the West, however, such a polity has been the end result of institutional and economic co-evolution rather than its beginning. In particular, central to this co-evolution were coercion-constraining institutions based on self-governance by the economic agents and widespread, yet locally organized, distribution of coercive power. The related constitutional polities had representative bodies that could effectively restrict the coercive power of rulers and each other by drawing on these resources. The creation of a western-style state with extensive administrative capacity and representative bodies in other parts of the world has been done in a different context. It therefore led, more often than not, to limited market expansion, crony capitalism, a high concentration of wealth among the politically well-connected, corruption, and predatory states.

Theory and history indicate the challenge of promoting welfare-enhancing market extension. Future research, however, will have to point to a better way to confront it. It is not merely the protection of property rights that matters. What matters to market expansion, and therefore to economic growth, are the details of the institutions that secure rights—contract-enforcement institutions and coercion-constraining institutions—whose rights they secure, in what products, and how these institutions are mapped into political institutions and policy.

Acknowledgement

In writing this paper I benefitted from discussions and comments from Yarone Greif, Saumitra Jha, Kivanc Karaman, Timur Kuran, John McMillan, and Yingyi Qian. Participants in seminars at FASID, Tokyo, CIAR, Canada, and Stanford Institute for International Studies provided helpful comments. The paper has been greatly improved, however, by the detailed comments on earlier drafts provided by the editors, Claude Menard and Mary M. Shirley, an anonymous referee, and, as usual, Joel Mokyr.

References

Acemoglu, Daron. 2003. "Why Not a Political Coase Theorem? Social Conflict, Commitment, and Politics". *Journal of Comparative Economics* 31(4): 620–652.
Acemoglu, Daron and James A. Robinson. 2000. "Political Losers as a Barrier to Economic Development". *American Economic Review* 90(2): 126–130.
Acemoglu, Daron, Simon Johnson, and James Robinson. 2002. "The Rise of Europe: Atlantic Trade, Institutional Change and Economic Growth". Working Paper, MIT.
Annen K. 2003. "Social Capital, Inclusive Networks, and Economic Performance". *Journal of Economic Behavior and Organization* 50(4): 449–463.
Aoki, Masahiko. 2001. *Toward a Comparative Institutional Analysis*. Cambridge, MA: MIT Press.
Arruñada, Benito. 2003. "Property Enforcement as Organized Consent". *Journal of Law, Economics and Organization* 19(2): 401–444.
Banner, Stuart. 1998. "The Origin of the New York Stock Exchange". *Journal of Legal Studies* 27: 113.
Barzel, Yoram. 1989. *Economic Analysis of Property Rights*. Boston, MA: Cambridge University Press.
Barzel, Yoram. 2002. *A Theory of the State*. Cambridge: Cambridge University Press.
Bates, Robert, Avner Greif and Smita Singh. 2002. "Organizing Violence". *The Journal of Conflict Resolution* 46(5): 599–628.
Bates, Robert H. 2001. *Prosperity and Violence: The Political Economy of Development*. New York: Norton.
Bellah, Robert N., Richard Madsen, William M. Sullivan, Ann Swidler, and Steven M. Tipton. 1985. *Habits of the Heart: Individualism and Commitment in American Life*. Berkeley, CA: University of California Press.
Berman, Harold J. 1983. *Law and Revolution*. Cambridge, MA: Harvard University Press.
Bernstein, Lisa. 1992. "Opting Out of the Legal System: Extralegal Contractual Relations in the Diamond Industry". *Journal of Legal Studies* 21: 115–157.
Bernstein, Lisa. 1996. "Merchant Law in a Merchant Court: Rethinking the Code's Secret Search of Immanent Business Norms". *University of Pennsylvania Law Review*.
Biggs T., M. Raturi, and P. Srivastava. 2002. "Ethnic Networks and Access to Credit: Evidence from the Manufacturing Sector in Kenya". *Journal of Economic Behavior and Organization* 49(4): 473–486.
Boot, Arnoud W., Stuart I. Greenbaum, and Anjan V. Thakor. 1993. "Reputation and Discretion in Financial Contracting". *American Economic Review* 83(5): 1165–1183.
Carlos, M. Ann. 1992. "Principal-Agent Problems in Early Chartered Companies: A Tale of Two Firms". *American Economic Review* 82(2): 140–145.
Carlos, M. Ann. and Stephen Nicholas. 1996. "Theory and History: Seventeenth Century Joint-Stock Chartered Trading Companies". *Journal of Economic History* 56: 916–924.

Clark, Gregory. 1996. "The Political Foundations of Modern Economic Growth: Britain, 1540–1800". *Journal of Interdisciplinary History* 26(4): 563–588.

Clay, Karen. 1997a. "Trade Without Law: Self-enforcing Institutions in Mexican California". *The Journal of Law, Economics, & Organization* 13(1): 202–231.

Clay, Karen. 1997b. "Trade, Institutions, and Credit". *Explorations in Economic History* 34(4): 495–452.

Conklin, James. 1998. "The Theory of Sovereign Debt and Spain under Philip II". *Journal of Political Economy* 106(3): 483–513.

De Soto, Hernando. 1989. *The Other Path*. New York: Harper & Row.

Dixit, Avinash. 2003. "On Modes of Economic Governance". *Econometrica* 71(2): 449–482.

Dixit, Avinash. 2003a. "Two-Tier Market Institutions". Working Paper, Princeton University.

Dixit, Avinash. Forthcoming. *Lawlessness and Economics:Alternative Modes of Governance*. Princeton, NJ: Princeton University Press.

Downing, Brian M. 1992. *The Military Revolution and Political Change*. Princeton, NJ: Princeton University Press.

Eggertsson, Thrainn. 1990. *Economic Behavior and Institutions*. Cambridge: Cambridge University Press.

Ellickson, Robert C. 1991. *Order Without Law*. Cambridge, MA: Harvard University Press.

Ellison, Glenn. 1994. "Cooperation in the Prisoner's Dilemma with Anonymous Random Matching". *Review of Economic Studies* 61(3): 567–588.

Ensminger, Jean. 1997. "Changing Property Rights: Reconciling Formal and Informal Rights to Land in Africa" in John N. Drobak and John V.C. Nye (eds.), *The Frontiers of the New Institutional Economics*. New York: Academic Press

Epstein, Steven A. 1996. *Genoa & the Genoese, 958–1528*. Chapel Hill, NC: The University of North Carolina Press.

Fafchamps, Marcel. 2004. *Market Institutions in Sub-Saharan Africa : Theory and Evidence*. Cambridge, MA: MIT Press.

Fafchamps, Marcel, Tyler Biggs, Jonathan Conning, and Pradeep Srivastava. 1993. "Enterprise Finance in Kenya". World Bank, Africa Region, Regional Program on Enterprise Development. Washington, DC: World Bank.

Fearon, James D. 1997. "Bargaining over Objects that Influence Future Bargaining Power". Working Paper, University of Chicago.

Fehr, Ernst and Simon Gächter. 2000. "Cooperation and Punishment in Public Good Experiments". *American Economic Review* 90: 980–994.

Fehr, Ernst and Urs Fischacher. 2004. "Third Party Punishment and Social Norms". Working Paper 106, Institute for Empirical Research in Economics, The University of Zurich.

Furubotn, Erik G., and Rudolf Richter. 1997. *Institutions and Economic Theory*. Ann Arbor, MI: The University of Michigan Press.

Galor, Oded and Omer Moav. 2003. "Das Human Kapital". Working Paper 2000–17, Brown University.

Gambetta, Diego. 1993. *The Sicilian Mafia: The Business of Private Protection*. Cambridge, MA: Harvard University Press.

Ghatak M. and Guinnane T.W. 1999. "The Economics of Lending with Joint Liability: Theory and Practice". *Journal of Development Economics* 60(1): 195–228.

Ghosh, Parikshit and Debraj Ray. 1996. "Cooperation in Community Interaction Without Information Flows". *The Review of Economic Studies* 63(3): 491–519.

Glaeser, L. Edward and Andrei Shleifer. 2002. "Legal Origi". *Quarterly Journal of Economics* 117: 1193–1230.

Glaeser, L. Edward and Andrei Shleifer. 2003. "The Rise of the Regulatory State". *Journal of Economic Literature* 41(2): 401–425.

Goetzmann, William and Elisabeth Köll. 2003. "The History of Corporate Ownership in China". Memo, Yale University.

Goitein, Shelomo Dov. 1955. "The Cairo Geniza as a Source for the History of the Muslim Civilization". *Studia Islamica* 3: 75–91.
Goitein, Shelomo Dov. 1971. *The Community. A Mediterranean Society*, Vol. 2. Los Angeles, CA: University of California Press.
Gonzalez de Lara, Yadira. 2002. "Institutions for Contract Enforcement and Risk-Sharing: from Debt to Equity in Late Medieval Venice". Memo, Ente Einaudi, Bank of Italy.
Goldstein, Markus and Christopher Udry. 2002. "Gender, Land Rights, and Agriculture in Ghana". Memo, Yale University.
Goody, J. 1983. *The Development of the Family and Marriage in Europe*. Cambridge: Cambridge University Press.
Granovetter. Mark S. 1985. "Economic Action, Social Structure, and Embeddedness". *American Journal of Sociology* 91(3): 481–510.
Greif, Avner. 1989. "Reputation and Coalitions in Medieval Trade: Evidence on the Maghribi Traders". *Journal of Economic History* XLIX: 857–882.
Greif, Avner. 1992. "Institutions and International Trade: Lessons from the Commercial Revolution". *American Economic Review* 82(2): 128–133.
Greif, Avner. 1993. "Contract Enforceability and Economic Institutions in Early Trade: The Maghribi Traders' Coalition". *American Economic Review* 83(3): 525–548.
Greif, Avner. 1994a. "Cultural Beliefs and the Organization of Society: A Historical and Theoretical Reflection on Collectivist and Individualist Societies". *The Journal of Political Economy* 102(5): 912–950.
Greif, Avner. 1994b. "On the Political Foundations of the Late Medieval Commercial Revolution: Genoa During the Twelfth and Thirteenth Centuries". *The Journal of Economic History* 54(4): 271–287.
Greif, Avner. 1995. Political Organizations, Social Structure, and Institutional Success: Reflections From Genoa and Venice During the Commercial Revolution". *The Journal of Institutional and Theoretical Economics* 151(4): 734–740.
Greif, Avner. 1996. "On the Inter-relations and Economic Implications of Economic, Social, Political, and Normative Factors: Reflections From Two Late Medieval Societies" in John N. Drobak and John Nye (eds.), *Frontiers of the New Institutional Economics*. New York: Academic Press.
Greif, Avner. 1997. "Contracting, Enforcement, and Efficiency: Economics Beyond the Law" in Michael Bruno and Boris Pleskovic (eds.), *Annual World Bank Conference on Development Economics*. Washington, DC: The World Bank.
Greif, Avner. 2000. "The Fundamental Problem of Exchange: A Research Agenda in Historical Institutional Analysis". *European Review of Economic History* 4(3): 251–284.
Greif, Avner. 2001. "The Islamic Equilibrium: Legitimacy and Political, Social, and Economic Outcomes". Working Paper, Stanford University.
Greif, Avner. 2002. "Institutions and Impersonal Exchange: From Communal to Individual Responsibility". *The Journal of Institutional and Theoretical Economics* 158(1).
Greif, Avner. 2004. "Impersonal Exchange without Impartial Law: The Community Responsibility System". *Chicago Journal of International Law*.
Greif, Avner. Forthcoming. *Institutions: Theory and History*. Cambridge University Press.
Greif, Avner, Paul R. Milgrom, and Barry R. Weingast. 1994. "Coordination, Commitment and Enforcement: The Case of the Merchant Gild". *The Journal of Political Economy* 102(4): 745–776.
Greif, Avner, and Eugene Kandel. 1995. "Contract Enforcement Institutions: Historical Perspective and Current Status in Russia" in Edward P. Lazear (ed.), *Economic Transition in Eastern Europe and Russia: Realities of Reform*. Stanford, CA: Hoover Institution Press.
Greif, Avner. 1998. "Self-Enforcing Political Systems and Economic Growth: Late Medieval Genoa," in *Analytic Narratives*, co-authored by Robert H. Bates, Avner Greif, Margaret Levi, Jean-Laurent Rosenthal, and Barry R. Weingast. Princeton, NJ: Princeton University Press.

Grossman, Herschel I. 1997. "Make Us a King: Anarchy, Predation, and the State". Working Paper w6289, NBER, Cambridge, MA.
Grossman, Herschel I. and Minseong Kim. 1995. "Swords or Ploughshares? A Theory of the Security Claims to Property". *Journal of Political Economy* 103: 1275–1288.
Guinnane T.W. 1994. "A Failed Institutional Transplant—Raiffeisens Credit Cooperatives in Ireland, 1894–1914". *Explorations in Economic History* 31(1): 38–61.
Gurevich, Aaron. 1995. *The Origins of European Individualism*. Oxford: Blackwell.
Haber S., N. Maurer, and A. Razo. 2003. "When the Law Does Not Matter: The Rise and Decline of the Mexican Oil Industry". *Journal of Economic History* 63(1): 1–32.
Hamilton, Gary. G. 1991. "The Organizational Foundations of Western and Chinese Commerce: A Historical and Comparative Analysis" in Gary G. Hamilton (ed.), *Business Networks and Economic Development in East and Southeast Asia*. Hong Kong: Centre for Asian Studies.
Hamilton, Gary G. 1994. "Civilizations and the Organization of Economies" in N. Smelser and R. Swedberg (eds.), *The Handbook of Economic Sociology*. Princeton, NJ: Princeton University Press, New York: Russell Sage Foundation.
Hardin, Russell. 1989. "Why a Constitution" in Bernard Grofman and Donal Wittman (eds.), *The Federalist Papers and the New Institutionalism*. New York: Agathon Press.
Harris, Ron. 2004. "Government and the Economy, 1688–1850" in R. Floud and P. Johnson (eds.), *Cambridge Economic History of Britain*. Cambridge: Cambridge University Press.
Hart, Oliver and John Moore. 1999. "Foundations of Incomplete Contracts". *Review of Economic Studies* 66: 115–138.
Head, Thomas F. and Richard Landes (eds.). 1992. *The Peace of God: Social Violence and Religious Response in France Around the Year 1000*. Ithaca, NY: Cornell University Press.
Helpman, Elhanan. Forthcoming. *The Mystery of Economic Growth*. Book MS.
Henley, David. 2004. "Conflict, Justice, and the Stranger-king: Indigenous Roots of Colonial Rule in Indonesia and Elsewhere". *Modern Asian Studies* 38(1): 85–144.
Herrmann-Pillath, Carsten. 1999. "On the Importance of Studying Late Qing Economic and Social History for the Analysis of Contemporary China, or: Protecting Sinology Against Social Science". Duisburg Working Papers in East Asian Studies, 3.
Hodgson, Geoffrey M. 1998. "The Approach of Institutional Economics". *Journal of Economic Literature* 36(1): 166–192.
Hodgson, Marshall G.S. 1974. *The Venture of Islam,* Vol. 2. Chicago, IL: Chicago University Press.
Hoffman, Philip T., Gilles Postel-Vinay, and Jean-Laurent Rosenthal. 2000. *Priceless Markets: The Political Economy of Credit in Paris, 1660–1870*. Chicago, IL: University of Chicago Press.
Hoffman, Philip T. 1991. "Land Rents and Agricultural Productivity: The Paris Basin, 1450–1789". *Journal of Economic History* 51: 771–805.
Hogue, Arthur R. 1996. *Origins of the Common Law.* Indianapolis, IN: Liberty Press.
Hsu, F.L.K. 1983. *Rugged Individualism Reconsidered*. Knoxville, TN: University of Tennessee Press.
Hughes, Diane Owen. 1974. "Toward Historical Ethnography: Notarial Records and Family History in The Middle Ages". *Historical Methods Newsletter* 7(2): 61–71.
Ingram, Paul. 1996. "Organizational Forms as a Solution to the Problem of Credible Commitment: The Evolution of Naming Strategies among U.S. Hotel Chains, 1896–1980". *Strategic Management Journal* 17: 85–98.
Irwin, Douglas A. 1988. "Welfare Effects of British Free Trade: Debate and Evidence from the 1840s". *Journal of Political Economy* 96: 1142–1164.
Israel, Jonathan I. 1995. *The Dutch Republic. It Rise, Greatness, and Fall, 1477–1806.* Oxford: Clarendon Press.
Johnson, Simon, R. La Porta, F. Lopez-de-Silanes, and Shleifer A. 2000. "Tunneling", *American Economic Review* 90(2): 22–27.

Johnson, Simon, John McMillan, and Christopher Woodruff. 2002. "Courts and Relational Contracts". *Journal of Law, Economics, and Organization* 18: 221–277.
Kali, Raja. 1999. "Endogenous Business Networks". *Journal of Law, Economics and Organization* 15(3).
Kambayash, Ryo. 2002. "The Registration System and the Grade Wage System, Coordination and Relative Performance Evaluation". Tokyo University.
Kandori, Michihiro. 1992. "Social Norms and Community Enforcement". *The Review of Economic Studies* 59: 63–80.
Klein, Daniel B. 1992. "Promise Keeping in the Great Society". *Economics and Politics* July: 117–136.
Klein, Daniel B. (ed.). 1997. *Reputation*. Ann Arbor, MI: The University of Michigan Press.
Klerman, Daniel. 2003. "Competition and the Evolution of Common Law". *Australia Journal of Legal History*.
Klerman, Daniel and Paul Mahoney. 2004. "The Value of Judicial Independence: Evidence from Eighteenth-Century England". Working Paper, USC.
Konrad, Kai, and Stergios Skaperdas. 1996. "The Market for Protection and the Origin of the State". Conference on Political Violence at Princeton University, Princeton, NJ.
Kranton, Rachel. E. 1996a. "The Formation of Cooperative Relationships". *Journal of Law Economics & Organization* 12(18): 214–233.
Kranton, Rachel E. 1996b. "Reciprocal Exchange: A Self-Sustaining System". *The American Economic Review* 86(4): 830–851.
Kreps, David. 1990. "Corporate Culture and Economic Theory" in James E. Alt and Kenneth A. Shepsle (eds.), *Perspectives on Positive Political Economy*. Cambridge: Cambridge University Press.
Lacher, Jeffrey M. and John A. Weinberg. 1989. "Optimal Contracts Under Costly State Falsification". *Journal of Political Economy* 97(6): 1345–1363.
Landa, Janet T. 1994. *Trust, Ethnicity, and Identity*. Ann Arbor, MI: University of Michigan Press.
Lane, Frederic C. 1973. *Venice: A Maritime Republic*. Baltimore, MD: Johns Hopkins University Press.
Lapidus, Ira, M. 1984. *Muslim Cities in the Later Middle Ages*. Cambridge: Cambridge University Press.
Levinson, Daryl J. 2003. "Collective Sanctions". *Stanford Law Review* 56: 345–428.
Li, Shuhe. 1999. "The Benefits and Costs of Relation-Based Governance: An Explanation of the East Asian Miracle and Crisis". Working Paper, City University of Hong Kong.
Lipset, Seymour, M. 1959. "Some Social Requisite of Democracy: Economic Development and Political Legitimacy". *American Political Science Review* 53: 69–105.
Ma, Debin. 2004. "Why Japan, not China, was the First to Develop in East Asia: Lesson from Sericulture, 1850–1937". Memo, Foundation for Advanced Studies in International Development. Forthcoming in *Economic Development and Cultural Change*.
Macaulay, Stewart. 1963. "Noncontractual Relations in Business: A Preliminary Study". *American Sociological Review* 23: 55–70.
Macfarlane, Alan. 1978. *The Origins of English Individualism*. Oxford: Basil Blackwell.
MacLeod, W. Bentley, and James M. Malcomson. 1989. "Implicit Contracts, Incentive Compatibility, and Involuntary Unemployment". *Econometrica* 57(2): 447–480.
McMillan, John. 2002. *Reinventing the Bazaar: A Natural History of Markets*. New York: W.W. Norton & Company.
McMillan, John and Christopher Woodruff. 2000. "Private Order under Dysfunctional Public Order". *Michigan Law Review* 98: 101–138.
Maskin, Eric S. and Jean Tirole. 1999. "Unforseen Contingencies and Incomplete Contracts". *Review of Economic Studies* 66: 83–114.
Menger, Carl. 1963 [1883]. *Problems of Economics and Sociology*. Translated by F.J. Nock. Urbana, IL: University of Illinois Press.

Machiavelli, Niccolo. 1990 [1532]. *Florentine Histories* (also known as *History of Florence*). Introduction by Harvey Mansfield, Jr. Translation by Laura F. Banfield Jr. and Harvey C. Mansfield. Princeton, NJ: Princeton University Press.

Milgrom, Paul R., Douglass C. North, and Barry R. Weingast. 1990. "The Role of Institutions in the Revival of Trade: The Law Merchant, Private Judges, and the Champagne Fairs". *Economics & Politics* 2: 1–23.

Moriguchi, Chiaki. 2003. "Implicit Contracts, the Great Depression, and Institutional Change: A Comparative Analysis of U.S. and Japanese Employment Relations, 1920–1940". *Journal of Economic History* 63: 1–41.

Morris, Colin. 1972. *The Discovery of the Individual 1050–1200*. London: S.P.C.K. for the Church Historical Society.

Moselle, Boaz and Ben Polak. 2001. "A Model of the Predatory State". *Journal of Law Economics and Organization* 17(1): 1–33.

Muldrew, Craig. 1998. *The Economy of Obligation*. London: MacMillan.

Munro, John H. 1990. "The International Law Merchant and the Evolution of Negotiable Credit in Late-Medieval England and the Low Countries" in Dino Puncuh (ed.), *Banchi Pubblici, Banchi Privati e Monti di Pietà nell'Europa Preindustriale*. Genoa: Società Ligure de Storia Patria.

Munz, Peter. 1969. *Frederick Barbarossa*. Ithaca, NY: Cornell University Press.

Muthoo, Abhinay. 2000. "On the Foundations of Property Rights, Part I: A Model of the State-of-Nature with Two Players", in typescript, Department of Economics, Essex, UK.

Nader, H. 1990. *Liberty in Absolutist Spain. The Habsburg Sale of Towns, 1516–1700*. Baltimore, MD: Johns Hopkins University Press.

Neal, Larry and S. Quinn. 2001. "Networks of Information, Markets, and Institutions in the Rise of London as a Financial Center in the Seventeenth Century". *Financial History Review* 7: 117–140.

North, Douglass C. 1990. *Institutions, Institutional Change and Economic Performance*. Cambridge: Cambridge University Press.

North, Douglass C. and Barry R. Weingast. 1989. "Constitutions and Commitment: Evolution of Institutions Governing Public Choice". *Journal of Economic History* XLIX: 803–832.

North, Douglass C. and Robert P. Thomas. 1973. *The Rise of the Western World*. Cambridge: Cambridge University Press.

Norwich, John Julius. 1989 [1977]. *A History of Venice*. New York: Vintage Books. (1989 ed. New York: Random House).

O'Brien, Patrick K. 2001. "Fiscal Exceptionalism: Great Britain and its European Rivals—from Civil War to Triumph at Trafalgar and Waterloo". Working Paper 65/01, Department of Economic History, London School of Economics.

Okazaki, Tetsuji. 2002. "The Role of the Merchant Coalition in Pre-modern Japanese Economic Development: An Historical Institutional Analyais". Memo, Faculty of Economics, University of Tokyo.

Olds K.B., Liu R.H. 2000. "Economic Cooperation in 19th-century Taiwan: Religion and Informal Enforcement". *Journal of Institutional and Theoretical Economics* 156(2): 404–430.

Olson, Mancur. 1993. "Dictatorship, Democracy, and Development". *American Political Science Review* 87(3): 567–576.

Pettengill, John S. 1970. "The Impact of Military Technology on European Income Distribution". *Journal of Interdisciplinary History* X(2): 201–225.

Polinsky, A. Mitchell and Steven Shavell. 2000. "The Economic Theory of Public Enforcement of Law". *Journal of Economic Literature* 38(1): 45–76.

Pomeranz, Kenneth. 2000. *The Great Divergence, China, Europe and the Making of the Modern World Economy*. Princeton, NJ: Princeton University Press.

Pomeranz, Kenneth. 2002. "Is There an East Asian Development Path? Long-term Comparisons, Constraints, and Continuities". AEA Annual Meeting.

Portes, Alejandro. 1994. "The Informal Sector and Its Paradoxes" in Alejandro Portes (ed.), *The Economic Sociology of Immigration*. New York: Russell Sage Foundation.

Przeworski, Adam, Michael E. Alvarez, Josè Antonio Cheibub, and Fernando Limongi. 2000. *Democracy and Development*. Cambridge: Cambridge University Press.

Quinn, Stephen. 1997. "Glodsmith-banking: Mutual Acceptance and Interbanker Clearing in Restoration London". *Explorations in Economic History* 34: 411–432.

Quinn, Stephen. 2001. "The Glorious Revolution's Effect on British Private Finance: A Microhistory, 1680–1705". *Journal of Economic History* 61(3): 593–615.

Rajan, Raghuram G. and Luigi, Zingales. 2003. *Saving Capatilism from the Capitalists*. New York: Random House.

Ramseyer, J. Mark. 1991. "Legal Rules in Repeated Deals: Banking in the Shadow of Defection in Japan". *Journal of Legal Studies* 10: 91–117.

Rauch, J.E. 2001. "Business and Social Networks in International Trade". *Journal of Economic Literature* 39: 1177–1203.

Redding, S. Gordon. 1991. "Weak Organization and Strong Linkages: Managerial Ideology and Family Business Networks" in Gary Hamilton (ed.), *Business Networks and Economic Development in East and Southeast Asia*. Hong Kong: Center of Asian Studies. University of Hong Kong.

Reynolds, Charles H., and Ralph V. Norman (eds.). 1988. *Community in America*. Berkeley, CA: University of California Press.

Richardson, Gary. 2002. "Christianity and Craft Guilds in Late-Medieval England". Working Paper 211, University of California at Irvine.

Root, Hilton L. 1989. "Tying the King's Hands: Credible Commitments and Royal Fiscal Policy During the Old Regime". *Rationality and Society* 1(2): 240–158.

Rose-Ackerman, Susan. 1999. *Corruption and Government*. New York: Cambridge University Press.

Ryser, Marc. 1997. "Sanctions without Law: The Japanese Financial Clearinghouse Guillotine and its Impact on Default Rate" in Daniel B. Klein (ed.), *Reputation*. Ann Arbor, MI: The University of Michigan Press.

Schaede, Ulrike. 1989. "Forwards and Futures in Tokugawa-Period Japan: A New Perspective on the Dojima Rice Market". *Journal of Banking and Finance* 13(4–5): 487–513.

Shiue, Carol H. and Wolfgang Keller. 2003. "Markets in China and Europe on the Eve of the Industrial Revolution". Memo, University of Texas.

Shleifer, Andrei and Robert W. Vishny. 1993. "Corruption". *The Quarterly Journal of Economics* 108(3): 599–617.

Skaperdas, Stergios. 1992. "Cooperation, Conflict, and Power in the Absence of Property Rights". *American Economic Review* 82(4): 720–738.

Skaperdas, Stergios and Constantinos Syropoulos. 1996. "Insecure Property Rights and the Stability of Exchange". Technical Report. Institute for Mathematical Behavioral Science, Pennsylvania State University.

Stringham, Edward. 2003. "The Extralegal Development of Securities Trading in Seventeenth-century Amsterdam". *The Quarterly Review of Economics and Finance* 43: 321–344.

Stulz Rm and Williamson R. 2003. "Culture, Openness, and Finance". *Journal of Financial Economics* 70(3): 313–349.

Sussman, Nathan and Yishay Yefeh. 2000. "Institutions, Reforms, and Country Risk: Lessons from Japanese Government Debt in the Meiji Period". *Journal of Economic History* 60(2): 442–467.

Sussman, Nathan and Yishay Yefeh. 2004. "Constitutions and Commitment: Evidence on the Relation between Institutions and the Cost of Capital". Memo, The Hebrew University.

Tadelis, Steve. 2002. "The Market for Reputations as an Incentive Mechanism". *Journal of Political Economy* 110(4): 854–882.

Tilly, Charles. 1990. *Coercion, Capital, and European States, AD 990–1992*. Cambridge, MA: Blackwell.

Tirole, Jean. 2001. "Corporate Governance". *Econometrica* 69(1): 1–35.
Townsend, Robert M. 1979. "Optimal Contracts and Competitive Markets with Costly State Verification". *Journal of Economic Theory* 21(2): 265–293.
Triandis, Harry C. 1990. "Cross-cultural Studies of Individualism and Collectivism" in J. Berman (ed.), *Nebraska Symposium on Motivation*, 1989. Lincoln, NE: University of Nebraska Press.
Udovitch, A.L. 1988. "Merchants and Amirs: Government and Trade in Eleventh-century Egypt". *Asian and African Studies* 22: 53–72.
Volckart, Oliver. 2001. "The Economics of Feuding in Late Medieval Germany". Working Paper, Institut fur Wirtschaftsgeschichte, Berlin.
Watson, Joel. 2002. "Starting Small and Commitment". *Games and Economic Behavior* 38: 176–199.
Watts, R.W. and J.L. Zimmermann 1983. "Agency Problems, Auditing and the Theory of the Firm: Some Evidence". *Journal of Law and Economics* 26: 613–633.
Weingast, Barry, R. 1997. "The Political Foundations of Democracy and the Rule of Law". *American Political Science Review* 91(2): 245–263.
Weingast, Barry. R. 1996. "Political Institutions: Rational Choice Perspectives" in Robert Goodin and Hans-Dieter Klingemann (eds.), *A New Handbook of Political Science*. Oxford University Press.
Williamson, Dean V. 2002. "Transparency and Contract Selection: Evidence from the Financing of Trade in Venetian Crete: 1303–1351". Memo, US Department of Justice.
Williamson, Oliver E. 1985. *The Economic Institutions of Capitalism*. New York: The Free Press.
Wong. R. Bin. 1997. *China Transformed. Historical Change and the Limits of the European Experience*. Ithaca, NY: Cornell University Press.
Woodruff, Christopher. 1998. "Contract Enforcement and Trader Liberalization in Mexico's Footwear Industry". *World Development* 26(6): 979–991.
Yang Li, Mu. 2002. "Essays on Public Finance and Economic Development in a Historical Institutional Perspective". Ph.D. dissertation, Stanford University.
Yarbrough B.V. and Yarbrough R.M. 2003. "The Contractual Role of Boundaries: Law and Economics Meets International Organization". *European Journal of International Relations* 9(4): 543–590.
Zelin, Madeleine, Jonathan K. Ocko, and Robert Gardella. 2004. *Contract and Property in Early Modern China*. Stanford, CA.: Stanford University Press.

SECTION VIII

Perspectives

29. Economic Sociology and New Institutional Economics

VICTOR NEE and RICHARD SWEDBERG

When economic sociology appeared on the academic scene in the mid-1980s its interactions with New Institutional Economics were soon plentiful as well as productive. Especially the ideas of Oliver Williamson and Douglass North were often discussed and found useful. That this was a fruitful interaction is exemplified not least by the fact that Williamson's notion of "hybrid" was developed in response to comments on his distinction between markets and hierarchies by some sociologists. The concept of "transaction cost" soon became part of the sociological language, and sociologists suddenly seemed more receptive to ideas of economists than they had been for a very long time.

A few years later, however, the interactions between new institutional economists and economic sociologists began to become less frequent and productive. A number of sociologists have continued to visit the annual meeting of ISNIE, and articles by sociologists occasionally appear in a journal such as *Journal of Institutional and Theoretical Economics*. There is also the recent anthology by Mary Brinton and Victor Nee—*The New Institutionalism in Sociology* (1998)—which represents a very successful attempt to bring together sociologists and economists around the issue of institutions. On the whole, however, since a decade or so there is considerably less interaction than one could have wished for.

This chapter represents an attempt to remedy this situation and further a two-way traffic between economic sociology and New Institutional Economics. We feel that economic sociology has enormously much to learn from New Institutional Economics and that this Handbook can play a constructive role in this process. We also feel that economists working in the tradition of New Institutional Economics may want to be better informed about what has been happening in economic sociology during the last few years, not least when it comes to such common interests as the concept of institution and the role of institutions in economic life. Reflecting these concerns, we have structured this chapter in the following way. We will first summarize developments in economic sociology since the early 1990s, when the link between the two fields started to become weaker. We shall the turn to the concept of institution and how it can be improved. We will also relate the concept of institution to norms, similarly trying to advance the discussion by introducing some new ideas.

C. Ménard and M. M. Shirley (eds.), Handbook of New Institutional Economics, 789–818.
© *2005 Springer. Printed in the Netherlands.*

1. ECONOMIC SOCIOLOGY: RECENT DEVELOPMENTS

The last ten to fifteen years have been characterized by an extremely dynamic growth in economic sociology and also by the gradual institutionalization of this field (see Table 1). Some new topics have been broached, such as wealth, entrepreneurship and the role of law in the economy. Earlier insights have been elaborated upon and developed in new directions. The latter is true, for example, for Mark Granovetter's well-known ideas about embeddedness and Harrison White's theory of production markets. There is also an ongoing attempt to consolidate the insights in economic sociology by going back to the classics and learn from these.

What struck economic sociologists as important in the mid-1980s differs to some extent from what they see as important today. The same is true for the relationship of economic sociologists to economic theory: what they saw as important two decades ago is not necessarily what they find suggestive and interesting today. The concern with transaction costs, for example, has grown

Table 1. Contemporary Economics Sociology

Programmatic Statements: Popular Classics: Max Weber, *Economy and Society* (1920); Karl Polanyi in *Trade and Market in the Early Empires* (1957); also Karl Marx, *Capital* (1867)
Modern Landmarks: Mark Granovetter, "Economic Action and Social Structure: The Problem of Embeddedness" (1985); also: Pierre Bourdieu, "Principles of Economic Anthropology" (1997, 2001).
Basic Approach: Economic phenomena can be analyzed with the help of the sociological apparatus (its ideas, concepts and methods). The relationship between economic phenomena and non-economic phenomena is central as well.
Central Conceptual Tools: embeddedness, networks (including actor-network-theory), an interest-based concept of institutions, fields (organizational and other), capital (social, cultural and so on).
Introductions to Economic Sociology: *Handbook of Economic Sociology* (1994, 2nd ed. forthcoming in 2005); *Sociology of Economic Life* (main reader); Sarah Babb and Bruce Carruthers, *Economy/Society* (undergraduate textbook); Richard Swedberg, *Principles of Economic Sociology* and Carlo Trigilia, *Economic Sociology* (medium-level introductions); Mary Brinton and Victor Nee (eds.), *The New Institutionalism in Sociology* (economists and economic sociologists, advanced introduction).
Current Strongholds: In the United States: major universities such as Cornell, Stanford, Berkeley, Princeton and Northwestern; also some business schools, such as the Sloan School of Management (MIT) and the University of Chicago Business School. In Europe, economic sociology is especially strong in France (Paris, Lille), Germany (Goettingen, Cologne), England (London, Cambridge) and Scotland (Edinburgh).
Key People: Wayne Baker, Jens Beckert, Nicole Woolsey Biggart, Luc Boltanski, Mary Brinton, Ronald Burt, Michel Callon, Bruce Carruthers, Gerry Davis, Frank Dobbin, Peter Evans, Neil Fligstein, Bai Gao, Gary Gereffi, Mark Granovetter, Mauro Guillén, Karin Knorr Cetina, Donald MacKenzie, Mark Mizruchi, Victor Nee, Joel Podolny, Walter Powell, Richard Swedberg, Laurent Thevenot, Brian Uzzi, Harrison White and Viviana Zelizer.
Recent Key Monographs: Pierre Bourdieu, *Social Structures of the Economy* (2004), Jens Beckert, *Unearned Wealth* (forthcoming), Bruce Carruthers, *City of Capital* (1996), Frank Dobbin, *Forging Industrial Policy* (1994), Neil Fligstein, *The Transformation of Corporate Control* (1990), Mark Granovetter, *Getting A Job* (1974, 1995), Richard Swedberg, *Max Weber and the Idea of Economic Sociology* (1998), Harrison White, *Markets from Networks* (2002), and Viviana Zelizer, *The Social Meaning of Money* (1994).

weaker; while the interest for work by economists on institutions has grown steadily in importance. While studies of markets in a decade or so ago routinely commented on transaction costs, this is not the case today. There is also a growing sense that that economic sociology and behavioral economics have quite a bit in common.

Theory and Theory Related Advances

When economic sociology was revived in the mid-1980s sociologists were basically at a loss when it came to theory. There was a strong sense that sociologists should develop their own approach, and that this approach should differ from that of mainstream economics—but that was about all. The heritage of economic sociology, especially the powerful ideas of Max Weber on *Wirtschaftssoziologie*, were not an option since they were little known (cf. Swedberg 1998). To draw on Marx's work did not seem much of an option either, since the days of radical sociology were over.

It was in this situation that Mark Granovetter came up with the suggestion that it might be possible to bring together the ideas of Karl Polanyi on embeddedness with those of networks analysis (Granovetter 1985). Following this suggestion, the task of economic sociology would primarily be to trace the way that economic actions are structured via networks. Economic actions, in brief, do not follow the short and direct paths of maximization, as the economists claim, but rather the considerably more complex paths of existing networks. Granovetter also suggested that networks can account for institutions, by conceptualizing the latter as "congealed" networks (Granovetter 1992:9).

This embeddedness project has met with some success; and during the recent decade it has, for example, been used quite a bit as well as added to by Granovetter, his students and some other scholars (e.g. Uzzi 1996, 1997; Portes and Sensenbrenner 1993). During the last ten years this perspective has, however, also been increasingly challenged by a number of economic sociologists; and one may even speak of a general discontent in contemporary economic sociology with the embeddedness perspective, accompanied by an attempt to go beyond it (e.g. Nee and Ingram 1998, Krippner 2001). One of those who have challenged the ideas of Granovetter et al is Pierre Bourdieu, who has criticized the embeddedness approach primarily for its exclusive focus on personal interactions and for its failure to deal with structural factors (e.g. Bourdieu 2000). As a remedy to this, Bourdieu himself has suggested that the concept of field is used, since it allows the analyst to handle macro issues as well as structural effects (e.g. Bourdieu forthcoming).

Several economic sociologists have also been less critical of mainstream economics than what Granovetter is; and these often draw on the work by various members of New Institutional Economics. They stress that Granovetter has difficulty in dealing with the role of institutions in economic life (as opposed to interpersonal networks), and that sociologists have much to contribute to clarifying the relationship between informal and formal elements of institutions (e.g. Nee and Ingram 1998). There also seems to be an affinity between those in favor of the embeddedness approach and a positive attitude to situations characterized by dense interpersonal relations, as opposed to situations where impersonal interactions predominate, as in much of modern capitalism (e.g. Uzzi 1996).

How much economic sociologists should draw on game theory represents another issue that has recently been raised, and for which the embeddedness approach provides little guidance (e.g. Swedberg 2001). Since a few years back the major journals in sociology regularly contain analyses that draw on game theory. Economic sociologists, on the other hand, have basically been suspicious of game theory. At the most they have shown sympathy for attempts to mix empirical analysis with game theory of the type that can be found in the well-known work of Avner Greif (e.g. Greif 1998). All in all, we may conclude that economic sociology is currently characterized by several theoretical approaches, and that a theoretical core is missing.

While sociologists have often been hostile to economics, it has gradually come to be understood that economics is a multifaceted science and that it also contains many ideas that are of relevance to economic sociology. Some economists, on their side, have also come to think that they can improve their own analyses by opening these up to sociological concepts and ways of thinking. The work of Herbert Simon has, for example, continued to be close in spirit to economic sociology (e.g. Simon 1997). This is also true for the work of George Akerlof and Jeffrey Sachs (e.g. Akerlof and Kranston 2000, Sachs 2000). Some economic sociologists have also been attracted by the attempts of Douglass North and Avner Greif to resurrect the concept of institution and improve upon it in the spirit of New Institutional Economics (e.g. Greif forthcoming, North 1990).

New Developments in Analyzing Old Topics (Networks, Markets and Firms)

In Granovetter's article on embeddedness from 1985 it was argued that economic activities were not simply embedded in social relations but in *networks*. Many of Granovetter's students at the State University of New York at Stony Brook in the 1980s would also use network analysis in their studies of the economy. Some of them focused on the kind of networks that develop around firms, while others analyzed the networks that are formed by directors sitting on several boards, so-called interlocks. While big hopes were initially attached to the latter type of study, it was eventually realized that research on interlocks had a rather limited potential (e.g. Mizruchi 1996).

One of the great strengths of networks analysis is that it represents a flexible and sophisticated tool with which a number of social phenomena can be approached, and recent developments in economic sociology tend to confirm this (e.g. Rouch and Casella 2001, Zuckerman 2003). Networks analysis has, for example, been used to explore various types of economic interactions which cannot be categorized either as customs or as some kinds of economic organization. These intermediary social forms are sometimes referred to as "network forms of organization" (e.g. Podolny and Page 1998). In a very influential work from the early 1990s Ronald Burt suggested that also entrepreneurship can be understood with the help of network analysis (Burt 1993). His basic idea is that an entrepreneur connects two groups of people who otherwise would be socially disconnected, say buyers and sellers. The entrepreneur, in his or her capacity as a middleman, straddles according to this argument a so-called "structural hole".

A special mention should also be made of business groups, which are typically studied with the help of networks. Through an article in the early 1990s Mark Granovetter gave great visibility to this topic, and since that time an increasing number of studies have been devoted to this phenomenon (Granovetter 1994; for an overview, see Granovetter forthcoming). One insight produced by this research is that in several countries in Europe, Asia and Latin America, business groups account for a significant part of the economy. In the United States, in contrast, this type of groups is much less common, probably because of anti-trust legislation.

Network analysis has also been used to analyze consumption, a development which can be exemplified by an interesting study by Paul DiMaggio and Hugh Louch (1998). Its focus is on a very special kind of consumer purchases, namely those for which people use their own networks of friends and acquaintances; and these purchases are then contrasted to purchases of the type where the buyer does not need to use a referral or network. Padgett and Ansell have finally carried out a very suggestive historical study with the help of networks analysis (Padgett and Ansell 1993). The famous Medici family, it is argued, held its power partly because of its great skill in building and activating various types of economic and political networks.

A special mention should also be made of a European version of networks theory, called actor-network-theory (ANT; e.g. Callon 1989, Law and Hassard 1999). The basic idea here is that not only individuals and firms can be actors but also objects. What is meant with this paradoxical statement is that the analysis should not exclusively focus on social relations but also include objects; and the rationale for this is that objects may be part of social interactions or steer social interaction in some distinct direction. As examples one can mention the way that, say, surveillance technology enables supervisors to track employees or how an assembly line presupposes that workers coordinate their actions.

Together with networks, *markets* have been one of the central topics in economic sociology from early on. One of the articles that helped to launch economic sociology in the 1980s was devoted to precisely this topic (White 1981). Its author was Harrison C. White, a physicist turned sociologist, and a major figure in 20th century sociology. After leaving the topic of markets for a period in the early 1990s, White resumed work on this topic, adding various features to his earlier model (e.g. White 2001). One of White's followers, it should also be mentioned, has followed up on his ideas about the relationship between market and identity (Aspers 2001).

According to White's theory, the typical (industrial) market has a small number of actors who, by signaling to one another through price and volume, form a coherent group with a stable social structure—in brief, a market. Complementing White's theory is Neil Fligstein's view that the characteristic feature of modern markets is their *stability* (Fligstein 1996, 2001). Market actors, according to this perspective, do not want volatility in price or cutthroat competition, but stable markets without any surprises. Fligstein has also recently analyzed the rise of the shareholder value-conception of the firm, which currently dominates corporate America (Fligstein and Shin 2004; cf. Dobbin and Zorn forthcoming).

Before leaving the topic of markets, a special mention should be made of an elegant study by Joel Podolny on the role of status in markets (Podolny 1992). The argument here is that buyers are willing to pay a premium for status, something which is obviously profitable for the seller. Having status, however, also restricts the seller to a small market, since he or she would otherwise lose status (and the earlier market).

Just like networks and markets have been on the agenda of economic sociology for two decades by now, so have *firms*. One major reason for this is that sociologists since long time back have done work in organization theory and, as part of this, studied firms. There is also the fact that many economic sociologists are employed in business schools, where organization theory is often seen as helpful. One important contribution that sociologists have made to the analysis of firms, and which has grown considerably in importance during the last decade, is that of population ecology (Hannan and Freeman 1988; Hannan and Carroll 1995). The main focus here is on populations of firms in some area of the economy (say railroads, newspapers or breweries), instead of on a single firm or on a few firms. The task then becomes to study how these populations of firms at some point in time come into being, expand, and gradually decline. Another contribution, which has developed forcefully during the last decade, has to do with the diffusion of ideas or various ways of doing things in a population of firms (e.g. Davis 1991). The way that the social relations between the firms are structured, will clearly influence the speed as well as the range of the diffusion.

The main novelty, when it comes to recent sociological research on firms, however, has to do with entrepreneurship. While this topic was occasionally touched on in the 1980s, one could not really speak of a sociology of entrepreneurship—something which is possible today (e.g. Thornton 1999, Swedberg 2000). Mark Granovetter, for example, has helped to explain why people who are not particularly entrepreneurial in their home countries may become successful entrepreneurs once they are in a foreign environment (Granovetter 1995). The secret, Granovetter suggests, is that extended family ties may prevent entrepreneurship in the home country, but will be absent in the new country—with forceful entreprenurship as a result. AnnaLee Saxenian has added to Alfred Marshall's ideas about industrial districts through her study of Silicon Valley (Saxenian 1996). By contrasting the decentralized and informal social structure of Silicon Valley in California to the centralized and formal social structure of Route 128 in Massachusetts, Saxenian has tried to get a handle on the factors that are conducive to entrepreneurship. In his study of village enterprises in China, Yusheng Peng (2004) confirmed empirically a sociological hypothesis on informal privatization which explains property rights as arising from social norms of close-knit entrepreneurial networks.

Some New Topics (Finance, Law, Stratification, Comparative-Historical Studies)

While one may speak of a certain continuity in the study of networks, markets and firms among economic sociologists, even if new and important contributions have been made during the last decade, this is much less the case with the topics that will now be discussed. In *finance*, for example, a number of important developments have taken place during the last decade. Sophisticated analyses of the social mechanisms that operate in this type of markets have begun to appear, as exemplified by the studies of Donald MacKenzie and Ezra Zuckerman (MacKenzie 2003, MacKenzie and Millo 2003, Zuckerman 1999). In a study conducted with Yuval Millo, Donald MacKenzie argues that option markets may have been partly created with the help of economic theory—which is then used to explain the workings of this very market (so-called performativity theory). Ezra Zuckerman analyzes the penalties that firms have to pay that are not tracked by security analysts.

First and foremost, however, economic sociology has brought ethnography and culture to the study of finance, and thereby altered the kind of questions that may be asked and also what kind of material to look for. This way, for example, Viviana Zelizer has discovered that people in their everyday lives do not look on money as some unitary kind of substance, as most social theoreticians do, but rather divide it up into different monies or currencies (e.g. Zelizer 1989). Karin Knorr Cetina and Urs Brügger (2002) have drawn on phenomenology to analyze what it means for people such as brokers, to interact with each other with the help of computers.

Law and economics emerged as a distinct field of inquiry many years before modern economic sociology came into being, and at first attracted little attention among economic sociologists. Slowly, however, it has been realized by economic sociologists that *law* constitutes a central part of the modern economy; and a broad program for how to analyze its role from a sociological perspective has recently been formulated (Swedberg 2003a, 2003b; cf. Edelman and Stryker forthcoming). This program outlines the tasks that an "economic sociology of law" may want to undertake; it also points to a small number of already existing studies that are highly relevant in this context.

One of the most important of these already existing studies has been authored by Lauren Edelman, who is the modern pioneer in introducing a sociological approach to law and economics. She has especially suggested that one should bring together the study of organizations with that of law; and one of her earliest studies that does precisely this, deals with due process in the workplace (Edelman 1990). The same approach can also be found in another study, in which a related subject matter is analyzed, namely the legalization of the workplace (Sutton et al. 1994).

But there is more to the current attempt to develop a sociological approach to law and economics. There exists, for example, an innovative attempt to show how networks analysis may be of help in analyzing the social structure of illegal cartels (Baker and Faulkner 1993). There is also a study that suggests that the privatization process in Eastern Europe may have created a new type of property (Stark 1996).

To claim that the study of *stratification and wealth*, would represent a new topic for economic sociology may seem strange to everybody, except perhaps sociologists. Is it not precisely these two topics that economic sociology is all about, from Marx and Weber to C. Wright Mills and beyond? Questions of inequality, however, are today exclusively handled in sociology in a special subfield called stratification, and not in economic sociology. And wealth, as it turns out, is rarely studied at all in contemporary sociology. Recently, however, stratification experts and economic sociologists have begun to study wealth and also to relate it to the workings of the economy (e.g. Keister and Moller 2000, Spilerman 2000). Another illustration of the attempt to bring together the study of stratification with the workings of the economy, can be found in the work of Victor Nee (1989). Using recent changes in China as his empirical example, Nee argues that when a society goes from redistribution to exchange via the market, this tends to be reflected in its stratification system. This so-called market transition theory has led to a lively debate among sociologists (e.g. Cao and Nee 2000), which has stimulated research by economic sociologists to clarify the state's role in instituting the rise of a market economy and sustaining economic development in transition economies (e.g., Nee 2000; Walder 1995; Peng 2001).

Before concluding this brief overview of recent developments in economic sociology, something also needs to be said about the recent attempt to develop *a historical and comparative economic sociology*. Sociologists have a long and successful tradition of analyzing historical and comparative topics, and it is sometimes argued that these two topics represent areas where economic sociologists have comparative advantages in relation to economists. However that may be, to exemplify this trend a few studies of this type should be mentioned.

Some of these are historical in nature, such as the study by Carruthers and Espeland (1991) of the evolution of accounting and the one by Granovetter and McGuire (1998) of the social construction of the electrical utilities industry in the United States. Others cover different countries and periods, basically arguing that the same economic activities can be organized in different ways, and that there consequently is little support for the argument that there only exists one optimal way of doing things. Marion Fourcade-Gourinchas, for example, makes this point for economic theory itself, by showing how economic theory reflects the social environment of the countries in which it has emerged (Fourcade-Gourinchas 2001). Jens Beckert (forthcoming) traces the evolution of inheritance law in the United States, Germany and France since the 18th century in an exemplary study. Frank Dobbin, finally, suggests that the industrial policy of various countries differ from each other, but also that they are deeply influenced by the way that political power is organized (Dobbin 2001).

2. NEW INSTITUTIONALISM IN ECONOMIC SOCIOLOGY

After this brief introduction to recent developments in economic sociology, we shall proceed to a discussion of the concept of institution and to the question of how institutions are related to norms and similar social mechanisms. We will not provide an overview of what sociologists have said about institutions during the last century, not only because this would take up far too much space but also because it has already been done a number of times (e.g. DiMaggio and Powell 1991, pp. 1-38, Stinchcombe 1997). We shall instead limit ourselves to the following summary observation. While early sociologists tended to restrict the concept of institution to central and key aspects of society (such as politics, the economy and the family), some sociologists use it in a considerably broader sense. According to the view of so-called new institutionalism in organizational analysis (Powell and DiMaggio 1991), where the role of culture, sense-making and the diffusion models of behavior are emphasized, pretty much anything is viewed as an institution, including a dance and a handshake (e.g. Jepperson 1991). Organizational new institutionalists also tend to downplay the concept of interest and prefer instead to focus on those aspects of institutions that are not related to interests (DiMaggio 1988).

This view of institutions, we argue, tends to take the edge out of the concept of institution, which in our opinion should be restricted to those areas of society where interests come into play in an important and direct manner—such as politics, the economy and the family. The strength of institutions, we also argue, comes precisely from the fact that they channel interests or, to put it differently, present dominant models for how interests can be realized. These models are typically surrounded by a sense of legitimacy or they would not be stable over time. They are also often enforced by law because of their very centrality to society. Institutions have in some cases been consciously designed—say in a constitution—but they may also develop in a gradual and largely unintended manner, along the lines that Hayek suggests (e.g. Hayek 1982). Since institutions regulate areas of society that are of great importance to individuals, they are often contested and reflect struggles in society.

We suggest the following definition:

An institution may be conceptualized as *a dominant system of interrelated informal and formal elements—customs, shared beliefs, norms, and rules—which actors orient their actions to when they pursue their interests.* In this view, institutions are dominant social structures which provide a conduit for social and collective action by facilitating and structuring the interests of actors and enforcing principal agent relationships. It follows from this interest-related definition that institutional change involves not simply remaking the formal rules, but requires the realignment of interests, norms and power.[1] Institutions that are seen as legitimate or valid are, to repeat, also more enduring than institutions that are directly based on say force. To this may be added that individuals and corporate actors, in pursuing their interests, will want to follow the existing rules or models for how to proceed—or their chances for realizing their interests will diminish dramatically. The existing rules or models for how to proceed constitute elements of two kinds: formal and informal. For example, in their study of high-tech firms in Silicon Valley, Baron and Hannan (forthcoming) examine the effect of the entrepreneur's vision on the organizational form of start-up firms. Formal organizational rules typically reflect the laws and regulations of the institutional environment, say of the type that exists about the status of workers in the in the modern corporation. Informal elements, on the other hand, emerge as soon as things go from the drawing board to reality, influenced by the entrepreneur's vision and the informal norms and culture of the network assembled for the core group of the start up firm. The end result is always a mixture of formal and informal elements which comprise the firm's organizational form, and this original imprint has a long lasting effect on organizational performance. To the extent that formal and informal elements are also seen as legitimate (valid or binding), the corporation will also be able to function without being challenged.

The concept of institutions that we advocate is especially close to that of Douglass North, and we advocate that economic sociology adopt what we term an institutionalist perspective in their analysis (e.g. North 1990). North's distinction between institutions as rules and organizations as players is especially useful to our mind; we also agree with him that institutions are related to incentive structures. We, however, are also of the opinion that one may proceed further than North on a few crucial points. One of these is that the concept of interest should stand at the very center of what we mean by institution; another is that the current literature on institutions makes a much too sharp distinction between actor and structure—to the detriment of our understanding of institutions. We will briefly elaborate on both of these points.

Interests

Interests represent the basic forces that motivate and drive the individual; and they must for this reason also be at the center of the concept of institution.

---

[1] Development of an interest related approach to comparative institutional analysis is being pursued by Nee and Swedberg at the Center for the Study of Economy and Society at Cornell University (see www.economyandsociety.org).

Interests can be of different types, say ideal or material.[2] One way of putting interests at the center of the analysis is to conceptualize institutions as dominant models for how interests should be realized. The individual who wants to realize her self-interest will, following this approach, typically orient her actions to the institution; meaning by this that if she wants to realize her interests she will have to follow the general rules or prescriptions for how to behave. As Raymond Boudon (1987) insists, rationality is context-bound insofar as institutions determine the incentive structure. The individual may also chose *not* to follow the institutional model, in which case sanctions will typically occur. Implicit in the choices made by individuals is consideration of costs and benefits entailed in a course of action. By emphasizing the independence of the actor (through the notion of "orienting oneself to rules", rather than simply "following rules"), we proceed in the spirit of methodological individualism.

When one presents the concept of institution as a dominant model for how to realize interests, it is important not to emphasize the element of model to the point that the individual disappears; hence new institutional economic sociology, like economics, focuses on self-interest as motivation for action. The reason for this is that society does not consist of models or rules but of ongoing activities, and similarly there are no institutions per se but only *institutions in action*. This means that ongoing institutions are invested with the power that comes from a number of individuals acting out their patterns of behavior in an effort to realize their interests, and it is precisely *this* that gives institutions their enormous force and importance in society. If institutions are hard to change, it is not only because models of behavior are hard to change because of inertia (an important topic in its own right), but because they are invested with the force that comes from interests-in-action (e.g., Nee forthcoming).

The concept of institution that we are proposing takes two key ideas of economics very seriously: the idea of interest and the idea of methodological individualism; and this is an important reason why we term it a new institutionalist perspective. As sociologists, however, we also want to highlight the role that social relations and norms play in the concept of institutions; and we shall now turn to the challenge of specifying and explicating the social mechanisms that determine the relationship between the informal social organization of close-knit groups and the formal rules of institutional structures monitored and enforced by organizations and states.

Informal Institutional Elements

It is clear that new institutional economics has forcefully contributed to explaining the emergence and maintenance of formal institutional arrangements that

---

[2] Economic sociologists and new institutional economists concur in assigning a huge importance to the role of political motives and ideology in social analysis. We differ, however, in that we suggest (with Max Weber) that this type of motives be termed "ideal motives" since they basically operate as driving forces, similar to economic interests. Also religious and altruistic motives qualify as ideal interests according to this terminology.

shape economic behavior. However, as North (1993:12) acknowledges, economics has largely "ignored the informal constraints of conventions and norms of behavior." Economists pose probing questions about the social dimensions of economic life as they encounter the limits of economic analysis of institutions (e.g. North 1991; Williamson 2000). Their questions address the manner in which informal social organization, formal rules and interests *combine* to shape the performance of organizations and economies. With recent advances in application of game theory, economists recently have also begun to incorporate informal institutional elements into their models of economic performance (Greif 2004; forthcoming). While economic sociologists may not have all the answers, clearly in cross-disciplinary research aimed at explaining the capacity of social institutions to facilitate, motivate and govern economic behavior, sociology's comparative advantage is to address questions that focus on the social mechanisms that channel economic interests and shape economic behavior. Such mechanisms are embedded in networks and norms, the informal institutional elements sociologists have emphasized in their studies of economic life.

While Figure 1 outlines the way institutions are sometimes seen in new institutional economics, Figure 2 provides a schematic representation of the multi-level causal model for the new institutionalism in economic sociology, which is related to but different from the new institutionalist models proposed by Williamson (1994). The institutional environment—the formal regulatory rules monitored and enforced by the state that govern property rights, markets

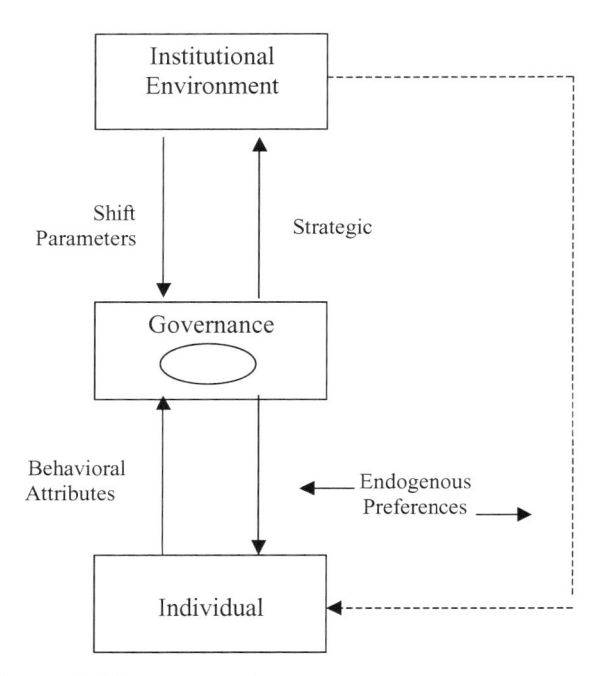

Figure 1. A model of new institutional economics.

Source: Williamson 1994: 80.

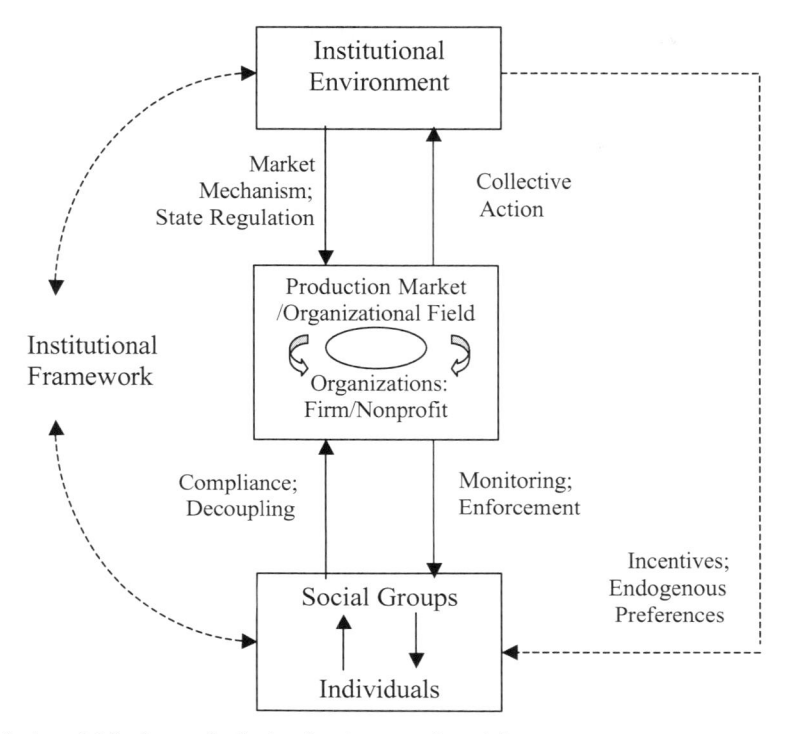

Figure 2. A model for the new institutionalism in economic sociology.
Source: Nee (Forthcoming).

and firms—imposes constraints on firms through market mechanisms and state regulation, thus shaping the incentives structure and the notions of how interests can be realized. The institutional mechanisms operating at this level are distal, as opposed to the proximate social mechanisms at the micro- and meso-levels of individuals and their interpersonal ties.

Institutional mechanisms encompass the deeper causes because they shape the incentive structure for organizations and individuals, and thereby the *contexts* in which proximate mechanisms operate and interests are realized. The institutional-level mechanisms posited by economists and sociologists, despite differences in behavioral assumptions and conceptual language, are not as far apart as is commonly perceived. New institutional economists emphasize incentives reinforced by the monitoring and enforcement of formal rules, a mechanism widely accepted by both political economy and sociology. The new institutionalism in economic sociology specifies the manner in which the norms of close-knit groups interact with formal rules in the realization of interests.

The variety of market mechanisms schematically represented in the downward arrow from the institutional environment to the organizations includes those embedded in labor markets, capital markets, raw material markets, and so on. Surprisingly perhaps, economists generally don't focus on markets as such, but just assume their existence in the neoclassical view of perfect competition in markets underlying the supply-demand curve. The institutional framework encompasses formal rules of the institutional environment and norms embedded in ongoing social relations, which interact to shape economic behavior. Whether conceived as an organizational field or a production market, sociologists tend to focus on the dynamics of interfirm relations to explain the behavior of individual firms. Paul DiMaggio and Walter Powell (1983) explain the surprising similarity of organizational practices in an organizational field of related firms by reference to the value of legitimacy to the firm's survival and success. Similarly, Harrison White (1981, 2001) models the social structure of so-called production markets as arising from firms competing and maneuvering for advantage and status with peer firms in a market niche. They are guided by the signals they read from the operations of their peers. In competitive markets, pressures on firms stemming from Darwinian selection processes necessitate an *interest-related* logic of strategic action, differing in emphasis from the *legitimacy-centered* orientation of nonprofit organizations—public schools, museums, day-care centers—which are dependent on state and federal government and philanthropy for resources.

Legitimacy is also important for enterprises, as manifest in firms' investments in promoting brand-name recognition, reputation for reliability and quality service or product, and compliance with federal and state laws, but legitimacy-seeking is driven mainly by the firm's interest in its survival and profitability in competitive markets. For nonprofit organizations, especially, legitimacy is an essential social capital increasing the chances for optimizing access to scarce resources. For both, legitimacy can be viewed as a condition of fitness which enables for-profit firms and nonprofit organizations to enhance their survival chances and secure advantages in economic and political markets. Processes of conformity with the rules of the game and cultural beliefs in organizational fields—*isomorphism*—motivate and guide organizations, endogenously giving rise to increasing homogeneity within an organizational field (DiMaggio and Powell 1983).

The bottom box of this multi-level causal model overlaps with the earlier embeddedness concept, which argue that the *nature* and *structure* of social relationships have more to do with governing economic behavior than do institutional arrangements for realizing interests and related organizational form. Specifically, Granovetter (1985: 490) refers to the "role of concrete personal relations and structures (or 'networks') of such relations in generating trust and discouraging malfeasance," which he attributes to the human preference for transacting with individuals known to be trustworthy and for abstention from opportunism. But what explains motivation for trustworthiness and abstention from opportunism in ongoing social relationships? Why is trustworthiness found more commonly in ongoing social relationships than in transactions between strangers?

The answer is to be found by specifying the *mechanisms* intrinsic to social relationships that develop and maintain cooperative behavior within close-knit groups, enabling actors to engage in collective action to achieve their interests. These mechanisms are rewards and punishment in social exchange and their use in the *enforcement* of social norms—shared beliefs and statements about expected behavior.[3] Peter Blau's (1955) classic field study of social exchange and networks in a federal bureaucracy, *The Dynamics of Bureaucracy*, confirms the efficacy of social rewards and punishment in facilitating, motivating and governing trustworthy behavior and group performance.[4] In his detailed account of the interactions in the work group he studied made up of a supervisor, sixteen agents and one clerk, Blau provides a rare illustration of *institutions in action*: how self-interested action of individuals endogenously produce the informal social organization of a close-knit work group. In the work group Blau studied, agents consult fellow agents about the appropriate legal rules that apply to their case, rather than bring their questions to the attention of their supervisor who evaluates their work. Blau observed that the informal interactions between agents involve a *social exchange* similar in logic to a decentralized market exchange:

"A consultation can be considered an exchange of values; both participants gain something, and both have to pay a price. The questioning agent is enabled to perform better than he could otherwise have done, without exposing his difficulties to the supervisor. By asking for advice, he implicitly pays his respect to the superior proficiency of his colleague. This acknowledgement of inferiority is the cost of receiving assistance. The consultant gains prestige, in return for which he is willing to devote some time to the consultation and permit it to disrupt his own work. The following remark of an agent illustrates this: 'I like giving advice. It's flattering, I suppose, if you feel that the others come to you for advice.'" (quoted from Homans 1974, p. 343).

Blau found that the more competent the agent, the more contacts she had with other agents, and the higher the esteem in which she was held. A few agents who were perceived as competent but who discouraged others from consulting them were disliked and had fewer contacts. These findings highlight the importance of social rewards and sanctions (e.g. esteem and disapproval) in the normative regulation of informal social organization (Homans 1974). Routine social exchanges, such as the one described by Blau, comprise the informal social organization that emerges and sustains the performance of formal organizations.

Norms are the informal rules that facilitate, motivate and govern joint action of members of close-knit groups, including attempts to realize their interests. They arise from the problem-solving activity of individuals as rule-of-thumb guidelines of expected behavior; and they are typically maintained through some sanction such as disapproval. Throughout history, norms have coordinated group action to improve the chances for success—the attainment of rewards and the realization of interests—through cooperation. As statements of shared beliefs about expected behavior, norms probably evolved together with language, as in the norms uttered by early hunting parties to coordinate action during the

---

[3] Social ties and norms do not themselves constitute mechanisms insofar as they are concepts referring to elements of social structure—the relationship connecting two or more actors and the informal rules governing the relationship (Homans 1974; Nee and Ingram 1998; Emerson 1962; Blau 1964).

[4] See Roethlisberg and Dickson (1939; Whyte (1943); Festinger, Schachter, and Back (1950); Schachter et.al. (1951); Jennings (1950); Seashore (1954); Bott (1957); Riley and Cohn (1958); Walker and Heyns (1962); Cook et.al. (1983); Ellickson (1991); Petersen (1992); Kollock (1994); Lawler and Yoon (1996).

course of the expedition. Norms presumably evolved through trial and error, with success the arbiter of why a particular norm persists in equilibrium across generations and diffuses to different groups.[5] Members of close-knit groups cooperate in enforcing norms not only because their interests are linked to the group's success, but their identity as well (White 1992).

The relationship between informal and formal institutional elements

In uncovering the social norms of Shasta County, a sparsely settled rural county of northern California, where local ranchers and suburbanites maintain multiplex relationships, Ellickson "was struck that they seemed consistently utilitarian;" from which he inferred that *"members of a close-knit group develop and maintain norms whose content serves to maximize the aggregate welfare that members obtain in their workaday affairs with one another"* (Ellickson 1991:167). Norms coordinating individuals' activities, as in the convention of arriving in a timely fashion at an agreed-upon social engagement, are not difficult to explain since it is easy to show that self-interested individuals share a common interest in complying with this convention. But the prisoner's dilemma norm is more difficult to explain since self-interested individuals derive a greater payoff for opportunism in a prisoner's dilemma game. What makes this game so important is that this type of dilemma is such a common feature of social and economic life. It is also the prisoner's dilemma aspects of human interaction that give rise to opportunism in contractual agreements and in ongoing social relationships. To some degree, all social exchange resembles the prisoner dilemma game insofar as there is always a temptation not to reciprocate a good turn provided by a friend or acquaintance (Hardin 1988). The prisoner's dilemma norm involves higher costs of monitoring and enforcement than coordination norms because it is always in the self-interest of individuals to free ride or defect. Hence, prisoner's dilemma norms must be welfare-maximizing in terms of the Kaldor-Hicks criterion in order to create sufficient rewards to individuals to overcome the temptation to do so (Ellickson 1991:171; Posner 1986:11-5).

The nature of the relationship between informal social groups and formal organizations can substantially affect the cost of monitoring and enforcement of formal rules in institutional and organizational environments. The norms of close-knit groups can contribute to the realization of the organization's goal if the interests embedded in welfare-maximizing norms are broadly speaking congruous with the incentives embedded in the formal rules. This condition is met when members of close-knit groups or networks perceive that their preferences and interests are aligned with the organization's capacity to survive and profit. It is strengthened when members of networks identify with the organization's goals.

---

[5] Shibutani (1978) provides detailed observations about the emergence and maintenance of norms of a close-knit group of Japanese American soldiers in a military base, documenting norm emergence as a product of collective problem-solving as members of the group socially construct a definition of the situation and course of action that optimizes their welfare.

This gives rise to endogenous motivation in networks to enforce formal rules, which substantially lowers the cost for organizations to monitor and enforce through formal sanctioning mechanisms, providing the necessary and sufficient conditions for high-level group performance in line with formal organizational goals.[6]

In contrast, when the formal rules are at odds with the interests and identity of individuals in close-knit groups, the welfare-maximizing hypothesis predicts the rise of so-called *opposition norms* that facilitate, motivate and govern the action of individuals in those groups. Opposition norms enable networks to coordinate action to resist either passively, through slow-down or non-compliance, or actively, in manifest defiance of formal rules and the authority of organizational leaders. This leads to increase in the cost of monitoring and enforcing formal rules as incidence of opportunism and malfeasance increases. There is also a higher level of uncertainty and information asymmetry as members of close-knit networks collectively withhold information that might lead to discovery of opportunism and malfeasance. When group performance facilitated, motivated and governed by opposition norms reaches a tipping point, the necessary and sufficient conditions for demoralization and oppositional movements at the organizational and institutional levels are met. *The incentives and disincentives emanating from the institutional environment, in combination with interests, needs and preferences of individuals, influence whether norms and networks give rise to a close coupling of informal and formal rules, or to a decoupling through opposition norms.*

In new institutionalist economic sociology purposive action by corporate actors and individuals (usually in close-knit networks) cannot be understood apart from the institutional framework within which interests have to be realized. For example, despite differences in local and regional history and culture, the laws and regulations monitored and enforced by the federal government apply to all regions of the United States, with very few exceptions. Variations in locality and region may limit the effectiveness of monitoring and enforcement, but they do not give rise to different underlying rules. Not only is the constitutional framework invariant, but federal rules aim to extend the power of the central state uniformly. As North's (1981) theory of the state emphasizes, the state is the sovereign actor specifying the framework of rules that govern competition and cooperation in a society. It has the power to enact and enforce laws and initiate institutional innovations to secure and uphold public goods and respond to changing relative prices (Stiglitz 1989).

Laws

Laws, like norms, are statements of expected behavior, backed by state power. Or, in Weber's formulation: when rules of expected behavior are enforced through

---

[6] However, close coupling between informal and formal rules does not necessarily give rise to success. Indeed, population ecologists argue that the environment selects adaptive organizational forms independent of the collective will and effort of individuals acting within the organization (Hannan and Freeman 1989).

the coercive actions by a specially created staff of people, we have a law (Weber 1978:34). Whether laws are seen as based on as ideology or cultural beliefs, they define the parameters of legitimate behavior to which organizations and individuals have to adapt and orient their actions. In keeping with their disciplinary traditions, economists emphasize the costs of opposing the coercive forces of the state, and organizational sociologists emphasize the value of legitimacy gained through recurrent compliance with the state's rules. But in actuality whether the price of noncompliance is perceived as costs imposed by fines and penalties or as a loss of legitimacy, is moot in the sense that both are costly to the firm.

The institutional mechanisms of monitoring and enforcement operate directly on firms and nonprofit organizations through the costs of penalties and withholding of federal grants and contracts, but also have indirect effects. The increase in costs of discrimination—loss of legitimacy and financial penalty—following the Civil Rights era and its institutional changes decisively opened U.S. mainstream organizations to formerly excluded ethnic and racial groups (Alba and Nee 2003). The civil rights movement and the legislative changes enacted by Congress created a normative environment in which legitimacy was conditioned on fair governance through formal protections of the principle of equality of rights (e.g. Edelman 1990, 1992). Equal Employment Opportunity Law (EEO) defined broad parameters and guidelines of legitimate organizational practices with respect to minorities and women.

Because the civil rights era laws have weak enforcement features and are ambiguously stated, organizations construct the meaning of compliance "in a manner that is minimally disruptive of the status quo" (Edelman 1992:1535). This enables organizations to gain legitimacy and resources through the appearance of abiding by civil rights legislation. However, "once in place, EEO/AA structures may produce or bolster internal constituencies that help to institutionalize EEO/AA goals" (Edelman 1992:1569). The civil rights era laws may have their largest impact indirectly through professionals who generate "ideologies of rationality" or cultural beliefs about how organizations should respond to the law. Not only do high profile landmark court cases (e.g., Texaco, Coca-Cola)impose direct costs through penalties and loss of legitimacy to specific firms, but a more far-reaching effect of these court decisions, along with legal advice about what organizations can do to insulate themselves from costly litigation, is to generate cultural beliefs about the rationality of self-monitored compliance with anti-discriminatory laws. This is manifested in the diffusion of EEO-specified grievance procedures in organizations (Edelman, Uggen and Erlanger 1999). Thus ideologies of rationality and cultural beliefs have combined with the incentives and disincentives of the institutional environment, mediated by state regulation and market mechanism. This is consistent with causal model in Figure 2, suggesting that mechanisms of isomorphism align with the structure of incentives stemming from formal rules of the institutional environment.

3. SOME ILLUSTRATIVE STUDIES IN NEW INSTITUTIONAL ECONOMIC SOCIOLOGY

The causal model in new institutionalist economic sociology integrates a microfoundation based on an account of the rational pursuit of interests as context-bound, influenced by social relations and norms, with the idea that each economy has an institutional framework. As Figure 2 indicates, causal mechanisms operate in both directions, from macro to micro and micro to macro levels of analysis. The multi-level causal model therefore moves well beyond the earlier embeddedness perspective towards a social relations *and* institutions-approach that can better explain the emergence, persistence and transformation of economic institutions and behavior. As a conceptual framework, the new institutionalism in economic sociology also offers an open architecture for generating theories at the middle range, extending in this manner the sociological approach to understanding economic behavior. The central challenge in new institutional economic sociology is to specify and explicate the nature of the relationships between elements at different levels of the multi-level causal model, in order to explain how informal social organizations interact with large institutional structures. Here are two illustrations of such use of a multi-level causal model.

Example # 1: A Weberian Model of Economic Growth

Evans and Rauch (1999) specify a multi-level causal model to examine the effect of Weberian state structures on economic growth in developing economies. They argue that the characteristic feature of the institutional framework of the development state, as opposed to the predatory state, is the presence of relatively well-developed bureaucratic forms of public administration. As Weber argued in his theory of bureaucracy, the introduction of merit-based recruitment offering predictable career ladders established the basis for long-term commitments to bureaucratic service. Whether in the Meiji era bureaucracy in Japan or in late-developing industrial economies like China, the development of modern bureaucratic capacity at the service of reform politicians was critical to the government's ability to monitor and enforce rules oriented to the promotion of economic development. At the level of individual action, close-knit groups of elite bureaucrats share norms and goals shaped by meritocratic rules for recruitment and promotion, which reduces the attractiveness of corruption. This Weberian model provides an alternative to Shleifer and Vishny's (1994:1023) "grabbing hand of the state"-model that conflates bureaucrats and politicians, showing that politicians invariably "try to influence firms to pursue political objectives" inconsistent with the objective of economic growth. In the Weberian model, bureaucrats are distinct from politicians insofar as they are vested with long-term careers governed by meritocratic rules of recruitment and promotion. Norms, shared belief in meritocratic service, and national development goals not only reduce the temptation of corruption but over time give rise to competence

808 Victor Nee and Richard Swedberg

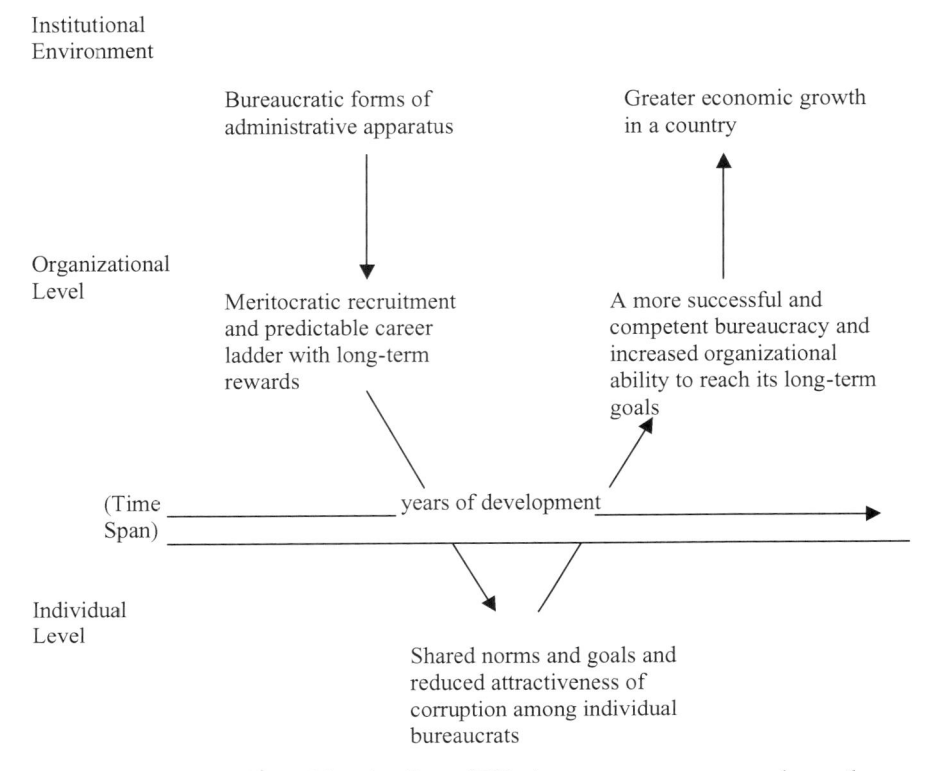

```
Institutional
Environment
                    Bureaucratic forms of              Greater economic growth
                    administrative apparatus           in a country
                                │                              ▲
                                │                              │
Organizational                  ▼                              │
Level               Meritocratic recruitment      A more successful and
                    and predictable career        competent bureaucracy and
                    ladder with long-term         increased organizational
                    rewards                       ability to reach its long-term
                                    ╲                 goals
                                     ╲                  ▲
                                      ╲                ╱
(Time _____ years of development _____▶
Span)   ───────────────────────────────────────────────────────────────────
                                     ╱  ╲
                                    ▼    ╲
Individual
Level
                    Shared norms and goals and
                    reduced attractiveness of
                    corruption among individual
                    bureaucrats
```

Figure 3. Evans and Rauch's model on the effects of Weberian state structure on economic growth.

and credibility of commitment to civil service dedicated to the public good. The result is increased organizational capacity of the state, which in turn enables and motivates reform-minded rulers to increase revenues through economic growth rather than predation.

Example # 2: A Dynamic Game Theoretic Model of De-institutionalization

A multi-level causal model provides analytic leverage for the understanding of the emergence of market economies in post-socialist China, Eastern Europe and the former Soviet Union. When Western economists traveled to Eastern Europe and the former Soviet Union to advise reformers at the onset of market reforms, their advice consistently emphasized big bang approaches to instituting a market economy by designing sweeping changes in the formal rules governing property rights and markets. They assumed that formal rules—i.e., constitution, civil law and other regulations—instituted by administrative fiat would succeed in establishing a modern capitalist economy (e.g. Sachs 1995). Such efforts at capitalism by fiat change in the rules of the game overlooked the realities of power and interests vested in the ruins of communism.[7]

By contrast, the incremental reform approach taken by reformers in China allowed economic actors to base their choices of institutions on trial-and-error that balanced speed with a credible record of success. This more evolutionary approach to market transition soon gave rise to the most dynamic economy in the world. In China, institutional change was driven not so much by top-down changes in the formal rules, as by bottom-up realignment of interests and power as new organizational forms, private property rights and market institutions evolved in an economy shifting away from central state control over economic activity to market-driven firm performance.[8] Changes in formal rules governing the emerging market economy tended to follow ex post changes in the informal business practices, and were therefore more in keeping with the real interests of political and economic actors.[9] As in the former Soviet Union, however, efforts to reform state-owned enterprises through formal rule changes in China also proved largely ineffectual because, in part, ex ante changes in formal rules often ran counter to the vested interests and conflicting sources of legitimacy of the communist party organization entrenched in state-owned firms.

Nee and Lian's dynamic game theory model (1994) of declining ideological and political commitment helps to explain the de-institutionalization of the communist party in departures from central planning in transition economies. The technological and military gap that grew during the Cold War between the advanced market economies and state socialist countries precipitated reform efforts by communist elites to narrow the gap through innovations that sought to incorporate in the institutional framework of central planning increased reliance on the market mechanism. But at the individual level of party bureaucrats and officials, the growth of economic and political markets increased the payoff for opportunism and malfeasance, which in turn sparked within close-knit groups of party members a group-based social dynamic leading to declining ideological and political commitment to the communist party. This is demonstrated in a tipping point model wherein opportunism and malfeasance among party members, initially small, eventually reaches a critical mass. The reform leaders in the party attempt to address the problem through campaigns aimed at punishing malfeasance.

Over time, however, declining commitment reaches a critical tipping point, precipitating demoralization and collapse of the communist party as an effective ruling organization. This in turn paves the way for de-institutionalization

---

[7] For analyses of how institutional change by administrative design and formal rule change faltered in Eastern Europe and Russia, see e.g. Stark (1996), Gray and Hendley (1997), Hellman (1997), Varese (2001).

[8] For analyses by economic sociologists of realignment of power and interests favoring economic actors in market transitions and institutional change in China, see e.g. Walder (1995), Nee (1996), Cao (2001), Guthrie (1999), Keister (2000).

[9] See e.g. Shirk (1993); Naughton (1995); Opper, Wong and Hu (2002) for analyses of how economic and political actors benefited from institutional change.

Figure 4

Level			
Institutional Environment	A rapid growing technological and economic gap between state socialist economies and the advanced market economies		Regime change in reforming state socialism
Organizational Level	Communist reformers' initiation of economic reform in state socialist economies		Deterioration and collapse of the communist party as an effective political organization
(Time Span)	years of market transition →		
Individual Level		Increasing opportunism and declining commitment to the communist party among agents of the state	

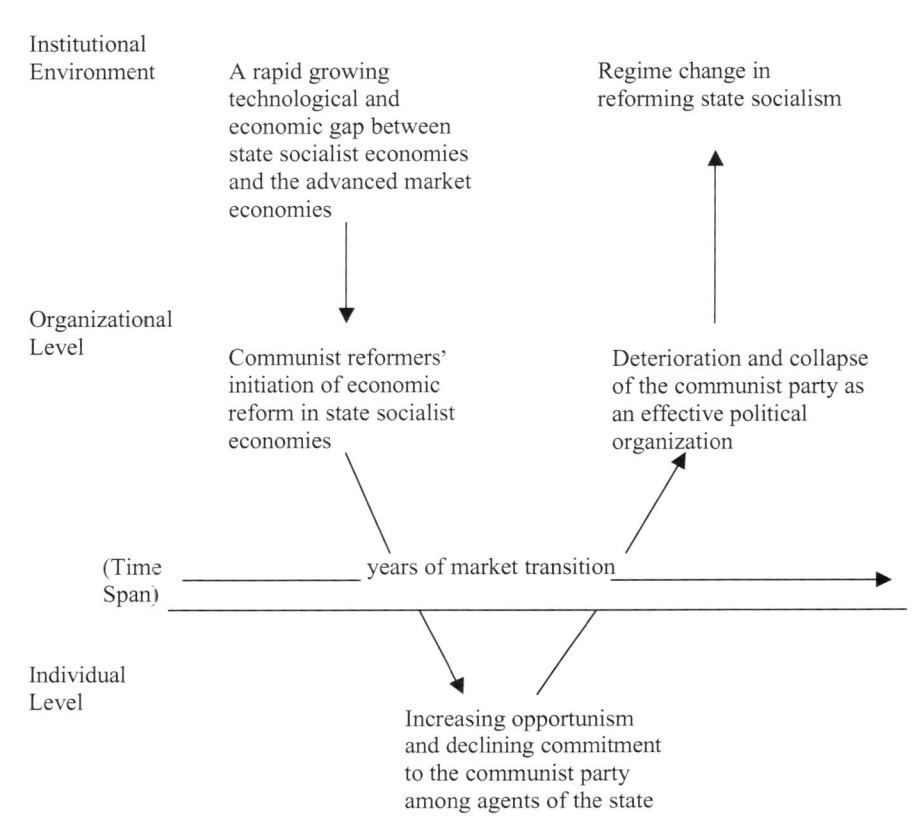

Figure 4. Nee and Lian's dynamic model of declining political commitment in state socialism.

of the party and far-reaching change in political institutions, including political revolution, in reforming state socialism. This model provides an explanation for declining organizational performance highlighting the embedded nature of ideological commitment among party members and specifying the social dynamics that produce the tidal shift from commitment to the party's rules and goals to widespread opportunism and defection. The model links change in the incentive structure of the institutional environment—from redistribution to market—to the emergence in close-knit party networks of belief in opportunism as the expected behavior, presently, in a ruling party founded on an ideology opposed to such behavior. This sociological explanation for the rapid and relatively nonviolent collapse of communist polities in Eastern Europe and the former Soviet Union is an alternative to standard economic and political interpretations (Aslund 1995; Beissinger 2002). In China and Vietnam, where communist parties still retain power, the model predicts a cumulative decline of ideological and organizational commitment to the party and a greater reliance on bureaucrats rather than politicians in state-crafted institutional change oriented to building a market economy.

4. Concluding Remarks

By way of concluding we would first of all like to note that the sociological analysis of the nature of the relationships between networks, norms and large institutional structures in economic life is still at an early stage. As economic sociology refines and deepens its explanation of the nature of these relationships, it will necessarily draw on a variety of methodological and theoretical tools. Insights from cognitive science, game theory and computer simulation of the emergence, diffusion and transformation of norms and beliefs can all contribute to a deepened understanding of the micro-macro links. These methods can also contribute to a better understanding of the joint stabilizing impact of customs, conventions, norms, beliefs and interests.

Central to the research agenda of the new institutionalist approach that we are advocating is to bring comparative institutional analysis back into economic sociology. Much of this work to date has involved qualitative historical analysis of one or two cases. While such work has led to some important advances in understanding the relationship between institutions and economic behavior, the use of quantitative methods moving beyond case studies to engage systematic cross-national firm-level studies is indispensable in the attempt to specify and explicate how variable features of the institutional environment affect firms' behavior in the global economy. Comparative institutional analysis of firm-centric data on sources of perceived costs in the institutional environment offers, for example, a promising approach to the measurement of transaction costs. Though transaction cost is the core theoretical concept of new institutional economics, economists have yet to measure this concept in a way that is useful for empirical analysis.[10] As it refers to the costs stemming from uncertainty and information asymmetry embedded in social relations (e.g., the principal agent relationship), it is a concept of significant interest to sociologists as well. The development of standardized indexes of transaction costs arising from a variety of institutional sources (i.e., property rights, uncertainty, transparency of rules, resource dependence, bureaucracy, government regulation, state predation) using firm-centric data opens the way for a more differentiated account of how the institutional environment influences economic behavior.[11] Economic sociologists can also fruitfully extend the ecological reasoning of organizational sociology to examine discrete patterns in institutional environments that support distinct organizational forms. For example, what features of the institutional

---

[10] North and Wallis (1986) estimated the size of the transaction sector of the American economy; however, their aggregate data is not very useful for empirical analysis.

[11] Firm-centric data, rather than aggregate national-level data, is needed to measure transaction costs, which are the costs to firms of negotiating, securing and completing economic transactions. The problem with national level aggregate data is that it does not measure the effect of variation in institutional conditions on the firm and entrepreneur.

environment—"institutional ecology"—support modern public-owned corporations as opposed to the traditional family-owned firms in the global economy?

The idea of path dependence, imported into economics from the physical sciences, has deepened social science understanding of institutional change (Nelson and Winter 1982; David 1986; Arthur 1988). Path dependence refers to the lock-in effects stemming from initial conditions on subsequent development and change in the institutional environment. Economic historians have used this idea in a productive manner to explain the stability of institutions and the persistence of institutional arrangements that may later be inefficient for economic actors, given changes in relative prices (North 1990; Greif [1994] 1998). Hamilton and Feenstra (1998:173) show that the idea of path dependence is adumbrated in Weber's theory of economic rationalization, which maintains that "entrepreneurial strategy is necessarily embedded in an array of existing economic interactions and organizations." Further research is also needed to deepen understanding of path dependent institutional change and especially of the relationship between the persistence of informal institutional elements and change in formal rules (Nee and Cao 1999). It is the very stability of informal institutional elements—customs, networks, norms, cultural beliefs—that together with a distinct constellation of interestsaccount for path dependence in institutional arrangements.

There is also the important issue that Douglass North in his recent work has drawn our attention to in a forceful manner, namely that shared mental models play an important but neglected role in economic life. His main sources of inspiration in this enterprise have been recent advances in cognitive science and Hayek's *Sensory Order* (e.g. Denzau and North 1994, Hayek 1952). To these sources we would like to add the century long attempt of Weberian-style sociology to introduce the perspective of the individual actor into the analysis in a stringent manner, which is known as "interpretive sociology" (Weber 1978; for an elaboration, see e.g. Schutz 1967). Weber was active long before the birth of modern cognitive science, but we would nonetheless argue that some of his ideas on this topic are still relevant. For a quick illustration we refer the reader toWeber's well-known argument about the way that the mental models of religion may channel and direct economic actions in various ways. In Weber's famous formulation:

> Not ideas, but material and ideal interests, directly govern men's conduct. Yet very frequently the 'world images' [of religion] that have been created by 'ideas' have, like switchmen, determined the tracks along which action has been pushed by the dynamic of interest. (Weber 1946:280)

Finally, just as economists may find it useful to incorporate the idea of networks into their models of the economy, so economic sociology can benefit from integrating economic ideas that are complementary to the modern sociological approach. Economic exchange, for example, can be seen as a specialized form of social exchange (Homans 1974:68); hence the mechanisms facilitating, motivating and governing social processes also extend to economic behavior. Cross-disciplinary trade with economics has been immensely useful to sociology in the past, as evident in the extensive borrowing from economics by the founders of modern sociology, and in the influence of imported ideas such as human capital, signaling and path dependence. New institutional economic sociology, we are convinced, is well positioned to benefit from and contribute to intellectual trade with economists, especially in light of their turn to sociology for understanding about the social dimension of economic life.

Acknowledgement

We want to thank Claude Ménard both for his patience and for his inspiration to write this chapter. We draw on some of the material in Nee (forthcoming) and Swedberg (forthcoming), but also add to our joint theoretical argument about institutions and norms.

References

Akerlof, George and Rachel Kranton. 2000. "Economics of Identity". *Quarterly Journal of Economics* 15: 715–753.
Alba, Richard, and Victor Nee. 2003. *Remaking the American Mainstream: Assimilation and Contemporary Immigration*. Cambridge, MA: Harvard University Press.
Arthur, Brian W. 1988. "Self-Reinforcing Mechanisms in Economics" in P.W. Anderson and Kenneth J. Arrow (eds.), *The Economy as an Evolving Complex System*. Menlo Park, CA: Assison-Wesley, pp. 9–32.
Aslund, Anders. 1995. *How Russia Became a Market Economy*. Washington, DC: The Brookings Institution.
Aspers, Patrik. 2001. "A Market in Vogue: Fashion Photography in Sweden". *European Societies* 3(1): 1–22.
Aspers, Patrik. Forthcoming. *A Market in Vogue: A Study of Fashion Photography in Sweden*. London: Routledge.
Baker, Wayne and Robert Faulkner. 1993. "The Social Organization of Conspiracy: Illegal Networks in the Heavy Electrical Industry". *American Sociological Review* 58: 837–860.
Baron, James N. and Michael T. Hannan. Forthcoming. "The Economic Sociology of Organizational Entrepreneurship: Lessons from the Stanford Project on Emerging Companies" in Victor Nee and Richard Swedberg (eds.), *The Economic Sociology of Capitalism*. Princeton, NJ: Princeton University Press.
Beissinger, Mark R. 2002. *Nationalist Mobilization and the Collapse of the Soviet State*. Cambridge: Cambridge University Press.
Blau, Peter. 1955. *The Dynamics of Bureaucracy*, 2nd edn. Chicago, IL: University of Chicago Press.
Blau, Peter. 1964. *Exchange and Power in Social Life*. New York: Wiley.
Bott, Elizabeth. 1957. *Family and Social Network*. London: Tavistock Publications.
Bourdieu, Pierre. 2000. *Les Structures Sociales de l'Economie*. Paris: Seuil.
Brinton, Mary C. and Victor Nee (eds.). 1998. *The New Institutionalism in Sociology*. New York: Russell Sage Foundation.
Burt, Ronald. 1993. "The Social Structure of Competition" in Richard Swedberg (ed.), *Explorations in Economic Sociology*. New York: Russell Sage Foundation, pp. 65–103.
Cao, Yang and Victor Nee. 2000. "Comment: Controversies and Evidence in the Market Transition Debate". *American Journal of Sociology* 105(2000): 1175–1189.
Cao, Yang. 2001. "Careers inside Organizations: A Comparative Analysis of Promotion Determination in Reforming China". *Social Forces* 80: 683–712.

Carruthers, Bruce and Wendy Nelson Espeland. 1991. "Accounting for Rationality: Double-Entry Bookkeeping and the Rhetoric of Economic Rationality". *American Journal of Sociology* 97: 31–69.

Cook, Karen S., Richard M. Emerson, Mary R. Gillmore, and Toshio Yamagishi. 1983. "The Distribution of Power in Exchange Networks: Theory and Experimental Results". *American Journal of Sociology* 89: 275–305.

David, Paul. 1986. "Understanding the Economics of QWERTY: The Necessity of History" in W. Parker (ed.), *Economic History and the Modern Historian*. London: Blackwell, pp. 30–49.

Davis, Gerald. 1991. "Agents without Principles? The Spread of the Poison Pill through the Intercorporate Network". *Administrative Science Quarterly* 36: 583–613.

Denzau, Arthur and Douglass North. 1994. "Shared Mental Models: ideologies and Institutions". *Kyklos* 47: 3–31.

DiMaggio, Paul and Hugh Louch. 1998. "Socially Embedded Consumer Transactions: For What Kind of Purchases Do People Most Often Use Networks?". *American Sociological Review* 63: 619–637.

DiMaggio, Paul J. and Walter Powell. 1983. "The Iron Cage Revisited: Institutional Isomorphism and Collective Rationality in Organizational Fields". *American Sociological Review* 48: 147–160.

DiMaggio, Paul J. and Walter Powell. 1991. "Introduction" in Walter Powell and Paul DiMaggio (eds.), *The New Institutionalism in Organizational Analysis*. Chicago, IL: University of Chicago Press, pp. 1–38.

DiMaggio, Paul. 1988. "Interest and Agency in Institutional Theory" in Lynn Zucker (ed.), *Institutional Patterns and Organizations*. Cambridge: Ballinger Publishing Company, pp. 3–21.

Dobbin, Frank and Dirk Zorn. Forthcoming. "The Rise of the Financial Officer in U.S. Corporations". *Social Forces*.

Dobbin, Frank. 2001. "Why the Economy Reflects the Polity: Early Rail Policy in Britain, France, and the United States" in Mark Granovetter and Richard Swedberg (eds.), *The Sociology of Economic Life*, 2nd edn. Boulder, CO: Westview, pp. 401–424.

Edelman, Lauren and Robin Stryker. Forthcoming. "Law and the Economy" in Neil Smelser and Richard Swedberg (eds.), *The Handbook of Economic Sociology*. 2nd rev. edn. New York and Princeton: Russell Sage Foundation and Princeton University Press.

Edelman, Lauren B., Christopher Uggen, and Howard S. Erlanger. 1999. "The Endogeneity of Legal Regulation: Grievance Procedures as Rational Myth". *American Journal of Sociology* 105: 406–454.

Edelman, Lauren. 1990. "Legal Environments and Organizational Governance: The Expansion of Due Process in the American Workplace", *American Journal of Sociology* 95: 1401–1440.

Edelman, Lauren. 1992. "Legal Ambiguity and Symbolic Structures: Organizational Mediation of Civil Rights Law". *American Journal of Sociology* 97: 1531–1576.

Ellickson, Robert. 1991. *Order without Law*. Cambridge, MA: Harvard University Press.

Emerson, Richard. 1962. "Power-Dependence Relations." *American Sociological Review* 22: 31–41.

Evans, Peter and James E. Rauch. 1999. "Bureaucracy and Growth: A Cross-National Analysis of the Effects of 'Weberian' State Structures on Economic Growth". *American Sociological Review* 64: 748–765.

Festinger, Leon; Schachter, Stanley; and Back, Kurt. 1950. *Social Pressures in Informal Groups*. New York: Harper.

Fligstein, Neil and Taekjin Shin. 2004. "Shareholder Value and the Transformation of the American Economy: 1984–2001". Center for the Study of Economy and Society, Cornell University, Working Paper Series # 19.

Fligstein, Neil. 1996. "Markets as Politics: A Political-Cultural Approach to Markets". *American Sociological Review* 61: 656–673.
Fligstein, Neil. 2001. *The Architecture of Markets: An Economic Sociology of 21st Century Capitalist Societies.* Princeton, NJ: Princeton University Press.
Fourcade-Gourinchas, Marion. 2001. "Politics, Institutional Structures, and the Rise of Economics: A Comparative Study". *Theory and Society* 30: 397–447.
Granovetter, Mark. 1985. "Economic Action and Social Structure: The Problem of Embeddedness". *American Journal of Sociology* 91: 481–510.
Granovetter, Mark. 1992. "Economic Institutions as Social Constructions: A Framework for Analysis". *Acta Sociologica* 35: 3–11.
Granovetter, Mark. 1994. "Business Groups" in Neil Smelser and Richard Swedberg (eds.), *The Handbook of Economic Sociology.* New York and Princeton: Russell Sage Foundation and Princeton University Press, pp. 453–475.
Granovetter, Mark. 1995. "The Economic Sociology of Firms and Entrepreneurs" in Alejandro Portes (ed.), *The Economic Sociology of Immigration.* New York: Russell Sage Foundation, pp. 128–165.
Granovetter, Mark. Forthcoming. "Business Groups and Social Organization" in Neil Smelser and Richard Swedberg (eds.), *The Handbook of Economic Sociology*, 2nd rev. edn. New York and Princeton: Russell Sage Foundation and Princeton University Press.
Gray, Cheryl W. and Kathryn Hendley. 1997. "Developing Commercial Law in Transition Economies: Examples from Hungary and Russia" in Jeffrey Sachs and Katharina Pistor (eds.), *The Rule of Law and Economic Reform in Russis,* Cambridge, MA: Westview, pp. 139–164.
Greif, Avner. [1994] 1998. "Cultural Beliefs and the Organization of Society: A Historical and Theoretical Reflection on Collectivist and Individualist Societies". *Journal of Political Economy* 102: 912–50; adapted for *The New Institutionalism in Sociology*, edited by Mary Brinton and Victor Nee, New York: Russell Sage Foundation.
Greif, Avner. 1998. "Self-Enforcing Political Systems and Economic Growth: Late Medieval Genoa" in Robert Bates et al., *Analytical Narratives.* Princeton, NJ: Princeton University Press, pp. 23–63.
Greif, Avner. Forthcoming. *Institutions and History.* Cambridge: Cambridge University Press.
Guthrie, Doug. 1999. *Dragon in a Three-Piece Suit: The Emergence of Capitalism in China.* Princeton, NJ: Princeton University Press.
Hamilton, Gary D. and Robert Feenstra. 1998. "The Organization of Economies" in Mary Brinton and Victor Nee (eds.), *The New Institutionalism in Sociology.* New York: Russell Sage Foundation, pp. 153–180.
Hannan, Michael and Glenn Carroll. 1995. "An Introduction to Organizational Ecology" in Glenn Carroll and Michael Hannan (eds.), *Organizations in Industry.* New York: Oxford University Press, pp. 17–31.
Hannan, Michael T., and John Freeman. 1989. *Organizational Ecology.* Cambridge, MA: Harvard University Press.
Hardin, Russell. 1988. *Morality within the Limits of Reason.* Chicago, IL: University of Chicago Press.
Hayek, Friedrich. 1952. *The Sensory Order.* London: Routledge.
Hayek, Friedrich. 1982. *Law, Legislation and Liberty.* London: Routledge.
Hellman, Joel S. 1997. "Constitutions and Economic Reform in the Post-Communist Transitions" in Jeffrey Sachs and Katharina Pistor (eds.), *The Rule of Law and Economic Reform in Russisa.* Cambridge, MA: Westview, pp. 55–78.
Homans, George C. 1974. *Social Behavior: Its Elementary Forms.* New York: Harcourt Brace Jovanovich.
Jenning, Helen Hall. 1950. *Leadership and Isolation*, 2nd edn. New York: Longmans, Green.

Jepperson, Ronald. 1991. "Institutions, Institutional Effects, and Institutionalism" in Walter Powell and Paul DiMaggio (eds.), *The New Institutionalism in Organizational Analysis*. Chicago, IL: University of Chicago Press, pp. 143–163.

Keister, Lisa and Stephanie Moller. 2000. "Wealth Inequality in the United States". *Annual Review of Sociology* 26: 63–81.

Keister, Lisa. 2000. *Chinese Business Groups: The Structure and Impact of Interfirm Relations during Economic Development*. New York: Oxford University Press.

Knorr Cetina, Karin and Urs Brügger. 2002. "Global Macro Structures: The Virtual Societies of Financial Markets". *American Journal of Sociology* 107: 905–950.

Kollock, Peter. 1994. "The Emergence of Exchange Structures: An Experimental Study of Uncertainty, Commitment, and Trust". *American Journal of Sociology* 100: 315–345.

Krippner, Greta. 2001. "The Elusive Market: Embeddedness and the Paradigm of Economic Sociology". *Theory and Society* 30: 775–810.

Lawler, Edward J. and Jeongkoo Yoon. 1995. "Commitment in Exchange Relations: Test of a Theory of Relational Cohesion". *American Sociological Review* 61: 89–108.

MacKenzie, Donald and Yuval Millo. 2003. "Constructing a Market, Performing a Theory: The Historical Sociology of a Financial Derivatives Exchange". *American Journal of Sociology* 109: 107–146.

MacKenzie, Donald. 2003. "Long-Term Capital Management and the Sociology of Arbitrage". *Economy and Society* 32(3): 349–380.

Mizruchi, Mark. 1996. "What Do Interlocks Do? An Analysis, Critique and Assessment of Research on Interlocking Directorates". *Annual Review of Sociology* 22: 271–298.

Naughton, Barry. 1995. *Growing out of the Plan: Chinese Economic Reform 1978–1993*. Cambridge: University of Cambridge Press.

Nee, Victor. 1989. "A Theory of Market Transition: From Redistribution to Markets in State Socialism". *American Sociological Review* 54: 663–81.

——. 1996. "The Emergence of a Market Society: Changing Mechanisms of Stratification in China". *American Journal of Sociology* 101: 908–949.

——. 2000. "The Role of the State in Making a Market Economy". *Journal of Institutional and Theoretical Economics* 156: 64–88.

——. Forthcoming. "The New Institutionalism in Economics and Sociology" in Neil Smelser and Richard Swedberg (eds.), *The Handbook of Economic Sociology*, 2nd edn. Princeton, NJ: Princeton University Press and Russell Sage Foundation.

——. Forthcoming. "The Organizational Dynamics of Institutional Change" in Victor Nee and Richard Swedberg (eds.), *The Economic Sociology of Capitalism*. Princeton, NJ: Princeton University Press.

Nee, Victor and Paul Ingram. 1998. "Embeddedness and Beyond: Institutions, Exchange, and Social Structure" in Mary Brinton and Victor Nee (eds.), *The New Institutionalism in Sociology*. New York: Russell Sage Foundation, pp. 19–45.

Nee, Victor and Peng Lian. 1994. "Sleeping with the Enemy: A Dynamic Model of Declining Political Commitment in State Socialism". *Theory and Society* 23: 253–296.

Nee, Victor and Yang Cao. 1999. "Path Dependent Societal Transformations". *Theory and Society* 28: 799–834.

Nelson, Richard and Sidney Winter. 1982. *An Evolutionary Theory of Economic Change*. Cambridge: Cambridge University Press.

North, Douglass C. 1981. *Structure and Change in Economic History*. New York: Norton.

North, Douglass C. and John J. Wallis. 1986. "Measuring the Transaction Sector in the American Economy, 1870–1970" in Staley L. Engerman and Robert E. Gallman (eds.), *Long-Term Factors in American Economic Growth*, vol. 51 of *The Income and Wealth Series*. Chicago IL: University of Chicago Press, pp. 95–148.

North, Douglass. 1990. *Institutions, Institutional Change and Economic Performance*. Cambridge: Cambridge University Press.

North, Douglass. 1991. "Institutions". *Journal of Economic Perspectives* 5: 97–112.

North, Douglass. 1993. "Institutions and Credible Commitment". *Journal of Institutional and Theoretical Economics* 149: 11–23.
Opper, Sonja, Sonia M.L. Wong, and Ruyin Hu. 2002. "Party Power, Market, and Private Power: Chinese Communist Party Persistence in China's Listed Companies" in K. Leicht (eds.), *The Future of Market Transition. Research in Social Stratification and Mobility* 19 Special Issue: 105–138.
Padgett, John and Christopher Ansell. 1993. "Robust Action and the Rise of the Medici, 1400–1434". *American Journal of Sociology* 98: 1259–1319.
Peng, Yusheng. 2001. "Chinese Townships and Villages as Industrial Corporations: Ownership, Governance, and Productivity". *American Journal of Sociology* 106: 1338–1370.
———. 2004. "Kinship Networks and Entrepreneurs in China's Transitional Economy". *American Journal of Sociology* 109: 1045–1074.
Petersen, Trond. 1992. "Individual, Collective, and Systems Rationality in Work Groups". *Rationality and Society* 4: 332–355.
Podolny, Joel and Karen Page. 1998. "Network Forms of Organization". *Annual Review of Sociology* 24: 57–76.
Podolny, Joel. 1992. "A Status-Based Model of Market Competition". *American Journal of Sociology* 98: 829–72.
Portes, Alejandro and Sensenbrenner, J. 1993. "Embeddedness and Immigration: Notes on the Saocial determinants of Economic Action". *American Journal of Sociology* 98: 1320–1350.
Posner, Richard A. 1986. *Economic Analysis of Law*. Boston, MA: Little Brown and Co.
Rauch, James and Alessandra Casella (eds.). 2001. *Networks and Markets*. New York: Russell Sage Foundation.
Riley, M.W. and R. Cohn. 1958. "Control Networks in Informal Groups". *Sociometry* 21: 30–49.
Roethlisberger, F.J. and W.J. Dickson. 1939. *Management and the Worker*. Cambridge, MA: Harvard University Press.
Rona-Tas, Akos and Alya Guseva. 2001. "Uncertainty, Risk, and Trust: Russian and American Credit Markets Compared". *American Sociological Review* 66: 623–646.
Sachs, Jeffrey D. 1995. "Consolidating Capitalism". *Foreign Policy*, Number 98, Spring.
Sachs, Jeffrey. 2000. "Notes on a New Sociology of Economic Development" in Lawrence Harrison and Samuel Huntington (eds.), *Culture Matters*. New York: Basic Books, pp. 29–43.
Saxenian, AnnaLee. 1996. "Silicon Valley: Competition and Community" in *Regional Competition: Culture and Competition in Silicon Valley and Route 128*. Cambridge, MA: Harvard University Press, pp. 29–57.
Schachter, Stanley, N. Ellertson, D. McBride, and D. Gregory. 1951. "An Experimental Study of Cohesiveness and Productivity". *Human Relations* 4: 229–238.
Schutz, Alfred. 1967. *The Phenomenology of the Social World*. Chicago, IL: Northwestern University Press.
Seashore, Stanley E. 1954. *Group Cohesiveness in the Industrial Work Group*. Ann Arbor, MI: Institute for Social Resaerch, University of Michigan.
Shibutani, Tomatsu. 1978. *The Derelicts of Company K: A Study of Demoralization*. Berkeley, CA: University of California Press.
Shirk, Susan L. 1993. *The Political Logic of Economic Reform in China*. Berkeley, CA: University of California Press.
Shleifer, Andrei and Robert W. Vishny. 1994. "Politicians and Firms". *The Quarterly Journal of Economics* 109: 995–1025.
Simon, Herbert. 1997. "The Role of Organizations in an Economy" in Herbert Simon (ed.), *An Empirically Based Microeconomics*. Cambridge, MA: Cambridge University Press, pp. 33–53.
Spilerman, Seymour. 2000. "Wealth and Stratification Processes". *Annual Review of Sociology* 26: 497–524.

Stark, David. 1996. "Recombinant Property in Eastern European Capitalism". *American Journal of Sociology* 101: 993–1027.
Stiglitz, Joseph E. 1989. *The Economic Role of the State*. Oxford: Basil Blackwell.
Stinchcombe, Arthur. 1997. "On the Virtues of the Old Institutionalism". *Annual Review of Sociology* 23: 1–18.
Sutton, John, Frank Dobbin, John Meyer, and Richard Scott. 1994. "The Legalization of the Workplace". *American Journal of Sociology* 99: 944–971.
Swedberg, Richard (ed.). 1996. *Economic Sociology*. Cheltenham, UK: Edward Elgar.
Swedberg, Richard (ed.). 2000. *Entrepreneurship: The Social Science View*. Oxford: Oxford University Press.
Swedberg, Richard. 2001. "Sociology and Game Theory: Contemporary and Historical Perspectives". *Theory and Society* 30(3): 301–335.
Swedberg, Richard. 2003a. "The Case for an Economic Sociology of Law". *Theory and Society* 32(1): 1–37.
Swedberg, Richard. 2003b. *Principles of Economic Sociology*. Princeton, NJ: Princeton University Press.
Swedberg, Richard. Forthcoming. "Introduction" in Richard Swedberg (ed.), *New Developments in Economic Sociology*. 2 vols. Cheltenham, UK: Edward Elgar.
Thornton, Patricia. 1999. "The Sociology of Entrepreneurship". *Annual Review of Sociology* 25: 19–46.
Uzzi, Brian. 1996. "The Sources and Consequences of Embeddedness for the Economic Perfomance of Organizations: The Network Effect". *American Sociological Review* 61: 674–698.
Uzzi, Brian. 1997. "Social Structure and Competition in Interfirm Networks: The Paradox of Embeddedness". *Administrative Science Quarterly* 42: 35–67.
Varese, Fedrico. 2001. *The Russian Mafia: Private Protection in a New Market Economy*. London: Oxford University Press.
Walder, Andrew G. 1995. "Local Government as Industrial Firms: An Organizational Analysis of China's Transitional Economy". *American Journal of Sociology* 101: 263–301.
Walker, Edward L. and Roger W. Heyns. 1962. *An Anatomy for Conformity*. Englewood Cliffs, NJ: Prentice-Hall.
Weber, Max. 1946. In Hans Gerth and C. Wright Mills (eds.), *from Max Weber*. New York: Oxford University Press.
Weber, Max. 1978. In Guenther Roth and Claus Wittich (eds.), *Economy and Society: An Outline of Interpretive Sociology*. Berkeley, CA: University of California Press.
White, Harrison. 1981. "Where Do Markets Come From?". *American Journal of Sociology* 87: 517–547.
White, Harrison. 1992. *Identity and Control: A Structural Theory of Social Action*. Princeton, NJ: Princeton University Press.
White, Harrison. 2001. *Markets from Networks: Socioeconomic Models of Production*. Princeton, NJ: Princeton University Press.
Whyte, William Foote. 1943. *Street Corner Society*. Chicago, IL: University of Chicago Press.
Williamson, Oliver E. 1994. "Transaction Cost Economics and Organization Theory" in Neil Smelser and Richard Swedberg (eds.), *The Handbook of Economic Sociology*. New York: Russell Sage Foundation, pp. 77–107.
Williamson, Oliver E. 2000. "The New Institutional Economics: Taking Stock, Looking Ahead". *Journal of Economic Literature* XXXVIII: 595–613.
Zelizer, Viviana. 1989. "The Social Meaning of Money: 'Special Monies'". *American Journal of Sociology* 95: 342–377.
Zelizer, Viviana. 2002. "Intimate Transactions" in Mauro Guillen et al. (eds.), *The New Economic Sociology*. New York: Russell Sage Foundation, pp. 101–125.
Zuckerman, Ezra. 1999. "The Categorical Imperative: Securities Analysts and the Illegitimacy Discount". *American Journal of Sociology* 104: 1398–1438.

30. Doing Institutional Analysis
Digging Deeper Than Markets and Hierarchies

ELINOR OSTROM

A major problem in understanding institutions relates to the complexity and diversity of contemporary life and the resulting specialization that has occurred within the social sciences. The central aim of the social sciences is to explain human behavior. But what kind of human behavior? Within which kinds of institutional settings?

As we go about our everyday life, we interact in a diversity of complex situations. Many of us face a morning and evening commute where we expect that others, who are traveling at great speeds, will observe the rules of the road. Our very lives depend on these expectations. Those of us who work in large organizations—universities, research centers, business firms, government offices—participate in a variety of team efforts. In order to do our own work well, we are dependent on others to do their work creatively, energetically, and predictably and vice versa.

Many of us play sports at noon-time, in the early evening, and on the weekends. Here, again, we need to learn the basic rules of each of the games we play, as well as finding colleagues with whom we can repeatedly engage in this activity. During the average week, we undertake activities in various types of market settings—ranging from buying our everyday food and necessities to investing funds in various types of financial instruments. And, we spend some hours each week with family and friends in a variety of activities that may involve worship, helping offspring with homework, taking care of our homes and gardens, and a long list of other activities undertaken with family and friends.

The formal study of institutions is typically divided into the study of separate kinds of situations. Students are confronted with the need to choose between the study of markets offered by Departments of Economics and the study of hierarchies or states offered by Departments of Political Science. The study of communities is sometimes offered in Anthropology or Sociology Departments, but may not be offered at all in some universities. Are markets and hierarchies entirely "different" structures? Do they, in turn, share little with families, neighborhoods, and committees? Are there no underlying universal building blocks of organized life analogous to the underlying universal building blocks of individual organisms?

In this chapter, I address the question of whether underlying components of markets and hierarchies (and, many other complex situations) constitute the elemental parts of multiple, complementary theories that explain regularities in human behavior across diverse and complex situations. In other words, I assert that there are universal components of all markets and other frequently encountered situations and provide a framework that can be used in analyzing any type of institutional arrangement.

Contemporary ways of organizing scientific knowledge have not encouraged pursuing this question. Whole disciplines have been built up around the presumption that they offer a *unique* perspective on the study of particular types of situations. Markets and hierarchies are presented in some courses as fundamentally different "pure types" of organization. Not only are these types of institutional arrangements perceived to be different but each is presumed to require its *own* explanatory theory. Recent works in transaction cost economics do, of course, bridge these structures in the discussion of choosing firms or markets to organize activities (Williamson 1991).

When we study or teach about these situations, behavior is presented as coming from separate worlds. Psychologists tend to study the way that single individuals acquire and process information and skills and how this affects individual choices. The theories of individual behavior developed in psychology are little known or used outside of psychology. Many economists develop their own theories of individual behavior that are not consistent with the work undertaken in contemporary psychology. Political scientists tend to study various kinds of collective-choice mechanisms (legislatures, executives, courts, and the selection of officials through voting) and are eclectic in the theories and approach they use. The discipline of law is taught in separate schools and usually made available only to those interested in becoming lawyers by profession. Social scientists rarely take any biology—and vice versa—even though recent developments in biology are highly relevant for understanding human behavior.

In each discipline, a separate set of languages is emphasized that makes diverse assumptions about the

- kinds of goals that individuals seek, the images they share, and the mechanisms they use in making decisions;
- variables that are important in affecting the structure of the situations in which individuals make choices;
- capabilities of individuals and the extent of freedom that individuals have to affect the structure of these situations; and
- range of outcomes that is likely to be achieved in the relevant situations.

The development of separate languages is a barrier to more general explanatory frameworks and closely related theories that help analysts make cross-institutional comparisons and evaluations.

What we have learned from all of our separate disciplinary work is that there is no single cause of human behavior—even though some scholars tend to push one or another all-encompassing cause such as poverty, population, or the division of labor. Even life itself is not dependent on one cause. To live, one needs at least oxygen, water, and minimum levels of nutrition. All of these are key parts of the explanation of life, but none is a sufficient explanation of living beings. Living beings also exist at multiple levels. The human genotype is a set of instructions for building human phenotypes. Natural selection processes operating primarily at an individual level, but also in multilevel processes, have selected for some genes and selected against others. Parsing the genetic code has been one of the major breakthroughs of contemporary scientific endeavors. Our biological foundations help to explain some aspects of all of our behavior, but much of our behavior is also affected by the structure of the diverse range of situations within which we interact with others.

After decades of moving further and further apart—and engaging in sometimes futile arguments about which discipline has the best approach to understanding human behavior—a very encouraging trend over the last several decades has been the growth of interdisciplinary approaches to the study of human behavior. The number of journals with two disciplines in the title has been growing:*The Journal of Law and Economics, Political Sociology, Ecological Economics*, and many others. The Public Choice Society was started in the 1970s—originally as the "no name society" by economists, political scientists, and sociologists (see V. Ostrom 1964). The International Association for the Study of Common Property was started in the mid-1980s to bring together anthropologists, economists, engineers, historians, political scientists, sociologists, and many others. The International Society for New Institutional Economics—while it has only economics in the title—includes a large number of noneconomists as key participants. This Handbook illustrates the diversity of formal disciplines that contribute to the study of institutions.

Thus, the time is ripe for an effort that attempts to draw on the foundations of many disciplines including anthropology, biology, economics, law, philosophy, political science, psychology, and sociology, to attempt to answer the core question of this chapter mentioned above. What are the underlying component parts that can be used to build useful theories of human behavior in the diverse range of situations in which humans interact? Can we identify the working parts of any kind of situation in which humans find themselves interacting on a repetitive basis? Can we use the same components to build an explanation for behavior in a commodity market as we would use to explain behavior in a university, or a religious order, or a transportation system, or an urban public economy? Can we identify the multiple levels of analysis needed to explain the regularities in human behavior that we observe? I give a positive answer to these questions based on years of work with colleagues developing the Institutional Analysis and Development (IAD) framework.[1]

The publication of "The Three Worlds of Action: A Metatheoretical Synthesis of Institutional Approaches" (Kiser and Ostrom 1982) represents the initial

---

[1] For earlier discussions, see Kiser and Ostrom 1982; E. Ostrom 1986; Oakerson 1992; E. Ostrom, Gardner, and Walker 1994; Crawford and Ostrom 1995.

published attempt to describe the IAD framework intended to help integrate work undertaken by political scientists, economists, anthropologists, lawyers, sociologists, psychologists, and others interested in how institutions affect the incentives confronting individuals and their resultant behavior.[2] During the two decades since this publication, the framework has been developed further[3] and applied to analyze a diversity of empirical settings. These include:

- the study of land boards in Botswana (Wynne 1989);
- the evolution of coffee cooperatives in the Cameroon (Walker 1998);
- the effect of rules on the outcomes of common-pool resource settings throughout the world (E. Ostrom 1990, 1992; Schlager 1990; Blomquist 1992; Tang 1992; E. Ostrom, Gardner, and Walker 1994; Lam 1998; National Research Council 2002);
- the study of local public economies in urban areas (McGinnis 1999);
- the evolution of banking reform in the U.S. (Polski 2003);
- the change from group ranches to private ranches among the Maasai of Kenya (Mwangi 2003); and
- the effect of formal decentralization laws on local-level outcomes (Andersson 2002).

Our confidence in the utility of the framework has grown steadily in light of the wide diversity of empirical settings where it has helped colleagues identify the key variables to undertake a systematic analysis of the structure of the situations that individuals faced and how rules, the nature of the events involved, and community affected (and were affected by) these situations over time. What is certainly true is that the number of specific variables involved in each of these empirical studies is very large, and specific values of variables involved in one study (or one location in a study) differed from the specific values of variables involved in another study.

1. FURTHER CHALLENGES INVOLVED IN STUDYING INSTITUTIONS

A set of further difficulties needs to be overcome in undertaking any form of institutional analysis. Some of these key difficulties involved in studying institutions include:

1. While the buildings in which organized entities are located are quite visible, institutions themselves are usually invisible.
2. The term "institution" is used to refer to many different types of entities including organizations as well as the rules, norms, and strategies used to structure patterns of interaction within and across organizations.

---

[2] Elements of the framework have been used in teaching both graduate and undergraduate courses at Indiana University since the mid-1970s. Sections of this chapter are based on E. Ostrom (1999b).

[3] E. Ostrom 1986; E. Ostrom, Gardner, and Walker 1994: chap. 2; Oakerson 1992; E. Ostrom 1999b.

Doing Institutional Analysis 823

3. Given the multiple languages used across disciplines, a coherent institutional framework is needed to allow for expression and comparison of diverse theories and models of theories applied to particular puzzles and problem settings.
4. Decisions made about rules at any one level are usually made within a structure of rules existing at a different level. Thus, institutional studies need to encompass multiple levels of analysis.
5. At any one level of analysis, combinations of prescriptions, attributes of the world, and communities of individuals involved work together in a configural, rather than an additive, manner.

Let us briefly discuss these issues.

Institutions are Invisible

One of the most difficult problems to overcome in the study of institutions is how to identify and measure them. Because institutions are fundamentally shared concepts, they exist in the minds of participants and sometimes are shared as implicit knowledge rather than in an explicit and written form. One of the problems facing scholars and officials is learning how to recognize the presence of institutions on the ground. The primitive physical structures that embed property-rights systems that farmers have constructed over time look flimsy to an engineer who considers only structures built out of concrete and iron to be real.[4] These flimsy structures, however, are used by individuals to allocate resource flows to participants according to rules that have been devised in tough constitutional and collective-choice bargaining situations over time.

Unlike physical structures that are immediately visible on the horizon, rules are invisible structures that can be deeply buried under the regularities of observed behavior. We see, for example, the regularities of human behavior involved in an election campaign, an open farmers' market, or among drivers on a major freeway. Many behavioral regularities result from the physical and technological world involved. The heavy use of television advertising in contemporary election campaigns in Western countries, for example, is due in part to the vast economies of scale involved in this mode of communicating. Some of what we see, on the other hand, results from rules. The rule that requires T.V. channels to give equal access to all candidates, the Equal Time Rule, affects the amount of broadcast time assigned to all candidates.

Multiple Definitions of Institutions

One of the most difficult problems to overcome in the study of institutions is how to identify and measure them. Because institutions are fundamentally

---

[4] An excellent example of what looks like "flimsy structures" that have lasted for centuries is the Banaue Rice Terraces in the Philippines (rice terraces curved from the top of mountain ranges to the valleys below and maintained for over 2,000 years and still working today). UNESCO has put them on its World Heritage List. I am thankful to Ed Araral for suggesting this example.

shared concepts, they exist in the minds of participants and sometimes are shared as implicit knowledge rather than in an explicit and written form. One of the problems facing scholars and officials is learning how to recognize the presence of institutions on the ground. The primitive physical structures that embed property-rights systems that farmers have constructed over time look flimsy to an engineer who considers only structures built out of concrete and iron to be real. These flimsy structures, however, are used by individuals to allocate resource flows to participants according to rules that have been devised in tough constitutional and collective-choice bargaining situations over time.

Unlike physical structures that are immediately visible on the horizon, rules are invisible structures that can be deeply buried under the regularities of observed behavior. We see, for example, the regularities of human behavior involved in an election campaign, an open farmers' market, or among drivers on a major freeway. Many behavioral regularities result from the physical and technological world involved. The heavy use of television advertising in contemporary election campaigns in Western countries, for example, is due in part to the vast economies of scale involved in this mode of communicating. Some of what we see, on the other hand, results from rules. The rule that requires T.V. channels to give equal access to all candidates, the Equal Time Rule, ensures that we will observe states granting equal broadcast time to each candidate.

In training researchers to identify and measure institutions, we stress the concept of rules-in-use rather than focusing on rules-in-form. Rules-in-use are referred to whenever someone new (such as a new employee or a child) is being socialized into an existing rule-ordered system of behavior. They are the "do's and don'ts" that one learns on the ground that may not exist in any written document. In some instances, they may actually be contrary to the "do's and don'ts" that are written in formal documents. Being armed with a set of questions concerning how is X done here and why is Y not done here is a useful way of identifying rules-in-use, shared norms, and operational strategies.

Multiple Definitions of Institutions

It is hard to make much progress in the study of institutions if scholars define the term to mean almost anything. A major confusion exists between scholars who use the term to refer to an organizational entity such as the U.S. Congress, a business firm, a political party, or a family, and scholars who use the term to refer to the accepted rules, norms, and strategies adopted by individuals operating within or across organizational settings. In this chapter, following the definition used by Douglass North (1990, 2004 [this volume]), I use the term "institution" in the latter sense to refer to the rules, norms, and strategies used by humans in repetitive situations. By rules, I mean shared prescriptions (must, must not, or may) that are mutually understood and enforced in particular situations in a predictable way by agents responsible for monitoring conduct and for imposing sanctions (see Crawford and Ostrom 1995). By norms, I mean shared prescriptions known and accepted by most of the participants themselves involving intrinsic costs and benefits rather than material sanctions or inducements.[5] By strategies, I mean the regularized plans that individuals make within the structure of incentives produced by rules, norms, and expectations of the likely behavior of others in a situation affected by relevant physical and material conditions.[6]

Multiple Levels of Analysis

When individuals interact in repetitive settings, they may be in operational situations that directly affect the world, or they may be making decisions at other levels of analysis that eventually impinge on operational decision-making situations (Shepsle 1989). Multiple sources of structure are located at diverse analytical levels as well as diverse geographic domains. Biologists took several centuries to learn how to separate the diverse kinds of relevant structures needed to analyze both communities and individual biological entities. Separating phenotypical structure from genotypical structure was part of the major neo-Darwinian breakthrough that allowed biologists to achieve real momentum and cumulation during the past century.

Besides multiple and nested action arenas at any one level of analysis, nesting of arenas also occurs across several levels of analysis. The nested structure of rules within rules, within still further rules, is a particularly difficult phenomenon to understand for those interested in institutions. Studies conducted at a macro level (see Kaminski 1992; V. Ostrom 1997; Loveman 1993; Sawyer 1992) tend to focus on a constitutional level of analysis (see below for further discussion of this level). Decisions made at this level affect collective-choice decisions as these impinge on the operational decisions of individuals (see Firmin-Sellers 1996; Agrawal 1998; Gibson 1999). Finding ways to communicate across levels is a key challenge for all institutional theorists.

Configural Relationships

Successful analysis can cumulate rapidly when scholars have been able to analyze a problem by separating it into component parts that are analyzed independently and then recombining these parts in an additive fashion. Many puzzles of interest to social scientists can be torn apart and recombined. Frequently, however, the impact on incentives and behavior of one type of rule is not independent of the configuration of other rules. Thus, the impact of changing one of the current rules that is part of a state "welfare system" depends on which other rules are also in effect. Changing the minimum outside-income that can be earned before losing benefits from one program, for example, cannot be analyzed

---

[5] Norms are viewed by institutional analysts drawing on sociological traditions as social facts that are not changeable by the individual (see Seo and Creed 2002; Scott 2001).

[6] When doing formal game-theoretical analysis, such strategies would be those identified as equilibrium strategies. Shared strategies may, however, take the form of heuristics adopted by most individuals in a society when they find themselves in particular situations.

independently of the effect of income on benefits derived from other programs. Similarly, analyzing the impact of changing the proportion of individuals who must agree prior to making an authoritative collective choice (e.g., 50 percent plus 1) depends on the quorum rule in force. If a quorum rule specifying a low proportion of members is in effect, requiring two-thirds agreement may be a less stringent decision rule than a simple majority rule combined with a quorum rule requiring a high proportion of members. *Ceteris paribus* conditions are always essential for doing any theoretical work involving institutions. In the case of institutional analysis, one needs to know the value of other variables rather than simply asserting that they are held constant. This makes institutional analysis a more difficult and complex enterprise than studies of phenomena that are strictly additive.

2. INSTITUTIONAL FRAMEWORKS, THEORIES, AND MODELS

Given the need for multiple disciplines, and hence multiple disciplinary languages, and the multiple levels of analysis involved in studying configural relationships among rules, relevant aspects of the world, and cultural phenomenon, the study of institutions does depend on theoretical work undertaken at three levels of specificity that are often confused with one another. These essential foundations include (1) frameworks, (2) theories, and (3) models. Analyses conducted at each level provide different degrees of specificity related to a particular problem.

The development and use of a general *framework* helps to identify the elements and relationships among these elements that one needs to consider for institutional analysis. Frameworks organize diagnostic and prescriptive inquiry. They provide the most general list of variables that should be used to analyze all types of institutional arrangements. Frameworks provide a metatheoretic language that is necessary to talk about theories and that can be used to compare theories. They attempt to identify the *universal* elements that any theory relevant to the same kind of phenomena would need to include. Many differences in surface reality can result from the way these variables combine with, or interact with, one another. Thus, the elements contained in a framework help the analyst generate the questions that need to be addressed when first conducting an analysis. In this chapter, I will present a framework for institutional analysis rather than specific theories.

The development and use of *theories* enable the analyst to specify which elements of the framework are particularly relevant for certain kinds of questions and to make general working assumptions about these elements. Thus, theories focus on a framework and make specific assumptions that are necessary for an analyst to diagnose a phenomenon, explain its processes, and predict outcomes. Several theories are usually compatible with any framework. Economic theory, game theory, transaction cost theory, social choice theory, covenantal theory, and theories of public goods and common-pool resources are all compatible with the IAD framework discussed in this chapter.

The development and use of *models* make precise assumptions about a limited set of parameters and variables. Logic, mathematics, game theory, experimentation and simulation, and other means are used to explore the consequences of these assumptions systematically on a limited set of outcomes. Multiple models are compatible with most theories. An effort to understand the strategic structure of the games that irrigators play in differently organized irrigation systems, for example, developed four families of models just to begin to explore the likely consequences of different institutional and physical combinations relevant to understanding how successful farmer organizations arranged for monitoring and sanctioning activities (Weissing and Ostrom 1991). This is one set of models we have developed to analyze, in a precise manner, a subpart of the theory of common-pool resources.

For policymakers and scholars interested in issues related to how different governance systems enable individuals to solve problems democratically, the IAD framework helps to organize diagnostic, analytical, and prescriptive capabilities. It is similar in structure and intent to the "Actor-Centered Institutionalism" framework developed by Renate Mayntz and Fritz Scharpf (1995) and applied to several national policy settings by Scharpf (1997). It also aids in the accumulation of knowledge from empirical studies and in the assessment of past efforts at reforms.

Without the capacity to undertake systematic, comparative institutional assessments, recommendations of reform may be based on naive ideas about which kinds of institutions are "good" or "bad" and not on an analysis of performance. One needs a common framework and family of theories in order to address questions of reforms and transitions. Particular models then help the analyst to deduce specific predictions about likely outcomes of highly simplified structures. Models are useful in policy analysis when they are well-tailored to the particular problem at hand. Models are used inappropriately when applied to the study of problematic situations that do not closely fit the assumptions of the model.

3. THE INSTITUTIONAL ANALYSIS AND DEVELOPMENT (IAD) FRAMEWORK

As indicated earlier, an institutional framework should identify the major types of structural variables present to some extent in *all* institutional arrangements, but whose values differ from one type of institutional arrangement to another. In all the analyses presented in this chapter, one can think about a core set of building blocks—which are themselves constructed of other building blocks and affected by multiple external variables. The simplest and most aggregated way of representing all situations is shown in Figure 1, where *actors* in *situations* together with exogenous factors generate *outcomes* that affect the actors in the situation and potentially others (see E. Ostrom, Gardner, and Walker 1994: chap. 2).

828   *Elinor Ostrom*

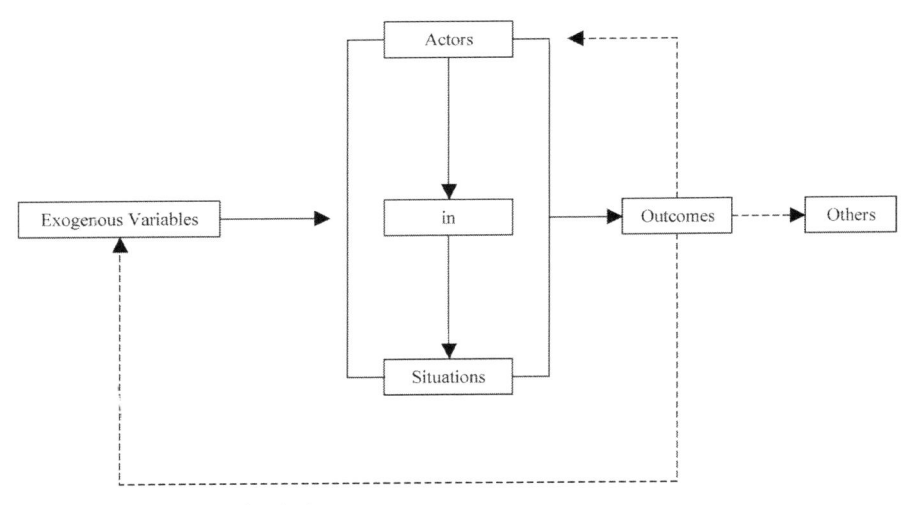

Figure 1. The focal level of analysis.

The outcomes that are achieved eventually feed back onto the actors and the situations and may transform both over time. When the outcomes are productive for those involved, they may increase their commitment to following the rules and norms that have evolved over time so as to continue to receive positive outcomes. When outcomes are perceived by those involved as of lower value than other outcomes that might be obtained, some actors will begin to raise questions about changing the structure of the situations through various changes in the exogenous variables or the structure of the situations themselves.

The IAD framework is a multitier conceptual map. The most basic schematic representation shown in Figure 1 will be unpacked, as shown in Figure 2. It can be further unpacked multiple times. The first step in using this framework to analyze a problem is to identify a conceptual unit—called an *action arena*—that can be utilized to analyze, predict, and explain behavior within institutional arrangements.[7] Action arenas include an *action situation* and the *actors* in that situation. An action situation can be characterized using seven clusters of variables: (1) participants, (2) positions, (3) outcomes, (4) action-outcome linkages, (5) the control that participants exercise, (6) information, and (7) the costs and benefits assigned to outcomes.

An actor (an individual or a corporate actor) includes assumptions about four clusters of variables:

1. the *resources* that an actor brings to a situation;
2. the *valuation* actors assign to states of the world and to actions;
3. the way actors acquire, process, retain, and use *knowledge contingencies and information;* and
4. the processes actors use for *selection* of particular courses of action.

---

[7] The concept of an action arena is analogous to the concept of fields as used by Bourdieu (1977), DiMaggio and Powell (1983), and Fligstein (1998).

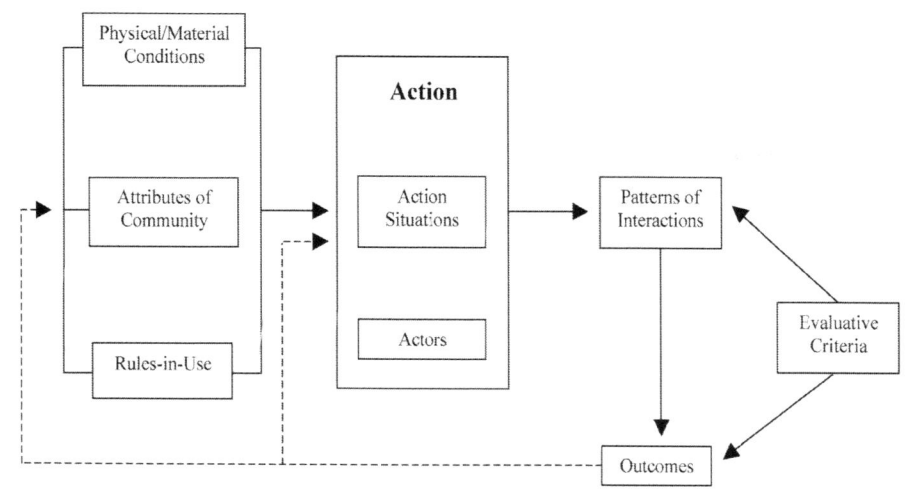

Figure 2. A framework for institutional analysis.

Source: Adapted from E. Ostrom, Gardner, and Walker (1994: 37).

The particular assumptions made by an analyst about each of these assumptions enable one to build a theory of self-centered rational choice, a theory of bounded rationality, or a theory of norm-driven behavior. All of these theories can be used to animate the "actor" module of the framework.

An action arena refers to the social space where individuals interact, exchange goods and services, solve problems, dominate one another, feel guilty, or fight (among the many things that individuals do in action arenas). Considerable ferment has been generated during the past several decades as a result of empirical studies—to a large degree, experimental studies—that have challenged some of the basic working assumptions used by many institutional analysts in predicting outcomes in various types of collective-action situations (E. Ostrom 1998). A major proportion of theoretical work stops after predicting outcomes from a particular action arena and takes the variables specifying the situation and the motivational and cognitive structure of an actor as givens. Analysis proceeds toward the prediction of the likely behavior of individuals in such a structure.

An institutional analyst can take two additional steps after an effort is made to understand the initial structure of an action arena. One step digs deeper and inquires into the factors that affect the structure of an action arena. From this vantage point, the action arena is viewed as a set of variables dependent upon other factors. These factors affecting the structure of an action arena include three clusters of variables: (1) the rules and norms used by participants to order their relationships, (2) the attributes of states of the world that are acted upon in these arenas, and (3) the structure of the more general community within which any particular arena is placed (see Kiser and Ostrom 1982). The second step examines how nested levels of rules affect behavior. I will now provide a brief introduction to how shared understandings of rules, states of the world, and nature of the community affect the values of the variables characterizing action arenas (see the left side of Figure 2) and then turn to a discussion of the linkage of action situations.

4. EXPLANATION VIEWING ACTION SITUATIONS AS DEPENDENT VARIABLES

Underlying the way analysts conceptualize action arenas are implicit assumptions about the *rules* individuals use to order their relationships, about attributes of *states of the world and their transformations*, and about the *nature of the community* within which the arena occurs. Some analysts are not interested in the role of these underlying variables and focus only on a particular arena whose structure is given. On the other hand, institutional analysts may be more interested in one factor affecting the structure of arenas more than they are interested in others. Sociologists tend to be more interested in how shared value systems affect the ways humans organize their relationships with one another. Environmentalists tend to focus on various ways that physical and biological systems interact and create opportunities or constraints on the situation human beings face. Political scientists tend to focus more on how specific combinations of rules affect incentives. Rules, states of the world, and the nature of the community all jointly affect the types of actions that individuals can take, the benefits and costs they attribute to these actions, and the likely outcomes achieved.

The Concept of Rules

The concept of rules is central to the analysis of institutions, but the term "rules" refers to many concepts with quite diverse meanings. In an important philosophical treatment of rules, Black (1962) identified four different usages of the term in everyday conversations. According to Black, the word "rule" is used to denote regulations, instructions, precepts, and principles. When used in its *regulation* sense, rules refer to something "laid down by an authority (a legislature, judge, magistrate, board of directors, university president, parent) as required of certain persons (or, alternatively, forbidden or permitted)" (ibid.: 115). The example of a rule in the regulation-sense that Black uses is: "The dealer at bridge must bid first." When using rule in its regulation-sense, one can meaningfully refer to activities such as the rule "being announced, put into effect, enforced (energetically, strictly, laxly, invariably, occasionally), disobeyed, broken, rescinded, changed, revoked, reinstated" (ibid.: 109).

When the term "rules" is used to denote an *instruction*, it is closer in meaning to an effective strategy for how to solve a problem. An example of this usage is, "In solving quartic equations, first eliminate the cubic term" (ibid.: 110). When speaking about a rule in this sense, one would not talk about a rule being enforced, rescinded, reinstated, or any of the other activities relevant to regulation. When rule denotes a *precept*, the term is being used as a maxim for prudential or moral behavior. An example would be: "A good rule is: to put charity ahead of justice" (ibid.: 111). Again, one would not speak of enforcing, rescinding, or reinstating a rule in the precept sense.

The fourth sense in which the term rule is used in everyday language is to describe a law or principle. An example of this usage is: "Cyclones rotate clockwise, anticyclones anticlockwise" (ibid.: 113). Principles or physical laws are subject to empirical test, and as such, truth values can be ascribed to them. But physical laws are not put into effect, broken, or rescinded.

Social scientists employ all four uses of the term that Black identifies. Scholars engaged in institutional analysis usually use the term to denote a regulation. Rules in the instruction-sense can best be thought of as the strategies adopted by participants within ongoing situations. It is better to use the term "strategy" rather than "rule" for these plans of action. Rules in the precept-sense are part of the generally accepted moral fabric of a community. I refer to these cultural prescriptions as norms. Rules in the principle-sense are physical laws and are considered as part of the events in the biophysical world.

Until recently, rules have not been a central focus of most of the social sciences. Even in game theory, where "the rules of the game" seem to play an important role, there has not been much interest in examining where rules come from or how they change. Game-theoretical rules include all physical laws that constrain a situation as well as rules devised by humans to structure a situation. The rules of the game—including both physical and institutional factors—structure the game itself, but have been irrelevant to many game theorists once a game can be unambiguously represented. Anatol Rapoport stated this position clearly:

> Rules are important only to the extent that they allow the outcomes resulting from the choices of participants to be unambiguously specified.... Any other game with possibly quite different rules but leading to the same relations among the choices and the outcomes is considered equivalent to the game in question. In short, game theory is concerned with rules only to the extent that the rules help define the choice situation and the outcomes associated with the choices. Otherwise the rules of games play no part in game theory. (1966: 18)

Rules are shared understandings about potentially linguistic entities (Ganz 1971; V. Ostrom 1980; Commons 1957) that refer to enforced prescriptions about what actions (or states of the world) are *required, prohibited*, or *permitted*. All rules are the result of implicit or explicit efforts to achieve order and predictability among humans by creating classes of persons (positions) who are then required, permitted, or forbidden to take classes of actions in relation to required, permitted, or forbidden states of the world (Crawford and Ostrom 1995; V. Ostrom 1991). Well-understood and enforced rules operate so as to *rule out* most occurrences of some actions.

Where do the rules that individuals use in action situations originate? In an open and democratic governance system, many sources of rules exist. It is not considered illegal or improper for individuals to self-organize themselves and craft their own rules if the activities they engage in are legal. In addition to the legislation and regulations of a formal central government, laws are considered passed by regional, local, and special governments. Within private firms and voluntary associations, individuals are authorized to adopt different rules for who is a member of the firm or association, how benefits are to be shared, and how decisions will be made. Each family constitutes its own rule-making body.

When individuals genuinely participate in the crafting of multiple layers of rules, some of that crafting will occur using pen and paper. Much of it, however, will occur as problem-solving individuals interact and try to figure out how to do a better job in the future than they have done in the past. Colleagues in a work-team are crafting their own rules when they say to one another: "How about if you do A and I do B in the future, and before we make a decision about C again, we both discuss it and make a joint decision." In a democratic society, problem-solving individuals do this all the time.

Thus, rules need not be written. Nor, do they need to result from formal legal procedures. Participants craft rules in order to change the structure of repetitive situations that they face so as to try to improve outcomes for themselves. Regardless of a rule's origin, however, it is always possible to rescind it or reinstate it—or it is not a rule.

Rules-in-use are the set of rules to which participants make reference if asked to explain and justify their actions to fellow participants. They are the "do's and don'ts" that one learns on the ground that may not exist in any written document. In some instances, they may actually be contrary to the "do's and don'ts" that are written in formal documents. While following a rule may become a "social habit," it is possible to make participants consciously aware of the rules they use to order their relationships. Individuals can consciously decide to adopt a different rule and change their behavior to conform to such a decision. Over time, behavior in conformance with a new rule may itself become habitual (see Shimanoff 1980; Toulmin 1974; Harré 1974). The capacity of humans to use complex cognitive systems to order their own behavior at a relatively subconscious level makes it difficult for empirical researchers to ascertain what the working rules for an ongoing action arena may be.

In a system governed by a "rule of law," the general legal framework in use will have its source in actions taken in constitutional, legislative, and administrative settings augmented by decisions taken by individuals in many different particular settings. In other words, the rules-in-form are consistent with the rules-in-use (Sproule-Jones 1993). In a system that is not governed by a "rule of law," there may be central laws and considerable effort made to enforce them, but individuals attempt to evade rather than obey the law. Rule-following or conforming actions are not as predictable as biological or physical behavior explained by scientific laws. All rules are formulated in human language. As such, rules share problems of lack of clarity, misunderstanding, and change that typify any language-based phenomenon (V. Ostrom 1980, 1997). Words are always simpler than the phenomenon to which they refer.

The stability of rule-ordered actions is dependent upon the shared meaning assigned to words used to formulate a set of rules. If no shared meaning exists when a rule is formulated, confusion will exist about what actions are required, permitted, or forbidden. Regularities in actions cannot result if those who must repeatedly interpret the meaning of a rule within action situations arrive at multiple interpretations. Because "rules are not self-formulating, self-determining, or self-enforcing" (V. Ostrom 1980: 342), it is human agents who formulate them, apply them in particular situations, and attempt to enforce performance consistent with them. Even if shared meaning exists at the time of the acceptance of a rule, transformations in technology, in shared norms, and in circumstances more generally change the events to which rules apply. "Applying language to changing configurations of development increases the ambiguities and threatens the shared criteria of choice with an erosion of their appropriate meaning" (ibid.).

The stability of rule-ordered relationships is also dependent upon enforcement (Gibson, Williams, and Ostrom 2005; Dietz, Ostrom, and Stern 2003). According to John R. Commons, rules "simply say what individuals must, must not, may, can, and cannot do, if the authoritative agency that decides disputes brings the collective power of the community to bear on said individuals" (1957: 138). Breaking rules is an option that is always available to participants in an action situation (as contrasted to players in a formal game), but associated with breaking rules is a risk of being monitored and sanctioned. If the risk is low, the predictability and stability of a situation are reduced. And, instability can grow over time. If one person can cheat without fear of being caught, others can also cheat with impunity. If the risk of exposure and sanctioning is high, participants can expect that others will make choices from within the set of permitted and required actions.

The simplifying assumption is frequently made in analytical theories that individuals in an action situation will take only those actions that are lawful given the rules that apply. For many purposes, this simplifying assumption helps the analyst examine important theoretical questions not related to how well the rules are enforced. Highly complicated games, such as football, can indeed be explained with more ease because of the presence of active and aggressive on-site referees who constantly monitor the behavior of the players and assign penalties for infraction of rules. And these monitors face real incentives for monitoring consistently and for applying fair and accepted penalties. Both the fans and the managers of the relevant sports teams may give a lot of attention to what the monitors are doing and the fairness of their judgments. In settings where a heavy investment is *not* made in monitoring the ongoing actions of participants, however, considerable difference between predicted and actual behavior can occur.

This is not to imply that the only reason individuals follow rules is because they are enforced. If individuals voluntarily participate in a situation, they must share some general sense that most of the rules governing the situation are appropriate. Otherwise, the cost of enforcement within voluntary activities becomes high enough that it is difficult, if not impossible, to maintain predictability in an ongoing voluntary activity. One can expect that it is usually difficult to maintain predictability in an ongoing activity where participants do not have the freedom to enter and leave the situation.

What rules are important for institutional analysis? A myriad of specific rules are used in structuring markets, hierarchies, committees, and other structures. Scholars have been trapped into endless cataloging of rules not related to a method of classification most useful for theoretical explanations. But classification is a necessary step in developing a science. Anyone attempting to define a useful typology of rules must be concerned that the classification is more than a method for imposing superficial order onto an extremely large set of seemingly disparate rules. The way we have tackled this problem using the IAD framework is to classify rules according to their impact on the elements of an action situation.

Rule Configurations

A first step toward identifying the working rules can be made, then, by overtly examining how working rules affect each of the components of an action situation listed above. A set of working rules that affect these variables should constitute the minimal but necessary set of rules needed to offer an explanation of actions and results based on the working rules used by participants to order their relationships within an action arena. Because states of the world and their transformations and the nature of a community also affect the structure of an action situation, working rules alone never provide both a necessary and sufficient explanation of the structure of an action situation and results.

Adopting this view of the task, seven groups of working rules can be said to affect the structure of any repetitive action situation, including markets, hierarchies, legislatures, common-property management systems, or competitive sports. These are: *boundary rules*, *position rules*, *scope rules*, *authority rules*, *aggregation rules, information rules*, and *payoff rules*. These seven groups of rules directly affect the seven components of an action situation.

Boundary rules directly affect the number of *participants*, their attributes and resources, whether they can enter freely, and the conditions they face for leaving. Position rules establish *positions* in the situation. Authority rules assign sets of *actions* that participants in positions at particular nodes must, may, or may not take. Scope rules delimit the *potential outcomes* that can be affected and working backwards, the actions linked to specific outcomes. Authority rules, combined with the scientific laws about the relevant states of the world being acted upon, determine the shape of the decision tree—the *action-outcome linkages*. Aggregation rules affect the level of *control* that a participant in a position exercises in the selection of an action at a node. Information rules affect the *knowledge-contingent information sets* of participants. Payoff rules affect the *benefits and costs* that will be assigned to particular combinations of actions

Table 1. Rules used to structure open, competitive market situations

---

Position Rules
- Positions of owner, seller, buyer, police, suspects, judge, and members of a jury are defined.

Boundary Rules
- Licensing requirements for individuals to become buyers and sellers are minimal.
- Buyers and sellers may enter and exit the market at their own initiative.

Authority Rules
- Sellers are authorized to decide how many legally owned goods to offer for sale at a price.
- Buyers are authorized to decide how much of a commodity to offer to buy at a price.
- Police are authorized to arrest those suspected of unlawful use of goods owned by others.
- Judges are authorized to determine rights and obligations of buyers and sellers in civil proceedings and of suspected thieves in criminal proceedings.
- Members of juries are authorized to determine guilt or innocence of those accused of theft.

Scope Rules
- Actors are limited in regard to the costs they can externalize on others. (Scope rules related to externalities vary substantially from market to market.)

Aggregation Rules
- Whenever any two actors agree to exchange goods they own, that transaction occurs.
- Police may make an arrest after a request or on their own initiative.
- Decisions made by a judge must be final unless challenged in a higher court.
- Members of a jury must vote before their decisions are official.

Information Rules
- Prices of current offers to buy and sell must be made available.
- No one is authorized to force information from others regarding preferences or costs.
- In some jurisdictions, seller may be required to provide specific information on content of goods.

Payoff Rules
- Seller retains profit, if any, after payment for inputs, interest, and taxes.
- Buyer retains consumer surplus, if any, after payment for goods.
- Suspects pay fines, or spend time in jail, if judged guilty of criminal acts.
- Buyers and/or sellers pay damages and costs to other parties if ordered to do so by judge.

---

and outcomes and establish the incentives and deterrents for action. The set of working rules is a *configuration* in the sense that the impact on actions chosen and outcomes of a change in one rule may depend upon the specific content of other rules-in-use.

Table 1 presents a simplified set of rules that could be used to constitute an open, competitive market. When a scholar makes the statement, "Let us assume an open, competitive market," the rules constituting a market are rarely enumerated. The statement, however, can be thought of as broadly encompassing the type of rules listed in Table 1. Substantial changes in any one of these rules affect the structure of a market and the resulting inferences that can be made about equilibria and market performance.

Change of only a few key rules would generate a situation that one would not call a market at all. A change in the aggregation rule, for example, which allocates goods to participants by officials, transforms the resulting action situation into something other than a market. (This is the rule that the military uses to assign uniforms to recruits.) A change in boundary rules affects the number of participants who enter and exit, and determines whether the resulting market is competitive, oligopolistic, or monopolistic. By affecting the structure of the market, changes in boundary rules affect predictions concerning the price at which goods will be sold, the quantity to be sold, and the relative distribution of producer and consumer surplus. Anderies (2002) uses these seven types of rules as initial steps in specifying a model of resource appropriation systems such as fisheries, rangelands, and forests. He then shows how changing position and boundary rules affects system dynamics over time.

Some colleagues are surprised at how many rules are needed to constitute a market. By simply manipulating the assumed components of action situations—e.g., the number of participants, the information they possess, the payoffs they face—a scholar using neoclassical economic theory is able to make predictions about probable interactions and outcomes that have considerable empirical support. Thus, for many aspects of theoretical and empirical research, we do not need to dig deeper than a set of assumptions about the structure of a particular type of situation.

When scholars, policy analysts, officials, and citizens try to change the structure of the action situations that exist in a particular firm, community, or region, however, they face a much more demanding task than simply "assuming law and order and an open, competitive market." They are facing the problem of how to create such a market (or an innovative, efficient firm or a sustainably managed resource). As the cases in Shirley (2002) demonstrate, finding the rule configuration to enhance the performance of urban water systems in regard to efficiency and distribution to the poor residents of a city presents an immense challenge. Privatizing water supplies turns out not to be one policy option. Each of the six major cities studied developed different contractual arrangements as among producers, regulators, consumers, and citizens. The performance of the reformed systems varied substantially across measures as well as across cities.

Changing the rules of a planned economy so as to constitute effective open markets has also proved to be a major challenge since the fall of the Berlin Wall. Policies intended to create open markets in many "transitional economies" have constituted monopolies or oligopolies instead! Given the recent experiences of failed efforts to improve the economies of the developing countries and many of those of Eastern Europe, the importance of understanding the deeper levels of institutional analysis is becoming more obvious. Further, as empirical studies of the linkages between rule configurations and action situations have shown, the actual number of rules-in-use in many typical situations is immense. At least 27 different boundary rules are in use in different locations in the management of common-pool resources, for example (E. Ostrom 1999a: 511). Similarly, a large number of authority rules, information rules, and payoff rules have been identified. The set of identified rules is large enough that no analyst can perform a complete analysis of the structure of resulting situations devoid from all combinations of these rules.

Consequently, the next frontier in doing institutional analysis is a much more self-conscious study of how rules combine with one another, as well as with the physical and material conditions and the nature of a community to create the situations in which participants interact. Janssen (2002) has taken major steps in opening that frontier with his analysis of lessons learned from languages and from immune systems for the study of resilient human-ecological systems. The use of agent-based models will enable scholars to tackle the study of complex adaptive systems in a coherent and cumulative manner.

Physical and Material Conditions

While a rule configuration affects all of the elements of an action situation, some of the variables of an action situation (and thus the overall set of incentives facing individuals in a situation) are also affected by attributes of the physical and material world. What actions are physically possible, what outcomes can be produced, how actions are linked to outcomes, and what is contained in the actors' information sets are affected by the world being acted upon in a situation. The same set of rules may yield entirely different types of action situations depending upon the types of events in the world being acted upon by participants. These "events" are frequently referred to as the "goods and services" being produced, consumed, and allocated in a situation as well as the technology available for these processes.

The attributes of states of the world and their transformation are explicitly examined when the analyst self-consciously asks a series of questions about how the world being acted upon in a situation affects the outcome, action sets, action-outcome linkages, and information sets in that situation. The relative importance of the rule configuration and states of the world in structuring an action situation varies dramatically across different types of settings. The rule configuration almost totally constitutes some games, like chess, where physical attributes are relatively unimportant. The relative importance of working rules to attributes of the world also varies dramatically within action situations considered to be part of the public sector. Rules define and constrain voting behavior inside a legislature more than attributes of the world. Voting can be accomplished by raising hands, by paper ballots, by calling for the ayes and nays, by marching before an official counter, or by installing computer terminals for each legislator on which votes are registered. However, in regard to organizing communication within a legislature, attributes of the world strongly affect the available options. The principle that only one person can be heard and understood at a time in any one forum strongly affects the capacity of legislators to communicate effectively with one another (see V. Ostrom 1987).

Considerable academic literature has focused on the effect of attributes of goods on the results obtained within an action situation. A key assumption made in the analysis of a competitive market is that the outcomes of an exchange are highly excludable, easily divisible and transferable, and internalized by those who participate in the exchange. Markets are predicted to fail as effective decision mechanisms when they are the only arena available for producing, consuming, or allocating a wide variety of goods that fail to meet the criteria of excludability, divisibility, and transferability. Market failure means that the incentives facing individuals in a situation where the rules are those of a competitive market, but the goods are not "private goods," do not motivate individuals to produce, allocate, and consume those goods close to an optimal level.

Let us briefly consider here several attributes that are frequently used to distinguish goods and services that are more effectively provided by a variety of nonmarket rules. A full elaboration of attributes of goods cannot be developed in this chapter given space limitations (see E. Ostrom, Gardner, and Walker 1994). Goods that are generally considered to be "public goods" yield nonsubtractive benefits that can be enjoyed jointly and simultaneously by many people who are hard to exclude from obtaining these benefits. Common-pool resources yield benefits where beneficiaries are hard to exclude, but each person's use of a resource system subtracts units of that resource from a finite total available for harvesting.

Excludability and the Free-Rider Problem

When it is difficult or costly to exclude beneficiaries from a good once it is produced, it is frequently assumed that such a good must be provided publicly, rather than privately. When the benefits of a good are available to a group, whether or not members of the group contribute to the provision of the good, that good is characterized by problems with excludability. Where exclusion is costly, those wishing to provide a good or service face a potential free-rider or collective-action problem (Olson 1965). Individuals who gain from the maintenance of an irrigation system, for example, may not wish to contribute labor or taxes to maintenance activities, hoping that others will bear the burden. This is not to say that all individuals will free-ride whenever they can. A strong incentive exists to be a free-rider in all situations where potential beneficiaries cannot easily be excluded for failing to contribute to the provision of a good or service.

When it is costly to exclude individuals from enjoying benefits from a common-pool resource or a infrastructure facility, private, profit-seeking entrepreneurs, who must recoup their investments through *quid pro quo* exchanges, have few incentives to provide such services on their own initiative. Excludability problems can thus lead to the problem of free-riding, which in turn leads to underinvestment in capital and its maintenance.

Public sector provision of common-pool resources or infrastructure facilities raises additional problems in determining preferences and organizing finances. When exclusion is low-cost to the supplier, preferences are revealed as a result of many *quid pro quo* transactions. Producers learn about preferences through the consumers' willingness to pay for various goods offered for sale. Where exclusion is difficult, designing mechanisms that honestly reflect beneficiaries' preferences and their willingness to pay is complex, regardless of whether the providing unit is organized in the public or the private sphere. In very small groups, those affected are usually able to discuss their preferences and constraints on a face-to-face basis and to reach a rough consensus. In larger groups, decisions about infrastructure are apt to be made through mechanisms such as voting or the delegation of authority to public officials. The extensive literature on voting systems demonstrates how difficult it is to translate individual preferences into collective choices that adequately reflect individual views (Arrow 1951; Shepsle 1979; Buchanan and Tullock 1962).

Another attribute of some goods with excludability problems is that, once they are provided, consumers may have no choice whatsoever as to whether they will consume. An example is the public spraying of insects. If an individual does not want this public service to be provided, there are even stronger incentives not to comply with a general tax levy. Thus, compliance with a broad financing instrument may, in turn, depend upon the legitimacy of the public-choice mechanism used to make provision decisions.

Subtractability of the Flow

Jointly used infrastructure facilities can generate a flow of services that is entirely subtractable upon consumption by one user; in other instances, consumption by one does not subtract from the flow of services available to others. The withdrawal of a quantity of water from an irrigation canal by one farmer means that there is that much less water for anyone else to use. Most agricultural uses of water are fully subtractive, whereas many other uses of water—such as for power generation or navigation—are not. Most of the water that passes through a turbine to generate power, for instance, can be used again downstream. When the use of a flow of services by one individual subtracts from what is available to others, and when the flow is scarce relative to demand, users will be tempted to try to obtain as much as they can of the flow for fear that it will not be available later.

Effective rules are required if scarce, fully subtractive service flows are to be allocated in a productive way. Charging prices for subtractive services obviously constitutes one such allocation mechanism. Sometimes, however, it is not feasible to price services. In these instances, some individuals will be able to grab considerably more of the subtractive services than others, thereby leading to noneconomic uses of the flow and high levels of conflict among users.

Allocation rules also affect the incentives of users to maintain a system. Farmers located at the tail end of an irrigation system that lacks effective allocation rules have little motivation to contribute to the maintenance of that system because they only occasionally receive their share of water. Similarly, farmers located at the head end of such a system are not motivated to provide maintenance services voluntarily because they will receive disproportionate shares of the water whether or not the system is well maintained (E. Ostrom 1996).

Consequently, for common-pool resources whose flows are highly subtractive, institutional arrangements related to the allocation of the flow of services are intimately tied to the sustainability of the resource. It is highly unlikely that one can achieve sustainability without careful attention to the efficiency, fairness, and enforceability of the rules specifying who can appropriate how much of the service flow, at what times and places, and under what conditions. Furthermore, unless responsibilities are linked in a reasonable fashion to benefits obtained, the beneficiaries themselves will resist efforts to insist that they take responsibilities.

Additional Attributes

In addition to these general attributes of physical and material conditions that affect the incentives of participants, resource systems are also characterized by a diversity of other attributes that affect how rules combine with physical and material conditions to generate positive or negative incentives. Whether resource units are *mobile* or *stationary*, and whether *storage* is available somewhere in a system, affect the problems that individuals governing and managing common-pool resources face (Schlager, Blomquist, and Tang 1994). The problems of regulating a lobster fishery, for example, are much simpler than those of regulating a salmon fishery. Similarly, allocating water in a predictable and efficient manner is easier to achieve when there is some storage in the system than when it is a run-of-the-river system.

If a natural resource system is renewable, such as many groundwater basins, the relevant time horizon for sustaining use is very long, and achieving appropriate rules may mean the difference between creating a sustainable conjunctive use system and destroying a groundwater basin. Devising an effective set of rules for regulating the use of an oil pool, on the other hand, involves determining an optimal path for mining a resource. The cost of withdrawing the last units of oil will be much higher if producers have not coordinated their withdrawal patterns. Since the oil field will eventually be used up, the lack of a future may not generate the incentives needed to achieve adequate regulation early in the development phase (Libecap 1978).

The size of a resource system can also have a major impact on the incentives facing participants. The length and slope of a main canal of an irrigation system not only affects the cost of its maintenance but also the strategic bargaining that exists between headenders and tailenders on an irrigation system (E. Ostrom 1996). Increasing the number of participants is associated with increased transaction costs. How steeply the costs rise depends, to a large extent, on the rules-in-use and the heterogeneity of the users.

The productivity, predictability, and patchiness of a resource affect the likelihood that private-property arrangements will be successful and enhances the likelihood that common-property arrangements will be necessary (Netting 1982). Similarly, the resilience of a multispecies ecosystem affects the sensitivity of the system to both the rules used to govern the particular system and to changes in economic or environmental conditions elsewhere (Holling 1994). These additional attributes are slowly being integrated into a body of coherent theory about the impact of physical and material conditions on the structure of the situations that individuals face and their resulting incentives and behavior. Analysts diagnosing resource problems need to be sensitive to the very large difference among resource settings and the need to tailor rules to diverse combinations of attributes rather than some assumed uniformity across all resources in a particular sector within a country.

Attributes of the Community

A third set of variables that affects the structure of an action arena relates to the community. The attributes of a community that are important in affecting the structure of an action arena include the norms of behavior generally accepted in the community, the level of common understanding potential participants share about the structure of particular types of action arenas, the extent of homogeneity in the preferences of those living in a community, and the distribution of resources among those affected. The term *culture* is frequently applied to this bundle of variables.

For example, when all appropriators from a common-pool resource share a common set of values and interact with one another in a multiplex set of arrangements, the probabilities of their developing adequate rules and norms to govern resources are much greater (Taylor 1987). The importance of building a reputation for keeping one's word is important in such a community, and the cost of developing monitoring and sanctioning mechanisms is relatively low. If the appropriators from a resource come from many different communities and are distrustful of one another, the task of devising and sustaining effective rules is substantially increased.

Whether individuals use a written vernacular language to express their ideas, develop common understanding, share learning, and explain the foundation of their social order is also a crucial variable of relevance to institutional analysis (V. Ostrom 1997). Without a written vernacular language, individuals face considerably more difficulties in accumulating their own learning in a usable form to transmit from one generation to the next.

5. Linking Action Arenas

In addition to analysis that digs deeper into the factors affecting individual action arenas, an important development in institutional analysis is the examination of linked arenas (see McGinnis and Williams 2000). Whereas the concept of a "single" arena may include large numbers of participants and complex chains of action, most of social reality is composed of multiple arenas linked sequentially or simultaneously (Hooghe and Marks 2001).

When individuals wish to intervene to change the structure of incentives and deterrents faced by participants in socially constructed realities to guide (or control) participants toward a different pattern of results, they do so by attempting to change the rules individuals use to order their interactions within particular types of action arenas. Some interesting and important institutional arrangements for coordinating complex chains of actions among large numbers of actors involve multiple organizations competing with one another according to a set of rules. Markets are the most frequently studied institutional arrangements that achieve coordination by relying primarily on rule-governed, competitive relationships among organizations. Rule-governed competition among two or more political parties is considered by many analysts to be an important requisite for a democratic polity. Less studied, but potentially as important a means for achieving responsiveness and efficiency in producing public goods and services, are arrangements that allow rule-ordered competition among two or more potential *producers* of public goods and services.

All rules are nested in another set of rules that define how the first set of rules can be changed. The nesting of rules within rules at several levels is similar to the nesting of computer languages at several levels. What can be done at a higher level will depend on the capabilities and limits of the rules at that level and at a deeper level. Whenever one addresses questions about *institutional change*, as contrasted to action within institutional constraints, it is necessary to recognize the following:

1. Changes in the rules used to order action at one level occur within a currently "fixed" set of rules at a deeper level.
2. Changes in deeper-level rules usually are more difficult and more costly to accomplish, thus increasing the stability of mutual expectations among individuals interacting according to a set of rules.

As discussed briefly above, it is useful to distinguish three levels of rules that cumulatively affect the actions taken and outcomes obtained in any operational setting (Kiser and Ostrom 1982). *Operational rules* directly affect day-to-day decisions made by the participants in any setting. *Collective-choice rules* affect operational activities and results through their effects in determining who is eligible and the specific rules to be used in changing operational rules. *Constitutional-choice rules* affect operational activities and their effects in determining who is eligible and the rules to be used in crafting the set of collective-choice rules that in turn affect the set of operational rules. One can even think about a "meta constitutional" level underlying all the others that is not frequently analyzed. One can think of the linkages among these rules and related level of analysis as shown in Figure 3.

For most practical applications, three or four levels are enough, but there is no theoretical justification for any specific number of levels. For the purposes of formal theory, we may need to assume as long a series of layers as is needed until we hit rock bottom—the physical world. Very deep layering—even infinite layering—turns out to be needed in many aspects of formal theory. Game theorists, for example, have had to assume that the common knowledge needed for one to assume that there is a game is nested infinitely. "Information is *common*

Doing Institutional Analysis 843

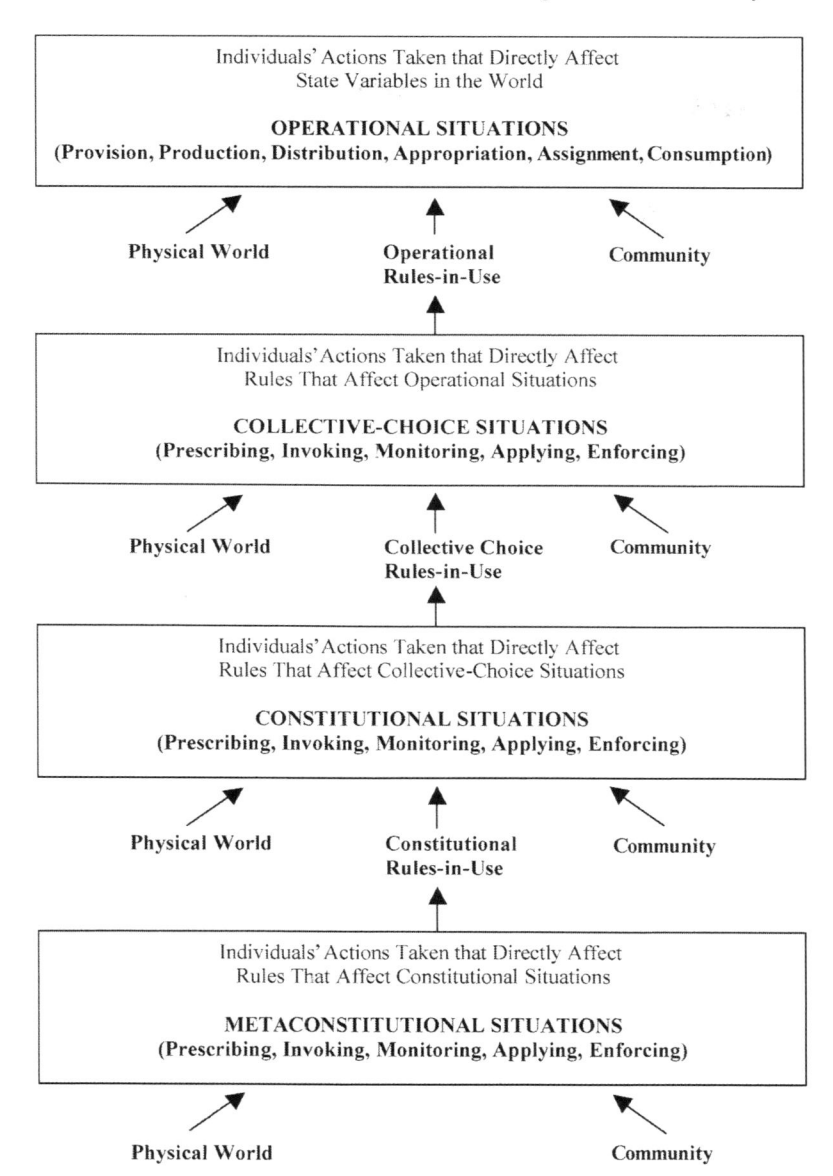

Figure 3. Levels of analysis and outcomes.

knowledge if it is known to all players, each player knows that all of them know it, and each of them knows that all of them know that all of them know it, and so forth ad infinitum" (Rasmusen 1989: 50). Thus, one can always assume that there are even more primitive rules underlying those that one is analyzing at any one level—thus our positing of a very general meta-constitutional level—until one gets to the constraints of a physical world.

The participants in collective-choice games may be the same participants as in linked operational-choice games (as when all firms in an industry agree upon a particular industry standard that they will all use in manufacturing goods). Or, participants in collective-choice games may differ from those in operational games. They may, for example, be legislative representatives selected in electoral games (themselves part of the collective-choice level of action) to be the agents of a set of principals—the citizens engaged in a wide diversity of operational games that will be affected over time by legislative policies. Participants in the third level can, again, either be participants in the other two levels or not. And, participants in constitutional choices may not recognize that they are making a constitutional rule—they may be simply trying to fix a problem with the way that they have been making policy choices over the last several years.

At each level of analysis there may be one or more arenas in which the types of decisions made at that level will occur. In the collective-choice, constitutional, and meta-constitutional situations, activities involve prescribing, invoking, monitoring, applying, and enforcing rules (Lasswell and Kaplan 1950; Oakerson 1994). The concept of an "arena" as described earlier does not imply a formal setting, but can include such formal settings as legislatures and courts. Policymaking (or governance) regarding the rules that will be used to regulate operational-level choices is usually carried out in one or more collective-choice arenas as shown in Figure 3.

6. Conclusion

When a theorist chooses to analyze a situation at any particular level, he or she must assume that the institutional rules at that level are temporarily fixed for the purpose of analysis. These rules form a part of the *structure* of the situation rather than the *solution* to the game created by that structure. When the purpose of analysis is to understand the origin of the rules at one level, knowing the structure of the situation at the next higher level is essential for that enterprise. The equilibria achieved at one level are thus supported by equilibria that have been achieved at higher levels.[8] Understanding the role of these nested levels does not, however, require that the analyst specify the full supporting infrastructure in eludicating how individuals are expected to behave at one level. Thus, assuming that there are multiple levels where decisions are made that affect actions at other levels actually greatly simplifies analysis rather than complicating it.

Some situations within any one of these levels may be simple enough that one can generate a clear and empirically supported prediction about outcomes.

---

[8] The decisions reached by members of a legislature are not stable if opponents of these decisions win a majority of seats in future elections on promises that they will reverse earlier decisions or change the constitutions so as to make the decisions unconstitutional. The stability of decisions in complex modern institutions is dependent not only upon the preferences and procedures used to organize decision making in one arena but upon the entire nested set of arenas (Shepsle 1989).

One can do this, for example, in a highly competitive market producing goods characterized by low costs of exclusion and subtractability. Here, one can rely on well-tested results from prior theoretical and empirical work. It is usually much more difficult to predict results when one is analyzing a collective-choice or constitutional-choice situation as it impacts on an operational-level setting. Existing theoretical results are frequently not available for predicting results in an operational situation whose rules are being changed at a collective-choice level. When new and unanalyzed situations are created by the process of changing parts of a rule configuration, institutional analysis needs to proceed to undertake a deeper analysis of how participants view the new rules, how they come to understand them, how they will be monitored and enforced, and what types of individual actions and collective outcomes are produced. This is frequently a challenging, difficult, and complex theoretical and empirical task.

Acknowledgements

The author is appreciative of the support of the "Institutions Project" of the Resilience Alliance and the comments of two reviewers of an earlier draft of this manuscript. Patty Lezotte has once again done a wonderful job of editing the manuscript.

References

Agrawal, Arun. 1998. *Greener Pastures: Politics, Markets, and Community among a Migrant Pastoral People*. Durham, NC: Duke University Press.

Anderies, J. Marty. 2002. "The Transition from Local to Global Dynamics: A Proposed Framework for Agent-Based Thinking in Socio-Ecological Systems" in Marco A. Janssen (ed.), *Complexity and Ecosystem Management: The Theory and Practice of Multi-Agent Systems*. Cheltenham, UK: Elgar, pp. 13–34.

Andersson, Krister. 2002. "Can Decentralization Save Bolivia's Forests? An Institutional Analysis of Municipal Forest Governance." Ph.D. dissertation, Indiana University, Bloomington.

Arrow, Kenneth. 1951. *Social Choice and Individual Values*. 2nd edn. New York: Wiley.

Black, Max. 1962. *Models and Metaphors*. Ithaca, NY: Cornell University Press.

Blomquist, William. 1992. *Dividing the Waters: Governing Groundwater in Southern California*. Oakland, CA: ICS Press.

Bourdieu, Pierre. 1977. *Outline of a Theory of Practice*. Cambridge: Cambridge University Press.

Buchanan, James M. and Gordon Tullock. 1962. *The Calculus of Consent*. Ann Arbor, MI: University of Michigan Press.

Commons, John R. 1957. *Legal Foundations of Capitalism*. Madison, WI: University of Wisconsin Press.

Crawford, Sue E.S. and Elinor Ostrom. 1995. "A Grammar of Institutions". *American Political Science Review* 89:3, 582–600.

Dietz, Tom, Elinor Ostrom, and Paul Stern. 2003. "The Struggle to Govern the Commons". *Science* 302(5652): 1907–1912.

DiMaggio, Paul and Walter Powell. 1983. "The Iron Cage Revisited". *American Sociological Review* 48(2): 147–160.

Firmin-Sellers, Kathryn. 1996. *The Transformation of Property Rights in the Gold Coast: An Empirical Study Applying Rational Choice Theory*. New York: Cambridge University Press.

Fligstein, Neil. 1998. "Fields, Power, and Social Skill: A Critical Analysis of the New Institutionalisms". Work. Paper. Berkeley, CA: University of California.

Ganz, Joan S. 1971. *Rules: A Systematic Study*. Paris: Mouton.

Gibson, Clark. 1999. *Politicians and Poachers: The Political Economy of Wildlife Policy in Africa*. Cambridge: Cambridge University Press.

Gibson, Clark, John Williams, and Elinor Ostrom. 2005. "Local Enforcement and Better Forests." *World Development* (forthcoming).

Harré, Rom. 1974. "Some Remarks on 'Rule' as a Scientific Concept" in Theodore Mischel (ed.), *Understanding Other Persons*. Oxford: Basil Blackwell, pp. 143–184.

Holling, C.S. 1994. "An Ecologist View of the Malthusian Conflict" in Kerstin Lindahl-Kiessling and Hans Landberg (eds.), *Population, Economic Development, and the Environment*. New York: Oxford University Press, pp. 79–103.

Hooghe, Liesbet and Gary Marks. 2001. *Multi-Level Governance and European Integration*. Lanham, MD: Rowman & Littlefield.

Janssen, Marco A. 2002. "Changing the Rules of the Game: Lessons from Immunology and Linguistics for Self-Organization of Institutions" in Marco A. Janssen (ed.), *Complexity and Ecosystem Management: The Theory and Practice of Multi-Agent Systems*. Cheltenham, UK: Elgar, pp. 35–47.

Kaminski, Antoni. 1992. *An Institutional Theory of Communist Regimes: Design, Function, and Breakdown*. Oakland, CA: ICS Press.

Kiser, Larry L. and Elinor Ostrom. 1982. "The Three Worlds of Action: A Metatheoretical Synthesis of Institutional Approaches" in Elinor Ostrom (ed.), *Strategies of Political Inquiry*. Beverly Hills, CA: Sage, pp. 179–222.

Lam, Wai Fung. 1998. *Governing Irrigation Systems in Nepal: Institutions, Infrastructure, and Collective Action*. Oakland, CA: ICS Press.

Lasswell, Harold and Abraham Kaplan. 1950. *Power and Society: A Framework for Political Inquiry*. New Haven, CT: Yale University Press.

Libecap, Gary D. 1978. "Economic Variables and the Development of Law: The Case of Western Mineral Rights". *Journal of Economic History* 38(2): 338–362.

Loveman, Brian. 1993. *The Constitution of Tyranny: Regimes of Exception in Spanish America*. Pittsburgh, PA: University of Pittsburgh Press.

Mayntz, Renate and Fritz W. Scharpf. 1995. *Steuerung and Selbstorganisation in staatsnahen Sektoren*. Frankfurt am Main: Campus-Verlag.

McGinnis, Michael (ed.). 1999. *Polycentricity and Local Public Economies: Readings from the Workshop in Political Theory and Policy Analysis*. Ann Arbor, MI: University of Michigan Press.

McGinnis, Michael and John Williams. 2000. "Policy Uncertainty in Two-Level Games: Examples of Correlated Equilibria" in Michael McGinnis (ed.), *Polycentric Games and Institutions: Readings from the Workshop in Political Theory and Policy Analysis*. Ann Arbor, MI: University of Michigan Press, pp. 202–236.

Mwangi, Esther. 2003. "Institutional Change and Politics: The Transformation of Property Rights in Kenya's Maasailand". Ph.D. dissertation, Indiana University, Bloomington.

National Research Council. 2002. *The Drama of the Commons*. Committee on the Human Dimensions of Global Change. Elinor Ostrom, Thomas Dietz, Nives Dolšak, Paul C. Stern, Susan Stonich, and Elke Weber (eds.), Washington, DC: National Research Council, National Academy Press.

Netting, Robert McC. 1982. "Territory, Property, and Tenure" in Robert M. Adams, Neil J. Smelser, and Donald J. Treiman (eds.), *Behavioral and Social Science Research: A National Resource*. Washington, D.C.: National Academy Press, pp. 446–501.

North, Douglass C. 1990. *Institutions, Institutional Change, and Economic Performance*. New York: Cambridge University Press.

Oakerson, Ronald J. 1992. "Analyzing the Commons: A Framework" in Daniel W. Bromley et al. (eds.), *Making the Commons Work: Theory, Practice, and Policy*. Oakland, CA: ICS Press, pp. 41–59.

———. 1994. "The Logic of Multi-Level Institutional Analysis". Paper presented at the Workshop on the Workshop conference, Indiana University, Workshop in Political Theory and Policy Analysis, Bloomington, IN, June 15–19, 1994.

Olson, Mancur. 1965. *The Logic of Collective Action: Public Goods and the Theory of Groups*. Cambridge, MA: Harvard University Press.

Ostrom, Elinor. 1986. "An Agenda for the Study of Institutions". *Public Choice* 48: 3–25.

———. 1990. *Governing the Commons: The Evolution of Institutions for Collective Action*. New York: Cambridge University Press.

———. 1992. "The Rudiments of a Theory of the Origins, Survival, and Performance of Common-Property Institutions" in Daniel W. Bromley, et al. (eds.), *Making the Commons Work: Theory, Practice, and Policy*. Oakland, CA: ICS Press, pp. 41–59.

———. 1996. "Incentives, Rules of the Game, and Development" in *Proceedings of the Annual World Bank Conference on Development Economics 1995*. Washington, DC: The World Bank, pp. 207–34.

———. 1998. "A Behavioral Approach to the Rational Choice Theory of Collective Action". *American Political Science Review* 92(1): 1–22.

———. 1999a. "Coping with Tragedies of the Commons". *Annual Review in Political Science* 2: 493–535.

———. 1999b. "Institutional Rational Choice: An Assessment of the Institutional Analysis and Development Framework" in Paul A. Sabatier (ed.), *Theories of the Policy Process*. Boulder, CO: Westview Press, pp. 35–71.

Ostrom, Elinor, Roy Gardner, and James Walker. 1994. *Rules, Games, and Common-Pool Resources*. Ann Arbor, MI: University of Michigan Press.

Ostrom, Vincent. 1964. "Editorial Comment: Developments in the 'No-Name' Fields of Public Administration". *Public Administration Review* 24(1): 62–63.

———. 1980. "Artisanship and Artifact". *Public Administration Review* 40(4): 309–317.

———. 1987. *The Political Theory of a Compound Republic: Designing the American Experiment*. 2d edn. Lincoln, NE: University of Nebraska Press.

———. 1991. *The Meaning of American Federalism: Constituting a Self-Governing Society*. Oakland, CA: ICS Press.

———. 1997. *The Meaning of Democracy and the Vulnerability of Democracies: A Response to Tocqueville's Challenge*. Ann Arbor, MI: University of Michigan Press.

Polski, Margaret M. 2003. *The Invisible Hands of U.S. Commercial Banking Reform: Private Action and Public Guarantees*. Boston, MA: Kluwer.

Rapoport, Anatol. 1966. *Two-Person Game Theory: The Essential Ideas*. Ann Arbor, MI: University of Michigan Press.

Rasmusen, Eric. 1989. *Games and Information: An Introduction to Game Theory*. Oxford: Basil Blackwell.

Sawyer, Amos. 1992. *The Emergence of Autocracy in Liberia: Tragedy and Challenge*. Oakland, CA: ICS Press.

Scharpf, Fritz W. 1997. *Games Real Actors Play: Actor-Centered Institutionalism in Policy Research*. Boulder, CO: Westview Press.

Schlager, Edella. 1990. "Model Specification and Policy Analysis: The Governance of Coastal Fisheries". Ph.D. dissertation, Indiana University, Bloomington.

Schlager, Edella, William Blomquist, and Shui Yan Tang. 1994. "Mobile Flows, Storage, and Self-Organized Institutions for Governing Common-Pool Resources." *Land Economics* 70(3): 294–317.

Scott, W. Richard. 2001. *Institutions and Organizations*. 2nd edn. Thousand Oaks, CA: Sage.

Seo, Myeong-Gu and W.E.D. Creed. 2002. "Institutional Contradictions, Praxis, and Institutional Change: A Dialectical Perspective". *Academy of Management Review* 27(2): 222–247.

Shepsle, Kenneth A. 1979. "Institutional Arrangements and Equilibrium in Multidimensional Voting Models". *American Journal of Political Science* 23: 27–59.

———. 1989. "Studying Institutions: Some Lessons from the Rational Choice Approach". *Journal of Theoretical Politics* 1(2): 131–147.

Shimanoff, Susan B. 1980. *Communication Rules: Theory and Research*. Beverly Hills, CA: Sage.

Shirley, Mary M. 2002. *Thirsting for Efficiency: The Economics and Politics of Urban Water System Reform*. Amsterdam: Pergamon.

Sproule-Jones, Mark. 1993. *Governments at Work: Canadian Parliamentary Federalism and Its Public Policy Effects*. Toronto: University of Toronto Press.

Tang, Shui Yan. 1992. *Institutions and Collective Action: Self-Governance in Irrigation*. Oakland, CA: ICS Press.

Taylor, Michael. 1987. *The Possibility of Cooperation*. New York: Cambridge University Press.

Toulmin, S. 1974. "Rules and Their Relevance for Understanding Human Behavior" in T. Mischel (ed.), *Understanding Other Persons*. Oxford: Basil Blackwell, pp. 185–215.

Walker, S. Tjip. 1998. "Both Pretense and Promise: The Political Economy of Privatization in Africa". Ph.D. dissertation, Indiana University, Bloomington.

Weissing, Franz J. and Elinor Ostrom. 1991. "Irrigation Institutions and the Games Irrigators Play: Rule Enforcement without Guards" in Reinhard Selten (ed.), *Game Equilibrium Models II: Methods, Morals, and Markets*. Berlin: Springer-Verlag, pp. 188–262.

Williamson, Oliver E. 1991. "Comparative Economic Organization: The Analysis of Discrete Structural Alternatives". *Administrative Science Quarterly* 36(2): 269–296.

Wynne, Susan G. 1989. "The Land Boards of Botswana: A Problem in Institutional Design". Ph.D. dissertation, Indiana University, Bloomington.

Subject Index

ABA (American Bar Association), 187
accountability, 528, 632, 677
action arena, 825, 828, 829, 830, 832, 834, 841, 842
adaptability, 200, 252, 253, 261, 262, 264, 266, 271, 272, 273
adaptation, 9, 47, 48, 51, 52, 53, 61, 197, 200, 216, 229, 233, 239, 246, 247, 285, 290, 291, 299, 300, 321, 322, 326, 327, 328, 329, 331, 337, 338, 377, 423, 426, 438, 492, 504, 524, 525, 591, 593, 595, 600, 601, 624, 629, 630, 632, 634, 646, 647, 661,
administrative costs, 286, 291, 293, 294, 311
Administrative Procedure Act, 535
administrative procedures, 13, 320, 520, 530, 532, 534, 535, 537, 684,
adoption of innovation, 417
adverse selection, 292, 365, 403, 734, 736
advertising, 54, 188, 189, 194, 215, 218, 328, 423, 425, 445, 501, 597, 602, 823
Africa, 93, 110, 223, 258, 259n., 575, 612, 616, 617, 618, 620, 622, 630, 639, 640, 733, 744, 773
agency
  problems, 11, 253, 254, 353, 361–2, 730, 738, 745
  relationship, 196
  theory, 281, 290
agenda control, 99, 107, 129, 131, 132, 133, 134, 137
agenda powers, 106–7, 131, 140
agricultural contracts, 12, 465–86
  features, 467
  structure, 12
  contracts, 473, 478–86

agriculture, 12, 58, 125, 128–9, 234n., 448n., 449, 455, 465–81, 486, 603, 615, 617, 619, 620, 625, 629, 620, 625
aid, 192, 368, 611, 621, 622, 631, 632, 633, 669, 765
air pollution, 564–8
  open-access problem, 564–6
  regulation, political economy of, 565n.
  transaction costs and solutions, 564–6
  tradable pollution permits, 566–8
Alcoa v. Essex, 495
alliances, 73, 76, 80, 81, 281, 295n., 296, 302, 389, 390, 412, 438, 447, 448, 449, 745, 845
Amazon, 552, 574, 575, 576, 580, 583, 584, 586, 587
Amerada Hess v. Orange & Rockland Utilities, Inc., 492, 506, 508
American federal system, 160, 164, 167, 168
American Law and Economics Association, 241n.
American Law Institute, 241
Anglo-American common law, 198, 199
aquifers, 14, 545, 546
arbitration, 16, 53, 192, 199, 206, 214, 216–18, 219, 224, 225, 291, 335, 678, 680, 740
Argentina, 102, 102n., 105, 116, 128, 159, 531n., 629, 634
  constitutional reforms, 111, 114
  democracy, 95
  macroeconomic imbalances, 154
  parliamentary system, 96
  presidential system, 115
  privatization, 521n.

Subject Index

arrondissement, 71, 72, 80
Asia, 93, 96, 110, 223, 374, 617, 618, 620, 621, 624, 639, 640, 773, 793,
asset specificity, 10, 12, 47, 51, 52, 53, 56, 310, 312, 321, 326–33, 338, 341, 342, 343, 402, 405, 412, 413, 437, 438, 439, 440, 442, 443, 444, 445, 446, 447, 448, 451, 452, 453, 454, 455, 456
  dedicated assets, 328
  human, 328
  intangible assets, 328
  physical, 327
  site specificity, 327
asymmetric information, 175, 208, 332, 502, 551, 745
auction, 57, 305
Australia, 93, 126n., 223, 246, 265
  settler colonies, 265
  system of registration, 246
  voting pattern, 128
Austrian civil codes, 258
authority, 5, 70, 91, 92, 96, 97, 98, 102–8, 116, 128, 131, 132, 136, 140, 150, 151, 153, 155, 156, 161, 162, 163, 165, 166, 169, 170, 180, 182, 188, 190, 194, 231, 234, 283, 287, 289, 301, 302, 309, 334, 335, 358, 359, 368, 371, 382, 403, 554, 560, 586, 737, 752, 772, 774, 805, 830, 834, 835, 836, 839

Bangladesh, 93, 624, 710, 719
Bank of San Giorgio, 759
bankruptcy, 11, 154, 195, 243, 253, 254, 349, 366, 377, 385, 386–7, 441, 500, 501, 629, 647, 682, 771
bargaining, 14, 44, 59, 99, 100, 101, 106, 108, 194, 195, 208, 321, 322, 326, 328, 329, 330, 332, 334, 335, 338, 379, 388, 391, 412, 426, 439, 444, 449, 452, 477, 478, 495, 549, 550, 556, 562, 563, 564, 565, 567, 568, 739, 760, 823, 824, 840
barriers to entry, 325, 591, 598
barter, 14, 35, 592, 594, 594n., 595, 604, 613
Bavaria, 256
Belgium, 71, 72, 80, 93, 393, 640
  legal system, 259
  electoral systems 72

beliefs, 1, 2, 3, 15, 21, 24, 26, 27, 179, 205, 305, 440, 580, 582, 587, 611, 612, 615, 617, 618, 622, 623–4, 625, 628, 629, 630, 631, 632, 633, 634, 734, 762, 797, 811
benevolent government, 150, 151, 154, 156, 169
Better Business Bureau, 216, 218, 713, 740, 744, 745
bicameralism, 81
black market activity, 626n.
blackboard economics, 33
Bloor v. *Falstaf*, 492, 500–503
Board, 56, 207, 267, 371, 372, 373, 374, 377, 379, 380–81, 383, 387, 388, 390, 396, 446, 792, 798, 822, 830
Bolivia, 93, 110, 115n., 598n., 657, 659
boundary rules, 633, 834, 835, 836
bounded rationality, 1, 12, 46, 282, 286, 322, 403, 407, 408, 409, 410, 416, 425, 426, 668, 829
Bourse of Amsterdam, 742
Brazil, 93, 95, 101, 102, 103, 104, 105, 107, 110, 113, 124, 133n., 154, 579, 582, 584, 585, 586, 599, 652, 653, 657, 659
  constitutional reforms, 111
  democracy, 95
  electoral rule, 124
  forest policies, 586
  macroeconomic imbalances, 154
  parliamentarism, 95
  property rights, 599
bribes, 69, 82, 85, 183, 185, 188, 376, 599, 611, 708
bright-line, 256, 273
Britain, 15, 74, 76, 126, 138, 139, 165, 384, 601, 639, 641, 642, 643, 644, 651, 652, 653
  broadcasting, 601
  constitutional structure, 139
British
  civil law, 257
  common law, 261, 266, 271
  electoral evidence, 76
  electorate, 138
  House of Commons, 74, 124, 126
  House of Lords, 133n.
  legal origins, 264, 265
  legal system, 219

Parliament, 137, 530
politics, 139
Tory Party, 138
Bulgaria, 93, 96, 110, 675
bureaucracy, 49, 51, 52, 53, 184, 185, 198, 210, 255, 290, 321, 323, 337, 338, 350, 357, 358, 359, 367, 368, 374, 438, 517, 527, 528, 529, 530, 531, 586, 591, 598n., 617, 621, 627, 630, 650, 677, 680, 687, 737, 752, 767, 803, 807, 808, 811
Byzantine Empire, 687, 731, 753

cabinet, 70, 92, 94, 95, 96, 99, 123, 124, 125, 126, 127, 132, 133, 134, 135, 138, 528
Canada, 77, 93, 163, 246, 468, 470, 471, 532, 575, 617, 619, 652, 653, 656, 657, 658, 659, 660
  administrative agencies, 532
  agricultural contracts, 468, 471
  federalism, 163
  system of registration, 246
Canon law, 236, 237
capital, 11, 12, 16, 24, 57, 152, 157, 166, 180, 183, 184, 185, 187, 189, 191, 194, 196, 209, 212, 214, 215, 236, 265, 266, 267, 269, 270, 271, 295, 297, 298, 302, 307, 326, 328, 333, 334, 365, 377, 378, 379, 381, 385, 386, 388, 393–6, 437, 439, 445, 448, 472, 484, 485, 486, 494, 519, 552, 558, 561, 604, 612, 616, 620, 624, 625, 634, 641, 642, 644, 651, 656, 660, 675, 676, 684, 686, 693, 701, 735, 748, 754, 760, 801, 802, 813, 838
  intensity, 439
  markets, 379
  structure, 385
capitalism, 175, 207, 401, 642, 642n., 650, 667, 678, 778, 792, 809
Caribbean, 536, 537, 617, 650, 652, 660
case law, 232, 236, 241, 242, 246, 255, 261, 271, 272
cash posters, 360, 362
cash rent, 12, 469, 470, 471, 476, 478, 480, 481, 482, 486
  contract, 469, 481
  cropshare leases and, 470
Charles IV, 771
Charles V, 772

Chile, 80, 93, 95, 102, 106, 110, 162, 521n., 598n., 630, 631, 653, 657, 658, 659
  Concertación, 80
  democracy, 95, 106, 162
  parliamentarism, 95
  Pinochet dictatorship, 629
  presidential budget authority in, 106
  presidential elections, 102
China, 28, 139, 159, 161, 259, 616, 625, 629, 630, 669, 676, 688–90, 692, 694, 708, 727, 729, 747, 752, 756, 764, 766–8, 777, 795, 807, 808, 809, 810
  commercial law, 259
  economic change, 28
  entrepreneurship, 773
  federal system, 629, 630
  fiscal decentralization, 161
  imperial China, 744
  low-trust societies, 708
  managerial incentives, 690
  Manchurian Qing dynasty, 752
  market preserving federalism, 630
  opium war, 746
  political development, 768
  sources of revenue, 159
  township and village enterprises, 631n.
  transitional institutions, 690
  Zhou dynasty, 766
choice and contract, 41–5
  sciences of, 42–5
Christian Democrats, 81
Churchill, Winston, 602
CIS (Commonwealth of Independent States), 672, 673n., 681, 682, 686
civil code law, 8,
civil code systems, 177, 195, 198, 200, 206, 585
civil law, 8, 9, 176, 182, 184, 190, 198, 219, 220, 229–33, 235, 236, 237–47, 256, 257, 259, 260–68, 272, 618, 619, 647, 808
  countries, 261
  jurisdictions, 245
  systems, 8, 9, 184, 191n., 198, 219, 241, 263, 229, 230, 232
  see also code law; common law
civil liberties, 8, 138n., 222, 626, 627, 626n., 627
Clean Air Act (1970), 565, 566

coal, 52n., 327, 337, 342, 343, 447, 455, 498, 500, 565, 595, 641
Coase theorem, 36, 208, 481, 491
code law, 8, 198, 206, 219–25
coercion, 16–17, 552, 592, 599, 613, 705–6, 727–76
  constraining institutions, 16, 705, 706, 725–39
coercive power, 16, 17, 181, 547, 564, 727, 728, 729, 737, 746, 747, 748, 749, 750, 751, 753–5, 757–9, 761, 763–78
cognitive science, 2, 26, 811, 812
Colombia, 93, 102, 104, 107, 110, 622
colonial heritage, 617–31
colonialism, 621, 624, 645, 752
command, 10, 24, 29, 137, 287, 289, 290–94, 297, 568
Commercial Code, 236, 241, 243, 258, 266, 492, 504, 629, 767
commercializing new products, 414, 416–25
commitment, 6, 13, 49, 51, 53, 55, 79, 111, 141, 175–200, 209, 213, 290, 294, 298, 300, 307, 343, 727–78
committee system, 126, 132, 133, 135, 136, 138, 139, 140
commodity contract, 496, 499
common and code law, 222–3
common forest and property rights, deforestation of, 547n.
common law, 8, 9, 176, 177, 195, 197, 198, 200, 217, 224, 229–31, 239, 239n., 240, 259, 263
  code law and, 219–23
  countries, 261, 264, 266n.
  evolution, 233–5, 240
  jurisdictions, 245
  legal systems, 177
  see also civil law; code law
common pool, 7, 14, 150, 153, 154, 158, 160, 161, 163–4, 166–7, 169, 545–68, 715, 822, 826, 827, 836, 838–41
  state regulation of, 564–8
  regulation of, 557–61, 566
  resources, 545–68
  wastes, 551n.
common property, 546, 547, 556, 821, 834, 840

common resource, regulation of, 561–8
commons, 14, 211, 403, 546–7, 549–57, 557, 559–62, 565, 568, 573, 577, 578
  information and measurement problems, 554
  tragedy of, 551
  transaction costs and solutions, 552
communalism, 762, 764, 766, 767, 776, 778
communism, 25, 28, 29, 34, 91, 96, 105, 109, 667, 676, 685, 809, 810
Compania Naviera Asiatic v. *The Burmah Oil Co.*, 499
compensation, 14, 56, 60, 179, 183, 185, 186, 213, 225, 335–7, 353–6, 362–3, 365, 367, 380, 383–4, 388, 390, 474, 494, 500, 502, 550, 554, 556, 585, 593, 655, 707
competition, 2, 7, 22–3, 25, 34, 37, 43, 57, 69–86, 91, 100, 117, 126, 150, 152, 155, 157, 169, 191, 221–2, 296, 387, 387, 536n., 602, 614, 625, 632, 682, 742, 753
competitive market, 10, 53, 193, 296, 302, 336, 617, 802, 835, 837, 838, 845
concentrated ownership, 270, 271, 390–91
confidence votes, 6, 94, 96, 99, 116, 134
conflict, 43, 55, 94, 95, 101, 104, 105, 107, 112, 116, 162, 182, 259, 295, 296, 299, 301, 335, 385, 435, 522, 554, 563, 584, 585, 586, 617, 621–3, 627, 654, 702, 749, 753, 767, 773
Congo, 110, 265
Congress, 91, 96, 100, 101, 104, 105, 106, 113, 114, 125, 127, 128, 130, 140, 165, 531–3, 586, 603, 824
Conseil d'Etat, 238
constitution, 6, 26, 91, 94, 95, 96, 99, 105, 106, 111–12, 115–16, 131, 155, 162, 164, 165–8, 532, 579, 585, 629, 656, 842
constitutional economics, 43
constitutional monarchy, 771, 772, 777
continental law, 235–6
contingency theory, 349, 359–60

contract, 45, 47, 320, 394–5, 445–9, 467, 469, 481, 484, 515, 605, 708
   complete, 175, 196
   contingent, 320, 322
   description, 468–74
   duration, 52n.
   enforcement, 16, 166, 176, 251, 491–510, 614, 727–47, 776
contract law 1, 48, 176, 177, 179, 192, 193, 195, 208, 209, 224, 335, 388–9, 493, 535–7
contractual arrangements, 12–13, 44, 46, 53–4, 197, 299–300, 308–9, 322, 333, 343, 447–9
contractual commitments, 175–200, 343, 366, 713
   problem of, 178–81
control, 10, 48, 51, 69, 83, 96–9, 107, 123–39, 155, 156n., 188, 220, 233–5, 253, 262–3, 269, 272, 283, 290–93, 299, 311, 334, 338, 392, 445, 467, 564–5, 593–7, 602n., 687, 760
convention, 17, 26, 99, 301, 405, 656, 702, 804, 811
cooperation, 47, 284, 292, 350, 362–7, 414–15
cooperatives, 22, 54, 295n., 741, 744, 822
coordination, 7, 34, 45, 69–81, 161–3, 182, 288–91, 295, 299, 302, 407, 435, 445, 452, 702
corporate finance, 251, 253, 261, 268, 269–71
corporate governance, 11, 16, 371–97, 670, 685–8
   basic institutions, 377–8
   problems, 372–7
corporate institutions, 376, 392, 393–6
corporate law, 11, 195, 244, 268, 372, 375, 384–5, 388–9, 396
   see also civil law
corruption, 7, 14, 113, 154, 183, 185, 186, 188, 199, 223, 583, 599–600, 673, 677, 678, 687, 738, 767
Costa Rica, 93, 102, 102n., 110, 622, 657, 658, 660
costs, 4, 10, 12–14, 21, 34–8, 49, 50, 52n., 54–5, 59–60, 105, 125, 165, 184, 194, 208, 231, 245, 261n., 272, 282, 284–6, 290–93, 299–300, 303–6, 310–11, 321–44, 360, 372, 374, 376, 378, 381, 390–91, 394, 404–5, 409, 423, 436, 438, 451, 454, 469, 474–86, 496, 506, 519–20, 525, 546–59, 561–6, 578–9, 596, 598, 604–5, 613, 615
courts, 13, 48, 134, 163, 176, 178, 181–6, 190–91, 192, 199, 206–8, 211, 213, 216, 219, 221, 222, 225, 231–2, 238, 255–9, 263, 272, 491, 499, 504, 508, 532, 533, 623, 678, 679, 680, 684–6, 756, 774
credible commitment, 49, 51, 53, 55, 307, 366–7, 404, 412, 414, 424, 426, 576, 600, 646, 662, 702, 706–11
credit, 195, 207, 209, 237, 253, 265, 266, 269, 494, 586, 592, 684, 711, 713, 733, 740, 741, 744, 745, 774
criminal law, 206, 207–9, 679
Croatia, 96, 110
cropshare vs. cash rent, 480–82
Cultural Revolution, 259
culture, 24, 260, 265, 269, 357, 368, 389, 614, 623, 641, 643, 709
Czech Republic, 29, 258, 683, 686, 687, 691

debt, 56, 164, 195, 253, 267, 311, 378, 385, 386, 718
debtors, 237, 267, 648, 706, 713
decentralization, 32, 140, 156, 159, 161, 231, 394, 647, 674, 689, 822
decree, 6, 103–5, 107, 132, 134, 217, 218, 586
dedicated assets, 297, 328, 439, 447
default rules, 196, 230, 236, 237, 479–80, 486, 505
delegation, 128, 129, 136–8, 196, 311, 334, 366, 527, 530–32, 756–7, 764
democracy, 5, 69, 70, 74, 76, 91, 94, 96, 97, 100, 111, 160, 167, 192, 366, 391, 626–9, 678, 709
Denmark, 93, 126n., 128, 129, 393, 640, 681, 703
deregulation, 57–60, 603
deterrence, 194, 732, 742, 749, 764

Subject Index

development, 7–9, 12–13, 15–18, 26–9, 31, 42, 56, 58, 95, 125, 166, 169, 175–7, 184–6, 188–9, 191–3, 196–9, 223, 229–30, 232–9, 243, 247, 251–73, 283, 286, 293–4, 305, 309–12, 328, 339, 402–3, 405–12, 414–15, 419, 422–4, 598–600, 611–34, 639–45, 652–6, 661, 676–81, 688–90, 720–21, 727–9, 747–8, 765–76, 790, 792, 795, 807, 821, 826–30
diffusion theory, 417–19, 421
discretion, 8, 105, 115, 133, 192, 229, 231, 233, 235, 237, 238, 246, 247, 255, 256, 261, 267, 385, 387, 492, 503–9, 515, 517, 524, 527, 529, 530
discrimination, 54, 323, 324, 592, 598–9, 806
dispute resolution, 4, 48, 53, 192, 199–200, 216
dissipation of rents, 579
distribution, 24, 37, 54–5, 70, 82, 116, 123, 164, 242, 267, 299, 321, 334, 335, 359, 380–81, 404–5, 422, 424, 444–5, 485, 503, 546, 548, 550, 560, 568, 649, 661, 668
divided governments, 100, 102, 530, 531, 534
division of labor, 282, 284, 325, 821
Dominican Republic, 93, 102
Dutch legal system, 259
Dutch Republic, 773

East Germany, 676
Eastern Europe, 16, 27, 29, 33, 37, 640, 667, 669, 673, 676, 677, 681, 684, 686, 690–92, 796, 808, 810, 836
EBRD, 676, 678, 680, 686, 690, 691
economic development, 2, 15, 21, 25–8, 58, 95, 166, 175, 177, 223, 265, 266, 596, 620, 641, 644, 652, 661, 677, 678, 691, 796
economic differences, 639–52
economic exchange, 706, 730, 812
economic growth, 15, 23, 149, 166, 169, 205, 211, 212, 213, 223, 243, 251, 401, 580, 627, 641, 691
economic planning, 34
economic power, 687, 729, 745, 753–9, 766
economic sociology, 17, 789–811

economies of scale, 153, 154, 293, 319, 372, 394, 422, 423, 518, 519, 536, 823, 824
Ecuador, 93, 95, 102, 104, 110, 113, 115, 657, 658
efficiency, 21, 22, 33, 54, 57, 108, 177, 191, 195, 206, 211, 216, 219–24, 229, 230, 239–45, 254, 270, 289, 292, 293, 321–3, 326, 334, 352, 358–9, 362, 381n., 448, 597, 630n., 689, 701n., 736, 744, 750
Egypt, 596, 616
El Salvador, 93, 102, 110, 622
election, 5, 16, 69, 70, 76, 77–80, 81, 85, 92, 94, 100–102, 112–14, 117, 139, 162, 167, 823–4
electoral coordination, 74–7
electoral cycles, 102
electoral district, 71, 73, 75, 78
electoral persuasion, 81–4
electoral rules, 5, 70, 71–4, 82–5, 97, 124, 128, 139, 526, 527, 611, 706
electoral system, 5, 70–75, 77, 81, 82, 83, 85, 97, 102, 139, 530
embeddedness, 600, 601, 790–92
empirical analysis, 4, 52, 205, 319, 339, 344, 345, 732, 792
empirical research, 51, 52, 285, 306, 320, 339, 354, 438–42, 451, 453, 836
employer and employee, 195, 236, 350, 353, 379n.
employment, 195, 288, 289, 336, 350, 351, 357, 368, 391–2, 600, 616, 682–3, 706, 735, 806
endogeneity, 244, 447, 478n., 646, 709
endowment, 212, 265, 269, 288, 289, 529, 576, 617, 620, 625, 649, 652, 656, 658, 767
enforcement, 4, 7, 9, 16, 17, 22, 28, 29, 166, 175, 176, 177, 178–81, 188, 191, 194, 195, 196, 197, 199, 200, 206, 208, 209, 214, 216, 218, 223, 231, 237, 245, 253, 267, 284, 302, 305, 322, 332, 396, 475, 479, 480, 491–509, 524, 527, 574, 586, 689, 708, 712, 714, 727–47, 766, 806, 833
England, 8, 187, 211, 231, 233, 235, 239, 246, 255, 257, 263, 268, 449, 482, 615, 617, 622, 764, 768, 771, 773

common law, 8, 231
  degree of discretion, 235
  institutional change in, 239
  institutional history of, 773
  political changes, 268
English common law system, 176, 216, 223, 233, 234, 257, 258
English Parliament, 234, 234n., 760
entrepreneur, 16, 22, 25, 26, 45, 269, 288, 290, 293, 303, 356, 367, 387–8, 426, 436, 600, 604, 693, 790, 793–5, 812
entry, 69, 70, 75, 85, 324, 325, 421, 422, 425, 546–8, 551–2, 558–9, 561, 598–9, 659, 745
environmental regulation, 153, 209, 337, 507, 565n.
Equal Employment Opportunity (EEO) Law, 806
equilibrium, 23, 70, 77, 84, 85, 98, 163, 304, 338, 361–5, 368, 402, 426, 450n., 515, 523–31, 534–5, 592, 600, 604, 612, 715, 732, 733n., 749–53, 757–9, 774, 804, 825n., 835, 844
equipment contracting, 471–3, 483–6
equity, 9, 56, 253, 267, 268, 269, 270, 311, 386, 425, 446, 447, 549, 561, 680
  finance, 56
  joint ventures vs. market contracts, 413
Erie Railroad v. *Tompkins*, 222
Estonia, 93, 675
Europe, 8, 16, 33, 37, 91, 93, 96, 98, 110, 125, 137, 179, 219, 223, 232, 234, 235, 239, 247, 254–60, 371, 376, 390–3, 482, 614, 615, 619, 621, 624, 631, 640, 690n., 727, 761, 770, 793
  legal systems, 254–8
  parliamentary systems, 98, 99
  politics, 390
exchange, 35, 36, 37
  economic, 706, 730, 812
  impersonal, 29, 592, 596, 614, 727, 736, 743–4, 746, 764–5, 774
  market, 48, 205–25, 475, 592, 595
  personalized, 592, 596
  voluntary, 42, 302, 491, 599, 730
Exchequer, 221
executive compensation, 356, 383–4
experimental evidence, 208, 703, 704, 708, 715, 717

expropriation, 212, 253, 270, 329, 338, 396, 451, 519, 520, 585, 586, 677, 748
externalities, 22, 153, 207, 209, 236, 242, 289, 323, 418, 423, 518, 549–50, 562–3, 576, 704, 711, 835

factor endowments, 620, 625, 644n., 651, 652, 654, 656
farm labor, 466, 474, 479, 485
farming, 465, 466, 470–75, 479, 484, 485
Federal Arbitration Act, 199
federal system, 6, 141, 149, 150, 153, 155, 157, 159,170, 225, 629
federalism, 6, 7, 81, 84, 149–64, 165, 167–8, 517, 616, 629, 630
  economic classics, 150–53
  economic performance, 149
  economic theories, 149, 151–5
  performance and stability, 149–70
  structure, 151
  theory, 169
  under New Constitution, 165–7
Federalist, 7, 154, 156, 161, 165, 167, 629
Federalist Papers, 165, 506
Feld v. *Hentry S. Levy & Sons, Inc.*, 505
Feld v. *Levy*, 492
FERC (Federal Energy Regulatory Commission), 448
fiduciary obligations, 196
finance, 17, 43, 54, 56–7, 59, 78, 158, 164, 209, 219, 251–73, 311, 385, 446, 457, 583, 630, 654, 686, 718, 752, 795
financial development, 251–73, 717
  legal institutions and, 251–73
  legal origin and, 266
  legal theories of, 253–66
financial markets, 230, 243, 251, 253, 254, 260, 261, 264, 268, 269, 273, 615, 646, 686
financial property rights, 689
firms, 4, 9, 10, 11, 22, 33, 34, 38, 48, 54, 55, 188–9, 214, 215, 218, 266–7, 269–71, 281, 282, 286–96, 307, 309, 310, 319, 323, 325, 335, 336, 343, 345, 349–67, 372, 374, 378, 379, 382, 386, 389, 390–92, 394–5, 401–27, 440, 443–4, 449, 453, 472, 494, 562, 594–7, 667–94, 740, 792–4, 798

firms (*cont.*)
  changing rules and behavior, 681–8
  cooperation and teamwork, 350
  principal-agent problems in, 349–69
  reaction to changing policies in the short-term, 681–8
  specific human capital investments, 365
fiscal federalism, 158, 161, 517
Fisher Body, 213, 309–10, 337, 345, 439, 442, 445, 456
fisheries, 545, 548, 551, 557–61, 568
formal institutions, 1, 22, 578, 599, 601, 629, 634, 667, 678, 702, 711–20, 804–5
  see also informal institutions
forward integration into distribution, 52n., 54–5, 444–5
Foss v. *Harbottle*, 271
France, 80, 93, 95n., 104, 109–10, 198, 244, 255–62, 268, 393, 482, 640, 708, 761, 771, 776
  civil law, 8
  common law, 258
  economic performance, 244
  legal system, 260
  level of influence on diffusion, 420
  political changes, 268
  presidential elections, 80, 109
  rule making power, 232
  traditionally unified governments, 534
  water regulation, 534n.
  see also French
franchising, 11, 295, 295n., 297, 342, 414, 448
Frankfurt Stock Exchange, 304
Frederic Barbarossa, 769, 770
free-rider, 374, 381, 754, 756, 838–9
French
  educational system, 630
  legal systems, 258–9, 264–5, 679
  Revolution, 255, 631, 760
  system of registration, 246, 257
  see also France
French Caribbean, 258
French civil code/law, 176, 223, 243, 255, 257, 258, 262, 263, 266–8, 272, 618, 640n.
Fujimori, 101, 104, 111–15

game theory, 731, 732, 732n., 792, 800, 809, 811, 826–7, 831
gatekeeper, 124n., 125, 409, 414, 576
gate-keeping, 136, 377, 380–81, 383
Genoa, 623, 749n., 759
Georgia, 96, 110, 659, 682
German civil code/law, 176, 223, 238, 243, 256, 258–62, 266, 268, 271, 272
German law, 184, 244, 258, 262, 264, 265, 679
Germany, 255–7, 382, 420, 582, 750, 776
  constitution, 134
  financial institutions, 383
  high-trust societies, 708
  parliamentary election, 80
  political changes, 268
  political system, 709
  voting pattern, 128
globalization, 612, 746
Glorious Revolution (1688), 621, 622, 768, 775
GM-Fisher Body
  case, 442
  relationship, 337, 345
good faith, 200, 217, 242, 412, 492, 493, 504–10
governance, 10–14, 43–6, 48–51, 55, 56, 57, 58, 282, 285–7, 290, 296, 297, 298, 299–302, 320–23, 326, 333–44, 371–95, 407, 412, 414, 437, 440–41, 445, 451, 516, 518, 521, 523–5, 529–37, 597, 681, 685–8, 756, 772
  forms of, 300–302
  modes of, 10
  structures, 48
government, 91–117, 149, 192–3
  benevolent, 150–51, 154, 156, 169
  crises, 108–16
  divided, 100, 102, 530–31, 534
  expenditures, 626n.
  traditionally unified, 534
government opportunism, 13, 517, 518, 522
  contrasting firm, 522–53
  performance implications of, 520–22
Grameen Bank, 746
Greece, 93, 258, 598n., 769
Grossman-Hart-Moore theory, 456
group membership, 614, 711, 718–20

Guatemala, 93, 101–2, 110, 113, 622
Guyana, 258

Habsburg Empire, 258
Hanseatic League, 745
hard budget constraint, 154, 163, 164, 165, 170
heterogeneity, 138, 295, 443–4, 452, 554, 559, 624, 702, 713, 715–18, 774, 840
  problem of, 559
  social, 715–18
hierarchy, 6, 10, 38, 47, 48–51, 135, 283, 287, 289, 293, 307, 357, 414, 446
  governance mechanisms, 333
  monitoring, 357–8
  organizations, 323, 336
holding companies, 320
holdup
  defined, 213
  problem, 436, 442, 446, 453, 454, 479
Hong Kong
  colonial heritage, 619
  low-trust societies, 708
  rent control system, 593, 594
human capital, 12, 24, 180, 183–5, 187, 189, 191, 194, 196, 199, 212, 328, 334, 365, 367, 439, 442, 444, 454, 578, 611, 615, 620, 625, 634, 656, 684, 693, 754
Hungary, 80, 93, 258, 686, 687, 691
hybrid arrangements, 6, 286, 294–302, 548
hybrid regimes, 92, 97, 104, 116–17
hybrids, 6, 49, 51, 53, 92, 95–7, 282, 294, 295–9, 301, 307, 309, 437, 438, 446, 448–9

Iceland, 93, 560, 561n.
illicit responses to regulation, 591–606
  discrimination, 598–9
  private coercion, 599
  underground economic activity, 598
imperfect information, 492, 605
Imperial Valley Water District, 583
impersonal exchange, 29, 592, 596, 614, 727, 736, 743–4, 746, 764–5, 774
incentives, 1–7, 11–12, 37, 43, 48, 51n., 81, 149–51, 156–60, 162, 169, 178, 179, 184, 190, 209, 290–91, 311, 322, 326, 329, 332–8, 350–60, 366–7, 381, 386, 517, 520–23, 806

income equality, 16, 621, 624, 721
incomplete contracts, 46, 47, 196, 319, 322, 326–33, 335, 435, 452, 456
independent judiciary, 27, 527, 533–4, 630
independent military organizations, 759, 760
India, 77, 93, 155, 159, 223, 619, 624, 625, 628, 631, 656, 707, 710, 720
individualism, 763, 764, 765, 769, 776, 799
Indochina, legal system, 258
Indonesia, 109, 110, 582, 718, 720
industrial organization, 31, 38, 52, 241, 302, 323, 339, 344, 453
Industrial Revolution, 233, 234, 639, 776
industrialization, 619, 623, 625, 768
inequality, 618, 625, 652, 656, 658, 660, 717, 796
informal agreements, 449–50, 455
informal economy, 598
informal institutions, 1, 22, 25, 578, 624, 628, 704, 713, 721, 799–804
  see also formal institutions
informal norms, 22, 25, 28, 191, 198, 592, 600, 604, 713, 721, 798
informal rules, 17, 266, 546, 592, 600, 630, 632, 701, 803
information, 127, 183, 292, 546, 554
  asymmetric, 175, 208, 332, 502, 551, 745
  disclosure, 11, 53, 55, 267, 383, 384, 387
  distribution, 381
  imperfect, 492, 605
  revelation, 100
institutional change, 4, 15–17, 22–4, 26, 29, 239, 311, 550, 553–4, 556, 575, 577, 600, 623, 629, 631, 706, 758, 842
institutional development, 247, 265, 269, 611–34, 645, 652, 656, 661, 669, 674, 676–81, 688–90, 692
institutional entrepreneurs, 16, 693, 694
institutional environment, 4, 10, 11, 180, 188, 190, 197, 282, 283n., 299, 426, 438, 516, 518, 523, 530, 601, 630, 667, 669, 684, 713
institutional frameworks, 15, 22, 24, 527, 629, 633, 644, 648, 674, 801, 807, 826–27
institutional legitimacy, 389–93, 397
institutional quality, determinants of, 625
institutional reform, 102, 630, 633, 670n., 676, 687–8, 694

institutionalism
  in economic sociology, 797, 800, 801, 805, 807
  in organizational analysis, 797
institutions, 21
  and organizations, interaction between, 22
  challenges involved in studying, 822–6
  corporate, 376, 392, 393–6
  definitions of, 802, 823
  development of, 678–81
  formal, 1, 22, 578, 599, 601, 629, 634, 667, 678, 702, 711–20, 804–5
  informal, 1, 22, 25, 578, 624, 628, 704, 713, 721, 799–804
  legal, 7–9, 175–200, 205, 206, 223–5, 244, 251–73, 391, 650, 684
  market, 229–47, 613, 623, 676–81
  political (Russian), 96, 104, 105, 163
  private-order, 16, 199, 208, 214, 731, 732–6, 739–47, 759, 760, 763, 776–7
  protect property and persons, 615–16
  public-order, 16, 728–9, 737–46, 761–5, 771–2, 774–5, 776–8
  under parliamentarism, 97
integration, 10, 34, 41, 45–6, 52–5, 60, 138, 150, 168, 179, 283, 293, 295, 297, 301, 307, 310, 319–44, 405, 408, 411, 414, 426, 437, 440–56, 494, 592, 595, 604, 739, 743, 764, 768
integration and R&D, 443
intellectual property, 189, 209, 211, 413, 615, 654
interdependence, 296
interest groups, 156, 198, 220, 261, 263, 518, 532, 534–5, 554, 592, 600–604
internal organization, 45, 50, 53, 128, 311, 320, 321, 327, 329, 332–41, 454, 667, 746, 773
international commercial law, 216
International Country Risk Guide (ICRG), 677
International Society for New Institutional Economics (ISNIE), 619n., 821
Investment, 23, 320, 322, 323, 326, 328–32
  distortions, 333, 343
  incentives, 327, 338
  underinvestment, 454

investor protection laws, 243, 251–4, 264, 265, 266, 269–71, 686
Irish parliament, 137
Israel, 80, 93, 95n., 772
Italy, 80, 252, 615, 624, 703, 772
  legal system, 258
  low-trust societies, 708
  political system, 709
  property rights, 599
  rule making power, 232
Ivory Coast, 265

Jamaica, 93, 536, 620, 655
Jamaican Public Utilities Act (1966), 537n.
Japan, 382, 557, 598n., 768
  civil code, 258
  common law, 259
  financial institutional, 383
  high-trust societies, 708
  LDP, 80, 125n., 528
  Meiji era, 807
  political system, 72, 73, 79, 139, 232, 536
  traditionally unified governments, 534
  voting pattern, 129
Japanese Diet, 124, 125
joint ventures, 196, 281, 320, 413, 425, 455
judge, 8, 9, 111, 181–6, 188, 190–94, 196–9, 217, 219, 220–22, 229–45, 255–6, 258–61, 271–2, 301, 385, 395, 403, 455, 491–3, 501, 503, 509, 680, 710, 738, 751, 835
  rulemaking discretion, 232
judicial bribery, 185
judicial discretion, 8, 192, 229–47, 255, 256
judicial failures, 183, 186
judicial human capital, 185, 199
judicial interpretation/discretion, 8, 135, 195
juries, use of, 232
jurisprudence, 231–3, 238, 242–3, 255–7, 258–9, 263, 272

Kenya, 575, 620, 717, 721, 822
Korea, 93, 110, 259, 600, 708

labor, 35, 55–8, 192, 195, 209, 284, 311, 358, 379, 391, 467, 579, 650–51, 655
  contracts, 473–4, 485

Subject Index 859

force, 24
law, 195
markets, 375
Labour Party, 76
Laredo Hides Co. Inc. v. H & H Meat Products Co., Inc., 499
Latin America, 93–6, 101, 102, 109, 111–12, 114–17, 163, 223, 264, 617, 629, 631, 640, 652, 658–60, 793
   democracies, 94, 95
   differences in federalism, 163
   French civil law countries, 264
   parliamentary system, 96
   countries, 629
law and finance, 219, 251–4, 263–6, 268, 270, 271–3, 385
Law Merchant, 175, 216, 218, 221, 222, 225, 774
Law of the Sea Convention (1982), 558n.
lawyer, 176, 182–3, 186–93, 197–9, 232, 349, 381, 479, 491, 493, 503, 774, 820
   corruption, 188
   courts and judicial oversight, 190–91
   direct government regulation and service provision, 192–3
   legal education, 187–8
   norms and practices of judicial reasoning, 191–2
   professional organizations, 188–90
learning, 22, 23, 24, 26, 28, 29, 328, 402, 411, 412, 422, 439, 443, 611, 612, 615, 631, 757–9, 767, 823, 824, 841
legal environment, 177, 193–9, 231, 455
   fees, 190
   formalism, 273
   laws governing the contracting environment, 194–7
   procedural laws, 193–4
   rulemaking and legal evolution, 197–9
legal institutions, 7–9, 175–200, 205, 206, 223–5, 244, 391, 650, 684
   financial development and, 251–73
   role in structuring an effective law of contracts, 181–200
legal system, 3, 7–9, 16, 29, 37, 176, 177, 188, 205–25, 229–31, 233, 237, 239–40, 243–7, 598, 619, 630, 642, 676, 679, 680, 683, 685, 689, 737–9, 742–4, 774

Ancient Regime, 244
   and finance, 251–73
   common law origin, 223
   competition among, 221–3
   components of, 206–7
   Europe's, 254–8, 258–60
   functions of, 207
   market-oriented, 8
   value of, 230
legislative, 5, 6, 70, 78, 80, 81, 91, 94–109, 113–17, 123–41, 193, 194, 198, 229, 231, 235, 241, 243, 256, 261, 268, 526–8, 530–33, 535, 536, 548, 573, 578, 644, 647, 737, 806, 832, 844
   cartel, 139
   controlling the agenda, 131–3
   delegation and legislative process, 136–8
   organization, 129, 131
   procedural control, 134–5
   resources and their allocation, 124–31
   reversion control, 133–4
legislatures, 6, 8, 22, 70, 91, 94, 96, 98, 99, 102–9, 113–14, 124–41, 158, 198, 206, 219, 220, 230, 231, 255, 257, 259, 261, 263, 517, 526, 527, 528, 530–33, 535, 628, 820, 830, 834, 837, 844
Lex mercatoria, 222
   see also Law Merchant
liberalization, 237, 671, 673, 674, 681, 689
licit responses to regulation, 592–8
Lithuania, 93, 96, 110
logrolls, 108, 124, 125, 136
long term contracts, 52n., 302, 320, 332, 337, 342, 437, 445, 449–52, 455, 494, 498, 503–9
Louisiana, 468, 470, 471, 472, 474, 479, 659
Low Countries, legal system, 258

macroeconomics, 154, 673
mafia, 599, 684
Maghribi traders, 17, 614, 623, 734, 735
majority system, 124, 138
make-or-buy, 11, 45, 50, 52, 294, 297, 435–57
maladaptation cost, 44, 47, 61, 436, 437n., 454
Mali, 109, 110
manager, 11, 33, 152, 176, 253, 270, 290–93, 298, 300, 303, 311, 333–5,

860 Subject Index

337, 349, 360, 365–8, 371–91, 393–6,
404, 408, 410, 425, 438, 440, 444, 446,
453, 474, 502, 548, 597, 687, 689, 690,
694, 706, 745, 833
market, 3–7, 11, 14, 16–17, 21, 32–9, 41, 43,
45–58, 105, 150, 151, 153, 155,
158–60, 165, 166, 169, 170, 176, 183,
186–9, 191–3, 195, 197, 198, 253, 254,
260–62, 264–73, 281, 302–8, 377–80,
445–57, 479, 484, 486, 494, 496–9,
502, 506–9, 536, 538, 566, 574–85,
597–8, 603, 605, 615–18, 626, 632,
641–2, 646–7, 651, 667, 673, 675,
679–80, 682, 686–7, 727–78
 contracting, 307–8, 340, 341, 492, 505
 culture, 368
 exchange, 48, 205–25, 475, 592, 595
 hierarchy, 38
 imperfections, 319
 mode of organization, 303–5
 new market creation, 401–27
 power, 12, 453, 456, 518, 522–3
 transaction, 306, 320–23, 335, 337
market economy, 1, 29, 33, 229, 281, 304,
611, 631, 672, 674, 729, 747, 755, 756,
768, 796, 808, 809, 811
 expansion and political development, 765
 institutions, 229–47, 613, 623, 676–81
 judicial system in, 8
 legal institution of, 7–9
 market-preserving federalism, 155, 630
 political institutions, 761
marketing, 11, 166, 350, 401, 421–5, 444–5,
465, 467, 468, 480, 501, 503
Mauritius, 74, 655
measurement, 12, 244, 292, 306, 344, 345,
440, 444, 451, 453, 486, 495–500,
554–5, 596–8, 628, 811
mental models, 17, 24, 26, 668, 812
Merchants' Law, 216, 218, 222, 225, 735,
774
methodological individualism, 799
Mexico, 93, 110, 129, 133n., 150, 155, 158,
159, 582, 629, 653, 657, 658, 659, 743,
754
 banking center, 157, 158
 colonial heritage, 619
 political system, 534, 536, 709
microeconomics, 31, 32, 36, 251, 269, 281,

304, 319, 323, 601, 668, 673
military technology, 615, 749n., 752, 757,
770, 778
mirroring principle, 123–41
Missouri Furnace Co. v. Cochrane, 498,
499
Moldova, 96, 110
monetary policy (inflation), 626n., 672
money, 14, 35–6, 152, 178, 181, 214, 352,
354, 379, 383–5, 396, 404, 495, 578,
579, 587, 591–5, 598, 604–5, 679, 703,
704, 706, 708, 714, 741, 745, 759, 795
monitoring, 11, 56, 183, 284, 290, 298–9,
301, 320, 322, 333, 335, 337, 350–52,
354–6, 357–60, 361–3, 366–8, 436,
475, 477, 483, 546, 558, 565, 595, 597,
611, 687, 708–10, 715, 736, 740, 757,
801, 804–6, 824, 827, 833, 841, 844
monopoly, 54n., 57–8, 156, 157, 187, 207,
209, 213, 254, 257, 258, 329, 332, 378,
379, 435, 452, 519, 520, 536n., 599,
602, 615, 622, 648n., 742, 745, 748,
756, 772
moral hazard, 12, 100, 292, 351, 352, 361–7,
403, 475–8, 481, 483–6, 491, 632, 733,
734
mutual dependence, 285, 291, 297–8, 301,
449

Napoleonic Code, 237n., 255, 256, 259, 260,
262
Nash equilibrium, 361, 362, 364, 365, 524,
530
National Research Council (NRC), 822
Nature, 4, 32, 33, 35, 38, 41, 42, 281, 352,
394, 466, 475, 477, 485, 486, 727
Navigation Act, 773
negotiation, 34, 36, 104, 105, 107, 117, 188,
195–6, 199, 284, 290, 296, 305, 321,
326, 334, 367, 447, 494, 495, 500,
508–9, 549, 550, 554–5, 563–4, 567–8,
594
neoclassical economics, 2, 3, 41, 319, 323,
324, 538, 591, 600
networks, 16, 17, 295, 295n., 297, 298, 301,
413, 438, 445, 448, 449, 596, 605,
613–15, 623, 629, 685, 701–2, 710,
712, 714, 721, 734, 762, 767, 769,
791–6, 800, 802–5, 810–12

Subject Index 861

New York Stock Exchange (NYSE), 304, 305n., 741
New Zealand, 265, 532, 560, 561n.
Nicaragua, 93, 102, 107, 110
Nipsco v Carbon Country, 495
non-standard contracting, 295, 323, 329, 340, 450
norms, 2, 3, 7, 8, 10, 11, 16–18, 22, 25–9, 178, 180, 191–2, 194, 197–8, 232, 241–2, 304, 363, 366–7, 384, 390–91, 421, 449–50, 474, 524, 545–7, 587, 592, 600–601, 604, 611–16, 616–25, 627–34, 701–22, 734, 762, 789, 795, 797–808, 822, 824, 825, 828, 829, 831, 833, 841
Norway, 93, 128, 560, 561n., 640, 703

OECD, 92, 97, 391
oil, 385, 404, 443, 499, 502, 506, 507, 545, 546, 551, 553–5, 561–6, 568, 582, 595, 754, 840
  open-access problem, 561–2
  transaction costs and history of regulation, 562–3
  unitization, 563–4
Oklahoma, 479n., 562, 563
old institutional economics, 2
open access, 14, 545–68, 573
opportunism, 11, 13, 46, 59, 213, 214, 299, 300, 322, 336, 389, 403, 412–14, 422, 426, 448, 522, 523, 555n., 809
optimality, 78–9, 127, 169, 207, 246, 330, 351, 352, 354, 360, 364, 497, 579–82, 670n., 736
Orange and Rockland Utilities, Inc. v. Amerada Hess Corporation, 492, 506, 508
organization
  arrangements, 1, 310–12
  construction, 41, 48
  incentives, 311
  mechanisms, 179
  structures, 605
  supporting transactions, 308
  theory, 281, 286
origin and dynamics of CCI and political institutions, 757
ostracism, 612, 613, 623, 702, 712, 715, 716, 719

outsourcing, 412, 435, 441, 444, 453, 456
ownership, 12–13, 53–4, 207–8, 212, 243, 245, 252, 264, 269–71, 288, 295, 311, 334, 359, 360, 364, 366, 368, 372–4, 381, 385, 388, 390–92, 395–6, 437, 438, 445–6, 454–5, 468, 471, 474, 476–7, 483–4, 501, 515, 518, 522, 536, 548–9, 552, 557, 560–61, 594, 597, 599, 681, 686–9, 693, 745

Papua New Guinea, 23, 77, 93
Paraguay, 93, 102, 110, 113
PARC (Policy Affairs Research Council), 125, 129, 132, 135, 139, 140
parliamentary system, 6, 80, 91–117, 132, 134–5, 527–8, 531, 534, 537
path dependence, 12, 22, 24–9, 406, 411, 414, 416, 420, 423, 426, 427, 600–604, 606, 668, 672, 812–13
payoff, 22, 23, 44, 61, 129, 179, 191, 331, 335, 351, 353, 358, 363, 402–3, 498, 526, 528, 529, 599–600, 615, 623, 625, 632, 690, 702, 715, 730, 750–51, 804, 809, 834–6
Peace of Constance, 771
per capita GDP, 639, 640, 653
personalized exchange, 592, 596
Peru, 93, 95, 96, 101–05, 110–15, 598, 653, 657, 658
Philippines, 93, 96, 110, 482, 523n.
planned economy, 304, 836
Poland, 93, 96, 110, 258, 684, 686, 674, 687, 691, 761
policy, 5–6, 29, 31, 41, 42, 46, 52, 57–60, 69, 70, 81, 98–100, 102–9, 114, 116–17, 124–9, 131–40, 150–57, 161–2, 166–70, 177, 183, 186, 192, 206, 224, 230, 237, 239, 246, 339, 375, 382, 494, 515–17, 522–38, 554, 566, 581, 582, 601, 602, 628, 629, 639, 643, 646, 648, 671, 672, 674, 677, 681, 682, 688, 706, 707, 720, 721, 738, 766, 775, 778, 797, 827, 836, 844
  flexibility vs. credibility of, 141
  public vs. private character of, 141
Policy Affairs Research Council (PARC), 125, 129, 132, 135, 139, 140
political economy, 21, 29, 52n., 560n., 561n., 672

Subject Index

political theory, 156
  cooperation, 525-9
  decision-making rights, 747
  democracy, 667
  incentives, 156-60
  institutions, 4, 727
  opportunism, 515, 524, 566
  parties, 123
  performance, 149
  political-economic system, 25
  political intervention, 738n.
  political rights, 626n.
  property rights, 582
pollution, 153, 154, 209, 551n., 564-8
Portugal, 93, 110, 232, 258, 259, 640, 652, 703
precedent, 8, 14, 104, 135, 186, 191, 194, 198, 217, 221, 231-5, 238, 263, 533, 552, 556-7, 752
presidential system, 80, 91-117, 124, 132, 534, 537, 633n.
  curtailment of, 113
  decree, 537n., 103, 104, 105
  election, methods of, 101, 109
  government, 91-117
  hybrids between , 6
  parliamentarization of, 112-16
  policymaking powers of, 102
  rules on reelection, 110
  stability, 94
presidentialism, 81, 91, 92, 94-5, 97, 99, 100, 108, 116
price, 2, 4, 6, 22, 31-4, 41-7, 53-4, 71-2, 187, 191, 197, 208-9, 213-15, 238, 269-70, 287, 289, 291, 295-7, 302-10, 323-31, 334, 336, 343, 367-8, 373, 380-84, 387-8, 391, 404-5, 408, 417-18, 421, 423, 436-8, 447-8, 453, 469-71, 492, 501-10 , 518-23, 536, 547-8, 564, 578, 583, 591-605, 628, 651, 673, 689, 742, 746, 760, 766, 794, 803, 805-6, 812, 835, 836, 839
  adjustment, 46, 493-5
  ceilings, 593, 707n.
  discovery, 46
  discrimination, 54, 323, 324
  property right in, 495-500

system, 33, 34, 289, 295, 303
  theory, 43, 321, 423
principal agent theory, 12, 349-52, 353, 355, 360-2, 368, 373, 475-6
private-order institutions, 16, 199, 208, 214, 731, 732-6, 739-47, 759, 760, 763, 776-7
  see also public-order institutions
private ordering, 4, 43, 196, 206, 213, 219, 491-510, 614
private ownership, 212, 536, 548-9, 557
private property rights, 8, 14, 166, 212, 229, 230, 234-5, 251, 253, 260-73, 547-9, 556-7, 573, 577, 809
  protection for, 8
  system of, 166, 233, 234, 547
privatization, 205, 206, 651, 671, 673, 674, 680, 681, 685-8, 693, 795-6
product development, 56, 402-8, 412, 415, 424
product market competition, 265, 682
  monopolistic, 378
  oligopolistic, 378
  product markets, 378, 387
production, 2, 4, 41, 42, 48, 58-9, 182, 184, 186, 194, 207, 209, 281-2, 286-7, 292, 294, 304, 307, 321, 323-5, 330, 332, 336-8, 342, 345, 355-7, 360-64, 367-8, 375, 387, 390, 394-5, 402, 407-9, 413-14, 435, 442-6, 449, 465-8, 472, 477, 484-6, 505-6, 548, 554-6, 561-4, 592, 595-6, 602-3, 611, 612, 643-6, 655, 673-5, 685, 689, 721, 738, 749, 754, 757, 773, 778, 790, 801-2
  institutional structure of, 31-9
productivity, 23, 177, 197, 210, 211, 355, 362, 367, 409, 482, 559, 613, 622n., 642, 675, 676, 840
profit, 7, 22, 24, 42, 45, 59, 196-7, 209, 212, 214, 219, 236, 269, 286, 291, 323, 324, 326, 330, 354, 356, 358, 364-7, 375, 378-9, 381, 384-7, 390, 391, 402, 405-8, 416, 437-8, 441, 475, 485, 492, 495, 498, 501-5, 509, 520-22, 560, 578, 592, 594, 597, 598, 614, 643, 654, 728, 730, 735, 739-42, 754, 761, 763, 772, 776, 794, 802, 804, 835, 838

Subject Index 863

property right, 10, 12, 14, 37, 208, 223, 282, 285n., 288, 291, 294, 303, 304, 319, 326, 328, 395–6, 399, 495, 548, 548n., 568, 573–88, 599, 605, 611, 614, 626n., 727, 739, 747, 748, 756, 763, 777
  alignment, 328
  definition, 208, 209, 573
  demand and supply of, 549, 576–87
  distribution, 739
  enforcement, 573
  evolution, 575, 576, 583–7
  informal, 581
  insecure, 579, 579n.
  laws protecting, 16, 237
  naive theory, 576n., 578
  price and measurement of damages, 495–500
  protection, 8, 9, 210, 211, 580, 587, 624, 626, 753
  rule of law, 209–13, 305
  tax, 157
  theory, 281
  vs. protection by private institutions, 213–19
Prussia, 256
public contract law, 199
public enterprises, 320, 371–3, 386, 394, 523
public goods, 7, 70, 81–5, 149–55, 158–9, 163, 165–7, 187, 192, 207, 223, 232, 567, 622, 628, 702, 706, 711–12, 715–18, 752–3, 755–6, 760, 766–8, 805, 807, 826, 838, 842
public order, 43, 731, 755, , 764
public-order institutions, 16, 728–9, 737–46, 761–5, 771–2, 774–5, 776–8
  see also private-order institutions
public policy, 42, 46, 52, 57–60, 156, 339, 375, 515, 516, 524, 707, 720
  antitrust, 58
  other public policy, 59
  regulation/deregulation, 58

quality standards, 300, 565, 597
quasi-rent, 178, 213, 238, 285, 301, 322, 327–9, 331, 334, 379, 437n., 451, 452, 454, 518–21, 523

reciprocity, 296, 301, 596, 716, 719
regulation, 13–15, 33, 36–7, 52, 54, 57–9, 166, 168, 192, 193, 195, 206, 209, 218, 223, 230, 243–5, 267, 337, 343, 391, 449, 455, 507, 515–38, 545–68, 581, 582, 591–606, 626n., 678, 708, 737–8, 752, 798, 801, 803, 805–6, 808, 811, 830–32, 840
  and natural monopoly, 57
  institutions, 524–5
  theory of, 516
regulatory governance, 13, 515–18, 521–3, 529–37
  origins of, 523
  transactions approach to, 523–9
relational contracts, 181, 198, 200, 266, 295–6, 333, 436, 449–50, 684
relationship-specific investments, 12, 319, 322, 326–9, 332, 337, 435–8, 442, 445, 447, 449, 451, 454, 456
religion, 264–5, 269, 600, 601, 614, 626, 642–3, 652, 762, 812
remediableness, 59, 630, 688, 689
rent seeking, 83–4, 156, 169, 187, 188, 190, 221, 240–41, 496, 516, 611, 632, 650
reputation, 16, 47, 82, 112, 114, 135, 138–40, 163, 178–81, 200, 209, 213–19, 298, 300, 307–8, 326, 333, 420, 423–4, 445, 449, 466, 479–80, 486, 520, 612, 614, 623, 628, 702, 711–20, 732–7, 740–46, 755, 775, 802, 841
revenue, 7, 157–60, 363–4, 405–8, 467, 469, 503, 506, 519, 563, 602–3, 615, 621, 660, 750, 755–7, 759, 766, 768, 773, 808
Rhodesia, 620
Rio conference, 567n.
risk, 6, 11–12, 24, 45, 53, 100, 128, 176–9, 185, 188–9, 195, 212, 214, 216, 219, 236, 246–7, 283, 289, 292, 296, 299, 310–11, 324–5, 349–57, 360–2, 368, 386, 390, 395, 396, 410, 413–14, 418–19, 422, 425–6, 436, 444, 451, 475–8, 481, 486, 493–5, 508, 612, 616, 620, 630, 677, 702, 706, 709, 716, 721, 740, 756, 760–61, 833
Roman Empire, 8, 615, 769, 771

Roman law, 8, 232, 234, 235, 236, 254, 255, 257, 614n.
Romania, 93, 96, 110, 684, 685
rule of law, 7, 205, 206, 209–13, 222, 224, 580, 587, 627, 628, 677, 679, 728, 754, 832
rulemaking, 197, 231–3, 236, 240
rules, 2, 3, 5–11, 14, 16–18, 22, 24–9, 43, 56, 69–71, 82–5, 91, 96–100, 110, 117, 124–40, 160–61, 164, 169, 179–87, 191, 193–9, 206–7, 209, 211, 217, 220, 221–2, 225, 230–46, 253, 256–7, 266–7, 270, 273, 299, 301, 304–7, 311, 358–61, 368, 380, 385, 388–9, 448–9, 479–80, 486, 505, 509, 515–16, 522, 525–30, 533, 536, 546–7, 557–9, 562–6, 600–601, 611–15, 616–20, 626–33, 643, 656, 668–9, 681–8, 701, 703, 706, 712, 727–8, 735–43, 747, 751–3, 771, 775, 797–812, 819–45
Russia, 34, 93, 103, 198, 206, 374, 376, 623, 631, 673–5, 680, 682–4, 687
  congress of people's deputies, 104
  economic system, 29, 208, 604
  Old Believers, 603–4
  Orthodox Church, 603
  political institutions, 96, 104, 105, 163
  presidential decree authority, 104
  rule to democracy, 96
  sort of economy, 208
  sources of revenue, 159
  trade barriers, 154

safeguards, 11, 53, 57, 282, 284, 286, 298–300, 307–8, 311, 412–13, 424–6, 448–50, 515, 524–5, 614, 759–61
sales force, 52n., 353–5, 415–16, 423–4, 435, 444
Scandinavian civil law, 175, 223, 243, 257, 259, 264, 266, 679
scarcity, 2, 14, 22, 24, 574–81, 594, 656
Securities and Exchange Commission (SEC), 9n., 712
selective intervention, 50, 291, 311
self-enforcement, 178, 181, 200, 215, 307, 527, 574
separation-of-powers, 6, 8, 98–100, 123, 128, 129, 141, 161, 167, 168

Serbia, 96
share contracts, 12, 469–71, 474, 476, 480–81, 482–3
shareholder, 9, 11, 57, 196, 243–5, 253–4, 264–7, 269–71, 364, 366, 371–95, 597, 646, 679–80, 686, 794
Sherman Act, 557
shipping industry, 449, 452, 499, 773
side payments, 14, 358, 555–6, 568, 576, 581–3
site specificity, 297, 327, 343, 438, 439, 442, 445, 447, 452–3
slavery, 162, 164, 167–8, 168n., 620, 622, 643n., 650–55, 661
Slovakia, 189, 684, 691
Slovenia, 691
social capital, 16, 266, 624, 642, 701–22, 802
social security, 134, 207, 532n.
social structure, 623, 639, 641, 734, 758, 762, 767, 769, 794–8, 802
social system, 414, 418, 421, 713
socialism, 162, 187, 198, 207, 618n., 650, 683, 810
soft budget, 150, 154, 681
South Africa, 93, 598n., 620
South Korea, 96, 110, 600, 621n.
Soviet Union, 96, 205, 596, 661, 667, 669, 677, 684, 690, 692, 808–10
Spain, 15, 74, 93, 420, 455, 482, 617, 620, 640, 652, 756–7, 766, 771, 772, 776
  Habsburg, 757
  legal system, 242, 259
  political system, 79, 162, 232
specific investment, 53, 283, 296–300, 310, 319, 322, 326–38, 341, 343–4, 411–13, 435–8, 445, 447, 449–56, 479n., 518, 521n., 522
spot market, 10, 48, 49, 51, 282, 302, 307, 320, 323, 325, 333, 342, 344, 435, 437, 446, 499, 706, 707
statute law, 9, 219, 221, 230, 231, 233, 238, 241, 245
stock markets, 251, 266–73, 391, 678–80, 686–7, 765, 772
sunk costs, 378, 519, 733, 744
Supreme Court, 112, 113, 134, 166, 271, 272, 529

Sweden, 93, 133, 640, 719
Switzerland, 93, 258, 622, 640

Taiwan, 77, 79, 93, 96, 110, 139, 140, 259, 621n., 708
take-or-pay, 52n., 447, 500, 508
takeover, 11, 196, 365, 374–7, 380–83, 386, 387, 388, 389, 396, 441, 519, 597
tax, 7, 36, 83, 104, 106, 124, 149, 151–2, 157–60, 162, 165, 170, 223, 234, 235, 367, 480–3, 502–3, 520, 548–50, 555–6, 560, 566–7, 583–4, 598, 600, 602, 615, 619, 646, 648, 659, 673, 687, 703, 707, 708, 721, 750–58, 761, 767, 770–75, 838, 839
TCE (transaction cost economics), 4, 41–61, 281, 302, 319, 320, 402, 403, 407, 410, 412, 435, 437, 440, 451, 455, 456, 597, 820
technology, 26, 32, 48, 53, 58, 178–80, 212, 284, 286, 297, 332, 337, 349, 371, 394, 406, 411–12, 415–16, 423, 435, 436, 443, 446, 448, 453, 475, 525, 565, 574–5, 578, 612–15, 643, 646, 648, 651, 662, 668, 736, 749, 752, 757, 770, 778, 793, 833, 837
temporal specificity, 439, 452
Thailand, 93, 575, 598n.
third-party, 81, 175, 179, 182, 200, 207, 216, 242, 335, 395, 403, 424, 450, 475, 486, 530, 549, 580–81, 614, 685, 702, 713, 737, 739, 742, 763
title, 185, 207, 289, 304, 445, 579, 584, 586, 745, 821
tort law, 207–9, 221, 242, 255
tournaments, 296, 355–6
township-village enterprises, 28, 630, 631n., 689
trade, 10, 11, 37, 80, 150, 154, 155, 165, 166, 199, 216–18, 231, 304–8, 321, 327, 329–34, 351–2, 360, 436, 438, 448–9, 491, 545, 564, 567, 580, 594–5, 602–5, 611–18, 622–6, 644, 651, 684, 706, 719, 733–49, 753–5, 758, 762, 767, 768, 770, 773–75
trade-off between firm and contract, 395
trade-offs, 229, 230, 293, 294, 311, 350, 395, 413, 475, 476, 501, 518

trade unions, 22
transaction, 4, 7, 10–11, 34, 42, 47, 54, 319, 411
transaction cost, 4, 10–14, 34–7, 18, 21, 36, 37, 52, 175, 281, 285n., 286, 302, 305n., 311, 435, 436, 475–6, 486, 492, 546, 547, 549, 581, 613, 653, 668, 683, 789
transaction cost economics (TCE), 4, 41–61, 281, 302, 319, 320, 402, 403, 407, 410, 412, 435, 437, 440, 451, 455, 456, 597, 820
transfer pricing, 253
transition, 16, 29, 55, 91, 94, 96, 176, 183–8, 197, 198, 207, 229–30, 239, 239n., 246, 247, 304, 363, 374, 376, 412, 449, 455, 502, 625, 629, 667–94, 744, 796, 809–10, 836
transport, 166, 195, 235, 239n., 367, 394, 438, 445, 552, 576, 577, 586, 649, 703, 821
trust, 13, 16, 52, 57, 58, 168, 178, 180, 207, 209, 213, 215, 218, 262, 266, 301, 308, 382, 384, 396, 409, 435, 448, 453, 456, 522, 604, 611, 612, 614, 617, 618, 624, 626–8, 642, 644, 684, 685, 701–2, 703–6, 709–12, 714, 718–21, 733, 793, 802–3
Turkey, 93, 232, 557n., 631

Uganda, 93, 627
Ukraine, 93, 96, 109n., 110, 675, 684
uncertainty, 10–13, 21–5, 28, 47, 53, 57, 81, 175, 208, 281, 284, 290, 298–9, 310, 319, 321, 325, 326, 332, 341, 353, 362, 380, 402, 406, 409–10, 415–17, 420, 423, 426, 437–40, 442–7, 451, 455–6, 477, 552, 554, 567–8, 579, 599, 805, 811
underdevelopment, 611, 616, 620, 622, 625, 629
underground economy, 592, 598
unions, 22, 55, 195, 371, 594, 711, 719, 744
United Kingdom, 93
   administrative agencies, 532
   contract law, 13
   corporate ownership, 252
   legal system, 9

United Kingdom (*cont.*)
  political system, 80, 132, 135, 530, 534, 536, 709
  social democrats and liberals, 80
United States, 24, 110, 152, 155, 160, 187, 216, 246, 265, 372, 383, 397, 580, 602–3, 617, 657, 658
  Civil War, 717
  common law, 222
  Congress, 98, 124, 125, 127, 130, 136, 137, 140, 824
  corporate governance, 375
  economy, 38, 157, 244, 343, 468, 471, 557, 563, 594
  legal system, 9, 13, 194
  farm production, 467n.
  federalism, 163–9, 199
  fisheries, 558
  high-trust societies, 708
  House of Representatives, 132, 134, 135
  National Labor Relations Act, 195
  political system, 13, 73, 79, 132, 134, 137, 530, 629, 709
  regulation, 154, 530, 567n.
  slavery, 162
Uruguay, 80, 93, 95, 102, 107, 100, 657, 658
utility, 13, 23, 83, 220, 360–61, 401–4, 407, 411, 516–23, 525, 605, 630, 712, 717, 822

Veblen effect, 403, 418
Venezuela, 93, 95, 96, 107, 110–13, 115, 116, 657, 658

vertical integration, 10, 41, 45–6, 52, 53, 58, 60, 179, 283, 297, 307, 310, 319–45, 394, 402, 405, 406, 411, 412, 414, 415, 426, 435–8, 440–52, 455–6, 494, 592, 595, 604, 739
veto, 6, 96–9, 103, 104, 107–8, 124, 132–41, 168n., 529, 536–7, 576, 581–2, 586
veto player, 98, 99, 129, 141, 268, 537
Vietnam, 627, 684, 733, 810
violence, 156, 162, 552, 573, 579, 581, 584–7, 599, 677, 679, 747, 751, 772
voluntary exchange, 42, 302, 491, 599, 730
voting, 6, 69, 70, 73–7, 85, 94, 101, 107, 125–8, 134, 138, 267, 366, 374, 388, 647, 649, 657–61, 709, 837, 839

wage, 351–5, 357–8, 360–63, 365, 368, 474, 485, 622, 735, 751, 7738
War of the Roses, 775
Wealth of Nations, The, 31, 32, 42n., 598
Weberian bureaucracy, 359
welfare, 59, 84, 86, 150, 153, 156, 169, 210, 352, 401, 529, 556, 564, 581, 593, 605, 624, 628, 634, 640, 662, 675, 689, 704, 711, 736, 738, 745, 748, 778, 804, 805, 825
West Indies, 620, 650, 654, 655, 661
Western individualism, 769
Western legal systems, 232, 233
World Bank, 27, 176, 183, 185, 225, 631, 632n., 671n., 685n., 722

Yugoslavia, 109n., 110, 258, 667

Zimbabwe, 93, 598n., 704

Author Index

Abbott, Keith, 234
Acemoglu, Daron, 205, 211, 212, 213, 225, 244n., 245n., 265, 273, 619, 620, 707, 729, 759n. *see also* AJR
Acheson, James M., 415, 449, 476n., 478n., 547n., 557n.
Afuah, Allan, 411, 412
Aganin, Alexander, 252, 271
Aggarwal, Rajesh, 384
Aghion, Philippe, 324
Agnello, Richard J., 557n.
Aitken, Murray, 423
Akerlof, George, 358, 360, 451n., 716, 792
Alarcon, Fabio, 115
Alatas, Vivi, 720
Alba, Richard, 806
Alcala, Humberto Nougueira, 95
Alchian, Armen, 125n., 178, 213, 283, 287, 288, 290, 292, 293, 307, 308, 309, 311, 311n., 322, 328, 337, 342, 395, 437, 437n., 442, 446, 452, 454, 456, 479, 594
Aldrich, John H., 129
Alemida, Heitor, 627n.
Alesina, Alberto, 69, 83n., 107, 141, 526n., 717
Alexander, De Alva Stanwood, 126
Allen, Douglas W.., 12, 13, 465–86, 579n.
Alston, Lee J., 14, 125n., 304, 305, 474, 547n., 552, 573–88, 599
Alt, James E., 141
Alvarez, Michael E., 784
Amorim Neto, 133n.
Anderies, J. Marty, 836
Anderson, Erin, 10–12, 298, 303, 342, 343, 401–27, 439, 444, 445, 450
Anderson, James H., 673

Anderson, Terry L., 474, 548n., 558n., 575, 577n.., 578, 580, 580n.
Andeweg, Rudy B.,132
Andonova, Veneta, 8, 9, 229–47
Annen, K., 736
Aoki, Masahiko, 288, 290, 292, 293, 311, 311n., 312, 730n.
Archer, Daniel, 104
Argote, Linda, 414
Argyres, Nicholas S., 416, 426
Armour, Henry O., 312, 443
Arnason, Ragnar, 558n.
Aron, Janine, 626
Arriagada, Genaro, 106
Arrow, Kenneth J. 2, 29, 98, 283, 323, 324, 335, 839
Arrunada, Benito, 8, 9, 229–47, 439, 443, 444, 737n.
Arthur, Brian W., 812
Asada, Y., 557n.
Aslund, Anders, 810
Aspers, Patrik, 794
Atack, J., 168
Attaturk, Mustafa Kemal, 631
Ayres, Ian, 199, 208

Bach, Stanley, 130
Back, Kurt, 803
Backhaus, Jürgen, 246, 263
Bagehot, Walter, 94
Bailey, Martin, 198, 210, 221, 240, 566, 567n.
Bain, Joe, 323, 422
Bajari, Patrick, 45, 61, 456
Baker, George, 296, 300, 436, 450, 484n.
Baker, Wayne, 796
Baldez, Lisa, 106

Bambaci, J., 531
Banfield, Edward C., 705n.
Banner, Stuart, 741
Baqir, Reza, 717
Barbarossa, Frederic, 769, 770
Bardhan, Pranab, 185, 600, 628
Barnard, Chester I., 47, 50, 283, 286, 288, 289
Baron, D., 516, 516n., 518n., 528
Baron, David P., 126n., 134
Baron, James N., 55
Barro, Robert, 211, 627n.
Barth, James, 264n.
Barzel, Yoram, 125n., 221, 305, 306, 475, 548n., 557, 593, 604, 729
Bass, Frank M., 419
Basu, Amiya, 353
Bates, Robert H., 615, 621, 622, 625, 634, 729, 749, 749n.
Bawn, Kathleen, 98, 133, 141
Bayus, Barry L., 402, 405
BDL, 265, 266n., 268, 269, 271
Bebchuk, Lucian A., 383
Beck, Thorsten, 8, 9, 245n., 251–73 see also BDL
Becker, Gary, 55n., 421
Beckert, Jens, 797
Beckmann, Martin J., 288–90
Bednar, Jennifer L., 163
Beissinger, Mark R., 810
Bellah, Robert N., 778
Benham, Alexandra, 597
Benham, Lee, 14, 591–606
Ben-Porath, Yoram, 595
Bensaou, Ben M., 413
Benson, Bruce L., 199, 216, 217, 222, 237n.
Bentham, Jeremy, 263
Bercovitz, Janet, 58, 448
Berg, Andrew, 674, 712
Bergen, M., 448
Berglof, Erik, 670, 686
Berkes, Fikret, 557n.
Berkowitz, Daniel, 177, 197, 223, 244n., 259, 264, 619
Berle, Adolf E., 311n.
Berman, Harold, 216, 221, 771
Berman, Sheri, 719, 722
Bernhardt, 83n.
Bernstein, David, 680

Bernstein, Lisa, 199, 218, 237n., 739, 743
Besley, Timothy, 83n., 575, 579, 580
Bethel, Jennifer E., 382
Bhagat, Sanjai, 380
Bial, Joseph J., 551n., 553n., 567n.
Bickers, Kenneth N., 126
Bigelow, Lyda, 439, 441
Biggs, Tyler, 762n.
Binder, Sarah A., 130, 133
Bindseil, Ulrich, 450
Birdzell, L., 211
Bismarck, 220, 256
Black, Bernard, 206, 375, 376, 380, 673, 687
Black, Duncan, 126n.
Black, Max, 830
Black, Sandra E., 367
Blair, Margaret, 376
Blais, André, 77, 84
Blanchard, Olivier, 674
Blanchard-Kremer model, 675
Blau, Peter, 803
Blomquist, William, 822, 840
Blume, Lawrence E., 263
Boeri, Tito, 670
Boerner, Christopher, 52, 436n., 455
Boger, Silke, 442, 455
Boix, Carles, 709
Bolling, Richard, 136
Bolton, Patrick, 291, 310, 324, 670, 686
Bonchek, 527n.
Boone, Peter, 270
Boot, Arnoud W., 737
Bork, Robert H., 241, 245
Bott, Elizabeth, 803
Botticini, Maristella, 476n., 478n.
Boudon, Raymond, 799
Bourdieu, Pierre, 791, 828
Bowler, Shaun, 76
Bowman, Douglas, 421
Boycko, Maxim, 681
Bradach, Jeffrey L., 414
Bradburd, Ralph E., 443
Bradley, Michael, 387
Brady, David W., 126n., 128, 136
Breach, Alasdair, 270
Brehm, John, 719
Brennan, G., 43, 156, 159
Breshnahan, Timothy F., 401
Brierley, John E. C., 266

Author Index

Brooks, Robin, 551n.
Brough, Wayne, 221
Brousseau, Eric, 308
Brown, Jacqueline, 418
Brown, James R., 450
Brown, Shona L., 408–11, 414
Browning, Robert X., 126, 128n.
Brudney, Victor, 389
Brugger, Urs, 795
Brunetti, A., 627n.
Bucarám, President, 115
Buchanan, James M., 42, 43, 151, 156, 159, 169, 551n., 564n., 582, 632, 839
Bullock, Charles S., 136
Burger, Joanna, 547n.
Burkart, Mike, 688
Burke, Mary A., 469
Burkhart, Barry G., 479n.
Burt, Ronald, 793
Butler, David, 76

Caenegem, R. C. van, 236
Cain, Bruce, 127n., 139n., 526n.
Caldwell, Michael, 98, 527n.
Cameron, Maxwell, 104
Campos, Nauro, 670, 677
Campoy, Abril, 238n.
Cao, Yang, 796, 809
Capon, Noel, 405
Caprio, Gerard, 264n., 269, 270
Capron, Laurence, 416
Cardoso, Fernando Henrique, 111, 586
Careaga, Maite, 158, 629
Carey, John M., 6, 82, 91–117, 125, 134, 139n., 530
Carlin, Wendy, 595
Carlsson, Fredrik, 212
Carlton, Dennis, 324, 325
Carmona, Juan, 482
Carpenter, Gregory S., 421
Carruthers, Bruce, 790
Carty, R. Ken, 84
Casadesus-Masanell, R., 443
Casella, Alessandra, 793
Catt, Helena, 76
Caves, Richard E., 383, 443
Chandler, Alfred D., 394, 404
Chattopadhyay, Amitava, 410
Chavez, Hugo, 111–12, 116

Cheffins, Brian R., 389
Cheibub, Jose Antonio, 100, 117
Chen, H., 450
Cheung, Steven, 31, 36, 287, 295, 481, 551, 593n., 594, 594n.
Chhibber, Pradeep, 81
Chiappori, Pierre Andre, 478n.
Chipty, Tasneem, 339
Christensen, Ray, 80
Chu, Wujin, 425
Churchill, Winston, 602
Claessens, Stijn, 269, 270
Claibourn, Michele P., 719
Clark, Ian N., 561n
Clark, Robert C., 374
Clay, Karen, 732n., 735, 762n
Coase, Ronald H. 4, 7, 10, 31–39, 41, 42, 45, 125n., 208, 254, 261, 282, 283–85, 287, 289, 293, 303, 305, 349, 367, 394, 435, 436, 446, 474, 546, 556, 565, 575, 601, 602n., 604, 605, 672
Coate, Stephen, 83n.
Coeurderoy, Régis, 340
Coffee, John C., 264, 389
Cohen, Linda, 139
Cohn, R., 803
Cohwey, P., 529n.
Coke, Edward, 257
Coleman, James, 701, 702, 712, 718
Collie, Melissa P., 125
Collor, Fernando, 101, 105
Colomer, Joseph, 97
Commons, John R., 43, 831, 833
Conklin, James, 756
Conlon, Edward J., 354
Cook, Karen S., 803
Cooper, Joseph, 126, 126n., 128, 130
Cooper, Richard N., 558n.
Cooter, Robert, 207, 221, 230, 232, 241, 455, 526n., 533n.
Coplin, William, 677
Core, John E., 384
Coricelli, Fabrizio, 670
Cosmides, Leda, 240, 241
Coughlan, Anne T., 414
Cowhey, Peter, 129, 139
Cox, Gary, 5, 70n., 72n., 73, 76n., 77, 79, 80, 97, 125, 126, 128–30, 133n., 134, 137–39, 139n., 141, 526n., 527n.

Crawford, Robert, 178, 213, 322, 328, 337, 342, 395, 437, 437n., 442, 446, 452, 454, 456, 479, 821, 831
Creed, W. E. D., 825
Cremer, Jacques, 163
Crew, Michael, 221, 240
Crewe, Ivor, 76
Crocker, Keith J., 52n., 340, 439, 447, 478n.
Crosby, Alfred W., 265
Croson, Rachel, 208
Cull, Robert, 686
Cungu, Azeta, 675
Cyert, Richard, 323

Dahl, Carol A., 447
Dahl, Darren W., 410
Dahl, Robert, 91
Dahlman, Carl J., 284, 306, 613
Dallago, Bruno, 672
Damaska, Mirjan R., 263
Damgaard, Erik, 129
Danet, Didier, 238, 243
Darr, Eric D., 414
David, Paul, 812
David, Rene, 266
David, Robert J., 436n.
Davis, Gerald F., 380, 794
Dawson, John P., 255, 256, 260, 264
De Alessi, Michael, 558n.
de Figueiredo, R., 149, 160, 161, 526n., 531, 533n., 535
De la Rua, F., 115
de Soto, Hernando, 223, 596, 598, 598n., 739
De Winter, L., 134
Deacon, Robert T., 547n.
DeCanio, Stephen J., 447
Deininger, Klaus, 474
Dekimpe, Marnik G., 420–23
Delios, Andrew, 455
Dell, Michael, 382
Demirguc-Kunt, 245n., 251, 265, 270, 271
 see also BDL
Demsetz, Harold, 31, 32, 57, 125n., 240, 283, 286n., 287, 288, 290–94, 303, 305n., 307, 308n., 309, 311, 422, 568, 575, 576
Denis, Diane K., 374
Dennen, R. T., 575
Denzau, Arthur T., 78, 812
DeSarbo, Wayne S., 420

Dev, C. S., 450
Dewatripont, Mathias, 650, 652
Di Virgilio, Aldo, 80
Diamond, Jared, 265
Diaz *see* González-Diaz
Dicey, Albert, 211
Dickhaut, John, 712
Dickson, W. J., 803
Diermeier, Daniel, 94,116, 134
Dietz, Thomas, 547n., 833
Dillinger, William, 154
DiMaggio, Paul, 793, 797, 802
Dion, Douglas, 130
DiPalma, Giuseppe, 95
Dixit, Avinash, 52, 59, 422, 526, 730, 732, 735, 739, 746
Djankov, Simeon, 176, 223, 224, 243, 262, 264n., 271, 273, 598, 670, 679, 681, 682, 686, 690n., 694
Dnes, Anthony, 297, 448
Dobbin, Frank, 794, 797
Dobrzynska, Agnieszka, 84
Dolsak, Nives, 547n.
Donnelley, Lawrence P., 557n.
Doring, Herbert, 133, 137
Dosi, Giovanni, 402, 406, 408
Dow, Gregory, 292
Downing, Brian M., 729, 769
Downs, Anthony, 126n.
Doyle, William, 236
Drobak, John N., 710
Druckman, James N., 141
Dubois, Pierre, 482
DuBow, Shane, 473
Duhalde, Eduardo, 115
Duman, Daniel, 234
Durlauf, Steven, 701
Dutta, S., 413, 448
Dutz, Mark, 682
Duverger, Maurice, 96, 101
Dwyer, F. Robert, 298, 301
Dyck, Alexander, 265, 270
Dyer, Jeffrey H., 296, 300, 413

Earle, John, 682
Easterbrook, Frank, 56, 254, 389
Easterly, William, 169, 264n., 611, 612, 717
Eberfeld, Walter, 325
Eccles, Robert, 295, 296, 300

Edelman, Lauren, 795, 806
Edwards, Steven F., 560n.
Edwards, William, 471n.
Eggertsson, Thrainn, 125n., 575, 576, 577n., 579
Eilat, Yair, 685
Eisenhardt, Kathleen M., 354, 408–11, 414
Ekelund, Robert B., 263
Eliashberg, Jehoshua, 420, 422
Ellerman, A. Denny, 567n.
Ellerman, David, 685n.
Ellickson, Robert C., 237n., 479n., 547n., 737, 803, 804
Ellison, Glenn, 732n., 734n.
Elster, Jon, 712
Emerson, Richard M., 803
Enelow, James, 126n.
Engerman, Stanley L., 15, 265, 269, 620, 621, 639–43
Ensminger, Jean, 304, 575, 778
Epple, Dennis, 159, 170, 414
Epstein, D., 526n., 527
Epstein, L., 533n.
Epstein, Richard A., 263
Epstein, Steven A., 749n.
Erickson, Gary, 402, 405
Erickson, John, 52n., 356, 439n., 494
Erin, Anderson, 52n.
Erlanger, Howard S., 806
Ertman, Thomas, 262n.
Eskeland, Gunnar, 154
Eskridge, William, 163, 533n.
Espeland, Wendy Nelson, 796
Estrin, Saul, 670, 682, 685
Eswaran, Mukesh, 364, 367, 368, 476, 481
Evans, Diana, 125
Evans, L., 522
Evans, Peter 807

Fafchamps, Marcel, 733, 734, 739, 744, 762n.
Falaschetti, Dino, 364, 366
Fama, Eugene F., 56
Farley, John U., 405, 419
Farrell, Joseph, 291, 295n.
Faulkner, Robert, 796
Faure, Michael, 240, 241, 242
Fearne, Andrew, 298
Fearon, James D., 759

Feddersen, Timothy J., 94, 134
Feder, Gershon, 474, 575, 579
Feenstra, Robert, 812
Feeny, David, 575, 579
Fehr, Ernst, 715, 716, 732, 734
Fein, Adam J., 298, 421, 424
Fenno, Richard, 127n., 139n.
Ferejohn, John A., 83n., 125, 126n., 127n., 128, 139n., 163, 533n.
Fernández, Alberto, 439, 443, 444
Ferreira, Daniel, 627n.
Festinger, Leon, 803
Figueiredo, Argelina C., 117
Finer, Samuel, 262n.
Fiorina, Morris, 100, 127n., 128n., 139n., 141
Firmin-Seller, Kathryn, 825
Fischbacher, Urs, 734
Fischel, Daniel R., 56, 254, 389
Fischer, David Hacket, 651n.
Fischer, Stanley, 676n.
Fishback, Price V., 450
Fligstein, Neil, 790, 828
Flores, Arturo A., 266
Fon, Vincy, 221
Fording, Richard C., 77
Fox, Gary W. 69–86
Fox, Kevin J., 560n.
Frank, S. D., 467n.
Franklin, Mark, 76
Franks, Julian, 252, 266, 380
Frazier, Gary L., 450
Frech, H. E., 447
Freeland, Robert F., 443
Freeman, John B., 441, 794, 805n.
Fried, Jesse M., 383
Friedman, Eric, 270
Friedman, Milton, 205, 441
Frye, Timothy, 96
Fudenberg, David, 526n.
Fujimori, Alberto, 101, 111, 115
Fukui, Haruhiro, 139
Fukuyama, Francis, 624n., 703, 704, 708, 708n.
Fulton, Murray, 467n.
Furubotn, Erik G., 731

Gächter, Simon, 715, 716, 732
Gaines, Brian, 77

Author Index

Galanter, Marc, 263
Gallagher, Michael, 72n.
Gallaher, Miriam, 130
Gallick, Edward C., 448
Gallo, Andres, 583
Galloway, George B., 126, 130
Galor, Oded, 759
Gambetta, Diego, 599, 710, 746
Ganz, Joan S., 831
Gardner, Roy, 821n., 822, 822n., 827, 829, 838
Garen, John, 354, 355
Garner, James, 365
Garoupa, Nuno, 242
Garvey, Gerald, 300
Gates, Bill, 372, 382
Gatignon, Hubert, 10, 12, 303, 401–27, 450
Gaucher, Severine, 300
Gaudet, Gerard, 560n.
Gavett, Earle E., 473
Gaynor, Martin, 363
Gelb, Alan, 676n.
Gelfer, Stanislav, 675, 679
Gely, Rafael, 52n., 526n., 533n.
Gertler, Paul, 708
Gertner, Robert, 199
Ghatak, M., 746
Ghosh, Mrinal, 299
Ghosh, Parikshit, 732n., 733, 734
Ghoshal, Sumantra, 453
Gibberd, 73n.
Gibbons, Robert, 338, 436, 443, 450
Gielens, Katrijn, 421, 422, 423
Gilligan, Daniel, 710, 719
Gilligan, Thomas W., 126
Gilson, Ronald J., 189, 380, 387
Ginsburg, T. B., 533n.
Gissurarson, Hannes H., 561n.
Glachant, Jean-Michel, 304, 308
Glaeser, Edward, 254, 254n., 256, 263, 264n., 273, 703, 704, 708, 714, 714n., 717
Globerman, Steven, 342, 443
Goetz, Charles, 196, 198
Goetzmann, William, 767, 768
Goitein, Shelomo Dov, 756, 769n.
Goldberg, Victor P., 13, 52n., 79, 283, 296, 436, 491–510, 519n.
Goldstein, Bernard D., 547n.
Goldstein, Markus, 778

Gonzalez de Lara, Yadira, 738n., 739
González-Diaz, M., 443, 444
Goodman, John, 221
Goody, J., 769
Gordon, H. Scott, 551
Gordon, Robert J., 401
Gorn, Gerald J., 410
Goss, Carol F., 128n.
Grafton, R. Quentin, 560n.
Graham, Carol, 106
Grajzl, Peter, 186
Gramlich, Edward, 153
Grandori, Anna, 297, 301
Granovetter, Mark, 292, 718n., 762n., 791–4, 796, 802
Green, Jerry, 324
Greif, Avner, 16, 175, 176, 199, 237, 305, 614, 623, 662, 705, 712, 727–9, 792, 800, 812
Griliches, Zvi, 402, 403, 416, 417, 419, 421
Grootaert, Christiaan, 718
Grossman, Herschel I., 749n.
Grossman, Sanford, 328, 334, 338, 386, 454, 456
Guay, Wayne R., 384
Gugerty, Mary Kay, 717, 721
Guinnane, T. W., 741, 746
Guiso, Luigi, 266
Gulati, Ranjay, 297, 412

Haber, S. N. Maurer, 754
Haber, Stephen, 157, 264
Hackett, Steven C., 476n.
Hadfield, Gillian K., 7, 8, 175–200, 221, 300
Hageboorn, John, 414
Haggard, Stephen, 141, 163, 522n., 526n.
Hahn, Frank, 23
Hahn, Robert W., 567n.
Hakansson, H., 301
Hall, Brian J., 383
Hall, Bronwyn, 402
Hall, Peter A., 376
Hall, Robert, 211, 626n.
Hallagan, William, 476n.
Hallwood, Paul C., 443
Hambrick, Donald C., 443
Hamilton, Barton H., 363, 453
Hamilton, Gary G., 767, 812
Hamilton, Gillian, 450

Han, Shin-Kap, 436n.
Hannan, Michael T., 794, 798
Hannesson, Rognvaldur, 558n., 561n.
Hansen, Zaynep K., 582
Hansmann, Henry, 195, 291
Hanson, Philip, 672n.
Hardin, Garrett, 552, 553
Hardin, Russell, 712, 716, 717, 729, 735n., 804
Harnay, Sophie, 241, 242
Harré, Rom, 832
Harrigan, Kathryn Rudie, 443
Harris, Jeffrey, 335
Harris, Milton, 352, 368
Hart, Oliver, 253, 324, 328, 334–36, 338, 386, 454, 456, 739
Hartog, Den, 126
Haspel, Moshe, 105
Haspeslagh, Philippe, 416
Hausmann, Ricardo, 107
Hay, Jonathan R., 176
Hayek, Friedrich A., 25, 27, 47, 150–52, 156, 159, 169, 219, 220, 238n., 252, 254, 283n., 293, 306, 615, 672, 797, 812
Hays, L., 367
Hazell, Peter, 579
Hazlehurst, Brian, 26
Heady, E. O., 483
Heath, Anthony, 76
Heide, Jan B., 414, 424, 425, 436n., 448–50
Heller, Michael, 208, 551n., 687
Heller, William B., 133, 133n.
Helper, Susan, 413, 414
Helsen, Kristiaan, 420
Henard, David H., 408
Henderson, D. R., 467n.
Henderson, Rebecca H., 374
Hendley, Kathryn, 176, 198, 684, 685
Henisz, V., 522n.
Henisz, Witold J., 450, 455
Henley, David, 752
Hennart, Jean-Francois, 443, 450
Henrich, Joseph, 715
Herbst, Jeffrey I., 621, 622, 625
Hermalin, Benjamin E., 380
Herr, Paul M., 418
Herrmann-Pillath, Carsten, 767
Hess, Charlotte, 547n.

Heyns, Roger W., 803n.
Hicken, Allen, 81
Hill, Peter J., 548n., 575, 577n., 578, 580
Hinich, Melvin, 126n.
Hirasawa, Y., 557n.
Hirshleifer, Jack, 221
Hobbes, 712, 747
Hobbs, Jill E., 442, 455
Hodgson, Geoffrey M., 732n.
Hoenig, Scott, 405
Hoffman, Philip T., 234n., 482n., 746
Hogue, Arthur R., 774
Holland, John H. 26
Hollick, Ann L., 558n.
Holling, C. S., 840
Holmstrom, Bengt, 32, 52, 288, 288n., 302, 311, 335, 336, 352, 353, 356, 357, 359, 360, 362–64, 367, 368, 445, 476n., 481, 485
Homans, Frances R., 558n., 560n.
Homans, George C., 360, 361, 803, 812
Hommes, Rudolf, 107
Hooghe, Liesbet, 841
Houser, Daniel, 553n., 567n.
Howse, Robert, 194
Hsieh, John, 77, 79
Hsu, F. L. K., 769
Hu, M., 450
Hubbard, R. Glenn, 447n.
Hubbard, Thomas N., 439, 452, 484n.
Huber, John, 98, 99, 116, 133, 134
Huberman, Gur, 365
Hughes, Diane Owen, 769
Huntington, Samuel, 91
Huq, Mainul, 710, 719
Hurley, Patricia, 128
Hutchins, Edwin, 26

Iaryczower, M., 159, 527n.
Ichino, Andrea, 243
Ingberman, 83n.
Inglehart, Ronald, 709
Ingram, James W., 137,
Ingram, Paul, 741, 791, 792, 803n.
Inman, Robert P., 158
Irwin, George D., 471n.
Isern, Thomas D., 473
Isham, Jon, 710
Ishiyama, J. T., 96

Jackman, Robert W., 84
Jackson, Tom, 498
Jacobides, Michael G., 293
Jacobson, Gary C., 78, 530
Jacobson, Robert, 402, 405
Janssen, Marco A., 837
Jap, Sandy D., 413
Jedidi, Kamel, 420
Jefferson, Gary H., 690
Jemison, David, 416
Jensen, Michael C., 56, 253, 354, 379, 384, 386, 391
Jepperson, Ronald, 797
Jevons, W. S., 36
Jin, Hehui, 159, 162
Johanson, J., 301
John, George, 52n., 298, 299, 413, 425, 440, 444, 449, 450
Johnson, D. Gale, 481
Johnson, Jason, 208
Johnson, Ronald N., 552, 558, 558n., 560n.
Johnson, Ryan, 545n.
Johnson, Simon, 176, 205, 211, 212, 244n., 245n., 254n., 265, 266, 269, 270, 273, 618n., 639n., 650n., 654n., 684, 688n.
Johnston, Richard J., 76
Jones, Charles, 136, 211, 626n.
Jones, Eric L., 265
Jones, Mark P., 101, 102
Jorde, T., 297
Joseph, Kissan, 357
Joskow, Paul L., 10, 11, 52n. 57, 294, 295, 297, 300, 309n., 319–45, 350, 436, 436n., 439, 443, 447, 450, 479n., 495, 517, 565n., 566, 566n., 567n., 682
Jütting, Johannes, 627

Kafka, Peter, 382
Kähkönen, Satu, 710, 718
Kahn, Charles, 365
Kahn, Matthew E., 710, 717
Kakalik, James S., 190, 194
Kali, Raja, 732n., 734, 736
Kalt, J. P., 128n.
Kalyanaram, Gurumurthy, 421, 422
Kaminski, Antoni, 825
Kanda, Hideki, 389
Kandel, Eugene, 176, 737, 739, 746
Kandori, Michihiro, 731n., 732n., 734n.

Kaplan, Abraham, 844
Karlan, Dean 718
Karpoff, John M., 558n.
Katz, Avery, 221, 229, 240
Katz, Elihu, 418
Katz, Jonathan, 130, 134
Kaufman, Robert R., 141, 522n.
Kaufmann, Daniel, 662, 677, 679, 691, 694n.
Kaul, Anil, 407
Kavanagh, Dennis, 76
Keefer, Philip, 16, 212, 624, 522n., 614, 624, 626, 628, 630, 633, 633n., 677, 701–22
Keister, Lisa, 796
Keller, Wolfgang, 766
Kelley, R. Lynn, 103
Kennedy, R., 96
Kenney, Roy, 52n., 450
Kerkvliet, Joe, 342
Kerr, Jeffrey, 368
Kerr, William A., 442, 455
Kessel, Reuben, 594, 599
Ketteringham, John M., 407
Keynes, John Maynard, 595n.
Khanna, Tarun, 299, 688
Kiewiet, D. Roderick, 105, 128, 133, 134
Kim, HeeMin, 77
Kim, John, 418
Kim, Minseong, 749n.
Kirmani, Amna, 423
Kiser, Larry L., 821, 829, 842
Kleibenstein, J. B., 467n.
Klein, Benjamin, 52n., 178, 213, 214, 283, 285, 295, 300, 301, 307, 309, 309n., 310, 322, 328, 329, 333, 337, 342, 395, 479
Klein, Peter G.., 13, 52, 340, 435–57, 478n.
Klerman, Daniel, 738n.
Knack, Stephen, 16, 212, 522n., 614, 623, 624, 624n., 644n., 677, 701–22
Knez, Marc, 366
Knight, Frank, 551
Knight, Jack, 533n., 534n.
Knoeber, Charles R., 300, 467n., 478n
Knorr Cetina, Karin, 790, 795
Kogut, Bruce, 415
Köll, Elisabeth, 767, 768
Kollman, Ken, 81
Kollock, Peter, 803n.
Kolstad, Charles D., 565n.
Konings, Jozef, 675

Konrad, Kai, 749n.
Kornai, Janos, 672, 674n.
Kornhauser, Lewis, 221, 229
Kotwal, Ashok, 364, 367, 368, 476, 481
Kötz, Hein, 255n., 257, 257n, 258, 263
Kraakman, Reinier, 195, 375, 380, 673
Kraay, Aaart, 677, 679, 691
Kranton, Rachel E., 732n., 733, 734, 736, 744, 763
Kreacic, Vladimir-Goran, 682
Krehbiel, Keith K., 126, 133, 133n.
Kremer, Michael, 674, 675, 721
Kreps, David M., 55
Krippner, Gretta, 791
Krishnamurthi, Lakshman, 421
Krishnan, V., 406, 407, 408, 408, 411
Krueger, Alan B., 417
Krueger, Anne O., 602, 605
Kuester, Sabine, 421
Kuhn, Thomas, 38
Kulatilaka, Nalin, 415
Kumar, Krishna B., 270
Kuran, Timur, 762n.
Kurland, Nancy, 443

La Croix, Sumner J., 578
La Ferrara, Eliana, 717
La Porta, Rafael, 220, 223, 230, 243, 244, 245, 251, 260, 262, 272, 385, 392, 619n., 623n., 708, 709, 709n., 710. See also LLS and LLSV
Lacher, Jeffrey M., 739
Laeven, Luc, 270
Laffont, Jean-Jacques, 175, 516, 516n.
Lafontaine, Francine, 295n., 296n., 297, 444, 448, 452, 476n., 478n.
Lagrone, William F., 473
Lam, Wai Fung, 822
Lamoreaux, Naomi, 263
Lamounier, Bolivar, 95
Landa, Janet, 214
Landes, William M., 217, 220, 221, 240
Langbein, John H., 184
Langlois, Richard, 337, 442
Lanoue, David J., 76
Larcker, David F., 383
Lasswell, Harold, 844
Lau, Lawrence, 689

Laver, Michael, 98, 116, 125n., 130, 134, 138, 141
Lawler, Edward, 363, 368, 803
Lawrence, Eric D., 128
Lawrence, John D., 467n.
Lazear, Edward, 355, 356, 365, 476n., 485n.
Lazzarini, Sergio G., 467n.
Le Pen, Jean Marie, 101
Leal, Donald R., 558n.
Lee, D. J., 450
Lee, Young, 176
Leffler, Keith B., 52n.,178, 214, 306, 322, 333, 476n., 478n., 479
Legler, John B., 157, 166n.
Lehmann, Donald R., 419
Leibowitz, Aleen, 363
Leonard-Barton, Dorothy, 411
Leshchenko, Larisa, 682
Lesi, Maria, 682
Levine, Daniel, 9, 103
Levine, David I., 708
Levine, Ross, 245n., 251–73, 717
Levinson, Daryl J., 778
Levitt, Steven D., 128n.
Levy, Brian, 52n., 305, 515, 516, 519n., 630
Levy, David, 439, 443
Lewis, C. A., 602n.
Li, Shuhe, 736, 737
Lian, Peng, 809
Libecap, Gary D., 14, 125n., 304, 305, 451n., 474, 545–68, 575, 576, 578, 579, 580, 582, 583n., 840
Lichtenstein, Peter M., 667n., 670n., 674n.
Lieberman, Marvin, 342, 443
Liebeskind, Julia Porter, 382, 416, 426
Lijphart, Arend, 73, 74, 77, 79, 86, 95, 97, 107, 116, 123, 138
Limongi, Fernando, 95, 117
Linz, Juan J., 94, 95, 100
Lipset, Seymour Martin, 393
Littleton, Thomas, 257
Litvack, Jennie, 154
Liu, R. H., 746, 762n.
Lizal, Lubomir, 683
Lizzeri, Alessandro, 84
Llewellyn, Karl, 51
LLS, 267, 270
LLSV, 252, 253, 257, 260, 261n., 262n., 266, 267, 269, 271

Loayza, Norman, 251n., 267, 268
Locke, John, 747
Loeb, M., 516
Lopez-de-Silanes, Florencio, 219, 243, 264n., 272 *see also* LLS and LLSV
Loredo, Enrique, 455
Lorsch, Jay, 380
Louch, Hugh, 793
Loveman, Brian, 825
Lowry, Robert C., 141
Lucky, Christian, 96
Lueck, Dean, 12, 13, 465–86, 557n., 559n., 560n.
Lunström, Susanna, 212
Lupia, Arthur, 116, 127
Lupia, S., 535
Luporini, Annalisa, 481
Lynch, Lias M., 367
Lyon, Thomas P., 476n.

Macaulay, Stewart, 283n., 300, 308n.
MacDuffie, John Paul, 442
Macey, Jonathan, 389
Macfarlane, Alan, 768, 769
Macher, Jeffrey, 52, 436n., 441n., 455
Machiavelli, Niccolo, 759
MacIver, Elizabeth, 380
MacKenzie, Donald, 790, 795
Macneil, Ian R., 197, 307, 309
Magat, W. A., 516
Mahajan, Vijay, 419
Mahoney, Paul G., 220, 223, 224, 230, 243, 389, 395, 738n.
Mahuad, Jamil, 115
Mainwaring, Scott P., 100, 101, 102
Major, Phillip J., 561n.
Makowski, L., 43
Maksimovic, Vojislav, 251, 270, 271
Malmgren, H., 283n., 293, 324
Maltzman, Forrest, 128
Manley, John F., 136
Manne, Henry, 235
March, James, 323
Marion, Fourcade-Gourinchas, 797
Marks, B., 533n.
Marks, Gary, 393, 841
Marks, Stephen, 455
Marshall, Alfred 281, 481, 595n., 795

Marshall, William, 52n., 124, 130, 527
Martens, Bertin, 632, 634
Martimort, David, 175
Martin, Lanny W., 116
Martin, Paul S., 719
Martin, Robert, 476n.
Martinez, Steve W., 452, 467n.
Marvasti, Akbar, 594n.
Mascarenhas, Briance, 421
Maskin, Eric S., 328, 739
Mason, Charles F., 339
Masten, Scott E., 52, 52n., 180, 294, 295, 297, 299, 306, 310, 328, 340, 342, 344, 436n., 439, 442, 443, 447, 452, 454, 478n., 597
Masters, John K., 439, 452n.
Mastruzzi, Massimo, 691
Matesova, Jana, 686
Mathewson, Frank, 180
Matsuzaki, T., 132
Mattei, Ugo, 243
Mauceri, Philip, 104
Mayer, Colin, 380
Mayhew, David, 127n., 139n.
Mazé, Armelle, 298
McCabe, Kevin, 712
McCay, Bonnie J., 547n.
McChesney, Fred S., 580n.
McConachie, Lauros G., 126n.
McConnell, John J., 374
McCormick, Richard P., 80
McCubbins, Mathew D., 6, 70n., 123–41, 517, 526n., 527n., 529n., 532, 533n., 534, 535
McGinnis, Michael, 822, 841
McGuire, Patrick 796
McKelvey, Richard, 98
McKinnon, Ronald, 154, 672, 674n.
McMillan, John, 176, 266, 269, 684, 728, 731n., 732, 762n.
McNeill, William H., 265
Meagher, Patrick, 176
Means, Gardiner C., 311n.
Mebane, Walter, 100
Meckling, William H., 253, 386
Meehan, James W., 52n., 342, 439, 442, 452, 454
Menard, Claude, 1–18, 281–312, 445, 449, 455, 612n.,

Menem, Carlos, 111
Menger, Carl, 729, 731
Merryman, John H., 182, 184, 198, 252, 255, 256, 259, 264
Merton, Robert, 50
Messick, Richard, 177, 186
Meyer, V., 471n.
Michelman, Frank I., 242
Michels, Robert, 50, 57
Migot-Adholla, Shem, 575, 579
Miguel, Edward, 708, 717
Miles, Grant, 439
Milesi-Ferretti, 84
Milgrom, Paul, 175, 178, 216, 218, 237n., 291, 306, 335, 336, 359, 360, 445, 476n., 481, 485, 614
Mill, John Stuart, 465, 480, 482, 716
Miller, David, 107
Miller, Gary J., 10, 11, 125n., 349–69
Miller, Merton, 253
Miller, Ross A., 84
Millo, Yuval, 795
Mills, C. Wright, 796
Miner, Anne S., 411
Minier, J. A., 627n.
Miwa, Yoshiro, 389
Mizruchi, M., 792
Mnookin, R., 455
Moav, Omer, 759n.
Modigliani, Franco, 253
Moe, Terry M., 98, 527, 527n.
Moenaert, Rudy K., 407
Mokyr, Joel, 762n.
Moller, Stephanie, 796
Mollett, Nina, 561n.
Monroe, Burt, 72n.
Monteverde, Kirk, 52n., 328, 342, 343, 439, 442
Montinola, G., 162
Moore, John, 328, 334, 338, 454, 456, 739
Moorhouse, John, 241n.
Moorman, Christine, 409, 410, 411
Moran, M. J., 531
Moran, Peter, 453
Morck, Randall, 270
Moreaux, Michel, 560n.
Morgenstern, Scott, 80, 128
Moriguchi, C., 762n.
Morris, Colin, 769

Morriss, Andrew, 241n.
Moselle, Boaz, 210, 749n.
Moser, Robert G., 81
Mueller, Bernardo, 14, 304, 305, 474, 547n., 552, 573–88
Muldrew, Craig, 769, 775
Mulherin, J. Harold, 52n.
Muller, W., 128
Munger, Michael C., 78, 129n.
Munro, John H., 775
Munz, Peter, 770
Muris, Timothy J., 219, 342, 445
Murphy, James T., 125, 128n.
Murphy, Kevin J., 354, 383, 436, 450, 600
Murphy, W. F., 533n.
Murray, Michael, 551n.
Murrell, Peter, 16, 176, 186, 625, 630, 667–94
Musgrave, Richard, 150, 151, 153, 155, 158, 166
Muthoo, Abhinay, 749n.
Mwangi, Esther, 822
Myatt, David, 76n.
Myers, R., 561
Myers, Stewart C., 386
Myerson, Roger, 70n., 76n., 82, 332, 516

Nadeau, Richard, 77
Nalebuff, Barry, 356
Narayan, Deepa, 710
Nayak, P. Ranganath, 407
Nechyba, Thomas, 152n., 153
Nee, Victor, 17, 287n., 601n., 789–813
Nelson, Richard R., 402, 408, 812
Nepstad, Daniel, 586
Nerlove, Marc, 417
Netting, Robert McC., 840
Newcomb, Peter, 382
Nickerson, Jackson A., 441, 443, 452, 453, 484n.
Niemi, Richard, 76, 77, 79
Nijzink, Lia, 132
Niou, Emerson, 79, 139n.
Noble, Gregory W., 135
Noboa, Jaime, 115
Noll, Roger G., 125, 139, 603n.
Nooteboom, Bart, 298
Norgaard, Richard B., 547n.
Norlin, Kara, 583

Norman, Ralph V., 772, 778
North, Douglass C., 1, 3, 4, 15, 21–30, 125n., 141, 166, 168, 175, 211, 216, 234, 236n., 264, 269, 283n., 284, 299, 304, 396, 519n., 575, 596, 598, 612, 612n., 614–17, 620–4, 629, 631, 634, 643, 644, 646, 672, 676, 691, 701, 729, 731, 732n., 747, 775, 789, 792, 798, 800, 805, 811n., 812
Nugent, Jeffrey B., 622, 622n.

Oakerson, Ronald J., 844
Oates, Wallace, 151, 153, 155, 158, 169
Octavio, Amorim Neto, 117
Oh, Sejo, 298, 301
O'Halloran, S., 526n., 527
Ohanian, Nancy Kane, 342, 439, 444
O'Hara, Erin, 224
Okazaki, Tetsuji, 760
Olds, K. B., 746, 762n.
O'Leary, Michael, 677
Oleszek, Walter, 133, 134
Olson, Mancur, 264n., 547, 554, 603, 708, 711, 719n., 750, 838
Opler, Tim, 382
Ordeshook, Peter C., 126n. 163
Ordover, Janusz, 324
Osborn, Richard N., 414
Osborne, Evan, 240
Osborne, Martin, 83n.
Ostrom, Elinor, 2, 7, 10, 17, 547n., 577n., 632, 633n., 634, 712, 715, 819–45
Ostroy, J., 43
Ouchi, William G., 295, 367, 368
Owen, Bruce, 603n.
Oxley, Joanne E., 297, 301, 413, 446, 449

Pagano, Marco, 252, 264, 393, 660
Page, Karen, 793
Pakes, Ariel, 402
Palay, Thomas, 52n. 295, 297, 298, 439n., 449, 455
Palfrey, Thomas, 76n., 163
Pantoja, Enrique, 705
Panunzi, Fausto, 688
Parente, Stephen, 213, 225
Pargal, Sheoli, 710, 719
Parigi, Bruno, 481
Parisi, Francesco, 221
Park, Seung Ho, 296, 301

Parker, Glenn R., 128, 420
Parker, Suzanne L., 128
Parks, McLean, 354
Parrish, Scott, 105
Parsons, Wes, 221
Passell, P., 168
Pattie, Charles J., 76
Patzelt, J. Werner, 128
Pauly, M., 363
Pawakapan, Niti, 403
Paxton, Pamela, 709
Payne, J. Mark, 632n.
Paz-Ares, Cándido, 242
Peltzman, Sam, 32, 57, 516
Pendlebury, Norman, 234
Peng, Yusheng, 773
Pennings, Johannes M., 443
Perez, Carlos Andres, 115
Peron, Juan, 629
Perotti, Enrico C., 84, 393, 675
Perry, Martin, 323, 467n.
Persico, Nicola, 84
Persson, Torsten, 83, 84, 86, 99, 100, 527n., 706
Peter Klein, 12, 340
Peter, Tsar, 631
Petersen, Trond, 803
Pettengill, John S., 758
Pfeil, Christian, 450
Pflueger, Burton W., 471n.
Phillips, Owen R., 339
Pigou, A. C., 36
Pintor, Lopez, 74, 79
Piore, Michael J., 394
Pipes, Richard, 211
Pirrong, Stephen Craig, 439, 452
Pisano, Gary P., 295, 416, 446
Pistor, Katharina, 177, 254n., 259, 260, 264, 619, 679, 680, 686
Plant, Arnold, 33, 34
Podolny, Joel, 793, 794
Polak, Benjamin, 210, 749n.
Polanyi, Karl, 769
Policansky, D., 547n.
Polinsky, A. Mitchell, 738
Pollak, Robert, 595
Polsby, Nelson W., 130
Polski, Margaret M, 822
Pomeranz, Kenneth, 766, 767

Poole, Keith T., 128
Pop-Eleches, Cristian, 272
Poppo, Laura, 453
Porath, Ben, 304
Porter, Michael E, 449
Portes, Alejandro, 701, 705n., 739, 791
Posner, Eric, 491, 509
Posner, Richard A., 56, 57, 207, 217, 232, 241
Postel-Vinay, Gilles, 234n.
Poterba, James, 158
Pound, Roscoe, 177, 264
Powell, G. Bingham, 84, 116
Powell, Major John Wesley, 582
Powell, Walter W., 297, 301, 797, 780, 802, 828n
Power, Timothy, 104
Prendergast, Canice, 363, 365, 476, 476n., 481
Prescott, Edward, 213, 225
Priest, George L., 52n., 221, 230, 242, 261
Pritchett, Lance, 625, 710, 720
Przeworski, Adam, 95, 162, 747
Puterman, Louis, 292n.
Putnam, Robert, 624, 642n., 701n., 702, 710, 714
Putsis, William P., 420

Qian, Yingyi, 154, 159, 162, 688n., 689, 768
Quibria, M.G., 632n.

Radford, R. A., 595
Radner, Roy, 288, 290, 361
Rae, Douglas, 77
Rahn, Wendy, 719
Raiser, Martin, 679
Rajan, Raghuram G., 251, 252, 261, 264, 268, 270, 393, 619, 775
Ramasastry, Slavova, 680
Ramseyer, Mark, 389, 533n.
Rao, Akshay R., 423
Rao, C. H. Hanamutha, 475
Rao, Vithala R., 407
Rapaczynski, Andrzej, 207
Raskov, Danila, 604
Rasmusen, Eric, 843
Rauch, James E., 807
Ravenscraft David J., 382
Raviv, Artur, 352, 368

Ray, Debraj, 732n., 733, 734
Raynaud, Emmanuel, 297–98, 448
Razo, Armando, 644n
Recanatini, Francesca, 675
Redding S. Gordon, 767
Reed, Steven, 72, 77, 79, 139n.
Regan, Laureen, 342, 424, 444
Reingen, Peter H., 418
Remington, Thomas, 105
Renate Mayntz, 827
Renneboog, Luc, 380
Revesz, Richard, 155
Reynods, Thomas H., 266, 439, 447, 778
Ribstein, Larry E., 224
Richard, Jean-Francois, 177, 259, 264
Richardson, Gary, 746
Richter, Rudolf, 731
Riker, William H., 98, 126n., 149, 150, 160, 162
Riley, M. W., 803
Rindfleisch, Aric, 52, 436n.
Ripley, Randall B., 133
Robbins, Lionel, 32, 42
Roberts, John, 302
Robertson, Paul L., 337, 342, 442
Robertson, Thomas S., 412, 418, 420, 421, 422
Robinson, James, 205, 211, 212, 225, 244n., 245n. 265, 622, 707, 759 *see also* AJR
Rochon, Thomas, 697
Rodden, Jonathan, 154, 159
Rodrik, Dani, 212, 620n., 627
Roe, Mark J., 9n., 11, 245, 264, 291, 371–97, 457, 619
Roethlisberg, F. J., 803
Rogers, Everett M., 418
Rohde, David, 126, 126n., 129, 136
Roland, Gérard, 99, 154, 672, 673n., 674n., 687, 689, 694n.
Roll, Richard, 626, 626n.
Romano, Roberta, 383, 389
Romer, Thomas, 99, 159, 170
Root, Hilton L., 759
Rose, Carol M., 567n.
Rose-Ackerman, Susan, 738
Rosen, Shewin, 356
Rosenberg, Nathan, 211
Rosenbluth, Frances M., 79, 80, 125, 139
Rosenstone, Steven J., 81

Rosenthal, Howard, 99, 128, 134, 139, 141, 234n., 263, 615
Rostagno, 84
Roth, Victor J., 450
Rothbard, Murray, 42n.
Rother, Larry, 116
Rauch, James, 793
Roumasset, James, 578
Rowley, Charles K., 221
Roy, Ewell Paul, 467n.
Rozenweig, Michael, 387
Rubin, Paul H., 8, 9, 198, 205–25, 230, 240, 243, 252, 261, 263, 295, 300
Rubinfeld, Danile, 153, 158, 263
Rucker, Randal, 52n., 476n., 478n.
Rundquist, Barry S., 130
Ryterman, Randi, 176, 675, 684

Saa, Rodriguez, 115
Sabel, Charles F., 394, 442
Sachs, Jeffrey, 654n., 685, 792, 808
Saiegh, 159
Sako, Mari, 414
Sala, Brian R., 130
Sala-I-Martin, Xavier, 625
Salanie, Bernard, 478n.
Salant, Stephen, 551n., 560n.
Saloner, Garth, 324
Salop, Steven, 324
Salter, Sir Arthur, 33
Salzberg, E. M., 533n.
Samuels, David J., 81, 95n.
Samwick, Andrew, 383
Sanguinetti, Pablo, 154
Sappington, David E. M., 465
Sarney, Jose, 105
Sartori, Giovanni, 95
Sarvary, Miklos, 420
Sato, Seizaburo, 132, 586
Satterthwaite, M., 332
Saussier, Stéphane, 52, 436n., 443, 446, 447
Sauvée, Loïc, 467
Sawyer, Amos, 825
Saxenian, AnnaLee, 795
Schachter, Stanley, 803
Scharfstein, David, 310
Scharpf, Fritz, 827
Scheffman, David, 342, 445

Scherer, F. M. 382, 422
Schickler, Eric, 130
Schindt, Richard, 443
Schlager, Edella, 822, 840
Schlesinger, Rudolph B., 255, 258
Schmalensee, Richard, 554, 565n., 566, 566n., 567n.
Schmidt, Gregory, 104
Schmittlein, David C., 52n., 298, 342, 343, 424, 439, 444
Schmitz, Patrick, 208
Schmookler, Jacob, 402, 405, 414
Schneider, Martin J., 191n., 198, 305, 547n., 576
Schofield, Norman, 98, 116, 141
Schrank, William E., 558n.
Schranz, Mary, 597
Schumpeter, Joseph, 69, 401, 403, 416n., 650, 672
Schutz, Alfred, 812
Schwartz, Alan, 198, 308
Schwartz, E. P., 527n., 533n., 535
Schwartz, Thomas, 127, 129, 136
Schwindt, Richard, 342
Scott, Anthony D., 551
Scott, Gordon H., 551
Scott, R. W., 50
Scott, Robert, 196, 198
Scott, W. Richard, 825
Scully, Gerald W., 211, 212, 219, 222
Sealy, Tom, 655
Sebenius, James K., 558n.
Sekhon, Jasjeet, 100
Selznick, Philip., 50
Sen, Amartya Kumar, 627n.
Sensenbrenner, J., 791
Seo, Myeong-Gu, 825
Sethi, S. Prakash, 419
Shaked, A., 188
Shamis, Hector, 115
Shankar, Venkatesh, 421
Sharon, Ariel, 95
Sharp, Basil, 561n.
Shavell, Steven, 198, 237n., 352, 353, 368, 738
Shaw, Kathrin, 297, 444
Shelanski, Howard A., 52, 340, 436n., 478n.
Shepherd, George B., 187

Shepherd, William G., 187
Shepsle, Kenneth, 98, 99, 116, 124, 125, 130, 134, 138, 527, 825, 839
Shimanoff, Susan B., 810
Shin, Taekjin, 794
Shipan, Charles, 116, 527, 533n.
Shirley, Mary M., 1–18, 603n., 611–35, 668, 721, 722, 836
Shirk, Susan L., 162, 809
Shiue, Carol H., 766
Shleifer, Andrei, 176, 219, 243, 251, 253, 254n., 256, 263, 264n., 264n., 272, 273, 365, 599, 681, 688, 738, 771, 807 *see also* LLSV and LLS.
Shotton, Ross, 560n., 561n.
Shugart, Matthew, 70n., 72, 72n., 73, 77, 80, 82, 95, 97, 100–104, 134, 139n., 526n., 530
Shvetsova, Olga, 105
Siermann, C. L. J., 627n.
Silva, S. C., 586
Silverman, Brian S., 441, 443, 452, 453, 484n.
Simester, Duncan, 366
Simon, Herbert A., 46–51, 283, 288, 290, 292, 323, 792
Simpson, Brian, 240, 482
Sinclair, Barbara, 129, 133, 135
Singer, Miroslav, 683
Singerman, Diane, 596
Singh, Harbir, 412
Sirks, Boudewijn, 236
Skach, Cindy, 95
Skaperdas, Stergios, 727n.
Slade, Margaret, 448
Slivinski, Al, 83n.
Slocum, John W., 368
Smith, Adam, 31, 32, 325, 465, 471n., 473, 480, 482, 483, 596
Smith, Henry E., 211, 577n.
Smith, James L., 562n., 563n., 564n.
Smith, Steven S., 105, 128, 130, 133
Smyth, David, 594n. Smyth, R., 667n., 670n., 674n.
Snyder, Edward A., 52n., 180, 328, 340, 342, 344, 439, 442, 452, 454
Snyder, James M., 128n.
Sobel, Joel, 701n.
Soda, Giuseppe, 297, 301

Sokoloff, Kenneth L., 15, 265, 269, 620, 621, 639–62
Solow, Robert, 60
Somanathan, E., 715
Sotomayer, Narda L., 479n.
Spence, Michael, 351, 422
Spilerman, S., 796
Spiller, Pablo T., 5, 13, 52n., 515–38, 629, 630, 634
Spitzer, M., 533n.
Sproule-Jones, Mark, 832
Spulber, Daniel F., 404, 443
Squires, Dale, 560n.
Stark, David, 672, 796, 809n.
Stein, Ernesto, 107
Stein, Robert M., 125
Stepan, Alfred, 95
Stern, Paul C., 547n., 833
Stevenson, Randolph, 116
Stewart, Charles H., 130
Stigler, George J., 36, 254, 306, 325, 516, 604
Stiglitz, Joseph, 356, 475, 481, 685n., 687, 805
Stinchcombe, Arthur, 797
Stockder, Archibald H. 595
Stolle, Dietlind, 719
Stone, Yasunori, 74, 79
Stonich, Susan, 547n.
Stout, Lynn, 376
Strauss, R., 153
Strausz, Ronald, 358
Strikler, 473
Strom, Kaare, 116, 125, 128
Stryker, Robin, 795
Stukey, John, 342, 443
Stulz, Rene, 264, 269, 762n.
Suárez, Eugenia, 455
Subramanian, Arvind, 212
Sultan, F., 419
Summers, Lawrence, 365
Sutton, John, 188, 796
Svejnar, Jan, 670, 673, 676, 683
Svenson, Palle, 129
Svetsova, Olga, 163
Swart, Koendraad W., 234, 236
Swedberg, Richard, 17, 789–812
Swinnen, Johan, 675
Sykuta, Michael, 595

Syropoulos, C., 749n.
Szymanski, David M., 408

Taagepera, Rein, 73, 77, 97, 526n.
Tabellini, Guido, 83, 84, 86, 99, 100, 527n., 706
Tadelis, Steven, 45, 61, 456
Talbott, John, 626, 626n.
Talley, Eric, 208
Tang, Shui Yan, 822, 840
Tapon, F., 415
Tarassova, Anna, 206, 375, 376, 673
Taylor, George, 236
Taylor, Michael, 841
Teece, David J., 52n., 289, 295, 297, 312, 328, 342, 343, 405, 409, 414, 415, 416, 439, 442, 443
Telser, Lester, 178, 215, 324
Temple, Jonathan, 626n.
Tennyson, Sharon, 424
Terpstra, Vern, 415
Terreborne, Peter, 221, 229, 240
Terrell, Katherine, 670
Thevaranjan, Alex, 357
Thies, Michael, 72, 125, 129
Thomas, Robert P., 211, 234
Thompson, James S., 54n.
Thornton, Patricia, 794
Thurman, Walter N., 467n.
Tiebout, Charles, 150–2, 155–6, 166, 169
Tiller, Emerson, 533n.
Tilly, Charles, 770
Tirole, Jean, 32, 52, 291, 323, 324, 328, 329, 331–3, 357–9, 516, 526n., 739
Tollison, Robert, 263, 363
Tommasi, Mariano, 5, 13, 159, 515–38, 629, 634
Tooby, John, 240, 241
Toulmin, Stephen, 832
Townsend, Robert M., 738, 739
Trebbi, Francesco, 212
Trebilcock, Michael, 194
Triandis, Harry C., 778
Troesken, W., 521n., 522
Tsebelis, George, 70n., 99, 98, 141, 526n., 527n.
Tsoodle, Leah J., 479n.
Tullock, Gordan, 43, 221, 263, 582, 839

Tutt, Tim, 125
Twight, Charlotte, 221, 240

Udovitch, A. L., 756
Udry, Christopher, 778
Uggen, Christopher, 806
Ulen, Thomas, 207, 232, 241
Ulrich, Karl T., 406–08, 411
Ulset, S., 443
Umbeck, John, 575, 577n.
Uphoff, 701
Urban, Glen L., 410, 421, 422
Urbiztondo, S., 527n., 531, 533n.
Useem, Michael, 380
Uzzi, Brian, 791, 792

Vagliasindi, Maria, 682
Vagts, Deltev, 391
Valenzuela, Arturo, 95
Valenzuela, J. S., 106
van Bastelaer, Thierry, 718n.
Van den Bulte, C., 407
Vannoni, Davide, 340, 436n.
Varian, Hal, 41
Varshney, Ashutosh, 719, 720
Vazquez-Vicente, Xose Henrique, 292n.
Vishny, Robert, W., 219, 243, 251, 253, 599, 681, 738, 807
Vogelsang, Igor, 530, 536n.
Volpin, Paolo, 252, 264, 271, 393
von Hagen, Jurgen, 158
Von Hippel, Eric, 410
von Savigny, Karl, 256n.
von Thadden, Ernst-Ludwig, 393

Wachter, M., 335
Wada, Tetsuo, 453
Wade, Robert, 624, 720
Wagner, Richard E., 240, 241, 246
Walder, Andrew G., 796
Walker, David I., 383
Walker, Edward L., 803n.
Walker, Gordon, 342, 439, 442, 473
Walker, James, 547n., 821n., 822, 827, 829, 838
Walker, T. G., 533n.
Wallis, John Joseph, 157, 160, 598
Walsh, Patrick Paul, 675
Wang, Yijiang, 674

Warwick, Paul, 116
Waterman, David, 339
Wathne, Kenneth H., 414, 424
Watson, Joel, 733
Wattenberg, Martin P., 72, 80
Weatherford, M. Stephen, 139
Webb, Steven B., 154
Weber, David, 342, 439, 442
Weber, Elke U., 547n.
Weber, Max, 623, 639n., 641n., 642, 642n., 790, 791, 796, 799n., 805, 806, 807, 812
Weber, Robert, 76n.
Weinberg, John A., 739
Weingast, Barry R., 5–7, 52n., 124, 125, 130, 141, 149–70, 175, 178, 216, 234, 237n., 306, 395, 479n., 522n., 526n., 527, 531, 533n., 580n., 616, 621, 622, 629, 630, 643n., 644n., 729, 732n., 738, 747, 754, 775
Weisbach, Michael S., 380
Weise, Jill C., 551n.
Weiss, Allen M., 443
Weiss, Andrew, 339
Weiss, Avi, 444
Weissing, Franz J., 827
Weitz, Barton A., 52n., 298, 414, 439, 444, 450
Weldon, Jeffrey, 103, 133n.
Wetterberg, Anna, 720
Whaples, Robert, 241n.
Whinston, Michael, 57, 285n., 324, 339
White, Harrison C., 304, 790, 793, 794, 802, 804
Whitford, Andrew B., 361
Whitten, Guy, 76
Whyte, William Foote, 803n.
Wibbels, 163, 164
Wiggins, Steven, 305, 451n., 553n., 563
Wildasin, David, 154
Wilen, James E., 558n., 560n.
Williams, Charles M., 484
Williams, John, 833, 841
Williamson, Oliver E., 1, 2, 4, 12, 17, 31, 35, 38, 41–60, 125n., 175, 179, 196, 213, 282–88, 290–97, 299–301, 303, 307–11, 311n., 320–22, 327, 329, 332, 333, 335–8, 375, 379, 394, 395, 403, 404, 409, 414, 425, 426, 436–42, 445, 452, 454–6, 479, 515, 517, 519n., 521n., 538, 597, 600, 601, 614, 630, 668, 671, 672, 676, 688, 692, 694, 712, 730n., 731, 737, 739, 789, 800, 820
Williamson, Rohan, 264, 269, 762n.
Willis, Eliza, 163
Wilson, Christine A., 479n.
Wilson, James A., 449
Wilson, Rick, 125
Wilson, Woodrow, 126n.
Wind, Yoram, 419
Winter, Ralph, 180, 324
Winter, Sidney G., 35, 293, 812
Witt, Ulrich, 293
Wolfensberger, Don, 133
Wong, R. Bin, 752, 756, 767
Woodruff, Christopher, 176, 266, 269, 684, 731n., 732, 743, 762n.
Woodward, Susan, 311, 311n., 312
Woolcock, M., 701, 720
Worm, Boris, 561
Wurgler, Jeffrey, 270
Wynne, Susan G., 822

Xu, Chen-Gang, 254n.
Xu, Colin, 690
Xuereb, Jean-Marc, 410

Yafeh, Yishai, 688
Yamagishi, Midori, 712
Yamagishi, Toshio, 712
Yamamoto, Tadashi, 557n.
Yang Li, Mu, 752, 756, 767
Yarbrough, Beth V., 286, 450, 746
Yarbrough, Robert M., 286, 450, 746
Yellen, Janet L., 358
Yeltsin, President, 105
Yen, Gili, 594
Yeung, Bernard, 270
Yoon, Jeongkoo, 803n.
Yoon, Yong J., 551n.
Young, Cheryl D., 126, 130
Young, H. Peyton, 469
Yu, Chwo-Ming J., 415
Yu, Wyane, 270

Zak, Paul, 703, 708, 716, 717
Zeckhauser, Richard, 351
Zelenitz, Alan, 159, 170
Zelin, Madeleine, 766

Zelizer, Viviana, 790, 795
Zelner, Bennett A., 455, 522n.
Zenger, Todd, 453
Zervos, Sara, 251
Zielinski, Jakub, 81
Zingales, Luigi, 251, 252, 261, 264, 265, 268, 270, 271, 379, 393, 619, 775

Zinnes, Clifford, 685
Zoido-Lobaton, Pablo, 677, 679
Zorn, Dirk, 794
Zucker, Lynne G., 308n., 713, 713n., 716
Zuckerman, Ezra, 793, 795
Zupan, M. A., 128n.
Zweigert, Konrad, 257, 258, 263
Zywicki, Todd J., 221, 222, 224, 235